W9-AHP-705

HISTORY OF LITERATURE SERIES
General Editor: A. NORMAN JEFFARES

HISTORY OF LITERATURE SERIES
General Editor: A. Norman Jeffares

OLD ENGLISH LITERATURE
Michael Alexander
ENGLISH GOTHIC LITERATURE
Derek Brewer
SIXTEENTH-CENTURY ENGLISH LITERATURE
Murray Roston
SEVENTEENTH-CENTURY ENGLISH LITERATURE
Bruce King
EIGHTEENTH-CENTURY ENGLISH LITERATURE
Maximillian Novak
NINETEENTH-CENTURY ENGLISH LITERATURE
Margaret Stonyk
TWENTIETH-CENTURY ENGLISH LITERATURE
Harry Blamires
ANGLO-IRISH LITERATURE
A. Norman Jeffares
THE LITERATURE OF SCOTLAND
Roderick Watson

HISTORY OF LITERATURE

THE LITERATURE OF SCOTLAND

Roderick Watson

FINKELSTEIN
MEMORIAL LIBRARY
SPRING VALLEY, N. Y.

Schocken Books · New York

862412

To my mother and father
and Olive Mackie

First American edition published by Schocken Books 1985
10 9 8 7 6 5 4 3 2 1   85 86 87 88
Copyright © Roderick Watson 1984
Published by agreement with Macmillan Publishers Ltd, London
All rights reserved.

Printed in Great Britain
ISBN 0–8052–3949–9

Library of Congress Cataloging in Publication Data
Watson, Roderick, 1943–
    The literature of Scotland.
    (History of literature series)
    Bibliography: p.
    Includes index.
    1. Scottish literature—History and criticism.
2. English literature—Scottish authors—History and
criticism.   3. Scotland—Intellectual life.   4. Scotland—
History.   I. Title.   II. Series.
PR8511.W38   1985   820'.9'9411   84–10707

Contents

List of plates

Editor's preface

THE study of literature requires knowledge of contexts as well as of texts. What kind of person wrote the poem, the play, the novel, the essay? What forces acted upon them as they wrote? What was the historical, the political, the philosophical, the economic, the cultural background? Was the writer accepting or rejecting the literary conventions of the time, or developing them, or creating entirely new kinds of literary expression? Are there interactions between literature and the art, music or architecture of its period? Was the writer affected by contemporaries or isolated?

Such questions stress the need for students to go beyond the reading of set texts, to extend their knowledge by developing a sense of chronology, of action and reaction, and of the varying relationships between writers and society.

Histories of literature can encourage students to make comparisons, can aid in understanding the purposes of individual authors and in assessing the totality of their achievements. Their development can be better understood and appreciated with some knowledge of the background of their time. And histories of literature, apart from their valuable function as reference books, can demonstrate the great wealth of writing in English that there is to be enjoyed. They can guide the reader who wishes to explore it more fully and to gain in the process deeper insights into the rich diversity not only of literature but of human life itself.

A. NORMAN JEFFARES

Preface

IN my researches for this book I owe a debt of gratitude to my colleagues at Stirling University, especially Felicity Riddy and Professor A. N. Jeffares; also Douglas Mack and the Stirling University Library, and Sarah Mahaffy of Macmillan. They were all most patient and helpful. Since many older translations of Gaelic poems adopted a rather tired poetic diction, I have quoted from the most contemporary available English versions whenever possible. In this respect I am indebted to translations made by Iain Crichton Smith, Ian Grimble, and Professor Derick Thomson in his book *An Introduction to Gaelic Poetry* (London: Gollancz, 1974). Finally, my thanks go to my wife Celia for her unfailing support during this project.

Acknowledgements

The author and publishers wish to thank the following who have kindly given permission for the use of copyright material:

Canongate Publishing Ltd, for the poems 'I Do Not See . . .', 'Calvary' and the extract from 'The Cry of Europe' from *Spring Tide and Neap Tide: Selected Poems 1932–72* by Sorley Maclean.

The Executors of the Hugh MacDiarmid Estate, for the poem 'The Eemis Stane'.

Ian Hamilton Finlay, for his poem 'The Cloud's Anchor'.

Macdonald Publishers, for the extract from 'Queer Ongauns' from Robert Garioch's *Collected Poems*; for the extracts from 'Old Woman' and 'What is Wrong' by Iain Crichton Smith from *Selected Poems 1955–1980*, and for the extracts from 'Steel', 'Between Summer and Autumn' and 'Coffins' by Derick Thomson from *Creachadh na Clàrsaich/Plundering the Harp: Collected Poems, 1940–1980*.

The Trustees of the National Library of Scotland, for the extract from 'Song' by William Soutar.

SHETLAND

Whalsay

Lerwick

20 m
30 k

ORKNEY

Kirkwall

Pentland Firth

Thurso
Wick

20 m
30 k

Thurso

Wick

Helmsdale

Dornoch

Moray Firth

Elgin

OUTER HEBRIDES

Stornoway

LEWIS

The Minch

HARRIS

N.UIST

Portree

SKYE

S.UIST

BARRA

RHUM

Mallaig

COLL

TIREE

MULL

IONA

Oban

NORTH WEST HIGHLANDS

GREAT GLEN

INVERNESS

Loch Ness

Ft. William

GLEN COE.

R. Spey

Huntly

Peterhead

GRAMPIANS

Braemar

R. Don

ABERDEEN

R. Dee

Stonehaven

Montrose

NORTH SEA

DUNDEE

PERTH

Firth of Tay

St. Andrews

ATLANTIC

Loch Lomond

STIRLING

Dunfermline

Firth of Forth

Dumbarton

Falkirk

Dunbar

Greenock

Paisley

GLASGOW

EDINBURGH

Berwick upon Tweed

Kilmarnock

Peebles

Galashiels

R. Tweed

ISLAY

ARRAN

Ayr

Melrose

SOUTHERN UPLANDS

CHEVIOTS

KINTYRE

Firth of Clyde

Langholm

HADRIAN'S WALL

Dumfries

Carlisle

Solway Firth

- - - - "Highland line"

- - - - Border

0   20   40 miles

0   20   60 kilometres

Scotland

Introduction: renewals and revivals

How we see literature, or a continuing cultural tradition, or even our own identity, depends upon an act of perception and hence of selection on our part. Different periods will make different selections from the available evidence according to the spirit of the times. Indeed, the music, literature and arts of the past are truly alive only because our understanding of them *has* to change in this way – from generation to generation, or even during the course of a single life. Literary and cultural history is especially fluid, because persuasive theories, let us say about what 'Scottishness' is, begin to influence how people think of themselves and hence how writers express themselves. Certainly, Scotland has expended enough effort over the centuries defending and defining a sense of national identity which has somehow refused to succumb to political or cultural pressures from her larger and more powerful neighbour to the south. The process started at least as long ago as the wars of independence in the early fourteenth century, and Barbour's *Bruce* and Blind Harry's *Wallace* did much to define the 'idea' of Scotland and to establish an independent-minded and egalitarian outlook as a characteristic part of the Scottish spirit. The fruits of this political identity, its close links with Europe, and the flowering of Scots came to full season in the poetry of Henryson, Dunbar, Douglas and Lindsay. A unique national identity seemed to be assured, not least because it was largely taken for granted.

The next most impressive period in Scottish cultural history was the 'Scottish Enlightenment' of the eighteenth and early nineteenth centuries. It too came from native stock, going back to the best of the Scots Presbyterian intellectual tradition, which

had always valued widely available academic teaching and
hence the primacy of philosophy, theory and analysis at the
heart of education, law and religion. The Enlightenment
produced figures of international standing such as David
Hume and Adam Smith, and a wealth of talent in engineering
and the physical sciences, very often among men who rose
from humble backgrounds. Clearly Scotland was flourishing,
and yet, paradoxically, the question of national identity arose
again, conjured up by the Union of 1707, the economic strength
of England and the tendency of educated Scots to look to the
metropolitan assumptions and opportunities of London. So the
eighteenth century saw a revival of literature in Scots, while
Gaelic poetry also came to a new vernacular strength. Antiquarians republished the verse of the great Makars, and they
collected and printed Scots songs and ballads from the folk
tradition, as a different 'Doric' inheritance just as valuable as
the intellectualism of an 'Athenian' Enlightenment. The voice
of the common people was heard and in part redefined by the
individual genius of Fergusson, Burns, Scott, Rob Donn and
Duncan Bàn Macintyre. Yet this mode was liable to decay and
by the end of the century its more self-conscious practitioners
had slipped into Victorian sentimentality, rural parochialism
and tartan stereotypes.

So the 'Scottish Renaissance' happened again in the 1920s,
as a political and critical effort to re-establish the native
heritage in a country which too many politicians, university
professors and popular newspapers were coming to regard as
merely 'North Britain'. There was a growing feeling, too, that
wider economic forces and the mass media were actually
eroding everything that was most distinctive and hence of most
value in all minority cultures in the modern world. Thus, it was
that the twentieth-century Scottish Renaissance contained a
new factor, for it realised that the country's Gaelic inheritance
was even more seriously in decline than the Scots, and, indeed,
it had been neglected and undervalued by the Lowland Scots
themselves. By the 1960s, hundreds of young men and women
were learning Gaelic and turning out to hear Gaelic poets with
all the enthusiasm once shown for Fergusson and Burns and
the renewal of the Lowland vernacular over a hundred years
before.

As always, this renaissance would have been stillborn

without the talents of great writers such as MacDiarmid and
Maclean, Grassic Gibbon and Gunn, but modern literary
histories and academics have played a small part too. T. F.
Henderson showed the way with his *Scottish Vernacular Literature*
(1898), just as the Revd Nigel Macneill had dealt with Gaelic in
The Literature of the Highlanders (1892) followed by the Revd
Magnus Maclean with *The Literature of the Highlands* in 1903,
updated in the 1920s. J. H. Millar ignored Gaelic but his
exhaustive *Literary History of Scotland* (1903) is still a *magnum opus*
on the subject, if very much a product of its time. More
recently, in 1977, Maurice Lindsay's *History of Scottish Literature*
has taken a similarly all-inclusive approach from a modern
point of view. By comparison with Millar's book, Gregory
Smith's *Scottish Literature: Character and Influence* (1919), was
briefer and more influential. This critical thesis tried to define
what might be called a national psychology or at least national
habits of expression, as they had appeared in Scottish literature
over the centuries. Hugh MacDiarmid was especially impressed and he incorporated many of these ideas in his own
poetry and used them as propaganda against the English
cultural establishment. Following Gregory Smith, he proposed
that the Scottish sensibility was characteristically extreme,
containing a combination of opposite tendencies – a
'Caledonian antisyzygy' – which manifests itself in a delight in
domestic realism and the accumulation of many small details
on the one hand, and a love of excess and wild and uncontrolled
flights of fancy on the other. These were 'the polar twins of the
Scottish muse', and MacDiarmid welcomed them as allies
against the Victorian conception of the Scotsman as a dull,
canny, parsimonious peasant. By 1936, Edwin Muir's *Scott and
Scotland* was suggesting that the 'Caledonian antisyzygy' was
exactly what was *wrong* with the national psyche, for it would
swing frantically from one extreme to the other without ever
reaching rest or resolution. For better or for worse, Smith's new
diagnosis of 'Scottishness' had entered the critical vocabulary
and the creative resources of the nation.

The natural inheritor of Gregory Smith's thesis was Kurt
Wittig, a German scholar whose work *The Scottish Tradition in
Literature* (1958) pursues still further what he takes to be the
most unique and persistent features to be found in writing from
Scotland. Our contemporary understanding of the Scottish

tradition owes much to this and two further books, both from 1961. George Elder Davie's *The Democratic Intellect* stresses the philosophical and egalitarian ideals of traditional Scottish education, and David Craig's *Scottish Literature and the Scottish People 1680–1830* makes a vigorous analysis of the social conditions and assumptions which influenced Scottish writers and readers during a crucial period of their history. David Daiches has also explored the special contradictions of eighteenth-century Scotland in his study *The Paradox of Scottish Culture* (1964). On the Gaelic front most recently, Derick Thomson has offered an invaluable *Introduction to Gaelic Poetry* (1974).

The present volume is not intended to present a selective thesis in the vein of Wittig, Davie, Craig or Daiches; nor can it lay claim to the comprehensiveness of Millar, Lindsay and Thomson. But perhaps there is still a need, as far as the general reader is concerned, for a path somewhere between these two approaches – a straightforward account of the lives, times and major works of Scotland's writers. The brief historical summaries at the start of each chapter have been chosen to reflect those aspects of Scottish history which feature most frequently, or contentiously, in Scottish literature. Whenever appropriate, I have tried to recognise the presence of factors such as the 'Caledonian antisyzygy', or the democratic intellect, or Craig's 'reductive idiom' in the Scottish heritage, without proposing these as necessary, or exclusive proofs of Scottishness. But there are at least two other major contributions to Scottish culture which have only occasionally received a proper recognition – although there are signs that this is changing at last. First, I would point to the *co-presence* of the Gaelic tradition and the mutual interactions between Highland and Lowland society and their conceptions and misconceptions of each other. There are as yet few major scholarly studies in this field. Secondly, it seems that the best of what might be called the Presbyterian intellectual inheritance in Scotland has been undeservedly obscured or denied, because the popular imagination has been so easily distracted (and understandably repelled) by the worst excesses of Calvinism. Thus, many Scots will tell enquiring visitors that the Reformation was the worst thing to happen in Scotland and that John Knox cast a permanent shadow on the Scottish face. This is a misleading myth because it hides the

truth about Scots from themselves – for better as well as for worse; and it is just as sentimental in the end as that other mythical Scotland where the wicked English are perpetually chasing Flora MacDonald and Bonnie Prince Charlie across the heather. Yet literature and history make lively and unscholarly bedfellows and some of Scotland's most enduring myths were created by her greatest writers – which brings us back again to the questions of how an author chooses his subject, and why he chooses to see it in a certain light. I hope that this book will help to explain some of these choices and how they came together to make the literature of Scotland.

1

The beginnings of Scotland: two cultures

SCOTLAND is a small place – even today her population is no more than that of Greater London – and she has been part of the United Kingdom for longer than North America has been a nation. But Scotland is a distinctively different country, with a culture, a church, a tradition in education and a legal system of her own. Few visitors can have left the place without being told this and having met a prickly sense of difference in the Scottish people. The national plant is a thistle, after all, whose motto, *Nemo me impune lacessit*, is translated as 'No one touches me with impunity', or, more vigorously, 'Wha daur meddle wi me?' The self-conscious assertion in these words reminds us that, as a small and often embattled country, Scotland has been much exercised over the centuries to protect a sense of identity, and this sense has regularly been stimulated or reflected or redefined and argued about in her literature. The thistle is a harsh talisman, and if it sometimes symbolises the libertarian Scottish ideal (as it does for the modern poet Hugh MacDiarmid), it can also look like a skeleton in an endless history of internal dispute and failure. MacDiarmid is not the first Scottish writer to have felt himself impaled on the national plant.

Many elements go to influence the history and the culture of a people; in Scotland perhaps the single most significant factor has been the geography of the land itself. Scotland is divided by major mountain chains and chopped into odd elbow-shapes by an irregular coastline. Thus isolated areas such as Moray to the north of the Grampians, or Fife between the rivers Tay and Forth, or Dumfries and Galloway between Ayr and the Solway Firth, not to mention the Western Isles, were almost independent little kingdoms of their own for many centuries. The mountains divide the country's resources even more radically. The Lowlands comprise the more open and fertile lands, which follow the southern coasts up to the central belt (where most of the mineral deposits also lie); then they take in Edinburgh, Glasgow, Stirling, Perth and Dundee, and follow the east coast up to Aberdeen and round to the Moray Firth. By comparison the centre of the country is wild and bleak, dominated by the Grampian mountains and the North and West Highlands, which look out to even more remote islands and a rugged western coastline. Many parts of the Highlands were accessible only by sea or by difficult trails until as late as the eighteenth century, when a few strategic military roads were driven into the fastness after the Jacobite rebellions.

Scottish cultural history is equally divided because it has a literary tradition in three languages – Gaelic, Scots and English – and there are a number of modern poets who still use at least two of these tongues to express themselves. Scots and English are cognate languages which belong to the dominant Lowland civilisation, which was agricultural, mercantile, urban, materialistic, literate and eventually industrial. Gaelic, on the other hand, belongs to an older and more warlike tradition of Highland boatmen, small crofters, herdsmen and hunters. These clans held strong family and regional loyalties and prided themselves on who they were, rather than on what they owned, and theirs was a sophisticated oral culture whose songs and poems and tunes were passed on from generation to generation usually without being written down. Not surprisingly, given such widely different values, these two cultures were often in conflict. But the densely populated Lowlands have encroached until Gaelic, once heard throughout the country, is now a minority language confined to the North-West, the Western Isles and the Hebrides, used by about 50,000 native speakers – 1 per cent of the population. Yet everything which the casual visitor most usually associates with Scotland – kilts, bagpipes, mountains and clansmen – stems from this Gaelic minority, even if it is usually promoted by Lowland businessmen. This is not the only paradox which Scotland has to offer and, like the others, it springs directly from the nation's various and changing origins. So, although this literary history will not formally begin until the later fourteenth century, the roots of a Scottish identity take us back much further, at least as far as the Celts and the mysterious Picts.

The Celts

The Celts belonged to a major 'barbarian' culture, the oldest in Europe next to Latin and Greek, whose greatest sphere of influence by the fifth and fourth centuries BC included north-west Germany, France, northern Italy and the Spanish peninsula. Linked by language, culture and custom, these confederated tribes spread from the Danube, and reached their most westerly point in Ireland, Wales and Scotland. The Celtic languages belong to the Indo-European family and are commonly subdivided into two branches – 'Q'-Celts, such as the Irish and Scottish Gaels, who retained the Indo-European 'qu' (later changed to 'c'); and 'P'-Celts, such as the Welsh, the Cornish and the Bretons, whose language changes 'qu' to 'p'. Heraclitus and the classical historians knew the *Keltoi* as tall warriors, fair-skinned, blue-eyed and moustached, who dressed in breeches, tunics and cloaks, wearing gold torcs and armlets with their hair stiffened and swept back like a horse's mane. They grew cereal crops, kept cattle and horses and valued hospitality, music, poetry, and feasts with plenty of fermented liquor to drink. Above all else they took pride in personal courage on the battlefield, where they favoured individual combats before the general mêlée and fought with spears and iron cutting-swords and light chariots. Celtic society was patriarchal, based on tradition and status within the tribe as well as loyalty to the family and its elaborate ties of kinship. All in all, these warrior values are strikingly similar to the ancient heroic mores of Homer's Greece. Songs and epics were composed and recited by privileged tribal bards; a Druid caste carried out the ceremonies of their ritual year; and Celtic artists and craftsmen excelled in fine metalwork and the elaborate decoration of bowls, jewellery, weapons and chariots. Celtic ornamentation is at once organic and abstract, with complex coils of strapwork which often terminate in stylised animal or human heads with fierce or comic little faces. This art is most familiar to us today in its much later Christian manifestation – in the Celtic crosses of Ireland and Scotland, or in the elaborate illuminations on the pages of the Book of Kells or the Lindisfarne Gospels. The Celtic heritage was a strong one, and its influence can still be found in the language, arts and social structures of Wales, Ireland and North-West Scotland. It lasted longest and changed least in these, the most isolated and far-flung outposts, because on the European mainland Celtic tribal culture eventually succumbed to the Roman Empire and evolved in different directions.

The Picts

In almost 400 years of settlement in Britain the Romans rarely penetrated north of the Antonine Wall, which ran from the Clyde to the Forth, nor did they establish their influence in Ireland. Classical writers of the late third century referred to the tribes in the North in only the loosest terms, calling them *Picti*, 'painted men', and in fact, we know very little about them. The Gaels of Ireland called then *Priteni*, 'people of the designs', which may refer to their liking for body-paint or tattoos, and they were most probably descended from a native Bronze Age people who intermarried with later P-Celtic arrivals. Their original tongue may have been non-Indo-European, for some of their inscriptions are in a language unknown to us. Furthermore, this society of tribes and minor kingships seems to have been matrilinear, with precedence given to males descended through the female line, and this, too, may derive from an indigenous Bronze Age population. The Picts and their precursors left vitrified forts (where the stones are fused as if by fire) and distinctive hollow, tower-like brochs all over Scotland, especially in Caithness and the islands. Their skilfully carved symbol stones – many of them in the North-East – testify to their love of animal designs and Celtic-style elaboration. We know little more about the Picts, except that their customs and something of their identity lasted until the ninth century, when they were submerged under pressure from the Norse in the north and the Irish Gaels in the west.

The Gaels

The Gaels arrived from Ireland in the fifth century and established a kingdom of their own, called Dalriada, in Argyllshire and the south-west of Scotland. These Q-Celts – called *Scoti* by the Romans – are the ancestors of the Gaelic-speaking Highland Scots. Christianity also crosses the water from Ireland, and Bede's history tells how St Ninian first showed the way and then how St Columba and his successors brought the Church to Iona in the sixth century and went on to convert more and more of the Picts and the *Scoti*. These early men of God were distinguished by their humble lives and by how humanely they accommodated Celtic mores and Celtic art to their Christian purpose.

Dalriada was not the only other kingdom within the Pictish sphere in the fifth and sixth centuries, for the Welsh-speaking Britons ruled Strathclyde, and Anglo-Saxon Angles from Northumbria held the south-east of Scotland, penetrating at one time as far as the Forth estuary. The epic Welsh (P-Celtic) battle-poem the *Gododdin* tells of a British raid out of Din Eidyn (Edinburgh) against the Angles, whom they fought near Catterick in Yorkshire about the year 600. But the Britons, like the Picts, gradually gave way to a Gaelic culture until the pattern of modern Scotland was finally set between the ascendant Gaels and the Old English-speaking Lowlanders from Northumbria – a minority whose time was yet to come. The Pictish kingdom was eroded still further in the eighth century when Norsemen came to colonise Orkney and Shetland and settled in the Western Isles and the north and west of Scotland.

The supremacy of Gaelic was finally assured in the ninth century when King Kenneth MacAlpin presented a legitimate claim to the Pictish throne and established himself as ruler of both Dalriada and Pictland, a kingdom later to be called Alba. The MacAlpin dynasty lasted almost 200 years, and when Malcolm II died in 1034 his country was called, for the first time, Scotia. There were struggles over the crown of Scotia, not least because MacAlpin's line had tried to favour direct succession instead of the Gaelic tradition of descent through brothers and uncles, or the Pictish preference for a matrilinear inheritance. Shakespeare's Macbeth was one of these claimants

and he ruled for seventeen years before the rise of Malcolm III
– Malcolm Canmore – established a dynasty which lasted for
another two centuries.

A Scottish nation

The new kingdom of Scotland was forged between the presence
of English Norman power to the south and the Norse occupation of the north and the Western Isles. Under the Canmores
the monarchy began to follow Anglo-Norman feudal customs,
for Malcolm's second wife came from the English royal line.
There were bloody wrangles over the disputed south-eastern
parts of Scotland and northern England, and internal disputes,
too, in the clash between Norman and Celtic mores. Still, the
Norman influence gained strength as intermarriage and
periods of peaceful trade consolidated the rule of King David I.
Edinburgh was established as the seat of royal power; Norman
forts, abbeys and monasteries were built throughout the
kingdom and the Church became an increasingly feudal
adjunct to the state. Gaelic Scotland did not succumb easily,
and the intransigently Celtic chiefs of the North-West
reclaimed their territory from the Norsemen and established
themselves as virtually autonomous lords of the isles. The
Anglo-Norman Lothian influence continued to rise, however,
and 'Inglis', the language at court, gradually prevailed over
native Gaelic and spread through the Lowlands and up the
east coast, taking the most fertile land and the most tradewor-
thy settlements into its sphere. Gaelic, the tongue of the original
Scoti, was now called 'Scottis', or 'Ersche' (Irish). The line
between Highland and Lowland Scotland was establishing
itself slowly but surely, although Gaelic did survive in remoter
parts of Galloway into the eighteenth century and in Perthshire
and the north-east almost until modern times.

The reign of Alexander III in the second half of the
thirteenth century was a period of exceptional peace, justice
and prosperity in early Scotland, but this 'golden age' ended
with his death. The succession was not obvious and there
followed a protracted struggle between many contenders, not
least the king's infant granddaughter, known as the Maid of
Norway; two Border lords, John Balliol and Bruce of Annan-
dale; and Edward I of England, who had recently subjugated

Wales and had an old claim of his own to be 'Lord Paramount of Scotland'. It was this claim which persuaded the northern lords to call on Edward to settle what was a very complicated feudal case. They eventually agreed on Balliol, who was crowned in 1292, swore fealty to Edward and promptly became his puppet. In the face of continuing unrest, however, and an alliance contracted between Scotland and France (the original 'Auld Alliance'), Edward reacted violently. He was at war with France, for he had feudal claims there himself, and he could not afford a threat from the north, especially since he was still faced with resistance in Wales. He took his army into Scotland in 1296 and penetrated to Perth, ravaging the Borders and killing thousands along the way. King John, ever since known as Toom Tabard ('empty coat'), ceded his realm to English governors and went south into comfortable captivity. Edward returned to London with much plunder, including the Stone of Destiny – the ancient Celtic throne-stone of Scotland – and the sworn allegiance of 2000 northern landowners. But he had behaved too savagely and it was not long before active revolt broke out and a certain William Wallace, son of a small landowner near Paisley, came to prominence during an uprising in Galloway in 1297. Over eighty years of fighting in what came to be known as the Scottish War of Independence had begun.

The War of Independence

Young William Wallace conducted a brilliant and ruthless guerrilla campaign and managed to join up with De Moray's Highlanders to control most of Scotland north of the river Tay. The great Scottish barons, the ruling Norman-feudal lords of the kingdom, had not as yet committed themselves, but Wallace was not leading a conventional Norman army, with emphasis on heavy troops, cavalry and siege-engines. In fact his forces were largely composed of footsoldiers and spearmen, made up from the Gaelic chiefs and their clansmen, middle-rank Lowland landowners with their followers, and the common people themselves. They could not attack castles, but they could move swiftly and control the countryside. Among men and women such as these a new sense of nationhood was growing – a sense that a country was defined by all those who lived in it and not just by the international family ties of a select few overlords. Wallace's hopes for Scotland were confirmed by a great victory at Stirling Bridge (1297), after which the English forces were driven beyond the Border and several isolated garrisons surrendered. He declared himself Guardian of Scotland on behalf of the exiled King John, but had to forfeit the title within a year when his forces were badly defeated at Falkirk, where they were overtaken by Edward at the head of a seasoned army shortly returned from the French campaign. The guardianship now passed to various members of the conventional nobility, and two in particular who had rival ambitions – John the Red Comyn and young Robert Bruce.

For the first five years of the new century Edward, 'the Hammer of the Scots', led a succession of campaigns across the Border, determined to establish English control by pressing his claim to be feudal overlord to the Scottish barons. Wallace was betrayed in 1305 and taken to London, where his execution provided a ghastly public spectacle. Parts of his body were displayed in Newcastle, Berwick, Perth and Aberdeen, but the example of his short life proved to be more potent than ever. Wallace's and Scotland's cause was taken up early the next year by Robert Bruce, who killed his rival Comyn in a church at Dumfries and had himself crowned king at the traditional site in Scone. Comyn's murder was such an ill-timed and sacrilegious act that it was almost certainly unpremeditated, but the desperation of the moment committed Bruce to the larger challenge of the throne.

Bruce's fortunes did not go well at first, for he had to flee to the Highlands, where he sought support in the west – a perennial haven for disaffected causes. Edward, aging and ill and set on vengeance, led one more army into Scotland, but died by the Solway. His son was less eager to pursue the issue, and Bruce and his brother Edward were granted valuable time to consolidate themselves in fierce internal strife against the Scottish supporters of Balliol and Comyn. Bruce's 'Rape of Buchan' – Comyn country – was particularly terrible; it swept away many of the local Gaelic-speaking lairds, but it secured the North-East for his cause as he gradually established a hold over more and more of Scotland in a campaign based on mobility, ruthlessness and surprise. Perth, Linlithgow and

Edinburgh were reclaimed, but the turning-point came in 1314 in two days at the Bannockburn outside Stirling castle. Here Bruce met a huge English army, brought from the south by Edward II himself, committed to defend his key garrison at Stirling and thereafter to re-establish English power throughout the land. The overwhelming Scottish victory at Bannockburn was the beginning of the end in the struggle for independence, but hostilities were to drag on for many more years.

At last Bruce had gained the support of most of his kingdom, and the Declaration of Arbroath in 1320 made a striking assertion of that nation's rights by appealing to the Pope not to side with the English against Bruce. This declaration, in Latin and signed by numerous earls and barons, is all the more unusual because it places an abstraction such as freedom and the liberty of individuals above the rights of any monarch. The right of subjects to select their king was believed to be part of the Pictish tradition, but this was a new and even a dangerous idea in the feudal world and one that was to endure for a long time in the Scottish people's conception of themselves:

> Yet if he should give up what he has begun, and agree to make us or our kingdom subject to the King of England or the English, we should exert ourselves at once to drive him out as our enemy and a subverter of his own rights and ours, and make some other man who was well able to defend us our King; for, as long as but a hundred of us remain alive, never will we on any conditions be brought under English rule. It is in truth not for glory, nor riches, nor honours that we are fighting, but for freedom – for that alone, which no honest man gives up but with life itself.

The English did not formally recognise Bruce's kingship and the sovereignty of Scotland until a treaty was signed with Edward III in 1328. Worn and sick after years of war, Bruce died the following year, to be succeeded by his five-year-old son David. In no time at all the old Balliol faction had revived – encouraged by Edward, despite his treaty – and a succession of regents and David II himself were once again caught up in internal strife and renewed warfare against the English. By mid century David was held hostage in England and the Black Death had arrived from Europe to ravage a land already laid waste by endless fighting. The absence of the king gave more power to the three Estates of barons, churchmen and burgesses

– the very people who had insisted on their independence at Arbroath – but the sufferings of the peasants had completely disaffected them from feudal lords and all their doings. French knights on Scottish soil were horrified at the 'impudence' of the common people, who chased them with hoes when they rode through their crops. Perhaps they had little left to lose, and perhaps the spirit of that declaration was seeding itself even among the scorched grass-roots. David returned to his kingdom for the last fourteen years of his reign to be succeeded by Robert II and Robert III, the 'Stewards' to his kingdom and the first, if undistinguished, members of a Stewart line which was to have more than enough problems in the centuries to come.

The Scots language

In Scotland, as in England and Europe throughout the Middle Ages, Latin was most commonly used for official purposes among the educated and governing classes. French was also used in England, but by the fourteenth century it had fallen out of use in Scotland and a new literature was growing up with original works and translations written in 'Inglis' – a version of Northern English speech which gradually took an even more distinctive character of its own. Within a hundred years this tongue was supplanting Gaelic – and came to be called 'Scottis' in its stead. Although James IV could speak Gaelic himself, the poet Dunbar at his court could safely taunt his rival Kennedy for coming from 'inferior' Highland stock and for using 'Irish'. The kingdom of Dalriada had slipped away.

Inevitably, in 400 years of development, Scots has very many words in common with English, although some are pronounced differently. Others come from older Anglo-Saxon forms which have dropped out of use in the south – words such as *dwine* (to decay or dwindle), *wersh* (insipid) and *thole* (to endure, suffer). Alternatively, Scots will take one form of a word from a Latin or French root when English takes another or leaves it altogether, as in *dispone* (dispose), or *dominie* (schoolmaster). Even common English words can be used in un-English ways, as in 'can I *get* to go' for 'may I go', or 'I *doubt* it's true' to mean 'I'm afraid it *is* true' – the opposite of what an English-speaker might assume.

Even for Scots themselves the writing, spelling and speaking of their language can provide special problems, not the least of which is the number of apostrophes which are often added, quite wrongly, as if it were simply English with letters missing – thus *a'* for 'all' instead of the more correct *aa*, and *fa'* for *faa*, and so on. The gutteral 'ch' is, of course, well known in Scots words such as *loch*, *licht*, *bricht*, and *nicht* and *heich* ('high'), but the Old English letter 3 (yogh, the name combining its two main sounds) was also retained, although later printers had to use the standard Roman letters 'y' , 'g' or even 'z' for it.* Thus Scots words such as *tulzie* (brawl) and especially proper names such as Menzies and Dalziel (and even MacKenzie) are often pronounced with an English 'z' when they should sound like 'toolye', 'Mingis', 'Dalyell' and even 'MacKingie'. By the same – mistaken – token, the unaccented syllables at the end of Scots words such as *pruvit* (proved) and *deavit* (deafened, bored) and *Scottis* itself, are often pronounced especially forcefully by modern readers, when they should be left relatively unstressed.

Some of the most distinctive and tricky features of Scots are to be found among the smallest words in its grammar. Among its pronouns Scots uses *ye* for 'you'; and *yon*, or *thon* as a variant of 'that' with *thae* for 'those'. English 'which' is usually rendered as *that* or *at* and the older form *whilk* (or *quhilk* – same pronunciation) is virtually obsolete. The indefinite article *a* and *an* is the same as English, but a scribal convention often writes them as *ane*, even although they should still be pronounced as usual. So Lindsay's play *Ane Pleasant Satyre of the Thrie Estaits* should simply be called *A Pleasant Satyre*. On the other hand *ane* in Scots is pronounced as it looks when used as an isolated numeral for 'one', as in *ane o them* (consider also *the tane and the tither*, for 'one and the other'); but when joined with a noun the form becomes *ae*, as in *ae weet forenicht* – one wet twilight. Finally, 'one' as an indefinite personal pronoun is not used as such, and the Scots idiom for 'if one thought so' is *gin a body thocht sae* ('if *a person* thought so'), or maybe *gin ye thocht sae*.

Scots had developed differently from English in the pattern of its borrowings from other languages. Thus Gaelic has given many loan words, such as *loch*, *glen*, *ben*, *caber* (originally a

* In quotations in this book, such 'z' spellings are avoided. Thus, where a text contained spellings such as *ze*, *zow*, the more familiar *ye*, *yow*, etc., are substituted.

roofbeam), *sonsie* (jolly or plump), *crine* (to shrivel), *partan* (crab) and, of course, *whisky* – *usquebae*, from the Gaelic for 'water of life'. This influence is less than might be supposed, given how widespread Gaelic place-names are throughout the country. Even so, it may well be that Gaelic patterns of expression have entered the speech-habits of Scotsmen, even when they think they are speaking English. Hence 'he's *away to the* fishing' for 'he has gone fishing', and 'Ian can't go to *the* school, he's got *the* measles', which follow Gaelic construction.

Old Norse made a particular contribution to Scots through Old English and its northern dialects, and then from the Viking settlement of the Northern Isles. Many common Scots words come from this source, such as *birk* (birch), *kirk* (church), *breeks* (breeches), and *skreich* (screech), as well as *big* (to build), *frae* (from), *gar* (to make, in the sense of persuade or cause to do), *tyne* (to lose), and so on. The original Anglo-Norman roots of Scots provided the language with a larger number of French-derived words, such as *douce* (quiet or gentle), *ashet* (dinner plate), *aumrie* (cupboard), *tassie* (cup), *houlet* (owl) and *mavis* (thrush), while later trade and the Auld Alliance brought further borrowings, such as *fash* (to bother) and *caddie* (originally *cadet*, a messenger). Finally, from the Netherlands, Scotland's other major source of foreign trade from the late fourteenth century onwards, came words such as *callant* (chap), *mutch* (a woman's cap), *kyte* (belly) and *dowp* (backside).

The literary Scots of the Makars was the dialect of mid-Scotland and this has been the basis of 'standard Scots', which developed as a versatile literary language from the fourteenth to the sixteenth century before meeting a renewed influx of English from south of the Border. By the late seventeenth century the interface with English usage and the availability of old forms, new forms and regional variations made Scots spelling very fluid indeed. The use of Scots itself came under threat when 'educated' people began to eradicate 'Scotticisms' from their writing – even if their accents remained resolutely Caledonian. There were many complicated reasons for this, and of course some shift in practice was inevitable after the two kingdoms were united. Then again, during the Reformation the Scots clergy had used an English translation of the Bible, and so English became associated with high and serious matters while Scots, by the eighteenth century, was linked with colloquial speech, the common folk and rustic life. Ever since then its full literary use has tended to be confined to poetry, for if it appears in prose it is as a 'speaking voice', as with Scott's characters or the 'narrators' of Galt's novels. Robert Burns's 'Lallans' was essentially mid-Scots from Ayrshire, but he introduced words from different dialects (his father came from the North-East, after all), and he also used anglified spellings for words which would still have been pronounced in the Scottish manner (e.g. 'ewes' for *yowes*). The nineteenth century saw a boom in sentimental dialect verses until modern poets in Scots set out to restore serious lyrical and intellectual status to the medium. They recognised that their language was a 'literary' construction to some extent, and MacDiarmid sometimes drew his inspiration from unusual dialect words which had long lain in the dictionary. Sydney Goodsir Smith stayed closer to what the Makars used, while Robert Garioch drew on his North-East roots and his life in Edinburgh in order to stay closer to contemporary spoken language. What exactly comprises 'standard Scots', after the eighteenth century or so, has become a debatable point, although common sense and common practice usually show the way. Scots is still potent in modern poetry, but it is doubtful if the evolution of the language can be reversed in other branches of literature. Its gradual 'vernacularisation' towards the eighteenth century and its literary history since then mean that it will always be associated with verse of colloquial expression. Nor will the formal stateliness of sixteenth-century Scots prose be seen again.

Gaelic literature

From the late twelfth century to the present day Gaelic has enjoyed a strong tradition of poetry, songs and prose tales, but its literature, whether memorised or written down, is most especially rich in poetry. This verse-tradition falls into two main periods. The first stems from the bardic schools, a 'classical' and conservative tradition which followed old Irish models going back to the ninth century. Bardic verse was slow to change, but by the sixteenth century Gaelic songs were flourishing in a more vernacular form of the language, and in the next century poets such as Iain Lom and Mary MacLeod heralded the second great period by beginning to use this language in place of bardic formality. Thus the slow development of a specifically Scottish Gaelic vernacular poetry reached its greatest expression in the eighteenth century among poets such as Rob Donn Mackay, Alexander MacDonald and Duncan Bàn Macintyre. Then the doors of the Gaelic world were flung wider still by such poets as Sorley Maclean, George Campbell Hay, Derick Thomson and Iain Crichton Smith of the twentieth-century Scottish Renaissance. These writers take a specifically modern outlook, yet their work is never far from their heritage. The spirit of Gaelic literature, with its characteristic strengths and subjects, is still remarkably consistent.

Not much survives of early bardic verse in Scotland, and the recitation of genealogies and chronicles is of little specifically literary interest anyway. In fact the classical schools were so stable that Gaelic bardic verse from the fourteenth to the sixteenth centuries can be usefully summarised at this point. The most substantial single source of early Gaelic poetry comes down to us in the Book of the Dean of Lismore, a manuscript from 1512 which was only discovered and published in 1862. The dean collected from oral sources in Argyll, and Perthshire, and these included bardic praise-poems along with much less formal satires, love-lyrics, Christian poems and mildly obscene verses. Most notably the collection includes Ossianic heroic ballads and verses in Irish, which demonstrate Scotland's continuing links with Ireland going back to their common roots. Indeed, one of the very oldest surviving texts to deal with Scotland, the *Duan Albanach* (most probably by an Irish poet at the end of the eleventh century), uses a mixture of legend and oral history to tell how the Irish Gaels first came to settle in the north, and the two countries continued to exchange contacts through bards and poems and patrons into the seventeenth century.

The Gaelic bardic system seems to have been well established by the thirteenth century. At first, this exclusive professional class produced learned and highly wrought verses along classical Irish lines, and bardic colleges were set up to teach the literary conventions, including as many as 300 different and complex metrical schemes. At the highest level these bards were fully literate and could aspire to the status of *filidh*. It is likely, however, that the common folk preferred tales and ballads outwith this antique, formal style and easier for them to understand. The task of the *filidh*, like the slightly less exalted position of bard, was 'eulogy and elegy' – to sing his leader's praises, recite his genealogy, chronicle his times and describe victories in battle. The bard's office was often hereditary, he had considerable prestige and could be a wealthy man in his own right, but he still depended on patronage and a stable aristocratic tradition.

Like all Celtic artists, the bards value impersonality and technical skill for their own sake and their verse is elaborate and conventional in its approach. Perhaps Dunbar's highly wrought aureate verses owe something to this heritage, despite his apparent contempt for things Gaelic. The traditional praise-poem could contain many elements – praise of a horse, a bow, the chief's ancestry, his land, his valour or the beauty of his lady. Other poems strike a more elegiac note with a lament for a leader's death or for the passing of glory. Bardic verses were based on the *rann*, a self-contained four-line stanza made up of two couplets of pre-determined syllabic lengths and a variety of rhetorical devices, including patterns of internal rhyme, assonance and alliteration. *Brosnachadh* poems, or versus as an 'incitement' to war, were also written, and an early example ascribed to Artur Dall MacGurcaigh and dating from about 1310 describes MacSween of Knapdale's fleet in terms which clearly show the parallels between Highland custom and the warriors and longboats of Scandinavia from 400 years before. (Gaelic chiefs from the north often boasted of their descent from Norse fighting-men.) In a later example from 1513, written for the Earl of Argyll before the Battle of Flodden, the unknown poet curses the English and asks the earl to punish their growing spite and power:

> The roots from which they grow, destroy them,
> their increase is too great,
> and leave no Englishman alive after you
> nor Englishwoman there to tell the tale.

> Burn their bad coarse women,
> burn their uncouth offspring,
> and burn their sooty houses,
> and rid us of the reproach of them.

Let their ashes float downstream
after burning their remains
show no mercy to a living Englishman
O chief, deadly slayer of the wounded.

(trs. K. H. Jackson)

Over 200 years later, the same bloodthirsty tradition was called up by Alexander MacDonald (Alasdair MacMhaighstir Alasdair), who wrote many poems in vernacular Gaelic to support the Jacobite rising of 1745.

Not all was war, however, and bardic metres were also used for laments or for gentler, more personal poems, such as the beautiful 'O rosary that recalled my tear' ('A phaidrín do dhúisg mo dhéar'), written in the 1460s by a non-professional poet, Aithbhreac Inghean Corcadail, in mourning for the death of her husband, Niall Og MacNeill:

O rosary that recalled my tear'
dear was the finger in my sight,
that touched you once, beloved the heart
of him who owned you till tonight.

I grieve the death of him whose hand
you did entwine each hour of prayer;
my grief that it is lifeless now
and I no longer see it there.

(trs. D. Thomson)

When the geographical isolation and the autonomy of the clans began to pass during the sixteenth century, the bards passed, too. Nevertheless, later Gaelic poets retained a high prestige, even if they came from humble stock without classical training, and, in fact, aspects of bardic style were to survive in a looser and more vernacular form for centuries to come.

Scots literature in the fourteenth century

After the *brosnachadh* poems of the Gaelic bards, it is appropriate that the first major literary achievement of the emerging Scots tradition should be John Barbour's *The Bruce*, a Lowland poem of war and victory. If Barbour had many predecessors, then they and their works are shrouded by time or hidden in the smoke of scholarly dispute. The oldest surviving fragment may date from the difficult years after 1286 and the end of Alexander III's 'golden age', but it comes to us as transcribed in 1424 by Andrew of Wyntoun from his *Origynale Cronykil of Scotland*:

Quhen Alexander our kynge was dede,	when
That Scotlande lede in lauche and le,	law and peace
Away was sons of alle and brede,	abundance of ale
Off wyne and wax, of gamyn and gle.	mirth
Our golde was changit into lede.	lead
Crist, borne in virgynyte,	
Succoure Scotlande, and ramede,	help
That is stade in perplexite.	beset

Also from Alexander's reign comes a long and relatively unskilled metrical romance called *Sir Tristrem*, often ascribed to Thomas of Ercildoune and later edited by Scott. But this, too, appears only in a fourteenth-century transcription and the authorship is disputed. Ercildoune is better known as 'Thomas the Rhymer' or 'True Thomas', the poet in the later ballads who became the Queen of Elfland's lover and was gifted with prophetic powers.

The *Awntyrs of Arthure* and *The Pistill of Susan* are two metrical romances, each with rhymed and alliterative thirteen-line stanzas, that survive in English transcriptions from the fifteenth century. The 'adventures' come from the stock of Arthurian tales, although they may be set around the Borders; and the epistle about Susan goes to the Apocrypha of the Bible for the moral tale of Susanna and the Elders. Andrew of Wyntoun ascribed these to someone called 'Huchown off the Awle Ryale' (although he puts 'Gawane' rather than Arthur in the title), and it has been suggested that this Huchown is 'Sir Hew of Eglinton', a Scot whom Dunbar lists among the dead poets of the past in his 'Lament for the Makaris'. ('Awle Ryale' has been rendered as 'the King's palace'.) Whether this connection holds or not, both poems belong to the same literary mode as later Scottish verses such as *Rauf Coilyear* and *Golagros and Gawane*, and these formed part of an 'alliterative revival' in the poetry of the north, even if the names of their authors cannot be convincingly established. 'Huchown' may or may not have been a Scot, but the nationality of John Barbour needs little proving.

John Barbour (1320?–95)

Barbour's famous poem survives in two manuscripts transcribed in the late fifteenth century, and the ubiquitous Wyntoun, a great admirer of *The Bruce*, confirmed its authorship and included 280 lines from it in his *Cronykil*. John Barbour was probably born in Aberdeen, and he is first mentioned in the records as archdeacon there in 1357. In the next eleven years he travelled to study at Oxford and then to Paris on at least two occasions each. Thereafter he was given a post as clerk of audit and was one of the auditors of the Exchequer for Robert II's household. He wrote *The Bruce* during the years 1374–75 and three years later he was granted a royal pension in perpetuity, most probably in recognition of his poem. A larger annual sum was awarded in 1388, and it is the cessation of this payment which marks his death in 1395.

From these slender details it can be seen that Barbour's long historical poem refers to events scarcely sixty years in the past, and it is likely that he had access to oral sources for many of the details in the work. These can be more reliable than might be supposed, although, typically, the odds against the Scots are multiplied for the sake of effect and at one point Bruce and his grandfather are conflated. In the same cause, Barbour's hero king is made of simpler stuff than the original, who suffered such divided Anglo-Norman loyalties and made a succession of broken promises to Edward and Balliol and Comyn. So *The Bruce* portrays an uncomplicated and noble epic from the start, and, although the English are allowed to be brave and chivalrous too, they are never seen as less than prideful and acquisitive enemies. Even so, Barbour's patriotism (and an awareness of his royal patron), does not lead him into mere propaganda or far-fetched romance. In fact *The Bruce* is most striking for its unelaborated narrative: twenty books full of the dispositions of troops, the vagaries of the campaign and the speeches and deeds of individuals, all of which are recounted in forthright style combined with a clerkly eye for the circumstantial details of time and place and equipment:

And went in hy towart the sea;	in haste
Quhar Schir Nele Campbell thaim met	where
Bath with schippis, and with meyte;	meat

Saylys, ayris, and othir thing,   oars
That was spedfull to thar passyng.
                    (v, 570–4)

The same dispassionate and documentary approach even
informs Barbour's account of the notorious 'Douglas larder',
when Bruce's fiercest young lieutenant surprised the occupying
English garrison at worship in the church of his family castle,
and flung their bodies and surplus supplies (and the feast they
had been about to eat) into the wine-cellar:

A foull melle thair can he mak;   mix
For meill, malt, blude, and wyne
Ran all to-gidder in a mellyne.
That wes unsemly for to se;
Tharfor the men of that cuntre,
For sic thingis that mellit were,
Callit it 'the Douglas Lardenere'.
                    (v, 404–10)

Barbour tells us that this master of guerrilla terrorism was
'meyk and sweyt in cumpany' and spoke with a lisp. Douglas is
a major character in the poem, and the tale ends with his death
in battle against the Saracens twenty-four years later, while
carrying Bruce's heart in a casket on a pilgrimage to the Holy
Land – a journey the king had long promised himself, but did
not live to make.
    True stories are a double pleasure, as the author observes in
his preface –

The fyrst plesance is the carpyng,   telling
    And the tothir the suthfastnes,   truthfulness
That schawys the thing rycht as it wes.
                    (i, 6–8)

– and one of the main things for Barbour, 'rycht as it wes', is the
spirit of liberty, famously evoked in the very first book with
lines which add a more than chivalric dimension to the tale:

A! fredome is a noble thing!
Fredome mayss man to haiff liking,   makes; pleasure
Fredome all solace to man giffis: gives
He levys at ess that frely levys.   lives at ease

A noble hart may haiff nane ess,
Na ellys nocht that may him pless,   [if freedom
Gyff fredome failyhe; for fre liking   fail; love of liberty
Is yharnyt our all othir thing.   yearned for over all
Na he, that ay hass levyt fre,
May nocht knaw weill the propyrte,
The anger, na the wrechyt dome,   doom
That is couplyt to foule thyrldome.   thraldom
Bot gyff he had assayit it,   if he had tried it
Than all perquer he suld it wyt;   by heart he should
And suld think fredome mar to pryss   more   [know it
Than all the gold in the warld that is.

(I, 225–40)

The unforced pace of such simple statement in Barbour's
octosyllabic couplets pervades the whole poem as well as the
character of its hero. Most notably, in comparison with Blind
Harry's *Wallace* of a century later, Barbour's work is not
suffused with blind hatred for the English. The same stable and
shrewd virtue is found in the mouths of the common people who
start to side with their king's cause:

He com soyn in the houss, and fand   soon; found
The gud wyf on the bynk sytand.   sitting on the bench
Scho askit him soyn quhat he wes   She; what
And quhyne he com, and quhar he gais.   when; where he
'A travelland man, dame', said he,   goes
'That travalys heir throu the cuntre.'
Scho said, 'All that travaland ere,   formerly
For saik of ane, ar welcom here.'
The King said, 'Gud dame, quhat is he
That garris yow have sic specialte   makes you have
Till men that travalis?' 'Schir, perfay,'   [such special liking
Quod the gud wif, 'I sall yow say;
Gud King Robert the Bruce is he,
That is rycht lord of this cuntre. . . .
'Dame, lufis thou him sa weill?' said he.
'Yea, Schir,' scho said, 'sa God me se.'
'Dame', said he, 'Lo! Him here the by,   he is by you here
For I am he;' – 'Sa ye suthly?'   truly
'Yea, certis, dame;' – 'And quhar ar gane
Your men, quhen ye ar thus allane?'
'At this tyme, dame, I have no ma.'   more
Scho said, 'It may no wiss be swa;   no way be so
I have two sonnys wicht and hardy,   vigorous
Thai sall becum your men in hy.'   in haste

(VII, 237–64)

Not surprisingly, the natural climax of the poem – after the accounts of Bruce's early sufferings – arrives with Bannockburn. Barbour's lengthy description of that two-day battle includes the tactical manoeuvres of the troops, the speeches of the leaders and courageous deeds on both sides; he also tells of the celebrated clash between Bruce and De Bohun, and how the humble camp-followers, determined to fight for Scotland in their own way, formed an army with sheets for banners, and convinced the faltering English that they were new and deadly reinforcements. The sober simplicity of Barbour's verses – and occasional shafts of grim humour – perfectly convey the purpose and the character of the Scottish cause as he sees it. Of course, it is the 'great folk' who stand most in the foreground, but the nobility of plain speech and simple dignity is shared by all. Thus Bruce's chivalric idealism has a sturdily domestic and practical foundation, as he addresses his men before Bannockburn and reminds them that, despite being outnumbered, they have three great advantages:

The first is, that we haf the richt;	
And for the richt ilk man suld ficht.	every man should
The tothir is, thai are cummyn heir,	[fight
For lypnyng in thair gret power,	trusting
To seik us in our awne land,	
And has broucht her, richt till our hand,	brought here
Richness in-to so gret plentee,	
That the pouerest of yow sall be	
Bath rych and mychty thar-with-all,	
Gif that we wyn, as weill may fall.	may happen
The thrid is, that we for our lyvis	
And for our childer and our wifis,	
And for the fredome of our land,	
Ar strenyeit in battale for to stand,	constrained/forced
And thai for thair mycht anerly . . .	only for their might

(xii, 235–49)

Professional knightly pride may have to give way in the face of men who are fighting to survive, but Bruce is king enough to know that the prospect of a little plunder helps, too.

Barbour concludes his account of Bannockburn with the understanding that a king must first earn and then maintain his people's loyalty, and he prays that 'thai that cummynge ar / of [Bruce's] ofspring, maynteyme the land, / And hald the folk . . . As weill as in his tyme did he!' Perhaps the poet had cause to worry, for Robert II was an aging and weak man when he came to the throne, and the Scots barons were, as always, ready to challenge his authority – not least the Douglases, who were fighting what was virtually a private war with England only three years after *The Bruce* had immortalised the loyalty of their most famous ancestor – 'that in his tyme sa worthy was'. The 'suthfast story' of Scotland was as complicated and bloody as ever.

2

The fifteenth century: the flowering

THE national and cultural confidence of Scotland came to fruition in the fifteenth century, but it was neither easy nor peaceful. A succession of Stewart minorities aggravated the power balance between crown and barons and each king had to struggle to establish his rule. The Stewarts made some headway, and yet Douglas and Percy still ruled the Borders, while in the North-West the Clan Donald line claimed and held their own kingly rights as Lords of the Isles. Nevertheless, the royal right of succession gradually became established and accepted by almost all factions in Scotland. It was dearly bought: from James I to James IV no Stewart king lived beyond his prime and all of them died violently. Relationships with England were muted for the most part, but the capture of James I gave early notice that England still nursed hopes of suzerainty. Thus, it was English policy to encourage malcontents in Scotland and particularly to support the ambitions of the Lords of the Isles.

The Scottish connection with France was more cordial and from time to time the Auld Alliance was invoked to enlist Scotland's aid against her southern neighbour. But the end result was usually unhappy, especially when James IV died in an entirely reluctant and futile bid to oblige French expectations by marching on England. Many Scotsmen travelled abroad to enlist as mercenaries in the armies of Europe: some fought for Joan of Arc and two of the elite corps in Charles VII's army were Scottish companies. In her turn, France's contribution was more cultural than military, and Pedro de Ayala noted how many young Scotsmen spoke French and made regular visits to the continent. The Scots pattern of education was based on the curriculum at Paris, and the universities of St Andrew's (1412), Glasgow (1451) and Aberdeen (1495) were all founded along European lines. By the end of the century James IV had established at Aberdeen the first chair of medicine in Britain and had passed an act to require the sons of all barons and landowners to attend school from the age of eight for the study of Latin, law and the arts. In 1507 the same king established Walter Chepman and Andrew Myllar as printers in Edinburgh. They published poetry by Henryson and Dunbar as well as the *Legends of the Saints* and the *Aberdeen Breviary* – a major project by the redoubtable Bishop Elphinstone of Aberdeen, whose intention was to preserve the Scottish form of worship against English influence.

By the second half of the century, in a period of peace with England, the burghs had gained in influence and wealth. Growing numbers of towns began to govern themselves in the pursuit of trade and to defend themselves too. Burgesses were obliged to provide weapons and armour and to turn out for home-guard service if necessary. Royal burghs could send representatives to parliament, and their trading-interests were another factor which maintained cultural links with Europe from Danzig to Spain. These connections and especially the one with France flourished in the architecture of this time. Falkland Palace, Linlithgow, the Border abbeys and the castles at Borthwick and Craigmillar show the full influence of northern 'perpendicular Gothic'. The Renaissance in Scotland could not match the glories of Italy – the national temperament, like the climate, tended to ruggedness rather than grace – but under James IV there was an energy and an excitement in the air.

The second half of the fifteenth century was a time of literary richness – one of the greatest that Scotland has seen. The outstanding poets were Robert Henryson and William Dunbar. Henryson has the finer spirit, but the period is characterised by Dunbar, although his poems actually date from the early 1500s. For this reason he has been included in the present chapter and also because the death of James IV and the psychological impact of his defeat at Flodden in 1513 makes a natural, if sad, conclusion to a century of high literary achievement.

The surface gorgeousness of Dunbar's poems contrasts with

the wilder and more brutal extravagance of his imagination, and these, in turn, play against a darker and more singular spirit of pessimism. Dunbar speaks of the prodigality of court life and he always speaks of himself. Henryson, on the other hand, has a broader and less selfish nature, a mature compassion for the spiritual plight of man and a practical sympathy for the common folk. He commends the values of peace and good order, values that were making difficult but discernible progress during his lifetime, and his poems frequently comment on how the common people are at the mercy of the rapacious and the powerful. There is a sense in which we hear the people in Henryson: a voice that will come to be the characteristic utterance of Scottish literature when the formal and courtly delights of *The Kingis Quair* and 'The Goldyn Targe' have faded. The same voice can be heard in parts of 'Rauf Coilyear' and 'Colkelbie's Sow' and most especially in the rougher folk energy of 'Peblis to the Play' and 'Christis Kirk of the Green'. *The Bruce* and Blind Harry's *Wallace* can be seen as the larger expressions of this force, because they too stem from the sense that a nation is simply its people. Scotland had not yet achieved political stability, and schisms still existed between Lowlands and Highlands; but the prominence of such writers as Henryson and Dunbar, or the distinctively local colouring which was given to traditional European romance subjects, or the technical confidence and verve to be seen in aureate and ballad verse – all these point to what came to be known as the golden age of Scottish poetry.

Inspired by the national spirit of *The Bruce*, **Andrew of Wyntoun** (1350?–1420?), prior to the monastery of Loch Leven, ushered in the new century with a long history of Scotland written in dogged verse couplets. *The Orygynale Chronykil of Scotland* (1424) sets out to establish the heritage of the Scots from 1408 right back to Adam and Eve, and woe betide any English monarch who does not recognise such a proud descent! As a historian Wyntoun is more dependable nearer to his own times, and one of the last events recorded in his book tells how an eleven-year-old boy, newly crowned king of Scotland, fell into English hands.

James I (1394–1437)

Young James I was captured by the English in 1406 while being shipped to France – ironically, for his own safety. He spent the next eighteen years of his life as a political pawn in England, although no doubt his captivity was comfortable enough. He is said to have written *The Kingis Quair* (the King's Book) during the last years of his sojourn, and it seems likely that this ornate allegorical poem does, indeed, describe the circumstances under which he fell in love with his future wife, Joan of Beaufort. There is little reason to suppose, as some scholars have maintained, that James is not the author. Yet the poem was not really 'discovered' until the eighteenth century, and so it had little contemporary influence and James is not one of the poets mentioned in Dunbar's 'Lament for the Makaris'.

The Kingis Quair is an allegorical dream vision framed by the poet's imprisonment and his despair at a 'dedely life full of peyne and penance'. As one might expect from the circumstances, the style is lightly Scotticised and markedly influenced by English models. It uses a seven-line rime-royal stanza similar to that of *Troilus and Criseyde*, and the mixture of realistic description and allegorical abstraction is reminiscent of Lydgate's *Temple of Glas*. The poet sees a beautiful woman outside his window and, rather in the manner of Palamoun in 'The Knight's Tale', he immediately falls in love with her. That night in a dream he presents his case to Venus before an emblematic assembly of all those who have felt the pangs of love. He meditates on free will in the manner of Boethius's *De Consolatione Philosophiae*, but the poem gains most force from its physical descriptions and from the ironies inherent in its theme of love as a kind of captivity which offers escape from literal physical imprisonment. The bright images of birds and the garden of crystal waters and little fish convey the poet's sense of exhilaration, clarity and gratitude when he feels that his fortunes have turned. Although still incarcerated, he begins to feel free. By comparison, although the autobiographical element is openly admitted, his loved one remains a collection of rather abstract virtues. The poet's meditation on Fortune is especially poignant, for James had been hostage to that fickle wheel all his life and yet could win free only by submitting himself once more to her macabre influence. This time she smiles on him, but the king cannot help noticing that her wheel revolves over a hellish pit. In a delightfully original touch he has the goddess give him a tweak on the ear as they part, and this teasing nip wakes him from his dream and serves as a sardonic reminder of Fortune's incorrigible and fatal playfulness. Nevertheless, the poet is now free – at least in spirit – and he can even bless the castle walls that keep him, because they provided the stage for his conversion to love.

It was not long before the king secured his release from Windsor and married Joan Beaufort. By 1424 he was restored to his throne in Scotland, where he determined to reassert his authority. But Fortune's wheel turned again, thirteen years later, when a discontented baron planned his assassination, and the author of *The Kingis Quair* met his death hiding in the privy of the royal bedchambers at Perth.

James's poem introduced the century with an allegorical work in courtly style. The literature which followed was, for the most part, less formal, less in the mode of Chaucer and Lydgate and closer to a more everyday vision of Scottish life. It was once the fashion to define the poets of this century as 'Scottish Chaucerians', but properly speaking only James owes the implied debt. The rest undoubtedly acknowledge Chaucer's greatness, but they draw as much from European and native influences as they do from the old master in England. At least three other poems have been ascribed to James I. 'Good Counsel' is a brief and sententious piece of advice to 'exil al vice and folow trewth alway', modelled after Chaucer's ballad of the same name, and there are few problems in accepting it as the king's work. It is not so, however, with 'Peblis to the Play' and 'Christis Kirk of the Green', and recent critical opinion favours a now unknown author for these pieces, from a time closer to the end of the fifteenth century.

Sir Richard Holland (fl. 1450)

If *The Kingis Quair* operates in the tradition of the dream vision and has moments reminiscent of 'The Knight's Tale', then Sir Richard Holland's *The Buke of the Howlat* (Book of the Owl) is a beast allegory after the fashion of Chaucer's *Parlement of Foules*. Holland's long poem was dedicated to Elizabeth Dunbar, wife to Archibald Douglas, Earl of Moray, and must have been written around 1450 to celebrate this powerful family and its history. The *Howlat* is written in the alliterative stanza used for 'Rauf Coilyear', *Golagros and Gawane* and the English *Awntyrs of Arthure*, but it is an allegory and an entertaining satire rather than a romance tale like the others. It is the first substantial poem of what was to become a Scottish revival of the use of alliteration in verse.

Holland makes innumerable connections between the world of birds and the pomp and circumstance of papal and regal power. Thus the peacock is the pope of birds and the swallow is his herald, while cranes (cardinals), swans (bishops) and common sea-birds (monks) throng his holiness's court. In similar fashion the birds of prey represent temporal power, with the eagle as emperor and gerfalcons, goshawks and sparrowhawks as the dukes, captains and knights of his retinue. In the middle of the poem, while describing the heraldry at the eagle's court, the poet takes some twenty stanzas to recite the arms and the prowess of the Douglas family, starting with the tale of Bruce's heart.

This elaborate poem has a simple moral about the dangers of pride (Blind Harry's *Wallace* refers to it, to make a timely warning to Sir William), for the allegory is set in motion by the owl's desire to be more beautiful. On a traditional May morning, the poet overhears the howlat's complaint against Dame Nature, and he follows its course from the papal congregation of birds to the assembled might of the emperor's court, where a feast, with juggling and recitations, is being held. Finally, the company prays for Dame Nature to appear, and she orders each bird to give one of its feathers to the ugly howlat. But, as soon as he is arrayed in finery, the owl becomes insufferably proud ('pomposs, impertinat, and reprovable') and the other birds waste no time in asking Dame Nature to return him to his former state – 'hidowis of hair and of hyde'. This accomplished, they all fly off, leaving the howlat, and the poet, to contemplate a moral directed at the rich and powerful:

> Now mark yow mirour be me, all maner of man,
> Ye princis, prentis of pryde for penneis and prowe   images; pennies;
> That pullis the pure ay,   exploit [profit
> Ye sall syng as I say,   [the poor
> All your welth will away,
> Thus I warn yow . . . .

The charm of *The Buke of the Howlat* lies in the way it miniaturises human society and dresses it in feathers, for neither the moral nor the celebration of the Douglases survives the test of time. Thus the Rook appears at the banquet as a Gaelic bard speaking gibberish, reciting genealogies, and demanding more food, all at the same time. It is a passage that Dunbar, with his prejudice against 'the ersche' tongue, would certainly have enjoyed:

	[shout and
Sa come the Ruke with a rerd and a rane roch,	a rough rann
A bard out of Irland with 'Banachadee'.	'blessing of God'
Said: 'Gluntow guk dynyd dach hala mischy doch;	('Gaelic' gibberish)
Raike hir a rug of the rost, or scho sall ryme the.	Reach me a chunk
Mich macmory ach mach mometir moch loch;	of the roast or I'll
Set hir dovne, gif hir drink; quhat Dele alis the?'	satirise you (he
O Deremyne, O Donnall, O Dochardy droch;	refers to himself as
Thir ar his Irland kingis of the Irischerye:	'she')
O Knewlyn, O Conochor, O Gregre Makgrane;	
The Schenachy, the Clarschach,	Gaelic bard; harp
The Ben schene, the Ballach,	
The Crekery, the Corach,	
Scho kennis thaim ilkane.	(I) know each one
	[of them

The lapwing and the cuckoo, a pair of clowns, eventually drive off the harsh-voiced rook, but not before he has said his piece: 'Mony lesingis [lies] he maid; wald let for no man / To spek quhill [while] he spokin had, sparit no thingis'.

Although it has a broader and more humorous aspect, the *Howlat*, like *The Kingis Quair*, belongs to the world of formal literary genres. When Henryson uses animals in his versions of Aesop's fables, they are more fully and more humanely characterised and their milieu is recognisably the place of everyday life and common experience, rather than a theatre of courts, castles and enclosed gardens.

Robert Henryson (1425?–1505?)

We know very little about Robert Henryson. If we believe Dunbar's 'Lament for the Makaris' then death must have had his way with the elder poet sometime before 1508. The honorific 'master' says that he was a university man and a graduate, perhaps of an institution in Europe. Among others, the title-page of the Bassandyne printing of *The Morall Fabillis* (done in 1571) refers to the author as a schoolmaster in Dunfermline. There is also evidence to suggest that he trained in law and operated as a notary public, and he does use legal terms and procedures in his poems. Henryson's fame rests on his fables and on *The Testament of Cresseid* – an extraordinary sequel to Chaucer's *Troilus and Criseyde*. Modern readers have come to value him highly and many would place his poetic achievement as second only to Chaucer, whom he acknowledged himself as the 'flower' of poets. Yet, although he shares something of the Englishman's compassion and sweet humour, Henryson has a terseness and sometimes a grimness of outlook that belongs to a harsher northern clime. Dunbar shows this temperament even more clearly and it is worth pointing out that it seems to be a part of the national psyche long before John Knox and Calvinism arrived to give it a doctrinal dimension.

A poem such as 'The Bludy Serk' suggests that the oral tradition was well established in the Scots canon, and this supernatural tale of how a doomed knight rescues a maiden from a giant shows that Henryson could easily match the laconic edge of the ballad style, even if he does add a literary moral which explains that it is an allegory of Christ and man's soul. In similar fashion the poet takes the old French *pastourelle* genre and, with a light touch, creates the rustic dialogue of 'Robene and Makyne', where canny Robene is concerned more with the welfare of his sheep than with Makyne's passion for him. (When he finally does warm to the idea, she has changed her mind.) Thus Henryson almost always works from established models and yet he so consistently transforms and vivifies his material that it seems as though Aesop's fables were always set in Scottish fields, or as though Troy were truly somewhere near Dunfermline. The poet's talent for realistic detail is expressed in succinct and unpretentious utterance – as though we were listening to the man himself speaking. These particular strengths in Henryson and later poets have done much to define the Scottish literary tradition even to the present day.

It is in his commitment to the human and the natural world that Henryson's Catholic faith and his wry and gentle imagination come together. 'Nane suld presume be ressoun

naturall / To seirche the secreitis off the Trinitie', he writes
in 'The Preiching of the Swallow': 'Yit nevertheles we may haif
knawlegeing / Off God Almychtie be his creatouris / That he is
gude, fair, wyis and bening.' Thus the separation of the
physical from the spiritual seems artificial to Henryson, for in
his view the natural world embodies the spirit quite plainly.
When winter comes it is the effect on the animals which the poet
visualises in his alliterated lines:

Than flouris fair faidit with froist man fall,	must
And birdis blyith changit thair noitis sweit	
In styll murning, neir slane with snaw and sleit.	
Thir dalis deip with dubbis drounit is,	dales; mud
Baith hill and holt heillit with frostis hair;	woods; hoar frosts
All wyld beistis than ffrom the bentis bair	heaths
Drawis ffor dreid unto thair dennis deip,	
Coucheand ffor cauld in coifis thame to keip.	coves/hollows

With the arrival of spring, man's work in the fields is celebrated
until the land, the beasts upon it and the labouring folk are all
equally present in the poet's eye and in the mind of God:

Sum makand dyke, and sum the pleuch can wynd,	plough
Sum sawand seidis fast ffrome place to place,	
The Harrowis hoppand in the saweris trace:	
It wes grit Joy to him that luifit corne,	
To se thame laubour, baith at evin and morne.	

'The Preiching of the Swallow' is one of thirteen poems in
'Eloquent and Ornate Scottish Meter' later compiled as *The
Morall Fabillis of Esope the Phrygian* (most probably written
around the 1460s), in which Henryson retells Aesop and other
animal tales from popular tradition. He uses rime royal
throughout – a seven-line stanza rhyming *ababbcc* with five
stresses in each line – and his sense of humour, whether gently
mocking, openly satirical or resolutely stern, is never absent. In
'The Taill How the Foxe Maid his Confessioun to Freir Wolf
Waitskaith', the fox wants to salve his conscience and so he
approaches Friar Wolf with these pious observations:

'Ye ar Mirrour, lanterne, and sicker way,	certain
Suld gyde sic sempill folk as me to grace.	
Your bair feit, and your Russet Coull off gray,	

> Your lene cheik, your paill pietious face.
> Schawis to me your perfite haliness.'

The wolf does seem surprisingly well versed in scriptural niceties, and for penance he forbids the fox to eat any meat. Temptation overcomes the sinner, however, and to escape the prohibition he catches a kid and 'christens' it a salmon by drowning it in the sea – 'Ga doun, Schir Kid, cum up Schir Salmond agane!' Stuffed with young goat the wily Tod lies dead to the world musing idly in the sun that it only needs an arrow-shaft sticking out of his belly to complete the picture. Whereupon the goatherd comes along and obliges him. The fox has just enough time to give us his last words: 'allace and wellaway! ... Me think na man may speik ane word in play / Bot now on dayis in ernist it is tane.' The moral of the tale is to beware the sudden stroke of death, lest it catch you unaware, but Henryson's wit gives it a crazier twist.

Many critics have commented on the division between the humorous realism of the fables and the formal virtues which are extolled in the concluding morals. It is tempting to enjoy the fable and to dismiss the moral, but it must be stressed that both elements are equally central to Henryson's vision. The *moralitas* may not always convince, but sometimes it can work with striking subtlety to give a broader, rather than a narrower account of the poem's meaning. In 'The Taill of the Cok and the Jasp', for example, *moralitas* and fable produce a kind of stalemate to trap the reader in real moral issues, quite different from simple maxims. A cock finds a precious jewel in the midden, but since he cannot eat it he leaves it there and goes his way:

> Thow hes na corne, and thairof haif I neid,
> Thy cullour dois bot confort to the sicht,
> And that is not aneuch my wame to feid.   enough; belly

In the fable the cock is a realist, yet the moral tells us he is a fool who prizes only his own ignorance, because the jewel symbolises knowledge and prudence – the only really enduring wealth – without which no one 'can Governe ane Realme, Cietie, or hous'. Alas, says the poet, the jewel is lost these days, still lying somewhere on a dunghill of disregard. While this allegory makes sense in its own terms, it does not mesh with the fable. The cock is not a swine who despises pearls because he knows only swill. On the contrary, he is aware of the Jasp's beauty and he recognises that it should be 'Exaltit in worschip and in grit honour' and set, perhaps, in a king's crown: 'Rise, gentill Jasp, of all stanes the flour, / Out of this midding, and pas quhar thow suld be'. But for himself, he observes that 'houngrie men may not leve on lukis'.

The reader is entirely convinced by this level-headed character and can scarcely blame him for leaving the stone, even if it does symbolise 'knowledge'. In fact, there need not be a contradiction between the two elements, and here again Henryson is using the moral to make his case more subtle. The final message which emerges from 'The Cok and the Jasp' is that knowledge and prudence belong in the first place with the king, and he must not expect too much of the common man, who has to struggle to find dry bread for his belly. If prudence is missing at court, why should it be valued in the farmyard? Moral and tale should not, therefore, be separated, for it is only through their conjunction that we reach the fullest insight into the frailties and contradictions of human existence.

In all aspects of his work Henryson's sympathies lie with the common folk. In ''The Taill of the Lyoun and the Mous' the king of the beasts spares an importunate mouse, but at a later date it is the tiny mouse and her relatives – the commoners – who gnaw through the nets to let the trapped lion escape. The *moralitas* extols mercy and vigilance in the great, not just as an abstract virtue, but as a matter of political prudence too, because 'Oftymis is sene' how 'ane man of small degre' can have his quittance of a nobleman. The message is clear: the mice may be small, 'wantoun' and 'unwyse', but they would have left the lion to die had he treated them too harshly at their first encounter: 'Bot King and Lord may weill wit quhat I mene'. The reader, too, will remember that the Declaration of Arbroath warned Robert Bruce that his subjects reserved the right to depose him if he betrayed their interests.

'The Wolf and the Lamb' makes the poet's position even more clear. The moral compares the lamb to the poor people and the wolf to those in power who pervert the laws to suit their own ends, particularly those feudal superiors who practice extortion on tenant farmers. Henryson provides details of how this is usually done and cries out at the plain injustice of a social and agricultural system which has the tenant labouring all day only to leave him 'lytill gude to drink or eit, / With his menye at evin quhen he cummis hame'. The abuse of power through the law is directly satirised in 'The Taill of the Scheip and the Doig' in which the poet observes all the technical niceties of legal procedure and places them in the mouths of a wolf as sheriff, a carrion-crow as beadle, a raven as coroner, a fox as clerk and a hawk as advocate. Little wonder, before such a court, that the sheep has to forfeit his fleece. This vivid and comic attack on the vested interests of authority does not hesitate to spell out its links with the human world.

The speech of the country sister in 'The Uponlandis Mous and the Burges Mous' is a model of native canny brevity, as when she is faced with the delicate titbits of her town sister's table and enquires

> '. . . how lang will this lest?'
> 'For evermair, I wait, and langer to.'   know/expect
> 'Giff it be swa, ye ar at eis' (quod scho).   If it be so

Henryson shares her sense of caution as well as a countryman's taste for understatement, and he reminds us, with a straight face, of the part played by Fortune in the affairs of mice – 'Eftir joye oftymes cummis cair' – and then, when the steward discovers the two creatures at their feast in the cupboard, the poet pauses at just the most dramatic moment to comment dryly, 'Thay taryit not to wesche, as I suppose'. The fable's intimate expertise is entirely convincing in the accents of the country mouse – spokesperson for 'blyithnes in hart with small possessioun' – as she cries to her more sophisticated sister,

> 'I had lever thir fourty dayis fast,   rather
> With watter caill, and to gnaw benis or peis,   cold water
> Than all your feist in this dreid and diseis.'

And with this she returns to her own humble home – undoubtedly situated somewhere in the 'kingdom of Fife'.

The same voice gives unique colouring to Henryson's tale of 'Schir Chantecleir and the Foxe'. In 'The Nonne Preestes Tale' Chaucer's narrative style creates a brilliantly extended parody of rhetorical techniques and chivalric virtues, but the Scots poet's version retains the swift colloquial pace of the other fables. The code of *amour courtois* is exploded simply by reporting what the hens say about their fallen lover. At first, Pertok strikes a high-flown note by lamenting 'our dayis darling / Our nichtingall', but Sprutok – a more practical lady – reminds her that 'als gude lufe cummis as gais', and resolves to 'Chant this sang, "wes never wedow sa gay!" ' As soon as Pertok is relieved of the burden of decorum, she too admits that the cock could not satisfy her and resolves to get within the week a fellow who 'suld better claw oure breik'. 'Schir Chantecleir' has been dismissed in three swift stanzas, and the hens' earthy honesty is a more telling judgement on his vanity than the main plot with the fox. Henryson's fables are full of such delights, demonstrating his ability to handle traditional materials as though the stories had never been told before.

Orpheus and Eurydice leaves the warmer world of the fables to make a grim Christian allegory out of that ancient myth, for the poet sees Orpheus's human and fleshly impatience as all too inevitable, despite his inheritance in the arts of celestial harmony and control. Henryson's most famous poem, about Cresseid's downfall, is equally unrelenting, although it shows a stern care too.

The earliest printed version of *The Testament of Cresseid* was added to Chaucer's *Troilus and Criseyde* in a 1532 edition of the English poet's works. While Henryson's poem (also written in rime royal) is, indeed, a sequel to the longer tale, it demonstrates a very different sensibility. Cresseid's failing is clear-cut – she is faithless and her sin is to blaspheme against Venus and Cupid, the fleshly deities to whom she has given her life. She has reason to be bitter in Henryson's version, for, having betrayed Troilus in favour of Diomede, she is herself discarded by her new lover. The Scots poet's view of the affair is sympathetic but clear-eyed and his spare introduction to her plight sets the mood for the whole poem:

> Quhen Diomeid had all his appetyte,
> And mair, fulfillit of this fair Ladie,
> Upon ane uther he set his haill delyte.

Henryson supplements the terse force of that phrase 'and mair' by noting that some men say that Cresseid became a common

prostitute. She pays dearly for this and for her repudiation of
Venus when the planets visit her in a dream trial, and Saturn
and the Moon afflict her with leprosy. Cresseid's complaint is
a passionate lament for the evanescence of wordly beauty and a
warning about the fickleness of Fortune.

'Nocht is your fairnes bot ane faiding flour,	Nothing
Nocht is your famous laud and hie honour	
Bot wind Inflat in uther mennis eiris.	ears
Your roising reid to rotting sall retour:	rosey skin; return
Exampill mak of me in your Memour!	

The medieval *ubi sunt* theme is evoked with a bitter power.
Cresseid's good looks have become abominable and her very
eyesight has been dimmed by disease, but Henryson's relentless and lucid fatalism makes her pay still more. Troilus passes
one day and drops some alms in her leper's cup. He does not
recognise her in her present state, but the pathetic figure
somehow evokes memories of his erstwhile lover and prompts
his charity. The moment is psychologically convincing. When
Cresseid is told who her benefactor was, she finally accepts
responsibility for her own failed honour, commends herself to
chaste Diana and dies: 'O fals Cresseid and trew Knicht
Troilus . . . Nane but my self as now I will accuse.' When he
hears of her fate, Troilus erects a tomb over her grave.

The bare bones of the plot can give only a hint of the
relentless concentration invested in the poem. It has the speed
and the grim concision of a ballad, conveying beauty, terror
and pity with masterly understatement. From the very start the
Testament is unmistakably the product of a northern sensibility.
Thus the opening lines are set in springtime – a traditional
beginning to a tale of love – but this fresh season has been
symbolically countered by harsh and inclement Scottish
weather:

Ane doolie sessoun to ane cairful dyte	A sad season to a
Suld correspond, and be equivalent.	[sorrowful tale
Richt sa it was quhen I began to wryte	
This tragedie, the wedder richt fervent,	
Quhen Aries, in middis of the Lent,	
Schouris of haill can fra the north discend,	
That scantlie fra the cauld I micht defend.	

The poet himself wants to honour the star of Venus that night, hoping that 'My faidit hart of lufe scho wald mak grene', but the cold air drives him indoors to the fire. This wryly informal and domestic note allows Henryson to express his pity for Cresseid, and yet it never loses sight of the fact that she is a pagan character in a book with her fate already long established and inescapable.

I mend the fyre and beikit me about,	wrapped
Than tuik ane drink my spreitis to comfort,	
And armit me weill fra the cauld thairout:	
To cut the winter nicht and mak it schort,	
I tuik ane Quair, and left all uther sport,	book
Written be worthie Chaucer glorious,	
Of fair Cresseid, and worthie Troylus.	

Of his distres me neidis nocht reheirs,
For worthie Chauceir in the samin buik
In gudelie termis and in Joly veirs
Compylit hes his cairis, quha will luik.
To brek my sleip ane uther quair I tuik,
In quihilk I fand the fatall destenie
Of fair Cresseid, that endit wretchitlie

Quha wait gif all that Chauceir wrait was trew?	Who knows if

Henryson sustains his objectivity by admitting that parts of the tale are not clear to him; thus Cresseid's pain is distanced from us and yet, paradoxically, the method actually increases the emotional effect: 'Gif scho in hart was wa [sad] eneuch, God wait!'; and then: '*Sum said* he maid ane Tomb of Merbell gray / And wrait her name. . . .' When Calchas sees his daughter's leprosy for the first time his lament is interrupted by the poet's curt comment, 'Thus was thair cair aneuch betwix thame twane'. The same succinct force can be found on Cresseid's lips, too, when she bewails the passing of her old life and realises her fate:

And for they Bed tak now ane bunche of stro,	
For waillit Wyne, and Meitis thou had tho,	choice
Tak mowlit Breid, Peirrie and Ceder sour:	mouldy
Bot cop and Clapper, now is all ago.	Begging cup and [leper's clapper

Chaucer's version of the tale involves itself brilliantly and at length with the sophisticated moods and trials of courtly love; but when Henryson has Troilus reflect on the affair he sums it up with a stunning simplicity: 'Siching [sighing] full sadlie, said, "I can no moir,/Scho was untrew, and wo is me thairfoir." ' Such brevity is only the mask of feeling and, indeed, there is a moving tenderness in how the characters treat one another, as when Calchas welcomes his fallen daughter, or when Troilus gives alms, or in how Henryson himself describes the leper folk and how they receive Cresseid with a loving and practical concern:

'Sen thy weiping dowbillis bot thy wo,	Since; doubles
I counsail the mak vertew of ane neid.	
To leir to clap thy Clapper to and fro,	learn
And leve eftir the law of lipper leid.'	leper people

The poet's narrative pace can be fast or lingering to equal effect, as when Cresseid, newly afflicted with her disease, is summoned to dinner by a serving-boy. She notices his good looks.

Quod scho: 'Fair Chyld ga to my Father deir,
And pray him come to speak with me anone'.
And sa he did, and said: 'Douchter quhat cheir?'

At other times the speed of the verse is greatly reduced, as the poet draws on the older alliterative-verse tradition and adds his talent for domestic realism in order to convey the full terror of Saturn's presence:

His face fronsit, his lyre was lyke the Leid.	frozen; skin; lead
His teith chatterit, and cheverit with the Chin,	
His ene drowpit, how sonkin in his heid,	
Out of his Nois the Meldrop fast can rin,	drips
With lippas bla and cheikis leine and thin.	blue

'Robene and Makyne', 'The Bludy Serk' and the *Morall Fabillis* have the same mastery of pace and ballad-like concision, but the humane irony of Henryson's always direct and colloquial presence reach their highest achievement in *The Testament* and have given us some of the finest passages in European literature.

> Sum said he maid ane Tomb of Merbell gray,
> And wrait hir name and superscriptioun,
> And laid it on hir grave quhair that scho lay,
> In goldin Letteris, conteining this ressoun:
> 'Lo, fair Ladyis, Crisseid, of Troyis toun,
> Sumtyme countit the flour of Womanheid,
> Under this stane lait Lipper lyis deid.'

Henryson has the final word and the last line of the poem vibrates with his strong and tenderly fatalistic charity: 'Sen scho is deid, I speik of hir no moir.'

Blind Harry (1450–93)

If Barbour's *Bruce* reads like a historical chronicle and a consideration of patriotism written by a priest of the Church, then Blind Harry's *Wallace* is a popular thriller in which the reader is caught up by the narrative to ask 'what happens next' through twelve books of verse. The *Wallace* is quite unlike *Golagros and Gawane* and other knightly romances of its time – for in place of tales of chivalry it offers a crude but forceful character study of its hero, full of circumstantial details and a heightened and bloody realism. *The Actes and Deidis of the Illustre and Vallyeant Campioun Schir William Wallace* must have been written around 1477 – 170 years after the events it describes – and it is instructive to compare it with the nearly contemporary *Morte d'Arthur*. Malory's great prose work looks back to an imagined world of knights and ladies, and even as he describes the break-up of the Round Table he enshrines the values of chivalry and purity symbolised by the quest for the Holy Grail. Harry's *Wallace* has no such spiritual dimension and little time for the melancholy nobility of Malory's conclusion. On the contrary, the Scotsman's many descriptions of split brains and arms hewn away re-create the details of combat as if from a footsoldier's point of view. For this reason the poem is much closer to the truth of warfare and the cruelty of the thirteenth, or indeed the fifteenth century. It is also closer to what we might assume to be the popular taste (then as now) for a succession of gory effects.

We have few details about the author. He seems to have been a professional poet and it is known that on various occasions he appeared at court and received money from James IV. He is mentioned in the 'Lament for the Makaris' and probably died about 1492; and, although he is traditionally referred to as 'Blind Harry', it is not certain that he was born blind. At least one scholar has argued that the poet's grasp of military action and his descriptions of the weather and the lie of the landscape suggest that he lost his sight late in life. Harry describes himself as unlearned – 'a burell man' – and late-eighteenth-century critics were keen to support him in the role of rustic Homer – a blind peasant bard. This underestimates the skills available within the oral tradition, nor does it accord with the plain and forceful versifying in Harry's heroic couplets, perhaps the earliest use of this measure in Scotland.

However composed, the *Wallace* became one of the nation's most popular books and, until Burns came on the scene, the most often reprinted. Indeed, the poem virtually 'invented' the heroic figure of William Wallace as it is known today, for, although Harry claimed to be following a Latin original written by Wallace's chaplain, it seems as likely that he compiled the work himself from surviving tales, folk sources and his own imagination. His purpose was unashamedly nationalistic and anti-English. At a time when James III was attempting to make peace with this southern neighbours, Harry speaks for perpetual opposition, for keeping faith with France and for warlike virtues in a leader. Wallace would rather kill Englishmen than ransom them, and this is entirely in keeping with the facts of battle as they have always been for the mere troops. Indeed, this lack of knightly graces probably established him even more securely as a fully fledged folk hero.

The poem is long and in places merely tedious, but gradually a genuinely impressive picture emerges of a martyr swordfighter who will rescue Scotland on three different occasions before going – treacherously betrayed – to his own death. Robert Burns testified to the power of this figure to 'pour a Scottish prejudice' in his veins even in William Hamilton's shortened paraphrased version of the original. From the very start we gain a sense of Harry's Wallace as a fated person, rather like one of Marlowe's granitic heroes. Thus the young man has the misfortune to be bullied by a succession of arrogant (and ill-advised) Englishmen, as when he is fishing peacefully by a river and gets into an argument with five of Percy's men who demand his catch for their lord. The teenage Wallace, armed only with a net on a pole and accompanied by a boy, is prepared to give them some but adds (too familiarly for the Englishmen), 'Gud frend, leiff part and tak nocht all away.' The retainer insists on having the lot and the vivid dialogue takes a more deadly turn:

'We serf a lord. Thir fische sall till him gang'.	
Wallace ansuerd, said, 'Thow art in the wrang.'	
'Quham dowis thow, Scot? In faith thow servis a	Whom do you
blaw.'	[address as 'thou'
Till him he ran and out a swerd can draw.	
Willyham was wa he had na wapynnis thar.	
Bot the poutstaff the quhilk in hand he bar.	netpole
Wallas with it fast on the cheik him tuk	
Wyth so gud will quhill of his feit he schuk.	
The suerd flaw fra him a fut breid on the land.	
Wallas was glaid and hynt it sone in hand,	glad and took it
And with the swerd ane awkwart straik him gawe,	
Wndyr the hat his crage in sondir drawe.	under; neck
Be that the layff lychtyt about Wallas.	the rest set about
He had no helpe only bot goddis grace.	

(i, 397–410)

When two English survivors escape to tell Percy of the fight, the lord laughs at their discomfiture and refuses to pursue the Scot further. All the same, the hero flees the neighbourhood and Harry comments that he never left his sword behind again.

The poem's short sentences, terse dialogue and detailed violence make it particularly active and dramatic. Although larger than life as a warrior, Wallace is not without some human qualities. He has a sense of humour (predictably grim) and his sufferings in battle and in sickness allow us to sympathise with him when his destiny and his own relentless will call him back to the practice of death after an all-too-brief spell of married happiness. At this point, the narrative takes a more tender and musical turn as it slips into ballat royal, an eight-line French stanza-form:

Now leiff thi myrth, now leiff thi haill plesance,	leave
Now leiff this blis, now leiff thi childis age,	
Now leiff thi youth, now folow thi hard chance,	
Now leiff thi lust, now leiff this mariage.	
Now leiff thi luff, for thow sall los a gage	lose a pledge
Quhilk neuir in erd sall be redemyt agayne.	

Folow fortoun and all hir fers outrage.   fortune
Go leiff in wer, go leiff in cruell payne,   live
(VI, 81–8)

The tale soon returns to heroic couplets, however, as Wallace's wife is killed and he dedicates himself to further slaughter with a righteous and savage efficiency. If the tale dwells too much on killing Englishmen and general mayhem, it draws a veil over the manner of its hero's actual death, for William Wallace was hanged, cut down while still alive and disembowelled before his own eyes. Wallace was a hero and a martyr to his contemporaries, but Blind Harry's poem made him a legend, until even William Wordsworth intones the name as though it were talisman for a later revolution, synonymous with freedom itself:

How Wallace fought for Scotland; left the name
Of Wallace to be found, like a wild flower,
All over his dear Country; left the deeds
Of Wallace, like a family of Ghosts,
To people the steep rocks and river banks,
Her natural sanctuaries, with a local soul
Of independence and stern liberty.
(*The Prelude*, I, 213–19)

'Anonymous' poets

If we lack details of Blind Harry, there are poems from the latter half of the fifteenth century whose authors cannot now be traced at all. *The Knightly Tale of Golagros and Gawane* might have been written by Clerk of Tranent, cited in Dunbar's 'Lament' as the man who 'maid the Anteris of Gawane', but we cannot be sure. The poem is most likely contemporary with the *Wallace* but, quite unlike Harry's work, it is a courtly fiction which belongs to the fabled past with a plot of twelfth-century French origins in *Le Conte du Graal*. The climax involves a battle between rival champions Gawaine and Golagros. To save his opponent's face, and because he cannot bear to kill him outright, Gawaine pretends to lose the match. In the light of his gentlemanly discretion the two knights and their factions are soon reconciled. The poem uses the same thirteen-line stanza-form as *The Buke of the Howlat* – a favourite for alliterative romances. The same measure appears in *Rauf Coilyear*, and other similarities between the two romances suggest that the poet of *Rauf* was at least familiar with the Gawain piece.

Rauf Coilyear goes back to the age of chivalry as well, but it gains a satirical or at least a humorous angle by making its short-tempered hero a charcoal-burner (collier) by trade. Rauf becomes involved with Charlemagne when the king gets lost in a storm while out hunting. The charcoal-burner offers shelter to the stranger but loses his temper with his anonymous guest when the latter's royal manners and polite hesitations make him slow to do his host's bidding. The great king receives buffets and a lecture on manners:

> 'Thow suld be courtes of kynd, and ane cunnand courteir.
>   Thocht that I simpill be,
>   Do as I bid the,
>   The hous is myne pardie,
>   And all that is heir.'

The host may be 'thrawin' but his table is generous with much game, taken, he explains, from the king's forest. Charles says he is one Wymond of the queen's wardrobe and they part the next day with an agreement that Rauf will be paid to deliver a load of coal to the court on Christmas Day. The fiery collier is somewhat abashed when he discovers the true identity of his guest, but Charles gives him armour, a retinue and makes him a knight. All the same, he must still win his spurs by combat and this leads to further complications, but the tale ends happily and Rauf is made Marshal of France.

The two parts of Rauf Coilyear's tale almost certainly come from French sources, although stories of incognito kings were common in England, too; but the setting, the weather and the bloody-minded independence of the hero have all been given a distinctively Scottish colouring. What begins as a rather pointed comment on manners, chivalry and the common man ends as an unlikely romance where everyone is rewarded with high office. Nevertheless, we appreciate the peppery Rauf of the earlier passages who proves with his fists the old French proverb that 'Charbonnier est maître chez soi' and who might have been a model for the medieval understanding that to be a Scot was to have *piper in naso*, pepper in your nose.

The world of romance joins with the supernatural in poems such as 'King Berdok', 'The Gyre-Carling' and 'Lord Fergus'

Ghost'. These pieces have an odd flavour, for they read less like magic and more like tall tales, and so they forfeit the sense of mystery and terror that the best of the great ballads have, not to mention that vital intimation of other planes of being. On the other hand, they take a matter-of-fact approach to the everyday and couple it with an unusual sense of the instability of the physical world. It is a grotesque and striking combination. Hence Berdok, king of Babylon, lives in a cabbage-stalk in summer while a cockle-shell keeps him warm in winter, because, as the unknown author patiently explains, 'Kingis usit nocht to weir clayis in tha dayis.' The burlesque is grosser but the dislocating effect is the same in 'The Gyre-Carling', which, among other unlikely things, explains that the distinctive conical shape of the hill known as Berwick Law was produced by a witch who expelled it as a turd in her mirth.

While 'The Gyre-Carling' is outlandish, the scatological anti-Gaelic humour of 'How the First Helandman, of God was Maid', is closer to the realities of social and racial prejudice. (The poem is sometimes attributed to Montgomerie but is most likely to be an earlier production.) The author's position is clear from the start, for the title notes that the hero was made 'of ane horss turd, in Argylle, as is said', and no sooner is he created than he steals God's gully-knife and promises that, for as long as he can get gear thus, he will never work. The whole outrageous slander is expressed in the most good-humoured way, evincing a sturdy Scottish familiarity with the supreme being and his saints:

> God and Sanct Petir was gangand be the way,
> Heiche up in Ardgyle, quhair thair gait lay.
> Sanct Petir said to God in a sport word,
> 'Can ye nocht mak a Helandman of this horss turd?'
> God turned owre the horss turd with his pykit staff,
> And up start a Helandman blak as ony draff.   dregs
> Quod God to the Helandman 'Quhair wilt thow now?'
> 'I will down in the Lawland, Lord, and thair steill a kow.'

The economic foundations for Lowland prejudice could not be more succinctly put.

The failings of the priesthood provided equally popular material for broad comedy in verse, and 'The Freiris of Berwick' is sometimes attributed to Dunbar, although it lacks technical incisiveness and his acerbic spirit. This lively piece tells how two friars outwit the adulterous wife of an innkeeper and enjoy a luxurious meal at her expense. 'Colkelbie's Sow' also mixes the domestic, and the far-fetched (with a rather ponderous sense of humour), by playing on the disparity between its subject and a plot loosely based on the biblical parable of the talents, complete with *sententiae*, a 'prohemium' and apologies for its 'mokking meteris and mad matere'. Its three parts, in rather anglicised Scots, tell what became of the three pennies that Colkelbie got when he sold his pig. The author claims that he learned these tales and their moral implications from his toothless great-grandmother who had many such stories fresh in her mind. The poem's loose structure and its succession of ingenious events are, indeed, very reminiscent of oral fireside tales, although its use of 'literary' apparatus suggests a self-conscious and bookish side to the narrator as well.

A vivid and hilarious sense of country life characterises 'Peblis to the Play' and 'Christis Kirk of the Green', the best of the anonymous poems of this period. They have been ascribed to James I, but a later author is much more likely. Both poems give a light-hearted account of the antics that took place on two holiday occasions. 'Peblis' happens at Beltane (the old Scots fire festival that ushers in the summer), and the description of the 'play' – of the wooing and dancing and drinking and fighting – is undoubtedly true to the life and spirit of that festival. 'Christis Kirk' sets out to cap even Peebles's distinction, with extravagant behaviour described at a local fair-day:

> Was never in Scotland heard nor seen
>   Sic dauncing nor deray,   disturbance
> Neither at Falkland on the green,
>   Nor Peblis at the play
> As was of wooeris, as I ween,   suitors
>   At Christ Kirk on ane day:
> There come our kitties washen clean
>   In their new kirtillis of grey,
>   Full gay,
> At Christis Kirk of the green.

Both poems are remarkable for their rollicking rhythms, and this pattern has been much copied, with variations, in later

Scots verse. The stanzas have ten lines each, the first eight of which rhyme *abababab* on alternate iambic tetrameter and trimeter. This provides a 'headlong' pace further emphasised by alliteration and the recurrence of the rhyme. Then there comes a 'bob-wheel' line of only two syllables to be clinched by a six-syllable refrain which is the title of the piece repeated at this point throughout the poem. The 'bob' line gives a most distinctive catch at the end of each stanza before precipitating the reader on to the next. This effect is especially well suited to recitation or singing and it does much to enhance the broad wit of the poems and to further their irresistible comic progress.

Fergusson and Burns learned much from these patterns and both use nine-line versions of them (without the 'bob') for their own accounts of the people at play: Fergusson in 'Hallow-Fair' and 'Leith Races' and Burns in 'The Ordination' and 'The Holy Fair'. What the later poets gain in satirical and social comment, their unknown predecessor makes up for with a boisterousness that recalls a Flemish Kermesse by Breughel full of fierce dancing, willing women, brawling men and some pretty wild play with bows and arrows:

A yaip young man that stude him neist	keen
Loused off a shot with ire;	
He ettled the bern in at the breist,	aimed at the man's breast
The bolt flew owre the byre;	over the cowshed
And cryit Fy! he had slain a priest	
A mile beyond ane mire;	
Than bow and bag fra him he kest,	cast
And fled as fierce as fire	
Off flint,	
At Christis Kirk of the green.	

'Symmie and his Bruder' is yet another of those popular verses about merry friars – notable for its use of the 'Christis Kirk' stanza – but 'The Thrie Tailes of the Thrie Priests of Peblis' is a longer and more conscientious affair, probably dating from the 1480s and commenting on the social ills and political failings in the reign of James III. It is a modest satire mainly concerned with telling its tales – and stories within the stories – as recounted by three priests after a particularly satisfying and worldly supper. Its cheerful vernacular uses homely couplets based on a pentameter line, and the tales, borrowed from older models or fablieux, have a simple domestic realism. It is possible to see an underlying unease in some of them about the growing power of money and the burgess class in the fifteenth century. In the last analysis, however, they remain a series of moral fables, and one has to look to Dunbar for the excitements of witty and acid criticism and to David Lindsay in the next century before social satire becomes a fully sharpened political weapon.

William Dunbar (1460?–1520?)

The fifteenth century ended with a 'second golden age' and a contemporary report from one Don Pedro de Ayala paints a picture of James IV as a gifted Renaissance prince. De Ayala was commissioned to his task because of Spain's eagerness to make an alliance with Scotland, and so in 1498 he sent off a document in cypher which described the king and his country. Doubtless the report is somewhat idealised, but Ayala had no reason to flatter or to lie outright. He tells of a well-read man with several languages, generous, handsome, popular and valiant to the point of recklessness in physical combat. He describes a country which is prosperous but not rich and a people who are extremely hospitable, bold, proud of appearances and quick to take offence. There is a contradictory side to the monarch, however, which de Ayala does not report, although it makes James even more a man of his times – a Renaissance prince whose temperament and whose kingdom, too, still retains something of a darker medieval past. The king was haunted by remorse all his life, perhaps for the part he felt he had played in his father's death, and so he went on religious retreats and was given to bouts of melancholy. He wore an iron chain around his waist in penance and yet he enjoyed an extravagant life, devoted to magnificent pageants, gambling, making love, good clothes and music. He shared these passions with equally strong intellectual pursuits, having an act passed in 1496 to make education compulsory for the offspring of men of substance and sending his own two illegitimate sons to be educated in Italy, where they studied for a while under Erasmus. By the end of his reign the extent of these enthusiasms and his practical excitement with artillery, alchemy, surgery and great warships had left the crown almost bankrupt. He was considerate and generous to religious orders and equally open-handed to passing musicians, jugglers and mountebanks. All his life he hoped to lead a crusade to the Holy Land, but at home he rewarded the most unsuitable men with powerful ecclesiastical positions. He was the last Scots ruler to speak Gaelic and he encouraged the commons to approach him and give him their opinions freely. In his strengths and failings, James is not unique among monarchs of his time, but the generous scope of his involvements and the number of his contradictions make him an especially colourful, headstrong and romantic figure – one of Scotland's most popular kings.

William Dunbar is the most significant literary figure of the late fifteenth and early sixteenth century, a poet whose technical skill is second to none. He mastered English stanza-forms from Chaucer and Lydgate and he was equally at home with French style, especially in the use of refrain. (His particular forte is to use refrains supported by strong alliteration carried over into two or three lines of the verse.) Despite his technical brilliance, his humour can be harsh and pessimistic at times, closer to the late medieval mood than to that of the Renaissance. And yet, in some of his wilder parodies and in moments of personal doubt, he seems much more modern – a spirit from the seventeenth or even the twentieth century. Because of these contradictions he epitomises more than any other writer the brilliance, the materialistic confidence and the spiritual unease of James's court and the stirrings of the Renaissance in Scotland.

We know little of Dunbar's life except that he was born around 1460 and educated at St Andrew's University; he may have become a Franciscan novice and he probably travelled a fair amount, visiting Paris and Oxford. For the last ten years of the century he seems to have served James as a notary and an ambassador, particularly in connection with the king's various plans for marriage. We know that Dunbar wanted a benefice as recompense for his services, but he had to settle for a series of pensions instead, probably given to him for his skill as a poet. Most of the poems which have survived date between 1490 and 1510 and they give a vivid picture of the court and its doings, unequalled in their colour and frankness.

Dunbar's commitment as a professional bard can be seen in formal, ceremonial works such as the poem which has come to

be known as 'The Thistle and the Rose', commemorating the
political marriage which James made with Margaret Tudor of
England, in 1503. It uses the dream-vision convention to tell
how the Thistle is crowned king of plants before celebrating its
marriage to the red and white (English) rose. In the same vein,
'Blyth Aberdeane' records the pageants with which this 'beryl
of all touns' greeted Queen Margaret when she visited the
North-East in 1511. The more ornate alliteration of 'Renounit,
ryall, right reverend and serene' is a flattering address to
Barnardus Stewart, who arrived at court in 1508 as ambassador from King Louis XII of France: 'B in thi name betaknis
batalrus, / A able in field, R right renoune most hie' and so on: a
poem doing what is expected of it and no more.

Dunbar admired Chaucer for his 'fresch anamalit termes
celicall', but the Scotsman's aureate verse has no equal and his
work abounds in brilliant and highly coloured descriptions. He
shows us less of the natural sphere than Henryson, whose
poems are closer to the world of fields and seasons, but his
images have a hard elaborate and jewel-like intensity which has
impressed many readers over the centuries. This richness is
especially evident in the divine poems, such as the address to
the Virgin Mary, 'Hale sterne superne, hale in eterne', where
the verse achieves a music-like abstraction wholly given over to
bright, clashing metallic effects of alliterative and assonantal
virtuosity – the verbal equivalent of a page from the Book of
Kells:

Empryce of prys, imperatrice,	Empress
Brycht polist precious stane,	
Victrice of vyce, hie genetrice	
Of Jhesu, lord soverayne:	
Our wys pavys fra enemys	shield
Agane the feyndis trayne,	fiend's followers
Oratrice, mediatrice, salvatrice,	
To God gret suffragane:	
Ave Maria, gracia plena,	
Haile sterne meridiane,	
Spyce, flour delyce of paradys	
That baire the gloryus grayne.	seed

When the poet dreams of Christ's passion on Good Friday
('Amang thir freiris within ane cloister'), it is the physical
details of the torment which immediately engage him, and he

even imagines that the soldiers let the cross fall deliberately, to hurt the saviour more, before they raise him above Calvary. The poem concludes with abstractions and the dreamer is assailed by personifications such as Compassion, Contrition, Ruth and Remembrance. In another poem it is the Resurrection on Easter Sunday and the harrowing of Hell that stir Dunbar to announce, 'Done is a battell on the dragon blak', where the lines resound like a gong with military triumph as the murk of the pit is suddenly penetrated by crystal-clear light:

> The grit victour agane is rissen on hicht
> That for our querrell to the deth wes woundit;
> The sone that wox all paill now schynis bricht,
> And, dirknes clerit, our fayth is now refoundit:
> The knell of mercy fra the hevin is soundit,
> The Cristin ar deliverit of thair wo,
> The Jowis and thair errour ar confoundit: Jews
> *Surrexit dominus de sepulchro.*

> The fo is chasit, the battell is done ceis,
> The presone brokin, the jevellouris fleit and flemit . . .   gaolers
> [fled and
> banished

The exalted orchestration of language and sound in these poems leaves little scope for empathy or a more personal approach to God and, despite its great artistic power, this achievement reveals quite a lot about Dunbar's sensibility. Perhaps he did have an affinity with the Celtic love of complex and elaborate organic patterns developed to the point of pure abstraction.

'The Goldyn Targe' demonstrates Dunbar's aureate and emblematic imagination at work in a secular vein. In a dream allegory of a tournament the golden shield of the poet's reason is eventually, inevitably, overcome by a congregation of all the feminine virtues, seasons and goddesses. The players are borrowed from the *Roman de la Rose* and the stanza from Chaucer's 'Compleynt of Faire Anelida'. (The same pattern crops up at the start of Book II of the *Wallace*.) The poem is set traditionally in the month of May. The sunlight becomes 'clear', 'purified', 'crystalline', an effect typical of Dunbar's vision, and reminiscent, too, of parts of *The Kingis Quair*:

The rosis yong, new spreding of thair knopis,   buds
War powderit brycht with hevinly beriall droppis;   beryl
     Throu bemes rede birnying as ruby sperkis
     The skyes rang for schoutyng of the larkis;
The purpur hevyn, ourscailit in silvir sloppis,   overflowing;
     Ourgilt the treis, branchis lef, and barkis   gilded over

Henryson's animals and plants have an individual existence as well as a place in the wider domestic ecology; but, for Dunbar, fish, fowl and flowers are turned to enamelled emblems of nature and set in a brilliant and Byzantine mosaic.

In a less elevated mode, the poet's skill with appearances provides a uniquely lively record of domestic behaviour at the court of King James. He describes a dance in the Queen's chamber ('Sir Jhon Sinclair begouthe to dance') and delights in exposing the antics of her retinue. Court physician Robert Shaw staggers like a hobbled cart-horse; Dunbar himself capers like a wanton colt until he loses his slipper; and in the extremity of the jig the Queen's almoner breaks wind 'lyk a stirk stackrand in the ry' [bullock staggering in the rye]. 'A mirrear dance mycht na man se', and Dunbar gleefully exposes the vulgar, mortal clay beneath the rich clothes and the pompous behaviour. From the evidence of such poems it becomes apparent that Dunbar's relationship with the court was at times a mixed and uneasy thing. He reminds the king that he has not yet received his expected advancement and begs him to listen to a petition from the Queen on his behalf ('Schir, for your grace bayth nicht and day'). Or he tells of his ambition to gain a benefice – 'Schir, yit remember as of befoir' – and presents James, and the reader, with a curious amalgam of slyly comic pathos and painful need: 'Jok that wes wont to keip the stirkis / Can now draw him ane cleik of kirkis . . . Worth all my ballatis undir the birkis [birch trees] / Exces of thoçht dois me mischief.' With the same wry mixture he portrays himself in another poem as an old grey horse, poorly clad and cast aside without a decent stall to winter in ('Schir lett it nevir in toun be tald'). Yet this is not Dunbar's only persona, and the mask of a faithful old steed is cast aside to reveal sharper teeth and a less venerable nature when he pays off old scores by attacking James Dog, or Doig, the keeper of the queen's wardrobe, who was rash enough to deny him a new doublet. ('The wardraipper of Venus boure' and 'O gracious princes, guid and fair'.)

Flyting and the Gaelic influence

Dunbar's acid and brilliant technique is given traditional scope under the guise of flyting. Literary flyting – 'scolding' – was a popular mode in fifteenth- and sixteenth-century Scotland. It is a disputation in verse between poets, and a licence for inspired and absurd invective. Sheer expressive extravagance and technical ingenuity is the thing, and, like a bout of professional wrestling, the contestants need not actually dislike each other before or even after the exercise. The genre owes much more to oral contests in medieval Gaelic verse than it does to anything in the European canon, and its heavily patterned hyperbolic abuse and its delight in the grotesque show the other side of the bardic praise poems. Indeed, the Gaelic bard's skill with words was truly a weapon in an oral society and he could threaten his enemies or a backsliding benefactor with verses which would confer on them an uncomfortable notoriety. A poet's curse was best avoided, and popular belief held that it could even raise blisters. The Bannatyne Manuscript contains examples of flyting such as 'The Flytting betwix the Sowtar and the Tailyar' – shoemakers and tailors being traditional enemies. In the 1580s Alexander Montgomerie and Sir Patrick Hume of Polwarth produced and delivered between them the 'Polwart and Montgomerie Flytting' and the story is that King James VI pronounced Montgomerie the victor. 'The Flyting of Dunbar and Kennedy' is the earliest surviving example of this genre. The two poets take turns at blast and counterblast, and it is likely that these originally went round the court as manuscripts or they may even have been performed as a verbal duel. Either way, they provide an outlet for the popular delight in grotes-querie already found in 'King Berdok' and 'The Gyre-Carling'.

Walter Kennedy (1460?–1508?), of noble descent, was a contemporary of Dunbar, and in his time he was almost as well known a poet as his adversary. He came from the Carrick district of Ayrshire, and Dunbar takes the opportunity to mock his knowledge of Gaelic and his country manners: 'Thy trechour tung hes ane Heland strynd; / Ane Lawland erse wald make a bettir noyis'; and 'The gallowis gaipis eftir thy graceless gruntill, [snout] / As thow wald for an haggeis, hungry gled' [hawk]. Regarding himself as a more sophisticated figure, Dunbar concentrates his attack on Kennedy's personal

appearance and on his gaucheness when he appears in the
capital: 'Stra wispis hingis owt quhair that the wattis [welts] ar
worne . . . Than rynis thow down the gait [street] with gild of
boyis, / And all the toun tykis hingand in thy heilis'. The poem
gains force like a terrible spell – 'I conjure the, thow hungert
heland gaist' – and ends with a veritable snare-drummer's
paradiddle of internal rhyme and alliteration:

> Baird rehator, theif of natur, fals tratour,   Bard enemy
>   feyindis gett;
> Filling of tauch, rak sauch, cry crauch, thow art
>   oursett;
> Muttoun dryver, girnall ryver, yadswyvar, fowll fell
>   the;
>   Herretyk, lunatyk, purspyk, carlingis pet,
> Rottin crok, dirtin dok, cry cok, or I sall quell
>   the.

Such virtuosity was not limited to flyting, of course, for it
appears as a kind of choral music in Dunbar's holy poems, such
as 'Hale sterne superne, hale in eterne', and indeed Henryson's
'Prayer for the Pest' concluded with just such a flourish:

> Superne / Lucerne / guberne / this pestilens,
> preserve / and serve / that we not sterve thairin.
> Declyne / that pyne / be they Devyne prudens.

Internal rhyme was a popular device on both sides of the
Border in medieval Latin verse and hymns, but its special
density in Scottish poetry, especially in the work of Dunbar,
and in the later poems of Alexander Scott and Alexander
Montgomerie, suggests a particularly northern predilection for
such effects. In fact the Gaelic bards delighted in the most
complex preset patterns of internal rhymes and alliterations,
usually set out in syllabic couplets and four-line stanzas.
Whether Dunbar knew Gaelic well or not, it seems very likely
that he and his audience responded to such effects, because
they were already present as a familir part of Scotland's Celtic
heritage. After all, his rival Kennedy and the practice of flyting
itself both came from these roots, and we know that James
could speak Gaelic and rewarded Gaelic poets for recitals at
court. On the other hand, Dunbar's overwhelming use of
strong initial stresses, and the harsh and explosive consonants

in his lines belong to the Lowland Scots tradition, with its links to Old English and Scandinavian sounds. By comparison, Gaelic verse lays greater emphasis on the softer chiming of assonance among internal vowels.

Despite his Gaelic heritage, Kennedy cannot quite rise to Dunbar's virtuosity in verse; on the other hand, it does lead him to attack his enemy's genealogy by giving his family a long tradition of cowardice and treachery and connivance with the English. He defends Gaelic as 'the gud language of this land' that 'sould be all trew Scottis mennis leid'. Such national feeling is significant, and we remember that Gaelic was still being spoken at this time in Galloway, Perthshire and the North-East, even if it was not the language of Lowland power.

Flyting is a hectic and specialised form, and Dunbar's comic gift is better displayed, at least to modern tastes, in his skill with burlesque and parody. In 'Ane Ballat of the Fenyeit Frier of Tungland' he satirises John Damian, an alchemist and 'sham friar' whom James had made abbot of Tungland in Galloway, much to Dunbar's disgust. Damian literally fell from royal grace, however, when he attempted to fly like Icarus from the battlements of Stirling Castle, only to plummet into a dunghill and break his thigh. In vain did he explain that he only failed because he had glued too many hen feathers among the eagle's plumes on his wings, and that hen feathers 'covet the mydding and not the skyis'. Dunbar tells the tale with undisguised glee, and the same colloquial gusto with which he scolds the merchants of Edinburgh for the noisy, crowded and smelly streets of their city ('Quhy will ye marchantis of renoun'). In other poems he follows French and Latin models by parodying the office of the dead in order to satirise a drunken court physician ('I, Maister Andro Kennedy'), or to persuade the king to stop doing penance with the Franciscans at Stirling, which is 'purgatory' compared to the heavenly delights of holding court in the capital ('We that are heir in hevins glory').

James was a part of this contradictory milieu, surrounded by brilliant men and importuned by place-seekers and charlatans. Dunbar hated the scene and yet he loves to depict it in poems which were written, after all, for the entertainment of the principal players. In 'Schir ye have mony servitouris' he points out that his own work will last as long as anything done by the king's company of diviners, philosophers, shipbuilders and 'uther gudlie wichtis'. Furthermore, he complains that other, much less worthy types seem to thrive at court – the 'fenyeouris, fleichouris, and flatteraris' (pretenders, coaxers and flatterers), the 'fantastik fulis bayth fals and gredy, / Of toung untrew and hand evill diedie', the gossips, spongers, parasites, shovers and pushers, jostlers and thrusters who scurry and crowd in the corridors of power and who respect learning in no man. Here is the darker side of the life described by Don Pedro de Ayala, and in a characteristically devastating use of the catalogue Dunbar assembles it for our delectation and conveys his contempt in a *tour de force* of accumulating alliterative epithets:

Cryaris, craikaris, and clatteraris,	
Soukaris, groukaris, gledaris, gunnaris,	
Monsouris of France, gud claret cunnaris,	
Inopportoun askaris of Yrland kynd,	
And meit revaris lyk out of mynd,	meat rustlers
Scaffaris and scamleris in the nuke,	
And hall huntaris of draik and duik,	
Thrimlaris and thristaris as thay war woid,	
Kokenis, and kennis na man of gude,	rogues
Schulderaris and schowaris that hes no schame,	
And to no cunning than can clame,	knowledge
And can non uthir craft nor curis	
Bot to mak thrang, schir, in your duris,	
And rusche in quhair thay counsale heir,	
And will at na man nurtit leyr	learn

The poet's heart nearly bursts when all these creatures reap favour and he is ignored. He is just at the point of crying 'fy on this fals world', when an outrageous afterthought prompts him to conclude that he might be more patient if he, too, had some reward with the rest:

Had I rewarde among the laif:	others
It wald me sumthing satisfie	
And les of my malancolie,	
And gar me mony falt ouerse	make; overlook
That now is brayd befoir myn e . . .	

The comic effrontery of this offer to write fewer satirical attacks if he is rewarded more is breathtaking, and yet curiously touching as well. We are moved because we sense that he probably means it. Dunbar's eye is unsparing when he regards the court; he mocks, chastises and derides it with all his considerable wit and technical dexterity, but ultimately he needs it, and he belongs to it body and soul.

Perhaps it is his dependence on the court that makes Dunbar's forays against it so successful; but there is a wilder, demonic side to his imagination, and this, too, must play a part in giving his work its special edge. 'The Dance of the Sevin Deidly Synnis' conjures up personifications of Pride, Anger, Envy, and so on, and sets them cavorting to the latest steps from France in a nightmarish version of that dance in the Queen's chamber. The seven sins were a common motif in medieval literature and art, but Dunbar's vision of their awful reel in Hell seems to be an original twist. They are brilliantly and specifically characterised, simultaneously comic and disgusting:

> And first of all in dance wes Pryd,
> With hair wyld bak and bonet on syd . . .

> Than Yre come in with sturt and stryfe,
> His hand wes ay upoun his knyfe,
>   He brandeist lyk a beir;
> Bostaris, braggaris, and barganeris
> Eftir him passit in to pairis . . . .

Syne Sweirnes, at the secound bidding,	Sloth
Come lyk a sow out of a midding,	
Full slepy wes his grunyie	snout

Each of them leads his human followers in a wretched babble of 'harlottis' and 'prestis', 'druncharts' and 'bakbyttaris in secreit placis', enough to grace the court of any king. The prideful skip in burning fires, the creatures of anger stab and cut each other with knives, the covetous vomit hot molten gold and the lecherous go through the dancing leading each other by the penis.

Than the fowll monstir Glutteny,	
Off wame unsasiable and gredy,	belly
To dance he did him dres;	begin
Him followit mony fowll drunckart	
With can and collep, cop and quart,	flagon
In surffet and excess;	
Full mony a waistles wallydrag	fat weakling

With wamis unweildable did furth wag	unmanageable
In creische that did incres.	fat
'Drynk', ay thay cryit with mony a gaip;	
The feyndis gaif thame hait leid to laip,	hot lead
Thair lovery wes na les.	

The whole terrible carnival continues until the Highlanders arrive, whereupon they take up so much room in Hell and make such a noise with their clatter in 'Ersche' that the Devil smothers the lot with smoke and ends the dance.

The poem has stunning verbal and imaginative force – a wild goliardic drive in the half-way house between horror and farce that is typical of the Scottish sense of humour. The same capacity for eldritch extravagance and all-too-specific physical realism lies at the heart of the sensibility which produced 'Tam O'Shanter' and *A Drunk Man Looks at the Thistle*. It is this precipitous imagination which gives a particularly furious barb to Dunbar's technical virtuosity, whether he is sending up the office for the dead or burlesquing the medieval *débat* on love.

'The Tretis of the Tua Mariit Wemen and the Wedo' begins in high style when the poet overhears three ladies discussing love in a garden on Midsummer Eve. The setting, the aureate terms and the alliterative blank verse all prepare the reader for a courtly poem on a matter of sophisticated interest. It is noticeable, however, that their enjoyment at table as they 'wachtit at the wyne' is just a little heartier than their dainty white fingers might lead one to expect. These suspicions are confirmed and the vision is shattered when they speak. One of the wives wants to be as free as the birds to show herself 'At playis and at preichingis and pilgramages', to move among men and 'cheis and be chosen, and change quhen me lykit'. Like May in Chaucer's 'Merchant's Tale', she is married to a crabbed old man: 'Ane bumbart, [dolt] ane dron bee, ane bag full of flewme, / Ane skabbit skarth [cormorant], ane scorpioun, ane scutarde [shitten] behind'. Unlike Chaucer, however, Dunbar allows no room for compassion at the plight of this 'amyable', so bawdily does she describe the chains of her condition. In response, the widow advocates utter hypocrisy: she has had two husbands and like the Wife of Bath she is a woman of broad experience and appetite. She advises the ladies to keep a lover and to dominate their husbands if they can; but widowhood is best of all – 'My mouth it makis murnyng, and

my mynd lauchis'. Like Henryson's Sprutok, she has a lively
sexual preference and, as she describes how she comforts and
flirts with several men at once, it becomes apparent to the
reader that her 'fair calling' is to run a brothel. Yet her speech
throughout is larded with the terms of courtly love while she
talks of her honour and advocates mercy as a 'meckle vertu' in
women, just in case some pining youth should die for want of
her. Finally, the poem slips back into its ideal and aureate
setting, as Dunbar distances his audience from what the ladies
are actually saying and returns to 'silver schouris' and 'the
sweit savour of the sward and singing of foulis'. It is a gay and
coarse exposure of womankind, very much in the tradition of
medieval anti-feminist literature, but without the subtlety and
sympathy of the 'marriage cycle' in *The Canterbury Tales*. The
Scots poet explodes the romance conventions, but his poem is
essentially a cruel laugh at the gullibility of men.

  The highly coloured scenes and the sometimes brutally
reductive eye at work in Dunbar's poetry have their source in a
darker aspect of his vision. He is never far from the 'malancolie'
which stems from a strong sense of his own impending
dissolution. The shadow provides a contrast which even further
heightens the glitter of his wit and the enamelled elaboration of
his style. 'Mutability' – the evanescence of man's earthly life –
is a constant theme in medieval literature, finding particularly
fine expression in Villon's *Testament*, where the general pathos
of the refrain from one of the ballades – 'Mais ou sont les neiges
d'antan?' (but where are the snows of yester year?) – mingles
with Villon's macabre but defiant awareness of the decay of the
physical flesh. Dunbar too writes in the vein of *memento mori*, but
he is equally prone to moods of highly personal anguish, and
these moments of despair give his poems a more modern, even
an existential aspect. 'I seik about this warld unstabile' begins
by admitting that despite all his wit he has failed to find even
one thought that is not ultimately deceitful:

  For yesterday I did declair
  Quhow that the seasoun soft and fair
    Com in als fresche as pako fedder;   peacock
    This day it stangis lyk ane edder,   adder
  Concluding all in my contrair.

All existence seems to offer him this personal affront, and he

judges life to be a violent succession of absolute contrasts:
'Yisterday fair up sprang the flouris, / This day thai are all slane
with schouris'. Not even in the closing stanza is there any hint
of Christian comfort or eternal assurance.

> So nixt to summer winter bein,
> Nixt eftir confort cairis kein,
>   Nixt dirk mednycht the mirthefull morrow,
>   Nixt eftir joye aye cumis sorrow:
> So is this warld and ay hes bein.

The masterly use of repetition makes its point and the contrasts
are stark and inescapable.

  Dunbar's poems in this mood show little of the bitter-sweet
pathos of the medieval sense of mutability, nor do they show the
compassion for erring man seen in Henryson's 'Preiching of the
Swallow'. Instead, his pessimism has a misanthropic and
sometimes a curiously triumphant note. His certainty may be
unpalatable, but it *is* certainty, and he has found 'ane sentence
convenabille' after all. He writes of despair with great intensity,
but such moments are almost always prompted by mental or
physical weaknesses with little hint of a solely spiritual or moral
dimension. He is a materialist and the images he chooses are
telling. When his spirit is utterly forlorn and 'no ladeis bewtie'
nor 'gold in kist [chest], nor wyne in coup' can help him, it is not
because he misses his saviour, but rather it is 'for laik of symmer
with his flouris' ('In to thir dirk and drublie dayis'). When he
muses on Fortune's wheel and on how we must always be ready
to leave this short life ('Full oft I mus'), he concludes that we
should enjoy ourselves – 'For to be blyth me think it best' – and
yet this last refrain is repeated so often in the poem that it
begins to lose all sense of conviction. When Dunbar commends
spiritual love over fleshly love in 'Now culit is dame Venus
brand', he sees it entirely as a matter of age over youth, made
possible only because 'Venus fyre' within him is nowadays
'deid and cauld'. The closing stanzas accept that, left to itself,
youth will never consider spiritual matters in the face of 'this
fals dissavand warldis blis'. The poet commends Christ's
cause, but again he sounds revealingly hesitant about it: 'He
suld be luffit agane, think me'. Finally, as an expression of
Christian morality, the poem's continuing refrain has an oddly
determinist and physiological bias: 'Now cumis aige quhair

yewth hes been / And trew lufe rysis fro the splene.' Even if we grant that the theory of humours would seem more apposite in Dunbar's time than it does now, these lines still seem strangely, even grotesquely indecorous, undoubtedly reflecting something of the unease in its author's spirit.

Dunbar's discontent and his materialistic cast of mind have resulted in some poems which seem almost modern, at least to post-Romantic eyes. The poet has suffered a migraine in 'My heid did yak yester nicht'; he can scarcely look on the light and he cannot find words to express his thoughts, trapped somewhere in his memory, 'Dullit in dulnes and distres'. He may rise in the morning but his spirit is still sleeping and it seems that nothing can stir it:

> For mirth, for menstrallie and play,
> For din nor danceing nor deray,
> It will nocht walkin me no wise.

The spirit of this poem is worthy of Coleridge, with its despair at a loss of imaging power, its inability to face the light, source of all illumination, and its failure to 'dyt thought'.

A conventional Christian note is allowed to appear at the very end of the famous poem 'Lament for the Makaris', but it seems like an abrupt and unconvincing afterthought:

> Sen for the deid remeid is none,   Since; death
> Best is that we for dede dispone   prepare
> Eftir our deid that lif may we:
> *Timor mortis conturbat me.*

If this is hope, it is quite outweighed by the force of the previous twenty-four stanzas, not to mention the internal rhyme 're-meid' and the repetition of 'deid' in each of the last three lines. Every stanza ends with that solemn Latin refrain from the Office for the Dead – 'the fear of death disturbs me' – conveying a personal terror which strikes like a funeral bell. By comparison, Henryson's 'Prayer for the Pest' is devoutly Christian, making supplication to God's mercy and power in every stanza. Death by plague was a familiar visitor at the beginning of the fifteenth century, yet Henryson's prayer shows no personal anguish and accepts it utterly in true 'medieval' humility as the justice of God: 'our syn is all the cause of thiss'. In contrast,

Dunbar draws on the medieval *danse macabre* for his poem
(Lydgate before him had used the same Latin line) as well as a
list of type-figures of those who must inevitably come to die:
'Princis, prelotis, and potestatis, / Baithe riche and pur of al
degre' – all are mortal, not forgetting the intellectuals of
James's court, 'Rethoris, logicianis and theologgis, / Thame
helpis no conclusionis sle' [cunning]. Death even takes 'on the
moderis breist sowkand, / The bab full of benignite'. For, with
that thin and relentless "ee' rhyme echoing down the poem,
there can be no suggestion of acceptance. Indeed, from the very
first lines the poem is a personal cry – 'I that in heill wes and
gladnes / Am trublit now with gret seiknes' – and this note is
confirmed when Dunbar begins to name all the other poets who
have played their part in the pageant and gone to the grave.
The toll contains twenty-four makaris – a most useful record for
the literary historian, although some remain unknown to us or
only a few lines by them survive. They and their works have,
indeed, been devoured by that 'strang unmerciful tyrand'.

I se that makaris amang the laif	rest
Playis heir ther pageant, syne gois to graif;	grave
Sparit is nocht ther faculte:	
Timor mortis conturbat me.	

He hes done petuously devour
The noble Chaucer of makaris flour,
The Monk of Bery, and Gower, all thre:
   Timor mortis conturbat me.

. . .

In Dunfermelyne he hes done roune	
With Maister Robert Henrysoun.	
Schir Johne the Ros enbrast hes he:	embraced
Timor mortis conturbat me.	

And he hes now tane last of aw	
Gud gentill Stobo and Quintyne Schaw,	
Of quham all wichtis hes pete:	whom; pity
Timor mortis conturbat me.	

Gud Maister Walter Kennedy
In poynt of dede lyis veraly;
Gret reuth it were that so suld be:
   Timor mortis conturbat me.

Sen he hes all my brether tane
He will nocht lat me lif alane;
On forse I man his nyxt pray be: Perforce
    Timor mortis conturbat me.

Sen for the deid remeid is none,
Best is that we for dede dispone
Eftir our deid that lif may we:
    Timor mortis conturbat me.

Starkly and unforgettably, the 'Lament' expresses one of the great themes of human existence. In this context the capacity to make poems was all important to Dunbar, for, when it fails, as in 'My heid did yak yester nicht', or when he foresees his extinction as a man, he is left with nothing else. Except, of course, that his work has given him a special kind of life after death – perhaps the immortality which meant most to him after all. The darker poems are the antithesis of Dunbar's commitment to the glitter of court life. His technical bravura, his satirical wit, his worldly cynicism and his inner terror make a potent and disturbing combination, and perhaps this is why he speaks so powerfully to modern readers.

James IV and the brilliance of Scotland's first steps into the Renaissance were soon to be swept away. The Scottish king had treaties with both England and France, but Henry VIII's increasingly hostile acts against France and across the border finally committed James to the Auld Alliance and led him, reluctantly, to invade England. The Scots army was defeated at the Battle of Flodden in 1513, where some 10,000 men were killed on Branxton hill. James himself died in the thick of the fighting along with members of his retinue, many nobles and hundreds of the lesser gentry and yeomanry. The English retired across the border, the king's infant son succeeded to the throne for yet another Stewart minority, and a peace was concluded the following year. The battle had served no military or political purpose whatsoever, and Scotland was shattered by the loss of her most popular king. Most households of note counted one or more members among the dead and Flodden Field passed into the folk memory, and remains to this day, a traumatic symbol of failure and grief. Dunbar lived on for another seven years at least, but we hear nothing more from

him or about him, and we do not even know where he was
buried.

Writing in prose

The works of James I, Henryson, Holland and Dunbar reach a
high order of accomplishment. In fifteenth-century Scotland
such powers of imagination and technique are solely the
province of the poet, and vernacular prose remains in its
infancy. The literature of most countries shows the same
pattern. **Sir Gilbert Hay** (1400?–1499?) provides the earliest
known literary prose in Scots with his translations from French
and Latin originals. Hay is also credited with the *Alexander*, a
lengthy verse translation from the French, and he is mentioned
as a poet in Dunbar's 'Lament'. His career also emphasises the
French connection, because he was at one time Chamberlain to
Charles VII. Back in Scotland in 1456, he made his manuscript
translations at the request of his host, the Earl of Orkney and
Caithness. *The Buke of Armys*, *The Buke of the Order of Knychthood*
and *The Buke of the Governaunce of Princis* all have to do with noble
models of philosophy, behaviour and belief. Caxton was to
publish his own translation of the *Livre de l'Ordre de Chevalrie*
almost thirty years later, so the taste for such topics survived for
quite some time and, of course, long after the chivalric order
itself.

The only other prose-writer of note is **John of Ireland**
(1440?–1496?), who, like Hay, had been to France, spending
thirty years there and ending up as confessor and counsellor to
Charles's successor, Louis XI. He produced an original piece of
Scots prose (again in manuscript only) for the edification of the
nineteen-year-old James IV. *The Meroure of Wysdome* is a rather
tedious treatise on political and personal wisdom, in which the
author is at pains to legitimise his saws by referring to the
authority of holy writ and to the scholarship of Paris. John
reveals something of the status of prose among academics in his
time by being anxious to point out that, for writing, he knows
Latin better than he does the 'commoune langage' of his
country. In fact a considerable tradition in vernacular historiography was soon to evolve in Scotland. The undistinguished verse of Wyntoun's *Orygynale Chronykil* of 1424 was

followed by a number of prose historians in the next era and then by a host of doctrinal historians in the seventeenth century. In the meantime, John of Ireland defends his use of the vernacular, even although he knows that 'mony errouris agane the faith and haly doctrine of iesu and of the kyrk ar writtin in this tounge and in inglis, at a part of the pepil of thi realme ar infekit with it'. It is not too fanciful to detect here already the rumblings of approaching Reformation and the major part that vernacular prose was to play in it.

3

The sixteenth century: John the Commonweill

WHEN the Renaissance came to Scotland it came as a spirit from abroad gradually making itself felt in the harsher climate of a Northern country. The spirit flowered until Flodden left the crown on the head of a two-year-old boy. Then, within only fifteen years, a new factor was added to the perennially shifting balance of power between king and barons. The scale was tipped in 1528 when Patrick Hamilton, a pupil of Erasmus and of Luther, was burned as a heretic at St Andrew's for preaching that man stands alone before God and is justified only by his faith. Hamilton argued that this faith is God's gift only and cannot be earned by good works, or interpreted or ameliorated by the hierarchy of any church. Soon this bare philosophical light, with all the hard clarity of the North, quite outshone the Mediterranean sunshine of that late spring at the court of King James IV. Nor was it simply a matter of religious belief, for kings, too, are only men before their maker, and soon the new church was reminding them of that fact and resisting all attempts at royal control. By the end of the century Andrew Melville was speaking for the very spirit of Scottish Presbyterianism when he reminded his ruler that 'there is twa kings and twa kingdomes in Scotland. Thair is Chryst Jesus the King, and his kingdome the Kirk, whose subject King James the Saxt is, and of whose kingdome nocht a king, nor a laird, nor a heid, bot a member.' This exhilarating and dangerous insight soon overtook the Renaissance in Scotland and absorbed almost all the intellectual and creative energy in the country for the next 200 years. It gave the Reformation a more revolutionary and democratic cast than it had in England, where the monarch remained as head of the Church, yet its fiercer elements would propose a far more total control over the individual spirit than any mere king could hope to achieve.

James V, 'the gudeman of Ballengeich', died in ineffectual despondency, yet at the beginning of his reign he had vigorously advanced the influence of the crown by taxation and military action. He provided funds for the Court of Session, annexed the power of the Lords of the Isles and led expeditions into the Borders to control the reivers there. In those debatable lands the barons still ruled like minor kings, doing nothing to discourage bandit families from raiding property and burning churches in England and Scotland alike. (One of these wild men, Johnny Armstrong, is remembered in tales and ballads; he and forty-eight of his men were hanged in 1530.) When Henry VIII split from Rome he was eager to make an alliance with his Northern neighbour, but James sided instead with Catholic Europe through a French marriage, although his sickly bride died within a year. His second wife was made of stronger stuff, and Mary of Guise, destined to be the mother of Mary Queen of Scots, was an especially staunch supporter of both the old religion and the absolute power of monarchs. This alignment established a tension between Scotland, England and France which was to dominate the century and make it impossible to separate the issues of religion and politics. Thus Protestant reformers would be supported by England against their own sovereign, while Scottish nobles took first one and then the other side according to their conscience and their sense of personal advantage. In such a context there was little hope that more moderate Catholic reformers would prevail, and the fiasco of the battle at Solway Moss further disillusioned both commons and nobles against the notion of military action in the French Catholic cause. 'It cam wi a lass, and it'll pass wi a lass', James is said to have murmured about the Stewart succession when he heard of his daughter's birth as he lay on his death bed.

For the next eighteen years Mary of Guise acted as queen regent. Henry pressed his plans to make an English marriage with the infant Scottish queen and when all else failed he tried brutal persuasion by ordering his armies to make deliberately destructive raids on southern Scotland, 'sparing no creature alyve'. But Henry's 'rough wooing' and his boast that he was

the 'very owner of Scotland' only strengthened the Auld
Alliance, and the baby Mary remained in France, betrothed to
the Dauphin. Meanwhile, the queen regent steadfastly
resisted the gathering changes of Reformation. She had a
potent ally in Cardinal David Beaton, but he only spurred on
the Reformers' cause and ensured his own death when he
burned Wishart at St Andrew's, thus launching an aging John
Knox into brief exile and a stormy career. Knox returned from
Europe inspired with Calvin's doctrinaire vision of a fighting
faith. He motivated a Protestant pressure-group among the
nobles, calling themselves the Lords of the Congregation of
Jesus Christ, and his passionate preaching around the country
encouraged his followers to see themselves as the Children of
Israel, engaged against an oppressor no less harsh than
Pharaoh himself. The country almost came to civil war before
the Treaty of Leith and the queen regent's death brought about
the first Reformation parliament in 1560, whereupon the
Confession of Faith and *The First Book of Discipline* set out the
Scottish ideals for a new Protestant kirk. When Mary Queen of
Scots landed from France in 1561, she found her mother's
religion out of favour and her own priest intimidated at court.
The first years of her reign passed off well enough, but hers was
a fraught existence, for in the eyes of Catholic Europe she, and
not Elizabeth I, was the legitimate heir to the English throne.
The young queen was soon submerged in a rising tide of
political, religious and sexual intrigue which her own headstrong nature did nothing to quell. After the murder of her
favourite, Rizzio, and the assassination of her effete husband
Darnley, she allowed herself to be abducted by Bothwell (who
was already suspected of complicity in Darnley's death), and
then, most ill-advisedly, she married him. In the ensuing
uproar Bothwell had to flee the country and Mary was forced to
abdicate in favour of her infant son. After a last desperate throw
of the dice, she retreated to exile in England, where her cousin
Elizabeth kept her in effective captivity for nineteen years
before finally resolving the threat of Catholic succession with
the edge of the headsman's axe.

James VI's inheritance was not an auspicious one, and his
early love of culture and his own pretentions to literature were
pursued in an uneasy and isolated context. In the Ruthven raid
of 1582 the sixteen-year-old king was actually kidnapped by

nobles who feared that his infatuation with the young lord of
Aubigny, the Duke of Lennox, would lead to dangerous
Catholic influence at court. Lennox fled and James escaped to
wage his long but circumspect tug-of-war with Presbyterianism
at home, while keeping an eye abroad on his prospects for the
throne of England.

After Knox's death it was Andrew Melville who had
consolidated Scottish Presbyterianism. The ideals of the Books
of Discipline were noble in many ways, although they were never
fully realised. The new church was to be based on a democratic
hierarchy beginning with each congregation and working up to
the General Assembly, a kind of church parliament which was
answerable only to God. At the grass roots, ministers had to be
elected by their own congregations and no landowner could put
his own man in the pulpit. At the same time the clergy were an
independent and influential moral authority in the parish and
could mete out punishments in public for the social misdemeanours of their flock. The new kirk set great store on the
Bible as the full expression of God's will, and so preaching and
the education of the masses became a worthy priority. Every
householder was to read the Bible to his family; there was to be
a schoolmaster skilled in the classics in every parish; bursaries
were to be made available for the talented poor, while there
were to be colleges in every large town, and divinity was to be
taught at the universities along with medicine and law. This
practical concern with the status and welfare of the common
man, both spiritual and temporal, was radical and humane,
yet, as so often happens, the revolutionary ideal contained the
seeds of authoritarianism. The Calvinist doctrine of the elect
led to exclusiveness, and a narrow literalism in the reading of
the Scriptures produced fanaticism and intolerance.

James VI was not slow to see the political implications of
such a structure, nor was Melville afraid to point them out, so
the king duly noted that 'Presbytery agreeth as well with a
monarch as God and the Devil', and gradually set about
regaining a degree of royal control. At the end of March in 1603
the news arrived in Edinburgh that Queen Elizabeth had died.
A week later, King James set off for the south and the throne of
England.

Gavin Douglas (1475?–1522)

In both his work and his life, standing divided between the Renaissance and the late Middle Ages, Gavin Douglas demonstrates something of the contradictions to be found in sixteenth-century Scotland. His greatest achievement was the translation of Virgil's *Aeneid*, and, although it is distinctly medieval in setting and interpretation, its commitment to the classical world and its concern to speak to a broader audience belongs to the new age. Douglas was born into the 'Red Douglases', the earls of Angus, who, with the 'Black Douglases' of Lanarkshire, were among the most powerful and ambitious families in Lowland Scotland, both boasting descent from the line of Robert Bruce's great champion and both with remote claims to the Scottish throne. Gavin, or Gawin, was the third son of the fifth Earl of Angus, Archibald 'Bell the Cat', who earned his nickname when he hanged six of the king's favourites at court. Young Gavin Douglas went to St Andrew's University in 1490 at the usual age of fifteen. He graduated after four years' study (conducted in Latin) of typical subjects such as grammar, rhetoric, Aristotle, mathematics, music and astronomy.

It is likely that he also went to Paris and visited the continent at least once more before settling in his native land. It was during these years that he wrote his poetry, completing the *Eneados* in 1513, scarcely two months before the Battle of Flodden. After the death of James IV all Douglas's energies were directed towards political affairs and to seeking an ecclesiastical appointment commensurate with his family's rank. He was eventually granted a bishopric at Dunkeld, but the French-connected factions of the regent Albany suspected him of political alignment with England. Matters came to a head and the poet had to resort to bribes and threat of arms to retain his place at Dunkeld and his standing in the tangled pattern of influence. But in the end he still had to flee to England, where he spent his days at court trying to arrange his return to the north. He died of the plague in 1522, exiled in London and a victim of the family influence which had promised so much.

Douglas's first poem, 'The Palice of Honour' (1501), is wholeheartedly within the medieval dream-allegory tradition.

The piece follows a French vogue for such subjects and expounds, in three books, the various ways in which honour may be obtained in life. When the poet finally does gain the palace, he is led to a keyhole where he glimpses Honour only to faint before his blinding glory. The style of the poem is aureate and 'enamelled' along the lines of Dunbar's near-contemporary pieces 'The Goldyn Targe' and 'The Thrissil and the Rois'. Thus Douglas delights in using an elaborate polysyllabic diction to 'amplify' or extend his descriptions, and he encourages the formal complexities of his craft by choosing a difficult nine-line stanza that depends on only two rhymes. These factors, and the author's own fluent Latinity, make the poem something of a young man's *tour de force*.

Douglas is often credited with another allegorical poem, called 'King Hart', but some doubt must remain about the attribution since it appears only once, in the Maitland Manuscript, added by a later hand. Such allegories belong to an earlier age, and it is Douglas's translation of the *Aeneid* which kept his name alive in the seventeenth and eighteenth centuries when greater makars were all but forgotten. It also contains, in the form of the prologues to each book, the best of his own original poetry.

Douglas worked on his *Eneados* for a year and half before abandoning literature in favour of his political career. Next to the *Wallace* it was the longest piece of verse yet sustained in Scots. It circulated in various manuscript copies, at least five of which have survived, but it was not published until 1553, thirty-one years after its author's death. (This was in an unsatisfactory edition made in London, anglicised and 'Protestantised'.) Nevertheless, it was common practice at the time for books to be copied by hand, for Chepman and Myllar's press – established in Edinburgh in 1507 – had not yet had time to fulfil the growing demand for Scottish books. Virgil's works were particularly popular throughout Europe, with over a hundred Latin editions printed by the beginning of the century and many others copied by hand. Some classical authors were also being translated and, indeed, in 1509 Octavien de Saint Gelais published an edition of the *Aenid* in French. Whether Douglas saw the French version or not, he felt himself to be in the forefront of the movement to make the classics available to a wider audience, and in the 'Conclusio' to his labours he encouraged fault-finders to do something more useful, like translating Ovid.

Douglas's was the first full-length translation of a major classical text to be made anywhere in Britain and it earns him a deserved place in the cultural history of the northern Renaissance. He was not unaware of the importance of his achievement. Accordingly, he castigates Caxton for inferior passages in his version (1490), which was based on a French paraphrase, and prides himself on keeping close to the 'fixt sentens or mater' of his original, so that 'all thocht my termys be nocht polisht alway, / Hys sentence sall I hald, as that I may'. Nevertheless, the poem is not exactly Virgil's, for the Latin hexameters have been rendered into heroic couplets and the text is expanded and explained in places with the aid of Ascensius's commentary as attached to his Latin edition of Virgil, first published in Paris in 1501. Furthermore, Douglas prefaces the thirteen books (one by Maphaeus Vegius) with original prologues of his own. In six of these (I, III, V, VI, IX and XIII), he gives serious attention to the problems of translation, which he solves by choosing contemporary equivalents in weapons, clothes, ships and manners. He asks for help if he has made errors, and warns against those who would spy out every 'falt and cruyk', even if he admits that he can see very few faults himself; after all, 'the blak craw thinkis hyr awin byrdis quhite'. This running commentary adds great charm to Douglas's version of the classical poem. Indeed his narrative couplets and Scottish settings provide a robust immediacy which may well be better suited to the primitive world of Aeneas than the decorous circumlocutions chosen by Dryden and later neoclassical poets.

Some of Douglas's finest poetry comes from the descriptions of the natural world which introduce Books VII, XII and XIII. These passages have become part of poetic history by anticipating James Thomson's *The Seasons* (1730) and something of what nature was to mean to the English Romantics. The Prologue to Book XII describes dawn on a May morning. Phoebus's chariot appears above the sea, dame Flora scatters flowers and the poet creates a conventional landscape of blossoms, animals and young people in a scene reminiscent of the more formal *Palice of Honour*. Yet there is physical particularity too, as every detail is brilliantly etched in the sun's early light:

Towris, turettis, kyrnellis, pynnaclys hie	battlements
Of kyrkis, castellis and ilke fair cite,	each
Stude payntit, euery fyall and stage,	little tower and
Apon the plane grund, by thar awyn umbrage.	shadow [storey

Plants and flowers are described with botanical specificity. Giddy young lovers pine and tease each other with whispered, oblique phrases:

Smyland says ane, 'I couth in previte	know how
Schaw the a bourd', 'ha, quhat be that?' quod he	jest [to
'Quhat thyng?' 'That most be secrete', said the tother.	

Here and everywhere Douglas catches a sense of movement with telling and realistic detail: 'So dusty pulder upstouris in euery streit, / Quhil corby [crow] gaspit for the fervent heit.' It was just this quality which Thomas Warton admired when he praised the passage for being 'the effusion of a mind not overlaid by the descriptions of other poets, but operating, by its own force and bias, . . . on such objects as really occurred' (*The History of English Poetry*, 1774–81).

If Douglas begins Book XII with a welcome to the May dawn, the Prologue to the following book describes a sunset in June – a luminous northern evening declining slowly into silence and darkness. In the night the poet dreams that Maphaeus Vegius chides him for not having translated his supplement to Virgil. Convinced by the ghost's argument (and the blows it rains on his head) Douglas agrees to satisfy his querulous visitor. Waking in the half-light before dawn he sees the stars quenched one by one – 'That to behald was plesans and half wondir' – until the workaday world gets under way and the spell is broken by a farm steward shouting to his men ' "Awaik! On fut! Go till our husbandry." '

The poet's delight in natural settings, described almost for their own sake, is most striking of all in his account of a northern winter in the Prologue to Book VII. In a scene reminiscent of the opening to *The Testament of Cresseid* we see the translator composing himself for sleep, wrapped in three layers 'fortil expell the peralus persand [piercing] cald', while outside, under the watery light of the moon, he hears 'the geiss claking eik by nyghtis tyde / Atour [around] the cite fleand'. In the morning he peeps from the window at the 'scharp hailstanys

. . . hoppand on the thak [thatch] and on the causay by' before withdrawing to the fireside to take up again the burden of his verses. Outside his window a typically Scottish countryside wrestles in the grip of the 'schort days', ruggedly evoked in harsh alliterative lines:

Thik drumly skuggis dyrknyt so the hevyn,	shadows
Dym skyis oft furth warpit feirful levyn,	hurled; lightning
Flaggis of fire, and mony felloun flaw,	deadly blast
Scharpe soppys of sleit and of the snypand snaw.	biting
The dolly dichis war all donk and wait,	dismal; dank
The law valle flodderit all with spait,	
The plane stretis and euery hie way	
Full of floschis, dubbis, myre and clay.	pools; puddles

Warton was right to find an almost Romantic spirit in such passages, but the poet was still a man of his time, and he was keen to draw acceptably Christian conclusions – 'ful of sentence' – from the 'pagan' world of classical literature.

Douglas distrusts learned Latinate terms, preferring them 'haymly playn' and 'famyliar' without 'facund rethoryk' so that his text will be 'braid and plane, / Kepand na sudron [southern speech] bot our awyn langage, / And spekis as I lernyt quhen I was page'. Indeed, he is the first of the makars to refer to 'Scottis' and 'the langage of Scottis natioun' to describe the tongue which Blind Harry would have called 'Inglis' (to distinguish it from Gaelic, the original 'Scottis'), and, although at times Douglas refers to the limitations of his chosen speech, he is prepared to use some 'bastard Latin', French or English to help out. He is consistently aware of the radical significance of this task and at the close of the thirteenth and final book he expresses the modest desire that his labour shall be a 'neidfull wark', especially 'to thame wald Virgil to childryn expone'. He hopes that the classics will not belong only to 'masteris of grammar sculys . . . techand on . . . benkis and stulys', but that Virgil will now be available to 'euery gentill Scot' – even to those who cannot read: 'And to onletterit folk be red on hight / That erst was bot with clerkis comprehend'. Such an outlook characterises the Renaissance and what was to be the best aspect of the slowly growing spirit of Reformation in Scotland.

Sir David Lindsay (1490–1555)

Like Dunbar and Douglas, but with somewhat more success, David Lindsay spent most of his life at the Scottish court. He was born in 1490, probably on his father's estate in Fife. By the age of twenty-two he was part of the royal household, employed as 'Keeper of the Kingis Grace's Person' – attendant and companion to the infant James V. He tells us in his poems how he used to sing to the royal baby and carry him on his back. In 1522 he married a girl at court, also in royal service. Lindsay's association with the young king was broken for four years when Archibald Douglas, nephew to Gavin and sixth Earl of Angus, became chancellor and assumed total power by holding the twelve-year-old James captive in Edinburgh Castle. In 1528, however, the king escaped to lead an army against his captor, and the Red Douglas had to forfeit his estates and go into exile in England. It is not certain what formal education Lindsay had, but he was undoubtedly an able man and his career prospered. In the 1530s he began to produce poems which presumed to advise the king, making satirical comments on the state of the nation and especially on the failings of the Church. James must have had some sympathy with these views, for he used the first performances of *The Thrie Estaits* as a warning to some of his recalcitrant bishops to reform themselves. Lindsay was made a royal herald and later he was knighted to become Lyon King-at-Arms, responsible for Scottish heraldry and the arranging of pageants, plays and farces for state occasions and the entertainment of the court. Schir Dauid Lyndesay of the Mount, as he was called, also served as an ambassador abroad and may well have visited Italy in his travels.

At home his anti-clerical views inevitably involved him with the cause of reform – he knew John Knox and is said to have encouraged him to take up preaching. In 1546 he acted as intermediary between the king and the group who had killed Cardinal Beaton and taken over St Andrew's Castle. (He called on them to surrender, but they held out until the following year.) 'The Tragedie of the Late Cardinal Beaton' does not leave Lindsay's sympathies in doubt, for the ghost of Beaton effectively condemns himself by describing his own career. The poem is a 'tragedy' only in the old sense that it concerns the fall of a powerful man:

> My gret ryches, nor rentis proffitabyll
> My Syluer work, Jowellis inestimabyll,
> My Papall pompe, of gold my ryche threasure,
> My lyfe, and all, I loste in half ane hour.

Lindsay concentrates in some detail on Beaton's great political influence and particularly on the commitments to France and Rome which would not allow him to countenance peace with England despite the high cost to everyone else:

> Had we with Ingland kepit our contrackis,
> Our nobyll men had leuit in peace and rest,
> Our Marchandis had nocht lost so mony packis,
> Our commoun peple had nocht bene opprest . . . .

On theological issues Lindsay has the cardinal admit that he did not read the Bible and did not encourage the teaching of it to the common folk, putting to great torment, indeed, the 'fauoraris of the auld and new Testament'. The poet does not mention the fire which consumed Wishart and directly fuelled Beaton's own death, although he does have a line where the ghost confesses to having destroyed many men, 'sum with the fyre'. This may seem a striking omission, but it was probably a well-considered one, for not even the Lord Lyon could challenge the authority of the spiritual arm with impunity. Douglas Hamer has suggested that the printer of 'the Tragedie' had to flee from arrest and that this was the poem of Lindsay's which we know to have been burned by the ecclesiastical authorities in 1549. In fact Lindsay's work does not bear an overtly Protestant doctrine, but it is fired by a hatred of unearned privilege, most especially in the established Church. He seems to have remained a Catholic, albeit a severely critical one who wished to see the Church give up wealth and temporal powers and return to its simple role as teacher of the Testaments to the people.

Beyond all matters of Christian doctrine, Lindsay's morality is founded on his sense of natural justice and his sympathy with the feelings and prejudices of the common people. In the spirit of *Rauf Coilyear* his hatred of oppression, his lurid anti-clericalism, and his ribald sense of humour have guaranteed a lasting and general popularity to his work. These forces find early expression in 'The Dreme' and 'The Papyngo' and come to fruition in *Ane Pleasant Satyre of the Thrie Estaits*. It is a measure of Lindsay's influence that he managed to stay at court during these turbulent times, for his views must have made him powerful enemies. Although he continued to write until just before his death at the age of sixty-five, his other work never matched the achievement of *The Thrie Estaits*. His poems were published and republished in subsequent years and a popular collected edition appeared in 1568, but *The Thrie Estaits* itself was not printed until 1602, over sixty years after its first performance.

Lindsay's purpose was clear from the start. 'The Dreme of Schir David Lyndesay' was probably written around 1528, when James V attained the throne. The Prologue describes how the poet used to play the lute and act the fool for his infant sovereign. Then the dream takes him on an elaborate tour of the cosmos from Hell to Heaven and back to Scotland again. 'Why are the people so poor', the poet asks, 'when they live in so pleasant a place?' The answer, of course, is misgovernment, and at this point John the Commonweill arrives in rags to describe how he has fled from oppression in the Borders and Highlands alike, without justice from the king or comfort from the Church. The dreamer awakes to point out the moral to his king.

'The Complaynt of Schir David Lindesay' celebrates James's escape from the bad influence of the Douglas family. It allows the poet to offer yet more advice to his monarch and to remind him along the way that he would appreciate a gift of money, or even a loan – 'Off gold ane thousand pound, or tway'. Clearly the poet enjoyed good relations with the king, and James was not above flyting his old companion in verses of his own, and tolerating a reply too, which warns him explicitly against his sexual adventures ('The Answer to the Kyngis Flyting', 1536). Lindsay wrote a number of other pieces satirising life at court, such as 'In Contemptioun of Syde Taillis' (c.1540) or 'The Confessioun of Bagsche' (c.1534) which has the king's old hound complain about the scuffling for preference, the backbiting and the dogfights which go on in the presence of power. Now that Bagsche is old and despised, he regrets his cruelty when he was on top. 'Belief weill', he reminds the current favourites, 'ye ar bot doggis.' The animal analogy provides Lindsay with further scope for satire in *The Testament and Complaynt of the Papyngo* (1538), in which the king's parrot, wounded by a fall from a tree, makes her last will and testament after setting down two epistles full of advice to the king and her fellow courtiers. The garrulous bird expounds on the follies of climbing too high, on good government, on the fate of the Stewart kings and on the mutability of human affairs – all with awesome fluency. The 'Papyngo' takes its place in what amounts to a Scottish penchant for animal satire, debate or epistle, running from the *Howlat* to Henryson's fables, to Hamilton of Gilbertfield's 'Last Dying Words of Bonny Heck' and Burns's 'Twa Dogs'. Notwithstanding the charms of his preaching parrot, Lindsay's finest satire remains *The Thrie Estaits*.

A short version of this play was performed in 1540 at the palace of Linlithgow on 6 January, the Feast of Epiphany, before James V and the court. Yule at the Scottish court was kept after the French fashion with the election of an 'Abbot of Unreason' to ensure entertainment for all. The ceremonies of Twelfth Night belonged to this tradition, with the choosing of a mock sovereign – the King or Queen of the Bean – to direct dances, games and burlesques. Great licence was allowed on such occasions, and it was in this context that Lindsay's merry exposure of folly and weakness amongst the powerful of this world was first performed. This is not to underestimate the author's seriousness, or his political intention, for when it was next performed, in Fife, at the Castle Hill in Cupar in June 1552, the satirical force had been strengthened and further elements of popular comedy, energetic caricature and vulgar farce were directed towards an audience in which, this time, the commons outnumbered the nobility. The third performance of the *Satyre* was equally public, on the sunny slopes of the Calton Hill in Edinburgh in 1554 in the presence of Mary of Guise, Queen Regent of Scotland. It had been fourteen years since the first performance, during which time James had died shortly after Solway Moss; Wishart and Beaton had both perished in windy St Andrew's and Henry VIII's troops had crossed the Border and even reached Edinburgh in their destructive zeal to persuade Scotland into an English marriage alliance. In this period of reform and counter-reform Lindsay's play must have been a potent instrument, and it was not to be performed again until 1948, when Tyrone Guthrie's memorable production rediscovered Lindsay's dramatic flair and the comic vigour of his verse.

The final version of *The Thrie Estaits* is in two parts separated by an interlude in which the 'rude mechanicals' provide comic relief by making comments on what has gone before. This was a common device between the acts of the early morality plays, and, since the whole performance must have taken many hours, it would have allowed the nobility some leeway to finish lunch and return to the play proper. Here and elsewhere Lindsay displays a shrewd stagecraft, derived no doubt from his experience with pageants and allegorical masques. Thus, when the Estates return to the stage in Part Two, they are led backwards by their ruling vices in a procession; or, at the end, when Falsehood comes to be hanged, his final speech summons all oppressors to follow him into death, until the rope tightens around his neck and a black crow is released to symbolise his soul. There are equally memorable scenes when the Pauper 'invades' the stage from the audience during the interlude and demands that his complaints be heard, despite the efforts of the players to stop him. At every turn, anarchic moments such as this are used, along with what must have been topical local references, to play against the more allegorical set pieces.

Lindsay also manages a number of sophisticated verse-forms and modes of address. The play's formal speeches are made in iambic pentameters with an eight-line stanza and a linking rhyme-scheme, a form used in Latin and French verse and in some early English mystery plays. There are swift-moving passages when single lines rhymed in couplets are exchanged between speakers (stychomythia), and moments when a jogging bob-wheel is used to set a three-stress line against a four-stress norm — a familiar effect and already a favourite with Scots poets:

> I haue sic pleasour at my hart,
> That garris me sing the treble pairt: makes
> Wald sum gude fellow fill the quart
>   It wald my hairt reioyce.

> Howbeit my coat be short and nippit,
> Thankis be to God I am weill hippit   padded
> Thocht all my gold may sone be grippit
>   Intill ane pennie pursse.

When John the Commonweill first speaks, his diction is appropriately plain and forceful: 'Out of my gait, for Gods saik let me ga'; and 'Gude maister I wald speir at you ane thing, / Quhair traist ye I sall find yon new cumde King?' But, when he accuses the Estates and their special sins, his couplets ring out in longer and sterner lines: 'And as ye se Temporalitie hes neid of correctioun, / Quhilk hes lang tyme bene led by publick oppressioun'. Such vigour and variety is remarkable for 1540, it is uncommon in contemporary morality plays and predates by at least twenty years the main body of notable pre-Shakespearean plays in England.

Lindsay's drama opens by showing how the young Rex Humanitas, encouraged by his minions, Wantonness, Placebo and Solace, is ensnared by Sensuality, the beautiful natural daughter of Venus. At such a court the aged adviser Good Counsel is ignored, while the vices of Flattery, Falsehood and Deceit dress up as friars and thrive as 'Devotion', 'Sapience' and 'Discretion'. The whole is played out in front of symbolic groups representing the assembled three Estates. Leaders of the Catholic Church, or the 'Spirituality', comprise the first Estate, the second is that of the lords and barons – the 'Temporality' – while the third Estate consists of established burgesses and merchants. Ordinary working folk without property or power have no place in this parliament and they are represented by the Pauper, who 'interrupts' the play, and by John the Commonweill, who comes forward in Part Two and testifies against all three arms of the establishment. Such an abstract gives little impression of the earthy nature of the satire, for the three vices are hilariously and broadly scurrilous and Flattery is a part for a leading comedian, who takes several disguises in the course of the play. Court and Church are his stamping-grounds, while Deceit reigns over merchants, and Falsehood thrives among the craftsmen. The first part of the play follows the promotion of these villains and parallels it with the misfortunes of the two maidens Verity and Chastity, who arrive on the scene only to be spurned by each Estate in turn. (Verity carries the New Testament 'in English toung' and is greeted with horror by the Spirituality and condemned as a heretic and a 'Lutherian'.) Before long, however, Divine Correction arrives to free the maidens from the stocks and assemble a parliament of all the Estates, at which he makes an examination of the condition of the kingdom. Correction strikes an old and familiar Scottish chord by asking 'Quhat is ane King?', and by giving the answer that he is 'nocht bot ane officiar, / To caus his Lieges liue in equitie'. Armed with God's truth, however, there is a new and thrilling resonance to his authority:

> I haue power greit Princes to doun thring,   throw down
> That liues contrair the Maiestie Divyne:
> Against the treuth quhilk plainlie dois maling   malign
>   Repent they nocht I put them to ruyne.

The political and philosophical impact of this insight must have been heady stuff for the commons in the audience, and one notices how often the word 'reformatioun' is repeated in the text.

The interlude provides a vulgar satire on the abuses of mendicant friars and the selling of remissions and relics, made all the more pointed because the audience knows that the corrupt Pardoner is Flattery in disguise. The second movement of the play presents John the Commonweill's case against the three Estates. The barons and the merchants submit to correction without demur, but the Spirituality resists and the parliament turns into a trial against corruption in the Church. Here Lindsay makes a vivid piece of propaganda drama in which many social and ecclesiastical abuses are specifically described, along with their painful effects on the commons and the country in general. The message is driven home at every turn, for the interlude and the epilogue repeat the arguments in burlesque terms; a 'learned Doctor' actually preaches a sermon from the stage, and, towards the end of the play, no less than fifteen acts of proposed reformation are read out formally and at length to the assembled audience. Such complaints are not unfamiliar; Chaucer's Pardoner led the way, after all; but Lindsay's case is outstanding because he links specific suggestions to his talent for drama and comedy.

From the very start *The Thrie Estaits* establishes a stirring and democratic truth about the nature of man, and the audience is brought to realise it on two radically different levels. All men are equal before their appetites; and all men are equal before God. Thus Dame Sensuality speaks to the Estates:

Paipis, Patriarks, or Prelats venerabill,
Common pepill and Princes temporall,
Ar subject all to me Dame Sensuall.

The play's impact depends on us being able to feel the essential truth of these and the following lines, even while we know that such feelings are sinful:

Quhat vails your kingdome and your rent,
      And all your great treasure,
Without ye haif ane mirrie lyfe,
And cast asyde all sturt and stryfe . . .
      Fall to and tak your pleasure.

And that pleasure is convincingly portrayed:

Behauld my visage flammand as the fyre.
Behauld my papis of portratour perfyte.
To luke on mee luiffers hes greit delyte.

In just the same way, Lindsay shows that Divine Correction applies to all classes – 'To rich and puir I beir ane equall hand' – and that Verity, a simple maid armed only with the New Testament, can dare to counsel kings.

These recognitions are at the heart of Lindsay's purpose. He is no puritan (as witness the bawdiness of his verses and Correction's approval of hunting and lawful merriness), but he believes in what would now be called public accountability. Good Counsel points out that, while cobblers and tailors are skilled workers at their trade, there are bishops and parsons who can neither read nor preach. Surely the Church should be no less craftsmanlike than the laity? It should recruit its members on merit alone: 'Cair thou nocht quhat estait sa ever he be, / Sa thay can teich and preich the veritie'. But the Spirituality's only defence is to attack the presumption of its critics – 'it is heresie, / To speik against our law and libertie' – until even the merchants see the weakness of such an argument from those who 'will correct and nocht be correctit'. Good Counsel, that shrewd courtier, adds that it is only common sense for a king to look after his humbler subjects, for 'the husband-men and commons thay war wont, / Go in the battell formest in the front', while John the Commonweill quotes from

St Paul to make a nobler case for the dignity of 'men that labours with thair hands':

> *Qui non laborat no manducet.*
> This is in Inglische toung or leit: language
> *Quha labouris nocht he sall not eit.*

John, Good Counsel, the merchants and the lords all agree that the first duty of churchmen should be to teach the people, and to clarify the Scriptures.

Confronted by Divine Correction and King Humanity, the Spirituality is made to discard its power and its rich robes as Bishop, Abbot, Parson and Prioress all stand nakedly revealed as 'verie fuillis'. They do not leave the stage, however, without a final telling shot – 'We say the Kings war greiter fuillis nor we / That us promovit to sa greit dignitie' – and Lindsay must have counted on these lines to produce a moment of gleeful recognition among the groundlings. John the Commonweill takes his seat in parliament, and in a sequence of light-heartedly brutal vignettes Theft, Deceit and Falsehood make their final speeches and are hanged. Flattery alone survives (by having testified against his fellows) and his escape serves as a reminder that the principle of duplicity and the appetite for fair words will never be extinguished from human society. As though to emphasise the point, the Epilogue reminds us that there is a kind of democracy among dunces, for 'the number of fuillis ar infinite' – and they thrive in every class.

Lindsay's other works are something of an anticlimax, although 'The Historie of Squyer Meldrum' (c.1550) is an enjoyable and rollicking account of the loves and valiant doings of a Fifeshire laird, probably written shortly after the real William Meldrum died. By comparison, *Ane Dialogue betwix Experience and ane Courteour, Off the Miserabyll Estait of the Warld* scarcely moves faster than a crawl. The four books of this poem, also known as *The Monarche*, were probably written between 1548 and 1553, and it seems that in Lindsay's later years his didactic impulse became merely pedantic. With *The Thrie Estaits*, however, he had created a unique form of propaganda drama, fully committed to the public forum, not too extreme in its doctrinal views, acceptably liberal and practical in its proposed reforms, and, above all, brilliantly tailored to influence the audience by the communal delights of laughter, anger and debate.

The theatre in Scotland

It seems very probable that there were precursors to *The Thrie Estaits*: Lindsay's grasp of stagecraft suggests as much; but no dramatic texts or reputations have survived. The Bannatyne Manuscript preserves a fragment from the early part of the century, sometimes attributed to Dunbar, and known as the 'Littil Interlude of the Droichis Part of the Play'. James Wedderburn, one of the brothers responsible for the *Gude and Godlie Ballatis*, is reported to have written comedies and tragedies around 1540, and it is known that the minor poet Robert Sempill had a play performed in 1568. (He also wrote a violently anti-Papist verse attack on the Archbishop of St Andrew's in 1584 – 'The Legend of the Lymmaris Lyfe'.) It seems likely, then, that there was a young dramatic tradition in Scotland and that it was not afraid to comment on the social and religious issues of the day. It is known that John Knox was mentioned in an anti-Catholic piece written by a friar called Kyllour and performed at Stirling in 1535. The older observances of folk festivals, guild processions, clerk plays, passion plays and pageants at court must all have contributed something to the growth of a theatrical understanding. In the course of the Reformation, however, the Kirk sessions came to oppose dramatic performances put on for public entertainment, and, although at first they remained content to ban only clerk plays based on interpretation of the Scriptures, they gradually came to suspect all plays as 'slanderous and undecent'. In 1599 the Kirk attempted to prohibit people from attending a comedy performed in Edinburgh by a group of English players, but James VI stepped in and assured his subjects that they could go to the show.

Even so, James could not make the theatre flourish in the second half of the century. A vernacular play called *Philotus* was published in 1603, but the author is unknown, although Robert Sempill is sometimes suggested. *Philotus* is a comedy after the Italian manner on sexual disguise, mistaken identity and the marriage between age and youth, but the plot moves from comic complexity to sheer confusion. As drama it scarcely compares with Lindsay's play, much less with a contemporary English piece such as *All's Well that Ends Well*. The contentious temper of the times in Scotland was not sympathetic to a theatre still in its infancy, and the success of the *Gude and Godlie Ballatis* speaks for a fairly unsophisticated popular taste. The final factor was that Edinburgh, unlike London, did not support a regular public playhouse nor any settled professional group of actors. Whether this was due to a lack of public interest or to the presence of public 'morals' it is difficult at this distance in time to tell. In either case, the early promise of *The Thrie Estaits* came to nothing. If the theatre never became a popular art in Scotland, the same cannot be said for songs and ballads, however. Of course the great ballads were born out of an oral tradition, as we shall see in the next chapter, and so their creators and the date of their first appearance cannot be identified in the usual way, but they would have been circulating through the sixteenth and seventeenth centuries, and in their own way they brought considerable colour and drama to the folk.

Writing in prose

David Lindsay's hopes that his verse would speak to 'Jok and Thome', like Gavin Douglas's concern for 'onletterit folk', reflect what was to be a growing commitment among prose writers of this period. Latin was still the tongue of learned discourse, and **John Major,** or **Mair** (1467–1550), a school-man of the old order who was educated at Cambridge and Paris, used it for his philosophical commentaries and for his influential *History of Greater Britain both England and Scotland* (1521). Major was distrustful of humanistic culture, but he numbered George Buchanan and John Knox amongst his pupils and something of his scholastic severity in disputation coloured the outlook of both men. Notwithstanding the con-tinued use of Latin at the universities, the spread of printing and the unfolding of the Reformation soon made both Protes-tant and Catholic writers acutely aware of the public power of their mother tongue. Some, such as Buchanan, retained a strong affinity with Latinate constructions, while others, such as Bellenden or Pitscottie, produced a more natural vernacular style. The most influential example was set by John Knox, who anglicised his Scots prose, with his eye on new readers south of the Border. This tendency was reinforced at the end of the century by James VI's move to London in 1603 and by the literary excellence of English writers such as Francis Bacon and Sir Thomas Browne. Back in Scotland, however, chronicles, pamphlets and theological disputations were more common, and by these means a nation was instructed about its individuality and how that manifested itself geographically, politically and spiritually.

The translation of the Bible into English, linked as it was with the spread of Protestantism, had a profound effect on the development of Scots vernacular prose. Murdoch Nisbet is credited with a Scots version of Wycliffe's fourteenth-century New Testament translation, but the work remained in manuscript and was not printed until 1901, so by far the most potent influence on the northern reformers came from testaments published in English. These began with the work of William Tyndale, undertaken at some personal risk (1525–34); officially tolerated versions followed, with Miles Coverdale's (1535) and the so-called Matthews Bible (1537), which was revised into Cromwell's Great Bible of 1539. The Calvinist Geneva Bible from 1560 came to hold a special place in Scottish hearts, and finally, of course, the Authorised Version appeared in 1611. Thus it was English prose which spoke to Protestant Scotland for the next three centuries, exerting an enormous cultural influence on a people who laid such emphasis on the reading and teaching of Scripture.

It was at James V's request that **John Bellenden** (1495–1550?), the archdeacon of Moray, undertook a free translation of Hector Boece's *Historia gentis Scotorum*, intended, no doubt, for the edification of the king's own barons and courtiers. *The History and Chronicles of Scotland*, in vigorous and straightforward Scots, was completed in 1533 and printed in Edinburgh no fewer than three times within the next fifteen years. Indeed, the current interest in history encouraged one William Stewart in 1535 to versify Boece into Scots. Bellenden also translated the first five books of Livy's *History of Rome* (1532) and prefaced the work with a rhymed prologue of his own.

The Complaynt of Scotland, sometimes ascribed to Robert Wedderburn, was printed and published in 1549 as an account of 'this affligit realme quhilk is my native countre'. The author's patriotism and his anti-English feeling can be explained by remembering that Solway Moss and Henry VIII's 'rough wooing' were still fresh and bitter memories. It is the most colourful early prose in vernacular Scots, and the nearest to imaginative writing in that it follows the allegorical-verse tradition by including a dream vision and using ornate descriptive language. Like Douglas before him, the writer adjusts his mother tongue to meet his needs and asks readers to forgive him if he has, in places, 'myxt oure langage witht part of termis dreuyn fra lateen, be rason that oure scottis tong is nocht sa copeus as is the lateen tong'. He claims that his intention is to speak as plainly as possible:

> For I thocht it nocht necessair til hef fardit ande lardit this tracteit witht exquisite termis, quhilkis are nocht daily usit, bot rather I hef usit domestic Scottis langage, maist intelligibil for the vulgare pepil.

In spite of its distrust of 'exquisite termis' and its purpose as propaganda, *The Complaynt* parades Latinate diction, highbrow prognostication and classical allusions across its pages as if to assure both author and reader of its intellectual respectability. Its main message is conveyed by an extended allegory in which the dire state of the country is explained through Dame Scotia's confrontation with her three errant sons, representing Church, nobles and the common people. This scheme was adapted from the original French prose of Alain Chartier's *Quadrilogue Invectif* (1422) – the most notable of several borrowings in the text – but *The Complaynt* still has a distinctively Scottish flavour of its own. It begins by philosophising on the fate of the nation, the mutability of temporal power and the forthcoming end of the world; then, fatigued by his efforts, the author repairs to the countryside for rest and relaxation. Strictly speaking, this 'Monolog Recreative' has nothing to do with the book's main purpose, but the author launches himself into a descriptive blizzard of detail like some forewarning of Sir Thomas Urquhart's own encyclopaedic muse. At dawn the sounds of the countryside begin to make themselves heard in this manner:

For fyrst furth on the fresche feildis, the nolt [cattle] maid noyis witht mony loud lou. Baytht horse and meyris did fast nee, and the folis nechyr. The bullis began to bullir, quhen the sheip began to blait, be cause the calfis began tyl mo, quhen the doggis berkit. Than the suyne [swine] began to quhryne quhen thai herd the asse rair quhilk gart [made] the hennis kekkyl quhen the cokis creu. The chekyns began to peu quehn the gled [hawk] quhissillit. The fox follouit the fed geise, and gart them cry claik. The gayslingis cryit quhilk, quhilk, and the dukis cryit quaik . . .

When the cacophony is finally documented, the author visits the seashore to witness a complicated naval engagement between two warships; he takes breakfast with a group of shepherds and reports on the joys of pastoral life and its contributions to science and astronomy; when the rustic company turns to recreation, the indefatigable scribe lists by name the forty-seven tales, thirty-eight songs and thirty dances they performed! Having survived this marathon, he wanders among the meadows and eventually falls asleep to have the allegorical dream vision, which is, after all, his main subject – but not before he has made an inventory of all the flowers and herbs and their medicinal properties. Over the centuries this recurring ennumerative exhaustiveness has a mad charm of its own in Scottish literature. But the sheer garrulousness of *The Complaynt* must have been something of a trial for the 'vulgar pepil' who were supposed to be reading it, even if future scholars have cause to bless its documentary zeal.

The most entertaining of the vernacular histories is by **Robert Lindsay of Pitscottie** (1532–90?). His *Historie and Cronikles of Scotland* was completed in the mid 1570s, but not published until 1782, when it went through three more editions at twenty- to thirty-year intervals. Many of the more colourful anecdotes in Scots history – from James II to James VI – come from Pitscottie, for, although his chronology is as uncertain as his sense of relevance, he has a splendid, gossipy journalist's eye for domestic detail, personal dramas and curious events. He knew men who had served at court or gone to war and so it seems likely that their reported experiences are not too far from the truth, even if they gained a little in the telling. Certainly the Scottish tapestry would be paler without the colour of Pitscottie's account of how James II was killed by a bursting gun, or the tragedy at Flodden, or the dying words of Border reiver and Stewart king, or the confusion and panic at the battle of Pinkie

in 1547, or dynastic betrayals and escapes, a ghost at Linlithgow, Siamese twins, strange portents, royal hunting-parties
and all the fascinating details of courtly fashion and behaviour.

By comparison with Pitscottie, **Bishop John Leslie**
(1527–96) is more austere and accurate, but much less
interesting. His ten-volume *History of Scotland* was written in
Latin during the 1570s, published in Rome in 1578, and
translated into Scots by Father James Dalrymple eighteen
years later. Both at home and in France, Leslie remained a
faithful ally to Mary Queen of Scots throughout her life. A more
contentious servant was **George Buchanan** (1506–82), almost
all of whose works were in Latin. In his thirties Buchanan
produced satires against the Franciscans, and, faced with the
charge of heresy, had to flee to Europe, where he spent twenty
years at various universities, including a spell as tutor to
Montaigne at Bordeaux and a scrape with the Inquisition in
Portugal, where he was imprisoned from 1550 to 1552.
Eventually Buchanan returned to Scotland to become an
adviser to Mary, a friend of John Knox's and a severe authority
on education and reformation. It was in this latter role that he
prepared virulent charges against Mary Queen of Scots and,
for the last twelve years of his life, acted as tutor to the young
James VI. Buchanan was famous throughout Europe as
scholar of the new humanism and a Latinist, in which language
he produced, among other pieces, translations from the Greek,
a verse paraphrase of the Psalms, metrical poetry of his own,
biblical and classical masques for the court, and two tragedies
in the Senecan style: *Jephthah* and *John the Baptist*. A lengthy
history of Scotland, *Rerum Scoticarum Historia* (1582), reminded
his royal charge that the people of ancient Gaeldom had had
the right to depose unsatisfactory kings. This was erroneous
but not by any means irrelevant, and *De Jure Regni apud Scotos*
(1579) pursued the same issue in contemporary terms through
seven editions, with translations in English, German and
Dutch, before the king suppressed it in 1586 and produced his
own *Basilikon Doron*, as a counterclaim for the divine right of
monarchs. Buchanan's vernacular prose includes a
propaganda-piece against the Hamiltons, and *The Chamaeleon*
(1570), a short satirical attack on William Maitland of
Lethington, the devious secretary to the queen, who was
accused of changing colours and religions daily. Buchanan's

vernacular prose is impeded rather than helped by his fluency in Latin, and it cannot match the simpler and more forceful style of his contemporary John Knox.

John Knox (1505–72) was born near Haddington, educated at the universities of Glasgow and St Andrew's, ordained as a priest and employed as a notary and tutor in his home district. He was in his forties before he joined himself to the Reformation movement in Scotland. A gradual intellectual commitment was catalysed by his meeting with George Wishart, who returned to Scotland from Switzerland to propose a new church, protected by the state but acknowledging only Christ as its leader. Knox carried a two-handed sword to protect the young preacher, but could not forestall Wishart's trial for heresy, within the year, at St Andrew's, where he was strangled and burned at the stake. Thenceforth Knox was caught up in the conflict. He only began to preach at the insistence of his fellows, and spoke his first sermon to the men who occupied St Andrew's after the revengeful murder of Beaton. When the castle finally surrendered in 1547, Knox was condemned with the other commoners to the French galleys, where he sat at an oar for almost two years before a petition from the English government brought about his release. He served in England as chaplain to Edward VI, but the accession of Mary Tudor in 1553 renewed the persecution of Protestants and Knox planned to go abroad, having married the young woman who was to bear him two sons before her death in 1560. He spent the next four years in Frankfurt and Geneva, where his early thoughts on election were powerfully influenced by Calvin's doctrines. Thus began his politico-religious war on behalf of a revolutionary democratic theocracy, a 'godly discipline' of behaviour to be guided at every turn by reference to the text of the Bible. He toured Scotland briefly in 1555 and savoured the public effectiveness of his preaching. During these years he also produced several pamphlets addressed to the people of Scotland and England, including a violent attack on 'bloody Mary' – *A Faythful Admonition unto the Professours of Goddis Truthe in England* (1554) – which did little to quench the fires of persecution in the South. The famous *First Blast of the Trumpet against the Monstruous Regiment of Women* (1558) had an equally backhanded effect. This treatise is informed with the misogyny of the times and coloured again by Knox's own cantankerous views about the female sex. (These did not stop him from marrying again in 1564 and, at the age of fifty-nine, taking a girl scarcely seventeen years old to be his wife. The disparity in their ages caused some talk, but Knox ignored it and eventually became the father of two daughters.) *The First Blast* turned out to be a rather loud tactical error, for, although it was directed at the political and religious policies of Mary Tudor in England and the queen regent in Scotland, it caused costly offence to Elizabeth I, who was, after all, a champion of Protestantism in her way, and a potential ally.

In 1559 Knox returned to Scotland and made another great preaching-tour – joining in what was now open conflict between the Lords of the Congregation and the forces of Mary of Guise. Each faction sought armed support from outside, the Protestants from England and the Catholics from France. Mobs rioted in Perth for two days after one of Knox's sermons and a situation of virtual civil war was only averted by the military impasse at Leith and by the death of Mary of Guise from dropsy. The spokesman for Christian Reformation hailed her painful end as a judgement from God. After the Treaty of Leith, the Reformation Parliament of 1560 and the Confession of Faith placed religious authority firmly in the hands of the new church and, as author of a treatise on predestination (1560) and as one of the writers of *The First Book of Discipline* (1560), it was John Knox whose vision helped to set the pattern for intellectual, social and religious life in Scotland, an iron mould which endured virtually until modern times. The arrival of Mary Queen of Scots heralded a turbulent seven years, and Knox had several private and public clashes with her, preaching that one Mass was more fearful to him than 10,000 armed enemies landed in the realm to suppress the whole religion. Events and eyewitnesses alike testify to the intemperate power of his rhetoric as he smote the pulpit as though to 'ding it in blads and fly out of it'. All the same, Knox found it prudent to retire from the court for a spell, during which time (1566–7) he completed *The Historie of the Reformation of Religioun within the Realm of Scotland*, published seventy-two years after his death. 'Here lies ane', said Morton at his graveside 'who never feared the face of man.'

It is impossible to warm to Knox's harsh, authoritarian nature, but it is equally difficult not to admit the forcefulness of his prose in *The Historie of the Reformatioun*. The energetic violence of his certainty, his grim sense of humour, his fluency in plain un-Latinate English and Scots colloquial speech, his eye for physical detail and his use of dramatic dialogue – all these testify to what must have been a truly powerful physical and political presence. He is an agitator rather than a philosopher, biased in his judgements and dogmatic in his opinions, yet there is something awesome in his unswerving adherence to what he saw as his duty. 'Madam,' he said to his queen, 'I am not master of myself, but must obey him who commands me to speak plain, and to flatter no flesh upon the face of the earth.' Carlyle saw him as a hero of private judgement, comparing him to some 'Old Hebrew Prophet', with the 'same inflexibility, intolerence, rigid narrow-looking adherence to God's truth, stern rebuke in the name of God to all that foresake truth', and he admired how Knox refused to do reverence to an image of the Virgin Mary when he was a prisoner in the galleys:

Mother? Mother of God? said Knox, when the turn came to him: This is no Mother of God: this is 'a pented bredd [board] – a piece of wood, I tell you with paint on it! She is fitter for swimming, I think, than for being worshipped, added Knox, and flung the thing into the river. It was not very cheap jesting there: but come of it what might, this thing to Knox was and must continue nothing other than the real truth; it was a *pented bredd*: worship it he would not.

('The Hero as Priest', *On Heroes and Hero-Worship*, 1841)

Knox's metaphysical audacity and grim-humoured, hard-nosed facticity speak for something in the Scottish spirit, and at least his prose is a stylistic advance on the laboured diction of *The Complaynt*. Here is his account of Cardinal Beaton's end:

And so he [James Melven] stroke him twyse or thrise trowght with a stog sweard; and so he fell, never word heard out of his mouth, but 'I am a preast; fy, fy: all is gone.'

Whill they thus occupied with the Cardinall, the fray rises in the toune. The Provest assembles the communitie, and cumis to the fowseis [moats] syd, crying, 'What have ye done with my Lord Cardinall? Whare is my Lord Cardinall? Have ye slayne my Lord Cardinall? Let us see my Lord Cardinall.' Thei that war within answered gentilye, 'Best it war unto yow to returne to your awin, houssis; for the man ye call the Cardinall has receaved his reward, and in his awin persone will truble the warld no more.' But then more enraigedlye thei cry, 'We shall never departe till that we see him.' And so was he brought to the East blokhouse head, and schawen dead ower the wall to the faythless multitude, which wold not beleve befoir it saw: How miserably lay David Betoun, cairfull Cardinall. And so thei departed, without *Requiem aeternam* amd *Requiescat in pace*, song for his saule. Now, becaus the wether was hote (for it was in Maij, as ye have heard) and his funerallis could not suddandly be prepared, it was thowght best, to keap him frome styncking, to geve him great salt ynewcht, [enough] a cope of lead, and a nuk in the boddome of the Sea-toore [tower] (a place whare many of Goddis childrene had bein empreasoned befoir) to await what exequeis his brethrene the Bischoppes wold prepare for him.

These thingis we wreat merrelie.

'This is superb,' wrote J. H. Millar drily, 'if not distinctively Christian', and, indeed, John Knox has remained patron saint and domestic demon in the Scottish psyche for 450 years. Knox's 'passion for truth', so admired by Carlyle, was really a passion only for his vision of the truth, with no patience for others or for the balanced judgement of philosopher or scholar. Yet his absoluteness could not have thrived had Scotland not been fertile ground for passionate personal conviction, and a delight in what MacDiarmid has called the 'hard fact', 'the inoppugnable reality'. It is one of history's ironies that equally uncompromising attitudes should be so much a part of left-wing commitment in modern Scotland, and that one of its popular manifestations should be to blame Knox alone for all the puritanical and constricting aspects of the national psyche.

James VI (1566–1625) should be mentioned as a prose-writer, although his work had far less political influence than that of his fiercest preacher. As patron of the poets who came to be known as the 'Castalian band', and at the tender age of seventeen, James produced sonnets of his own prefaced by a short treatise on poetic forms. Three years later he wrote *Daemonologie* as a proof of the dangerous existence of witchcraft. He is no less than a man of his time in this belief, but it is a shameful fact that the persecution and the burning of 'witches' – mostly female commoners – reached appalling heights in post-Reformation Scotland. These epidemics of social hysteria used to break out for a few years at a time, lasting into the mid seventeenth century. In 1588 and 1589 James produced two theological essays – 'meditations' – on verses from the Bible, while the *Basilikon Doron* (1599) was a defence of kingship written for the instruction of prince Henry and informed by James's determination not to allow the Presbyterian Church to dictate to him. About this time, he began to write only in English, as in *A Counterblaste to Tobacco* (1604). A collection of his works was published in London in 1616 and a comparison with earlier texts shows that where possible James replaced Scots words with the English equivalents. This process characterises the development of Scots prose from now on.

Minor poetry of the Reformation

Doctrinal conflict, disputatious pamphleteering, Knox's unyielding personality, the puritanism and religious persecution of subsequent years, all these darken our view of the early Reformation in Scotland. It is easy to miss the revolutionary exhilaration of a new movement which proposed a return to fundamentals, to the philosophical importance of individual judgement and to the surprising, unasked for, unearned, unacquirable descent of God's grace upon the faithful. Something of this Lutheran spirit of celebration is caught in a collection of hymns and lyrics directed to the Protestant cause, mostly collected and composed by **Robert Wedderburn** (1510?–1557) a priest of Dundee, assisted by his older brothers John, also a priest, and James, a merchant. *Ane Compendious Buik of Godlie Psalms and Spirituall Sangs* contains a calendar, the catechism, and metrical psalms and hymns in the Lutheran style, some translated from German. The collection, usually known as the *Gude and Godlie Ballatis*, is mostly notable, however, for the way it rearranges popular and courtly material – 'changeit out of Prophane Sangis in Godlie Sangis, for avoyding of sin and harlotrie'. The lively spirit of many of these pieces, and doubtless their thinly concealed worldliness too, made them a considerable popular success. Editions (also commonly called the *Dundee Psalms*), were published in 1567, 1578, 1600 and 1621. Along with the list of shepherds' songs in *The Complaynt*, they provide useful evidence of a vigorous musical tradition, except that the perennial themes of love, courting and the chase have been assimilated into a spiritual context. The process is not exactly one of bowdlerising or parody, but more like a mimicry of popular airs, especially directed at 'young personis . . . as are not exercisit in the Scriptures':

> Quho is at my windo, quho, quho?
> Go from my window, go, go,
> Quha callis thair so lyke ane stranger?
>   Go from my windo, go.
>
> Lord I am heir ane wratcheit mortall
> That for thy mercy dois cry and call
> Unto the my Lord Celestiall,
>   Se quho is at my windo, quho.

If these lines look rather thin, it must be remembered that they would have been set and sung to old tunes. A certain parallel suggests itself with Gospel songs or spirituals:

> Downe be yone Riuer I ran,
> Downe be yone Riuer I ran,
>   Thinkand on Christ sa fre,
> That brocht me to libertie,
>   And I ane sinful man.

The practice of 'spiritualising' secular lyrics was not confined to Protestantism, for an earlier Roman Catholic version of the following old love-song also survives, and would have been sung in church on selected occasions.

> My lufe murnis for me, for me,
> My lufe that murnis for me, for me,
> I am not kynde, hes not in mynde
> My lufe that murnis for me.
>
> Quha is my lufe, bot God abufe,
> Quhilk all this world hes wrocht;
> The King of blis, my lufe he is,
> Full deir he hes me bocht.

Other pieces are considerably less lamb-like, as in this rowdy attack on God's vicar, an original song, if scarcely original in sentiment:

> The Paip, that Pagane full of pryde,
> He hes us blindit lang,
> For quhair the blind the blind dois gyde
> Na wounder baith ga wrang;
> Lyke Prince and King he led the Regne
> Of all iniquitie:
> Hay trix, tryme go trix, under the grene wod tre.

The *Godlie Ballatis* have little in the way of literary merit, but they do convey an often-forgotten side to the Reformation, evoking as they do a hint of the revivalist meeting, with its willing submergence of the self, and perhaps of the critical faculties too, in cheerful congregational singing. Calvin's conception of the elect and his absolutist arrogance have not yet dampened this group celebration.

The rowdier side to the Reformation continued to be expressed in verse, and numerous political and ecclesiastical broadsheets were circulating in the second half of the century, mostly published by Robert Lekpreuik's Press in Edinburgh. The most notable of these satirists is **Robert Sempill** (1530–95), who wrote secular pieces such as 'Margaret Fleming' and 'Johnet Reid', as well as satirical attacks on the Old Church, including a famously abusive diatribe against the Archbishop of St Andrew's: 'The Legend of the Lymmaris Lyfe'.

It is a pleasing paradox that 'godlie' versions may have helped to save 'prophane' originals from oblivion, but two other major verse-collections of the period deliberately set out to record and preserve old Scottish poetry. Without the Bannatyne and Maitland manuscripts, the store of fifteenth- and sixteenth-century Scots verse would be much impoverished, for they contain poems by Henryson, Dunbar and Douglas as well as many anonymous or disputed pieces which would otherwise have been lost. **George Bannatyne** (1545–1608), was an Edinburgh merchant who returned to his home in Forfarshire in 1568 to escape an outbreak of plague in the capital. During his year's sojourn he transcribed many poems from old and tattered copies and prints and even included in the collection some unremarkable verses of his own. Allan Ramsay drew on this source for his *Ever Green* collection in 1724, and editors ever since have had cause to be grateful for the fruits of Bannatyne's enforced retreat. **Sir Richard Maitland of Lethington** (1496–1586), was a legal judge of noble birth and long-standing service who also collected old poems over the years and arranged to have them compiled in two manuscript anthologies. (The next most important manuscript collection in Scottish letters is also from the sixteenth century: the Asloan Manuscript of 1515.) Maitland was himself a poet (a better one than Bannatyne), but he did not start composing until he was in his sixties with failing sight: his verses are seldom cheerful.

Alexander Scott (1525?–1584?) did not share Maitland's personal and political gloom, although his poems date from the 1560s and the turbulent years of the Reformation Parliament and Mary Stewart's reign. Scott's only political poem, 'Ane New Yeir Gift to the Quene Mary quhen scho Come First Hame, 1562', is full of dull advice and reflections, but it includes the worthy wish that the queen will ban all disputations on holy writ by anyone other than qualified scholars, for these days even 'lymmer lawdis and little lassis lo / Will argun bayth with bischop, preist, and freir'. 'The Justing and Debait up at the Drum betwix Wa. Adamsone and Johine Sym' has these two worthy commoners in a burlesque of knightly combat and shares both its earthy vivacity and its metre with the older 'Christis Kirk' and 'Peblis' poems. With the exception of a couple of psalms, the rest of Scott's work (or what was preserved of it in the Bannatyne Manuscript), consists of love lyrics. Some of these follow a medieval ethos by giving a coarse recital of the sexual weaknesses of women ('Ane Ballat Maid to the Derisioun and Scorne of Wantoun Wemen'), while others are more sophisticated in a playfully cynical, Ovidian way, as in 'Of Wemenkynd', where the poet begins by posing himself a problem:

> I muse and mervellis in my mind,
> Quhat way to wryt, or put in vers,
> The quent consaitis of wemenkynd . . . .

Scott's verse is technically various: he can use short, simple lines, rather in the manner of Skelton, or metrical gymnastics reminiscent of Dunbar. The following lines from 'A Rondel of Luve' use the old French rondel form, with an epigrammatic succinctness:

> Lufe is an fervent fyre
> Kendillit without desyre:
> Schort plesour, lang displesour;
> Repentence is the hyre;
> Ane pure tressour without mesour:
> Lufe is an fervent fyre.

In all cases Scott's muse explores the pain of sophisticated love affairs expressed in a worldly, sometimes facile manner, not unlike Wyatt's love poems, but technically more polished. It is physical attraction that Scott pursues, and, if there is little sense of the ideal in his work, he can still rise to an erotic directness.

The 'Castalian band'

The poetry of the sixteenth century closes with the productions of Alexander Montgomerie and James VI's 'Castalian band'. When the boy king escaped from the Protestant nobles who had kidnapped him on the 'Ruthven Raid', he re-established himself at court (in 1583) surrounded by more sympathetic lords. James produced his own poems in *Poetical Exercises* (1591), and the *Essayes of a Prentise in the Divine Art of Poesie* (1584), prefaced by the 'Reulis and Cautelis'. James's pretensions allowed him to style himself as 'Apollo' ruling a court where poetry and song were to prevail. The play *Philotus* was probably a part of the court's entertainment during these years, but the little group could not support a wider theatrical tradition. Among these courtly practitioners of the muse, Alexander Montgomerie is the most distinguished, having taken the king's fancy by challenging another writer – Patrick Hume of Polwarth – to a flyting-match and defeating him in floods of ingenious invective. The other poets remain resolutely minor, including James himself. The king came to call his circle 'brothers of the Castalian band', after the fountain of Castalia, sacred to Apollo and muses. During this special decade of music and poetry, models were sought and works translated from France and Italy, many Petrarchan-style love-sonnets were written in the English manner or after Ronsard, and always the qualities of smoothness and sophisticated lightness were prized.

Although not Castalian 'brothers', Robert Sempill and 'old Alexander Scott' would have visited the court and had a ready audience there, while another poet of the period, **Alexander Hume** (1557–1609) grew tired of seeking royal favour and withdrew to become a minister of the church at Logie, near Stirling. Hume renounced his early secular work in favour of worthier themes and prefaced his collection *Hymns and Sacred*

Songs (1599) with the sour remark that 'In princes' Courts . . . the chief pastime is to sing prophane sonnets, and vaine ballads of love.' Despite this moral tone, his best-known poem, 'Of the Day Estivall', is a beautiful description of a Midsummer's Day, celebrating domestic, rural observances and every natural detail bathed in heat and a brilliant light:

> What pleasour were to walke and see
> Endlang a river cleare,
> The perfite forme of everie tree,
> Within the deepe appeare?

> The Salmon out of cruifs and creels
> Up hailed into skowts,   cobles (fishing boats)
> The bells, and circles on the weills,
> throw lowpping of the trouts.   jumping

> O: then it were a seemely thing,
> While all is still and calme,
> The praise of God to play and sing,
> With cornet and with shalme.

Alexander Montgomerie (1545?–1610?) met the favour of his king – he was a distant blood relation – and came to prominence in his mid thirties. He had quite a large poetic output, although much of his work was not published until relatively modern times. The seventeen-year-old monarch enjoyed Montgomerie's poetry, hailed him as a master in the craft and awarded him a pension in 1583 (although it took the poet some ten years of manoeuvring to collect it). For his part, Montgomerie took care to admire his royal patron without fear of excess, even if, at times, he saw quite clearly what life at court entailed: 'First thou mon preis thy Prince to pleiss, / Thoght contrare Conscience he commands'. Montgomerie left Scotland in 1586, perhaps on business for James, which took him to Flanders, France and Spain. He was a Catholic involved with Catholic interests at court, and this connection may explain his mission and the fact that he got into unspecified trouble abroad and was imprisoned there for some years. He returned to Scotland in 1591, but by this time his fortunes were ebbing, for he had slipped from James's favour. When he was implicated in a Catholic plot in 1597 – apparently to do with a Spanish invasion – he more or less disappeared from public ken.

Montgomerie wrote many love-sonnets without particular distinction, showing the influence of Scott, Ronsard and the English models of Wyatt and Sidney. Although he affects the conventional pose of complaint both as a man of affairs and as a lover, there is at times a genuinely pessimistic and irritable cast to his poems, a note which the affliction of gout and the instability of his financial status probably did nothing to dispel. A coarser and wilder delight, reminiscent of Dunbar's technique, informs the 'Flyting betwixt Montgomerie and Polwart', a sustained and lengthy exercise in the old-fashioned duel of invective 'by ryme' – 'anger to asswage, make melancholy lesse.' Montgomerie begins in relatively mild terms:

> POLWART, yee peip like a mouse amongst thornes;
> Na cunning yee keepe; POLWART, yee peip;
> Ye look like a sheipe an ye had twa hornes:
> POLWART, ye peip like a mouse amongst thornes.

In due course Polwarth replies, and forcefully, too. Enraged that he should be 'bitten' in verse by another, and especially bitten by such 'a duck' as Polwarth, Montgomerie promises to drive him from the 'kings chimney nuike', but not before his adversary delivers a few raspberries more:

> Thou was begotten, some sayes mee,
> Betwixt the devil and a dun kow,
> An night when that the fiend was fow.

Since Montgomerie seems to have spent part of his youth in Argyll, Polwarth chides him for having Highland connections, showing, like Dunbar, a courtier's contempt for life in the west. Tradition has it that James gave the victory to Montgomerie, but it is Polwarth who has the exhaustive last word, sustained for sixty-six lines in lavatorial strain:

> Fond flytter, shit shytter, bacon byther, all defyld!
> Blunt bleittar, paddock pricker, puddin eiter, perverse!
> Hen plucker, closet mucker, house cucker, very vyld!
> Tanny cheeks, I think thou speiks with thy breeks, foul-erse!

In complete contrast to the rude extravagances of the flyting, the aureate lines of 'The Bankis of Helicon' celebrate the beauty of the poet's lady; but they, too, suggest echoes of

Dunbar and really belong to an earlier mode of writing. The same stanza-form (invented by Montgomerie) and the same somewhat antique mode of expression are seen to better effect in *The Cherrie and the Slae*, Montgomerie's longest and most famous work. It was published in 1597 and by the end of the eighteenth century it had gone through twenty-two editions, making it the most widely read Scots poem next to the *Wallace* and the verses of Burns. Allan Ramsay included it in *Ever Green* and copied the form for his own 'The Vision', while Burns later adopted the complex fourteen-line 'quatorzain' stanza for his 'Epistle to Davie' and the recitative parts of the 'The Jolly Beggars'.

The Cherrie and the Slae opens on a May morning whose crystal clear light beams down on a landscape typical of the old dream allegories. Although Montgomerie uses some 'enamelled' terms and peoples the scene with classical references, he also draws on images from nature and manages to imbue the scene with a sense of idyllic freshness. In this setting, the poet accidentally wounds himself with one of Cupid's darts and finds himself possessed not only by Courage, Desire and Hope, but also by their counterparts, Dread, Danger and Despair. Too late he realises that his peace of mind has left him:

> To late I knaw quha hewis too hie
> The spail sall fall into his eie,   chips; eye
>   To late I went to Scuillis:
> To late I heard the swallow preiche,
> To late Experience dois teache,
>   The Skuil-maister of fuillis:
> To late to fynde the nest I seik,
>   Quhen all the birdis are flowin:
> To late the stabill dore I steik,   shut
>   Quhen all the steids are stowin:
>   To lait ay, their stait ay,
>   All fulische folke espye:
>   Behynd so, they fynd so,
>   Remeid and so do I.

Montgomerie's quatorzain is at its best with these wry and *triste* epigrams. In this state of mind the poet comes to a stream before a precipitous crag with a cherry-tree growing at the top, while below, on his side of the water, a bush of sloe-berries offers itself to any passer-by. He is divided between a sweet, impossible ideal, and the humbler, sourer, more attainable fruit of expediency. As a love-allegory the symbols ask him to choose between a high-born lady and a common mistress, and the young lover's divided feelings engage in a symbolic debate before he finally decides to seek the cherries. No sooner has the allegorical company arrived at the unclimbable cherry-tree, than the ripe fruit drops into the poet's hands. When he tastes the cherries he finds himself relieved of every care and offers up praises to God.

The descriptive opening scenes are detailed, charming and in the familiar love-allegory mode, but the debate that follows is lengthy, abstract and rather tedious, despite classical allusions and many familiar proverbs done in telling rhyme. Indeed some critics have maintained that the argument is an addition prompted only by an impulse to moralise. The allegory, too, is undoubtedly odd, for it conveys a fable about erotic experience with all the conventional trappings of the *Roman de la Rose*, and then turns into an extended sermon. Helena Shire explains the predominance of the *débat* by making the convincing case that at one level the choice between cherry-tree and sloe-bush is, for Montgomerie, a choice between the Catholic and the Reformed churches. This fits what we know of the poet's sympathies and it certainly explains why the option is discussed at such length and in such weighty terms. Whatever the complexities of the allegory, the poem most probably earned its wide popularity through the freshness of those opening scenes and because of the epigrammatical impact of dozens of quotable saws, such as 'Quhat can thou losse, quhen honour lyvis?', or 'Brunt bairn with fyre the danger dreidis', or 'als guid drinking out of glas, / As gold in ony wise' and the marvellously 'oratorious' 'Tak time in time or time be tint [lost] / For tyme will not remaine' – worthy of Polonius at his most lugubrious. Montgomerie has been called the 'last of the makars', but, notwithstanding the partial success of *The Cherrie and the Slae*, he cannot really match the earlier work of Henryson, Dunbar, Douglas or Lindsay, and with him the golden age of Scottish poetry undoubtedly declines and comes to a close.

The contest between Montgomerie and Polwarth reminds us that in flyting, at least, Gaelic forms were still present in court life, although it is possible that the wildness of the mode was granted a special tolerance by the sophisticates of the 'Castalian band'. In the oral tradition of Gaeldom at large, bardic measures were still as formal as anything in the classical canon of the Renaissance, but it is not clear if this was ever fully appreciated by that courtly group of musicians and writers with their sights set on England and Europe. In fact the period from the sixteenth to the eighteenth centuries was particularly rich in Gaelic music and songs and the latter introduced a shift towards a more vernacular Gaelic which began to penetrate formal bardic practice later in the following century. A popular tradition in Scots songs and ballads was beginning to stir as well, but it seems appropriate to end this chapter with a closer look at something of the culture which Montgomerie must have left behind him in Argyll.

Gaelic song and music

Gaelic songs derive from the community in the most direct way, and all their values, in both technique and outlook, stem from a conservative society, isolated, clan-based and bound by strong family ties and an enduring sense of place. Thus there are many songs celebrating place – islands, hills and favourite glens, and traditional themes and approaches prevail even in accounts of human relationships. The song-style often uses the first person and offers many striking details and yet it retains an objective and unselfconscious dignity, more elevated than the voice of the Scots ballads but similarly impersonal in its progress, even when involved (as in the Scots tradition too) with songs of betrayal and longing and supernatural encounter.

Many Gaelic songs take a 'functional' context. For instance, the *iorram* or rowing-songs use the rhythms of the oars to deal with battles or laments – for the clans often sailed to war, and a dead chieftain would be carried to burial in his boat. Some of the earliest surviving vernacular songs deal with war, and the Jacobite risings ensured that this particular genre was heard well into the nineteenth century, even if its expression varies from direct incitement to romantic nostalgia. On the distaff side there are innumerable songs connected with the task of reaping, spinning, weaving, waulking and milking, not to mention love-songs, lullabies, and ballads from the point of view of the jealous woman. Early examples of these show all the signs of an oral art by which songs are retained in the memory, performed and transmitted with the help of repetition, traditional images and more or less stock epithets. At the same time, such 'work songs' or songs for particular occasions became a recognised mode within which poets could seek a more literary expression.

The *oran luadhaidh*, or waulking-song, was sung by women, often in a call-and-response pattern, while they 'waulked' lengths of wet cloth by pulling and rubbing on it to thicken the fibres. One such early Gaelic waulking-song, 'Seathan, Son of the King of Ireland' ('Seathan Mac Righ Eireann'), may date from the sixteenth century, and in one version at least, is almost 200 lines long. The singer of 'Seathan' laments the death of her lover in long rhyming paragraphs in which her memories and desires accumulate extraordinary emotional force by way of repetition and a host of details:

But Seathan is in the lonely chamber,
without drinking of cups or goblets,
without drinking of wines from splendid silver tankards,
without drinking of ale with his cronies and gentlemen,
without drinking to music, without kiss from seductive woman,
without music of harp, without listening to melody,
but strait bands on his shoulders,
and looped bands on the bier poles.

I am a sister of Aodh and yellow-haired Brian,
I am a kinswoman of Fionn son of Cumhall,
I am the wife of brown-haired Seathan, the wanderer,
but alas! for those who said I was a joyous wife,
I am a poor, sad, mournful, sorrowful wife,
ful of anguish and grief and woe. . . .

If Seathan could be but redeemed
The ransom could be got like rushes,
silver could be got like ashes,
gold could be got on the fringe of meadows,
wine could be got like spring water,
beer could be got like a cool verdant stream;
there would not be a goat in the rock or stony upland,
there would not be a young she-goat in meadow,
there would not be a sheep on rocky shelf or mountain top,
there would not be cattle on plain or in fold,
there would not be pig or cow in pastures;
the salmon would come from the seas,
the trout would come from the river-banks,

the geldings would come from the rushes;
there would not be a black or white-shouldered cow
high or low in the fold,
at the edge of the township or in stall,
that I would not send, my love, to redeem thee,
even to my green plaid,
though that should take the one cow from me,
and it was not the one black cow of my fold,
but herds of white-shouldered cattle,
of white-headed, white-backed, red-eared cattle.

But Seathan is to-night in the upper town,
neither gold nor tears will win him,
neither drink nor music . . .

(trs. Alexander Carmichael; rev. J. C. Watson, A. Matheson)

(The use of exhaustive catalogues in this way has been a powerful and common device in Gaelic and Irish literature through the ages. The same penchant appears in Scots work such as *The Complaynt of Scotland*, or even Urquhart's *Rabelais*, as well as in the modern world-language poems of MacDiarmid, or in the prose of Irish writers such as James Joyce and Samuel Beckett, who delight in presenting the reader with lengthy and all-inclusive lists.)

The Gaelic song-book has ballads, religious verses, nonsense pieces, drinking-songs and lullabies, but it is especially rich in love-songs and laments – *cumha*. Many love-songs celebrate courting and physical beauty, others have a more melancholy edge of loss or betrayal. The ritual practice of keening over the dead body of a loved one has produced a context for some particularly moving songs, and sometimes chilling images. 'Brown-haired Allan, I would go with you' ('Ailein Duinn, shiubhlainn leat') is a lament from the eighteenth century, composed by Ann Campbell of Scalpay in Harris, and like 'Seathan' it uses long rhymed verse-paragraphs of irregular length. It was made for the death of her fiancé, who was lost at sea on his way to their wedding:

It is a sale tale I have tonight,
not of the death of the cattle in want,
but of the wetness of your shirt,
and of the porpoises tearing at you.

Brown-haired Allan,
I heard that you had been drowned,
would that I were beside you,
on whatever rock or bank you came ashore,
in whatever heap of seaweed the high tide leaves you.
I would drink a drink, whatever my kin say,
not of the red wine of Spain
but of your breast's blood, I would prefer that . . .

(trs. D. Thomson)

If song and music can be said to thrive in Scotland from the sixteenth to the eighteenth centuries, then there is particular genius to be found in the essentially folk-based traditions of Gaelic and the Scots ballads. By comparison, the songs of James VI's Castalian poets belong to a shallower and more urbane genre which looks to European models in form and music and never achieves the penetrating cry of the Gaelic *cumha*, or the grim concision of the Border ballads. And, of course, the full effect of these native songs is not felt until their haunting melodies are heard with all the incisive delivery of the traditional singer, whose sense of timing and use of grace notes far transcend in passion and power the politer classical training of the *salon*.

Gaelic songs can be sung on their own, like the ballads, or they can be accompanied by the little Celtic harp, the *clarsach* – also a solo instrument in its own right for quiet melodies. The *clarsach* goes back to the early society of aristocratic Gaeldom; Highland bards would be sent to Ireland to learn its use, and chiefs of the old style would keep a harper in their entourage, along with a bard, a piper and even a fool. Among the last of these minstrels in Scotland was Roderick Morison – 'the blind harper' – from Lewis, who lived in Lochaber and Skye in the seventeenth century under the protection of the Clan Mac-Leod. Airs to his songs have survived, but little of his purely instrumental work remains. In general the fiddle took over from the harp in succeeding generations, and indeed, some harp tunes were only preserved through fiddle adaptations, until the nineteenth century saw a revival of interest in the *clarsach* as an instrument for ladies in the drawing-room.

As though reflecting the fiercer side of the Highland sensibility, the bagpipe is a more disturbing and warlike instrument. Like the harp, its origins are too ancient to be specifically Scottish, and in the Middle Ages it was widely known throughout Europe. In the isolation of the Highlands, however, pipe-music continued to develop well into the nineteenth century, and thrives today in marches and dances (strathspeys, reels and jigs) as well as the more melodic slow airs. The finest pipe-music is not to be found with the massed bands and tartans of modern times, but with the solo pipes playing *ceòl mór* ('the big music') – unique to Scotland and originally called simply 'pipe-playing' (*piobaireachd*, or, in English, pibroch). This, the 'classical music' of the bagpipe, first states a simple theme as the *urlar*, or ground, and moves to *siubhal*, or variation, the variations increasing in complexity until *crunluath*, the climax, is reached and the progression ends with a return to the bare ground. The rules of construction and variation are highly developed, and pipe-tunes and their proper fingering can be passed on only by personal tuition, so a system of mimetic chanting called *canntaireachd* was evolved as a level of aural notation – although it could also be written down as 'words'. Conventional musical notation only came to be used in the mid nineteenth century and it still cannot give a complete account of the subtleties of the grace notes and how the instrument should be fingered. Like Celtic carving or the art of the Book of Kells, pibroch favours complication and technical virtuosity as the tune is gradually embellished with repetition or variation through the multiplication of notes, all within a fixed framework. Yet the melody too is vital, for these deceptively simple pentatonic lines are the ground or 'floor' upon which everything else is built. Tunes from the pipe-tradition can equal the finest melodies in European music, and it has been suggested that Dvořák first heard the slow movement of the 'New World' symphony in the beautiful air of 'MacIntosh's Lament'. Pibrochs can be stirring war-tunes, or boasts and challenges in the *brosnachadh* vein, but some of the finest tunes of glory have been the laments, poignant and strong, sad and yet somehow exultant.

We know little about early pipe-music except that it existed, and even the development of pibroch is unclear until the sixteenth century, when an almost legendary family called the MacCrimmons appeared as hereditary pipers to the Macleods of Skye, where they are reputed to have run a piping-college at

Boreraig. Some of the finest pibrochs were composed by MacCrimmons during the seventeenth and eighteenth centuries, when pibroch really came into its own, and the same family had pipers in it for another hundred years. Other families made significant contributions too, often beginning with MacCrimmon tuition, and two in particular stand out. The Mackays of Gairloch were descended from Iain Dall MacKay (1656–1754), the blind piper whose masterpiece, 'Lament for Patrick Og MacCrimmon', was composed in honour of his old teacher. The MacKays of Raasay, on the other hand, stem from John MacKay (1767–1845), who mastered about 250 tunes in *canntaireachd* and passed on a large part of the MacCrimmon heritage. In turn his son Angus (1813–58) recorded over 180 tunes in manuscript, to make a link with piping in modern times. Perhaps it is in pibroch, more than in any other art from a relatively remote Highland society, that the autonomy and the sophisticated intensity of Gaelic culture developed to its furthest and purest expression.

4

The seventeenth century: crown and Covenant; the ballads

AFTER the union of the crowns, Scotland was disrupted by conflict for almost ninety years as the struggle between Presbyterians, Episcopalians, Catholics and extreme dissenters continued. For the people in the northern part of the kingdom, the Civil War, the Restoration and the Revolution Settlement were only further episodes in a cause which had started, as far as they were concerned, with the triumph of the Kirk in Mary's reign and the Declaration of Faith in 1560. These disputatious years devoured the intellectual and creative energies of two generations to the exclusion of almost everything else. Among Scottish writers, Drummond and Urquhart are of some note, and of course the oral ballad-tradition must not be forgotten, but, even so, there are no Scots writers to equal Donne, Marvell, Milton and Bunyan. Perhaps the best poetic expression of the turbulent times everywhere in the north came from the biting verses of Iain Lom, who used a more vernacular Gaelic than the old bards had favoured, and whose work looks forward to the flowering of Gaelic verse in the next century.

From the vantage-point of his new throne in London, James VI and I,* began to reconsolidate his authority. He used his powers to restore episcopacy in Scotland, and when Charles I acceded in 1625 he continued his father's policy by reclaiming for the crown all those Church lands which had been redistributed by the Reformation. After the coronation at Edinburgh in 1633, Charles passed acts of parliament to establish

* Henceforth the old line of 'Stewards' were to spell their name 'Stuart'.

Anglican forms of worship – on pain of excommunication. The communion-table was turned back into an altar, confession was restored and a new prayer-book imposed. Popular unrest spread and in 1637 a famous riot broke out in St Giles' Cathedral, when a band of serving-women attacked the priest for following the new ways. At a more responsible level a plebiscite was organised to declare support for the 1560 Confession of Faith. This 'National Covenant' was drawn up at Greyfriars' Churchyard in 1638 and signed by thousands of people from all classes amid scenes of delirious fervour. The Covenant declared loyalty to the king, but requested him to re-establish the goals of Presbyterianism and not to interfere with the proper business of a free parliament and the General Assembly. The next two years saw the spasmodic 'Bishops' Wars' until Montrose's tactics with the volunteer Covenanting armies eventually persuaded Charles to make concessions to the Scots by calling an English parliament – only to have that parliament take away his right to terminate it. (Indeed, the 'Long Parliament' was eventually to depose him.) When the Civil War broke out in the south the Scottish extremists pressed their case and the 'Solemn League and Covenant' was drawn up in 1643 to force the king to stamp out Catholicism and Episcopacy throughout Britain. At this point Montrose's conscience led him to side with Charles, and he was not alone in his belief that the Solemn League had gone too far. The Highlands had never been too enthusiastic, even about the relatively mild National Covenant, and so Montrose found support there to wage a brief and brilliant military campaign. His forces began to dwindle, however, and after defeat at Philiphaugh in 1645 he had to escape into exile. Inspired by their ministers' battle-cry of 'Jesus and no quarter!', the unforgiving Convenanters massacred the beaten clansmen and all their wives and children for days. Despite his defeat, when it finally came at Naseby, Charles still refused to sign the Solemn League and Covenant and by this time the Independents in the New Model Army had become equally uncomfortable with the notion of universal compulsory Presbyterianism. Nevertheless, the Covenanters were still convinced that their faith could be imposed by royal decree, and after Charles's execution in 1649 they took their cause to his nineteen-year-old exiled son. He too refused, and once again Montrose was prevailed upon to take up arms on behalf of kingship and his king, only to be betrayed and captured within a few months. 'Arrayed like a bridegroom' in fine linen and ribbons, he was executed at the Mercat Cross in Edinburgh in 1650 – and only a month later his young Stuart prince signed the Covenant after all. With a bloody reversal only too typical of the times, the Scots Presbyterian forces duly marched south to fight against Cromwell on behalf of what was now the Royalist cause. They were defeated at Worcester in 1651; Charles escaped to France, and Scotland was subdued under English judges and troops commanded by General Monck. Peace prevailed for the next eight years, although after two decades of civil and religious turmoil it had an air of exhaustion about it.

The Restoration in 1660 was welcomed by the Scots – after all, Charles was still a Stuart monarch; but the more radical Presbyterians from the south-west (called 'Whiggamores' during the Civil War) resented the return of bishops, not to mention the king and his favoured lords. Some 300 dissenting ministers left their parishes and held services with their congregations on the open hillsides, despite attempts by troopers to disperse them. It was not long before an armed rising of dissenters from Galloway declared for the Covenant and marched on Edinburgh, only to be routed at Rullion Green in the Pentlands by Sir Thomas Dalyell of the Binns. Many were transported to Barbados and a few were hanged at the gibbet, but the hillside conventicles continued to grow – even after it was made a capital offence to attend them. These were 'the Killing Times', when radical preachers carried weapons and their congregations were harried by the mounted dragoons of Dalyell and John Graham of Claverhouse, who noted that 'there were as many elephants and crocodiles in Galloway as loyal or regular persons'. Walter Scott's novel *Old Mortality* deals with what happened after 1678 when Archbishop Sharp of St Andrew's was brutally murdered by a party of Covenanters who came across his coach outside the city. The dissenters' ambitions were further aroused by a confused engagement at Drumclog, during which an armed conventicle put the dragoons of 'bluidy Clavers' to flight. Flushed with success, but divided by internal disputes, the Covenanters raised an army of 5000 which was eventually defeated by the king's forces at Bothwell Brig. Yet every death was a martyrdom which added to their resolve. Militant working-class groups such as Richard Cameron's 'Society Folk' refused to make allegience to any ruler other than Christ himself, and so they were outlawed and persecuted. Some Cameronians were killed on the spot for refusing to acknowledge the king, and, although such brutal acts were not widespread, they provided powerful moral and political ammunition which the Covenanters were not slow to use in comparing themselves to the Children of Israel under the oppression of a godless Pharaoh.

Paradoxically, the cause of Presbyterianism was best served by James II when he came to the throne in 1685 and proceeded, against advice, to restore Catholics to power throughout the realm. In both England and Scotland this amounted to political suicide, and within three years, faced with widespread revolution, James had to forfeit the crown to his sister Mary and her husband from Protestant Holland, William of Orange. John Graham of Claverhouse ('Bonnie Dundee' to his supporters) came out for James's cause and led some of the clans to victory at Killiecrankie, but he himself was killed on the field. Without his leadership his dispirited forces were finally defeated at Dunkeld at the hands of a Protestant 'Cameronian' regiment who had so recently been outlaws themselves, fleeing from 'Clavers' when he, in his turn, had been the arm of established authority. A similar rising in Ireland was defeated by King William and his army at the Battle of the Boyne, and to this day the date '1690' and the epithet 'King Billy' have been rallying-cries for intransigently anti-Catholic 'Orangemen' in Ulster and Scotland.

The Highland clans were required to sign an oath of fealty to William, and, when the MacDonalds of Glencoe were late to do so in 1692, the Secretary of State in Scotland decided to make an example of them. In due course Campbell soldiers descended on winter-bound Glencoe and sought hospitality from the MacDonalds. After several days of food and shelter, the soldiers turned on their hosts in an act of planned terrorism, killing nearly forty MacDonalds and driving the rest out into the snow. The 'Massacre of Glencoe' outraged public opinion, and, although it encouraged other chiefs to recognise William, they did not forget the matter, nor the treachery of the Campbells. Nor was the Jacobite question resolved, for, when James II died in exile in 1701, his son James (the 'Old

Pretender' and father to 'Bonnie Prince Charlie') was recognised by Louis XIV as the rightful and Catholic heir to the British throne.

The rest of Scotland returned to a semblance of stability, with the wheel of prejudice now turned against the Episcopalians as the General Assembly recovered its influence and restored the heritage of Knox and Melville. In material terms the last twenty years of the century saw a growth in trade and prosperity and Scots capital began to look for investments abroad. Plans were made for expansion to Africa and the East Indies, but, when these were blocked by the influence of the East India Company, Scottish businessmen came up with the optimistic 'Darien Scheme' (1698) to form a trading-company of their own in central America. The chosen site was ridden with fever, however, and when things began to go wrong the English trading-interests in Jamaica refused to help, and even hindered the project. The Darien adventure ended with many deaths, a resounding commercial loss to the country and much bitterness against the English.

The seventeenth century seemed determined to end badly as a series of poor harvests brought poverty and famine to Scotland and most of northern Europe. But Scotland's hardship had been more than material, and, after almost a hundred years of civil, constitutional and religious strife, the cost in psychological and cultural terms can scarcely be calculated. On the one hand the Presbyterian ideal enhanced the status of every individual citizen as he or she stood, literate and alone, before God and the word of God in the Bible. On the other hand, the Kirk could not allow such freedom to lead to licence and unorthodoxy, and so the parish minister and his elders played an influential part in social and moral guidance and control. When narrow Calvinism was in the ascendancy, as it was from 1690 until about 1720, such men had the baleful power of commissars in a one-party state and, indeed, in 1696 an Edinburgh student was actually executed for the crime of blasphemy. In cultural terms the humane spirit and the vigorous language of the makars had all but disappeared. Many Scots intellectuals were turning to London, to English and even to Latin for their models, and gradually Scots was becoming regarded as the vernacular speech of country people. This sad process of 'vernacularisation' continued into the next century, but its results were not entirely negative. If Scots was associated with 'vu̇lgar' directness, then it also spoke with the very voice of the people – vigorous, swift, violent, earthy, realistically in touch with hardship and the seasons and yet capable, too, of romance and a sense of wonder at the supernatural. James's 'Castalian band' had quite lost touch with such forces, but they were burgeoning nevertheless without need of courtly patronage in the great Scottish ballads – some of the finest and most popular examples of the oral tradition to be found anywhere in the world. It was not until the end of the century and the beginning of the next that this colloquial energy was to flourish again in a more peaceful world of books and publishing.

Poets at court

When King James took the road to London in 1603 he retained his role as patron of the muse and was soon joined by a number of Scottish poets. William Alexander and Robert Ayton received knighthoods and positions of favour; Sir David Murray (fl. 1620) later joined the short-lived Prince Henry's retinue, and the sonneteer Robert Kerr (1578–1654) received an earldom from Charles I and became an intimate of the London *literati*. **Sir William Alexander** (1577?–1640) wrote sonnets in the fashion of a gentleman of the day. An admirer of Spenser, he knew Drummond in the north and befriended Michael Drayton in England, but there is little of lasting value in *Aurora*, his collection of sonnets published in 1604. A venture into Jacobean verse drama resulted in four 'Monarchicke Tragedies' (1603–7) outlining the perils of ambition; and a sustained exercise in verse produced over 10,000 moral and unexciting lines in *Doomesday* (1614). Alexander rose to be Secretary of State for Scotland, but he was an unpopular and profit-seeking politician who eventually lost everything and died in poverty.

Sir Robert Ayton (1569–1638) was a better poet with a degree of skill in English verse as well as in Latin, French and Greek. Ayton, from a prosperous Fife family, joined the court shortly after the king's arrival in London, and within eight years he had been knighted and made a member of the royal household. He made friends of Ben Jonson and Hobbes and appears in Aubrey's *Brief Lives*. In common with many of his accomplished contemporaries, however, he was not published in his own lifetime, nor did he consider himself to 'affect the name of a poet'. His best work is probably to be found in songs for the lute rather like Thomas Campion's, and it is possible that he was the author of the original version of the piece which Burns turned into 'Auld Lang Syne'. Only a few of his early poems were in Scots, while almost half his output was in Latin, with verses addressed to the king on all the issues of the day, including some lines on the Gunpowder Plot of 1605.

Many contemporary Scottish writers were similarly fluent in Latin, and they too chose to eschew the vernacular tradition in favour of the scholarly example of George Buchanan. Among these were the gallant James Crichton (1560–83), later hailed by Sir Thomas Urquhart as 'the admirable Crichtoun', and Arthur Johnston (1587–1661) who edited and contributed to an anthology of many other Scottish Latin poets – *Delitiae Poetarum Scotorum* (1637). **James Graham, the Marquis of Montrose** (1612–50), is mainly remembered for the brilliance of his brief military career, but he too produced civilised verses. The best known of these is addressed to his mistress as 'My Dear and Only Love', but four lines from it could well apply to the author's own grim end:

> He either fears his Fate too much,
>   Or his Deserts are small,
> That puts it not unto the Touch,
>   To win or lose it all.

William Drummond of Hawthornden (1585–1649)

Unlike his friend Montrose, William Drummond tried to avoid public life and religious dispute. Educated in Edinburgh and a student of law in France, he inherited his father's estate at Hawthornden near Lasswade, just outside Edinburgh, and decided to settle there at the age of twenty-four on his own terms as a man of letters. He collected books avidly and expanded Hawthornden's already substantial library; he read widely in French and Italian and showed a taste for epigrams, anagrams, ephemera and curiosities of all sorts. Drummond's first poem, 'Teares, on the Death of Moeliades' (1612), was a conventional lament on the death of Prince Henry, James's eldest son, infused with the influence of Sir Philip Sidney. Before long he had compiled a collection of songs and a sequence modelled on *Astrophel and Stella*, with other sonnets translated or adapted from French and Italian, all in a sad neo-Platonic vein. This romantic colouring does seem to have been a genuine part of Drummond's temperament, later reinforced by the early death of his fiancée in 1616. Drummond's collection was first published probably in 1614 and then again in 1616, finely bound and expensively set, just as he insisted all his works should be.

Drummond was especially keen to be appreciated in England, and his manuscripts show his many literary debts and the care he took to excise all Scotticisms of expression and spelling from his verse. Within formal modes his elegant lines aim for a smooth and decorative flow of sound, rather than for the strenuous dialectic of Donne or the wit of Marvell. Nevertheless, Drummond's fellow writers thought highly of his erudition and, like them, we can admire his particular penchant for sweet and sensuously melancholy accounts of loneliness:

> Sound hoarse sad *Lute*, true Witnesse of my Woe,
> And striue no more to ease self-chosen Paine
> With Soule-enchanting Sounds, your Accents straine
> Vnto these Teares vncessantly which flow.
> Shrill Treeble weepe, and you dull Basses show
> Your Masters Sorrow *in a deadly Vaine*,
> Let neuer ioyfull Hand vpon you goe,
> Nor Consort keepe but when you doe complaine.
> Flie Phoebus Rayes, nay, hate the irkesome Light,
> Woods solitarie Shades for thee are best,
> Or the black Horrours of the blackest Night,
> When all the *World* (saue Thou and I) doth rest:
> Then sound sad Lute, and beare a mourning Part,
> Thou *Hell* may'st mooue, though not a Woman's *Heart*.

(Sonnet xxviii of 'The First Part')

Despite his declared preference for Hawthornden, the 'sweet solitarie Place, Where from the vulgare I estranged liue', Drummond was not a complete recluse. He corresponded with Michael Drayton in England and with Alexander and Kerr, his fellow Scots at court in London. Ben Jonson particularly admired Drummond's work, visiting Scotland late in 1618 to stay at Hawthornden for three weeks. The host made notes on his guest's table talk and his *Conversations with Ben Jonson* (1711) have become well known and widely quoted, not least for the portrait they paint of the bibulous playwright as a 'contemner and Scorner of others' and a 'great lover and praiser of himself'.

Drummond developed the melancholy of his earlier poems to produce *Flowres of Sion* (1623), a collection of madrigals, sonnets and hymns all of which reflect on human frailty, on the instability of the world and on the 'contemplation of invisible excellences above by the visible below' (Sonnet xviii).

> O Sunne invisible, that doest abide
> Within thy bright abysmes, most faire, most darke,
> Where with thy proper Rayes thou dost thee hide;
> O euer-shining neuer full seene marke,
>   To guide mee in Lifes Night, thy light mee show,
>   The more I search of thee, the lesse I know.
>
> (Sonnet xvii)

Once again the poet praises the lonely life, but now his sonnets have a more philosophical dimension, named after spiritual solitaries and outcasts – 'For the Prodigal', 'For the Magdalene' and 'For the Baptiste'. Drummond's best poems are in this mode, and if some of them have been translated from other sources then the work has been well and fully assimilated into the poet's own character. In the same volume he developed his theme in prose with *A Cypresse Grove*, a meditation on death derived from Italian models and especially from the French of Montaigne's *Essais*. Written almost twenty years before Sir Thomas Browne's *Religio Medici* was published, *A Cypresse Grove, or Philosophical Reflections Against the Fear of Death* anticipates and matches the latter's achievement with a musical and weighty prose written largely for poetic effect. Perhaps Drummond is the more sober of the two, for he lacks the conjurer's adroitness with which the Norwich man makes to dance the heavy furniture of his style.

Despite *A Cypresse Grove*, 'wormewood' was not Drummond's only food, nor 'Teares his Drinke', and during the course of his life he produced satirical and sexually comic verses as well as various proverbs and epigrams. He is usually credited with a Macaronic jest called 'Polemo-Middinia', where Scots and English words are mixed with dog Latin and given Latin endings to lampoon a countryside quarrel over rights of way on a footpath. He had a mistress and three children and at forty-five he married and fathered another large family. In 1627 he had invented and patented plans for numerous ingenious weapons of war and by 1633 he had become well enough known to be put in charge of the pageant for Charles I's visit to Edinburgh. He found politics uncongenial and had little sympathy with the more extreme Presbyterians, although he had signed the National Covenant in 1638. His pamphlets in favour of peace and toleration on all sides were not published during his lifetime. *Irene, A Remonstrance for Concord, Amitie and Love amongst His Majesties Subjects* (1638) praises Charles I for making concessions to the Covenant and lectures the commoners on the virtues of obedience: 'Good Princes should be obeyed, yea evill Princes should be tollerated . . . they are not to be judged by their Subjectes.'

Perhaps the author's peaceful seclusion on the banks of the North Esk would not have survived the broadcasting of such sentiments; but, in any case, events moved on without Drummond. A lengthy *History of Scotland* covering the period 1423–1542 was published six years after his death and has little to distinguish it. Drummond ended his days at Hawthornden with his wealth greatly reduced, engaged in litigation and embittered by the times in which he lived. He left an unfinished satire about a country 'latlie turned most part Mad' by the worshipping of a golden 'calfe anant' (Covenant) which was really only made of paper after all. His youthful taste for solitude had turned a little sour in the mouth, and, as a conservative who looked back to the Elizabethan England of Sidney and Spenser for his literary values, his isolation in the Scotland of the turbulent 1640s was never more poignantly acute.

Writing in prose

Alas, the music of *A Cypresse Grove* is not typical, and for the most part Scottish prose in the seventeenth century consists of treatises on religious doctrine, church politics, histories, memoirs, letters, or contumacious and wordy mixtures of all these. Whatever their sectarian views, almost everyone followed Knox's example in avoiding overtly Scottish expressions. The historian David Hume (1560–1630) supported the use of Scots but confessed that he too had 'yielded . . . to the tyranny of custom and the times' by 'not seeking curiously for words, but taking them as they came to hand'. His equivocal feelings about Scots may be gathered from the fact that he changed the name of his house from 'Gowkscroft' (Cuckoo farm) to 'Godscroft'. Unlike his namesake (he was no relation), the grammarian Alexander Hume (1558–1631?) did use a diluted Scots to propound his theories on orthography in *Grammatica Nova* (1612); but the title of one of his later pamphlets refers only to 'the Britan Tongue'. Scots was used, again rarely, by Abacuck Bysset (fl. 1610) for a catalogue of ancient historical sites called *The Rolement of Courtis* (1622), in which he defended his 'awin . . . mother tung' as 'pithie and schorte'; although it must be admitted that his own practice does not always attain brevity:

> I haue nocht bene copius in langaig be far drevin, uncouth evill placed termis, and multiplicatioun of wordis be paraphraces of circumlocutioun of speich, silogismes, and refutatioun of argumentis be parablis or comparesonis; nor haue I adhered to auld proverbis or bywordis, fair, flattering, fenzeit [invented], and counterfuit fictionis, uttered be archadicienis, maid up, counterfuit, and phrasing langaige; neither haue I . . . used minzeard [mincing] nor effeminate tantting invective nor skornefull wordis, vane, saterick, or louse wowsting and wanting [boasting and vaunting] speeches; nor haue I . . . .

Most prose at the time was characterised by exactly this tendency to be 'copius'. John Brown (d. 1679), for instance, an exiled Covenanter, could produce a 'pamphlet' of 400 pages on the sufferings of godly ministers in Scotland, while the even more extreme Alexander Shields (d. 1700) produced 700 pages of his *Hind Let Loose* for the Cameronian viewpoint in 1687, including an argument for the assassination of uncovenanted and unrightful authority. On the other hand, **Sir George Mackenzie of Rosehaugh** (1636–91), defended national eloquence in his Preface to *Pleadings* (1673) by claiming that Scots was best suited for arguing in the law court, because 'our pronunciation is like ourselves, fiery, abrupt, sprightly and bold'. As Lord Advocate, Mackenzie founded the Advocates' Library in Edinburgh (now the National Library) and produced several more books on the Law as well as political studies, a novel (*Aretina*, 1660) poems, moral essays and *Religio Stoici* (1663), which contained his reflections on the schisms within the Church. He was a gifted man who abhorred fanaticism and was strongly opposed to the obscene witchcraft trials in his time. He was equally forcefully in favour of the proper authority of the king, and his prosecution of dissenting Covenanters, although legal and humane by his lights, earned him the nickname of 'bluidy Mackenzie'. His *Memoirs of the Affairs of Scotland from the Restoration* was not published until long after his death.

If Mackenzie's legal training made him shun casuistry, the same cannot be said of most of the religious controversialists who took it upon themselves to expound the words of God. Yet there were some divines of great expressive ability and the church-going public relished their demonstrations of dialectical eloquence, whether simple and passionate, or decked in the sesquipedelian flowers of classical rhetoric. Godly debate was as 'forensic' as any lawyer could desire. Men such as Robert Bruce and the unfortunately named Andrew Cant were famous for the power of their preaching, while others were noted more for erudition. Best regarded of all was the extempore composition of complex arguments, redolent with learned references and cunning strophes. Publications in both Latin and English abounded, with titles such as *Instructiones Historico-Theologicae* (1645), by John Forbes, a moderate Episcopalian who was the professor of Divinity at Aberdeen University; *Aaron's Rod Blossoming* (1646), by George Gillespie, a member of the Presbyterian camp; or *Lex Rex* (1644), Samuel Rutherford's case against the king, a work 'stuffed with positions, that in the time of peace and order, would have been judged damnable treasons'. Indeed, seventeen years later, the pamphlet was burned in public by the hangman.

Among the outstanding divines of the day, **Robert Baillie** (1599–1662) was a man of shrewd and moderate temper who possessed a 'golden' Latin style and became known for his intellectual excellence in twelve or thirteen languages. He was a determined Presbyterian, an ecclesiastical diplomat with some service abroad and several publications in defence of his beliefs;

but it is his *Letters and Journals* (1637–62) that provide an invaluable insight into the contemporary world of political and ecclesiastical affairs. They begin in 1637, the year of the riot in St Giles' against the Anglican prayer-book. Baillie was equally opposed to 'Laud's liturgy', but he feared the worst for Scotland:

> What shall be the event, God knows: there was in our Land ever such ane appearance of a sturr; the whole people thinks Poperie at the doores; the scandalous pamphlets which comes daily new from England adde oyl to this flame; no man may speak any thing in publick for the King's part, except he would have himself marked for a sacrifice to be killed one day. I think our people possessed with a bloody devill, farr above any thing that ever I could have imagined. . . . For myself, I think, God, to revenge the crying sinns of all estates and professions . . . is going to execute his long denounced threatnings, and to give us over unto madness, that we may every one shoot our swords in our neighbours hearts.

Within a year the National Covenant was signed to make, in effect, a direct challenge to the power of kings.

A vivid picture of subsequent events can be found in other diaries and memoirs, such as those of Sir John Lauder and Sir James Turner – Presbyterians who gradually came to support the king, or at least the cause of the crown. (Turner was one of the models for Walter Scott's Dugald Dalgetty in *A Legend of Montrose*.) Henry Guthrie (?1600–76), whose opinion of *Lex Rex* has already been heard, was a moderate Episcopalian, and, although he had signed the Covenant, like Montrose he eventually took the king's side. The waters of dissent were certainly muddy enough, and Guthrie maintains that the 'spontaneous' St Giles' riot had actually been planned three months in advance, so that women 'might give the first affront to the book, assuring them that men should afterwards take the business out of their hands'. The diaries of John Nicoll (1590–1667) testify to the confusions of the day in a different sense, for he left blanks in his pages so that he could adjust his views in retrospect and insert 'God save the King!' at appropriately prophetic points! Nicoll's accounts of the passing scene are more reliable, but his belief in witches and his interest in witch trials testify to troubled times and a thoroughly unlikeable character.

History and doctrinal dispute became inseparable, and many chroniclers were intent only on a vindication of their particular church. John Spottiswoode (1565–1639), the Bishop of St Andrew's, had to flee for London when his cause was defeated, but his *History of the Church of Scotland* (1655) shows a relatively generous recognition that 'popular fury once roused can keep no measure, nor do anything with advice and judgment'. The Episcopalian historian Gilbert Burnet (1643–1715) was amazed by another side to the common people when he toured the country in the 1660s to meet

> a poor commonality, so capable of arguing upon points of government, and on the bounds to be set on the power of Princes, in matters of religion: upon all these topicks they had texts of scripture at hand; and were ready with their anssers, to anything that was said to them. This measure of knowledge was spread even among the meanest of them, the cottagers and their servants.

David Calderwood (1575–1650) shows a Presbyterian bias, and his *History of the Kirk of Scotland* (1678) is vividly anecdotal, as when he describes how Bishop Spottiswoode (the rival historian) deprived reformer David Dickson of his ministry:

> 'The will of the Lord be done', said Mr David. 'Though you cast me off, yit the Lord will take me up. Send me where ye please. I hope my Master sall goe with me; and as He hath beene with me heirtofore, He will be with me still as with His owne weake servant.'
> 'Sweith away!' said the bishop, as if he had been speaking to a dogge; 'Pack, you swinger!' and crying to the doorekeeper, he sayes, 'Shoote him out!'

It is difficult not to sympathise with the bold Spottiswoode in the face of Dickson's pious complacency, and we shall let him have the last word.

Witchcraft and superstition

It was the Presbyterian extremists who were most committed to the discovery and extirpation of witchcraft, as if the fear of the Lord had turned to a paranoid fear of the Devil as well. Perhaps, too, the Kirk's insistence on rigid paternal authority led to barely submerged resentment against the implications of female sexuality, for witches' covens were widely suspected of the most promiscuous behaviour. James VI's *Daemonologie* had first pursued these various fears in 1597, and towards the end of the seventeenth century two further books on the occult proved to be particularly popular. George Sinclair (1618–87), one-time professor of Philosophy at Glasgow, had already produced studies on engineering and hydrostatics, but in *Satan's Invisible World Discovered* (1685), he set himself equally seriously to the tasks of recounting all the instances he could gather of supernatural events and apparitions, including the evidence heard at contemporary witchcraft trials. *The Secret Commonwealth of Elves, Fauns, and Fairies* (1691), written by **Robert Kirk** (1641–92), is quite another matter, however. Like his father before him, Kirk was a minister at Aberfoyle; he translated the Psalms into Gaelic and in *The Secret Commonwealth* he set about writing a 'natural history' of Celtic fairy lore. The *Sidh* (pronounced 'Shee') are not like the gauzy-winged creatures of Victorian sentiment, but are more likely to appear as full-sized good-looking beings dressed as mortals, though with a preference for green and silver. Nevertheless, they are capricious folk with supernatural powers, so it is not safe to speak ill of them and they are best referred to as 'the good people'.

> [They] are said to be of a midle Nature betwixt man and angel, (as were daemons thought to be of old); of intelligent studious spirits, and light changable bodies, (lik those called astral) . . . they are sometimes heard to bake bread, strike hammers, and to do such like services within the little hillocks where they most haunt. . . . They remove to other Lodgings at the beginning of each quarter of the year. . . . 'Tis one of their tenets that nothing perisheth, but (as the sun and the year) everything goes in a circle, less or greater, and is renewed or refreshed in its revolutions.

James's *Daemonologie* had been less sympathetic to the Sidh, referring to them as 'one of the sortes of illusiones that was rifest in time of *Papistrie*', when the Devil 'illuded the senses of sundry simple creatures, in making them beleeve that they saw and hearde such thinges as were nothing so indeed'. Without doubt, the king regarded himself as the voice of reason in this matter, yet more suffering was caused in James's kingdom by Christian belief in the power of the Devil than can ever be laid at the feet of the fairies.

As a seventh son, Robert Kirk was reputed to have second sight, and, when he collapsed at the age of fifty-one on the Hill of the Fairies in Aberfoyle, the tale went round that he was not really dead, but finally captured by the 'good people'. Walter Scott records how his likeness is reputed to have been seen after the funeral on two occasions. The spiriting away of mortals is the very stuff of the popular supernatural ballads, and these songs of beauty and awe and Kirk's book too, which is a repository of folk belief in itself, make a refreshing change from the blighted fields of dogmatic theology.

Ballads and ballad-collectors

The Scots ballads derive from an oral tradition in narrative songs which flourished during the sixteenth and seventeenth centuries. Since they were not published as 'literature', it is difficult to establish their authorship or when they first appeared, and these matters have led to much speculation ever since. Whatever their origins, the ballads were 'discovered' by antiquarians and literary enthusiasts in the eighteenth century, when many examples were collected and transcribed. In Scotland this appetite for old songs followed the union of parliaments in 1707, and a key part was played by their appearance in Allan Ramsay's *Tea Table Miscellany* anthologies (1724–37). As early as 1711, Joseph Addison had praised 'Chevy Chase' in the *Spectator* for its 'majestic simplicity', while Bishop Thomas Percy's collection, *Reliques of Ancient English Poetry* (1765 *et seq.*) did even more to create the pre-Romantic craze for 'old, unhappy far-off things and battles long ago'. Percy's interest was aroused when he found a manuscript collection of ballads being used by servants to light fires in a friend's house. He saved the sheets and began to gather ballads from enthusiasts around the country, although it can be difficult to distinguish between songs recorded verbatim and pieces 'improved', or patched from older fragments, or specially written for the occasion. Others soon followed. David Herd published *Ancient and Modern Scottish Songs* in 1776, and in the 1780s John Pinkerton produced two collections of old Scottish ballads, although he was not above including forgeries of his own. The irascible Joseph Ritson was a better scholar and his many volumes stressed the importance of recording the melody as well as the words. Sir Walter Scott tells of his excitement at the age of thirteen when he first came across

Percy's *Reliques* and how this youthful delight led him to become a collector himself. The two volumes which he called *Minstrelsy of the Scottish Border* (1802–3) contain some unscholarly editorial improvements which he came to regret in later years (he may even have composed most of 'Kinmont Willie') but nevertheless his work was sympathetic and very influential. Jamieson's *Popular Ballads and Songs* followed in 1806, and Motherwell's *Minstrelsy Ancient and Modern* (1827) took Ritson's line by insisting that collectors should seek authenticity.

The modern study of ballads owes most to the long dedication of an American scholar, Francis J. Child, whose life's work, *The English and Scottish Popular Ballads*, appeared from 1882 to 1898 in five volumes. Alas, Child died before he could produce the critical introduction which was to summarise his findings. Child accumulated and numbered 305 ballads and many variants, which he classified with letters, so that it is now usual, for example, to refer to the twenty-seven different versions of 'The Twa Sisters' as 'Child 10A, B, C', and so on. (In fact there are even more versions of this tale than Child printed.) In Denmark, Grundtvig and Olvik made a similarly extensive gathering of Danish ballads in *Danmarks Gamle Folkeviser* (6 vols, 1853–1920) and the groundwork was laid for what has now become a subject of international expertise drawing on philology, anthropology, comparative literature and folk-life studies. Thus, if doubts exist about the authenticity of 'Edward' as it appeared in the *Reliques*, these can be dispelled by the realisation that the same tale is told in Swedish, Danish and Finnish ballads. The spelling of Percy's version (got from Lord Hailes in Edinburgh) may be contrivedly 'antique', but its narrative patterns clearly belong to authentic tradition. 'Lord Randal' (Child 12), is an equally famous ballad, first collected in Edinburgh in 1710; but versions of it are found in Czechoslovakia, Hungary, Sweden and, a hundred years earlier, in Italy. Thus although there is not enough information to chart when or where the 'Lord Randal' tale first appeared in Scotland, it is clear that the oral tradition can prove to be surprisingly robust and far-travelled. In a more esoteric vein, Stith Thompson has classified the motifs which appear in folk tales from many countries (*Motif-index of Folk Litereature*, 6 vols, 1932–6), and it can be shown that many of these motifs are, indeed, international, and that some of them also occur in a few Scottish ballads. Recent theories on the nature of oral composition and transmission have derived from work done by Milman Parry and Albert Lord on Yugoslavian folk epic (Lord, *The Singer of Tales*, 1960), and comparisons have been established between Yugoslavian composition and that of Homer's ancient epic verse. It is also recognised that the ballad-singer is of primary importance in any study of the form, and modern students give full attention to these sources. Thus an early and invaluable contribution to Child's collection was provided by Mrs Anna Brown of Falkland (1747–1810), who came from the North-East and knew thirty-eight ballad stories, no less than one-eighth of all the 'classic' Anglo-Scottish themes ever recorded. Today, the School of Scottish Studies in Edinburgh (founded in 1951) has a huge archive of material gathered from traditional singers over the years, and the advent of the tape-recorder has added a vital dimension to the collection of ballads, songs and tales. The oral tradition still survives in Scotland, especially among the 'travelling people', who lead their itinerant, gipsy-like lives despite society's attempts to make them conform. Some of the finest traditional singers have come from these families, most notably the late Jeannie Robertson (1908–75) a 'sweet and heroic' voice, and her daughter Lizzie Higgins.

Since few ballads were written down or published when they first appeared, problems immediately arise about the date and the 'authenticity' of their eventual texts. In fact the very notion of an 'authentic text' is misguided, and such literary considerations cannot apply to an oral tradition in which the bare bones of the tale remain more or less constant while settings, proper names and other such details vary according to circumstances. The Robin Hood tales come from some of the oldest known ballads, circulating in the fifteenth century, and in this case a link can be made back to the late medieval minstrels who sang and recited the long narrative works so popular in the fourteenth century. Carols, religious lyrics, riddles and folk songs joined the canon and began to disseminate among the people, and it seems likely that the ballad-forms as collected by Child, with their distinctive quatrains and their use of refrain and repetition, had began to appear by the sixteenth century. The author of *The Complaynt of Scotland* (1549) names many tales, dances and old songs as performed by shepherds, and his list includes what must have been versions of 'The Battle of Harlaw' (Child 163), and 'The Battle of Otterburn' (Child 161), and 'The Hunting of the Cheviot' or 'Chevy Chase' (Child 162), which date from at least the beginning of the century and tell about a border conflict which took place as long ago as 1388. Sir Philip Sidney testified to the power of 'Chevy Chase' in 1595, writing in his *Apology for Poetry* that it moved his heart 'moore then with a trumpet: and yet it is sung by some blinde crouder'. *The Complaynt* also mentions the 'dance' called 'Johnne Ermistrang', and, from the 1570s, Pitscottie's *Historie and Chronicles of Scotland* gives an account of that reiver's fate (only forty years before) which uses phrases identical to those found in the ballad of 'Johnie Armstrong' (Child 169) as transcribed in the 1650s. The conclusion to be drawn is that the oral tradition can be remarkably stable, despite our contemporary and literate lack of confidence in the powers of memory and recitation. By the seventeenth century the professional minstrel class was disappearing and ballads had become the property of singers among the common people. At the same time these ballads were beginning to appear more frequently in print and manuscript and, indeed, the old folio which provided Bishop Percy with so many of his 'reliques' was just such a collection, copied out in the 1650s from other written and perhaps some oral sources.

The nature of ballads

If the literary history of the ballads cannot help but be obscure in places, then the question of how they were composed has been a matter of outright disagreement. 'Communalists' held that a ballad is evolved by accretion from tales and the folk consciousness; while 'individualists' made a case for a single 'begetter', at least at first, whose composition might then be gradually disseminated and changed by others as time passes. A version of the latter view has prevailed among modern scholars, although it is not necessary to suppose, as some 'individualists' did, that the process of transmission is always one of decline. On the contrary, it has been held that ballads are sustained by a process of re-creation and not just by simple feats (or lapses) of memory. Thus a singer will reconstruct the song from his or her knowledge of the key moments of the tale, as well as from a deep familiarity with the patterns of ballad expression and their many stock phrases and rhymes. Perhaps that singer's 'best' version of the song would tend to become fixed in his repertoire, but the process of oral re-creation would still play a part between singers, down the generations, or from district to district. Inevitably, some versions are poorer than others and the spread of literacy and printed copies must also be a factor; nevertheless the theory of oral re-creation does help to explain the variations which occur in different versions of a ballad, and how these differences can sometimes be equally effective, sustaining the tale and its artistic impact over the generations. It follows that the 'typical ballad' contains many elements which are of structural help to the singer in remembering and telling the tale effectively, and, by the same token, these features lend themselves to dramatic and poetic results.

The ballad is a song which tells a tale by letting the events and the characters speak for themselves. It focuses on a single crucial dramatic situation; the narrator almost never makes a personal comment, and little time is spent in setting the scene or explaining motives. Even the longest ballad is comparatively brief when compared to verse romance or folk epic, and, of course, it is sung to a distinctive melody. The ballads tell of fated lovers, or battles and blood feuds or visitations from the other world – the very stuff of popular taste; and yet their presentation of this romantic, violent or uncanny material is realistic, objective and concise. In fact it is just this trenchant impersonality which produces effects of great emotional power. Ballad melodies are often appropriately stately and plaintive, repeating themselves hypnotically with each short verse, but they manage to avoid monotony by the singer's use of variations and grace notes at suitably expressive points. A typical stanza uses four lines, with a rhyme scheme such as *abcb*, often alternating between four and three stresses:

> The king sits in Dumfermling toune,
>   Drinking the blude-reid wine:
> 'O whar will I get a guid sailor,
>   To sail this schip of mine?'

('Sir Patrick Spens', Child 58A)

Another common form uses a constant refrain or refrains in lines three and four:

> There was three ladies playd at the ba,
>> *With a hey ho and a lilie gay*
> There cam a knight and played oer them a'.
>> *As the primrose spreads so sweetly.*

('The Cruel Brother', Child 11A)

These opening stanzas from two different ballads show how quickly the songs get to the point as they unfold their tales with a characteristic mixture of immediacy and artful delay, a movement well named 'leaping and lingering'. Here the demands of art and those of oral performance compliment each other most fruitfully, and the ballads are full of stock phrases such as 'then up and spak' or 'loud, loud lauched (or cried) he'; colours come with traditional epithets, such as '*blude*-reid', '*milk*-white' or '*berry*-brown'; and numbers are usually 'magic' quantities such as three and seven. Antithetical sets of questions and answers accumulate in the songs, or whole phrases recur in an incremental repetition which makes the tale 'linger' and yet at the same time produces a sense of steadily advancing inevitability. All these devices bear witness to the ballad's origins, in which an act of oral re-creation meets with an act of memory to recognise the dramatic need for a telling delay before surrendering to sudden and inevitable denouement.

The Scottish ballads

The Scottish ballads are among the finest, for, while the tale may be internationally familiar, the particular form it takes within the genre will be dictated by the cultural and historical forces which shaped the singer. The forces in Scotland up until the sixteenth and seventeenth centuries were particularly well-suited to songs about violent, romantic and eerie encounters, all told with succinct wit and an enduring sense of fatalism. Such qualities were already deep within the Scottish sensibility, from the warlike celebration of Barbour and Blind Harry to the grimly tender understatement of Henryson when he describes how Cresseid's father discovers her leprosy – 'then was thair care enough betwixt them twain'; or, again, to the terrible, witty cruelty of Knox's account of the death of Beaton. The courtly poetry of the early seventeenth century and the studied melancholy of Drummond had completely lost touch with these tough roots, and it is the many anonymous singers of the ballad tradition who carried them over: from the makars to the vernacular revival in the eighteenth century and, ultimately, to Scottish poets of more modern times.

Although the divisions are fluid, the Scottish ballads are concerned with three perennially popular topics – violent history, tragic romance and the supernatural. All of these elements, like the songs themselves, belong in special measure to the Border country – from Edinburgh and Newcastle in the east to Dumfries and Penrith in the west. It is a wild, rolling landscape scattered with old battlefields, castles, towers and fortified houses. Loyalties were fiercely local, and Border barons had long regarded themselves as rulers of their own small kingdoms with no allegiance to politics or boundaries or even the king himself. Equally independent lesser lairds, with notorious family-names such as Armstrong, Ker and Scott, sallied forth as reivers to capture cattle and horses – the wealth of the district – from the English or, with equal facility, from their Scottish neighbours. James V led an expedition against the Borders in 1530 (when he hanged Johnie Armstrong), before having to move north to pacify the equally troublesome clans. It is no accident that the great songs of fighting, loving and terror should have arisen from such conditions: they occur again in the North-East of Scotland, where Lowlands and Highlands met along a different border, but the true crucible of the ballad-tradition lies to the south and particularly towards the centre and west of the country. Here the more open ground of Teviot and Tweed and the route from Berwick to Edinburgh begins to give way to the pass at Carter Bar in the hills above Jedburgh, to the tangled outlawed valleys of the 'debatable lands' at Eskdale and Liddesdale above Carlisle, and to the treacherous boglands of Solway Moss. The 'historical' ballads in particular are full of names, places and events from this part of Scotland.

Tales of violent history

'The Battle of Otterburn' (Child 161) and 'The Hunting of the Cheviot' or 'Chevy Chase' (Child 162), both tell of a raid the Scots made on Northumberland in 1388 and of how the Scotsman Sir Hugh Douglas perished on the sword of Sir Harry Percy, who was in his turn killed or captured by Douglas's nephew Montgomerie. 'Chevy Chase' tells the story from the English point of view, and 'Otterburn' favours the Scots. The latter was sent to Walter Scott by James Hogg, and is best known for the lines in which Douglas has an eerie premonition that the battle will be won only after his own death:

> 'My nephew bauld,' the Douglas said,
>   'What boots the death of ane?
> Last night I dreamed a dreary dream,
>   And I ken the day's thy ain.

> I dreamed I saw a battle fought
>   Beyond the isle of Sky,
> When lo, a dead man wan the field,
>   And I thought that man was I.'

> (Child 161C)

The Battle of Harlaw was fought north-west of Aberdeen in 1411, between Donald of the Isles and Lowland forces from Angus and the Mearns. The ranting ballad of the same name (Child 163), with its parodies of the Highland accent ('Yes, me cam frae ta Hielans, man'), must date from considerably after the conflict. On the other hand, 'The Battle of Philiphaugh' (Child 202) is probably contemporary with the defeat of Montrose, 'our cruel enemy', outside Selkirk in 1645. 'The Bonny Earl of Murray' (Child 181) laments how, in 1592, James Stewart of Doune was killed by his old enemy the Earl of Huntly, who had been instructed to convey him to the king without harm. As with almost all the ballads, this tale of the doings of great people is seen from the point of view of the common folk. In fact Murray was burned out of his mother's house and killed while trying to escape, but one version of the song has him admit his 'brother' Huntly in a trusting way, only to be stabbed in his bed like King Duncan in *Macbeth*. The best-known version has a beautiful melody, simultaneously rousing and tender, which opens with the verses

> Ye Highlands, and ye Lawlands,
>   Oh where have you been?
> They have slain the Earl of Murray,
>   And they layd him on the green.
>
> 'Now wae be to thee, Huntly!
>   And wherefore did you sae?
> I bade you bring him wi you,
>   But forbade you him to slay.'
>
> He was a braw gallant,
>   And he rid at the ring;
> And the bonny Earl of Murray,
>   Oh he might have been a king.

(Child 181A)

In the ballads, historical accuracy always takes second place to heroic figures and dramatic events, and so John Armstrong's deserved execution at the hands of James V is retold as a treacherous betrayal, and one version (copied, according to Allan Ramsay from a descendant of Armstrong's) even manages to be patriotic:

> John murdered was at Carlinrigg,
>   And all his galant companie:
> But Scotlands heart was never sae wae,
>   To see sae mony brave men die
>
> Because they savd their country deir
>   Frae Englishmen; nane were sae bauld,
> Whyle Johnie livd on the border-syde,
>   Nane of them durst cum neir his hald.

(Child 169C)

Another version ends more convincingly, on a note chillingly reminiscent of revenge plays by Tourneur or Webster:

> O then bespoke his little son,
>   As he was set on his nurses knee:
> 'If ever I live for to be a man,
>   My father's blood revenged shall be.'

(Child 169B)

In more recent years an equally unlikely folk hero has been made of a small American murderer called William Bonney, but we still listen to tales of Billy the Kid, and we thrill to Armstrong's grim and cutting retort when his sovereign refused to spare his life:

> To seik het water beneth cauld yce,
>   Surely it is a great folie;
> I haif asked grace at a graceless face,
>   But ther is nane for my men and me.

The memorable history behind 'Mary Hamilton' (Child 173), is equally cloudy when it comes to facts. There are nearly forty variants of the tale, also known as 'The Queen's Marie' and 'The Four Maries', and almost all of them have the poignant lines

> Last nicht there was four Maries,
>   The nicht there'l be but three;
> There was Marie Seton, and Marie Beton,
>   And Marie Carmichael, and me.

(Child 173A)

The tale has it that Mary Hamilton was executed because she drowned her illegitimate baby, whose father was Darnley, 'the hichest Stewart of a' and the queen's unworthy husband. Mary Queen of Scots did, indeed, have four Marys attending her, but they were ladies of gentle birth from the families of Seaton, Beaton, Fleming and Livingston. There *was* a scandal at court in 1563, but it involved an apothecary and a French lady of the chamber, with no mention of any Mary Hamilton. In fact, there was a Mary Hamilton who suffered a fate similar to that recounted in the ballad, but she was an attendant to the wife of Peter the Great of Russia at the end of the seventeenth century. All these names and events have merged in the popular imagination to fit a sad and lilting melody full of memorable lines and images. Consider how Mary goes to her death in the following verses, in which the action is typically heightened and delayed by the incremental repetitions of statement and reply, and by the antithesis between laughter and tears:

'O Marie, put on your robes o black,
  Or else your robes o brown,
For ye maun gang wi me the night,
  To see fair Edinboro town.'

'I winna put on my robes o black,
  Nor yet my robes o brown;
But I'll put on my robes o white,
  To shine through Edinboro town.'

When she gaed up the Cannogate,
  She laughd loud laughters three;
But whan she cam doun the Cannogate
  The tear blinded her ee.

When she gaed up the Parliament stair,
  The heel cam aff her shee;   shoe
And lang or she cam doun again
  She was condemned to dee.

Atmosphere, setting, and intense feeling are all conveyed in
these lines, but only through direct speech and direct action.
Her bold decision to wear virginal white, and the ill omen of her
broken heel – these are exactly the kind of details at which the
ballads excel, and they strike the listener with the simple force
of a bolt of electricity.

The creative versatility of oral tradition can be gauged by
comparing what is functionally the same stanza, drawn from
five different versions of the song:

'Last night I washed the queen's feet,
  And gently laid her down;
And a' the thanks I've gotten the nicht
  To be hangd in Edinboro town.'

(Child 173A)

'Yestreen I wush Queen Mary's feet,
  And bore her till her bed;
This day she's given me my reward,
  This gallows-tree to tread.'

(Child 173B)

'Yestreen I mad Queen Mary's bed,
  Kembed doun her yellow hair;
Is this the reward I am to get,
  To tread the gallows-stair.'

(Child 173C)

'Seven years an I made Queen Mary's bed,
  Seven years an I combed her hair,
An a hansome reward noo she's gien to me,
  Gien me the gallows-tow to wear!'

(Child 173N)

'O wha will comb Queen Mary's heed?
  Or wha will brade her hair?
And wha will lace her middle sae jimp,   slender
  Whan I am nae langer there?'

(Child 173W)

It is not possible to advance critical reasons for preferring any one version over the others: they all focus on past services as compared to present fate, and, although the details change, each stanza is effective in its own way.

An equally poetic power, and something of the same historical uncertainty, is at work in 'Sir Patrick Spens' (Child 58). In typical 'leaping and lingering' fashion, the singer goes directly to the beginning and then to the end of the ill-fated voyage, pausing only to record Sir Patrick's reactions, and an old sailor's premonition of disaster:

The first line that Sir Patrick red,
  A loud lauch lauched he;
The next line that Sir Patrick red,
  The teir blinded his ee.

. . .

'Late late yestreen I saw the new moone,
  Wi the auld moone in her arme,
And I feir, I feir, my deir master,
  That we will cum to harme.'

(Child 58A)

When the storm has had its way, the ballad focuses on small details in a series of poignantly understated 'snapshots':

O our Scots nobles wer richt laith
   To weet their cork-heild shoone;
But lang owre a' the play were playd,
   Thair hats they swam aboone.

O lang, lang may their ladies sit,
   Wi thair fans into their hand,
Or eir they se Sir Patrick Spence
   Cum sailing to the land.

O lang, lang may the ladies stand,
   Wi their gold kems in their hair
Waiting for thair ain deir lords,
   For they'll se thame na mair.

Haf owre, haf owre to Aberdour,
   It's fiftie fadom deip,
And thair lies guid Sir Patrick Spence,
   Wi the Scots lords at his feit.   (Child 58A)

If the functional reason for such repetition in oral art is by now familiar, it still remains to point to the extraordinarily moving symbolic effects which it creates at the same time. Our attention is seized by those fashionably cork-heeled shoes, by the fans and gold combs and all the genteel accoutrements of a privileged class. The physical movement of the ladies, when they switch from sitting to standing, has an equally dramatic eloquence, and this is matched in turn by a contrasting vision of Sir Patrick Spens under fifty fathoms of water with their drowned husbands laid at his feet – like those stone dogs carved on a knight's tomb.

Tales of tragic romance

'Mary Hamilton' and 'Sir Patrick Spens' could almost belong to the 'tragic romance' category of ballads, except that the latter are more fiercely suffused with the passions of love, jealousy or betrayal. 'The Dowie Howms of Yarrow' (Child 214) tells how a Border laird is killed by his brother-in-law after a drunken quarrel, and the first two stanzas, when the tale is 'leaping' at its swiftest, provide an extraordinary example of ballad concision:

> Late at een, drinkin the wine,
>   Or early in a morning,
> They set a combat them between,
>   To fight it in the dawin'.
>
> 'O stay at hame, my noble lord!
>   O stay at hame, my marrow!   partner (spouse)
> My cruel brother will you betray,
>   On the dowie houms o' Yarrow.   dreary low river-banks

(Child 214E)

Jealous brothers, sisters and mothers abound in these tales and, not surprisingly, there are many international variants on the same themes. 'The Twa Sisters' (Child 10) exists in over sixty versions from Scotland, England, Denmark, Norway, Iceland, the Faeroes and Sweden. In most of these versions a musical instrument is made from the bones of the drowned girl, and when it is played it reveals that she was murdered by her sister – clearly a folk tale of wide and enduring force. In another ballad, it is a brother who kills his sister, because, although the rest of the family were consulted, his particular consent to her marriage was not asked. Like so many of its kind, 'The Cruel Brother' (Child 11) ends with a dying person leaving their goods to those around them, until the final bequest is made:

> 'What will you leave to your brother John?'
>   *With a hey ho and a lillie gay.*
> 'The gallows-tree to hang him on!'
>   *As the primrose spreads so sweetly.*

(Child 11A)

The world of the ballads revolves around sudden contrasts between tears and laughter, peace and war, love and hatred, marriage and death; and contrast is found again in the juxtaposition of the dying girl's curse and the sweet refrain which has accompanied the grim narrative from the start. 'Lord Randal' (Child 12) and 'Edward' (Child 13), are among the best-known ballads to use the device of a surprise last bequest, and they too have many international variations. In each case a heavily structured and repetitiously patterned duologue is set up between the hero and another person, until it produces a sense of inevitable process, a painful journey towards death or a final, ghastly revelation. Lord Randal leaves 'hell and fire' to his true love, who has poisoned him, while Edward curses his mother for persuading him to kill his father. Incremental repetition and the melody's slow pace are vital to the overall effect, and in 'Lord Randal' only the first half of the third line in each stanza actually advances the plot, while everything else, rhymes and line-endings included, is said over and over again.

> 'O where ha you been, Lord Randal, my son?
> And where ha you been, my handsome young man?'
> 'I ha been at the green wood; mother, mak my bed soon,
> For I'm wearied wi hunting, an fain wad lie down.'
>
> 'An wha met ye there, Lord Randal, my son?
> An wha met you there, my handsome young man?'
> 'O I met wi my true-love; mother, mak my bed soon,
> For I'm wearied wi hunting, an fain wad lie down.'
>
> (Child 12A)

In this fashion, the story of how he has been poisoned is haltingly revealed, as though the tale were taking three steps forward in every verse, and two steps back again: 'lingering' has become massively static.

When asked what he will give to his wife and children before he flees into exile, Edward's answer is succinct: 'the warldis room, late them beg thrae life, / For thame nevir mair wil I see O', and his cruel realism is characteristically Scottish. It is instructive to compare 'The Three Ravens', an English ballad, with 'The Twa Corbies' (Child 26), a counterpart from north of the Border. 'The Three Ravens' has a refrain, 'Downe a downe, hay down . . .', and it tells how a slain knight is protected from predators by his faithful hounds and his hawks, until his lady, in the symbolic form of a pregnant fallow doe, comes to bury him and then to join him in death. 'The Twa Corbies' is half the length and much less comforting. The crows have the knight to themselves:

'His hound is to the hunting gane,
His hawk to fetch the wild-fowl hame,
His lady's ta'en another mate,
So we may mak our dinner sweet.

'Ye'll sit on his white hause-bane,
And I'll pike oot his bonny blue een;
Wi ae lock o his gowden hair
We'll theek our nest when it grows bare.

'Mony a one for him maks mane,
But nane sall ken where he is gane;
Oer his white banes, when they are bare,
The wind sall blaw for evermair.'

(Child 26)

The same fatalism reigns with particular force in the ballads of the supernatural.

Tales of the other world

The 'other world' in Scotland has many of its origins in Celtic lore, with tales of seal men and kelpies who delight in the downfall of poor mortals, or of the fairy folk, ruled by a beautiful queen on a milk-white horse with silver bells in its mane. The 'good people' live in mounds or under the hills, and the Eildon Hills are particularly famous as one of the doors to their kingdom. Mortals enter this realm at their peril, but they can ensure their return by leaving iron or a dirk at the gate, for the fairies are afraid of steel. (Another passport to their land is said to be the branch of an apple-tree, and perhaps there is a connection here with the apples of the Hesperides, the golden fruit from the magic West which Hercules had to find in Greek myth.) The border between the natural and the supernatural is a misty one, and even the human dead can cross it as revenants from their home in Tir nan Og – the Isle of the Blest – which is neither Heaven nor Hell but a pagan Celtic paradise, the land of the ever-young, somewhere over the western horizon.

When the Queen of Elfland describes her kingdom to Thomas the Rhymer, it is a middle state where magical awe meets with sexual danger, quite distinct from the after-worlds of Christian teaching:

'O see not ye yon narrow road,
  So thick beset wi thorns and briars?
That is the path of righteousness,
  Tho after it but few enquires.

'And see not ye that braid braid road,
  That lies across yon lillie leven?   lea
That is the path of wickedness
  Tho some call it the road to heaven.

'And see not ye that bonny road,
  Which winds about the fernie brae?
That is the road to fair Elfland,
  Where you and I this night maun gae.   must go

'But Thomas ye maun hold your tongue,
  Whatever you may hear or see,
For gin ae word you should chance to speak,   if one
  You will never get back to your ain countrie.'

('Thomas the Rhymer', Child 37A)

Yet there are still some religious elements in the ballad, and
shades of sexual guilt too, for when Thomas first sees her he
mistakes the Elf Queen for the 'Queen of Heaven'. Again,
during their desperate journey to fairyland – 'For forty days
and forty nights,/He wade thro red blude to the knee' –
Thomas is stopped just in time from picking an apple, no less
than the fruit of man's first sin. Thus Christian and Celtic
themes are intermingled along with hints of the romance tales,
for the story of a knight abducted by the Elf Queen also features
in the Arthurian cycle, which, too, contains in its turn echoes
from earlier Celtic sources. Seven years pass before True
Thomas returns to the Eildon Hills, although it seems but a
brief time to him, and he brings back the gift of second sight –
the ability to see aspects of the future. In fact Thomas of
Ercildoune seems to have been a real person, living about 1320,
and various prophecies of his have been preserved, along with
verses from the early fifteenth century which tell of his
adventures in the first person:

Als I me wente this Endres daye,
ffull faste in mynd makand my mone,
In a merry mornynge of Maye,
By Huntle bankkes my selfe allone,

I herde the jaye, and the throstyll cokke,
The mawys menyde hir of hir songe,   thrush lamented
The wodewale beryde als a belle,   woodlark sang like
That alle the wode abowte me ronge.

The fairies might promise erotic adventure or ambiguous
gifts, but it can be fatal to deal too closely with the other world.
Clerk Colvill (Child 42) dies because he has made love with a
mermaid, while Tam Lin (Child 39) seduces an earthly girl
while still himself under the power of the Queen of Fairies. His
human lover must reclaim him by pulling him down from his
fairy horse at midnight, and by holding him fast, despite the
several frightening shapes he will assume. Lady Isabel manages to outwit her eerie seducer by killing him at the last minute
('Lady Isabel and the Elf-Knight', Child 4); but the Daemon
Lover (Child 243), is not so easily denied as he lures his former
love aboard ship, only to show her 'where the white lilies
grow,/ In the bottom o' the sea'.

The finest of the supernatural Scots ballads deal with those
moments when the other world and the everyday world come
together, if only for a brief time. When the three drowned sons
return to their mother in 'The Wife of Usher's Well' (Child 79),
their birch-bark hats announce that they have come from the
Celtic isle of the dead and, like all ghosts, they cannot stay past
the dawn. When the youngest brother says goodbye to home
and hearth, the simplicity of his words strikes the listener with
the full force of that final, inexorable separation from the
common earth and all human warmth:

The cock he hadna crawd but once,
    And clapped his wings at a',
When the youngest to the eldest said,
    'Brother, we must awa.

'The cock doth craw, the day doth daw,
    The channerin worm doth chide;   whining
Gin we be mist out o our place,
    A sair pain·we maun bide.

'Fare ye weel, my mother dear!
    Fareweel to barn and byre!
And fare ye weel, the bonny lass,
    That kindles my mother's fire!'

                    (Child 79A)

The same sweetly painful grief pervades 'The Great Silkie of Sule Skerry' (Child 113), which is known in only one version collected from an old lady in the Shetlands. The 'silkies' are seal folk who can take human shape and earthly lovers, but this tale is especially poignant for its sense of the inevitable parting of all human ties, whether made with the fairy folk or not. The wider symbolic reverberations of this remarkable ballad tell how the saddest thing is not that the heart will eventually stop, but that, sooner than that, it will come to change its affections:

Now he has ta'en a purse of goud,
   And he has pat it upo' her knee,
Saying', 'Gie to me my little young son,
   An' tak thee up thy nourrice-fee.   *nurses fee*

'An' it sall pass on a simmer's day,
   When the sin shines het on evera stane,
That I will tak my little young son,
   An' teach him for to swim his lane.   *on his own*

'An' thu sall marry a proud gunner,
   An' a proud gunner I'm sure he'll be,
'An' the very first schot that ere he schoots,
   He'll schoot baith my young son and me.'

Technical concision and grim realism meet here with insight and tender fatalism, to capture the timelessly popular poetic voice of the Scottish ballads and their many anonymous singers – a timely reminder that great art is not the exclusive property of educated or literary circles.

Robert and Francis Sempill

The energy of the oral tradition in Scots was not entirely lost to written verse, for it makes a brief appearance in the works of **Robert Sempill of Beltrees** (1595?–1665?). Robert's father was Sir James Sempill (1566–1625), the author of several pro-Presbyterian pamphlets and a satirical drama in English called *A Picktooth for the Pope, or the Packman's Paternoster*. (Sir James had been educated with James VI under George Buchanan, and he later served his king as an ambassador in London and Paris.) Robert, laird of Beltrees in Renfrewshire, was a loyalist who fought for Charles I and supported the Restoration. He did not produce much poetry, nor did his son Francis, but the Sempills represent a new class of author, drawn from the educated minor gentry, who were destined to inherit the Scots literary tradition from the clerics, scholars and courtiers who had gone before. At the same time, their resolutely colloquial spirit makes a link between Scots verse in the sixteenth century and the vernacular revival 200 years later. Robert's fame rests on the verse-form which he chose for a naïve elegy called 'The Life and Death of the Piper of Kilbarchan, or the Epitaph of Habbie Simson'.

> At Clark-plays when he wont to come,
> His Pipe played trimly to the Drum
> Like Bikes of Bees he gart it Bum,   made
>   And tun'd his Reed:
> Now all our Pipers may sing dumb,
>   Sen Habbie's dead.

> And at Horse Races many a day,
> Before the Black, the Brown, the Gray,
> He gart his Pipe when he did play,
>   Baith Skirl and Skreed,
> Now all such Pastime's quite away
>   Sen Habbie's dead.

Sempill's six-line stanza with its two emphatic short lines produces a notable rhythmic effect. The scene is set and the rhyme sustained by a galloping four-stress rhythm in the opening three lines; then the pace is checked, picked up again and abruptly concluded by a second rhyme appearing in two short lines of only two stresses each. This second rhyme and the entire last line are repeated throughout the poem. The same delight in a lilting metre with its checks and refrains is found in the 'bob and wheel' effects of 'Christis Kirk' and 'Peblis to the Play', and they too seem well suited to the movement of popular dances and reels in celebration of the ordinary domestic scene. Passages with a similar rhythm – also used for satirical effect – appeared in Lindsay's *Thrie Estaits* and in popular airs such as 'Hey Tuttie Taittie' (later sanctified in the *Gude and Godlie Ballatis*). Kurt Wittig has suggested that the pattern may owe something to Gaelic octosyllabic metres, *ochtfhoclach mór*, used for elegies, and *ochtfhoclach beag*, used for verses to dance tunes.

Whatever its precursors, the stanza-form of Sempill's verses became so popular among later Scots poets that it has been known ever since as 'Standard Habbie', or sometimes, slightly varied, as the 'Burns stanza'.

'Habbie Simson' was first published in 1706 in James Watson's *Choice Collection*, and subsequently Allan Ramsay, Robert Fergusson and Burns himself were to make more of its distinctive jig-time measure than ever Sempill achieved with his naïve, but touchingly direct, lament for a dead piper. Fergusson and Burns found 'Habbie' particularly suited to comedy, satire and social comment, for its short lines can produce a variety of ironic, or sly, or sententious effects. Sempill is usually credited with another mock elegy, called 'Epitaph on Sanny Briggs, Nephew to Habbie Simson and Butler to the Laird of Kilbarchan', but it is unlikely that either poem would be remembered had their distinctive pattern not taken fire in the hands of later and better poets.

Francis Sempill (1616?/25?–1682) is said to have shared his father's talent for vernacular verse, and 'Sanny Briggs' is sometimes attributed to him, as well as 'The Banishment of Poverty', a rather contrived account of how the poet was followed everywhere by 'poverty' – like a stray dog at his heels – until he reached the debtor's sanctuary at Holyrood and the Duke of Albany's generosity freed him. The fine song 'Maggie Lauder' is tentatively attributed to Francis, although he may only have reworked it from an earlier popular source. 'The Blythsome Wedding' is an odd and lively piece which juxtaposes a hilarious account of the grotesque guests at a country wedding with an equally extensive list of what there was to eat. The poem's vulgar and encyclopaedic zest belongs to the tradition of 'Christis Kirk' joined to that of *The Complaynt of Scotland*, and the end result is like a peasant feast recorded by Breughel down to the last and grossest detail. If such comprehensive grotesquerie seems to be a Scottish characteristic, it is by no means confined to the peasant world, for Sir Thomas Urquhart, knight and word-spinner extraordinary, must be its undisputed champion.

Sir Thomas Urquhart of Cromarty (1611–60)

The knight of Cromarty was a stout supporter of the Stuart crown, a flamboyant cavalier, a proud and patriotic Scot and the possessor of a uniquely eccentric mind and manner. He began his studies at Aberdeen University at the age of eleven, and, although he left without a degree, he retained fond memories and a taste for esoteric learning. During his travels abroad he describes (typically innocent of modesty) how he gained friends and 'vindicated his native county' by fighting three separate combats of honour in the lists. At home, his father refused to sign the Covenant and Thomas returned to fight for the Royalists. Despite initial successes in the north, the Cavaliers who opposed the Covenanters in the 'Bishops' Wars' were gradually dispersed. Urquhart went to London, was knighted by Charles, and produced an excruciatingly banal book, *Epigrams: Divine and Moral* (1641). His father's lack of business-sense had almost ruined the estate in the far north of Scotland, and when Sir Thomas inherited it in 1642 he was quick to resume his travels. After three years abroad he returned to Cromarty determined to achieve fame as a writer, inventor, scholar and mathematician. Urquhart was an admirer of his countryman John Napier (1550–1617), the inventor of logarithms (whom the famous German astronomer Kepler regarded as the greatest mathematician of his day), and he decided to produce a treatise of his own which would help students to memorise and calculate the theorems of trigonometry. He seems to have known his subject well enough, but *The Trissotetras* (1645) is made almost completely unintelligible by a language crammed with abstract terms and neologisms. The glossary throws even more darkness on the subject: '*Amfractuosities*; are taken here for the cranklings, windings, turnings, and involutions belonging to the equisoleary scheme. . . .'

Immediately after the execution of Charles I, Urquhart took part in an ill-fated Royalist uprising in the north and was declared a traitor – although he was leniently treated by the Covenanters. Within two years he was supporting Charles II's cause (in line with Covenanting policy this time) and marching south with the Scottish army which was eventually defeated by Cromwell at Worcester in 1651. Urquhart travelled with a full wardrobe and writing-desk and many of his manuscripts and papers were looted or lost after the battle, although once more he himself was spared. After a spell in the Tower of London, he was held at Windsor Castle and, to prove his merit to his captors and avoid the confiscation of his estates, he set about the demonstration of his intellectual prowess. *Pantochronochanon* (1652) traces the descent of the Urquharts back to Adam (with Eve, too, on the female side) and promises in a future volume, if the writer is released, to explain why the shire of Cromarty alone in Britain has all its place-names derived from 'pure and perfect Greek'. Equally Greek, if not quite so pure, *Ekskybalauron, or The Discovery of a Most Exquisite Jewel* (1652) attempts to vindicate the honour of Scotland from the canting image given it by the rigid Presbyterian party. Along the way it makes another plea for its author's freedom, as well as a proposal for a universal language which will be easier to learn than any other, despite having eleven genders, ten tenses, and words which can be read just as meaningfully backwards as forwards (This seems to have been a species of code, and not quite as mad as it sounds, although Urquhart never actually perfected it.) The *Jewel* is chiefly notable for its enthusiastic account of many brave and learned Scots, in particular 'the admirable' James Crichtoun (1560–83), soldier, scholar, duellist, polyglot and lover extraordinary – a fitting hero for the knight of Cromarty.

Urquhart was paroled in 1652 and returned to Scotland only to find his creditors awaiting him. The following year saw him back in London, from where he published a many-sided diatribe against those 'stinging wasps' and another proposal for his universal language, *Logopandecteision* (1653). As always, Urquhart's prose is elaborately and relentlessly euphuistic, but it does have a manic energy and, at its best, it is the hilariously inventive and exhaustive text itself which turns out to be the main subject and hero of the piece. Even so, when faced with the cosmic grandeur of his schemes and with a style which occasionally slips into complete gobbledegook, it is difficult not to suspect that the author was a little mad.

Urquhart's peculiar genius found its true *métier* in 1653 with his translation of the first two books of Rabelais's *Gargantua and Pantagruel*. (A third book was published in the edition of 1694, along with Books IV and V as translated by Motteux.) Rabelais is notoriously difficult to translate, because he mixes pompous and learned diction with earthy phrases and accumulates long lists of objects, epithets and synonyms. Such a challenge might have been specially made for Urquhart, and he met it by outdoing the Frenchman, and even himself, with a translation almost twice the length of the original: more compendious in its lists, more outrageous in its vulgarities and more hyperbolic in its hyperboles. When Rabelais notes the animal-noises which spoil the peace of his countryside, he manages to name the calls of dogs, wolves, lions, horses, elephants, snakes, asses, crickets and doves. Urquhart's version contains seventy-one species and their increasingly unlikely cries, including the 'drintling of turkies, coniating of storks, frantling of peacocks . . . rantling of rats, guerieting of apes, snuttering of monkeys, pioling of pelicans', and so on – truly a list worthy of the catalogues to be found in *The Complaynt of Scotland*. Notwithstanding his flamboyant expansions, a good case can be made for Urquhart's essential accuracy, for his version catches the spirit of Rabelais with an immense and greasy gusto:

HOW GARGAMELLE, BEING GREAT WITH GARGANTUA, DID EAT A HUGE DEAL OF TRIPES

The occasion and manner how Gargamelle was brought to bed, and delivered of her child, was thus: and, if you do not believe it, I wish your bum-gut fall out, and make an escapade. Her bum-gut, indeed, or fundament escaped her in an afternoon, on the third day of February, with having eaten at dinner too many godebillios. Godebillios are the fat tripes of coiros. Coiros are beeves fattened at the cratch in ox stalls, or in the fresh guimo meadows. Guimo meadows are those, that for their fruitfulness may be mowed twice a year. Of those fat beeves they had killed three hundred sixty-seven thousand and fourteen, to be salted at Shrove-tide, that in the entering of the spring they might have plenty of powdered beef, wherewith to season their mouths at the beginning of their meals, and to taste their wine the better.

They had abundance of tripes, as you have heard, and they were so delicious, that every one licked his fingers. But the mischief was this, that for all men could do, there was no possibility to keep them long in that relish; for in a very short while they would have stunk, which had been an undecent thing. It was therefore concluded, that they should be all of them gulched up, without losing anything.

Ezra Pound preferred Douglas's *Eneados* to Virgil and many readers have found Urquhart's *Rabelais* equally special: it joins that select company of translations which have achieved their own creative identity, along with Chapman's *Homer*, Fitzgerald's *Omar Khayyam*, some of Pound's Chinese poems, and the Authorised Version itself.

Little is known of Sir Thomas's last years. He is said to have died of a fit of laughing when he heard of the Restoration of Charles II; and, if that is not true, as one writer puts it, then it certainly should be.

Urquhart was not the only distinguished writer to support the Stuart crown, for, of course, the Gaelic Highlands espoused the Catholic cause as well, and the poet Iain Lom (who had been a friend of Montrose's) honed the edge of his Gaelic verse to comment fiercely on the political events of his day.

Gaelic poetry in the late seventeenth century

The second half of the century was a period of transition and renewed activity in Gaelic verse, and, although Iain Lom was probably the most radical and influential poet of the time, there were many others, especially among women, who composed fine songs too. The formal patterns of bardic verse were finally changing, and syllabic metres, high diction and learned historical allusions were giving way to a more colloquial Gaelic with metres based on stress. This had been a gradual change which can be traced to the previous century, and, after all, the modes of eulogy, elegy and bardic satire were to continue unabated into the next. Yet the work of this period stands as a watershed between the bardic schools and what was to become, in effect, modern Gaelic poetry.

Niall MacMhuirich (1637?–1726)

If Iain Lom's verse looks towards modern Gaelic, then Niall stays almost entirely with the old style. This is scarcely surprising, since he and his distinguished predecessor Cathal came from a long line of MacMhuirich bards going back to the thirteenth century, and much of their poetry is in the learned tradition of elegy and panegyric for their patrons in the Clanranald branch of the MacDonalds. Niall was almost the last of the literate bardic school with Irish connections, and his elegy for Donald, son of John of Moidart, who died in the late 1640s, shows his clear and vigorous style and also the extreme formalism of the genre:

> The son of big bodied spirited John of Moidart, the shortness of his life has wounded me sharply; wretched is my state now that this man is dead: that has consumed [as with fire] my flesh and my blood. . . .

> He was a lion in the fierceness of his exploits, but would not indulge in anything shameful, a man who was foremost in showing the way to peace, my beloved was he who gave protection to the destitute and to the learned poets.

> (trs. D. Thomson)

Niall's verses and his prose history of the Montrose wars were gathered, along with other pieces from the MacMhuirich bards, in a manuscript collection known as the Red Book of Clanranald. Niall wrote very little in vernacular Gaelic, but two poems do survive, both on the death of Allan of Clandranald after the battle of Sherrifmuir in 1715. He laments the passing of the traditional learning of the Gael as if he knew that the aftermath of the Jacobite risings was indeed to change their customs for ever.

Roderick Morison (1656?–1714?)

Known as 'an clàrsair dall' ('the blind harper'), Morison served the MacLeod chiefs at Dunvegan and has often been called (not quite accurately), the last of the old minstrel-class. Tradition has it that he left Lewis to study for the ministry at Inverness, where he caught smallpox and lost his eyesight. He turned to music to survive and visited Ireland to further his craft before roving the Highlands to earn his living. In Edinburgh in 1681 he met Iain Breac MacLeod, who took him under his care at Dunvegan in Skye, although Morison was never the official bard there. Iain Breac was among the last chiefs to keep the old style of establishment, for, as well as his harper, he had a bard and a jester and his piper was the famous Patrick Og MacCrimmon himself, the roar of whose drones, according to blind Roderick, would stir the whole household into cheerful activity every morning. Morison performed the usual eulogies, but in 1688 he fell out of favour at Dunvegan and was 'banished' to Glenelg – perhaps on account of his outspoken Jacobite sympathies at a time when his chief was studiously trying to remain neutral. The harper found another patron at Talisker for a while before returning to his travels and relative obscurity.

When Iain Breac died in 1693 the blind harper composed a unique 'Song to MacLeod of Dunvegan', which begins as a lament for his former patron with a lovingly detailed picture of happy days under his roof. Then the poem turns into a scathing attack on Roderick, the son and heir who went south to live at court, spent money on gambling and clothes and ignored Skye and the old culture. The harper had cause for alarm, for in the six years before he died of consumption the young chief raised loans of £45,000 against an annual income of only £9000 – 'then does the boil fester on the thigh', sings Morison, 'with its pain at the root'. The original uses rhyme in its eight-line stanzas:

> He comes out of the shop
> with the latest fashion from France,
> and the fine clothes worn on his person
> yesterday with no little satisfaction
> are tossed into a corner –
> 'The style is unmodish, not worth a plack.
> On the security of a townland or two,
> take the pen and sign a bond.'
>
> The page will not be regarded
> unless his clothes are in the current fashion;
> though it should cost a guinea a yard,
> that can be got for a mart given in lieu of rent.
> As much again in addition
> will got to the purchase of a doublet for him,
> and breeches of soft velvet
> to wrap up gusts at his rear.

(trs. W. Matheson)

A bard's satire could be fearsomely specific, but in this case it was not enough to stop young MacLeod, and many others after him, from breaking the kinship ties and becoming an absentee landlord in Edinburgh or London.

There was another bard with the MacLeods of Skye during

Morison's time, although she was an unlettered and 'unofficial' one.

Mary MacLeod (1615?–1706?)

Mary MacLeod (Màiri Nighean Alasdair Ruaidh) first came from Harris to be a nurse at Dunvegan, and she looked after several members of the family during her long life there. She too fell into disfavour for a while and spent some years in the Hebrides and Mull before being recalled to Skye. This may have been during young Roderick's six years as chief, or perhaps during his father's time, and so it is not certain if Mary ever met with the blind harper in the 'wide mansion' where she spent her last days as an old lady with a taste for whisky and snuff. Mary's laments and eulogies for members of the clan follow the usual bardic form, but she enlivens her verse with freer stress-patterns (often in a three-line stanza) and her vernacular Gaelic is more spontaneous in feeling, music and rhythm than the old schools would have had it.

Much more radical departures were made by our next poet.

John MacDonald ('Iain Lom') (1620?–1707?)

Mary's outlook was limited to Dunvegan and the doings of the family, but Iain Lom lived a more mobile life, with a political eye on the wider world. Descended from the chiefs of Keppoch, Iain was involved in the clan feuds which grew up around Montrose's campaigns. He supported the Royalist cause passionately and was present when the Covenanters and the Campbells were defeated at the battle of Inverlochy in 1645. 'Iain Lom', as the name suggests, was a lean 'bare' man, known for his quick and scathing wit. It is said that the Campbells, all too aware of his talent for invective, offered a reward for his head. Tradition has it that he arrived at Inverary castle to claim the bounty himself and was indeed rewarded for his nerve by being entertained as a guest for a week. The Campbells had cause to fear this bard's tongue, for his account of the battle of Inverlochy shows his impressionistic and ferociously exultant verse in action – a vernacular Gaelic honed to hard, succinct and cruel images all leading to an absolutely merciless conclusion:

> Alasdair of sharp, biting blades,
> if you had the heroes of Mull with you,
> you would have stopped those who got away,
> as the dulse-eating rabble took to their heels.
>
> Alasdair, son of handsome Colla,
> skilled hand at cleaving castles,
> you put to flight the Lowland pale-face:
> what kale they had taken came out again.
>
> You remember the place called the Tawny Field?
> It got a fine dose of manure;
> not the dung of sheep or goats,
> but Campbell blood well congealed.
>
> To Hell with you if I care for your plight,
> as I listen to your children's distress,
> lamenting the band that went to battle,
> the howling of the women of Argyll.

(trs. D. Thomson)

An indefatigable Royalist, Iain Lom took Charles II fiercely to task for not claiming his kingdom – 'let not your soft tin sword/be in a fair sheath that is gilded' ('Lament for the Marquis of Huntly'). The king does not seem to have held a grudge, for with the Restoration he made Iain Lom his poet laureate in Scotland and the bard delivered a eulogy for the coronation. The poet was true to his appointment, for, when the Revolution of 1688 arrived, he did not hesitate to denounce William of Orange as a 'borrowed king' and flayed him and his queen in the bitterest possible terms.

Vituperation was not the poet's only voice, and the 'Lament for Montrose' shows a more tender note as he describes his depression at his leader's end; and an early lament for Angus MacRanald Og of Keppoch shows his typically economical images fired with a sense of personal loss. Iain Crichton Smith's translation tries to catch this terse, bright restraint in the rhythms of the Gaelic:

> I'm a goose that is plucked
> without feather or brood,
> or like Ossian condemned by Saint Patrick.

> Or a tree that is stripped,
> without apple or nut,
> the sap and the bark having left it.
>
> That raid to Loch Tay
> has darkened my way:
> Angus lay dead by its waters.
>
> . . .
>
> What wrung tears from my eyes
> was the gap in your side
> as you lay in the house of Cor Charmaig.
>
> For I loved your gay face
> (branched with blood and with race)
> both ruthless and graceful in warfare.

The 'bard of Keppoch' also produced a number of conventional stock elegies, but his most memorable verse deals with his turbulent times and his own incisively 'ruthless and graceful' feelings. Nor did he lose his sharpness in old age, as testified by the bawdy virulence of his 'Song against the Union' ('Oran an Aghaidh an Aonaidh'), on attack on those Lowlanders who promoted the parliamentary union of 1707 for personal gain:

> Lord Dupplin, without delay
> the vent to your throat opened,
> a turbulence rose in your heart
> when you heard the gold coming;
> you swallowed the hiccoughs of avarice,
> your lungs inflated and swelled,
> control over your gullet was relaxed,
> and the traces of your arse were unloosed.

> (trs. D. Thomson)

Iain Lom was far from alone in his distrust of the Commissioners, but Andrew Fletcher, the most outspoken Lowland critic of the Union, would not have welcomed him or his support.

Andrew Fletcher of Saltoun (1655–1716)

As a member of parliament at the beginning of the century, Fletcher is especially remembered for his opposition to the proposed union with Westminster. Scots of all persuasions were equally disturbed. After all, the Highlands still sustained a Jacobite interest, and, as far as the Lowlands were concerned, the failure of the Darien scheme had done little to convince Scottish businessmen of England's good faith. From an English point of view, the union of the parliaments would help to promote much-needed security for the Hanoverian succession after Queen Anne. The 'seven ill years' at the close of the century had left Scotland in terrible straits, with an acute shortage of money and resources and over a quarter of the population dead of hunger and disease. Factions both for and against Union were not slow to make the most of this failure in their arguments. In 1698 Fletcher produced *Two Discourses concerning the Affairs of Scotland*, the second of which contained a passionate denunciation of the state of affairs which had produced a permanent population of some 100,000 vagabonds, 'who have lived without any regard or subjection either to the laws of the land, or even those of God or nature'. The recent famines doubled this number, and, since Fletcher believed in a citizen militia, he condemned the keeping of a standing army when such poverty was rife:

> we had more need to have saved the money to have bought bread, for thousands of our people that were starving afford us the melancholy prospect of dying by shoals in our streets, and have left behind them reigning contagion which hath swept away multitudes more, and God knows where it may end.

Although Fletcher had Highland Jacobite allies in his opposition to Union, as a stout Presbyterian he had little sympathy with their cause or their culture. No Swiss burger could have had a more vehement concern for freedom, peace and healthy trade, and the kin-based, warlike and essentially unmaterialistic nature of clan society was anathema to him. He complained that half of Scotland was occupied 'by a people who are all gentlemen only because they will not work; and who in everything are more contemptible than the vilest slaves, except that they always carry arms, because for the most part they live upon robbery'. Fletcher's patriotism looked back to the great times of the Declaration of Arbroath; and the twelve 'limitations' which he proposed to parliament in 1703 all had to do with making sure that no king could act against the interests, or without the sanction of the Estates of Scotland. He was equally passionately opposed to what he took to be the erosion of wealth and cultural identity, which a parliamentary union with England could only accelerate. To this end he wrote an essay called *An Account of a Conversation concerning a Right Regulation of Governments for the Common Good of Mankind* (1704), which includes his famous saying on nationhood and the ballads. The essay was written in the form of a letter to the marquis of Montrose and other Whig nationalists, and it strikes a surprisingly contemporary note to any reader familiar with the debates on devolution which took place in Scotland in the late 1970s:

> That London should draw the riches and government of the three kingdoms to the south-east corner of this island, is in some degree as unnatural, as for one city to possess the riches and government of the world. . . . And if the other parts of government are not also communicated to every considerable body of men; but that some of them must be forced to depend upon others, and be governed by those who reside far from them, and little value any interest except their own . . . I say, all such governments are violent, unjust and unnatural.

If nothing else, the contemporary recurrence of these opinions suggests that Fletcher's diagnosis of Scotland's condition was more far-sighted than the successful Unionists of 1707 could ever have realised or admitted.

5

The eighteenth century: new Athenians and the Doric

On 28 April 1707 Chancellor Seafield concluded the last meeting of the last Scottish parliament with the words, 'Now there's ane end of ane auld sang', but these were far from the final words on the subject, for Scotland had been so deeply divided over the issue that debates and accusations of bribery and corruption raged for years. Many landowners had been in favour of what they saw as a profitable partnership, and the vested interests of Church and law had been protected by separate acts in both parliaments; but the boroughs feared a reduction in their status and the volatile urban crowds rioted at the prospect of their rulers moving to London, capital of the 'auld enemy'. It was not long before their fears were realised, agreements were broken, and even the Unionists began to have second thoughts as English businessmen denied them the expected benefits in trade and exports. Rises in taxation hit the poorer classes in Scotland much harder than their more comfortable counterparts in the south. The Kirk saw Episcopalian forms return under the new Toleration Act and the principle of lay patronage was introduced contrary to the Acts passed at the Union. Parliamentary action in far-away London was difficult and tedious to implement, and the forty-five new members and the Scottish nobility too found themselves outnumbered and diminished when they moved to the larger stage. For a while these disappointments seemed to have little to do with the Highlanders, who expected to live in their old society much as before. Yet it was only a matter of time before disaffection with the Union and the death of Queen Anne fanned the ashes of Jacobite hopes into a last fitful, destructive flame.

The 1715 rebellion was an abortive campaign despite a fair measure of support with 10,000 men from the clans. At Braemar in September, the Catholic cause of King James VIII was declared by 'Bobbing John', the sixth Earl of Mar, a man who had lost his position as Secretary of State when Queen Anne died. Mar and the clans expected more support from France and the south than they got, for the Hanoverian succession of George I was by no means universally popular and crowds in England had rioted at the prospect. Yet Mar would not commit himself and had to be persuaded to allow 2000 of his men to join English sympathisers on the road to the capital. The Jacobites reached Preston before they were encircled by superior numbers and surrendered. By this time Bobbing John had finally brought himself to Stirling to tackle the Duke of Argyll and his Campbells, who remained loyal to the government although outnumbered two to one. The Battle of Sherrifmuir was confused and indecisive, but in effect it was a defeat for Mar, because he failed to gain access to the south and his Highlanders began to go home. In late December the Old Pretender arrived in Scotland only to return to France in little over a month, leaving money for restitution and a plea for the approaching Argyll to be merciful. In fact the disillusioned rebels were treated relatively mildly, because Scots juries were reluctant to convict Jacobites for anti-Union sentiments. Nevertheless, Lowland Scots and English prejudices against the Highlanders had been reinforced once again, and groups such as the Society for Propagating Christian Knowledge continued to link the spread of schools and Presbyterian Christianity in the north-west with the deliberate extirpation of 'heathenish customs' and the speaking of what they still called 'Irish'. Garrisons were established at Fort William, Fort Augustus and Inverness, and General Wade built a network of roads which finally began to open the Highlands to trade, travel and the military presence of the state. At the same time soldiers were recruited from the north and the Black Watch was formed to deter the clansmen from cattle-raiding and the extortion of 'black mail' – a traditional form of 'protection money'. By 1745 the new Black Watch regiment was in the Netherlands fighting bravely in the service of King George.

Their absence from the home front and the French victory at Fontenoy encouraged Prince Charles Edward Stuart to revive the ambitions of the Stuart dynasty for one last throw of the dice.

The twenty-three-year-old prince was a more daring and attractive personality than his exiled father, but he landed near Arisaig with only a handful of followers and it took all his charm and his assurances to persuade the chiefs to join him – anti-Union sentiment was fading and the last Stuart had left the throne over forty years before. Nevertheless, moved by old loyalties or the threats of their chiefs, encouraged by an early victory at Prestonpans, or by the prospect of settling old scores against the Campbells, or even by a bad harvest at home, the clansmen gradually rallied to the prince's cause, until by November he was on his way south with 5000 men. This time the Jacobites reached Derby and put all London in a panic before their momentum ran out and Charles's advisers persuaded him that their position was too extended and vulnerable. The army returned to Scotland, met a few French reinforcements and won another victory at Falkirk; yet its supplies were dwindling and more and more clansmen were slipping away to spend the worst of the winter at home. Meanwhile the young Duke of Cumberland was pressing north with 9000 men, an army composed of twelve English battalions supported by artillery, horse-troopers and militia, as well as three battalions of Lowland Scots and one from Clan Campbell. On 16 April 1746, and against all advice, Charles insisted on a confrontation at Culloden on the moors outside Inverness. His exhausted and outnumbered troops with their claymores, pistols and shields were torn apart by artillery and decimated again when they finally charged a modern army trained to fire its muskets in alternating volleys. Charles escaped into the west, where he was gallantly (if sometimes reluctantly) hidden from his pursuers until he could set sail for France in September; but the wounded at Culloden were killed on the field where they lay. In the savage aftermath of the battle more than 3000 men, women and children were imprisoned and shipped to the south, where 120 were executed and over a thousand more banished and transported. Even although many were eventually set free, hundreds more died in captivity of hunger, wounds or disease. Meanwhile, as a matter of government policy, 'Butcher' Cumberland began to implement the most brutal repression throughout the Highlands. Clansmen were forbidden to carry arms, to play the pipes, or to wear tartan or the kilt, on pain of death or transportation; their music, their customs and their language were reviled and the glens given over to desultory bouts of terror and killing for over five years. Charles peddled his cause around Europe to increasingly little effect and died forty-two years later, a drunken and disillusioned man whose hopes had ended with the last land battle to be fought on British soil.

In the second half of the century, Scotland began to embark on better times, with a long overdue expansion in agriculture, trade and industry and a powerful and confident middle class. Even the Highlands came to share in this prosperity as rising cattle-prices encouraged clans to keep the peace and to trade with a Lowland society whose growing appetite for fish, timber, wool and latterly kelp, to serve the soap and glass industries, meant still more wealth in the north. Highland regiments became part of the British Army tradition, and men were raised by their clan-chiefs, clad in (legal) tartan and sent out to ply their warlike skills on behalf of a government and culture scarcely less foreign to them than that of the French, Spanish or Americans they were fighting. All these factors resulted in something of a boom for the hitherto underprivileged clans, and when the potato was introduced as a staple crop in times of peace and plenty, the population began to grow dramatically. Trade was accelerated again by the Napoleonic Wars, but it left the Highlands dreadfully vulnerable when peace came in 1815 and prices dropped. Lowland Scotland was less extended: it had coal and industrial resources on the east coast, with the Carron ironworks (which made the famous 'carronade' guns) and linen-manufacture and trade with the Baltic, while, on the west, Glasgow was becoming a major seaport where tobacco and sugar 'barons' made their fortunes from the Americas. It seemed as if the Union was bearing fruit at last and Scotland ready to match the Augustan culture of her new partner to the south.

The 'golden age' of the Scottish Enlightenment began in the 1740s and lasted for a hundred brilliant years, but its origins go back long before the Union, to those more humane aspects of the Reformation which had stressed breadth, accessibility and utility in education. So it was the Kirk's hopes for learning as a route to the word of God which initiated – ironically enough – the flowering of philosophy and the sciences in eighteenth- and nineteenth-century Scotland. Yet the old cultural tensions and insecurities were still there. If Highland mores were being undermined by well-meaning Lowland 'improvers', so the Scots tongue was being increasingly associated with all that was 'characterful' in Scots life – rustic or antique at best, and provincial at worst. The painful ambivalence that had been felt by many over the Union was replayed in cultural terms a generation later. In the 1780s Burns's vernacular muse was ecstatically received by the Edinburgh *literati* – the very people who had made a success of a little guide-book called *Scotticisms*, intended 'to put young writers and speakers on their guard against some of those Scotch idioms', much less broad Scots words, for 'the necessity of avoiding them is obvious'. So it is that there are two contrasting strains in eighteenth-century Scottish letters. The period opened with a marked revival of interest in ballads, songs and the poetry of the makars, and closed with the vernacular genius of Fergusson and Burns. In the mid century, however, the Scottish Enlightenment had also achieved a European scope and a thoroughly Augustan critical stance which led to the major literary periodicals of the 1800s. This extraordinary melting-pot produced Edinburgh as 'the Athens of the North' and it is fitting that the very fabric of the city itself should symbolise the contradictions and the creative vigour of the age, bubbling with the vulgar satirical energy of the 'Doric' and cooled again with hopes for an 'Athenian' clarity and control.

A vivid picture of life in mid-century Scotland can be found in the autobiography of Alexander 'Jupiter' Carlyle (1722–1805), a 'moderate' minister of the Kirk who wrote satirical pamphlets, attended the theatre, and enjoyed dancing and the company of the *literati*. Among the artists of the time, John Kay produced bold likenesses of the many characters to be seen walking in the Edinburgh streets, as did David Allen – 'the Scottish Hogarth', who illustrated 'The Gentle Shepherd' and 'The Cottar's Saturday Night'. Young Allan Ramsay (1713–84), the poet's son, became a well-known painter, a contemporary of Gainsborough and an early influence on Reynolds. He travelled widely, studied in Italy and settled in

London, where he became portrait-painter to George III. By the end of the century Sir Henry Raeburn (1756–1823) was Scotland's best-known portraitist. His most interesting works are divided between studies of Highland chiefs, now become a new class of landowner, clad in romantic tartan and keen to see a grandiose image of themselves in oils, and more sober portraits of his Lowland friends in law, literature, Kirk and sciences.

The boundaries of eighteenth-century Edinburgh were scarcely changed from two hundred years before, and so everyday life was crammed into the high tenement buildings or 'lands' which ran down the Royal Mile from the Castle to Holyrood Palace and spilled over each side of the ridge on the way. These tenements rose ten or twelve storeys high, creating ravine-deep vennels and lanes between them, darkened by overhanging gables and stinking with sewage and slops flung from the windows every evening at ten o'clock. Tenement life had long prevailed in Edinburgh, Stirling and Glasgow, producing a characteristically Scottish mixture of the classes by which elegant apartments were sandwiched among crowded attics, cellars and workshops, all linked by steep and narrow stairs. Advocates, craftsmen, beggars, butchers, porters, churchmen and academics all lived on top of one another in old Edinburgh and continued to do so until the 1780s. At first there was little in the way of formal entertainment, for the Kirk frowned on anything to do with theatre and even the richest apartments were small and cramped, so the life of society, and many professional and business transactions too, took place in the streets and, of course, in innumerable drinking-'howffs'.

A visiting Englishman remarked that Edinburgh streets were as crowded as a perpetual fair – and it was indeed a carnival of vivid contrasts, with St Giles' Cathedral and the town prison facing each other in the High Street, flanked by Parliament House and market-stalls; yet, despite the crowding, burglary, robbery and violent crime were relatively rare events, and the most common misdemeanours were drunkenness and falling into debt. Nevertheless the Edinburgh mob could be a political force to be reckoned with, as in the Porteous riot of 1736, when an army officer of that name opened fire in an attempt to disperse an unruly crowd attending an execution, only to be lynched himself; or when enraged citizens protested against the repeal of the anti-Catholic laws in 1779, by wrecking the house of the Moderator of the General Assembly and burning his library. Walter Scott compared life in these old streets and crowded rooms to 'the under deck of a ship. Sickness had no nook of quiet, affliction no retreat for solitary indulgence.' Yet there was a fierce energy to be found as well (at least for the survivors) in a milieu where everyone knew everyone else's business and where there was no room and little mercy for pretensions or class barriers.

English visitors admired an open-mindedness about Scottish intellectuals and noted that they had a wider range of acquaintances and intimates than was common in 'polite society' and the more rarefied circles of Dr Johnson's London. The talents of mid-eighteenth-century Scotland swung from the abstruse to the intensely practical: from divines, advocates and professors of moral philosophy to no-less-distinguished surgeons, chemists, inventors and civil engineers, many of whom came from humble origins and parish schools. By the 1760s, the School of Medicine at Edinburgh had replaced Leyden as the leading European centre for teaching and research. Glasgow too was an important centre, producing, among others, the famous Hunter brothers, who went to London to revolutionise surgery and anatomy. Chemistry was an equally distinguished field, with William Cullen as one of the great teachers of the subject, as was his successor Joseph Black, who befriended and helped the young James Watt. Black's work on carbon dioxide and latent heat was followed by Rutherford's on nitrogen and Hope's on strontium. The Edinburgh mathematician David Gregory had been friend and colleague to Newton and Halley at the beginning of the century, and James Hutton, who had studied under Gregory's successor, virtually founded modern geology.

These were the days before the need arose for narrow specialisation in the sciences, and in the traditional Scots term such men were all students of 'natural philosophy'. In applied technology James Watt is best known for his invention of the steam condenser. A merchant's son from Greenock, he had an equally learned interest in chemistry, architecture, music, law, metaphysics and language. By the mid seventies he had founded a firm with Boulton in Birmingham to manufacture his new improved steam engines. The next decade saw paddle steamships pioneered by Millar in Dumfriesshire, experiments which bore fruit with Symington's *Charlotte Dundas*, constructed in 1801 to tow barges on the new Forth–Clyde canal – the first practical steam vessel in the world. John Rennie from East Lothian served with Boulton and Watt for a while before becoming the most highly regarded civil engineer in the country, building harbours and canals throughout Britain; while Thomas Telford, a shepherd's son and a parish school-boy from Dumfriesshire, made himself a household name by the end of the century, constructing over a thousand bridges and hundreds of miles of roads and canals, including the Caledonian Canal, a vast system of waterways in Sweden and the Menai suspension bridge. Men such as these founded what was to become a nineteenth-century tradition of Scottish success in engineering and the applied sciences – witness McAdam, who gave his name to an improved road surface; Mackintosh, who waterproofed cloth; and Robert Stevenson, the second in three generations of civil engineers (and the grandfather of Robert Louis Stevenson), who built twenty-three lighthouses round the Scottish coast, including one on the notoriously wave-torn Bell Rock in 1810. Such respect for practical knowledge, and a belief that it should be available to all, was dear to the Presbyterian ethic and the Scots carried it into publishing with the *Encyclopaedia Britannica*, founded in 1771, while in 1810 the *Edinburgh Encyclopaedia* set out to summarise the whole of natural science and technology.

'Auld Reekie' was becoming seriously overcrowded, even by Scottish standards, but the growth in prosperity allowed better-off families to move south to new suburbs and more spacious houses, such as the ones in the homely neoclassical style of George Square. By the 1760s plans were made to expand in the opposite direction across the Nor' Loch (now Princes Street Gardens), and the poet James Thomson's nephew, a young architect called James Craig, won a gold medal for his plan of a 'New Town' to be built in the European neoclassical manner. At last Edinburgh was to have buildings appropriate to the spirit of the Enlightenment, and the old capital, which had been so shaken by the departure of crown and parliament, could express its new-found confidence and ambition in the geometrical symmetries and the grand scale of George Street, flanked by Princes Street and Queen Street and closed by a magnificent square at each end. It did not matter that at first the site was remote and exposed to the notorious Edinburgh winds, for it soon became the most fashionable place to live. Many of the men of the Enlightenment – including David Hume, Lord Kames, Lord Monboddo, Hugh Blair and William Robertson – had been familiar figures in the Canongate, the Lawnmarket and the old High Street, but they all ended their careers in the new and more stately surroundings of 'Georgian' Edinburgh. With buildings such as Register House, designed by Robert Adam, the New Town continued to expand into one of the finest neoclassical cityscapes in the world. If modern literary critics have found the combination of opposites to be a feature of Scottish culture, then no more striking physical example can be found than the two faces of Edinburgh, as clearly defined today as they were in the late eighteenth century, when those spacious Palladian and Grecian symmetries were overlooked by the towering, seething, chaotic tenements and wynds of the vernacular town – new Athens and Auld Reekie, indeed.

By the end of the century egalitarian feeling was afoot once again in Scotland. Stirred by social changes, the American War of Independence and particularly the French Revolution, the newly industrialised working classes and many middle-class liberals sought to extend the franchise to all men over twenty-one. The reform movement was beginning, many 'Societies of Friends of the People' were started, and the Edinburgh mob, never slow to express itself, rioted for three days after the king's birthday in 1792, to cries of 'Liberty, equality and no king!' The notorious Lord Braxfield presided over intolerant trials of freethinkers, sentencing Thomas Muir, a young advocate, to transportation for fourteen years and doing the same for three English delegates who attended a national convention in Edinburgh the following year. Outright republican sentiment gained force in Scotland, to the gradual alarm of liberal sympathisers. Tom Paine's *The Rights of Man* (1790) was especially sought after and even translated into Gaelic. The weavers – the most skilled and educated workers – were particularly active in radical circles and in the proto-revolutionary 'United Scotsmen' movement, whose Calvinist and dissenting roots went back to Rullion Green. However, the terror in France and the eventual rise of Napoleon dampened republican sympathies in the country at large and allowed the government to supress the 'United Scotsmen' by transporting many of them to Botany Bay in His Majesty's newest colony.

'If a man were permitted to make all the ballads,' wrote Fletcher of Saltoun in 1704, 'he need not care who should make the laws of a nation.' When, despite his best efforts, the lawmakers actually went to London, Scotland was left alone with her ballads to test the truth of Fletcher's claim. The result was a revival of interest in the vernacular tongue, especially among the educated middle classes, and literary and creative ambitions began to stir again, despite the Church's puritanical attitude towards 'profane' books and plays. Between 1706 and 1711 an Edinburgh printer and bookseller called James Watson produced three separate anthologies to satisfy the literary nationalism of new readers. The first volume of Watson's *Choice Collection of Comic and Serious Scots Poems both Ancient and Modern* began with a special plea: because the book was 'the first of its nature which has been published in our own native Scots Dialect', the editor hoped that the candid reader may 'give some charitable grains of allowance if the performance come not up to such a point of exactness as may please an over nice palate.' In fact *The Cherry and the Slae* needed no such apology, but for the most part the Scots poems are self-consciously homespun pieces such as 'Habbie Simson', 'Sanny Briggs' and 'The Country Wedding'. A mock elegy by Hamilton of Gilbertfield was especially influential, and when Watson published 'The Last Dying Words of Bonny Heck, A Famous Grey-Hound in the Shire of Fife' it sired an entire menagerie of philosophical talking animals. The convention had come from noble beginnings, and Burns was to rescue it again, but in the meantime the acute social observation of Henryson's animal fables had given way to pastiche and easy pathos:

> 'Alas, alas, 'quo' Bonny Heck,
> 'On Former days when I reflect!
> I was a Dog much in Respect
>   For doughty Deed:
> But now I must hing by the Neck
>   Without Remeed.

William Hamilton of Gilbertfield (1665?–1751) was a retired army lieutenant who assisted Allan Ramsay in compiling and 'improving' songs for his *Tea Table Miscellany*. Ramsay was so impressed by the aptness of standard Habbie in 'Bonny Heck' that he adopted it forthwith and popularised it in many of his own poems, including the 'familiar verse epistles' which the two enthusiasts exchanged, thereby establishing yet another mode which was to catch on widely. It was Hamilton's 1722 edition of Blind Harry's *Wallace* which excited Burns so much with a sense of national pride, and, since the text was abridged and anglicised, the ironic implications of this say a lot about the times. Scots pride was evoked again by Dr George Mackenzie (1669–1725), who produced three volumes of dubious biographies – *The Lives and Characters of the Most Eminent Writers of the Scots Nation'* (1708–22) – while Thomas Ruddiman (1674–1757), a better scholar and a Jacobite sympathiser, produced and glossed an edition of Douglas's *Eneados* in 1710. A developing taste for antiquarian romance was met by Lady Elizabeth Wardlaw (1677–1727), who wrote and published 'Hardyknute' as if it were an old, anonymous ballad 'fragment', and, although her deception did not endure, the poem appeared as such in the *Ever Green* collection. In a more contemporary vein, Lady Grizel Baillie (1665–1746) chose Scots to speak to a polite audience about the love-life of swains – 'Were na my heart licht I wad die'. The romance of 'ancient' poems, national pride, the vernacular comedy of common manners and rustic sentiment – these were the varied and swelling currents upon which a wigmaker in Edinburgh launched what has come to be known as the eighteenth-century revival of Scottish verse.

Allan Ramsay (1685–1758)

Sometime in his middle teens Allan Ramsay left his native Lanarkshire and arrived in Edinburgh to seek his living as a maker of periwigs. In 1710 he became a burgess of the town and two years after that he was married, established as a master wigmaker, and beginning to express an enthusiasm for the world of letters. Brought up on *The Bruce*, *Wallace* and the poems of David Lindsay, he was one of the many Scotsmen of his time who felt indignant at the loss of the Scottish parliament and at what he took to be a subsequent decline in the old capital city. He determined to master English literature and make Edinburgh less provincial. Thus the emblem of his new bookshop at the Luckenbooths in 1726 was a sign with two heads on it – Drummond of Hawthornden for Scotland and Ben Jonson for England. Yet for Ramsay, as for many of his countrymen, England was still the 'auld enemy' in a sentimental sense, even if his Lowland respect for trade and 'the frugal arts of peace' could not envisage reversing the Union. Such contradictions convey the essence of the eighteenth-century Scottish condition, and to some extent they survive in the popular consciousness to the present day. Thus Ramsay and his values play a significant part in the history of Scottish culture, even although he is a much less gifted poet than either Fergusson or Burns.

In 1712 Ramsay helped to found 'the Easy Club' – a group of mild Jacobites dedicated to 'mutual improvement in conversation' and to reading the *Spectator* aloud at each meeting. By 1718 he was calling himself poet and publisher on the strength of a collection of Scots songs and a piece called 'Tartana' – English heroic couplets in praise of the humble plaid. He also published an edition of 'Christis Kirk on the Green' with two extra Scots cantos of his own – added, he said, to show 'the Follies and Mistakes of low life in a just Light, making them appear as ridiculous as they really are.' Ramsay next adopted the form and manner of 'Habbie Simson' for a lively series of Scots poems on the notables of Edinburgh street life. These early 'elegies' celebrated 'Maggie Johnston' and 'Lucky Wood', who kept low alehouses, not to mention 'John Cowper', the Kirk's watchdog on wanton girls and professional ladies. 'Lucky Spence's Last Advice' plays to another convention, with the dying words of one of the city's most famous bawds providing her girls with the benefit of long experience:

> O black Ey'd Bess and mim-Mou'd Meg,   affected prim in speech
> O'er good to work, or yet to beg;   Too
> Lay sunkots up for a sair leg,   something
>   For whan ye fail,
> Ye'r face will not be worth a feg,   fig
>   Nor yet ye'r tail.

. . .

Whan e'er ye meet a fool that's fow,   *drunk*
That ye're a maiden gar him trow,   *make him believe*
Seem nice, but stick to him like glew;
    And whan set down,
Drive at the jango till he spew,   *fornicate*
    Syne he'll sleep soun.

  Whan he's asleep then dive and catch
His ready cash, his rings or watch . . . .

Although the author seems to be in love with his own vulgar daring, there is, at least, plenty of life and good humour in such character-studies. By comparison the invocation to 'Tartana' is impossibly stilted, and, although the *double entendre* in the last line would be worthy of Lucky Spence, the dullness of the rest of the poem suggests that it was an accident only:

Ye Caledonian Beauties, who have long
Been both the Muse, and subject of my song,
Assist your Bard, who in harmonious Lays
Designs the Glory of your Plaid to raise.

By 1719 Ramsay and William Hamilton were exchanging elaborate compliments in the standard Habbie of their 'familiar epistles', reflecting, among other things, that

The chiefs of London, Cam and Ox,
Ha'e rais'd up great poetick stocks
Of *Rapes*, of *Buckets*, *Sarks* and *Locks*,
While we neglect
To shaw their betters . . . .

If there is a hint of insecurity in these lines, then a similar instability marks the 'Pastoral on the Death of Joseph Addison', in which Ramsay constructs a dialogue between 'Richy' and 'Sandy' – none other than 'Sir Richard Steele and Mr Alexander Pope' – discoursing like Lowland shepherds in an excruciating amalgam of broad Scots and Augustan English. Pastoral dialogue in rhyming couplets was used to better effect in 'Patie and Roger', which gains an unforced freshness from Ramsay's vernacular realism:

Last morning I was unco airly out,	very early
Upon a dyke I lean'd and glowr'd about;	wall
I saw my *Meg* come linkan o'er the lee,	tripping
I saw my *Meg*, but Maggie saw na me:	
For yet the sun was wadin throw the mist,	
And she was closs upon me e'er she wist,	
Her coats were kiltit, and did sweetly shaw	petticoats; tucked up
Her straight bare legs, which whiter were than	
snaw	

The popularity of his poems encouraged Ramsay to produce a proper volume, and this duly appeared in 1721, pretentiously provided with a portrait of the author, dedications by other writers, footnotes, a glossary and a preface which defended the use of Scots in pastoral verse as no less appropriate than the Doric dialect used by Theocritus. Thus the language of Henryson and Dunbar was to become increasingly associated in Ramsay's mind, and in the minds of his readers, with bucolic simplicity, rustic topics and a dialect of Greek noted for its old, simple, solemn utterance. This assumption survived up to and beyond the time of Burns, and, indeed, it complimented the Edinburgh intelligentsia's picture of themselves as citizens of a new Athens – urbane and educated and yet conversant, too, with what they took to be 'Doric' from the countryside beyond.

The 1721 edition was a success and Ramsay gave up wigmaking to become a full-time writer and bookseller. He started his new career by editing 'A Collection of Choice Songs' (some of them his own) and publishing them as *The Tea Table Miscellany* in 1724. Ramsay was no scholar, he did not include the music to the songs and he frequently 'improved' the originals – 'so that the modest voice and ear of the fair singer might meet with no affront'. (The first collection of airs for Scots songs appeared the following year in William Thomson's *Orpheus Caledonius*, but the first fully responsible edition of texts and music was not produced until David Herd's collection of 1769.) The *Miscellany* was popular and influential, eventually running to four volumes (including English songs) and twenty-four reprintings in the next eighty years. Ramsay promptly followed it with two volumes of older Scottish poems 'wrote by the ingenious before 1600' and culled mostly from the Bannatyne Manuscript. *The Ever Green* (1724) contained superior ballads and many fine poems by Henryson and

Dunbar, but never achieved anything like the commercial success of the *Miscellany*. Once again Ramsay interfered with the texts, censoring some lines, paraphrasing others and even adding a verse prophecy of his own birth at the end of Dunbar's 'Lament for the Makaris'!

The success of 'Patie and Roger' encouraged Ramsay to produce a sequel in 1723, written from the point of view of the shepherds' girlfriends. The gentle satire of 'Jenny and Meggie' is more pointed than in the earlier piece, perhaps because Jenny's pessimism is closer to the reality of woman's lot:

O! tis a pleasant thing to be a bride;	
Syne whindging getts about your ingle-side	whining offspring
Yelping for this or that with fasheous din,	troublesome
To make them brats then ye maun toil and spin.	rags
Ae we'an fa's sick, ane scads itsell wi broe,	scalds; broth
Ane breaks his shin, anither tynes his shoe;	
The deel gaes o'er John Wobster, Hame grows Hell,	
When *Pate* misca's ye war than tongue can tell.	

Nevertheless, Patie's girlfriend eventually persuades Jenny to yield to romance by presenting the other side of the old coin:

Yes, 'tis a heartsome thing to be a wife,
When round the ingle-edge young sprouts are rife.
Gif I'm sae happy, I shall have delight,
To hear their little plaints, and keep them right.

These two eclogues gave birth to Ramsay's best-known work and provided him with the first two scenes of *The Gentle Shepherd* (1725) – a dramatic pastoral comedy in five acts. The author was persuaded to add songs in 1728 and to expand it into a ballad opera, whereupon it proved very popular for the next 150 years. The text saw many editions, some of them anglicised, performed by both amateur and professional groups all over Britain, making its author wealthy and famous at last.

The Gentle Shepherd perfectly encapsulates the strengths and weaknesses of Ramsay's muse, and the divided loyalties of his countrymen. The play's rural setting is idealised, but the plain Scots speech of the characters adds a physical conviction to the place and the people in it. Jenny's description of the woes of marriage and poverty is realistic, and yet the plot is an unashamed confection of Arcadian love-matches and hidden blue blood. Patie, the gentle shepherd, turns out to be the son of an exiled Cavalier gentleman, but still he refuses to forsake his milkmaid lover. The conflict between his lineage and his heart need not last long, for Peggy is an aristocratic foundling too, and in next to no time the shepherd and his lass are exchanging Augustan clichés in stilted Anglo-Scots, to the effect that 'Good manners give integrity a bleez [glow] / When native vertues join the Arts to please'. By this stage, not surprisingly, what vitality the play still possesses has passed to the low-life subplot, in which Bauldy seeks witchcraft to make Jenny love him instead of Roger. His energetic descriptions of the uncanny are firmly within a tradition that runs from Dunbar to Burns's 'Tam O' Shanter':

She can o'ercast the night, and cloud the moon,	
And mak the deils obedient to her crune.	devils; croon
At midnight hours, o'er the Kirk-yards she raves,	
And howks unchristen'd we'ans out of their graves;	digs
Boils up their livers in a warlock's pow.	skull
Rins wither shins about the hemlock low;	anti-clockwise
And seven times does her prayers backward pray,	
Till Plotcock comes with lumps of Lapland clay,	
Mixt with the venom of black taids and snakes	toads

(II. ii)

Notwithstanding the 'black taids', enlightenment prevails, and the poor peasant is disabused with: 'What silly notions crowd the clouded mind, / That is thro' want of Education blind!', and then he is chastised 'because he brak good breeding's laws'. The modern readers will be forgiven for preferring the imaginative force of Bauldy's fantasies to the vapid moralising of Ramsay's gentlefolk, and yet later in the century Adam Smith and Hugh Blair spoke for educated Edinburgh by decrying the passages using a 'homely' style which was 'rustic' and 'not intelligible'. 'It is the duty of a poet', opined Smith, 'to write like a gentleman', and his assumption that this was not possible in Scots was even shared at times by Burns. In this context the wide success of *The Gentle Shepherd* ensured that Scots would continue to present an exclusively bucolic face.

Ramsay moved to new premises at the Luckenbooths – a group of lockable shops near the Mercat Cross and St Giles' – and began the earliest known circulating library in Britain, from which readers could borrow books at twopence a night. The narrow-minded took exception to such pleasures, particularly his interest in the theatre, and on at least two occasions Ramsay's shop was raided by the righteous, who claimed that 'villainous profane and obscene bookes and playes printed at London by Curle and others, are gote downe from London by Allan Ramsey, and lent out, for an easy price, to young boyes, servant weemen of the better sort, and gentlemen, and vice and obscenity dreadfully propagated'. The publisher was not to be deterred from his cultural convictions, and when his teenage son showed a talent for drawing and painting he helped to found the 'Academy of St Luke' (1729) for the graphic arts and the training of students. In due course young Allan continued his studies in Italy and became a famous and respected painter in London.

A new collection of poems appeared in 1728, including 'The Last Speech of a Wretched Miser' in what was now a thriving genre of character monologue. ('Holy Willie's Prayer' owes something to this particular poem.) Ramsay also supported various theatrical ventures in their struggle against Presbyterian prejudice and opened a theatre of his own at Carruber's Close, only to have it threatened in 1737 by those who feared its popularity and invoked the new Licensing Act to try to shut it down. The poet resisted for three years and gave vent to his rage in the (unpublished) 'Epistle to Mr H. S.' (1738):

> Thus whore, and bawd, doctor and pox
> The tavern and a large white ox,
> Are the whole sum for Lord or clown
> Of the diversions of our town,
> Since by a late sour-snouted law
> Which makes great heroes stand in awe
> The morall teachers of broad Truths
> Have golden padlocks on their mouths . . . .

At the age of fifty-five Ramsay withdrew from active business and retired to his fine new house – an octagonal dwelling on

Castle Hill, nicknamed 'the goose pie' by irreverent locals who had to live in the teeming streets below it. Ramsay and his bookshop at the Luckenbooths had been a vital focus for the liberal arts in the early years of the century and the cultural flowering of Edinburgh could no longer be much delayed by frosts from the pulpit. The Licensing Act, for example, was soon countered by the gambit of selling theatre tickets as 'concert' tickets followed by a 'free' play, and numerous Edinburgh lawyers – an influential new audience – supported the deception and enjoyed a night at the theatre.

Pre-Romantics and others

Ramsay had committed himself and the best of his writing to the Edinburgh he loved, but other men looked elsewhere and **James Thomson** (1700–48) left for the south just two months before *The Gentle Shepherd* was completed. The son of a minister in the Borders, Thomson abandoned his career as a divinity student in favour of a literary life in London. He found a job as a tutor, joined circles in which Pope moved, and made an early reputation for himself with four poems begun in 1725 and collected as *The Seasons* in 1730. (They were to be revised quite extensively over the next sixteen years.) Thomson's neoclassical blank verse is conventional enough with poetic diction, personification and echoes of Milton's elevated tone, but a more original note is struck by his painterly eye for the play of weather and light on the landscape and a host of moral, patriotic and scientific observations, all determined to prove that the harmony of God can be shown in the natural world. Such views owe something to the Earl of Shaftesbury's writings at the beginning of the century and were promoted in Scotland by Frances Hutcheson. Thomson's 'philosophy of nature' was an untidy mixture but it proved to be a popular one, and *The Seasons* is often said to anticipate the Romantic 'discovery' of nature. With this, Thomson passes into the history of literature in England, although his descriptions of landscape were also to influence the Gaelic poetry of Alasdair MacMhaighster Alasdair. Of Thomson's later works *The Castle of Indolence* (1748) is a pleasant Spenserian pastiche; *Liberty* (1735–6) is thankfully forgotten; and *The Masque of Alfred* (1740), co-written with Malloch, is remembered only for the words of 'Rule Britannia'.

If the author's Scottish origins can be identified in *The Seasons*, they appear in his didactic Christian rationalism and in a tendency to add more and more examples to his account of the countryside and its weather. 'Winter', published in 1726, was the first of the poems to be completed and it joins a long Scottish line – going back to Henryson and Douglas – in the poetic description of bad weather:

> At last, the muddy deluge pours along,
> Resistless, roaring; dreadful down it comes
> From the chapt mountain, and the mossy wild,
> Tumbling thro' rocks abrupt, and sounding far:
> Then o'er the sanded valley, floating spreads,
> Calm, sluggish, silent; till again constrained,
> Betwixt two meeting hills, it bursts a way,
> Where rocks, and woods o'erhang the turbid stream.
> There gathering triple force, rapid, and deep,
> It boils, and wheels, and foams, and thunders thro'.

(1726 edn)

Thomson's words, punctuated with weighty pauses, establish a chain in the development of the Romantic imagination which stretches from the actuality of the Scottish Borders to Wordsworth's spirit in the Alps and the full-blown symbolism of Coleridge's sacred river.

Another small link in the evolution of the pre-Romantic sensibility was contributed by **Robert Blair** (1700?–46) with the publication of *The Grave* (1743), a blank-verse meditation on mortality. (The 1808 edition was illustrated by Blake.) Blair was a Kirk minister in East Lothian, and, although the pulpit voice can be heard in most of his verse, *The Grave* enjoyed a considerable following. He featured in the so-called 'Graveyard School', along with the Englishman Edward Young, whose *Night Thoughts: On Life, Death and Immortality* (1742–4) influenced the Gaelic poet Duguld Buchanan and catered to a vogue for religiose melancholy. This genre was refined in Gray's 'Elegy' (1751) and popularised by the Gothic novel at the end of the century.

Fourteen years after Thomson, a young surgeon's apprentice called **Tobias Smollett** (1721–71) left Glasgow with a verse tragedy in his luggage, and set out for London to try to get the play performed. He had little luck, and 1741 saw him enlisted in the navy as a surgeon's mate, serving in the West Indies in the war against Spain. Five years later he was back in London with a moneyed wife and a not very successful practice, for surgeons were regarded as the tradesmen of the medical profession in those days. Smollett turned to satirical fiction and achieved success at last with a picaresque semi-autobiographical novel about the travels of a young Scotsman. *The Adventures of Roderick Random* (1748) assured him of an early place in the development of the English novel (*Clarissa* appeared the same year) and Smollett happily joined the *literati* of London to become another of those Scotsmen whose noblest prospect, according to his friend Samuel Johnson, was the high road leading him to England. Yet Smollett did not entirely forget his native country, for he came north on various occasions and was prompted to write an indignant poem against the slaughter at Culloden. His last visit, a trip of some seven months in search of health, provided him with material for the tour undertaken by Matthew Bramble in the final novel, *The Expedition of Humphrey Clinker* (1771).

As editor of the *Critical Review*, Smollett had fallen foul of the Scottish establishment in 1759 by criticising a long Homeric epic which had been produced by **William Wilkie** (1721–72), a Kirk minister from just outside Edinburgh. No less a man than David Hume wrote in defence of the poem, but it must be admitted that his judgement as a critic was unduly influenced by patriotism, friendship and an overdeveloped respect for classical learning done out in English heroic couplets. Nevertheless, Wilkie was a remarkable person: he came from a peasant farming family, and his devotion to learning and his erudition eventually gained him a chair in the sciences at St Andrew's University, even if his eccentric behaviour made him equally notable. He produced fables in verse, including 'The Hare and the Partan' in Scots, but his *magnum opus*, nine books on the siege of Thebes called *The Epigoniad* (1757), remains as dead as the seven heroes who razed that ancient city.

Another of Hume's enthusiasms was a blank-verse tragedy called *Douglas* by his cousin **John Home** (1722–1808) which had scored a notable success on the Edinburgh stage in 1756 before going on to London and Covent Garden. Home was a minister in Berwickshire, a lively, generous, romantic and popular man, remembered with affection by Henry Mackenzie, who wrote a biography of him. Home's next five verse tragedies were not so well received, but his namesake, the famous philosopher, still maintained that *Douglas* was better than Shakespeare and Otway because the Scots play was 'refined from the unhappy barbarism of the one, and the licentiousness of the other'. The tragedy is Romantic in spirit, for it concentrates on evoking wonder at the wild landscape and pity at the plight of the characters; but its structure is essentially neoclassical – elevated, stately and completely static. Notwithstanding its less-than-inflammatory style, there was scandal at the Edinburgh performance when the 'unco guid' heard that some ministers, including the liberal thinker 'Jupiter' Carlyle, had been seen in the theatre. It must be admitted that time has not been kind to the literary judgements of Hume and his educated friends, for most of their favourites are now forgotten, including Professor James Beattie's Spenserian imitation *The Minstrel* (1771–4) and the Augustan verses of blind Dr Thomas Blacklock (1721–91), equally praised by Dr Johnson. But fortunately Hume's taste is not the only yardstick of the man, and a closer look at his milieu and at his contemporaries from the 1720s to the 1770s will show where the real strengths of mid-century Edinburgh were to be found.

The Scottish Enlightenment

Francis Hutcheson (1694–1746) an Irishman who took the chair of moral philosophy at Glasgow in 1729, was the first professor to teach in English instead of Latin. His thinking was developed from Shaftesbury's philosophy, which linked man's moral nature to his aesthetic responses. Hutcheson stressed individual experience and our responses to beauty and happiness, and he believed in a social, caring person whose common humane feelings, rather than any exercise of logic, would encourage them to act for 'the greatest happiness of the greatest number'. (The phrase predates Bentham's more rational utilitarian system by some forty years.) He held that the existence of this moral sense reveals the essence of mankind and the goodness of God. More than an echo of these beliefs can be heard in Burns's call for 'Ae spark o' Nature's fire, / That's a' the learning I desire.' Indeed, the primacy of instinctive sympathetic feeling as a gauge of morality became central to how northern writers understood themselves, the common people and the Scottish psyche in general. This tendency reached a peak of sorts with Mackenzie and degenerated into sentimentalism by Victorian times, but Burns, Scott, Hogg and Galt all testify to its healthier influence. Given the holiness of the heart's affections in their original sense, it follows that Hutcheson, like Burns, Keats or Shelley for that matter, was against external authoritarianism, whether on the part of governments or landowners or even in the family.

Professor Hutcheson was one of the first to contribute to what became known as the 'Scottish Enlightenment' and to what was to become a particularly northern exploration of moral philosophy, the nature of man and the nature of knowledge itself. Such interests are not entirely divorced from the intellectual inheritance of Calvinism and the Reformation, but the new direction was more speculative and humane, being broadly applied to society at large, and, indeed, Hutcheson was influential in the growth of a moderate party within the Church of Scotland itself.

The greatest figure of the time, however, was most certainly not a Christian moderate, for all that he was a mild and amiable man with many friends. **David Hume** (1711–76) dismissed all religion in his works and even struck at the foundations of reason itself. As a result Presbyterian reaction ensured that he never did become a university professor, despite at least two promising opportunities. Hume was the impecunious son of a small Berwickshire laird. He studied briefly at Edinburgh, but his enthusiasm for literature overcame his more sober intention to follow law. He then tried a post as a merchant's clerk in Bristol before escaping to France, where he stayed for the next three years. There, still in his middle twenties, he completed his most important book, three volumes published in London as *The Treatise of Human Nature* (1739–40). The work had little immediate effect, however, and so on returning to his home at Ninewells in Berwickshire he produced a more accessible series of essays on moral and political issues. After another two years abroad he established himself in Edinburgh, became Keeper of the Advocate's Library and started on his monumental *History*

of Great Britain under the Stuarts (1754–62). The first volume was
not well received, partly because his account of the country's
religious disputes treated both factions with equal contempt,
but eventually the project gained favour not least because of its
interest in cultural changes, and it brought him useful income
over the years.

Further philosophical works appeared: the *Political Discourses*
(1751) prepared the way for Adam Smith's economics, and *An
Enquiry Concerning Human Understanding* (1748) and *An Enquiry
Concerning the Principles of Morals* (1752) further advanced a
radical critique of the age's confidence in reason. Hume's
scepticism follows Locke, Shaftesbury and Hutcheson in so far
as he too stresses the empirical evidence of our individual
experience, but his conclusions take him much further. Thus,
for example, in dismissing the possibility of miracles, he
undermines religion too by defining the act of Christian faith in
an individual as a process 'which subverts all the principles of
his understanding, and gives him a determination to believe
what is most contrary to custom and experience' (*Enquiry
Concerning Human Understanding*). Hume's scepticism is fundamental, for it derives from a radical reassessment of the nature
of reason itself. From his earliest work he insists that what we
call 'cause and effect' is really only based on our own
psychological expectations. Thus, to invent a simplified example, when one billiard ball strikes another it always makes it
move, and from repeated observation of the fact we infer certain
'laws' of physics. But Hume says that such 'laws' are only
upheld by 'custom' – that is, by our supposition that the future
will be conformable to the past. A statistician may assure us
that colliding billiard balls have imparted motion in every
recorded instance, but the only *cause* he has really identified is
the cause of our own *expectations* that such events should always
continue to be so. Thus Newton's 'laws of motion' depend on no
less than an act of imaginative faith on our part – not so very
different, after all, from a belief in miracles. Admittedly this
imaginative act does not *feel* the same to us as, say, the idle
notion that the billiard balls will turn into hedgehogs when they
meet; but the apparent difference between these two expectations is simply a matter of what we used to and not a matter of
reason. Therefore, according to Hume, 'logic' itself turns out to
be upheld only by reference to what he calls 'custom'.

It is not surprising that such 'notorious' ideas were publicly attacked in 1752 by the General Assembly of the Kirk of Scotland. Nevertheless, Hume was well-enough received in Edinburgh circles, even by some of the more liberal churchmen. By all accounts the philosopher was a calm, genial and sociable man, whose shattering scepticism was not at all dogmatic nor in the least consonant with his comfortable girth and a face, seen in the Allan Ramsay portrait, which was described as that of 'a turtle-eating alderman'; indeed, in the world of practical politics he was a Tory who could see no reason why men could not organise society so that it ran quietly and efficiently. The academic reaction to Hume's books was led by **Thomas Reid** (1710–96), an Aberdeen graduate who succeeded Adam Smith in the chair of moral philosophy at Glasgow. Reid's *Enquiry into the Human Mind, on the Principles of Common Sense* (1764) set out to refute Hume by maintaining that his system (like Bishop Berkeley's) reduces our certitude about the world to a matter of mental sensations and ideas. In place of this Reid invokes 'common sense' to point to the experential difference between the *idea* of touching something and the actual physical act itself – thus Newton's world of actual objects and causal relationships is restored to us. These views were influential in establishing a 'Scottish School' of philosophy which managed to bypass, if not to bridge, the abyss of Hume's scepticism.

In the meantime Hume lived in Paris for two years, where he was lionised by intellectual society and recognised as one of the most trenchant thinkers in Europe. In 1766 he returned to London with Rousseau, whom he befriended until the Frenchman's paranoia led to a parting of the ways. Two years later Hume returned to Edinburgh, where he spent his last eight years and where he died calmly in the sure expectation of eternal extinction. His final demolition of Christian orthodoxy was published posthumously, and the *Dialogues on Natural Religion* (1779) show that the old man kept his wry doubts to the end. Not so the establishment, where the 'common sense' school prevailed, popularised by **James Beattie** (1735–1803), professor of moral philosophy at Aberdeen, minor poet and author of the book against Scotticisms. Beattie's *Essay on Truth* (1770) attacked Hume's 'sophistical arguments' and offered in their place a blindingly inane definition of truth as that 'which the condition of our nature determines us to believe'.

Notwithstanding Beattie's comfortable definition of truth, Hume's clashes with the Kirk, as well as his historical writing and his interests in politics and economics, are characteristic of the Scottish scene at a time when new ideas were afoot and moral philosophy was taken to be central to an understanding of man and society. The Kirk no longer had the monopoly on such issues and was itself divided over matters of internal and external policy and doctrine. Philosophical historians followed, such as **Adam Ferguson** (1723–1816), yet another Edinburgh professor of moral philosophy, who has been called the founder of sociology. His *Essay on the History of Civil Society* (1766) proposed a comparative, almost anthropological, approach to the study of man as a being who creates social structures and moral imperatives for himself – the complete opposite of Rousseau's view of man as an isolated being who is best when least tainted by 'civilisation'. **William Robertson** (1721–93), a minister who became Principal of Edinburgh University and Moderator of the General Assembly, published a successful *History of Scotland* (1759), followed by a *History of the Reign of the Emperor Charles V* (1769) and a *History of America* (1777); next to Gibbon, perhaps, he was the most outstanding historian of his day. Unlike Hume, Robertson could see beyond the excesses of the Scottish Reformation to sympathise with the democratic impulse behind the Presbyterian ideal. He was a sociable and upright character and, although he could be forceful enough in the General Assembly, he employed his eloquence in support of the moderate cause in the Kirk. **Sir David Dalrymple, Lord Hailes** (1726–92) went to original sources to provide his *Annals of Scotland* (1776–9). A Law Lord and an antiquarian, he also collected ballads and edited the Bannatyne Manuscript. A fellow advocate and judge, **Henry Home, Lord Kames** (1696–1782) combined all the interests of philosopher, historian and literary critic. His *Historical Law Tracts* (1758) established a common historical pattern in the links between the evolution of man's institutions and his economic condition. Friend of Hume, Boswell and Benjamin Franklin, patron to Adam Smith and John Millar, Kames took an active and varied part in Edinburgh life, espousing literary criticism, crossing swords with the Kirk and then with Voltaire, publishing tracts on agricultural improvements, and all with equal panache. Kames's engagement is typical of the breadth of interest shown by professional men at the time, and they formed a 'Select Society' to provide an appropriate forum in which the only taboo subjects were religion and Jacobitism. Also in the Select Society was **James Burnett, Lord Monboddo** (1714–99), a famously lively man of the Law, keenly interested in ancient Greek philosophy and the origins of language and primitive societies. His anthropological theories were seriously limited by his dependence on second-hand sources and by his own enthusiastic gullibility, but he is remembered now, as he was ridiculed then, for his theory that the orang-outang is a primitive member of the human species, a form of the noble savage not quite evolved enough for speech.

The philosophical study of society came to fruition in the works of **Adam Smith** (1723–90), who held the chair of logic and then of moral philosophy at Glasgow. In fact it was Smith who founded the Select Society, along with Kames and Hume and Allan Ramsay's son in 1754, as well as contributing to the *Edinburgh Review* in its first short-lived incarnation the following year. The financial success of his *Theory of Moral Sentiments* (1759) allowed him to leave the university to travel in France as tutor and companion to the duke of Buccleuch, who rewarded him with an annuity. In 1766 Smith returned to his birthplace in Kirkcaldy to produce the *Inquiry into the Nature and Causes of the Wealth of Nations* (1776). The modern study of political economy was virtually begun by this book, with its penetrating observation of the conflicts and balances between the individual's urge to accumulate wealth and the wider needs of society, or between the benefits of material prosperity and the needs of workers condemned to labour at monotonous tasks. Smith's prose is succinct and clear-eyed, just as his view of the moral case for social equity is wryly practical:

Is this improvement in the circumstances of the lower ranks of the people to be regarded as an advantage or as an inconveniency to the society? The answer seems at first sight abundantly plain. Servants, labourers and workmen of different kinds, make up the far greater part of every great political society. But what improves the circumstances of the greater part can never be regarded as an inconveniency to the whole. No society can surely be flourishing and happy, of which the greater part of the members are poor and miserable. It is but equity, besides, that they who feed, clothe, and lodge the whole body of the people, should have such a share of the produce of their own labour as to be themselves tolerably well fed, clothed, and lodged.

One of Smith's students at Glasgow went on to make his own study of class-structure in a book called *Observations Concerning the Distinction of Ranks in Society* (1771). **John Millar** (1735–1801), who became professor of civil law at Glasgow, was more radical than many of his fellow intellectuals, for he openly upheld the early egalitarian principles of the French Revolution and joined the Society of the Friends of the People in 1792 at a time when the establishment was bent on their suppression. Millar was a brilliant lecturer and his classes were packed with enthusiastic students.

Romanticism and the cult of feeling

By the 1770s the influence of Rousseau was making itself widely felt in the emergence of the pre-Romantic sensibility. It is ironic that, in using reason to undermine the supremacy of reason itself, even Hume contributed something to a popular interest in personal and passionate experience, uninfluenced by education and society and everything that the Scottish Enlightenment valued so highly. Even Adam Smith seemed to have endorsed the importance of sensibility in an early book, *The Theory of Moral Sentiments* (1759), in which he pleaded for the power of imaginative empathy as a form of moral control. John Home's *Douglas* had invoked the heroic and the pathetic in a wild setting, and Thomas Gray struck another early chord with the Celticism of his poem 'The Bard' (1757). But it was a farmer's son from Inverness who spoke most directly to the new taste, and his 'translations' of Gaelic epic verse entranced the drawing-rooms of Britain and Europe, throwing them open to vistas from another world – Celtic, heroic, ancient and sublime.

James Macpherson (1736–96), encouraged by John Home's support, made his literary reputation in 1760 with a little book called *Fragments of Ancient Poetry Collected in the Highlands of Scotland and Translated from the Gaelic or Erse Language*. These purported to be a few love-poems and battle-verses from the Ossianic tales of the third century, handed down in the Bardic oral tradition, or copied by later scribes and now translated by Macpherson. In an unsigned preface Hugh Blair announced that the young man was keen to translate still more pieces – 'if encouragement were given to such an undertaking'. The *literati* were excited by the evidence of such native genius and encouragement duly came in the form of a subscription. Macpherson, a handsome tutor and schoolteacher in his mid twenties, became a full-time writer and surrendered himself to fame. *Fingal* (1762) was followed by *Temora* and finally in 1765 the *Works of Ossian* were collected in two volumes.

Home and Beattie were enthusiastic and in 1763 Hugh Blair, the professor of rhetoric at Edinburgh, wrote a critical dissertation in praise of 'Macpherson's Ossian'. The Germans were even more impressed – an edition appeared in Frankfurt in 1773 – and 'Ossian' joined Rousseau's 'noble savage' as a key figure in the evolution of Romanticism from Goethe to the Gothic novel. Yet, when all is said and done, the poems were neither very good nor very authentic, although some of them were at least based on the Fenian cycle of heroic tales which came to Scotland with the Irish Gaels. As a boy in Inverness when the Forty-five broke out, Macpherson did know some Gaelic and he had contact with the oral tradition, as well as considerable sympathy for Highland culture. But he could never produce the manuscripts he claimed he had seen and the poems remain essentially his own work: a vision of a lost age of gentle and valiant warriors. (He had already tried his hand at sentimental heroism in 1758 with an unsuccessful poem called 'The Highlanders'.) 'Ossian's' style turns out to be a form of neoclassical prose poetry mixing Homeric action with love, noble pathos and a melancholy landscape. Now at last the 'Athens of the North' could lay claim, in Madame de Stael's phrase, to 'l'Homère du Nord':

> By the side of a rock on the hill,
> beneath the aged trees, old Ossian
> sat on the moss; the last of the race
> of Fingal. Sightless are his aged eyes;
> his beard is waving in the wind. Dull
> through the leafless trees he heard
> the voice of the North.

Dr Johnson also heard a voice from the North and he denounced it as a forgery by a man who loved Scotland more than the truth, whereupon Ossian's translator threatened to beat him with a stick if they should meet. But Johnson's judgement could not impede the astonishing success of the poems – Burns, Scott and Byron were all devotees and Napoleon is said to have carried a copy with him everywhere.

Authentic or not, Ossian also spoke to antiquarian interests and was as influential in this as Bishop Percy's *Reliques* (1765 *et seq.*) and Lord Hailes's *Ancient Scottish Poems* (1770). Ironically, nine years before 'Ossian' appeared, the verses of the great Gaelic poet MacMhaighstir Alasdair had been banned in Edinburgh as Jacobite propaganda. The final irony is that Macpherson's popularity created a vogue among lesser Gaelic poets for compositions in its archaic style, and some of his 'fragments' in English were 'retranslated' into Gaelic.

The heart began to claim its own in the second half of the so-called Age of Reason, and by the 1770s the novel-reading public had acquired a powerful appetite for pathos, nobility and sentiment. Richardson's books started the vogue in England. Similar ingredients impressed the Parisians who read Rousseau's novel *Julie, ou la Nouvelle Héloise* (1761) and the genre was brought to new intensities by the first novel of a young Edinburgh lawyer called **Henry Mackenzie** (1745–1831). Mackenzie was a blithe and practical person, a keen sportsman who could remember hunting for hare and ducks on the ground where the New Town had just been built, but he too in his younger years liked to experience the luxury of vicarious feeling. His novel *The Man of Feeling* (published anonymously in 1771) purports to be the biography of a sensitive youth called Harley, except that its 'manuscript' has been broken up and only odd chapters and sections remain. This device gives Mackenzie a certain episodic freedom, for his main intention was to introduce 'a man of sensibility into different scenes where his feelings might be seen in their effects, and his sentiments occasionally delivered without the stiffness of regular deduction.' Indeed the 'sentiments' are regularly delivered in a whole series of affecting scenes as the hero on his first visit to London makes his way among the streets and confidence-tricksters of the metropolis. His adventures include a visit to a madhouse and a brothel, where he saves a young lady by reuniting her with her father. The key term is 'sensibility', for Harley wears his sympathies on his sleeve and Mackenzie's prose invites readers to establish their own emotional credentials by feeling for the sad lives and 'complicated misfortunes' of those he meets on his travels. (The tale is not without satirical irony and echoes of Sterne and Goldsmith.) Harley is absent-minded and more than a little green, yet his generous nature conveys a silent rebuke to his fellow

men, who clothe their selfish interest and self-deceit in what
Harley sees as a 'fabric of folly', as they pursue 'delusive ideas',
which range from sexual seduction to the expansion of the
British Empire. Harley is not made for this world; he retreats to
his father's house, where he pines with unrequited love, catches
a fever and expires with a sigh in the arms of his beloved.
Eschewing 'the intricacies of a novel', the biographer is left to
tell the tale of a 'few incidents in a life undistinguished, except
by some feature of the heart'.

There was a positive fashion for weeping over the sad
passages of *The Man of Feeling*, and Burns had two copies,
calling it 'a book I prize next to the Bible'. In his turn
Mackenzie praised the first collection of Burn's poems in 1786,
marvelling at the 'unimitable delicacy' and the 'rapt and
inspired melancholy' of the 'heaven-taught ploughman, from a
humble and unlettered station'. This gentle creature scarcely
sounds like the Burns we know, but it does testify to the
contemporary propensity for adopting a sentimental attitude to
what Adam Smith called 'the language of nature and simplicity
and so forth' – a process started by Ramsay and equally in line
with the European fashion for the primitive. Mackenzie's next
book, *The Man of the World* (1773), introduced a counterpart to
Harley; a play called *The Prince of Tunis* appeared the same year
and four years later he produced an epistolary novel, *Julia de
Roubigné*. But his best writing is to be found in the later essays
and tales, and his sketches of Scottish life and character
prepared the way for Galt and Scott. Indeed, the latter
dedicated *Waverley* to him as 'the Scottish Addison'. By the late
1780s Mackenzie was a successful lawyer and a well-known
figure in Edinburgh and London. He founded the *Mirror*
(1779–80) and then the *Lounger* (1785–7), both periodicals in
the manner of the *Spectator*, and he became an honoured and
popular elder statesman in the arts, linking the age of Hume
and Smith with that of Burns and Scott – the 'second
generation' of the Enlightenment. As a critic Mackenzie
fostered an interest in Schiller and German literature and was
one of the first to appreciate Byron, Scott and Chatterton. He
welcomed Burns too, mostly for the elements of sentiment in his
work, but his Addisonian bias led him to underestimate the
broader reductive comedy of Fergusson, seeing it as somewhat
tainted by 'blackguardism'. In other respects, too, he demon-

strated a genteel insecurity about the essentially populist spirit of his native city, for he felt that the locals knew the author too well to credit him with wit and confessed that the name of the Canongate seemed to him to lack the sense of 'classic privilege' conveyed by 'the Strand'.

James Boswell (1740–95) is often taken to be the quintessential example of the busy, confident Scot determined to make his name in the Strand and to ingratiate himself with the literary giants of London. Yet this picture does not do justice to a gifted and complicated writer, prey to fits of heavy drinking and plagued by depression. As the son of Lord Auchinleck, a Court of Session judge, Boswell was ordered to become an advocate in Edinburgh, but his heart was given to a life of letters and travel. He had met Johnson in London while still in his twenties, and his appetite for fame and foreign places took him to Europe and to a somewhat contrived acquaintanceship with Rousseau and Voltaire. He produced pamphlets and articles, and a visit to Corsica in 1765 led him to champion the cause of Corsican independence three years later, when General Paoli raised his countrymen against French occupation. The *Account of Corsica* was published in 1768 and brought the young Scot a literary reputation as well as a certain notoriety (partly because of the dress he affected) as 'Corsica Boswell'. In the 1770s he wrote many essays for the *London Magazine* and visited the capital whenever he could, becoming the friend and confidant of Dr Johnson and eventually persuading the old man to undertake their famous trip to Scotland in 1773. The *Journal of the Tour to the Hebrides* (1785) demonstrates Boswell's talent as a gossipy and good-humoured *raconteur* and reveals him, despite the good doctor's frequent discouragements, as a proud Scot eager to show his country in a favourable light. Gradually he gave himself less to Law and more to his biography of Johnson, and four years after the great man died he moved to London to further his researches. Boswell's voluminous letters, notebooks, diaries and journals (many of them available only in this century) testify to an unflagging industry as he documents absolutely everything that caught his fancy. At times he seems breathlessly naïve and tasteless, as when he pestered the dying Hume with questions about his atheism and whether he wanted to change his mind about it in the face of eternity; but his value as a writer also lies in this openness and in his ability to make even the most trivial of encounters vivid, entertaining and revealing. *The Life of Johnson* appeared in 1791 to become the most famous biography ever written, and there is a strong case for saying that the Dr Johnson so popularly known and widely quoted today was actually assembled (if not created) by Boswell's fluent, vain and paradoxically selfless talent.

Gaelic poetry

Bardic verse declined because Highland society was changing, as the blind harper had found when his young chief set out for London. Poets still celebrated clan loyalties of course, and still addressed their work to men who were likely to help them eat, but the old aristocratic tradition was dead, and, when Mac-Donald of Sleat made John MacCodrum his bard in 1763, it was a historical gesture rather than a cultural obligation. The new poets were writing for a more popular audience, and, as ordinary people themselves, were open to new influences and a wider range of subjects than ever before. Alasdair Mac-Mhaighstir Alasdair produced Jacobite poems with all the old warlike swagger, but he was impressed enough by James Thomson's *Seasons* to write poems of natural description as well. Like many of his contemporaries he called his verses 'songs', and specified, like Burns, the airs to which they could be set. From now on the term 'bard' lost its strict technical sense and came to mean simply a composer of poems. Duncan Bàn Macintyre followed Alasdair's lead in nature description; William Ross shows a familiarity with Burns and the Augustan neoclassical tradition, and even Rob Donn, an unlettered man, has echoes of Pope in his poems. Comedy, satire, lampoon, Evangelical religion, everyday community life and love-poems all join the Gaelic canon in the eighteenth century.

This vernacular Gaelic was much less formal than the bardic syllabic metres with their 'high style' of address, but technique was still valued. The new poems emphasise stressed rhythms – often with four stresses to a line – and internal rhymes, or assonances, are carried over from line to line throughout the verse. A brief example from John MacCodrum's 'Duan na

Bainnse' ('A Wedding Rime') will show how this works, with the different rhyming vowels italicised in the Gaelic text:

Chaidh mi sìos do Ph*a*ibil
   Ann am m*a*duinn 's i ro fh*ua*r;
Chomhdhalaich mo gh*o*istidh mi,
   E fhéin is L*o*chlann R*ua*dh;
Ghabh sinn chum na t*u*laich
   Far 'n robh cr*ui*nneachadh math sl*ua*igh:
Ma rinn iad dearmad b*ui*deil oirnn
   So m'*ui*rsgeul dhuibh g'a l*ua*idh.

I went down to Paible
   One morning when 'twas very cold;
My boon companion met me,
   He and Lachlan Ruadh;
We made for the knoll
   Where there was a goodly gathering of people:
As they missed us with the bottle
   Here is my tale to tell of it.

(trs. W. Matheson)

If the internal rhymes are schematised, their pattern makes two quatrains with the 'ua' sound (shown as rhyme *b*) appearing at the end of every second line and the other rhymes distributed as follows:

line 1	$-a-$
line 2	$a-b$
line 3	$-c-$
line 4	$c-b$
line 5	$-d-$
line 6	$d-b$
line 7	$-e-$
line 8	$e-b$

Reputed to be MacCodrum's first effort in verse, this song caused great offence in his small community by lampooning a wedding-party at which the poet got nothing to drink because he turned up as an uninvited guest.

   The first-ever publication of contemporary Gaelic verse was

a collection of MacMhaighstir Alasdair's work which he had
printed in Edinburgh during a brief visit in 1751. Religious
poems by Duguld Buchanan were next to appear in book form
in 1767, and in the following year, also in Edinburgh, Duncan
Bàn Macintyre's poems were copied out for him (he was
unlettered) and published in the city which was now his home.
Despite the contemporary enthusiasm for Macpherson's
Ossian, the authentic genius of these poets passed relatively
unnoticed in Lowland literary circles; but, as far as Gaelic
speakers were concerned, the availability of work in print was a
most welcome affirmation of cultural identity, and this modest
growth continued, even after the Forty-five. MacMhaighstir
Alasdair had already had a hand in the publication of a
Gaelic–English vocabulary in 1741; Duguld Buchanan helped
produce a Gaelic New Testament in 1767; Alasdair's son
produced an anthology of older Gaelic verse (and some more
poems of his father's) in 1776; and Macintosh's collection of
Gaelic proverbs appeared in 1785. Gaelic prose, on the other
hand, remained scarce and mostly confined to religious tracts,
a state of affairs which lasted almost until modern times.

Alexander MacDonald (Alasdair MacMhaighstir Alasdair, 1695?–1770?)

MacMhaighstir Alasdair called his collection of poems *Ais-
eiridh na Sean Chánain Albannaich* ('The Resurrection of the
Ancient Scottish Language') as a deliberate gesture towards
the widening of his art and the promotion of Gaelic. He studied
bardic verse, lamenting his lack of 'chiselled stones and
polished words', and wrote a praise-poem to vaunt Gaelic as
the language of Adam and Eve, no less, which deserved to
thrive 'in spite of guile/ and stranger's bitter hate'.

MacMhaighstir Alasdair came from an educated Episcopalian family in Moidart, where his father, 'master Alasdair',
was minister. He went to Glasgow University to study for law
or the Church, but married young and had to abandon his
degree. Little else is known of his early life until 1729, when he
appears as a teacher in the Highlands, working at various
schools run by the Society for Propagating Christian Knowledge. Alasdair's Gaelic–English word-book was produced for

this society, whose aim was to bring literacy, English and the Reformed Church to the North-West. His salary was little more than a pittance, but for the next sixteen years he ran a croft, became an elder of the Kirk, taught the children and composed love-songs, satires and nature-poems.

Alasdair's satires included scurrilous attacks on various local figures and rival bards, and the explicit imagery in these and in some of his love-poems gave such offence to later collectors and editors that even today there is not a complete and unexpurgated edition of his works. Yet the spirit of his famous 'Praise of Morag' ('Moladh Mòraig') is a fine and joyful catalogue of feminine delights, rapidly delivered in an elaborate imitation of pibroch, with 'ground' and 'variation', and making play with *double entendres* drawn from the language of piping itself:

> There's one thing that I'm certain of,
> I'd better not tell Jane of her,
> and how I've fallen headlong,
> and am going at the knees now;
> there isn't enough water
> in Loch Shiel, or snow on Cruachan,
> to cool and heal the raging fire
> that burns away within me.
>
> When I heard the melody
> played on Morag's chanter
> my spirit danced with merriment,
> an answering most joyous:
> the stately ground, most elegant,
> of her tune, with fingers tapping it,
> a music with fine setting,
> the rocks providing bass for it.
> Ah! the chanter with its grace-notes,
> a hard sharp, clean-cut music,
> sedate now, and now quavering,
> or smooth, controlled, soft, tender;
> a steady, stately march then,
> full of vigour, grace and battle-zest,
> a brisk and strutting *crunluath*
> played by sportive swift–soft fingers.
>
> (trs. D. Thomson)

The poem ends with the bard waking up 'on fire' beside his wife and making love to her. Fantasy or not, his jealous wife is supposed to have prompted him to write the 'Miomholadh Mòraig' ('Dispraise of Morag') in which, with equal extravagance, he gives his dream girl red eyes and the face and sexual habits of a monkey.

If MacMhaighstir Alasdair's Gaelic nationalism was somewhat at odds with his employers' preferences for English, the bawdy, sly and passionate love-songs were even more unbecoming in an elder of the Kirk. The curious tensions and contradictions of this career came to a head in 1744 when the SPCK noted that the schoolmaster at Ardnamurchan was 'an offence to all Sober Well-inclined persons as he wanders thro' the Country composing Galick songs, stuffed with obscene language'. In fact Alasdair's son was doing the teaching for him by this time, and in 1745 the old man, now in his fifties, threw over his post completely, converted to Catholicism and joined up as a captain fighting for Clanranald in the Jacobite army.

Almost half of MacMhaighstir Alasdair's poems are dedicated to the Jacobite cause, not just to the prince, although he wrote many songs to him, but to a vision of resurgent Gaeldom, free at last from the taint of Lowland manners and values:

How I welcome the thunder of sweetly-tuned organs,
And the dazzling bonfires the streets all alighting,
While the market resounds with 'Great Charles, our own Prince!'
While each window shines with the light that is streaming
From high-burning candles fair maidens are tending,
    Every thing that is fitting to hail him with pomp!
The cannon all booming and belching their smoke-clouds
Making each country shake with the dread of the Gaels,
While we o'er-exultant, lightly, o'er-weening,
At his heels march in order, embued with such rapture
    That no one weighs more than three fourths of a pound!

('Charles Son of James' ['Tearlach Mac Sheumas'], trs. J. L. Campbell)

Alasdair invoked the old incitement-poetry and wrote the most scathing and bloodthirsty verses against King George and the Clan Campbell – those perennial enemies of the MacDonalds. He maintained his fervour even after Culloden, and a piece such as 'A Waulking Song' ('Oran Luaidh no Fucaidh') symbolises the exiled prince as a beautiful girl – 'Morag of the ringlets' – and hopes for her return against the English with 'maidens' (French soldiers) 'to waulk the red cloth firmly'. Poems such as these renewed for almost the last time the old vaunting warrior-spirit of the clans, and this was why, no doubt, the unsold copies of his book are said to have been burned as seditious documents by the hangman in Edinburgh in 1752. By comparison, John Roy Stewart (1700–52) has a quieter voice as a Jacobite bard, and his two fine songs on Culloden are eloquent with pain and the sorrow of defeat.

From bardic praise-poems to the 'songs' of the eighteenth-century revival, the spirit of Gaelic poetry is objective, detailed and descriptive. It responds to the physical world with such a disinterested but passionate observation of the surface of things that it positively discourages subjectivity or the symbols and philosophical reflections so favoured by the English Romantic poets. Prompted by James Thomson's *Seasons*, it was Mac-Mhaighstir Alasdair who brought this Gaelic love of passionate catalogue to bear for the first time on poems of natural description, until he, and Duncan Bàn Macintyre after him, created some of the finest and most influential poems in the whole body of Gaelic verse.

Poems such as Alasdair's 'Song to Summer' ('Oran an t-Samhraidh'), 'Song to Winter' ('Oran a'Gheamhraidh') and 'Sugar Brook' ('Allt an t-Siùcair'), were most probably written around the early 1740s, and, although they follow Thomson's descriptive lead, they do not share his sentimental and didactic bias. Instead the Gaelic displays intellectual precision and a characteristically crystalline excitement:

> The lithe brisk fresh-water salmon,
> lively, leaping the stones;
> bunched, white-bellied, scaly,
> fin-tail-flashing, red-spot;
> speckled skin's brilliant hue
> lit with flashes of silver;
> with curved gob at the ready
> catching insects with guile.
>
> May, with soft showers and sunshine,
> meadows, grass-fields I love,
> milky, whey-white and creamy,
> frothing, whisked up in pails,
> time for crowdie and milk-curds,
> time for firkins and kits,
> lambs, goat-kids and roe-deer,
> bucks – a rich time for flocks.

('Song to Summer', trs. D. Thomson)

The descriptive detail of nature-pieces such as these, and the fierce spirit of the later Jacobite songs come together in *Birlinn Chlann Raghnaill* ('Clanranald's Galley'), which was probably written after 1751. As MacMhaighstir Alasdair's most famous poem (and one of the longest in modern Gaelic), it is a *tour de force* among oar-songs. Attentive to the individual tasks of the crew, and all the lengthy preparations needed for a voyage to Ireland, the poem is filled with exact technical detail and inspired by the rhythms of the sea in both storm and calm. This is how the storm begins in Hugh MacDiarmid's translation of the poem, in which he attempts to convey something of the original metre and the impacted energy of the verse:

> Now they hoisted the speckled sails
>   Peaked and close-wrought,
> And stretched out the stubborn shrouds
>   Tough and taut
> To the long resin-red shafts
>   Of the mast.
> With adroit and firm-drawn knotting
>   These were made fast
> Through the eyes of the hooks and rings;
>   Swiftly and expertly
> Each rope put right of the rigging;
>   And orderly
> The men took up their set stations
>   And were ready.
> Then opened the windows of the sky
>   Pied, grey-blue,
> To the lowering wind's blowing,
>   A morose brew,
> The sea pulled on his grim rugging   tugging (Scots)
>   Slashed with sore rents,
> That rough-napped mantle, a weaving
>   Of loathsome torrents.
> The shape-ever-changing surges
>   Swelled up in hills
> And roared down into valleys
>   In appalling spills.
> The water yawned in great craters,
>   Slavering mouths agape
> Snatching and snarling at each other
>   In rabid shape.

If heroism still thrives in MacMhaighstir Alasdair's verse,

his contemporaries John MacCodrum and Rob Donn Mackay look more to the everyday life of small communities.

John MacCodrum (Iain Mhic Fhearchair, 1693?–1779)

John MacCodrum was married three times in the course of a long and quiet life on North Uist. His many songs make a wry commentary on domestic themes and local personalities – from his own problems with eager widows, to grasping tacksmen and landlords, to his last wife, who did not look after him as well as she should – at least, according to 'A Complaint about his Wife' ('Gearan air a Mhnaoi'):

> 'Tis no small cause of displeasure,
> When I am not short of sheep,
> To be buying cloth,
>   Though my wife is alive;
> And though it is not much to say,
> I am ashamed at times
> To be reduced to thigging sewing thread,
>   Though my wife is alive.

(trs. W. Matheson)

MacCodrum was famous for the sharpness of his wit and the refrain of his complaint becomes more pointed with every repetition. Most of his poems were composed when he was in his fifties or older, and, although he was not a literate man, he belonged to an oral tradition which was capable of remarkable feats of memory. When James Macpherson arrived in Uist in 1760, MacCodrum was recommended to him as a man who could recite at length from the old Ossianic cycle, but the visitor's bad Gaelic and his bad manners evinced only a dry evasion from the bard. MacCodrum's own verses, so often based on village events, are far from Macpherson's notion of the antique sublime, as witness the descriptive comedy of such pieces as 'Macaskill's Wedding' ('Banais Mhicasgaill'), or a rhymed debate on the delights and pitfalls of drinking, 'The Friend and Foe of Whisky' ('Caraid agus Namhaid an Uisge-bheatha'), or 'A Song to Fever' ('Orain do 'n Teasaich') in which he characterises fever as the *cailleach* – an old crone:

> She planted confusion in my head;
> a host of men, both alive and dead,
> like those whom the Trojan Hector led,
> and Roman warriors, thronged my bed;
>   that dismal, dark and hunch-backed crone,
>   to scandal and lying tales too prone,
>   reduced my speech to delirious moan
>   and left me stripped of sense, alone.
>
> . . .
>
> Your coat has grown too big, and throws
> into relief your wrinkled hose,
> your splayed, pathetic ankle shows,
> long as a wild-cat's the nails of your toes.
>
>   (trs. D. Thomson)

The poet's classical references, and his remarks on European politics in other poems, remind us that an oral culture need not be a parochial one; nor are Gaelic poets unaware of each other's work, whatever their geographical isolation. MacMhaighstir Alasdair visited MacCodrum on at least two occasions, and his poem 'The Mavis of Clanranald' was very probably composed in emulation of the Uistman's famous 'Mavis of Clan Donald'. The tradition was swift and fluid, for MacCodrum's 'Dispraise of Donald Bàn's Pipes' ('Diomoladh Pioba Dhomnaill Bhain') was his reply to another poet's extravagant praise of an inferior piper. Such interchanges were common when poems were recited and their composers valued as a part of communal experience. A skilled bard could memorise a song after only one hearing, and, indeed, MacMhaighstir Alasdair recalled two of MacCodrum's songs well enough to print them complete and without acknowledgement in his own book. Then again, Rob Donn, another unlettered poet, had such a grasp of Mac-Mhaighstir Alasdair's 'Song to Summer', that he could produce a complex parallel to it in line after line of his own 'Song to Winter', entirely composed in his head. The tale of how MacCodrum came to be bard to the MacDonalds of Sleat also testifies to the potency of verse in an oral culture.

Tradition has it that MacCodrum satirised the itinerant tailors of Uist for being unwilling to travel to his remote house; and when they heard his lampoon ('Aoir nan Tailleirean') they retaliated by swearing to boycott him for ever more. The bard's ragged condition subsequently attracted the attention of Sir James MacDonald, who was on a visit from Skye, and when he heard the reason (and the poem) he gave MacCodrum a pension and made him his bard on Uist. The old man duly produced many praise-poems and elegies on behalf of Sir James and the heroes of Clan Donald – that 'death-dealing bright company of keen blades'. But the clan-system had been irrevocably damaged at Culloden, and its close ties of kinship were breaking down at all levels.

In the 1770s the more prosperous farmers and tacksmen began to emigrate, many of them choosing to go to South Carolina. (Tacksmen used to be responsible to the chief for raising so many armed men, and they sublet their holdings to clansmen lower down the hierarchy.) When they left, their places at home were taken by strangers who did not hesitate to raise the rents until the poorer subtenants were forced to leave their crofts in turn. Thousands departed the western Highlands during these years and MacCodrum's late poem 'Song to the Fugitives' ('Oran do na Fogarraich') lamented what was happening:

'Tis a sad matter to consider,
The land is being made dearer;
Our people have swiftly left,
    And sheep have come in their place:
A weak host they and ineffective
At going into quarrel and strife,
Full of braxy and leanness,
    At the mercy of a guileful fox;
Smearing will not save you
In presence of battle on a field,
Nor will the moorland shepherd's whistle
    Change your misfortune a whit;
And though you were to gather
Fifty wedders and hornless rams,
Never would one of them lift up
    An edged sword of steel.

(trs. W. Matheson)

In fact the 'edged sword of steel' was to be lifted again, but this time the Highland regiments were fighting for a British cause. Among the first of them were MacDonald troops from Skye raised by Sir James's successor to fight the American 'rebellion' in 1776.

Robert Mackay (Rob Donn MacAoidh, 1714–78)

Rob Donn lived in Sutherland on the far north coast of Scotland, remote from the traumas of Culloden. He came from a humble Presbyterian family (the Reformed Church was well established in the north), and like John MacCodrum, he was not literate. Rooted in his home community, he occasionally drove cattle to Falkirk or Carlisle, and a brief spell as a regimental bard took him to most Scottish cities in the early 1760s. As a boy Rob Donn ('Brown Robert') had a precocious gift for rhyming, encouraged by John Mackay of Musal, who took him under his care and gave him his first job as a herdsman. An early failure in love is remembered with bawdy sweetness in 'The Shieling Song' ('Is Trom Leam an Airigh'):

> Fair Anna, daughter of Donald,
>   If you only knew my condition,
> It is unanswered love,
>   That took away my reason:
> It's alive in me yet
>   As if you were here.
> It teases and squeezes
>   In my heart like a spear
>   All though the day
>   It's an uproar for me
>   Trying to quell it
>   While it grows like a tree.

(after a translation by I. Grimble)

The shieling was a hut in the high pastures where village boys and girls would take the cattle for summer grazing. Many would associate the first pangs of adolescent love with their long days at the shieling.

Rob Donn's heart survived to write other love-poems, as well as verses on his passionate fondness for hunting deer, but most of his poems reflect on the events and personalities around him. He celebrated his native glen in verses which had young Isabel

Mackay defend the delights of Strathmore against the attractions of Thurso, where her sister had been sent to school. When Isabel was married in 1747, her mother slighted the bard by not inviting him to the wedding. He turned up anyway with a light-heartedly bawdy lampoon on the family and their guests in which he puzzled over the fate of a supposedly missing pair of trousers. The bride's mother makes her appearance in the fourth 'verse of 'MacRory's Trousers' ('Briogais Mhic Ruairidh'):

> Catherine, William's daughter,
> Make some trousers for the lad
> And don't take a penny
>   In payment for them.
> Who knows but it was your father
> Who took them to wear?
> He needed as much
>   And time was when he would have done it.

(trs. I. Grimble)

No doubt the community enjoyed such pieces immensely, but Rob Donn also took a more general view of character, morality and politics, as with his long poem against the government ban on the wearing of the kilt. John MacCodrum's piece on the same theme had simply complained about the discomfort of trousers, and called up the old vision of a warrior in a plaid – and 'not a Saxon in the world but will blench at the sight of him'; but Rob Donn's 'The Black Cassocks' ('Na Casagan Dubha') takes a more astute and dangerous line:

> So, so King George!
> What a mockery of your good faith
> To make new laws
> That double the bondage.
> But since they are fellows without honour
> It would be better to strike than spare,
> And there will be fewer to support you
> When the same thing happens again.
>
> If your enemy and your friend
> Receive the same punishment in Scotland,
> Those who rose against you
> Made the better choice. . . .

(trs. I. Grimble)

This was so pointed that he was called to task before the sheriff and the (Hanoverian) chief of the Mackays.

Rob Donn's verse can rise to virtuoso effects, as in 'Song to Summer' ('Oran an t-Samhraidh') or the pibroch poem to young Isabel Mackay, both of which follow the technical dazzle of MacMhaighstir Alasdair. But for the most part his muse speaks more plainly on his own and his neighbours' foibles. There is a grave, reflective quality in many of his commentaries which has been likened to the balance in Pope's couplets. In fact we know that Rob was familiar with the English poet's work through his local minister's habit of translating it into Gaelic and quoting it in his sermons. When the minister died in 1763, Rob Donn's 'Elegy to Master Murdoch Macdonald' ('Marbhrann do Mhaighstir Murchadh Macdhomhnaill'), made a truly Augustan homage to the old man, if tempered with an appropriately Calvinist sternness:

> What has grieved me in spirit
> And those who loved and followed you
> Is the magnitude of your labour before you left us
> And the scantiness of its traces that remain after you.
> Some profitable lessons will flow
> From the fringes of your grace,
> That fools did not heed
> By listening to your teaching. . . .
> You made the reluctant willing
> And the ignorant wise,
> And the absolute joy of your life
> Was in imparting more light to them.
> You were gentle to those in need,
> You were generous with reasonable people,
> You were shrewd of aspect, hard
> As stone towards the miscreant,
> You were bountiful in giving,
> You were a diligent preacher,
> You gave timely advice
> And even your hostility turned to love in the end.

(trs. I. Grimble)

Like the poet, Macdonald enjoyed the unaccompanied singing of metrical psalms in church. These 'long tunes' are a kind of Gaelic Presbyterian plainsong, with each line chanted by the precentor and then sung at length and freely embellished by the congregation. The effect is one of wild and chilling grandeur.

The Presbyterian tradition was strong in the poet's community and in his own outlook. His verse did not hesitate to reproach Lady Reay (wife of the fifth Lord) when she tried to secure his silence over a marriage of convenience which she had forced upon two of her servants:

> With sharp command and counsel
> There was placed in my mouth a gag like a skewer
> Concerning the incident to be spoken of,
> Which did not resemble a love-affair so much as a hunt,
> Indeed I am sorry for the pair of them. . . .

('Lady Reay and her maid': 'Ged a thuit mi' n car iomraill . . .', trs. I Grimble)

He took morality seriously, but Ron Donn was no prude. His wry sense of humour had enjoyed singing the praises of Sally Grant – the darling of his Sutherland regiment – and his satires and lampoons were bluntly spoken and reinforced with a typically Gaelic awareness of family-history:

> Your grandmother was lustful
> And bore children to twelve men,
> And your mother did not refuse
> One single man apart from her husband
>
> . . .
>
> Your mother was illegitimate
> And a great strumpet of a wench
> And she bore you a bastard
> To a lout of a fellow.
> Many a lamentable day
> They punished her on the stool of penitence,
> And you yourself got a yelping little creature
> In the usual way before you were married.

('Barbara Miller': 'Tapadh leat a Bharb'ra . . .', trs. I. Grimble)

Perhaps Rob Donn's most powerful poetry lies in his elegies – which were as likely to be for ordinary men as for chiefs. His wry 'Lament for Ewan' ('Marbhrann Eoghainn') compares the approaching end of an old man in a remote cottage with the reported death of a head of state – only to have the ancient revive at the last gasp in a rage at the poet for his presumption. 'The Rispond Misers' ('Marbhrann, do Thriuir Sheann

Fhleasgach') uses its subjects to reflect on the uselessness of hoarding gold. In poems such as these, and in the verses to the fourth Lord Reay, Murdoch Macdonald and his old friend John Mackay (Iain Mac Eachainn), Rob Donn reshaped the Gaelic tradition of almost uncritical lament, in order to make his own more sombre commentary on men and the times.

Duguld Buchanan (Dùghall Bochanan, 1716–68)

Born and brought up in Strathyre, near the Trossachs in Perthshire, Duguld Buchanan, like Rob Donn, also came from a Presbyterian family. His mother's excessive devoutness, however, gave him morbid religious fears as a boy, and these visions marked his nature and his poetry for the rest of his life. He completed his education at Stirling and Edinburgh and spent some restless years as an apprentice carpenter for various masters. He moved from job to job as he alternated between wild escapades and the acute religious depressions which he described in his diary. He worked as an itinerant teacher before settling as schoolmaster at Kinloch Rannoch, where the General Assembly recognised his religious fervour by confirming him as a lay preacher and catechist. A later move to have him appointed as minister was frustrated by his lack of university qualifications, and by fears that his style was too inflammatory. The poems which he was beginning to write were disturbing enough – replete with images from the Book of Revelation and racked by a morbid empathy with suffering and damnation. His most famous poem, 'The Day of Judgement' ('Là a 'Bhreitheanais'), is over 500 lines long. It describes the sublime and terrible descent of Christ on the last day, and the doom that all the sinners of history have to endure:

> On fiery chariot he sits
> with roars and thunder all around,
> calling to Heaven's outmost bounds,
> and ripping clouds tempestuously.

> From out his chariot's wheels there comes
> a stream of fire aflame with wrath,
> and that flood spreads on every side,
> until the world is flaming red.

The elements all melt with heat,
just as a fire can melt down wax;
the hills and moors are all aflame,
and all the oceans boil and seethe.

(trs. D. Thomson)

No doubt Dante, and Robert Blair's 'graveyard school' or Young's *Night Thoughts* were influences on Buchanan. By the same token his poem in forty-four stanzas 'The Skull' ('An Claigeann') most likely borrowed its outlook from Hamlet's speech on Yorick. Nevertheless, Buchanan's terse Gaelic and his visionary imagination create a special intensity.

Towards the end of his life Buchanan studied in Edinburgh, where he met David Hume and compared notes with him on the sublime. He helped the Revd James Stewart produce the New Testament in Gaelic for the SPCK, and published a small collection of his own poems, *Spiritual Songs* (1767). These had a wide influence within the Evangelical movement, and many other minor Gaelic writers were to produce hymns and religious poems over the next hundred years.

William Ross (Uilleam Ros, 1762–90)

Towards the end of the century William Ross produced a number of wryly personal and elegaic love-poems. This was a new departure for the Gaelic muse, and perhaps it owes something to Ross's education in the classics and his familiarity with the poems of Burns. He was born in Skye and spent his boyhood in Strath Suardal between Broadford and Torrin, where, indeed, Dr Johnson and Boswell had stayed during their tour of the Hebrides in 1773. Ross's poem on whisky 'The Son of Malt' ('Mac-na-Bracha') pays testimony to its effect on the good doctor, who was for once in his life 'tongue-tied', despite his English 'and his Latin and Greek speech beside'. William was sent to the grammar-school in Forres on the mainland, where he excelled as a scholar. Then the family moved to Gairloch and the young man accompanied his father as travelling pedlar, carrying a pack of sundry goods throughout Scotland and recording his travels in verse. After some years at this trade he returned to Gairloch to settle as the schoolmaster there. He became a popular member of the community, but died of tuberculosis at the age of twenty-eight.

Ross was more than familiar with the Gaelic tradition in poetry and some of his own pieces follow the pattern of praise-poems – to his native glen, a Highland maiden, or to whisky, not to mention the by now almost obligatory 'Song to Summer' and an 'Elegy for Prince Charlie'. His Lowland education appears in the classical allusions which he makes in comparing his beloved to Venus or Diana, or in his references to Cupid as 'the Black Laddie' in a lightweight piece ('Oran air Cupid') which has a priest smitten with love for a pretty cowherd. It may be that he had found something of this spirit in Burns, and certainly his 'Toothache Reprimanded' ('Achmhasan an Deideidh') looks familiar; but at the same time it is likely that vernacular Gaelic was evolving the personal lyric in its own right. (And of course Burns and Ross could draw on the folk-song tradition in each of their cultures.) Whatever their antecedents, it is Ross's love-songs which are best remembered, along with the romance which grew up around his unrequited affair with a girl called Marion Ross.

The poet must have met Mòr Ros in Stornoway during his youthful travels. He fell in love with her but she married a sea captain in 1782 and went to live with him in Liverpool. Tradition has it that she was unhappy and sent for the poet in later years. He got as far as Stirling before deciding that the affair was hopeless, and turned back only to catch the chill which killed him. His best poems do deal with this girl, and her image crops up indirectly in other verses. 'Love Song' ('Oran Gaoil') – also called 'Monday Evening' ('Feasgar Luain') – is the poet's recollection of seeing Marion at a ball in Stornoway. The formality of the occasion is matched by the verse with its classical allusions and rather highly wrought compliments. 'Song of Lament' ('Oran Cumhaidh') involves oblique references to a traditional tale of Cormac – an Irish harper who cured his love-pains with his own music. But Ross has no such consolation:

Why was I not born sightless,
dumb, without power to see,
before I saw your modest face
that dimmed a hundred's light;

since first I ever saw you
your virtues were renowned,
and death to me were easier
than to live now you are gone.

(trs. D. Thomson)

This poem was followed by 'Another Song on the Same Theme' ('Oran Eile, air an Aobhar Cheudna'), an even barer expression of personal anguish. The Gaelic tradition had seldom attempted such confessional force, although of course the impersonal lament was well established. The verse begins with the shocking image of a maggot hatching in the poet's chest:

I am lonely here and depressed
No more can I drink and be gay.
The worm that feeds on my breast
is giving my secret away.
Nor do I see, walking past,
the girl of the tenderest gaze.
It is this which has brought me to waste
like the leaf in the autumn days.

Iain Crichton Smith's verse translation catches Ross's sense of desperate vulnerability very well, especially in the closing stanzas:

Ill-wishers who hear of my plight
call me a coward and worse.
They say that I'm only a poet
whose fate is as dead as my verse.
(His father's a packman. You know it.
His father, in turn, couldn't boast.)
They'd take a good field and plough it.
I cut better poems than most.

My spirit is dulled by your loss,
the song of my mouth is dumb.
I moan with the sea's distress
when the mist lies over the foam.
It's the lack of your talk and your grace
which has clouded the sun from my eyes
and has sunk it deep in the place
from which light will never arise.

> I shall never praise beauty again.
> I shall never design a song.
> I shall never take pleasure in tune,
> nor hear the clear laugh of the young.
> I shall never climb hill with the vain
> youthful arrogant joy that I had.
> But I'll sleep in a hall of stone
> With the great bards who are dead.

The oblique and brooding pain in William Ross's love-poetry was to be recalled in modern times by Sorley Maclean's *Songs to Eimhir*. By comparison the last great Gaelic poet of the century composed hardly any love-poems, for his work returned to the older descriptive tradition and shows no trace of introspection or personal unhappiness.

Duncan Bàn Macintyre (Donnchadh Bàn Mac an t-Saoir, 1724–1812)

Duncan Bàn Macintyre lived half his life in Edinburgh, and he and his family are buried in Old Greyfriars' churchyard, but he is remembered above all Gaelic poets as a composer of songs about the remote hills and the running deer. His poems were more popular than any others and his printed collection went through two editions in his own day and three more in the following century.

Born and brought up in Glen Orchy, Duncan Bàn was unlettered and without formal education, but he could recite his own work by heart and much more again from the older Gaelic tradition. He served reluctantly in the Forty-five, for the Argyll Militia on the government side, and from 1746 to 1766 he worked as a gamekeeper for the Earl of Breadalbane and then the Duke of Argyll, walking the hills and forests of Glen Lochay, Ben Dorain and Glen Etive. His great descriptive verses were composed in these years, as well as dutiful praise-poems to various members of the Glen Orchy Campbells.

Duncan Bàn wrote few love-poems, but his marriage to 'fair-haired young Mary' prompted a long praise-poem called 'Song to his Bride' ('Oran d'a Cheile Nuadh-Phosda'), as a fine and elaborately courtly compliment to Màiri Bàn Òg. Macintyre's strength as a poet lies in his observation of nature, so, while a reference to Cupid in his poem remains pretty stock stuff, some of his other similes are truly fresh and unexpected. He compares his bride's skin to white quartz, or her soft body to moor cotton-grass, or he thinks of her like a slender tree:

> I went to the wood where grew trees and saplings
>   that were radiant to view all around;
> my eyes' desire was a branch outstanding
>   in the dense growth of twigs overhead –
> a bough from top to base in blossom,
>   which I tenderly bent down:
> 'twere hard for others ever to cut it,
>   as this shoot I was destined to pluck.

(trs. A. MacLeod)

The other side of this coin can be found in the relentless flyting against Donald MacNaughton, a tailor who had dared to lampoon the bard – 'Song to the Tailor' ('Oran do 'n Tàillear'). The poor man paid a high price for his presumption, measured in long lines of frightful attributes, worthy of Dunbar's satire or a warlock's curse. The image of the tree is used again:

> Thou art the rotten tree, withered,
> full of decay and microbes,
> grown scraggy and stunted,
> short, hump-backed, distorted;
> a stump bound for the embers art thou,
> who didst deserve to be burned as sacrifice:
>   thou hast grossly neglected the gospel,
>   thou hast grossly neglected the gospel.

(trs. A. MacLeod)

Much of Duncan Bàn's output, especially in later years, is cheerfully occasional. He loved deer-hunting and he sang about what he knew and saw around him – Glen Orchy, a gift sheep, a favourite gun, an unsuccessful hunt, or, in mock elegy, a cockerel that was shot by mistake. He was an uncomplicated extrovert, unlike the fiercely touchy MacMhaighstir Alasdair; nor did he share Rob Donn's moral nature or the capacity for pain to be found in the works of Buchanan and William Ross. Nevertheless, it is with Macintyre that the Gaelic passion for objective observation reaches its highest point.

'Song to Summer' ('Oran an t-Samhraidh') is an overly formal and elaborately crafted attempt to match MacMhaigh-stir Alasdair, but with 'Song to Misty Corrie' ('Oran Coire a' Cheathaich') and 'Praise of Ben Dorain' ('Moladh Beinn Dòbhrain'), Macintyre is – literally – on his home ground and he charts it with loving detail. Verse after verse of 'Misty Corrie' moves to a measured pace, reading like some lyrically precise botanical catalogue, bringing together the life of plants and then fish, birds and deer:

> Thy genial braes, abounding in blaeberries and cowberries,
>   are studded with cloudberries of the round, red head,
> with garlic forming pads in the angles of ledges,
>   and fringed rock stacks, not a few;
> the dandelion and penny-royal,
>   soft, white cotton sedge, and sweet grass are there
> in every part of it, from the lowest hill foot
>   to the crested regions of the highest reach.
>
> . . .
>
> Around each spring that is in the region
>   is a sombre brow of green water-cress;
> at the base of boulders is a clump of sorrel,
>   and sandy gravel, ground fine and white;
> splashing gurgles, seething, not heated,
>   but eddying from the depth of smooth cascades,
> each splendid rill is a blue-tressed plait,
>   running in torrent and spiral swirls.
>
> In that rugged gully is a white-bellied salmon
>   that cometh from the ocean of stormy wave,
> catching midges with lively vigour
>   unerringly, in his arched bent beak. . . .
>
> (trs. A. MacLeod)

Such intensely focused observation is a kind of sublime passion, and it clearly influenced Hugh MacDiarmid who from the 1940s came to see his later English work as a scientifically based 'poetry of fact' dedicated simply and entirely to the material world for its own sake. The 'Song to Misty Corrie' is 'nature-poetry' of the purest sort, entirely free of personal or symbolic reflection; perhaps some of John Clare's verses come close, but there is nothing else in the English tradition quite like it. The clarity of Macintyre's eye belongs to what Kenneth Jackson has called 'the high sunlight of the Celtic vision', and it is deeply ironic that within the next century the Gaelic muse would be associated – as far as Lowland culture was concerned – with glamorous shadows in a Celtic twilight.

'Praise of Ben Dorain' is based on a pipe-tune, and like MacMhaighstir Alasdair's 'Praise of Morag' its light and lively rhythms imitate the pibroch changes between theme and variation (*urlar* and *siubhal*). In over 500 lines Duncan Bàn is attentive to the minutiae of grasses and streams on Ben Dorain's slopes; but the poem is particularly dedicated to the herds of deer which he had watched and hunted there for years. He is no sentimentalist, for, if he admires their delicate movements, he also takes delight in describing the intricacy of the flintlock on the gun which will kill them. The poem ends, moreover, with dogs pulling the deer down to die in moorland pools, and these last scenes are described by means of unstressed extra syllables in imitation of *crunluath*, the most complex movement in pibroch which marks the climax of the tune. Iain Crichton Smith's English catches something of the Gaelic's hectic excitement, and also the way the poem suddenly stops just like a pipe-tune. Perhaps, like pibroch again, the effect is to bring us back to the beginning in an endless cycle:

> Erratic was the veering then
> and rapid in its motion
> when they would go sheering on
> short cuts with exertion.
>
> Tumultuous the baying and
> echo of the crying as
> the hairy-coated violent
> dogs would show their paces.
>
> Driving them from summits to
> lakes that are unplumbable
> bleeding dying swimming and
> floundering in water.
>
> Hounds hanging to their quarries while
> they sway and toss and rock and kill –
> their jaws will never let them feel
> their haughty style again.

The little that I've sung of them
is not enough to tell of them
O you'd need a tongue for them
of a most complex kind.

The bloody water where the deer met their end comes from the
same fresh springs praised earlier in the poem, in the quieter
pace of *urlar*:

Transparent springs that nurse
the modest water cress –
no foreign wines surpass
these as drink for her.

. . .

The spotted water-cress
with forked and spiky gloss;
water where it grows
so abundantly

This is the good food
that animates their blood
and circulates as bread
in hard famine-time.

That would fatten their
bodies to a clear
shimmer, rich and rare,
without clumsiness.

It is characteristic of Duncan Bàn's muse that he should
celebrate the deer's diet with such tenderness and expertise.
More than anything else, however, his poem is full of the
movement of these graceful animals, with what Crichton Smith
has called a pagan spirit which is absolutely free from any
moral dimension. Here the movement is the quicker *siubhal*:

The hind that's sharp-headed
is fierce in its speeding:
how delicate, rapid,
its nostrils, wind-reading!
Light-hooved and quick limbèd,
she runs on the summit,
from that uppermost limit
no gun will remove her.
You'll not see her winded,
that elegant mover.

Her forebears were healthy.
When she stopped to take breath then,
how I loved the pure wraith-like
sound of her calling,
she seeking her sweetheart
in the lust of the morning.

By 1768 other men were employed on Duncan Bàn's favourite estates and he found himself and his family in Edinburgh. With the help of his former captain in the Argylls he joined the City Guard – a local police-force largely composed of Highlanders. As a member of what Fergusson called 'the black banditti' he wrote songs in praise of his halberd, his musket and whisky and brandy – those indispensable items of company equipment. A volume of his poems was published by subscription and sold well, but he had already done his best work. In the 1780s he composed a series of prize-winning poems on pibroch and Gaelic – to be recited at an annual piping-competition in Falkirk as organised by the London Highland Society. The same society gave him a modest grant in recognition of his status as a poet. In preparation for a second subscription volume, Duncan Bàn and his wife spent a couple of years, sometime after 1786, touring the Highlands and islands. Dressed in the plaid with a sword and a fox-skin cap, the bard was widely welcomed. He left the City Guard in 1793 and served as a soldier for six years with the Breadalbane Fencibles, although exactly what duties were asked of a man in his seventies is not clear. His last poems, musing on death and advancing age, adopt an untypically moralistic tone; but a livelier note in the old vein is struck by his 'Song to the Foxes' ('Oran nam Balgairean'), which praises them for killing the sheep that were taking over the hillsides from his beloved deer. His lines stand for the experience of many at the beginning of the nineteenth century, puzzled by social changes beyond their control as an old, old way of life finally found itself in the modern world:

The villages and shielings
where warmth and cheer were found,

have no houses save the ruins,
and no tillage in the fields.

Every practice that prevailed
in Gaeldom has been altered,

and become so unnatural
in the places that were hospitable.

(trs. A. MacLeod)

Even so, some of these changes had produced the culture's finest achievements in Gaelic verse, and in the second half of the eighteenth century Lowland Scotland too was about to enjoy a vernacular revival.

Robert Fergusson (1750–74)

If Mackenzie and his respectable friends had doubts about the 'classic' status of the Canongate, they were never shared by young Robert Fergusson, whose poems immortalised the vulgar intimacy of the streets in his native 'Auld Reekie'. Fergusson's parents came to Edinburgh from Aberdeenshire and 'The Farmer's Ingle' shows his familiarity with North-East Scots. As the fourth in a family of five, young Robert went to St Andrew's University at the close of 1764 and enjoyed a lively undergraduate life despite poor health. While at university he wrote two acts of a tragedy on Wallace and then abandoned it because he felt it was not original enough. Fergusson's sympathies were patriotically Scottish, even Jacobite, and his ambitions were set on a literary career, but the sudden death of his father meant that he had to leave St Andrews in 1768 and find work to support the family. He ended up as a copying-clerk – a dull-enough job, but one which kept him in Edinburgh and gave him some freedom to write for himself. He soon made friends in theatrical and musical circles by producing English words to Scots tunes, and these pieces were included in two operas performed at the Theatre Royal in 1769. In 1771 the *Weekly Magazine or Edinburgh Amusement* began to publish Fergusson's English poems, which were pastorals, mock heroics and complaints in the prevailingly genteel Augustan manner. Fergusson continued to produce such verses for the rest of his life, but his energetic genius was only to be realised in Scots when 'The Daft Days' appeared in January 1772. This seasonal piece heralded an extraordinary two years during which Fergusson produced poem after poem in the *Weekly Magazine* – almost his entire output before he collapsed and died at the age of twenty-four. The magazine's owner, Walter Ruddiman, continued to promote his poet over the next twelve years by publishing no fewer than three editions of the collected works.

'The Daft Days' hailed the Scottish custom of celebrating the New Year with drinking and dancing. Other poems soon followed in the same vein – lamenting the decline of Scots music, laughing at the noise made by 'The Tron-kirk Bell', or praising the virtues of 'Caller Oysters' and 'Braid Claith' – all expressed in vigorous Scots and standard Habbie. These verses offered a vision of Edinburgh street-life that had not been matched since Allan Ramsay or Dunbar. It was a world of lawyers, farmers, Highland porters, change-house keepers, magistrates, stall-owners, police, maids, whores, servants, men of fashion and the ubiquitous cadies (guides and errand boys), who were intimates to the whole town. The citizens were delighted to find themselves and their activities so hilariously and irreverently reflected:

On Sabbath-days the barber spark,	
Whan he has done wi' scrapin wark,	
Wi' siller broachie in his sark,	shirt
Gangs trigly, faith!	finely dressed
Or to the Meadow, or the Park,	
In gude Braid Claith.	
Weel might ye trow, to see them there,	believe
That they to shave your haffits bare,	cheeks
Or curl an' sleek a pickle hair,	
Wou'd be right laith,	reluctant
When pacing wi' a gawsy air	stately
In gude Braid Claith.	

. . .

Braid Claith lends fock an unco heese,	folk; considerable help
Makes mony kail-worms butter-flies,	caterpillars
Gies mony a doctor his degrees	
For little skaith:	expense
In short, you may be what you please	
Wi' gude Braid Claith.	

Readers from Edinburgh, the Borders and Fife wrote letters to Ruddiman in praise of Fergusson's 'auld words' in a 'sonsy canty strain' and he became a well-known figure, greeted as the 'new Ramsay'. He joined the Cape Club, one of the wilder of the many drinking- and debating-clubs which were so popular at all levels of society. Fellow-member David Herd must have encouraged his love of Scots songs, and Fergusson (unlike Burns) was known for his good voice. (Later members of the Cape included the painter Henry Raeburn and William Brodie, a respectable deacon by day and a robber by night who was eventually hanged in 1788.) Fergusson became the very patron poet of Edinburgh tavern-life:

When big as burns the gutters rin,	
Gin ye hae catcht a droukit skin,	If; soaked
To *Luckie Middlemist's* loup in,	Mistress/Goodwife; jump
And sit fu snug	
Oe'r oysters and a dram o' gin,	
Or haddock lug.	ear
When auld Sanct Giles, at aught o' clock,	
Gars merchant lowns their chopies lock,	blokes; shops
There we adjourn wi' hearty fock	folk
To birle our bodles,	ring our copper coins
And get wharewi' to crack our joke,	
And clear our noddles.	heads

('Caller Oysters')

No doubt the poet's rowdy pranks led him to fall foul of the City Guard, for he never misses an opportunity in his verses to satirise the 'black banditti' and their Highland accents.

Ruddiman published a collection of Fergusson's poems in 1773 and it sold moderately well, but polite literary taste had been otherwise engaged for the past fifty years and the established critics were slow to report on the work. 'Auld Reikie', which appeared separately the same year, was greeted with a similar silence, and perhaps this is why Fergusson never developed it beyond 'Canto i'. Then again, the young poet had parodied the melodrama of Henry Mackenzie's *The Prince of Tunis* by putting a highly rhetorical lament, full of 'sensibility', into the mouth of an English-speaking and neoclassically inclined pig. 'The Sow of Feeling', as he called it, would scarcely have endeared him to Mackenzie, and that influential literary figure could see little but 'coarse dissipation' in such a bohemian muse. In fact the poet's health was beginning to collapse under the pressures of late nights and heavy drinking, and his wild behaviour and unkempt appearance became ever more conspicuous. He gave up his job at the end of 1773 because of increasing physical illness and bouts of religious melancholia. It is possible that he was suffering from syphilis, and, although he made a brief recovery in the summer of 1774, a fall in which he struck his head broke his health completely and plunged him into morbid fears and virtual insanity. In the end he had to be taken from his mother's home and lodged in the Bedlam next to the Edinburgh poorhouse, where he died in a straw-littered cell in October 1774. He was buried in Canongate churchyard in an unmarked grave.

Fergusson's life was short and his poetic output relatively small, but he had considerable literary influence, not least on his successor, Robert Burns. The Ayrshire man's direct debt can be established in various specific poems, but his true inheritance comes from the integrated comic spirit of the younger writer, whose vigorous and racy tongue expressed a complete personality enlivened by an ironic eye for the pretensions of his fellow citizens. Fergusson's range is limited by the topics he chooses, but never by literary or class-conscious preconceptions, for he is not concerned with appearing genteel nor with making points about 'simple' life and pastimes. Thus Fergusson's 'dialogue' poems, such as 'Mutual Complaint of Plainstanes and Causey' and 'A Drink Eclogue', are used to make satirical reflections on the world in general, and, although the debates are personified and the 'road' and the 'pavement' or 'brandy' and 'whisky' are revealed in speech as the broadest of Scottish characters, this alone is not Fergusson's subject. Poems such as 'Hallow Fair' and 'Leith Races' have a more local focus and they are certainly satirical and even downright impudent, but they are never condescending. In this vein Fergusson's masterpiece is 'Auld Reikie', a poem of over 300 lines in octosyllabic couplets in which he conjures up the institutions and the lively folk and the crowded, odiferous streets of his native city:

Now some to Porter, some to Punch,
Some to their Wife, and some their Wench,
Retire, while noisy Ten-hours Drum
Gars a' your Trades gae dandring Hame.   makes
Now mony a Club, jocose and free,
Gie a' to Merriment and Glee,
Wi' Sang and Glass, they fley the Pow'r
O' Care that wad harrass the Hour:
For Wine and Bacchus still bear down
Our thrawart Fortunes wildest Frown: obstinate
It maks you stark, and bauld and brave,
Ev'n whan descending to the Grave.

Fergusson's spirit is bold, ribald, cheerful or stark, but
never in the least 'polite'. He lived the life he wrote about, even
if 'Wine and Bacchus' did serve him sadly in that last descent.

Robert Burns (1759–96)

Thirteen years after Fergusson's death, Robert Burns commissioned a headstone in memory of a poet whom he generously acknowledged as his 'elder brother in misfortune, by far
my elder brother in the muse'. At this time (February 1787) the
twenty-eight-year-old Burns was newly famous after a winter
season in Edinburgh literary society. The Kilmarnock edition
of his poems had appeared the previous year and Henry
Mackenzie in the *Lounger*, the blind poet Dr Blacklock, Hugh
Blair, Professor Duguld Stewart and even 'plough boys and
maid-servants' were all 'delighted, agitated, transported' by
what the *Edinburgh Magazine* saw as 'a striking example of
native genius bursting through the obscurity of poverty and the
obstructions of laborious life'. The critics underestimated
Burns's education, but they were not wrong about his poverty
at the time. Indeed, he had prepared the Kilmarnock collection
under the most pressing need for money and, until the volume's
success, had planned to emigrate to Jamaica. Things were not
going well at home: he already had an illegitimate daughter by
a servant girl and now his mistress Jean Armour was pregnant.
Jean's father was determined that they should not marry (and
she seems to have agreed with him at the time), because, with
the death of his father in 1784, the poet was having to support
his mother, three brothers and three sisters and his farm at

Mossgiel was failing. Burns and Jean had made public repentance in church according to Kirk law and her father was seeking support for what turned out to be twins. To cap it all, in the aftermath of Jean's rejection Burns seems to have become involved with a Highland girl called Mary Campbell, who features in some of his tenderest poems and songs but who died of a fever (perhaps in child-birth) later in 1786. The details of the 'Highland Mary' affair remain conjectural, for Burns was understandably reticent about a painful memory. Along with the other pressures upon him it may explain a letter written at the height of his literary fame in Edinburgh in which he confessed to 'secret wretchedness':

> The pang of disappointment, the sting of pride, with some wandering stabs of remorse, which never fail to settle on my vitals like vultures, when attention is not called away by the calls of society or the vagaries of the Muse. Even in the hour of social mirth my gaiety is the madness of an intoxicated criminal under the hands of the executioner.

The 'heaven-taught ploughman' was a more dynamic and complicated personality than Mackenzie's epithet implies, or than the *literati* realised in their eagerness to see Burns as the gifted offspring of Rousseau's savage and the Gentle Shepherd. Yet the time was right for Burns's success and there is no doubt that he was aware of his role as a 'rustic bard': after all, the Preface to his poems craved the reader's indulgence by assuming just such a persona. But literary and critical fashions cannot detract from his exciting debut, and the Kilmarnock edition and the 1787 Edinburgh edition which followed it reveal a young writer leaping straight to the height of his powers with astonishing assurance. Almost all of his most famous poems appeared in these collections (the exceptions are 'Holy Willie's Prayer', which was omitted; 'The Jolly Begars' which Hugh Blair persuaded him to leave out; and 'Tam o' Shanter', which was yet to be written).

Burns's book revitalised the Scots language as a medium for verse – it had not been so potent since the days of Lindsay and Montgomerie – but at the same time its success virtually 'type-cast' poetry in Scots until modern times. His was the genius which crowned and concluded the domestic, 'Doric' vein to be found in the works of the Sempills, Hamilton, Ramsay and even in such a city poet as Fergusson. For the next hundred years and more 'poetry in Scots' meant 'poetry like Burns's', and as late as the 1920s Hugh MacDiarmid could curse the influence of a writer whose brilliance set the mould for so many inferior imitations.

Burns's background was genuinely close to the spirit of 'Christis Kirk on the Green', and in this sense his convivial muse belongs to the world of small farms and market towns with their local gossip and a tradition of occasional verse. On the other hand, he had also read the makars, and his vernacular approaches a standard literary Lowland Scots – he called it 'Lallans' – for he used Scots words from dialects other than his own. In 'The Vision' Burns uses an eloquent Scots, well worthy of the makars, to set the scene and to talk of his own sombre feelings. But, when his muse appears as an idealised girl, it is, significantly, English which both she and her bard adopt as the most appropriate language in which to discuss 'the dignity of Man'. Like most educated men of his day, Burns was inclined to abandon his mother-tongue when he sought what he took to be a sophisticated or 'literary' voice.

Robert Burns was born the first of seven children on 25 January 1759 at Alloway in Ayrshire. His father, William Burns or Burnes, married a local girl after coming south from Kincardineshire in search of work. But the land at Mount Oliphant farm was unproductive and at forty-four Burns found himself bound to a life of lonely toil until his health was damaged by the effort. By the age of fifteen Robert too was labouring in the fields, and despite his natural sturdiness he contracted a rheumatic heart-condition that eventually killed him. Even in hardship, Burns wanted a good education for his two eldest boys and so he and four of his neighbours arranged for a young tutor called Murdoch to teach their children. These arrangements were known as 'adventure schools' and meant that in areas where parish schooling was not practicable most of Scotland's rural population could still read and write. Thus Robert was introduced to English literature in selections from Shakespeare, Milton, Dryden, Addison, Thomson, Gray and Shenstone.

During the summers when he could be spared from the farm, Burns was sent away to continue his studies, and at Kirkoswald near the coast he met Douglas Graham of Shanter farm, said to be a model for Tam o' Shanter, and 'Soutar Johnnie', who was the local cobbler. He made a start at Latin, trigonometry and French, and took pride in the letters which he sent home. His commonplace book records his early rhymes and the first stirrings of what was to be a lifetime's infatuation with girls. The lease at Mount Oliphant expired when Burns was eighteen, and the family moved some ten miles to Lochlie farm in the parish of Tarbolton. Here Robert befriended the apothecary John Wilson, an innocent model for the fatal 'Dr Hornbook', as well as John Rankine and 'brother poet' David Sillar, who were to feature in his later epistle poems. In the company of such lively young men Burns became first president of the 'Bachelor's Club' – a debating-society dedicated to the fair sex and 'honest-hearted' male friendship. The farm was failing, however. William Burns's goods were impounded to pay for back rent, and only his death in 1784 saved him from being arrested for debt. It is not difficult to explain the poet's lifelong hatred of landlords and the kind of factor who 'thinks to knit himsel the faster/In favour wi' some gentle Master' by seeing that 'decent, honest, fawsont [seemly] folk,/Are riven out baith root an' branch,/Some rascal's pridefu' greed to quench' ('The Twa Dogs'). Robert and Gilbert leased a farm less than three miles away at Mossgiel and they took the rest of the family there in 1784. This time their landlord, Gavin Hamilton, proved to be a good friend and Burns dedicated the Kilmarnock edition to him.

Now in his early twenties, Robert was set on a literary career. By this time he had read and admired *The Man of Feeling*, as well as Thomson, Sterne, Macpherson's *Ossian* and Hume and Locke. Moreover, he had discovered an enthusiasm for old Scots songs and for the works of Ramsay and Fergusson. It was the latter's 'Scotch poems' in particular which encouraged him to persevere with his own verse and to 'string anew', as he put it later, his 'wildly-sounding, rustic lyre, with emulating vigour'. Accordingly, the next two years were extraordinarily full as Burns produced poem after poem and made several songs to traditional airs. No doubt the setting of words to old tunes (as well as his delight in dancing) helped to develop an early facility with strong rhythms and internal rhymes, for Burns's verse is characterised by such qualities, and the onward, reel-like thrusting of standard Habbie became such a favourite of his that it is also known as 'the Burns stanza'. The poet's energies were more than fully engaged, for he committed himself to farming and flouted his shaky health by adopting an equally hectic social life. With his talent for friendship he was not slow in becoming well known and liked in the nearby village of Mauchline, where his landlord Gavin Hamilton worked as a lawyer and where he met Jean Armour and began an affair with her. Mauchline people went straight into his poems, and, when Hamilton's free behaviour was reprimanded by the local Kirk, Burns took his side and claimed that he would rather be damned in his friend's company than saved among such 'canting wretches'. One of the 'wretches' was an elder called William Fisher, whose vindictive hypocrisy is immortalised in 'Holy Willie's Prayer'. When Hamilton came before the presbytery at Ayr it was 'glib tongued' Robert Aiken who demolished Holy Willie's case, and this distinguished senior lawyer became the poet's close friend and something of a patron in influential circles. (Burns dedicated 'The Cottar's Saturday Night' to him.)

In this most creative period the poet's emotional life was complicated; furthermore, the family depended on him, but Mossgiel was not flourishing and he needed money badly. Hamilton, Aiken and others helped to collect subscriptions for a volume called *Poems, Chiefly in the Scottish Dialect*, which was published at Kilmarnock in July 1786, and the immediate success of this book catapulted him into fame and allowed him to give funds at last to Gilbert and the family. That winter Burns went to meet his reputation in Edinburgh, where plans were immediately made for an expanded 'Edinburgh' edition, which appeared in April 1787. This volume contained extra poems, including more work in English, but, if his Augustan verses pleased his new literary friends, they seem merely imitative and conventional today. The most significant additions are poems such as 'The Ordination', 'The Calf' and the 'Address to the Unco Guid', which give openly satirical accounts of the Kirk and its doings. More personal attacks such as 'The Holy Tulzie' or 'The Twa Herds' were left in manuscript circulation only, and, indeed, 'Holy Willie's Prayer' did not see print until 1801.

In Burns's time it was not possible in a small community (as Gavin Hamilton found out) to ignore the church's mandates on everyday social behaviour. Yet the Kirk was divided on several doctrinal matters, including lay patronage. The 'Moderates' were in favour of tolerating other creeds and of accepting the law which allowed the local landowner to propose a minister for the parish. However, the minority 'Popular party', or 'Evangelicals', took a harder line and were becoming more influential in country districts. Some seceded to form a separate presbytery, and before long the seceders split and split again, reviving all the fanaticism of the old Covenanters. The history of these changing alliances, of Burghers and anti-Burghers, 'Auld Lichts' and 'New Lichts', serves to demonstrate once again the Scottish preference for theoretical or organisational disputes over what should be spiritual issues. Burns and his friends in Edinburgh regarded themselves as liberal Christians, and scoffed at the 'three mile prayers and hauf-mile graces' of the extreme faction; yet they still had to accept the Kirk's authority in a society where elders could act like moral policemen with the right of access to people's houses to ensure that the Sabbath was being kept. As a fallible lover of women, Burns had little sympathy with the 'unco guid', nor was he slow to draw attention to their hypocrisies and excesses. Thus 'The Holy Fair' satirises the annual Communion at Mauchline, a custom common in rural parishes where, in what usually became a tent show and a rowdy picnic, hundreds gathered once a year in the open air to hear the preaching, to drink ale and see the sights, and – officially – to prepare for Communion:

> Here, some are thinking on their sins,
>   An' some upo' their claes;   clothes
> Ane curses feet that fyled his shins,
>   Anither sighs an' prays:
> On this hand sits a Chosen swatch,   sample
>   Wi' screw'd up grace-proud faces;
> On that, a set o' chaps, at watch,
>   Thrang winkan on the lasses   busy
>   To chairs that day.

This easy, loping verse was borrowed from Fergusson, who cast a similarly genial eye on public holidays in 'Hallow-Fair' and 'Leith Races'. The Breughelian spirit goes back to 'Christis Kirk' and 'Peblis to the Play', but Burns's more modern eye is quicker to note the contradictions of the scene and to use the antitheses towards a wider and wittier satirical end:

> How monie hearts this day converts,
>   O' Sinners and o' Lasses!
> Their hearts o' stane, gin nicht are gane   at nightfall
>   As saft as ony flesh is.
> There's some are fou o' love divine;   full
>   There's some are fou o' brandy;   drunk
> An' mony jobs that day begin,
>   May end in Houghmagandie   fornication
>   Some ither day.

The barbed subtlety of Burns's educated punning can be more
fully appreciated if the original passage from Ezekiel 36:26 is
recalled: 'A new heart also will I give you, and a new spirit will I
put within you: and I will take away the stony heart out of your
flesh, and I will give you an heart of flesh.'

Burns's knowledge of the Bible and his familiarity with the
language of God's Presbyterian spokesmen makes 'Holy Willie's Prayer' particularly potent. Here the high-flown diction of
Evangelical fervour bumps and tangles with standard Habbie
and parochial Scots to lay bare the unctious vindictiveness of
the speaker.

> Lord, mind Gau'n Hamilton's deserts!
> He drinks, an' swears, an' plays at cartes,   cards
> Yet has sae mony taking arts
>   Wi' great and sma',
> Frae God's ain Priest the people's hearts
>   He steals awa.
>
> And when we chasten'd him therefore,
> Thou kens how he bred sic a splore,   quarrel
> And set the warld in a roar
>   O' laughin at us:
> Curse Thou his basket and his store,
>   Kail an' potatoes!   cabbage

The poet dons the flesh of his enemy to explode him from
within, and Willie's rolling syntax falters only when he has to
confess his own failings, even if his complacency remains
unmoved:

> But yet – O Lord – confess I must –
> At times I'm fashed wi fleshly lust; . . .   troubled
> O Lord – yestreen – Thou kens – wi' Meg –
> Thy pardon I sincerely beg! . . .

1. Carved Pictish cross at Aberlemno, 12 miles east of Montrose. The cross is filled with an intricate interlacing, while the surrounding symbols (some of them similar to those in the Lindisfarne Gospels) show horses, hounds and a deer to convey a delight in hunting. The other side of the slab has a battle scene.

2. Craigievar Castle, Aberdeenshire, 5 miles south of Alford, a 'Scots Baronial' fortified house from the 1620s. The great fireplace has an inscription: 'Doe not vaiken sleeping dogs'.

3. A street in old Edinburgh. The scene would not have been much different from the seventeenth to the nineteenth century when this was painted by Henry Duguid.

4. *The Black Stool*, by David Allan, 1784. An unwed mother takes the 'cutty stool' in the foreground, while the minister rebukes her lover in a crowded and noisy kirk.

5. The General Assembly of the Kirk of Scotland (1783) is a more sober body of men, but David Allan still notices plenty of fringe activity.

6. The 'lands' of James' Court, a typical Scots tenement at the Lawnmarket above the Mound in early nineteenth-century Edinburgh, painted by Henry Duguid.

7. Ainslie Place in the 'Athenian' New Town of Edinburgh in the early nineteenth century, painted by Thomas H. Shepherd.

8. Country life at 'Pitlessie Fair', by Sir David Wilkie (*detail*).

9. The Revd Robert Walker skating on Duddingston Loch, by Sir Henry Raeburn (1784).

10. Crofter's house (1889).

11. Planting potatoes (1890) with the help of the *cas-chrom* ('crooked spade'), a kind of foot-plough.

12. Herring gutters at Ullapool. The Scottish fleets followed the herring from the east to the west coast and then to the Shetlands and East Anglia.

ROBERT BURNS

13. David Hume, by Allan Ramsay, the poet's son.

14. Robert Burns, from the 1787 Edinburgh edition and considered a good likeness by the poet himself.

15. Sir Walter Scott, by Andrew Geddes (1823).

16. James Hogg, by William Bewick.

17. Thomas Carlyle.

18. Robert Louis Stevenson.

19. *Left to right:* Norman MacCaig, Sorley Maclean, Hugh MacDiarmid and Sydney Goodsir Smith in Edinburgh (1972). The portrait of MacDiarmid on the wall is by R. H. Westwater.

Besides, I further maun avow   must
Wi' Leezie's lass, three times – I trow –
But Lord, that friday I was fou   drunk
    When I cam near her!

The characterisation is repulsively convincing, but Burns's
satire expands to attack the whole system of Calvinist belief
which allows such a self-styled elect to set themselves apart
from the majority of folk, who will be damned no matter how
they behave:

O Thou that in the Heavens does dwell,
Wha, as it pleases best Thysel,
Sends ane to Heaven an' ten to Hell
    A' for Thy glory,
And no for ony guid or ill
    They've done before Thee!

I bless and praise Thy matchless might,
When thousands Thou hast left in night,
That I am here before Thy sight,
    For gifts an' grace
A burning and a shining light
    To a' this place.

Burns satirised the Auld Lichts again in 'The Ordination', and
in a letter of 1788 expressed his opposition to the Calvinist
doctrine that we are born 'wholly inclined' to evil. He believed
instead that we come into the world 'with a heart and a
disposition to do good for it', and this conviction explains his
affinity with Rousseau's ideals and his lifelong preference for
'the social, friendly, honest man/Whate'er he be' ('Second
Epistle to J. Lapraik').

On a broader note, Burns enjoyed hearty companionship,
like Fergusson before him, and in Edinburgh he joined a
drinking-club called the 'Crochallan Fencibles'. He goes
further than his 'elder brother', however, by celebrating a
Blakean faith in energy as eternal delight. The fullest expression of this anarchic, disreputable but always gloriously alive
spirit comes in 'Love and Liberty – A Cantata', more familiarly
known as 'The Jolly Beggars'. This sequence of poems and
songs seems to have been a little too potent for his intellectual
friends in Edinburgh, and Hugh Blair persuaded him to leave it
out of the 1787 collection. Like 'Holy Willie's Prayer', the piece

was never published in Burns's lifetime, and in fact the version that has survived may be incomplete. As so often in his work, Burns owed the initial conception to an already-established genre, for a song-sequence called 'The Happy Beggars' was featured in the *Tea Table Miscellany* and John Gay had drawn on the romance of thieves and vagabonds with his *Beggar's Opera* in 1728. Burns went further to produce an anti-pastoral (the very reverse of *The Gentle Shepherd*) which Matthew Arnold later hailed as a world of 'hideousness and squalor' and yet a 'superb poetic success' with a 'breadth, truth and power . . . only matched by Shakespeare and Aristophanes'.

Arnold's analogy with drama is appropriate, because Burns enters into the lives and voices of others as he describes a wild autumn night of merriment and song amongst a gang of wandering beggars and their doxies in Poosie Nansie's tavern. The effect of the whole is greater than any one section, for the 'Cantata' alternates between narrative passages to set the scene, and songs in which the various characters lay bare their lives and loves in a variety of stanza forms and traditional airs. The poem's diction keeps changing, too, as Burns swings from rich Scots to a cooler English and back again, so that the juxtapositions heighten the effectiveness and expand the field of his satire. The beggars, raddled, drunk, noisy and boastful, dance and fight and sing in a greasy dive; yet their antics also cast wild and telling shadows which ape the wider world outside, the world of social pretension and sexual gallantry, of political expediency, business-affairs and wars. An old soldier and his lover pledge themselves to drink and fornication, and their songs tell how he has lost an arm and a leg, while she has been through the regiment from drummer boy to chaplain; a tiny fiddler and a tinker fight over a raw-boned widow who earns her living as a pickpocket – the caird wins but the musician soon consoles himself with another lady:

> The Caird prevail'd – th'unblushing fair   tinker
>   In his embraces sunk;
> Partly wi' LOVE o'ercame sae sair,
>   An' partly she was drunk:
> Sir VIOLINO with an air,
>   That show'd a man o' spunk,   spirit
> Wish'd UNISON between the PAIR,
>   An' made the bottle clunk
>   To their health that night.

> But hurchin Cupid shot a shaft,
>   That play'd a DAME a shavie –   trick
> The Fiddler RAK'D her, FORE and AFT,
>   Behint the Chicken cavie.   coop

Burns's diction switches contexts with a speed and irreverence which anticipates Byron's *Don Juan*. A positively Augustan epithet such as 'th' unblushing fair' is matched with abstractions such as 'LOVE' and 'UNISON' and other elements from Cupid's vocabulary. These phrases are almost serviceable, if slightly shop-soiled (entirely appropriate to the would-be sophistication of 'Sir VIOLINO'), but Burns dynamites them and all their romantic conventions with the brutality of an ugly rhyme ('drunk' / 'spunk' / 'clunk') and the outrageousness of the shaft and the shavie played out behind a hen-house.

The little fiddler's *amour* is one of three ladies in tow with a 'bard of no regard', and it is this night-town version of Burns himself who sings a closing song which shakes the rafters of Poosie Nansie's and strikes at the foundations of the establishment's respect for property, religion and order itself;

> Here's to Budgets, Bags and Wallets!
>   Here's to all the wandering train!
> Here's our ragged Brats and Callets!   children and wenches
>   One and all cry out, Amen!
>
> CHORUS
> *A fig for those by Law protected,*
>   *Liberty's a glorious feast!*
> *Courts for cowards were erected,*
>   *Churches built to please the Priest.*

The political implications of these lines are reinforced because the song and chorus are written almost entirely in English – as if the poet means to generalise. Burns's sympathies are not just fashionably radical; they are fundamental to his background, to his optimistic and humanitarian nature and to that sense of dour pride and self-respect so important to his class. This attitude appears repeatedly in those letters and poems where he protests his independence and the honesty of his feelings with a telling and even excessive emphasis. 'The Twa Dogs' comments pointedly on the superficiality of rank in human society just as the early 'Epistle to Davie' predicted another kind of democracy by insisting on the primacy of the heart and its affections.

> It's no in titles nor in rank;
> It's no in wealth like Lon'on Bank,
>   To purchase peace and rest;
> It's no in makin muckle, mair: much, more
> It's no in books; it's no in lear,   learning
>   To make us truly blest:
> If Happiness hae not her seat
>   And centre in the breast,
> We may be wise, or rich, or great,
>   But never can be blest.

The terms may be hedonistic but the spirit of these lines is not far removed from that of Presbyterian dissent (substitute 'Grace' for 'Happiness' in the seventh line); and Burns is certainly speaking from a tradition of sturdy independence within his own milieu of crofters, tenant farmers and 'bonnet lairds'. The same dignity is at the heart of the song 'Is there for honest poverty', and it is the source of Burns's sympathies with the American fight for independence and, later, with the early stages of the French Revolution:

> What though on hamely fare we dine,
>   Wear hodden grey, and a' that.
> Gie fools their silks, and knaves their wine,
>   A Man's a Man for a' that.
> For a' that, and a' that,
>   Their tinsel show an' a' that;
> The honest man, though e'er sae poor,
>   Is king o' men for a' that.

The popular success of Burns's work, with its many expressions of universal brotherhood speaks volumes for the change in outlook, both political and personal, which was to accompany the Romantic movement in literature. By 1795, however, the Reign of Terror, the threat of invasion and perhaps his new responsibilities as an excise-officer combined to put revolution in a different light for the poet, and, like Wordsworth and many others, he became disillusioned with the French experiment. He helped to organise the Dumfries volunteers and even wrote a song for them which rather uneasily combines his distaste for authoritarian rule, whatever its origins, with a jingoistic British patriotism:

> The wretch that would a Tyrant own,
>   And the wretch, his true-sworn brother,
> Who'd set the mob above the Throne,
>   May they be damned together.

As far as his celebrity in Edinburgh was concerned, the poet remained the 'man of independent mind' who refused to have his head turned by the admiring salons. He took pleasure in meeting and corresponding with influential friends but he foresaw the day when he would return to his 'rural shades', recognising that at least part of his fame came from what he called the 'novelty of his character' among learned and polite people. As 'To a Louse' and 'The Twa Dogs' testify, Burns was too sensitively aware of social pretentiousness and class-differences to be blind to these currents at work in the tide of his own reputation:

> O wad some Pow'r the giftie gie us
> To see oursels as ithers see us!
> It wad frae mony a blunder free us
>   An foolish notion.

> ('To a Louse')

In 'The Twa Dogs' the poet's sympathies are openly with the labouring classes, and although he does not underestimate their hardships he allows them the satisfaction of stout hearts and simple pleasures and feels, too, that it is their toil which supports the restless hypochondria and the corrupt activities of their idle masters. Neither Luath, the poor man's collie, nor Caesar, the rich man's Newfoundland, has a complete picture of the human world, but it is not long before one emerges from their conversation. Caesar gives a hilarious version of the propertied classes at play abroad: but Burns has not forgotten how his father died trying to pay rent and feed his family.

> At Opera an' Plays parading,
> Mortgaging, gambling, masquerading:
> Or maybe in a frolic daft,
> To Hague or Calais takes a waft,
> To make a tour an' take a whirl,
> To learn *bon ton* an' see the worl'.

> There, at Vienna or Versailles,
> He rives his father's auld entails;   grabs/robs; mortgages
> Or by Madrid he takes the rout,
> To thrum guittares an fecht wi' nowt;   cattle (bullfights)
> Or down Italian Vista startles,
> Whore-hunting amang groves o' myrtles:
> Then bowses drumlie German-water,   drinks muddy
> To make himsel look fair an' fatter,
> An' clear the consequential sorrows,
> Love-gifts of Carnival Signioras.

The poet's gaiety never curdles and yet at times its ferocious intensity hints at the pain of injustice and the pressures and resentments felt by the labouring poor. The coarser pleasures of Poosie Nansie's and the groaning excesses of Evangelical fervour both bear witness to how these pressures were so often sublimated in small Scottish communities. There are hints of a similar strain behind the male vaunting with which Burns so often declares his passion for the 'lasses'. Thus in 'Epistle to James Smith' the poet makes a fine allegiance with the 'hare-brained sentimental' 'ramstam boys' and scoffs at 'douse [prudent] folk that live by rule, / Grave, tideless-blooded, calm and cool', whose hearts 'are just a standing pool'. But it is less easy to admire the 'Epistle to John Rankine', a favourite poem of his, in which he tells how he was fined for 'poaching' Elizabeth Paton like a partridge, leaving her pregnant because 'ae night lately, in my fun, / I gaed a rovin wi' the gun':

> The poor wee thing was little hurt;
> I straiket it a wee for sport,
> Ne'er thinkan they wad fash me for't . . .   bother
>
> As soon's the clockin-time is by,   hatching
> An' the wee pouts begun to cry,   young partridges
> Lord, I'se hae sportin by an by,
>   For my gowd guinea . . .

In contrast to his coarser moments, Burns's taste for sentiment was understandably popular in Henry Mackenzie's sophisticated circle. 'The Cottar's Saturday Night' was praised by contemporaries for giving Augustan dignity and 'the true flavour of natural tenderness' to rustic life; but modern readers often find the poem too condescending and prone to moralise, as well as marred by an uneasy mixture of Scots and English.

Burns wanted to depict the virtues of artless, common folk and to this end his descriptive passages are more successful than has sometimes been allowed, but the barer, sterner language of Wordsworth's 'Michael' (1800) succumbs less to the cult of feeling and makes a better job of the same subject. The Scot achieved an even-toned and successful combination of natural tenderness and moral reflection with 'To a Mouse'; but the very similar 'To a Mountain Daisy' contains a hint of self-pity, easy sentiment and that use of the Scots diminutive that was to multiply like frogspawn in so many luckless imitations. Nevertheless, the poem was highly regarded, not least by Mackenzie and the poet himself. A more robust comic talent finds expression in 'To a Haggis' and especially in 'Address to the Deil', where Milton's fallen archangel has to endure Burns's cheery familiarity and sceptical good wishes. Satan seems to have been something of a cronie of Scottish poets since at least Dunbar's time, and Calvinist Hell-fire has obviously done nothing to curb their presumptions:

An' now, auld Cloots, I ken ye're thinkan,
A certain Bardie's rantin, drinkin,
Some luckless hour will send him linkan,   tripping along
      To your black pit;
But faith! he'll turn a corner jinkan,   dodging
      An' cheat you yet.

The same irreverent spirit is directed at Death in 'Death and Dr Hornbook' and finds its high point in 'Tam o' Shanter', written three years later.

Burns's life was unsettled after the triumph of his first winter in Edinburgh. He left two lovers behind him and returned to Mauchline a hero; there was a reconciliation with the Armours and Jean became pregnant again, although he still did not want to marry her (he was nursing an affection for Peggy Chalmers, another new friend in Edinburgh, but she married someone else the next year). The 'Edinburgh edition' appeared in April 1787 and thereafter Burns took various tours through Scotland, being awarded the freedom of Dumfries and visiting relatives in the North-East. Creech, his Edinburgh publisher, was always slow in paying royalties, but the prospects were good and the poet arranged for half the profits to go to Gilbert and the family. Still, he was not sure how he should live and that winter saw him back in the city again. His arrival was not the social sensation it had been in 1786. He found himself involved with the beautiful Nancy M'Lehose, a married lady separated from her husband, and they conducted an impassioned and sentimentally spiritual affair, mostly through their many letters to each other as 'Sylvander and Clarinda'. Burns's major literary commitment was now entirely given to songs, for he had begun to help James Johnson with *The Scots Musical Museum*, which appeared in six volumes from 1787 to 1803. Burns became the literary editor of most of these books, although he refused payment for the work, collecting and altering old songs and writing completely new ones to old airs and fiddle-tunes. He was very enthusiastic about the task and before his death he had created over 200 songs of his own.

Leaving Edinburgh in the spring of 1788, Burns returned once more to Mauchline. Jean had borne him twins for the second time but the two little girls died within weeks. The poet arranged to lease a new farm at Ellisland and finally married the girl who had endured more from him and for him than ever Clarinda had, but it was never to be a marriage of minds and he had other affairs, including one with Anne Park, who bore him a child. Jean produced a second and then a third son and Burns was given a post at last with the Excise. He did well in the service but the long miles he had to ride did not help his health. His last literary poem was 'Tam o' Shanter', written in the winter of 1790. It is a brilliant and corruscating summation of all the vigour, local comedy, satirical irreverence and the driving technical virtuosity which he had inherited from the tradition and made his own. The poem incorporates the mock heroic, the bawdy and the tender; it relishes a local ghost story well told and presents a 'proper' eighteenth-century moral conclusion with a poker face; it focuses on domestic rural life with convincing realism only to leap to the grotesquerie of a hallucinatory encounter with sexuality and diabolism. 'Tam o' Shanter' is a unique poem in European culture, for it straddles literary and cultural gulfs by combining an earthy peasant *joie de vivre* with the more rarefied possibility of individual imaginative transport: in it 'The Miller's Tale' meets the world of 'Kubla Khan'.

When Ellisland eventually failed at the end of 1791 (not through lack of effort on Burns's part) the poet fell back on his

Excise appointment and moved to Dumfries with his family. Jean gave him a daughter and he brought Anne Park's little girl into the household as his own. Here, despite uncertain health and official suspicion about his liberal views, he found the energy to continue his commitment to old songs and song-writing. The popular appetite for songs, whetted by Ramsay's *Tea Table Miscellany*, had been fed by many writers. Among the best known were two men from Aberdeenshire, Alexander Ross (1699–1784), a schoolmaster who produced lively pieces such as 'The Rock and the Wee Pickle Tow' and 'Woo'd and Married an' A''; and John Skinner (1721–1807), an Episcopalian minister whose racy, reeling 'Tullochgorum' was held by Burns to be 'the best Scotch song ever Scotland saw'. Burns's own editorial work for *The Scots Musical Museum* was not unscholarly, but David Herd (1732–1810) was more exacting and published fragments without embellishment. Herd's *Ancient and Modern Scots Songs* (1769; 1776) includes some of the first printings of the old ballads, and, although Burns had copies of the book, the ballads rarely influenced him in his own songs, which concentrate on tender love-lyrics, drinking-verses such as 'O Willie Brew'd a Peck o' Maut', and sturdy airs such as 'Scots Wha Hae', 'Is there for honest poverty' and (refined from several originals) 'Auld Lang Syne'.

The love-songs and their beautiful tunes are particularly memorable. 'The Lea Rig' and 'Corn Rigs are Bonie' celebrate the bitter-sweetness of first assignations and the joys of sexual meeting, while 'Mary Morison', 'Ae Fond Kiss' and 'Highland Mary' are songs of parting and death suffused with the poet's sense of mortality. These intimations of inevitable ending invade love-lyrics such as 'A Red, Red Rose' and 'O wert thou in the cauld blast', while others (such as 'Whistle O'er the Lave o't') take a bolder, gayer note, and an old and bawdy complaint about fading potency was rewritten as an expression of simple companionship between ageing lovers – 'John Anderson my Jo'. Even with optimistic words, the plangent tunes chosen by Burns give the force of a lament to songs such as 'The Young Highland Rover' and 'Where braving angry winter's storms'. The latter was set to a fiddle-tune by Neil Gow and so, like several of Burns's airs, it provides the singer with a fairly severe challenge to his or her vocal range. The poet's affinity with the age's taste for honest sentiment is seen at its clearest in these songs and Burns was by no means the only writer to work in the genre. As a popular art-form it is closer to pastoral in its moods and expression than it is to the oral traditions of the folk tale and the ballads. Lady Grizel Baillie pointed the way at the beginning of the century and she was followed by other educated women who wrote and adapted material to their view of humble life. These include Jean Elliott (1727–1805) and her 'The Flowers o' the Forest'; Lady Anne Lindsay (1750–1825), 'Auld Robin Gray'; Joanna Baillie (1762–1851), 'Tam o' the Lin'; and, in the next century, Lady Nairne's 'The Land o' the Leal'. Such pieces were usually touching, sometimes comic and always decorous. Later writers, such as Scott and Stevenson, felt that Burns's songs were a lesser achievement than his early poems, but modern critics have come to emphasise the high level of their musical success. Indeed, his best Scots poems were never far removed from the rhythms of popular dancing and the traditions of sentiment and humour in song.

By 1793 Creech's second 'Edinburgh' edition – with some additional poems – was published, and on top of his contributions to the *Musical Museum* Burns was sending songs to George Thomson's *Select Scottish Airs*. (The poet's private collection of Rabelaisian verses, later known as *The Merry Muses of Caledonia*, was never intended for publication.) Burns kept up his editorial tasks until a few weeks before his death at the age of only thirty-seven. He could not have foretold the international fame which was to come, nor the ambiguous influence which his work was to have on Scottish life and culture for the next hundred years.

6

The nineteenth century: history, industry, sentiment

In Scottish cultural history the writers of the late eighteenth and early nineteenth century contribute to a single period of change and unusually creative activity. Walter Scott made Scotland and its past famous throughout Europe, periodical literature flourished in the capital, and there was a massive expansion of cities and industry. The population of Edinburgh doubled, with a powerful middle class to confirm its supremacy in law, medicine, the Church, banking, brewing and publishing. Farming and fishing were equally well established, on the east coast, along with heavier industries in coal, textiles, paper and especially the manufacture of linen. Great streets and houses in London were built with Aberdeen granite, and the finest American clippers were matched by sailing-ships from yards in the North-East.

The north's most significant export was people, and the economic and cultural life of the area was dominated by emigration to Canada and America. Estate-owners and clan-chiefs had been enclosing the land from the 1770s, and the ancient runrig style of strip cultivation, with its emphasis on subsistence farming shared by the community, had finally begun to disappear. Sheep-farming made a profitable appearance in the South-West, where there was plenty of grazing and urban markets close to hand, but in the Highlands, where the poorer land could no longer support an expanding population, the arrival of sheep only added to their problems. Landowners in search of grazing encouraged tenants to leave their crofts by offering them new jobs or assisted passage and emigration. In the second decade of the century the vast Sutherland estate set about 'improvement' in this manner, planning to resettle families on the coast, where the herring industry was enjoying a boom. (Neil Gunn's novel *The Silver Darlings* is set in this period.) The Countess of Sutherland intended these developments for the best, but old customs and loyalties could not be uprooted without pain. The evictions carried out by her agents, and the particular cruelty of Patrick Sellar in the small glen of Strathnaver made the Sutherland 'Clearances' and Sellar's name notorious. Many Gaelic poems were written about the pains of eviction, and the small crofters conceived a hatred of sheep and the English language alike:

> Not sweet the sound that waked me from slumber,
> coming down to me from the mountain tops:
> the Lowland shepherd whose tongue displeases,
> Shouting there at his lazy dog.

> (Iain MacLachlainn, 'Alas my State' ['Och, och mar tha mi'],
> trs. D. Thomson)

The use of Gaelic in Highland schools was officially permitted, but, in practice, the Education Act of 1872 set up a system of national control and inspection which inevitably favoured English. For the most part the Highlanders offered only passive resistance to changes forced upon them; but there were outbursts from time to time between evicted crofters and the police, the militia and even the army. Women often joined in these skirmishes, and their leading part in the famous 'Battle of Braes' in Skye in 1882 gained the support of public opinion and helped to bring about the Crofters' Act, which finally offered secure tenure and controlled rents. Not the least effective in this campaign were the songs and poems of Mary Macpherson of Skye, who spoke out fearlessly on behalf of the old culture and land-reform.

For the first half of the century, however, the poorer parts of the North-West Highlands had no protection from the demands of capital and the burgeoning of market-forces elsewhere. When wool-prices declined, or when the demand for kelp collapsed in the face of cheaper imports and chemical substitutes, many old families went bankrupt and landownership fell into new, perhaps less caring, hands. The pattern of clan obligations had not survived the aftermath of the 1745 rising, and many chieftains now regarded themselves as landowners in the capitalist mould, spending their time and their money elsewhere. When the potato-crop failed in 1846 there was no government relief for famine in the north, and thousands of impoverished Highlanders went abroad or came in search of work, like their Irish fellows, to the Lowland cities of Scotland. Little wonder that many Gaelic verses of the period, composed in Glasgow or in the settlements of Nova Scotia, are steeped in nostalgia for the communities, customs and girls left behind in the 'homeland'. Yet it is difficult to imagine how even the most enlightened of policies could have solved all the problems of the Highlands, in the face of their limited resources and a growing population.

If the brash and confident heart of the industrial nineteenth century belongs to any one area of Scotland, it belongs to Paisley, Greenock, Glasgow and the South-West. The groundwork was done by many small merchants who had invested in the weaving of cotton imported from the Americas. Their business had begun as a scattered rural industry with hand-looms for linen and cotton; next it developed with water-powered mills until, finally, steam-driven factories with large work-forces were concentrated near the cities. This led to an increased demand for coal, more industrialisation and higher wages for the miners, who had only recently been emancipated from virtual slavery on the estates of mine-owners. Iron foundries began to produce steam engines to pump the mines and power the mills. Chemical works developed new techniques in bleaching and dyeing for the textile-trade, and the production of coal-tar and gas brought advanced lighting to many factories and towns. The Industrial Revolution saw Glasgow's population increasing faster than that of any other town in Britain. Thousands of labourers arrived from Ireland and the Highlands, and under such pressure the old fabric of the city could not cope. By the 1850s half the children born in Glasgow died before the age of five, and there were outbreaks of cholera until the new Loch Katrine water-supply was brought into service ten years later. The Scottish Act of the great Reform Bill of 1832 was welcomed by everyone, but gradually it became apparent to the new labourers that their lot had hardly improved at all. The Chartist movement's demand for universal male suffrage found ready support in industrial Scotland,

and its struggles in the 1840s confirmed a radical sensibility in the South-West and a sense of solidarity among the working class. But early attempts to gain better wages when times were hard had failed. In later years unions such as the Coal Miners' Association did better for their members, but it was 1867 before most workers got the vote and the Factory Act afforded some protection and a limit to the hours worked by women and children.

After the expansion of the railways in order to transport coal and then manufactured goods and passengers, the second half of the century saw an astonishing growth in heavy industry. Blast furnaces, fuelled by cheap coal and ore, supplied the raw material for engineering and ship-building. For twenty years after 1850 nearly three-quarters of all the iron vessels launched in Britain came from Clydeside, and the developing British Empire ensured that these ships, locomotives, boilers, pumps, marine engines and the engineers themselves went into service all around the world. 'Clyde-built' became synonymous with advanced technology and durability. Glasgow was called the 'second city of the Empire', middle-class ironmasters and ship-building families made their fortunes and beautiful new terraces and parks were created in the city. But a shortage of housing for the proletariat meant that social problems got worse and worse. In 1880 a quarter of the city's families lived in one-room apartments, and many took lodgers as well. New tenements in the Scottish style were erected, and life in these crowded buildings had a special sense of community; but they were also subject to overcrowding and decay, until by the end of the century the slums of Glasgow were among the worst in Europe, breeding-grounds of violence, drunkenness and vice. Yet the booming city bred a native resilience in its people, and, if the influx of families from Ireland led to religious prejudices between Protestants and Catholics, it also contributed a unique humour and vitality to the working population, not to mention a healthy scepticism about the British establishment.

As far as the Kirk was concerned, the old Presbyterian principles were once again in arms against centralised government control and patronage by landowners, while fundamentalist Evangelical preachers were coming to the fore, especially in the crowded cities, where there was a fear of Catholic emancipation. Ten years of wrangling between the state and various Church factions came to a head at the General Assembly of 1843, when nearly 40 per cent of the establishment broke away from the 'Auld Kirk' on a matter of principle and formed the Free Church, claiming to represent the true values of Presbyterianism. The 'Disruption' caused considerable hardship to the rebel congregations and their ministers, for in the early days they were harried by their landlords and forced to worship on the open hillside. They survived, however, to form a General Assembly and a parallel organisation of their own, even down to schools and overseas missions. The Free Kirk was particularly successful in the Highlands, much to the dismay of the landowners, and its radical tendency immediately made itself felt in votes for the Liberal Party which unseated many established Tory members. In other respects, however, the Protestant ethic was entirely in tune with the pursuit of profit and the age's materialistic belief that every man should make his way by dint of personal initiative, 'respectability' and hard work. Thousands of Scots took this course by leaving home, and skilled, unskilled, Highland and Lowland alike, they spread throughout the British Empire to become a byword – both loved and hated for their ambition, hardiness and ingenuity.

By the 1880s Scotland was indisputably part of British Victorian industrial society, yet the Scots' own sense of their cultural differences from England had not died out. Thus, when the country's prosperity was most fully centred on heavy industry in the urban areas, there grew up a vogue for 'cabbage-patch' literature – backward-looking and sentimentally rustic tales extolling simple 'Scotch' folk, pawky humour and 'honest' feeling. When Queen Victoria built Balmoral in 1855, it confirmed an English vogue for tourism, tartan and turrets in the north, and 'Scottish baronial' architecture in the same style appeared throughout the country in a rash of railway-stations and hotels. A monument to Wallace towered over the plain at Stirling; the new railway-station at Edinburgh was called 'Waverley', and the Scott monument commanded Princes Street like a mislocated cathedral spire. Burns had his monument in Auld Reekie too, and Burns Associations were formed throughout the world to promulgate his works and to consume a ritual supper each year on the anniversary of his birth. The typical 'canny Scotsman' began to appear in the press with a famous *Punch* cartoon in 1860 along the lines of 'I hadna been in London mair than half-an-hour, when bang! went saxpence!' This northern counterpart to John Bull – staid, bewhiskered and famously cautious with his money – has more in common with his *petit bourgeois* Victorian inventors than he has with an older, prouder and more volatile Scottish spirit.

Not all was tartan ribbons and bardolatry, however, and national feeling took a political dimension too, for the Association for the Vindication of Scottish Rights was formed in 1853, and, of course, the Disruption of the Kirk had already served to remind folk of old Scottish values. When those crofters on Skye resisted eviction by physical force, they were aware that similar action had made nationalism a potent political issue in Ireland, and so the Highland Land League was formed along Irish lines to press for reform. In the face of the 'Irish question' to the west and the so-called 'Crofters' War' to the north, the Liberal government was pleased to make concessions by passing the Crofters' Act. When the government fell after the failure of the Irish Home Rule Bill in 1886, Liberal and nationalist opinion in Scotland was further stimulated and an all-party Home Rule Association was formed to promote political independence. Their case did not have the urgency or the violence of the Irish movement, but it contained a separatist and a nationalist feeling which has played a part in Scottish politics ever since.

Although the century began in Scotland with Walter Scott's verse romances, there was no poet to match the achievement of Burns, nor was there any Scottish equivalent to the English Romantic poets, unless, of course, **George Gordon, the sixth Lord Byron** (1788–1824) is seen as a Scottish writer. This claim is not as eccentric as it may seem, for Byron's early childhood was spent in Scotland – he attended Aberdeen Grammar School and his mother was Elizabeth Gordon of Gight, an unstable member of an unstable family from Donside. He himself claimed to be 'half a Scot by birth and bred / A whole one' (*Don Juan*), and T. S. Eliot believed there was a particularly Calvinist element in his delight in posing as a damned creature. Gregory Smith identified Byron's mercurial temperament with the 'clean contrair' spirit of the Scottish sensibility, and it must be admitted that the poet's swift transitions from pathos to mockery, or from moral satire to self-deflating parody, scarcely correspond to an English conception of literary decorum. The case can be developed at greater length, but for present purposes Byron's career must be left to the realm of English letters, where he came to prominence with *Childe Harold's Pilgrimage* in 1812 to join Walter Scott as one of the most famous writers in Europe.

Notwithstanding Byron's fame and Scott's early success in verse, the medium of the age in Scotland was undoubtedly prose, and the spread of literacy, of circulating libraries and the book-buying habit created an enormous appetite for books and periodicals of all sorts. Writers came to depend on the periodical scene to make their living, and, of course, many novels appeared there in serial form. Edinburgh became a most influential publishing-centre, largely due to Archibald Constable and William Blackwood, whose presses, along with the *Edinburgh Review* and *Blackwood's Magazine*, made them household names throughout the kingdom. The phenomenal popularity of Scott's fiction was intimately bound up with Constable's firm and it exactly matches the expansion of what was coming to be known as 'the reading public' – a new critical conception and a new market.

Scott, Hogg, Galt, Ferrier, Lockhart and Moir were all writing at the same time, and this talented *'Blackwood's'* group played a large part in the growing status of prose fiction throughout urban Britain. Yet their work is curiously divided, not least because they rarely deal with city life. Scott and Hogg look to an earlier and still potent Romantic tradition; while Galt, Moir and Ferrier, with their novels of small town or rural society, foreshadow the *petit-bourgeois* provincialism of late-Victorian Scottish culture. In fact the essence of this latter vision had first appeared as early as 1806 in the work of the painter David Wilkie (1785–1841). In that year Wilkie, a son of the manse from Fifeshire, made his reputation at the Royal Academy in London with a picture called 'Village Politicians'. He produced genre paintings in similar vein for the next two decades – all distinguished by a novelistic desire to imply a story and to portray humour, pathos and sturdy 'Scottish' character-types, rather in the style of 'The Cottar's Saturday Night' or Wordsworth's poems about Cumbrian folk. When Galt and Moir wrote for *Blackwood's* they confirmed a whole country's view of its own nature in terms which were not essentially different from Wilkie's genre painting. This is not to undervalue Galt's keen documentary eye and his sense of comedy, character and irony, but in the hands of lesser men and women the inheritance became 'provincial' in the worst sense of the word, leading to the 'Kailyard' at the end of the century, with its vision of Scotland as a charming rustic backwater.

Unaware of these future developments, Scott's contemporaries felt themselves to belong to the 'second generation' of the Scottish Enlightenment. John Pinkerton (1758–1826) had tried to repair the public neglect of poets such as Barbour and Dunbar with his collection of *Ancient Scotish Poetry* (1786), and the Revd Dr John Jamieson (1759–1838) produced his *Etymological Dictionary of the Scottish Language* (1808, 1825) a work which remained a substantial scholarly reference until modern times. As antiquarians, Sibbald, Irving and Laing wrote biographies and literary histories, and Scott founded the Bannatyne Club in 1823 to publish rare historical texts. In the field of moral philosophy, Duguld Stewart (1753–1828) succeeded Adam Ferguson as professor at Edinburgh, and, while Stewart was not an original thinker, being content to follow Thomas Reid's 'common sense' school, his personality, eloquence and liberal views influenced a whole generation. Most prominent among his peers were Henry Thomas Cockburn (1779–1854), and his friend Francis Jeffrey (1773–1850), two middle-class lawyers who played a part in establishing the Reform Bill and went on to become Whig law lords. Cockburn's *Life of Jeffrey* (1852) and his own various memoirs, published posthumously, give an attractive account of his life and times. Francis Jeffrey started the *Edinburgh Review* in 1802 with the support of Henry Brougham and the English clergyman and wit Sydney Smith – former pupils of Duguld Stewart – and the new quarterly immediately made a name for itself. Within ten years the *Review* had a circulation of over 13,000 and its publisher Constable could attract the best writers in the country with astonishing fees of up to 20 guineas a sheet for anonymous reviews and £1000 or more for a single poem or article. Cockburn wrote on matters of law, and during the twenties and thirties Macaulay and Carlyle contributed regularly with some of their most famous essays.

The *Edinburgh Review* was never more successful than during its early years. Jeffrey was sympathetic to the literature of feeling, but it had to be supported by formal style and moral content, so that Burns, for example, was criticised for espousing 'vehement sensibility' without 'decency and regularity'. In this sense Jeffrey's values are neoclassical and it is not surprising that he began a famous review of Wordsworth's *The Excursion* on a typically proscriptive note – 'This will never do.' The *Review* was celebrated for the scathing and superior tone of its criticism, and, while it allowed Wordsworth and the English 'Lake School' to have 'a great deal of genius and of laudable feeling', it did not hesitate to chastise the poets for 'perverseness and bad taste'. Scott's *Marmion* was pruned with equal rigour, as if the task were an irksome duty – 'because we cannot help considering it as the foundation of a new school, which may hereafter occasion no little annoyance both to us and to the public'. Little wonder that Byron satirised Jeffrey and his 'critic clan' in *English Bards and Scotch Reviewers* by referring to them as the 'bloodhounds of Arthur's Seat'!

It was not long before Scottish Tories lost patience with the dominance of the *Review* and its Whiggish politics. Walter Scott helped to found the (London) *Quarterly Review* in 1809, but Jeffrey's periodical did not meet its match until 1817, when William Blackwood, Constable's rival in publishing, produced the *Edinburgh Monthly Magazine*, which was soon changed to *Blackwood's Edinburgh Magazine*. The revised 'Maga' or 'Ebony', as it came to be known, was edited by John Gibson Lockhart and John Wilson, two young lawyers determined to make their mark on the cultural scene. This they did without delay, helped by James Hogg, in a mock biblical 'Translation from an Ancient Chaldee Manuscript', which satirised the 'war' between Constable and Blackwood and provided malicious caricatures of their Whig enemies and literary rivals. There was an immediate scandal, the October issue sold out, new readers were left panting for more, and the (anonymous) authors found it expedient to leave town. Over the next two years the publisher had to pay out £1000 in damages, but he stood by his 'wild fellows' and *Blackwood's* flourished, to be published without a break until 1980. Under Wilson and Lockhart, and an Irishman William Maginn, 'Maga' continued to make a stir, particularly in its wholehearted opposition to the poetry of Leigh Hunt, Shelley and Keats, motivated, perhaps, by the fact that Francis Jeffrey had greatly praised Keats in the *Edinburgh*

Review. Whatever the reason, *Blackwood's* roasted 'the Cockneys' with a vituperative glee virtually indistinguishable from snobbish and personal spite. Of course, Keats's fiery mind was not 'snuffed out' by any such 'article', as Byron has it in *Don Juan*, nor was he the only writer to suffer from the critical hostilities declared between Constable and Blackwood. Wilson and Lockhart were not above petty lies and libels and political prejudices and old scores were settled forcefully on all sides.

John Wilson (1785–1854) continued as contributing editor to *Blackwood's*, and as 'Christopher North' he produced many of the 'Noctes Ambrosianae' (1822–35), a long-running series of essays in the form of conversations or monologues supposedly overheard by the scribe. (They were published in four volumes in 1885.) These often featured a version of his friend James Hogg somewhat broadly sketched as the 'Shepherd', a bibulous and loquacious countryman, spokesperson for common sense, but given to tall tales or sudden flights of philosophising:

Tickler: James, would you seriously have North to write dramas about the loves of the lower orders – men in corduroy breeches, and women in linsey-woollen petticoats –

Shepherd: Wha are ye, sir, to speak o' the lower orders? Look up to the sky, sir, on a starry nicht, and, puir, ignorant, thochtless, upsettin' cretur you'll be, gin you dinna feel far within, and deep down your ain sowl, that you are, in good truth, ane o' the lower orders – no, perhaps, o' men, but o' intelligences! and that it requires some dreadfu' mystery, far beyond your comprehension, to mak' you worthy o' ever in after life becoming a dweller in those celestial mansions. Yet think ye, sir, that thousan's, and tens o' thousan's o' millions, since the time when first God's wrath smote the earth's soil with the curse o' barrenness, and human creatures had to earn their bread wi' sweat and dust, haena lived and toiled, and laughed and sighed, and groaned and grat, *o' the lower orders*, that are noo in eternal bliss, and shall sit above you and Mr. North, and ithers o' the best o' the clan, in the realms o' heaven!

Tickler: 'Pon my soul, James, I said nothing to justify this tirade.

The 'Noctes' proved very popular, and other writers, most notably Lockhart and Hogg, contributed, while De Quincey featured as a character in them and wrote for *Blackwood's* in his own right. (Wilson had befriended him and Wordsworth during a stay in the Lake District in his earlier years.)

Sir Walter Scott (1771–1832)

Scott's career belongs to the nineteenth century but his links
are with the earlier Edinburgh of Burns and Mackenzie, and it
was his interest in ballads and Romantically 'medieval'
adventure-poems which led him to prose fiction and the virtual
invention of the 'historical novel'. He was born in a house in
College Wynd among the crowded, disease-ridden streets of
Old Edinburgh, where only six of his parents' twelve children
survived infancy. Walter was the third of three healthy boys,
but at eighteen months a bout of infantile paralysis left him
weak with his right leg permanently lamed. His next eight years
were spent at his grandfather's farm in the Borders, where he
regained his health and acquired a taste for tales and ballads
and stories of the Jacobite rebellion. He never did lose his
lameness, but he thrived among doting elders, turning into a
robust lad, forthright and full of confidence.

Back with the family at a new house in George Square, he
attended the old High School in Edinburgh and read Shakespeare, Macpherson's *Ossian*, Pope's Homer, Ramsay's *Ever
Green* and Spenser, all of which developed his appetite for 'the
wonderful and the terrible', as he put it – 'the common taste of
children . . . in which I have remained a child even unto this
day'. Little wonder that he came to admire the Stuart cause,
with the Cavaliers and Montrose and his Highlanders, and yet
his private tutor was a Whig and a Presbyterian and so their
amicable wrangles ensured that Scott also heard about the
history of the Kirk and the sufferings of the Covenanters.
Summer holidays were still spent in the Borders, where he
discovered Bishop Percy's *Reliques* and the 'historical incidents and traditional legends' associated with the ruins of
castles and abbeys all around.

Apprenticed as a copy-clerk to his father's law-practice in
1786, he learned to produce hundreds of pages of legible
manuscripts to short order, and business travels to Perth and
the Trossachs (once with an escort of armed soldiers) gave him
tales and settings enough for his later fiction. The young clerk
attended the theatre and mixed with literary people, leaving a
memorable description of Robert Burns, whom he met briefly
in the home of Professor Adam Ferguson. But it was decided
that Walter should follow his father's profession, so he

graduated as a qualified advocate in 1792, although his studies did not preclude him from the city's convivial drinking-habits, nor from joining various clubs and debating-societies. Despite his withered leg, Scott had matured into a strong, raw-boned man who could ride, walk or drink with the hardiest farmer or sportsman. When French invasion threatened in 1797, he joined the Royal Edinburgh Volunteer Light Dragoons, delighting in the uniform and the dashing practice with horse and sabre on the sands of Portobello.

A predilection for boisterous, manly company was characteristic of his class and countrymen, and Scott was equally typical in his more sentimental longings. For five years in the early 1790s he had nursed passionate feelings for Williamina Stuart-Belsches of Fettercairn, a young and beautiful heiress whom he called the 'lady of the green mantle' – the model for a character of the same name in *Redgauntlet* and for several more of his gentle and rather pallid heroines. Williamina married someone else in 1797, but within the year Scott had met Charlotte Margaret Charpentier, of French extraction, who became his loyal and affectionate wife until her death in 1826.

The young advocate harboured literary ambitions and under the spur of the Romantic Gothic craze he translated Gottfried Bürger's 'Lenore' and 'Der Wilde Jäger'. In fact the German poet had already been influenced by ballads in Percy's *Reliques*, and so Scott's versions brought the wheel of fashionable influence full circle. A meeting with 'Monk' Lewis led to a translation of Goethe's *Götz von Berlichingen* – the essence of Romantic medievalism – and a visit to London to see the volume published in 1799. Scott's links with the Borders were renewed when he was appointed Sheriff-depute of Selkirkshire, shortly after his father's death in 1799, and he needed no further encouragement to roam among the hills and rivers of Ettrick, Tweed and Yarrow. In a sense he had been preparing all his life for such a collection as *The Minstrelsy of the Scottish Border* (3 vols, 1802–3), and it seems equally inevitable that he should have followed its success by writing poems of his own, suffused with the romance of antique battles in a benevolent wilderness.

As an editor Scott was inclined to collate what he regarded as the 'best' text from different versions, but he also collected from oral sources and sought the help of better scholars and local people too, including the redoubtable James Hogg, whom he met in the summer of 1802. The *Border Minstrelsy* was an immediate success, beautifully printed by his old friend James Ballantyne, with an enthusiastic introduction and footnotes full of history and quaint details. A third volume was projected for the following year and the work was reprinted several times thereafter, to become a milestone in the Scottish literary world's rediscovery of its own past.

Scott contributed to the newly founded *Edinburgh Review*, encouraged Hogg in his hopes of being published and received William and Dorothy Wordsworth on their Scottish tour. He persuaded James Ballantyne to move to Edinburgh and entered into a secret partnership which ensured that Ballantyne got plenty of printing-commissions, including legal work, Scott's own books and other antiquarian projects from various different publishing-houses. Scott lent money, took a share of the profits and thought it a good scheme, although it put him in an ambiguous position sometimes, and eventually went badly wrong. At first, however, business thrived and Archibald Constable took a commercial interest as well. Preferring to leave the Bar, Scott managed to get appointed as one of the clerks of Session who sit below the judge in the High Court at Edinburgh. His duties as Sheriff of Selkirkshire encouraged him in 1804 to set up a house at Ashestiel in that county, and henceforth he spent half the year sitting at the Court of Session and the rest of the time in travel, or living happily by the Tweed as a 'rattle skulled half-lawyer, half-sportsman' surrounded by his children, his dogs and various family retainers.

Prompted by the Countess of Dalkeith's enthusiasm for a local story of supernatural mischief, *The Lay of the Last Minstrel* was originally intended as an imitation ballad for the third volume of the *Minstrelsy*. It grew considerably, however, under Scott's compulsion to spin a tale of love, magic and chivalry, with English and Scottish armies in conflict, and many descriptions of Border lore and 'scenery and manners'. Whatever he learned from the ballads, it was not concision, and the poem is a typically Romantic confection of that glamorous 'medieval' world already familiar from the poems of Spenser, Chatterton and Coleridge. (Scott acknowledged a metrical debt to 'Christabel' and used much the same pattern of octosyllabic iambic couplets for his other long poems.) *The Lay* was an unprecedented popular success throughout Britain in 1805, with several editions and over 21,000 sales in the first four years, rising to almost 44,000 copies by the time the collected poems appeared in 1830. Francis Jeffrey gave it an enthusiastic review, although he felt that it was too 'local', and opined that 'Mr Scott must either sacrifice his Border prejudices, or offend his readers in the other parts of the empire' – a revealing point of view from the leading critic in 'the Athens of the North', and completely blind to what made Scott's poem special. The author's literary ambitions were thoroughly aroused and he started on a novel which was to deal with Highland life of sixty years earlier. But public acclaim demanded another metrical romance, and so Scott put away prose fiction and set to work on *Marmion*, which was promptly purchased by Constable – unseen and still unfinished – for 1000 guineas.

The Lay was essentially an old legend, but *Marmion* is closer to a novel in conception. Set in 1513 as 'a tale of Flodden field', it visualises the melancholy end of James IV and his army in rather the same spirit as Malory describes the fate of Arthur's Round Table. Marmion is an English knight, an anti-hero with a complicated and treacherous love life. His peace-mission to the Scottish court fails just as his private affairs catch up with him disastrously, and he dies on the battlefield with 'repentance and reviving love'. The melodrama is relieved by a wealth of geographical and historical detail, drawn from Scott's own youthful memories and his reading of the chronicles of Froissart and Pitscottie. He never did take Jeffrey's advice to eschew the 'local', and there are striking set descriptions of the abbey at Lindesfarne, or the battle at Flodden, or Marmion's first sight of Edinburgh. It was another huge success, and after his work on Dryden Scott accepted a further contract with Constable to produce an edition of Swift which was to take him six years to complete. He was unpretentious enough to compare such editorial work to a good cash crop of 'turnips and peas', but a growing dissatisfaction with the Whig politics of the *Edinburgh Review* led to a split with Constable. Scott had Ballantyne form his own publishing-house under the name of his younger brother John, an entertaining but somewhat dilettante character, who was also to act as Scott's agent. The rival business did not last much beyond 1813, for the principals were not good enough judges of what would sell, but it did produce Scott's best and most popular poem.

The Lady of the Lake (1810) takes place in the reign of James V, some twenty-five years after Flodden, and it turns on the king's habit of travelling incognito among his people. (Popular legend refers to him as 'the Gaberlunzie man' – a travelling beggar.) Here the Gothic furniture of knightly chivalry is abandoned in favour of the excitements of stag-hunting, and the real romance of the tale lies with the beauty of the wild countryside around Loch Katrine and 'the ancient manners, habits and customs' of the Highlanders. Scott was sensitive to trends in popular taste and he knew that Anne Grant's *Highland Memoirs* (1806) and *The Cottagers of Glenburnie* (1808), a novel by Elizabeth Hamilton, had already stirred an urban interest in Highland life. He was no expert in Gaelic culture, however, despite a liking for talking to old Jacobites, and it is an oddly bitter reflection that when he was visiting the country around Loch Katrine, convinced that 'the old Scottish Gael' was a subject 'highly adapted for poetical composition', Duncan Bàn Macintyre, one of the greatest Gaelic poets of the eighteenth century, was far from his beloved Ben Dorain and passing the last years of his life virtually unknown to polite Edinburgh as a retired member of the City Guard in the narrow streets of the old town. Yet Scott's 'discovery' of the 'aboriginal race by whom the Highlands of Scotland were inhabited' took lowland Britain and Europe by storm. In fact his romantic and selective view of the clansmen as a warrior-class, volatile, proud, loyal to their own and cruel to others, still prevails in the popular consciousness. In a confrontation between Roderick Dhu and the disguised King James, Scott has the Highlander justify his clansmen's raids in exactly the same terms as a North American Indian chief might have used when speaking to the white man. (Fenimore Cooper came to be known as 'the American Scott' fifteen years later, for his leatherstocking novels proposed a very similar vision of native Americans living in the wilderness.)

These fertile plains, that soften'd vale,
Were once the birthright of the Gael;
The stranger came with iron hand,
And from our fathers reft the land.

Where dwell we now? See, rudely swell
Crag over crag, and fell o'er fell. . . .
Pent in this fortress of the North,
Think'st thou we will not sally forth,
To spoil the spoiler as we may,
And from the robber rend the prey?
Ay, by my soul! While on yon plain
The Saxon rears one shock of grain,
While of ten thousand herds there strays
But one along yon river's maze,
The Gael of plain and river heir,
Shall with strong hand redeem his share.

(v. vii)

In another striking scene, 'Black Roderick' only has to give a whistle and the bare hillside comes alive with armed men, springing up like Satan's minions in *Paradise Lost*:

And every tuft of broom gives life
To plaided warrior arm'd for strife. . . .
As if the yawning hill to heaven
A subterranean host had given.
Watching their leader's beck and will,
All silent there they stood, and still.
Like the loose crags, whose threatening mass
Lay tottering o'er the hollow pass.

(v. ix)

These are not the only Miltonic aspects which Scott ascribes to James's fierce antagonist, for earlier in the poem the 'waving of his tartans broad' and his 'darken'd brow' had, indeed, made him seem like the 'ill Demon of the night', and even on his death-bed he is described with an epic simile worthy of the fallen angel:

As the tall ship, whose lofty prore
Shall never stem the billows more,
Deserted by her gallant band,
Amid the breakers lies astrand
So, on his couch, lay Roderick Dhu!

(vi. xiii)

Thus the chieftain is revealed as a Romantic anti-hero in the

Satanic/Byronic mould – arrogant, intractible and yet honour-able according to his own lights. Nevertheless, Roderick must die to leave the way clear for a bitter-sweet reconciliation between *Lowland* lords – the exiled Douglas, whose daughter Ellen is the 'Lady of the Lake' herself, and the stag-hunting 'Fitzjames', now revealed as an enlightened and forgiving monarch. The future is clearly theirs.

The poem concludes somewhat in the spirit of *A Winter's Tale* as identities are revealed and the opposing values of country and court set aside (if not reconciled) with the promise of a noble marriage and a happy ending. Another Shakespearean analogy is suggested by the way Scott intersperses ballads and songs throughout the poem – a device he was to use to even greater effect in the novels. Scott's octosyllabic measure is not markedly better than in his previous verses, but for once the plot avoids Gothic elaboration, and so the hunt-scenes and the beautiful landscapes are given room to stand forth as swiftly paced and effectively unified symbols of freedom and daring, to convey a strikingly ritualised, almost balletic, vision of heroic conflict: as if war, too, were sport on the shores of Loch Katrine – a remote Arden in the north.

The Lady of the Lake was Scott's greatest success to date. A few critics, and Coleridge in particular, continued to dislike his loping couplets ('prose in polysyllables'), but the public had no doubts and bought over 20,000 copies within the year. Even Jeffrey changed his tune about 'local subjects' and hoped in the *Edinburgh Review* that the poet would turn to 'a true Celtic story':

There are few persons, we believe, of any degree of poetical susceptibility, who have wandered among the secluded valleys of the Highlands, and contemplated the singular people by whom they are still tenanted – with their love of music and of song – their hardy and irregular life, so unlike the unvarying toils of the Saxon mechanic – their devotion to their chiefs – their wild and lofty traditions – their national enthusiasm – the melancholy grandeur of the scenes they inhabit – and the multiplied superstitions which still linger among them – without feeling that there is no existing people so well adapted for the purposes of poetry, or so capable of furnishing the occasions of new and striking inventions.

We are persuaded, that if Mr Scott's powerful and creative genius were to be turned in good earnest to such a subject, something might be produced still more impressive and original than even this age has yet witnessed.

Scott's poem and Jeffery's new-found enthusiasm show how strongly a Highland version of 'Scottishness' seized the popular imagination. Here at last was the formula for a national identity uncomplicated by the rigours and the old pains of Presbyterianism, and most gratifyingly separated from the everyday political and commercial facts of the Union. At last 'Scottishness' could be glamorous and noble and fashionable – and 'safe'. Before the publication of *The Lady of the Lake*, Loch Katrine and surrounding hills were little known and virtually inaccessible. After 1810, thousands of visitors flocked to the Trossachs to see the place for themselves, and innkeepers and pony-hirers never knew such trade. As if inspired by his own subject, the author himself set out on a trip through the Hebrides to collect more old customs and 'legends of war and wonder'.

Scott felt that he could now afford a home of his own in the Borders, and so he bought a little farmhouse called Cartley Hole situated on the Tweed between Melrose and Galashiels, builders were engaged to add to it, and the famous poet and his family, his horses, dogs and fishing-rods, arrived in the summer of 1812. He called it Abbotsford and spent the next twelve years buying property, planting trees and developing the building until it grew into a huge mansion – a maze of wings and towers filled with antiques, ancient arms and armour. In order to finance these baronial ambitions, Scott took on heavier and heavier commitments, borrowing, mortgaging and spending advances on books not yet written. The laird of Abbotsford was not ashamed of financial success – indeed, he saw it as a merit – yet, when the Waverley novels first appeared, he kept his authorship secret, and, although it was a well-known secret for years, he did not publicly acknowledge them until 1826. Scott's sense of honour and his material ambitions brought him much heartache in the end, but his generous temperament remained unspoiled. In the early hours of every morning he worked hard at his desk – scorning 'artistic' affectations and taking pride in his capacity for workmanlike, profitable toil. Later in the day he was an outgoing host to many friends and famous visitors – the very image of a sporting country laird and a spokesperson for the culture of romantic Scotland.

Rokeby, a poem of the Civil War, appeared at the beginning of 1813 but it could not match the economy and force of *The Lady of the Lake*. Besides, Byron had burst on the scene with the first two cantos of *Childe Harold's Pilgrimage* – a publishing-sensation scarcely less glamorous than its young creator. The elder poet recognised *Childe Harold* as 'a piece of most extraordinary power', and he and Byron entered into an amicable and respectful correspondence, despite the public's desire to see them as bitter rivals. They met each other frequently in London during two months in 1815 and parted good friends. Byron's romances, such as *The Giaour* (1813), *The Bride of Abydos* (1813) and *The Corsair* (1814), owe something to the genre created by Scott, but his settings were even more wildly exotic, and the modern misanthropical psychology of Childe Harold quite overtook the antiquarian romance and the chivalric code of the 'last minstrel'.

Scott recognised that his vogue was over, and later romances – *The Bridal of Triermain* (1813), *Harold the Dauntless* (1817) and *The Lord of the Isles* (1815) – were never to recapture his early triumphs. 'Well, well, James, so be it', he remarked to Ballantyne with typically pragmatic modesty; 'but you know we must not droop, for we can't afford to give over. Since one line has failed, we must just stick to something else.' 'Something else' was prose fiction, with the resumption of *Waverley*, the novel he had conceived in 1805 and never finished. At the age of forty-three Scott embarked on an entirely new creative career.

In a 'postscript which should have been a preface' the author of *Waverley* explained his point of view, giving notice, in effect, of the themes which were to inspire and guide him in all the later novels. He felt that the most extreme historical and social changes had taken place in the Highlands and Lowlands during the last two generations, as if the sixteenth century had led straight to the nineteenth century, so that 'the present people of Scotland [are] a class of beings as different from their grandfathers as the existing English are from those of Queen Elizabeth's time'. Scott thought that he had come to terms with these changes, but his feelings were crucially ambivalent. As a Lowland Tory and a Unionist, he was half in love with a warlike Stuart cause. As a man of aristocratic prejudices, and a lifelong opponent of the Reform Bill, he delighted in the oral tradition and the sturdy independence of common Scots folk. These are the conflicting claims at the heart of his novels, in which he places ordinary people at a time of violent change. His young heroes, whose inheritance is progress and the United Kingdom, learn to accept what Scott calls 'the prose of real life', but it seems colourless by comparison with the old ways and the 'poetry' of a lost Scotland.

Conflicts between 'emotional' and 'rational' responses to the Union had been manifest in Ramsay's time; but their sublimation in Scott's novels raised what might otherwise have been adventure-fiction to a penetrating exploration of loyalty and historical change. It is as if the author's own contradictory feelings were being replayed through his account of the characters and events of the past, and the difficulties of his position may well be reflected in the nature of his young protagonists. Thus it is that a typical Scott hero seems rather passive: he is often cast as a stranger and an observer from 'outside' who is caught up in events, so that the scenes and actions of the novel are introduced to the readers in just the same way as they are introduced to him. This allows the author to describe at length the landscape and manners of his native country in what amounts to an act of recognition, translation and explanation – not just for his readers, but for himself too. Edward Waverley in the novel of that name is a young Englishman whose father is a Whig interested in commercial and political advancement in the city of London, but whose uncle is a Tory cavalier of the old aristocratic school. Young Captain Waverley despises his father's values, and when he is posted to Scotland and visits Baron Bradwardine he becomes involved in the freebooting life of the Highlands, falls in love with a Highland girl, is cashiered from the army and ultimately joins the Jacobite rising of the Forty-five. (He returns to the fold in the end, however, and is granted a pardon.) In Waverley's case it is psychologically convincing that his sentimental and romantic nature should have been stirred by the charm of Charles Edward Stuart and his cause, just as he was fascinated (like his creator) with the clansmen, so strange and fierce in their loyalties and wild as the countryside they inhabit.

Of course, Scott's glamorous settings are part of the popular Romantic taste for the 'picturesque', but they also touch on the wellsprings of his inspiration, for he frequently makes his landscapes play a part in the workings of plot and denouement, and they relate to his understanding of mood and character too. A chapter from *Waverley*, 'The Hold of a Highland Robber', perfectly displays the author's talent for combining the awe-somely picturesque with detailed observation and a lively sense of contrast:

> The party preserved silence, interrupted only by the monotonous and murmured chant of a Gaelic song, sung in a kind of low recitative by the steersman, and by the dash of the oars, which the notes seemed to regulate, as they dipped to them in cadence. The light, which they now approached more nearly, assumed a broader, redder, and more irregular splendour. . . . As he saw it, the red glaring orb seemed to rest on the very surface of the lake itself, and resembled the fiery vehicle in which the Evil Genius of an Oriental tale traverses land and sea. They approached nearer, and the fire sufficed to show that it was kindled at the bottom of a huge dark crag or rock, rising abruptly from the very edge of the water; its front, changed by the reflection to dusky red, formed a strange and even awful contrast to the banks around, which were from time to time faintly and partially illuminated by pallid moonlight. . . .
>
> The principal inhabitant of this singular mansion . . . came forward to meet his guest, totally different in appearance and manner from what his imagination had anticipated. . . . Waverley prepared himself to meet a stern, gigantic, ferocious figure, such as Salvator would have chosen to be the central object of a group of banditti.
>
> Donald Bean Lean was the very reverse of all these. He was thin in person and low in stature, with light sandy-coloured hair, and small pale features, from which he derived his agnomen of *Bean*, or white. . . . He had served in some inferior capacity in the French army, and in order to receive his English visitor in great form, and probably meaning, in his way, to pay him a compliment, he had laid aside the Highland dress for the time, to put on an old blue and red uniform, and a feathered hat, in which he was far from showing to advantage, and indeed looked so incongruous, compared with all around him, that Waverley would have been tempted to laugh, had laughter been either civil or safe.

Waverley, or 'Tis Sixty Years Since (1814) was an immediate success and it remains one of Scott's best novels. Critics and readers admired the colourful minor characters and enthused about the use of 'Daft Davy Gellatly' as a kind of Shakespearean fool. They expressed enlightened relief that the pains of discord and civil war were now in the past, and the author (often surmised as Scott) was congratulated on his portrayal of a northern race which was assumed without question to have 'vanished from the face of their native land . . . within these few years'. Here and in succeeding novels the reading public found action, adventure and morality tied to outdoor places and 'real' historical events – a great relief from the contrived settings and overheated horrors of the prevailing Gothic school. Maria

Edgeworth's Irish novels, such as *Castle Rackrent* (1800), had pioneered the use of regional settings, and Scott acknowledged their influence on him, but his version of the Highlands was even more intriguing for a growing urban readership. On top of this, his many colourful secondary characters provide a comedy of manners less fine than Jane Austen's, but broader and more various, for Scott delights in robust contrasts between Highlanders and Lowlanders, Englishmen and Scotsmen, young and old, rich and poor, noble and devious, all to great effect. By comparison, the love-interest in these novels is a more conventional thing and his heroes and heroines are not without a flavour of the juvenile lead. Even so, the 'passive hero' so familiar in Scott's fiction does allow him to concentrate on the pressure of events and on how social, political or religious influences manifest themselves. In the last analysis these influences, and Scott's evocation of travel, landscape and local history all drive the novels along just as effectively as any more unique or dominant hero could. Indeed, the reader may find it easier to empathise with a protagonist who is caught up in events in the same way that he, or she, is caught up in reading the book. This sort of empathy is common to many popular novels, then as now, and no doubt it was yet another factor in the extraordinarily wide appeal of the 'wizard of the North'. *Waverley* went through four editions in as many months and sold 40,000 over again when the complete 'Waverley Novels' edition appeared with notes in 1829. Scott returned from a tour of the Northern Isles to find himself famously suspected of being 'the Great Unknown', and he gave himself up to fiction with a complete concentration of his remarkable energies.

Constable published *Guy Mannering* in 1815 and *The Antiquary* in 1816, both 'by the author of Waverley', as well as *Paul's Letters to his Kinsfolk* (1816), which appeared under Scott's own name as an account of his visit to Europe and the battlefield of Waterloo. In the same year two more novels, called *The Black Dwarf* and *Old Mortality*, from a series to be called 'Tales of my Landlord' were published by Blackwood as apparently collected and retold by an old schoolmaster named Jedediah Cleishbotham. It seems to have been John Ballantyne who persuaded Scott to go to another publisher with this scheme. In the face of this prolific output Scott explained how the first three Waverley novels were to fit together:

The present Work completes a series of fictitious narratives, intended to illustrate the manners of Scotland at three different periods. *Waverley* embraced the age of our fathers, *Guy Mannering* that of our youth, and *The Antiquary* refers to the last ten years of the eighteenth century.

(Introduction to *The Antiquary*)

Compared to *Waverley*, *Guy Mannering or the Astrologer* is something of a disappointment to the modern reader; being closer to a conventional romance of its day, it lent itself well to stage-adaptation, with a lost heir, supernatural agencies and a happy ending. Yet the novel still gains from its setting and its evocation of country life in the Borders, and characters such as the lawyer Pleydell, Dandie Dinmont and the wild old crone Meg Merrilies – a fated instrument of fate herself – give it life and charm. *The Antiquary*, more nearly contemporary, is Scott's best comedy of manners. It involves a melodrama – also about a lost heir – but the elaborations of this plot about unsung noble birth and its eventual discovery are the least important elements in a novel rich with sympathetic humour and charged with topographical, psychological and social details. As with many of Scott's novels, it is possible to trace originals for some of the more entertaining characters: Jonathon Oldbuck, the eccentrically enthusiastic 'antiquary', owes something to old George Constable, a friend from the author's boyhood, and Edie Ochiltree the travelling beggarman had a real counterpart too. These figures are not isolated creations, however, for they fit into a wider portrait of a small Scots coastal community of fishermen, modest gentlemen and landed aristocrats, and Scott drew on his own upbringing to show that the spirit of such a place belongs most enduringly with the common folk. They are the ones who transmit the tales and legends from old times; they meet poverty and bereavement with strength and dignity and their opinions, prejudices and sufferings are a sturdy yardstick against which we measure the unlikely Gothic entanglements of the better-born, or the enthusiasms and hobby-horses of the better-educated. Among his many novels it was Scott's own favourite.

While such figures as Edie Ochiltree are drawn with a generosity which rescues them from caricature, Scott is not, on the whole, a novelist who explores the psychological depths of motivation and introspection; nor do his characters evolve much or stray from their original casting in the course of his books. Yet, if he does not seek a directly analytical depth, he still achieves subtlety by the telling juxtaposition of events, scenes and characters. When the Earl of Glenallan, for example, has to face error, cruelty and shame in his own past, he hears of it in a fisherman's cottage from the mouth of old Elspeth, a singer of ballads and one time lady's maid to his mother. She spins a complicated tale of hatred, intrigue, suicide and a posthumous baby heir since lost. Glenallan is plunged into frozen gloom. By direct and deliberate contrast, the fisher family has just lost its eldest boy to the sea, and old Saunders Mucklebackit, stiff and grim with grief, stands on the beach repairing the shattered boat that drowned his son – even as Glenalmond hears how his own mother arranged to kill the baby daughter he never knew he had. The sentimental Gothicism of these tangled webs is highly contrived, to say the least, but Scott manages it by having it told by a storyteller who is herself implicated in guilt and half-crazed with age, and it is distanced again by comparison with the silent, clumsy pain of Saunders as he fumbles blindly with his repairs:

> 'And what would ye have me to do,' answered the fisher gruffly, 'unless I wanted to see four children starve, because ane is drowned? It's weel wi' you gentles, that can sit in the house wi' handkerchers at your een when ye lose a friend; but the like o' us maun to our wark again, if our hearts were beating as hard as my hammer.'

Scott has a dramatist's grasp of how to use such juxtapositions to sustain powerful effects in pathos and in comedy too, and he may well have learned it from his early love of Shakespeare. Indeed, Edie Ochiltree, the garrulous and dignified old beggar who links the various strands of the plot together, is a truly Shakespearean creation. Licensed by his age and humble station, he moves between cottage and manor like some unlikely, interfering Prospero whose native wit, tricks and compassion are all mobilised to help the other characters, and the author himself, to achieve a proper resolution:

> '. . . what wad a' the country about do for want o' auld Edie Ochiltree, that brings news and country cracks fae ae farm-steading to anither, and gingerbread to the lasses, and helps the lads to mend their fiddles, and the gudewives to clout their pans, and plaits rush-swords and grenadier caps for the weans, and busks [dresses] the laird's flees [fishing flies], and has skill o' cow-ills and horse-ills, and kens mair auld sangs and tales than a'

the barony besides, and gars ilka body laugh wherever he comes? Troth, my leddy, I canna lay down my vocation; it would be a public loss.'

The final factor in Scott's realisation of comedy and drama is to be found in his selective use of the spoken vernacular. This sinewy and lively idiom (never too dense for the average reader) varies the narrative and illuminates character and society with such impact that the author hardly needs to comment more. For thousands of delighted readers, it was Scott rather than Wordsworth who revealed the democracy of plain values and common sense among humble folk, and reaffirmed, not least in Scotland itself, a sense of native character with all its strengths and its terrible blind spots too.

For the theme of *Old Mortality* (1816) Scott returned to civil strife, this time between Cavalier and Covenanter in the late seventeenth century. The novel, from the 'Tales of my Landlord' series, is a much plainer and grimmer work than *The Antiquary* and it was Scott's first attempt to re-create an historical past quite beyond living memory and his own boyhood roots. True to his muse, he seizes on the voices and features of the commons to measure his vision of the divided times, so that it is the old widow Mause Headrigg, expelled from her house and out on the hillside with the open-air conventicles, who speaks for the pride of ordinary folk, keeping to the harsher demands of their faith despite all consequences. Her son Cuddie is less convinced, however, and his hopes for a comfortable life are constantly and comically frustrated by his mother's insatiable need to testify, at the drop of a Bible, against 'popery, prelacy, antinomianism, erastianism, lapsarianism, sublapsarianism, and the sins and snares of the times'. 'Hout tout, mither', he complains as he drags her away from yet another confrontation, 'ye preached us out o' our canny free house and gude kale-yard . . . sae ye may haud sae for ae wee while, without preaching me up a ladder and down a tow.' We enjoy the exchange and yet in this novel it is likely that Scott's tendency to equate passionate principles with comic or grotesque characters goes some way towards defusing and disguising the fundamental divisions which caused so much unhappiness in seventeenth-century Scotland.

Old Mortality works well enough as a warning against extremism, or as an adventure among the Covenanters, but, despite Scott's researches in the writing of it, its historical and philosophical insight is very limited. Undoubtedly he intended to make a case for moderate Presbyterianism, for his hero Henry Morton comes from dissenting stock and when circumstances make him a leader in the Covenanters' camp he stands by the cause, even when his sympathies are divided because his sweetheart, Edith Bellenden, and some of his friends are Royalists from old families. He retains his humanity and disowns the men of perpetual violence, such as the daemonic Balfour of Burley, one of the murderers of the archbishop of St Andrew's. Yet Morton remains unconvincing because he never expresses intellectual conviction about his religious or political principles, and Scott surrounds him instead with a host of wild and curious figures with such names as Habakkuk Mucklewrath – a fanatical madman – or Poundtext, Kettledrummle and Macbriar, all of whom are satirical figures who expatiate on their cause in endlessly pedantic or comic fashion. Like Waverley before him, Morton is pardoned for his beliefs and reconciled with conventional authority in the end. He marries Edith Bellenden and the book ends happily, even if the more truly revolutionary issues of these times were never to be so easily reconciled or dismissed.

Scott's next novel, *Rob Roy*, published in December 1817, returned to the Highlands. It is not particularly well constructed but Scott compensated by creating some memorable characters, most especially Baillie Nicol Jarvie, that most pragmatic of Glasgow traders, who within a year became the star of a stage-adaptation which was packing theatres in Edinburgh and Glasgow. Six months after *Rob Roy*, despite severe stomach pains from gallstones, Scott completed the book which many critics hold to be best of all his novels.

The Heart of Midlothian (1818) is set in the Edinburgh of 1736, the year of the Porteous riots, and its central theme is the moral and physical journey which Jeanie Deans undertakes to save her pretty young half-sister from the death penalty. Eighteen-year-old Effie is accused of murdering her illegitimate baby – it has, indeed, disappeared – and in the absence of an infant body the complicated case against her depends on the fact that she kept her pregnancy secret from everyone because her lover, implicated in the killing of Captain Porteous, has had to flee and leave her unsupported. She does not know it, but she is innocent of the child's death, for it was stolen away from her while she was in a fever. Even so, she would probably be acquitted if only her sister Jeanie would testify that she had told her she was pregnant, for this is the key point in a law intended to stop heartless infanticides. But Jeanie, the daughter of 'Douce David Deans', a stern and moral old Covenanter, cannot tell a saving lie, despite the agony it brings to them all. It is a classical conflict between two kinds of good – the inviolable nature of truth as opposed to family love and natural justice. In this case stern Kirk morality and the unshakable strictness of the letter of the law are shown to be equally absolute and inescapable imperatives – a very Scottish pairing. The truth prevails and Effie is condemned to death. Jeanie sets out on an epic walk to London and has to experience several adventures and setbacks along the way before she succeeds in winning clemency for her sister at the court of Queen Caroline.

Jeanie Deans is quintessentially Scottish but there is no trace of the colourful 'Scotch character' about her, and at last Scott has created a positive hero, central to the novel, who makes things happen and takes responsibility firmly into her own hands. Indeed, Jeanie and her father embody the Presbyterian strengths and the moral seriousness which Scott had failed to evoke in Henry Morton and the Covenanters of *Old Mortality*. The central debate between law and conscience is pursued and renewed at many levels, not least in setting it against the Porteous riots and the Tolbooth prison – the so-called 'Heart of Midlothian' itself. The issues are discussed again at a comic level in the inspired gobbledegook of Bartoline Saddletree, a harness-maker with legal pretensions, while the novelist's talent for wild and touching scenes creates Madge Wildfire, a demented creature who dies singing 'Proud Maisie' and acts as an instrument of fate in the same mould as old Elspeth or Meg Merrilies. Madge too is caught up in the theme of guilt and compassion, for the poor creature is accused of witchcraft and subjected to the 'justice' of a mob near Carlisle.

Scott continues the tale of Effie and her lover beyond the more obvious conclusion which would seem to have arrived with her pardon. The unhappy pair are eventually reunited and return to high society as 'Sir George and Lady Staunton'. Sir George meets a violent end at the hands of a wilful young bandit whom he comes upon by accident in the Highlands, without ever knowing that he is Effie's lost child and the son he has, himself, so long sought. This latter part of the book is often criticised for slipping into melodrama and it is usually accepted that Scott was under pressure to make the novel long enough for four volumes. This is not the whole story, however, for the conclusion does try to continue the unifying theme of guilt, mercy and justice, a topic which Scott pursues far more consistently in this book than any other theme in his other novels. He was not often so single-minded and was given to dismissing the extent of his labours and the importance of unity in them. 'I am sensible', he wrote in his journal, 'that if there be anything good about my poetry or my prose either, it is a hurried frankness of composition, which pleases soldiers, sailors and young people of bold and active dispositions.' Beneath his bluff disclaimers he was genuinely clear-sighted about the strengths and weaknesses of his art. He could make complicated plans for the structure and evolution of his novels, but characters and incidents seemed to lead him astray of their own accord:

> When I light on such a character as Bailie Jarvie, or Dalgetty, my imagination brightens, and my conception becomes clearer at every step which I make in his company, although it leads me many a weary mile away from the regular road, and forces me to leap hedge and ditch to get back into the route again. If I resist the temptation, as you advise me, my thoughts become prosy, flat, and dull; I write painfully to myself, and under a consciousness of flagging which makes me flag still more; the sunshine with which fancy had invested the incidents, departs from them, and leaves everything dull and gloomy. I am no more the same author, than the dog in a wheel, condemned to go round and round for hours, is like the same dog merrily chasing his own tail, and gambolling in all the frolic of unrestrained freedom.
>
> (Introductory Epistle, *The Fortunes of Nigel*)

Scott was to provide plenty more sunshine in his novels, but the image of that dog condemned to toil for hours was to become all too grimly apposite of his later creative life. In the meantime he continued to be extraordinarily productive and, despite a severe illness which only slowly retreated, he turned out two and sometimes three multi-volume novels a year. The manuscripts show virtually no signs of revision or hesitation, and in 1819 the most part of *The Legend of Montrose*, *The Bride of Lammermoor* and *Ivanhoe* were actually dictated during convalescence. Thus he managed, once more, to pay various debts and bonds, even if the expenses of Abbotsford more than kept pace with his considerable earnings. He wrote essays and reviews and took part in the launching of *Blackwood's*, through which he made friends with John Wilson and John Gibson Lockhart, his future biographer and son-in-law. He was made a baronet in 1818 and his place in established society was confirmed when he was asked to organise King George IV's visit to Scotland in 1822. Still Scott poured out books – 'let us stick to him', wrote Constable's partner, 'let us dig on and dig on at that extraordinary quarry'. For southern readers *Ivanhoe* (1819) was the greatest success yet, and although its history is faulty it opened a whole new seam of picturesque romance in a 'medieval' English setting. *The Monastery* and *The Abbot* (both 1820) returned to sixteenth-century Scotland, while *The Pirate* (1821) drew on earlier visits to the Shetlands, and *Kenilworth*, from the same year, took readers to the English court of Queen Elizabeth. Scott's daughter Sophia had married Lockhart in 1820, and, when young Walter married five years later, his father made a will which settled the whole of Abbotsford on his favourite son and his bride. These were happy and varied years for 'the Great Unknown', now in his fifties and recovering something of his former strength. He had become the most celebrated writer in Britain and a famously generous host at Abbotsford, where he entertained guests in a setting which brought Gothic interiors together with the most modern of gadgets, including pneumatic bells and gas lighting.

The Fortunes of Nigel (1822) was followed a year later by *Peveril of the Peak*, *Quentin Durward*, set in fifteenth-century France, and *St Ronan's Well*. Jacobite themes returned with *Redgauntlet* (1824) – a fine novel made even more memorable by 'Wandering Willie's Tale', a *tour de force* of the supernatural told in broad Scots and often published as if it were a separate short story. The Middle Ages featured once again in lesser novels called *The Betrothed* and *The Talisman* (1825), and Scott also began a lengthy nine-volume *Life of Napoleon Bonaparte* not published until 1827. Despite his industry, however, his financial affairs were finally and disastrously overextended. For years now, Constable the publisher, Ballantyne the printer and Scott, that 'extraordinary quarry', had erected an ever-more-complex tower of mutually supportive credit and bills of exchange. In the meantime Constable's London agent had been speculating on the volatile money-market of the day, and when he was finally swept away the financial backwash brought down the Edinburgh partners as well. Scott was faced with private debts of £30,000 and a further call for over £96,000 owed through Ballantyne, Constable and various other parties. Not even his closest friends knew of his financial involvement with these businesses, and so the news of his ruin at the beginning of 1826 fell on Edinburgh, in Cockburn's words, like a thunderbolt: 'if an earthquake had swallowed half the town, it would not have produced greater astonishment, sorrow and dismay. . . . How humbled we felt when we saw him – the pride of us all, dashed from his honourable and lofty station, and all the fruits of his well-worked talents gone.' Even so, Scott refused to accept bankruptcy, just as he resisted various subscriptions which were proposed to help him. A trust was formed for his creditors, he took lodgings and sold his Edinburgh house, but was allowed to live at Abbotsford rent-free, despite the fact that he had only recently mortgaged the estate for a further £10,000 in a futile attempt to help Constable just before the crash.

So Scott, bound by his sense of honour in the matter, set about the massive task of clearing his debts by the further labours of his pen. At first his spirits were stimulated by the immediate controversy which surrounded his *Letters of Malachi Malagrowther* (1826), a lively pamphlet in opposition to the government's plan to do away with the distinctive paper currency of the Scottish banks. Such emblems of national identity were important to him, and he felt equally strongly about threats to the unique character of Scots law, just as he had revered the old Scottish regalia when they were discovered in 1818. The Malagrowther letters carried the day, but Scott was becoming increasingly isolated. The splendid years were over and the establishment at Abbotsford much reduced. Lady Scott died in the early summer of 1826, leaving her husband shaken with grief and melancholy. He had just begun a private journal and this intimate work provides a unique record of his last years. Bothered with rheumatism and palpitations of the heart, he seemed almost to welcome the routine of endless writing. He completed *Woodstock* in 1826 and the next year produced his *Life of Napoleon*, a set of short novels called 'Chronicles of the Canongate', and the first series of *Tales of a*

Grandfather – a retelling of Scottish history for children, written for his frail grandson, who had only four more years to live. Three further volumes in this series appeared between 1828 and 1830, along with *The Fair Maid of Perth* (another of the 'Chronicles'), and what he called his 'Opus Magnum', a complete new edition of the Waverley novels furnished with introductions and notes. After *Anne of Geierstein* (1829) a serious stroke finally broke his strength. He retired as clerk of the Court of Session, but refused to give up writing, although he was sorely extended by his *Letters on Demonology and Witchcraft* (1830), and two further short novels (*Count Robert* and *Castle Dangerous* from 1831) show only a failing hand. His all-too-limited energies were further expended by more Malachi letters against the various Reform Bills which were dividing parliament and country in those years. The redistribution of political seats and the extension of franchise were long overdue, but Scott could only see anarchy and an end to the values he loved, and even his more conservative friends thought his views were intemperate. They persuaded him to burn the Malachi manuscript, but they could not stop him from speaking for the Tory candidate at an election in Jedburgh, where he was shouted down and his carriage stoned.

By now Scott was markedly frail and prematurely old. Ironically, perhaps, it was a Whig government which helped the novelist to escape from a Scottish winter, by arranging for a frigate to take him to Malta and Naples. He saw the sights and struggled with another novel, to be called *The Siege of Malta*, as if the old dog could not give up the wheel to which he had been bound so long. But his mind was fading and his main anxiety was to reach Abbotsford before the end. Another stroke threw him into a coma, but he gained a few days of clarity by Tweedside in the early autumn, before dying at the age of sixty-one on 21 September 1832. He is buried among cloisters in the ruins of Dryburgh Abbey.

The 'wizard of the North' was one of the best-loved and most famous writers in Europe and America – a figure along with Goethe and Byron who dominated the literary scene of his day, moving and influencing thousands of readers and dozens of writers who were to be famous in their turn. Yet the years to come belong to Dickens, Balzac, Flaubert, Tolstoy or Dostoevsky, for Scott strikes an older balance between the robust and rational world of the Enlightenment and a Romantic love for the fabric of Scotland and her people. Conservative, nationalistic, antiquarian, sentimental and yet down to earth, his spirit, and the contradictions within it, belongs to the Edinburgh of the late eighteenth century – divided as always between a United Kingdom and the call of an 'auld sang'.

Scott's own life became part of the song too, largely owing to Lockhart's massive biography (1837–8), a long and entertaining study which made full use of his journals and thousands of letters, thus earning a place in all subsequent studies despite an account of Hogg which was coloured by personal dislike. Educated at Glasgow and Oxford, **John Gibson Lockhart** (1794–1854) was another of those advocates who took to literature in Edinburgh. He wrote a somewhat genteel life of Burns in 1828 and so the book on Scott was not his first biography. After the scandal of the 'Chaldee Manuscript' in his youth, *Peter's Letters to his Kinsfolk* (1819) was a much more illuminating, although still scathing, series of sketches on the intelligentsia and Scottish manners. Lockhart's contributions to 'Maga' included many poems, and in the early 1820s he began writing novels. *Valerius* and *Reginald Dalton* have less to commend them than *Adam Blair* (1822) and *Matthew Wald* (1824), which manage to hint at darker psychological tensions in northern society. Adam Blair is a Presbyterian minister who eventually makes love to a married cousin, a girl who enters his life after his wife's death. Blair is tormented by what they never doubt to be a sin, most especially against the cloth, and he can find peace again only through public atonement and long suffering. *Matthew Wald* is a less satisfactory novel, but a similar involvement with crime and the Presbyterian conscience reminds us that Hogg's *Justified Sinner* was not the only book to explore this aspect of the country's psyche. Lockhart's early success with *Blackwood's* in Edinburgh was followed by his editorship of the Tory *Quarterly Review*, a post he held in London from 1825 until the year before his death.

The best of the women novelists whose works appeared during Scott's reign is **Susan Ferrier** (1782–1854), who looks to the novel of manners in the vein of Jane Austen or Maria Edgeworth. Earlier writers such as Anne Grant and Elizabeth Hamilton brought social life in the Highlands to the public eye, and **Mary Brunton** (1778–1818) chose the same setting for her second novel, *Discipline* (1814). These writers intended to instruct and 'improve' their readers, and Susan Ferrier shares something of this aim – her last work was called *Destiny* (1831), and it too was set in the north with a Highland heroine. Nevertheless she writes with more humour and penetration than her predecessors. Her themes were established from the first in *Marriage* (1818), probably her best novel, in which social observation and comedy are used to explore the condition of young women in contemporary society. In her books (*The Inheritance* followed in 1824) she sets the fashionable world of London or Bath against the provincial life of Scotland, where her heroines find the virtues of peace, piety and common sense, even if the accents and the behaviour of the Scots – well caught in her prose – are finally judged to be uncultivated. After *Destiny* she wrote no more novels and in later years her religious convictions led her to disapprove of her early work. No such polite qualms ever occurred to James Hogg, her fellow *Blackwood's* writer, whose roots were inextricably bound to the vernacular tradition.

James Hogg (1770–1835)

When Hogg's father's sheep-farm failed, his seven-year-old son was obliged to leave school and go to work. As a shepherd in his teens the boy taught himself to play the fiddle and laboured to develop his rudimentary grasp of reading and writing. One employer, a Mr Laidlaw of Blackhouse, gave Hogg access to his library, and the shepherd stayed with him for ten years, befriending his son William, who was later to be steward of Scott's estate at Abbotsford. At the age of twenty-seven, 'ravished', as he put it, by 'Tam o' Shanter', Hogg resolved to be a poet like Burns, and before long his 'Donald MacDonald', a war song against Napoleon, became well known throughout the country. His *Scottish Pastorals* appeared in 1801 – a small collection of songs and poems in the style of Ramsay's *Gentle Shepherd* – 'sad stuff, although I judged them to be exceedingly good'. In 1802 Scott's *Border Minstrelsy* inspired Hogg to set old tales into rhyme, and his friend William Laidlaw was instrumental in introducing Hogg's mother to Scott as a source of further traditional material. The 'Ettrick Shepherd' and the Sheriff of Selkirkshire became friends.

Hogg was never to be a successful farmer, and when a plan to run sheep on Harris came to nothing he lost his savings and had to turn again to shepherding in the Borders. His ballad-imitations were published as *The Mountain Bard* (1807), prefaced by a romantic account of his humble origins, but a treatise on the diseases of sheep proved more profitable. By 1810 he was finally out of work and came to Edinburgh to try his luck as a writer. Constable was persuaded to publish *The Forest Minstrel* (1810), an unsuccessful anthology – 'but the worst of them are all mine', as Hogg reflected later. He started a weekly paper called the *Spy*, mostly written by himself, which lasted for a year before closing. Disappointed at his inability to emulate Burns's success, Hogg used the last issue of his paper to publish a 'Memoir of the Author's Life' which deliberately encouraged the popular image of the 'Ettrick Shepherd' as some illiterate native genius who 'ran away from his master' to seek his fortune in the arts. He lived to regret this role, but for the moment he was at the mercy of his insecurity, and his responses to the educated society which he longed to join could be naïve, vain or aggressive by turns.

The popularity of Scott's narrative verse was at its height and Hogg determined to try a long poem in the same style, choosing a framework which allowed him to offer several different poems as 'recited' by bards in a competition before Mary Queen of Scots. *The Queen's Wake* finally appeared in 1813 and it was successful enough for Blackwood to take it onto his lists. Two of the best and most popular 'songs' were 'The Witch of Fife' a Scots ballad full of grotesque misadventures, somewhat in the spirit of 'The Gyre-Carling'; and 'Kilmeny', a supernatural lay in antique Scots, later anglified. Both poems are enlivened by Hogg's familiarity with folk tales and the uncanny, but 'Kilmeny' makes something more original and disturbing out of its account of how a young virgin is spirited away, perhaps to Heaven, by the fairies and given an allegorical vision of the future. Hogg's unsophisticated taste adds a chaste eroticism and a spiritual idealism to the bare bones of the ballad, and the result, with echoes from Ramsay's 'The Vision', is prophetic of the mystical other realms in George MacDonald's books

'O, bonny Kilmeny! free frae stain,
If ever you seek the world again,
That world of sin, or sorrow and fear,
O, tell of the joys that are waiting here;
And tell of the signs you shall shortly see;
Of the times that are now and the times that shall be.'

They lifted Kilmeny, they led her away,
And she walked in the light of a sunless day:
The sky was a dome of crystal bright,
The fountain of vision, and fountain of light:
The emerald fields were of dazzling glow,
And the flowers of everlasting blow.
Then deep in the stream her body they laid,
That her youth and beauty never might fade;
And they smiled on heaven, when they saw her lie
In the stream of life that wandered bye.

The narrative links in *The Queen's Wake* are weak, and Hogg was satisfied in later years to acknowledge Scott's supremacy in 'the school o' chivalry'. But he would not relinquish his own claim to be 'the king o' the mountain an' fairy school', and his poem 'Superstition' (1814) testifies to the impact of folk lore on his young imagination.

At last the poet had 'arrived', and the Duke of Buccleuch was so impressed that he gave Hogg Altrive Lake Farm, rent-free for the rest of his life. He was introduced to Wordsworth in Edinburgh and toured with him in the Borders before visiting Rydal Mount to join John Wilson, and De Quincey too. The little gathering was not without its tricky moments, as Hogg later recalled in typical style. The party was viewing a meteor in the night sky when Hogg ventured a pretty remark to Dorothy:

'Hout, me'm! it is neither mair nor less than joost a treeumphal airch, raised in honour of the meeting of the poets.'
   'That's not amiss. – Eh? Eh – that's very good', said the Professor [Wilson], laughing. But Wordsworth, who had De Quincey's arm, gave a grunt and turned on his heel, and leading the little opium-chewer aside, he addressed him in these disdainful and venomous words: – 'Poets? Poets? – What does the fellow mean? – Where are they?'

Hogg produced further long poems in English over the next two years, but they offered only derivative romance or contrived philosophising. *The Poetic Mirror*, however (1816), did show his considerable talent for imitating his famous contemporaries, including Scott, Byron, Coleridge and – sweet revenge – Wordsworth, whom he hilariously parodied.

These volumes had a mixed reception, but the 'Ettrick Shepherd' was established as a kenspeckle figure, even if it is difficult not to suspect a certain condescension among his friends when they refer to their 'good honest shepherd' and his 'quaint originality of manners'. The *Blackwood's* connection encouraged Hogg to return to prose with essays and tales for this and other periodicals. He needed the money, for his verse was flagging and *Dramatic Tales* (1817) for the stage had been a failure. Accordingly *The Brownie of Bodsbeck* appeared in 1818, a rather long-winded novel, yet a book which touches the tap-roots of Hogg's imagination by linking folk superstitions with tales of the Covenanters. As a stout Presbyterian, brought up on the sufferings of the just under 'bloody Clavers', Hogg was bound to differ from Scott's more gentlemanly preferences in *Old Mortality*. The Shepherd claimed that his manuscript predated Scott's novel (published at the end of 1816) and defended it against the great man's displeasure. Hogg was no liberal – 'the great majority o' shepherds are Conservatives', according to his *alter ego* in 'Noctes', 'no to be ta'en in by the nostrums o' every reformer'. But on the issue of religion, his sympathies belonged with the common people and the folk-history of their persecution by the establishment – a theme he was to return to in later stories such as 'The Edinburgh Baillie', 'A Tale of Pentland' and 'A Tale of the Martyrs'. *The Brownie of Bodsbeck* is set after the Battle of Bothwell Brig, telling how a shepherd is arrested for secretly helping Covenanters to escape from Claverhouse, and how his daughter, suspected of conniving with evil spirits, is denounced by the local curate, who has his own designs upon her. Even the father himself comes to fear that his Katherine is in league with the shambling 'Brownie' before it is revealed that the 'spirit' is really an injured Covenanter and that the odd happenings have been owing to her tending the wounded at night. Yet Hogg's evocation of the uncanny has been so successful that the possibility of magic survives his realistic 'explanation'. He was to use this double vision again.

Hogg married in 1820 and took a nearby farm at Mount Benger for nine years until the lease expired and his finances failed again. In the meantime he edited collections of his own and other stories and worked on his most ambitious novel yet, *The Three Perils of Man: War, Women and Witchcraft* (1822). The subtitle does indeed set the main topics for this ramshackle, picaresque book, mobilising allegory, fantasy, historical romance, coarse comedy and mock epic in a series of adventures in which knights and border reivers rub shoulders and tangle with wizards, magic and old-fashioned skulduggery. It includes a set of tales told by characters within the tale – each in an appropriate style – and it is all set against Robert II's determination to besiege the English in Roxburgh castle in the fourteenth century. The book is lively, savage and longwinded by turns, and its anachronistic history owes more to ballads and the oral tradition than to any notion of scholarship. Pressed by Scott to try for 'a little more refinement, care and patience' in his work, Hogg admitted that he was inclined to let his imagination sail on 'without star or compass'. The *Blackwood's* circle did not appreciate the wild vigour of his inspiration, and in the face of such gentility, Hogg's next book, *The Three Perils of Women, or Love, Leasing and Jealousy* (1823), rashly attempted the novel of manners and emotional entanglement. Written 'as if in desperation', it was roundly condemned by the critics – not least by Christopher North, whose 'Noctes Ambrosianae' had just begun to fix Hogg in the role of an aboriginal worthy, to the delight of thousands of *Blackwood's* readers. There is a telling irony in the fact that a man on the point of writing one of European literature's earliest masterpieces of the divided psyche should have been so caught up in the doings and sayings of 'the Shepherd', or 'the Caledonian Boar' – his own familiar, vulgar and profitable *Doppelganger*. The tensions in Scottish cultural identity, already felt by Ramsay and Scott, were about to take a stranger, darker twist.

The Private Memoirs and Confessions of a Justified Sinner (1824) was published anonymously because its author was particularly concerned that his identity be kept from his friends at the 'Maga'. He need scarcely have worried, for it made very little critical impact and the *Westminster Review* took him to task for 'uselessly and disgustingly abusing his imagination'. Yet it is a novel of extraordinary force, economically written and darkly modern in its psychological insights, so that some critics, more familiar with the 'Noctes', perhaps, have wondered whether

Hogg actually wrote it at all, as if the Shepherd were suddenly revealed as a Raskolnikov. Yet the book contains so many thematic and stylistic elements already used in Hogg's earlier work – however imperfectly – that his authorship is not in serious doubt, even if it does stem from the tradition of Hoffmann or from Lockhart's novels of religious anguish. Louis Simpson has also noted a possible documentary seed in the real confessions of a religious-minded murderer called Nicol Muschet, which were published in Edinburgh in 1818.

The *Justified Sinner* is told in three parts: the 'editor's' narrative; the sinner's confession; and finally a brief account of how the editor and his friends had a hand in recovering the middle part of the tale from the sinner's grave. The book opens as a story of rival brothers in the early eighteenth century. Their parents are mismatched, for the father is an easy-going sensualist and his wife is a narrow-minded Presbyterian, much under the influence of the Revd Robert Wringhim, a fanatically Calvinist minister. The elder son is called George Colwan, but his father disowns the younger boy, Robert, because he suspects him to be the natural son of Wringhim. Cut off from his inheritance, Robert is brought up by the minister and even baptised as a Wringhim. He is more intelligent and intense than George, whom he hardly ever sees, but his mother and the minister educate him to hate his father and his brother, and they fill him with extreme antinomian doctrines. This creed takes Calvinist predestination a step further by arguing that, since good works and faith alone are not enough to get to Heaven (for that would be like purchasing salvation), then good works may not even be *necessary* for the 'justified' – like Burns's Holy Willie – who are already chosen for heaven. Still more startling is the possibility that sins committed by the justified may not be sins at all, but merely a part of God's higher plan.

Fired by a mission to chastise the unbelievers, young Robert begins to haunt his brother like a dark counterpart to George's cheerful, generous and athletic nature –a political counterpart too, for, whereas Wringhim looks to the Covenanters, old Colwan is a Tory MP given to sentiments in favour of the Cavaliers. The turning-point between the two brothers comes early one morning on the hill known as Arthur's Seat which overlooks Edinburgh. George has gone for a walk on the cliffs and is admiring the brilliant morning when a huge threatening shadow appears in the mist. He turns away in panic only to stumble into Robert, who is right behind him, and George strikes him in the ensuing confusion. Robert soon recovers his usual disdainful composure and prosecutes George for attempted fratricide, but he loses the case when his habit of following George everywhere is revealed in court. George goes off to celebrate with his boisterous friends, but quarrels with a Highlander called Drummond, and is found stabbed later that night. Drummond flees. The bad news kills George's father and Robert inherits everything. The first half of the novel ends when eyewitnesses to George's death are tracked down and persuaded to tell how it was Robert who stabbed him in the back while his brother was duelling with another figure, who only resembled Drummond. The Highlander's name is cleared, but now Robert cannot be found.

The second part of the novel is Robert's 'confession', recovered from his grave, in which the events already described are told all over again to show him in a noble and righteous light. The unbalanced intensity of this narrative inspires the novel and draws the reader into another world, utterly alien to the comfortable and shallow assumptions of young bloods such as George and his companions. We discover that Robert has a friend and religious mentor called Gil-Martin – a 'brother' in the revealed truth – who haunts him just as he himself has pursued George. Gil-Martin instructs him in godly doctrine at every step and it is he who encourages and aids Robert in seeking justified vengeance on sinners and on George in particular. The reader soon suspects that Gil-Martin is the Devil. On the other hand, Robert's state seems strangely alienated, and in a fit of illness he feels himself to be two people, Gil-Martin and his brother, between whom he has somehow lost himself. The extreme subjectivity of Robert's tale would certainly suggest that he is deluded, except that Hogg produces independent witnesses to testify to Gil-Martin's actual physical presence at crucial times. Robert may profit through his shadowy companion, but his mental state deteriorates. He conceives a mortal fear of Gil-Martin, until, alcoholic, amnesiac and still raving in his belief that he is one of the elect, he publishes his confession as a moral pamphlet and ends it with a promise to take his own life.

The novel concludes with how the editor tracked down the author's grave from an essay published in *Blackwood's* in which James Hogg (no less) had given an account of an unknown suicide and strange events associated with his burial site in the country. The editorial party seeks the aid of the Shepherd himself, but he proves unhelpful and too busy to 'houk up hunder-year-auld banes'. It is left to the editor to exhume the text and to republish *The Private Memoirs and Confessions*. He explains it as an 'allegory', born out of 'dreaming or madness', in which the unfortunate author came to believe that he was his own fictional character. This is the final sophisticated twist to the novel's capacity to set tales within tales, as different narrators come up with different explanations for the same events.

Hogg's discovery of the mirror mazes of subjectivity takes him beyond these merely relative differences, however, and his use of 'the double' anticipated Dostoevsky's Golyadkin by more than twenty years to give dramatic and psychological depth to a study of obsession and madness. On the other hand, Gil-Martin's role as the Devil suggests an unearthly rather than a psychological explanation, and it is not easy to choose between them, for the book provides evidence for both points of view, allowing Hogg to reconcile his domestic realism with a penchant for the supernatural and the grotesque. This combination becomes especially potent given the Presbyterian Church's historical obsession with witchcraft and demonology and the paradox that puritanism has always been prone to imagining the personifications of temptation and evil. In this case the 'shadow' may throw light on the 'substance' of all such religious convictions based on fear. Yet there are no easy answers, for in the face of such mysteries George's complacent Tory rationality is almost as unattractive as Robert's fanaticism and both are bound together in a complicity of unhappiness. The novel can be called a moral and cultural allegory as well as a supernatural tale or a study of psychotic delusion, for it offers a searching analysis of the nature of the Scottish psyche as it engages with its own religious history, divided loyalties and lost inheritance. Hogg's book goes far deeper into such matters than the author of *Old Mortality* could comprehend. He was never to achieve its like again, however, and, as far as literary Edinburgh was concerned, he returned to his role as 'Maga's' favourite Shepherd.

When the poem *Queen Hynde* eventually appeared in 1825 it was found to be a lengthy failure and Hogg settled for tales and sketches, including the notable 'Brownie of the Black Haggs' (1829). He visited London for three months in 1832 and was a considerable social success while organising a collected edition to be called *Altrive Tales*, only one volume of which ever appeared. Two years later he produced essays on good manners and *The Familiar Anecdotes of Sir Walter Scott*, which Lockhart found so very offensive because Hogg dared to recall his old friend's undignified end, and remarked on Scott's 'too strong leaning to the old aristocracy of the county' – namely those families descended from 'old Border Barbarians'. 'In Wilson's hands the Shepherd will always be delightful', wrote Lockhart, putting the Chaldee manuscript and his old collaborator firmly behind him, 'but of the fellow himself I can scarcely express my contemptuous pity'. Undaunted by the quarrel, Hogg continued to select and revise his prose, and a three-volume collection of previously unpublished stories appeared as *Tales of the Wars of Montrose* in the spring of 1835. That November he died of a liver-disease at the age of sixty-five. The *Tales and Sketches of the Ettrick Shepherd* were published two years later, but Hogg had abridged the *Justified Sinner* to 'The Confessions of a Fanatic' and his greatest novel was not printed again until 1895, nor appreciated by literary critics until at least the 1920s. The French novelist André Gide set the book in a European perspective with an enthusiastic preface to the edition of 1947.

John Galt (1779–1839)

Although it was *Blackwood's Magazine* which serialised his early novels, John Galt did not seek out or belong to the Edinburgh milieu of Scott, Hogg and Ferrier. He was born in Irvine on the coast of Ayrshire and brought up in Greenock, the seaport to the west of Glasgow where his father was a shipmaster to the West Indies. Galt left for London when he was twenty-five, but by 1809 his business-plans in the capital had foundered and he took a two-year tour through the Mediterranean and the Near East, befriending the young Lord Byron along the way (and eventually publishing a biography of him in 1830). Back in London he wrote about his travels and produced a biography of Cardinal Wolsey and a volume of five tragedies. He turned to writing full-time after his marriage in 1813, and offered Constable a book looking back to an old-fashioned Scotland to be called *Annals of the Parish*. The publisher turned it down as too local and too Scottish, but the success of *Waverley* was soon to change such assumptions. Galt drew on his voyages again for a book of poems and an equally unsuccessful novel called *The Majolo* (1816), and he persevered with a variety of articles and projects, including text-books, further biographies and two more novels. But these were dull, hard years and critical success eluded him until he entered his forties and *Blackwood's* began to serialise *The Ayrshire Legatees* in 1820. Galt may have taken his pattern from Lockhart's *Peter's Letters to his Kinsfolk*, or from Smollett's *Humphrey Clinker*, for the work comprises a series of letters in which an Ayrshire family tell their friends at home all about their visit to London. The exchanges are full of topical details, and the Scots family – naïve and level-headed by turns – is used as an affectionately comic and ironic touchstone for the sophistication of London. This anonymous series proved very popular; William Blackwood made it a book in 1821 and asked Galt for more. The author sent him *Annals of the Parish* and this time it was published straightaway.

Galt did not consider these books to be true novels, preferring to call them sketches, observations or 'theoretical histories' which outlined the manners and the changes in provincial society, often through the voice of a single character. The *Annals* purports to be the chronicles of the country parish of Dalmailing from 1760 to 1810 as recorded in the Revd Micah Balwhidder's journal. Its companion volume *The Provost* (1822) reminisces about small-town politics and public events over the same period, all recounted in the revealingly opportunistic and blithely unself-conscious tones of Provost James Pawkie. ('Pawkie' in Scots means artful, with suggestions of country cunning.) These ironic 'autobiographies' owe their success to Galt's capacity for sympathy with his narrators, even while he uses their voices to cast indirect reflections on their own failings. 'What happened in my parish was but a type and index to the world', Balwhidder assures us serenely, and no doubt Galt's urban readers allowed themselves a smile at his parish-pump priorities:

> The Ann. Dom. 1763, was, in many a respect, a memorable year, both in public and in private. The king granted peace to the French, and Charlie Malcolm, that went to sea in the *Tobacco* trader, came home to see his mother.

Yet Galt has the eye of a social historian, and these amusing chronicles accumulate a host of minor but significant details in fashion, economics, manners and politics as the old ways of speaking and living gradually changed during the second half of the eighteenth century. Galt's intention was to chart the recent past just as Scott claimed to have done with *Waverley*, *Guy Mannering* and *The Antiquary*, and it can be argued that his diaristic approach allowed him to do a better job.

The autobiographical style suited Galt's strengths as a writer because it allowed him to use the distinctive rhythms of Lowland speech (in Scots or English) as his central narrative medium, with plenty of scope for broad Scots and proverbial expression. He uses a denser dialect than Scott allowed himself – amounting to a *tour de force* in the case of Lady Grippy in *The Entail* – and this oral flow, with its encapsulation of regional and national attitudes, lies at the ironic heart of Galt's understanding of how 'voice' reveals character, and how that 'local' voice can be used to make double-edged social comments on the wider world of his more sophisticated readers.

The Entail (1832) completes Galt's sequence of major Scottish books and it is closer to a conventional novel in that it abandons the autobiographical mask and follows the fortunes of a single family over three generations and a forty-year period. As a study of the ties of property, avarice and affection in the rise and fall of a self-made man, and in the legal disputes within the family after his death, *The Entail* has been seen as a forerunner in the line of Balzac, Dickens, Zola, Hardy and Galsworthy. It has a claim to be Galt's most powerful novel, if less fully realised than *Annals*; yet, while Scott, Byron, Coleridge and Jeffrey had all admired the Scottish series, there were also complaints about the latest book's 'sordidness' and its impenetrable dialect. It was not reprinted in the author's lifetime. Galt stepped up his output of fiction with four more novels using Scottish settings and three historical novels all within four years of 1822, but, not surprisingly, these works seem hastily written and were less successful than their precursors.

Ringan Gilhaize (1823), however, is notable as another imaginative autobiography, this time in a grim and tragic mode. It was written to vindicate the Covenanting spirit, 'hugely provoked', in Galt's words, by *Old Mortality* and by what he felt to be Scott's ridicule of the defenders of the Presbyterian Church and their sufferings over more than three generations. This time Galt immersed himself totally in the mind and voice of his narrator – full of long phrases, ringing with biblical rhythms and echoes, as he asserts, 'I have not taken up the avenging pen of history, and dipped it in the blood of martyrs, to record only my own particular woes and wrong.' There is no hint of comic or ironic distance in Ringan's savage experiences and in his ultimately successful quest to shoot Claverhouse down. Galt's achievement is to let that iron-hard, obsessive nature speak for itself, without apology and without entirely forfeiting the reader's sympathy. He was particularly proud of this technique of imaginative 'transfusion', but it was not fully understood by readers and the novel got little credit for a serious attempt to come to terms with some of the most painful themes in the Scottish inheritance.

Galt's success was on the wane and his best books were behind him. Between 1825 and 1829 he worked in Ontario as superintendent for the Canada Company, but his health was poor and problems with the board of directors led to resignation, bankruptcy, and a spell in debtors' prison in London. He continued to write, but a series of strokes in his mid fifties left him an invalid, and in 1834 he returned to Greenock, where he died five years later.

Perhaps the popularity of Galt's early Scottish novels obscured the subtleties of his approach to imaginative biography, and the importance of sympathy in the ironic distances which he established between author, 'narrator' and reader. His successors settled for much broader effects, almost exclusively in the vein of domestic comedy. The first step in this direction was taken by **David Macbeth Moir** (1798–1851), a friend and biographer of Galt's and a doctor in Musselburgh near Edinburgh. Moir contributed regularly to *Blackwood's* with both prose and poetry under the *nom de plume* of 'Delta', or Δ. His best-known book, *The Life of Mansie Wauch, Tailor of Dalkeith*, 'written by himself', began as a series for the magazine in 1824 and was published as a book four years later. These small-town 'memoirs' were dedicated to Galt, but they lack the older man's sense of perspective and social irony. The result is genre literature, and the pattern was set for the 'Kailyard' and a Victorian vogue in Scottish 'worthies'.

Sentimentalists and Spasmodics

By the 1850s nationalism had become a revolutionary force in Europe, but Lowland Scottish culture was to remain remarkably complacent for the rest of the century. Of course, the patriotic appeal of Scott's novels had always been romantic and conservative. On the other hand, Patrick Fraser Tytler's *History of Scotland* (1823–43) gave scholarly support to a popular understanding of how the nation had evolved and defended its frontiers, while the Disruption had done much the same for the old values of the Kirk, and movements such as the Association for the Vindication of Scottish Rights were formed to attack the centralisation of government around Westminster interests. Yet somehow these scholarly, religious and political stirrings never came together to achieve any truly effective cultural or political expression. With poetry in particular, the distinctively Scottish tradition seems to have completely lost its way.

Carolina Oliphant, Lady Nairne (1766–1845), disguised as 'Mrs Bogan of Bogan', had written and adapted many Scots songs for *The Scottish Minstrel* in the early 1820s. Her work is genteel and pastoral or suffused with the nostalgic parlour Jacobitism which Hugh Millar characterised as 'a sort of laughing gas' agreeably exciting to the feelings. 'Will ye no' come back again?', 'Caller Herrin'', 'The Hundred Pipers' and 'The Land o' the Leal' are still sung today. The various *Whistle-Binkie* anthologies from 1832 to 1890, subtitled 'A Collection of Songs for the Social Circle' have lasted less well (with the possible exception of 'Wee Willie Winkie') and the title has provided a generic label for all such milk-and-water vernacular verse, in a sentimental, complacent and utterly trivialised notion of what poetry might be. On the other hand, the only alternative seemed to be the sub-Miltonic rhetoric of epics such as *A Life-Drama*, which appeared in 1851. Its author, **Alexander Smith** (1830–67), a working-class lace-pattern-maker from Kilmarnock, was immediately hailed by the critics for the portentous ambition of his English verse, although he was accused of plagiarising from Tennyson after his second collection, *City Poems*, appeared in 1857. Smith also wrote essays and a novel, but he died young and neglected. His vein of extravagant Byronic expression had a certain vogue, however, even if it did keep dropping into flat and turgid lines. This was a failing shared by his English contemporaries, Philip Bailey and Sydney Dobell, so that they all came to be known as the 'Spasmodic school'.

The 'Spasmodics' were christened and parodied by **W. E. Aytoun** (1813–65), yet another Tory Edinburgh lawyer, son-in-law to John Wilson and a contributor to 'Maga'. Aytoun became professor of Rhetoric at Edinburgh in 1845, he supported the Scottish Rights Association and wrote solemn poems on national topics such as 'Edinburgh after Flodden' and 'The Execution of Montrose'. He is best remembered for humorous short stories and his satirical verse parodies. The mock-tragical *Firmilian* (1854) tells us enough about the Spasmodics to justify their oblivion, and the *Bon Gaultier Ballads* (1855), a collaboration with Theodore Martin, show a good critical ear at work, closer to burlesque than to any more pointed satire. There is one indisputably great writer of this period, however, who would have nothing to do with parody, rustic sentiment or the likes of Mansie Wauch, and he came from a small village in Dumfries whose name might have been invented on the pages of *Whistle-Binkie*.

Thomas Carlyle (1795–1881)

Born in Ecclefechan, about ten miles from the Border, Carlyle came from a strongly Presbyterian family, and this early theological discipline, along with his philosophical disposition and an intense romantic idealism combined to make him one of the most complicated and intransigent thinkers and cultural critics in Victorian Britain. Carlyle lived and worked in

London after the age of thirty-nine, yet his roots were deeply Scottish; he kept in touch with family and home through regular visits and correspondence, and before he died in February 1881 he declined a place in Westminster Abbey and asked that his body be returned to Ecclefechan in the plainest of coffins.

Carlyle's father was a stonemason–builder, a grim and taciturn man who was largely self-educated. He and his family belonged to the 'Burghers', a branch of the secession Church which had condemned the Church of Scotland for lax doctrine, and so his son grew up with a creed which stressed the power of preaching and solemn exposition, and the importance of individual acts of will and judgement in the face of eternity. Inevitably destined for the Church, Carlyle set off for Edinburgh University in 1809. He was excited by science and mathematics, but become disillusioned with university life just as his faith in the religious doctrine of his childhood began to falter, along with his health. He supported himself by working as a tutor and teacher – which he hated – and made abortive plans to study law. He learned German, undertook translations and reviews and corresponded with Goethe. The German Romantics made a deep impression on his idealistic, mandarin and uncouth temperament. Dyspeptic, sleepless and prone to depression, he seems to have undergone something of an existential crisis at this time – later described in *Sartor Resartus* as a sense of the 'Everlasting NO':

> To me the Universe was all void of Life, of Purpose, of Volition, even of Hostility: it was one huge, dead, immeasurable Steam-engine, rolling on, in its dead indifference, to grind me limb from limb.

He was not the only Victorian to be so haunted.

By the mid 1820s translations and his life of Schiller were gaining Carlyle a place in the world of letters, and he had met, and clumsily wooed, a doctor's daughter called Jane Welsh, a witty and beautiful middle-class girl who became his lifelong companion. Jane's *Letters and Memorials* (1883) provide a fascinating insight on their liaison. The couple married in 1826 and had two happy years in Edinburgh before financial constraints took them to remote Dumfriesshire. Their life was isolated at Craigenputtock and Jane had to cope with Carlyle's intense, restless and hypochondriac nature, which required absolute silence as he struggled with his thoughts, his journal and his highly-wrought prose style. Among the essays of this period, 'Signs of the Times', which appeared in the *Edinburgh Review* in 1829, launched a prophetic attack on the evils of Victorian materialism and the cool calculation inherent in Utilitarian ideas. In the 1830s Carlyle continued to develop a complex and transcendental analysis of his own relationship with the world in what was to be his first major work.

The extraordinary, nearly unreadable prose of *Sartor Resartus* was serialised in 1833, but it did not appear as a book until an American publisher took the risk in 1836, and it was a further two years before it was published in London. The title – literally, 'The Tailor Retailored' – refers to an elaborate disquisition on the philosophy of clothes, or of 'appearances', supposedly edited from the life and writings of 'Herr Teufels-dröckh' ('Devil's cast-off') a fictional German philosopher and mystic. 'Rightly viewed,' he tells us (in a sentence which sums up his creator's hopes for cultural criticism), 'no meanest object is insignificant; all objects are as windows, through which the philosophic eye looks into Infinitude itself.' The alter ego of Teufelsdröckh, and his peculiar brand of pedantic whimsy (as much a Scottish failing as a German one), allows Carlyle to air his transcendental views in an unashamedly prophetic style. Yet his account of the 'Everlasting NO' is conveyed with passionately autobiographical force. (His black depression was eventually dispelled by 'the Everlasting YEA', a dynamic, if unclear, revelation of hope in man's urge always to seek light in the beauty and mystery of the universe.)

The couple moved to London in 1834 and set up house in Chelsea. Carlyle wrote with difficulty, and his sentences are highly crafted and rugged at the same time, full of biblical echoes, repetitions, allusions and antitheses. At his best this method of address is bold, jagged and direct as he seeks to persuade the reader by the very passion of his own conviction, using tones of intimacy, irony or open scorn as he seeks to achieve rapport, agreement or downright surrender. Here is his lively defence of the transcendental, but it is not an argument in any sense of the word at all:

Thou wilt have no mystery or mysticism; wilt live in the daylight (rushlight?) of truth, and see the world and understand it? Nay, thou wilt laugh at all that believe in a mystery; to whom the universe is an oracle and temple, as well as a kitchen and cattle stall? *Armer Teufel!* Doth not thy cow calve, doth not thy bull gender? Nay, peradventure, doest not thou thyself gender? Explain me that, or do one of two things: retire into private places with thy foolish cackle; or, what were better, give it up and weep, not that the world is mean and disenchanted and prosaic, but that thou are vain and blind.

Is anything more wonderful than another, if you consider it maturely? I have seen no men rise from the dead; I have seen some thousands rise from nothing. I have not force to fly into the sun, but I have force to lift my hand, which is equally strange.

(*Early Life*, II, 1830)

And no Scottish Presbyterian Whig divine could be firmer than Carlyle in his praise of the humble labourer (such as his own father), or more convinced of the power of work as an existential act of faith: 'Whatsoever thy hand findeth to do, do it with thy whole might. Work while it is called Today; for Night cometh, wherein no man can work' (cf. Ecclesiastes 9: 10).

Carlyle's historical writing is haunted by that 'Night' – a poignant sense of the 'pastness' of the past – and a furious sympathy for the unsung plight of the common people who remain in the shadows while the same few aristocrats strut in the limelight of posterity's attention: figures such as 'Mary Stuart, a Beauty, but over light-headed; and Henry Darnley, a Booby who had fine legs'. Like his contemporary Macaulay, a fellow contributor to the *Edinburgh Review* and equally fierce in his opinions, Carlyle preferred what would now be called social history and he looked for moments of what he took to be evolutionary change in the spirit of the times. The Reformation was such a moment, when 'all Scotland is awakened to a second, higher life ... convulsed, fermenting, struggling to body itself forth anew'; or the turmoil in France, which threw new ideals and a new fanaticism into the world. For the writing of *The French Revolution* (1837) Carlyle's research drew on the memoirs of other men, but it is supremely his own imagination and his rhetorical use of the present tense which transforms his material to the atmospheric immediacy of an eye-witness account. 'History, after all, is the true Poetry', he had proposed in 1832. 'Reality, if rightly interpreted is grander than Fiction; nay, that even in the right interpretation of Reality and History does genuine Poetry consist'. Some critics were puzzled by the style of *The French Revolution*, but for most it established Carlyle as a major writer and historian, one of the most sought-after intellectual figures in London. As 'the sage of Chelsea', he became friends with J. S. Mill, Emerson, Browning, Arnold, Tennyson and Dickens. Mill called *The French Revolution* the 'truest of histories . . . not so much a history as an epic poem', and its author was pleased to concur.

With *Chartism* in 1839, and in *Past and Present* (1843), Carlyle once more brooded angrily on *laissez-faire* economics and the plight of the poor and the working classes; and showed bitter contempt, too, at the inadequacies of Reform, which could only tinker with a rotten system. Yet sympathy for the oppressed did not make Carlyle a democrat. He mistrusted the emancipated masses and, when he extolled new directions and a new humanity in the evolving spirit of the times, he looked for them to be manifested in 'heroic' individuals. These thoughts were taken further with *On Heroes and Hero Worship* (1841), which began as a set among his many public lectures. The 'forerunners of history', according to Carlyle, included Odin, Mahomet and Napoleon; and his Scottish bias appears in his choice of Burns and Rousseau and in his respect for the authority of Luther, Knox and Cromwell. Such heroes, like the Calvinist elect, were chosen above others to lead or to show the way.

As he grew older, however, Carlyle's bracing prophesies of needful transformation and turmoil gave way to fears of anarchy and led him to equate heroic authority with control as a bulwark against change. He spent the latter part of his life working on an exhaustive and sterile act of homage with a *History of Frederick the Great* (1858–65), and the gross insistence of such pieces as *The Nigger Question* (1853) caused controversy and offence by maintaining that slaves (in the spiritual as well as the literal sense) are deemed slaves by the 'Supreme Powers' and should remain so. The harsh prophetic urgency of his early voice had become strained, hysterical and intolerant of all but its own views. Like the pattern of the Reformation in his native land, it is as if Carlyle's philosophy moved from an iconoclastic striving of the highest spirit, to a death grip of the most rigid and gloomy sort.

Hugh Millar (1802–56)

Hugh Millar never aspired to Carlyle's stature, but he came from a similar background and was an influential figure, by precept and example, in his own right. Essayist, journalist and geologist, he embodies the independence and the didacticism of the Scottish dissenting tradition. A self-educated stonemason from Cromarty, near Inverness, he became a local journalist and entered the national lists with a pamphlet letter against Church patronage. On the strength of this he was brought to Edinburgh to edit the *Witness*, the newspaper which became the voice of the Free Church after the Disruption. Millar was a moderate in Free Kirk circles and played a worthy part in their concern to bring education, self-advancement and self-expression to the labouring classes. He and his newspaper roundly condemned the clearances in Sutherland, for example, and protested against landowners who would not allow the Free Kirk – with its radical overtones – to build on their land. Atheist John Maclean and the Independent Labour Party workers of the next century were to lay similar emphasis on the education of the working classes as the route to social justice, but Millar's sturdy Presbyterian respectability was never revolutionary. He opposed Chartism and the formation of unions as too violent a step for the times, even although his own lungs had been damaged by stone-workers' silicosis in his youth. In the end his health did collapse, and exhausted and depressed, he took his own life with a gun. Among his books, the succinct prose of *The Old Red Sandstone* (1841) is something of a geologist's classic, even if he did try to reconcile the biblical account of creation with his scientific observations in a later work called *Footprints of the Creator* (1849). *Scenes and Legends of the North of Scotland* (1835) and an autobiography called *My Schools and Schoolmasters* (1854) testify to the life of the times and his constant interest in the landscape around him. Carlyle commended Millar as a genial fire 'tempered down into peaceful radical heat' and described the natural stateliness of his prose as 'luminous, memorable, all wholesome, strong and breezy' – an image of the man himself that outlasted his poor end.

William Alexander (1826–94)

The Disruption was a major historical and personal event in the life of Millar and thousands like him in parishes throughout the country. It revived communal ideals and redefined, if only through opposition, the traditional centres of authority in village life balanced as they were between minister, schoolteacher and laird. The dialect novel *Johnny Gibb of Gushetneuk* (1871) describes just such a community. Its author, William Alexander, worked on farms in Aberdeenshire until an accident in his twenties cost him one of his legs and he turned to journalism as a career. He became editor of the *Aberdeen Free Press* and published his memoirs and the collection *Sketches of Life among my Ain Folk* (1875), both dedicated, like his novel, to preserving a record of the life, manners and speech in the countryside of his birth. Then, as now, he spoke to a potent sense of pride and regional identity in his North-East readers. Alexander uses formal English for passages of objective narrative and comment, and this tends to distance him from his creation, but the true life of the novel comes from the density of its dialect speech – a repository of wit, scorn, gossip and common wisdom. This oral inheritance is the social and moral focus of the book – weighty, considered and drily alert to pretension, it is the voice by which a community knows and guides itself.

Alexander's tendency to explain his characters at every turn was part of his documentary intention, for he was looking back some thirty years and his little community already seems frozen in time. Of course, change did not come quickly to the remoter parts of Scotland, and, even when it did, few writers seemed able to manage more than nostalgia at the prospect. This was particularly evident in the Highlands, where continuing and considerable changes failed to produce literature that was equal to the occasion, although some poets did manage political commitment and a fine rage in their verse. Perhaps new forms were needed to respond to the times, and most Gaelic poets were still loyal to the old communities and the old ways of looking at the world.

Gaelic literature

In search of opportunity, faced with rising rents, or simply
cleared off their lands, thousands of Highlanders set sail for
America in the opening years of the century. The oral treasury
of Gaelic verse, music and tale-telling went with them and the
old propensity for elegy and lament found new scope in their
leavetaking. The homeland verses from the Gaelic-speaking
settlements of Nova Scotia, South Carolina or the cities of
Lowland Scotland all speak of exile, parting lovers, childhood
and a simplified past. Popular songs poured out on these
themes – typified by the 'Canadian Boat Song' in a translation
sent back to *Blackwood's Magazine* by John Galt in 1829:

> From the lone shieling of the misty island
>   Mountains divide us and the waste of seas;
> Yet still the blood is strong, the heart is Highland,
>   And we in dreams behold the Hebrides.
>
> CHORUS
> Fair these broad meads – these hoary woods are grand;
> But we are exiles from our fathers' land.

There were many competent voices singing in these nostalgic
pastures, but they did not produce any poets to equal those of
the previous century.

In the very years when so many Gaels were leaving for
America, tartan was breaking out like a rash, thanks to the
'wizard of the North', all over Britain and France. Fashionable
society endured a craze for extravagantly formal 'Highland
dress', and McIan's still popular clan prints or the formal,
plaid-ridden portraits of Raeburn all testify to the glamour of
the kilt. The uniform dress of the Highland regiments was
gradually adapted to civilian purposes and mill-owners and
chieftains got together to define 'recognised' clan tartans and to
associate them with Lowland families so that any Scot with any
surname could be told to which clan he or she 'belonged'. The
respectability of the kilt and all things tartan was finally
assured when Queen Victoria sojourned at Balmoral and
Prince Albert, that worthy Hanoverian, bared his knees and
appeared in public as a Jacobite pretender.

In the meantime native Gaelic-speakers were coming to
terms with life in modern urban society. The Free Church, the

Society for Propagating Christian Knowledge, and the rise of Evangelical Christianity all played a part in promoting literacy and the publishing of hymns and religious verses in Gaelic as well as homilies and sermons in prose. Yet the true fluency and power of Gaelic prose was largely unrecorded, for it came from the extempore oral tradition of the Free Church pulpit, and the passionate address of these sermons was to influence later Gaelic poets even if they were not church-goers or Christians. Prose fiction, on the other hand, remained almost unknown, and the market had little chance of developing for as long as Gaelic speakers lacked the leisure, the spending-power or the literacy to read novels in their own language. Songs and poems were published successfully, however, because they had the strength of the oral tradition behind them, and for the same reason folk stories and proverbs were collected in books such as John F. Campbell's four-volume *West Highland Tales* (1860–2). Gaelic periodicals were established to speak to the growing Highland communities in Glasgow and the west of Scotland. **The Revd Norman Macleod** (1783–1862), called 'the friend of the Gael', was an influential editor and contributor to these magazines. He worked on a Gaelic dictionary (1831) and composed the beautiful song 'Farewell to Fiunary'; his short essays and dialogues were particularly widely appreciated and were collected posthumously in a volume called after him – *Caraid nan Gaidheal* (1867). His pieces such as 'The Emigrant Ship' ('Long mhór nan Eilthireach') extracted the maximum pathos from the leave-taking of the young who crossed the Atlantic and the grief of the elderly left behind. Such tales of piety and sentiment were equally popular in the Lowland Scots 'Kailyard' school, most of whose authors reached a large urban readership through the Revd William Robertson Nicoll's Evangelical *British Weekly*.

By the end of the century anthologies and collections of Gaelic poems were being published, popularised and translated by journalists such as Henry Whyte ('Fionn', 1852–1914) who was particularly keen on the song tradition. From 1909 into the 1920s Marjory Kennedy-Fraser produced *The Songs of the Hebrides* in several volumes, although she was inclined to 'improve' her folk sources to meet what she felt to be more refined standards of taste. Alexander Carmichael spent the last forty years of the century collecting the vast storehouse of anonymous Gaelic tales, songs, hymns and incantations which was finally published in six invaluable volumes as *Carmina Gadelica* (1900–69). Highland societies flourished in Glasgow and Inverness, while Gaelic churches, ceilidhs, concerts and shinty-matches all established themselves as part of Scottish city life. Under the same stimulus amateur dramatic societies performed short Gaelic plays, and An Comunn Gaidhealach was formed to promote Highland culture and music. The first National Mod was held in 1893, and before long regular competitions were arranged, with Gaelic choirs assembled and an official 'bard' crowned as if to bring concert-hall status to the informality of the old oral ways.

Gaelic literature was not entirely given over to sentiment and respectability. **William Livingstone (Uilleam MacDhunléibhe,** 1808–70) looked back to a heroic past and wrote battle-poems dramatising old conflicts against the Norse or the wars of independence against England. A self-educated man with a fierce hatred for everything English, he brought his rage to bear on the problem of depopulation in the Highlands. In 'A Message to the Bard' ('Fios thun a'Bhàird') he paints a loving picture of his native Islay and then upsets the convention by crying out against the absence of people in the scene. His refrain 'carry this clear message / as I see it, to the Bard' comes to seem increasingly bitter as the poem progresses.

John Smith (Iain Mac a' Ghobhainn, 1848–81) composed lampoons and humorous verses about village life in Lewis, but his best poems are directly political. 'Song for Sportsmen' ('Oran Luchd an Spòrs') attacks the Scots themselves for allowing their lands and their heritage to fall into the hands of sportsmen and industrialists, and its scathingly radical outlook is prophetic of Hugh MacDiarmid's disgust for the 'pickle makers' who now 'own' the hills.

> Some of them trafficed in opium,
> they gathered a great deal of riches,
> their vice made the Chinamen suffer,
> their people destroyed by the poison;
> men without kindness or mercy,
> who were hard to prick in the conscience;
> in payment for all of their plunder
> they deserved to be stabbed with a whinger.   short sword

(trs. D. Thomson)

Smith was thinking of James Matheson, a native of Sutherland who had made his fortune in the disgraceful opium-trade with China and purchased the whole island of Lewis in 1844. He and his factors were not popular, most especially Donald Munro, whose autocratic rule – he held almost every official post on the island – earned him the title of 'the Shah'. The poet recognised that the poor man can be arrogant, too, and he mocks the unco guid of the Free Church in 'The Spirit of Pride' ('Spiorad an Uamhir'). But his finest rage is reserved for the world of social injustice and misused privilege. Among other lines in favour of *caritas*, 'The Spirit of Kindness' ('Spiorad a' Charthannais') speaks on behalf of the Highland regiments at Waterloo to make a complaint which Scotland, and Lewis in particular, was to hear again at the end of the First World War:

What solace had the fathers
of the heroes who won fame?
Their houses, warm with kindliness,
were in ruins around their ears;
their sons were on the battlefield
saving a rueless land,
their mothers' state was piteous
with their houses burnt like coal.

While Britain was rejoicing
they spent their time in grief.
In the country that had reared them,
no shelter from the wind;
the grey strands of their hair were tossed
by the cold breeze of the glen,
there were tears upon their cheeks
and cold dew on their heads.

Smith reminds his oppressors that death is a landlord who comes to us all, and he saves his most vehement hatred for the factor Munro:

The wriggling worm will praise you then
for your flesh's enticing taste,
when it finds you placed before it
on its table, silent now,
saying 'This one's juicy flesh
is good for earthy worms,
since he made many hundreds thin
to feed himself for me.'

(trs. D. Thomson)

Smith's images are strong, concrete and uncomfortably savage, with something of the spirit of Iain Lom in place of the nostalgia which prevails in so many of the 'homeland' verses.

The struggle for land-reform in Skye in the 1880s motivated many of the poems of **Mary Macpherson** (**Màiri Nic a' Phearsain**, 1821–98). Màiri Mhór lived latterly in Inverness and Glasgow, and some of her songs, such as 'Farewell to the New Christmas' ('Soraidh leis an Nollaig ùir'), for instance, evoke longing for the island of her youth; but her popular songs in support of land-reform made her something of a legend, and she became known for her outspoken and earthy expression, made doubly impressive by her energy and her huge size. Imprisoned at Inverness on what she insisted was a false charge of shoplifting, she explained in 'The Oppression I Suffered' ('Na dh'fhuiling mi de dh'fhòirneart') that the injustice of the experience was what turned her talents to verse. In the cause of land-reform she composed 'Incitement of the Gaels' ('Brons-nachadh nan Gaidheal') and listed the movement's heroes in 'Song of Ben Lee' ('Oran Beinn-Lì'). It is entirely fitting that 'Big Mary of the songs' should have become one of the heroes herself, for it was, after all, the crofting womenfolk who had driven off the police in the 'battle of Braes'.

Margaret Oliphant (1828–97)

In complete contrast to Mary Macpherson, the many books of Margaret Oliphant returns us to the Lowlands and to a politer provincial scene. Born near Edinburgh and brought to Liverpool as a girl, Mrs Oliphant's sympathies remained with small dissenting communities and her northern origins. The heroine of her first novel, *Margaret Maitland* (1849), encapsulates all the Scottish Victorian spinsterly virtues of piety, good sense, reticence and industry. The author herself had to draw on these strengths soon enough, for she was widowed while scarcely in her thirties and had to turn to writing to support herself, her family and an alcoholic brother, too. Her career in England spans forty-five years of extraordinary industry during which time she produced innumerable articles and reviews for 'Maga' as well as biographies, criticism, literary histories, an auto-biography, a history of *Blackwood's* and over sixty two- and three-volume novels. She prided herself on being a *Blackwood's* author, as well she might, but her life's work did not make her particularly rich or famous.

Margaret Oliphant wrote several Scottish novels, including *Merkland* (1851), *Katie Stewart* (1853) – an historical piece – and *Kirsteen: A Story of a Scottish Family Seventy Years Ago* (1890). In some other novels and short stories she focuses on supernatural or theosophical intimations of a realm of spirits beyond death – a growing Victorian obsession; but the bulk of her work concerns itself with the more mundane tribulations of provincial life and manners. Q. D. Leavis has cited these novels as a useful link between the worlds of Jane Austen and George Eliot, and indeed Oliphant's *Miss Marjoribanks* (1866) may have been a direct influence on *Middlemarch* (1871–2). (George Eliot was suspected of being the author of *Miss Marjoribanks* because it was serialised in *Blackwood's*, where her own *Scenes of Clerical Life* had first appeared.) *Miss Marjoribanks* belongs to a series of novels and stories set in England which were collected as 'The Chronicles of Carlingford' (1863–6) after the style of Trollope's 'Barchester' books and Mrs Gaskell's 'Cranford' sketches. By the end of the sixties, however, Mrs Oliphant had to support another of her brothers and his family, and her increased literary output led to a decline in quality for the rest of her life as a professional author. Even so, she was a respected friend of Carlyle's, and Barrie and Henry James admired her best work for the potential they saw in it, just as they acknowledged her good humour and her indomitable spirit.

James Thomson (1834–82)

Among the other Scots working in London at this time, James Thomson was to make a grimmer indictment of late-Victorian life and belief than even Carlyle had attempted. Thomson's father was a merchant seaman in Port Glasgow until a stroke paralysed him when James was six. The family moved to London, but Thomson's mother died within two years and he went to an asylum for the children of poor Scottish servicemen. With his limited means he joined up as an army schoolmaster, but after eight years his drinking led to dismissal and in 1862 he found himself back in London looking for a new livelihood. He turned to literature and journalism, having published some poems and articles while he was still in the army, and eventually gained a post with the *National Reformer* – a periodical directed at freethinkers who wanted to keep up with the views of Darwin, Spencer and Huxley.

Thomson's mother had been an Irvingite and no doubt he assimilated some of her passionate Christianity along with a youthful enthusiasm for Shelley and Novalis – the late-eighteenth-century German Romantic poet. (Thomson used 'BV' – Bysshe Vanolis – as a pseudonym for his verses.) Early poems and articles suggest a struggle between idealistic and mystical beliefs and a conviction that the profit-motive and the old ways of worship have corrupted and enslaved mankind. He attacked Christianity for ignoring the vital present in favour of rewards and punishments in an afterlife, and proposed a kind of pantheism in which each man's duty is to realise the true freedom of his spirit before it returns to the infinite, impersonal evolutionary flow of matter. Thomson gradually came to atheism and a philosophical pessimism which recognised the disparity between human hope and man's imperfectibility, and he published these views in the *National Reformer*. He also produced a memoir of the Italian pessimist Giacomo Leopardi and translated his dialogues and discourses.

Thomson's drive to show 'the bitter, old, and wrinkled truth, stripped naked' culminates in *The City of Dreadful Night*, published in parts during 1874 and as a book in 1880. The poem is often cited as a 'modern' vision of the city as nightmare, but it is essentially a Dantesque allegory, a symbolic rather than a realistic visit to a cold Inferno of streets, squares and graveyards. (In fact earlier poems such as 'Sunday up the River' and 'Sunday at Hampstead', from 1865, are markedly more 'realistic' and more modern in their use of colloquial English. They also show London in a cheerful and sunny mood, to remind us that Thomson was not entirely given over to gloom.) Even so, *The City of Dreadful Night* does look forward to T. S. Eliot's vision of London as a wasteland, and Thomson's empty squares have a strange and menacing calm, which seems to anticipate surrealism and the modern paintings of De Chirico. For the most part, however, the echoes are of Dürer and Shelley, and the poet's atheism is suffused with a

melancholy which might have been drawn from Fitzgerald or
even Drummond of Hawthornden:

> And now at last authentic word I bring,
> Witnessed by every dead and living thing;
>   Good tidings of great joy for you, for all:
> There is no God; no Fiend with names divine
> Made us and tortures us; if we must pine,
>   It is to satiate no Being's gall.
>
> . . .
>
> This little life is all we must endure,
> The grave's most holy place is ever sure,
>   We fall asleep and never wake again;
> Nothing is of us but the mouldering flesh,
> Whose elements dissolve and merge afresh
>   In earth, air, water, planets, and other men.

Even the readers of the *National Reformer* were startled by the
sustained threnody of Thomson's 'comfort', and, although he
received encouraging letters from George Eliot and Meredith,
most reviewers accused the poem of insincerity or heresy or
both, and they preferred the other pieces in the 1880 collection.
Thomson despaired of finding favour with the prestigious
literary periodicals, and a break with his editor saw him
reduced to writing reviews and biographical essays for *Cope's
Tobacco Plant* – a journal subsidised by a Liverpool tobacco firm.

Increasingly given to bouts of excessive drinking, the poet's
health and morale declined until a particularly destructive
episode killed him in June 1882. He had achieved a modest
reputation, but *The City of Dreadful Night* spoke more clearly to a
later generation. If its images of despair look rather romantic to
readers used to Eliot and Kafka, we can still sympathise with
his courageous attempt to face the indifference of the universe
without flinching. At least he felt that poetry should tackle
serious philosophical issues, and in this he shared his idealism,
and a preference for evolutionism too, with John Davidson.
Hugh MacDiarmid's later poetry can also be seen to have a
place in this company, going back to Carlyle himself, in what
amounts to a school of Scottish writers who have followed a
'metaphysical' direction with polemical urgency.

By comparison, the desperate plight of poetry in Scotland
may be judged by the continuing success of the *Whistle-Binkie*

anthologies and the vogue which grew up for the verse of
William McGonagall (1825?–1902), 'poet', 'tragedian' and
public performer from Dundee. McGonagall himself was
sincere (or deluded) in his ambitions to be a great poet, but his
audiences came mostly to laugh. His naïve verses on all the
issues of the day – preferably 'tragedies' such as the Tay Bridge
disaster in 1879 – do have a kind of genius for the banal, stuffed
with prosaic details and hilariously contrived rhymes.
McGonagall undertook poetry-readings throughout Scotland
(in a variety of striking costumes) and even visited London and
New York. His *Poetic Gems* (1890) have seldom been out of print
– a reflection that would have given poor Thomson little
comfort.

Robert Louis Stevenson (1850–94)

Thomson's confrontation with the problems of modernity –
urban despair and scientific materialism – scarcely features
in the fiction of Robert Louis Stevenson, whose best-known
books belong to an extrovert tale-telling tradition which looks
back to Scott. He was not alone, and for the rest of the century
the preferred modes of Scottish novelists will be Stevensonian
romance, symbolic fantasy, or nostalgic rusticism. While these
forms undoubtedly represent a reaction to the materialistic face
of the contemporary world, they cannot be said to deal with it
directly. It would be wrong to accuse Stevenson of escapism,
however, for his mercurial personality had a most complicated
relationship with Scotland and his own Scottishness. Critical
and nostalgic by turns, he wrote about his homeland from exile
in the South Seas, seeking to express a vision shaped by the
rigours of Calvinism and yet self-consciously dedicated to the
free life of art and the imagination. Such internal divisions fuel
the best of Stevenson's fiction, as if he were replaying in
psychologically ambiguous terms Walter Scott's own conflict
between Unionist stability and Jacobite romance. He had
scarcely begun to fulfil his deepening grasp of these old themes
when a brain haemorrhage ended his life at the age of
forty-four.

Stevenson's health was perpetually at the mercy of acute
lung-troubles and tuberculosis, and the damp and windy

climate of Edinburgh plagued his boyhood with coughs and chills which put him to bed for weeks of fever and sleepless nights. As an only child, he would not have survived if he had not come from a well-off and caring family, for his father was a harbour engineer and lighthouse-builder, like his grandfather, who had constructed the 'impossible' light on Bell Rock. Stevenson senior was a devout and conservative man, whose sense of duty had led him in his father's footsteps to be a civil engineer, despite his own rather intense and imaginative nature. He was fond and affectionate with his son and encouraged his youthful writing. So often confined to bed, the boy thrived on escapist tales and delighted to create plots with cut-out figures from his toy theatre – a pastime he recalled in his essay 'A Penny Plain and Two Pence Coloured' (1883). Many of his poems in *A Child's Garden of Verses* (1885) – assembled while he was convalescing as an adult – relate to this imaginative life of bedside dreams and games on the counterpane, and he dedicated the collection to Alison Cunningham, the devoted young nurse of his childhood whom he never forgot as 'My second Mother, my first Wife'. 'Cummie' came from strict Presbyterian stock and, although she disapproved of plays and novels, she still fired her charge's imagination with stories of the Covenanters and tales of righteousness.

Stevenson entered Edinburgh University at the age of seventeen, but his studies in civil engineering (to please his father) took second place to new friends, new books and the bohemian life. He declared a romantic preference for the low life of Edinburgh – 'the lighted streets and the swinging gait of harlots' – so excitingly different from a New Town background in middle-class bourgeois respectability. When engineering failed to enthuse him he attempted law, but growing differences with his father came to a head over his professed agnosticism and his bohemian friends – notably his lively cousin Bob Stevenson. Louis's parents (his name was pronounced 'Lewis') were disproportionately frightened and dismayed by their son's loss of grace and he was made to feel extremely guilty. Life at home became tense, and a very early story only recently published – 'The Edifying Letters of the Rutherford Family' – deals with this crisis. The young man found relief in letters to Mrs Francis Sitwell, an older woman whom he had met at a cousin's house in Suffolk. She believed in his talent, and she and

Sidney Colvin – later her husband – helped him to make London contracts in journalism and publishing. The following year saw something of a reconciliation with the family, who never ceased to support him financially, and he was back in Edinburgh studying Scots law again. His father gave him £1000 when he finally became an advocate in 1875, but had to accept that his son's career was henceforth to be a literary one. Stevenson began his peripatetic adult life with regular visits to London and the continent, especially to the forest of Fontainebleau, where his cousin Bob spent the summers painting in congenial artistic company, away from the cold winds and the sterner expectations of the North.

A few essays and book-reviews had already appeared under Stevenson's name, including a piece on what he took to be John Knox's two-faced attitude to women. At Edinburgh Infirmary he met the English poet W. E. Henley, who had come to have the tubercular bones of his foot treated by Joseph Lister. Stevenson based Long John Silver's better qualities on his rumbustious friend, and they wrote four plays together in the 1880s, without much stage success. The two writers remained close for thirteen years until a quarrel over a slight to Stevenson's wife parted them. Neither gave in to their ailments, and both seemed determined to pursue an actively physical life. Indeed, Louis's first book – *An Inland Voyage* (1878) – describes a canoe holiday he took through the canals of Belgium in the summer of 1876. Later that year at a hotel in Fontainebleau he met the woman he was to marry.

Fanny Osbourne was an American in Europe with her children, where she intended to study painting and make a break from her husband. Stevenson was struck by this resourceful and intelligent lady – ten years his senior – and she was intrigued by his physical frailty combined with an extraordinarily vital and volatile personality. They became lovers, but Fanny's money finally ran out and she had to return to America. That autumn Stevenson set out on a twelve-day mountain-walking tour in the south of France, travelling alone with his pack, his notebook, a revolver and a donkey called Modestine. By now his delight in France and the free life had produced a study of François Villon and a short story featuring him – 'A Lodging for the Night' (1877) – as well as 'The Sire de Malétroit's Door' (1878). He had made friends with Andrew

Lang and Edmund Gosse and produced a number of essays for Henley's *London*, later collected in *Virginibus Puerisque* (1881). In the winter he completed *Edinburgh: Picturesque Notes*, and in June 1879 *Travels with a Donkey in the Cévennes* became a minor classic among travel-books. His literary career was under way at last.

Then Stevenson received a cable from Fanny Osbourne in California, and, to the absolute consternation of friends and family, he decided to go to Monterey to join her, though she was not yet divorced. Excited by the prospect of America, he expected to meet the energy and optimism which he had found in the works of Walt Whitman; but the rigours of the journey and the strain of his arrival nearly killed him. *Across the Plains* (1892) and *The Amateur Emigrant* (1895) give a rawly realistic account of the sufferings he shared with his fellow voyagers, but neither piece appeared in his lifetime. Louis's fiction was more successful, and 'The Pavilion on the Links' (1880) was published as an atmospheric short story set on the bleak sands of the Scottish east coast – full of convincing detail, mysterious doings at night and the lore of tides and winds. His youthful visits to lighthouses with his father had not been forgotten, and many later works show the same delight in shores, islands, harbours and coastal inns.

Louis and Fanny were married in May 1880. With limited means, but tough and resourceful in her own way, Fanny took her husband into the mountains for the sake of his health, and their experiences in an abandoned shack at an old silver-mine produced *The Silverado Squatters* (1883). Fences were mended with Edinburgh and by August the new couple and twelve-year-old stepson Lloyd Osbourne were in Heriot Row, where Fanny succeeded in befriending Louis's parents and friends. As ever, the approach of a Scottish winter drove them abroad, but the following summer saw them back in Pitlochry and Braemar, and Stevenson began to write again, using Scots for the first time as a major narrative voice. 'Thrawn Janet' (1881) is a gripping account of supernatural possession with its roots in the oral tradition – not unlike Scott's 'Wandering Willie's Tale'. It tells how the Revd Murdoch Soulis is forced to recognise the power of the Devil, although as a college-educated and liberal young minister he used to scoff at such superstition and to chide the locals for their cruelty to Janet, the local witch. The community's beliefs are vindicated when Janet is found to be a reanimated corpse and, on the imaginative level at least, Stevenson joins Hogg in accepting the intimate proximity of the Devil and all his works. Fired by his theme and its native setting, Louis followed it with 'The Body Snatcher' and then 'The Merry Men' (1882) as a tale of Cameronian piety and guilt among the shipwrecks on an elemental Scottish coast in the eighteenth century. Not far from the spirit of Hawthorne and Poe (whom he had read and admired), 'The Merry Men' is made surprisingly subtle by Stevenson's mastery of atmospheric description. The same expertise, and memories of the California coast, came to fruition when he began to write *Treasure Island*.

Conceived in Braemar and finished in Switzerland, where they wintered again, 'The Sea Cook' began as a tale around a map drawn for young Lloyd's amusement. It followed a genre already established by Captain Marryat (1792–1848) and popularised by a fellow Edinburgh writer, **R. M. Ballantyne** (1825–94), whose dozens of books include *Martin Rattler*, *The Coral Island* (both 1858) and *The Gorilla Hunters* (1861). Yet *Treasure Island* (1883) was more than another adventure serial in *Young Folks*, for Stevenson had uncovered a theme which spoke to his life-experience and his imagination with equal force. Indeed, its psychological and moral patterns were to reappear in all his mature works. The typical Stevenson hero is an untried young man faced with formative experience: Jim Hawkins is a teenager, while the protagonist of 'The Merry Men' and David Balfour of *Kidnapped* are scarcely older – lads of university age at a time when studies started young. Archie Weir also fits this pattern, although he is less typical in other respects. On leaving home, or travelling, these young heroes are freed from the security of convention and routine, much as the author himself threw over Heriot Row in favour of Fontainebleau and Silverado. Impressions of the world are heightened in such new surroundings – an effect which the readers share – and the protagonists have to make judgements on people and events entirely from their own resources. Having lost their fathers (a motif of interest to the psychoanalytical critic, perhaps) the heroes look to friends for guidance instead, or to charismatic strangers or distant uncles, only to be shocked by what they find. The world of their elders, like the elders themselves, is not what it seemed to be from the security of childhood. Nevertheless, when Jim Hawkins finally realises that Silver is a lot less than the 'best of shipmates', he still cannot condemn him. Dr Livesy, Squire Trelawney and Captain Smollett belong to the world of gentlemen – the world Jim will enter after these rites of passage – but it is Silver who strikes a strange note of sympathy and complicity with the boy, and it is Silver, like a dangerous mixture of Iago and Falstaff, who dominates the stage with his power to charm. Thus Jim and Long John, like David Balfour and Alan Breck, or the two Duries in *The Master of Ballantrae*, or the two sides of Dr Jekyll, represent opposed tendencies in a shifting balance between stability and adventure, or social responsibility and individual freedom. If Walter Scott proposed a similar polarity, he always ended with the *status quo*, but for Louis the condition is psychological and less easily resolved – a struggle within the hearts and minds of his heroes, who are still haunted by the booming surf, or by nights on the bare hillside, even after they have accepted a settled future. In this way Stevenson transcends the adventure novel by using its uncomplicated lines to say some rather complicated things about the tensions between imagination and convention, and the changes which take place, for better and for worse, between youth and maturity.

When Stevenson chooses the past – and almost all his stories do – it is imaginative freedom which he is choosing – as if the past were another kind of exotic location, more appropriate for such deeds and dilemmas than late-Victorian Edinburgh. A moment's comparison with Dostoevsky or James will show his limitations in this respect, yet the landscapes of *Treasure Island* or *Kidnapped* are so vividly realised, and the reader is so involved with the physical immediacy of vicarious experience, that all is made contemporary again. Despite his favourite eighteenth-century settings, Stevenson is not a historical novelist at all, certainly not in the style of Scott or Galt, who were so keen to explore the differences between 'then' and 'now'. Nevertheless, Louis was sensitive about his standing as a conscious and serious artist. He explained his theories about fiction and defended prose romance in an essay called 'Gossip on Romance' (1882), and again in 'A Humble Remonstrance' (1884), which was offered as a reply to Henry James's essay

'The Art of Fiction'. The Scot maintained that truth to life was not enough in fiction, for life is inchoate, while the novelist's job is to construct order by subsuming character, setting and incident to an overriding creative conception. At the same time he must meet the challenge to convey a sense of 'real' and dazzling experience in his prose. This concern with style and the writer's craft gave him common ground with James, and the two men met and corresponded and became admirers of each other's work.

Further collections of essays and short stories and the book-publication of *Treasure Island* brought critical status and much-needed royalties; but Stevenson's health forced him abroad again, where he completed a lesser romance, *Prince Otto* (1805), and began *The Black Arrow* (1888). After a year, the family returned to Britain for the last time, settling in Bournemouth at 'Skerryvore', where Stevenson wrote 'Markheim' and the novels *Kidnapped* and *Jekyll and Hyde*, both of which appeared in 1886.

As a novel of travel and the Scottish landscape *Kidnapped* has few equals, yet its fascination comes as much from character as from action, although its main protagonists need to be considered together to realise the author's theme in this respect. David Balfour is the canny heir to Walter Scott's Lowland, Presbyterian, Unionist world, while Alan Breck Stewart epitomises the wilful courage and Jacobite romance of the Highlands – still potent five years after Culloden. Yet, even although David is carried along by events, rather like a Scott hero, Breck's loyal, vain and dangerous spirit seems to echo something within himself. When their escapade is over, Alan Breck must go into exile in France and David must turn to the gentlemanly responsibilities of his inheritance. This is symbolised by his passing through the doors of the British Linen Bank at the end of the adventure, and all the time 'there was a cold gnawing in my inside like a remorse for something wrong'. The remorse is not unlike J. M. Barrie's regret for the loss of boyhood – Peter Pan's kingdom of ruthless innocence and amoral imaginative freedom. Peter Pan crows like a cock at the defeat of his enemies, with just the same untrammelled spirit as Alan Breck does when he claims staid and earnest Balfour for his own:

> He came up to me with open arms. 'Come to my arms!' he cried, and
> embraced and kissed me hard upon both cheeks. 'David,' said he, 'I love
> you like a brother. And O, man,' he cried in a kind of ecstasy, 'am I no' a
> bonny fighter?'
>   Thereupon he turned to the four enemies, passed his sword clean
> through each of them, and tumbled them out of doors one after the other.
> As he did so, he kept humming, and singing, and whistling to himself . . .

Such is the 'brother' David must learn to leave behind, but his
call is felt from within and it cannot be denied without that
feeling of 'remorse for something wrong'.

Stevenson had already realised that duality was the true
and underlying theme of his fiction, for he had just given an
overtly psychological focus to it in *The Strange Case of Dr Jekyll
and Mr Hyde* (1886). Its origins as a Gothic 'shilling shocker' are
obvious and Louis had already written a play about the good
Deacon Brodie's secret career of crime in Edinburgh. But this
novel's interest in the unconscious and interior nature of good
and evil give it a more serious moral dimension, just as it also
symbolises a social truth about Victorian society and the
anonymity of its great cities, where depravity and respectability rub shoulders. Although the tale is set in London, it has
deeply Scottish roots, and true to the ethos of the *Justified Sinner*
it shows the principle of evil as a kind of double which threatens
the upright personality from within. Jekyll's experiments were
originally intended to remove this unworthy self, but they
released him instead, and it is the experience of pleasure which
subverts the doctor's Calvinist ideal of 'a life of effort, virtue
and control'. At first he rejoices in his new ability to slip off
'genial respectability', as he puts it, like a schoolboy who sheds
his clothes to 'spring headlong into the sea of liberty'. But he
discovers that he cannot escape from his freer and darker side
without killing himself.

Stevenson's long and complicated relationship with his
father – resentful, affectionate and dependent by turns – finally
came to an end when the old man died, and the writer decided
to leave Britain once and for all with his mother, Fanny and
Lloyd in 1887. They went to the Adirondacks near the
Canadian border, where he could attend a TB clinic. His
American royalties alleviated his perpetual money-problems at
last, until wanderlust and a longing for the sun took them all to
California, where they chartered a schooner for an extended

cruise in the South Seas. *The Master of Ballantrae* (1889) was completed in Hawaii, shortly after the new year.

This time Stevenson symbolised the divisions of eighteenth-century Scotland in the lifelong struggle between two brothers. Staid and worthy Henry Durie is briefed to support the Hanoverian cause, while his younger brother James – a charming and amoral character – becomes a Jacobite adventurer. Their father's plan is that the house should survive, whatever the outcome of the rising. Here the differences between a Balfour type and a Breck type are exacerbated by rivalry in love, moral obsession and fraternal betrayal. At first our judgement of the two brothers is biased because the most part of the tale is told by Ephraim Mackellar, an educated and dogmatic servant, jealous on behalf of his 'Mr Henry' and prone to see things from his point of view. Mackellar is a limited narrator worthy of Galt, and the quality of the novel flags without his distinctive voice. Thus we only slowly come to realise that young James is neither a Byronic chevalier in exile, nor the Devil incarnate, although the Durie family casts him in both roles. The rather colourless and pious Henry is obsessed with his 'Satanic' brother, but it is his own sense of grievance, justification and wounded pride which takes over his sanity and ruins him. In the end, the old religious fears and the old Stuart romances have killed them both, and Stevenson's novel has made a more subtle point about Scottish character and history than its melodramatic moments might suggest.

The Stevenson family found itself on another sea trip, on a trading-schooner through the Gilbert Islands, and these voyages on the fringes of respectable commerce provided the material for the author's best South Sea stories. In his fortieth year he was making a growing commitment to life in the Pacific, and when they came to Samoa again they bought a large estate at Upolu and built a house there. Thinking to visit Britain just one more time, they travelled to Sydney in 1890, but Louis's health collapsed, and collapsed again even after another convalescence. The little party returned to Vailima, where they remained for the last four years of Louis's life. Slowly the estate established itself, and Stevenson became a respected figure in the community as a champion of native rights and a 'Tusitala' – a storyteller.

Louis's thoughts turned to Scotland, which he never

expected to see again. He corresponded with J. M. Barrie and invited him to Samoa, longing to talk to a fellow Scot; and he began *Weir of Hermiston*. Faced with more immediate demands for money, he fell back on David Balfour and wrote *Catriona* (1893) as a sequel to *Kidnapped*, substituting moral complications and a love interest for the topographical brilliance of the earlier book. Further adventure stories were in order, so he worked on *St Ives* (finished by Quiller-Couch in 1897) and started books on the Covenanters and Prince Charlie. In the meantime, the South Seas featured in a collaboration with his stepson, while *Island Night's Entertainments* (1893) included 'The Beach at Falesa', perhaps his plainest and finest South Sea story. *The Ebb Tide* followed in 1894 as a picture of moral decay and the seamy side of island existence. It is ironic that Stevenson was so resolutely unromantic about his exotic surroundings while the Kailyard school was reinventing Scotland as a homespun Eden. At the end of 1894 Louis was working once more on *Weir of Hermiston*, excited by its exploration of the doomed relationship between an overbearing father and his sensitive son. It was his practice to read passages aloud to the family at the end of each day, but on 3 December he suffered a sudden cerebral stroke and died in the evening with the story unfinished.

Weir of Hermiston (1896) might have been Stevenson's greatest work, or it might have turned to melodrama in its closing stages like *The Master of Ballantrae*. What survives is a magnificent beginning in which the author's fascination with the duality of Scottish character and the mysterious influences of inheritance and history, are expressed as a conflict between father and son, with the very spirit of Calvinist authority set against the frailer virtues of imagination and empathy. Loosely based on the real Lord Braxfield, judge Adam Weir is an unforgettable fictional creation. A brutally plain-spoken Lord Advocate of the early nineteenth century, he faces harsh truths about the world with a cruel relish for absolute exposure. He cares for his son Archie, but is suspicious of his own tenderness as if it were a weakness to be despised. Yet Stevenson manages to make us thrill to the savage flair and the awkward, granite integrity of his crushing and grim humour: ' "Weel it's something of the suddenest" ', he comments when he hears of his ineffectual wife's unexpected death, ' "But she was a

dwaibly body from the first. . . . It was a daftlike marriage."
And then, with a most unusual gentleness of tone, "Puir bitch,"
said he, "puir bitch!" ' '

Weir fears that his son will take after his weak mother, and
certainly the young man's excitable, imaginative and sentimental nature is as yet unformed and untried. Stevenson was
setting a green version of his own impulsive sensibility against
archetypal Scottish mores, whose fascination and whose kinship he could not deny, even from the distance of Samoa. Could
these two elements ever be at peace with each other, or within
one nature? The stage is set for a terrible confrontation, which
will come about when the son has to be sentenced by his own
father for the murder of the man who betrayed him with his girl.
The psychological drama of the Weirs, father and son, is set
against the remoter backdrop of oral tradition associated with
the Weaver's Stone – where the lovers meet, where a Covenanter was once brutally murdered and where murder will be
done again. This ballad-like sense of community history and
fate is emphasised by Stevenson's narrative distance and the
ironic compassion with which he treats the sweetly foolish
love-games of the young people. Archie and Christina are
infatuated with the idea of being in love, and Frank Innes, the
rival suitor, toys with their affections and his own impulses like
a cruel boy. Their sentimental idyll at Archie's country home
will come to a bad end, and Archie will soon have to face his
father in a suddenly and tragically adult world.

The violent folk-history of the Borders and a symbolic model
of Scottish society are brought together in the four 'black
Elliott' brothers – a businessman, an improving farmer, a
radical weaver and a poet – who rode down the robbers who
killed their father in years past. It is likely that Stevenson would
have had them ride again to free Archie for the sake of their
niece, but we cannot tell whether this would have led to a
melodramatic rescue or a more mature and less predictable
outcome. Stevenson was not immune to the dangers of
romance, but the ironic 'folk-historical' distance of his narrative style in *Weir of Hermiston* suggests a new control in his
treatment of it. If the novel had come to show the limitations of
swashbuckling solutions, it would, indeed, have been his
greatest work.

Stevenson's talent for telling a tale gained him a considerable popular audience, and in this respect his skills were shared by his compatriot **Arthur Conan Doyle** (1859–1930). Both writers, incidentally, admired the stories of Émile Gaboriau, the inventor of the French detective-novel in the 1860s. Conan Doyle, who was born in Edinburgh nine years after Stevenson, took a medical degree in 1881 and turned to writing to help his finances as a struggling doctor in Portsmouth. Sherlock Holmes was introduced to the world in *A Study in Scarlet* (1887) and thereafter on the pages of *Strand Magazine* throughout the nineties. (His deductive talents were based on those of Dr Joseph Bell, one of Doyle's teachers at Edinburgh and a pioneer of forensic medicine.) Historical adventure-novels, the Professor Challenger stories and books on the Boer War, the First World War and, latterly, on spiritualism, all added to Conan Doyle's reputation, but Holmes and Watson remain his best-loved and best known creations, forever associated with the atmospheric streets of late Victorian London.

Conan Doyle's interest in spiritualism was not unconnected with the death of his son in the First World War, but the late Victorian age had already seen many such responses to a prevailing sense that established religion had somehow failed to give comfort in the face of scientific materialism, industrialisation, and the anonymity of the great cities. This urge to restore the primacy of the imagination and the spirit manifested itself in the Oxford Movement or in the Evangelical fervour of the 'Irvingites', who encouraged 'speaking in tongues' at their meetings. There was a wide interest in theosophy, while William Morris's fantasy novels and the Pre-Raphaelite artists all speak to the public's longing for other realms and modes of being. One of the most striking literary exponents of this tendency was a large dandified Scot with a black beard, whose mythopoeic novels and fairy stories prompted G. K. Chesterton to declare him the most original writer of his age.

George MacDonald (1824–1905)

Brought up on an Aberdeenshire farm, MacDonald went to his home university, where he studied German and graduated with an MA in 1845. Unable to afford a medical career, he worked in

London as a tutor for three years, until, encouraged by his future wife, he became a minister of the Congregational Church – a moderately Calvinist dissenting body, more numerous in England than in the north. He was invited to take the pulpit at Arundel in 1850 and married in the spring of the following year, despite a severe lung-haemorrhage. MacDonald was to be haunted by the spectre of tuberculosis all his life: it had killed his beloved mother when he was eight, his father lost a leg to it, his brother and a half-sister died young and his wife shared the condition too. Not surprisingly, perhaps, he conceived an early interest in Novalis, who had died of TB at twenty-nine and held a mystical conception of death as the doorway to another existence – a doorway his fifteen-year-old fiancée had already passed through. Before long, MacDonald's unorthodox views in this regard forced him to resign from the ministry, and he set about establishing himself in the world of journalism and letters. He became a popular lecturer in the Manchester area, and a rather 'spasmodic' blank-verse drama achieved a modest success. A collection of poems was completed in 1857 after a winter in Algiers for the sake of his health, and the following year saw the publication of his first novel – 'a faerie romance for men and women'.

The hero of *Phantastes* (1858) is called Anodos ('pathless'), and the book follows his dream-fantasy journey into fairyland. MacDonald's imagination shows the influence of Novalis, Hoffman, Dante, Spenserian allegory, Celtic lore and Victorian sentiment, but in the end this eclectic realm is a place of his own devising. The book is suffused with a search for maternal love along with an almost erotic surrender to death, and, in a startlingly Freudian world of dream-like transformations, mysterious prohibitions and stifled sexual longings, it is difficult to be sure that the author is in full control of his imagination. Yet later readers have praised MacDonald's intuitive grasp of the inner logic of dreams, and this aspect of his work has taken his reputation into the twentieth century, with a direct influence on such writers as C. S. Lewis, Charles Williams and David Lindsay.

Still much in demand on the popular lecturing-circuit, MacDonald moved to London in 1859 to take up a professorship of English at Bedford College. He made friends with many writers and started another novel and several fairy stories.

David Elginbrod (1863) was the first of three novels to be set in the author's native Aberdeenshire. Poorly constructed and inclined to preach, it has many faults, but MacDonald used it to reassess his own background and to argue for the need for every man to rediscover human and divine love, free from false sophistication and free from the strictures of Calvinism. MacDonald himself had been persuaded of this by F. D. Maurice – a controversially popular Christian socialist – and had joined the Church of England. The same search occupies *Alec Forbes of Howglen* (1865), perhaps his best book on this theme and his most consistent picture of regional life. The third novel in the series, *Robert Falconer* (1868), is less unified and more didactic.

MacDonald continued to publish fairy-stories during the 1860s – 'Works of Fancy and Imagination', which were collected in ten volumes in 1871. One story in particular, 'The Golden Key' (1867), has a rare imaginative power. Much more coherent than *Phantastes*, it is probably MacDonald's best work, with disturbing images of search and fulfilment through death in some other world. *The Princess and the Goblin* (1872) and its sequel *The Princess and Curdie* (1883) are still popular with young readers, while *At the Back of the North Wind* (1871) was an even more successful children's novel about the 'land of everlasting dream' once visited, as the boy hero discovers, by James Hogg's fated girl Kilmeny. MacDonald balanced these mystical experiences with social realism and a concern for reform, a cause close to his heart and fuelled by vicarious descriptions of the sufferings of poor children. This very Victorian taste for a mild sentimental sadism can be disturbing to the modern reader, and episodes of abasement and whipping feature rather too vividly in some of MacDonald's later adult novels. It is difficult not to suspect several such unhealthy tensions in Victorian fantasy literature in general, and MacDonald's Scottish inheritance left him uneasily balanced between sentimental realism and mystical idealism, always with the harsher shadows of Calvinist authority in the background.

By the late sixties MacDonald had become a well-known figure in nonconformist and spiritualist circles and he was the friend and confidant of Ruskin, Arnold, Carlyle, Browning, Tennyson, Kingsley and Lewis Carroll. He made a lecture tour of America in 1872 and dazzled his audiences with charismatic eloquence and a taste for cloaks, white suits, or the kilt and plaid – not exactly the expected dress for a farm boy from Aberdeen. His American friends included Emerson and Mark Twain. During the rest of his career MacDonald produced a further eighteen novels – ten of them with Scottish settings – but they tend to cover already-established themes and he admitted that he saw them as a popular substitute for preaching. His last book, however, is notable because it returns once more to the mode of dream fantasy.

Lilith (1895) offers a strange other-dimensional world which is grimmer and more frightening than his earlier versions of fairyland. This realm, a place without tears or rain, lies beyond a looking-glass in the house of 'Mr Vane' and he visits it several times in the attempt to understand why skeletons slowly regrow their flesh there, or why lost babies turn into rapacious giants. The land is terrorised by Lilith, a beautiful vampire demon princess who kills children and assumes the shape of a spotted leopardess. MacDonald's metaphoric images are strange and cruel, or sweet and sickly sentimental – for example, the lisping baby-talk of 'the little ones' – and the author's mystical optimism is juxtaposed with morbid visions of horror and pain. MacDonald was never afraid to give his imagination free reign, and perhaps in this book above all it took its colouring from a life experience in which tuberculosis had now killed his favourite grandchild and five of his own children. His own disease was arrested, but that was little consolation. The last eight years of his life were spent in virtual silence, waiting for the death he had thought to welcome in his younger days.

The Celtic twilight

MacDonald was not alone in his hatred of industrial capitalism. Matthew Arnold proposed 'culture' as a weapon against the spiritual sterility of the times, and in the 1860s he had identified a 'Celtic' spirit as the antithesis of narrow materialism. William Morris and Ruskin advocated a new art and utopian socialism in the 1870s, while the more aesthetic bias of the 1890s, with Dowson, Lionel Johnson, Symons and Yeats, looked to French Symbolism or the hermeticism of the 'Golden Dawn' as some sort of alternative to materialism. The

Irish Celtic revival sought a renewal of poetic force and imagination in myth and legend, and, from a more conventional academic direction, two Scots scholars did much to further this new interest in mythology and primitive societies. J. G. Frazer (1854–1941), a Glasgow man who became a fellow in classics at Cambridge, began his monumental study *The Golden Bough* in the 1890s; while Andrew Lang (1844–1912), from Selkirk and St Andrew's University, and a classics don at Oxford, had been one of anthropology's pioneers in the eighties with his own studies of myth and comparative religion. Lang also worked at poetry, fiction, history, biography and literary journalism, and his *Fairy Books*, published under various colours, are still enjoyed by children today.

There was a vogue for Celticism in Scotland, with a self-conscious preference for France rather than England, and an interest in Breton and Belgian cultural minorities. This outward-looking nationalism was supported by Patrick Geddes (1854–1932) a polymath biologist and architect who established the Outlook Tower in Edinburgh in 1892, as a focus for his new ideas in sociology, ecology, and environmental planning. His views brought him fame abroad, but they never flowered in his native country. Geddes and his friends wanted to publish 'Celtic' work, and so they established a periodical and a Celtic library series in an attempt to match the Irish revival. The 1890s saw a new outburst of 'Ossianism' which influenced craft and design, with art-nouveau style and organic abstractions of a decoratively 'Celtic' sort being produced in Glasgow by the Macdonald sisters, Herbert MacNair and the brilliant young architect and designer Charles Rennie Mackintosh (1868–1928).

Scottish Celticism never produced a writer to compare with Yeats, but its best exponent was **William Sharp** (1855–1914), whose self-consciously musical prose is not unlike the cadences of Synge in *Riders to the Sea*. Sharp was born in Paisley and cut short a degree in Glasgow University to go to London to work as a journalist, biographer, art-critic and essayist. His dashing bohemian looks and nervous intensity gained him admission to the Rossetti circle, where he espoused the Pre-Raphaelite cause and met most of the writers of the day, including Walter Pater, who impressed him greatly, and the young Yeats, with whom he shared an interest in spiritualism and the occult. He was informed about the art and literature of many countries and travelled widely all his life, spending short spells in Europe, the Middle East and America. As a cosmopolitan journalist and a lively, dandyish figure, Sharp had a curious relationship with his own identity, for he came to perceive a sensitive, secret and feminine side to his personality, coloured by hints of a mystical Catholicism quite different from his Presbyterian roots in Paisley. He associated this side of his nature with visits to the Highlands and psychic experiences from childhood, and he identified his sense of passive poetic fatedness with what he took to be the Celtic inheritance. Eventually this *persona* entered his writing under the name of 'Fiona Macleod', whom he pretended was a cousin of his and something of a recluse. *Pharais* ('Paradise') appeared in 1894, the *Mountain Lovers* and *The Watcher of the Ford* in the following year. These books dealt with timeless and archetypal patterns of love and death in remote Highland settings. They sold well, and further novels, essays and short stories appeared in the next ten years as 'Fiona Macleod' gradually took over literary production from William Sharp. This was more than a successful pseudonym, and Sharp took elaborate steps to maintain the fiction of Fiona's existence and dreaded exposure and the disillusionment of his readers.

Sharp's Celticism lacked the linguistic, political and nationalistic direction which fuelled the Irish movement. His ideal was to seek a mystical expression of the eternal feminine which would add a much needed leaven to Anglo-Saxon pragmatism and the Presbyterian work-ethic. But he belongs to the 'Celtic twilight' because his world of hills and islands is sentimentally charged by the conviction that it is already passed or doomed to pass. He paints a 'golden age' that never existed in Gaelic culture, and its popular appeal depended on the fact that it was far from industrialisation and the gaslights and tenements of Glasgow streets. Even so, a similar belief in archetypal values is very marked in the work of Edwin Muir, Lewis Grassic Gibbon, Neil Gunn and George Mackay Brown, and all these writers from the next century could be said to form a distinctively Scottish school of 'mythopoeic realism' whose origins go back to these earlier movements in anthropology and the 'Celtic' ideal.

Apart from Stevensonian romance or symbolic fantasy, Scottish fiction ended the century with a vision of itself which was parochial, sentimental and almost entirely given over to nostalgia. Late-Victorian readers seem to have refused to countenance the industrial and urban growth around them, and, although the prolifically popular novelist 'Sarah Tytler' (Henrietta Keddie, 1827–1914) touched on the poverty and disease of Glasgow in *St Mungo's City* (1884), the theme was not central to her tale of a self-made businessman who learns charity and recovers his holdings. For most other novelists the honourable tradition of domestic realism had not advanced beyond the hearthside piety of 'The Cottar's Saturday Night'. Fiction in just this vein by J. M. Barrie, S. R. Crockett and Ian Maclaren achieved widespread success in the 1890s, as if Lowland Scots were longing, like their Gaelic-speaking compatriots, for their own 'homeland' literature of childhood memories and maternal security.

The Kailyard

The term comes from the verse epigraph to a collection of tales published by Ian Maclaren in 1894:

> There grows a bonnie briar bush in our kail-yard,
> And white are the blossoms on't in our kail-yard.

Within a year W. E. Henley's *New Review* attacked the genre as cabbage-patch – 'kailyard' – writing, and J. H. Millar, the critic in question, renewed the assault in 1903 in his *History of Scottish Literature*. Perhaps the most scathing comments over the years have been made by other creative writers, such as the novelist George Blake, who contributed *Barrie and the Kailyard School* in 1951. Critics have found it difficult ever since to say anything positive about these tales, for their vogue, like the Victorian appetite for tearful death-scenes, has undoubtedly passed away. Yet the case of the Kailyard reveals much about the complicated nature of Scottish cultural identity, going back at least as far as the genteel insecurities of Alan Ramsay.

The best works of Scott, Hogg, Galt and Stevenson were derived from the passions of the past, the difficulties of change, or from their authors' grasp of psychological or moral tensions. But the Kailyard is against change, and when it looks to the past – usually one generation back – it describes a timeless stasis of isolated rural communities whose dramas revolve around the doings of the minister or the dominie – arrivals, departures, weddings, funerals and the pitfalls of petty presumption. It must be admitted that these themes belong within the Scottish tradition of feeling and domestic realism, but it has sadly dwindled to a sentimentalised subgenre.

As *Blackwood's* was the forum for so many influential writers earlier in the century, so the *British Weekly* and a number of liberal Presbyterian ministers were the patrons of the Kailyard. This Evangelical periodical was edited in London by **the Revd William Robertson Nicoll** (1851–1923). Born and educated in the North-East, Nicoll trained as a Free Church minister like his father before him, and from him he inherited a vast library and a voracious appetite for books. He served as a minister for twelve years before moving to London to establish a career in journalism with Hodder and Stoughton, one of the Kailyard's principal publishers. He founded the *British Weekly* in 1896, aimed at a nonconformist market where Christian doctrine was leavened by humorous sketches and articles on moral issues such as the 'temptations of London'. On literary subjects *The Bookman* followed in 1891 and *Woman at Home* (1893) spoke to married women with fashion-notes, advice and popular fiction-serials. Nicoll championed the young J. M. Barrie and persuaded Ian Maclaren to take up writing. Anne S. Swan (1859–1943), the redoubtable creator of innumerable romantic stories, was an early contributor and became the mainstay of *Woman at Home*, subtitled 'Annie S. Swan's Magazine'. The *British Weekly* and the *Christian Leader* – a Baptist weekly from Glasgow – were particularly responsive to Kailyard fiction, in which sentimental piety was so conveniently packaged. On the strength of this market Ian Maclaren toured America with lectures and sermons in 1896, followed by Nicoll and **J. M. Barrie** (1860–1937) who were well received in their turn by large audiences in Boston and New York.

Only the initial stages of Barrie's career properly belong to the Kailyard school, but his sketches of village life in 'Thrums', most of which appeared in the *St James's Gazette* and the *British Weekly* were among the earliest and most successful publications in the genre. Barrie came from a large working-class family in Kirriemuir, where his father was a linen-weaver, working the loom from his own home. The children – five daughters and three sons – (two more died as infants) were all brought up in the Free Kirk, although their mother Margaret Ogilvy came from a more puritanical sect called the 'Auld Lichts', who objected to hymns, religious music and even to written prayers and sermons. True to type, the family was determined that the boys should gain advancement through education, so the eldest son became a teacher and David, Mrs Barrie's favourite, was destined for the ministry. But David was killed in a skating-accident at the age of thirteen and his mother fell into an obsessive grief which at first entirely excluded her youngest son. Wracked with jealousy, sympathy and guilt, James Matthew Barrie, scarcely seven years old, tried very hard to take David's place in his mother's heart. He spent long afternoons with her, telling stories and listening to tales and memories from her own childhood, and the pair grew very close. When eventually she died Barrie was compelled to relive their intimacy publicly in a loving memoir called *Margaret Ogilvy and her Son* (1896). His complicated feelings for this emotionally smothering and puritanical little woman almost certainly led to the failure of his marriage, and it is tempting to find the roots of his affection for children, his fear of ageing and his fascination with death in the overwhelming nature of this early relationship.

Barrie graduated with an MA from Edinburgh in 1882 and set his mind on a literary career. He reviewed plays and worked as a journalist in Nottingham for two years before moving to London, where he placed articles with the *St James's Gazette* and various other periodicals (sometimes using the name 'Gavin Ogilvy') and made friends with W. E. Henley and Robertson Nicoll. A light novel called *Better Dead* was published at his own expense in 1886, but his sketches of 'Scotch' life for the magazines were so popular that he was encouraged to assemble them in book form. *Auld Licht Idylls* appeared in 1888 and *A Window in Thrums* was ready the following year. Both derive from his mother's recollections of an isolated community of farmers and nonconformist weavers, a world of parish-pump politics, proud, pious and obsessed with keeping up appearances. Barrie's descriptive prose is well realised and his observant and cutting humour can rise to bleak irony, for he remembered enough about Kirriemuir to know that 'Thrums' was not entirely idyllic. Yet he 'miniaturises' its society in a way that Scott or Galt would not have done, and in place of a changing social scene he writes a series of brief vignettes and invites us to eavesdrop upon them. As vignettes do, these depend on single moments of pathos or comic discomfiture, and the result is static, knowing and patronising.

If these sketches have any wider scope, it comes from Barrie's awareness of change and mortality – we have already been told that such communities died away in the last fifty years – and the opening piece of *A Window in Thrums* evokes Jess McQumpha's cottage, now empty and fallen into disrepair. Hers is the window where she sat 'for twenty years or more looking at the world as through a telescope'. In the narrator's reminiscences we share this window with Jess, but the telescope is the wrong way round, and what we really see is Barrie's sense of his own lost childhood – suspended in time, and ever so far away. Thrums exists like Shangri-La in a charmed circle and Barrie is overcome by pathos whenever characters have to leave it, for, in this nostalgic light, death or a departure for London seem equally final; and any hint of the outside world would certainly be fatal.

The Thrums books were popular and even Stevenson admired them (although the folk at Kirriemuir were not so sure), but Barrie's greatest success in the mode came with two later novels. *The Little Minister* (1891) was originally serialised in the *British Weekly* as the improbable tale of a minister's love for a gipsy girl; and *Sentimental Tommy* (1896) draws on Barrie's childhood with rather more insight to describe how his character's intensely sensitive and imaginative inner life fits him for artistic creativity and prevents him from achieving maturity. The theme became still more pointed in *Tommy and Grizel* (1900), which raised the question of marriage. By this time the author had been married for six years, but he found it easier to work in his study for hours, or to visit his club, than to share his thoughts or his physical affections with his beautiful actress wife. His chronic shyness, the emotional tensions of his childhood and his elegiac sense of Thrums as a place one cannot return to were all to achieve their fullest expression in the disturbing network of symbols behind *Peter Pan*.

'Thrums' renewed a vogue for pawky Scotchness and what *The Times* admired as 'unstrained pathos'. **The Revd John**

Watson (**'Ian Maclaren'**, 1850–1907), was a Free Kirk minister who was persuaded to recount his experiences of Perthshire for Robertson Nicoll's magazine. Henceforth the collections *Beside the Bonnie Briar Bush* (1894) and *The Days of Auld Lang Syne* (1895), the village of 'Drumtochty' and the name Ian Maclaren all became widely known. Watson was a minister in Liverpool when he began writing and produced as many religious works as fiction. He also helped to found the University of Liverpool and Westminster College, Cambridge, and was much in demand as a public speaker and preacher. A Drumtochty novel called *Kate Carnegie and those Ministers* appeared in 1896, and other collections followed in the next six years, including the sketches in *St Jude's* (1907), set in the Glasgow where he had preached for three years before 1880.

The Drumtochty tales came from three happy years at a church in Glen Almond, and they are suffused with longing for a country life left behind. Not surprisingly, perhaps, the narratives revolve around the kirk and many of the stories focus on either man's chief end (to glorify God) or man's mortal end:

'Ye can hae little rael pleesure in a merrige,' explained our gravedigger, in whom the serious side had been perhaps abnormally developed, 'for ye never ken hoo it will end; but there's nae risk about a "beerial".'

In this, and indeed in general, the author shares the views of the community, for, unlike Barrie, Maclaren writes from within its values and does not erect the former's affectionately satirical and ultimately condescending distance between his creatures and himself. On the other hand, his prose is often weak and sentimental and his piety has an untried, naïve air, especially when it is exercised over the frequent deaths which occur in the tales. Like most Kailyard fiction, it is as if all the more profane human passions which Presbyterianism was so intent on stifling could be rechannelled and respectably expressed only through vicarious grief at one fictional death after another. Such green pathos cannot appeal to modern readers, but in its day the evocation of Drumtochty as another lost Eden proved to be extraordinarily popular – especially in the United States, where over 500,000 copies were sold in the first few years. Maclaren died in America during his third tour of readings and lectures.

S. R. Crockett (1860–1914) was yet another Free Church minister, although he gave up his charge in 1895 once his success seemed assured and became a productive best-seller with over forty novels and adventure romances in the mode of Stevenson. The Kailyard sketches from his native Galloway first appeared in the *Christian Leader* and were collected in 1893 as *The Stickit Minister*. Crockett's descriptive style is ambitious in its evocation of place and atmosphere, and at their best the energy of stories such as 'The Lammas Preaching' makes the 'idylls' of Drumtochty seem naïve in execution. But most of Crockett's tales are too obviously designed to move his readers to laughter, or pity and horror, although they always manage to come to a comforting conclusion. To this end he mobilises sentimentality with ruthless insistence. In 'The Tragedy of Duncan Duncanson', a drunken schoolmaster, once a minister himself, strikes one of his pupils with a poker – quite forgetting that he had it in his hand. But the wounded boy protects him, for love of his young daughter, and swears that he hurt himself in a fall. 'Oh, Flora but yer e'en are terrible bonny!' the lad whispers as he regains consciousness. In another tale an old spinster who aspires to be a poet dies with tears of happiness in her eyes just as she sees her work mentioned in the newspaper. She does not know that the review was a savage one concocted by a smart young reporter. 'God is more merciful than man', intones Crockett at the end of 'The Heather Lintie'. Such is his preferred method – to evoke pain and then to 'kiss it away' with anodyne conclusions. The device is especially noticeable in *Cleg Kelly, Arab of the City* (1896), which does at least recognise the harshness of Victorian Edinburgh, but an insistently idyllic sentimentality entirely overwhelms the love story behind *The Lilac Sunbonnet* (1894). Crockett's talent for vigorous description does better with his later historical romances such as *The Raiders* (1894) and *The Men of the Moss Haggs* (1895), but they lack the psychological tensions of Stevenson's work and remain popular adventure fiction.

John Davidson (1857–1909)

If the Kailyard failed to acknowledge the modern world altogether, the same cannot be said of the poetry of John

Davidson, and it is fitting that this chapter should end with the only Scottish writer of his generation who tried to find a voice for the coming century. Davidson was a contemporary of William Sharp, and, although the two Scots were very different in outlook, they both came to prominence in the London of the nineties. Davidson contributed early lyrics to the *Yellow Book*, mixed with the Rhymers' Club at the Cheshire Cheese and had some of his novels illustrated by Beardsley. He made friends with Max Beerbohm, Richard Le Gallienne and Edmund Gosse, and he crossed swords with Yeats on one occasion. As a writer, however, he did not really belong to their circle. Outwardly conservative in appearance and manners, he was often contemptuous of his bohemian friends, preferring to see himself as a more truly intellectual rebel.

As the son of an Evangelical minister, Davidson was brought up in Glasgow and Greenock. He was an enthusiastic reader and soon tried his hand at poetry, but had to leave school early to earn a living, first as a laboratory assistant and then as a pupil teacher. He went to Edinburgh University in 1876, but his student career, or his money, or perhaps his patience, lasted only a year. He returned to teaching, with a post in Glasgow where he met John Nichol, professor of English at the university, a friend of Swinburne's and a freethinker. Davidson's absolutist nature and his impatience with his father's creed responded to the Carlylean fervour of Nichol's mind, and his literary ambitions must have been greatly stimulated when Swinburne admired his youthful verses and pronounced him poet. After getting married in 1884 he worked for a while as a clerk, but soon found himself teaching again, although he did not enjoy it. During these years in Glasgow, Perth and Crieff, his output of prose, verse and drama received very little recognition, but he nevertheless decided to commit himself to journalism and set out for London in 1888 with his young son and his pregnant wife.

His first collection of poems, *In a Music Hall* (1891), made little impact, but the next two, *Fleet Street Eclogues* (1893) and *Ballads and Songs* (1894), were rather well received. Sadly, he was never to regain this early success, although he produced further collections of eclogues and ballads in the next five years. His impressionistic poetic sketches of cityscape and country scenes are not untypical of their time, with Kiplingesque ballads and 'ninetyish' mood pieces with titles such as 'Nocturne'. Yet some of the ballads strike a new note of barely-suppressed rage at the futility and humiliations of daily urban life as suffered by Britain's equivalent of Gogol's clerks and the 'superfluous persons' of Russian fiction. 'In a Music Hall' reflects his own experiences as a clerk in Perth and it catches the fevered and sleazy excitements of popular entertainment as seen from both sides of the footlights. 'Thirty Bob a Week' is equally animated by a ferociously ironic spirit raging at the material difficulties of making ends meet on a pittance. Yet these poems are not merely 'social realism', for they offer a vision of the individual spirit – a spirit capable of a metaphysical destiny – somehow trapped and sullied in the ordinary world. The effect is startling – as if Kipling were suddenly to speak like Shelley, or Carlyle.

During the early nineties Davidson wrote several light novels somewhat in the manner of Beerbohm or Chesterton. *Baptist Lake* (1894), for example, lampooned the pretensions of aristocrats and aesthetes alike and there are moments in some of his books when the writer's humour can seem disconcertingly sadistic or ironically wild, rather like the later satire of Huxley or Wyndham Lewis. Since he always wrote slowly and with difficulty, Davidson found the demands of journalism particularly exhausting. Yet he needed the work, for he had to support his mother in Edinburgh as well as his wife, children and a younger brother too, whose alcoholism and irrational violence had brought him to an asylum. Towards the end of the century he tried his luck with adaptations and plays for the London theatre, with only short-lived success. His *New Ballads* (1897) were given bad reviews in the *Athenaeum*, and his spirits and general health – he suffered from chronic bronchitis – began to decline. He particularly resented his lack of poetic success, yet the rough-hewn and ambitious scope of a poetry so full of abstruse ideas could never have appealed to popular taste and his critics began to call it chopped-up journalistic prose. Even so, despite their imperfections, these verses were his most original achievement.

Davidson was beginning to evolve a vitalist philosophy of how the universe and consciousness emerge out of matter as if driven by an evolutionary will. He linked a growing fascination with scientific materialism with the romantic spirit of assertion to be found in Carlyle and especially in Nietzsche. This was his answer to the Victorian crisis of faith and his own bouts of terrible depression. Thus he celebrates the crystalline structure and the 'purpose' of a snow-flake – which is to achieve form for its own sake ('Snow'); or he commands his soul to do the same by casting-off bourgeois values and conventional notions of good and bad in favour of being 'haughty, hard, / Misunderstood' ('The Outcast'). There can be harsh inconsistencies in voice and craft in some of Davidson's verses, but an awkwardly powerful and original poetry does emerge from the assertive violence and confusion of his metaphysics. In the last ten years of his life he pursued this vision into longer and longer blank-verse poems, knotted with argument and ideas, increasingly idiosyncratic, increasingly unsuccessful with the public.

'The Crystal Palace' (1908), one of Davidson's last poems, was constructed – like several others – from an article he had already written in prose. It is a long, low-key, Browningesque monologue on the urban crowd as it throngs through the Victorian age's most famous monument to modernity. The juxtaposition it makes between aristocratic cultural values and vulgar entertainment anticipates something of the spirit of Pound and Eliot:

> A dense throng in the central transept, wedged
> So tightly they can neither clap nor stamp,
> Shouting applause at something, goad themselves
> In sheer despair to think it rather fine:
> 'We came here to enjoy ourselves. Bravo,
> Then! Are we not?' Courageous folk beneath
> The brows of Michael Angelo's Moses dance
> A cake-walk in the dim Renascence Court.

T. S. Eliot admitted to being influenced by 'Thirty Bob a Week' as well as by the poet's eye for 'dingy urban images', for Davidson was one of the few poets of his generation (along with Thomson, whose work he admired) to portray the squalor, despair and grim beauty of the modern city:

> Now wheel and hoof and horn
> In every street
> Stunned to its chimney-tops,
> In every murky street –
> Each lamp-lit gorge by traffic rent
> Asunder,

Ravines of serried shops
By business tempests torn –
In every echoing street,
From early morn
Till jaded night falls dead,
Wheel, hoof and horn
Tumultuous thunder
Beat
Under
A noteless firmament
Of lead.

('Yuletide', 1905)

The Scot also wanted poetry to 'certify the semi-certitudes of science', and he brought the very stuff of the sciences into his verse. The result was not always successful but there are original and striking passages too:

The other atoms, as the planets cooled,
Became; and all the elements, how much
So ever differing in appearance, weight,
Amount, condition, function, volume (gold
From iodine, argon from iron) wrought
Of the purest ether, in electrons sprang
As lightning from the tension filling space.
Forms of the ether, primal hydrogen,
Azote and oxygen, unstable shapes,
With carbon, most perdurable of all
The elements, forthwith were sifted out
To be the diverse warp and woof of life,
The lowest and the highest, louse and man.

(*The Testament of John Davidson*, 1908)

Hugh MacDiarmid also acknowledged a debt to this aspect of Davidson's vision, and his own later world-language poems are equally laden with esoteric scientific ideas. Davidson's long monologues and dialogues, darkly Spasmodic poetic tragedies and his polemic testaments – there were five of them – were his last achievements. They can be disturbingly desperate: *The Testament of a Vivisector* (1901), for example, revels in images of sado-masochistic pain, and yet manages to convey, too, the author's sensitive anguish at the material plight of our bodies. Uneven as they are, passages from Davidson's later works did genuinely enlarge the subject-matter of poetry, and Davidson certainly pushed his vision and his grasp well beyond the comfortable and accepted limits of his day.

The poet's sense of isolation was not helped by a move to Penzance in 1907. When *The Testament of John Davidson* appeared the following year, he became angry and depressed at the incomprehension and hostility of the critics, and in the belief that he had contracted cancer he took a revolver and disappeared from home in March 1909. His body was recovered from the sea after six months.

7

The twentieth century: the Scottish Renaissance

When the French critic and philosopher Denis Saurat wrote an influential essay on the 'Scottish Renaissance' in 1924, he was thinking mainly of the writers associated with Hugh Mac-Diarmid's *Northern Numbers* anthologies and his magazine the *Scottish Chapbook*, started two years earlier. Yet the notion of a renaissance was not a new one, and signs of a revival in culture and politics can be traced to the beginning of the century. Of course, MacDiarmid's creative example, not to mention his nationalism and his indefatigable propaganda, soon became the heart of the matter, just as the insistence on a European outlook and his satirical attacks on his own countrymen gave the movement a necessary international and critical dimension. Today 'the Scottish Renaissance' is used more generally to describe the remarkable outpouring of cultural activity which has gone towards making this the third major period of literary achievement in Scotland's history. It has become convenient to refer to a 'second wave' in the Renaissance to describe those writers who came to prominence in the forties and fifties, and after that we can talk of a third generation as well, even if some of the younger writers discussed briefly at the end of this chapter would deny any direct literary debt to MacDiarmid, Gibbon, Gunn, Muir or Maclean, or, indeed, any connection with each other. Thus, while some of the sixties' writers looked to Europe or America or England for their models, others, especially in Glasgow and the west, turned to a lively appreciation of working-class Scottish speech and topics. These three 'waves' of literary activity can also be found in the country's periodicals, with MacDiarmid's *Chapbook* leading the way from

1922. In the thirties and forties J. H. Whyte's *Modern Scot* and Maurice Lindsay's *Poetry Scotland* were among the more influential publications, with the *Saltire Review* and then the *New Saltire* taking over between 1954 and 1964. (Among the little magazines *Lines Review*, which started in 1952, Duncan Glen's *Akros*, David Morrison's *Scotia Review* and *Chapman* have all been particularly constructive.) Finally, the 'third generation' was heralded by the publication of magazines such as Bob Tait's *Scottish International* (1968–74), the *New Edinburgh Review* from the same year, and *Cencrastus* from 1979.

The century began with the popular success of Charles Murray's vernacular verse in *Hamewith*, while Professor H. J. C. Grierson had begun to teach Scots literature and language at the University of Aberdeen. Literary histories by Millar and Henderson followed in the next ten years, while Gregory Smith's *Scottish Literature, Character and Influence* (1919) provided MacDiarmid with just the argument he needed to propose a dynamic and contradictory spirit in the Scottish sensibility – a psychology worthy of Dostoevsky himself – and utterly opposed to the sentimental dilutions of the Kailyard. MacDiarmid tried to align even the vernacular tradition with the swift collisions of imagery in modernist verse, or claimed that Scots was well suited to the spirit of D. H. Lawrence's prose. The Irish literary revival had impressed Scotsmen at the turn of the century, and by the 1920s James Joyce was being cited as a figure who could achieve international status and universal significance for books which were still deeply rooted in his native Dublin. The local need not be parochial, and MacDiarmid stressed the point by insisting that true internationalism could not even exist without small nations. The unique identity of such countries and the need to resist their slide into the anonymity of larger political and economic bodies became an early concern of Scottish nationalism and was to be revived in the seventies, after the spirit of E. F. Schumacher's *Small is Beautiful* (1973) – a 'study of economics as if people mattered'. The First World War had played a part in this understanding, for it was fought – so the population was told – 'to preserve the right of small nations', and yet many servicemen returned to a Scotland whose cultural and economic identity seemed to be at a very low ebb indeed. MacDiarmid and Saurat were not slow to adopt the motto of the Belgian literary revival – 'Soyons nous mêmes'

– although, surprisingly, the Irish example was seldom used. For the 'Renaissance group' at least, cultural and political identity were inseparable.

In fact political nationalism and the demand for 'Home Rule' go back to Liberal politics of the previous century, and also featured in the thinking of the Scottish Left in the Independent Labour Party and the trade-unions. Labour-tensions had come to a head in Clydeside during and immediately after the war – under the influence of internationally minded socialists on the shop-floor, and the ordinary worker's recognition that the ailing heavy industries of the central belt had been ruthlessly expanded to meet the war-effort only to face decline again in the years of peace. The anti-war speeches of John Maclean, strikes, mass meetings, and his imprisonment with James Maxton on charges of sedition all led to real fears of revolution and 'Red Clydeside' on the part of the establishment, especially during the famous mass strike for a forty-hour week in 1919, when armoured cars and troops policed the streets of Glasgow. Maclean's hopes for a form of Scottish republican communism (free of Moscow) were not to be realised, but his many trials and his early death in 1923 made him a martyr for the cause and a potent symbol of it ever since. Sorley Maclean, MacDiarmid, Edwin Morgan, Hamish Henderson and Sydney Goodsir Smith were all to write verses about him, for the old Covenanting spirit had not lost its power to move – most especially as reflected in the secular but evangelical intensities of Sorley Maclean's political poems.

After the initial euphoria at the coming of peace, the post-war slump took hold with particular force in the heavy industries and coal-mines of Scotland, Tyneside and south Wales, and these areas suffered disproportionate hardships in the Depression years to come. By 1922 the Left and the ILP had made major advances in Scotland, sending twenty-nine Labour MPs to Westminster, with ten 'Red Clydesiders' headed by John Wheatley and including Maxton, Mannie Shinwell, Tom Johnston and one Communist – Willie Gallacher. The Labour movement continued to grow during the years around the General Strike in 1926, and many figures from Scotland's radical tradition played leading parts on the national stage. After all, social conditions in the post-Victorian Scottish cities and especially in the industrial west were truly appalling. Yet internal strife, dispute between the ILP and the Labour Party, widespread fears of communism, and simple dread at the prospect of the Depression getting worse, all helped to put Ramsay MacDonald's essentially conservative National Government into power in the 1930s. The radical 'Red Clyde' entered the realms of legend, although Glasgow and the west continue to be a heartland of left-wing politics in Britain.

Meanwhile a more culturally centred drive for nationalism had led to the foundation of the National Party of Scotland at Stirling in 1928, with R. E. Muirhead and John MacCormick as chairman and secretary (both from the ILP), and a spectrum of support from workers, liberals, students and radical intellectuals such as MacDiarmid and their president, Cunninghame Graham. In the 1930s the National Party amalgamated with the more liberal Scottish Party to form the Scottish National Party, and the movement began to gain strength during and after the Second World War, when the tendency once again had been to submerge Scotland's economic and social problems for the sake of Britain as a whole. It was popularly believed that, for as long as power was centralised in Westminster and in the massive population of the Home Counties, government would never come to grips with matters in Scotland and the north of England, which continued to suffer from unemployment, industrial decline, inadequate housing and high emigration. By the more prosperous sixties the case for 'devolution' had attracted widespread interest, and after the winning of Hamilton by Winnie Ewing in 1967 the SNP began to influence Westminster, if only because its presence as an electoral threat stimulated both Labour and Conservative parties to accommodate themselves to Scottish needs. (The Liberal Party had continued to support decentralisation but made less of a threat to the *status quo* in parliament.)

The discovery of oil in the North Sea heralded a boom for the SNP as well, typified by the opportunistic slogan 'It's Scotland's Oil'. The widespread success of John McGrath's play *The Cheviot, the Stag and the Black, Black Oil* in 1973 had as much to do with sentimental nationalism as it had with his own brand of republican socialism, but, even so, it seemed that a devolved socialist Scotland was just around the corner. Had not Scotland voted Labour since the war? Was there not a bill before parliament for moderate devolution? The bill passed at the close of 1976 only to die the death of a thousand cuts in committee-stage. Then Westminster decreed that the referendum result could not be valid unless 40 per cent of all registered Scottish voters voted 'yes', which meant that none of the parties could agree on how to interpret the result in 1979, when only 33 per cent of the total electorate voted 'yes' to Scottish devolution, with a majority of 80,000. In any case the bill died, and in the face of world economic recession the political popularity of devolution or separation died as well. These matters from the twenties and the seventies are worth recounting at length, for to many it seemed as if the 'auld sang' had been heard again – in two different keys – only to be lost again, twice in one century.

If MacDiarmid's hopes for a Scottish republic never bore fruit, his vision of a broader cultural revival fared better. His own poems were set to music by his friends F. G. Scott (1880–1958) and Ronald Stevenson (b. 1928), both of whom played leading parts in the Renaissance by developing modern music from aspects of traditional Scottish sources. At a less academic level – although MacDiarmid himself hated 'folk music' – there has been a notable revival in traditional playing, singing and song-writing, while the School of Scottish Studies, since 1951, has developed the field of folk-life studies and promoted a new and wider appreciation of traditional and oral culture. Of course, institutions do not make art, but the foundation of the two major Scottish-language dictionaries and the Scottish Gaelic Text Society in the years between 1929 and 1937 helped to make up for the past neglect. The publications of the Porpoise Press and William Maclellan and then, in the sixties, the popularity of public poetry-reading, the rise of small presses, the growth of interest in Gaelic and the availability of the Traverse Theatre in Edinburgh and the Third Eye Centre in Glasgow have all helped to bring new Scottish creative work to a wider audience.

Among painters the 'Scottish Colourists' at the beginning of the century had looked to Europe and the 'Fauves', most notably J. D. Fergusson (1874–1961), who had lived abroad until the outbreak of the Second World War. The 'Edinburgh School' also remained true to the expressive and poetic use of colour and pattern – from its formation in 1922, with William Gillies (1898–1973) and William MacTaggart (b. 1903), into the post-war years, and the appearance of Anne Redpath (1895–1965), John Maxwell (1905–62) and Robin Philipson (b. 1916). These painters represent what was to be the mainstream of Scottish art in the mid-century period, as opposed to the more surreal and abstract works of James Cowie (1886–1956) and William Johnstone (b. 1897). The brilliant work of Joan Eardley (1921–63) combined an eye for colour, landscape and abstract textures with an equal commitment to the social surface of the cities. Elizabeth Blackadder (b. 1931), James Morrison (b. 1932), John Knox (b. 1936) and Willie Rodger (b. 1930) all have established reputations, as have John Bellany (b. 1942), whose sparse realism contrasts with the primitive naturalism of Alexander Moffat (b. 1943), who has painted many portraits of Scottish writers – in complete contrast to the photographically realised but brooding and dreamlike images of Neil Dallas Brown (b. 1938).

If a Renaissance exists at all, however, its most developed expression has been achieved in the literature of the last eighty years as writers have sought to express themselves in a modern Scotland where more than ever before they have felt the need to evaluate and to remake an understanding of their own present nature and past history. No two writers have taken the same route, but the polarity between MacDiarmid and Muir is suggestive of two broadly different responses, in which the materialist and extrovert energy of the one contrasts with the more inward and mythopoeic response to life from the other. The same distinction can be seen between the poetry of Edwin Morgan and that of George Mackay Brown; while Neil Gunn, Sorley Maclean, Iain Crichton Smith and most especially Lewis Grassic Gribbon tried to bring both modes together with varying degrees of success. Their work, however, speaks best for itself. The modern period really begins with a young journalist who wrote one good novel before he died; but first we must pick up the later career of J. M. Barrie, by far the most famous and successful Scottish writer of his day.

J. M. Barrie (1860–1937): later career

Following the success of the Thrums stories and *Margaret Ogilvie*, Barrie made a triumphal visit to America with

Robertson Nicoll. In 1897 he adapted his Kailyard novel *The Little Minister* for the stage and it was such a hit on both sides of the Atlantic that he turned all his considerable energies to the theatre, producing twenty-nine more plays in the next two dozen years. These brought him a knighthood, wealth and public status, yet he was a complicated and withdrawn personality, reclusive, hard-working, small of stature and intensely shy. Barrie had made friends with Shaw – a vigorous supporter of Ibsen and 'Ibsenism' at the time – but the Scotsman's social comedies rarely attempted Shaw's didactic wit, and they settled, like *The Admirable Crichton* (1902), for comfortable endings within the *status quo*. Thus *What Every Woman Knows* (1908) proposed that a briskly competent wife – his ideal woman – is the real power behind a successful man; but the point is painlessly made and in flattering both sexes the play entertained large audiences who were not quite ready for *A Doll's House*.

Barrie never allowed his own wife to share his inner life or his physical attentions and she left him for a more generous man in 1909. He was still in emotional bondage to memories of his boyhood and his mother. Plays such as *Dear Brutus* (1917) and *Mary Rose* (1920) are full of hints of death, eternal childhood, and the poignant divisions between inevitable age (or maturity) and carefree youth. Innocent of Freud, and without the capacity for sophisticated self-analysis, Barrie, like George MacDonald, can still create moments of disturbing symbolic power, and perhaps this innocence makes their work even more startling for the modern reader. Barrie's first and most enduring achievement in this vein was, of course, *Peter Pan, or The Boy Who Never Grew Up* (1904).

The play sprang from a friendship which he had formed with the neighbouring Llewelyn Davies family and their three (later five) sons. It was as if this famous writer, with his gruff manner and an unprepossessing pale face, had adopted another man's family – somewhat to the consternation of his own wife, not to mention Arthur Llewelyn Davies. The stories in *The Little White Bird* (1902) grew from the fairy-tales he began to spin about Kensington Gardens, and *Peter Pan* soon followed. No one was really sure at first if it was a play for adults or one for children, but it was a huge success in any case, going on to become a family Christmas treat for year after year. Even so, its dreamlike evocation of flight, the plight of the lost boys, the motherly comfort offered by a child, and paternal authority burlesqued as 'Captain Hook' seem like hints of a fable from the unconscious. Most memorable of all is the relationship between Peter and Wendy, in which her motherly, fussy and yet loving character hopes for some deeper bond only to be betrayed in the end by the innocently cruel forgetfulness of Peter's eternally immature nature. Barrie's earlier novels *Sentimental Tommy* and *Tommy and Grizel* had shown that he understood something of this betrayal in his own innermost being.

The playwright's relationship with the Llewelyn Davies family was deepened when Arthur died in 1907, and became closer still when Barrie's marriage broke up. Within three years Sylvia Llewelyn Davies died as well and Barrie became guardian and unofficial father to 'my boys', paying for their education at Eton and taking a great interest in their careers. Nevertheless, he could not avoid Wendy's fate, for the Davies boys, and then other young friends, inevitably matured and left him behind. Viewed in this light Sir J. M. Barrie seems a rather lonely figure, and, although he continued to write successful plays for years, few of these later works have been worth reviving. He died in 1937, but developments in Scottish literature had long left him behind – almost from the moment of his early theatrical success in London. Indeed, the first expression of the new spirit in the north had been a howl of anger at the sentimentality of Thrums and all its Kailyard imitators.

George Douglas Brown (1869–1902)

George Douglas Brown is remembered on the strength of only one novel – his second attempt at the form – and he died of pneumonia at the age of thirty-three within a year of its publication. *The House with the Green Shutters* (1901) was greeted by many critics and readers as a savage attack on the Kailyard, and Brown agreed but also maintained that he had wanted to picture small-town Scottish life accurately, and then to 'get inside the heads' of old John Gourlay and his son. The book does show a community undergoing social and economic changes – quite unlike the static nostalgia of Thrums and

Drumtochty, and in this, as with his desire to catch the humour
and strength of Scots speech, Brown follows his admired John
Galt. Yet he also explores several personally sensitive and
autobiographical themes.

Brown must have known small communities well enough,
not to mention their propensity for gossip, for he was born as an
illegitimate child in the little village of Ochiltree – in the heart
of Burns and Galt country near Mauchline in Ayrshire. His
mother was the unlettered daughter of an Irish labourer, and
his father, a local farmer renowned for his dour independence
and his colourful Scots speech, never did marry her. Young
George moved from the village school to Ayr Academy – with
the help of the rector there – and William Maybin's confidence
in his new pupil was rewarded when the boy excelled in English
and Classics and won a bursary entrance to Glasgow University, where he became a favourite student, and later the
assistant, of young Professor Gilbert Murray. Brown's mixed
feelings about his father appear in the matriculation forms from
these days, in which he sometimes listed him as a farmer and at
other times claimed he was dead. Artistic rather than scholarly,
Brown's temperament was given to bursts of energy and vivid
intuitive insights, but he graduated with first-class honours and
won the Snell Exhibition Scholarship, which took him to Balliol
College, Oxford. Brown's years as a student in the south were
fruitful, and he took a lively part in college life, but his studies
were erratic with periods of intensive activity followed by spells
of depression and poor health – a familiar pattern in his later
life. He read Balzac, Tolstoy and Dostoevsky – without liking
the Russian giants – and began to think of writing a novel which
would say something about his own background and the
Scottish character. Perhaps such themes were in his mind
because he had finally confronted his father before leaving for
England, only to find a tired and peppery old man in place of
the hard-hearted creature he must have imagined in his youth.
Whatever the reasons, Brown's classical studies began to
suffer, and when his mother's health collapsed – she had been
ill for years – he returned home to nurse her. She died in 1895
and he graduated later in the year with a third-class degree and
a certain sense of failure, despite his recognition that such
matters were no longer so important to him. He was later to
modify these experiences in his portrait of young John Gourlay

as a boy who finds himself out of his depth at university – a disappointment to a domineering father and his dying mother.

Set on a literary career, Brown took up freelance journalism in London, using the pen-names 'William Douglas' and 'Kennedy King' for short stories and a boy's adventure novel called *Love and Sword* (1899). He became involved in a small publishing-scheme with friends and continued to produce what he regarded as hack work. He was more serious, however, about a long story written in June 1900 which features a powerful character named Gourlay in a village to be called Barbie. His friends encouraged him to develop the theme, so at the end of the year he retreated to a cottage in Haslemere, bought a supply of exercise books and began to write his novel.

The House with the Green Shutters, by 'George Douglas', appeared in October 1901 and was widely and well reviewed. Andrew Lang – himself a distinguished Snell Scholarship man before Brown's time – likened Gourlay to Weir of Hermiston and compared Brown to a Scottish Balzac or Flaubert 'with a bitter sense of humour'. Other reviews invoked Galt and the power of Greek tragedy, and indeed Brown had drawn on his classical education for the 'bodies' – the common folk of Barbie, whose gossip responds like a Greek chorus to the doings and the sufferings of the Gourlay family. Most of the gossip is malicious, and the grimness of Brown's picture of village life derives from the fact that the few decent voices are seldom heard against the spiteful and cowardly backbiting of the majority, led in specially loathsome fashion by the lisping hypocrite Deacon Allardyce. Compared to these uncharitable nonentities, John Gourlay – the self-made carter – stubborn, brutal and tyrannical though he is, strides like a tiger among worms. Like Stevenson's Adam Weir, old Gourlay is imbued with all the absolutist paternal authority of Calvinism, although he is a more limited and stupid man than the judge. Thus Brown's study of a mother's son in conflict with such a father follows the psychological symbolism of Stevenson's novel, as if the Scottish sensibility were torn between broadly feminine and masculine outlooks, between what it owes to the muse and what to Jehovah. Stevenson, Brown and Lewis Grassic Gibbon all make use of the struggle between fathers and sons (or a daughter, in the case of Chris Guthrie) and the same late Victorian battle with puritanical authority motivated

Edmund Gosse's powerful study *Father and Son* (1907). Brown's sympathies are not easily given, however, for, although he paints Barbie and Gourlay in hellish colours, young John is little better – ending up as a weakling and a drunk.

Old Gourlay, like the house of which he is so proud, dominates the little town on the brae below, but times are changing because of the railway and the coal-mines nearby, and he begins to lose commercial supremacy to a wilier businessman called Wilson who diversifies from a general store to take over Gourlay's monopoly as a goods-carrier – the only trade the older man knows. Like his business, Gourlay's personality is monolithic and inflexible, and when his rival's son is sent to university he insists that young John should go as well – as a 'lad o'pairts' whose success will reflect credit on his father. But John's weak and sensitive character cannot cope, and he fails, just as his father's business is failing, and returns home to sulk in disgrace. He takes to drink, kills his father in a drunken fit and then commits suicide, only to be followed into death by his tubercular sister and his mother – an abused creature who has nursed a fear of Gourlay all her life just as she nurses the secret cancer gnawing at her breast. Before they take poison, Mrs Gourlay and her daughter turn to the Bible and read the famous passage on charity from 1 Corinthians.

The conclusion is excessively unrelenting – not formal enough for Greek tragedy and too melodramatic for realism. Yet the earlier parts of the novel are well controlled, with a forensic detachment in the narrative style, in effective contrast to descriptive passages which might have been written with the nervous excitation of young John Gourlay himself. Brown's prose is frequently criticised for a tendency to analyse his creatures, pontificating on them and on Scottish failings in general; but this is a deliberate device against the cosy familiarity of Scots speech and the Kailyard setting. Contemporary readers familiar with post-modernist fiction may find this authorial position less intrusive than did earlier critics:

When we think of what Gourlay did that day, we must remember that he was soaked in alcohol – not merely with his morning's potation, but with the dregs of previous carousals. And the dregs of drink, a thorough toper will tell you, never leave him. He is drunk on Monday with his Saturday's debauch. As 'Drucken Wabster' of Barbie put it once, 'When a body's hard up, his braith's a consolation.' If that be so – and Wabster, remember, was an expert whose opinion on this matter is entitled to the highest credence – if that be so, it proves the strength and persistence of a thorough alcoholic impregnation, or, as Wabster called it, of 'a good soak'. In young Gourlay's case, at any rate, the impregnation was enduring and complete. He was like a rag steeped in fusel oil.

Brown defended such ironic objectivity in his notes for *The Novelist* – a study he never completed – and in the 'Rules for Writing' collected during 1901, in which he described the artist as an 'Observer of Humanity *from the outside*'. Thus he aspired to be philosophically aloof, as if *sub specie aeternitatis*, and even 'callous', for ''tis the weakling-artist who invites his lachrymose readers to a petty whine over the merited sorrows of the human race'. If there is a young man's arrogance to such a programme, it is not so very different from Stephen Dedalus's theory that the writer should be like God – indifferent and beyond his handiwork. The device is not always successful, but it was an original effort to bring a crystal-clear, hard-edged definition to the flattering mists of 'Scotch' setting and sentiment. It is especially fitting that his forensic tones – reminiscent of a pedantically precise Scots advocate – should be used to reinforce an equally Scottish taste for Old Testament retribution as it came to be visited on the Gourlays at the end. Without Brown's ironically inhumane distance, *The House with the Green Shutters* would be a more predictable book, and certainly less disturbing in its effect – at least until he relaxes his steely grip and melodrama takes over in the final scenes.

At the age of thirty-three George Douglas Brown was delighted with the success of his first serious novel. He visited friends in Ayrshire, assembled notes on his theories of writing and contemplated another novel, to be called 'The Incompatibles'. But pneumonia, left untreated for too long, killed him in August 1902. His novel became a special milestone in Scottish letters because it used the Kailyard's own ingredients to blight the bonnie briar-bush itself. Hay's *Gillespie* followed in 1914, but it was overtaken by the Great War and, despite enthusiastic reviews, it never became as well known as *The House with the Green Shutters* and it was 1963 before it was published again.

John MacDougall Hay (1881–1919)

Hay was born and brought up in Tarbert at the mouth of Loch Fyne to the west of Glasgow. It was a community with Highland roots, but he did not speak Gaelic. He graduated with an ordinary MA at Glasgow University, where he had begun, even as student, to write creatively and to earn money as a freelance journalist. He worked as a teacher in the west until a severe attack of rheumatic fever changed his plans and he determined to train as a minister for the Church of Scotland, returning to university in 1905 and graduating five years later. He supported himself during this time and kept up his writing with a succession of reviews and articles for various Glasgow newspapers and London magazines. He made friends with Neil Munro, already an established novelist, and he started to think of the book that was to become *Gillespie*. In 1909, after a probationary period, Hay became minister at Elderslie, a largely urban parish on the outskirts of Glasgow, between Paisley and Johnstone. He married and settled down to a reticent life as minister and author, working late into the night on his bulky and intractable manuscript.

Hay had few pastimes, beyond reading and fishing, but his imaginative life must have been dramatic enough, for he said in a later interview that the intense sensations experienced by his character young Eoghan were based on his own visions and on memories of childhood. Certainly *Gillespie* is remarkable for the hallucinatory richness of its style, and it caused a sensation when it appeared in 1914, being highly praised by Hardy and particularly well received by American critics. A second novel, *Barnacles*, followed in 1916 and a collection of free verse called *Their Dead Sons* was published in 1918, but neither volume recaptured the impact of the first book, and *Gillespie*'s unrelenting grimness must have seemed less and less palatable after the war. Hay's health had never been very strong since his early illness, and he succumbed to TB in the winter of 1919. His son is the Gaelic poet George Campbell Hay.

There are obvious similarities between the stories of Gillespie Strang and John Gourlay. Both novels paint a savage picture of Scots community life and Hay's Brieston is also based on his home town – namely Tarbert. Both books have a tyrannical father who dominates all those around him, including his suffering wife and a fey and sensitive son. Both end with death and destruction. Clearly Hay had read Brown, but his literary tastes owe nothing to his predecessor, nor does he attempt the embryo modernism of a detached prose style. In this respect it is significant that Hay liked Dostoevsky – a writer Brown considered exaggerated and obscure. There is an extravagant symbolic richness to Hay's outlook and on every page he elevates the Scottish penchant for descriptive detail to overpowering heights – like a development of Mannerism in prose. Consider this description of herring-gutters at work:

> Those beautiful fish, silk-shot with a greenish-blue through the scales, are the strongest hostages against penury. From the cold deep they have come to brighten the hearth; fashioned in silver in the dark, as diamonds in the bowels of the earth. The burnishing of knives was a labour of love in the Back Street. What a sight it was to see again the big fishing-boats laced with scales and the shining pile in the Square. The women sat on empty herring boxes by the pile, their arms bared and dappled with blood. . . . When the dusk came the work was continued within the store, whose interior, lit with torches, presented a weird spectacle. Beneath the glare of the torches mingled with smoke, the gutters with blood-stained hands sat around, their faces starting out of the reek in the murky light and falling again into shadow. The pile of herring smouldered in pools of dull gold. . . . The big guttings of former days were recalled when the splendid fishing lured gutters from Stornoway and Peterhead to Brieston. Old times were restored; the old dead were resurrected; the aged were seen as young.
>
> 'Many's the guttin' ye hae sang at noo, Flory'; and as the torches flicker and the knives grow idle, and the weary hands are at rest a moment, a sweet treble voice sings the Scottish ballad:
>
> > 'Last night there were four Maries,
> > To-night they'll be but three',
>
> and fifty women take up the haunting air, making it swell beyond the rafters and the roof to the night and the stars. In that song the hungry days are ended, and the sorrows of the sea.

Scene after scene is illuminated in this portentous light, rising to moments of apocalyptic intensity, for Hay's outlook is genuinely metaphysical or theological, and he conceives Gillespie Strang as a demonic force whose very birth was heralded, in unashamedly Shakespearean fashion, by evil omens. Gillespie's soul is like an iceberg, and yet he wears the outward guise of a hearty self-made businessman. Unlike John Gourlay, Hay's clever protagonist turns the law, technical progress and other people's cupidity all to his own advantage, destroying everything around him (and finally himself) in the successfully calculated pursuit of profit and self-interest. Hay reported that his target was the growing spirit of materialism in Scotland, and in true Evangelical fashion he gave its spokesman a Mephistophelian stature, a capitalist convinced that 'the stars were fighting for him in their courses', a figure who even seems to have chance and natural disaster on his side. Overcharged with physical detail and portents, Gillespie looks back to the Gothic Romanticism and the folk energy of Hogg's visions of evil and uses this spirit to give an eldritch animation to the nineteenth-century world of commerce and bourgeois materialism.

Neil Munro (1864–1930)

Like his young friend Hay, Neil Munro came from the Central Highlands lying to the west of Glasgow. Following a spell in a lawyer's office he turned to journalism and for two years after the First World War he was editor of the *Glasgow Evening Times*, where George Blake also came to know him. Although Gaelic was in decline in Inverary, where Munro was born, his own familiarity with the language and its speech-patterns is clearly reflected in the spare English prose of his early stories. In a sense the bitter-sweet short stories of *The Lost Pibroch* (1896) belong with the Celtic twilight, except that Munro regards Highland culture and the destructively romantic pull of its old loyalties with gentle irony. Beyond the Stevensonian romance of his historical novels, Munro shows an ironic fatalism which recognises that the love of 'romance' is dangerous, just as the melancholy narrator of *John Splendid* (1898) looks back to the tragic futility of Montrose's bitter campaign in Argyll, and recalls how he was caught up in it by an adventurer in the mould of Alan Breck. *Doom Castle* (1901) is an ironically Gothic tale set in the years after the Forty-five, while Munro's excellent sense of landscape and the excitements of eighteenth-century travel make *The New Road* (1914) an adventure in the footsteps of *Kidnapped*. The young hero is harried across Scotland only to discover that the story of his father's distant death in the

Jacobite cause is a lie – a lie concocted to conceal a sordid murder for simple gain at home.

As a journalist Munro wrote short stories and newspaper sketches calling himself 'Hugh Foulis', and it was under this name that he created the droll characters 'Archie' and 'Jimmy Swann'; but his most famous comic achievement was 'Para Handy', the skipper of a puffer called *Vital Spark*. The 'puffers' were tiny tramp steamers – like sea-going trucks – which used to operate out of the Clyde estuary, and the adventures of Para Handy and his eccentric crew are full of sly humour and delight in the manners and affairs of small townships up and down the west coast. Munro was reluctant to own up to these tales, but their popularity has quite overshadowed his more serious ambitions as a poet and they inspired a television comedy series in the 1970s.

John Buchan (1875–1940)

If Munro's historical fiction followed Stevenson's example, then the novels of John Buchan brought the same approach to contemporary settings. Buchan spent his teenage years in Glasgow, where his father – a Free Kirk minister – had his parish in the Gorbals. From Glasgow University Buchan won a classical scholarship to Oxford, where he arrived just as George Douglas Brown left for London. By the end of his student days he had produced a first-class degree, two historical novels and three other volumes, making a splash, too, as a Union president who made contributions to *The Yellow Book*. *John Burnet of Barns* (1898) looks to Covenanting times with lovingly detailed descriptions of Buchan's favourite Tweedside, where the holidays of his youth were spent, and this use of landscape set the pattern for most of his later fiction. After Oxford, Buchan turned to law in London and managed another couple of novels before going to South Africa for two years to work for the British High Commission at the end of the Boer War. He returned to London and the Law in 1903, accepted the post of literary adviser to Nelson's publishing-house and eventually became a director in 1915.

The novelist drew on his African experience for *Prester John* (1910) – a boys' adventure which begins on the Fife coast and takes its protagonist to a veritable heart of darkness where warring tribesmen follow a charismatic black leader who speaks with all the old passion of the Covenanters – the distorted religious inheritance of 'Prester John'. Buchan's enthusiasm for the original ideals of Presbyterianism and his hatred of its latent fanaticism illuminates his study of *The Marquis of Montrose* (1913), a subject he returned to with *Montrose* in 1928. The marquis's lightning campaigns over wild country particularly appealed to him and confirmed his belief that every man should be prepared to support his convictions or his social privileges by direct action. A simplified version of this creed motivated the exploits of Richard Hannay, who first appeared in 1915 with *The Thirty-nine Steps*. Indeed, Buchan's 'shockers', as he called them, show a strongly Calvinist sense of the presence of evil and savagery just beneath the 'civilised' surface of the everyday world, and they are equally alert to the dangers of fanaticism – just as extreme Calvinism was prone to what he saw as 'dark and vehement emotions'. Against such forces Buchan, like his heroes, values success born of hard effort, a simple clarity of purpose and a stubborn unwillingness to give up, rather than subtlety of insight or any more profound philosophical motivation. Such was the Presbyterian work-ethic of a Scottish gentleman conservative and, no doubt, there were thousands like him in the colonial service. If these values seem naïve in the face of the terrible sophistication of con-temporary dilemmas, at least they made for grand adventure tales, as another Scot, Ian Fleming, was to discover – although his James Bond is a more cynical creation reflecting the consumerism of the sixties.

By the early twenties Buchan was living in Oxford and commuting to London to work for Reuters and Nelson, for whom he had written a huge history of the war. He took an interest, too, in the new stirrings in Scottish poetry and contributed to Grieve's *Northern Numbers*. Although Buchan's own verse rarely strays from the ordinary, his taste was sound, and in 1924 he compiled an excellent anthology of old and new Scots poems which he called *The Northern Muse*, prefaced with an essay on how Scots vernacular literature had sunk to a provincial genre. Fond of walking and fishing, Buchan took regular holidays in Scotland and these settings feature in many of the thrillers he produced – one a year – between 1922 and

1936. The last five years of his life were spent as Governor General of Canada – with the title of Baron Tweedsmuir. As a confidant of Franklin D. Roosevelt, Buchan tried to mobilise American opinion to support Britain against Hitler and hence to forestall the outbreak of war. He failed, and in 1940 he died of a cerebral stroke. During the course of his life he had produced over a hundred books.

As far as his 'shockers' were concerned, Buchan was content to entertain, and, although they lack the historical or psychological depth of Scott and Stevenson, their approach, like Buchan's own craft, is honourably descended from that line. The historical novel itself, with the glamour of Scottish history and landscape, has continued to thrive. Its later exponents include Nigel Tranter (b. 1909), a professional writer for most of his life who has used his enthusiasm for Scottish history and architecture to give authentic detail to his fictionalised biographies, scholarly publications and local guides. By comparison Dorothy Dunnett (b. 1923) has developed character and atmosphere in a sequence of six books beginning with *The Game of Kings* (1961), featuring a charismatically Byronic Scottish soldier of fortune called Francis Crawford of Lymond. These long novels use the most densely realised dialogue and settings to evoke the cruel and glittering brilliance of sixteenth-century Europe and the north.

R. B. Cunninghame Graham (1852–1936)

Among the remaining prose writers from the first twenty years of the century, the fiery, dandyish and Quixotic Graham might have been invented in some unlikely collusion between Oscar Wilde, John Buchan and Hugh MacDiarmid. With Spanish blood on his mother's side and remote connections with Robert the Bruce, Graham came from a privileged background and got an early taste for foreign parts by going to Argentina at the age of eighteen to spend most of the next seven years living as a rancher, dressed like a gaucho and known as 'Don Roberto'. He returned to London, eloped with a Chilean girl whom he met in Paris, and roamed around Texas and Mexico before returning to Scotland to become a radical Liberal MP. This did not prevent him from being imprisoned after the riots in Trafalgar

Square in 1887 and suspended from Parliament more than once for his support of nationalisation, socialism or communism on a platform which demanded free education, a better deal for women, stronger trade-unions and more wages for a shorter day's work. A friend of Keir Hardie, Graham became first president of the Scottish Labour Party when it was founded in 1888. During the 1890s he began to write and came to know literary figures such as Conrad – whom he helped with *Nostromo* – Edward Garnett, Henry James, Oscar Wilde, Masefield, Hardy and Shaw. (He was the model for Saranoff in *Arms and the Man*, although Shaw felt that he was so much larger than life that a full account would never be believed on stage.) Don Roberto cultivated his own piratical and idealistic personality to an unusual degree. His South American background and fresh adventures as a latter-day explorer and gold-prospector in Morocco and Spain gave him material for his first travel books in the 1890s and then in the 1920s and 1930s he published biographies and historical studies of the conquistadores.

Several of Graham's first short stories and sketches were set in Scotland, for he was proud of his nationality but contemptuous of the vogue for Kailyard parochialism: 'Today a Scotsman stands confessed a sentimental fool . . .', he wrote in *The Ipané* (1899), 'oppressed with the tremendous difficulties of the jargon he is bound to speak, and above all weighed down with the responsibility of being Scotch.' Never afraid to put his spurs to sacred cows, Graham was equally scathing about the Kirk and all its doings. English imperialism fared little better, for he had a natural sympathy with foreign peoples, however distant their mores were from his own. His prose is succinctly and vigorously set down with telling and original details. Often hovering somewhere between sketch, free reminiscence and fiction, it is usually controlled by his own alert and astringent sense of irony – a style admired by many of his more famous writer friends. Further stories were collected in *Faith* (1909), *Hope* (1910), *Charity* (1912) and *Scottish Stories* (1914). In the post-war years Graham became critical of the Labour Party and renounced his socialism to campaign as a Liberal. He became president of the National Party in 1928 and of the Scottish National Party when it was brought together in 1934. In these circles he met with Hugh MacDiarmid, who criticised his retreat from the radical Left but shared his delight in slashing artistic mediocrity and bourgeois values whenever possible.

Norman Douglas (1868–1952)

As a cultivator of personality, a 'writer's writer' and an iconoclast in his own way, Douglas was as cosmopolitan as Graham. He became famous for his loving evocation of the southern tip of Italy in *Old Calabria* (1915) and for the sardonic zest of his first novel, *South Wind* (1917), which is replete with the hedonistic spirit of Capri – fictionalised as 'Nepenthe' – and full of the author's favourite topics and disquisitions. Douglas's family came from Tilquhillie Castle to the west of Aberdeen, but his father managed cotton-mills in Austria and Norman was born there with German as his first language. Young Douglas disliked the damp castle on Deeside and hated his English public school even more, regarding himself as a sophisticated European. At the age of twenty-eight he abandoned his short-lived career in the Foreign Service and settled in Italy as an amateur enthusiast – producing short stories with his wife before their marriage broke up. He had early fallen in love with Capri and the civilised ease of the Mediterranean, where he felt that his classical hedonism, and a cheerfully pagan interest in adolescent boys, was validated by past cultural history and the unsentimental brilliance of the light – all very far away from the puritanism of the North or the stuffiness of English society. Douglas became a professional writer relatively late in life, and was forty-eight before *South Wind* brought him fame by speaking for wit and sophisticated freedoms against the greyness that was post-war Europe. Two further books of fiction – both fantasies – appeared during the twenties, but Douglas's real talent was for the evocation of place in the celebration of a sun-drenched world and his own spiky nature – defined again in *Alone* (1921), *Together* (1923) and *Looking Back* (1933).

Urban writing in the early twentieth century

Nothing could be further from the spirit of Cunninghame Graham or Douglas's Mediterranean than the popular literature which still prevailed on the home front in Scotland. George Douglas Brown's savage detachment may have shaken the Kailyard's more serious pretensions, but he did not dent the market for parochial light comedy – the literary equivalent, as MacDiarmid put it, of cold haggis and ginger beer. Neil Munro's friend J. J. Bell (1871–1934) was among the best of these pawky humorists and his work is not without charm. His *enfant terrible* 'Wee Macgreegor' made his debut in the *Glasgow Evening Times* at the beginning of the century, but Bell mined the same vein of working-class character comedy for over thirty years. This 'urban kailyard' lived on through the forties and fifties, with Helen W. Pryde's 'McFlannels' series on Scottish Radio, and D. C. Thomson of Dundee had already founded a considerable publishing-empire on dozens of periodicals aimed at a working-class and lower-middle-class market for conservative values, sentiment, piety, true-love romances and droll Scots humour. MacDiarmid and other writers of the early Renaissance came to regard the comedian Harry Lauder as the patron saint of this version of Scottishness – a music-hall figure of fun, swathed in surrealistic tartans, sporting bare knees and a knobbly walking stick. Yet Lauder and the other 'Scotch comics' were undeniably popular with their audiences, representing an absurd stereotype that had come to be loved for its own sake.

Some writers, however, particularly in Glasgow, did attempt a more realistic picture of Scottish city life. John Blair gave an unusually direct account of the life of a factory girl in *Jean* (1906); while twin novels by Patrick MacGill (1890–1963), called *Children of the Dead End* (1914) and *The Rat-pit* (1915), spoke of the Irish immigrant experience in Scotland and Glasgow, with grim details of life in the slums and lodging-houses of the city. As the son of a Glasgow manufacturer, **Frederick Niven** (1878–1944) turned to writing, and, after early ambitions to become a painter, he led a restless life between Scotland, Canada and London before finally settling in British Columbia shortly after the First World War. Several of his many novels – most notably *The Justice of the Peace* (1914) and *The Staff at*

Simson's (1937) – give a detailed account of bourgeois and commercial Glasgow society in the first years of the century. Not surprisingly the first stirrings of urban realism in this 'Glasgow school' were confined to prose, and it was to be many years before Scottish poetry could turn to city life, and even longer before it took a distinctively Glaswegian accent.

The Renaissance of poetry in Scots: MacDiarmid's precursors

As far as poetry in Scots was concerned, the Kailyard strain went back at least as far as the *Whistle-Binkie* anthologies, fifty years before the new century. Stevenson's Scots poems were better, but linked the language with nostalgia or bairn rhymes. As for the rest, the sentimental rustification of Scots had left it frozen in time and place as a language apparently reserved for the 'poetry corners' of local newspapers and hundreds of talentless imitators of Burns. Even James Logie Robertson (1846–1922), who had edited many valuable popular collections of the works of Ramsay, Scott, Dunbar and Burns, could produce little more than pastoral pastiche when he wrote as 'Hugh Haliburton', with titles such as *Horace in Hamespun* (1882) and *Ochil Idylls* (1891). The language seemed lost to serious use. Yet it did retain some credibility in the hands of authentic dialect poets, and in this respect it was Charles Murray, Violet Jacob and several other North-East poets who showed what could be done in Scots a significant number of years before MacDiarmid took up Lallans for himself.

Born in Alford, trained as an engineer in Aberdeen, and working in South Africa for most of his life, **Charles Murray** (1864–1941) was completely at home with North-East speech and his poems move with the easy flow of oral expression – often as dramatic monologues. His taste for pithy epigrams, like his eye for landscape, weather and the trappings of country life, all stem from a folk tradition which had remained particularly rich in Aberdeenshire and Angus. Alexander's *Johnny Gibb of Gushetneuk* was first published as a serial in the Aberdeen newspaper, and Gavin Greig (1856–1914), with the help of the Revd J. B. Duncan, had spent the last ten years of his life making a monumental collection of oral lore and ballads from the region. To this day North-East Scots has retained an unforced linguistic confidence. *Hamewith* (1900) made Murray's reputation, and it was enlarged, reprinted three times and then collated with two later collections to make the complete works of 1927. After a distinguished career in South Africa the poet returned home to a considerable degree of local fame. 'Gin I were God' and 'The Whistle' ('He cut a sappy sooker from a muckle rodden tree') are widely anthologised, but poems such as 'Dockens afore his Peers', 'The Three Craws' and 'A Green Yule' give a better sense of his sardonic wit, while the lyrical conclusion to the last-named poem goes beyond dialect verse to the voice of the ballads infused with the grim weight of Dunbar:

Bring them alang, the young, the strang,	
The weary an' the auld;	
Feed as they will on haugh or hill,	low meadow
This is the only fauld.	fold
Dibble them doon, the laird, the loon,	Plant; boy
King an' the cadgin' caird,	travelling tinker
The lady fine beside the queyn,	girl
A' in the same kirkyard	

Violet Jacob (1863–1946), came from the Kennedy-Erskine family, who had held the lands near Montrose since the fifteenth century. Her first books (1902 and 1904) were historical novels, and she went on to write short stories and three main collections of poems – *Songs of Angus* (1915), *Bonnie Joann* (1921) and *Northern Lights* (1927). She is more prone to sentimentality than Murray, partly because her focus is on the pains of love, the fears of children, or the onset of old age. Even so, her Scots is rarely coy and her sense of muted sexual shame, like her sympathy with landscape or the supernatural, is often illuminated by particularly effective small-scale images – a broken stone and black nettles ('The Jaud') or brambles and toadstools among dark fir-trees ('Craigo Woods') or a thistle going to seed on a river-bank ('The End o' t'). Jacob contributed to MacDiarmid's *Northern Numbers* anthologies at a time when he himself was still writing in English, and she was generously represented in Buchan's *Northern Muse*.

Marion Angus (1866–1946) and **Helen Cruickshank** (1886–1975) also had their roots in the North-East, and, although most of their poems were not published until after

MacDiarmid had shown what the Scots lyric could achieve, they qualify as forerunners along with Violet Jacob. Cruickshank also appeared in *Northern Numbers*, and Angus's *The Lilt and Other Poems* dates from 1922, followed by *The Tinker's Road* (1924) and four further collections during the twenties and thirties. Within her chosen range Marion Angus is technically the most accomplished of her generation, and a later English piece on Mary Stuart – 'Alas! Poor Queen' – might have been constructed by a young Ezra Pound. She also learned from the ballads, and, although the lilting sadness of her lines can become excessively fey, her best lyrics are terser and genuinely disquieting – 'The Can'el', 'Ann Gilchrist' and 'The Blue Jacket'. Angus lived most of her life in Aberdeen, away from the storms of literary Edinburgh. Helen Cruickshank's poems, by comparison, are nearer once more to a vernacular muse with its interest in landscape and reminiscence, although she uses this to make political points, too. She succeeded MacDiarmid as secretary of the Scottish PEN Club and proved to be a loyal supporter of most of the younger Renaissance poets and a particularly good friend to MacDiarmid and his family during their difficult years in the thirties.

The North-East connection was continued with Mary Symon (1863–1938) from Banffshire, another contributor to *Northern Numbers*, who published her work in *Deveron Days* (1933) and with **Pittendrigh MacGillivray** (1856–1938), the sculptor who made the statues of John Knox in St Giles' and Byron at Aberdeen Grammar School. Born near Inverurie, MacGillivray was an enthusiast for eighteenth-century Scots verse, but for the most part it is his own native voice which controls poems such as 'Observances' – drawing on folk-customs for greeting a new baby – or 'Mercy o' Gode', a finely sardonic account of two old men sitting in a churchyard. His first publication was *Pro Patria* (1915), but his best Scots work appeared in *Bog Myrtle and Peat Reek* (1922) – a privately produced and expensive little book. **Alexander Gray** (1882–1968) was born in Dundee and worked for the Civil Service before becoming professor of political economy in Aberdeen and Edinburgh. He too drew on North-East Scots for his poems, and used a modified version of it to translate pieces from Danish and German, including *Songs and Ballads Chiefly from Heine* (1920) and German ballads and folk-songs done into an efficient Scots verse for *Arrows* (1932). **Lewis Spence** (1874–1955) came from Dundee, working for the *Scotsman* and the *British Weekly* before becoming a full-time writer. In forty years he produced almost as many books, on legends and mythology from the Celts to the civilisations of Mexico, South America and 'Atlantis'. Spence championed the cause of new writing in Scots and, although most of his own poems use a rather poetical diction in English, he chose an archaic Scots for some of them. 'The Queen's Bath-house, Holyrood', 'The Prows o' Reekie' and 'The Firth' catch the dour strength he was seeking, even if they are mainly descriptive and backward-looking.

Most of the above-mentioned poets using Scots were featured in three anthologies called *Northern Numbers*, which appeared between 1920 and 1922. Edited by a writer in his late twenties called C. M. Grieve, these planned to do for contemporary Scottish poets what Edward Marsh's *Georgian Poetry* collections had already achieved in England. Indeed, these little books from Montrose do mark the first stirrings of what was to be a renaissance in Scottish poetry, as well as the first significant appearance of its most energetic proponent. At this stage, however, Grieve's own poems were all in English and for his part he doubted if Scots would ever be an effective medium for modern poetry. 'Hugh MacDiarmid' was soon to change all that.

Christopher Murray Grieve ('Hugh MacDiarmid', 1892–1978)

C. M. Grieve launched *Northern Numbers* when he was twenty-eight years old – married and recently demobilised from the Army Medical Corps, he was a self-confessed 'late ripener'. Now that he was working as a journalist in Montrose he set about taking the first serious steps towards a literary career planned during the long watches as a quartermaster sergeant in military hospitals in Salonika and near Marseilles. He had shown creative promise from the start, and throughout the war and after he kept up a correspondence with George Ogilvie, his English-master from Broughton Student Centre in Edinburgh, pouring out his doubts and ambitions and sending him examples of the many sonnets which he was writing at the time. These poems in English tended to deal with death, eternity and God in a rather studiously crystalline poetic diction

Grieve was working in prose too, and since 1919 he had been assembling material written or planned during the war, to be called *Annals of the Five Senses* – a series of psychological studies or sketches, each of them laying bare, under various personae, the author's sense of his own enthusiastic mental life. The collection was ready by 1921, but could not be published until 1923, and, although it is not about the war, *Annals* does relate to some of Grieve's experiences in Greece and France. He contracted cerebral malaria in Salonika and had been invalided home as a chronic case in 1918 (it was during this leave that he married Margaret – Peggy – Skinner) and it is possible that the positively feverish intensity of the consciousness described in *Annals* stems at least in part from this illness. Every character in each of the six stories has a 'brain like a hall of mirrors in which he caught countless reflections of every theme in as many shapes and sizes', and those themes are evoked in long and lovingly elaborated lists of the most esoteric details culled from his own sensations or the world of books and newspapers to make 'a swift, beautiful catalogue of the most delightful and unexpected of interests'. (Grieve had been a compulsively omnivorous reader since his early boyhood, when the family lived in rooms beneath the Langholm public library, where his mother worked as a caretaker.) The *Annals* stories mix a furious sense of physical detail with unacknowledged quotations from dozens of writers and a tendency to abstruse or metaphysical speculation – a striking combination, even when the young man's prose style cannot quite support the strain. Nevertheless, in view of the poems which he was to write in the late thirties, these first studies are of great interest.

The Montrose years were among the most productive in Grieve's life, despite his commitments to many other fields as well. Apart from working for the *Montrose Review*, he sat on the town council as an Independent Socialist, becoming a parish councillor as well and, in 1926, a justice of the peace. After *Northern Numbers* his next project was to found a literary monthly called the *Scottish Chapbook*, which appeared in August 1922 and managed fourteen issues before the end of 1923. By then he was also publishing and editing the *Scottish Nation*, a weekly dedicated to Scottish nationalism, and the *Northern Review*, which appeared for four months in the summer of 1924. These short-lived periodicals mark the beginning of the 'Scottish Renaissance' as a defined modern literary movement, and for the next twenty years Grieve promoted the cause of literary and political self-awareness with a constant stream of newspaper-articles, books, reviews, essays, letters and public speeches, all of which made him one of the most vociferous and best-known cultural figures in Scotland. Some of his more influential and contentious essays, from a regular series in the *Scottish Educational Journal*, were collected as *Contemporary Scottish Studies* in 1926, to be followed by *Albyn, or Scotland and the Future* in 1927.

The first *Chapbook* contained a playscript by Grieve and a visionary poem called 'A Moment in Eternity' dedicated to George Ogilvie. Subsequent numbers embarked on 'A Theory of Scots Letters', which developed Gregory Smith's definition of 'antisyzygy' to show what Scots could offer to the modern poet – especially in its 'reconciliation of the base and the beautiful' and in its potential for creating images drawn from physical and psychological states no longer available, so Grieve claimed, to an urbane and oversophisticated English tradition. He found these strengths particularly evident in Jamieson's *Scottish Dictionary* and used many words and phrases from its pages to make his point. Grieve cited the works of Dostoevsky, Lawrence and Joyce as writers who had felt the need to overthrow the old modes in order to express their vision, and for him Scots should be equally capable of contributing to the modernist movement. He had no time, therefore, for Scots as an exercise in nostalgia, nor for the Victorian stereotype of Scottish 'dourness', and he redefined the 'true Scot' as a figure possessed by Gregory Smith's combination of opposites – 'dominated by the conception of infinity, of the unattainable, and hence ever questioning, never satisfied, rationalistic in religion and politics, romantic in art and literature' – a figure not unlike 'Hugh MacDiarmid', in other words. Grieve's desire to follow Pound and to 'make it new' is central to his conception of the Renaissance, and from the start his periodicals and essays looked outwards to Europe and beyond. The *Chapbook*'s motto was 'Not Traditions – Precedents' and, if its editor cried 'Back to Dunbar!', it was because he hoped that Dunbar's complex spirit and technique would be a salutary antidote to the bucolic sentimentality of the post-Burns tradition. Yet all this activity would have come to nothing from a literary point of view were it not for the poems which Grieve produced in four extraordinary years from 1922 to 1926.

Grieve published his first poems in Scots in the *Dunfermline Press* in September 1922, but he pretended that they were written by a friend – later named as 'Hugh M'Diarmid'. He now admitted an interest in the poetic potential of 'obsolete' or 'distinctively local' words and opined that his friend's verses had a 'descriptive potency otherwise unobtainable'. One of the poems was 'The Watergaw' and Grieve was right. It was as if the vocabulary and idiom of Scots with its long tradition of colloquial utterance and domestic detail added a special and much needed physical body to the metaphysical inspiration of his early work. This was a voice which could express both the sublime and the vulgar, moving from one to the other with speed, wit and the appearance of ease. Gregory Smith had described this 'medieval . . . freedom in passing from one mood to another', and it turned out to be exactly right for the author of *Annals of the Five Senses* and his volatile sensibility, so wildly idealistic and materialistic by turns. Struck by this insight, Grieve immediately explained it in his 'Theory of Scots Letters', and acknowledged the debt by adopting the name Hugh MacDiarmid for all his poems thereafter.

MacDiarmid's first two collections of Scots poems were called *Sangschaw* (1925) and *Penny Wheep* (1926) and both were enthusiastically received. Edwin Muir admired 'a crazy economy' in the language, 'which has the effect of humour and yet conveys a kind of horror', and he saw this as 'truly Scottish' and as distinct from the English ethos as was the prose of George Douglas Brown or Carlyle. The reviewer for *The Times Literary Supplement* praised 'an unusual sense of the movement and changing aspects of the earth in its diurnal round', and Professor Denis Saurat of the University of Bordeaux, who had taken such an early critical interest in the Scots revival, translated many of them into French. Danish versions were made, and the poet's former schoolteacher from Langholm, a composer called Francis George Scott (1880–1958), set several of the lyrics, and ultimately about seventy of MacDiarmid's poems, to music. *La Renaissance ecossaise* was off to a properly

international start. Scott and MacDiarmid renewed their old
acquaintance and became close friends, for 'F. G.' helped the
poet assemble the long sequence which became *A Drunk Man
Looks at the Thistle* and the book was dedicated to him.

Some of the early lyrics use a vernacular voice – 'Crowdie-
knowe' and 'Focherty', for example, might have been conceived
by Charles Murray – but for the rest the domestic realism of the
Scots is astonishingly transformed, as if their landscapes have
become charged with a strange energy – like Expressionist
paintings by Munch or Soutine. MacDiarmid creates a world
of vivid contrasts, of 'Cloudburst and Soarin' Mune', or of wind
and light where the trees fatten and thin themselves like turkeys
screaming ('Sunny Gale'). Even the filthy gutter in the
cowshed is transmuted – 'The aidle-pool is a glory o' gowd' –
and we seem to cling to the surface of the planet with an
exhilarating sense of the vastness of time and infinite distance:

> The moonbeams kelter i' the lift,   waver in the sky
> An' Earth, the bare auld stane,
> Glitters beneath the seas o' Space,
> White as a mammoth's bane.

> ('Au Clair de la Lune')

Other poems in this vein include 'Ex Vermibus', 'Country Life'
and 'Farmer's Death', and their hallucinatory intensity is
charged again by MacDiarmid's choice of not-quite-familiar
Scots words or by the succinct and subtle breaks which he
makes from what would otherwise be fairly predictable ballad-
like stresses. (In this respect his handling of rhythm is
reminiscent of Wordsworth's 'Lucy' poems, or some of Hardy's
pieces on his wife.) A sense of cosmic scale characterises also
'Au Clair de la Lune', 'The Innumerable Christ', 'Servant
Girl's Bed' and 'Empty Vessel'. 'The Eemis Stane' is rightly
famous:

> I' the how-dumb-deid o' the cauld hairst night   harvest
> The warl' like an eemis stane   insecure, wobbling
> Wags i' the lift;   sky   [stone
> An' my eerie memories fa'
> Like a yowdendrift.   blizzard with snow
>   [rising from ground

Like a yowdendrift so's I couldna read	
The words cut oot i' the stane	
Had the fug o' fame	moss
An' history's hazelraw	lichen
No' yirdit thaim.	buried

The specific earthiness of Scots words such as 'fug' and 'hazelraw' contrasts with the more English abstractions 'fame' and 'history', while the planet teeters like a rocking boulder in the sky. If there is some primal message or meaning to be found there, the poet cannot read it, because it has been hidden by his own memories and by all the experience of the world itself – like moss and lichen on the surface of a gravestone.

These poems, and others such as 'Moonstruck', 'The Watergaw', and 'The Bonnie Broukit Bairn', reach a truly extraordinary imaginative compression of image, language and ideation. They meet the requirements of Imagist verse more effectively than any of the poems written by Pound, HD, or T. E. Hulme, and in this respect MacDiarmid took the Scots tradition to a new and truly modern expression. Even so, the poet's mercurial sensibility, his polemical humour and his enthusiasm for metaphysical flights, had further to go and he turned his energies to a much more ambitious project.

A Drunk Man Looks at the Thistle (1926) is MacDiarmid's single most famous book and one of the great poems of modernist literature – a testament to creative energy and optimism at a time when Yeats, Pound and Eliot could see only cultural decline and spiritual failure all around them. The poem's setting is simple enough – a drunk man lies gazing at a thistle on a moonlit hillside. His intoxicated state and the fickle and deceptive light of the moon send him on an imaginative odyssey as strange as any undertaken by Tam o' Shanter or Thomas the Rhymer. Operating somewhere between dramatic monologue and stream of consciousness, the poem's technique is fairly conventional – he uses simple ballad-like rhyme-schemes and the language is a lightly colloquial Scots. Yet this familiarity is deceptive, for MacDiarmid creates and juxta-poses so many startling images, and makes so many swift changes of pace and tone – from broad satire to tender lyrics to ribaldry, metaphysical anguish and back again – that the poem is electric with energy and exhilaration. The drunk man finds that the world around him and his own thoughts seem to mix and change with alarming fluidity, and the whole universe is destabilised by whisky, moonlight and his own overheated cerebration.

The poem has little formal structure beyond its individual rhyme-schemes and it can be bewilderingly garrulous and repetitious, but particular images do recur to give it a certain thematic coherence. Most notably the thistle is a deeply ambivalent symbol – representing some ideal beauty or fulfilment by its purple flower (the thistle's 'rose') but conjuring up sterility, failure and pain in its ugly stalks and spikes. It seems that we are fated always to be caught between the two: 'Man torn in twa / And glorious in the lift and grisly on the sod'. The drunk man finds this division within himself, his country (it is the national plant, after all) and the fate of all humankind. He is obsessed with it, just as Ahab was obsessed with the mystery and menace of Moby Dick, and the thistle takes a dozen different shapes throughout the poem – comic, vulgar or terrifying – as he wrestles with its personal, social and philosophical implications:

> A black leaf owre a white leaf twirls,
> A grey leaf flauchters in atween,   flutters
> Sae ply my thochts aboot the stem
> O' loppert slime frae which they spring.   clotted
> The thistle like a snawstorm drives,
> Or like a flicht o' swallows lifts,
> Or like a swarm o' midges hings,
> A plague o' moths, a starry sky,
> But's naething but a thistle yet,
> And still the puzzle stands unsolved.
> Beauty and ugliness alike,
> And life and daith and God and man,
> Are aspects o't but nane can tell
> The secret that I'd fain find oot
> O' this bricht hive, this sorry weed,
> The tree that fills the universe,   (Yggdrasil, the tree of life)
> Or like a reistit herrin' crines.   dried herring shrivels

In the course of this Dionysian exploration, the broadest satirical attacks are delivered on Burns Clubs, Harry Lauder and all the conventional trappings of bourgeois 'Scottishness'. MacDiarmid also created hundreds of the most startling poetic images, where the abstractions of his theme are embodied in the concrete particularities of Scots speech: 'nocht but a chowed core's left whaur Jerusalem lay / Like aipples in a heap!' If Grierson and Eliot admired a quality of 'felt thought' in the poetry of John Donne and the Metaphysicals, this is no less than MacDiarmid achieves in almost every page of his long poem:

> I tae ha'e heard Eternity drip water
> (Aye water, water!), drap by drap
> On the a'e nerve, like lichtnin', I've become,
> And heard God passin' wi' a bobby's feet   policeman's
> Ootby in the lang coffin o' the street
> – Seen stang by chitterin' knottit stang loup oot   paroxysm;
> Uncrushed by th'echoes o' the thunderin' boot,   [shivering
> Till a' the dizzy lint-white lines o' torture made   flax-white
> A monstrous thistle in the space aboot me,
> A symbol o' the puzzle o' man's soul.

These lines make broad comedy collide with the most intense spiritual longing, as if Fergusson and Shelley were united in profound grotesquerie – a new category of literary taste.

Unlike Yeats and Eliot, MacDiarmid welcomes the insignificance of man and the vastness of the universe, just as he welcomes the myriad conflicting sensations and impulses within himself. In this he is a truly post-Romantic modernist with absolutely no hankering for the balance or the certitudes of some idealised classical past:

> I'll hae nae hauf-way hoose, but aye be whaur
> Extremes meet – it's the only way I ken
> To dodge the curst conceit o' bein' richt
> That damns the vast majority o' men.

Thus he gives himself up to change, fluidity and perpetual opposition, and embraces – rather like Walt Whitman – the *élan vital* of the universe itself.

If *A Drunk Man* rings with MacDiarmid's special brand of optimistic modernism, fuelled by his interests in materialism, socialism and Scottish nationhood, it also has moments of visionary intensity when he glimpses some spiritual or neo-platonic ideal of peace and enlightenment beyond the endless whirl of the world or his own introspection.

And O! I canna thole	endure
Aye yabblin' o' my soul,	gabbling
And fain I wad be free	
O' my eternal me.	

This ideal is symbolised by the bride carrying a bunch of thistles, or by the 'silken leddy' who drifts into a crowded and noisy tavern to create a moment of stillness and insight. For the drunk man the mystery of existence and the challenge 'to be yersel's – and to mak' that worth bein'', is an imperative that goes beyond Scottish national identity (although that is the first step), for he believes that human consciousness is an integrated part of universal evolution and that an outstanding effort must be made to *realise* it – in every sense of the word. This is what he refers to as the 'seamless garment' or the 'diamond body' in later poems. For the moment, however, the drunk man can solve nothing in a world where the only constant seems to be eternal change. But at least for one glorious, intoxicated night he has given himself up to the flux of the universe and joined the dance in his own wild and fantastical imagination. If he comes to silence in the closing lines of the poem, it is the silence of human experience, or repletion, or even exhaustion, but never the stillness of extinction, blind faith, acquiescence or despair – those common ailments of the modern spirit.

MacDiarmid's drunk caused a critical sensation in Scotland – at last a fully modern poem in Scots had appeared, bursting on the nation with all the force, in one incomparable phrase, of a childbirth in church. Yet already some readers were regretting his move away from the lyric. The poet remained in Montrose for the next three years, as prolific as ever with reviews and innumerable articles on Scotland and all things Scottish. He worked on another long poem, to be called *To Circumjack Cencrastus* (1930), in which the puzzle of the thistle is pursued yet again in the form of 'Cencrastus', which Mac-Diarmid associated with the Celtic curly snake with its tail in its mouth – a symbol of eternity – and with the mythological serpent whose coils surround the world. But the mode had been better realised in *A Drunk Man*, and, although the theme is central to MacDiarmid's poetry, the new book had passages where he seems bitterly dissatisfied with his life and his job as an underpaid journalist in Montrose. By the 1930s the poet was looking for a new direction and for a way of more overtly expressing his socialist principles in verse.

When Compton Mackenzie suggested that he edit *Vox*, a recently founded arts magazine for the radio, MacDiarmid seized the chance and moved to London with his wife and two children late in 1929. But London proved to be an unhappy experience. Towards the end of the year he fell from a bus and suffered severe concussion – experiencing headaches for some years afterwards – and *Vox* had died before he recovered. The poet's marriage was under strain and, when he eventually found a job as a publicity officer in Liverpool, Peggy refused to go with him and they agreed to separate. The Liverpool appointment did not last long and MacDiarmid found himself back in London. *First Hymn to Lenin and Other Poems* appeared in 1931 with an introduction and a portrait of the author by 'AE', but it was limited to only 500 copies. Many of the poems looked back to his roots in Langholm as if seeking a new stability there. He was drinking heavily and estranged from his wife, for she had found someone else, and in the middle of an economic depression he had no job and no savings at all. (The couple were finally divorced at the beginning of 1932.) 'My story', he was to write later, 'is the story of an absolutist whose absolutes came to grief in his private life.' The one good thing that happened to him at this time was his meeting with a Cornishwoman called Valda Trevlyn, a creative lady in her own right, who became his wife and an unfailing source of support and courage for the rest of his life. They lived in a cottage in Sussex and then moved back to Scotland with a new baby, Michael, who had been born in the summer.

When *Scots Unbound and Other Poems* appeared in 1932, MacDiarmid explained that it was to join *First Hymn to Lenin and Other Poems* as part of an extended sequence in five books to be called 'Clann Albann' – 'the children of Scotland'. The first book, 'The Muckle Toon', would consider his years in Langholm and the influence of parents, childhood, socialism and the Church on his growing sensibility. The project was never realised, but most of the poems and some short stories of the period do, indeed, relate to autobiographical themes. He chose a light colloquial Scots, for pieces such as 'At my Father's Grave', 'Charisma and my Relatives', and 'Kinsfolk'; and his home town and the surrounding country feature in poems such as 'Whuchulls' and 'Tarras'. Langholm is a place where three rivers meet, and MacDiarmid's fascination with water in all its changes appears as a symbol of life itself in 'Prayer for a Second Flood', 'Water of Life', 'Excelsior' and 'The Oon Olympian', reaching a climax with 'Water Music', a Joycean extravaganza which uses a plethora of the most obscure Scots words to imitate the sound and the movements of his favourite rivers.

Socialism was a further theme in MacDiarmid's poems of the early thirties, and in this, of course, he was in line with most other left-wing writers of the day. Yet his polemical roots are deeper and narrower than those of Auden, Spender, MacNeice and Day Lewis, and his idealism is more far reaching. His father was a country postman and a socialist (as well as an elder in the United Free Kirk) and MacDiarmid had joined the Fabian Society and the ILP when he was sixteen. As a young journalist in South Wales in 1911 he had worked for a miners' newspaper, witnessed police baton charges, and made speeches in support of the Labour cause. Thus in later years he took a hardliner's delight in opposing 'bourgeois liberalism', and his overtly political poems often adopt a harshly polemical stance. The three 'Hymns to Lenin' celebrate Lenin's heroic ruthlessness, as if he were one of Carlyle's heroes who represents 'the flower and iron of the truth' and has the courage to stand apart from 'the majority will that accepts the result'. Even so, MacDiarmid's brand of millennial socialism has little to do with 'bread and butter problems', for he regards all political goals and structures as merely the first steps towards a far more radical – evolutionary – reorganisation of man's physical and spiritual resources. 'The Seamless Garment', set in a Langholm woollen-mill, makes just this point in a good-humoured way, using a low-key colloquial Scots to explain it to a 'cousin' who works there:

> The haill shop's dumfoonderin'
>   To a stranger like me.
> Second nature to you; you're perfectly able
>   To think, speak and see
> Apairt frae the looms, tho' to some
> That doesna sae easily come.

Lenin was like that wi' workin' class life,
  At hame wi't a'.
His fause movements couldna been fewer,
  The best weaver Earth ever saw.
A' *he'd* to dae wi' moved intact
  Clean, clear, and exact.

A poet like Rilke did the same
  In a different sphere,
Made a single reality – a' a'e 'oo' –   all one wool
  O' his love and pity and fear;
A seamless garment o' music and thought
But you're ower thrang wi' puirer to tak' tent o't.   too caught up with
                                                            [poverty to heed it
What's life or God or what you may ca't
  But something at ane like this?

In Christian doctrine the seamless garment represents the
unity between Christ's life and his divine being, but 'Second
Hymn to Lenin' recognises the practical difficulties of reaching
that state ourselves without being 'Unremittin', relentless, / Organised to the last degree'. Thus he extols the ruthless
concentration of Lenin's vision – those 'lizard eyes' – and the
cold and granite-hard creed which will be necessary to realise
'The Skeleton of the Future'. In the meantime the poet could
not earn enough to support his family and they were practically
destitute until friends rallied to their support in the spring of
1933 and found them a cottage in the Shetlands. At last
MacDiarmid had made a break with his problems in Scotland
and London, and for the next nine years he committed himself
to living and writing on the remote island of Whalsay.

MacDiarmid was stunned by the Shetlands. His health was
poor and they were living at little more than subsistence level,
but the remote beauty of this treeless landscape, caught
between the sea and the vast northern skies, offered an austere
peace and a return to fundamentals. Letters to William Soutar
and Neil Gunn, and a chapter in *The Islands of Scotland* (1939) all
testify to this new inspiration:

the vivifying element of water breaking up the land everywhere, and the
strange glories of the displays of the Aurora Borealis; and beautiful when
these are absent, in an awe-inspiring way, like a foreglimpse of the end of
the world! – bedrock indeed! – Earth's final state to which all else has been
tending under all the veils of Maya – a world of stone, water, and light. . . .

The family ate seagull-eggs and mackerel, cut peat for their fire, and MacDiarmid began to write longer poems, 'valuable new departures' he thought, in a cool and icily controlled English diction. He undertook prose too, in order to earn a living, and in 1934 his essays appeared in *At the Sign of the Thistle* (1934), while a collaboration with Lewis Grassic Gibbon resulted in an irreverent and entertaining book called *Scottish Scene or The Intelligent Man's Guide to Albyn*. In 1938 he founded the *Voice of Scotland*, a quarterly dedicated to 'Scottish Workers' Republicanism *à la* John Maclean', which published work by several of the younger poets – the 'second wave' of the Renaissance – including Norman MacCaig, George Bruce, Sorley Maclean and George Campbell Hay. The magazine reached five issues before the outbreak of war stopped it.

Stony Limits and Other Poems (1934) was the poet's most substantial and challenging collection for years. It contained fine work in Scots, including a set of 'Shetland Lyrics', 'Harry Semen' and 'Ode to All Rebels', but he was using English for political poems such as 'The Belly Grip' and 'John Maclean', and most especially for those 'new departures'. These turned out to be long meditations on scientific, geological and philosophical themes, full of obscure technical terms and a deliberately intellectualised diction – verses as austere and hard as the Shetland coast itself. There are poems in memory of Rilke and Charles Doughty (of *Arabia Deserta*), whose visions had also taken them into remote and desert landscapes of the spirit; and in the same vein 'Lament for the Great Music' welcomes pibroch as the sternest and loveliest art of all – 'like the metaphysics of light . . . in the grey life of these islands.' The most outstanding of these productions is 'On a Raised Beach', a meditation on death, truth and the 'bedrock' of the world, and one of the finest existential poems in modern literature.

If one can compare MacDiarmid's career with that of T. S. Eliot, then the energy of *A Drunk Man* would correspond to *The Waste Land*, and the philosophical restraint of 'On a Raised Beach' would stand on equal terms with *Four Quartets*, except that the Scot, unlike Eliot, gives himself up to the absolute and unrelenting materiality of the world:

What happens to us
Is irrelevant to the world's geology
But what happens to the world's geology
Is not irrelevant to us.
We must reconcile ourselves to the stones,
Not the stones to us.
Here a man must shed the encumbrances that muffle
Contact with elemental things, the subtleties
That seem inseparable from a humane life, and go
    apart
Into a simpler and sterner, more beautiful and
    oppressive world,
Austerely intoxicating; the first draught is
    over-powering;
Few survive it . . . .

The 'raised beach' in question is an ancient shoreline left far from the movements of any contemporary tide, and the 'otherness' of this strange world is literally conjured up in the poem's opening lines with an incantation of magically unapproachable words – 'Deep conviction or preference can seldom / Find direct terms in which to express itself':

All is lithogenesis – or lochia,
Carpolite fruit of the forbidden tree,
Stones blacker than any in the Caaba,
Cream-coloured caen-stone, chatoyant pieces,
Celadon and corbeau, bistre and beige,
Glaucous, hoar, enfouldered, cyathiform,
Making mere faculae of the sun and moon,
I study you glout and gloss . . . .

'These stones are one with the stars' writes the poet, with the same imaginative leap from domestic to cosmic which characterised the early lyrics. He insists too that 'This is no heap of broken images', and, if the phrase reminds us of *The Waste Land*'s spiritual despair, it serves to emphasise MacDiarmid's refusal to submit to the comfort of organised religion – 'Let men find the faith that builds mountains / Before they seek the faith that moves them'. In place of faith the poet asks only that we 'Be ourselves without interruption / Adamantine and inexorable', although the task may well require that men become like stones themselves by some 'immense exercise of will, / Inconceivable discipline, courage, and endurance, / Self purification and anti-humanity'. MacDiarmid celebrates the 'deadly clarity' of this materialism throughout, even if his tone is unmistakably reminiscent of Knox and the rock-hard inheritance of Scottish Calvinism: 'Listen to me – Truth is not crushed; / It crushes, gorgonises all else into itself. . . . Do not argue with me. Argue with these stones.' The poem ends with a call to 'participate' in material life – which 'is nearest of all and easiest to grasp'; except that man may have to come face to face with the inevitability of his own death before he sees that 'barren but beautiful reality' clearly enough: 'I lift a stone; it is the meaning of life I clasp/ Which is death . . . .'

It seems likely that his philosophical confrontation with a universe of stones, not to mention years of strain and the hardships of life on the island, took a considerable toll on MacDiarmid's health, and he suffered a complete nervous and physical collapse in the summer of 1935. His condition was serious and friends arranged for him to enter hospital in Perth, where he spent seven weeks in care. Recovery was slow and a photograph of the time shows an emaciated and exhausted figure, like a prisoner of war who has just been released from some frightful camp. Back on Whalsay, he soon picked up the threads of his indefatigable correspondence and renewed contacts with the outside world. But he had not lost his sense of literary and political isolation, and his contentious absolutism, which had an air of desperation about it, led him to break with many old friends and fellow writers. Edwin Muir had been a friend since the twenties, when they both contributed to the *New Age*, but now that Muir had come to live in St Andrew's he was reassessing his views on the future of literature in Scots. Despite his early enthusiasm for the language (and a few ballad-like poems of his own), he had come to believe that the use of Scots only encouraged a split between thinking and feeling, and offered no hope for a national literature for as long as English prevailed as well. He thought that Scots poets would do better to use English, and worse still, from the point of view of MacDiarmid's hopes for creative contradiction, he held that the 'Caledonian antisyzygy' could only result in a sterile cultural impasse. When Muir expressed these views in *Scott and Scotland* (1936), MacDiarmid felt betrayed and launched a bitter personal attack which ended their friendship and emphasised his own isolation as a John Maclean socialist at odds with what he took to be liberal or reactionary tendencies in Scottish culture and politics. On these grounds too he parted company with Neil Gunn, whose success as a novelist was about to be confirmed with *Highland River*.

More prose projects were planned, and although some fell by the wayside others, such as *Scottish Eccentrics* (1936) and *The Islands of Scotland* (1939), brought in much-needed royalties. He also wrote *Lucky Poet. A Self-Study in Literature and Political Ideas* (1943), in which he set out to explain himself by way of an infuriating and entertainingly wayward chronicle of his multitudinous interests and opinions. The book also contained passages from unpublished long poems and a new assessment of the Gaelic spirit. MacDiarmid had already produced 'Lament for the Great Music', and a translation of MacMhaighstir Alasdair's *Birlinn Chlann Raghnaill* had followed from his meeting with Sorley Maclean in 1934; now the 'Gaelic Muse' and three 'Dìreadh' poems appeared in *Lucky Poet*. In these and other verses, MacDiarmid invoked the Celtic spirit, and an 'East–West synthesis' with Russia, as necessary opposition to what he saw as the commercial values and the cultural imperialism of an English-speaking ascendancy in the Western world. The same resistance to received values and literary modes inspired his plans for an epic poetry which would cast off the 'irresponsible lyricism in which sense impressions / Are employed to substitute ecstasy for information' ('The Kind of Poetry I Want'). In the cause of that 'information' MacDiarmid redefined Celtic complexity and developed Duncan Bàn Macintyre's penchant for lengthy objective description, until his own verses became vast extended catalogues, full of borrowings from a host of unacknowledged prose sources, as if he were determined to list everything that interested him in the material universe. MacDiarmid spent the rest of his life working over these epic poems from the late thirties and early forties. They were supposed to come together in a *magnum opus* to be called 'Mature Art', only sections of which – such as *In Memoriam James Joyce* (1955) – have ever appeared.

Even if 'Mature Art' did not materialise, the poems that were written under its influence offer an extraordinary 'vision of world language', as if the poet has decided to relinquish his creative and image-making power in favour of merely listening to the details of the world as it 'speaks' itself, choosing only to select examples, perhaps, from that fascinating monologue:

> They are not endless these variations of form
> Though it is perhaps impossible to see them all.
> It is certainly impossible to conceive one that doesn't
>   exist.
> But I keep trying in our forest to do both of these . . . .
>
> ('In Memoriam James Joyce'; also 'In the Caledonian
>   Forest', from *Stony Limits*)

The principle behind these catalogue poems was anticipated by one of the characters in *Annals of the Five Senses*, who observed that, 'if every opinion is equally insignificant in itself, humanity's bewilderment of thought is a mighty net which somehow holds the whole truth'. The 'world language' poems were MacDiarmid's mightiest 'net' ever in the attempt to match the thistle, to capture Cencrastus, or to achieve 'the diamond body'. Scientific detail and detachment has not dimmed the poet's sense of sudden wonder at the unity of all things when 'time whuds like a flee' and microcosm and macrocosm come together before his eyes:

> What after all do we know of this terrible 'matter',
> Save as a name for the unknown and hypothetical
>   cause
> Of states of our own consciousness? There are not two
>   worlds,
> A world of nature, and a world of human
>   consciousness,
> Standing over against one another, but one world of
>   nature
> Whereof human consciousness is an evolution,
> I reminded myself again as I caught that sudden
>   breathless glimpse,
> Under my microscope, of unexpected beauty and
>   dynamic living
> In the world of life on a sliver of kelp
> Quite as much as the harpooning of a forty-two foot
>   whale shark.
>
> ('Diamond Body', 1939)

MacDiarmid called such works a 'poetry of fact'. Truly he had abandoned 'lyricism' in favour of 'information', often culled from other sources, and perhaps he had abandoned poetry altogether. The literary status of these works still provokes controversy, and analogies might be made with Ezra Pound, who devoted the latter half of his life to the *Cantos* only to question their worth in the end. MacDiarmid managed to sustain faith in his project, but it did get increasingly unrealisable and perhaps more and more unreadable as the years went by.

The Second World War imposed its own priorities on the poet and MacDiarmid was conscripted in 1941, leaving Whalsay to become a fitter in a munitions-factory in Glasgow, later transferring to work as first engineer on a Norwegian vessel servicing ships in the Clyde estuary. When the war ended, MacDiarmid found himself, at the age of fifty-three, without regular work and with poems too long and too abstruse for easy publication. Undaunted, he threw himself back into public life by standing as an independent Nationalist candidate for Kelvingrove during the 1945 general election. He lost his deposit and parted company once again with the SNP. Few political parties could satisfy or tolerate his contentious, contradictory and idealistic nature for long. He himself saw no necessary conflict between his communism and his Scottish nationalism, but neither of the two parties concerned was very happy about his affiliations with the other and he continued to fluctuate between them.

MacDiarmid revived the *Voice of Scotland* and renewed his friendship with the younger writers on the literary scene. In 1950 he was awarded a Civil List pension and visited Russia – the first of several visits to Eastern European countries, where his status was high. In 1951 a small farm cottage became available at Brownsbank, near Biggar, some twenty-six miles from Edinburgh, and the Grieve family moved in. Edinburgh University students helped to modernise it and Valda Grieve still lives in this comfortable little house, which is lined with books and portraits of the poet.

As the last of the early modern giants in the generation of Eliot, Pound, Yeats and Joyce, MacDiarmid enjoyed the stimulation of controversy to the end, and his spirit, intellect and courage were unimpaired until in September 1978 cancer killed him at the age of eighty-six. He is buried on a hillside cemetery above Langholm. He was the first Scottish poet for generations to draw on the full canon of his country's literary tradition and to add a substantial contribution of his own. Thus his poetry embraces lyrical subtlety and the simple force of the ballads, the goliardic glee of Dunbar and the bitter polemic of Iain Lom. He unites Duncan Bàn's loving catalogue of the familiar landscapes of Scotland with John Davidson's scientific and philosophical abstractions, just as his poetic voice moves from colloquial Scots to the elitist and passionate tones of Carlyle. Whatever the outward style, his work shows a Blakean delight in the movement of the spirit and a materialistic delight in the physical universe, as he tries to show us 'the fundamental similarity of all activities', or the mystery to be found in the chemistry of water – 'aye, and ilka drap a world / Bigger than a' Mankind has yet unfurled'.

Edwin Muir (1887–1959)

As if to satisfy the principle of 'Caledonian antisyzygy', MacDiarmid's position as the major poet of the Renaissance movement is balanced by the life and work of Edwin Muir, a quiet, shy man five years his senior, who came from the Orkney Isles. For a time, in fact, Muir was better known to English and American readers than his friend from the Borders. MacDiarmid's rejection of him in the 1930s had to do with Muir's political and cultural opinions, but the two men always did possess radically different poetic sensibilities. MacDiarmid's work is charged with lyrical, linguistic, intellectual or polemical energy, while Muir adopts an English verse of calm and neutral tone to meditate on time and the timeless by way of classical allusions or images drawn from the realms of childhood, mythology or dreams.

Muir's first book of poetry appeared in the same year as *Sangschaw*. He was living in London at the time and had already made a small reputation as a journalist and literary critic, writing as 'Edward Moore', for Orage's *New Age* – an idiosyncratically radical journal which numbered Pound and MacDiarmid among its contributors. Muir had come to the capital in 1919 with his new wife, a Shetland girl called Willa

Anderson (1890–1970) who was to become a novelist in her own right with *Imagined Corners* (1931) and *Mrs Ritchie* (1933). The couple worked together in translating German literature, and are particularly remembered for their versions of Kafka. At first Muir was oppressed by London, and his already insecure psychological state was made worse by the size and anonymity of the city. His marriage was a happy one, however; he made friends and began to adjust; and Orage encouraged him to undertake Jungian analysis. This experience led to the unlocking of his creative capacity, as he kept a dream diary and began to reconstruct the meaning of his life with the help of images and archetypes from his subconscious. Such insights were to become central to his poetry, with its neo-Platonic sense of some timeless pattern beyond the contingent everyday. The couple moved to Europe in 1921 and lived and travelled there for three years before returning to England. Muir remembered Prague, Italy and Austria with gratitude – 'everyone should live his life twice', he wrote, and indeed he went over his old life and exorcised old griefs during that happy time abroad. Free at last, he began to write poetry at the age of thirty-five.

First Poems (1925) shows the influence of the Scots ballads and Heine, with the adoption of ballad stanzas (he experimented with Scots only briefly) to convey a childlike sense of simplicity and suspended wonder. Time seems to stand still and the world shrinks to a toy in 'Childhood':

> Grey tiny rocks slept round him where he lay,
>   Moveless as they, more still as evening came,
> The grasses threw straight shadows far away,
>   And from the house his mother called his name.

The mood is characteristic, and further insight can be gained into Muir's mature work from his account of how the 'Ballad of Hector in Hades' came to him:

> I must have been influenced by something, since we all are, but when I try to find out what it was that influenced me, I can only think of the years of childhood. . . . These years had come alive, after being forgotten for so long, and when I wrote about horses they were my father's plough horses as I saw them when I was four or five, and a poem on Achilles pursuing Hector round the walls of Troy was really a resuscitation of the afternoon when I ran away, in real terror, from another boy as I returned from school. The bare landscape of the little island became, without my knowing it, a

universal landscape over which Abraham and Moses and Achilles and Ulysses and Tristram and all sorts of pilgrims passed; and Troy was associated with the Castle, a mere green mound, near my father's house. (*An Autobiography*, 1954)

It is not difficult to understand the origins of Muir's unhappiness as a young man, nor the sense of mythopoeic timelessness which haunts his verse. They both go back to his childhood on Orkney, and in a sense all his poems, although they never speak directly about himself, stem from a single biographical and metaphysical insight which he rediscovered there. As the youngest of six children, the poet was raised in the loving shelter of his father's farm on Orkney, and from his sixth to his eighth year the family lived on the little island of Wyre. He never forgot this idyllic experience of freedom and innocence, and in later life he came to see his childhood as a dream of Eden itself. The dream was all the more vivid when it stopped, for his father was evicted when Muir was fourteen and the family had to move to Glasgow in 1901.

It was as if they had travelled forward in time from a place whose seasonal and communal pattern of life went back to earliest days. Muir used to say that he was born 250 years ago, and when he finally met the industrial and urban age it came as a grim shock. Within four years both his parents died and two of his brothers as well, from consumption and a tumour in the brain. Muir was on his own at the age of nineteen. He earned his living as a clerk in a variety of offices, and in his own time he taught himself German, read Nietzsche, joined the ILP and educated himself as best he could. Latterly he spent two years in the office of a factory at Fairport where rotting bones were rendered down to make charcoal and fat. Already nervous and in poor health, he conceived a lasting dread of the place, and it seemed the very image of his unhappiness. Things improved towards the end of the war when he began to write for the *New Age*, and in Glasgow he made friends with Denis Saurat and the musician F. G. Scott. Then he met and married Willa – 'the most fortunate event in my life' – and the pair of them set off for London. He did exorcise the bone factory in the end, for he used his poetry as a means of personal reintegration: to discover a glimpse of Eden beyond the stench, and the stray dogs fighting over railway trucks of rancid bones.

In the late twenties the Muirs translated Kafka's *The Castle* and began to write novels for themselves. Edwin produced *The Marionette* (1927), a historical piece called *The Three Brothers* (1931) and *Poor Tom* (1932), which was closely based on his grim years in Glasgow and Greenock. A rather diffuse poem-sequence called *Variations on a Time Theme* (1934) did not escape echoes of T. S. Eliot's style. By 1935 the Muirs and their son were in St Andrew's, and Edwin made a sympathetic but curiously detached analysis of his country in *Scottish Journey* (1935) and then offered his controversial reassessment of its culture in *Scott and Scotland* (1936). He diagnosed something like Eliot's 'dissociation of sensibility' in which the Scots had long been divided between Lallans and English without a 'homogenous language' to convey thought as well as feeling. He admired MacDiarmid as an exception to this rule, but his general opinion was that Scots writers should settle for English. The fact that MacDiarmid was beginning to write in English himself at just this time did not save Muir from his fury.

The poet was fifty years old when his second collection, *Journeys and Places* (1937), developed its imagery of time and fate as a 'stationary journey' endlessly repeated by poets, heroes, lovers or Trojan slaves. These poems reflect the distinction which he liked to make between the 'story' and the 'fable' (this was to be the title of his autobiographical study in 1940) to show how the archetypal pattern of a fable can be discerned within the everyday, historical details of the 'story'. So his symbols become emblems, or heraldic devices on a shield – one of his favourite images – and 'Merlin' and 'The Enchanted Knight' share the same road with 'Ibsen' and 'Mary Stuart', all somehow on the way back in search of some 'Solitary' or 'Unattained' or 'Dreamt of Place' before, or beyond, man's fall from grace. Muir uses simple ballad-forms and a dispassion-ately plain diction for this elusive metaphysical theme and a lightly and skilfully measured lyricism:

> There is a road that turning always
> Cuts off the country of Again,
> Archers stand there on every side
> And as it runs time's deer is slain,
> And lies where it has lain.

('The Road')

In St Andrew's the poet felt frustrated and isolated and began once again to review his life, having come to realise that his creative vision was essentially religious. When war broke out, he and Willa made ends meet as best they could until 1942, when Edwin was offered a post in Edinburgh with the British Council. In 1946 he went to Prague for three years as Director of the British Institute, but post-war Czechoslovakia was an unhappy place in the throes of a Communist take-over, and Muir felt that one kind of oppression had merely been supplanted by another. The couple were glad to return to London and take another British Council post in Rome, where Edwin found himself deeply moved by the Catholic Church's emphasis on incarnation and mystery. Muir's *Essays on Literature and Society* (1949) confirmed his reputation as a literary theorist and critic, and in 1950 he returned to Scotland to become the much-admired warden of Newbattle, an unconventionally creative college for adult education just outside Edinburgh.

The three volumes of poems from these years – and especially *The Labyrinth* (1949) – contain most of Muir's finest work, and his last collection, called *One Foot in Eden*, followed in 1956. The inwardly metaphysical themes of 'The Journey Back' – age, guilt, redemption, mystery and sweetness – are still pursued, but the grimmer historical experience of the forties, and his own frustrations with Scotland, gave a needed edge to other poems. 'Scotland 1941' rises to rage at what he saw as the pernicious influence of Knox and Presbyterianism on his country and its long history of futile internal strife – 'Such wasted bravery idle as a song, / Such hard-won ill . . . .' (He had taken a similar line in the study of Knox which he wrote in 1929.) 'The Incarnate One' and 'Scotland's Winter', from the last collection, offer a vision of his homeland crippled by 'the fleshless word' where 'all the kings before / This land was kingless, / And all the singers before / This land was songless' lie locked under ice 'content / With their poor frozen life and shallow banishment'. Muir also drew on his post-war European experience in poems such as 'The Refugees', 'The Good Town' and 'The Interrogation', and gains a typically understated power – not unlike the spirit of Kafka in places – by refusing to be specifically biographical or documentary:

> My old friends
> (Friends ere these great disasters) are dispersed
> In parties, armies, camps, conspiracies.
> We avoid each other. If you see a man
> Who smiles good-day or waves a lordly greeting
> Be sure he's a policeman or a spy.
> We know them by their free and candid air.

('The Good Town')

Stranger images of dread, confusion or loss appear in 'The Combat', which was directly based on a dream, or 'The Horses', which describes the symbolic return of the old ways after some future holocaust, or 'The Return', which develops his understanding of our life as if it were a strange journey back to reconsider childhood. Muir's vision reached one of its most evocatively mysterious expressions in 'The Labyrinth', in which his theme is mirrored by the Kafkaesque and labyrinthine extension of his syntax in an opening sentence which unwinds for thirty-five lines without a break. Theseus seems to have emerged from the Minotaur's maze, but nothing is certain, and he still sees the mark of the labyrinth in the landscape all around:

> all the roads
> That run through the noisy world, deceiving streets
> That meet and part and meet, and rooms that open
> Into each other – and never a final room –
> Stairways and corridors and antechambers
> That vacantly wait for some great audience,
> The smooth sea-tracks that open and close again,
> Tracks undiscoverable, indecipherable,
> Paths on the earth and tunnels underground,
> And bird-tracks in the air – all seemed a part
> Of the great labyrinth.

He is haunted by a vision of a perfect, toy-like world, or perhaps it was the truly real world – a Platonic ideal beyond the shadows of the cave – but, then again, nothing is certain. The difficult double negatives of lines such as 'I could not live if this were not illusion', and the poem's brooding last lines, epitomise the tale which precedes them (and the experience of trying to read it) so that by implying a familiar context which we cannot place, they throw everything into doubt again:

Oh these deceits are strong almost as life.
Last night I dreamt I was in the labyrinth,
And woke far on. I did not know the place.

After a year as Norton Professor at Harvard in 1955, Muir retired to Swaffham Prior near Cambridge, where he died in the first week of 1959. *An Autobiography* (1954) gives a memorably sensitive and unegocentric account of the poet's travels and his absorption with his inner vision, and Willa Muir's memoir *Belonging* (1968) adds further details of their life together.

Muir's concern to find the 'fable' as a state of grace beyond the circumstance of history is absolutely contrary to MacDiarmid's furious dedication to the specific material details of the world. Yet the Orcadian does have affinities with other Scottish writers, and most notably with the mythopoeic patterns which Grassic Gibbon and Neil Gunn sought to establish in their novels during the thirties. Perhaps the impulse to seek a place outside time has been an attempt to escape the pressure of past history on the Scottish psyche, or to evade the problems of present politics; or perhaps it has been an attempt to reassess that history and to align it towards more creative developments in the future. Gibbon and Gunn were the most outstanding novelists of the Scottish Renaissance, the two figures whose books most surely complement the poetic achievements of MacDiarmid, Muir and Sorley Maclean, and yet, of course, they were not alone.

Compton Mackenzie (1883–1974)

Among the first to support the new political feeling in the north was Compton Mackenzie, who moved from London to Barra in 1928. Born in England and educated at London and Oxford, Mackenzie abandoned his studies in law to write for the stage – his father was an actor and his sister Fay Compton was a star in Barrie's plays in the 1920s. Mackenzie's youthful milieu was Edwardian literary London, in which he cultivated a romantic and dashing personality. Success did not come, however, until he turned to prose fiction and embarked on a long and prolific career. Life behind the scenes of a variety theatre provided him with the best-selling material for *Carnival* (1912), followed by *Sinister Street* (1913), which was particularly admired by Henry James and Ford Madox Ford. The book is a lengthy semi-autobiographical 'development novel' which tells of Michael Fane's growth to maturity from childhood to Oxford, and from there to London and experiences in the shadier parts of society. It is a long novel with atmospheric settings, and its approach to sexual frankness made it something of a *cause celèbre* when circulating-libraries tried to restrict access to it. Mackenzie developed the scenario by carrying characters over into four further books.

The First World War took Mackenzie – now in his thirties – to the campaign in the Dardanelles (*Gallipoli Memories*, 1928) and thence to a leading role in British Intelligence in Greece and the Aegean, recounted in *Extremes Meet* (1928). He delighted in the Mediterranean and continued to produce novels after the war, visiting Norman Douglas at Capri, where he renewed a friendly acquaintance with D. H. Lawrence. The Englishman could not quite approve of Mackenzie's theatrical manner, and satirised him later in 'The Man who Loved Islands'. Certainly the Scot was a flamboyant and patrician figure, and it was typical of his romantic nature that he should express his commitment to Scotland in the post-war years by setting up home in the remote island of Barra. He was a founder member of the National Party, and in those early years Mackenzie, MacDiarmid and the party's first president, Cunninghame Graham, made a formidably eclectic trio on political platforms throughout the country. Mackenzie remained an enthusiastic nationalist to the end of his life, but up to this point he had not dealt with questions of Scottish character or politics in any of his novels. These issues finally appear, if indirectly, in *The Four Winds of Love*, a series of six volumes published between 1937 and 1945.

With a truly Scottish didactic exhaustiveness, Mackenzie's *magnum opus* is a lengthy romance of travel, ideas and, once again, semi-autobiographical character-development. The hero of the sequence is Juan Pendarves Ogilvie – public-schoolboy, playwright, traveller, lover, philosopher, politician and pedagogue – and each book adds a few more years to his odyssey, from the beginning of the century to the outbreak of the Second World War. Mackenzie explained that his plan was to equate the four winds with 'four love stories and four philosophies of love and four decades of a man's life', and he associated different seasons, political motifs and different countries from his own travels with each 'wind' in turn. The action starts with early life and love in England from 1900 to 1911 and moves to Poland (*The East Wind of Love*); then it shifts to love and war under the South Wind of the Mediterranean from 1912 to 1917; thence to the post-war years in America and the plight of Ireland and Ogilvie's hopes for nationalism in the rise of Mussolini (*The West Wind of Love* and *West to North*); finally the sequence comes round to the North Wind, with Ogilvie's home on a Hebridean island and his (and Mackenzie's) hopes for a Catholic Christian confederation of small Celtic nations. The hero renews his travels in Europe until Hitler's increasingly grandiose vision of Nordic nationalism makes him flee from the coming of a new winter to seek the sunshine of the Greek isles. *The Four Winds of Love* offers over three thousand pages of travel, complicated love-affairs and political, personal and philosophical discourse, and in the end the tireless eloquence of its hero–spokesman may overwhelm all but the most dedicated reader.

After the 1940s, Mackenzie became best known and loved for a light-hearted series of Highland farces, featuring a cantankerous, English-educated laird called 'Ben Nevis' (*The Monarch of the Glen*, 1941), or the natives of the island of 'Todday', most famous in *Whisky Galore* (1947). The author was knighted in 1952, an honour entirely in keeping with his colourful role as a literary personality, dividing his time between Edinburgh and the south of France. *Thin Ice* (1956), his last serious novel, was a sympathetic treatment of public scandal in the life of a homosexual. In later years Mackenzie dedicated himself to ten volumes ('Octaves') of exhaustively detailed personal reminiscence in *My Life and Times* (1963–71).

Eric Linklater (1899–1974)

Less directly involved with Scottish nationalism, Eric Linklater still shared Mackenzie's view that democracy and culture were best served by preserving the identity of small nations in the face of larger and more anonymous forces. He outlined these theories, very much in the spirit of the times, in *The Lion and The Unicorn* (1935) and Mackenzie dedicated the first volume of the *Four Winds* sequence to Linklater as his 'junior contemporary'. Linklater's father was a master mariner, and the novelist was actually born in Wales, but they were an Orkney family and he spent his childhood in the islands and later returned to live there for a number of years, before settling in the North East. Educated at Aberdeen Grammar School, Linklater joined the Black Watch in the last years of the First World War to serve as a private soldier in the trenches of France, where he nearly died from a bullet wound in the head. He went on to take a degree at Aberdeen University, changing from medicine to English literature, before going to Bombay for two years as a journalist on *The Times of India*. 1927 saw him back in the granite city as an English assistant at the university, where he began his first novel and gained a Commonwealth Fellowship which allowed him to travel through America from 1928 to 1930.

White-Maa's Saga, published in 1929, drew on the author's own background in Aberdeen and Orkney to tell of his student hero's growth to maturity and love, while *Poet's Pub* (1929), a light comedy in Chestertonian vein, was conceived as 'sheer . . . invention', an exercise in the craft of fiction. With its acceptance Linklater determined to earn his living as a writer, and his presence in America had already given him the material for what was to be his most successful and possibly his best book. He later describd *Juan in America* (1931) as a 'historical novel' about the United States during Prohibition – 'a country and a society which were vanishing even as I left them'. Juan Motley, descended from Byron's Don Juan, is Linklater's picaresque foil for a series of grotesque and hilarious adventures through the length and breadth of a nation apparently given over to college football, gangsterdom, bootlegging, movie-making and West Coast cults. Everywhere he goes Juan creates disorder, like a Byronically amorous but still innocent Candide. Linklater moves with linguistic precision from an ironically classical detachment, through straight-faced lampoon, to episodes of wild, chaotic farce, and this preference for absurdity and irreverent laughter was to become essential to his conception of satire.

Linklater took pride in his professional ability to suit style to subject-matter, and his next book was radically different, for

The Men of Ness (1932) adopted a stripped and austere prose as the most appropriate voice for the epic Norse past and a bare saga of Viking fate – although it is significant that it is the 'little man', Gauk, who survives when grim heroes die at the end. The author returned to live in Scotland, and a short-lived involvement with the National Party saw him adopted as their candidate for an East Fife by-election in 1933. He was 'resoundingly defeated' and *Magnus Merriman* (1934) gives a satirical account of the affair from the point of view of its hero. Magnus is a sexual and political adventurer who moves from the ambitious social circles of London to end up as an inefficient crofter on his native Orkney, where he is trapped in marriage by the shy guiles of a young, beautiful and pragmatically unimaginative farm girl. She may represent his punishment or the making of him, but it is difficult to tell, for he is a romantic chameleon who changes his stripes to suit his situation whatever it may be – city sophisticate or island poet. Linklater himself seems unsure, as if he were divided between his plain love of Orkney and a delight in travel and smart company. In later years he liked to describe himself as a 'peasant with a pen', but his sharp talent for society farce is very far from the worlds of Grassic Gibbon or George Mackay Brown. In this sense the impasse of Magnus Merriman's fate may be revealingly honest about Linklater's position in Scotland, and even his own careless brush with politics. Given the satirical portraits in his novel, it is not surprising that he soon broke with the Nationalists, although MacDiarmid remained delighted with his incarnation as 'Hugh Skene' and liked to quote it with approval.

More novels followed, including an exuberant comedy of upper-class manners exploded by gross farce in *Ripeness is All* (1935), and *Juan in China* (1937), which did not match the success of his American adventures, despite Linklater's actual visit to China. Long aware of the brutality of fascism in Germany, Linklater's liberal imperialism was equally critical of communist ideology, and his essays and novels from the late thirties and early forties reflect a concern to oppose oppression and find values worth fighting for. The outbreak of war found him in uniform again, helping to establish land defences for the fleet at Scapa Flow. He renewed his regard for what he saw as the simple decency of ordinary men in the ranks and helped to run a service newspaper for the Orkneys. Later he travelled widely as a freelance correspondent for the War Office, ending up with the campaign in Italy for which he wrote the official history. Among his autobiographical books *The Man on my Back* (1941) records his early life as a writer, and the travails of two wars are described in *Fanfare for a Tin Hat* (1970).

Linklater's Italian experiences produced *Private Angelo* (1946) in celebration of a peasant soldier's good sense in knowing when to run away. This is his most gently controlled statement in favour of the fallible individual, innocent of ideology and the 'serious' abstractions by which large organisations seek to control him. The novelist shows compassion for those who are fated to be maimed by life, and Angelo has to lose a hand before the war is done with him. 'Without irony history would be intolerable', a character remarks in a later novel, and to some extent Linklater's stance does depend on a rather precarious balancing-act between grotesque farce and melodrama, and sometimes his irony seems to slip into a rather heartless and mechanical process without final commitment. His later works include *Laxdale Hall* (1951), *The House of Gair* (1953) and *The Dark of Summer* (1956); he considered *Position at Noon* (1958) to be his wittiest novel and certainly, along with *A Man Over Forty* (1963), it recovers the wilder satirical exuberance of his earlier work.

By comparison with Linklater and Mackenzie, who wrote many entertaining best-sellers, the few works of David Lindsay and Fionn MacColla take a darker and more metaphysical twist. Lindsay's fantasy novels have affinities with the painful world of John Davidson or the strange landscapes of George MacDonald; while Fionn MacColla's angry muse has a vision of Scotland inherited from Douglas Brown or John MacDougall Hay.

David Lindsay (1878–1945)

David Lindsay is best known for *A Voyage to Arcturus*, a philosophical fantasy novel of considerable power, yet his writing-career ended in obscurity and for years he enjoyed only an 'underground' reputation. Born in London, Lindsay lived most of his life in the south but took regular holidays with his father's relatives near Jedburgh, for it pleased him to maintain the connection despite the fact that his Scottish father had abandoned his wife and children without support, thus forcing his youngest son to give up hopes of university in order to earn a living as an insurance-broker. Lindsay became a shy and puritanical person, deeply interested in music and philosophy but largely self-educated in these fields. It is difficult not to identify the marks of this early history in his mature work and thought, with its almost Calvinistic distrust of pleasure and its urge to confront the face of God, and then to unmask and go beyond that ultimate figure of paternal authority. Lindsay's books are haunted by the need to identify a reality beyond reality, and the metaphysical fantasies of George MacDonald were a potent early influence on him. His rather unbending and cerebral nature responded equally to the writings of Schopenhauer and Nietzsche, who seemed to support his convictions about the importance of will in the universe, and of the need for the individual to adopt a lonely and prophetic stance in his quest for a truth beyond the mob. In this respect his affinities also lie with the unhappy spirits of James Thomson and John Davidson.

Lindsay led a life of bachelor routine in his his city office for over twenty years. When he was finally conscripted to help the war-effort, at the age of thirty-eight, he managed to find an administrative post with his regiment in yet another London office. The move led to a meeting with a vivacious eighteen-year-old, and within two months they were married. Spurred by his bride's enthusiasm, Lindsay determined to take up full-time writing. The couple found a house in Cornwall and by 1919 Lindsay had embarked on his first novel – derived from the notes and reflections of many years. His practical inexperience as a writer betrays itself in a clumsy pedantic prose, and he never did perfect his style or the ability to handle plot and character smoothly. Nevertheless, *A Voyage to Arcturus* (1920) is a work of such conceptual originality that it was accepted by the first publisher to read it.

Usually referred to as a fantasy, and sometimes mistaken for crude science-fiction, Lindsay's book is more properly an allegory of spiritual and philosophical search. The opening chapters depend on contrivances to do with a seance in Hampstead, and a crystal torpedo which takes off from a tower on the North-East of Scotland to fly its passengers to the planet Tormance under the double star of Arcturus. Once there, the protagonist Maskull begins his quest to confront the nature of the universe. He has already received premonitions of his fate back on earth, where he knew Nightspore, who will later be revealed as the *alter ego* of his spirit, and Krag, their mysterious guide on the voyage. After landing, Maskull is separated from his friends and sets out to look for them, like Bunyan's pilgrim in some nightmarishly precise but undecipherable allegory. He finds new colours on Tormance and grows extra organs for his senses. He meets people whose names – Joiwind, Crimtyphon, Panawe and Spadevil – might have come from one of Blake's more obscure prophetic books. Nothing will turn out to be quite what it seems in this world under a double star – the very image of duality. Tormance is a stark place of strange sexuality bound up with kindness, pain, nameless sensations, beauty, shame, terror and successive deaths. Its ultimate nature is only gradually and indirectly revealed to the reader as Maskull journeys through grim landscapes and makes ambiguous encounters with various semi-human creatures. When Maskull finally arrives at the end of his quest it is only to meet death to the sound of the eerie drumbeats, or heartbeats, which he had first heard on the Scottish coast before parting. Yet through death he rejoins his 'double', Nightspore, and moves to a confrontation with Muspel, the source of all light. He finds that Muspel is locked in Manichean conflict – like some eternal symbiosis – with Crystalman, the shaping-force of worlds, whose advocacy of pleasure, art and beauty turns out to be a deceitful masquerade covering a shameful, vulgar, leering grin. This, the true aspect of the material universe, has haunted the novel from the start, for it has appeared on the face of every creature in the moment after death. When Nightspore realises this, he almost despairs, but Krag is there to assure him that they will continue the moral combat, and that Crystalman will not prevail. Maskull's journey is over. Nightspore's has only begun. The book ends at this point, and Krag reveals that his true name on Earth is 'pain'.

C. S. Lewis acknowledged the influence of *Arcturus* on his own Perelandra novels, and successive readers and critics have testified to the disturbing power of Lindsay's universe, suffused as it is with symbols of music, repressed sexuality, shape-changing, death, pain and moral effort. Against such a vision even his awkward prose comes to seem curiously effective. It is Lindsay's finest book and, although reviews were mixed and sales small, it achieved a serious critical reputation. Lindsay was encouraged and in the next three years he produced two further metaphysical fantasies, this time set in the contemporary everyday world. *The Haunted Woman* (1922) evokes the proximity of other times and realms of being with some brilliantly memorable and ambiguous images; *The Sphinx* (1923) is less effective, however, and neither book did very well. Lindsay immediately wrote *The Adventures of M. de Mailly* as a historical-romance potboiler, but it was not published until 1926. For the next five years he struggled with the drafts and revisions of his next novel, *Devil's Tor* (1932), but most readers found it humourless and wordy. The family moved to Sussex and eventually to Hove, near Brighton, where Mrs Lindsay ran a boarding-house to help support them. Her husband persevered with his writing and his philosophical notes, but his publishing-career was over and he died in 1945, in great pain from an abscess in the jaw for which he refused treatment. *The Violet Apple* (1976) did not find a publisher in Lindsay's lifetime, and his last book, *The Witch* (1976), was left unfinished. In the light of more recent studies, however, the later books still offer valuable insights into the unique and underrated imagination which produced *A Voyage to Arcturus*.

Tom Macdonald ('Fionn MacColla', 1906–75)

Tom Macdonald had only a little more luck with publishers during his career, and he shares something of Lindasy's austere and philosophical bias. A native of Montrose, Macdonald trained and worked as a teacher in the North-East before going to Palestine to teach in a Church of Scotland college at Safed. He had a happy childhood brought up as a member of the Plymouth Brethren – an extremely severe Presbyterian sect – but he later came to reject everything to do with the Reformed Church and eventually joined the Catholic faith. His critique of Protestantism is one of the themes of his first novel, *The Albannach* ('The Highlander'), which he began when he returned to Scotland in 1929. The condition of his country at the height of the Depression made him an active member of the National Party, and he went to Glasgow University to study Gaelic. Henceforth 'Fionn MacColla' dedicated himself to a vision of a transcendent Highland culture, which would be utterly opposed to the Kirk and the bourgeois interests of Scottish establishment and English imperialism alike. He defined Protestantism as the historical expression of a desire to control mankind by negating individuality and creativity, and hence he saw Knox as the first in a line of dictators leading to Lenin and Hitler. For Macdonald, history was the by-product of malign or benevolent forces in the human spirit, and as an imaginative writer he possessed a powerfully empathetic understanding of the negative pleasures to be gained from the Calvinistic exercise of the will.

The Albannach (1932) describes how Murdo Anderson grows away from the repressive faith of his home, only to be recalled from Glasgow University when his father dies. Returned to the narrow confines of life in a Highland village, he succumbs to an unwise marriage and comes close to alcoholism and suicide before he learns compassion and rediscovers his creative balance and a place in the community, too, by way of crofting, piping and traditional poetry. In typical style, Macdonald's prose adopts Murdo's point of view, and the physical details of local places and faces are brilliantly charged with his subjective intensity. The same effect characterises *And the Cock Crew* (1945), a novel of the Clearances whose central scene is a long debate between an old Gaelic bard and the local minister, Zachary Wiseman. 'Maighstir Sachairi' is the protagonist who first defends and then betrays his parishioners by encouraging them to submit to the most brutal of evictions as 'the will of God'. (The novel's title refers to Peter's betrayal of Christ.) The minister's tortured moments of certainty and doubt and his melodramatic death dominate the tale; and, although the quieter tones of the poet Fearchar imply a kinder vision, there is no sign of it at the end. If Gunn's *Butcher's Broom* was a poetically controlled protest against the Clearances, *And the Cock Crew* is a Gothic cry of philosophical anger.

The descriptive intensities of Macdonald's prose, and his occasional melodrama, recall aspects of *Gillespie* and *The House with the Green Shutters*, and his fiction gains further force through his fascinated and polemical hatred of Protestantism as part of a more universal 'nay-saying'. In this sense Macdonald's case against the Presbyterian conscience goes further than Hogg did, or Lockhart's *Adam Blair*. His theories were published in *At the Sign of the Clenched Fist* (1967), and a short autobiography, *Too Long in this Condition*, appeared posthumously in 1975. Macdonald worked as a head teacher in the Highlands in later years, but came to believe bitterly that fate, critics and other writers had been less than kind to his creative development, especially during his hard times in the thirties. His case is complex, for he was a flamboyant and unhappy personality whose real gift for vivid writing was fuelled and ultimately overwhelmed by his own philosophical obsessions. *Scottish Noël* (1958) and the debate *Ane Tryall of Heretiks* (1962) were potent fragments from what was to be a larger historical novel. After his death several other unpublished manuscripts were found among his papers, including a novel from the late fifties, *The Ministers* (1979).

Lindsay and Macdonald had a long struggle to find an audience for a few brilliantly flawed books, but the single most sustained and innovative achievement in modern Scottish fiction was made by a man who died when he was thirty-four, after only seven years as a serious writer.

James Leslie Mitchell ('Lewis Grassic Gibbon', 1901–35)

The three books in *A Scots Quair* were Mitchell's last and finest work. They give a powerful account of history and social change in Scotland between 1911 and 1932, and at the same time they explore the fate of a particular spirit, ancient, free and intuitive, in the face of the modern world. Mitchell found this spirit in the enduringly feminine psyche of his heroine Chris Guthrie, as she grows up in the rural North-East, and he associated it with his own mythopoeic vision of Scotland's past. Neil Gunn and Edwin Muir shared a similar understanding of how timeless values were to be found within the tradition – for Gunn they were Celtic, because he himself came from the Highlands, while Muir looked to the Eden of his childhood in Orkney. Mitchell is unique, however, in bringing his poetic vision into contact with life in the modern city and in confronting it with his own fiercely socialist principles – a conflict which led to difficult tensions which made the elegiac note of his art all the more poignant.

The author's sense of place could not have been more authentic, for *A Scots Quair* sprang from his own upbringing on crofts in the Howe of the Mearns, especially at Bloomfield above Inverbervie, later fictionalised as 'Blawearie' in the parish of 'Kinraddie'. Here is the heart of the rich farming-land which lies to the south of Stonehaven between the Grampians and the coast. The author liked to recall that he was 'of peasant rearing and peasant stock', and expressed pride 'that the land was so closely and intimately mine (my mother used to hap me in a plaid in harvest time and leave me in the lee of a stock while she harvested)'. Yet he was not fitted for farm work, and grew to be a sensitive and bookish boy, interested in archaeology and astronomy, with thoughts of becoming a journalist or an editor. Mitchell's village schoolmaster – a friend in later years – preserved his brightest pupil's early compositions and encouraged him to take secondary education at Mackie Academy in Stonehaven. But he was not to be a 'lad o' pairts', for Mitchell's teenage years were disturbed and unhappy and he walked out of school at the age of sixteen, to work as a junior reporter for the *Aberdeen Journal*. Stirred by the promise of the Russian Revolution in 1917 he became an enthusiastic communist; and when he went to work for the *Scottish Farmer* in Glasgow in 1919 his experiences of the unrest on Clydeside, and the terrible urban poverty which he found there, reinforced his commitment to revolutionary socialism. His career in journalism was cut short, however, when a minor scandal over the padding of expenses led to his dismissal without references. Greatly disturbed by the experience, he made a clumsy attempt at suicide and had to return home – under something of a cloud – to recover his bearings.

All too aware that his parents could not support him, and driven by the need to escape from his home background, he decided to join the army. He enlisted in August 1919 and spent the next three and a half years working for the Service Corps in Persia, India and Egypt; and his letters to Rebecca Middleton – who came from the croft next to Bloomfield – are full of a young man's enthusiasm for the romance of these distant countries and their ancient ruins. When Mitchell left the army in 1923,

Hugh MacDiarmid had just started his own literary campaign from Montrose, but they were not to meet until later and the younger man's own efforts brought him no success at all. After six months during which he 'nearly starved to death', Mitchell settled once again for the security of enlistment, joining the Royal Air Force this time, in which he served as a clerk on various stations in England until 1929. He tried his hand at poetry without finding a publisher, but one of his short stories won a magazine competition and, although it was to be another four years before he saw himself in print again, Mitchell was duly encouraged. He renewed contact with Rebecca Middleton – she was a civil servant in London – and the couple took a holiday together in the Mearns and married in the summer of 1925. Rebecca, or Ray as he called her, had to leave her job and times were hard for them during the next few years.

Mitchell persevered with more stories, planned a book on exploration, and worked on a novel to be called *Stained Radiance*, closely based on his ideas and experiences. Its heroine foreshadows the later Chris Guthrie and his own ambivalent feelings of pride in and distaste for peasant life in Scotland, but is is an ironic and often an angry work, and many publishers rejected it. He continued to work at the manuscript while pursuing his interests in archaeology, anthropology and the culture of the Mayans and the Incas in America. He was particularly keen on 'Diffusionism', a theory which held that civilisation began with the discovery of agriculture in ancient Egypt and spread throughout the world, sweeping away a 'golden age' of primitive nomadic hunters in the process and bringing all the ills of property, nationalism and the slavery of labour in its place. The theory appealed to Mitchell's communist ideals and he associated the golden age in Scotland with the lost era of the aboriginal and matriarchal Picts, whose remote descendants were still, he felt sure, to be found among the peasants of his native North-East – far from the slums and factories of 'progress'. (He summarised this idiosyncratic account of prehistory and Scottish culture – including his regard for the Reformation as a people's cause – in a later essay called 'The Antique Scene' written for *Scottish Scene* in 1934.)

Mitchell's fortunes began to change when his speculative book *Hanno, or the Future of Exploration* was published in 1928. Early next year another of his Middle East stories was accepted for *Cornhill Magazine* – after the recommendation of H. G. Wells – and this led to the publication of twelve more in a cycle of tales later collected as *The Calends of Cairo* (1931). Mitchell could now leave the RAF with some hopes at last for his future as a writer. Articles on the Mayans had appeared in *Antiquity* and he already had a small reputation in this field. *Stained Radiance* came out in 1930, and Jarrold's, who were to publish nearly all his work, accepted his next novel too. *The Thirteenth Disciple* is another thinly disguised autobiographical book, filled with his interest in Diffusionism and particularly frank about his unhappy schooldays and his troubles in Glasgow. A daughter, Rhea, was born to the couple, and in 1931 they all moved to Welwyn Garden City, a genteel new town outside London. Leslie Mitchell poured his energies into more and more work, composing straight onto the typewriter, as was his habit, with few revisions. Within a year he produced two novels on the romance of Diffusionism – *Three Go Back* (1932), which was a time-travel fantasy about Atlantis, and *The Lost Trumpet* (1932). Both were well received by writers such as Compton Mackenzie and H. G. Wells, one of Mitchell's boyhood heroes. But Leslie's thoughts had already turned back to his native Mearns, enhanced by a sense of perspective gained in the south, and encouraged, perhaps, by the critical success being accorded at home to Neil Gunn's *Morning Tide* (1930).

Mitchell wrote *Sunset Song* (1932) in a single and remarkably sustained creative effort which lasted less than two months. It was published under his mother's name as the first in a planned trilogy of novels on the life of a girl called Chris Guthrie. These books were to give the definitive account of the land he loved and hated, with Chris as its spokesperson and the vessel for his own imaginative spirit. The second volume, *Cloud Howe*, appeared in 1933 and the series ended with *Grey Granite* in 1934. Early in the following year Mitchell suffered a perforated ulcer, and after an emergency operation he died on 7 February. He was a man of vivacious and unusually intense energy, but not even he could sustain the pressure of work to which he had committed himself at the end. In those last two years he produced seven more books, including a fine historical novel, *Spartacus* (1933), which shows his sympathy for the oppressed and the exploited. Then in 1934 there appeared a life of Mungo Park; *The Conquest of the Maya*; another time-travel adventure,

Gay Hunter; the collaboration (as Grassic Gibbon) with Hugh MacDiarmid in *Scottish Scene*; and, finally, nine short biographies of famous explorers published as *Nine against the Unknown*. Part of a further novel on North-East life was left unfinished when he died, and this was published in 1982 as *The Speak of the Mearns*. The trilogy remains his finest achievement, widely popular among Scottish readers and televised as three major serials.

The voice and personality of Chris Guthrie lies at the heart of all three books in *A Scots Quair*, but it is felt most strongly in *Sunset Song*, which deals with her upbringing and young womanhood. For all its failings and the occasional brutality of country folk, her home parish of Kinraddie still offers the security of an extended family circle. It stands for 'the Scots countryside itself', as the minister remarks wryly, 'fathered between a kailyard and a bonny briar bush in the lee of a house with green shutters', but the spell of the sunset will not last and all the kailyard securities will be swept away. In fact Gibbon had few illusions about country life: Chris's mother commits suicide, worn out by childbirth and terrified of another pregnancy, while her father, brutalised by toil and made still more severe by his religion, drives his son to emigrate and eventually suffers a paralysing stroke which leaves his daughter to struggle with the farm and to ward off his delirious sexual advances. In such circumstances Chris comes to physical and intellectual maturity, determined to be her own woman, divided between the two Chrisses 'that fought for her heart and tormented her':

> You hated the land and the coarse speak of the folk and learning was brave and fine one day and the next you'd waken with the peewits crying across the hills, deep and deep, crying in the heart of you and the smell of the earth in your face, almost you'd cry for that, the beauty of it and the sweetness of the Scottish land and skies.

This passage is typical of Gibbon's internalised colloquial narrative method, in which the impersonal but familiar 'you' encloses Chris, the community and the reader in an easy assumption of shared experience. To the same end, the novelist italicises speech and includes it in the narrative without breaking the flow of description or reported thought. In this way the whole book is integrated within Chris's sensibility as she recalls the key events of what passed before, advancing the story chapter by chapter, like a retrospective diary which returns to the 'present' at the end of each section. Chris carries out these acts of recollection while resting among standing stones beside a loch on the hill above her home. As her favourite private spot, this place sets her experiences against the passage of epochs, and allows Gibbon to express his Diffusionist feelings for the timeless value and innocence that once prevailed when the world was young. She has an affinity with these mysterious perspectives, and is haunted, in all three novels, by a sense that nothing endures but change itself, and beyond it all, the land which made her:

> The wet fields squelched below her feet, oozing up their smell of red clay from under the sodden grasses, and up in the hills she saw the trail of the mist, great sailing shapes of it, going south on the wind into Forfar, past Laurencekirk they would sail, down the wide Howe with its sheltered glens and its late, drenched harvests, past Brechin smoking against its hill, with its ancient tower that the Pictish folk had reared, out of the Mearns, sailing and passing, sailing and passing, she minded Greek words of forgotten lessons, Παντα'ρει *Nothing Endures*.
>
> And then a queer thought came to her there in the drooked fields, that nothing endured at all, nothing but the land she passed across, tossed and turned and perpetually changed below the hands of the crofter folk since the oldest of them had set the Standing Stones by the loch of Blawearie and climbed there on their holy days and saw their terraced crops ride brave in the wind and sun. Sea and sky and the folk who wrote and fought and were learnéd, teaching and saying and praying, they lasted but as a breath, a mist of fog in the hills, but the land was forever, it moved and changed below you, but was forever, you were close to it and it to you, not at a bleak remove it held you and hurted you. And she had thought to leave it all!

Not surprisingly, the land and its elegiac and seductive voice features most strongly in *Sunset Song*, for the novel deals, after all, with Chris's sexual growth from girlhood to maturity and with her decision to stay at home to work the croft with her new husband Ewan Tavendale – a boy of Highland descent with a darker and more fragile temperament than her own. In this respect the book is indeed a 'song' which combines Hardy's sense of season, place and rural custom with a Lawrentian insight into the sexual and psychological intensities between two young people making a life together. But the novel has a social dimension as well, for modern transport and city life are making their presence felt, and finally the Great War – at first so little heeded by Kinraddie – marks or destroys everyone in the little community. All the trees in the neighbourhood are felled for timber, and larger and more commercial farming takes over until the old peasant crofter-class finally passes away. Ewan is brutalised by barrack-room life long before he is shot for desertion at the Front, and the fighting kills kindly Chae Strachan and even Long Rob of the Mill, who finally enlisted, despite his socialism and the objections of his conscience.

Chris herself heralds a more peaceful social change, for Long Rob was one of the few people in Kinraddie who was her intellectual equal (he was modelled on Ray Mitchell's father), and she is distinguished by her determination to remain spiritually and mentally her own person in the face of a community which offers only the narrowest and most domestic of roles to women. But her pride and her poetic sense of change make her a solitary figure too, and she finds another love, and a father for her young son Ewan, in the new minister of the parish, an idealistic young man called Robert Colquhoun. Chris cannot promise him her old self – for that belongs to her first husband – but she offers him 'maybe the second Chris, maybe the third'. The novel ends with Colquhoun's sermon at the dedication of a memorial to those who died in the war. Set among the standing stones, and followed by the playing of 'Flowers of the Forest' on the pipes, this scene serves to recall once again, older perspectives on mutability and human loss.

Sunset Song is not without its sentimental side, but Gibbon shows that subtle and mature art can be achieved beyond the Kailyard genre. In setting and development it has several striking similarities with a German novel called *Jörn Uhl* (1901) by Gustav Frenssen, and Gibbon may have read it in earlier years, although some similarities are inevitable in so far as both books deal with a common fund of peasant experience. Nevertheless, Gibbon's voice and his wider use of symbolism is decidedly his own, and his prose style is redolent of North-East Scots, for, although relatively few dialect words are used, his narrative rhythms remain distinctively local. Yet *Sunset Song* has no difficulty in communicating with its readers, and its evocation of the seasons and rural life has made it by far the most popular of the three novels, even in America, where it was widely praised. But the full scope of Gibbon's complex and disturbing vision is lost if the novel is studied on its own, for Chris will not find happiness in the end, and the world beyond Blawearie will offer little comfort. (Gibbon followed the success of his novel with three stories in the same vein for the *Scots Magazine*, and 'Smeddum' and 'Clay' were published again, along with 'Greenden' and two others, as part of the author's contribution to *Scottish Scene*.)

Appropriately enough, perhaps, since she has left the scenes of her childhood, Chris's sensibility is less central to the town of Segget, where her husband takes her in *Cloud Howe*. The doings and the gossip of the place, and the strike among the linen-spinners there, give a more social and political focus to their life together as the new minister and his wife, and the voice of the community can be heard more often as it joins Chris's voice in the narrative flow – not unlike the spiteful reports from the 'bodies' of Barbie.

Colquhoun calls his wife 'Chris Caledonia', observing wryly that he has 'married a nation', and indeed she does have a symbolic part to play in her progress from the setting sun of Kinraddie to the township of Segget and eventually – in *Grey Granite* – to the industrial city of 'Duncairn' at the height of the Depression, where her son will become a communist organiser. This movement towards a more immediate historical awareness is foreshadowed by her fascination with the Kaimes and the ruined castle there, which replaces the standing stones as her favourite vantage-point, evoking years of bloodshed, fallen barons and the sufferings of the Covenanters. Robert Colquhoun is an idealistic liberal socialist who preaches about the thousands of Christs who died in the war, supports the miners in the General Strike of 1926, and tries to assuage the cynicism and the political violence of the linen-workers. These spinners have always been an exploited class, for they were cannon-fodder in the war and are little more than that now to the owners of the mills. They are equally despised by the petty bourgeoisie, for Segget has lost men such as Long Rob and Chae – if it ever had them – and it is a community largely without wisdom, conscience or charity. Colquhoun starts well, but the struggle is too great for him. The General Strike fails and Chris's new baby dies at birth. She recovers, but her husband suffers a crisis of personal faith and terror – haunted by a vision of Christ and by the memory of an evicted worker's baby which was gnawed by rats. Finally his health collapses, for his lungs were gassed in the war, and when he dies Chris finds herself alone once again at the end of a grimmer book than *Sunset Song*.

She will survive, for beyond the social surface of the novel Gibbon shows us a woman grappling with her identity as if she were a succession of different Chrisses, each reacting to different men in her past and yet always remaining herself and, in some vital sense, untouched. This ancient spirit stands aloof from politics or her husband's religion, symbolised by the 'clouds' whose various formations are used to name the chapters of the book, just as the chapters of *Sunset Song* used the farming-seasons. Ewan and Chris's father were men of the earth, but Colquhoun's idealism has taken her beyond those fertile cycles to a more elevated and abstract point of view. Yet she cannot find substance in any of the doctrines of men, and, for her, even love itself is only another mirage from their busy world:

> Once Chris and Robert came to a place, out in the open, here the wind blew and the ground was thick with the droppings of sheep, where a line of the ancient stones stood ringed, as they stood in Kinraddie far west and below, left by the men of antique time, memorial these of a dream long lost, and hopes and fears of fantastic eld.
>
> Robert said that they came from the East, those fears, long ago, ere Pytheas came sailing the sounding coasts to Thule. Before that the hunters had roamed these hills, naked and bright, in a Golden Age, without fear or hope or hate or love, living high in the race of the wind and the race of life, mating as simple as beasts or birds, dying with a like keen simpleness, the hunting weapons of those ancient folk Ewan would find in his search of the moors. . . .
>
> And she thought then, looking on the shadowed Howe with its stratus mists and its pillars of spume, driving west by the Leachie bents, that men had followed these pillars of cloud like lost men lost in the high, dreich hills, they followed and fought and toiled in the wake of each whirling pillar that rose from the heights, clouds by day to darken men's minds – loyalty and fealty, patriotism, love, the mumbling chants of the dead old gods that once were worshipped in the circles of stones, christianity, socialism, nationalism – all – Clouds that swept through the Howe of the world, with men that took them for gods: just clouds, they passed and finished, dissolved and were done, nothing endured but the Seeker himself, him and the everlasting Hills.

The chapters of *Grey Granite* are named after the silicates and crystals to be found in that durable rock, reflecting the hardships of the Depression years in Duncairn, a big city on the east coast, modelled on the granite of Aberdeen with aspects of Dundee and Glasgow. Gibbon may not have been entirely at ease with an urban setting, and certainly the book, like *Cloud Howe* in places, bears the evidence of hasty work, for it came from that last and most desperate year of writing. It is a harsh and unsettling novel and many readers have found it difficult after the lyricism of the first volume. Yet it was clearly Gibbon's intention to disturb us in this way, for the granite imagery also charts young Ewan's commitment to communism as he comes to develop the same flinty dedication which MacDiarmid had admired in his hymns to Lenin. In fact, the book was dedicated to MacDiarmid, and Gibbon shared the poet's convictions, but his picture of Ewan has a darker side, for he appears to be an activist who will sacrifice his girl, his friends, and the truth itself to the cause of revolution. Ewan loses his idealism when he is physically beaten by the police for his part in a labour demonstration. He experiences a vivid identification with all suffering humanity, and from then on he has stone in his soul and the quiet and precocious child who collected flint arrowheads in the hills around Segget has died within him. The passage is disturbing, masochistic and suffused with hatred:

> He was one with them all, a long wail of sobbing mouths and wrung flesh, tortured and tormented by the world's Masters while those Masters lied about Progress through Peace, Democracy, Justice, the Heritage of Culture. . . .
> And a kind of stinging bliss came over him, knowledge that he was that army itself – that army of pain and blood and torment that was yet but the raggedest van of the hordes of the last of the Classes, the ancient Lowly, trampling the ways behind it unstayable: up and up, a dark sea of faces, banners red in the blood from the prisons, torn entrails of tortured workers their banners, the enslavement and oppression of six thousand years a cry and a singing that echoes to the stars. No retreat, no safety, no escape for them, no reward, thrust up by the black, blind tide to take the first brunt of impact, first glory, first death, first life as it never yet had been lived – . . . .

Grey Granite offers no deliverance, nor could its author see an easy conclusion to the work. The city of factories, owners, shopkeepers, workers and sheer drudgery is seen through Chris's eyes as she helps to keep Ma Cleghorn's boarding-house, but the narrative is shared with Ewan and one of his worker friends, and, when the voices of various characters in the boarding-house are heard as well, the result is a comic and sometimes savage satire; but it means that the warmth of Chris's sensibility no longer infuses and controls the book. She marries again, but her husband, Ake Ogilvie – an old acquaintance from Segget – realises that he does not have her true self, and he grants her freedom by emigrating to Canada. Chris is finally alone and wholly given over to her vision of changeless change and independence in 'a world without hope or temptation, without hate or love, at last, at long last'. She moves to another cottage, in the countryside where her family lived before they moved to Blawearie, and she finds another vantage-point on the site of an ancient Pictish fort on the Hill of Fare. Here she reflects on the journey of her life and on the role of change as 'Deliverer, Destroyer and Friend in one', and she seems to die away in the closing sentence of the trilogy.

It is difficult not to feel that Chris has been somehow defeated – she is only in her forties and yet her life seems over. Ewan is left planning a workers' hunger march on London and his story is still to be decided. Perhaps Gibbon could see no further, for the novel ends in virtually contemporary times, with all the issues of the thirties necessarily unresolved and a heroine already much older in experience than he was himself. On the other hand, Chris's end returns us to a vision of the land in which she is the harbinger of a fundamentally feminine and disinterested faith in existence, simply for its own sake. The vision grew from Gibbon's poignant sense of his own lost past, and it sustains the trilogy at a poetic level, more moving, profound and problematical than any of his more 'masculine' and intellectual allegiances to Diffusionism or communism. Yet Chris simply drops out of history, and, although the future must belong with Ewan, Gibbon's heart seems to stay behind with the rain and the lapwings and the eternal stasis of Scotland's empty spaces. Thus *A Scots Quair* belongs with the several great books in Scottish literature which have dealt with the theme of the divided self and the spiritual antithesis between 'masculine' authority and 'feminine' sensitivity. Most of these novels forced a confrontation and ended tragically, but Gibbon's gift seems to be suspended between the two, although it is possible that Chris's early death tells us that it is time to leave the enduring power of 'Kinraddie' and all its sister villages in the heartland of Scottish letters.

The genre survives, however, for it is derived from common Scottish experience, and, like Chris Guthrie herself, it has great strength. It appears without ambiguity in the work of Fred Urquhart (b. 1912), whose first and autobiographical novel, *Time Will Knit* (1938), showed his interest in the stream-of-consciousness technique. His short stories contain strong Scots speech and a particularly realistic evocation of rural life – collected in *The Dying Stallion* (1967) and *The Ploughing Match* (1968). Vivid sentimental realism thrives in the work of Jessie Kesson (b. 1916), who re-creates a past North-East town and country scene in *The White Bird Passes* (1958) and *Glitter of Mica* (1963), while the stories and novels of John Reid, ('David Toulmin', b. 1913), a farm worker from the same region, revive the world of Grassic Gibbon in more melodramatic and emotive terms – *Hard, Shining Corn* (1972), *Blown Seed* (1976). Further novels of growth and development in the same vein include *The Taste of Too Much* (1960) by Cliff Hanley (b. 1922) and *The Magic Glass* (1981) by Anne Smith.

If Mitchell's fiction looks through Chris's spirit to find a golden age of free hunters long ago, Neil Gunn's origins offered him a similar ideal rather closer to home, and he was to develop this single vision of Highland landscape and culture through a long and productive literary career.

Neil M. Gunn (1891–1973)

Gunn grew up as a fisherman's son, the fifth of seven boys in a family of nine, living in Dunbeath near Helmsdale on the far north-east coast of Caithness, and, although he was not a native Gaelic speaker, he was always very aware of the Gaelic, Norse and Pictish influences in the region. He valued a Celtic inheritance in the face of the modern world and his first short stories were in the style of 'Fiona Macleod' and Neil Munro. He soon threw over their twilight fatalism, however, and his best work has a clarity of style and focus which relates to the Gaelic delight in the actuality of things, and then points to universals beyond them. This tendency is also evident in his treatment of character and of women in particular. The result might be called 'Celtic Platonism' if it were a philosophy, and 'symbolic realism', or even allegory at times, in fiction. Gunn shares this mythopoeic tendency with Grassic Gibbon, but the two writers arrive at radically different conclusions. Hence Chris and Ewan represent an impasse of irreconcilable spiritual and political values at the end of *A Scots Quair*, while Gunn's intention was to try to restore completeness to the individual and to offer Scottish culture at least the possibility of regeneration from within.

This search for self-development and wholeness motivates most of the characters in Gunn's books, and, like Wordsworth, he feels that the philosophical implications of this quest can be found in the journey to maturity from the landscapes and exploits of childhood. He was an athletic and adventurous boy who loved to go exploring, fishing and poaching in the sheltered strath of Dunbeath water. The central symbols in his later fiction come from these years when he watched the men go to sea in their little boats while the women waited at home, and he saw a wider meaning in the search for herring – 'the silver darlings' – or in clandestine expeditions after salmon – that ancient Celtic symbol of wisdom, now reserved for the gentry and protected by gamekeepers. Like Wordsworth, too, Gunn made a creative act of recollection at the end of his life in an autobiography called *The Atom of Delight* (1956), and in a key passage he remembers cracking hazelnuts as a boy, and how a sudden moment of insight and unity gave him the ideal which he sought so long in later adult experience:

I can't remember now how I got on to the boulder in the river but I was there. It was a large flattish boulder and I was sitting on it with my legs stuck out in front at the angle which is wide enough both to give complete comfort and to crack nuts within it. I had picked a stone from the bed of the stream and was using it as a cracking hammer. . . .

The shallow river flowed around and past with its variety of lulling monotonous sounds; a soft wind, warmed by the sun, came upstream and murmured in my ears as it continuously slipped from my face. As I say, how I got there I do not remember. . . .

Then the next thing happened, so far as I can remember, for the first time. I have tried hard but can find no simpler way of expressing what happened than by saying: *I came upon myself sitting there.*

Within the mood of content, as I have tried to recreate it, was this self and the self was me.

The state of content deepened wonderfully and everything around was embraced in it.

There was no 'losing' of the self in the sense that there was a blank from which I awoke or came to. The self may have thinned away – it did – but so delightfully that it also remained at the centre in a continuous and perfectly natural way. And then within this amplitude the self as it were became aware of seeing itself, not as an 'I' or an 'ego' but rather as a stranger it had come upon and was even a little shy of.

Transitory, evanescent – no doubt, but the scene comes back across half a century, vivid to the crack in the boulder that held the nut.

This passage is typical of how Gunn approaches the world as a writer, for he insists on a local and scrupulous clarity and on the difficulty of describing inner experience in words. Yet in Scottish folk lore hazelnuts are associated with the putting-on of wisdom or prophetic ability, and so the little scene is also invested with intimations of magical or symbolic power. Gunn's fondness for such archetypes tends to place his vision outside history and politics, just as Chris's standing stones are remote from the injustices of the factory floor which Ewan had to face. Yet Gunn would claim that his espousal of wholeness, traditional wisdom, communal care, courage and loyalty is exactly what is needed to redeem the sad vacuum of modern life, even if Gibbon would have felt that such gains were meaningless without an economic revolution too. In either case, these two novelists tackle universal questions about man's spirit, just as they draw on a poetic sense of the past to confront the central issues of modern alienation. In their books the regional setting of the 'Scottish novel' is redeemed, and Caithness and the Mearns, like Auchtermuchty in MacDiarmid's *Drunk Man*, become part of a continuing concern with the 'timeless flame'.

At Dunbeath the fishing-industry was in decline and times were hard; so Gunn left home when he was twelve, to stay with his married sister in Dalry. At fifteen he went to London and worked as a bank clerk for a couple of years before coming to Edinburgh to prepare for a career as a Customs and Excise officer. He passed his Civil Service exams in 1911 and was posted to Inverness, from where he travelled as an 'unattached' junior to a variety of offices and distilleries all round the north. Gunn spent the war-years working with shipping from Kinlochleven and was just about to be called up when the conflict ended. This was a considerable relief to his mother (his father had died in 1916), for, among her sons, Ben had been killed on the barbed wire, John was badly gassed (their stories are used in *Highland River*) and the twins who had gone to Canada also lost their lives as a result of their army service. Prompted by a posting to the south, Neil married his Dingwall girlfriend Daisy Frew in 1921 and the couple set up house in Wigan. During a year there Gunn had to assess pension-claims on behalf of miners who were suffering the worst of poverty as a result of wage-cuts and lockouts by the owners – for the coal mines had been returned to private hands after the war. Such experience, so close to the sacrifices of the Front, marked him deeply and confirmed his socialist sympathies. He was glad to return to Lybster and then to Inverness, for, even if the Highland economy was in ruins too, there was always the familiar countryside and a sense of surviving community life. He settled in a permanent post as Excise officer for the Glen Mhor distillery and began to write seriously.

Gunn corresponded with MacDiarmid in Montrose and soon placed short stories in the *Scottish Chapbook* and other periodicals. The best of these pieces suggest a darker version of the Celtic twilight or hint at themes to come, and a collection, *Hidden Doors*, appeared in 1929 from the Porpoise Press in Edinburgh – a new Scottish Renaissance publisher which was to produce most of his books in the thirties until Faber and Faber took over. Grieve was enthusiastic about Gunn's talent, and, although he criticised a predictable 'anti-Kailyard' impulse in parts of the first novel, he detected the arrival of an original vision and 'a purely Scottish use of English'. The two men became close friends. *The Grey Coast* (1926) is an account of rivalry in love set against Highland life in a small fishing- and crofting-community. Coloured 'grey' indeed by Gunn's hatred of poverty, avarice and lust, it offers a bitter and gloomy account of the fate of the Gael in the generations after the Clearances. He developed the same theme more melodramatically in his next work, *The Lost Glen* (serialised in the *Scots Magazine* in 1928, but not published in book-form until 1932), in which a failed university student returns home – a disgrace to his family – to work as a gillie and to see his people as a depressed peasant-class, slyly subservient to southern incomers with superior airs. Depressed by this bleak book, and by his inability to find a publisher for it, Gunn turned to drama for a spell, with the help of John Brandane and James Bridie. But the three-act symbolic drama *The Ancient Fire* was not well received and he settled for a lasting friendship with Bridie and a return to prose. His hopes were greatly rekindled by the success of his third book.

Morning Tide (1930) is a happier thing than its predecessors. Prompted by the recollections of his brother John, Gunn turned back to the scenes of his childhood in Dunbeath – as if to recover optimism by means of the story of a growing boy, Hugh, and how he comes to terms with his parents, his sisters and the dangers of the sea. It is the first of four notable novels in Gunn's output (*Highland River*, *The Silver Darlings* and *Young Art and Old Hector* are the other three) which deal with the growth of a boy's mind, looking to childhood as an age of primitive and intuitive truths. When *Morning Tide* was selected as a Book Society choice, Gunn followed it with a revision of *The Lost Glen*, whose grimmer theme was less popular, and then plunged into a more symbolic and philosophical vision of the ancient past with *Sun Circle* (1933). Here another young protagonist, Aniel, has to learn about Viking power and the 'civilising' influence of Christianity, both of which will sweep away his ancient Pictish–Celtic world; and yet its spirit will survive in the Highlands beyond the reach of history and change – in the imaginative wholeness and timeless affirmation symbolised by the sun circle:

> As the Sun puts a circle round the earth and all that it contained, so a man by his vision put a circle round himself. At the centre of this circle his spirit sat, and at the centre of his spirit was a serenity for ever watchful.

The next book turned to more immediate history, and *Butcher's Broom* (1934) describes how the values of Highland life – personified by the healer Dark Mairi – were betrayed by the Clearances at the beginning of the nineteenth century. The Strathnaver events were still a matter of bitter folk-memory in Gunn's Caithness, and English-speaking 'improvers', such as the factor 'Heller' (Patrick Sellars) can see nothing but poverty and 'gibberish' in the community, because the Gaelic tongue is not available to them. In fact Gaelic's graceful sensitivity to minute discriminations (paralleled by Gunn's talent for subtle detail and inner states in prose) is the real cultural and philosophical wealth of the place – uncountable, of course, by those who can think only in material terms. *Butcher's Broom* spoke directly to the political and nationalist issues of Scotland in the thirties, and Gunn himself was active for the Scottish National Party behind the scenes in Inverness. The book was a great success and Grassic Gibbon wrote to marvel at how Gunn had managed to control his rage at the fate of 'those people of yours'. Faber and Faber were interested in Gunn, and T. S. Eliot and the American publisher Alfred Harcourt came north to visit him at home. Up in Shetland, however, Neil's old friend MacDiarmid was becoming rather cool, and naming Fionn MacColla as the true Gaelic novelist of the future. Gunn's next book was one of his finest.

Highland River (1937) returns once more to Dunbeath and the river strath where the author spent his childhood – a simple landscape in which a boy's struggle to land a poached salmon with his bare hands becomes an initiation into life's mystery, wisdom, fear and secret delight. Gunn dedicated the book to his brother John, for it encapsulated their youthful adventures together, and his hero, Kenn, becomes a scientist as John had done and shares his experiences of gas and a brother's death at the Front. Gunn found unexpectedly deep resonances in this book, and his imagination was profoundly stirred. The story is told in a series of overlapping presents which annihilate the apparent passage of time, so that Kenn's childhood and his wartime and adult experiences coexist and reflect on each other through a series of witty and moving associative links. Finally, he revisits the river of his boyhood in order to trace it, and the nature of his own being, back to the source. The river-mouth and its shallows are associated with infancy, just as it was the middle reaches which he frequented as an older boy; but he never did find the source before he left home and, indeed, he could not truly have attained it or understood its nature until the end of the book, when he returns as a mature and solitary man. The theme is very evocative, with traditional overtones of the 'river' of life and time; and yet its style imitates the scientific precision of Kenn's trained intellect, and this dispassionate and analytical enquiry is very different from the poetic surrender to mood and the flow of dialect which Gibbon chose to use for his Chris:

> The heath fire and the primrose: the two scents were jotted down by Kenn as simple facts of experience, without any idea of a relationship between them.

And then suddenly, while the mind was lifting to the cold bright light of spring, to the blue of birds' eggs and the silver of the first salmon run, there came out of the tangle in a soft waft of air the scent of primroses.

An instant, and it was gone, leaving a restlessness in the breast, an urgency that defeats itself, an apprehension, almost agonising, of the ineffectiveness of the recording machine. Finally nothing is jotted down and the mind is left exhausted. . . .

But the grown Kenn knows quite exactly one quality in the scent of the primrose for which he has an adjective. The adjective is innocent. The innocency of dawn on a strath on a far back morning of creation. The freshness of dawn wind down a green glen where no human foot has trod. If the words sound vague, the pictures they conjure up for Kenn's inner eye are quite vivid. The grasses and green leaves in the clear morning light have a quality of alertness like pointed ears. And they sway alive and dancing-cool and deliciously happy.

As a scientist, Kenn – whose name suggests the act of knowing – also finds this elusive delight in art and good action. It is the very spirit of Duncan Bàn's 'Ben Dorain' – a pagan realism quite removed from the strictures of organised religion or politics or official dogma of any kind. He remembers when he first found it in science, too, in an exam question on how 'the principal forms of energy are traceable to the sun':

Forests of dead trees turn into coal. . . . Sun takes up water into clouds; clouds fall and form rivers and waterfalls; falling water directly used for making electricity. . . . The cycles of action were cosmic wheels, opening fanlike, each spoke glittering in Kenn's mind. The excitement of apprehension made his brain extraordinarily clear; his sentences were factual and precisely written.

The 'sun circle' has been rescued from the Celtic twilight to be redefined as the 'energy cycle' with a scientific clarity which actually enhances its symbolic force. The 'salmon of knowledge' and this 'excitement of apprehension' (in both senses of the word) lie at the heart of Gunn's novels, and Kenn emerges into the sunlight as a new kind of sensibility – a solitary atheist, ready for laughter at the unexpectedness of the universe, and yet coolly detached, too, for his war-experiences have marked him with a ferocious sense of irony:

The blowing of gaps in the advancing Germans on that early morning towards the end of 1917 on the Somme was coarse unskilled work, though its sheer devastating efficacy had its fascination, because – apart from the joyous potting of church steeples and such – even observers saw little of the actual results of the gun-teams' labours. On this particular morning, however, precision in its trigonometrical sense was almost entirely confined to the exquisite narrowness of the shaves by which death passed them by or the instant and annihilating manner in which it got them. Escape was a matter of pure chance.

After his brush with death and a near blinding by gas, Kenn goes back to memories of the river, and eventually, years later, at the age of thirty-seven, he reaches the source and comes to understand the humour and the beautiful indifference of being:

> Bow to it, giving nothing away, and pass on the moor like sunlight, like shadow, with thoughts hesitant and swift as a herd of hinds. In this way one is undefeatable – until death comes. And as death is inevitable, its victory is no great triumph.

Yet beyond the watershed he sees a mountain; and, beyond that, 'the grey planetary light that reveals the earth as a ball turning slowly in the immense chasm of space'. In the end, there is no end and no goal – only the quality of the moment.

Gunn's prose achieves a memorably cool expression of the elusive, considering nature of the human mind, where symbolic insights meet the Gaelic poetic genius for impersonal and detailed actuality. This is a Scottish novel which is entirely free from 'Celtic' twilight, not to mention the old penchant for rural sentiment. *Highland River* has a claim to be Gunn's finest book: it was awarded the James Tait Black Memorial Prize for 1937, widely acclaimed and frequently reprinted; and as a novel of individual development it bears comparison with Joyce's *Portrait of the Artist*. Encouraged by Eliot and the directors of Faber, Gunn committed himself to full-time writing by resigning from his job at the age of forty-six and taking his wife to live at Braefarm House near Dingwall, to the north of Inverness. *Off in a Boat* (1938) gives an autobiographical account of that summer of freedom. Essays, plays and two more novels followed in the next two years, but they seem to be marking time somewhat before the appearance of his most popular book.

The Silver Darlings (1941) links the theme of personal development in *Highland River* with an account of the growth of the herring-industry after the Highland Clearances in the early nineteenth century. It is Gunn's most fully researched historical novel. Based on his own Dunbeath, now fictionalised as 'Dunster', it is founded on two generations of economic and social change and filled with fine descriptions of local character, landscape and the thrill and danger of the sea. Against this densely realised setting, Gunn relates the inner odyssey of the boy Finn, growing up without a father, coming to terms with his mother's affection for another man, finding a girlfriend himself and eventually a boat of his own and a place in the working community of men. These simple themes are filtered through the Lawrentian intensity of young Finn's pride and innocence, but the book begins with his mother Catrine, who was forced to the shore by the Clearances. Her inexperienced young husband is press-ganged by the navy while he is fishing in his little boat, and eventually he dies abroad. In later years Catrine's suitor Roddy is one of the most successful skippers on this dangerous coast, but she fears and hates the sea, to which he, with now her son, is so inevitably drawn. Thus Finn comes to realise that his home embraces polarities beyond the obvious truths of everyday, just as Gunn himself describes his own background as 'the boy' in *The Atom of Delight*:

> As his existence had two parents, so it had the earth and the sea. If his mother was the earth, his father was the sea. In fact he could hardly think of his father without thinking of the sea. Out of the sea came the livelihood of the household. They depended on the sea, and of all the elements in nature it was the least dependable. You could never be sure of it as you could be sure of the earth.

Here the presence and authority of all those Scottish fathers – Weir, Gillespie or Gourlay – has come down to its most elemental role. Yet, despite the terrors of the waves, a man at peace with himself can approach them and work in harmony, although he must never take anything for granted. On the other hand, the land is always there, comforting, stable and feminine. In figurative terms, Finn's achievement is to reach maturity by bridging the gap between the empathetic and land-oriented spirit of Chris Guthrie and the unrelentingly harsh universe of Adam Weir, symbolised by the capricious sea. More conventionally, Gunn likens the sea to a mistress and the land to a wife, and Finn has to learn to share the sea, and his mother too, with Roddy, whom he greets at first with jealousy and suspicion. Finn's rite of passage is made during a voyage to Stornoway when the crew of Roddy's boat comes close to shipwreck and starvation until the boy makes a courageous ascent of an impossible cliff to fetch water and raw food to sustain them all. When the tale is retold it is as if it has become a part of folk history, linking Finn with Finn MacCoul, his heroic namesake in an epic past; but Finn's real victory comes later in the book, in the quiet moment when he finds peace within the circle of his own heart and a place within the circle of the community. Only now can he enter the bustle of history, and the book ends by recognising that Finn is at last truly ready to begin: a properly whole person with a part to play in the world and plans for a family of his own. The novel's closing words are 'Life had come for him', and the optimism of this conclusion makes a marked contrast with the melancholy diffusion which overtakes Chris Guthrie at the end of *Grey Granite*.

The popularity of *The Silver Darlings* is not unrelated to its foundation in social history and realistic detail, but later novels would seek an increasingly symbolic exploration of his favourite themes. At first *The Serpent* (1943) marked time with another plea for the whole individual in the face of a narrow-minded, Kirk-ridden village, but Gunn's new direction is particularly clear in the development from *Young Art and Old Hector* (1942) to *The Green Isle of the Great Deep* (1944). These are two separate but linked narratives which move from the gently light-hearted and instructive vignettes of the first to an anti-utopian fantasy novel which casts reflections on the nature of totalitarian rule. As a wilful eight-year-old, young Art gains 'instruction' and exasperation in the company of Hector, an old poacher with his best years behind him but still wise in the insights of folk lore and tradition. Their first book together has a grave whimsy which can stray dangerously close to sentimental 'philosophy'. Naomi Mitchison suggested as much in a letter to the author which initiated a friendly debate over the years, in which Gunn stubbornly defended his case for simplicity and individual self-realisation in the face of her more conventionally socialist enthusiasm for concerted action and political involvement. The indirect result of their wrangle was *The Green Isle of the Great Deep* – a different kind of book altogether, in which Art and Hector fall into a salmon-pool and find themselves in a version of Tir nan Og which is run like an enlightened totalitarian state. An early reference to Nazi concentration-camps reminds us of the date when the two protagonists 'drown', but the main target of this anti-utopian allegory is the rational arrogance of faceless 'scientific' authority, which presumes to know best and attempts to tranquillise and control us for our own good. Gunn had read Koestler's *Darkness at Noon* (1940) and been dismayed by recent reports of 'brainwashing' in Stalin's Russia. At an imaginative level he saw the materialistic assumptions of corporate decision-makers as a more real menace for the future than the Gothic horror of Nazi fascism, currently approaching its end in the ruins of Europe. The question was, how would the quiet, interior wisdom of his two unlikely Highland heroes fare against these 'Administrators'? The answer is worked out through humour, surprise and Art's anarchic boyish spirit, which his captors seem to be incapable of suppressing or trapping. He becomes a 'legend', until God returns to investigate and put things right in the domain he left long ago. In the end it is Art's understanding that beyond 'knowledge' there is 'wisdom', and beyond that 'magic', which returns them to the real and imperfect world where they are fished out of the salmon-pool, dripping wet and alive. It may be debatable whether 'magic' is enough in the face of the power of the corporate state, but Gunn's defence of what MacDiarmid called 'the shy spirit that like a laich wind moves' would be to say, as anarchists do, that, if every individual had such quality within them, then external coercion would indeed wither away.

In the last six years of his writing-career, Gunn's novels tried to realise the quest for intuitive wholeness in more contemporary settings, for he was determined to avoid a return to the 'chronicle novel' and he could do little more with the overt allegory of *The Green Isle*. Besides, he was sensitive to accusations that his spiritual outlook was mystical or escapist. Thus in a realistic setting the symbolism of *The Drinking Well* (1947) relates to earlier work, looking back to the paternal conflicts in *The Serpent* and *The Lost Glen*, as does the more melodramatic psychological thriller *The Key of the Chest* (1945).

The post-war years were difficult ones in Gunn's personal life, and, like many of his friends, he had become increasingly pessimistic about the future of socialism in the light of Stalin's tyranny. The novels of this period – *The Shadow* (1948), *The Lost Chart* (1949) and *Bloodhunt* (1952) – take a darker look at the split between the rational intellect and the wholeness of feeling, with symbols which often relate to the intuitive power of women as opposed to the reductive habits of the masculine mind, and images which conjure up the atavistic thrills of violence and the hunt. A lighter-hearted book, *The Silver Bough* (1948), had been well received – Edwin Muir particularly admired it – but Gunn had not recaptured his earlier sucesses and he began to feel a sense of literary and geographical isolation in his beloved north. He was fifty-nine years old and his career as a writer was nearly at an end; yet, if his last novels relate to themes and books which had gone before, they were still to be transmuted in significant ways.

The Well at the World's End (1951) follows the spirit of *The Silver Bough* to make a triumphant return to the archetypal innocence and humour of the world of *Highland River*, but this time it is experienced by a middle-aged academic, a man who already knows the wider world and the horrors of history. He comes to moments of comedy, mystery and near death in the course of a picaresque camping-holiday in the everyday Highlands, and the world is renewed by his experience of delight and laughter, even laughter at himself, just as his own inner being and his relationship with his wife is refreshed. The protagonists are not unlike Gunn and Daisy themselves, and the novel is the sweetest of the late works, for it manages to catch the ineffable 'nothingness' of interior insight – clear as water in a well, transparent as the Caithness light itself. There is a stranger humour and affirmation too in *The Other Landscape* (1954), in which an anthropologist narrator struggles to understand the archetypally mischievous nature of existence in the vision of a gifted and eccentric musician who has lived as a recluse ever since his wife died in childbirth, cut off from help. This novel, as 'metaphysical' as any by David Lindsay, was followed by Gunn's autobiography – his last book.

The Atom of Delight (1956) is the author's defence of a lifelong preference for personal unity and insight in the face of fashionable pessimism, collectivism and the aesthetic and political violences of the 'modern' world. In retrospect he found affinities between the pagan spirit of freedom in his boyhood and the irreverent teachings of the Zen masters who demonstrate a letting-go of self in moments of intuitively integrated action. This was the single vision which Gunn had pursued in various forms through all his novels:

Without consciously thinking or striving, 'It' is achieved, spontaneity comes into its own, the arrow lands in the bull. Musical composers, scientists, painters, writers, know how in the midst of their striving 'It' takes charge, strife ceases, and the 'marked passage' is born. In that moment of delight freedom is known; as, not to be high falutin, its rare moment is known in archery, cricket and putting the shot, not to mention the way a rosebush looked at the boy when he had landed his fish.

The future remains open to this kind of freedom.

Neil Gunn lived for another seventeen years, actively engaged in local affairs, literary magazines and broadcasting, until he died after a short illness in January 1973. The Neil Gunn International Fellowship has since been awarded to many distinguished overseas novelists, including Heinrich Böll, Chinua Achebe and Saul Bellow.

Other novelists of the early twentieth century

Among the other novelists who were prominent in the 1930s, **Naomi Mitchison** (b. 1897) heralded a wave of interest in the myths and rituals of primitive societies, especially with *The Conquered* (1923) and her twelfth book, *The Corn King and the Spring Queen* (1931). Following her own interests in ancient history and anthropology after the manner of J. G. Frazer, the later novel revolves around the rituals of kingship and fertility in the ancient world of Scythia and the Mediterranean. Linklater's *Men of Ness* and Gunn's *Sun Circle* followed within two years. Closer to home, *The Bull Calves* (1947) drew on her family-history – she was a member of the distinguished Haldanes – to tell a tale set in Perthshire after the Forty-five. She has played a leading part in left-wing politics and women's rights and has travelled widely and written many novels. **Ian Macpherson** (1905–44) anticipated aspects of *Sunset Song* in his first novel, *Shepherd's Calendar* (1931), based on his own youth and education in the rural North-East. Occasionally overwritten, the book charts an adolescent's painful farewell to the farm he loves in order to satisfy his mother's desire to see him 'succeed' at university. Macpherson's next two novels took the Clearances for their theme, but his last and best work, *Wild Harbour* (1936), was a more original tale about a young married couple trying to live in the Highlands away from the universal future war which has broken out in '1944'. Their love for each other, the summer wilderness of remote Speyside, and the skills of stalking and lonely survival are all economically recounted before the anarchic world catches up with their idyll and sweeps them to random and meaningless deaths. The author himself was killed in a motorcycle accident in 1944.

A. J. Cronin (1896–1981) began a long career as a popular author with *Hatter's Castle* (1931), re-creating some of the themes of *The House with the Green Shutters* in a vein of sentimental realism. His own medical expertise and his interest in politics and social problems enlivened several of his books and made *The Citadel* (1937) a best-seller. Based on his own experiences as a doctor in the mining-towns of Wales, it was successfully translated into a TV serial, like the adaptations which went to make the series *Dr Finlay's Casebook*.

Other novelists at this time looked to modern city life for their material, in what might be called a 'Glasgow school'; and, although there was no formal movement as such, their devotion to urban realism in the west of Scotland makes a significant counterbalance to the symbolism of Gibbon and Gunn. In the later 1920s, Dot Allan had placed several stories of family life in a Glasgow setting from the First World War or during the Depression, and a later novel called *Hunger March* (1934) dealt with the plight of the city's unemployed workers. Chief among these writers was **George Blake** (1893–1961), a Law graduate who turned to journalism after the war, becoming a colleague of Neil Munro at the *Glasgow Evening News* and later the editor of *Strand Magazine* in London. He returned to Scotland in the 1930s to join George Malcolm Thomson at the Porpoise Press when it amalgamated with Faber. Throughout his career, Blake made a sustained effort to write about Scotland's mercantile and working classes in the face of industrial decline in the Clyde and Greenock from the 1920s to the Second World War. His first book, *Mince Collop Close* (1925), was a melodramatic tale about a female gang-leader in the slums, but *The Wild Men* (1925) and *Young Malcolm* (1926) – dealing with revolutionary politics and the education of a young man – were less sensational, if still inclined to sentimental realism. Blake is best known for *The Shipbuilders* (1935), a major attempt to evoke Glasgow during the Depression by following the problems, the family-ties and the different fortunes of two men who formed a friendship during the Great War. Ex-soldier and officer's batman Danny Shields is now a riveter at Pagan's shipyard, working for his admired 'Major' – the owner's son and manager, Leslie Pagan. But the yard has taken its last order. Pagan bows to economic forces, although he keeps his wealth, and before he leaves for England he offers the riveter a job on his estate there. Danny's proud nature decides to 'stick to his trade' and seek work among the other yards on the Clyde. He does not know it, but his skills are already made obsolete by the new electric welding.

The Shipbuilders is notable for its evocation of a grimy and beloved city, with its lively culture of tenements and trams, street gangs, pubs and football-matches. But Danny is sentimentalised as a loyal and stalwart type-figure, as if the author himself saw the workers from the point of view of Pagan's officer-class. The human interest of the friendship with Pagan, like the latter's fatalism, is neither developed nor shaken by circumstances, and this draws the centre of the novel well away from any more crucial psychological, political or economic understanding. Even so, Blake handles the urban scene well. David and Joanna (1936) and Late Harvest (1938) developed his understanding of the strength and the plight of women tied to frailer menfolk, and the resignations of life in a declining industrial town. The latter book painted a particularly detailed picture of shabby respectable existence in a fictionalised Greenock, and this paved the way for a series of later works set in 'Garvel'. These include The Constant Star (1945) and The Westering Sun (1946), which follow the dynastic history of the shipbuilding Oliphant family, from the early nineteenth century to the fate of the last daughter of the line, who struggles through the Depression in Glasgow to die in a wartime air raid. Blake's personal commitment to the history of his home region led him to produce several books on ships, shipbuilding and the lighthouses of the Clyde – a fascination which also featured in his autobiographical study Down to the Sea (1937).

Edwin Muir's unhappy years in Glasgow are reflected in his third and last novel, Poor Tom (1932), in which the painful relationship between alcoholic Tom, who is dying of a brain tumour, and his brother Mansie, is used to convey all Muir's distaste for the slums and the cultural and political shallowness of lower-middle-class life in the city. Among the novels of

James Barke (1905–58) *The Land of the Leal* (1939) tells the epic story of a peasant family's progress through various jobs in nineteenth-century rural Scotland, to finish in Glasgow during the Depression. The book draws on Barke's own background and socialist sympathies to make popular fiction out of social history – full of humour, dialect, and admiration for the indomitable strength of his heroine, Jean Ramsay. His play *Major Operation* (1936) explored the dialectics of labour and capital by placing a union-organiser and a businessman in the same hospital-ward. Barke also edited the poems of Burns, and from the late forties he produced five novels based on the life of the poet. Alexander McArthur and H. Kingsley Long became famous for their collaboration on *No Mean City* (1935), a lurid semi-documentary novel on slum life and gang-warfare in the Gorbals of the 1920s. **Edward Gaitens** (1897–1966) was born in that once-notorious district and with the support of James Bridie he sought publication for stories based on his life there before the First World War. Some of these were collected as *Growing Up and Other Stories* (1942), and six of them appeared again as chapters of a novel called *Dance of the Apprentices* (1948). These books are notable for handling domestic realism and working-class vitality without the usual pitfalls of melodrama or sentimentality. By comparison the novels of **Guy McCrone** (1898–1977) belong to a popular mode of domestic history and family romance. His second novel introduced readers to a middle-class family in Victorian Glasgow, and their saga was completed as the *Wax Fruit* trilogy in 1947, and then extended by two further sequels. McCrone was deeply interested in opera and singing, and as a cousin of James Bridie he also became involved with the Glasgow Citizens' Theatre, which was to play such an influential part in modern Scottish drama.

Theatre, plays and playwrights

Barrie's successes on the London stage offered little support to the idea of a literary renaissance in the north, nor were there to be any truly outstanding Scottish playwrights in the modern period. Nevertheless, new growth did appear in a field which had lain fallow for a very long time. Paradoxically, it is this lack of a theatrical tradition which may explain why most Scottish writers have been content to work within already-established genres and conventions. Even in the 1970s – a boom-time for Scottish plays – the prevailing and most popular mode was a proletarian social realism which had done well in the twenties, and a stagecraft which Ibsen would have found loose and predictable. On the other hand, it could be argued that dramatic naturalism has now *become* the tradition.

It was the example of the Irish National Theatre which stirred theatre lovers north of the Border. If the Abbey Theatre in Dublin had managed to nurture a native Irish drama, might not the same be accomplished in Scotland? The formation of the Glasgow Repertory Theatre in 1909 marked one of the first steps, and, if it lacked a fully Scottish programme, at least it provided a stage for northern actors which lasted until the outbreak of war. In the 1920s **Dr John McIntyre ('John Brandane'**, 1869–1947) started the Scottish National Players and wrote their first production, which was a piece called *Glenforsa* (1921), set on a Hebridean island and suffused, rather like Synge's plays, with the rhythms of Gaelic speech. The Scottish National Theatre Society followed and for the next twenty-five years the National Players provided a forum for a succession of writers, including George Blake, George Reston Malloch, Donald Carswell and the plays of Robert Kemp. 'If anything becomes of the Scottish Drama,' wrote Bridie, 'John Brandane is its begetter. He spent more time . . . on raw young dramatists than he spent on work that might have made him famous.' Brandane's best-known play was *The Glen Is Mine* (1923), set once again in the Hebrides, where the old ways have to meet with the new – not without sentiment – while his one-act comedy *Rory Aforesaid* (1928) is still a regular favourite with amateur companies. Yorkshire-born Dr Gordon Bottomley (1874–1976) was equally committed to theatre in Scotland and became a leading light in the Community Drama Association which started in the thirties. His rather antique verse play *Gruach* – a prelude to *Macbeth*, no less – made a hit in 1923 and shared the bill with *The Glen Is Mine*. In complete contrast, the plays of **Joe Corrie** (1894–1968) introduced urban domestic realism and political issues to the National Players' repertoire. Corrie was a coal-miner who gradually turned to full-time writing, and his best play, *In Time of Strife* (1929), deals with the fate of a mining-family during the General Strike. He wrote poems too, and dozens of one-act plays for amateur productions. Corrie's stylised working-class speech was a brave new experience on stage in the 1920s, although it can seem rather stilted when asked to bear the full literary burden of dramatic description and evocation.

O. H. Mavor ('**James Bridie**', 1888–1951) was a young friend of Brandane's and a fellow doctor, who joined the board of the Scottish National Theatre Society in 1923 and played a generous role himself in helping young playwrights, including Neil Gunn. Mavor's interest in writing went back to his student days at Glasgow, for he had enjoyed them enormously and taken a long time to graduate. He served in the Royal Army Medical Corps (as he did in the Second World War) and when he returned to general practice and hospital work he resumed his enthusiasm for the stage as well. Brandane and a brilliant young producer called Tyrone Guthrie helped Mavor with *The Sunlight Sonata* (written by 'Mary Henderson') at the Lyric Theatre, Glasgow, in 1928. This was the first of over forty plays by Mavor, who became much better known as 'James Bridie' and gave up practising medicine in 1938. He was a popular and witty character with a droll sense of humour, who liked to conceal considerable energy and commitment behind a pretence of laziness and irreverent frivolity. One of the best early plays and his first London success was *The Anatomist* (1930), a study of the egocentric Dr Knox's involvement with the Burke and Hare body-snatching scandal in Edinburgh. In *Tobias and the Angel* (1930) Bridie's use of colloquial speech and his experience of the Middle East during the First World War help to transform the story in the Apocrypha of an archangel's visitation into a lively comedy of modern attitudes. *A Sleeping Clergyman* (1933) was a more innovative play: it follows the sorry family history of a medical researcher back through three generations in order to refute the suggestion that we are slaves to heredity. The tale is told by means of 'flashbacks' from a chat between medical men in a respectable Glasgow Club in the 1930s, but the clergyman of the title – like God, perhaps, in the modern world – sleeps throughout the whole play.

Bridie has a very Shavian delight in the excitement of debate, and his talent for this and for novel conceptions and confrontations on stage helps to make up for the structural imbalances in many pieces. Thus *Mr Bolfry* (1943) – one of his wittiest works –

draws on the Scottish penchant for religious dualism and diabolerie to conjure up the Devil on a dull Sunday evening in a Free Kirk manse in the contemporary Highlands. When 'Mr Bolfry' appears, he is dressed like the minister himself and the two engage in a ferocious debate, before the man of God finally suspects that he is confronting an aspect of himself and learns to find strength in simple faith rather than disputation. Bridie's plays were regularly produced in the West End but he kept in touch with the arts in Scotland, helping to establish the Glasgow Citizens' Theatre in 1943 and involving himself with the Edinburgh International Festival, and in particular with the Robert Kemp and Tyrone Guthrie production of Lindsay's *Satire of the Three Estates* in 1948. In 1950, the year before he died, he helped to establish a College of Drama at the Academy of Music in Edinburgh.

Bridie's best later plays include a telling study of the hopes and despairs of a middle-aged teacher (*Mr Gillie*, 1950), while *The Queen's Comedy*, from the same year, is set among the gods and mortals assembled around Troy. It is given a modern bias, however, and its satire on war and power is contemporary enough. The author called *The Baikie Charivari* (1952) a 'miracle play', mixing together fantasy and symbolism, with the stories of Punch and Judy and Pontius Pilate in a contemporary setting, to make his most experimental work.

Although Bridie was the most notable and successful playwright of his day, there have been no successors to his style. It can be argued that the formation of a Glasgow branch of the Unity Theatre in 1946 was more influential while it lasted, because its working-class socialist dramas, such as George Munro's *Gold in his Boots* (1947) look forward to the 1970s and the plays of Bill Bryden and Roddy McMillan (who began his acting career with Unity). Bridie's achievement is equally isolated from the other main tendency in Scottish theatre, which has been to produce dramas in broad Scots, and here the most prominent names from the 'second wave' of the Renaissance are Robert McLellan and Alexander Reid.

Not surprisingly, historical themes prevail in broad Scots drama, and the reductive spirit of the language delights in bringing great men and great events down to earth. **Robert McLellan** (b. 1907) grew up among Scots-speaking farm people in Lanarkshire, and his book *Linmill and Other Stories*

(1977) evokes that milieu with considerable linguistic and personal sensitivity. His first play, the one-acter *Jeddart Justice* (1934), was a comedy based on Border feuds in the sixteenth century, as were *The Changeling* (1935) and his first full-length play, *Toom Byres* (1936). His best and most popular work was the 'historical comedy' *Jamie the Saxt* (1937), distinguished by the pace and humour with which it recounts the struggle between the scheming Earl of Bothwell and King James, 'the wisest fool in Christendom' – harried on all sides, weak, wily and finally triumphant. McLellan's Scots is vividly concrete in its idioms, colloquial, versatile and unstrained – the perfect vehicle for a comedy of character and deflation. Such free and vernacular skill is more than a pasing delight in McLellan's plays, for it encapsulates a literary tradition and a habit of mind which in itself makes an indirect critique of affairs of state and fallible human beings, however lordly their dress. Other plays followed, including *Torwatletie* (1946) and *The Flouers o Edinburgh* (1947), which are set in the eighteenth century. McLellan has three volumes of collected plays to his credit, but he stopped writing for the stage in the 1950s. Given the fluency of his Scots and the importance of its spirit to his meaning, he became understandably depressed at the difficulties which arose in finding enough native actors who could speak it well. *Jamie the Saxt*, however, has enjoyed frequent revivals, and the late Duncan Macrae is particularly remembered for his brilliance in the leading role.

The two Scots comedies of **Alexander Reid** (1914–82) placed legendary medieval figures in humble settings among the common folk of the Borders. *The Lass wi' the Muckle Mou'* (1950) features Thomas the Rhymer returned from fairyland, while *The Warld's Wonder* (1953) became another hilarious vehicle for Duncan Macrae, as the wizard Michael Scott. It was the skill of actors such as Andrew Keir and Roddy McMillan at the Glasgow Citizens' which first inspired Reid to write in Scots, and he made a sturdy defence of it in the Foreword to the 1958 edition of his plays. Yet, to meet a wider audience, he anglicized the texts of that edition and sadly diluted the spirit of his work. Sydney Goodsir Smith used an entirely stiff and rhetorical language for *The Wallace* (1960), which is more of a political pageant than a play. Robert Kemp (1908–67) also used Scots for his stage and radio drama, while the poet

Alexander Scott followed his flair for the language in three rumbustuous verse plays in the 1950s. In more recent years, however, broad Scots has declined in favour of the wit and violence of colloquial urban speech in a notable resurgence of proletarian drama.

The link with earlier days at the Glasgow Citizens' is provided by Roddy McMillan (1923–79), whose first play in a naturalistic mode, *All in Good Faith*, was a success there in 1954. Stewart Conn (b. 1936), poet and radio-producer for the BBC, wrote *I Didn't Always Live Here* (1967), evoking the humour and harshness of Glasgow life and speech from the Depression to the post-war years through a series of flashbacks from its two female protagonists. Then **Bill Bryden** (b. 1942) came to the Edinburgh Lyceum, where he assembled an extremely talented company of Scottish actors, many of whom were already stars. With such a cast, *Willie Rough* (1972) was an enormous success. Set in Bryden's native Greenock, it follows the political education of a moderate shop-steward on 'Red Clydeside', whose increasingly radical commitment costs him his freedom and his job, but not his spirit. It is a story of working-class life and sentiment with a naturalistic succession of scenes from 1914 to 1916. Bryden is a skilful and successful director, but the limitations of his writing became clearer with *Benny Lynch* (1974) and clearer still with *Civilians* (1981). Nevertheless, *Willie Rough* was the vanguard of a revival in urban realism and a new popular interest in the Scottish stage.

The very name of the 7:84 Company proclaims the political purpose of its founder, John McGrath, who came north in 1973 to start a Scottish branch of the theatre company he had first conceived in London. (The numbers claim that 7 per cent of the population owns 84 per cent of Britain's wealth.) McGrath developed a style of Brechtian propaganda drama which mixed together documentary material, music-hall routines, folk-song, jokes and satirical ditties to make fast moving and hilarious shows, full of melodrama, pathos and didacticism. The actors were encouraged to help to construct the play, and audiences were encouraged to sing along with them on the stage. The company's Scottish debut was *The Cheviot, the Stag and the Black, Black Oil* (1973), which argues for Scottish republicanism against English and American influences from the time of the Clearances to the present day. It arrived at just the moment when devolution and North Sea oil were the hottest topics in the country, and the play was taken on tour to community centres and remote town halls before it ever saw the major theatres. Visibly fuelled by the talent and conviction of the actors themselves, *The Cheviot* was an enormous popular and critical success, with a tour of Ireland and two appearances on national television. Subsequent plays adapted different themes and different social problems to the same political end, and perhaps inevitably the message became predictable, despite individually brilliant actors and the high energy of the group's demotic style. Nevertheless, a vital new contribution to theatrical experience and community involvement had been made, linking a long standing polemical tradition in Scotland to the popular arts of variety theatre, folk-song and protest-songs.

Looking back to the more conventional drama of the Citizens' Theatre, Roddy McMillan's second play, *The Bevellers* (1973), is a sympathetic study of an apprentice's initiation into life on the shop-floor of a glass-bevelling works where the language is anything but polished, and Hector MacMillan (b. 1929) used a similar freedom in exploring the internal horrors of Protestant bigotry in Glasgow with *The Sash* (1973). In 1976 the Traverse Theatre presented *The Jesuit* by the poet Donald Campbell (b. 1940), set in the seventeenth century at the trial of Catholic martyr John Ogilvie. Like much of Campbell's work, the play focuses on an historical moment of personal crisis, but the modern style of the common soldiers' speech gives it a place in what was fast becoming a vogue in Scottish plays for colloquial coarseness and 'hard man' attitudes. Thus a play called *The Hard Man* (1977) by Glasgow writer Tom McGrath (b. 1940) was based on the life and times of his collaborator Jimmy Boyle to paint a grim picture of street violence and prison oppression.

It is difficult to deny the immediate impact of such plays, although it can be argued that some of them create a new Kailyard sentimentality out of urban deprivation, or that they use sensationally brutal speech and action merely as a substitute for dramatic force. Nevertheless, they also brought the demotic immediacy of Scots street speech to the stage, and to thousands of playgoers it seemed like a breath of salty air. John Byrne (b. 1940), from the 7:84 Company, rose to the occasion with the banter of *The Slab Boys* (1978), set in a carpet-factory in Paisley. Here 'patter' reigns supreme, appropriately enough for teenagers in the 1950s, and Byrne was encouraged to produce a sequel about the staff dance called *The Loveliest Night of the Year* (1979). A grimmer mixture of comedy and violence in speech and action, and the same depressed urban setting in the west of Scotland, characterised several gripping television plays by Peter Macdougall while on the wider screen this new Scottish confidence had already made its mark with the pioneering 'My Childhood' trilogy – an austere set of films by Bill Douglas, later followed by the gently humane comedy of Bill Forsyth, whose films *That Sinking Feeling*, *Gregory's Girl* and *Local Hero* have become internationally famous. On an equally popular note the gritty Chandleresque anti-romance of Edward Boyd (b. 1916) created entertaining Glasgow thrillers and serials for radio and television – a line also followed in Hugh C. Rae's fiction and William McIlvanney's 'Laidlaw' books – while the nationwide success of Billy Connolly the comedian brought the creative wit and the broad irreverence of Glasgow humour to a wider audience than ever before.

More experimental drama has yet to gain wide recognition in Scotland, but the roots are there in plays by Cecil Taylor (1929–81), Tom Gallacher (b. 1934), Stanley Eveling (a Newcastle man who lives and works in Edinburgh) and Tom McGrath, whose play *Animal* (1982) depends largely on brilliant mime. There is promise too in the fact that younger poets than the more established figures of Stewart Conn, George Mackay Brown and Donald Campbell have found it possible to write for the theatre, and Liz Lochhead, Alan Spence and Catherine Lucy Czerkawaska have all had work produced in close co-operation with director and players.

The 'second wave' of the Scottish Renaissance

It remains now to turn back to those writers after MacDiarmid, Gibbon and Gunn who made up the 'second wave' of the Renaissance. One man in particular – the Gaelic poet Sorley Maclean – might be ranked with the first generation, but his poetry did not reach a wider audience until relatively late in his lifetime and so he joins the many fine poets in Scots, English and Gaelic who came to prominence between 1940 and 1960. Quite apart from MacDiarmid's propaganda for a renaissance, the number of writers who achieved a high literary standard in this period speaks for itself.

Poetry in Scots

Poets were not slow to follow the example of MacDiarmid's early lyrics, as Albert D. Mackie (b. 1904) acknowledged in *Poems in Two Tongues* (1928). Even **William Soutar** (1898–1943), whose first three collections were all in English and who was not to return to Scots until the 1930s, sent four 'Triolets in the Doric' to be published in *Scottish Chapbook* in 1923. Soutar's health had started to deteriorate during his service in the navy, and when he graduated after the war he had to live at home in Perth because of recurring pain in his feet, legs and back. He turned to private study and writing poetry, influenced by Romantic and Georgian models. Initially opposed to MacDiarmid's polyglot energy (he produced a satire called 'The Thistle Looks at a Drunk Man'), Soutar's nationalist sympathies were aroused and he began to formulate his own theories about making Scots available to children. By 1928 he was writing 'bairn rhymes' for Evelyn, the little girl his parents had adopted, for he was more or less housebound and much in her company. He had contracted a progressive disease of the spine and by 1930 he found himself confined to bed in a ground-floor room which he was not to leave for the rest of his life. His journals and dream-books are a testament to the courage with which he faced a painful fate. Resettling his life around books and visits from friends and fellow writers, he developed an eye for detail and a love of nature from what he could see of the world beyond his window, and a selection from his journals was published as *Diaries of a Dying Man* (1954). Four further collections of his English poems were published in his lifetime, and his socialist and pacifist beliefs illuminate verses such as 'Beyond Country', 'The Children' and 'The Permanence of the Young Men'. But Soutar is chiefly remembered as a poet in Scots, for he found a colloquial ease, humour and pathos there which escaped the precision of his English work. The first Scots poems were for children, and *Seeds in the*

Wind (1933) was dedicated to young Evelyn. 'If the Doric is to come back alive,' he wrote to MacDiarmid, 'it will come back on a cock horse', and he based the rhythms of his animal fables and rhymes on playground chants and dance games. He had discovered the ballads, too, and learned a lot from them, as in 'The Whale', which spins a fantastic tale in ballad stanzas, or 'The Lanely Mune', which catches a moment of uncanny simplicity in only six lines.

Soutar came to believe that it was in the ballads 'that we hear the voice of Scotland most distinctly' and he hoped for a 'new age in which the people shall regain their articulateness and art has an anonymous character'. At times his own ballad poems can seem rather too 'anonymous', but the best of them rediscover the true eerie note, and then add a powerful sense of anguish that never states its personal origin. 'Song' and 'The Tryst' from his second collection of *Poems in Scots* (1935) are rightly famous:

> Whaur yon broken brig hings owre;
> Whaur yon water maks nae soun';
> Babylon blaws by in stour: dust
> Gang doun wi' a sang, gang doun . . . .

('Song')

A collection of riddles followed in 1937, but the rest of Soutar's work in Scots comes from manuscripts which were first published posthumously in an otherwise unsatisfactory *Collected Poems*, edited by MacDiarmid in 1948. The poems in 'Theme and Variation' move away from bairn rhymes to offer a sequence of variations and imitations of English poems and translations from European literature, while the 'Whigmaleeries' contain some of his most humorous verses, such as 'Ae Nicht at Amulree' and 'The Philosophic Taed' – deceptively small pieces infused with an irreverent philosophical glee that refused to submit to his illness.

Soutar's example lived after him in the work of J. K. Annand (b. 1908), a teacher whose delightful bairn rhymes are widely used in Scottish schools. *Sing it Aince for Pleisure* first appeared in 1965; two further collections followed suit; and *Poems and Translations* (1975) covers the work of nearly fifty years, going back to his early contacts with MacDiarmid. The Scots of the next poet, however, is far removed from the simpler tongue of Annand and Soutar, or the more colloquial language of his other contemporaries.

Sydney Goodsir Smith (1915–75)

Born in New Zealand of a Scottish mother, Smith did not arrive in Edinburgh – where his father had been appointed professor of Forensic Medicine – until his late teens. After an unsuccessful start as a medical student, he completed his education at Oxford before returning to Auld Reekie, the city he loved and was to celebrate for the rest of his life. *Skail Wind* (1941) contains poems in English and his first awkward verses in Scots, but by the time his third book appeared – *The Deevil's Waltz* (1946) – he had attained a characteristic literary voice. Indeed, he launched himself into the world of the middle-Scots makars as if he had found his own spirit and enthusiastic appetites reflected there. Beginning with obvious debts to Dunbar, Montgomerie and Douglas, Smith created a modern poetry of his own, just as Pound had done with the echoes from his interest in Provençal, Old English and Chinese poets. Smith's vocabulary and his cultural references can be arcane enough, but the energy of his expression becomes increasingly colloquial as the years go by. *The Deevil's Waltz* placed poems to John Maclean alongside a hymn to Venus, while its allusions link Prometheus, Beethoven, Pompeii, Tchaikovsky, Delacroix and the Declaration of Arbroath to the fall of Warsaw and the struggle at El Alamein. The whole war-torn world has become a Devil's waltz in the poet's eyes.

Most of Smith's best poetry was written in the post-war period, although his main collections did not appear until the fifties, with *So Late into the Night* (1952) and *Figs and Thistles* (1959). At the heart of his work at this time there are two outstanding books. The first is *Carotid Cornucopius* (1947), a prose extravaganza that reads as if Sir Thomas Urquhart had got Rabelais to describe the joys of drink and fornication in Edinburgh after the style of *Finnegans Wake*. Begun in 1945 – 'Anno Dambomini' – it is an ultimately exhausting *tour de force* of scatological and creative etymology with the author himself –

known as 'the Auk' to his friends – as the thinly disguised hero of the title page:

> Caird of the Cannon Gait and Voyeur of the Outlook Touer, his splores, cantraips, wisdoms, houghmagandies, peribibulatiouns and all kinna abstrapulous junketings and ongoings abowt the high toun of Edenberg, capitule of Boney Scotland.
>
> A drammantick, backside, bogbide, bedride or badside buik . . . .

Smith's undoubted masterpiece, however, is *Under the Eildon Tree* (1948), a linked series of twenty-four love-poems, meditations, satires and elegies, and the only other long Scots poem of the period to match *A Drunk Man*. By now his poetry, and his life too, had come to celebrate a Villonesque vision of man's fate, with himself cast as a bard at the mercy of love and drink, swinging between exaltation and fornication as if to drive home the glorious fallibility of a human condition utterly opposed to Presbyterian respectability, material possession and industrial progress. His setting was Auld Reekie in the spirit of Fergusson, except that for Smith it becomes a timeless place where Diana and Eurydice haunt the streets along with Bothwell and Huntly and 'fair Montrose and a the lave / Wi silken leddies doun til the grave' – not to forget sixteen-year-old 'Sandra', picked up in a pub, 'drinkan like a bluidie whaul' with her 'wee paps, round and ticht and fou / Like sweet Pomona in the oranger grove' (XIII: 'The Black Bull o Norroway').

This ribald, goliardic spirit is constantly qualified by the poet's sense of that moment when all the merry music 'turns to sleep' and 'The endmaist ultimate white silence faas / Frae whilk for bards is nae retour' (I: 'Bards Hae Sung'). In the meantime, as he sees it, there is only love, whose spiritual or carnal delights bind us to our physical natures and undermine the 'serious' world of politics and public affairs. Yet, even so, in post-coital sadness or romantic partings the ties of love bring us to a sense of death again. Hence the title of the poem refers to Thomas the Rhymer's eerie encounter with the Queen of Elfland, and Smith's elegies reflect on the unhappy fates of 'Highland Mary', Orpheus, Cuchulainn, Dido, Tristram and Antony. Elegy XII from Orpheus is a particularly fine example of the poet's capacity to move between mockery, pain, rage and tenderness in the space of a few lines. Such pace is reminiscent of the 'jostling of contraries' in MacDiarmid's *Drunk Man*, but

Smith has more confidence in handling free verse in Scots and a Poundian breadth of reference:

– Euridicie stummelt.	stumbled

(*Lauchter cracked abune, Jupiter leuch*;
    – And richtlie sae!
Och, gie the gods their due,
They ken what they're about.
    – The sleekans!)
	above; laughed
	
	crafty ones

She stummelt. I heard her cry. And hert ruled heid again.
– What hert could eer refuse, then, siccan a plea?   such a
    I turned –
        And wi neer a word,
            In silence,
Her een aye bricht wi the joy o' resurrectioun,
She soomed awa afore my een intil a skimmeran wraith
And for a second and last time was tint for aye   lost
Amang the gloams and haars o Hell   shadows
    – Throu my ain twafauld treacherie!   [and mist

      'Quhar art thou gane, my luf Euridices!'

        iv

Sinsyne I haena plucked a note	Since then
Nor made a word o a sang	

    The same dramatic and technical confidence appeared in *Figs and Thistles* in the unlikely form of a poem written 'To Li Po . . . *in memoriam* Robert Fergusson', and in 'The Twal', which is the liveliest available translation of Alexander Blok's long visionary poem in which the dispossessed of the earth drive towards revolution through the snowstorm of history with Christ in the lead. The play *The Wallace*, however, was less successful and *Kynd Kittock's Land* (1965), written for television, and *Gowdspink in Reekie* (1974) were longer poems which covered already familiar ground without refreshing it. Smith also wrote for radio and edited a number of Scottish literary texts. Among his last poems there are several fine lyrics as well as 'Three', 'The Riggins of Chelsea' and 'Spring in the Botanic Gardens', which recaptured the ironical swagger and the brave melancholy of a generous, comic and genuinely anarchic spirit who lived like some reincarnation from the vulgar and scholarly howffs of eighteenth-century Edinburgh.

More scholarly still, and almost as unconventional, **Douglas Young** (1913–73) was one of several of the new makars (including Smith) who met in Edinburgh in 1947 to formulate rules for the spelling of modern literary Scots. (They were well intended, but poets soon went their own way again.) A polyglot enthusiast and Oxford scholar, Young taught classics at the universities of Aberdeen and St Andrew's before accepting a chair in North America. Over six feet tall, with a large black beard, he was a notably extrovert figure in Scottish Nationalist circles, and during the war he refused conscription on a point of politics and served a term in prison. He produced two volumes of his own poems in the mid forties and, although his Scots is not always smooth, it included verses taken from Russian, German, French, Italian and Latin originals, as well as translations of Gaelic poems by Maclean and Hay. His *Selected Poems* appeared in 1950 with *The Puddocks* (1957) and *The Burdies* (1959) as Scots versions of the comedies by Aristophanes.

Robert Garioch (1909–81)

A quieter and more retiring personality than his friend the Auk, **Robert Garioch Sutherland** (1909–81) graduated from the University of Edinburgh with a degree in English and spent the next thirty years as a schoolteacher – rather unhappy with the drudgery of the task and with the necessity for keeping discipline. He first appeared on the literary scene in 1933, with a column in the *Scots Observer* and 'The Masque of Edinburgh' – a satirical scenario of life in his native city, complete with famous figures from past and present. (An expanded version was published in 1954). Garioch (he rarely used his last name) committed himself to his main subject and to what he called 'artisan Scots' from the very start, and declared in 'The Masque' that 'a man who'd write in Edinboro / maun seek his language in a pub'. It was to be many years, however, before he found a publisher for his work, and his first two slim pamphlets were printed by himself. During the war Garioch was captured in North Africa in 1942, and *Two Men and a Blanket* (1975) gives an anti-heroic account of his time as a prisoner of war in Italy and Germany, bored and obsessed with food, like all the other prisoners. When peace came, he lived in London for thirteen years before returning to Edinburgh. Thenceforth Garioch adopted the position of a sceptical bystander in all his poetry. He felt a strong affinity with Robert Fergusson's outcast fate, making his own tribute to him in the fine sonnet 'At Robert Fergusson's Grave' and imitating his manner in a light-hearted satire on the Edinburgh Festival, called 'Embro to the Ploy'.

Garioch had a scholarly grasp of literature, for he translated George Buchanan's *Jephthah* and *The Baptist* from Latin into Scots in 1959, as well as poems from Apollinaire and many sonnets from the nineteenth-century Roman dialect of Giuseppe Belli. Nevertheless, the most frequent voice in his own poetry is that of the disaffected common man. Thus a brilliant sequence of 'Saxteen Edinburgh Sonnets' deflates the Athens of the North and its International Festival by describing it from the sidelines:

> Some dignitaries in the cawrs, gey posh   cars
> in queer, auld-farrant uniforms, were haean   old-fashioned; having
> a rare auld time, it looked a lot of tosh
>
> to me, a beadle of some sort displayin
> frae ilk front sait a muckle siller cosh: each; seat; great silver
> shame on them aa, whativer they were daean!   doing

('Queer Ongauns')

If the speaker in 'Heard in the Gairdens' is newly unemployed, he is also free at last, for 'nae gaffer, boss nor beak / can touch me ferder . . . And nou I drop my guaird, / bide still in my ain neuk, lift up my heid'. The poet's own experience as a schoolteacher is never very far away in these and other pieces, and the comedy of 'Sisyphus' shows the teacher as a man who actually chooses the pointless labour of heaving boulders endlessly up a hill, simply for the sake of job security – 'shair of his cheque at the month's end'. 'Repone til George Buchanan' warns any would-be poets to avoid a profession in which 'ilka weekend, month and year / his life is tined [lost] in endless steir, / grindan awa in second gear'. At such moments there is a

hint of rage and pain beyond the light comedy, and, if a belief in
God, work and education lies at the heart of the Scottish
Presbyterian ethos, then many of Garioch's verses are subtly
subversive. 'A! Fredome is a noble thing!', cries 'The Canny
Hen', but then she adds 'and kinna scarce, to tell the truth, / for
naebody has muckle rowth [much to spare] / of fredome gin
[if] he warks for wages'. Another thoughtful bird, 'The
Percipient Swan', has 'ideas and notions and aïbstract conceptions', but is still condemned to swim round and round in its
pond because its wings have been clipped 'to keep me good':

> soumin roun
> like a mous in a well,
> glowred at by ratepeyers
> bored like masel.   myself

Henryson's beast fables and the romantic debasement of
Baudelaire's 'Le Cygne' have been redefined in typical Garioch
fashion. Yet even while going through the motions 'laid doun
for me / by the Parks Committee', the bird plans a 'swan-song'
that 'sall rhyme the end / of your hale stupid faction'. 'Brither
Worm' describes the stone slabs of the New Town, whose
neoclassical squares and crescents are the epitome of property
and propriety; yet here the poet finds a worm, like a messenger
of lowly life from another world:

> I was abaysit wi thochts of what was gaun-on ablow my feet,
> that the feued and rented grund was the soil of the naitural Drumsheuch
>   Forest,
> and that life gaed on thair in yon soil, and had sent out a spy . . . .

The realisation brings him to the wonders of Nature and 'the
deeps of the soil, deeper nor the sea' until the mood is broken by
the arrival of a rat – 'he leukit at me, and wes gane'.

  Robert Garioch was very popular in public readings on the
strength of his gently comic personality, and so the subversive
nature of his humour and the darker vision which lies beneath it
has sometimes been underestimated by his many admirers.
'The Wire' offers a nightmare allegory of entrapment and death
on some vast moor, perhaps a Scottish grouse moor, where the
heather, blaeberries and gossamer spider webs are overtaken
by barbed wire and guard towers – images from his own

imprisonment during the war, and more clearly universal ever since. 'The Muir' is a more ambitious attempt to write a discursive verse in Scots which can describe relativity, atomic physics, gravity and light, but Garioch's final mastery of free verse in Scots came with the longer poems from slightly later in his career. Verses such as his translations from Apollinaire, or 'Lesson' or 'The Big Music', are effectively weighty but still colloquial, with his own unique voice balanced between sober judgement and a kind of sadness at the small limitations of life and art:

> The piobaireachd comes til an end, gin we my cry it
>   end,
> the grund naukit again, as tho it had aye been sae.   *naked*
> Gin it werenae a competition, wi international rules,
> there seems nae reason why it sudnae stert owre again,
> gin the piper has braith eneuch, and there's nae dout
>   about that,
> but he neatly thraws the thrapple of the deil in his   *rings the*
>   pipes,   *[throat*
> that dees decently, wi nae unseemly scrauch.
> He taks leave of us wi dignity, turns, and is gane.
> The judges rate him heich, but no in the first three.

('The Big Music)

The poetry of **Alexander Scott** (b. 1920) is equally colloquial – he grew up speaking Scots in his native Aberdeen – but his own bold and vigorous nature, and a preference for alliterative effects, gives his work a rough-hewn formality – a paradoxical combination which suits his resolutely physical and anti-sentimental stance. This began with an early translation of the Anglo-Saxon 'Seafarer' and it characterises poems such as 'Haar in Princes Street' and 'Heart of Stone', a notable long poem on his native city. Scott has championed Lallans and the teaching of Scots throughout his long career at the Department of Scottish Literature at Glasgow University, and as a well-known critic and editor his opinions are as forthright as his verse. His own writing in both English and Scots has remained consistent ever since *The Latest in Elegies* appeared in 1949, but his best work is in Scots. Poems such as 'Dear Deid Dancer' and 'To Mourn Jayne Mansfield', from *Cantrips* (1968), show his extrovert and sometimes cruelly sardonic outlook – 'Cauld is thon corp that fleered sae muckle heat, / Thae Babylon breists . . . .' Yet he shows a kind of brutal sympathy for the fate of such 'beautiful people', as if his real topic were to rage against mortality itself – a theme first raised in 'Coronach', a fine poem for the dead of the Gordon Highlanders with whom he served in the war.

The earliest poems of **Tom Scott** (b. 1918) were in English after the style of the New Apocalypse. He came to write Scots while he was a research student in the fifties, and his work reflects his scholarly involvement with the European cultural world of Villon, Dante and especially Dunbar – the subject of a book by him. Scott's *Seevin Poems o Maister Francis Villon* (1953) manage an effective balance between the colloquial and a sense of the originals' medieval nature. In *The Ship and Ither Poems* (1963) he produced verses on Ahab, Orpheus, Adam and Ulysses ('Ithaka'), all of which pursued the theme of freedom and renewal through pain and worldly experience. As a poet and an 'old fashioned utopian socialist' Scott deplored the egocentricity of modern 'confessional' verse and argued for the older and more culturally stable literary forms of allegory and epic. Thus 'The Ship' is a long symbolic piece on the plight of our materialistic culture, using the *Titanic* as the model for a modern ship of fools. His didactic impulse and the poetic problems of describing actions and speech eventually overburden the poem, but Scott has persevered with what he describes as 'symphonic verse' in *The Tree* (1977). The moments of excitement in this massive verse meditation on evolution do not offset dull pages of scientific and moral philosophising in English, but Scott has determined to follow the example of the later poems of MacDiarmid and Davidson with a lonely and acerbic integrity rather similar to that of his friend Fionn MacColla. Most critics have preferred the colloquial Scots in 'Brand the Builder', from a series of St Andrew's studies which he began in the fifties.

The publication of *Clytach* (1972) and *Back-Green Odyssey* (1980) came relatively late in life for **Alastair Mackie** (b. 1925) but they show a sensitive use of conversationally unforced Scots in his wry and humane reflections on family history, the nature of parenthood and middle age, or nostalgia for boyhood in Aberdeen. Mackie makes the ordinary world new again with a plain dignity and a growing craft free from sentiment or bombast. **Duncan Glen** (b. 1933) seeks a similar end with a low-key Scots in deliberately prosaic and transparent lines, at its best in the poems of personal recollection from *In Appearances* (1971) and *Realities* (1980). Glen founded and edited the poetry-magazine *Akros* from 1965 to 1983, and through many books from the Akros Press and his extensive work on Hugh MacDiarmid he has made a valuable contribution to Scottish letters for the last twenty years. From the younger generation a rougher urban Scots can be found in the work of Donald Campbell (b. 1940) – well suited to express the life of the streets in Edinburgh, where he lives, and this gift for dramatic speech has led him to work increasingly for the theatre. In the west of Scotland Stephen Mulrine (b. 1938), Tom McGrath (b. 1940), Alan Spence (b. 1947) and most notably Tom Leonard (b. 1944) have used the idiosyncratic aspects of Glasgow speech (and spelling) for their poetry, and although it may not be a purist's definition of literary Scots there is no doubt that they are writing succinct and witty poems in a valid colloquial idiom, in a movement whose work stems from the same upsurge of cultural confidence which characterised the Glasgow novel of the sixties and the new wave of proletarian plays ten years later.

Poetry in English

The works of Linklater, Gunn, Muir, Goodsir Smith and Sorley Maclean all testify to the fact that the 1940s were a productive period, despite the exigencies of war, and many new poets writing in English made their mark during these years. Figures such as J. F. Hendry, Maurice Lindsay, G. S. Fraser and Norman MacCaig had all had early contacts with the 'New Apocalypse' movement in the south, while William Soutar, MacDiarmid, Muir, Maclean, Alexander Scott, George Bruce and Douglas Young also featured with them in *Poetry Scotland* – an influential set of four magazine-format anthologies founded and edited by Maurice Lindsay between 1943 and 1949. R. Crombie Saunders and the artist J. D. Fergusson followed suit with five issues of *Scottish Art and Letters* from 1945 to 1950. Both these annuals were published by William Maclellan, whose fine press produced some of the best poetry-books of the period.

Among the poets whose works appeared in these volumes were William Jeffrey (1896–1946) and R. Crombie Saunders (b. 1914), both of whom wrote in Scots as well; and Joseph Macleod ('Adam Drinan', 1903–84), who worked in theatre and wrote poems for broadcasting before retiring to live in Florence. Ruthven Todd (b. 1914) was educated in Scotland and spent the war years in London before returning to his native America. Many of his verses reflect toughly or tenderly on his own northern inheritance and the Scottish landscape. Like Todd and Macleod, William Montgomerie (b. 1904) has spent many years abroad, and he and his wife also followed Soutar's lead by collecting and editing Scottish nursery-rhymes. Norman Cameron (1905–53) lived mostly abroad and in London, and he is especially remembered for his poems on the war in the desert.

The same campaign gave **Hamish Henderson** (b. 1919) his one, most remarkable book of verse – *Elegies for the Dead in Cyrenaica* (1948), based on his service there with the Highland Division. As an intelligence officer he played a role in the invasion of Italy, and his love for the country and his socialist convictions led him to translate Antonio Gramsci's *Letters from Prison*. The *Elegies* offer an effective documentary, sometimes rhetorical, picture of the desert war, but Henderson takes in a larger perspective too. In his Foreword he noted how frequently vehicles would change hands in the 'deceptive distances' of the desert, and how the landscape and dust seemed to turn their enemies into mirror images of themselves. Thus he sees the ordinary soldiers of both sides united in death, and united against death – a metaphysical and egalitarian theme for which he uses colloquial slang as well as more austere passages coloured by Gaelic speech-patterns:

> There were our own, there were the others.
> Therefore, minding the great word of Glencoe's
> son, that we should not disfigure ourselves
> with villainy of hatred; and seeing that all
> have gone down like curs into anonymous silence,
> I will bear witness for I knew the others.
> Seeing that littoral and interior are alike indifferent
> and the birds are drawn again to our welcoming north
> why should I not sing *them*, the dead, the innocent?

(First Elegy, 'End of a Campaign')

Henderson joined the School of Scottish Studies in 1951 and is widely known and respected among traditional musicians, not least for his own songs, such as 'The Banks o Sicily', 'The Freedom Come All Ye', 'The John Maclean March' and 'Free Mandela'. Morris Blythman ('Thurso Berwick', 1919–82) belongs to the same radical tradition, with songs such as 'The Scottish Breakaway', but his roots as a writer go back to the socialism of Glasgow in the thirties.

The short-lived Apocalypse movement reacted against overtly political commitment by following a programme of much more inward-looking, symbolic or surrealistic verse. One of the leading lights of this movement, along with Henry Treece and G. S. Fraser (their theorist) was **J. F. Hendry** (b. 1912), who coedited all three Apocalypse anthologies. His novel *Fernie Brae* (1947) describes life in Glasgow and the west from his own childhood, but his verse has a much more abstract and intellectual style, with staccato lines and a crystalline coolness, especially in the visionary title-poem, called a 'polar sonata', in *Marimarusa* (1978). **G. S. Fraser** (1915–80) was born in Glasgow and educated in Aberdeen, but after the war he spent most of his time in England working as a freelance journalist, a critic and then a lecturer at Leicester. His own verse had never been truly Apocalyptic and, indeed, he became an influential figure with the 'Movement' poets in London in the fifties. Some of his best early poems took the form of 'letters home' during the war, which he spent in the Middle East ('A Winter Letter'), and this mode continued to suit his relaxed, civilised and wryly self-deprecating verse. He admired the selfless mildness of Edwin Muir's poetry, but mental tensions of his own gave new urgency to the work of the late sixties – 'Speech of a Sufferer', 'The Insane Philosophers'. Fraser never truly lost his gently sceptical neoclassical balance, however, as can be seen in *Poems of G. S. Fraser* (1981), which reprints all four of his earlier collections.

Norman MacCaig (b. 1910)

Although this poet wrote his first two collections in the Apocalyptic vein, he has taken care to disown them in later years, having come to value clarity, compassion and a certain humane elegance of the mind above all else – fitting qualities for a classics graduate of Edinburgh University. MacCaig returned to schoolteaching after the war – his abhorrence of killing made him a conscientious objector – and he has lived in Edinburgh ever since. He was the first 'writer in residence' at the university there in 1967, and three years later he joined the English Department at the University of Stirling, subsequently becoming Reader in Poetry until his retirement in 1978. He was a friend of Goodsir Smith's and had a close relationship with Hugh MacDiarmid in the poet's later years. Greatly in demand at public poetry-readings, MacCaig has produced a book every one or two years since *Riding Lights* in 1955. The most recent selection of his work is *Old Maps and New* (1978), and a *Collected Poems* will appear in 1985.

Despite his long career in Edinburgh, the spiritual fulcrum of MacCaig's work is to be found nearer to Lochinver, where he retreats from the city every summer. 'Return to Scalpay' – the island where his Gaelic-speaking mother was born – affirms his love for the people and the landscapes of the North-West, from which he derives the gaiety, the penetrating understatement and the wry modesty which characterise him. MacCaig's poetry grows from the delight with which he greets the world, but the images which he creates to describe people, animals and landscapes also reflect back on language and his own observing mind. So MacCaig is never simply a 'nature' poet, and his preference for linking precise observation with creative wit can be seen in an early poem, 'Summer Farm': 'A hen stares at nothing with one eye, / Then picks it up'. He recognises that this is a perception which depends on his own eye, as if he could lift the farm 'like a lid and see / Farm within farm, and in the centre, me'. MacCaig's work came to full maturity of expression and technique with his move to free verse in the mid sixties, and in a succession of poems over the years he has delighted readers with his deftness in creating likenesses which seem so just, but were never there before – frogs die on the roads 'with arms across their chests . . . like Italian tenors' ('Frogs'), or a toad is told to 'stop looking like a purse' ('Toad'). In such a world the poet has cultivated his capacity for surprise ('Country Dance') or even sudden terror ('Basking Shark'), while a quiet rage at the fact of human suffering is found in 'Assisi'. Nevertheless, the reflective–reflexive habit of mind is not an unmixed blessing, and in other poems MacCaig has explored the more awkward implications of the relationship betwen himself, language and other people. 'A Man in My Position' and 'Private' recognise that there is a 'comfortable MacCaig whose / small predictions were predictable', while 'Equilibrist' tells how the radio can be switched from tortures in foreign prisons 'to a sonata of Schubert (that foreigner)'. He draws his own conclusions from the juxtaposition with typical reserve: 'Noticing you can do nothing about. / It's the balancing that shakes my mind'. Since he does not accede to Christian or political dogma of any kind, he has to achieve that balance on his own, just as he had to reconcile himself to the death of MacDiarmid and to that of a close friend in Inverkirkaig. That effort led to a collection called *The Equal Skies* (1980), which contains some of his most moving and finely controlled poems.

A more theoretical involvement with the problems of creative language can be found in the poetry of **W. S. Graham** (b. 1948), a Greenock man who has lived in Cornwall for many years. As a friend of Dylan Thomas and George Barker, Graham showed affinities with the Apocalyptic writers in his early work, although verses such as 'The Children of Greenock' were more autobiographical. He became well known with *The Nightfishing* (1955), a long poem which makes fishing and the sea (which features in much of his work) a symbol for the creative process. The making of poetry and the nature of language itself have been consistent themes in Graham's work ever since. Thus the cerebral wit of 'Malcolm Mooney's Land' associated the awful spaces of arctic exploration with the terrifying whiteness (for a writer) of blank paper, and 'The Dark Dialogues' brought this more abstract concern with the place 'where I am, between / This word and the next' into closer touch with his childhood in Greenock. This welcome biographical directness returns in such fine poems as 'Loch Thom' and 'To Alexander Graham', from *Implements in their Places* (1977). In the same collection 'Joachim Quantz's Five Lessons' uses a well-realised historical setting to consider the disciplines of art, and he reintroduces 'Malcolm Mooney' to ask 'What is the Language Using Us For?', in a witty sequence on the elusive, illusive, nature of syntax and sentences.

Graham's more speculative poems show that he has long recognised what contemporary critics have had to say about the artificial status of the word. On the other hand, the bare and telling verses of **George Bruce** (b. 1909) see the word and the world as inescapable verities. He grew up in the fishing town of Fraserburgh to the north of Aberdeen, and the stern religious faith of the place, its clear light and its harsh coast are all reflected in the linguistic austerity which he chose for his first collection, *Sea Talk* (1944). 'Inheritance' maintains that 'This which I write now / Was written years ago. . . . It was stamped / In the rock formations / West of my home town'. The longer lines of the title-poem describe the culture of the place, using the sand-blown fields, the boney-faced fishermen and a beach of stones, crabs, bones and splinters of shell for his images and setting them against the terrors of the sea and the shapelessness of salt fog. Bruce has written fine occasional poems on the social scene and political events, but his best later work has always seemed to come from the originally stark themes of *Sea Talk*. 'A Man of Inconsequent Build' remembers his father as cooper in Fraserburgh, while a set of four poems on 'Tom' mixes the pathos of childhood with more chilly premonitions of the future – 'We hold out our hands to History / Then ask not to be taken'.

George Bruce's *Collected Poems* appeared in 1970, the year he retired from a long career as talks-producer for the BBC, during which time he did much to encourage younger authors. Since retiring he has been even more active as a visiting writer in Scotland, America and Australia. **Sidney Tremayne** (b. 1912) also worked in the media, as a journalist, but has taken little active part in literary circles. His *Selected and New Poems* (1973) shows how he achieves an unselfish descriptive purity which grows from his observational delight in the countryside with its animals and the weather in all its moods. His is a genuine 'nature poetry', thoughtful, but without the metaphysical stress which Bruce finds in his landscapes.

All the foregoing poets appeared in *Poetry Scotland* during the forties. It is appropriate to close that particular group with the work of **Maurice Lindsay** (b. 1918), who had so much to do with the series and who has continued an active career as journalist, editor, critic and literary historian ever since. He became director of the Scottish Civic Trust in 1967 and his contacts with television have kept him in the public eye. His early experiments with Scots (*Hurlygush*, 1948) did not master the medium, but by the 1960s his own polished and urbane responses to the social scene had come into their own. His essentially conservative nature has more in common with Philip Larkin, perhaps, than with many of his Scottish contemporaries, and, if he lacks Larkin's capacity for flashes of sudden rage or despair, he has a more companionable enjoyment of the world. No slave to fashion, and certainly not a modernist, Lindsay explains in the Preface to his *Collected Poems* (1979) that he has been glad to write as 'an enjoyable poet'. This stance was further celebrated in a long autobiographical poem in *ottava rima* called *A Net to Catch the Winds* (1981).

The last four figures to be considered in the 'second wave' of poets who used English could not be more different from each other. They come from the four corners of the country and embrace literary and philosophical views almost equally far apart.

George Mackay Brown (b. 1921)

Born in Orkney, Brown worked as a local journalist until he was in his thirties, before becoming one of Edwin Muir's mature students at Newbattle College. It was through Muir's direct encouragement that his first major collection, *Loaves and Fishes*, was published in 1959. Brown suffered badly from tuberculosis, which was to interrupt and curtail his studies more than once; nevertheless he persevered and graduated from Edinburgh in 1960, continuing with research for a couple of years before returning to Orkney, where he has lived ever since. From the very first, Brown's poems have presented a consistent vision of Orkney life in a style derived from the sagas and reduced to its archetypal essentials, so that the little community of 'fishermen with ploughs' becomes a model for all life, and especially of the 'good life' which he prizes. He is deeply opposed to the values of industrial materialism, which he sees as an inheritance from the Reformation, being influenced in these views by Muir's autobiography and the friendship he formed with the older poet. Mackay Brown goes much further than Grassic Gibbon and Gunn as a writer who seeks to evoke timeless values and mythopoeic patterns in his work, and, like Muir and Fionn MacColla, he

found these qualities in Catholicism and joined the Church in
1961. The very title of *Loaves and Fishes* relates to the sacramental symbols in his ideal vision of life on Orkney, while a poem
such as 'Our Lady of the Waves', from his next collection, uses
the simple ritual of labour among the brothers at Eynhallow in
order to reflect all experience:

> Queen of Heaven, this good day
> There is a new cradle at Quoys.
> It rocks on the blue floor.
> And there is a new coffin at Hamnavoe.
> Arnor the poet lies there
> Tired of words and wounds.
> In between, what is man?
> *A head bent over fish and bread and ale.*
> *Outside, the long furrow.*
> *Through a door, a board with a shape on it.*
>
> Guard the plough and the nets.
>
> Star of the sea shine for us.

Such pure images and terse lines are typical of Mackay Brown's
lucid, gentle inspiration, and his feeling for reverence and ritual
in the humble acts of life has produced memorable work. His
best and most innovative poems appear in *Fishermen with
Ploughs* (1971), a linked 'poem cycle' which records, very
obliquely, the rise and fall of the community of Rackwick on
Hoy. Different sections take it through the ages from the epic
days of its foundation to modern decline, and then on to a
resettlement which is described in prose journals after some
unknown future cataclysm. It is characteristic of Brown's
historical position that he should explain that 'the same people
appear and reappear through many generations . . . all are
caught up in "the wheel of bread" that is at once brutal and
holy'. This is not to say that he does not have a dry sense of
humour in some of these verses, as also in, for example, the 'Tea
Poems' from *Winterfold* (1971). Even so, after several collections, the poet's cyclical themes do tend to lead always to the
'same people', until the timeless is in danger of becoming
merely static.

Brown's short stories bring him back into contact with the
world, and they may yet be judged to be his finest achievement.

The title-story from *A Calendar of Love* (1967) takes place in modern times, but the author calls on episodic cycles of fertility, birth, shame and forgiveness, to set the stage for a succession of such tales from different eras. He is closest to contemporary life in *A Time to Keep* (1969), and his studies of alcoholism and loneliness in 'Celia' and 'The Eye of the Hurricane', and of the cruelty of fate in 'A Time to Keep', show that his prose can rise to an outstanding tact and sensitivity. 'Celia' was made into a memorable television production and Brown has written many other plays and radio plays, not least through his association with the composer Peter Maxwell Davies and their work together for the Orkney Festival. His book *Magnus* (1973) establishes a pared-down, epic quality to the life and martyrdom of St Magnus, operating somewhere between a saga and a devotional mediation. Brown's prose is effective, but the work is not a novel in the conventional sense, unlike its predecessor, *Greenvoe* (1972), which describes the end of an island community on 'Hellya' in the 1960s.

Greenvoe is taken over by an unspecified military-research or defence project called 'Black Star'. Brown assembles a picture of the community by revealing the foibles of its various inhabitants from different points of view, but the reader may be forgiven for feeling that it is rather close to the Kailyard, despite the author's obvious affection for it. Hellya is no sooner cleared of its inhabitants than the project closes down, although in the larger perspective of history and with the survival of the old rituals of the 'Lord of the Harvest' the saga continues. Brown could be describing several such military and industrial projects in modern Scotland, but the author's mythic and fatalistic habit of mind will not let his theme develop to tragedy or anger, nor does it always do justice to the tensions and complexities inherent in the contemporary world.

Iain Crichton Smith (Iain Mac a'Ghobhainn, b. 1928)

In a different sense, Crichton Smith is equally at the mercy of a metaphysical point of view, for his upbringing on Lewis brought him into contact with the absolutism of the Free Kirk and his poetry has reflected that meeting ever since. Caught between discipline and freedom, or 'Thistles and Roses', or

'The Law and the Grace' (the titles of his first two collections), Smith is divided again between Gaelic and English, for he has written poetry and prose in his mother tongue, and translated some of it into what he has called a 'foreign language'. Nevertheless, it was as an English teacher that he worked in Oban for twenty-two years. A complex, sensitive and intelligent poet, Smith is a compulsive and sometimes too prolific writer, with over eighteen volumes of verse to his name, as well as plays, short stories and several novels.

MacDiarmid saw excitement in the thrilling clash of contraries, but Smith finds it a more personal and painful thing, closer, perhaps, to Edwin Muir's diagnosis of a Scottish division between the head and the heart – 'I am tied to the Highlands', he wrote in the Gaelic poem 'Eight Songs for a New Ceilidh', 'that is where I learnt my wound'; and, again, 'it was the fine bareness of Lewis that made the work of my mind'. If he paraphrases Sidney's advice to poets to ' "Look in your own heart and write" ', then his heart is a divided place. Translations of his two main Gaelic collections can be found in *The Permanent Island*, 1975. They are *Biobuill is Sanasan Reice* ('Bibles and Advertisements'), 1965; and *Eadar Fealla-dha is Glaschu* ('Between Comedy and Glasgow'), 1969. Smith seems able to speak more directly in his Gaelic verse, and many poems in the 1965 collection offer invaluable insights into his work as a whole – from his love of the stark landscapes of his native island and his desire for the 'bareness of the knife's blade' to the sense of desolation which he finds there, too, and an awareness of Nagasaki, Hiroshima and Belsen set against the standing stones of Callanish. He writes of division in his relationship with language, seeing himself 'In the dress of the fool, the two colours that have tormented me – English and Gaelic, black and red, the court of injustice, the reason for my anger': 'The Fool' ('An t-Amadan'), and he concludes that the result is a motley 'so odd that the King himself will not understand my conversation'.

Crichton Smith is a poet haunted by images, sometimes almost beyond his capacity to comprehend them; thus, in the Gaelic poem 'What is Wrong' ('Dé tha Ceàrr'), he feels once again divided between head and heart, until a characteristic moment of insight occurs:

But one day I saw a black pit in green earth, a gardener kissing flowers, an old woman squeaking in her loneliness, and a house sailing on the water.

> I don't know whether there is a language for that, or, if there is, whether I
> would be any better breaking my imagination into a thousand pieces. . . .

His many volumes of poetry in both Gaelic and English
describe a continuing search to find 'a language for that' and,
sometimes too, the breaking of his imagination into a thousand
pieces. Thus the sequence 'Am Faigh a' Ghaidlig Bas?' ('Shall
Gaelic Die?', 1969), links a passionate concern with the future
of his native tongue with a more philosophical understanding of
the nature of all language-systems as limited conventions
standing between the real and the abstract – and yet they still
encapsulate untranslatable subtleties.

The bareness of Lewis and the starkness of Calvinism come
together in Smith's early work to make a complicated weave of
love and hate – 'Here they have no time for the fine graces of
poetry', he wrote in 'Poem of Lewis', from his first collection in
1955. His admiration for the stoic strength of such an
inheritance and his equal alarm at its grim narrowness feature
in his many poems about old women, who become symbols of
mortality for him, as well as key figures in the daily life between
hearth and Kirk. He can describe the 'thorned back' and the
'set mouth' of righteousness which 'forgives no-one, not even
God's justice/perpetually drowning law with grace' ('Old
Woman'); yet at the same time he understands this spirit and
shares its delight in hard certainties. 'There is no metaphor', he
concludes in *Deer on the High Hills* (1962); 'The stone is
stony./The deer step out in isolated air. . . . Winter is wintry,
lonely is your journey.' The deer are symbols for the spirit
which moves him in this long poem, because 'A deer looks
through you to the other side,/and what it is and sees is an
inhuman pride'. He knows compassion too, and the importance of dignity in the face of death, and 'Old Woman', from
Thistles and Roses (1961), is one of the finest and most lyrically
moving studies of old age in modern literature:

> And she being old, fed from a mashed plate
> as an old mare might droop across a fence
> to the dull pastures of its ignorance.
> Her husband held her upright while he prayed
>
> to God who is all-forgiving to send down
> some angel somewhere who might land perhaps

in his foreign wings among the gradual crops.
She munched, half dead, blindly searching the spoon.

Outside, the grass was raging. There I sat
imprisoned in my pity and my shame
that men and women having suffered time
should sit in such a place, in such a state

and wished to be away. . . .

Crichton Smith chose an old woman as the protagonist of his first novel, *Consider the Lilies* (1969), giving a grim account of the Clearances through her consciousness. His memories of his mother – he lived with her for many years and married relatively late – add to his insight into such themes, and he has reflected on the harshness of her youth as a fish-gutter following the herring fleet around Britain, compared to his own sheltered education at Aberdeen University (*Love Poems and Elegies*, 1972). In other poems his compassion for young girls may well grow from his awareness of the hardships which the world will probably bring to them.

While many of Smith's poems respond to the physical beauty of the hills and the islands, other verses, in *From Bourgeois Land* (1968) and in sequences such as 'By the Sea' and 'The White Air of March', convey his scathing impatience with much of Lowland Scottish life – stifled by respectability, given over to third-rate jokes and music, or cluttered with souvenirs for the tourist trade. His novels produce a similarly critical, but less savage, account of bourgeois life and the limitations of a timidly intellectual middle class – especially schoolteachers. *My Last Duchess* (1971) and *An End to Autumn* (1978) make their points by exteriorising the inward states of such characters, rather than through any broader social analysis. Despite the rather grey world of these books, it would be wrong to suppose that Crichton Smith lacks humour, for his dry wit can be found in English and Gaelic alike, most notably in the poems of *Eadar Fealla-dha is Glaschu*, an entertaining series of epigrams, 'Gaelic stories' and 'haikus' in affectionate mockery of his own background. In prose, too, *Murdo and Other Stories* (1981) expresses a wilder and hilariously absurd side to his nature, which was always there, along with an elusive and fey quality,

among the darker intensities of his work in both the languages
of his inheritance.

Edwin Morgan (b. 1920)

Edwin Morgan might be said to epitomise MacDiarmid's
hopes for a cosmopolitan and outward-looking culture in
post-Renaissance Scotland. As an academic and poet, his
interests range widely, turning more often to Europe and
America than they do to London and the south, and he has
translated verse by Mayakovsky, Montale, Voznesensky,
Quasimodo, Brecht, Neruda, Weöres, Juhasz and many
others. His own poetry is equally varied, for he is a man whose
essentially private and optimistic nature is attuned to the face
of the contemporary world, very often as it comes to us by way
of newspapers and television. Where other writers see only
confusion, decay or empty technology, Morgan discovers
growth, change, flux and delight. He uses his poetry to report
back on these discoveries or to push our imaginations a little
further beyond them. With over 400 pages (excluding his books
of translations), Morgan's *Poems of Thirty Years* (1982) testifies
to his witty engagement with science fiction, sound poetry and
concrete verse, and his grasp of dramatic and imaginative
narrative verse. Among more than twenty books and pamphlets the major collections have been *The Second Life* (1968),
From Glasgow to Saturn (1973) and *The New Divan* (1977).

As a lecturer and then a professor of English at the
University of Glasgow, Morgan has spent his working life in the
city of his birth, and it features in many of his poems. 'King
Billy', 'Death in Duke Street', 'Glasgow Green' and a sequence
of ten 'Glasgow Sonnets', describe a grim and sordid world of
urban decay, old age, religious bigotry, and muttered threats of
violence or desire, all very much in the popular image of 'No
Mean City'. Yet 'King Billy' ends with an admonition to
'Deplore what is to be deplored,/and then find out the rest',
and 'Glasgow Green' comes to sympathise with the hunter and
the hunted and the violent demands of the flesh 'as it
trembles/like driftwood through the dark'. Morgan can find
compassion and a kind of beauty in his city, for he sees energy

and a superb carelessness in the drunks of 'Saturday Night', or he celebrates the 'happy demolition men' in 'For Bonfires', who tear down an old slum 'stacking and building/their rubbish into a total bonfire . . . they all stand round,/and cheer the tenement to smoke'. Anonymous encounters in the city can lead to fear or the thrill of sexual danger ('The Suspect', 'Christmas Eve'), but there is redemption too, in the ordinary charity of people ('Trio'), or in the almost unbearable, dull courage of a blind hunchback ('In the Snack-Bar'), just as there is beauty in a Joan Eardley painting of decayed shop-fronts and city urchins – 'Such rags and streaks that master us!' ('To Joan Eardley'). Morgan's Glasgow poems do try to 'find out the rest', and his unsentimental eye for beauty and compassion in the grimy streets makes him unique among British poets of his generation.

If the tenements and the 'rags and streaks' are transformed into smoke – or poetry – in the Glasgow verses, then Morgan's many sound-poems and 'computer' poems also have to do with transmutation, especially as it occurs when information is transmitted. 'Message Clear' and 'The Computer's First Christmas Card' act out a painful progress towards some final statement – a telling theme for any poet to choose. Thus a succession of broken lines are slowly reconstructed from scattered letters down the page to end with 'I am the resurrection and the life' ('Message Clear') or a manic ticker-tape of worthy attempts is churned out only to fail at the last line, by wishing the programmer

```
merryChris
ammerryasa
Chrismerry
asMERRYCHR
YSANTHEMUM
```

Morgan has written many poems around similar effects, including sound-poems such as 'The Shaker Shaken', in which a stanza of nonsense syllables is repeated five times – each time with a few more real words substituted until the listener begins to experience a poem with strangely beautiful surreal images as it emerges from the abstract rhythmical noise. Morgan called his early ventures in such modes 'Emergent Poems', and the same process features in many of his 'science fiction' pieces. 'In

Sobieksi's Shield', 'The Gourds', 'Memories of Earth' and the hilarious 'The First Men on Mercury' all deal with confusions, transmissions or transmutations when the world of matter and of words is suddenly seen to be mutable, frightening, beautiful or insecure. This understanding lies at the core of all Morgan's art, and it links the Glasgow poems to the science-fiction verses, just as it runs through the computer and the concrete poems to go back to language itself and the world that language creates, whether it be on Glasgow, Saturn or the printed page. Morgan's fine talent for the evocative and elusive image transcends all categories, especially in the exotic and opaquely personal meditations in the sequence of 'The New Divan' – 'Let matter/envy you the metamorphoses a/dancer steals and cannot stay'.

Ian Hamilton Finlay (b. 1925)

Finlay is a writer who has gone beyond the page to become known as one of Europe's leading concrete poets. His work began with short stories, a radio-play and a collection of more or less conventional poems, *The Dancers Inherit the Party* (1960), although their odd humour and deliberately small scale was already rather original. A set of animal haikus followed in urban patois, but after *Glasgow Beasts, and a Burd . . .* (1961), Finlay became involved with the international movement known as 'concrete poetry'. There are many kinds of concrete verse, but essentially it is a move away from egocentrically romantic self-expression towards a poetry which concentrates on the import, or even the shape, of individual words and how they are spaced out on the page. Edwin Morgan's concrete verse often plays on witty shapes, puns and acrostics: for instance, his poem to Isambard Kingdom Brunel is shaped like a bridge made out of lines which ring the changes on his name – 'I am bard/I am Isobar/I am Iron Bar', etc. By comparison Finlay has taken a quieter and more classical line towards his declared goal of 'lucidity, clarity, resolved complexity'. *Poems to Hear and See* (1971) uses coloured inks and graphic effects, such as the word 'a c r o b a t s' printed over and over to fill the page as if the letters are standing on each others' shoulders. Alternatively the word 'STAR' is repeated in a wavering column down the page until it suddenly becomes 'STEER' at the last line. In these examples the conceptual implications within and beyond what the words mean have been explored in an engagingly unpretentious way. He also wrote 'one-word' poems which operate rather like the Japanese haiku in that they depend on an imaginative leap between the title and the verse. Thus the poem called 'The Cloud's Anchor' consists of a single word – 'swallow'.

In 1969 Finlay and his wife settled in a remote farmhouse, 'Stonypath' at Dunsyre, to set up a small press and produce dozens of booklets and over 200 cards and poem-prints in this vein. He uses favourite images of fishing-boats, nets, waves, canals, sailing-ships, stars, sundials and the seasons, and his poems and constructions share a simple and beautiful integrity – a welcome alternative to the then prevailing vogue for agonisingly 'confessional' verse. Finlay's work has continued to evolve and much of it is now realised in stone, wood and glass constructed to his designs by different artists and craftsmen. His work has been more widely exhibited and commissioned in Europe than in Britain, and the carefully landscaped garden which he has created around his house has become another kind of artistic statement, expressed through plants, sundials and inscribed stones. The link with eighteenth-century landscape gardening is not accidental, for Finlay takes a learned and resolutely classical approach to his art, enlivened by his fondness for apparently iconoclastic, but ultimately satisfying, images – such as a nuclear submarine's sail (conning-tower) in black slate, which serves as a worldless *memento mori* at the edge of an ornamental pond. In this at least, Hamilton Finlay has passed beyond the conventional definition of 'poetry', although he has never lost touch with its essence in surprise, illumination and delight.

Poetry in Gaelic

Although MacDiarmid's programme for the Renaissance began with Lowland Scots, it was not long before he included Gaelic in his vision of how a truly distinct Scottish culture should develop. By 1930 specifically Gaelic references were appearing in his work, and major poetic statements such as

'Lament for the Great Music' and 'Island Funeral' soon followed. Nevertheless, it was the poetry of Sorley Maclean which most truly brought the Gaelic tradition into the twentieth century, and in this respect he has been as vital an example to his fellow writers as ever MacDiarmid was to poets in Scots and English. As with the Kailyard, comic Gaelic verses and sentimental 'homeland' themes had persisted into the new century, while other poets were content to stay within the traditional modes – as, for example, the Skye man Angus Robertson (Aonghas MacDhonnchaidh, 1870–1948), who also wrote a novel (*An t-Ogha Mor*, 1913) set between the Jacobite risings. All this changed when Maclean's first collection of poems appeared in 1943.

Sorley Maclean (Somhairle MacGill-Eain, b. 1911)

Maclean was born on the island of Raasay, between Skye and the mainland, coming from a family with strong roots in the tales, music, songs and poems of the Gaelic tradition. Studying for a degree in English at the University of Edinburgh in the 1930s, the young man came into contact with the poems of Eliot, Pound and the seventeenth-century metaphysicals. In his final year he came across MacDiarmid's lyrics and the *Drunk Man*, and they left a lasting impression on him, crystallising many of his feelings about Scottish culture and how a poet could encompass both intellect and passion in his work. By 1934 Maclean had met the older poet and was helping him with his translations of MacMhaighstir Alasdair's *Birlinn Chlann Raghnaill* and Duncan Bàn Macintyre's 'Moladh Beinn Dòbhrain'. Maclean's pursuit of what he called 'the lyric cry' in verse took him in a completely different direction from MacDiarmid, and he was never a fully convinced Scottish nationalist; nevertheless, the two men found much in common – they were both committed socialists, after all – and they remained close friends for many years.

Maclean was one among many writers in the thirties to be deeply concerned by the rise of fascism and the outbreak of the Spanish Civil War. Social justice at home seemed equally important, and the poem 'Calvary' ('Calbharaigh') from his student years reflects his outrage at the slums of the Depression:*

> My eye is not on Calvary
> nor on Bethlehem the Blessed,
> but on a foul-smelling backland in Glasgow,
> where life rots as it grows;
> and on a room in Edinburgh,
> a room of poverty and pain,
> where the diseased infant
> writhes and wallows till death.

Employment as a schoolteacher took the poet to Mull for two years, where he saw the effects of cultural decline and the Clearances on every beautiful and barren hillside. This experience led him to compose more poems and to seek publication for them. The bitterness of 'A Highland Woman' ('Ban-Ghàidheal') belongs to this period: 'Hast Thou seen her, great Jew, who art called the One Son of God?' Then, in the later thirties, Maclean underwent an extremely intense and tortured love-affair, and the pressure of events in the world at large joined with his own heightened emotional state to produce the creative outpouring of the poems to 'Eimhir' and other works, in his first and most famous collection. (He had already shared a little booklet with Robert Garioch – *17 Poems for 6d*, 1940.) The new manuscript was complete by 1941, when Maclean left Scotland to serve in the desert campaign in North Africa, but the problems of wartime publishing were such that the book did not appear until 1943, by which time its author was in an English hospital, convalescing from serious wounds suffered at the battle of El Alamein. The publication of *Dain do Eimhir agus Dain Eile* (*Poems to Eimhir and Other Poems*, 1943) was a milestone in modern Gaelic poetry, assuring Maclean of a lasting reputation, even although it was to be twenty-seven years before his next book was published.

Among the 'other poems' in the collection there are pieces, such as 'Glen Eyre' ('Gleann Aoighre') and 'The Island' ('An t-Eilean'), which celebrate his own family history and the beloved landscapes of Skye; others focus on his political convictions. 'Cornford' is an agonised lament on the Spanish

---

* All the modern Gaelic poems in this chapter have been translated by the poets themselves – usually in their own dual text editions.

Civil War, in which John Cornford, Julian Bell and Garcia Lorca died, and the poet feels that he should himself have made some more active commitment. The heart of the book, however, is to be found in the forty-eight lyrics to 'Eimhir', although they are not conventional love-poems at all. It is as if Maclean's mixed feeling about the affair, his thoughts on his Gaelic heritage, his political awareness of the agony of Europe and a passionately spiritual idealism have all been heated and brought to almost unbearable intensities by the catalyst of love. Poem IV, 'The Cry of Europe' ('Gaoir na h-Eorpa'), is terribly divided between personal desire and a more general awareness:

> Girl of the yellow, heavy-yellow, gold-yellow hair,
> the song of your mouth and Europe's shivering cry,
> fair, heavy-haired, spirited, beautiful girl,
> the disgrace of our day would not be bitter in your kiss.
>
> Would your song and splendid beauty take
> from me the dead loathsomeness of these ways,
> the brute and the brigand at the head of Europe
> and your mouth red and proud with the old song?

In poem XLIII, 'The Blue Rampart' ('Am Mùr Gorm'), she becomes 'my reason and the likeness of a star', or he celebrates her as a 'dawn on the Cuillin' (LIV: 'Camhanaich') or he muses on the pointlessness of writing anything at all:

> I do not see the sense of my toil
> putting thoughts in a dying tongue
> now when the whoredom of Europe
> is murder erect and agony;
> but we have been given the million years,
> a fragment of a sad growing portion,
> the heroism and patience of hundreds
> and the miracle of a beautiful face.
>
> (LV: 'I Do Not See . . .': 'Chan Fhaic Mi . . .')

Maclean creates an extraordinary tension in these poems, and, although they are still based on traditional Gaelic metres and modes of expression (he admired William Ross and Mary Macpherson), he brings many other elements from beyond the native canon. Thus he has been influenced by his reading of Yeats and the Metaphysicals, there are echoes of Sidney's plight in *Astrophel and Stella*, and he uses musical and opaque images in the manner of European Symbolism. Driven by his own urgent socialism, mixed with feelings of desire and guilt, Maclean's verse is haunted by images of hurt and desolation, as when the 'knife' of his brain 'made incision, my dear, on the stone of my love,/ and its blade examined every segment' (XLV: 'The Knife': 'An Sgian'); or his unwritten love-poems come to seem like dogs and wolves with the spoor of their paws dappling the snows of eternity, 'their baying yell shrieking/ across the hard bareness of the terrible times' (XXIX: 'Dogs and Wolves': 'Coin is Madaidhean-Allaidh'). In the end Eimhir becomes a symbol of beauty and pain, as if the poet were struggling to reach an aspect of his own ideal spirit against the world itself and the inevitability of defeat and loss. This metaphysical dimension also appears in 'The Woods of Raasay' ('Coilltean Ratharsair'), and, although it is not one of the love-lyrics, this long celebration of the woods shifts from the detailed descriptive tradition of Gaelic praise-poems to a more complex and symbolic meditation on the tangles of love and idealism, concluding,

> There is no knowledge of the course
>   of the crooked veering of the heart,
>   and there is no knowledge of the damage
>   to which its aim unwittingly comes.
>
> There is no knowledge, no knowledge,
>   of the final end of each pursuit,
>   nor of the subtlety of the bends
>   with which it loses its course.

After the war Maclean returned to teaching in Edinburgh, and from 1956 until he retired he was headmaster at the school in Plockton on the mainland to the east of Skye. He published fine poems in *Poetry Scotland* and other periodicals from time to time, but the emotional storm of *Dain do Eimhir* had passed, and it was 1970 before a substantial selection of his work appeared again. His *Selected Poems* from 1932–72 were published in two languages as *Reothairt is Contraigh/Spring Tide and Neap Tide* (1977). The poet's war experiences in the desert feature in poems such as 'Heroes' ('Curaidhean'), 'An Autumn Day' ('Latha Foghair') and 'Death Valley' ('Glac a Bhàis'), but there are no polemics against fascism here, rather a resigned wisdom and compassion for the living and the dead of either side. From such experience, perhaps, Maclean's socialism has not retained the bitter certainties of his youth, and in this respect he makes better poems from the modulated and complex insights of 'At Yeats's Grave' ('Aig Uaigh Yeats'), 'Palach', and 'The National Museum of Ireland' ('Ard-Mhusaeum na h-Eireann'). In 1939 he abandoned 'The Cuillin', a long symbolic poem as a meditation on communism and only sections of it have been published since.

Maclean's later work has come to have the power of a threnody or incantation sustained through a web of historical, cultural and family references within which traditional metaphors and his own singular and haunting images take their place. The elegy for his brother Calum Maclean takes a modern form to raise the old tradition of lament (*cumha*), while 'Hallaig' invokes an eerie beauty in a long deserted township on Raasay where his own ancestors lived before the place was cleared to make a sheep-farm in the 1850s. In this outstanding poem the trees become like girls in some vision of the past and its verses end with the symbolic death of Time, like a deer in the woods.

> and when the sun goes down behind Dun Cana
> a vehement bullet will come from the gun of Love;
>
> and will strike the deer that goes dizzily,
> sniffing at the grass-grown ruined homes;
> his eye will freeze in the wood,
> his blood will not be traced while I live.

As the son of the author of *Gillespie*, **George Campbell Hay** (**Deòrsa MacIain Deòrsa**, 1915–84), taught himself to speak Gaelic and wrote in English and Scots as well, which is a relatively unusual combination, although William Neill (b. 1922), was to take a similar route in the late sixties. Not surprisingly, given his scholarly nature and his nationalistic convictions, Hay's poems in Scots and Gaelic show interest in traditional modes, metrical structure and rhymes. Many of them celebrate the natural world, as in 'To a Bonny Birch Tree' 'Do Bheithe Boidheach' or 'Song' ('Oran'), and especially the sea in all its moods ('Pleasure and Courage'). Hay also follows classical themes with a ballad-like narrative approach in 'The Return of Ulysses' ('Tilleadh Uiliseis'), or a supernatural tale of shipwreck in the Scots poem 'The Three Brothers'. This delight in formal pattern, and his patriotic care for Scotland, is evident in 'The Four Winds of Scotland' ('Ceithir Gaothan na h-Albann'), while his feeling for weather and landscape features in 'An Ciùran Ceòban Ceò', for which he also has a most musical version in Scots – 'The Smoky Smirr o Rain':

A misty mornin' doon the shore wi a hushed an' caller air,   fresh
an' ne'er a breath frae East or West tae sway the rashes there,
a sweet, sweet scent frae Laggan's birks gaed breathin' on its ain,
their branches hingin' beaded in the smoky smirr o rain.

The hills aroon war silent wi the mist alang the braes.
The woods war derk an' quiet wi dewey, glintin' sprays.
The thrushes didna raise for me, as I gaed by alane,
but a wee, wee cheep at passin' in the smoky smirr o rain.

(Other Gaelic poems of Hay's were translated into Scots by his friend Douglas Young.) A much more agonised vision of the world, however, characterises 'Bisearta', based on his unhappy experiences during the war, when he saw Bizerta in flames in the distance while he stood night guard:

What is their name tonight,
the poor streets where every window spews
its flame and smoke,
its sparks and the screaming of its inmates,
while house upon house is rent
and collapses in a gust of smoke?
And who tonight are beseeching
Death to come quickly in all their tongues,
or are struggling among stones and beams,
crying in frenzy for help, and are not heard?
Who tonight is paying
the old accustomed tax of common blood?

A similarly impassioned empathy for the underdog informs 'Atman', a poem on behalf of an Arab convicted for theft by a well-fed judge, and he developed this concern in a distinguished long poem *Mochtar and Dougal* (*Mochtàr is Dùghall*), which was not published until 1982. Hay's peace of mind was damaged by the war, and he wrote at infrequent intervals, but recent work showed no diminution of his powers.

Derick Thomson (Ruaridh MacThómais, b. 1921)

As critic, scholar, and founder-editor of the quarterly *Gairm* since 1952, Derick Thomson has played a leading part in Scottish Gaelic studies, and most of his own poems from previous collections can be found in *Creachadh na Clàrsaich / Plundering the Harp* (1982). His language is more colloquial than Maclean's and he uses freer verse-forms, although of course he still draws on Gaelic's capacity to use subtle rhymes and assonances in the vowels within a sequence of words. Over the years his work has shown a sustained engagement with his origins in Lewis in relation to the wider world beyond. As an academic educated at Aberdeen and Cambridge, and after years as a professor of Celtic at Glasgow University, Thomson cannot look back on the distant island of his boyhood without recognising that there is no longer a working-place for him in it. The poem 'Coffins' ('Cisteachan-laighe'), from his second collection, describes what has happened to him and others like him by remembering his grandfather as a carpenter making coffins. He associates the process with his own education, in which English was compulsory, and, indeed, until a generation ago Gaelic children were actively dissuaded from speaking Gaelic in the classroom at any time:

> And in the other school also,
> where the joiners of the mind were planing,
> I never noticed the coffins,
> though they were sitting all around me;
> I did not recognise the English braid,
> the Lowland varnish being applied to the wood,
> I did not read the words on the brass,
> I did not understand that my race was dying.
> Until the cold wind of this Spring came
> to plane the heart;
> Until I felt the nails piercing me,
> and neither tea nor talk will help the pain.

The same sad recognition informs the plaintive cadences of 'When This Fine Snow is Falling' ('Triomh Uinneig a' Chithe'), but there is a sharper edge to poems such as 'Steel?' ('Cruaidh?') and 'Strathnaver' ('Srath Nabhair'), which manage a bitter wit at the recollection of the Clearances:

> And throw away soft words,
> for soon you will have no words left;
> The *Tuatha De Danann* are underground,
> the Land of the Ever-young is in France,
> and when you reach the Promised Land,
> unless you are on your toes,
> a bland Englishman will meet you,
> and say to you that God, his uncle, has given him a title to the land.
>
> ('Steel')

(The Tuatha De Danann are a supernatural race in Ireland, sometimes said to be progenitors of the fairies.) 'Donegal' and 'Budapest' extend this wry rage beyond Scotland's borders, while the fine movement of 'Between Summer and Autumn' ('Eadar Samradh is Foghar') shows the music of Thomson's Gaelic in a quieter mood:

> Up from the sea, in a lonely hollow
> is a patch of grass where the shoots were bruised,
> on a summer's day I can never forget;
> but when I garner both grass and corn,
> autumn stays not for me in the stacks,
> nor will summer return though I will it so.
>
> The sea lay below me, white and red,
> white-skinned wave-crest and dark-blue trough,
> receding and nearing,
> joy with its breath held,
> swelling and breaking,
> with healing in its hurting;
> and I grasped a moment
> to think of the mutability
> that lay below me,
> and to think of the constancy
> that I see now I utterly lacked.

The bitter-sweet and intimate relationship between Thomson and his homeland becomes the central theme of *An Rathad Cian / The Far Road* (1970), a collection of fifty-six linked lyrics in free verse. The poet's clear images seem to rise in the most unforced way from the natural landscape or from casual memories, and yet they accumulate to make the book his most sustained statement to date – timeless as Mackay Brown's *Fishermen with Ploughs*, but more in touch with the contemporary world and with his own wry distance from the island he is visiting. Thomson does not make Lewis into Edwin Muir's remembered Eden, but there is a strongly elegiac note in many of his poems; and somewhere between the shafts of his anger and the eloquent music of memory and longing there is an acceptance and a submission to fate which Maclean, for example, resists by turning to the more strenuous tradition of recollection. For Maclean, the evocation of dates, places and names in family or cultural history (as in the lament for his brother, or 'Screapadal') becomes an act of affirmation, with implications for community memory and an understanding of history. Thomson's, by contrast, is a more personal sense of history, with an essentially lyrical and *triste* vision. This seems to lie at the heart of his work even if he has produced topical and satirical verses, or political allegories such as 'The Eagle' ('An Iolaire') or 'The Plough' ('An Crann').

Aspects of Iain Crichton Smith's Gaelic poetry have already been discussed, but the example of his Gaelic short stories and novels should not be underestimated, for this is a small but growing development in Highland publishing, to which John Murray (Iain Moireach) and the Revd Colin Mackenzie (Cailein MacCoinnich) have also contributed.

Donald MacAulay (**Domhnall MacAmhlaigh**, b. 1930), is yet another Lewis man (it seems to be an island of poets) whose work looks to his origins, critically and otherwise. He is moved by traditional psalm-singing and by the 'liberating, cascading melody' of Gaelic prayer, which is 'my people's access to poetry' ('Gospel 1955': 'Soisgeul 1955'); or he deplores the narrowness of religion, as in 'Self-righteousness' ('Fèin-Fhìreantachd'). A spell in Turkey led him to recognise the social intolerance of the small community which is his home ('Amasra, 1957' and 'Holiday': 'Latha Fèill'), while his poem 'For Pasternak, for Example . . .' ('Do Phasternak, mar Eiseamplair . . .') reflects on how a poet must sustain his art against the 'contrary wind'. MacAulay is professor of Celtic at Aberdeen, and his work features in an anthology edited by himself, *Nua-bhàrdachd Ghaidlig / Modern Scottish Gaelic Poems* (1976), which contains work by all the above-mentioned writers as well. Among the younger generation notable poetry has been published by Angus Nicolson (Aonghas MacNeacail, b. 1942), Catriona Montgomery (Catriona Nic-Gumaraid, b. 1947) and Fergus MacKinlay (Feargus MacFionnaigh, b. 1948).

Contemporary writing

As a coherent movement the Scottish Renaissance probably ended somewhere in the sixties, although of course the liveliness of the contemporary literary scene cannot be separated from those strong foundations. Some younger writers still see themselves as part of that tradition, while others would deny the fact, or are happily unaware of it. There are older writers, too, such as Muriel Spark and James Kennaway, whose Scottish origins can be discerned in their work, although they have taken little active part in the world of Scottish letters and have spent most of their lives out of the country. Robin Jenkins, on the other hand, has returned to Scotland, and, his Scottish novels, and even his books set in the Far East, show a sensibility deeply affected by the culture and the ethos of his native land. Even more notably, the 'Glasgow novelists' in the sixties and the new dramatists of the seventies have set out to express and to reassess the local and national character of Scottish life, usually in terms which combine a psychological or moral analysis of native inhibitions with a grim urban naturalism. George Douglas Brown's legacy of love and rage is still with us, and, if the house with the green shutters has been sublet and transported to the big cities, there is plenty of desperate life in those rooms yet, as well, perhaps, as a tendency to haunt already familiar ground.

Muriel Spark (b. 1918) spent the first eighteen years of her life in Edinburgh before moving to London and then to Rome. She feels herself to be a 'constitutional exile' in Edinburgh, and yet she recognises that certain habits of mind have survived from her youth. Several critics, too, would claim a distinctively Scottish strain in her work. *The Prime of Miss Jean Brodie* (1961) relates to a clash between different kinds of authority –

indirectly Calvinist and Catholic – as played out between a schoolteacher and the disciple who will eventually betray her. Other readers see a Scottish flavour in Spark's 'mordant irony', and, in either case, the complex moral fate of Jean Brodie, and her confusions between liberal and elitist values, gave Muriel Spark one of her best and best-known novels.

Robin Jenkins (b. 1912) did not identify himself with the Renaissance writers, and having worked as a schoolteacher and travelled widely, he was forty-eight before his first book was published. Nevertheless, most of his novels are set in Scotland (although he has written fiction set around Afghanistan and the Middle East) and they take issue with central problems of morality and the nature of innocence, goodness and maturity in a world seemingly hostile to such qualities. Jenkins sees the urban west of Scotland as a place of crumbling streets or stifling gentility, brutal crowds and lonely individuals, and he sets this against the nearby Highlands as a place of remote beauty, old estates or isolated forests. Of course, good and evil can be found in either scene, but Jenkins's novels gain power from his use of such settings where he finds the symbols which suit the poetic or metaphysical nature of his vision. *The Thistle and the Grail* (1954) describes its Scottish town as a crowded place where all the petty frustrations and hopes of the narrow spirits who live there are given over to football, while *The Cone Gatherers* (1955), has a simpler and more poetic sense of tragic inevitability. It takes place on a country estate during the Second World War, as if a parable of that wider evil were being acted out among the trees and cones, which symbolise both darkness and seed for the future. The action unfolds between a retarded, kindly and hunchbacked forestry worker and the obsessed and unhappy gamekeeper who comes to hate him as he hates his sick wife and his own dire nature. The simpleton's brother and the aristocratic lady owner of the estate are left shaken at the end, after the murder of the poor fellow and the gamekeeper's suicide – as if they had witnessed some cathartic ritual act. Jenkins's predominantly ethical imagination finds one of its best expressions in *A Would-be Saint* (1978), an understated study of the ambiguities of unforced goodness and the problems which it brings to Gavin Hamilton's life as he grows up during the Depression. When war breaks out he becomes a conscientious objector, leaving town to work in the forests, which become the stage for his confrontation with himself and what he owes to a world which cannot understand him. The novelist's most virulent and ambivalent account of cultural life and spiritual failure in Scotland is given in *Fergus Lamont* (1979), the 'autobiography' of a soldier and poet during the 'Renaissance' period. It charts the rise and fall of an egocentric, creative, self-destructive and hypocritical man in a career of repeated petty betrayals and lost love.

It was the failure of another military career through psychological and class conflict which distinguished *Tunes of Glory* (1956), the accomplished first novel by **James Kennaway** (1928–68). The book centres on the characterisation of Colonel Jock Sinclair, a hard-drinking, hard-fighting, vain, coarse, immature, obsolete old soldier, who seems doomed to destroy himself in a clash with the Sandhurst officer who arrives to replace him as acting head of a Highland regiment. In the end it is the new commander who commits suicide and Jock survives to suffer a final breakdown. Kennaway's own restless emotional life was something of a struggle in between bouts of obsessively hard writing. His subsequent novels often deal with destructive marital or emotional conflicts within a family or between lovers, and he gave a specifically Scottish setting to *Household Ghosts* (1961).

By comparison the novels and stories of **Elspeth Davie** (b. 1919) offer a much quieter, but no less sensitive, account of bourgeois life within the daily setting of the city – most usually Edinburgh, where she lives. The stories in *The High Tide Talker* (1976), contain memorable images of the lonely and unique nature of ordinary people conveyed in a clear and subtly polished style. Her novel *Creating a Scene* (1971) deals with the relationship between two art-students and their teacher during a project to help to 'humanise' a housing-scheme. Grimly urban settings in the crowded west of Scotland feature in many novels of the sixties, which set out to explore the nature of 'Scottishness' and the difficulties of achieving any kind of creative life in such an environment.

Alan Sharp (b. 1934) worked in the Clydeside shipyards when he left school before going on to university and eventually to London and America, where he is now a successful screen-writer. *A Green Tree in Gedde* (1965) and *The Wind Shifts* (1976) are the first two volumes of a triology which was never completed. They follow the lives, thoughts and journeys of four characters in search of 'home' in an effort to understand and explore existential questions of sexuality and identity. Sharp set himself a large scale task with these picaresque novels, and under the influence of Henry Miller and Joyce he adopted a highly-wrought and various prose, moving from impersonal narrative to impressionism, terse dialogue and elaborately poetic evocations. It was a brilliant and ambitious debut, but Sharp seems to have left it unfinished with something of an air of relief. **Gordon Williams** (b. 1934) has a clearer and more professionally economical prose style, and a sharper rage at the nature of Scottish failings – especially in matters of drink, sexual guilt and physical violence. *From Scenes Like These* (1968) accumulates these aspects of the national inferiority-complex in the life of young Dunky Logan, to create one of the darkest pictures of Scottish life since *Gillespie*. *Walk Don't Walk* (1972) is more cheerfully scathing about national limitations, as it tells how a Scots novelist copes with a promotion-tour of America, when all his images of that country have come to him from his boyhood love of Hollywood films. The novels of George Friel (1910–75), on the other hand, have stayed in Glasgow to chronicle the lives of lonely individuals against the pressures of the city – most notably in his grimmest and last novel, *Mr Alfred, MA* (1972).

William McIlvanney (b. 1936) explored the environmental and family tensions of life in the urban west with his first two novels – *Remedy is None* (1966) and *A Gift from Nessus* (1968). His third book, *Docherty* (1975), links the 'hard man' theme to expressive naturalism in order to describe the hardship and courage of his hero's life as a coal-miner, seen from the point of view of his son in the years before and during the Depression. An equally deeply felt and indirectly autobiographical account of working-class aspiration is sustained in *The Dear Green Place* (1964) by Archie Hind (b. 1928), in which its protagonist's unsophisticated commitment to his own talent and his dreams of being a novelist are described against the hardships of his background and social circumstances. The well-written stories of Alan Spence and Carl MacDougall derive from similar roots in colloquial realism, and an equally humorously bizarre development from this mode has appeared in the collection *Not Not While the Giro* (1983) by James Kelman. The most striking and far-reaching achievement in recent fiction has been *Lanark* (1981), the work of many years, written and illustrated by **Alasdair Gray** (b. 1934). It is a large, complex, nightmarish and witty novel, which takes its hero beyond sordid urban realism, and beyond life itself, to explore the author's surreal and anti-utopian vision of modern society. With a very Scottish combination of scholarly weight and flippancy, this extraordinary book follows in the modernist tradition of Kafka, Burroughs and Borges, and yet it belongs equally convincingly to the allegorical visions of *The City of Dreadful Night*, *A Voyage to Arcturus* or the fantasy-worlds of George MacDonald. Further prose-writers who show a welcome awareness of modern European and American literature would include Giles Gordon, Alan Massie and John Herdman whose *Pagan's Pilgrimage* (1978) explored the pains and perversities of the Scottish Presbyterian sensibility with an acerbically philosophical and satirical style.

These writers bring us to an immediately contemporary generation whose work is still in the process of defining what the map of Scottish literature will look like in the last thirty years of the century. Tom Buchan and Alan Jackson came to prominence in the late sixties as poets who made their muse a medium for popular expression and social comment. The plainer political and personal verses of Alan Bold are equally accessible, as are the poems of Ken Morrice, Robin Bell, Valerie Gillies and the spritely wit with which Liz Lochhead recounts personal relationships and the female condition. Stewart Conn makes a sparer and more reflective verse out of his thoughts on family life, while Alasdair Maclean derives a darker and more personal vision from his west Highland background. Douglas Dunn's poems have been widely published and broadcast, and since his return to Scotland Northern themes – especially in *St Kilda's Parliament* (1981) – have begun to engage him more. Kenneth Whyte and Alastair Reid have lived mostly in France and America, and their poetry, especially Whyte's, has a sparer intellectual focus – reminiscent, perhaps, of the fine poems of Burns Singer (1928–64), and equally notable in the analytical reserve of Robin Fulton, a long-time editor of *Lines Review* who is currently working in Scandinavia. George Macbeth has taken a much more surreal vein, although his recent poetry has abandoned black humour in favour of a gentler response to nature. On the other hand, the finely modulated longer verses of David Black have created a remarkably consistent fantasy-world out of his interest in archetypal images and Grimm-like tales, while the poems of Roderick Watson meditate on how landscapes and objects are marked by the past and permeated by memory. Walter Perrie shows a similar interest in modernist techniques in the linked themes of his longer poems, as do Ron Butlin and Andrew Greig. The story – and the fable too – is still unwinding in all three of Scotland's languages, but let us 'mak up work heirof', as Douglas says, 'and clos our buke'.

Further reading

Literary history

BOLD, ALAN: *Modern Scottish Literature* (London: Longman, 1983).
—— *The Ballad* (London: Methuen, 1979).
BUCHAN, DAVID: *The Ballad and the Folk* (London: Routledge and Kegan Paul, 1972).
CAMPBELL, IAN: *Kailyard: A New Assessment* (Edinburgh: Ramsay Head Press, 1981).
—— (ed.): *Nineteeth Century Scottish Fiction* (Manchester: Carcanet, 1979).
CRAIG, DAVID: *Scottish Literature and the Scottish People, 1680–1830* (London: Chatto and Windus, 1961).
DAICHES, DAVID: *The Paradox of Scottish Culture* (London: Oxford University Press, 1964).
—— (ed.): *A Companion to Scottish Culture* (London: Edward Arnold, 1981).
——: *Literature and Gentility in Scotland* (Edinburgh: Edinburgh University Press, 1982).
FULTON, ROBIN: *Contemporary Scottish Poetry* (Edinburgh: Macdonald, 1974).
GLEN, DUNCAN: *Hugh MacDiarmid and the Scottish Renaissance* (Edinburgh: Chambers, 1964).
HART, FRANCIS: *The Scottish Novel* (London: John Murray, 1978).
HENDERSON, T. F.: *Scottish Vernacular Literature*, 3rd rev. edn (Edinburgh: John Grant, 1910).
HUTCHISON, DAVID: *The Modern Scottish Theatre* (Glasgow: Molendinar Press, 1977).
LINDSAY, MAURICE: *History of Scottish Literature* (London: Robert Hale, 1977).
MACLEAN, MAGNUS: *The Literature of the Highlands* (London and Glasgow: Blackie, 1925).
MILLAR, J. H.: *A Literary History of Scotland* (London: Fisher Unwin, 1903)
ROYLE, TREVOR: *The Macmillan Companion to Scottish Literature* (London: Macmillan, 1983).
SMITH, G. GREGORY: *Scottish Literature, Character and Influence* (London: Macmillan, 1919).
THOMSON, DERICK: *An Introduction to Gaelic Poetry* (London: Gollancz, 1974).
—— (ed.): *A Companion to Gaelic Scotland* (Oxford: Blackwell, 1983).
WITTIG, KURT: *The Scottish Tradition in Literature* (Edinburgh: Oliver and Boyd, 1958).

BIBLIOGRAPHY

AITKEN, WILLIAM R.: *Scottish Literature in English and Scots* (Detroit, Mich.: Gale Research, 1982).

BURGESS, MOIRA: *The Glasgow Novel 1870–1970* (Glasgow: Scottish Library Association, 1972).

History

CAMPBELL, R. H.: *Scotland since 1707* (Oxford: Blackwell, 1965).

—— and SKINNER, A. S.: *The Origins and Nature of the Scottish Enlightenment* (Edinburgh: John Donald, 1982).

CHITNIS, ANAND, C.: *The Scottish Enlightenment: A Social History* (London: Croom Helm, 1976).

DAICHES, DAVID: *Scotland and the Union* (London: John Murray, 1977).

DICKINSON, W. C.: *Scotland from the Earliest Times to 1603* (Edinburgh: Edinburgh University Press, 1965).

FERGUSON, WILLIAM: *Scotland 1689 to the Present* (Edinburgh: Oliver and Boyd, 1968).

HARVIE, CHRISTOPHER: *Scotland and Nationalism* (London: Allen and Unwin, 1977).

KERMACK, W. R.: *The Scottish Highlands: A Short History, 1300–1746* (Edinburgh: Johnston and Bacon, 1957).

LENMAN, BRUCE: *An Economic History of Modern Scotland 1660–1976* (London: Batsford, 1977).

RENDALL, JANE: *The Origins of the Scottish Enlightenment* (London: Macmillan, 1978).

SMOUT, T. C.: *A History of the Scottish People 1560–1830* (London: Collins, 1969).

General

AITKEN, A. J. and McARTHUR, T. (eds): *Languages of Scotland* (Edinburgh: Chambers, 1979).

ASH, MARINELL: *The Strange Death of Scottish History* (Edinburgh: Ramsay Head Press, 1980).

CAMERON, DAVID KERR: *The Ballad and the Plough* (London: Gollancz, 1978).

COLLINSON, F. M.: *The Traditional and National Music of Scotland* (London: Routledge and Kegan Paul, 1966).

CRAWFORD, THOMAS: *Society and the Lyric: A Study of the Song Culture of Eighteenth Century Scotland* (Edinburgh: Scottish Academic Press, 1979).

DAVIE, GEORGE ELDER: *The Democratic Intellect* (Edinburgh: Edinburgh University Press, 1964).

DUNBAR, JOHN TELFER: *Highland Costume* (Edinburgh: William Blackwood, 1977).

FYFE, J. G. (ed.): *Scottish Diaries and Memoirs 1550–1746* (Stirling: Eneas Mackay, 1928).

—— *Scottish Diaries and Memoirs 1746–1843* (Stirling: Eneas Mackay, 1942).

GRAHAM, HENRY G.: *The Social Life of Scotland in the Eighteenth Century* (London: A. and C. Black, 1909).

HAY, GEORGE: *Architecture of Scotland* (Northumberland: Oriel Press, 1977).

MACAULAY, DONALD (ed.): *Modern Scottish Gaelic Poems* (Edinburgh: Southside, 1976).

MACNEILL, SEUMAS: *Piobaireachd* (Edinburgh: BBC, 1968).

McNEILL, F. MARIAN: *The Silver Bough*, 4 vols (Glasgow: William Maclellan, 1957–68).

MILLER, KARL (ed.): *Memoirs of a Modern Scotland* (London: Faber and Faber, 1970).

MILLMAN, R. N.: *The Making of the Scottish Landscape* (London: Batsford, 1975).

MUIR, EDWIN: *Scott and Scotland* (Edinburgh: Polygon Books, 1982).

MURISON, DAVID: *The Guid Scots Tongue* (Edinburgh: William Blackwood, 1977).

ROSS, ANNE: *Folklore of the Scottish Highlands* (London: Batsford, 1976).

SCOTTISH GAELIC TEXTS SOCIETY: The works of almost all the older Gaelic poets, usually with translations and helpful introductions, can be found in the publications of this society in Edinburgh.

SHIRE, HELENA M.: *Song, Dance and Poetry at the Court of Scotland under James VI* (Cambridge: Cambridge University Press, 1969).

THOMPSON, HAROLD W.: *A Scottish Man of Feeling: Some Account of Henry MacKenzie Esq. of Edinburgh and of the Golden Age of Burns and Scott* (London: Oxford University Press, 1931).

WATSON, W. J. (ed.): *Bàrdachd Ghàidhlig: Specimens of Gaelic Poetry 1550–1900* (Glasgow: An Comuun Gaidhealach, 1959).

Chronological table

Abbreviations: *d.* = dies; D = drama; P = prose; *r.* = reigned; V = verse

DATE	AUTHOR	EVENT
500		*Scoti* established in Dalriada
c.600	*Gododdin* (V)	Battle between Welsh and Angles at Catterick
1058		Malcolm III Canmore (*r.*1058–93)
1093	*Duan Albanach* (V)	
1124		David I (*r.*1124–53)
1200	Scottish Gaelic bardic poetry well established	
1249	The 'golden age'	Alexander III (*r.*1249–86)
1286		Disputes over Scottish succession
1297		Wallace; Battle of Stirling Bridge The War of Independence (1296–1328)
1305		Wallace executed in London
1306		Bruce kills Comyn; crowned king (*r.*1306–29)
1314		Battle of Bannockburn
1320		Declaration of Arbroath
1374–5	Barbour, *The Bruce* (V)	
1394		James I *r.*1394–1437)
1400		Chaucer *d.*
1406		James I captured by English

DATE	AUTHOR	EVENT
1411	Lachlann MacMhuirich, *Harlaw Brosnachadh* (V)	Battle of Harlaw
1412		University of St Andrews founded
c.1424	James I, *The Kingis Quair* (V)	
1437		James II (*r.*1437–60)
c. 1450	Holland, *Buke of the Howlat* (V)	
1451	Sir Gilbert Hay, *The Buke of Armys* (P)	University of Glasgow founded
1460	Corcadail, 'O rosary that recalled my tear' (V)	James III (*r.*1460–88)
c.1460	Henryson, *The Morall Fabillis* and *Testament of Cresseid* (V)	
1470		Malory, *Morte d'Arthur*
c.1477	Blind Harry, *Wallace* (V)	
1478		Caxton prints *Canterbury Tales*
1488		James IV (*r.*1488–1513)
1495	Dunbar, poems at court	University of Aberdeen founded Erasmus at Oxford W. Indies discovered by Columbus
1509		Henry VIII takes throne of England
1512	Book of the Dean of Lismore (collection of Gaelic verse)	
1513	Gavin Douglas, *Eneados* (V)	Battle of Flodden James V (*r.*1513–42)
1520		Luther, 'On Christian Freedom'; Papal ban
1533	Bellenden translates Boece's *History and Chronicles of Scotland* (1527) into Scots (P)	
1542		Mary Queen of Scots (*r.*1542–87) Copernicus, *De Revolutionibus* (1543)
1549	*The Complaynt of Scotland* (P)	

DATE	AUTHOR	EVENT
1552	Sir David Lindsay, full performance of *The Thrie Estaits* (D)	
1557	George Buchanan, *Jephtha* (Latin D)	
1558		Elizabeth I takes throne of England
1560	Knox *et al.*, *First Book of Discipline*	Reformation Parliament
1567	Wedderburn brothers, *Gude and Godlie Ballatis* (V)	James VI (r. 1567–1625)
1568	Bannatyne Manuscript (V)	
1570		Donald Mor MacCrimmon born; family piping-dynasty established in Skye
c.1575	Robert Lindsay of Pitscottie, *History and Chronicles of Scotland* (P)	
1580s	James VI and 'Castalian band' at court (V) Poems of Alexander Scott	University of Edinburgh founded (1582) Montaigne, *Essais* Shakespeare, *Love's Labours Lost*
1597	Montgomerie, *The Cherry and the Slae* (V)	
1603		UNION OF CROWNS; James VI goes to London
1605		Bacon, *Advancement of Learning* Shakespeare, *King Lear.*
1611		King James Bible Galileo discovers moons of Jupiter
1614	Drummond, *Poems* (V)	
1620		Mayflower sets sail for America
1623	Drummond, *Flowers of Sion* (V) and *A Cypresse Grove* (P)	
1625		Charles I (r. 1625–49)
1637–8		Riot in St Giles'; National Covenant Descartes, *Discourse on Method*
1639		Civil War (1639–49)

DATE	AUTHOR	EVENT
1643		Solemn League and Covenant
1649–51		Charles I executed; Montrose hanged; Commonwealth established
		Charles II crowned at Scone; Scotland subdued under Monck
c. 1650	Robert Sempill, 'Habbie Simson' (V)	
1653	Urquhart translates Rabelais (P)	
1660	Gaelic poetry on Montrose wars and exhortations to Charles, by Iain Lom	Restoration of Charles II (r. 1660–85)
		Royal Society established
1666		Covenanters march on Edinburgh; Battle of Rullion Green
		'The Killing Times'
1667		Milton, *Paradise Lost*
1679		Covenanters defeated at Battle of Bothwell Brig
1685		James VII and II (r. 1685–1701)
1686		Newton, *Principia*
1688		'The Glorious Revolution'; James dethroned
		William and Mary (r. 1689–1702)
1690		William defeats James at Battle of the Boyne
1692		Massacre of Glencoe
1698		Darien scheme
1701	Gaelic poems by Niall MacMhuirich and Morison ('An clàrsair dall')	James II dies; his son the 'Old Pretender' recognised by Louis XIV as heir to British throne
		Queen Anne (r. 1702–14)
1704	Fletcher of Saltoun opposes Union (P)	
1707		UNION OF PARLIAMENTS

DATE	AUTHOR	EVENT
1706–11	Watson (ed.), *Choice Collection* (V)	Pope, *Essay on Criticism* Shaftesbury, *Characteristics of Men, Manners* (1711)
1715		George I (*r.*1714–27) Jacobite rising for Old Pretender
1721	Ramsay, *Poems* (V)	
1722		Bach, *Well-tempered Clavier*
1724	Ramsay (ed.), *Tea Table Miscellany* and *The Ever Green* (V)	Swift, *Drapier's Letters*
1725	Ramsay, *The Gentle Shepherd* (D)	
1727		George II (*r.*1727–60)
1729		Swift, *A Modest Proposal*
1730	James Thomson, *The Seasons* (V)	
1736		Porteous riots in Edinburgh
1739–40	Hume, *Treatise of Human Nature* (P) 'The Scottish Enlightenment'	Richardson, *Pamela* Handel, *Messiah* (1742)
1745		Jacobite rising for Charles Edward Stuart
1746		Battle of Culloden
1748	Hume, *An Enquiry Concerning Human Understanding* (P)	Smollett, *Adventures of Roderick Random* Richardson, *Clarissa*
1751	Gaelic poems of MacMhaighstir Alasdair published in Edinburgh	
1756	Home, *Douglas* (VD)	
1759	Adam Smith, *Theory of Moral Sentiments* (P)	Voltaire, *Candide* Sterne, *Tristram Shandy*
1760s	'Gaelic vernacular revival' Poetry of Rob Donn	

DATE	AUTHOR	EVENT
1760	James Macpherson, *Fragments of Ancient Poetry* ('Ossian') (V)	George III (*r.* 1760–1820)
1761		Rousseau, *Julie, ou la Nouvelle Héloise*
1764–5		Walpole, *Castle of Otranto*
1767–8	Gaelic poems by Duncan Bàn Macintyre and Duguld Buchanan published in Edinburgh Gaelic poems of MacCodrum	Percy's *Reliques*
1770		Watt's steam condenser; Industrial Revolution Rousseau, *Confessions*.
1771	Henry Mackenzie, *The Man of Feeling* (P) *Encyclopaedia Britannica* published in Edinburgh	
1773	Fergusson, *Poems* (V)	Goethe, *Werther* (1774) Priestley discovers oxygen
1766	Adam Smith, *Wealth of Nations* (P)	American War of Independence
1780s	Gaelic poems of Ross	Kant, *Critique of Pure Reason* (1781)
1785	Boswell, *Tour of the Hebrides* (P)	
1786	Burns, *Poems, Chiefly in the Scottish Dialect*, Kilmarnock edn (V)	
1787– 1803	Burns (ed.), *Scots Musical Museum*	Mozart, *Don Giovanni* (1787) Charles Edward Stuart dies (1788)
1789		French Revolution Blake, *Songs of Innocence*
1790		Paine, *Rights of Man*
1791 1798	Boswell, *Life of Johnson* (P)	Wordsworth and Coleridge, *Lyrical Ballads*

DATE	AUTHOR	EVENT
1800		Napoleon in power
		Beethoven, First Symphony
1802	Jeffrey starts *Edinburgh Review*	
	Sir Walter Scott (ed.), *Border Minstrelsy*	
		Battles of Trafalgar and Austerlitz
1805	Scott, *Lay of the Last Minstrel* (V)	
1810	Scott, *The Lady of the Lake* (V)	
1811		Luddite riots
1812		Byron's *Childe Harold*, I and II
		Austen, *Pride and Prejudice*
1813	Hogg, *The Queen's Wake* (V)	
1814	Scott, *Waverley* (P)	
1815		Battle of Waterloo
1816	Scott, *The Antiquary* and *Old Mortality* (P)	Beethoven, Fifth Symphony
1817	*Blackwood's Magazine* founded	Keats, *Poems*
1818	Scott, *The Heart of Midlothian* (P)	
1819	Scott, *Ivanhoe* (P)	'Peterloo Massacre'
		Schopenhauer, *The World as Will and Idea*
1820		George III (*r.*1820–30)
1821	Galt, *The Ayreshire Legatees* and *Annals of the Parish* (P)	Constable, *The Hay Wain*
		Napoleon *d.*
1823	Galt, *Ringan Gilhaize* (P)	
1824	Hogg, *Confessions of a Justified Sinner* (P)	
1830		William IV (*r.*1830–7)
		Stendhal, *Le Rouge et le Noir*
1832		First Reform Bill
1836	Carlyle, *Sartor Resartus* (P)	Dickens, *Pickwick Papers*

DATE	AUTHOR	EVENT
1837	Carlyle, *The French Revolution* (P)	Victoria (*r.* 1837–1901)
1841	Carlyle, *On Heroes and Hero Worship* (P)	Edinburgh–Glasgow railway-line opens (1842)
1843		Disruption of the Church of Scotland: United Free Church formed
1840–60	Gaelic poetry of Livingstone *Whistle-Binkie* antholgies (V) and 'Spasmodics' (D, V) Novels of Mrs Oliphant	'Year of Revolutions' in Europe (1848) Marx–Engels, *Communist Manifesto* (1848) Tennyson, *In Memoriam* 1850) Melville, *Moby Dick* (1851) Crimean War (1854–6) Baudelaire, *Les Fleurs du Mal* (1857) Darwin, *Origin of Species* (1859)
1858	George MacDonald, *Phantastes* (P)	
1870s	Gaelic poetry of John Smith	
1879	Stevenson, *Travels with a Donkey* (P)	Ibsen, *A Doll's House* Tay Bridge disaster
1880–1	James Thomson, *City of Dreadful Night* (V)	Dostoevsky, *The Brothers Karamazov*
1882	Gaelic poetry of Mary Macpherson	The 'battle of Braes' on Skye Highland Land League
1883	Stevenson, *Treasure Island* (P)	
1886	Stevenson, *Dr Jekyll and Mr Hyde* and *Kidnapped* (P)	Daimler Benz motor car Seurat, *La Grande Jatte* English translation of *Das Kapital*
1888	Barrie, *Auld Licht Idylls* (P)	Scottish Labour Party formed with Keir Hardie and Cunninghame Graham
1889	Stevenson, *The Master of Ballantrae* (P) Barrie, *A Window in Thrums* (P)	Yeats, *The Wanderings of Oisin*
1890	MacGonagall, *Poetic Gems*	Forth rail bridge completed
1893	Davidson, *Fleet Street Eclogues* (V)	

DATE	AUTHOR	EVENT
	Crockett, *The Stickit Minister* (P)	
1894	Maclaren, *Beside the Bonnie Briar Bush* (P) Sharp, *Pharais* (P)	The Yellow Book Debussy, *L'Apres-midi d'un faune*
1895	George MacDonald, *Lilith* (P)	Trial of Oscar Wilde
1896	Stevenson, *Weir of Hermiston* (P) Munro, *The Last Pibroch* (P)	
1898	Buchan, *John Burnet of Barns* (P)	
1900	Charles Murray, *Hamewith* (V) Cunninghame Graham, *Thirteen Stories* (P)	Freud, *Interpretation of Dreams* Sibelius, *Finlandia* Chekhov, *Uncle Vania*
1901	George Douglas Brown, *The House with the Green Shutters* (P)	Edward VII (r. 1901–10)
1904	Barrie, *Peter Pan* (D)	Rennie Mackintosh designs Willow Tea Rooms in Glasgow Synge, *Riders to the Sea*
1907	Davidson, *Testament of John Davidson* (V) John MacDougall Hay, *Gillespie* (P)	Picasso, *Les Demoiselles d'Avignon* Bergson, *Creative Evolution*
1910		George V (r. 1910–36) Marsh (ed.), *Georgian Poetry* (1911)
1913	Compton Mackenzie, *Sinister Street* (P)	Stravinsky, *Rite of Spring* Lawrence, *Sons and Lovers*
1914		First World War (1914–18) Yeats, *Responsibilities* Joyce, *Dubliners*
1915	Buchan, *The Thirty-Nine Steps* (P) Norman Douglas, *Old Calabria* (P)	Einstein, General Theory of Relativity

DATE	AUTHOR	EVENT
1916		Easter Rising in Dublin
1917	Norman Douglas, *South Wind* (P)	Russian Revolution Jung, *The Unconscious*
1919		'40 Hour' strike in Glasgow. Troops called out; 'Red Clydeside'
1920	Grieve ('Hugh MacDiarmid') (ed.), *Northern Numbers* (1920–2) David Lindsay, *A Voyage to Arcturus* (P)	Prohibition in America (until 1933)
1922	Grieve (ed.), *Scottish Chapbook*	Eliot, *The Waste Land* Joyce, *Ulysses* Mussolini marches on Rome and forms Fascist government
1923		John Maclean *d.*
1925	MacDiarmid, *Sangschaw* (V) Muir, *First Poems* (V)	
1926	MacDiarmid, *Penny Wheep* and *A Drunk Man Looks at the Thistle* (V) Gunn, *Grey Coast* (P)	General Strike Kafka, *The Castle*
1928		National Party of Scotland formed Women get vote in Britain
1929	Linklater, *White Maas Saga* (P) Grant and Murison, *Scottish National Dictionary* (1929–76)	Trotsky expelled from Russia Wall Street crash Labour government in Britain
1930	Bridie, *The Anatomist* (D)	Gandhi starts civil disobedience in India
1931	Linklater, *Juan in America* (P) MacDiarmid, *First Hymn to Lenin* (V)	Scottish Party formed MacDonald forms National Government to balance budget Riots in Glasgow and London; Naval mutiny at Invergordon
1932	Gibbon, *Sunset Song* (P) MacDiarmid, *Scots Unbound* (V) Muir, *Poor Tom* (P) MacColla, *The Albannach* (P)	Hunger marches in Britain

DATE	AUTHOR	EVENT
1933	Gibbon, *Cloud Howe* (P) Bridie, *A Sleeping Clergyman* (D) MacDiarmid, *Second Hymn to Lenin* (V)	Reichstag fire. Hitler takes power; Jews persecuted in Germany Orwell, *Down and Out in Paris and London*
1934	Gibbon, *Grey Granite* (P) Linklater, *Magnus Merriman* (P) MacDiarmid, *Stony Limits* (V)	Scottish National Party formed
1935	George Blake, *The Shipbuilders* (P) Soutar, *Poems in Scots*	
1936	Muir, *Scott and Scotland* (P) Craigie, Aitken and Stevenson, *Dictionary of the Older Scottish Tongue*	Edward VIII abdicates George VI (r. 1936–52) Spanish Ciivil War (1936–9)
1937	Gunn, *Highland River* (P) Muir, *Journeys and Places* (V) Compton Mackenzie, *The Four Winds of Love* (P) (1937–45) McLellan, *Jamie the Saxt* (D)	Scottish Gaelic Text Society
1939		Second World War (1939–45)
1941	Gunn, *The Silver Darlings* (P)	Battles of El Alamein and Stalingrad Pearl Harbor; America enters war
1943	Sorley Maclean, *Dain do Eimhir* (V) Lindsay (ed.), *Poetry Scotland* (V) (1943–9) MacDiarmid, *Lucky Poet* (P) MacCaig, *A Far Cry* (V)	
1944	Gunn, *The Green Isle of the Great Deep* (P) Bruce, *Sea Talk* (V)	D-Day Normandy landings Construction of atomic bomb Eliot, *Four Quartets*
1946	Linklater, *Private Angelo* (P)	
1948	Goodsir Smith, *Under the Eildon Tree* (V) Henderson, *Elegies for the Dead in Cyrenaica* (V)	Lindsay's *Satire of the Three Estates* performed at second Edinburgh International Festival

DATE	AUTHOR	EVENT
1949	Muir, *The Labyrinth* (V)	Orwell, *1984*
1950		Korean War (1950–3)
		Pound, *Cantos*
1951	Derick Thomson, *An Dealbh Briste* (V)	School of Scottish Studies founded
	Gunn, *The Well at the World's End* (P)	
1953		Coronation of Elizabeth II
		Stalin *d.*
		Beckett, *Waiting for Godot*
1954	Muir, *An Autobiography* (P)	
1955	MacCaig, *Riding Lights* (V)	
	MacDiarmid, *In Memoriam James Joyce* (V)	
	Graham, *The Nightfishing* (V)	
1956	Jenkins, *The Cone Gatherers* (P)	Suez crisis
	Gunn, *Atom of Delight* (P)	Russia invades Hungary
1959	Brown, *Loaves and Fishes* (V)	
	Goodsir Smith, *Figs and Thistles* (V)	
1960	Muir, *Collected Poems* (V)	Oil discovered in North Sea
1961	Crichton Smith, *Thistles and Roses* (V)	Berlin Wall built
	Jenkins, *Dust on the Paw* (P)	Mass CND rally in Trafalgar Square
		Gagarin in space
1962	MacDiarmid, *Collected Poems* (V)	Cuban missile crisis
		Solzhenitsyn, *One Day in the Life of Ivan Denisovich*
1963		Assassination of President Kennedy
1965	Crichton Smith, *Biobull is Sanasan Reice* (V)	
	Sharp, *A Green Tree in Gedde* (P)	
1966	McIlvanney, *Remedy is None* (P)	Rise of SNP popular support
	Garioch, *Selected Poems* (V)	

DATE	AUTHOR	EVENT
1967		Scottish Arts Council established
1968	Morgan, *The Second Life* (V) Crichton Smith, *Consider the Lilies* (P) Williams, *From Scenes Like These* (P)	Oil rigs in North Sea Moves towards Devolution proposed Martin Luther King assassinated
1970	Derick Thomson, *An Rathad Cian* (V) Crichton Smith, *Selected Poems* (V)	
1971	Davie, *Creating a Scene* (P) MacCaig, *Selected Poems* (V) George Mackay Brown, *Fishermen with Ploughs* (V)	

Index

A Mirror for Modern Scholars

A Mirror
for
Modern Scholars

Essays in Methods of Research in Literature

Edited by

LESTER A. BEAURLINE

UNIVERSITY OF VIRGINIA

The Odyssey Press, Inc., New York

CARL A. RUDISILL LIBRARY
LENOIR RHYNE COLLEGE

801.95
B38m

56722
Jan. 1967

© COPYRIGHT 1966

THE ODYSSEY PRESS, INC.

ALL RIGHTS RESERVED

Printed in the United States

Library of Congress Catalog Card Number 65-26779

A 0 9 8 7 6 5 4 3 2 1

ACKNOWLEDGMENTS

Don Cameron Allen, STYLE AND CERTITUDE, reprinted from *ELH: A Journal of English Literary History*, XV (1948), 167–175, by permission of The Johns Hopkins Press.

William Arrowsmith, A GREEK THEATRE OF IDEAS, reprinted from *Ideas in the Drama: Selected Papers from the English Institute*, ed. John Gassner, pp. 1–41, copyright © 1964, Columbia University Press, by permission.

Donald C. Baker, THE DATE OF *MANKIND*, reprinted from *Philological Quarterly*, XLII (1963), 90–91, by permission of the State University of Iowa and the author.

R. C. Bald, EVIDENCE AND INFERENCE IN BIBLIOGRAPHY, reprinted from *English Institute Annual, 1941*, pp. 159–183, copyright 1942, Columbia University Press, New York, by permission.

G. E. Bentley, Jr., THE DATE OF BLAKE'S *VALA* OR *THE FOUR ZOAS*, reprinted from *Modern Language Notes*, LXXI (1956), 487–491, by permission of The Johns Hopkins Press.

Morton W. Bloomfield, SYMBOLISM IN MEDIEVAL LITERATURE, reprinted from *Modern Philology*, LVI (1958), 73–81, by permission of The University of Chicago Press, copyright 1958 by The University of Chicago Press.

Wayne C. Booth, CONTROL OF DISTANCE IN JANE AUSTIN'S *EMMA*, reprinted from *The Rhetoric of Fiction* by Wayne C. Booth by permission of The University of Chicago Press, © 1961, The University of Chicago Press.

Fredson Bowers, SOME RELATIONS OF BIBLIOGRAPHY TO EDITOR-IAL PROBLEMS, reprinted from *Studies in Bibliography*, III (1950–51), 37–62, by permission of the author.

James B. Colvert, THE ORIGINS OF STEPHEN CRANE'S LITERARY CREED, reprinted from *The University of Texas Studies in English*, XXXIV (1955), 179–188, by permission of the University of Texas Press and the author.

R. S. Crane, THE HOUYHNHNMS, THE YAHOOS, AND THE HISTORY OF IDEAS, reprinted from *Reason and the Imagination: Studies in the History of Ideas, 1600-1800*, ed. J. A. Mazzeo, pp. 231–253, copyright © 1962, Columbia University Press, by permission.

Leon Edel, PSYCHOANALYSIS [and Literary Biography], reprinted from *Literary Biography* by permission of the author, copyright © 1959 by Leon Edel.

Richard Ellmann, THE BACKGROUNDS OF 'THE DEAD,' from *James Joyce* by Richard Ellmann, copyright © 1959 by Richard Ellmann, reprinted with permission from the Oxford University Press, Inc.

W. W. Greg, THE RATIONALE OF COPY-TEXT, reprinted from *Studies in Bibliography*, III (1950–51), 19–36, by permission of Lady Greg.

Bruce Harkness, BIBLIOGRAPHY AND THE NOVELISTIC FALLACY, reprinted from *Studies in Bibliography*, XII (1959), 59–73, by permission of the author.

Harrison Hayford, MELVILLE'S FREUDIAN SLIP, reprinted from *American Literature*, XXX (1958), 366–368, by permission of the Duke University Press.

Graham Hough, GEORGE MOORE AND THE NINETIES, reprinted from *Edwardians and Late Victorians: English Institute Essays, 1959*, ed. Richard Ellmann, pp. 1–27, copyright © 1960, Columbia University Press, by permission.

Frank Kermode, 'DISSOCIATION OF SENSIBILITY': MODERN SYMBOLIST READINGS OF LITERARY HISTORY, reprinted from *The Romantic Image*, copyright 1957 by the Chilmark Press, by permission.

F. O. Matthiessen, METHOD AND SCOPE [of *American Renaissance*], from *American Renaissance* by F. O. Matthiessen, copyright 1941 by Oxford University Press, Inc., reprinted by permission.

R. B. McKerrow, FORM AND MATTER IN THE PUBLICATION OF RESEARCH, reprinted from *Review of English Studies*, XVI (1940), 116–121, by permission of The Clarendon Press, Oxford.

S. Schoenbaum, INTERNAL EVIDENCE AND THE ATTRIBUTION OF ELIZABETHAN PLAYS, reprinted from the *Bulletin of the New York Public Library*, LXV (1961), 102–124, by permission.

A. J. Smith, THE METAPHYSIC OF LOVE, reprinted from *Review of English Studies*, n. s. IX (1958), 362–375, by permission of The Clarendon Press, Oxford.

Hallett Smith, PASTORAL POETRY: THE VITALITY AND VERSA-
TILITY OF A CONVENTION, reprinted by permission of the publishers from Hallett Smith, *Elizabethan Poetry,* Cambridge, Mass.: Harvard University Press, copyright, 1952, by the President and Fellows
of Harvard College.

Ernest Tuveson, THE IMPORTANCE OF SHAFTESBURY, reprinted from
ELH: A Journal of English Literary History, XX (1963), 267–299, by
permission of The Johns Hopkins Press.

F. P. Wilson, SHAKESPEARE AND THE DICTION OF COMMON LIFE,
reprinted from *Proceedings of the British Academy,* XXVII (1941), 167–
197, by permission of The British Academy.

Preface

"The scholar is the guardian of memories . . . The choice is *not* between knowledge of the past and the concern for the future; if it were that it would be a hard choice. It is between the search for truth and the acceptance of falsehood. For every community insists on . . . 'the Story that must be told' about its own past, and where scholarship decays myth will crowd in."[1] An art historian, E. H. Gombrich, made these remarks, but they are just as appropriate to literary studies. Each of the following essays attempts to show that the truth really matters. Literary interpretation is not just the endeavour of a generation to read its own preoccupations into the documents of the past. When scholarship is at its worst, we create new myths out of our memories; when it is at its best, we recover a part of the lost or forgotten.

There is a factual substratum beneath every poem or play, a substratum about which assertions can be made, and the assertions are open to investigation of their truth or falsity. Karl Popper suggested that the difference between knowledge and pseudo-knowledge lies in the possibility of refutation—if a theory may possibly be disproved, it may also be verifiable; but a theory that seems to explain everything, such as Freudian pyschology or Marxian historicism, can never be refuted: it is a faith, a pseudo-science.[2] So, in literary study, we might ask what interpretations are more or less verifiable, and what theories such as the nearly universal appeal to irony or symbolism may never be refuted because they are permanently insulated from attack, perfectly self-fulfilling. Most scholars' assertions try to go back to the facts, the primary sources, and most of their assertions are in the form of narrative propositions concerning causes, influences, sources, or corruptions of a work or a tradition, and most of them lead to a scholar's

[1] E. H. Gombrich, *Meditations on a Hobby Horse* (London, 1963), p. 107.
[2] K. R. Popper, *Conjectures and Refutations* (New York, 1962), pp. 33-37.

attempt at reconstruction. He assumes that a work was written by an author with certain determinate purposes, within certain literary conventions, for a certain audience. And although he may never know the full truth, he tries to recover as much as he can.

The selections here do not attempt to represent various periods or genres but to show the methods or problems that scholars must consider. Thus it is no accident that many of these have been read before the English Institute, an organization that takes a special interest in method. Most of the essays address a particular problem, but often they enunciate general principles along the way. Most of these pieces have never been reprinted, and, so far as I know, are not available in a form suitable for a text in advanced literature courses.

A word about the obvious imbalance in the choice of essays. If a clear distinction between scholarship and criticism ever existed, recent writers have blurred and nearly obliterated it, much to the benefit of all concerned. Consequently it has seemed neither desirable nor possible to choose only examples of "pure scholarship" (a species about as rare as "pure poetry"). According to the cliché, criticism depends upon sound scholarship, but we have come to see that good scholarship presupposes good criticism. The articles in sections VI-X illustrate this truth clearly enough. I have nevertheless put emphasis on the factual side of the study of English and American literature, and I was especially generous in the inclusion of elementary problems. Writings of this kind are usually buried in learned journals, an awkward place to inter a large class of students. The standard books on method are old; even R. B. McKerrow's *Introduction to Bibliography* is outdated. Various fields have changed radically since the 1920's, and since most students of literature at one time or another try to edit a text, identify an author, or claim a literary source, and since they all must evaluate the performance of writers who pretend to do these things, they should study some precepts and examples. When, as in sections IV-X, the articles are more reticent concerning theory, I have tried to include contrasting pairs that will provoke thought about their methods, but when pairing was not possible, I settled for two good examples. Several essays could just as easily have fitted in some other section of the book because they illustrate two or three problems, but I was satisfied to place them where they seemed most significant. A special effort was made to secure readable prose, clear exposition, and apt use of detail, so that students may see how some of the best writers present their arguments. All the articles are complete except for the exclusion of the last half of Hallett Smith's chapter on pastoral poetry.

Styles of footnotes remain the same as in their original publications, since it is useful to see the various conventions; footnotes appear at the end of each article.

I am grateful to my students in English 297 at the University of Virginia, whose reactions to many of these essays helped me decide upon their worth, and to my colleagues who suggested several of the pieces to be included. I thank each of the distinguished authors for their kind permission to print their work.

L. A. B.

Charlottesville, 1965

Contents

xiv   *Contents*

VI STYLE

VII HISTORICAL PERIODS

VIII HISTORY OF IDEAS

IX HISTORICAL INTERPRETATION

X FORM AND CONVENTION

APPENDIX

A Mirror for Modern Scholars

Evidence and Inference in Bibliography

R. C. Bald

An important branch of the law, especially for the courtroom lawyer, is the law of evidence. Legislators and judges have decided that evidence must be presented to the courts in strict accordance with certain principles which they have laid down and that there are certain types of evidence which they will refuse to accept. Hearsay evidence is rejected, not because it is necessarily untrue, but because it is unreliable; the chances against its being accurate are too great for the courts to allow it to influence their decisions. Again, there are certain crimes for which a man cannot be condemned by the unsupported evidence of one person alone, and the definition of what constitutes corroboration has been worked out by lawyers with extraordinary care and thoroughness.

I have no doubt that many readers of so-called scholarly papers have often wished that a body of law of evidence had been drawn up for scholarship. However, I have no intention of advocating any such course of action. Hearsay is inadmissible in the courtroom, but it may be invaluable to the criminal investigator and may put him on a line of investigation that will produce evidence that can be presented in court. But the legal analogy can be pressed no further, for if there is insufficient evidence of the right kind, the case for the prosecution will lapse. Scholarship, on the other hand, refuses to be thus circumscribed. Scholars are curious people who will not let a problem rest; if a murder has been committed, and there is not enough evidence to send

1

anyone to the gallows, they still preserve the right to speculate on the identity of the murderer.

Yet there is no doubt that scholarship should examine its procedures and question the bases for its conclusions more frequently than it does. My own complacence was rudely jolted some time ago by a classroom incident which I shall relate even at the risk of exposing myself as a teacher. I had asked an unusually good and experienced graduate student to prepare a paper on a minor seventeenth-century figure. He was to make the best use of all the material he could find in our library, though that, as I well knew, was scanty, for I had spent some time in London trying to see what I could add to it. In due course we met in class; he read his paper, and then I went over the ground again to show what fresh light new facts could throw on the old material. My victim's paper was good—and exceedingly plausible—but practically every time he attempted to interpret the facts he had collected or to fill in a gap with a reasonable conjecture he was wrong; I was able to produce facts unknown to him which disproved his interpretations. Yet I felt sure that almost any learned journal would have printed his paper; its conjectures and conclusions would have been generally accepted, and it would unquestionably have been regarded as the most authoritative treatment of the subject. If this were so, it was inevitable that I should feel that the limitations of this particular paper, of which I was aware, should be shared by dozens of others, of whose limitations I was unaware.

It has sometimes been stated, and by the highest authorities, that bibliography is a study not subject to such shortcomings. "Such discoveries as we may make are real discoveries, not mere matters of opinion, provable things that no amount of after-investigation can shake," says McKerrow at the end of the first chapter of his *Introduction to Bibliography*, and Greg, in that genuinely epoch-making address of his in 1912, entitled "What Is Bibliography?"[1], claims for the study the rank of a science. "Critical bibliography is the *science* of the material transmission of literary texts," he asserts, and one of its aims is "the construction of a *calculus* for the determination of textual problems."[2] "Science" is a word with a variety of meanings, more or less precise, but Greg is one who habitually uses words with precision, and the appearance of "calculus" in his next sentence removes any doubt that he is using it loosely or that he would at that time have refused to endorse McKerrow's statement.

Yet, whatever bibliography may or may not be, it is not an exact science, if one understands by an "exact" science a branch of study which arrives at its conclusions through experiment and observation and can reproduce the conditions of an experiment so that the results can be repeated and checked at any time. The making of books is a human activity, and the human factor is the incalculable with which we must always reckon. We might conceivably be able to reproduce a seventeenth-century printing house down to the last detail. But we could not reproduce its probably unwritten "Manual of Style," much less a harassed author, a testy master printer, a stupid proofreader, a love-sick compositor, a drunken pressman, or a newly-articled apprentice—all in the states of mind which affected their relations to a book on, let us say, the first of April, 1625.

Bibliography, therefore, cannot claim for its conclusions the same universal validity as belongs to those of the exact sciences. If it could, then some of its rules, such as McKerrow's rules for determining the order of editions, would have the same force as scientific laws.[3] One of those rules, you will remember, is that an edition of a given book "in which the signatures are all of one alphabet, beginning with A and proceeding regularly, is likely to be later than an edition in which the preliminary leaves have a separate signature."[4] Yet the collation of the first edition of Sir William Berkeley's play *The Lost Lady*, a small folio in 2's, is A-O², with the title-page on [A]1 and the beginning of the text on A2; in the second edition, on the other hand, the text beings on B1 and is preceded by the title page on a single unsigned leaf. What happened can be explained easily enough. The first edition was published without the author's consent, and the printer knew when he started printing that there would be no preliminaries after the title page. Then the author interposed, and a corrected edition was published with his authorization; in setting to work the printer decided he ought to allow for preliminaries, although none were actually forthcoming.[5] This example shows, as McKerrow realized when he formulated it in the terms he did, that the rule cannot be expected to hold for every case.

It is clear, then, that if bibliography is the study of "the material transmission of literary texts," it is concerned both with the material objects by which they are transmitted—printers' tools as well as books and their components—and with the human activities which transmit them. This is obvious, because the material objects could not have existed without the relevant human activities, which must accordingly be regarded as basic. Now the studies which deal with the various types of organized human activities *per se* are the group loosely known as "history and the social sciences," and it is to them that bibliography belongs. As Greg himself has stated, in a later address than that which has already been quoted from, "Bibliography is an historical study, or perhaps I should rather say a method of historical investigation."[6]

Without embarking on any profitless arguments as to how far the social sciences are sciences and whether history is a science or an art, we can all agree, I fancy, that the procedures of these studies cannot be identical with those of the exact sciences. Writers on historical methodology have made a distinction, which indicates how their study differs from the exact sciences, between two classes of sources, namely, between remains, or "monuments," as they rather clumsily call them, and documents. The distinction is between material objects, used for instance as indexes of culture or civilization, on the one hand, and written records on the other. The latter, they aver, are subject to all the defects of human inaccuracy—of which imperfections of observation or recollection are the least—in a way that the first class is not. A similar tendency can be observed in criminal jurisprudence to prefer the concrete evidence (fingerprints, the rifling on a bullet, and such like) to the inevitable conflicts and inaccuracies of oral testimony. Bibliography is concerned with the interpretation of material "remains," or books, and this is why Greg referred to it as "a method of historical investigation," but in its task of interpretation it cannot base its conclusions solely on books as material objects—it will make use of any other relevant evidence as well. For this reason the determination of printing-house practice in the sixteenth and seventeenth centuries is a historical enquiry and will be conducted according to the recognized principles of historical investigation.

I do not deny that bibliography, owing to the richness of its "remains," can often achieve a far greater measure of certainty than many other branches of study. We can prove beyond any reasonable doubt that certain Shakespearian quartos dated 1600 and 1608 were actually printed in 1619 and that there was an interruption in the printing of the First Folio. The evidence for these statements is stronger than that for many a "fact" in the history books.

I should not deny, either, that bibliography offers opportunities for thinking and reasoning of a kind that have distinguished much of the best scientific work, though I should hesitate to affirm that such thinking and reasoning are exclusively scientific. One of the most illuminating bibliographical papers ever written is McKerrow's article on "The Elizabethan Printer and Dramatic Manuscripts."[7] It is a paper which can legitimately be compared to the one in which Darwin first formulated the theory of evolution, even though it is admittedly not of equal importance in the history of human thought. Both were the fruit of long and patient observation; both reveal a remarkable capacity for sound generalization; both achieve hypotheses of far-reaching scope. Above all, both have that touch of greatness which expresses itself by asking a question about something which had always seemed a commonplace; as Whitehead says, "It requires a very unusual mind to undertake the analysis of the obvious." McKerrow pointed out that Elizabethan dramatic texts as a class are far worse than any other class of texts in the period. We had all known in a vague way that dramatic quartos, especially Shakespeare's, contained an unusual number of obscurities and cruxes, to say nothing of lesser errors, but no one had demonstrated the fact before so clearly or attached any special significance to it. McKerrow then went on to argue that the printer's copy for plays must have been much worse than for other kinds of printed matter. But the manuscripts used in the theaters were, and had to be, both reasonably correct and legible. Therefore, except when we can show, as we sometimes can, that the prompt copy came into the printer's hands, it is likely that he usually set up his text from the only other manuscript available—the author's "foul papers." A brilliant and illuminating hypothesis, and the more likely to win acceptance from its simplicity! Yet alongside a scientific hypothesis it has one grave disadvantage: it cannot be proved. Einstein's theory inaugurated series after series of experiments, and for years sent expeditions to remote parts of the world to observe each fresh eclipse. But how can confirmation of McKerrow's theory be secured? Scholarship can investigate the premises, but cannot finally test the conclusion. The past is an experiment that cannot be repeated.

Another weakness of bibliography, from the point of view of the exact sciences, is the use which it has to make of analogy. Argument from analogy is not necessarily unscientific, but some of the so-called social sciences rely on it to such a degree as to make a chemist or physicist doubt their right to be called sciences at all. Anthropology, for instance, is founded almost entirely on the assumption that human behavior under certain circumstances at one time and place is related to somewhat similar behavior under altered circumstances at other times and places. Such an assumption is not unknown in bibliography, but fortunately its use is not so extensive.

"An argument from analogy," it has been said, "is an argument basd upon *untested* resemblances,"[8] but, as we have already emphasized, the past cannot be reproduced for testing. Thus our analogies can never be complete; all we can maintain is that their strength depends upon their closeness, and that the nearer similarity approaches identity, the nearer are the conditions of scientific experiment approximated. In his monograph on the printing of the Shakespeare First Folio Dr. E. E. Willoughby found it necessary to estimate the rate at which the type was composed. Suppose that such things as compositors' time sheets for work in Jaggard's shop on books other than the Folio were extant for 1621 and 1622; they would furnish as close an analogy as anyone could hope to find. Actually, Dr. Willoughby had to rely for his estimate on two sorts of evidence: the amount of type a present-day compositor is expected to be able to set by hand, and a number of statements definitely mentioning the rates at which certain seventeenth-century books were set up.[9] Anyone will feel that the second analogy is stronger, or closer, than the first. It is valuable as a check to know what a modern compositor can do, so that there will be no danger of crediting the seventeenth-century compositor with physical impossibilities; but it is more convincing to know what seventeenth-century compositors actually performed under the conditions in which they worked. In this particular case the two analogies led to virtually the same conclusions; nonetheless the distinction between them is not to be ignored.

One of the drawbacks of arguing by analogy is that the validity of the analogy may be challenged. Suppose, for instance, that it is essential to a hypothesis to show that seventeenth-century compositors were accustomed at the end of a day's work to distribute the formes that had been in the press during the day; and suppose, further, that the only available evidence is a passage in Benjamin Franklin's *Autobiography:*

> Breintnal particularly procured us from the Quakers the printing of forty sheets of their history, the rest being done by Keimer, and upon these we worked exceedingly hard, for the price was low. It was a folio, *pro patria* size, in pica, with long primer notes. I composed a sheet a day and Meredith worked it off at press. It was often eleven at night, and sometimes later, before I had finished my distribution for the next day's work; for the little jobs sent in by our other friends now and then put us back. But so determined I was to continue doing a sheet a day of the folio that one night, when having imposed my formes I thought my day's work over, one of them by accident was broken and two pages reduced to *pi.* I immediately distributed and completed it over again before I went to bed; and this industry, visible to our neighbors, began to give us character and credit. [10]

The bibliographer who relied on this anecdote might try to strengthen it as evidence by pointing out that: (1) this incident occurred fairly early in the eighteenth century, namely, in 1728; (2) Franklin had received part of his training in one of the best London printing houses; (3) most of the practices in force there would almost certainly go back to the seventeenth century; and (4) Franklin was a methodical man who would unquestionably have been industrious in following the best practices of his trade. An opponent, however, might well counter such arguments by asserting that (1) Franklin was a methodical man to the extent of being able to improve on the London trade practices if they were capable of improvement; (2) at the time of the incident Franklin by his own admission was working under pressure, and trying to give proof of his industry, so he is not describing normal practice; and (3) to suppose that there would be a regular amount of type ready for distribution every evening is to take no account of accidents (such as the one Franklin describes), human frailties, and the varying sizes of editions.

Such argumentation, I fear, is to be found in almost every scholarly journal, and the extent to which it is beside the point in our hypothetical case is shown by the relevant passage from Moxon:

> The *Compositor*, if conveniences suit, chuses to *Destribute* his *Letter* over Night, that he may have a *dry Case* (as he calls it) to work at in the Morning, because Wet *Letters* are not so ready and pleasant to pick up as Dry; and besides are apt to make the Fingers sore, especially if the *Ly* be not so well *Rinc'd* from the *Letter* as it should be.[11]

After reading Moxon the iconoclast would probably press for a law of evidence to exclude from scholarship anything resembling the previous discussion. But unhappily there is not always a Moxon to fall back on; gaps in historical evidence are inevitable. To fill them the scholar may be driven to all sorts of shifts: he will be forced to extract the last drop of implication from the merest hint or to press a conjecture to extremes. An unfounded assumption or a rough working hypothesis is probably necessary at some stage of every investigation, but it must be judged by the results it can produce, that is, by the extent to which it actually works. And if it seems capable of opening up new possibilities of knowledge it will need to be tested before progress can be assured.

An example of what I have in mind is to be found in Greg's study of *The Variants in the First Quarto of "King Lear."* In that quarto, it will be remembered, an exceptional number of variants has been found, and Greg has made a minute examination of the twelve surviving copies. Twelve out of any number between five and fifteen hundred is a very small proportion, and the problem first to be settled is whether any generalizations can be hazarded from these copies, even though they are liable to differ from one another in the number of corrected and uncorrected sheets they contain. Greg decides that certain propositions are significant: (1) At least 50 percent of the pulls from formes in which variants occur were from the corrected forme. (2) Though it cannot be assumed when a sheet is found in only one state that no other state ever existed, it can be assumed that the corrected, not the uncorrected, state has survived. (3) Variants usually appear on only one side, not on both sides, of a sheet. These are largely *a priori* assumptions, based in part on mathematical probabilities and confirmed by the existing copies of the First Quarto of *Lear,* but they are extraordinarily fruitful and enable Greg, with the aid of the variants themselves, to work out more thoroughly than anyone has done previously the way in which proofs were corrected and revised in an early seventeenth-century printing house. In other words, the assumptions work. Greg's *a priori* case is essentially reasonable, and, as I have said, it is supported by the twelve copies of the Quarto. But twelve out of even five hundred is a distressingly small number on which to lean for support; and, well—we all know what erratic things bridge hands can sometimes be.

Anyone who has read this part of Greg's study will admire the brilliance and cogency of his reasoning, but will, I think, also wish to find some way of checking his assumptions. Of *Lear* itself there is not much left to be said; but would it not be possible to fall back on analogy and to study variants over a much larger number of copies in order to obtain results that might have something approaching experimental validity? Of course, it is quite unlikely that the complete edition of any Elizabethan book has survived, and even if it had there would still be the fantastic task of finding all the copies. Yet if only a quarter of the edition had survived and the copies could be located, some survey of the variants would be of real value. The only book of the period of which such a proportion of copies could be located is unquestionably the Shakespeare First Folio. I am not suggesting that someone should spend his whole life collating the two-hundred-odd known copies—Heaven forbid!—but at most that a few sheets in which variants are known to occur should be concentrated upon. Professor R. M. Smith might undertake the task in connection with his revised census of Folios. Even a review on such lines of the 79 Folger copies might well be profitable.

But to return to the main argument. Conjecture and assumption obviously have their place in building a hypothesis, and it would be foolish to plead for their suppression in scholarship. I do, however, plead for a clearer recognition in each instance of the foundations on which such speculations and assumptions rest, and to that end I propose to present for rigorous examination some bibliographical speculations.

Once again the First Quarto of *King Lear* will furnish a convenient point of departure. In his Introduction to the facsimile of the Folio text of the play Dover Wilson drew attention to an interesting feature of the Quarto:

> while one third of the play is printed in lines 3¼ inches broad, with words tucked in, above, below the end of the line whenever they would otherwise cause it to exceed this breadth; the rest of the play runs between 3¾ inch limits and pays no attention to the narrower restrictions. In other words, the printer of the Q must originally have assumed that the whole copy was in verse (which would naturally fall into a 3¼ inch setting), and only later have discovered his mistake. What this betokens I have no notion, never having had occasion to examine the Q closely; but assuredly it has some bearing upon the provenance and character of the copy used in 1608.

This is inaccurate, because, though it does not state it in so many words, it gives the impression that the 3¼-inch line was used for the first third of the play and the longer line for the rest of it; whereas the play actually begins with the longer line, and the two of them alternate all the way through for passages of varying length. This is not as important at the moment, however, as the attitude of the investigator, who produces a clue with a great flourish and then blandly tells us he has no idea what it means.

The significance of the clue was indicated, not by Dover Wilson, but by Greg, in an article entitled "*King Lear*—Mislineation and Stenography,"[12] in which he politely remarked:

> The other cause of mislining . . . is more complicated and has puzzled some careful observers a good deal. It is found only in quartos, and is particularly common in *Lear*. . . . This is the use of two distinct measures (i. e. line-lengths); the wider being usually reserved for prose, and another narrower one for verse. That the composi-

tor actually used two composing-sticks of different lengths is clear from the fact that he frequently turned over long lines of verse although there was plenty of room to print them out in the width of the page. . . . The compositor, when he came to a passage of verse in a play, sometimes took a shorter stick, thus producing a column of type narrower than the full measure of the page, and made up the difference in the galley with furniture.[13] Moreover, it is not always whole pages that are in wider or narrower measure: the width of the column of type sometimes alters within the page.

This is final as far as it goes. Greg here shows that there is a bibliographical cause for mislineation in quartos; and he goes on to show that there is another bibliographical cause for mislineation in folios, when it occurs at the beginning of speeches. This part of the article is incontrovertible, but at the risk of seeming to digress I wish to demur against an assumption underlying the rest of it. Greg is engaged in replying to a paper in which it had been suggested that much of the mislineation in the Quarto was due, not to shorthand reporting, but to the compositor's attempts to save space. He shows that this is not an entirely satisfactory explanation, and suggests that the mislining arose from the attempts of "two or more compositors of different ability making what they could of copy that presented no metrical division at all." In other words, both Greg and his opponent assume that the compositor was not following his copy—was, in fact, departing from it fairly extensively. Such studies as have been made—and there is plenty of material extant for a thorough investigation of the topic—scarcely suggest that compositors were liable to modify their copy to this extent. A great deal of the most fruitful textual and bibliographical research of the last twenty years rests on the assumption that compositors *did* follow copy, and the assumption has abundantly justified itself. To depart from it now would merely reinstate the old belief that Shakespeare's texts had, as Dr. Johnson put it, "suffered depravation from the ignorance and negligence of the printers."

To return to *Lear*. Greg's explanation of the reason for the two lengths of line still leaves room for the discussion of two relevant topics. In the first place, can we, knowing the reason for the use of the two measures, make any inference, as Dover Wilson hoped, about the nature and source of the copy for the Quarto? Very little, I fear; merely, perhaps, that the compositor used the shorter length when he thought he had a longish stretch of verse ahead of him, and the longer one when there was a fair admixture of prose to be expected. Conceivably one might suggest that the use of the two lengths argues that the compositor was more than usually interested in distinguishing verse and prose and that therefore his treatment of the two throughout the play reflects pretty accurately his impressions of his copy. But even this would be speculative. Argue if you will that it is a compositor's business to follow his copy and that confusion occurs in the printed text because it occurred in copy too, but do not argue that he had special reasons for following his copy more closely than usual.

Secondly, if careful measurements are made throughout the Quarto of the lengths of the two measures it will be found that each varies to the extent of about three millimeters. This fact might suggest that more than one composing stick of each length had been used and therefore that more than one compositor was at work on the book. Greg, it will be recalled, allowed for this possibility, though he made no attempt to prove it. But an attempt to prove by such means that there was more than one compositor involves two assumptions: first, that composing sticks would be likely to vary in this way and, second, that a different composing stick means a different compositor, or, in other words, that each workman had his own tools.

As to the first, there is some uncertainty as to the exact form of composing stick in use in 1608, but we know from Moxon that in 1683 composing sticks were still made individually by hand,[14] so that minor variations in size would be almost bound to occur. The second is also no difficulty. It is unnecessary to argue that in many trades down to the present day the workman is expected to supply his tools; Moxon specifically states that journeyman compositors had to provide their own composing sticks.[15]

As far as the assumptions are concerned the hypothesis that there was more than one compositor is still a possible one, but alternative hypotheses will doubtless have already occurred to the reader. The variations may be due to the fact that the type worked loose during printing, and on one or two pages this has probably happened, though I doubt if it would have been likely to affect more than one or two pages. They may also be due, as a printer has suggested to me, to deliberate action on the part of a compositor if he happened to find it easier on certain pages to justify the lines by lengthening them by an en or even by a mere hairspace. The variations may also be due to the shrinkage of the paper during drying. Actually, the last is the most probable explanation of the majority of the variations in the *Lear* quarto, since vertical, as well as horizontal, measurements reveal proportionate variations.

I should like to point out, however, that theoretically shrinkage and one of the other explanations are not mutually exclusive. The principle of the forme-unit should be operative here, too. If the variations occurred within the same forme, where one would be justified in presuming fairly uniform conditions of damping and drying, it would seem necessary to have recourse to one of the other explanations as well.

It is unlikely that much progress could be made with an investigation along the lines we have just been considering; there are too many possibilities, and they are too difficult to isolate.[16] On the other hand, in speaking a moment ago about the shrinkage of paper a presumption about damping and drying was made, and it is interesting to find that there is apparently some uncertainty as to the early printers' practice in these matters. "The drying of the sheets," says McKerrow, *"between the printing of the first and second side,* and after the second, was done by hanging them on strings or wooden battens across the room."[17] But this by no means tallies with Moxon's account. Moxon first describes how the paper was dampened and continues:

> having Wet his first *Token* [or half-ream] he doubles down a great corner of the upper sheet of it . . . This Sheet is called the *Token-Sheet,* as being a mark for the *Pressman* when he is at Work to know how many *Tokens* of the *Heap* is *Wrought-off.*[18]

Then, describing the pressman at work, he tells in detail how he takes a sheet from the top of the heap, puts it on the tympan, makes the pull, and removes it from the press

> and so successively every Sheet till the whole *Heap* of *White-paper* be *Wrought off.*
>
> As he comes to a *Token-sheet* , he un-doubles that, and smoothes out the Crease . . . that the *Face* of the *Letter* may Print upon smooth Paper. And being Printed off, he folds it again, as before, for a *Token-sheet* when he works the Reiteration.
>
> Having *Wrought off* the *White-paper,* he turns the *Heap.* . . .
>
> Having now turned the *Heap,* and made *Register* on the *Reteration Form* . . . he Works off the *Reteration.* . . . Only, the *Token-sheets,* as he meets with them, he Folds not down again, as he did the *White Paper.*[19]

McKerrow, then, asserts that as the first side was being printed the damp and freshly-inked sheets were taken off to dry; that they were damped again before being perfected and dried again before folding. Moxon plainly states that the pressman made a pile of the damp and freshly-inked sheets as they came off the press, turned the heap upside down, and, as soon as the new forme was in the bed of the press, proceeded to perfect. In face of this conflict of authority further information seemed necessary, so I consulted *The Printer's Grammar*, by C. Stower, Printer (London, 1808); *Typographia; or, The Printer's Instructor*, by J. Johnson, Printer (London, 1824); *Typographia; or, The Printer's Instructor; second edition with numerous emendations and additions*, by Thomas F. Adams, Typographer (Philadelphia, 1844); and *The American Printer: a Manual of Typography*, by Thomas Mackeller (Philadelphia, 1867). I found with ever-growing surprise that one and all they repeated Moxon's words verbatim. By then the resources of our library were exhausted, but I was still unsatisfied, although I could not help feeling that these good gentlemen, who boasted of their credentials on their title pages, would not have carried their plagiarism so far as to incorporate uncorrected all Moxon's errors. There was only one thing left to do—ask a present-day printer; and I was fortunate enough to find one who had had experience of printing on dampened paper. I put the problem to him and asked him who was right; he laughed and said "Both," but went on to explain, "It depends on the quality of the ink." A cheap ink, he said, dries quickly and will not offset unless under heavy pressure; the very best inks take a long time to dry, and offset easily. McKerrow must have had in mind the practice of printing houses such as the Kelmscott Press, and probably some of the famous fifteenth-century presses. Moxon, however, complains that the usual quality of English ink was bad and describes how much better it was made in Holland in his day.[20] But even the seventeenth-century Dutch methods of manufacturing ink arouse the contempt of De Vinne in his reprint of Moxon,[21] so we can take it that English ink throughout the seventeenth century was far from good, as anyone familiar with the cheaply printed quartos of the period will not hesitate to admit. Ink of better quality was doubtless used sometimes for other classes of books, but very rarely, I should say, in those that are of most interest to the student of literature. Hence we need have no hesitation in accepting Moxon in preference to McKerrow if we wish to know the normal practice of seventeenth-century English printing houses.

Now, if this practice can be regarded as established, one consequence follows: sheets were perfected in exactly the same order as that in which the first side had been printed. This fact is of some importance, for instance, in relation to variants in the forme, and Greg is forced to presume it in a general way on *a priori* grounds, even though he accepts McKerrow's account instead of Moxon's. It also strengthens considerably his contention that when one variant forme appears, the other must, except under abnormal circumstances, be invariant; since if this were not so we should expect to find two uncorrected states or two corrected states appearing together on the same sheet in a large majority of copies.[22]

Earlier in this paper I animadverted on an indiscretion of Professor Dover Wilson in printing what he might better have kept to himself, so I hope no one will make the mistake of supposing that the foregoing discussions are examples of the sort of thing I consider should adorn the pages of our learned journals. Far from it; they are meant as an attempt to bring into the light some of the processes that, fortunately, are generally concealed from the public view—to illustrate, in other words, the processes of testing and elimination that must go on behind the scenes rather than to emphasize the one positive conclusion eventually reached. Perhaps this paper should have been entitled "Some Suggestions towards a Methodology for Bibliography." Yet the title is better as it is; there has been enough pedantry here already without emphasizing it. Methodology is at best a short cut for the inexperienced. The great historians, for instance, have in most cases left such academic trifling to lesser men. In bibliography, as in all other studies, what counts is the trained, alert, and ingenious mind which can cope with its difficulties as it meets them. And the vitality of bibliography today lies not so much in its having, except incidentally, formulated for itself a methodology as in having been guided by practitioners of consummate skill. If in this paper I have seemed here and there to take issue with Greg and McKerrow, it is not from any sense of disrespect; it is rather from a sense of wonder that it should be possible to disagree with them. For bibliography owes its present status almost entirely to their efforts; and one's most earnest hope can only be that a generation of comparable caliber will rise to succeed them. To the bibliographer of the new generation, experienced or still inexperienced, there is but one word of advice to give, and that is "Follow them."

NOTES

[1] *Transactions of the Bibliographical Society*, XII (1911-13), 39-53.

[2] In fairness to Dr. Greg it should be added that in his later writings he has shown a tendency to recede from the more extreme implications of these statements. See especially, "The Present Position of Bibliography," *The Library*, XI (1930-31), 256-58.

[3] The nearest approximation to a scientific law in bibliography is prob-

ably the principle of the forme-unit, and the apparent exceptions to it, due to single-page or two-color printing, are apparent only, not real.

[4] *Introduction to Bibliography for Literary Students*, p. 188.

[5] R. C. Bald, "Sir William Berkeley's *The Lost Lady*," *The Library*, XVII (1936-37), 395-426, at 402-4.

[6] "The Present Position of Bibliography," at p. 256.

[7] *The Library*, XII (1931-32), 253-75.

[8] L. S. Stebbing, *A Modern Introduction to Logic*, p. 255.

[9] *The Printing of the First Folio of Shakespeare*, pp. 54-55.

[10] *The Writings of Benjamin Franklin*, ed. by A. H. Smith, I, 300-301.

[11] *Moxon's Mechanick Exercises*, ed. by T. L. De Vinne, II, 210.

[12] *The Library*, XVI (1936-37), 181-82.

[13] But see Greg in *The Variants in the First Quarto of "King Lear,"* p. 56n, where this is somewhat modified.

[14] *Op. cit.*, I, 32-33.

[15] *Ibid.*, I, 32.

[16] Another, and somewhat different, example of the use of two different measures is worth recording. In *The Knave in Graine*, a play published in 1640, a measure of 92 millimeters is used until the end of sheet H; in the remaining three-and-a-half gatherings one of 97 millimeters is used and the normal number of lines to the page is increased from thirty-seven to thirty-nine. The change comes too soon to assert that there was a definite attempt to get the rest of the play into any specific number of pages, and the increase in the number of lines to the page was probably as much for aesthetic reasons as for economy; that is, thirty-

seven lines of the shorter measure and thirty-nine of the longer gave a properly balanced quarto page and represented the normal practice of the printing house. The change, incidentally, has nothing whatever to do with the difference between prose and verse. It looks as if a different compositor took over at the beginning of sheet I and that he simply went on using the stick he had been using for another quarto without realizing that a shorter measure had been used for the part of the play already set up.

[17] *Introduction to Bibliography*, p. 23.

[18] *Op. cit.*, II, 305.

[19] *Ibid.*, II, 325-27.

[20] *Ibid.*, I, 76-77.

[21] *Ibid.*, II, 412-13.

[22] Apparently these combinations do occur in folios, and it seems likely that what has been said above is applicable only to quartos and to books of smaller size. Greg's assertion that one forme is invariable rests on the postulate that both formes of the sheet were made up at about the same time and that one was in the press while the other was waiting and still available for corrections. In a folio, however, printing could begin as soon as the inner forme of the inner sheet had been set up, and thus it might be in the press before the composition of the outer forme was complete. Hence the printing of the outer forme might also have to be interrupted so that the final corrections could be made. This, rather than exceptional care, would explain the combination of corrected or uncorrected formes in the 1616 edition of Ben Jonson's *Works* to which Greg draws attention on pp. 46-47.

Some Relations of Bibliography to Editorial Problems

Fredson Bowers

Bibliography concerns itself with editorial problems not as a usurper of the functions of legitimate criticism, but instead as the necessary foundation on which, in certain investigations, textual criticism must be based and to which criticism must constantly refer for more or less definitive judgments. Bibliography, in W. W. Greg's acute phrase, is the grammar of literary investigation. This position was strikingly advanced in Greg's classic address on the relations of bibliography to literature which appeared some time ago in *Neophilologus*, and, again, in his "Bibliography—An Apologia" (*The Library*, 4th ser. XIII [1932], 113 ff.). Any attempt merely to restate Greg's views here would be quite superfluous. For some years, at least among scholars, the inferential identification of bibliography with textual criticism has been so firmly established that to talk about the contribution of one to the other might appear to be like a solemn discussion of the usefulness of the arm to the hand.

Nevertheless, it is possible to suspect that, as more and more scholars have come to deal with these twin methods, the popularizing of their disciplines may have led, by subtle degrees, to a rather over-simplified view of the basic provinces of bibliography and textual criticism, especially as applied to editorial problems. Certainly the theory that every bibliographer is professionally qualified to be a full-fledged textual critic and editor is quite wrong. Correspondingly, there are a number of distinguished textual critics whom, according to any strict accounting, we might hesitate to call bibliographers.

Some fortunate scholars like Pollard, McKerrow, Greg, and Percy Simpson may happily combine in themselves both functions, although perhaps in unequal proportions; but this two souls in body one is certainly the exception rather than the rule. On the other hand, the most prominent Elizabethan textual critic now living—I refer to Mr. Dover Wilson—often operates in that dark region of the ur-state of a text which McKerrow rightly hesitated to identify with bibliography. One should comment, however, that not all of Wilson's readers—or his critics—are completely aware of the distinction. It is somewhat perturbing, for example, in Hereward Price's admirable "Towards a Scientific Method of Textual Criticism in the Elizabethan Drama"[1] to find his chief whipping boy, Dover Wilson, consistently referred to as representing the bibliographical school. Save for his impatience at various of Wilson's well-known aberrations, Mr. Price—no more than the rest of us—would, I should think, completely discount such investigations. But we may agree with McKerrow and Greg that this scholarship is not usually bibliographical in any sense in which we should be prepared to use the term.

Bibliography is likely to be a vague and misused word because it has come to be employed for too many different purposes. For the present discussion we may rule out enumerative bibliography—the making-up of finding or reference lists of books on various subjects—and use the term to mean analytical bibliography, the investigation and explanation of a book as a material object. Yet even within this narrower limitation there are various strata and subdivisions of research. For example, we have such forms of bibliographical spadework as the identification and recording of type-faces as by Haebler, or of STC printers' ornaments as is now in progress by F. S. Ferguson, with their dates and history.

But when we move from such essential preliminary investigation, and from the recording of material data as a part of publishing history, to another sort of bibliography, more specifically of the kind we designate as *analytical,* we come to a field in which all our accumulated knowledge of printing practice and history is devoted to the examination of individual or related books as material objects, with a view to determining the facts of their production. Is there or is there not a cancel in a certain gathering; were the various sheets of a book printed *seriatim* or simultaneously in two or more sections; did one or two compositors, one or more presses, work on this book, and if so which parts did they do; was a cancel title-page or a cancel in the text printed later or as a part of the continuous printing of the book. Are variants in the sheets of the book the result of different impressions, or do they result from different typesettings or from simple correction at the press. If some of the sheets are of a single impression but certain others exhibit variant typesettings, which setting is the original, and why was the resetting made. If there are variant imprints, which was first through the press. And so on. It will be seen that correct answers to some of these questions depend not only on the simple discovery of the facts themselves, but more particularly on the satisfactory explanation of the ascertained facts. From specific analyses of this kind, some speculatively minded bibliographers may endeavor to evolve new techniques for bringing to light yet further secrets in printed books, techniques which may enable us to attack successfully some general problems which have heretofore been thought insoluble.

Such technical examinations of individual books for their own sake are proceeding very swiftly these days, and they are being matched step by step by the parallel development of techniques for determining with greater precision the relation of the printed book to its underlying manuscript.[2] No textual critic can afford to ignore the results of these investigations. From Willoughby's and Hinman's explorations of spelling tests,[3] assisted in certain cases by evidence from the varying length of the compositor's stick,[4] we are now able to distinguish with some certainty in the *STC* period and the following years the precise pages of a book set by different compositors. By an equation of these compositors' habits we can thereupon make certain assumptions about the characteristics of the manuscript from which they were setting. The cooperative efforts which have been made in the analysis of the evidence of headlines[5] have opened up possibilities, in combination with this compositor evidence, for determining sometimes quite minute but necessary questions of the presswork and proofreading. To these may be added—among many other investigations—the classic Carter and Pollard examination of paper and type which exposed the Wise forgeries, Hazen's use of identified paper to detect Strawberry Hill forgeries, and Stevenson's technique for aligning watermarks with presswork.[6] The unexpected uses of bibliography have been demonstrated in Bond's assignment of authorship to certain doubtful *Spectator* papers, the whole argument resting ultimately on type left standing in advertisements and headings.[7]

Astonishing results have recently accrued from certain research on eighteenth-century press figures, which had been earlier dismissed by McKerrow as of little bibliographical significance. Knotts[8] has added a chapter to the work of Sale, Chapman, and others; and W. B. Todd's latest interpretation of the evidence of these figures in a number of books demonstrates some most exciting things one can learn of printing.[9] From this evidence a whole new area of research has been opened up of such importance for distinguishing impressions, partial re-impressions, and editions, as well as various other important textual matters, that we may well believe in many cases press figures alone will come to be the most valuable tool for penetrating the extreme difficulties of textual problems in frequently reprinted popular eighteenth-century authors.

I should be less than candid if I tried to pretend that the immediate or even the chief aim of these and of many other bibliographical scholars was to serve as the sons of Martha to textual criticism. Without question, a number of bibliographical investigations which eventually proved invaluable to textual criticism were not undertaken with this end immediately in view and almost by accident arrived at their textual applications. Thus a real difference from textual criticism must always be felt, I suspect, in bibliographical research in its purest aspect. To defend themselves against doubters, bibliographers are accustomed to argue that the ultimate aim of all bibliographical research, and therefore its justification, is the definitive account of books in a descriptive bibliography, or the direct application of their findings to textual criticism. But I make bold to say that—at least as I view it—the *immediate* end of a great deal of research is no such thing. Although I believe that the conventional justification is valid for the ultimate aims, and that this rationale is deeply felt by almost every bibliographical student, nevertheless, even though eventual application is the ideal, ordinarily textual criticism has not provided the immediate spur to the investigation and no specific textual use is often anticipated, at least in the early stages of the work. This attitude develops, in part, because many technical studies that are absolutely necessary yet require no interest in textual criticism on the part of the investigator. In part, because various of these studies are concerned only with a fragment of some total problem, the whole of which must be unraveled before any of it can be made of practical use to textual criticism.

Nonetheless, in spite of the various legitimate reasons which may be advanced to explain the rationale for much technical work in bibliography, the point of view does in fact serve to separate many bibliographers from textual critics; indeed, it would be tempting to say *most* bibliographers were it not an increasing tendency for a number of analysts, with or without due training, to cross over the line and to concern themselves directly with the editing of texts. Others, though not editors, may develop so great an interest in textual questions that they direct their research specifically towards bibliographical problems which do have an immediate textual application and thus underlie accurate criticism. The record, while respectable, has not been one of unalloyed success, perhaps, and when bibliographers have concerned themselves with matters of textual criticism that were not primarily bibliographical, they have sometimes floundered pitifully if they lacked the training and the qualities of mind which are necessary for textual criticism in *its* purest state.

I use this statement of a point too often overlooked, in our current tendency to exalt the bibliographer, as an aid towards a cursory glance at the nature of textual criticism, a subject on which I can speak with little authority and on which I shall anticipate correction. It is perhaps absurd to set up too sharp a distinction between textual critics and textual bibliographers. Anyone, we may suppose, who is concerned with the origin, derivation, authority, and correctness of a text, in whole or in part, is a textual critic, no matter what his method of approach. Some scholars tackle problems through bibliography, some through what Greg has called metacriticism, some through an attempted or actual combination of bibliography and criticism. For purposes of distinction I must deal in blacks and whites more starkly than is perhaps realistic. Nevertheless, I am sure that when we distinguish between a McKerrow and a Dover Wilson, both brilliant examples of different schools, we are in fact implying a greater fundamental difference than exists between the conservative and speculative wings of the same method.

Greg—and in this he is frequently misunderstood—insists that the bibliographer must view a book only as a material object.[10] This is a far cry from the aims of a textual critic. Historically, textual criticism developed long before analytical bibliography; and it evolved its own rules, especially for dealing with manuscripts, both classical and vernacular, according to certain principles which are outside the strictly bibliographical range, if for our purposes we continue to limit the definition of bibliography to analytical bibliography. These principles, or something like them, were also applied to printed books, again before bibliography was more than a gleam in the eye, and—as Greg has shown in his paper for this series—they are still in part applicable to certain problems. Thus there has been established in the past a firm tradition for dealing with texts; and it would be foolish for us to believe that analytical bibliography has displaced this tradition, or even that in many cases it could. Nevertheless, analytical bibliography has demonstrated that in some circumstances the classical tradition is not completely self-sufficient. We may put it, therefore, that bibliography is neither a usurper nor a poor relation in the field of textual criticism, but rather its foundation, the grammar of the subject.

If, in the interests of brevity, we pass over the important field of manuscript texts and concern ourselves with textual criticism based chiefly on printed books, we may, perhaps, discern three main but by no means mutually exclusive lines of endeavor. The first concerns itself with the authorship, origin, and characteristics of the lost manuscript behind a printed book both in whole and in part. I am thinking first of various studies in the attribution of anonymous works, or of the solution of problems in multiple authorship as in the Beaumont and Fletcher plays, Massinger, and Dekker; and secondly of such studies as Mr. Duthie has made in the bad quarto of *Hamlet* and more recently in the Pide Bull *King Lear*. Dover Wilson's reconstructions of the manuscript copy for *Hamlet* and other texts should be placed here, as also various studies such as Hoppe's of *Romeo and Juliet* but especially Greg's of *Doctor Faustus*. As with the *Faustus* and *Lear* investigations, according to the circumstances this division may merge imperceptibly with the second, which I take to be concerned with the critical analysis of texts in known manuscripts or printed exempla. Here we might place studies like Grierson's on the text of Donne, Wolf's on commonplace books, Shaaber's on *2 Henry IV*. The determination of the order and authority of printed texts after the first also applies, and we must certainly include the very difficult task of separating from compositor's, proof-reader's, and printing-house editor's alterations those true revisions from an authoritatively corrected copy used as the basis for a later edition. The relation of the variants in the Quarto and Folio of *King Lear* or *Troilus and Cressida* is such a problem. In all of these divisions various special studies may enter in one form or another. I list as examples a few of the inquiries which Mr. Price sets up as among the subjects for textual criticism: vocabulary tests of authorship, and also of plagiarism, metrical tests including study of broken lines, deficient lines, redundant syllables, feminine endings, prose as blank verse, and so on, applied to form an opinion of a text.

Finally, perhaps we may assign as a third general division the orderly bringing together of all this information in an editorial capacity, and the consequent evolution of a modern critical text designed to represent the intentions of the author more faithfully than any single preserved manuscript or printed copy. Whereas the findings of analytical bibliography may or may not be applicable in the first two divisions, the claims of analysis enter full force in the editorial third.

In the first two divisions, it is true, the investigations lead hopefully towards the ideal of a definitive text, but, as with pure bibliography, much textual criticism is undertaken either for its own sake or else to attack only a fragment of the total problem, so that the immediate end of the research may not be the formation of a text. For example, Mr. Duthie did not edit *Hamlet* after he had solved the problem of the bad quarto. It will be convenient, however, to treat textual criticism and its relations to bibliography in its narrower application to the evolution of an edited text and to the various delicate problems that arise before this text can eventually be fixed. Moreover, the limitation may be extended to cover only the specific problem of old-spelling critical texts, for—as Greg's paper has shown—these are subject to certain criteria which do not always apply to modernized versions, even though the basic problems are shared in common.

At the start one should distinguish certain editorial problems that have no necessary connection with bibliography. An editor of the literature of the past must have considerable linguistic attainments, or ready access to professional advice. Through long familiarity he must grow to be a native in the characteristic thought, usage, speech patterns, and customs of his period. Although bibliography may occasionally assist in the solution of some problems, or offer a convincing after-the-event confirmation, much emendation—or refusal to emend—much estimate of authenticity, must be made quite independently of bibliographical considerations and instead on a philological basis. This aspect has no relation to bibliography, and it requires a discipline and study which leave little time for bibliographical investigations not concerning the problem immediately at hand. Moreover, if we speak of only one characteristic, the great emendations have been inspired art and not systematic science. One can give a rational palaeographical explanation to derive "a table of green fields" set in type from the crabbed script of "a' babld of green fields," but I beg leave to doubt that this famous emendation would to the present day ever have been arrived at by strictly palaeographic reasoning. Greg, I believe, has no very high opinion of palaeography as giving more than a hint for emendations,[11] although its confirmation is often most valuable. Usually, I suspect, one arrives at an emendation of any subtlety by inspiration, memory, and a strong sense of analogy, and then one brings in palaeography if possible to justify one's conclusions.

Many other considerations of text are too frequently confused as soluble by bibliography. For example, bibliography can establish that edition *B*. was printed from edition *A*., and not from an independent manuscript; but if revisions appear in *B*., there is no bibliographical technique for determining except in isolated cases whether they derive from the author himself, a scribe revising the text of *A*. from a manuscript, or an editor of some kind. Such problems in one way or another involving emendation or the acceptance of variant readings fall to the lot of the textual critic once bibliography has cleared his way to the limit of its ability.

This critical acumen, which we cannot value too highly as applied to text, is, of course, the product of a keen and imaginative mind; but, again, it is materially aided by a very close acquaintance with one's period in general philological considerations. This acquaintance gradually develops an opinion about speech and imagery which, in mature and thoughtful hands, has its own authority not only in questions of emendation but in any division of textual criticism. We may note that even the conservative, bibliographical McKerrow does not disdain in certain circumstances to write about the authority of variants between editions which best seem to have the greatest internal harmony with an author.[12]

This strong and subtle imagination necessary for close inquiries into texts may apply itself to studies in attribution, plagiarism, or multiple authorship, or to studies in an author's speech and metrical characteristics, or it may be found in Dover Wilson's various attempts—whether rightly or wrongly—to discover layers of revision in the pre-printing history of a manuscript, or it may be utilized in the scrupulous examination of the sources and methods of corruption in a text which Duthie has demonstrated in *Hamlet* and in *King Lear*. Such striking deductions as those Duthie makes about the composition of memorial texts from tag ends of general recollections exhibit a critical virtuosity which has its own discipline and rigorous training.

If I were a textual critic concerned with such matters as I have been sketching, problems involving my total powers as a critic, I fancy I should be rather impatient with a bibliographer who insisted that I should be all this and McKerrow too. And I should be strongly inclined to reply: you are a technician—you do the technical part of this business and I shall apply your findings, taking care that I have studied the principles and general methods of your craft seriously enough so that I can follow your arguments and understand the applicability of what you are saying.

This is roughly what has happened, and as a consequence something like the following rationale is commonly accepted. The bibliographer's function is to prepare the general material of the texts, when bibliographical investigation is necessarily involved; and the textual critic, in the light of bibliographical findings, can then proceed to apply the discovered relationships, and to add his own art, to achieve the finished, definitive result.

Since we are an age of specialists, this separation of function seems reasonable to us. Indeed, in various cases it may work very well, and in some it may even be positively necessary. Yet I must confess it is a position I held with more conviction in the past than I do today, and I anticipate holding it with even less conviction in the future, especially if certain far-reaching bibliographical speculations and experimental techniques for dealing with the accidentals in an old-spelling text ever reach success. This change in attitude, I am conscious, may have been dictated too much by various experiences with amateur editors, from whom the good Lord deliver us, by a tendency to over-emphasize the importance of a close reconstruction of accidentals, and by allowing the special problems of distinctly unusual texts to bulk too large in my mind so that the uncomplicated, run-of-the-mill variety is obscured.

Whatever the cause, I have here what is only a selection of examples to illustrate that a textual critic, when he is himself incapable of applying advanced bibliographical techniques to every detail of an old-spelling text, can seldom achieve absolute authority in his results, and may indeed be led into serious error through the false confidence induced in him by the notion that bibliography has sufficiently prepared the way before his labors have begun.

This hypothetical critic can ordinarily be prepared only to follow and apply bibliographical arguments: his training has not prepared him to evaluate their correctness on technical grounds. A small but rather interesting example occurs in Thomas Southerne's *Disappointment* of 1684. Here the case for a cancel to abridge a censored scene was very plausibly advanced in 1933, and in 1946 was vetted by a good bibliographer who made some necessary modifications but in no way questioned the central thesis. Yet in the last sixteen years if any textual critic had treated the scene in the light of this apparently authoritative evidence, without testing it bibliographically for himself, he would have been quite wrong, for no cancel exists and the scene is not abridged.[13]

Secondly, this critic may often be forced to enter upon subjects where rigorous bibliographical investigation has not yet been made, although he may not be aware of that fact. A really egregious case of false bibliography has only recently been corrected by W. B. Todd's study of *The Monk*.[14] The full story is very involved, but the point is brief. If between 1935 and 1949 any critic had blindly relied on the accepted ordering of the publishing history which pseudo-bibliography had set up, he would have been led to evolve a text which treated Lewis's revisions as the original readings, and the readings which Lewis had discarded as in fact his later revisions. *Q. E. D.* Don't trust all the bibliographers.

This is a pretty fix for a textual critic, since he is damned if he does and damned if he doesn't. And in fact, in many cases no solution for his dilemma is possible unless he is himself also a trained bibliographer who is capable of re-examining technically a fouled-up problem. Yet he must do something. One course is to trust only *some* bibliographers. The very best butter. Nonetheless we may well remember in this connection Curt Bühler's favorite quotation of the observation made by A. W. Pollard on his colleague Robert Proctor, a great pioneer in incunabula studies, "that in matters of bibliography he would not have taken the results of an archangel upon trust." As an example we may survey two specific but fortunately minor instances in which Mr. Duthie in his new edition of *King Lear* was misled by untested bibliography. A small part of his arguments concerning certain peculiarities of the quarto rests on Greg's speculation that two compositors with different habits might have been engaged with the book. Now in this case Greg was not speaking *ex cathedra* as the result of a detailed bibliographical examination, but only in terms of possibilities. Fortunately the point was of no very great consequence for Duthie's conclusions, because he accepted the speculation on trust and did not test it. We know now, however, from a recent bibliographical study, which can be confirmed by even stricter bibliographical evidence,[15] that only one compositor set the book. These peculiarities, therefore require another explanation.

In the second instance the point of discussion is the mislining of the verse at the opening of Act III, Scene 2, the great storm scene. Greg took the view that the early part is mislined because the compositor was setting the text as prose, and it was not until he reached a certain point that he recognized he was dealing with verse and thereafter proceeded to line correctly. Duthie, naturally, accepted Greg's explanation as 'bibliographical,' and quite properly added that of course the compositor must have gone back to insert capitals at the beginning of each line in the prose section to give it the appearance of verse that it assumes in the printing. However, a single piece of bibliographical evidence demonstrates the mechanical impossibility of such a proce-

dure. Throughout *Lear* the compositor of the quarto used a short stick
for verse and a longer stick for prose; and he never sets prose in his
short or verse measure. Since the opening lines of this scene were set
in the verse measure, not the prose, the explanation for the mislineation must be sought elsewhere, for from the start the compositor intended to set verse. But other consequences resulted from this failure to
see the bibliographical evidence. Because the implications of the short
measure were not recognized, in these lines Duthie over-conservatively
retained a corrupt lack of punctuation which succeeds in destroying,
almost completely, not only a successful flower of rhetoric but also one
of the mightiest images of this great storm scene.[16]

If the critic finding himself thus abused hurls a curse on this treacherous science of bibliography and betakes himself to his own estimates
—to what Greg calls metacritical evidence—he may find himself in a
rather vulnerable position. A simple, though typical, case occurs in
The Dumbe Knight of 1608 which is preserved with either one of two
title-pages, the major difference between them being that one gives
the author's name whereas the other does not. Metacritics worked up
a pretty romance about this play, conjecturing that Gervase Markham,
the author, was so disgusted when he found his play printed with an inferior underplot by another hand that he withdrew his name from the
title. On the contrary, bibliography demonstrates that the title with the
name is the true cancel leaf so that the name was added rather than
excised.[17]

Vulnerability increases when the problem is one of any complexity.
Here is a small problem yet one in which an old-spelling editor must
make a decision. The inner forme of text sheet A of George Sandys's
Christs Passion, a translation in 1640 from Grotius, was reset in the
course of enlarging the edition. One typesetting of this inner forme
agrees largely with the invariant outer forme in making up capital W's
from two V's, whereas the other uses regular W's. Aha, says the critic,
I'm not so bad at bibliography myself: obviously the setting of inner A
which is consistent with outer A must be the original for me to reprint. The only trouble is, he is wrong. A rather technical interpretation
of the evidence of the headlines demonstrates that this setting must
have been printed a sheet or so later.[18] The inconsistent forme is the
authoritative original which must be taken for the copy-text, and it is
probably inconsistent because we may be dealing with two compositors casting off copy and setting by formes in order to get the book
started in a hurry.

We do not need the example of nineteenth-century editors basing

Shakespeare texts on the Pavier Quartos to indicate some of the larger dangers of inferences about the relations of texts made on purely metacritical grounds. But lest we feel too confident about our present abilities to cope with matters more properly the province of textual criticism, such as our ability to construct a correct family tree of editions on the basis of their readings alone, we may consider the case of the ninth edition of Dryden's *Indian Emperour* in 1694. Certain of its readings are drawn apparently at random from those which are unique in the seventh edition and are not found in the eighth. Others derive from equally random readings unique in the eighth and not found in the seventh. There are three reputable critical interpretations of this phenomenon: (1) the ninth edition comes from an independent manuscript; (2) the seventh and eighth editions were collated at the printing house and the conflation of readings thus results from editorial intervention—or one might even introduce collation of one of these editions against a prompt copy or other manuscript; (3) the ninth is set from a lost edition which may be placed in between the seventh and eighth and on which the eighth is also based. This last would be a favorite with critics accustomed to dealing with manuscripts, and it is certainly the most plausible.

At least the first two of these quite reputable explanations might cause some critical perturbation, since fresh authority could have been introduced into the text, and the various new readings in the ninth not found in either the seventh or eighth might demand critical acceptance on their merits. However, when analytical techniques are applied, the answer is not hard to find. Two compositors were employed on the ninth edition, but—perhaps because only one press was available—instead of chopping the reprint up into two sections to be set and printed simultaneously, they set the book *seriatim* but working in relay. One would compose from four to five type-pages, or only one or two, and then be relieved by the other while he distributed this type, and so on in turn. Since the eighth edition was a paginal reprint of the seventh, what actually happened was that one compositor set from a copy of the seventh, and the other from a copy of the eighth, and so they worked merrily along in relay to the confusion of scholarship, conflating the two editions to form the ninth. The answer is very easy after bibliographical analysis.[19]

I do not wish to infer that in all cases bibliographical evidence is applicable. To be properly bibliographical, evidence must concern itself with only certain relations between preserved printed or inscribed pieces of paper. For example, a form of textual criticism linked with bibliography can usually decide on an over-all basis whether variations in a later edition are compositors' variants or editorial revisions; and pure bibliography can demonstrate whether or not this later edition was otherwise set from a copy of an earlier. But whether these revisions were the author's or someone else's can never be decided by bibliography under ordinary circumstances; that is for textual criticism pure and simple. The case is usually not demonstrable by any form of bibliographical evidence. Some critics may deal extensively with evidence which is probably bibliographical at bottom because it is founded on the peculiarities of printed inscriptions on paper; but the inferences they draw may have no relation to the laws of bibliographical evidence. As I shall indicate in a moment, strictly bibliographical deduction is not always possible from bibliographical facts. It is this common confusion about the difference between the strictly bibliographical and the metacritical interpretation of the evidence offered by a book as a material object which places, wrongly I believe, a number of Dover Wilson's ingenious arguments in the field of bibliography. Larger examples may be cited. The *Taming of the Shrew* problem can have no bibliographical basis, for whatever relation existed between *A Shrew* and *The Shrew* antedates their printing, and the manuscripts behind the printed copy of each have no bibliographical relation. Somewhat less clearly, perhaps, the formation of a critical text of *Hamlet* is not, basically, a bibliographical investigation. There is no direct relationship between the three printed texts.

But when pure textual criticism concerns itself with problems in which bibliographical investigation is possible, it can seldom be equally definitive as in this other field, for critical interpretation of evidence is at best inferential, and the logic of the argument is frequently reversible. Until the problem was directly tackled by bibliographical methods, the question of whether *Troilus and Cressida* in the Folio was set from an annotated copy of the quarto or from an independent manuscript had yielded no convincing answer from the critical approach. Yet Mr. Williams has made the problem seem like child's play,[20] and we may find his study very illuminating for the relative validity of bibliographical and critical methods in such situations. Similarly, Mr. Hinman's authoritative study of *Othello* and its second quarto contains a most ingenious bibliographical solution of another long-vexed critical problem.[21]

There are other problems involving the relations between editions. Greg, I think, has remarked that given two editions only, the critical method could never satisfactorily establish their relationship or indeed, if they are similarly dated, as with certain of the Pavier quartos, their priority. I may be making this more positive or detailed than his original statement, but when we realize that Greg is not thinking in terms of inferences establishing high probability but instead of absolute proof, then we must admit that true demonstration is impossible because of the reversibility of the critical evidence. Is a variant a correction or rationalization in one edition, or a corruption in the other—frequently the case may be argued either way.

An example is Dryden's *Wild Gallant,* which has two editions in 1669, the year of its first appearance in print. One is clearly a paginal reprint of the other, but the question is—which? On the one side we have Macdonald setting up his number 72a as the first edition, whereas Griffith, backed by Osborn, argues for 72b, or Macdonald's second edition. As a part of a fresh bibliographical examination of this play I have elsewhere tried to show in detail too lengthy to be summarized here that while the basic fact on which each hinges his argument is bibliographical, the arguments from this fact are only inferential and therefore do not conform to the strictest requirements of bibliographical reasoning, that is, to a mechanical demonstration for which there is no possible alternative save in the realm of purest fantasy.[22]

It will be pertinent, however, to consider more fully in this play certain kinds of evidence which, for a very good reason, have not been published. The exposé, I hope, will offer an enlightening example, though at my own expense, of what bibliographical evidence is and what it is not. I can speak very feelingly on the subject because when I came to the problem as an editor I was completely booby-trapped, and at first I arrived at certain conclusions on grounds which I gullibly persuaded myself were bibliographical only to have the whole argument blow up in my face when at length the true evidence became apparent.

A textual collation of the two editions quickly established that there had been no real rewriting between them, but that in a score of places —if 72a were first—corrections, possibly even revisions, had certainly been made in 72b, a few of which could have come only from the author himself. On the other hand, if 72b were first, in various readings the text had undergone a corruption rather more serious than one might expect in a first reprint. Mr Osborn in his notes to Griffith's argument had confidently pronounced *B.* the first on the evidence of this textual degeneration in *A.*[23] This is a critical touchstone which experience has shown to be sound, provided the further inference is made that the author had no part in producing the reprint. However, I approached the *Gallant* fresh from a study of *The Indian Emperour*, in which without question Dryden had directly concerned himself with revising not only the second but also the third edition, the year before and after *The Wild Gallant* respectively. With this example before me, I felt hesitant to accept Osborn's conclusions without further inquiry, for the second inference could not be automatically applied. Indeed, I came to feel that there was just about as much chance that the careless errors of A. had been rectified in B. by an errata list sent to the printer as that A. represented a careless and unauthoritative reprint of B. And I still do not think that the priority of one or other edition can be positively demonstrated on the readings alone. Whether one is corruption or the other correction is not demonstrable in the very strictest sense once we know that Dryden had concerned himself at this date with correcting reprints of at least one other play.

I approached the two editions, therefore, not on the basis of the respective 'goodness' of their readings, but in search of some material evidence that one had been printed from the other. Here are some of the highlights of the preliminary case I evolved for the priority of A.

In the A. edition, the shortened name *Will* is almost invariably followed by a period to indicate that it is an abbreviation for *William*, and this period substitutes for other necessary punctuation such as commas, semi-colons, or even question marks. In B., *Will* is treated as a simple familiar name and no period is ever found except once—and significantly this once is the first time the name appears. Inadvertent following of copy by B. in this single initial instance seemed the best answer.[24] Given this hint, I continued looking for what one might describe as fossils in B. of strong characteristics present in A. but not in B. Twice in A. one compositor set the extreme contraction *h's* for *he's*, and, once later, *h'll* for *he'll*. In B. the two *h's* are normalized to the conventional *he's*, but the fossil *h'll* retained. More evidence appeared of what was apparently inadvertent following of copy. For example, the two compositors of A. spelled the conjunctive adverb *than* indifferently as *then* or as *than*. In B. the invariable spelling is *than*, even when *then* appears in A., except for two cases, and one of these turned out to be in the uncorrected state of a press-variant forme in B. where the A. spelling *then* originally appeared in B. but was changed by the proof-reader to *than*. There were various other instances in which the isolated appearance in B. of marked characteristics in A. seemed significant, especially since the two pairs of compositors were different in each edition. Moreover, on the textual principle that the 'harder' reading is the original, there were at least two cases which seemed to point to the priority of *A*. In the first, the form *wall* in the phrase in *A*. "she wall write" seemed to derive more plausibly from a manuscript collo-quialism *wall* or *wull* than from a misprint of the *B*. "she shall write." In the second, Constance is deceiving Lord Nonsuch that she is with child, and when he demands the name of the father she responds that she does not know. He exclaims, "Not know! went there so many to't?" and in *A*. she answers, "So far from that, that there were none at all, to my best knowledge, Sir." In *B*. the repetition *went* substitutes for *were*, and it seemed a plausible hypothesis that the 'harder' reading was *were*, and that memorial failure in the *B*. compositor carried over the repeti-tion of *went* from Nonsuch's line. That the *A*. compositor in such a circumstance, where the repetition seems most natural, saw *went* in his *B*. copy and set *were* seemed more difficult to believe.

There is not time to go into this next evidence, but in the light of general experience that irregularities between catchword and follow-ing word in an original edition usually tend to be normalized in re-prints, it seemed to me at first highly probable that certain irregularities in the *A*. catchwords were much better explained on the belief that it was the first edition rather than the second.

Finally, I attacked the gap of eight pages in the pagination which appears between sheets G and H in both editions. In one edition this identical error could have resulted only from slavish following of copy. Hence if I could establish a reason for the gap in one edition, but no reason in the other, I felt I should have my original. Analysis disclosed that edition *A*. was set by two compositors in sections of one or more full sheets and that their respective sections can be identified not only by the different lengths of their sticks but also by the difference in the use of skeleton-formes which is associated with each.[25] In *B*. there is no evidence for any interruption in the presswork between sheets G and H, and indeed it seems likely that one compositor set the last pages of G and continued over into the first pages of H as part of his stint. On the contrary, in *A*. the gap in pagination occurs between one of the clearly marked sections where the compositors shifted, and it seemed a reasonable inference that when the compositor of sheet H returned to duty and came to make his first impositions, he forgot the system under which he was working and miscalculated the pag-ination.

I had, then, among various other pieces of evidence, the apparent survival in unique forms in *B*. of strongly marked compositorial habits manifested in *A*., among such fossils being the abbreviation of *Will*, the survival of the form *h'll* and of a random *then* spelling. I may also mention a few cases in *B.* of the very common practice in *A.* of using a semi-colon for a question mark, the setting in *A.* of a period in over a dozen cases where a necessary question mark was used in *B.*, and a very odd but marked use of the full *-ed* ending in *A.* for the elided form *apostrophe d* in *B.*, an expansion difficult to account for with such frequency in a reprint. Then there were such cases as this. The colloquial form *u'm* for *them* is absolutely consistent throughout both editions except for one single late use of *them* in *A.* where *u'm* appears in *B.* The probability seemed much higher that *B.* had normalized *A.* than that *A.* had wilfully departed from its copy *B.* There were also two cases where proper names were found in italic in *B.*, as customary, but in roman in *A.*, a reversal hard to account for. Finally, the evidence of the catchwords possibly, but almost certainly that of the mispagination, seemed to point to *A.* as the original.

I hope I have made this case reasonably convincing, even in an incomplete and digested form, because I am ashamed to confess that initially—before I began to prepare the text for an edition—it had me thoroughly convinced. Yet I hasten to point out that all these conclusions are quite wrong, that Griffith and Osborn are right. Edition *B.* indeed precedes *A.;* and this case I have presented for Macdonald's order, though based mostly on 'bibliographical' facts, has been one only of inference and probability but never of true bibliographical demonstration.

This, briefly, is the real evidence for *B.* as the first edition which my subsequent investigation revealed. Only one press-variant forme emerged from collation of eleven copies of *A.*, but from ten copies of *B.* I finally turned up seven formes which had undergone stop-press correction. Of these, two are indifferent since the uncorrected state agrees with *A.* for one, and the other is the variant act-heading noticed by Professor Griffith in the apparently unique Texas copy. Of the remaining five, all—in their significant *B.* readings—have an agreement between the *corrected* state of the formes and *A.* There is no need to elaborate the bibliographical argument here.[26] Almost inevitably, *A.* must have been set from *B.*

Finally, to clinch the case, this evidence developed. On one occasion in *A.* the verb *tells* in the phrase *she tells me* is misprinted as *tel's.* We can demonstrate the source of this misprint in *A.* when we find that in the corresponding place in *B.* the second letter *l* in *tells* inks so very slightly in all observed copies that only its tip is visible without a magnifying glass; and since this inked tip would almost inevitably be taken as an apostrophe, the compositor of *A.* read it as one and faithfully followed what he thought was the spelling of his copy. Correspondingly, in three places in *A.* where rather essential punctuation is missing, we find that the actual commas are so lightly inked in some copies of *B.* as scarcely to be seen. The evidence of the *tel's* alone is sufficient on which to rest one's whole case for the order of the editions; but especially when so powerfully confirmed by the evidence of the press-variant formes in *B.* followed by *A.*, one could take the dispute to a court of law and secure a judgment for the priority of *B.*

From this detailed example I draw a moral which applies to much of what I have been trying to say in this paper. Textual and pseudo-bibliographical evidence can seldom if ever afford more than a high degree of probability, and this is essentially different from positive demonstration. A very plausible chain of inferences can be built up, if the person is as stupid as I seem to have been; and if only the same line of evidence is employed to attack such a case, nothing but an indecisive stalemate can result. On the contrary, strictly bibliographical evidence such as that about the *tel's* and the press variants—evidence which usually appears in texts if one digs deep enough—crosses the line of probability into something close to the field which in science would be regarded as controlled experiment capable of being reproduced. Instead of high probability we have, in fact, practical demonstration on physical evidence of a mechanical nature, demonstrable by a mechanical process, evidence like the prose and verse measures of *King Lear*, and this is what Greg means by bibliography's treatment of a book as a material object. To every point in my construction of the case for 72a as the first edition, alternatives could have been suggested, and therefore any credibility it possessed depended on the cumulative bulk of the inferences. Yet when actual bibliographical evidence enters the scene, one little *tel's* sweeps all before it.

I draw the further moral as this applies to editing. Such minute yet crucial evidence on which the case hinges would normally be discoverable only by an editor. For example, the ordinary tests which a descriptive bibliographer would apply could not determine the truth; hence, if a textual critic, faced with the problem of corruption versus correction, felt that the standard bibliography of Dryden had sufficiently set up the material for him to proceed with 72a as his copy-text (and he could very well do so), he would be most seriously misled if he failed to come upon the bibliographical points which destroy Macdonald's case.

In this paper I seem to have given a considerable number of examples where bibliographers were wrong. I have not intended to cast doubts on the validity of bibliographical findings, or to speak in a way to discourage the faint-hearted from depending upon bibliographical evidence. Quite the reverse. What has been paramount in my mind is, first, that bibliography may sometimes be imperfectly practised; and unless a textual critic is himself enough of a bibliographer to make his own discoveries independently, or else to submit existing bibliographical conclusions about his material to the acid test of his own bibliographical re-evaluation—unless he can do this, in many cases he will be living in a fool's paradise, either believing that there are no bibliographical problems, or else that the bibliographers have authoritatively worked over the material for him and he can go ahead on his own line without further consideration.

Secondly, this principle seeps down from the very top, or the choice and treatment of the copy-text, to the very bottom of the last, minute detail of an old-spelling critical edition which must be exhausted bibliographically before pure criticism can properly operate.

Thus I think we may freely say that the bibliographer's text is by no means always the best that can be contrived if the editor has not got the mind of a true textual critic—only perhaps that such a text does the minimum of harm. On the other hand, as a practising bibliographer I do object mightily to critics who often nullify the brilliance of their substantive text by failing to observe bibliographical principles when they engage themselves to an old-spelling edition. I should be inclined to set up four operations which an old-spelling editor should perform, for the interpretation and application of the evidence discovered by these investigations lie at the heart of a sound edition. It is astonishing to a bibliographer to find how often various of these have been omitted by an editor who otherwise has exhibited every desire to be scrupulous in the details of his work. First, the determination of authority in all early editions and, on this evidence, the proper choice and treatment of the copy-text as we have heard it described by Greg. Second, the collation of multiple copies of each authoritative edition to disclose proof-corrections for analysis. Third, the analysis of running-titles for the interpretation of the presswork, a matter which is closely linked with the fourth, or compositor analysis, this last being positively essential, at least in Elizabethan texts, for any consideration of the variants between two or more authoritative editions in a direct line of derivation.

These few demands are not especially severe and need not require any extraordinary technical training. But I place them as the basis for any bibliographical preparation of an individual text by an editor once the larger questions have been settled. And until they become standard procedure, at least in cases of any complexity where their chief value is found, our old-spelling texts are not going to be definitive in any real sense. Critical brilliance can settle many a substantive crux, although by no means all of them; but if these excellent major substantives are placed in a semi-substantive old-spelling background which is not itself accurate, then the reason for old-spelling texts degenerates into sentimentality or ostentation. Moreover, by an accurate background of accidentals and minor substantives, much more should be implied in many cases than the mechanical ability to copy and then proofread accurately from an old edition. If we are to learn to reconstruct the accidentals and minor substantives of an author's manuscript with as much care as we labor over reconstructing his correct major substantives, a whole new and delicate biblio-critical art is involved in which criticism by itself can never be a sufficiently scientific instrument.

I shall try to summarize the main points at which I have glanced. First, both textual criticism and analytical bibliography in their purest states are, in my opinion, independent arts which have no necessary relation in their disciplines, or frequently in the subjects with which they concern themselves. Textual criticism must deal with words and their meanings, with stylistic and linguistic considerations, and with the basic quesions of authority in texts, both in whole and in part. Pure analytical bibliography, on the other hand, deals with books as material objects formed by the mechanical process of printing. In many investigations it is not concerned with texts as such; but when it does approach texts it endeavors to treat them not from the literary or critical point of view, which is that of the 'goodness' of readings, but instead as pieces of paper mechanically impressed with certain symbols. The mechanical relation between these sets of symbols is thereupon its chief concern.

Second, although the two methods are essentially independent, textual criticism cannot controvert accurate bibliography in its findings when the subject is one on which bibliography can properly operate. However, the two often join in attacking certain problems of texts. These problems are by no means limited to editing, but nevertheless the construction of a critical text is most commonly the point at which the two methods cross.

Third, even though the first and the last approach to a text must be the bibliographical one, neither method can achieve definitive textual results in any detailed manner if utilized without reference to the other. On a broad scale it is bibliography which establishes the physical facts of the derivation of texts from one another and which wrings from a given book every last drop of information about the mechanical process of its printing that may be of service in determining the relation of the printed result to the manuscript or printed copy used by the printer. Still on a broad scale, it is the function of textual criticism to evaluate the authority of this manuscript and then to proceed to the correctness and the authority of the words in the text in the light of the ascertained physical facts which bibliography has furnished. Thereupon, in the process of fixing the text of a modern critical edition in every possible detail, the two methods are often so closely conjoined that an attempt to separate their respective functions would be futile.

When we come to criticize the average edited text produced today, we find that the usual source of error lies in the insufficient bibliographical training of the editor. Either he has little concept of textual problems, and—scornful of the minutiae which sometimes concern the bibliographer—is content to have any kind of a text, because what he really wants is only a peg on which to hang his annotations; or else he is overconfident in his purely critical abilities to solve any problems which may arise. In either case he has ventured on a delicate literary task without knowing his grammar, and hence his results can seldom be definitive. Sometimes even greater harm is caused by a little knowledge than by none. It is enough to make the angels weep to find Saintsbury, for example, throwing out various correct readings in Scott's text of *The Wild Gallant,* derived from edition 72b through the Folio and a later edition, to substitute absolute corruptions from 72a under the illusion he was restoring the purity of the text from the first edition. Or to find Davenport in the new edition of Joseph Hall's *Poems* declining the editorial responsibility to make a choice of readings, and basing his text on the derived reprint of 1598 for the first six books of *Virgidemiarum,* even though it was slightly revised, rather than the purer 1597 first edition.[27] It is really the hardest job in the world for a bibliographer to convince a critic who is beginning to be conscious of old-spelling problems that an author did not set his own type, seldom proof-read his book and if he did cannot be taken as approving every minute detail of its accidentals, and that a printed book is a fallible second-hand report of the author's manuscript, not a facsimile of it set in type.[28] One of the chief functions of textual bibliography is to try to pierce this veil of the printing process and to restore, however imperfectly, the authority of the manuscript, which we know only through its printed and thus secondary form.

On the other hand, a bibliographer who tackles the problems of text with insufficient critical and philological training is also in danger of false judgments in decisions which are not material and are therefore not strictly the business of bibliography. The usual result is that he may retreat to the narrowest conservatism to avoid having to face up to problems which are not wholly factual. And this timidity is as unbalanced as a critic's rashness in proceeding without the counterweight of bibliography. Such critical uncertainty may lead to good reprints of a single authority for a text but by no means to a true edition of the best text of an author.

It seems to me that for an ideally definitive work an editor must combine in himself the knowledge of both methods, and the training to put both into practice, or else he must resort to an almost impossible attempt at collaboration. Collaboration can be effective between a bibliographer and a literary critic who will handle all problems of biography, attribution of authorship, literary estimates, and who will write the critical introductions and illustrative notes. In such a case each has his relatively independent responsibilities; and indeed Greg is inclined to recommend this procedure for many editions. But I find it harder to imagine save in the most exceptional circumstances an effective collaboration of bibliographer and critic on the minutiae of the text.

I disclaim bibliography as the usurper of editorial privilege, and indeed I am concerned to aid the textual critic against the increasing pressure which editor-bibliographers are exerting on him. But if this potentially most valuable kind of an editor is to produce texts which in every detail will stand up under the increasingly exact and rigorous standards which are now being applied to this form of scholarship, he must learn his bibliography with a thoroughness not previously thought necessary. Only by this wider extension of scholarship can texts be achieved which will not need to be done all over again by the next generation.

NOTES

This paper was read before the English Institute on September 9, 1949.

[1] *Journal of English and Germanic Philology*, XXXVI (1937), 151-67.

[2] In this connection one must al-

ways recall W. W. Greg's searching monograph on *Orlando Furioso* and *The Battle of Alcazar*.

³ E. E. Willoughby, *The Printing of the First Folio of Shakespeare* (1932); C. J. K. Hinman, "Principles Governing the Use of Variant Spellings as Evidence of Alternate Setting by Two Compositors," *The Library*, 4th ser., XXI (1940), 78-94; see also P. Williams, "The Compositor of the Pied-Bull *Lear*," *Papers Bibl. Soc. Univ. Virginia*, I (1948), 61-68.

⁴ *Studies in Bibliography*, II (1949), 153-67.

⁵For a number of references, see J. G. McManaway's footnote in *Standards of Bibliographical Description* (1949), pp. 88-89. See also *The Library*, 4th ser., XIX (1938), 315-38; 5th ser., II (1947), 20-44, 5th ser., III (1948), 124-137; *Papers Bibl. Soc. America*, XLII (1948), 143-48; XLIII (1949), 191-95.

⁶ J. Carter and G. Pollard, *An Enquiry into the Nature of Certain Nineteenth Century Pamphlets* (1934); A. T. Hazen, *A Bibliography of the Strawberry Hill Press* (1942); A. H. Stevenson, "New Uses of Watermarks as Bibliographical Evidence," *Papers Bibl. Soc. Univ. Virginia*, I (1948), 151-82.

⁷ D. F. Bond, "The First Printing of the *Spectator*," *Modern Philology*, XLVII (1950), 174-77.

⁸ W. E. Knotts, "Press Numbers as a Bibliographical Tool: A Study of Gay's *The Beggars' Opera*, 1728," *Harvard Library Bulletin*, III (1949), 198-212. See also, P. Gaskell, "Eighteenth-century Press Numbers: Their Use and Usefulness," *The Library*, 5th ser., IV (1950), 249-61.

⁹ "Observations on the Incidence and Interpretation of Press Figures," *Studies in Bibliography*, III (1950-51), 171-205.

¹⁰ "Bibliography—An Apologia," *op. cit.*, pp. 121 ff.

¹¹ "Principles of Emendation in Shakespeare," *Proceedings of the British Academy*, XIV (1928), 154-55.

¹² *Prolegomena for the Oxford Shakespeare* (1939), p. 18.

¹³ *The Library*, 4th ser., XIII (1933), 395-98; 5th ser., I (1946), 67-69; II (1947), 64; and finally "The Supposed Cancel in Southerne's *Disappointment*," forthcoming in *The Library*, vol. V (1950).

¹⁴ "The Early Editions and Issues of *The Monk*," *Studies in Bibliography*, II (1949), 3-24.

¹⁵ P. Williams, *loc. cit.*; see also *Studies in Bibliography*, II (1949), 164.

¹⁶ For a detailed consideration of this passage, see G. W. Williams, "A Note on *King Lear*, III. ii. 1-3," *Studies in Bibliography*, II (1949), 175-82.

¹⁷ W. W. Greg, *A Bibliography of the English Printed Drama to the Restoration*, I (1939), no. 277.

¹⁸ *Papers Bibl. Soc. America*, XLII (1948), 146-48.

¹⁹ J. S. Steck, "Dryden's *Indian Emperour*: The Early Editions and their Relation to the Text," *Studies in Bibliography*, II (1949), 147.

²⁰ P. Williams, "Shakespeare's *Troilus and Cressida*: The Relationship of Quarto and Folio," *Studies in Bibliography*, III (1950-51), 131-43.

²¹ C. J. K. Hinman, "The 'Copy' for the Second Quarto of *Othello*," *Joseph Quincy Adams: Memorial Studies* (1948), pp. 373-89.

²² "The First Edition of Dryden's *Wild Gallant*, 1669," *The Library*, 5th ser., V (1950), 51-54.

²³ J. M. Osborn, "Macdonald's Bibliography of Dryden," *Modern Philology*, XXXIX (1941), 83-85.

²⁴ The reverse seemed, and still seems to me, almost incredible. With A. the reprint, both compositors of A. (for two compositors can be readily established) agreed in treating the name as an abbreviation and in sub-

stituting the abbreviating period for other punctuation found in *B.*, their copy, perhaps rigidly following the single hint of the initial abbreviation of the name in *B.*

[25] One identifiable compositor used only one skeleton to impose both formes of his sheet; the other, seemingly the quicker workman, used two.

[26] The full argument is provided in the article mentioned above in fn. 22, but no bibliographer will need the details. If *B.* were set from *A.*, we should have to believe that in these five corrected formes in *B.* the proof-reader made only changes in minutiae which helped to bring the reprint into conformity with its copy, and no other alterations. Moreover,

an error in the uncorrected state of one forme in *B.* could under no circumstances have originated in a misreading of *A.*

[27] Davenport's theory of editing and its contracitory results are touched on in my "Current Theories of Copy-Text, with an Illustration from Dryden," *Modern Philology,* August, 1950.

[28] Apparently this unbibliographical view is held by Richard Flatter, *Shakespeare's Producing Hand* (1948), and the error succeeds very thoroughly in turning his textual criticism into absurdity. For an analysis of his position, see my review in *Modern Philology,* August, 1950.

The Rationale of Copy-Text

W. W. Greg

When, in his edition of Nashe, McKerrow invented the term 'copy-text', he was merely giving a name to a conception already familiar, and he used it in a general sense to indicate that early text of a work which an editor selected as the basis of his own. Later, as we shall see, he gave it a somewhat different and more restricted meaning. It is this change in conception and its implications that I wish to consider.

The idea of treating some one text, usually of course a manuscript, as possessing over-riding authority originated among classical scholars, though something similar may no doubt be traced in the work of biblical critics. So long as purely eclectic methods prevailed, any preference for one manuscript over another, if it showed itself, was of course arbitrary; but when, towards the middle of last century, Lachmann and others introduced the genealogical classification of manuscripts as a principle of textual criticism, this appeared to provide at least some scientific basis for the conception of the most authoritative text. The genealogical method was the greatest advance ever made in this field, but its introduction was not unaccompanied by error. For lack of logical analysis, it led, at the hands of its less discriminating exponents, to an attempt to reduce textual criticism to a code of mechanical rules. There was just this much excuse, that the method did make it possible to sweep away mechanically a great deal of rubbish. What its more hasty devotees failed to understand, or at any rate sufficiently to bear in mind, was that authority is never absolute, but only relative. Thus a school arose, mainly in Germany, that taught that if a manuscript could be shown to be generally more correct than any other and to have descended from the archetype independently of other lines of transmission, it was 'scientific' to follow its readings whenever they were not manifestly impossible. It was this fallacy that Housman exposed with devastating sarcasm. He had only to point out that 'Chance and the common course of nature will not bring it to pass that the readings of a MS are right wherever they are possible and impossible wherever they are wrong'.[1] That if a scribe makes a mistake he will inevitably produce nonsense is the tacit and wholly unwarranted assumption of the school in question,[2] and it is one that naturally commends itself to those who believe themselves capable of distinguishing between sense and nonsense, but who know themelves incapable of distinguishing between right and wrong. Unfortunately the attractions of a mechanical method misled many who were capable of better things.

There is one important respect in which the editing of classical texts differs from that of English. In the former it is the common practice, for fairly obvious reasons, to normalize the spelling, so that (apart from emendation) the function of an editor is limited to choosing between those manuscript readings that offer significant variants. In English it is now usual to preserve the spelling of the earliest or it may be some other selected text. Thus it will be seen that the conception of 'copy-text' does not present itself to the classical and to the English editor in quite the same way; indeed, if I am right in the view I am about to put forward, the classical theory of the 'best' or 'most authoritative' manuscript, whether it be held in a reasonable or in an obviously fallacious form, has really nothing to do with the English theory of 'copy-text' at all.

I do not wish to argue the case of 'old spelling' *versus* 'modern spelling'; I accept the view now prevalent among English scholars. But I cannot avoid some reference to the ground on which present practice is based, since it is intimately connected with my own views on copy-text. The former practice of modernizing the spelling of English works is no longer popular with editors, since spelling is now recognized as an essential characteristic of an author, or at least of his time and locality. So far as my knowledge goes, the alternative of normalization has not been seriously explored, but its philological difficulties are clearly considerable.[3] Whether, with the advance of linguistic science, it will some day be possible to establish a standard spelling for a particular period or district or author, or whether the historical circumstances in which our language has developed must

always forbid any attempt of the sort (at any rate before comparatively recent times) I am not competent to say; but I agree with what appears to be the general opinion that such an attempt would at present
only result in confusion and misrepresentation. It is therefore the modern editorial practice to choose whatever extant text may be supposed
to represent most nearly what the author wrote and to follow it with
the least possible alteration. But here we need to draw a distinction
between the significant, or as I shall call them 'substantive', readings
of the text, those namely that affect the author's meaning or the essence of his expression, and others, such in general as spelling, punctuation, word-division, and the like, affecting mainly its formal presentation, which may be regarded as the accidents, or as I shall call them
'accidentals', of the text.[4] The distinction is not arbitrary or theoretical,
but has an immediate bearing on textual criticism, for scribes (or compositors) may in general be expected to react, and experience shows
that they generally do react, differently to the two categories. As regards substantive readings their aim may be assumed to be to reproduce exactly those of their copy, though they will doubtless sometimes
depart from them accidentally and may even, for one reason or another, do so intentionally: as regards accidentals they will normally follow
their own habits or inclination, though they may, for various reasons
and to varying degrees, be influenced by their copy. Thus a contemporary manuscript will at least preserve the spelling of the period, and
may even retain some of the author's own, while it may at the same
time depart frequently from the wording of the original: on the other
hand a later transcript of the same original may reproduce the wording with essential accuracy while completely modernizing the spelling.
Since, then, it is only on grounds of expediency, and in consequence
either of philological ignorance or of linguistic circumstances, that we
select a particular original as our copy-text, I suggest that it is only in
the matter of accidentals that we are bound (within reason) to follow
it, and that in respect of substantive readings we have exactly the
same liberty (and obligation) of choice as has a classical editor, or as
we should have were it a modernized text that we were preparing.[5]

But the distinction has not been generally recognized, and has
never, so far as I am aware, been explicitly drawn.[6] This is not surprising. The battle between 'old spelling' and 'modern spelling' was
fought out over works written for the most part between 1550 and
1650, and for which the original authorities are therefore as a rule
printed editions. Now printed editions usually form an ancestral series,
in which each is derived from its immediate predecessor; whereas the

extant manuscripts of any work have usually only a collateral relationship, each being derived from the original independently, or more or less independently, of the others. Thus in the case of printed books, and in the absence of revision in a later edition, it is normally the first edition alone that can claim authority, and this authority naturally extends to substantive readings and accidentals alike. There was, therefore, little to force the distinction upon the notice of editors of works of the sixteenth and seventeenth centuries, and it apparently never occurred to them that some fundamental difference of editorial method might be called for in the rare cases in which a later edition had been revised by the author or in which there existed more than one 'substantive' edition of comparable authority.[7] Had they been more familiar with works transmitted in manuscript, they might possibly have reconsidered their methods and been led to draw the distinction I am suggesting. For although the underlying principles of textual criticism are, of course, the same in the case of works transmitted in manuscripts and in print, particular circumstances differ, and certain aspects of the common principles may emerge more clearly in the one case than in the other. However, since the idea of copy-text originated and has generally been applied in connexion with the editing of printed books, it is such that I shall mainly consider, and in what follows reference may be understood as confined to them unless manuscripts are specifically mentioned.

The distinction I am proposing between substantive readings and accidentals, or at any rate its relevance to the question of copy-text, was clearly not present to McKerrow's mind when in 1904 he published the second volume of his edition of the Works of Thomas Nashe, which included *The Unfortunate Traveller*. Collation of the early editions of this romance led him to the conclusion that the second, advertised on the title as 'Newly corrected and augmented', had in fact been revised by the author, but at the same time that not all the alterations could with certainty be ascribed to him.[8] He nevertheless proceeded to enunciate the rule that 'if an editor has reason to suppose that a certain text embodies later corrections than any other, and at the same time has no ground for disbelieving that these corrections, *or some of them at least*, are the work of the author, he has no choice but to make that text the basis of his reprint'.[9] The italics are mine.[10] This is applying with a vengeance the principle that I once approvingly described as 'maintaining the integrity of the copy-text'. But it must be pointed out that there are in fact two quite distinct principles involved. One, put in more general form, is that if, for whatever reason, a particular authority be on the whole preferred, an editor is bound to accept all its substantive readings (if not manifestly impossible). This is the old fallacy of the 'best text', and may be taken to be now generally rejected. The other principle, also put in general form, is that whatever particular authority be preferred, whether as being revised or as generally preserving the substantive readings more faithfully than any other, it must be taken as copy-text, that is to say that it must also be followed in the matter of accidentals. This is the principle that interests us at the moment, and it is one that McKerrow himself came, at least partly, to question.

In 1939 McKerrow published his *Prolegomena for the Oxford Shakespeare,* and he would not have been the critic he was if his views had not undergone some changes in the course of thirty-five years. One was in respect of revision. He had come to the opinion that to take a reprint, even a revised reprint, as copy-text was indefensible. Whatever may be the relation of a particular substantive edition to the author's manuscript (provided that there is any transcriptional link at all) it stands to reason that the relation of a reprint of that edition must be more remote. If then, putting aside all question of revision, a particular substantive edition has an over-riding claim to be taken as copy-text, to displace it in favour of a reprint, whether revised or not, means receding at least one step further from the author's original in so far as the general form of the text is concerned.[11] Some such considerations must have been in McKerrow's mind when he wrote (*Prolegomena,* pp. 17-18): 'Even if, however, we were to assure ourselves . . . that certain corrections found in a later edition of a play were of Shakespearian authority, it would not by any means follow that that edition should be used as the copy-text of a reprint.[12] It would undoubtedly be necessary to incorporate these corrections in our text, but . . . it seems evident that . . . this later edition will (except for the corrections) deviate more widely than the earliest print from the author's original manuscript. . . . [Thus] the nearest approach to our ideal . . . will be produced by using the earliest "good" print as copy-text and inserting into it, from the first edition which contains them, such corrections as appear to us to be derived from the author.' This is a clear statement of the position, and in it he draws exactly the distinction between substantive readings (in the form of corrections) and accidentals (or general texture) on which I am insisting. He then, however, relapsed into heresy in the matter of the substantive readings. Having spoken, as above, of the need to introduce 'such corrections as appear to us to be derived from the author', he seems to have feared conceding too much to eclecticism, and he proceeded: 'We are not to regard the "goodness" of a reading in and by itself, or to consider whether it appeals to our aesthetic sensibilities or not; we are to consider whether a particular edition taken *as a whole* contains variants from the edition from which it was otherwise printed which could not reasonably be attributed to an ordinary press-corrector, but by reason of their style, point, and what we may call inner harmony with the spirit of the play as a whole, seem likely to be the work of the author: and once having decided this to our satisfaction we must accept *all* the alterations of that edition, saving any which seem obvious blunders or misprints.' We can see clearly enough what he had in mind, namely that the evidence of correction (under which head he presumably intended to include revision) must be considered *as a whole;* but he failed to add the equally important proviso that the alterations must also be *of a piece* (and not, as in *The Unfortunate Traveller,* of apparently disparate origin) before we can be called upon to accept them *all.* As he states it his canon is open to exactly the same objections as the 'most authoritative manuscript' theory in classical editing.

McKerrow was, therefore, in his later work quite conscious of the distinction between substantive readings and accidentals, in so far as the problem of revision is concerned. But he never applied the conception to cases in which we have more than one substantive text, as in *Hamlet* and perhaps in 2 *Henry IV, Troilus and Cressida,* and *Othello.* Presumably he would have argued that since faithfulness to the wording of the author was one of the criteria he laid down for determining the choice of the copy-text, it was an editor's duty to follow its substantive readings with a minimum of interference.

We may assume that neither McKerrow nor other editors of the conservative school imagined that such a procedure would always result in establishing the authentic text of the original; what they believed was that from it less harm would result than from opening the door to individual choice among variants, since it substituted an objective for a subjective method of determination. This is, I think, open to question. It is impossible to exclude individual judgment from editorial procedure: it operates of necessity in the all-important matter of the choice of copy-text and in the minor one of deciding what readings are possible and what not; why, therefore, should the choice between possible readings be withdrawn from its competence? Uniformity of result at the hands of different editors is worth little if it means only uniformity in error; and it may not be too optimistic a belief that the judgment of an editor, fallible as it must necessarily be, is likely to bring us closer to what the author wrote than the enforcement of an arbitrary rule.

The true theory is, I contend, that the copy-text should govern (generally) in the matter of accidentals, but that the choice between substantive readings belongs to the general theory of textual criticism and lies altogether beyond the narrow principle of the copy-text. Thus it may happen that in a critical edition the text rightly chosen as copy may not by any means be the one that supplies most substantive readings in cases of variation. The failure to make this distinction and to apply this principle has naturally led to too close and too general a reliance upon the text chosen as basis for an edition, and there has arisen what may be called the tyranny of the copy-text, a tyranny that has, in my opinion, vitiated much of the best editorial work of the past generation.

I will give a couple of examples of the sort of thing I mean that I have lately come across in the course of my own work. They are all the more suitable as illustrations since they occur in texts edited by scholars of recognized authority, neither of whom is particularly subject to the tyranny in question. One is from the edition of Marlowe's *Doctor Faustus* by Professor F. S. Boas (1932). The editor, rightly I think, took the so-called B-text (1616) as the basis of his own, correcting it where necessary by comparison with the A-text (1604).[13] Now a famous line in Faustus's opening soliloquy runs in 1604,

> Bid *Oncaymæon* farewell, *Galen* come

and in 1616,

> Bid *Oeconomy* farewell; and *Galen* come . . .

Here *Oncaymæon* is now recognized as standing for *on cay mæ on* or ὂν καί μὴ ὄν: but this was not understood at the time, and *Oeconomy* was substituted in reprints of the A-text in 1609 and 1611, and thence taken over by the B-text. The change, however, produced a rather awkward line, and in 1616 the *and* was introduced as a metrical accommodation. In the first half of the line Boas rightly restored the reading implied in A; but in the second half he retained, out of deference to his copy-text, the *and* whose only object was to accommodate the reading he had rejected in the first. One could hardly find a better example of the contradictions to which a mechanical following of the copy-text may lead.[14]

My other instance is from *The Gipsies Metamorphosed* as edited by Dr. Percy Simpson among the masques of Ben Jonson in 1941. He took as his copy-text the Huntington manuscript, and I entirely agree with his choice. In this, and in Simpson's edition, a line of the ribald Cock Lorel ballad runs (sir-reverence!),

Allw^{ch} he blewe away with a fart

whereas for *blewe* other authorities have *flirted*. Now, the meaning of *flirted* is not immediately apparent, for no appropriate sense of the word is recorded. There is, however, a rare use of the substantive *flirt* for a sudden gust of wind, and it is impossible to doubt that this is what Jonson had in mind, for no scribe or compositor could have invented the reading *flirted*. It follows that in the manuscript *blewe* is nothing but the conjecture of a scribe who did not understand his original: only the mesmeric influence of the copy-text could obscure so obvious a fact.[15]

I give these examples merely to illustrate the kind of error that, in modern editions of English works, often results from undue deference to the copy-text. This reliance on one particular authority results from the desire for an objective theory of text-construction and a distrust, often no doubt justified, of the operation of individual judgement. The attitude may be explained historically as a natural and largely salutary reaction against the methods of earlier editors. Dissatisfied with the results of eclectic freedom and reliance on personal taste, critics sought to establish some sort of mechanical apparatus for dealing with textual problems that should lead to uniform results independent of the operator. Their efforts were not altogether unattended by success. One result was the recognition of the general worthlessness of reprints. And even in the more difficult field of manuscript transmission it is true that formal rules will carry us part of the way: they can at least effect a preliminary clearing of the ground. This I sought to show in my essay on *The Calculus of Variants* (1927); but in the course of investigation it became clear that there is a definite limit to the field over which formal rules are applicable. Between readings of equal extrinsic authority no rules of the sort can decide, since by their very nature it is only to extrinsic relations that they are relevant. The choice is necessarily a matter for editorial judgement, and an editor who declines or is unable to exercise his judgement and falls back on some arbitrary canon, such as the authority of the copy-text, is in fact abdicating his editorial function. Yet this is what has been frequently commended as 'scientific'—'streng wissenschaftlich' in the prevalent idiom —and the result is that what many editors have done is to produce, not editions of their authors' works at all, but only editions of particular authorities for those works, a course that may be perfectly legitimate in itself, but was not the one they were professedly pursuing.

This by way, more or less, of digression. At the risk of repetition I should like to recapitulate my view of the position of copy-text in editorial procedure. The thesis I am arguing is that the historical circumstances of the English language make it necessary to adopt in formal matters the guidance of some particular early text. If the several extant texts of a work form an ancestral series, the earliest will naturally be selected, and since this will not only come nearest to the author's original in accidentals, but also (revision apart) most faithfully preserve the correct readings where substantive variants are in question, everything is straightforward, and the conservative treatment of the copy-text is justified. But whenever there is more than one substantive text of comparable authority,[16] then although it will still be necessary to choose one of them as copy-text, and to follow it in accidentals, this copy-text can be allowed no over-riding or even preponderant authority so far as substantive readings are concerned. The choice between these, in cases of variation, will be determined partly by the opinion the editor may form respecting the nature of the copy from which each substantive edition was printed, which is a matter of external authority; partly by the intrinsic authority of the several texts as judged by the relative frequency of manifest errors therein; and partly by the editor's judgement of the intrinsic claims of individual readings to originality—in other words their intrinsic merit, so long as by 'merit' we mean the likelihood of their being what the author wrote rather than their appeal to the individual taste of the editor.

Such, as I see it, is the general theory of copy-text. But there remain a number of subsidiary questions that it may be worthwhile to discuss. One is the degree of faithfulness with which the copy-text should be reproduced. Since the adoption of a copy-text is a matter of convenience rather than of principle—being imposed on us either by linguistic circumstance or our own philological ignorance—it follows that there is no reason for treating it as sacrosanct, even apart from the question of substantive variation. Every editor aiming at a critical edition will, of course, correct scribal or typographical errors. He will also correct readings in accordance with any errata included in the edition taken as copy-text. I see no reason why he should not alter misleading or eccentric spellings which he is satisfied emanate from the scribe or compositor and not from the author. If the punctuation is persistently erroneous or defective an editor may prefer to discard it altogether to make way for one of his own. He is, I think, at liberty to do so, provided that he gives due weight to the original in deciding on his own, and that he records the alteration whenever the sense is appreciably affected. Much the same applies to the use of capitals and italics. I should favour expanding contractions (except perhaps when dealing with an author's holograph) so long as ambiguities and abnormalities are recorded. A critical edition does not seem to me a suitable place in which to record the graphic peculiarities of particular texts,[17] and in this respect the copy-text is only one among others. These, however, are all matters within the discretion of an editor: I am only concerned to uphold his liberty of judgement.

Some minor points arise when it becomes necessary to replace a reading of the copy-text by one derived from another source. It need not, I think, be copied in the exact form in which it there appears. Suppose that the copy-text follows the earlier convention in the use of *u* and *v*, and the source from which the reading is taken follows the later. Naturally in transferring the reading from the latter to the former it would be made to conform to the earlier convention. I would go further. Suppose that the copy-text reads 'hazard', but that we have reason to believe that the correct reading is 'venture': suppose further that whenever this word occurs in the copy-text it is in the form 'venter': then 'venter', I maintain, is the form we should adopt. In like manner editorial emendations should be made to conform to the habitual spelling of the copy-text.

In the case of rival substantive editions the choice between substantive variants is, I have explained, generally independent of the copy-text. Perhaps one concession should be made. Suppose that the claims of two readings, one in the copy-text and one in some other authority, appear to be exactly balanced: what then should an editor do? In such a case, while there can be no logical reason for giving preference to the copy-text, in practice, if there is no reason for altering its reading, the obvious thing seems to be to let it stand.[18]

Much more important, and difficult, are the problems that arise in connexion with revision. McKerrow seems only to mention correction, but I think he must have intended to include revision, so long as this falls short of complete rewriting: in any case the principle is the same. I have already considered the practice he advocated (pp. 44–45)— namely that an editor should take the original edition as his copy-text and introduce into it all the substantive variants of the revised reprint, other than manifest errors—and have explained that I regard it as too sweeping and mechanical. The emendation that I proposed (p. 46) is, I think, theoretically sufficient, but from a practical point of view it

lacks precision. In a case of revision or correction the normal procedure would be for the author to send the printer either a list of the
alterations to be made or else a corrected copy of an earlier edition. In
setting up the new edition we may suppose that the printer would incorporate the alterations thus indicated by the author; but it must be
assumed that he would also introduce a normal amount of unauthorized variation of his own.[19] The problem that faces the editor is to distinguish between the two categories. I suggest the following frankly
subjective procedure. Granting that the fact of revision (or correction)
is established, an editor should in every case of variation ask himself
(1) whether the original reading is one that can reasonably be attributed to the author, and (2) whether the later reading is one that the author can reasonably be supposed to have substituted for the former. If
the answer to the first question is negative, then the later reading
should be accepted as at least possibly an authoritative correction (unless, of course, it is itself incredible). If the answer to (1) is affirmative
and the answer to (2) is negative, the original reading should be retained. If the answers to both questions are affirmative, then the later
reading should be presumed to be due to revision and admitted into
the text, whether the editor himself considers it an improvement or
not. It will be observed that one implication of this procedure is that a
later variant that is either completely indifferent or manifestly inferior,
or for the substitution of which no motive can be suggested, should be
treated as fortuitous and refused admission to the text—to the scandal
of faithful followers of McKerrow. I do not, of course, pretend that
my procedure will lead to consistently correct results, but I think that
the results, if less uniform, will be on the whole preferable to those
achieved through following any mechanical rule. I am, no doubt, pre-
supposing an editor of reasonable competence; but if an editor is really incompetent, I doubt whether it much matters what procedure he
adopts: he may indeed do less harm with some than with others, he
will do little good with any. And in any case, I consider that it would
be disastrous to curb the liberty of competent editors in the hope of
preventing fools from behaving after their kind.

I will give one illustration of the procedure in operation, taken again
from Jonson's *Masque of Gipsies*, a work that is known to have been
extensively revised for a later performance. At one point the text of
the original version runs as follows,

> a wise Gypsie . . . is as politicke a piece of Flesh, as most Iustices in
> the County where he maunds

whereas the texts of the revised version replace *maunds* by *stalkes*. Now, *maund* is a recognized canting term meaning to beg, and there is not the least doubt that it is what Jonson originally wrote. Further, it might well be argued that it is less likely that he should have displaced it in revision by a comparatively commonplace alternative, than that a scribe should have altered a rather unusual word that he failed to understand—just as we know that, in a line already quoted (p. 47), a scribe altered *flirted* to *blewe*. I should myself incline to this view were it not that at another point Jonson in revision added the lines,

And then ye may stalke
The *Gypsies* walke

where *stalk*, in the sense of going stealthily, is used almost as a technical term. In view of this I do not think it unreasonable to suppose that Jonson himself substituted *stalkes* for *maunds* from a desire to avoid the implication that his aristocratic Gipsies were beggars, and I conclude that it must be allowed to pass as (at least possibly) a correction, though no reasonable critic would *prefer* it to the original.

With McKerrow's view that in all normal cases of correction or revision the original edition should still be taken as the copy-text, I am in complete agreement. But not all cases are normal, as McKerrow himself recognized. While advocating, in the passage already quoted (p. 44), that the earliest 'good' edition should be taken as copy-text and corrections incorporated in it, he added the proviso, 'unless we could show that the [revised] edition in question (or the copy from which it had been printed) had been gone over and corrected *throughout* by' the author (my italics). This proviso is not in fact very explicit, but it clearly assumes that there are (or at least may be) cases in which an editor would be justified in taking a revised reprint as his copy-text, and it may be worth inquiring what these supposed cases are. If a work has been entirely rewritten, and is printed from a new manuscript, the question does not arise, since the revised edition will be a substantive one, and as such will presumably be chosen by the editor as his copy-text. But short of this, an author, wishing to make corrections or alterations in his work, may not merely hand the printer a revised copy of an earlier edition, but himself supervise the printing of the new edition and correct the proofs as the sheets go through the press. In such a case it may be argued that even though the earlier edition, if printed from his own manuscript, will preserve the author's individual peculiarities more faithfully than the revised reprint, he must nevertheless be assumed to have taken responsibility for the latter in respect of accidentals no less than substantive readings, and that it is therefore the revised reprint that should be taken as copy-text.

The classical example is afforded by the plays in the 1616 folio of Ben Jonson's Works. In this it appears that even the largely recast *Every Man in his Humour* was not set up from an independent manuscript but from a much corrected copy of the quarto of 1601. That Jonson revised the proofs of the folio has indeed been disputed, but Simpson is most likely correct in supposing that he did so, and he was almost certainly responsible for the numerous corrections made while the sheets were in process of printing. Simpson's consequent decision to take the folio for his copy-text for the plays it contains will doubtless be approved by most critics. I at least have no wish to dispute his choice.[20] Only I would point out—and here I think Dr. Simpson would agree with me—that even in this case the procedure involves some sacrifice of individuality. For example, I notice that in the text of *Sejanus* as printed by him there are twenty-eight instances of the Jonsonian 'Apostrophus' (an apostrophe indicating the elision of a vowel that is nevertheless retained in printing) but of these only half actually appear in the folio, the rest he has introduced from the quarto. This amounts to an admission that in some respects at least the quarto preserves the formal aspect of the author's original more faithfully than the folio.

The fact is that cases of revision differ so greatly in circumstances and character that it seems impossible to lay down any hard and fast rule as to when an editor should take the original edition as his copy-text and when the revised reprint. All that can be said is that if the original be selected, then the author's corrections must be incorporated; and that if the reprint be selected, then the original reading must be restored when that of the reprint is due to unauthorized variation. Thus the editor cannot escape the responsibility of distinguishing to the best of his ability between the two categories. No juggling with copy-text will relieve him of the duty and necessity of exercizing his own judgment.

In conclusion I should like to examine this problem of revision and copy-text a little closer. In the case of a work like *Sejanus,* in which correction or revision has been slight, it would obviously be possible to take the quarto as the copy-text and introduce into it whatever authoritative alterations the folio may supply; and indeed, were one editing the play independently, this would be the natural course to pursue. But a text like that of *Every Man in his Humour* presents an entirely different problem. In the folio revision and reproduction are so blended that it would seem impossible to disentangle intentional from what may be fortuitous variation, and injudicious to make the attempt. An editor of the revised version has no choice but to take the folio as his copy-text. It would appear therefore that a reprint may in practice be forced upon an editor as copy-text by the nature of the revision itself, quite apart from the question whether or not the author exercized any supervision over its printing.

This has a bearing upon another class of texts, in which a reprint was revised, not by the author, but through comparison with some more authoritative manuscript. Instances are Shakespeare's *Richard III* and *King Lear*. Of both much the best text is supplied by the folio of 1623; but this is not a substantive text, but one set up from a copy of an earlier quarto that had been extensively corrected by collation with a manuscript preserved in the playhouse. So great and so detailed appears to have been the revision that it would be an almost impossible task to distinguish between variation due to the corrector and that due to the compositor,[21] and an editor has no choice but to take the folio as copy-text. Indeed, this would in any case be incumbent upon him for a different reason; for the folio texts are in some parts connected by transcriptional continuity with the author's manuscript, whereas the quartos contain only reported texts, whose accidental characteristics can be of no authority whatever. At the same time, analogy with *Every Man in his Humour* suggests that even had the quartos of *Richard III* and *King Lear* possessed higher authority than in fact they do, the choice of copy-text must yet have been the same.

I began this discussion in the hope of clearing my own mind as well as others' on a rather obscure though not unimportant matter of editorial practice. I have done something to sort out my own ideas: others must judge for themselves. If they disagree, it is up to them to maintain some different point of view. My desire is rather to provoke discussion than to lay down the law.

NOTES

This paper was read before the English Institute on September 8, 1949, by Dr. J. M. Osborn for W. W. Greg.

[1] Introduction to Manilius, 1903, p. xxxii.

[2] The more naive the scribe, the more often will the assumption prove

correct; the more sophisticated, the less often. This, no doubt, is why critics of this school tend to reject 'the more correct but the less sincere' manuscript in favor of 'the more corrupt but the less interpolated', as Housman elsewhere observes ('The Application of Thought to Textual Criticism,' *Proceedings of the Classical Association*, 1921, xviii. 75). Still, any reasonable critic will prefer the work of a naive to that of a sophisticated scribe, though he may not regard it as necessarily 'better.'

[3] I believe that an attempt has been made in the case of certain Old and Middle English texts, but how consistently and with what success I cannot judge. In any case I am here concerned chiefly with works of the sixteenth and seventeenth centuries.

[4] It will, no doubt, be objected that punctuation may very seriously 'affect' an author's meaning; still it remains properly a matter of presentation, as spelling does in spite of its use in distinguishing homonyms. The distinction I am trying to draw is practical, not philosophic. It is also true that between substantive readings and spellings there is an intermediate class of word-forms about the assignment of which opinions may differ and which may have to be treated differently in dealing with the work of different scribes.

[5] For the sake of clearness in making the distinction I have above stressed the independence of scribes and compositors in the matter of accidentals: at the same time, when he selects his copy-text, an editor will naturally hope that it retains at least something of the character of the original. Experience, however, shows that while the distribution of substantive variants generally agrees with the genetic relation of the texts, that of accidental variants is comparatively arbitrary.

[6] Some discussion bearing on it

will be found in the Prolegomena to my lectures on *The Editorial Problem in Shakespeare* (1942), 'Note on Accidental Characteristics of the Text' (pp. l-lv), particularly the paragraph on pp. liii-liv, and note 1. But at the time of writing I was still a long way from any consistent theory regarding copy-text.

[7] A 'substantive' edition is Mc-Kerrow's term for an edition that is not a reprint of any other. I shall use the term in this sense, since I do not think that there should be any danger of confusion between 'substantive editions' and 'substantive readings'.

I have above ignored the practice of some eccentric editors who took as copy-text for a work the latest edition printed in the author's life-time, on the assumption, presumably, that he revised each edition as it appeared. The textual results were naturally deplorable.

[8] He believed, or at least strongly suspected, that some were due to the printer's desire to save space, and that others were 'the work of some person who had not thoroughly considered the sense of the passage which he was altering' (ii.195).

[9] Nashe, ii.197. The word 'reprint' really begs the question. If all an 'editor' aims at is an exact reprint, then obviously he will choose one early edition, on whatever grounds he considers relevant, and reproduce it as it stands. But McKerrow does emend his copy-text where necessary. It is symptomatic that he did not distinguish between a critical edition and a reprint.

[10] Without the italicized phrase the statement would appear much more plausible (though I should still regard it as fallacious, and so would McKerrow himself have done later on) but it would not justify the procedure adopted.

[11] This may, at any rate, be put

forward as a general proposition, leaving possible exceptions to be considered later (pp. 51 ff.).

[12] Again he speaks of a 'reprint' where he evidently had in mind a critical edition on conservative lines.

[13] Boas's text is in fact modernized, so that my theory of copy-text does not strictly apply, but since he definitely accepts the B-text as his authority, the principle is the same.

[14] Or consider the following readings: 1604, 1609 'Consissylogismes', 1611 'subtle sylogismes', 1616 'subtle Sillogisms'. Here 'subtile', an irresponsible guess by the printer of 1611 for a word he did not understand, was taken over in 1616. The correct reading is, of course, 'concise syllogisms'. Boas's refusal to take account of the copy used in 1616 led him here and elsewhere to perpetuate some of its manifest errors. In this particular instance he appears to have been unaware of the reading of 1611.

[15] At another point two lines appear in an unnatural order in the manuscript. The genetic relation of the texts proves the inversion to be an error. But of this relation Simpson seems to have been ignorant. He was again content to rely on the copytext.

[16] The proviso is inserted to meet the case of the so-called 'bad quartos' of Shakespearian and other Elizabethan plays and of the whole class of 'reported' texts, whose testimony can in general be neglected.

[17] That is, certainly not in the text, and probably not in the general apparatus: they may appropriately form the subject of an appendix.

[18] This is the course I recommended in the Prolegomena to *The Editorial Problem in Shakespeare* (p. xxix), adding that it 'at least saves the trouble of tossing a coin'. What I actually wrote in 1942 was that in such circumstances an editor 'will naturally retain the reading of the copy-text, this being the text which he has already decided is *prima facie* the more correct'. This implies that correctness in respect of substantive readings is one of the criteria in the choice of the copy-text; and indeed I followed McKerrow in laying it down that an editor should select as copy-text the one that 'appears likely to have departed least in wording, spelling, and punctuation from the author's manuscript'. There is a good deal in my Prolegomena that I should now express differently, and on this particular point I have definitely changed my opinion. I should now say that the choice of the copy-text depends solely on its formal features (accidentals) and that fidelity as regards substantive readings is irrelevant—though fortunately in nine cases out of ten the choice will be the same whichever rule we adopt.

[19] I mean substantive variation, such as occurs in all but the most faithful reprints.

[20] Simpson's procedure in taking the 1616 folio as copy-text in the case of most of the masques included, although he admits that in their case Jonson cannot be supposed to have supervised the printing, is much more questionable.

[21] Some variation is certainly due to error on the part of the folio printer, and this it is of course the business of an editor to detect and correct so far as he is able.

Bibliography and the Novelistic Fallacy

Bruce Harkness

It is a truth universally acknowledged, that a critic intent upon analysis and interpretation, must be in want of a good text.[1] It is also universally acknowledged that we live in an age of criticism, indeed of "new criticism"—which means that we as critics are dedicated to a very close reading of the text. Sometimes, it is true, that critical principle leads to abuses. The symbol-hunting, the ambiguity-spinning become wonders to behold. As one objector has put it, "nose to nose, the critic confronts writer and, astonished, discovers himself."[2] Nonetheless, the principle of close reading is held central by us all. Immediately that one contemplates novel criticism, however, an oddity appears: the last thing we find in a discussion by a new critic is some analysis of the actual text.

The modern critic is apt to be entirely indifferent to the textual problems of a novel. He is all too prone to examine rigorously a faulty text. As Gordon Ray and others have pointed out, even the Great Cham of British Criticism errs in this respect. F. R. Leavis defends the early Henry James in *The Great Tradition:* "Let me insist, then, at once, . . . that his [James's] 'first attempt at a novel,' *Roderick Hudson* (1874), in spite of its reputation, is a very distinguished book that deserves permanent currency—much more so than many novels passing as classics." Professor Ray adds that "Mr. Leavis goes on to quote three long paragraphs to illustrate the novel's 'sustained maturity of theme and treatment. . . .' These remarks are amply warranted by the passage that Mr. Leavis cites. But unhappily he has quoted, not the text of the first edition of 1877 [while carefully dating it from the time of composition to make it appear all the more precocious], which is simple enough, but that of the New York edition of 1907, revised in James's intricate later manner. This leaves him," concludes Leavis's critic, "in the position of having proved at length what nobody would think of denying, that James's writing at the age of sixty-four has all the characteristics of maturity."[3]

Unhappily, few of us can afford to laugh at the poor new critic. We all know the truth that we must have a good text, but most of us do not act upon it. A commonplace? Yes, and unfortunately, I have only that commonplace to urge; but I claim good company. Jane Austen, with whom I started, recognized that *Pride and Prejudice* had no profoundly new meaning. She ironically developed upon commonplaces: don't act on first impressions; don't interfere in your best friend's love affair; don't ignore your younger daughters. My point is that, ironically, everyone ignores the bibliographical study of the novel. People who would consider it terribly bad form to slight the textual study of a play or poem—or even doggerel—commit bibliographical nonsense when handed a novel. It seems that the novel just doesn't count. A key error in many studies of the novel is simply this, that the novel is unconsciously considered a different order of thing from poetry—a poem's text must be approached seriously. I shall illustrate by mentioning the sins of editors, reprinters, publishers, scholars, and, alas, bibliographers. Then, after discussing a few of the many reasons for this bibliographical heresy, I shall turn to my main illustration of the need for textual bibliography, *The Great Gatsby*.

II

A list of representative errors, by no means exhaustive, by sound men whom I admire in all other respects will make clear how faulty the texts of novels are, and how little we care. A good editor has put *The Nigger of the "Narcissus"* in *The Portable Conrad,* an excellent volume the introductions to which contain some of the best Conrad criticism. But what, one may wonder, is the copy-text for *The Nigger?* A search through the book discloses two references, the less vague of which reads as follows: "It is from the editions published and copyrighted by the latter [Doubleday and Company] that the texts reproduced in this volume have been drawn" (p. 758).

After a spot of searching the reader can discover for himself that the copy-text for *The Nigger of the "Narcissus"* is not the collected English edition, which as is well known was Conrad's major concern. The copy-text was an early American publication, which Conrad habitually did not supervize. The new critic immediately asks, does it make any difference?

The collected English edition was, as one might suspect with an author who was constantly revising, changed in many ways. This final version cuts down Conrad's intrusive "philosophizing," and corrects Donkin's cockney accent, among other shifts.[4] I yield to no man in my admiration for Conrad, but if he has a fault, it lies in that adjectival "philosophy" which is admired by some, charitably overlooked by others, and condemned by a few as pipe-sucking old seadog-talk. Surely the following, from the early part of Chapter Four, is inappropriate in the mouth of the sailor-narrator: "Through the perfect wisdom of its grace [the sea's] they [seamen] are not permitted to meditate at ease upon the complicated and acrid savour of existence, lest they should remember and, perchance, regret the reward of a cup of inspiring bitterness, tasted so often, and so often withdrawn before their stiffening but reluctant lips. They must without pause justify their life. . . ." Most of this passage, and much similar sententiousness, were cut by Conrad from the collected English text; but they all stand in *The Portable Conrad*.

As for the class of books known loosely as "reprints," I suppose that no one expects a good text for twenty-five or thirty-five cents. These books I am not concerned with, but the more serious paperbacks, obviously intended for use in colleges, are sometimes faulty. For example, Rinehart Editions' copy of *Pride and Prejudice* reprints Chapman's excellent text—but suppresses the indication of three volume construction by numbering the chapters serially throughout.[5] Though three volumes are mentioned in the introduction, this misprinting of such a tightly constructed novel can only be regretted, for the effect on the college reader must be odd.

What of the publisher of more expensive novels? It can easily be seen that errors are not limited to the paperback field. Consider, for example, the one-volume Scribner edition of James's *The Wings of the Dove*, dated 1945 or 1946. Here is no scrimping for paperback costs, but the book is not what one would think. It is not a reprint of the famous New York edition; it is another, unacknowledged impression of the 1902 first American edition, dressed up with a new-set New York preface—an odd procedure the reason for which is not apparent. The publisher nowhere tells the reader that this is like some wines—an old text with a new preface. Yet one line of print would have made the matter clear. It is only by his own efforts of collation of the preface and the text itself that the reader knows where he is.[6]

To turn to the errors of scholarship, take F. O. Matthiessen's lengthy appreciation of Melville's phrase "soiled fish of the sea" in

White Jacket. Melville's narrator says of himself, after he had fallen into the sea, "I wondered whether I was yet dead or still dying. But of a sudden some fashionless form brushed my side—some inert, soiled fish of the sea; the thrill of being alive again tingled. . . ." This section Matthiessen acclaims as being imagery of the "sort that was to become peculiarly Melville's . . . hardly anyone but Melville could have created the shudder that results from calling this frightening vagueness some 'soiled fish of the sea'!" Then follows a discussion of the metaphysical conceit and its moral and psychological implications.

As has been pointed out, the genius in this shuddering case of imagery is not Melville, who wrote *coiled* fish, not *soiled* fish. "Coiled fish" stands in the first editions of *White Jacket,* and to an unknown Constable printer should go the laurels for soiling the page with a typographical error.[7]

Matthiessen's error does not concern me now, but it does concern me that the scholar who first caught the mistake has a strange but perhaps understandable attitude toward textual matters. Recognizing that such an error "in the proper context" might have promulgated a "false conception," the scholar feels that the slip does not actually matter in Melville's case. Furthermore, he feels that Matthiessen's position is essentially sound—he was merely the victim of "an unlucky error." While sympathizing with common sense and professional etiquette, one may still wonder, however, how many such slips in illustration are allowable. Could the critic, if challenged, produce as many sound illustrations as one would like? Does not Matthiessen, in his categorizing of conceits, virtually admit that this particular kind is rare in *White Jacket?*

When we look at the texts of novels from the other way, how many good editions of novelists do we have? How do they compare with the poets? We know a good bit about the bibliographies of Scott, Trollope, Meredith, but those of Dickens, Thackeray, Conrad, Hawthorne, and many more are completely out of date.[8] How many collected editions can be put on the same shelf with Chapman's 1923 Jane Austen? "We have virtually no edited texts of Victorian novelists," says Mrs. Tillotson in the introduction of *Novels of the Eighteen-Forties* (1954). How slowly we move, if at all.

Take Hardy for example. In 1946 Carl Weber said that "many scholars have apparently made no attempt to gain access to Hardy's definitive texts." In March, 1957, a scholar can complain that "As late as November 1956, sixty full years after the publication of the book, the only edition of *Jude* printed in the United States took no account of either of the two revisions which Hardy gave the novel. . . . The New Harper's Modern Classics edition . . . [however] is *almost* identical with that of the definitive 1912 'Wessex Edition.' "[9] One is hardly surprised that Professor Weber is the editor.

Sixty years is a long time, but American literatue is no better off. *Moby-Dick*, our greatest novel, presents no problem of copy-text. Yet more than 100 years went by after publication before we had what a recent scholar called the "first serious reprint," by Hendricks House. Before that, the careful reader did not even know, for example, the punctuation of the famous "Know ye, now, Bulkington?" passage. But how good is this reprint? The same scholar—not the editor—asks us to consider it a definitive edition. His reasons? It contains only 108 compositor's errors and twenty silent emendations.[10] Would anyone make such a claim for a volume of poems?

So much for editors, publishers, scholars. The sins of the bibliographer are mainly those of omission. For well-known reasons he tends to slight 19th- and 20th-century books in general, and in consequence most novels.[11]

The critic therefore needs convincing that novels should be approached bibliographically. The critic appreciates the sullied-solid-sallied argument about Shakespeare, but not that of 108 typos for *Moby-Dick*. A false word in a sonnet may change a fifth of its meaning; the punctuation at the end of the "Ode on a Grecian Urn" can be considered crucial to the meaning of the whole poem; but who, the critic argues from bulk, can stand the prospect of collating 700 pages of Dickens to find a few dozen misplaced commas? Like the "soiled fish" reading of *White Jacket*, a few mistakes seriously damage neither novel nor criticism. They are swallowed up in the vast bulk of the novel, which by and large (and excepting a few well-known oddities such as *Tender is the Night* in which case one must be sure which text one is attacking) is decently printed and generally trustworthy. The critic feels that a mistake here or there in the text is immaterial. "It doesn't *really* alter my interpretation," is the standard phrase.

This attitude has long since been defeated by bibliographers for all genres except the novel. One wonders indeed, if the critic would be willing to make his plea more logical. Could not the attitude be extended to some formula for trustworthiness versus error? It ought not to be difficult to arrive at a proportion expressing the number of errors per page, exceeding which a novel could be condemned as poorly printed.

Amid bad reasoning, there is some truth to the critic's defence against bibliography. The argument can be shifted from the ground of a novel's size and a reader's energy to the aesthetic nature of the novel. The critic is certainly right in maintaining that novels are more loosely constructed, even the best of them, than poems or short stories. The effects of a novel are built through countless small touches, and the loss of one or two—whether by error in text or inattention in reading—is immaterial. Putting aside the counter claim that this truth is damaging to the critical and crucial premise of close reading, surely all is a matter of degree. And what is more, the theory applies mainly to character portrayal. If we fail to recognize Collins as a fawning ass on one page, we will certainly see him aright on another.

That much must be granted the critic. In other concerns, however, the novel may not be repetitive. To give just one illustration: F. Scott Fitzgerald's *Last Tycoon* as published in unfinished form contains a boy whom the reader should compare to the "villain" of the piece, Brady (or Bradogue as he was called in an earlier draft). In Fitzgerald's directions to himself left in his MSS, he says "Dan [the boy] bears, in some form of speech, a faint resemblance to Bradogue. This must be subtly done and not look too much like a parable or moral lesson, still the impression must be conveyed, but be careful to convey it *once* and not rub it in. If the reader misses it, let it go—don't repeat."[12]

My last and painful reason why virtually no one is concerned with the texts of novels is this: most bibliographers are also university teachers and many of them suffer from schizophrenia. I do not refer to that familiar disease which makes us scholars by day and diaper washers by night, but that split in the man between Graduate Seminar number 520 in Bibliography and Freshman "Intro. to Fic.," 109. How many of us make bibliographical truths part of our daily lives or attempt to inspire our graduate students so to do? In this respect many bibliographers are like socialists and Christians: walking arguments for the weakness of the cause.

Let me give one or two illustrations from experience. Not very long ago I sat in a staff meeting while we worried over a sentence of Conrad's introduction to *Victory* in the Modern Library edition. The sentence contained the odd phrase "adaptable cloth," used about mankind. It made no sense until it was finally pointed out that "adap-table" was divided at the end of the line in both American collected edition and reprint—a domestically minded compositor was talking about a table cloth, while Conrad was saying that Man is "wonderfully adaptable both by his power of endurance and in his capacity for detachment."

And our silly discussion had gone on despite long teaching, and one's natural suspicion of the cheaper reprints that perforce must be used in college classes.

More seriously, consider Dickens' *Great Expectations*, taught to freshmen at many universities, by staffs composed of men nearly all of whom have been required to "take" bibliography. Yet how many of these teachers have turned to the facts of serial publication to explain the figure of Orlick, extremely puzzling by critical standards alone? One immediately sees that Orlick's attack on Mrs. Joe, which ultimately causes her death, is used by Dickens to pep up a three instalment sequence the main purpose of which is simply to let Pip age. This sequence would have been too dull, too insistent on domestic scenes round the hearth while Pip gradually withdraws from Joe, were it not for the Orlick subplot.[13] The novel apparently had to have thirty-six weekly units, and Dickens therefore could not simply skip this period of Pip's life. The figure of Orlick may not be critically acceptable, but he is at least understandable when one views him in the light of publishing history.

I am also indicting myself for not understanding this point; for it was not many months ago that I looked up the weekly issues of *All the Year Round* and now have far more detail than, as the saying goes, "the short space of this article will permit the discussion of." I was derelict in my duty partly because life is short and bibliography is long, but also partly because I unconsciously resented the editor of my paperback *Great Expectations* whose job I was having to do.

For I am more familiar with the schizophrenia than most people, though mine takes a different form. With critics I am apt to claim to be a bibliographer; among bibliographers, I proclaim myself a critic.

The critic, one must recognize, can argue on aesthetic grounds against working on the texts of novels. He can produce the *tu quoque* argument. And he can say that the bibliographer neglects *what* he is working on. Of 244 articles on textual bibliography in the *Studies in Bibliography* list for 1954, only three were related to novels.[14] "What has the bibliographer been doing?" asks the new critic.

It may be that under the aspect of eternity George Sandys' *Ovid* is more important than Conrad's *Nostromo* or Melville's *Moby-Dick*, but it would be hard to convince the novel critic of that.

III

For these reasons I have chosen F. Scott Fitzgerald's *The Great Gatsby* as my main illustration. It brings out nearly all my points: inconsistent editing, an unknown or unidentified text, a publisher who is good but vague, important errors in an important book, schizophrenia in the bibliographer-teacher. Not only is *Gatsby* a fine novel, but it is taught so often because it contains many of the basic themes of American literature: West versus East; the search for value; the American dream; crime and society; and in young Jim Gatz's "General Resolves," it even reaches back to Ben Franklin and Poor Richard.

How many know, however, what they have been teaching?

The Great Gatsby exists in print in three main versions: the first edition, beginning in April, 1925; a new edition in the volume with *The Last Tycoon* and certain stories, beginning in 1941; and a sub-edition of the latter text in the Modern Standard Authors series (*Three Novels*) together with *Tender is the Night* and *The Last Tycoon*, beginning in 1953.[15] Though *Gatsby* in the *Three Novels* version is another impression of *The Last Tycoon* plates I call it a sub-edition because *Gatsby's* position is different, coming first in the volume, and there are many changes in the text.[16]

So far as I know, the only available information about the text of *Gatsby* is buried in the notes to Arthur Mizener's *The Far Side of Paradise*. Mizener says that Fitzgerald found a misprint in the first edition: the future Nick Carraway speaks of at the end of the novel should be "orgiastic," not "orgastic".[17]

> It was one of the few proof errors in the book [adds Mizener], perhaps because Scribner's worked harder over *Gatsby* than over Fitzgerald's earlier books, perhaps because [Ring] Lardner read the final proofs. The only other proof error Fitzgerald found was the reading of "eternal" for "external" on p. 58 [of the first edition]. . . . Edmund Wilson's reprint in his edition of *The Last Tycoon* corrects all it could without access to Fitzgerald's personally corrected copy.[18]

Let us couple these comments with Matthew Bruccoli's interesting article on Fitzgerald's *This Side of Paradise*. Bruccoli is surprised that thirty-one errors are corrected in later impressions of the novel. He concludes that "the first printing was an inexcusably sloppy job," although Fitzgerald was himself in part responsible for the difficulty. We might infer two things, therefore: far fewer errors in *Gatsby's* first edition, and a correction of the word "eternal," in *The Last Tycoon*.

Not so. The correction to "external" is not made in the second impression of the first edition, nor in any impression of *Last Tycoon* (202.2, TN 38.2). Though there are only four changes from the first to second impression of the first edition, there are no less than twenty-seven changes between *First* and *Last Tycoon.* Between *First* and the 1953 *Three Novels,* there are more than 125 changes. Of these changes about fifty are quite meaningless. They change "to-morrow" with a hyphen to "tomorrow," for example. Or they change "Beale Street Blues" to *Beale Street Blues.* This class of change will not be commented upon nor included in statistics, except to add that the publisher was not at all consistent in making such alterations.[19]

There are, in other words, 75 changes of moment between the first edition and *Three Novels*—forty-four more than in *This Side of Paradise.* Many of them are more important. Of the changes the August, 1925, first edition brought, the most important was the substitution of the word "echolalia" for "chatter" in the phrase "the chatter of the garden" (*First* 60 line 16).[20]

But we must remember that *Last Tycoon* and *Three Novels* are both posthumous, and that of the twenty-seven changes from *First* to LT, twelve are clearly errors, seven are dubious improvements, and only eight are clearly better readings. Of them all, the word "orgiastic," apparently, alone has the author's authority. What's more, the sub-edition *Three Novels* retains all but two of these bad changes. An example of an error begun in LT and continued in TN occurs on page 209.6 of *First* (296.8 of LT and 132.8 of TN). The sentence of Nick's, "It just shows you." is dropped from the text, thereby making the punctuation wrong and leading the reader to confuse speakers.

Between *First* and *Three Novels* the changes are of several kinds. In addition to the fifty or so "meaningless" changes, there are (a) fifteen changes of spelling, including six that change the meaning of a word and others that affect dialect; (b) seventeen changes in punctuation, including quotation marks, paragraph indication, and so on; (c) six incorrect omissions of a word or sentence or other details; (d) six proper deletions of a word or more; (e) thirty-one substantive changes—the substitution of a word or the addition of a phrase or sentence. For instance, Gatsby is transferred from the Sixteenth to the Seventh Infantry during the war. (See *First* 57.17, LT 201.12, TN 37.12.)

For when we turn to *Three Novels* we must move out of the camp of strict bibliography into the field of its important ally, publishing history. Fitzgerald's own copy of the first impression, with pencilled notes in the margins, is now located at the Princeton University Library and was used to make the sub-edition.

Of the seventy-five changes between *First* and TN, thirty-eight are with Fitzgerald's sanction and thirty-seven are without. Most of the thirty-seven changes not recommended by Fitzgerald are "corrections" made by a publisher's staff editor or by Malcolm Cowley, who supervized the sub-edition. However, some of this group are clearly errors, many of them having crept into the text by way of the *Last Tycoon* version. The noteworthy thing is that no reader knows the authority for *any* of the changes. The sub-edition itself does not even announce that it takes into account Fitzgerald's marginal comments—which, one would have supposed, would have been good business as well as good scholarship.

Furthermore, some of the thirty-eight "sanctioned" changes were only queried by Fitzgerald: no actual rewording was directed. An example is the phrase "lyric again in." Fitzgerald questioned "again" and the editor dropped it. But in five instances of Fitzgerald's questioning a word, no change was made—as, for example, Fitzgerald was unhappy to note that he had used the word "turbulent" twice in the first chapter.[21] There is also one instance in which Fitzgerald expressly asked for a change that was not made. At *First*, 50.1, Fitzgerald corrected "an amusement park" to "amusement parks," but the later version does not record the request (TN 32.32).

On the whole, one can say this, therefore: that about sixty of the changes from *First* to *Three Novels* are proper. That is, they either have the author's authority or are stylistic or grammatical improvements or are immaterial. I speak just now as a devil's advocate—a critic with a jaundiced eye toward bibliography. He would call the deletion of a comma from a short compound sentence "immaterial," though it was not done by the author.[22] I am trying, in other words, to make the text sound as good as I can. Problems arise, however, from the fact that awkward readings sometimes come from purely typographical errors, sometimes from editor's decision, and sometimes from Fitzgerald's own notes. Everyone would accept such changes as "an Adam study" for "an Adam's study," (*First* 110.26, LT 233.30, TN 69.30); but by the same token few critics will be pleased by a Fitzgerald marginal correction reading "common knowledge to the turgid sub or suppressed journalism of 1902," instead of "common property of the turgid journalism of 1902" *First* 120.11, TN 76.5).

We are left then with fifteen or sixteen errors begun or continued in *Three Novels*, errors which I trust even the newest of new critics would accept as having some degree of importance. That degree of course varies. The dedication "Once again, to Zelda," is left off, for example. Dialetical words are falsely made standard English, or half-doctored-up, as in this sentence where the word in *First* was "appendicitus": "You'd of thought she had my appendicitis out" (*First* 37.4,

LT 188.37, TN 24.37). Sentences start without a capital[23] or end without a period[24] or are dropped altogether.[25] Quotation marks appear or disappear[26] and awkward readings come from nowhere. To illustrate that last: on page 149.10 of *First* Nick says that "the giant eyes of Doctor T. J. Eckleburg kept their vigil, but I perceived, after a moment, that other eyes were regarding us with peculiar intensity from less than twenty feet away." The eyes are Myrtle Wilson's but in *Three Novels* 95.1 (and LT 259.1) the sentence is confused when "the" is added without any reference and "from" and "with peculiar intensity" are dropped: "the giant eyes of Doctor T. J. Eckleburg kept their vigil, but I perceived, after a moment that *the* other eyes were regarding us less than twenty feet away" (italics added). Another dubious change is this: a joking slip or drunken mistake by Daisy is corrected—"Biloxi, Tennessee" becomes academically placed in its proper governmental locality.[27] One hardly needs to add that none of these changes have Fitzgerald's sanction.

The biggest errors, critically speaking, are ones that also occur in *Last Tycoon*. The principle of order in *The Great Gatsby* is a simple one: Nick Carraway, the narrator, tells his story wildly out of chronological order, but *in* the order that he learned it—with one exception.[28] The first half of the book is concerned with the development of the outsiders' illusions about Jay Gatsby—he is "nephew to Von Hindenburg," and so on (TN 47). The second half is a penetration in depth of Gatsby's illusion itself. The shift in the theme of the book is marked by the one major sequence which Nick gives the reader out of the order in which he himself learned it. I refer to the Dan Cody episode from Gatsby's early days.[29]

Now the most important structural unit in the book below the chapter is the intra-chapter break signified by a white space left on the page.[30] In *Last Tycoon* and *Three Novels* four of these important indications of structure are suppressed.[31] Oddly enough, it is the one following the Dan Cody story that is the first one missing. The detail that divides the book into its two structural elements is botched.

In the *Three Novels* version of *Gatsby*, then, we have a book quite well printed—surprisingly so when we look at the galley proofs. They are filled with changes—with page after page added in long hand, with whole galleys deleted or rearranged. (I would estimate that one-fifth of the book was written after the galley stage.) And we have a book that tries to take into account the author's latest stylistic revisions. Unfortunately, it is also a book that has far too many errors.

Perhaps this is the place to mention the third Scribner edition of

Gatsby, the paperback Student's Edition, which uses TN as copy text. Have matters been improved? Some have, but more errors have been added. There are twelve changes from TN to SE: it makes two distinct improvements, including the replacement of the dedication; but it adds three places in which intra-chapter breaks are suppressed.[32] The other changes are "immaterial" typographical errors such as "turned to be," instead of "turned to me" (SE 71.17 and TN 54.20) and *"police,"* instead of "po*lice*" (SE 27.27 and TN 22.19).

I hope it is clear, then, that *Three Novels* represents the best present text of *Gatsby.* No doubt it and the Student's Edition will be the ones most used in colleges for some time. It should also be clear that in *Three Novels,* we have this kind of book:

1. A book which nowhere gives the reader the authority for seventy-five changes, all of them posthumously printed.

2. One which fails to make use of all of Fitzgerald's corrections.

3. One which contains thirty-seven changes which Fitzgerald did not authorize—some of which are of most dubious value.

4. A book which contains at least fifteen quite bad readings, one of which is of the highest structural importance.

So, armed with this mixed blessing, or with the worse one of *Last Tycoon,* or worst of all, with a reprint by another publisher which has none of Fitzgerald's corrections and additions, many students unwittingly face the next semester with their prairie squints. Only a nonexistent, eclectic text, combining the best of the August, 1925 first edition and the *Three Novels* text of *The Great Gatsby* would be proper.[33]

Could we not as critics pay more attention to Bibliography, and we as Bibliographers to criticism? Can not we somehow insist that editing actually be done—instead of the practice of putting a fancy introduction on a poor text? Can not we have sound texts reproduced and publisher's history stated by the editor? Can not we know *what it is* we have in our hands? For it is simply a fallacy that the novel does not count.

NOTES

[1] This article represents an expanded form of a paper read at the Bibliography Section of the 1957 Modern Language Association meetings.

[2] Marvin Mudrick, "Conrad and

the Terms of Modern Criticism," *Hudson Review,* VI (1954), 421.

[3] Gordon N. Ray, "The Importance of Original Editions," in *Nineteenth-Century English Books,* by Gordon N. Ray, Carl Weber, and John Carter (1952), p. 22. See also "Henry James Reprints," *TLS,* Feb. 5, 1949, p. 96.

[4] C. S. Evans of the editorial department of Heinemann wrote Conrad on 2 Sept., 1920, about Donkin's inconsistent dialect: "I have queried spelling of 'Hymposed,'" and so on. (See *Life and Letters* [London: Heineenn, 1927], II, 247-248, for the exchange with Evans.) J. D. Gordon in *Joseph Conrad: The Making of a Novelist* (1940), p. 139, et passim, discusses many of the revisions of the text.

It might be possible to defend the use of an early text for *The Nigger,* but no reason is given in *The Portable Conrad.*

[5] Though I cannot pretend to have examined them all, I know of only one independently produced paperback novel with good textual apparatus. This is Rinehart Editions' *Lord Jim,* which contains a collation of the four main texts. Riverside's *Pride and Prejudice* has a good text, but again Chapman's edition lies behind it. There must be, I am sure, many more good texts beside *Lord Jim* in the higher class of paperbacks, and even in the cheaper ones. But what publishers draw them to our attention, and what publisher doesn't (apparently) feel that a properly edited paperback novel will frighten away the common reader by its appearance?

[6] Furthermore, it would be difficult to defend the choice of first-edition text, as one might for *The Nigger of the "Narcissus,"* or *Roderick Hudson,* since James was writing in his intricate manner by 1902.

[7] See J. W. Nichol, "Melville's 'Soiled Fish of the Sea,'" *AL,* XXI (1949), 338-339.

[8] See John Carter, *op. cit.,* p. 53 et passim; reasons for the lack of bibliographical study are also discussed.

[9] Robert C. Slack, "The Text of Hardy's *Jude the Obscure,*" *N-CF,* XI (1957), 275. Italics added.

[10] William T. Hutchinson, "A Definitive Edition of *Moby-Dick,*" *AL,* XXV (1954), 472-478.

[11] See Fredson Bowers, *Principles of Bibliographical Description* (1949), p. 356 ff, for a discussion of these reasons on the part of the bibliographer. One should admit, furthermore, that the non-professional bibiographers, the scholarly readers and editors, may have reasons which are indefensible, but are nevertheless *reasons.* I daresay one would be shocked to know how many trained men feel today that novels aren't really "literature"; or that modern printing is either perfect or too complicated ever to be fathomed.

[12] F. Scott Fitzgerald, *The Last Tycoon,* in *Three Novels* (1953), p. 157. Italics added.

[13] See instalments 8, 9, 10 (Chapters XII and XIII, XIV and XV, XVI and XVII). The Pip-Magwitch strand is early developed as much as can be without giving away the plot. Pip loves Estella early, but is apprenticed back to Joe by the beginning of chapter XIII. The glad tidings of Great Expectations don't come until instalment 11. Without Orlick, more than four chapters would have to deal with domestic bliss and withdrawal. Orlick is introduced and attacks Mrs. Joe, all in the ninth instalment.

At the other end of the book a similar situation obtains. The reconciliation with Miss Havisham comes in instalment 30; that with Joe is brief enough not to be needed until after instalment 33. Estella is not brought in until the end. Instalments 31, 32, 33 are needed, therefore, to make the 36 weekly unit structure complete—but they cannot all contain the secret plan to get Magwitch down stream. The reader cannot go boating with Pip, Startop, and Herbert for two entire instalments before the disastrous attempt to get Magwitch out of the country; so instalment 32 is devoted to Orlick's attempt to kill Pip.

In other words, serial publication took Dickens to melodrama, but not quite in the crude form that one's unsubstantiated suspicions would indicate.

[14] There are, it is encouraging to note, signs of change. In the last year or two, one has the feeling that perhaps six or eight articles appeared on the texts of 19th- or 20th-century novels. For example, see Linton Massey, "Notes on the Unrevised Galleys of Faulkner's *Sanctuary*," *SB*, VIII (1956), 195-208 or Matthew J. Bruccoli, "A Collation of F. Scott Fitzgerald's *This Side of Paradise*," *SB*, IX (1957), 263-265. The latter article is especially interesting in pointing out changes between impressions of editions.

Having mentioned Dickens, I must add that Mrs. Tillotson has followed up her remark (*op. cit.*) that we have no Victorian texts, and "no means, short of doing the work ourselves, of discovering how (and why) the original edition differed from the text we read." I refer of course to John Butt and Kathleen Tillotson, *Dickens at Work* (1957); on the importance of part publication, it deals mainly with novels other than *Great Expectations*. While it also illustrates how long it takes for a general appreciation of the importance of bibliographical facts to culminate in a specific study, the book makes my comments on Dickens, so to speak, unspeakable.

[15] The first edition has had three impressions: April, 1925, August, 1925, and August, 1942. I have collated three copies of the first impression, including Fitzgerald's personally corrected volume now located at Princeton. The August, 1942 impression I have not examined. I would like to record here my special thanks to Lawrence D. Stewart of Beverly Hills, California, for most kindly checking my collation against his copy of the rare second impression.

The second edition of *Gatsby* is that printed with *The Last Tycoon* and certain stories, as supervized by Edmund Wilson. It uses as copy-text the August, 1925 first edition. I have collated three impressions, 1941, 1945, 1948.

The sub-edition of *Gatsby*, as printed with *Tender is the Night* and *The Last Tycoon*, in the *Three Novels* volume, has been collated in three impressions, 1953, 1956, 1957.

The parent company, Scribner's, has permitted several reprints, which I have not examined thoroughly. There is also a recent (1957), third edition of *Gatsby*, by Scribner's, a paperback, called "Student's Edition."

I shall refer to these editions of *Gatsby* by the short but obvious forms of *First, Last Tycoon* or LT, *Three Novels* or TN, Student's Edition or SE. For convenience I shall give the line in a page reference by a simple decimal; as TN 31.30, for *Three Novels*, p. 31, line 30. [Matthew J. Bruccoli, "A Further Note on the First Printing of *The Great Gatsby*," *SB*, XVI (1963), 244, supplements this information. *Editor's note.*]

[16] My thanks are due to Princeton University Library for permitting me to examine both Fitzgerald's own copy of *Gatsby* and the surviving manuscripts. Doubtless I should add

that since my special concern is the printed texts, I did not rigorously collate the mass of MS, TS, and galleys.

I would like also to thank Wallace O. Meyer of Scribner's, Harold Ober, Edmund Wilson, Malcolm Cowley, and Dan C. Piper for their advice and for patiently answering my queries about the changes in the texts.

[17] The comment is a trifle misleading, because the reading "orgastic" stands in MS, galleys, and first edition. Perhaps this is another example of Fitzgerald's well-known weakness in matters of spelling, grammar, and so on; at any rate, it can hardly be called a "proof error."

[18] Arthur Mizener, The Far Side of Paradise (1951), p. 336, n. 22. Mizener points up the generally sad fate of Fitzgerald's texts by mentioning that the reprints of The Modern Library, New Directions, Bantam (first version), and Grosset and Dunlap all have the word "orgastic." One therefore assumes they reprint the first edition, though at least the Modern Library reprints the second impression. The later Bantam edition and The Portable Fitzgerald both use the faulty Last Tycoon as copy-text.

[19] See, for example, the word "to-day," in LT, p. 280 line 36 and TN, p. 116 line 36; but "to-day" (as in First, p. 184 lines 7 and 10) is kept three lines later—LT p. 281.1, TN p. 117.1. In addition to forty-two such changes, there are six more which are nearly as minor: the word "sombre" is changed to "somber"; "armistice" to "Armistice," as examples. All these, and the change in the spelling of a name (Wolfshiem to Wolfsheim) which was usually but not always wrong in the first edition, are not included in my statistics.

[20] See LT 203.4 and TN 39.4. The

other changes in the August, 1925 First are as follows:
April, 1925 it's driver p. 165.16
    August 1925 its driver
April some distance away p. 165.29
    August some distance away.
April sick in tired p. 205. 9 & 10
    August sickantired
All four are, presumably, authorial.

[21] See "lyric again in," First 62.17, LT 204.12. "lyric in," TN 40.12. Cf. "turbulent," First 20.17, LT 178.25, TN 14.25; "turbulence," First 7.28, LT 171.3, TN 7.3.

[22] See First, 35.21: Her eyebrows had been plucked and then drawn on again at a more rakish angle, but the efforts of nature. . . . LT 188.7 and TN 24.7 remove the comma.

[23] First 111.14 and LT 234.5 When I try . . . TN 70.6 when I try . . .

[24] First 115.25 generating on the air. So LT 236.33. TN 72.33 generating on the air.

[25] The sentence "It just shows you," mentioned above as an error begun in LT.

[26] First 141.6, LT. 253.38, TN 89.38. Tom Buchanan is speaking and by closing a paragraph with quote marks, LT and TN give the reader the momentary impression that the next sentence and paragraph beginning "Come outside . . ." is by someone else.

First 139.26, LT 253.7, TN 89.7 represent the obverse. "The bles-sed pre-cious . . . spoken by Daisy loses the quotation mark in LT and TN.

[27] See First 153.8, LT 261.14, TN 97.14. TN alone reads "Biloxi, Mississippi." I realize that the line can be interpreted in other ways, that for example, Fitzgerald wished an obviously fictional town. But I cannot agree that Fitzgerald was so ignorant of Southern geography as to put the city in the wrong state. I am all the more certain that Fitzgerald meant it as a joke because

there is other geographical word-play in the same scene, and it is only four pages earlier that Tom snorts that Gatsby must have been an Oxford man—"Oxford, New Mexico."

[28] The statement is not quite accurate: there are one or two other violations of this order, minor ones very late in the book. For example, the giving of the Michaelis's testimony, p. 124 of TN is apparently after the scene on pp. 119 ff.

[29] The scene was, in the manuscript, at the place where it is referred to in the chapter now numbered VIII, pp. 112 of TN. Fitzgerald then changed it to its present position, ending at TN 76, LT 241, *First* 121—Chapter VI.

[30] Since I have mentioned Conrad so often, it might not be amiss to add Conrad's name to the list of influences mentioned by Cowley in the introduction to *Three Novels*. (See Fitzgerald's introduction to the Modern Library *Gatsby* and *The Crack-Up* for his interest in Conrad.) The time scheme of *Gatsby* is, of course, Conradian, as well as the narrator. And there are quite a few passages that echo Conrad—the closing section on the old Dutch sailors' feelings in New York might be a twist on parts of "Heart of Darkness." "In the abortive sorrows and short-winded elations of men," p. 4 of TN's *Gatsby*, is just one of the verbal echoes of Conrad. More pertinently, the intra-chapter break was a device very much used by the older author. For a detailed examination of this relationship, see R. W. Stallman, "Conrad and *The Great Gatsby*," *TCL*, I (1955), 5-12.

[31] See *First* 121.26, LT 240 foot, TN 76 foot; *First* 163.26, LT 267 foot, TN 103 foot; *First* 192.16, LT 285 foot, TN 121 foot; *First* 214.21, LT 299.21, TN 135.21. In all but the last of these the break in the page comes at the turn-over of the page and, unfortunately, no space was left for it.

[32] For the suppressed intra-chapter breaks, see TN 126.31 and SE 167.26; TN 132.24 and SE 175.19; TN 136.24 and SE 181.7. The other improvement is at TN 89.7 and SE 117.3, where SE returns to *First* to get the quotation marks of "The bles-sed . . ." as spoken by Daisy, correctly once more. SE 175.1 does not restore Nick's sentence "It just shows you." but it does "correct" the quotation marks that were wrong in the preceding sentence in TN 132.9.

[33] I should add that the collation of these three editions has of course not been reproduced in full here—and there are several places in the text that call for emendation though there are no changes between editions. For example, Tom brings the car to a dusty spot under Wilson's sign. (So in *First* 147 and TN 93.23 and SE 123.7). Should it be a dusty stop?

Internal Evidence and the Attribution of Elizabethan Plays

S. Schoenbaum

In the field of Elizabethan drama, attribution studies based on internal evidence—chiefly the evidence of style—command little respect these days, and present serious inconveniences.[1] They are associated with eccentricity, amateurism, and irresponsibility; with error, contradiction, and wild surmise; with Fleay and the heritage of Fleay. They have added to the burdens of the editor, who must determine which plays to include in his edition; the critic, who must trace the course of a dramatist's development; and the historian, who must evaluate previous scholarship on authenticity and attribution. G. E. Bentley is constrained to write:

> After working painfully through the attributions of an anonymous play like *The Revenger's Tragedy* to Webster and to Tourneur and to Middleton and to Marston, the disgusted historian is tempted to lay down this principle: Any play first published in a contemporary quarto with no author's name on the title page and continuing without definite ascription of authorship for twenty-five years or more should be treated as anonymous world without end Amen.[2]

The almost 1500 pages of volumes III to V of *The Jacobean and Caroline Stage* tell a melancholy story of the fate of a large number of attempted attributions. Yet such studies, which are a necessary part of our discipline, continue to appear regularly in the pages of journals and the appendices of monographs. But certainly they should be better than they are; the same follies are committed again and again. "The

72

problem," Chambers shrewdly observed in his famous British Academy lecture on the disintegration of Shakespeare, "seems to me one which calls for exploration upon a general and disinterested method, rather than along the casual lines of advance opened up by the pursuit of an author for this or that suspected or anonymous play."[3] Few have followed this excellent advice in the thirty-five years since it was offered, and this essay may be regarded, at least in part, as an act of belated homage. In it I shall be concerned necessarily with past errors and illusions, but also, and more important, with first principles and particular tests, and with inherent difficulties and shortcomings of the method. This is broad coverage, perhaps rather too broad for a single paper; but there may be compensatory advantages to a wide-ranging discussion of a topic usually given narrow or perfunctory notice—when it is given notice at all—as a preface to specific authorship investigations.

I

Just half a century ago, in the Golden Age of Attribution Studies, Oliphant could survey the land and find it good. In his essay on "Problems of Authorship in Elizabethan Dramatic Literature," he cited the large number of plays of anonymous, uncertain, or disputed authorship that had survived, and he recommended, with the delicious casualness of a departed era, that "students with time and inclination for such pursuits" make "a selection from amongst the problems that await solution."[4] In the years following, the selection was duly made. Lawrence, Lloyd, Wells, and others urged the merits of their author-candidates; Sykes published the studies later assembled as the *Sidelights;* Oliphant himself turned to the Beaumont and Fletcher canon, *The Revenger's Tragedy,* and other plays. Meanwhile the disintegrators disintegrated Shakespeare.

These men knew and loved the old plays, and were fertile of ideas and intuitions. They ransacked scenes for parallel passages; they counted nouns, adjectives, and interjections, rhymes, end-stopped lines, and double and triple endings; they strained their ears to catch the elusive notes of the "indefinite music" permeating the verse.[5] Yet by 1932 Miss Byrne could remark, in the course of her devastating arraignment of Sykes, that "it is extraordinarily difficult to persuade most people to examine serously the so-called 'stylistic' attributions of anonymous or acknowledged collaborate plays."[6] Her statement has lost none of its relevance. It is no easier—perhaps, indeed, it is more difficult—to persuade Bentley than it was to convince Chambers.

Why did Oliphant, Sykes, and the rest come to grief? After all, they were not, like Fleay, fantastics unwilling to support their theories with argument, prone to dizzying improvisations and changes of mind, possessed by demons of inaccuracy.[7] Their great failing is revealed inadvertently by Oliphant in the concluding paragraph of his essay of fifty years ago. "As to how the detection of the presence of unknown writers . . . is to be effected and their identity determined," Oliphant writes, "that is a matter which every investigator must settle for himself."[8] It is this astonishing indifference to method that is their fatal weakness, and the source of the anarchy still prevalent in attribution work. These enthusiasts set vigorously to work without troubling about the essential preliminaries. They established no basic principles of procedure. They made no attempt to define the nature of evidence. They applied the various tests indiscriminately. They often ignored relevant external information about the plays they scrutinized so minutely. They failed to grasp the significance of the bibliographical revolution taking place around them: they were indifferent to the fortunes of copy in the printing-house, they did not discuss compositors. Oliphant and his co-workers were essentially literary amateurs unable by training or temperament to subject their investigations to the tedious rigor of scholarly discipline. Their approach—subjective, intuitive, ardent—differs little from that of the impressionist critics with whom they were contemporaneous. But the canonical impressionists were mischievous in a way that the critics were not. For in rationalizing their intuitions and presenting them as evidence, they bequeathed a legacy of confusion and error. Little is to be gained by attempting—as R. H. Barker has recently tried to do—a belated resurrection of Oliphant's reputation, on grounds that the strictures of our most distinguished authorities merely reflect the vagaries of scholarly fashion.[9] The gesture in the direction of Oliphant's memory may have sentimental appeal, but the strictures themselves are not easily dismissed, and indeed Barker makes no effort to refute them. If a case is to be made for the legitimacy of employing internal evidence to determine authorship, it must be made with a full awareness of past failures and present limitations.

II

The limitations are considerable. The investigator's task, as I see it, is to isolate and describe the special character of a literary work of unknown or doubtful authorship, to show the extent to which a known writer's work partakes of that special character, and from this evidence to arrive at an appropriate conclusion. The enterprise is hazardous, for an author's individuality never exists as pure essence, but is subtly alloyed by many interrelated factors: literary conventions and traditions; personal, professional, social, religious influences. And of all writers the dramatist is most elusive, as he appears not in his own persona but in the manifold guises of the personages that are his imaginative creations. All plays, furthermore, are in a sense collaborations, shaped from conception to performance by the author's awareness of the resources of actors and theatre, the wishes of impresario or shareholders, and the tastes and capacities of the audience.

The investigator working with the Elizabethan drama faces additional difficulties. Far removed in time from his materials, he may be easily misled into fancying as original what a contemporary would have instantly recognized as imitation. His task is not eased by the fact that a great many plays of the period have perished, or by the related fact that plays generally were not held in very high literary esteem, expecially before the appearance of the great Jonson Folio in 1616. Artistic individuality is scarcely to be expected in artifacts manufactured for a commercial market. That individuality nevertheless blossomed—that the age produced not only Shakespeare, Marlowe, and Jonson, but also Chapman, Marston, Webster, and a number of other distinctive voices—is a remarkable assertion of the creative principle. But it should not blind the investigator to the parlous conditions of his labor: conditions that favor not the establishment of facts but the proliferation of conjecture.

I cannot then accept Arthur Sherbo's "basic premise" that, in questions of authorship, "internal evidence deals with essentials while external evidence deals with accidentals," and that "short of an unequivocal acknowledgment by the author himself, the value of internal evidence outweighs any other."[10] External evidence can and often does provide incontestable proof; internal evidence can only support hypotheses or corroborate external evidence. So far as the Elizabethan drama is concerned, the justification for the use of internal evidence in determining a canon lies primarily in the inadequacy of the available outward evidence. Our primary sources of information—the title-pages of plays, the Stationers' Register, the Office Book of the Master of the Revels, the seventeenth-century catalogues—are pitifully incomplete, misleading, or inaccurate. Famous "standard" attributions at times rest on remarkably fragile foundations. No record, for example, survives from Kyd's lifetime to connect his name with *The Spanish Tragedy*. The only external evidence that he wrote the age's most sensationally popular melodrama is Heywood's statement in his *Apology for Actors,* which appeared eighteen years after Kyd's death.

Yet *The Spanish Tragedy* is linked inseparably with Kyd's name. Justly so. For we recognize, with the play's most recent editor, that it stands in "a peculiarly intimate relation" to the closet drama *Cornelia,* translated by Kyd from Garnier, and that "the only reasonable way of accounting for the relationship is to say that the same man was responsible for both works."[11] In this case, as in others, the external evidence—by itself hardly overwhelming—is buttressed by the evidence of style. The responsible historian is of course aware of the gaps and contradictions in the records with which he works. Thus it is that Bentley cannot subscribe to his own tempting formula, already quoted, of everlasting anonymity after twenty-five years. Such a principle, he is quick to note, would not only deprive Marlowe of *Tamburlaine* but Beaumont and Fletcher of *The Woman Hater;* it would thrust *The Thracian Wonder* upon Webster and *The London Prodigal* upon Shakespeare.

Internal evidence used in fruitful conjunction with the meagre external facts stirs no controversy but provides, rather, welcome illumination of the obscurity in which we must too often work. But it is another matter to suggest authors where the external evidence is pathetically insufficient, as in the case of *The Bloody Banquet,* with its 1639 title-page ascription to "T.D."; or non-existent, as with *The Fairy Knight, Dick of Devonshire,* and many other plays. It is risky to attempt the allocation of scenes in collaborations, even when all the partners are known—Middleton, Rowley, and Massinger's *The Old Law,* for example, which has come down in a wretched text; riskier still when not all the collaborators are specified, as in the Beaumont and Fletcher corpus, amply dissected by the disintegrators. Fraught with even greater perils are the investigator's attempts to transform into collaborations plays for which the outward evidence points to single jurisdiction: Eberle finding Dekker in *The Family of Love,*[12] Lucas and others seeing Webster in *Anything for a Quiet Life.*[13] But most dangerous of all is the attempt to overthrow, by the weight of internal evidence alone, an attribution for which there is external support; and here we have the famous case of *The Revenger's Tragedy,* to which I shall return at the conclusion of this essay.[13a]

III

The investigator who works without external evidence to bolster his conclusions assumes the full burden of proof; he must anticipate that his assumptions, methods, and claims will undergo the severest scrutiny. It is a measure of the amateurism of Sykes and Lawrence and the rest that they did so little to fortify themselves against this inspection. But even today, when there is less excuse, attribution studies frequently offer little or nothing in the way of description or defense of the methods employed. In some cases apparently no thought *has* been given to methodology, or so one would conclude from the cavalier violations of ordinary principles of logical procedure. Recently one investigator has even, by implication, expressed impatience with the rigors of methodological discipline; but the vague standard of doing "the best one can," offered instead, may seem inadequate to the conscientious student faced with the frustrating complexities of a canon.[14] I cannot, therefore, really apologize for the elementary character of the procedures that I now recommend to canonical investigators. Such interest as these principles may have will lie primarily in the fact that they have to be stated at all. That they do need stating, the illustrations will, I trust, demonstrate.

(1) *External evidence cannot be ignored, no matter how inconvenient such evidence may be for the theories of the investigator.*

The Spanish Gypsy, claimed wholly or in part for Ford by Sykes, Sargeaunt, and others,[15] is credited to Middleton and Rowley on the title pages of the 1653 and 1661 Quartos. There is no reason to suspect fraud on the publisher's part: the flaunting of the names of the dramatists on the title page would not have stimulated sales, if one can judge from their contemporary reputations.[15a] The attribution is, moreover, in keeping with the fact that the play was licensed for acting by the Lady Elizabeth's men (9 July 1623). In the previous year the same company had performed the same authors' *Changeling*, which indeed is advertised by an allusion in the second act of *The Spanish Gypsy*.[16] The outward evidence of authorship is then fairly strong, and the play cannot be dislodged from the Middleton canon on the basis of subjective critical impressions—especially since some Middletonians have no difficulty in reconciling the play, on critical grounds, with the dramatist's acknowledged later work. Other instances might easily be cited of the too casual treatment of relevant external facts. Most striking perhaps is Lucas's work on *The Fair Maid of the Inn*, which was licensed by Herbert in 1626 as Fletcher's composition and printed in the 1647 Beaumont and Fletcher Folio. Lucas includes the play in his standard edition of Webster, and divides it among Webster, Ford, and Massinger—thus eliminating Fletcher entirely.[17] It is Bentley's painful duty to point out that, contrary to Lucas's theories, the Master of the

Revels was not an advertising agent, and the King's men, who produced the play and took a direct part in the preparation of the 1647 Folio, knew their business.[18]

(2) *If stylistic criteria are to have any meaning, the play must be written in a style.*

"Very few writers," remarks Miss Byrne (22-23), "are capable of anything so distinguished as a recognizable style, and the minor Elizabethan dramatists are definitely not among that happy band. Men like Munday and Chettle used blank verse as quickly, as slickly, and in as unremarkable a manner as the modern journalist uses his so-called prose." The editors of the Oxford *Jonson* make much the same point about Jacobean prose dialogue.[19] Collaborations (which prompted the foregoing observations) and revisions are less likely to have stylistic individuality than the unrevised work of a single author. The partners may adjust their styles to one another; the reviser may imitate his predecessor. In *Eastward Ho*, Jonson, Marston, and Chapman—three of the age's most individualistic writers—pooled their talents to produce a play with remarkable consistency of texture. Whoever added to *The Spanish Tragedy* acquired, as Prior points out, mannerisms and characteristic images of the original author.[20] I do not envy the future investigator who attempts, on the basis of style, to distinguish between the work of William Faulkner and his collaborators on the screen play of *Land of the Pharaohs*.

Yet a recognizable style, and hence one that may be described, is perhaps rather less rare than Miss Byrne would have us believe. Even hacks like Chettle and Munday, with whom she is concerned, may have occasional strange quirks of individuality. And when she suggests that style is likely to answer our question only when we are dealing with genius, Miss Byrne overlooks the startling distinctiveness that really bad writing can have. Marston at his worst, for example.

The principle holds, however: no style, no stylistic evidence. A collection of stylistic commonplaces isolates nothing and persuades only the gullible or those already convinced. Such collections—Sykes's stock in trade—have unfortunately been the rule rather than the exception (*vide* Bentley). As preposterous as any are the attribution studies of William Wells who, after expressing learned disagreement with Sykes, goes on to use similar "evidence" to assign *King Leir, Alphonsus Emperor of Germany, The Troublesome Reign of King John, Edward II*, and other plays to Thomas Kyd.[21] The number of curious additions to the Kyd canon is, Wells grants, "large enough to evoke hilarious incredulity among leading authorities with a too conservative bent."[22] With this point I hesitate to quarrel.

(3) *The investigator must always work with reliable texts, preferably directly with the early editions or manuscripts.*

As in canonical investigations the closest and most scrupulous study of texts is required, the validity of this principle should be apparent. Yet Sykes evidently trusted to whichever edition came first to hand. He used Hazlitt's *Webster* for *Appius and Virginia* and *The Fair Maid of the Inn,* and the same editor's *Dodsley* for *The Second Maiden's Tragedy, Lust's Dominion,* and other plays. He relied on Dyce's *Middleton* for *Anything for a Quiet Life,* Pearson's reprint of Chapman for *Alphonsus,* and (not without amply justified misgivings) the Mermaid *Webster and Tourneur* for *The Revenger's Tragedy.* Of these editions one, the Dyce *Middleton,* was an admirable achievement for its own time; but that time was 1840. Yet T. S. Eliot defers to Sykes as "perhaps our greatest authority on the texts of Tourneur and Middleton."[23] So much for our greatest. Investigators continue, however, to rely upon unsuitable texts. In two recent books concerned with the Dekker canon, the data—often involving small details of style—are taken from the miserable Shepherd reprint of Dekker's plays, despite the fact that the first volumes of the superb Bowers edition have for several years been readily available.[24]

(4) *Textual analysis logically precedes canonical analysis.*

The wise investigator knows his own text and what evidence it may afford of corruption, revision, or collaboration. Apparently Lawrence did not know the Quarto of *Eastward Ho* when he proposed that before publication the play underwent authorial revision, presumably by Jonson, so that offensive passages might be deleted and the gaps "neatly" closed.[25] The editors of the Oxford *Jonson* have since shown that the cuts were almost certainly the work of the publisher, and that, with the exception of the notorious passage on the Scots in Act III, they were in fact not closed.[26]

Thus the canonical question bears an intimate relation to the textual problem. Further, an apparent matter of style may conceivably be an actual matter of text. Because the only extant early edition of Shakespeare's *Pericles* falls into sections of unequal merit, some authorities have assumed that the play is a collaboration. According to this view, the second author took over with the third act, when the style suddenly improves. But if Edwards is correct in suggesting that the 1609 Quarto represents a memorial reconstruction by a pair of reporters—

the first responsible for the first two acts; the second, better skilled, for the last three—then we have no basis for regarding the original play of *Pericles* as anything but the work of a single dramatist.[27] Edwards' suggestion is of course only one hypothesis of many that have been offered to explain a particularly difficult problem. But it illustrates a possibility that other canonical investigators have failed even to consider.

In dealing with the minute features of a dramatic text—spelling, linguistic forms, punctuation, and the like—the investigator has a special problem. He must recognize the possibility of compositorial intervention in the case of printed texts, and scribal intervention in the case of manuscripts. We know that compositors and scribes were capable of exercising considerable autonomy over certain features of the manuscripts they were reproducing. The impressionists—as I shall refer hereafter to the school of Oliphant and Sykes—do not often trouble themselves with considerations so hostile to romance, and it is not surprising that the skeptical reader should trouble himself as little with data gathered in a vacuum. On the other hand, an investigator like Cyrus Hoy, aware of the relevant bibliographical considerations, disarms us at the outset of his study of the Beaumont and Fletcher canon by forthrightly discussing the role of compositors and scribes.[28] Hoy's criteria for authorship—the presence or absence of certain pronominal and verbal forms and contractions—are simple enough and have been employed by previous students. Certainly they are not equally serviceable for all the collaborators traced in the Beaumont and Fletcher corpus. But these tests have never been handled with the like judgment and discretion, and for this reason Hoy's monograph has from the first commanded respect.[29]

(5) *For any author proposed, a reasonable amount of unquestioned dramatic writing, apart from collaborations, must be extant.*

The more plays the better; better yet if some precede and others follow the work under consideration, as a theory of imitation is then with more difficulty maintained. Oliphant suggests the possibility that Thomas Watson had a hand in *Thorney Abbey* (printed in 1662 as by "T. W."), and he goes on to advise that "Anyone who wants a quite new field of Elizabethan study might first steep himself in a knowledge of Watson's poetry and then read the dramas (and especially the unattached dramas) of the period prior to the middle of 1592, with an eye to determining his presence."[30] The value of the advice is lessened by the fact that not a single play survives that is known to be the work, in whole or in part, of Thomas Watson. Thus a whole new field of study remains unexplored.[31]

(6) *Intuitions, convictions, and subjective judgments generally, carry no weight as evidence.* This no matter how learned, perceptive, respected, or confident the authority.

An anonymous reviewer in *The Times Literary Supplement* writes: "Tourneur's case [for *The Revenger's Tragedy*] has rested partly on historical evidence (admittedly flimsy), but far more upon the judgment of critics such as Mr. Eliot or Professor Ellis-Fermor or Professor Nicoll, who write with a special sensibility for such matters as the poetic style of the two authors, their range of characterization and their dramatic idiom and texture. 'Middleton,' says Mr. Eliot, 'has a different feel of the relation of the tragic and the comic.' This is of course the kind of view which a critic may hold with an instinct bordering on certainty, but which is quite unsusceptible of proof."[32] But a case cannot rest upon "judgment," and a view "unsusceptible of proof" has no binding authority. The keenest sensibility may go astray. To show that Middleton is at times "a great master of versification," our greatest living man of letters, T. S. Eliot, singles out the passage beginning, "I that am of your blood was taken from you / For your better health. . . ."[33] The speech occurs in the last scene of *The Changeling*—a scene which, according to all the evidence and all the reputable authorities, is the unaided work of William Rowley.

The value of intuitions is that they are sometimes right. Their correctness is determined by the evidence. Nothing else counts.

(7) *Wherever possible, stylistic evidence should be supplemented by textual evidence.*

A playwright's individuality may find expression in a number of accidentals: his idiosyncrasies with regard to speech prefixes, stage directions, act divisions, the recording of entrances, etc; his peculiarities of spelling, punctuation, and abbreviation. As with linguistic preferences, the usefulness of the data depends entirely upon the fidelity with which scribe or compositors have followed the author's manuscript—provided they worked from author's manuscript. Because so little autograph dramatic manuscript has survived from the Elizabethan period, it is often impossible to do more than theorize about a playwright's habits with regard to these minutiae. Yet bibliographical evidence may at times provide a valuable corroboration of an attribution already probable on critical grounds. This is demonstrated in Bowers' textual introduction to Dekker and Massinger's *The Virgin Martyr*.[34]

For Massinger there survives the holograph manuscript of *Believe As You List;* for Dekker we have only a single scene from *Sir Thomas More,* but valid inferences can be made from Dekker's printed texts. The 1642 Quarto was set by a single compositor, probably from the holograph papers of the two authors. Guided by such minute features of the text as the spellings *Cesarea* and *Cæsarea* and the use of hyphens in compounds, Bowers effectively supplements the stylistic evidence for scene allocation.

Such textual evidence has not often enough been brought to bear on canonical problems. *The Puritan,* to cite but one example, has for long puzzled scholars. Printed in 1607 as by "W. S.," it is certainly not by Shakespeare. A number of authorities feel it may be a Middleton work. The play is a comedy of London life acted by the Children of Paul's about 1606; at that time Middleton was the chief Paul's dramatist, and he was writing London comedies. There is some stylistic evidence for Middleton. No other plausible candidate for authorship has been proposed. But the case, as it stands, is inconclusive; further evidence is badly needed if the play is to be given even a conjectural place in the Middleton canon. Yet, although a number of investigators have made pronouncements about *The Puritan,* and although we have a sufficient quantity of dramatic manuscript in Middleton's hand, the 1607 Quarto has never been studied for spelling, punctuation, and other textual clues to authorship. Nor, for that matter, has it been studied for the related evidence of linguistic preferences.

The seven principles I have outlined do not exhaust the possibilities for cautionary advice to canonical investigators. Other strictures, at least equally wholesome, will no doubt occur to readers who have concerned themselves with attribution questions. The principles I have suggested derive from my own experience with particular problems and with the literature of attribution, which I have had to explore rather systematically in revising Alfred Harbage's *Annals of English Drama.* All seven reflect my dissatisfaction with the casual methodlessness of stylistic impressionism, the dominant mode of investigation during the past half century. That methodlessness is, I feel, largely responsible for the disesteem in which authorship studies are now held, at least in the area of Elizabethan drama.

IV

It is not possible, in the compass of a single essay, to deal with very many—let alone all—of the tests by which investigators in their wisdom or folly have sought to prove authorship by style. Some of the criteria that have been employed are, in any case, too feeble even to require citation. But one or two tests, particularly that of parallel passages, certainly call for serious discussion, while still others, such as metrical investigations, may for present purposes be briefly considered.

"The danger of metrical evidence is that it is too often believed." So wrote Lucas some years back in his edition of Webster (IV 250). After giving entirely persuasive reasons for regarding the tests with profound distrust, he goes on to apply them himself to *Anything for a Quiet Life* and *The Fair Maid of the Inn,* with results no happier than those of his predecessors. Today little danger exists of metrical statistics being too easily believed, except perhaps by their compilers. If the use of such evidence can be justified at all, it is only as corroboration for the assignment of scenes of collaborate plays in which the partners have been identified, and are known to have widely differing metrical habits (e.g., Middleton and Rowley's *Fair Quarrel* and *The Changeling*). But even with such cases previous results testify to the need for extreme caution.[35]

Imagery studies have also yielded much dubious evidence. The hazards are nicely illustrated in the work of Marco Mincoff and the late Una Ellis-Fermor. Each made, unaware of the other, a detailed study of the imagery of *The Revenger's Tragedy.*[36] Mincoff concluded that the play was Middleton's; Ellis-Fermor, that it must be Tourneur's. Mincoff avoids certain pitfalls: he does not use imagery as the basis for pseudo-biographical reconstructions, which must be reckoned as evidentially worthless. But skeptical readers will hardly be persuaded by his data, and the conflicting results achieved by two well-known scholars working on the same play and concerned with the narrowest possible field of author-candidates do not inspire confidence in the method. The strictures (discussed below) relevant to the test for parallels may be held to apply to image tests as well, and may provide some discipline. But the image-hunter faces special difficulties. The need for selection—few words do not convey an image of some kind— and classification inevitably enlarges the subjective factor in attribution work. The investigator is, moreover, hampered by our very limited knowledge of the images and image-patterns favored by the various minor Elizabethan dramatists. Detailed study of imagery is a relatively recent critical preoccupation, and misgivings about applying its techniques prematurely to authorship problems would seem to be fully warranted.[37]

The foundation of most stylistic attributions during the past fifty years has not, however, been imagery or metrics, but the testimony of parallels: unusual correspondences of language and thought, generally in brief passages, between the doubtful play and the acknowledged works of the suggested dramatist. This test too has occasioned doubts and skeptical protests. "There is nothing more dangerous," Chambers declared, "than the attempt to determine authorship by the citation of parallels."[38] More recently, the editors of the Oxford *Jonson* have remarked upon "the illusory test of parallel passages" (IX 636), and Bentley has deprecated, with customary vigor, the "parallel-passage 'evidence' of modern enthusiasts."[39] But in this instance the difficulties are, I feel, different in character and significance from those presented by the tests I have already touched upon. Most conservative editors, the Simpsons included, are able to use the evidence of parallels, and most conservative historians, Bentley included, can accept attributions based chiefly on such evidence.

In his account of the disintegration of Middleton's *Anything for a Quiet Life* by the impressionist quartet of Sykes, Oliphant, Lucas, and Dunkel, Bentley provides (IV 859-860) an at times almost farcical but essentially sad chronicle of the misuse of stylistic evidence. That evidence consists mainly of parallel passages. Bentley's chief complaint is that "Most of the passages are not parallel, and the words and phrases are by no means peculiar to Webster [Middleton's proposed collaborator]." The objection to commonplace or unparallel parallels occurs often in *The Jacobean and Caroline Stage*. It is a legitimate objection, but applies less to a method than to its abuses. For if the parallels are not parallel and the words and phrases are commonplace, the test, in a very real sense, has not been employed.

The abuses that Bentley properly deplores did not pass with the impressionists of the Roaring Twenties. In 1948 G. J. Eberle published a study of *The Family of Love*, a comedy issued anonymously in 1608 and assigned to Middleton in Archer's 1656 playlist. The aim of the study is to demonstrate that the play "is a revision by Dekker and Middleton of an early play written by Middleton with considerable help from Dekker."[40] A thesis as complicated as this is difficult either to prove or disprove; unfortunately for Eberle, the burden of proof rests upon him. To support his argument, he assembles a number of parallels, or "touchstones," as he calls them. "Even distant echoes in Middleton" are cited. "Commonplaces and proverbial expressions" are "included as confirmatory evidence if Dekker uses them often and Middleton never" (725). Thus Middleton's collaborator—if he had one—is from the outset presumed to be Dekker. Eberle assumes also that *The Puritan* and *The Revenger's Tragedy* are Middleton's, and he gives to

Dekker all or part of *Blurt, Master Constable; The Weakest Goeth to the Wall; The Bloody Banquet; The Merry Devil of Edmonton;* and *The Black Book.* All these ascriptions are the proposals of modern critics, and all are controversial. To parallels from these works, Eberle adds others from collaborations: *The Changeling; The Honest Whore, Part I* (a Dekker-Middleton collaboration!); *The Roaring Girl* (also by Dekker and Middleton); *The Old Law* (where the authorities disagree on the assignment of some scenes); and *A Fair Quarrel* (where an episode almost certainly by Rowley is cited as evidence for Middleton). Despite the catholic variety of sources Eberle has to draw upon, many of his parallels are not parallel. The entire essay is, indeed, a fine illustration of the inadequacy of good intentions alone. "This study," Eberle had assured his readers at the beginning, "attempts to approach the ideal set down by Bentley for studies in attribution" (725).

If Eberle's study falls short of his own ideal, it is because he has set up no *a priori* rules of procedure for his own guidance in collecting data, and has made no effort to classify and evaluate the evidence once gathered. Rather he has amassed ungraded parallels. The amassing of ungraded parallels proves nothing. This truth was stated almost three decades ago by Miss Byrne.[41] At the same time she offered five Golden Rules, as she reasonably described them, for the improvement of parallel hunting. Miss Byrne observed that parallels vary in quality, and that correspondences of thought and phraseology are greatly superior to simple verbal parallels. She reasoned that parallel collectors may pass logically from the known to the anonymous or from the known to the collaborate play, but less securely from the collaborate to the anonymous work. She did not skirt the problem that even striking parallels may admit of more than one explanation: they may testify to common authorship, but they may also be the result of coincidence or of imitation, conscious or unconscious. Above all, Miss Byrne stressed the necessity for the careful grading of parallels, and for submitting them to negative checks to show that they cannot be duplicated as a body in acknowledged plays of the period.

The impressionists have not questioned the validity of any of Miss Byrne's tenets. Instead they have left her article severely alone. Although in my work of revising the *Annals of English Drama,* I have had occasion to examine a number of attribution studies involving the citation of parallels, I cannot recall one that referred to Miss Byrne's paper. Eberle's study of *The Family of Love* does not stand alone as an unhappy reminder of the dangers faced by the investigator unacquainted with her untarnished Rules.

Allied to verbal parallels, and subject to some of the same strictures governing the admissability of evidence, are the larger correspondences of thought and theme, characterization and dramatic technique. But parallels of this kind—which for convenience I shall call literary correspondences—also make special demands of their own. Their usefulness depends closely upon the investigator's capacities for literary analysis, and the precision with which he can formulate critical distinctions. In practice the canonical impressionists have been, as we might expect, critical impressionists, and the subjective element present in all criticism has been in their work pervasive and detrimental. Their inclination, insufficiently resisted, is to make oversimplified descriptive pronouncements and pass oversimplified value judgments. A scene is by Jonson because it is "masterful," by Middleton because "it has his irony," by Peele or Greene or Heywood because it is not very good. As evidence for Dekker's authorship of Blurt, Master Constable, Lawrence suggests that two songs in the play "have a good deal of that careless grace of style, what one might characterise artful artlessness, which marks Dekker's lyrics."[42] Apparently it did not occur to Lawrence that precisely the same observations might be made about any tolerable Elizabethan lyric, and the age produced a number of tolerable lyrics. The limited critical value of this kind of impressionism is sufficiently obvious. As evidence its value is nil.

Yet verbal parallels and literary correspondences—defined correspondences, not mere impressions—may provide a basis for attributions acceptable to the responsible historian, critic, and editor. The evidence of style—largely of parallels—for the assignment of The Queen to Ford is most impressive.[43] Archer surely erred in assigning the play to Fletcher in his 1656 playlist, and the error is satisfactorily explained by Greg. The attribution has gone unchallenged since Bang proposed it over half a century ago. An equally successful argument for attribution was made by Cyrus Day, who pointed out striking resemblances of phraseology, dramatic situation, and character portrayal between an anonymous seventeenth-century comedy, The Drinking Academy, and the known writings of Thomas Randolph, a distinctly minor dramatist who habitually pillaged his own works.[44] The literary correspondences are in this case satisfyingly concrete: the characters of Worldly, Knowlittle, and Cavaliero Whiffe in The Drinking Academy are equivalent to Simo, Asotus, and Ballio in The Jealous Lovers. The verbal parallels with nine of Randolph's acknowledged pieces are numerous and often unusual. There are no external facts to contradict the evidence of style, and Randolph's authorship of the play has been accepted by (among others) Hyder Rollins, Fredson Bowers, and G. E. Bentley.

V

The results of any single test of authorship have to be viewed, of course, as part of a larger design. An investigator like Hoy, applying a limited number of linguistic criteria to the Beaumont and Fletcher canon, must at times supplement his findings with other kinds of evidence, and he recognizes fully that his own work depends in part upon the work of others before him. A case for attribution may well represent the patient efforts of a number of scholars over a long period of time. Each contributes his particular bits of evidence. The ultimate effect sought is a cumulative one, in which all the internal evidence—stylistic, bibliographical, and linguistic—converges inexorably upon a single possible author-identification: an identification compatible with the known external information.

This cumulative effect no doubt is, as Sherbo and others have urged, something apart from and greater than the individual pieces of testimony of which it is composed, just as a building transcends the materials—the steel, concrete, wood, and plaster—that have gone into its making. But the architect of attributions must beware lest his materials be merely of the air, airy—the formulas of style and expression that are the common currency of an age. Thus the word "dilling," as the Simpsons complain with understandable irritation, "is not 'a Marston word' because it occurs once in the text of Marston . . . and 'well-parted' . . . is not exclusively a Jonson phrase when it is found in Shakespeare, Webster and Rowley, and Field."[45] Zeros, Ephim Fogel neatly puts it, no matter how great their number, add up to zero.[46]

Yet proper methods, employed by disinterested seekers after truth, may yield inconclusive results. Attribution proposals as firmly supported as those for *The Queen* or *The Drinking Academy* are after all rare, and the successful identification of the authors of collaborate plays rarer still. The investigator may find himself, sooner than he anticipated, at the frontiers of ignorance, which after so much expenditure of sweat and ink, remains a spacious domain. The words with which Baldwin Maxwell concludes his study of *A Yorkshire Tragedy* apply equally well to a number of other plays of anonymous or doubtful authorship. "A convincing identification of the author or authors . . . ," Maxwell writes, "if it is ever to be accomplished, must await our clearer knowledge of what were the peculiar characteristics of the var-

ious Jacobean dramatists."[47] The trend away from simple impressionism to a more analytical criticism (well exemplified by such recent
work as Jonas Barish's *Ben Jonson and the Language of Prose Comedy*)
may help to provide that knowledge with regard to the larger aspects of dramatic art. Electronic calculating machines will make possible on a wide scale the compilation of valuable statistical data—information about spelling, linguistic preferences, and other accidentals of
style. They will also facilitate work on concordances. The few such
tools now readily available—the Shakespeare, Kyd, and Marlowe concordances—have demonstrated how vulnerable is some of the vocabulary evidence put forward by the impressionists. Further shocks will
no doubt be felt as the stock of source materials for negative checks is
increased. Cornell University has led the way in the pioneering application of electronic computers to literary research; others may be expected to follow.

But it would be excessively hopeful to assume that, even with better tools and more refined methods, students will be able to find answers—plausible explanations, I should say—for the majority of our
vexing attribution problems. The investigator may be halted by unbridgeable gaps in his evidence; he may find himself faced with the
stubborn reluctance of facts to dispose themselves conveniently in support of hypotheses. This brings us to the extraordinary question of *The
Revenger's Tragedy*. The most important Elizabethan play of disputed
authorship, it may serve as an object lesson in the perplexities and
frustrations of canonical research.

Printed anonymously in 1607 and assigned to Cyril Tourneur by the
early cataloguers, *The Revenger's Tragedy* has become in the present
century the subject of an exasperatingly protracted controversy. In
1926 Oliphant, in what was probably his best performance, made a
detailed argument for attributing the play to Middleton, whom he had
tentatively proposed some years earlier.[48] Since then the literature on
the subject has reached staggering dimensions, as scholars have supported or rejected Oliphant's contention.[49] In 1955 I summarized the
case for Middleton in my book on the tragedies, and I concluded then
that, while the evidence was not definitive, it justified a provisional
assignment of the play to Middleton. This conclusion received, it is
fair to say, a mixed reception. Against this background, Barker's announcement in 1958, in the Preface to his *Thomas Middleton*, has
more than ordinary interest. "I have given new evidence," he writes,
"that will, I think, settle the controversy about authorship once and
for all." The new evidence is a literary correspondence, supported by

a verbal parallel, between *The Revenger's Tragedy* and Middleton's *A Mad World, my Masters*. Barker suggests that the two plays are companion pieces: Vindice and Follywit, their protagonists, are examples of "the clever man who is blinded by his own cleverness, the self-satisfied hero who turns out to be anything but a hero in the end."[50] This is of course the classic peripeteia of drama, tragedy and comedy alike. The fate that overtakes Vindice and Follywit, as one reviewer was quick to note, also overtakes the clever and self-satisfied Volpone, and the list of complacent heroes thus undone might be indefinitely extended. Several articles on the authorship of *The Revenger's Tragedy* have followed upon Barker's book. Two (by one student) support Tourneur; a third favors Middleton.[51] Thus the deadlock continues.

The view to which my concern with attribution problems during the past five years has led me is that the question remains unanswered because it is unanswerable. This despite the considerable labors of a number of scholars—labors that have yielded a rather massive accumulation of evidence. A full review of that evidence here is not feasible, but the chief issues may be stated briefly.

First, the external evidence. It is not very satisfactory—if it were, the controversy would not have arisen—but such information as we have favors Tourneur. The lists of Archer and Kirkman do not command respect for their accuracy, but it is more difficult to account for a mistake in the assignment of *The Revenger's Tragedy* to an obscure figure like Tourneur than it is to explain the erroneous ascription of, say, *The Queen* to Fletcher or *A Trick to Catch the Old One* to Shakespeare. The play was, moreover, printed "*As it hath beene sundry times Acted, by the Kings Maiesties Seruants.*"[52] There is no evidence to contradict this title-page statement which, as Miss Ekeblad points out, is supported by the use in Act V of a blazing star, a stage effect for which the Globe theatre was noted.[53] Nor is there any evidence that Middleton had a connection with the King's men at the time, about 1604-1606, that *The Revenger's Tragedy* was written. He was then the leading playwright for Paul's boys, providing them almost singlehandedly with a comic repertory. He is not likely to have undermined his own efforts by contributing plays to the powerful company with whom his own troupe was waging an increasingly desperate competitive struggle. A possible explanation—if Middleton wrote the play—is that *The Revenger's Tragedy* was originally performed by the children, and somehow afterwards passed, like Marston's *The Malcontent,* into the repertory of the adult company; but this is merely speculation.

The internal evidence is more complicated. In some ways *The Revenger's Tragedy* is a unique product of the Jacobean stage, and hence unlike either Tourneur or Middleton. It bears, however, enough general resemblance of theme and dramatic technique to *The Atheist's Tragedy*, Tourneur's only unquestioned extant play, for the attribution to Tourneur to be acceptable to many. But on the basis of other considerations, involving minute details of style and linguistic preferences, it is difficult to accommodate the two works with one another as the achievement of a single author. Indeed, our severest authorities have expressed their qualms: Chambers was skeptical enough about Tourneur's claim to *The Revenger's Tragedy* to classify the play as an anonymous work in *The Elizabethan Stage;* Greg doubted that it would have been assigned to Tourneur at all were it not for the seventeenth-century catalogues.[54] On the other hand, the stylistic evidence for Middleton is extensive and varied, and it has recently been supplemented by George R. Price's very welcome bibliographical study of *The Revenger's Tragedy.*[55]

Still the internal evidence does not sweep all before it, and the situation, as it stands, is that neither Middleton's nor Tourneur's advocates have been able to bring forward the kind of proof to which one party or the other must submit. Hence the seemingly endless exchanges of replies and counter-replies in our journals. Whatever his own personal *feeling* about the attribution may be, the task of the historian is, as I see it, to record the fact of uncertainty, which is in this case the only certainty. In the "Authors" column of the revised *Annals of English Drama,* the entry for *The Revenger's Tragedy* will read: Anonymous (Tourneur, C.? Middleton, T.?).

Does this inconclusive conclusion mean that the efforts of a number of scholars over the past thirty-five years represent so much wasted labor? I think not. By focusing intensively on so many manifestations of style, the work on *The Revenger's Tragedy* has fostered a more sensitive awareness of the distinctive characteristics of two dramatists, one of whom is a major dramatist. It has raised questions that needed raising. Less than a century ago, Churton Collins could edit Tourneur without any sense of the limitations of the evidence for the authenticity of the play on which the dramatist's fame chiefly rests. This uncritical certainty has been superseded by a reasonable doubt, and a serious hypothesis of alternative attribution has been proposed—an hypothesis that the responsible historian cannot safely ignore. Our understanding of the nature of a particular problem has been to some extent modified. That is a legitimate accomplishment of scholarship. However much we may yearn for certainties, and for grander and more romantic achievements, we recognize—or we should recognize—that the scholarly process usually proceeds by the slight modification of already existing knowledge.

There is a place for hypothesis as well as for demonstration, and in the field of Elizabethan drama, where the factual records are far from satisfactory, hypothesis assumes an especially important role. We want to know; something there is that doesn't love an anonymous play. And so scholars use internal evidence as a basis for attribution. Some of their hypotheses are much better supported than others; some, and I have noted one or two in this paper, are almost certainly correct. But all of them remain hypotheses. Despite the safeguards devised, a subjective element resides in all attribution work, and even the utilization of electronic computers will not eliminate the need for the exercise of scholarly judgment. Bentley, in including *The Queen* in his section on Ford, judiciously adds the proviso that the play "may be accepted as his until evidence of its composition be a very clever imitator is forthcoming."[56] The proviso is justified. Still we would be the poorer without Bang's hypothesis, as indeed we would without a number of others.

But if hypothesis is to be accorded its full value it must be recognized and presented as such. Not only in authorship studies but in almost every specialty, we have encountered studies in which the evidence does not support the claims which the scholar's enthusiasm has led him to make. No doubt many a worthwhile speculation has been too easily dismissed because of the impatience that undue partisanship arouses. It is good, I believe, that we pay tribute now and then to the virtue of recognizing our limitations.

"Several things dove-tailed in my mind," writes John Keats in perhaps the most famous passage of his correspondence, "and at once it struck me what quality went to form a Man of Achievement, especially in Literature, and which Shakespeare possessed so enormously—I mean *Negative Capability*, that is, when a man is capable of being in uncertainties, mysteries, doubts, without any irritable reaching after fact and reason. . . ."[57] The scholar no less than the poet must have his own kind of negative capability. He must know and accept the often frustrating limitations of the methods available to him if, in his quest to dispel illusions and errors, he is not to create new ones in their place.[58]

NOTES

This paper was read, in a somewhat different form, at the English Institute in New York on September 8, 1960.

[1] I use the term *Elizabethan* loosely, but conveniently, to include the period until the closing of the theatres in 1642.

[2] G. E. Bentley, "Authenticity and Attribution in the Jacobean and Caroline Drama," *English Institute Annual 1942* (New York 1943) 102.

[3] E. K. Chambers, "The Disintegration of Shakespeare," *Shakespeare Gleanings* (Oxford 1944) 12.

[4] E. H. C. Oliphant, "Problems of Authorship in Elizabethan Dramatic Literature," *MP* VIII (1911) 413.

[5] Oliphant, *The Plays of Beaumont and Fletcher* (New Haven 1927) 31.

[6] M. St. C. Byrne, "Bibliographical Clues in Collaborate Plays," *The Library* 4th ser XIII (1932) 23.

[7] On Fleay, see Chambers, "Disintegration of Shakespeare," 4-5.

[8] Oliphant, "Problems of Authorship," 459. It is true that years later, when the reaction had begun to set in, Oliphant prefaced his study of the Beaumont and Fletcher canon with an account of the way in which he approached the task of disintegration; but the account breaks down into rationalization and emotional self-justification, and is further marred by an ill-conceived and intemperate attack on Chambers, in the course of which Oliphant offers the quaint suggestion that Chambers was not a scholar (*Plays of Beaumont and Fletcher* 10-12).

[9] Richard Hindry Barker, *Thomas Middleton* (New York 1958) 166. On attribution procedures I am sorry to have to differ with Mr.

Barker, the virtues of whose stimulating book I have elsewhere much commended. When Mr. Barker discusses Middleton's plays, his enthusiasm—readily communicated—has a positive value of its own.

[10] Arthur Sherbo, "The Uses and Abuses of Internal Evidence," *Bulletin of The New York Public Library* LXIII (1959) 6.

[11] Philip Edwards, ed, Thomas Kyd, *The Spanish Tragedy* (London 1959) xvii.

[12] Gerald J. Eberle, "Dekker's Part in *The Familie of Love*," *Joseph Quincy Adams Memorial Studies*, ed McManaway, Dawson, and Willoughby (Washington, D.C. 1948) 723-738.

[13] F. L. Lucas, ed, John Webster, *Works* (London 1927) IV 66-68; H. Dugdale Sykes, *Sidelights on Elizabethan Drama* (Oxford 1924) 159-172; Barker, *Thomas Middleton* 191-192.

[13a] For a balanced view of the whole problem of attribution, whether by internal or external evidence, see W. W. Greg's brief, disinterested statement in *A Bibliography of the English Printed Drama to the Restoration* (London 1939-1959) IV xxi-xxii.

[14] Barker writes: "I have avoided enumerating Middleton's 'characteristics,' partly because this has often been done before, and partly because I feel that to do so here would be to misrepresent the process of determining authorship, which is anything but deductive. One just does the best one can. One reads and forms, or tries to form, impressions; finally a play or a scene or a passage gets to 'sound like' Middleton or Dekker or Rowley. Then one looks for somewhat more objective evidence that can be used

to convince other readers" *(Thomas Middleton* 155). Oliphant, on the other hand, thus describes the same process: "However strong the internal evidence may be, it is after all only a matter of deduction: because the style of a play, the literary form, the vocabulary, the phraseology, the dramatic technique, the characterization, the philosophy, the outlook on life, are characteristic of a certain writer, we assume his authorship" *(Plays of Beaumont and Fletcher* 13). Yet Barker, as noted, pays tribute to Oliphant, and both men approach attribution study in essentially the same way. That they should disagree on so fundamental a matter as whether the method they employ is inductive or deductive would seem to indicate that they have not fully considered the nature of their own assumptions and procedures.

¹⁵ Sykes, *Sidelights* 183-199; Oliphant *Shakespeare and His Fellow Dramatists* (New York 1929) ɪɪ 18; M. Joan Sargeaunt, *John Ford* (Oxford 1935) 41-57; Barker, *Thomas Middleton* 208-209. I have myself in the past accepted too easily the arguments for Ford (Schoenbaum, *Middleton's Tragedies: A Critical Study*, New York 1955, 202, 247).

¹⁵ᵃ It should be noted, however, that the same publisher, Richard Marriott, is responsible for the attribution of *Revenge for Honor* to George Chapman on the title page of the 1654 Quarto—although he had previously entered the play on the Stationers' Register as the work of Henry Glapthorne. The most plausible explanation *is*, in this instance, a dishonest commercial intention on the part of Marriott: the name of the famous translator of Homer, thus displayed, might well have been expected to spur the play's sales. But Middleton and Rowley are another matter.

¹⁶ This point is made by Bentley, *The Jacobean and Caroline Stage* (Oxford 1956) ɪᴠ 894.

¹⁷ Lucas, Webster's *Works* ɪᴠ 148-152.

¹⁸ *Jacobean and Caroline Stage* ɪɪɪ 338; ᴠ 1252-53.

¹⁹ "From the beginning of the seventeenth century there was a tendency for individual dramatic styles in prose dialogue to converge on one more or less established type; somewhat as a modern journal acquires a distinctive style to which all who write for it tend to conform" (C. H. Herford and Percy and Evelyn Simpson, eds, Ben Jonson, *Works*, Oxford 1925-52, ɪx 637). And Jonas Barish, who has studied Elizabethan dramatic prose more closely than most students, similarly finds that "Elizabethan style, in the theatre particularly, tends toward anonymity" *(Ben Jonson and the Language of Prose Comedy*, Cambridge, Mass 1960, 281).

²⁰ Moody E. Prior, "Imagery As a Test of Authorship," *SQ* ᴠɪ (1955) 383.

²¹ William Wells, "The Authorship of 'King Leir,'" *N&Q* cʟxxᴠɪɪ (1939) 434-438; "Thomas Kyd and the Chronicle-History," *N&Q* cʟxxᴠɪɪɪ (1940) 218-224 and 238-243; and "'Alphonsus, Emperor of Germany,'" *N&O* cʟxxɪx (1940) 218-223 and 236-240.

²² "Thomas Kyd and the Chronicle-History" 219.

²³ T. S. Eliot, "Cyril Tourneur," *Selected Essays* (London 1951) 186.

²⁴ M. T. Jones-Davies, *Un peintre de la vie londonienne, Thomas Dekker* (Paris 1958) 2 vols; Barker, *Thomas Middleton*.

²⁵ W. J. Lawrence, *Pre-Restoration Stage Studies* (Cambridge, Mass 1927) 363-364.

²⁶ Herford and Simpson, Jonson's *Works* ɪᴠ 495-498; ɪx 637.

27 Edwards, "An Approach to the Problems of *Pericles*," *Shakespeare Survey* 5 (Cambridge 1952) 25-49. In his New Cambridge edition of *Pericles*, J. C. Maxwell considers and rejects the arguments in Edwards' "important article" (1956 xvi-xviii). Greg, however, regards them more favorably (*The Shakespeare First Folio* [Oxford 1955] 98).

28 Cyrus Hoy, "The Shares of Fletcher and His Collaborators in the Beaumont and Fletcher Canon," *Studies in Bibliography* VIII (1956) 137-142. Installments of Hoy's study have appeared in *Studies in Bibliography* VIII (1956) 129-146; IX (1957) 143-162; XI (1958) 85-106; XII (1959) 91-116; XIII (1960) 77-108.

29 It must be said, however, that Hoy is most effective when he relies upon linguistic criteria. When he turns (as indeed he must) to other kinds of evidence to supplement inconclusive linguistic findings, he drifts into stylistic impressionism. See, for example, Hoy's discussion of *The Laws of Candy* (XIII 97-100), which he gives entirely to Ford. Hoy goes on to assign Ford a share in Act II, Sc. 1, of *The Fair Maid of the Inn*, on the very doubtful basis that "one passage therein echoes fairly closely a passage of similar import from III, 2 of *The Laws of Candy* . . ." (102-103). Thus, as so often in the work of Oliphant and company, one inference leads to another, supposition is based upon supposition.

30 "Problems of Authorship" 439.

31 The next—and ultimate—step is to attribute plays to persons for whom we have no literary remains whatsoever. That step has, indeed, been taken more than once. Several students have proposed Sebastian Westcott as the author of various extant and lost Tudor plays; see

H. N. Hillebrand, "Sebastian Westcote, Dramatist and Master of the Children of Paul's," *JEGP* XIV (1915) 568-584; C. W. Roberts, "The Authorship of *Gammer Gurton's Needle*," *PQ* XIX (1940) 97-113; and James Paul Brawner, "Early Classical Narrative Plays by Sebastian Westcott and Richard Mulcaster," *MLQ* IV (1943) 455-464. But, as Arthur Brown points out, "there is neither music nor literature extant which can with certainty be attributed to him [Westcott]," and "until we know a good deal more about Master Sebastian, we must continue to treat his claim to any of these plays as *not proved*" ("A Note on Sebastian Westcott and the Plays Presented by the Children of Paul's," *MLQ* XII [1951] 134-136). Marjorie L. Reyburn has recently suggested that Owen Gwyn —for whom, similarly, we have no surviving writings of any kind— collaborated in the Parnassus trilogy ("New Facts and Theories about the Parnassus Plays," *PMLA* LXXIV [1959] 325-335).

32 Review of Schoenbaum, *Middleton's Tragedies*, *TLS* LV (1956) 102.

33 Eliot, "Thomas Middleton," *Selected Essays* 169.

34 Fredson Bowers, ed, Thomas Dekker, *Dramatic Works* (Cambridge 1958) III 368-374.

35 Metrical statistics for Rowley's plays have been derived from texts in which printers and editors have misdivided lines and printed prose as verse and verse as prose; see Dewar M. Robb, "The Canon of William Rowley's Plays," *MLR* XLV (1950) 9-10. Robb justly concludes that "Metrical tests based upon such texts are worse than useless."

36 U. M. Ellis-Fermor, "The Imagery of 'The Revengers Tragedie' and 'The Atheists Tragedie,'" *MLR* XXX (1935) 289-301; Marco K. Min-

coff, "The Authorship of *The Revenger's Tragedy*," *Studia Historico-Philologica Serdicensia* II (1939) 1-87.

[37] Certain of the pitfalls are usefully discussed by Prior in "Imagery As a Test of Authorship" 381-386. The complexities of definition and classification are ably surveyed by Edward B. Partridge in *The Broken Compass: A Study of the Major Comedies of Ben Jonson* (London 1958) 19-36. Partridge believes that "imagery cannot be safely used to settle questions about the canon of an author" (p 14).

[38] Chambers, *William Shakespeare: A Study of Facts and Problems* (Oxford 1930) I 222.

[39] *Jacobean and Caroline Stage* IV 860.

[40] Eberle, "Dekker's Part in *The Familie of Love*" 726.

[41] Byrne, "Bibliographical Clues" 24.

[42] Lawrence, "Dekker's Theatrical Allusiveness," *Speeding Up Shakespeare* (London 1937) 118.

[43] See W. Bang, ed, *The Queen, Materialien* (Louvain 1906) vii-ix, 41-57; also Sargeaunt, *John Ford*, Appendix I; Sykes, *Sidelights* 173-182; and Bentley, *Jacobean and Caroline Stage* III 457-458.

[44] Cyrus L. Day, "Thomas Randolph and *The Drinking Academy*," *PMLA* XLIII (1928) 800-809.

[45] Jonson's *Works* IX 636-637.

[46] Ephim G. Fogel, "Salmons in Both, or Some Caveats for Canonical Scholars," *Bulletin of The New York Public Library* LXIII (1959) 304.

[47] Baldwin Maxwell, *Studies in the Shakespeare Apocrypha* (New York 1956) 196.

[48] Oliphant, "The Authorship of *The Revenger's Tragedy*," *SP* XXIII (1926) 157-168.

[49] The discussion up to 1954 is summarized in Schoenbaum, *Middleton's Tragedies* 153-182.

[50] Barker, *Thomas Middleton* 70-71.

[51] I.-S. Ekeblad, "An Approach to Tourneur's Imagery," *MLR* LIV (1959) 489-498, and "On the Authorship of *The Revenger's Tragedy*," *ES* XLI (1960) 225-240; George R. Price, "The Authorship and the Bibliography of *The Revenger's Tragedy*," *Library* 5th ser XV (1960) 262-277.

[52] R. A. Foakes makes this point in his important article, "On the Authorship of *The Revenger's Tragedy*," *MLR* XLVIII (1953) 129-138. I have previously dismissed Mr. Foakes's paper too lightly, and I am pleased to have an opportunity to comment upon it again.

[53] Ekeblad, "A Note on 'The Revenger's Tragedy,'" *N&Q* CC (1955) 98.

[54] Greg, "Authorship Attributions in the Early Play-lists, 1656-1671," *Edinburgh Bibliographical Society Transactions* II (1946) 317-318.

[55] See note 51.

[56] *Jacobean and Caroline Stage* III 457.

[57] John Keats, *Letters*, ed M. B. Forman (Oxford 1947) 72.

[58] I wish to thank Mr. J. H. P. Pafford, the Goldsmiths' Librarian, for generously permitting me to make use of the facilities of the Library of the University of London during the summer of 1960, when this essay was written. I also owe a debt of gratitude to his very capable staff.

The Date of Blake's *Vala* or *The Four Zoas*

G. E. Bentley, Jr.

Blake's long manuscript poem, which he first entitled *Vala* and later altered in pencil to *The Four Zoas,* was never published by him even in the limited sense in which most of his prophecies were published. Blake left the poem in manuscript, and the first attempt at a published transcript was in the late nineteenth century. Consequently the dating of the poem is extremely difficult, since there are no contemporary references to it. Blake himself wrote after his first title "by William Blake   1797," but it is difficult to be sure just what this means. The first part of the poem (about thirty-four pages) is written in an elegant large hand which must be a fair copy of Blake's rough draft. However, eighty-six percent of the poem is in a distinctly different hand, and to this have been added about eight hundred lines of corrections. It is impossible to be certain which stage of the poem the date 1797 refers to, though it is generally assumed that since the date is written in Blake's copperplate hand it refers to his fair copy.

Several of Blake's engraved prophecies are dated 1795. His next public literary productions, *Milton* and *Jerusalem,* are dated 1804 on the engraved titlepages, but, largely on the evidence of the paper used in the only surviving copies, the usually accepted dates for these are about 1808 and 1820 respectively. It seems likely that Blake was engaged during much of the interim from 1795 to 1808 on *Vala,* though there has never been any definite evidence relating to its date other than the 1797 on the titlepage.

There is now definite evidence to prove at least that Blake took the poem with him to Felpham, and there is every reason to believe that he worked on it while he was there from September 1800 until September 1803. On the second page of the fourth Night of *Vala*[1] there is a very faint impression of printing, which has not been commented on before. It is mirror-printing, every letter backwards, and the type gets fainter towards the left-hand side of the page. The type must have been transfered when the print was still fresh,[2] probably when the page with the print was laid on the *Vala* page.

The print transfered is from page nine (the last page) of the first of the Ballads about animals which were written by Hayley and for which Blake made engravings in 1802.[3] Hayley wrote at some length of these Ballads in his letters to Lady Hesketh, who was collaborating with him, more or less, on his biography of Cowper. On May 24th, 1802 Hayley warned her:

> Do not be surprised if you receive in about a Fortnight a Bundle of Ballads, for I have a wicked project of turning your Ladyship into a Ballad Monger for the sake of serving the excellent friendly artist, who has been working so long & so patiently by my side on our Portraits of Cowper.—He has drawn & engraved some very ingenious designs of his own to a series of singular Ballads, one of which He proposes to publish every Month with three prints annexed to it.—for the moderate price of half a Crown.—His first number will be ready in a week or two, delicately printed on a fine quarto paper, & if I send you one dozen to dispose of among yr friends I know you will not think yrself overloaded by
> > your sincere &
> > > affectionate   Hermit[4]

All the engravings for this first Ballad are actually dated June 1, 1802, and they were evidently published by about this date, for, according to his letter of June 10th, Hayley expected them to have reached Lady Hesketh by the second week of June.

Seagrave, the Chichester printer who was printing Hayley's biography, was responsible for the text of the Ballads, but Blake himself printed the engravings. As Hayley explained in his June 10th letter to Lady Hesketh,

> you receive a *smaller number,* than I led you to expect: not from our apprehension that you might find it difficult to metamorphose them into Half Crowns for the ingenious Artist . . . but in Truth, because the busy artist had not Time to furnish a larger number of these interesting animals for his distant Friends *immediately*—He & his excellent Wife (a true Helpmate!) pass the plates thro' a rolling press in their own Cottage together; & of course it is a work of some Time to collect a Number of Impressions.—But if you find, that you are likely to have *many Customers* in *your new Trade of*

> *Ballad Monger,* He will take care that you shall not want *a stock in Hand.* . . .

Probably Blake collected a large number of printed sheets from Seagrave and took them home to put the engravings in the spaces left empty on the appropriate sheets. Evidently he laid a freshly printed sheet on a page which is now part of the *Vala* manuscript.

This page which transfered print to the *Vala* manuscript has, in the published form, an engraving of an elephant at the foot. There is no trace of this engraving transfered to the manuscript page, but instead there is an indentation in the *Vala* paper of the size and in the position of the engraving which appears in the published Ballad.[5] Hayley does not say so directly, but Blake must have added the engravings to the already printed page rather than vice versa.[6] It seems probable that Seagrave printed up all the necessary copies of the first Ballad, and delivered them fresh from the press to Blake in late May.[7] If so, we can, I think, safely assume that the impression in question was transfered in late May of 1802;[8] the demand for this Ballad was certainly not such as to require Seagrave to make a second printing.

The crucial question is, however, whether the writing is on top of the print, or vice versa. I can give no satisfactory clear-cut solution to this problem; the print itself is so extremely faint that it is impossible to be certain which was added last. However, a minute examination of the manuscript leads me to believe that the writing is on top of the printing.

A number of other probabilities support this conclusion. In the first place, it seems highly unlikely that Blake would have been so careless as to leave a freshly printed page on his carefully written manuscript. Secondly, the pages of the manuscript have tiny holes in the margin, as if they had been stitched, and if they were stitched in 1802 it would be most surprising to find Blake putting a sheet or stack of sheets into his manuscript which he had bound with such care. Thirdly, it is very likely that Blake kept a large number of proofs of his *Night Thoughts* engravings, on which *Vala* is largely written, as scratch paper.[9] Some of the engravings exist in at least three states, and consequently Blake had a considerable number of sheets which, because of the space left in the center for the type, were unsaleable as separate engravings, and which were useful and usable only for scratch paper. It seems likely that the clean *Night Thoughts* engravings were among the "Sixteen heavy & portfolios full of prints"[10] which Blake took with him to Felpham.

I believe that all the evidence points toward the conclusion that the print is underneath the handwriting, and consequently that all of *Vala* from the fourth Night on was written or transcribed in its present state after May, 1802. The least that the evidence indicates, if the print must have been wet when transfered, is that Blake had his *Vala* manuscript with him at Felpham, and that he could have been making additions to it during those years.

NOTES

[1] This page is written in Blake's usual letter-writing hand on the back of a proof of his engraving for Young's *Night Thoughts* which was published in 1797. On the fourth page of the eighth Night (which is also a *Night Thoughts* verso) is a faint impression similar to that described above. It was transfered from the engraving which appeared as page twenty-three of the published *Night Thoughts;* the figure transfered is a sitting cherub or angel.

[2] I think the possibility that the paper was later accidentally moistened, and the print transfered then, is negligible.

[3] These Ballads about animals appeared in two sets; the first was issued in the summer of 1802, every Ballad (to the number of four) being sold separately; and the second was published as a small book in 1805.

[4] Quoted from an article, soon to appear in *Review of English Studies*, in which are transcribed the references to Blake in the correspondence of William Hayley and Harriet Lady Hesketh, now in the British Museum, Adds 30,803.

[5] The Ballad page was laid neatly in the center of the *Night Thoughts* proof, leaving an even border of about two inches all around it. The indentation of the *Vala* page is one

quarter inch lower than the engraving on the Ballad page (British Museum copy), but presumably there was a significant variation in every print. The left margin of the indentation is quite firm, but the right margin made several ridges, as if Blake were positioning the copperplate on the Ballad page. Perhaps the *Night Thoughts* proof was used as a backing cushion when the Ballad engravings were printed. Creases on this page of *Vala,* and on the one preceding it, but on no others in the manuscript, lend credit to this suggestion.

[6] Some reasons why one would expect the engravings to have been added to the printed Ballad page are: engraving is more expensive than type; wear on engraving is more significant than wear on type; it would be easy for Blake to run as few sheets through his press as desired, but uneconomical for Seagrave to print off sheets as demand called for them; and Hayley suggests that the production of more copies of the Ballads depends on Blake alone.

[7] Later in these letters Hayley mentions frequently going to a friend who lived nearer Chichester, so he could meet and correct the proofs of his Cowper biography. Blake usually went with him, and perhaps in late May he took, as a

piece of stray paper to protect the Ballad proofs or final printing, the proof of his *Night Thoughts* engraving on which the second page of the fourth Night of *Vala* was later written.

[8] Therefore, whether or no Blake later printed off more engravings for this first Ballad after the first week in June, that fact would not relate to the date at which the printing was transfered to the *Vala* man-

uscript, as the print can only have been fresh in May.

[9] Forty-seven proofs of these engravings were used in *Vala*, and twenty more are in the possession of Philip Hofer. An examination of these trial proofs reveals that Blake must have made hundreds of proofs of his *Night Thoughts* engravings.

[10] *Poetry and Prose of William Blake*, ed. G. Keynes (London, 1948), p. 844.

The Date of *Mankind*

Donald C. Baker

No great mystery surrounds the date of the so-called "Macro" morality play *Mankind*. It has long been assigned to "around" 1475 on linguistic evidence and because of a rather clear reference in the play to "Edward" as a reigning monarch. Thus scholars have with some confidence placed the play in the reign of Edward IV, the date "around" 1475 being in the second reign of the Yorkist king.

I believe, however, that attention to other internal evidence can improve upon the accuracy of the date, giving a very precise *terminus a quo* and a very likely *terminus ad quem*. This internal evidence consists of the many references to current money found in the play. This example of an early professional play abounds with references to coin, in keeping with the spirit of the later moralities.

In line 458 occurs the sentence "Gyf us rede reyallys, yf ye wyll see hys abhomynabull presens."[1] The phrase "rede reyallys" is, of course, a reference to the "royal" or "ryal," the gold coin valued at ten shillings which Edward IV caused to be coined to replace the traditional noble. It was also called the "rose-noble" because of the institution of

the York rose in the reverse design of the coin. This coin was first issued in Edward's second coinage of 1464/5.[2] No previous coin bore
this popular name, and therefore the reference in the play is clearly of
a date later than 1464/5, probably at least two years later, giving the
term some time to gain popular currency.

The second piece of evidence is negative. It begins with the observation that every piece of coin current in England in the second half
of the fifteenth century is mentioned in the play with a lone exception.
That one exception is rather glaring in view of the fact that this coin,
the angel, was first minted in Edward IV's reign, and furthermore,
judging from popular and literary references, quickly became the most
popular of the gold coins.[3] Literary references to the angel abound, as
every student of the field knows, and, after having made a study of its
uses in literary works, I feel that it is quite inconceivable that, considering the profuse allusions to current coin found in *Mankind,* a reference to, or pun upon the name of the angel would not have appeared
in the play if the coin had indeed been current at the time of its composition.

The angel made its appearance in the last two years of the first
reign of Edward IV (1468-69 or 69-70). Its popularity with the people
was so great and its value as a symbol of royal authority was so
impressive,[4] that, when Henry VI was restored, the only gold coin issued in his short six-month reign (1470-71) was the angel, and upon
Edward's regaining the throne, he once again minted the angel, and,
as a matter of fact, minted no other gold for the remainder of his
reign. The angel, then, quickly became the standard gold of England
(ca. 1468) and was the only gold minted until the reign of Henry VII.

To sum up the evidence presented, I feel that a *terminus a quo* of
1464/65 because of the "royal" reference is unquestionably established. Further, I feel that a date for *Mankind* in the second reign of
Edward IV (1471-83) is highly unlikely because of the absence of references to the most popular gold coin, the angel, in the midst of a
profusion of allusions to current coin. Clearly, the reference to Edward
in the play itself rules out the period 1470-71, at least for the six
months in which Henry VI had regained the throne. This reference,
considering the dependence of the professional players upon popular
sympathy, was not likely, further, to have been written in a period of
extreme uncertainty as to which of the contestants would win out. Therefore I would rule out on general grounds the period 1469-71. For
these reasons, I would argue that *Mankind* is very likely a product of

CARL A. RUDISILL LIBRARY
LENOIR RHYNE COLLEGE

the years 1464-69. Giving the name "royals" time to gain acceptance, and setting the date before the introduction of the angel, and before the restoration of Henry VI would have made a reference to Edward as king impossible, I would assign a tentative date of 1466, being reasonably confident that the date could not be at the most more than a year or two off either way.

NOTES

[1] F. J. Furnivall and A. W. Pollard, *The Macro Plays, EETSES* (London, 1904), xci, 17.

[2] J. J. North, *English Hammered Coinage* (London, 1960), ii, 63-68.

[3] See my essay, "The Angel in English Renaissance Literature," *Studies in the Renaissance,* vi (1959), 85-93.

[4] *Ibid.,* p. 87.

Psychoanalysis and Literary Biography*

Leon Edel

I

In these discourses I have tried to suggest that modern biography—and in particular the biography of imaginative writers—has undergone a marked development in our century. From the undocumented life, speculatively erected around a few meagre facts, more straw than bricks, we have come to the life of documentary surfeit, and the biographer has had to learn how to keep from putting up biographical skyscrapers. I have shown how his quest has been altered as a result of man's growing consciousness of himself as a figure in a continuum of history, and the strange and even macabre duel that can occur between subject and biographer—a matching of wits in an unequal battle between the dead and the living. We have looked into the relations between biography and criticism and seen that the biographer is committed at every turn to the act of criticism. And now I should like to examine the newest and most significant of all the biographer's relationships: his as yet uneasy flirtation with psychology.

It would be somewhat more accurate to speak of it as psychoanalysis rather than psychology, formidable and forbidding though that sounds. Psychology is the study of human behaviour: it is an all-inclusive term. Psychoanalysis is the term applied to the special techniques developed by Sigmund Freud and elaborated by his successors for the study of the symbols evoked by man which can explain his behavior.

* Retitled here. The author's chapter heading is "Psychoanalysis."

Neither term is altogether satisfactory for our purposes; the one is too large and the other too narrow. In the psychoanalytic process the analyst has constant access to the symbol life of his subject—dreams; modes of expression (such as slips of the tongue and the pen); association; the interconnections of experience; rationalization; involuntary memory, the events of everyday life. A biographer also deals in such materials: they are the ones I have pictured to you as cluttering his large table. But what a difference there is between having such inert data on a desk and having the subject in front of you in a chair or on a couch! A biographer can never, in reality, psychoanalyse his documents; and yet he is concerned with the same kinds of symbols as the psychoanalyst.

The many confusions and misunderstandings which arise between literature and psychology begin in the fact that psychoanalysts have found—as Freud did from the beginning—that the life of the imagination, and especially of great figures in literature, is highly illustrative. When they look for archetypes or universals they discover them in such figures as Oedipus or Hamlet. The result is that they venture frequently upon literary ground and sometimes indeed into places where angels fear to tread, leaving (from the point of view of the student of literature) large muddy footprints in their wake. Possessing neither the discipline of criticism nor the methods of biography, they import the atmosphere of the clinic and the consulting room into the library. And what they write is not, in reality, so much a contribution to the study of literature—I do not believe they make any such extravagant claim—but an illustration of this or that aspect of their own technical work.

The other side of the picture has been, inevitably, the venture, on the part of critics and biographers, upon psychoanalytic ground, where they have been no less inexpert than the psychoanalysts on *our* ground. The use of the psychoanalytic tool involves high skills, some quasi-scientific; a deep saturation in the problems of the mind and of the emotions; and a grasp of certain phenomena—such as "projection" or "distortion" or "malevolent transformation." We have thus a common problem: that of certain individuals who are perfectly competent in their proper field but who seem prepared to blazon forth their incompetence on ground where they do not belong.

It is not difficult to understand therefore that there has been, in the academy, a vigorous resistance to "psychologizing" and a tendency to stop up one's ears the moment a psychoanalyst arrives on the scene and tries to explain that what was wrong with Robert Louis Stevenson was that he had a feeding problem; that having as an infant been denied his mother's breast he sought ever after to gratify his oral needs—which was why he dreamed up *Dr. Jekyll and Mr. Hyde* and hinged the story on the swallowing of a potion, or why he could hold his own so splendidly at the prodigious day-long feasts in Hawaii and Samoa. This, they further tell us, meant that he never really became a mature adult. It so happens that they are not entirely wrong. Mrs. Stevenson kept a diary when Louis was an infant; and certain of his problems could be traced in psychoanalytic terms to his infantile difficulties there recorded. But isn't the important thing in all this *not* that Stevenson, for deep reasons about which we can only speculate, retained certain childish elements in his make-up—but that out of these grew the eternally youthful *Treasure Island?* And if there was this duality within him, how admirably equipped he was to trace the double sides of man's nature, as he did in the story of Jekyll and his hideous counterpart! In a word, the process of applying psychoanalysis to literature in a purely diagnostic sense invariably ends up by reducing the artist to a neurosis. Perhaps the artist *was* "neurotic." We are interested, however, in how he not only triumphs over his wound, but acquires, because of it, a kind of second sight. I need not go here into the whole troubled question of art and neurosis, which would take us far afield. Mr. Lionel Trilling has written one of his most measured essays on this subject and we have had Edmund Wilson's book *The Wound and the Bow* before us for almost two decades. The literature is large and important. Indeed, Charles Lamb, as Mr. Trilling reminds us, wrote a penetrating essay "On the Sanity of True Genius" long before the advent of psychoanalysis. Men, Lamb observed, "finding in the raptures of the higher poetry a condition of exaltation, to which they have no parallel in their own experience, besides the spurious resemblance of it in dreams and fevers, impute a state of dreaminess and fever to the poet. But the true poet dreams being awake. He is not possessed by his subject but has dominion over it. . . . Where he seems most to recede from humanity, he will be found the truest to it."

Art is the result not of calm and tranquillity, however much the artist may, on occasion, experience calm in the act of writing. It springs from tension and passion, from a state of disequilibrium in the artist's being. "His art is happy, but who knows his mind?" William Butler Yeats asked in speaking of Keats. The psychoanalyst, reading the pattern of the work, can attempt to tell us what was wrong with the artist's mental or psychic health. The biographer, reading the same pattern in the larger picture of the human condition, seeks to show how the negatives were converted into positives: how Proust translated his allergies and his withdrawal from the pain of experience, into the whole world of Combray, capturing in language the very essences which seemed illusory and evanescent in man's consciousness; how Virginia Woolf, on the margin of her melancholy, pinned the feeling of the moment to the printed page as the hunter of butterflies pins his diaphanous and fluttering prize to his; and how James Joyce, visioning himself as Daedalus, soaring over a world he had mastered, created a language for it, the word-salads of *Finnegans Wake*—but where the schizophrenic patient creates world-salads because of his madness, Joyce created them with that method in madness which Lamb was describing when he spoke of the artist's dominion over his subject. These are the triumphs of art over neurosis, and of literature over life, as I have had occasion to say elsewhere, and they illustrate Henry James's assertion to H. G. Wells that "it is art that *makes* life, makes interest, makes importance . . . and I know of no substitute whatever for the force and beauty of its process."

In one supreme instance in recent times, the psychoanalyst and the biographer have become one. I refer to Dr. Ernest Jones and the three substantial volumes in which he recorded the life of Sigmund Freud. Dr. Jones wrote out of a deep friendship and a Boswellian knowledge of his subject's life; he wrote also from extensive documents made available to him by the Freud family and as a disciple who had himself arrived at a mastery of psychoanalysis. He ran the inevitable biographical risk of apotheosizing his dead leader; but having himself been analyzed he could say at the outset (as he did) that "my own hero-worshiping propensities had been worked through before I encountered [Freud]." Dr. Jones had fewer difficulties in his quest for data than many biographers, although Freud, like Henry James, leveled the approaches to certain areas of his early life by destruction of personal papers. The remaining mass was considerable, however, and more important still, there was available to Dr. Jones in Freud's voluminous writings—the writings of a man with a profound literary sense—much of his subject's self-exploration and his dream life.

The result was a biography of major scope as befitted the luminous mind it celebrated; and a work which uses psychoanalysis constantly while being in itself a partial history of psychoanalysis. *The Life and Work of Sigmund Freud* will probably stand as an archetypal study, illustrating the relation of psychoanalysis to biography—and in negative as well as positive ways. Its shortcomings, for the literary biographer, are fairly obvious: they reside in Dr. Jones's ready use of that language —the concepts, assumptions, conclusions—to which he was accustomed and which had become second nature to him, but which is confusing to the uninitiated reader. The reader without psychoanalytic orientation is asked to make too many leaps and to hurdle ideas that by everyday standards appear strange and inconsistent, and indeed are still open to debate within the psychoanalytic disciplines. One example will suffice. In the first chapter Dr. Jones describes the emotional problems which beset the two-year-old Freud upon the impending birth of another child in the family:

> Darker problems arose when it dawned on him that some man was even more intimate with his mother than he was. Before he was two years old, for the second time another baby was on the way, and soon visibly so. Jealousy of the intruder, and anger for whoever had seduced his mother into such an unfaithful proceeding, were inevitable. Discarding his knowledge of the sleeping conditions in the house, he rejected the unbearable thought that the nefarious person could be his beloved and perfect father.

One needs to be more than merely conversant with Freudian theory to grasp this picture of a childish consciousness told in the terms of adult sexuality. Dr. Jones was inevitably much less concerned with the *translation* of his specialized concepts into the language of everyday life. The literary biographer, when he borrows the psychoanalyst's code, is obliged to decipher it and render it into the language proper to literature and literary discussion.

II

Literature and psychology are not necessarily antogonistic, as they have been made to seem. They meet on common ground. We have for decades used psychology in criticism and in biography. When we study the motivations of Hamlet, is not this psychology? When we try to understand and speculate upon symbols in a work, are we not "psychologizing"? And in our time, when creative writers have been exposed directly to the works of Freud and Jung and their disciples, and use them in their writings, we must treat them for the sources that they are. How can we understand William Faulkner's *Light in August* without at least a glance at certain modern theories of "conditioning" and behavior? Can we deal adequately with *Finnegans Wake* without looking into Jung and his theory of the collective unconscious? What meaning can Eugene O'Neill's *Strange Interlude* and *Mourning Becomes Electra* have if they are divorced from the popular Freudian misconceptions of the 1920's? Freud himself acknowledged that Sophocles and Dostoevsky and Ibsen had those glimpses into the unconscious which were vouchsafed to him in his consulting room. The answer to the misguided use of psychoanalysis is not to close our ears, but to ask ourselves: how are we to handle this difficult material while remaining true to our own disciplines—and avoid making complete fools of ourselves?

Well, it is fairly obvious that we can handle it only after we have studied and mastered that part of psychology useful to us, as we must master any learning. Our success will depend entirely on the extent to which we know what we are about and the way in which we learn to use these shiny new tools. We must not run amuck; above all we must beware of the terminology and jargon of the psychoanalysts. What we must try to do is to translate the terms in a meaningful way and into language proper to our discipline. Critics who babble of the Oedipus complex and who plant psychoanalytical clichés higgledy-piddledy in their writings do a disservice both to literature and to psychoanalysis. Biographers who take certain arbitrary symbols and apply them rigidly to the wholly volatile human personality, inevitably arrive at gross and ludicrous distortions. These are matters highly complex and difficult to explain and I have accordingly devised an illustrative problem in an effort to demonstrate what I would deem to be the use—and the abuse—of psychoanalysis in the writing of biography.

I intend to draw upon certain material presented in the Alexander Lectures of 1949-50 in E. K. Brown's discussion of *Rhythm in the Novel*. I am going to take that portion of the third lecture in which Brown discussed Willa Cather's novel *The Professor's House*, a passage later incorporated into his biography of Miss Cather. The passage in question shows Brown at his best as critic and explicator; he evokes the central symbol of the novel—the house—and illuminates it wholly in the light of his own critical intelligence. I will then try, as fairly as I can, to show how the psychoanalyst would handle this same material in a broad diagnostic sense; and finally I will try to show how the biographer, using the material offered by the critic and the psychoanalyst, can more deeply illuminate the work by seeking to determine what the house symbol meant to Miss Cather herself. First, however, let us look at the story.

III

The Professor's House, published in September 1925, is the story of a professor in a Midwestern university who has achieved success but derives no particular pleasure from it. The novel is a record of his mental depression. With the money received from a prize he was won for a monumental historical work, Professor St. Peter has built a new house, to please his wife and daughters. He would prefer to remain in the rented house in which he has shaped his career for thirty years. Indeed he cannot bring himself to move out of his old study, located in the attic, where still stand the wire forms on which a dressmaker fitted the clothes for his wife and growing daughters. The attic sewing-room is lit by an oil lamp. It is heated by a stove. Professor St. Peter has scorned cushion-comforts. He had a "show" study downstairs and has one in the new house. But the attic room, with its silent dummies, is comfort enough for him. He clings to the old place even after the rest of the house has been emptied and the moving is over. Since the lease still has some months to run, he decides he will keep his former workroom until he has to give it up.

His elder daughter is Rosamond, an attractive girl who has married a suave, fast-talking, pretentious but cultivated young man named Louie Marsellus. Marsellus has, with great practicality, turned to commercial use in aviation a certain discovery made by one of the professor's former students, Tom Outland, who was Rosamond's financé but who was killed during the First World War. Outland bequeathed his patent to Rosamond, and since her marriage to Marsellus it has become a source of wealth. The professor loves his daughter very much, but intensely dislikes the upstart qualities of her husband and accordingly feels a certain alienation from her. The professor's wife, however, is extremely fond of her son-in-law and his European affectations. She feels that her husband, in his withdrawal from the entire family, does not sufficiently recognize how materially its fortunes are being altered by Louie Marsellus's business acumen. There is a second daughter who is married to a newspaper columnist named McGregor. They tend to side with the father against the somewhat vulgar *nouveau riche* world of Louie and Rosamond. The latter are also building a house—in the style of a Norwegian manor, set incongruously in this Midwestern community.

The first part of the book, titled "The Family," sketches for us the

professor's alienation from those closest to him because of his feeling
that his wife and daughters do not really understand his deeper emotional life, and his rebellion against the crass materialism of the college
town. He has set himself apart rather successfully over the years. He
has made for himself a French garden in this prairie setting, he has
cultivated his love for French wines and delicate sauces; he has a
beach house on the lake and spends long lonely hours in the water.
He is a Gallic epicure isolated, like his garden, in surroundings to
which he cannot ever wholly belong. He has had only one student in
all the years of his teaching who has meant anything to him—Tom
Outland. He dislikes the new generation of students. He dislikes college politics. He has no real friends among his colleagues. He feels
himself oppressed by the prosaic, mediocre world of the town of
which his wife and daughters are so much a part. Material values
have been exalted here over those he cherishes: the rich fabric of art
related to the rich fabric of the old religion in which great cathedrals
and the drama of Good and Evil exalted men to a high creativity.

The second part of the book is called "Tom Outland's Story." Here
Miss Cather attempts a risky technical device, which is nevertheless
time-honored in fiction. In the manner of Cervantes or Smollett she
interpolates a story within a story: she gives us an autobiographical
fragment written by Tom Outland and confided to Professor St. Peter.
It describes a crucial episode in the young man's life. Miss Cather explained that in writing this part of the novel she had in mind those
Dutch paintings in which interiors are scrupulously rendered; in many
of these there was "a square window, open, through which one saw
the masts of ships, or a stretch of gray sea"; the effect is that of an
inset, a picture within a picture. Having given us the interior of the
professor's family life, she directs our attention to the one important
window in it—the one that looks out upon Tom Outland's adventure.

The crucial episode had been his discovery of a Cliff Dwellers' village tucked into a wall of rock high in a New Mexico canyon. Here
was beauty at once primitive and sophisticated. Here were houses that
let in wind and sun and yet sheltered an unfathomable past. Here also
was a great tower: "It was still as sculpture. . . . The tower was the
fine thing that held all the jumble of houses together and made them
mean something. . . .That village sat looking down into the cañon
with the calmness of eternity." The Cliff Dwellers' houses are never
overtly contrasted with the houses in the professor's town, but they
invite contrast. In the modern town the emphasis, as E. K. Brown ob-

serves, is on the individual buildings. In the ancient village it is on the architectural as well as the social unity.

Tom made his discovery with the aid of a fellow cowpuncher, Roddy. He travelled to Washington in great excitement to inform the Department of the Interior, bringing with him samples of the ancient pottery he had found in the long-deserted houses. In the capital he is promptly wrapped up in heedless red tape; he sits in impersonal outer offices; he is met with general indifference. Civil servants seem to him strange modern cave dwellers living in rows of apartments as if in rabbit warrens; and their careerism and arrogance blot out all his hopes. He turns his back on Washington, disillusioned; he had felt he had done the proper thing as a citizen, but the petty officials did not share his interest in his country's distant past. However, a still greater disappointment awaited him. Roddy, during his prolonged absence, had profited by the arrival of a German anthropologist to sell the entire contents of the cliff town. The ancient relics had been packed and shipped to Europe and Roddy had deposited the money for Tom in a bank thinking he had driven a good bargain. Tom, in anger at what he considered a betrayal, broke with Roddy and then returned to the cliff town to spend a few days in magnificent solitude, hiding in the high tower his notes and records of the entire adventure. Then, descending again, he withdrew the money from the bank and used it to go to college, there meeting the professor who became his guide and mentor.

The final part of the novel is a mere sketch. Titled "The Professor," it returns to the dilemma of St. Peter's isolation in his attic. Lonely and depressed, he remains there while his family is away during the summer, living a monastic dream-life, with the old sewing-woman turning up to act as charwoman. One day, on awakening from a nap, he discovers the room filled with fumes from the stove, but he is incapable of making the effort to arouse himself and to throw open the window. He has lost the will to live. The fortuitous arrival of the sewing-woman saves him, and there the novel ends. We can only speculate that the professor will go on living in isolation amid his family.

IV

What are we to make of this novel—if we can call it a novel? It is a stitching together of two inconclusive fragments about a professor, his family, and his wish for death, and the adventures of a young man alone with the past on a mesa and briefly in touch with the modern urban life of Washington. The two episodes relating to the professor hardly constitute a novel: they convey a picture of his deep depression which nothing in the book really explains. Why does he wish for death at a time when his life has been crowned with success and when his family flourishes as never before; when indeed there is the promise of a grandchild, for Rosamond expects a baby as the book ends? The Tom Outland story fills in the background of Rosamond's wealth and gives us the strange story of the intense young man who altered the whole course of the professor's life; this does not illuminate, however, the professor's final state of mind. His wish to die is at no point sufficiently motivated by the facts of the small-town life, the general hopelessness of the Philistine surroundings. To believe so intensely in art and the religion of art, and to have created so fully, and yet at the same time to be overpowered by a sense of futility and ineffectuality—these are the contradictions we discern within the professor.

E. K. Brown, in his Alexander Lecture, found an inner unity which he explained in terms of the symbolism of houses within the book. It is a striking passage. There are, he points out, the two houses of the professor, and of these the old house is the significant one. The new house is wrong for him. The Marsellus-Rosamond Norwegian manor house is wrong too. It is a product of pretension and materialism, without regard for the style of the town and the essential dignity of human dwellings. The homes of the Cliff Dwellers—for these are houses also—primitive and wind-swept on their high perch, possessed that dignity. In the third portion of the book the link between these houses is established. Brown continues, speaking of this final part:

> The first and second parts of the book which have seemed so boldly unrelated are brought into a profound unity. It is in this third part of the novel that the large background of emotion, which demands rhythmic expression if we are to respond to it as it deserves, becomes predominant. In the first part it was plain that the professor did not wish to live in his new house, and did not wish to enter into the sere phase of his life correlative with it. At the beginning of the third part it becomes plain that he cannot indefinitely continue to make the old attic-study the theatre of his life, that he cannot go on prolonging, or attempting to prolong his prime, the phase of his life correlative with that. The personality of his mature

years—the personality that had expressed itself powerfully and in the main happily in his teaching, his scholarship, his love for his wife, his domesticity—is now quickly receding, and nothing new is flowing in. What begins to dominate St. Peter is something akin to the Cliff Dwellers, something primitive which had ruled him long ago when he was a boy on a pioneer farm in the rough Solomon valley in northwestern Kansas. To this primitive being not many things were real;. . . what counted was nature, and nature seen as a web of life, and finally of death.

For the professor remembers an old poem he has read, Longfellow's translation of the Anglo-Saxon *Grave*. He doesn't recall it quite accurately (that is, Miss Cather didn't) but this is what is given in the novel:

> For thee a house was built
> Ere thou wast born;
> For thee a mould was made
> Ere thou of woman camest.

And Brown concludes:

All that had seemed a hanging back from the future—the clinging to the old attic study, the absorption in Tom Outland and the civilization of the Cliff Dwellers, the revival of interest in the occupations of his childhood and its pleasures—was something very unlike what it had seemed. It was profound, unconscious preparation for death, for the last house of the professor.

This seems to me quite admirable literary criticism; the critic has seen the unity of the book created by the central symbol; he has penetrated to the professor's state of mind and grasped that his interest in the occupations of childhood is a stepping backward—or forward—to old age and death. But the story, as told by Miss Cather, in reality leaves the critic helpless in one respect: there is no way to explain why the professor should at this moment of his middle years lose his will to live. We are given no clue. Miss Cather records merely the professor's despair.

V

And now let us apply the tools of psychoanalysis to this material. I want to look at it through the understanding of people and of symbols offered us by Sigmund Freud and, more recently, by Harry Stack Sullivan. The first striking element in the story is the professor's strange attachment to his attic room, high up, old, and cramped, but safely away from the family life in the house below. Now, people do form attachments to rooms and to houses, but the professor's attachment here verges upon the eccentric. He clearly thinks of his attic as a place of—and Miss Cather's words express it—"insulation from the engaging drama of domestic life . . . only a vague sense, generally pleasant, of what went on below came up the narrow stairway." And later he thinks that "on that perilous journey down through the human house, he might lose his mood, his enthusiasm, even his temper."

This is much more than a professor seeking a quiet corner for his working hours. The room is "insulation." The professor withdraws from his family and at the same time makes demands on it, for care, food, attention. There is decidedly something infantile here, the security a baby feels in its possession of the mother and the breast for which it need make no return. In this attic room, tiny and snug as a womb, cradled in a warm and alive household, but safe from any direct contact with the world outside, Professor St. Peter can feel taken care of and as undisturbed as an embryo.

The room, furthermore, is used by one other person—the motherly sewing-woman, Augusta. Adjuncts to this mother figure are the two dressmakers' dummies. Seen as part of the sewing-woman, the mother figure, these two dummies express opposite experiences of the mother: one is described as matronly, of a bulk suggesting warm flesh and reassuring physical possession; the other is of sophisticated line suggesting spirit and sexual awareness and interest. So the professor has in his secluded place the beloved mother, who cares for and protects him but is also of some sexual interst to him. He wants his mother to be both a mother and an erotic stimulus and above all he wants to possess her exclusively.

Willa Cather now weaves a second story, but it is in reality a repetition of the same theme. Her hero, again a man, yearns for a high mesa, a sun-beaten plateau, and when he conquers it he finds a cave city. Caves are feminine sexual symbols. These caves are for him inviolate and untouched, like a seemingly virginal mother preserved from others, a mother of long ago, of the infant years, who belonged only to the child greedy at her breast. There is also beautiful pottery. Pottery is again a feminine symbol. The hero cherishes these artifacts and comes to regret that he has a male companion with whom he must share them. The disinclination to share might be seen as sibling jealousy for the mother, or the kind of rivalry a boy, in his Oedipal phase, has for the father who possesses the mother in the sexual way the boy aspires to have her. The hero is disillusioned first when his mother country, symbolized by Washington, is not interested in his discoveries and, in effect, rejects him, and then when his male friend puts the pottery to some practical use: so that we might say the boy is disillusioned when he first learns that in reality his mother is not a virgin and that his father is the cause of her having been thus despoiled. The hero angrily drives the male friend—father or sibling—away and spends a period among the caves—that is with his mother—as blissful as a babe in full possession of the breast. He preserves a record of his narcissistic-infantile paradise, the paradise of life in the womb, of possessing the mother physically, in a notebook which he carefully secretes in the tower. Like the professor's attic room, the tower is still higher and more secluded than the dwellings, where the mother can be preserved, if not in actuality (the pottery), at least in the diary describing his intimate life with her (Outland's detailed account of the caves and their contents as he first found them). Life, its rude events and passage of time, its insistence on moving forward and routing the infant from the womb and the breast, also disrupts the hero's blissful eternity on his hidden mesa, in his caves, with his pottery. He has been disturbed. He seeks stubbornly at least to preserve the memory of days with mother (the mesa, etc.) even as the professor cannot leave his cubbyhole study and would not want the dressmaker's dummies removed.

But life does move on, and in moving on it demands that we follow. The professor seeks a solution to this problem. The family which sustained him in the house below, while he took attic refuge, moves to the new house. If he follows he must accept a new room, a modern room, a room on a lower floor; he must take his place in the family on a different basis; his daughters are now married; they will have children. He must change and grow too, accept his new role as father-in-law and eventually as grandfather. He must, in other words, meet life in an adult way and recognize the demands which are being made on him to take a more active part in the lives of his grown-up children. But the professor clings as long as he can to the old attic room, and with the life gone from the house beneath he is actually threatened with greater isolation than ever before. He has a choice: he can maintain this state of alienation from his family, or he can emerge from his passive dependency and assume the active life expected of him. Appropriately enough, Willa Cather ends her story with the professor nearly suffocating in his room. To remain in the womb beyond one's time is indeed to suffocate. The tenacity of the professor's—and the writer's—determination to maintain this *status quo ante,* if only in fantasy, is illustrated in the ending of the story. It is the sewing-woman—who, by the way, was sensibly eager to move to her new, bigger sewing-room, to a new life, a new relationship, and cannot understand the professor's infantile attachment to the old room, the old relationship—it is the sewing-woman who rescues the professor from suffocation. A mother figure has once more appeared upon the scene for the professor, who thus hangs on to his fixation even though it has brought him an immense threat. The book ends with the professor's problem unresolved, save in the sense that ultimately Mother Earth will enclose him in her womb.

VI

Psychoanalysis, by singling out certain primal elements in the picture, has illuminated our story and offered answers to some of our questions. The professor's death-wish, undefined by the author, would appear to be due to lingering infantile needs, so strong that this successful adult teacher and writer, otherwise a figure of dignity and maturity, adheres to a pattern of behavior which belongs to his childhood. This he masks by rationalization: a love for the past, a dislike of the present. But how are we to handle this material, so heavy with Freud's ideas about infantile sexuality—its insistence upon the attic as a womb symbol, its incestuous fantasies and Oedipal situation—a kind of "psychologizing" which can have meaning only to those who have worked with these concepts on a clinical level? And does this interpretation, fascinating and incredible though some of it is, tell the layman anything about the novel as novel? Or is he being offered a virtually meaningless diagram, highly speculative, of the unconscious fantasies of the professor, derived though it may be from the overt material placed in the book by the author? We all live in some form of house and doubtless, for some of us, on some unconscious level, caves and attics may be wombs and houses mothers, and the smooth curves of pottery may suggest the curves of women. But houses, and the rooms within them, are also universal facts and a universal reality. They testify to man's need for shelter and warmth. It is true that we are thrust out of the womb into the world and must inevitably acquire some shelter, by stages that start with the basket and the cradle and end in adult dwellings. And it is true that there are certain individuals who, instead of welcoming the shelters of this world, long for the unattainable state of the embryo where one was sheltered from everything, that state which James Joyce, mimicking the cradle-tones of our literature, described as "Before born babe bliss had." Wombs are for blissful embryos; houses for growing children and adults. We juggle, so to speak, with the obvious when we invoke such universal symbols.

And what has become of the fine social criticism in the novel? In tracing such a diagram of the professor's neurosis, it is seen as a mere desire to cling to the past for infantile or infantile-sexual reasons. Yet the social criticism is perhaps the best part of Miss Cather's novels. They record the protest of a gifted woman against the ever increasing conformities and clichés of American life. Her voice is never more resonant than when she shows how the capital of the pioneers was converted into the small change of standardization; and that while the original settlers wrested fom the land the glory of America, the sons of the settlers became real-estate agents parcelling this land out and dealing in mortgages, or front-office men—like Louie Marsellus. The anguish of Tom Outland in Washington (whatever neurotic traits he may thereby reveal) is still the genuine anguish of someone who wants government to meet its responsibilities to the past, to history.

And what of criticism of the novel itself? To label the symbols within it in terms of Freud or to describe the "interpersonal" relations between the professor and his family after the manner of Sullivan, gives us no help in assessing the work as work of art. We have merely used psychoanalytic ideas as instruments of quasi-clinical diagnosis. Has Miss Cather successfully carried out her general intention? What is the explanation of the professor's happiness in the past? Why does he experience malaise in the present—a present in which, even without neurotic motivation, the malaise can certainly be held to be genuine?

I have given you the point of view of one critic about this novel, and a psychoanalytical approach to the material. It is my contention that the method used in this approach leads us to a "diagnosis" which can have little meaning unless it is translated into different terms. And I hold that this translation is possible only by calling upon the resources of biography. Let us therefore pursue our inquiry on this third level.

Psychoanalysis is concerned with what goes on in the unconscious and how this is reflected in conscious thoughts and actions. It deals always with a given consciousness. A dream cannot be truly interpreted, as we have seen, unless it is attached to the dreamer, although it may be a pretty story and have distinct meanings for someone to whom it is narrated. These meanings, however, are not necessarily those of the dreamer, who has put into the dream his personal symbols. The personal symbols can be understood only after a close study of their recurrent use in the weaving of that person's dream structures. As with dreams, so with the work of art. Ernest Jones has significantly said:

> A work of art is too often regarded as a finished thing-in-itself, something almost independent of the creator's personality, as if little would be learned about the one or the other by connecting the two studies. Informed criticism, however, shows that a correlated study of the two sheds light in both directions, on the inner nature of the composition and on the creative impulse of its author. The two can be separated only at the expense of diminished appreciation, whereas to increase our knowledge of either automatically deepens our understanding of the other.

It is true that sometimes we have no alternative but to cling to our shreds of evidence and to speculate endlessly. But with a writer so recently in our midst as Willa Cather, we have abundant biographical material relating to her actual experience. We can try to determine—what she at best may have only glimpsed—how this was incorporated into the imagination by which she created.

VII

Our data are derived from E. K. Brown's biography of Willa Cather and from the valuable memoir written by her friend of four decades, Edith Lewis. In these works we discover how intensely Willa Cather suffered as a little girl from an initial displacement from one house to another. She was born in Virginia and lived in a large house. At ten she was torn from the east and taken to the Divide, to a new house. Here she discovered also the sod houses of the early settlers, even as she was later to observe the cave houses of the Cliff Dwellers in the Southwest. We note that the professor in her novel was "dragged" to Kansas from the east when he was eight, that he "nearly died of it."

In Nebraska Willa Cather discovered that nearly all the inhabitants were displaced from somewhere else, and some had been involved in a transatlantic displacement. Her later novels were to depict with deep emotion the meaning of this displacement of the pioneers from Europe and civilization to the rugged prairie. Willa Cather could show empathy with them; their anguish was hers. Then, in Red Cloud, in Nebraska, where the adolescent girl began to discover the life of the frontier, there was a neighboring house in which lived a childless couple. In her own house there was the clash of temperaments and the rivalries of a large family of boys and girls; in their midst was a refined Southern-bred mother, a gentlewoman somehow strangely aloof and exhausted by repeated pregnancies. And so this other house became a retreat; the cultivated Mrs. Wiener from France served as a kind of second mother to Willa Cather. She provided books and quiet surroundings; the future author could lie for hours on the parlor rug, reading and dreaming. A fairly circumstantial account of the two houses may be found in Miss Cather's late story, "Old Mrs. Harris." From the small town Miss Cather went to Lincoln, Nebraska, to attend the university, and here she discovered still another house. It was filled with robust young men, over whom there presided an Old World mother. Miss Cather had again found a home, this time as an escape from the dreariness of a furnished room. The house was that of the Westermann family, and the late William Lynn Westermann of Columbia University, a distinguished Egyptologist, testified to the accuracy of Willa Cather's picture of life in his early home as portrayed in her novel *One of Ours.*

In 1895 Miss Cather went to Pittsburgh and worked on a newspaper. She lived in a series of depressing boarding houses. The way in which she escaped from these into the world of the theatre and music is reflected in her ever-popular short story, "Paul's Case." After five years of drab existence she met a young woman who changed the course of her life. This was Isabelle McClung, the daughter of a prominent and wealthy Pittsburgh judge, a strikingly handsome woman interested in the arts. So attached did she become to Willa Cather, the radiance of her personality and the promise of her art, that she invited her to come and live in the McClung family mansion. The gesture might be described as protective and motherly, and Isabelle became, indeed, during these years, a patron of Miss Cather's art. Her house was many times more elegant and spacious than the Wiener house or the house of the Westermanns. Here Willa Cather put together her first book of verse, began to publish short stories, and finally her first volume of tales. She was given a quiet room to work in at the rear of the McClung mansion. It had been a sewing room. Still standing in it were some dressmaker's dummies.

Willa Cather remained deeply attached to this house. It represented security and peace. From it she was able to face the world and build her career. Even after she had moved to New York and taken up a new abode in Greenwich Village—thus establishing her own home—and was the successful managing editor of *McClure's Magazine,* she would dash off to Pittsburgh for periodic stays with Isabelle and uninterrupted work in her favorite room.

In the midst of the First World War there came a break. It followed Isabelle McClung's decision to marry a violinist she had known for some years, Jan Hambourg, who with his father and brother had a school of music in Toronto. This happened in 1917 when Miss Cather was in her late forties. Isabelle too was no longer young. Thus a significant change was introduced into the fixed pattern of the years. And it is from this moment that the biographer can date a change in Willa Cather's works. They reflect an increasing tension and deep inner anxiety. Her novel *One of Ours,* written in the early twenties, is an anxious book; on the surface the anxiety is related to the disillusion and malaise that followed the war and to a strong sense of betrayal by the new generation in Nebraska, which was watering down the achievements of the pioneers. For all its defects it won the Pulitzer Prize. The title of the next novel clearly conveys the state of mind of the author: it is the story *A Lost Lady*—and it tells of a woman who clings to a vanished past in a changing world. After this Miss Cather wrote *The Professor's House.*

But just before she set to work on this novel, before she had even had the idea for it, she had gone to France to visit Isabelle and Jan Hambourg. Isabelle, in her French home at Ville-D'Avray, had set aside a study for her friend. The new house would incorporate in it this essential feature of the Pittsburgh mansion. Miss Lewis testifies: "The Hambourgs had hoped that she would make Ville-D'Avray her permanent home. But although the little study was charming, and all the surroundings were attractive, and the Hambourgs themselves devoted and solicitous, she found herself unable to work at Ville-D'Avray. She felt indeed that she would never be able to work there."

Why? Miss Lewis does not tell us. But she does tell us what we already have suspected: that there are some traits of Jan Hambourg in the character of Louie Marsellus. Hambourg was a cultivated musician, deeply read in French literature and apparently as good a conversationalist as Marsellus. Miss Cather had dedicated *A Lost Lady* to him, thereby welcoming him to the circle of her intimate friends. The strange thing is that she dedicated *The Professor's House* as well: "For Jan, because he likes narrative." As we collate the somewhat pretentious figure of Louie with the figure of the real-life musician, we recover so many similarities, or exaggerations, of certain traits that we are prompted to speculate whether the novelist did not find it necessary to write this flattering dedication—the second book in succession to bear his name—to mitigate the effect of the unflattering portrait she had painted. A dedication is by its nature so friendly an act that it is difficult to think of it as masking a concealed animus. It is clear that Miss Cather was charmed by one side of Jan Hambourg; but like the professor, she would have welcomed him as a friend rather than as the husband of Isabelle-Rosamond.

We can now see what life itself contributed to *The Professor's House*. Willa Cather's early uprootings have more meaning in explaining the attachment to a fixed abode than the universal uprooting from the womb; her mother's aloofness, and her search for substitute houses, can also be readily fitted into the novel. The Pittsburgh house with its sewing-room has been transferred into the professor's frame house. Like the professor of her fiction, Miss Cather won a prize during her middle years; like him, she achieved success. The new house at Ville-D'Avray has become the new house built by the professor's family; it too was no substitute for the old one, since in France Isabelle could no longer function for Willa Cather as a maternal figure exclusively possessed by her; she now had to share Isabelle with Jan— as she had had to share her mother with her brothers; as the professor, though he dislikes it, must share Rosamond with Louie; and as Outland shares his caves and pottery with Roddy, only to lose them.

And here we touch the heart of our problem. We can now see what motivated the depression of Willa Cather's middle years when she wrote that "the world broke in two in 1922 or thereabouts," for we know that to her search for inner security, going back to childhood, was added the deeper sense, irrational from an adult point of view, that she had been rejected. Of course this was not so: but our emotions have a way of clinging, in the teeth of adult reality, to patterns fixed at an earlier time. The reality was that Isabelle had moved forward in life, and had married; Willa Cather had not been able to move forward and adapt herself to this situation. In *The Professor's House* Miss Cather had so identified herself with the professor that she could not supply any "rejection motif" for his depression. All she could do was to say that the world was out of joint for him, as it was for herself. This depression of spirit is expressed in her first section, in her account of the professor who cannot keep pace with his family, although his life has been crowned with fame and success.

But such is the nature of our inner fantasies that they persist in seeking expression. In the first part of the novel which emerged from these fantasies, the professor in reality is the one who, by clinging to his attic, has rejected his family. Willa Cather accordingly opens a window into a second theme, after the manner of the Dutch painters, and here she can incorporate her deepest feelings. The Tom Outland story is linked to Isabelle in a curious way. It would seem that in Willa Cather's consciousness the Pittsburgh house, standing on high ground, could be identified with the mesa and the tower. For, some years earlier, when she published *The Song of the Lark,* her first novel to draw upon the southwest, she dedicated it to Isabelle McClung with the following verses:

> On uplands,
> At morning,
> The world was young, the winds were free;
> A garden fair
> In that blue desert air,
> Its guest invited me to be.

Uplands had become Outland. The world in the "blue desert air" of the mesa is a re-creation of the feeling of freedom Willa Cather had experienced in her life with the maternal Isabelle, patroness of the arts, and in the sewing-room sanctuary of the Pittsburgh mansion. But Tom Outland is rejected twice: the maternal-paternal Government rejects him, and when he returns home he finds that Roddy, his boon companion, has denuded his cliff sanctuary of all that was precious to him. The fantasy of rejection is thus incorporated into the novel.

The Tom Outland story is complete. That of the professor is not. By merging the insights gained from psychology with the biographical data that give us clues to the workings of the author's imagination, we are able to render a critical evaluation: we can see the failure of *The*

Professor's House as a work of fiction. The professor lives for us as a man who has given up his good fight and takes the world as preparation for the grave. He has retreated into a vale of misanthropy and despair. He has everything to live for; and for reasons unexplained and unresolved he does not want to live. The materialism of an age, the marrying off of one's children to persons we may like or dislike, the process of growing old—these are not sufficient motives for a depression as deep and as all-consuming as the professor's. The world is never all that we would want it to be, and lives are lived in a constant process of doing, and of ups and downs. The novel is thus incomplete because of Miss Cather's inner problems, which did not permit her to resolve clearly the problems of the character she had projected in her novel. Therefore the professor was not given a clear-cut motivation: his state of mind was described but not explained. The truth was that Willa Cather was incapable of admitting to herself—who can?—that what was troubling her was not the departure of Isabelle but what it symbolized: the re-assertion of an old need to have an "other house" and the security of a mother figure all to herself within it. In the guise of Outland, and with a theme further removed from herself, she could project the deeper anxiety resulting from her sense of rejection. The professor was too close to herself. His story could not be told without emotional involvement on the part of the author. Tom Outland was farther away: and his story is told with complete success.

All Willa Cather's later works can be read in the light of this deep feeling of insecurity: her choice of the Rock as the symbol of endurance, her rigidity in the face of her nation's growth and change, her gradual regression in her writings to childhood situations—these spring from the same overpowering isolation, the same death wish yet struggle to live, acted out in the suffocating attic by the professor. I could find other episodes in her life to amplify what I have said. Not least is the one in which she had to uproot herself from her Bank Street apartment in Greenwich Village because a subway was being run through the area. She took refuge for a few days in a Lower Fifth Avenue hotel, and remained there for several years. Whatever rationalizations might be offered, it was clearly difficult for her to move and a sheltering hotel, ministering to her needs, seems to have made her reluctant to search out an apartment and re-establish her home. I am told that Miss Cather intensely disliked being in the hotel—all the more reason, we might suppose, for her to have left it sooner than she did. The world did break in two for Miss Cather. One part of it moved on; she remained stranded in the other. And *The Professor's House*, in its very structure, contained this break. It is an unsymmetrical and unrealized novel because Willa Cather could not bring the two parts of her broken world together again.

To arrive at this view the biographer has had to unite the qualities of critic and psychoanalyst. By penetrating more deeply into the life it has been possible to penetrate more deeply into the work.

The Backgrounds of 'The Dead'

Richard Ellmann

The silent cock shall crow at last. The west shall shake the east
  awake.
Walk while ye have the night for morn,
  lightbreakfastbringer. . . .

—*Finnegans Wake* (473)

The stay in Rome had seemed purposeless, but during it Joyce became aware of the change in his attitude toward Ireland and so toward the world. He embodied his new perceptions in 'The Dead.' The story, which was the culmination of a long waiting history, began to take shape in Rome, but was not set down until he left the city. The pressure of hints, sudden insights, and old memories rose in his mind until, like King Midas's barber, he was compelled to speech.

Although the story dealt mainly with three generations of his family in Dublin, it drew also upon an incident in Galway in 1903. There Michael ('Sonny') Bodkin courted Nora Barnacle; but he contracted tuberculosis and had to be confined to bed. Shortly afterwards Nora resolved to go to Dublin, and Bodkin stole out of his sickroom, in spite of the rainy weather, to sing to her under an apple tree and bid her goodbye. In Dublin Nora soon learned that Bodkin was dead, and when she met Joyce she was first attracted to him, as she told a sister, because he resembled Sonny Bodkin.[1]

Joyce's habit of ferreting out details had made him conduct minute interrogations of Nora even before their departure from Dublin. He was disconcerted by the fact that young men before him had interested her. He did not much like to know that her heart was still moved, even in pity, by the recollection of the boy who had loved her. The notion of being in some sense in rivalry with a dead man buried in the little cemetery at Oughterard was one that came easily, and gallingly, to a man of Joyce's jealous disposition. It was one source of his complaint to his Aunt Josephine Murray that Nora persisted in regarding him as quite similar to other men she had known.[2]

A few months after expressing this annoyance, while Joyce and Nora Barnacle were living in Trieste in 1905, Joyce received another impulsion toward 'The Dead.' In a letter Stanislaus happened to mention attending a concert of Plunket Greene, the Irish baritone, which included one of Thomas Moore's *Irish Melodies* called 'O, ye Dead!'[3] The song, a dialogue of living and dead, was eerie enough, but what impressed Stanislaus was that Greene rendered the second stanza, in which the dead answer the living, as if they were whimpering for the bodied existence they could no longer enjoy:

It is true, it is true, we are shadows cold and wan;
And the fair and the brave whom we loved on earth are gone;
       But still thus ev'n in death,
       So sweet the living breath
Of the fields and the flow'rs in our youth we wandered o'er,
       That ere, condemn'd, we go
       To freeze, 'mid Hecla's snow,
We would taste it awhile, and think we live once more!

James was interested and asked Stanislaus to send the words, which he learned to sing himself. His feelings about his wife's dead lover found a dramatic counterpart in the jealousy of the dead for the living in Moore's song: it would seem that the living and the dead are jealous of each other. Another aspect of the rivalry is suggested in *Ulysses*, where Stephen cries out to his mother's ghost, whose 'glazing eyes, staring out of death, to shake and bend my soul, . . . to strike me down,' he cannot put out of mind: 'No, mother. Let me be and let me live.'[4] That the dead do not stay buried is, in fact, a theme of Joyce from the beginning to the end of his work; Finnegan is not the only corpse to be resurrected.

In Rome the obtrusiveness of the dead affected what he thought of Dublin, the equally Catholic city he had abandoned, a city as prehensile of its ruins, visible and invisible. His head was filled with a sense of the too successful encroachment of the dead upon the living city; there was a disrupting parallel in the way that Dublin, buried behind him, was haunting his thoughts. In *Ulysses* the theme was to be reconstituted, in more horrid form, in the mind of Stephen, who sees corpses rising from their graves like vampires to deprive the living of joy. The bridebed, the childbed, and the bed of death are bound to-gether, and death 'comes, pale vampire, through storm his eyes, his bat sails bloodying the sea, mouth to her mouth's kiss.'[5] We can be at the same time in death as well as in life.*

By February 11, 1907, after six months in Rome, Joyce knew in general what story he must write. Some of his difficulty in beginning it was due, as he said himself,† to the riot in Dublin over *The Playboy of the Western World*. Synge had followed the advice of Yeats that Joyce had rejected, to find his inspiration in the Irish folk, and had gone to the Aran Islands. This old issue finds small echoes in the story. The nationalistic Miss Ivors tries to persuade Gabriel to go to Aran (where Synge's *Riders to the Sea* is set), and when he refuses twits him for his lack of patriotic feeling. Though Gabriel thinks of defending the autonomy of art and its indifference to politics, he knows such a defense would be pretentious, and only musters up the remark that he is sick of his own country. But the issue is far from settled for him.

'The Dead' begins with a party and ends with a corpse, so en-twining 'funferal' and 'funeral' as in the wake of Finnegan. That he began with a party was due, at least in part, to Joyce's feeling that the rest of the stories in *Dubliners* had not completed his picture of the city. In a letter of September 25, 1906,‡ he had written his brother from Rome to say that some elements of Dublin had been left out of his stories: 'I have not reproduced its ingenuous insularity and its hos-pitality, the latter "virtue" so far as I can see does not exist elsewhere in Europe.' He allowed a little of this warmth to enter 'The Dead.' In his speech at the Christmas party Gabriel Conroy explicitly commends Ireland for this very virtue of hospitality, though his expression of the idea is distinctly after-dinner: 'I feel more strongly with every recur-ring year that our country has no tradition which does it so much hon-our and which it should guard so jealously as that of its hospitality. It is a tradition that is unique as far as my experience goes (and I have visited not a few places abroad) among the modern nations.' This was Joyce's oblique way, in language that mocked his own, of begin-ning the task of making amends.

The selection of details for 'The Dead' shows Joyce making those

---

* The converse of this theme appears in *Ulysses* (113[107]), when Bloom, walking in Glasnevin, thinks 'They are not going to get me this innings. Warm beds: warm fullblooded life.'

† See p. 248 [of Ellmann's book].
‡ See p. 239 [of Ellmann's book].

choices which, while masterly, suggest the preoccupations that mastered him. Once he had determined to represent an Irish party, the choice of the Misses Morkans' as its location was easy enough. He had already reserved for *Stephen Hero* a Christmas party at his own house, a party which was also to be clouded by a discussion of a dead man. The other festive occasions of his childhood were associated with his hospitable great-aunts Mrs. Callanan and Mrs. Lyons, and Mrs. Callanan's daughter Mary Ellen, at their house at 15 Usher's Island, which was also known as the 'Misses Flynn school.'[6] There every year the Joyces who were old enough would go, and John Joyce carved the goose and made the speech. Stanislaus Joyce says that the speech of Gabriel Conroy in 'The Dead' is a good imitation of his father's oratorical style.*

In Joyce's story Mrs. Callanan and Mrs. Lyons, the Misses Flynn, become the spinster ladies, the Misses Morkan, and Mary Ellen Callanan becomes Mary Jane. Most of the other party guests were also reconstituted from Joyce's recollections. Mrs. Lyons had a son Freddy, who kept a Christmas card shop in Grafton Street.[7] Joyce introduces him as Freddy Malins, and situates his shop in the less fashionable Henry Street, perhaps to make him need that sovereign Gabriel lent him. Another relative of Joyce's mother, a first cousin, married a Protestant named Mervyn Archdale Browne, who combined the profession of music teacher with that of agent for a burglary insurance company. Joyce keeps him in 'The Dead' under his own name. Bartell d'Arcy, the hoarse singer in the story, was based upon Barton M'Guckin, the leading tenor in the Carl Rosa Opera Company. There were other tenors, such as John McCormack, whom Joyce might have used, but he needed one who was unsuccessful and uneasy about himself; and his father's often-told anecdote about M'Guckin's lack of confidence† furnished him with just such a singer as he intended Bartell d'Arcy to be.

The making of his hero, Gabriel Conroy, was more complicated. The root situation, of jealousy for his wife's dead lover, was of course Joyce's. The man who is murdered, D. H. Lawrence has one of his characters say, desires to be murdered;[8] some temperaments demand the feeling that their friends and sweethearts will deceive them. Joyce's conversation often returned to the word 'betrayal,'[9] and the entangled innocents whom he uses for his heroes are all aspects of his

---

* He excepts the quotation from Browning, but even this was quite within the scope of the man who could quote Vergil when lending money to his son.[11]

† See p. 14 [of Ellmann's book].

conception of himself. Though Gabriel is less impressive than Joyce's other heroes, Stephen, Bloom, Richard Rowan, or Earwicker, he belongs to their distinguished, put-upon company.

There are several specific points at which Joyce attributes his own experiences to Gabriel. The letter which Gabriel remembers having written to Gretta Conroy early in their courtship is one of these; from it Gabriel quotes to himself the sentiment, 'Why is it that words like these seem to me so dull and cold? Is it because there is no word tender enough to be your name?' These sentences are taken almost directly from a letter Joyce wrote to Nora in 1904.[10] It was also Joyce, of course, who wrote book reviews, just as Gabriel Conroy does, for the *Daily Express*.[11] Since the *Daily Express* was pro-English, he had probably been teased for writing for it during his frequent visits to the house of David Sheehy, M. P. One of the Sheehy daughters, Kathleen, may well have been the model for Miss Ivors, for she wore that austere bodice and sported the same patriotic pin.[12] In Gretta's old sweetheart, in Gabriel's letter, in the book reviews and the discussion of them, as well as in the physical image of Gabriel with hair parted in the middle and rimmed glasses, Joyce drew directly upon his own life.

His father was also deeply involved in the story. Stanislaus Joyce recalls that when the Joyce children were too young to bring along to the Misses Flynns' party, their father and mother sometimes left them with a governess and stayed at a Dublin hotel overnight instead of returning to their house in Bray.'[13] Gabriel and Gretta do this too. Gabriel's quarrels with his mother also suggest John Joyce's quarrels with his mother, who never accepted her son's marriage to a woman of lower station.[14] But John Joyce's personality was not like Gabriel's; he had no doubts of himself, in the midst of many failures he was full of self-esteem. He had the same unshakable confidence as his son James. For Gabriel's personality there is among Joyce's friends another model.[15] This was Constantine Curran, sometimes nicknamed 'Cautious Con.' He is a more distinguished man than Joyce allows, but Joyce was building upon, and no doubt distorting, his memories of Curran as a very young man. That he has Curran partly in mind is suggested by the fact that he calls Gabriel's brother by Curran's first name Constantine, and makes Gabriel's brother, like Curran's, a priest.[16] Curran has the same high color and nervous, disquieted manner* as Gabriel, and like Gabriel he has traveled to the continent and has cultivated cosmopolitan interests. Curran, like Conroy, mar-

* See Joyce's letter, p. 234 [of Ellmann's book].

ried a woman who was not a Dubliner, though she came from only as far west as Limerick. In other respects he is quite different. Gabriel was made mostly out of Curran, Joyce's father, and Joyce himself. Probably Joyce knew there was a publican on Howth named Gabriel Conroy; or, as Gerhard Friedrich has proposed,[17] he may have borrowed the name from the title of a Bret Harte novel. But the character, if not the name, was of his own compounding.*

Joyce now had his people, his party, and something of its development. In the festive setting, upon which the snow keeps offering a different perspective until, as W. Y. Tindall suggests,[19] the snow itself changes, he develops Gabriel's private tremors, his sense of inadequacy, his uncomfortable insistence on his small pretensions. From the beginning he is vulnerable; his well-meant and even generous overtures are regularly checked. The servant girl punctures his blithe assumption that everyone is happily in love and on the way to the altar. He is not sure enough of himself to put out of his head the slurs he has received long ago; so in spite of his uxorious attitude towards Gretta he is a little ashamed of her having come from the west of Ireland. He cannot bear to think of his dead mother's remark that Gretta was 'country cute,' and when Miss Ivors says of Gretta, 'She's from Connacht, isn't she?' Gabriel answers shortly, 'Her people are.' He has rescued her from that bog. Miss Ivors's suggestion, a true Gaelic Leaguer's, that he spend his holiday in the Irish-speaking Aran Islands (in the west) upsets him; it is the element in his wife's past that he wishes to forget. During most of the story, the west of Ireland is connected in Gabriel's mind with a dark and rather painful primitivism, an aspect of his country which he has steadily abjured by going off to the continent. The west is savagery; to the east and south lie people who drink wine and wear galoshes.

Gabriel has been made uneasy about this attitude, but he clings to it defiantly until the ending. Unknown to him, it is being challenged by the song, 'The Lass of Aughrim.' Aughrim is a little village in the west not far from Galway. The song has a special relevance; in it a woman who has been seduced and abandoned by Lord Gregory comes with her baby in the rain to beg for admission to his house. It brings together the peasant mother and the civilized seducer, but Ga-

---

* The name of Conroy's wife Gretta was borrowed from another friend, Gretta (actually Margaret) Cousins, the wife of James H. Cousins. Since Joyce mentioned in a letter at the same time that he was meditating 'The Dead,' the danger of becoming 'a patient Cousins,'[18] this family was evidently on his mind.

briel does not listen to the words; he only watches his wife listening. Joyce had heard this ballad from Nora; perhaps he considered also using Tom Moore's 'O, Ye Dead' in the story, but if so he must have seen that 'The Lass of Aughrim' would connect more subtly with the west and with Michael Furey's visit in the rain to Gretta. But the notion of using a song at all may well have come to him as the result of the excitement generated in him by Moore's song.

And now Gabriel and Gretta go to the Hotel Gresham, Gabriel fired by his living wife and Gretta drained by the memory of her dead lover. He learns for the first time of the young man in Galway, whose name Joyce has deftly altered from Sonny or Michael Bodkin to Michael Furey. The new name suggests, like the contrst of the militant Michael and the amiable Gabriel, that violent passion is in her Galway past, not in her Dublin present. Gabriel tries to cut Michael Furey down. 'What was he?' he asks, confident that his own profession of language teacher (which of course he shared with Joyce) is superior; but she replies, 'He was in the gasworks,' as if this profession was as good as any other. Then Gabriel tries again, 'And what did he die of so young, Gretta? Consumption, was it?' He hopes to register the usual expressions of pity, but Gretta silences and terrifies him by her answer, 'I think he died for me.'[*] Since Joyce has already made clear that Michael Furey was tubercular, this answer of Gretta has a fine ambiguity. It asserts the egoism of passion, and unconsciously defies Gabriel's reasonable question.

Now Gabriel begins to succumb to his wife's dead lover, and becomes a pilgrim to emotional intensities outside of his own experience. From a biographical point of view, these final pages compose one of Joyce's several tributes to his wife's artless integrity. Nora Barnacle, in spite of her defects of education, was independent, unself-conscious, instinctively right. Gabriel acknowledges the same coherence in his own wife, and he recognizes in the west of Ireland, in Michael Furey, a passion he has himself always lacked. 'Better pass boldly into that other world, in the full glory of some passion, than fade and wither dismally with age,' Joyce makes Gabriel think. Then comes that strange sentence in the final paragraph: 'The time had come for him to set out on his journey westward.' The cliché runs that journeys

---

[*] Adaline Glasheen has discovered here an echo of Yeats's nationalistic play, *Cathleen ni Houlihan* (1902), where the old woman who symbolizes Ireland sings a song of 'yellow-haired Donough that was hanged in Galway.' When she is asked, 'What was it brought him to his death?' she replies, 'He died for love of me; many a man has died for love of me.'[20]

westward are towards death, but the west has taken on a special meaning in the story. Gretta Conroy's west is the place where life had been lived simply and passionately. The context and phrasing of the sentence suggest that Gabriel is on the edge of sleep, and half-consciously accepts what he has hitherto scorned, the possibility of an actual trip to Connaught. What the sentence affirms, at last, on the level of feeling, is the west, the primitive, untutored, impulsive country from which Gabriel had felt himself alienated before; in the story, the west is paradoxically linked also with the past and the dead. It is like Aunt Julia Morkan who, though ignorant, old, grey-skinned, and stupefied, seizes in her song at the party 'the excitement of swift and secure flight.'

The tone of the sentence, 'The time had come for him to set out on his journey westward,' is somewhat resigned. It suggests a concession, a relinquishment, and Gabriel is conceding and relinquishing a good deal—his sense of the importance of civilized thinking, of continental tastes, of all those tepid but nice distinctions on which he has prided himself. The bubble of his self-possession is pricked; he no longer possesses himself, and not to possess oneself is in a way a kind of death. It is a self-abandonment not unlike Furey's, and through Gabriel's mind runs the imagery of Calvary. He imagines the snow on the cemetery at Oughterard, lying 'thickly drifted on the crooked crosses and headstones, on the spears of the little gate, on the barren thorns.' He thinks of Michael Furey who, Gretta has said, died for her, and envies him his sacrifice for another kind of love than Christ's. To some extent Gabriel too is dying for her, in giving up what he has most valued in himself, all that holds him apart from the simpler people at the party. He feels close to Gretta through sympathy if not through love; now they are both past youth, beauty, and passion; he feels close also to her dead lover, another lamb burnt on her altar, though she too is burnt now; he feels no resentment, only pity. In his own sacrifice of himself he is conscious of a melancholy unity between the living and the dead.

Gabriel, who has been sick of his own country, finds himself drawn inevitably into a silent tribute to it of much more consequence than his spoken tribute to the party. He has had illusions of the rightness of a way of life that should be outside of Ireland; but through this experience with his wife he grants a kind of bondage, of acceptance, even of admiration to a part of the country and a way of life that are most Irish. Ireland is shown to be stronger, more intense than he. At the end of *A Portrait of the Artist*, too, Stephen Dedalus, who has been so resolutely opposed to nationalism, makes a similar concession when he interprets his departure from Ireland as an attempt to forge a conscience for his race.

Joyce did not invent the incidents that conclude his story, the second honeymoon of Gabriel and Gretta which ends so badly. His method of composition was very like T. S. Eliot's, the imaginative absorption of stray material. The method did not please Joyce very much because he considered it not imaginative enough, but it was the only way he could work. He borrowed the ending for 'The Dead' from another book. In that book a bridal couple receive, on their wedding night, a message that a young woman whom the husband jilted has just committed suicide. The news holds them apart, she asks him not to kiss her, and both are tormented by remorse. The wife, her marriage unconsummated, falls off at last to sleep, and her husband goes to the window and looks out at 'the melancholy greyness of the dawn.' For the first time he recognizes, with the force of a revelation, that his life is a failure, and that his wife lacks the passion of the girl who has killed herself. He resolves that, since he is not worthy of any more momentous career, he will try at least to make her happy. Here surely is the situation that Joyce so adroitly recomposed. The dead lover who comes between the lovers, the sense of the husband's failure, the acceptance of mediocrity, the resolve to be at all events sympathetic, all come from the other book. But Joyce transforms them. For example, he allows Gretta to kiss her husband, but without desire, and rarefies the situation by having it arise not from a suicide but from a memory of young love. The book Joyce was borrowing from was one that nobody reads any more, George Moore's *Vain Fortune;* but Joyce read it,* and in his youthful essay, 'The Day of the Rabblement,' overpraised it as 'fine, original work.'[21]

Moore said nothing about snow, however. No one can know how Joyce conceived the joining of Gabriel's final experience with the snow. But his fondness for a background of this kind is also illustrated by his use of the fireplace in 'Ivy Day,' of the streetlamps in 'Two Gallants,' and of the river in *Finnegans Wake*. It does not seem that the snow can be death, as so many have said, for it falls on living and dead alike, and for death to fall on the dead is a simple redundancy of which Joyce would not have been guilty. For snow to be 'general all over Ireland' is of course unusual in that country. The fine description:

---

* He evidently refreshed his memory of it when writing 'The Dead,' for his copy of *Vain Fortune,* now at Yale, bears the date 'March 1907.'

'It was falling on every part of the dark central plain, on the treeless hills, falling softly upon the Bog of Allen and, farther westward, softly falling into the dark mutinous Shannon waves,' is probably borrowed by Joyce from a famous simile in the twelfth book of the Iliad, which Thoreau translates:[22] 'The snowflakes fall thick and fast on a winter's day. The winds are lulled, and the snow falls incessant, covering the tops of the mountains, and the hills and the plains where the lotus-tree grows, and the cultivated fields, and they are falling by the inlets and shores of the foaming sea, but are silently dissolved by the waves.' But Homer was simply describing the thickness of the arrows in the battle of the Greeks and Trojans; and while Joyce seems to copy his topographical details, he uses the image here chiefly for a similar sense of crowding and quiet pressure. Where Homer speaks of the waves silently dissolving the snow, Joyce adds the final detail of 'the mutinous Shannon waves' which suggest the 'Furey' quality of the west. The snow that falls upon Gabriel, Gretta, and Michael Furey, upon the Misses Morkan, upon the dead singers and the living, is mutuality, a sense of their connection with each other, a sense that none has his being alone. The partygoers prefer dead singers to living ones, the wife prefers a dead lover to a live lover.

The snow does not stand alone in the story. It is part of the complex imagery that includes heat and cold air, fire, and rain, as well as snow. The relations of these are not simple. During the party the living people, their festivities, and all human society seem constrasted with the cold outside, as in the warmth of Gabriel's hand on the cold pane. But this warmth is felt by Gabriel as stuffy and confining, and the cold outside is repeatedly connected with what is fragrant and fresh. The cold, in this sense of piercing intensity, culminates in the picture of Michael Furey in the rain and darkness of the Galway night.

Another warmth is involved in 'The Dead.' In Gabriel's memory of his own love for Gretta, he recalls incidents in his love's history as stars, burning with pure and distant intensity, and recalls moments of his passion for her as having the fire of stars. The irony of this image is that the sharp and beautiful experience was, though he has not known it until this night, incomplete. There is a telling metaphor: he remembers a moment of happiness, standing with Gretta in the cold, looking in through a window at a man making bottles in a roaring furnace, and suddenly calling out to the man, 'Is the fire hot?' The question sums up his naïve deprivation; if the man at the furnace had heard the question, his answer, thinks Gabriel, might have been rude;

so the revelation on this night is rude to Gabriel's whole being. On this night he acknowledges that love must be a feeling which he has never fully had.

Gabriel is not utterly deprived. Throughout the story there is affection for this man who, without the sharpest, most passionate perceptions is yet generous and considerate. The intense and the moderate can meet; intensity bursts out and declines, and the moderated can admire and pity it, and share the fate that moves both types of mankind towards age and death. The furthest point of love of which Gabriel is capable is past. Furey's passion is past because of his sudden death. Gretta is perhaps the most pitiful, in that knowing Furey's passion, and being of his kind, she does not die but lives to wane in Gabriel's way; on this night she too is fatigued, not beautiful, her clothes lie crumpled beside her. The snow seems to share in this decline; viewed from inside at the party, it is desirable, unattainable, just as at his first knowledge of Michael Furey, Gabriel envies him. At the end as the partygoers walk to the cab the snow is slushy and in patches, and then, seen from the window of the hotel room, it belongs to all men, it is general, mutual. Under its canopy, all human beings, whatever their degrees of intensity, fall into union. The mutuality is that all men feel and lose feeling, all interact, all warrant the sympathy that Gabriel now extends to Furey, to Gretta, to himself, even to old Aunt Julia.

In its lyrical, melancholy acceptance of all that life and death offer, 'The Dead' is a linchpin in Joyce's work. There is that basic situation of cuckoldry, real or putative, which is to be found throughout. There is the special Joycean collation of specific detail raised to rhythmical intensity. The final purport of the story, the mutual dependency of living and dead, is something that he meditated a good deal from his early youth. He had expressed it first in his essay on Mangan in 1902, when he spoke already of the union in the great memory of death along with life;[23] even then he had begun to learn like Gabriel that we are all Romes, our new edifices reared beside, and even joined with, ancient monuments. In *Dubliners* he developed this idea. The interrelationship of dead and living is the theme of the first story in *Dubliners* as well as of the last; it is also the theme of 'A Painful Case,' but an even closer parallel to 'The Dead' is the story, 'Ivy Day in the Committee Room.' This was in one sense an answer to his university friends who mocked his remark that death is the most beautiful form of life by saying that absence is the highest form of presence. Joyce did not think either idea absurd. What binds 'Ivy Day' to 'The Dead' is that in both stories the central agitation derives from a character who never appears, who is dead, absent. Joyce wrote Stanislaus that Anatole France had given him the idea for both stories.[24] There may be other sources in France's works, but a possible one is 'The Procurator of Judaea.' In it Pontius Pilate reminisces with a friend about the days when he was procurator in Judaea, and describes the events of his time with Roman reason, calm, and elegance. Never once does he, or his friend, mention the person we expect him to discuss, the founder of Christianity, until at the end the friend asks if Pontius Pilate happens to remember someone of the name of Jesus, from Nazareth, and the veteran administrator replies, 'Jesus? Jesus of Nazareth? I cannot call him to mind.' The story is overshadowed by the person whom Pilate does not recall; without him the story would not exist. Joyce uses a similar method in 'Ivy Day' with Parnell and in 'The Dead' with Michael Furey.

In *Ulysses* the climatic episode, *Circe*, whirls to a sepulchral close in the same juxtaposition of living and dead, the ghost of his mother confronting Stephen, and the ghost of his son confronting Bloom. But Joyce's greatest triumph in asserting the intimacy of living and dead was to be the close of *Finnegans Wake*. Here Anna Livia Plurabelle, the river of life, flows toward the sea, which is death; the fresh water passes into the salt, a bitter ending. Yet is also a return to her father, the sea, that produces the cloud which makes the river, and her father is also her husband, to whom she gives herself as a bride to her groom. Anna Livia is going back to her father, as Gabriel journeys westward in feeling to the roots of his fatherland; like him, she is sad and weary. To him the Shannon waves are dark and mutinous, and to her the sea is cold and mad. In *Finnegans Wake* Anna Livia's union is not only with love but with death; like Gabriel she seems to swoon away.[*]

That Joyce at the age of twenty-five and -six should have written this story ought not to seem odd. Young writers reach their greatest eloquence in dwelling upon the horrors of middle age and what follows it. But beyond this proclivity which he shared with others, Joyce had a special reason for writing the story of 'The Dead' in 1906 and 1907. In his own mind he had thoroughly justified his flight from Ireland, but he had not decided the question of where he would fly *to*. In Trieste and Rome he had learned what he had unlearned in Dublin, to be a Dubliner. As he had written his brother from Rome with

[*] See also pp. 724-6 [of Ellmann's book].

some astonishment, he felt humiliated when anyone attacked his 'impoverished country.'[25] 'The Dead' is his first song of exile.

NOTES

[1] Letter to me from Mrs. Kathleen Barnacle Griffin.

[2] See p. 222 [of Ellmann's book].

[3] S. Joyce, 'The Background to "Dubliners,"' *Listener*, LI (March 25, 1954), 526-7.

[4] *Ulysses*, p. 12 (8).

[5] Ibid. p. 48 (44).

[6] Interview with Mrs. May Joyce Monaghan, 1953.

[7] Idem.

[8] Birkin in *Women in Love*.

[9] Information from Professor Joseph Prescott.

[10] At Cornell.

[11] See p. 116 [of Ellmann's book].

[12] Interview with Mrs. Mary Sheehy Kettle, 1953.

[13] *My Brother's Keeper*, p. 38 (58).

[14] See p. 17 [of Ellmann's book].

[15] Interview with S. Joyce, 1953.

[16] Suggested to me by Professor Vivian Mercier.

[17] Gerhard Friedrich, 'Bret Harte as a Source for James Joyce's "The Dead,"' *Philological Quarterly*, XXXIII (Oct. 1954), pp. 442-4.

[18] Letter to S. Joyce, Feb. 1907.

[19] W. Y. Tindall, *The Literary Symbol* (New York, 1955), p. 227.

[20] I am indebted to Mrs. Glasheen for pointing this out to me.

[21] *Critical Writings*, p. 71.

[22] Professor Walter B. Rideout kindly called my attention to the similarity of these passages.

[23] *Critical Writings*, p. 83.

[24] Letter to S. Joyce, Feb. 11, 1907.

[25] Letter to S. Joyce, Sept. 25, 1906.

Melville's Freudian Slip
Harrison Hayford

In the course of his researches for *The Melville Log*, Jay Leyda discovered an error made in the official birth record of Melville's son Stanwix, in the office of the City Clerk of Pittsfield, Massachusetts. The maiden name of the child's mother was recorded not as Elizabeth Shaw (Melville's wife) but erroneously as Maria G. Melville (his own mother). In the *Log* Mr. Leyda reported this error without attributing it to anybody.[1] But on the assumption that it was Melville himself who filled out the official form or reported the birth and supplied the misinformation, this error has been used by two able biographers to support evidence of a mother-complex of some sort.[2] By them the error is regarded as due to a revealing slip of Melville's pen. Since otherwise Melville's emotional attitudes toward his mother must be mostly inferred from his semi-autobiographical fiction, especially *Pierre,* and since such inferences are pretty hazardous, any authentic external evidence beyond fugitive family traditions would be valuable indeed.[3]

For this reason I wrote some time ago an inquiry to the City Clerk of Pittsfield, Mr. John J. Fitzgerald, explaining the exact bearing of the facts. Mr. Fitzgerald made the following admirably explicit reply, which seems to me to account for the error conclusively upon other grounds than a "Freudian slip" of Melville's own pen. Two points discussed by Mr. Fitzgerald reveal additional errors in the official record: the erroneous birthdate October 25 for October 22, and the misspelling "Stanwicks" for "Stanwix," which certainly cannot be attributed to Melville, however wildly he spelled upon occasion.[4] Finally, in any case, as Mr. Fitzgerald indicates, the birth was reported not at the time of its occurence but at the beginning of the following year, 1852. This fact negates the implied assumption that Melville's emotional distraction at the time of the birth contributed to a slip of his pen. Mr. Fitzgerald's letter follows:

> In Massachusetts city and town clerks receive reports of births from three sources—the parents, the attending physician and the hospital authorities when the birth is in the hospital. The official record of birth is compiled from these three sources and entered in the Register of Births. More often than not the three reports will vary in detail and it is up to the town clerk to do the best he can in ascertaining which of the various versions is the correct one. Oftentimes his final choice is nothing but a blind guess.
>
> Since the original reports for 1851 births have been lost there is no way of determining definitely from what sources the birth record of Stanwicks Melville was compiled. From what knowledge I have of the birth registration system in effect in those days I would say that the particular record in question was based upon the annual "baby census" taken by the town clerk. Each one of the 221 births registered in 1851 bears January 31, 1852, as the date of record (the date when the birth was registered) and that indicates to me that the records all came from one source at one time.
>
> Assuming that Stanwicks Melville's birth record found its way to

our books through the town clerk's annual census, and drawing an analogy between that census and canvasses of a similar nature which I have seen in actual operation in modern times, I would say that the error in the mother's name could be attributed to any one of a dozen causes, the least probable of which would be a mother fixation on the part of Herman Melville. For example, it is known that in one year back in the 1870's the town refused to appropriate any money for the annual baby census, and the birth records for that year were apparently made by the clerk without leaving his office. In the censuses of that nature the information is often given by servants or neighbors or by others not in a position to have accurate knowledge of all the details.

For whatever bearing it may have on the problem I would like to point out that we also have the record of birth of an unnamed daughter of Herman Melville who was born in 1855 (month and date not given) in which the mother's name is given as Eliza. Her birthplace is given as Boston whereas the Maria G. named in the other record was recorded as having been born in Albany, N. Y.

Incidentally the name of Herman Melville's son appears in our books as I have given it above and not as Stanwix. If Stanwix was the spelling favored by Herman Melville it would be hard to resist the conclusion that he had nothing to do with the making of the record that appears on our book. Also our book gives October 25 as the date of birth and not October 22. For whatever interest it may have for you I am pleased to send you herewith certified copies of the complete records of both births.[5]

NOTES

[1] *The Melville Log* (New York, 1951), I, 430.

[2] *Pierre,* ed. Henry A. Murray (New York, 1949), p. xxxvii. Newton Arvin, *Herman Melville* (New York, 1950), p. 204. Leon Howard, *Herman Melville* (Berkeley and Los Angeles, 1951), p. 184, says that the error may have been Melville's but draws no psychological inferences. The supposed slip has been referred to in a number of articles as well.

[3] See William H. Gilman, *Melville's Early Life and Redburn* (New York, 1951), p. 342 note 154, for a mordant comment on the other "evidence" of Melville's relationship to his mother.

[4] Family records fix the birth date as October 22.

[5] Letter dated May 8, 1950. Mr. Fitzgerald has consented to its publication.

The Metaphysic of Love

A. J. Smith

Recent discussions of 'The definition of Love', as Marvell is conceived to have attempted it, turn one's mind back quizzically to the hoary old controversy over a still more sizeable treatment of the theme, never satisfactorily resolved. On Donne's much-teased 'The Extasie' opinion seems nowadays to have settled—out of sheer weariness one supposes. We content our minds with the comforting assumption that Donne in that poem quieted once for all the long tug of war between soul and body in human love, which so exercised Sidney and Spenser, to mention no more. Grierson's taut note is reassuringly behind us:

> This is one of the most important of the lyrics as a statement of Donne's metaphysic of love, of the interconnexion and mutual dependence of body and soul.[1]

'Donne's metaphysic of love.' The poem is significant as the statement of a personal philosophical view; and by implication which we have not failed to draw, a revolutionary view at that. Take this with Grierson's further dicta—'a record of intense, rapid thinking', 'a . . . natural utterance of passion'[2]—and we are but a step from the emotional apprehension of thought. It was the late Professor G. R. Potter who added the indispensable Eliotian trimmings for us, in rebutting Legouis's heretical 'Don Juan' reading:

> It seems to us the poem in which Donne came as close as he ever did to putting in words those subtle relations between the body and the mind of which he was conscious continually, and most keenly when he was most in love.[3]

Now we are given the record of an intense personal experience; and the 'metaphysics' become the product of a keen habit of introspection, the analysis of consciousness at the moment of an emotion which heightens it. How very modern, we all conclude, was Donne, and what a piece of original thinking the poem is! It is true that he expressed quite contrary notions of love elsewhere, at a time when he had much more claim to be considered as a thinker—the very notions he is here supposed to be scouting finally.[4] But that was on a public occasion; and a preacher learns to temper the wind.

Yet Professor Tuve has made it more difficult than it used to be, to consider Donne as a startling revolutionary phenomenon. We are at last becoming aware, in general, that our primary office for this poet is not to invest him with current aims and seek covert reports on his psychological condition, but discarding our determinedly inward-focused modern spectacles, to establish a full technical context, and to trace material sources. And if we seek sources for the attitudes to love set out in 'The Extasie', we shall find them in plenty. Indeed, without the varied setting these provide, we may not hope to read the poem aright.

For the theory of love, as it was developed in sixteenth-century Italian writing, was by no means all of a Neoplatonic piece. As well as the Platonic Florence of Ficino there was the Aristotelian Padua of Sperone Speroni, not a whit less in following; and besides both there was the great synthetic source on which all subsequent sixteenth-century theorists, of all complexions, drew heavily, the *Dialoghi d'Amore* of the Spanish-born Italian Jew, Leone Ebreo (Jehudah Arbabnel). Between these schools (if one can call them anything so definite) there was a good deal of common ground, and where they differed was precisely in the degree of importance assigned to the body in love. Thus they were all agreed that love can be of several kinds, varying enormously in operations and effects. For Ficinians the general division tended, of course, to be between those whose love was a contemplation of the beauty of the soul alone—and ultimately an ascent to, and uniting with, the Divine Beauty—and those who cared for the body only, gross and bestial natures. Usually there was an intermediary condition, that of those who tried to love both body and soul. Some found two further species, making five in all. The Florentine Varchi divided the intermediary into 'courteous, or virtuous', when both are loved but the soul more than the body, and only with the senses of sight and hearing; 'human, or civil', when such lovers pass to the other, less spiritual senses as well; and 'plebeian, or vulgar', when both are loved, but the body more than the soul.[5] Aristotelians, on the other hand, tended to restrict themselves to two broad categories—the vulgar love whose end is simply the enjoyment of the body; and, to quote Tullia d'Aragona,

> honest love, which is proper to noble men, that is those who have a gentle and virtuous soul, whether they are poor or rich; and which is not generated in desire, as the other, but by the reason.[6]

Nevertheless, the two 'schools' were close enough in their overall view to permit a fairly general agreement on characteristics.

The characteristic commonly ascribed to the vulgar love was instability. 'All the things that delight our material sentiments, of their nature, when they are possessed are sooner abhorred than loved', said Leone Ebreo,[7] and Tullia tells us that it was the nature of the lower love in particular to be 'past reason hunted', and then 'past reason hated':

> I say, that the carnal desire gratified, there is no one who does not instantly lose that will and appetite which so tormented and devoured him . . . not only does it put an end to love, but turns it to hate.[8]

There could be no permanency or fidelity, for revulsion immediately followed on attainment of the sole end. In higher conditions, on the other hand, the satisfaction of physical desire actually increased, not destroyed love—'And if the appetite of the lover is quite sated with the copulative union, and that desire, or properly, appetite, continently ceases, in no way is cordial love thereby diminished, rather is the possible union bound the closer.'[9] Some, Tullia among them, held that in good love the very physical appetite might increase by what it fed on, seeking bodily union all the more ardently for the pleasure once proved.

There was general agreement that the chief effect of the higher kinds of human love was the conjoining of the souls of the two lovers to make a perfect union, or unity. Indeed, love itself was commonly defined as a 'desire to unite oneself with the thing esteemed good', which 'would be the soul of the beloved'.[10] Speroni put it neatly when he said that lovers in a perfect love were joined so completely that they lost their proper semblance and became a strange third species, neither male nor female, resembling a hermaphrodite.[11] But the standard conceit was that such lovers' souls, transformed into each other by a kind of miracle, become 'one soul in two bodies',[12] and, as the younger Tasso put it, 'the lovers are not two, but one and four'.[13] This arithmetical juggling originated in Ficino's Commentary on the Symposium, and is elaborated at length by such Neoplatonists as Betussi. In essence it means simply that two souls, 'transformed together, the one into the other',[14] are made one; while each at the same time, having another soul added to it, becomes two, making four in all. Strange to think that so crudely sophistical an idea was quite literally intended! But at least its point was the emphasis on a conjoining of souls so perfect that 'they are united together in every part, and become mixed and intermingled'.[15]

Such a union of souls could not be consummated in a normal state; nor could the lovers, having achieved it, remain as they had been in their singleness. It required what Leone Ebreo called 'the ecstasy, or else alienation, produced by amorous meditation'.[16] This love-ecstasy was sometimes said to be brought on above all when 'we direct our eyes in the face, and in the eyes of the person who so much pleases us . . .', the effect of which was that, 'for the marvel of it we become as persons stupefied'. The spirit, 'almost fomented by the continued power of the fixed cogitation', continues Cattani, whose description this is, 'is no sooner affected by that effluence than it all but changes itself into the nature of the other'.[17] The state of 'privation of sense and movement'[18] thus induced permitted a condition of ecstatic mutual contemplation, in which one's soul left its body and remained 'outside the self, in that which it contemplates and desires':

> For when the lover is in ecstasy, contemplating that which he loves, he has no care or memory of himself, nor does he perform any work in his own benefit, whether natural, sensitive, motive, or else rational. Rather is he quite alien to himself, and belongs to the object of his love and contemplation, into which he is totally converted.[19]

We are presented, in fact, with an analogy often explicitly confessed, and as exact as it could be made, between this secular state and the ecstasy of Divine Contemplation, 'when as the Servants of God were taken up in spirit, separate as it were from the body, and out of the body, that they might see some heavenly mystery revealed unto them'.[20] And as the outcome of the 'divine vision' which temporarily united the soul with the great Fount of Truth, was that 'all things are seen most perfectly',[21] so in a suitably humbler way of this. Sometimes the increase of knowledge was material. Following Ficino, writers describe a general exchange and mixing of the beauties of bodies and souls, in which love either 'levels every inequality, and reduces them to parity, to unite them perfectly, and make not union, but unity',[22] or produces a third thing 'finer than they had been separately made', as in 'a compounding of the voice with the lute, of perfume with perfume'.[23] The virtuous lover, knowing that 'love raises souls to high things',[24] might indeed deliberately seek this condition 'to make himself more perfect in the union with the soul of the beloved', for 'always the lover desires to be made participant in that which he lacks, and knows or believes to abound in the beloved'.[25] But some writers describe as well a superior illumination, produced 'when the superior loves the inferior in all the first semicircle, from God down to the prime material'.[26] Again the necessary step to it was the uniting of loving souls. 'There is no perfection or beauty that does not increase when it is communicated, for the fruitful growth is always more handsome than the sterile', said Leone Ebreo; and he made the essence of his ecstatic intercommunion a mystical sharing of some part of the Divine Beauty and Wisdom:

> And so it happens of man with woman; that knowing her in exemplary fashion he loves and desires her, and from love passes to the unitive cognition, which is the end of desire. . . . This great love and desire causes us to be abstracted in such contemplation that our intellect is raised up; and in such a way that, illuminated by a singular divine grace, it comes to know things above human power and speculation; as happens in such union and copulation with the Highest God. . . .

Moreover, this exalted state achieved, the love was thereby irrefrangibly proof against decline, for 'without end is the perfect desire, which is to enjoy union with the loved person'.[27]

Here was the more important ground, and in the main it was common. Some account of the body's part, and therefore of its relation to the soul, was needed. There were in fact few writers on love who steadily discounted the body. Ficino was one. For him the soul is the whole man, and the body its poor instrument—or as the figure was, its prison. But if this was a rare severity, the Florentine account of the vital linking of two such different essences was generally followed. The linking agent, the 'knot between the soul and the elemental body',[28] was the 'spirit', which was 'a certain extremely subtle and lucid vapour, generated by the heat of the heart from the most subtle part of the blood'.[29] This 'spirit' at once 'transfuses the life' from the soul to the body, and, 'being spread through all the members, takes the *virtu* of the soul, and communicates it to the body'. Conversely, it 'takes again, by the instruments of the senses, the images of outside bodies', which the soul is not gross enough to contact directly, and presents them to it 'as in a mirror', for judgement.[30]

Such spirits were thus necessary intermediary agents between the soul and each of the senses, and each of the faculties of the man. The purer Ficinians drew no corollary which might diminish the essential independence of soul. The limit of their admission concerning the two elements was that 'a powerful alteration of the one' might 'make its way to the other'.[31] With the renewed favour of Aristotle in the sixteenth century, however, and following the strong example of Leone Ebreo, writers tended to be syncretic. Even professing Neoplatonists discarded Ficino's strict separatism. Leone's own view was eccentrically non-Christian, founded in the common notion that the soul is 'mixed of elements, or else principles, discontinuous and separate the one from the other',[32] but affirming this mixture to be of elements of intellect and body, which fitted it to mediate between the two. Christian Aristotelians had Aquinas behind them.

The vital Thomist denial of the position that the body is dross is grounded precisely in the Aristotelian affirmation of the absolute interdependence of soul and body. Man is not 'a combination of the two substances but a complex substance which owes its substantiality to one only of its two consecutive principles'. An intellect without a body would be impotent, cut off from the sensible world, and in order to communicate with matter must 'descend, so to speak, into the material plane'. For these Aristotelian intellects Aquinas substitutes immortal souls, whose imperative need of the co-operation of sense-organs he thus affirms:

> in order to obtain this co-operation they acutalise matter; it is due wholly to them that this matter is a body; and yet they are not themselves save in a body; the man, therefore, is neither his body, since the body subsists only by the soul, nor his soul, since this would remain destitute without the body: he is the unity of a soul which substantialises his body and of the body in which this soul subsists.[33]

To trace the wash of this teaching in sixteen-century writings on love, one need hardly canvass extreme opinions—the heretical Giordano Bruno's denial of the essential contrariety of body and soul,[34] or even Tullia's affirmation that self-evidently, 'all the compound, that is the soul and the body together, is more noble and more perfect than the soul alone'.[35] Equicola, a standard authority, found 'the great friendship and union which is seen between the body and the soul' to be so close that 'while this organic member is in being, one cannot think of the action of the soul apart from the body, much less separate them; nor can that of the body be considered without the soul'.[36] Aristotelian Padua naturally approved a close integration of the hypostatic union, and consequent raising of the status of the flesh. 'I say then', said its spokesman, the revered Speroni, 'that our soul, in understanding, has already used the organs of the external and internal sentiments, nor may it understand without those; but those serve it in understanding, supplying it with the species, without which it does not understand. And therefore it is said, and truly, that the man understands and not the soul.'[37] It is more impressive that writers in the other camp should have concurred to the extent of following this crude empiricism, even if it was 'as philosophers and not as Christians'. Varchi starts from just Speroni's position—'our soul being incapable of understanding anything without the sense'; and his conclusion would have won Locke's applause:

> all those things which sense cannot feel and apprehend, the intellect cannot treat of or understand, for there is never anything at all in the intellect which has not first been in sense.[38]

The part Neoplatonists assigned to the body in love was that described in the famous notion of the steps. One ascended by stages from the lowest to the highest, at each stage seeking the appropriate form of union with the loved object. Pleasure in the physical beauty of one's mistress led to the contemplation of her true beauty—that of her soul—and this, ultimately, to the ecstatic vision of the Eternal Beauty. Every step transcended the previous one, which was then rejected. The body was the lowest step, and only beasts and the vulgar went no higher; nevertheless, it was still initially necessary, 'as prospect of truth',[39] physical beauty in some way shadowing forth the beauty of the soul. This splendidly impossible view was certainly influential, but in Italian writing it could not long remain undiluted, or indeed uncontradicted. Petrarchans, predisposed to the sublimated love of Neoplatonism, yet commonly admitted that in love 'one does not love the soul alone', saving their allegiance by adding 'but principally, and more the soul than the body'.[40] Torquato Tasso himself had maintained as a youth the vanity of the opinion that one could love the soul, or virtue alone, and in his soberer age would say only that if bodily intercourse was not necessary to the union of souls, it could be desired as an accessory and sign of that.[41]

But in fact there was authority as considerable as Ficino's for quite another view than his. Leone Ebreo, owing as little to a celibate as to a courtly tradition, had provided an account which satisfied less rarefied demands. While not conceding in the slightest that physical union might be the final end of a perfect love, he was emphatic that it is for a number of reasons to be sought. Amorous acts bind the knot faster. They are signs that the love is fully reciprocal. They allow the consummation of the union, which is not complete with the fusion of souls but requires the coupling of bodies, 'to the end that no diversity may remain'. Above all, the spiritual condition itself is deficient until the bodies are united, for

> with the correspondence of the bodily union, the spiritual love is augmented and made more perfect, just as the understanding of prudence is perfected when it is answered with due works.[42]

This was not the first time that physical conjunction had been recognized as a means to the higher union. The great Bembo himself had remarked the power of the kiss to draw forth souls by the lips, and in chaste love, to join them.[43] But here, in the most quoted and praised of all sixteenth-century writers on the subject, was the theoretical justification of lovers whose 'every love is desire, and very desire is love',[44] an account of the body's part which held good for the common state of secular love. Ficino had seemed to find no connexion between love and the procreation of kind, and was concerned with human relationships only as a means of achieving mystical states. If later writers had followed him they would never have thought of praising love for its work in drawing mankind to temperate coitus, as did even Betussi,[45] nor of adding with Equicola that abstention is actually bad, and for women in especial.[46] But beyond easing such adjustments in the name of practical sense, Leone's view lent weight to the balance at a decisive point. There was a calculated rejection of Ficino behind subsequent reaffirmations that, together with spiritual union, a lover desires also the union of bodies 'to make himself, to the limit of his power, one selfsame thing with the beloved'.[47] Aristotle in fact now supplanted Plotinus as the philosopher in vogue. It was to be a severe stricture on Leone himself that he 'said many things which were not peripatetic'.[48]

One further step was possible, the making of the perfect love of souls actually inseparable from, or dependent upon, the love of bodies. It was taken; and became as a matter of course the standard Aristotelian teaching. The entire philosophy of 'that prince of philosophers Aristotle', declared Equicola, shows that the man is soul and body together, constituents whose actions are indivisible in love as in all else.

To love truly is necessarily to love both, for 'Love is of soul and body, and the operations of the soul depend on the body'. It follows that 'the one ministers to the other in voluptuousness, and to delight the one without the other is impossible'.[49] Such a view was bound to recommend itself beyond the study walls of Padua and Ferrara. Nothing better shows the syncretism of later writers than that a Florentine Platonist should have recommended it to his own Accademia in expounding Petrarch—though without altogether denying his birthright. Varchi's unusually refined analysis of the types of love enabled him to declare that it was just the human sort, 'when some man loves some woman again, in good love', which could not be perfected unless the union was total, and entire, 'that is, if as one first conjoins the souls, one does not conjoin the bodies too'. But his reason hardly admitted of practical distinction, for it was that body and soul are so united while we live that no entity could be more one.[50]

This being the Aristotelian response to the notion of the stairs, Speroni's adoption of that figure in his assault on spurners of the body is particularly pointed. The senses, he says, provide 'stair and path' to the reason, but all the senses and not just sight and hearing. Moreover, it is a step that you have to take every time you want to get there:

> Whoever is such a fool in love that he has no care of his appetite, but as simple disembodied intelligence seeks solely to satisfy his mind, can be compared to him who, gulping his food without touching it or masticating it, more harms than nourishes himself.

Human beings in love are 'centaurs', their reason and desires inextricably mixed.[51] Love's hermaphrodite, ultimate perfection of human lovers, will not be made with souls, or minds, alone.

Such were the ideas which the Italians passed to the rest of Europe, providing in this field, as in so many others, a varied and malleable body of public material. Donne, whether or not he actually read any of the quoted writers, was patently among their beneficiaries. My concern now is to see how he drew on and handled these common positions in 'The Extasie'—that is to say, taking account of the circumstances of his day in England, by what means he made them into a witty poem.

Donne's individual contribution to the theory of love in this poem is, to all appearances, not great. He confines himself to an eclectic use of sources; and one's attention is on the whole less usefully directed to what he used than to how he used it. In other words, it is in that measure a typical piece of witty writing.

What this meant for Donne's age one sees at once in the first episode, lines 1 to 12. The matter is a treatment of the ecstasy-inducing disposition of the lovers' bodies, as Cattani and others described it; but it is tricked out with every convenient quirk of current poetic wit. It seems that Donne's is here an art of embellishment, no less than that of the courtliest Petrarchist, different in that he preferred another means to the elegances, flowers, harmonies, and the like recommended by the Italian theorists of Imitation. The situation is, of course, stereotyped and emblematic[52]—what the rhetoricians called a *topothesia*—and it serves to introduce the general theme. 'Pillow' and 'Pregnant banke' provide erotic motivation, while the violet, 'pleasing flower dedicated to Venus',[53] is emblem of faithful love. A little play on some stock Petrarchan properties touches off the description of the ecstatic posture in lines 5-8, to the end of showing the depth and fixity of the trance. The sweat of the conventionally-joined hands becomes an immovable cement, and the adaptation of an extravagant form of the old play on eye-beams permits the coupling of the contemplating eyes. One surely need not cavil at this latter figure. It is ridiculous only if treated as an 'image', and quite adequately performs its near-emblematic function, while not being markedly different from those common witty plays of the time in which a figurative account is treated as though it were literally intended:

> So with the course of Nature doth agree,
> That Eies which Beauties Adamant do see
> Should on Affections line tremblying remayne.[54]

At all events, this form of coupling would have satisfied an Aristotelian only as a preliminary, and in concluding his first section Donne unambiguously motivates his latter position. A deft exploitation of the even more familiar Petrarchan play of the picture in the eye enables him to refer to the normal end of physical union, and the whole extent of the present deficiency is shown. Moreover, his 'as yet', in line 9, promises a remedy.

The description of the emanation and coupling of souls properly follows that of the bodies, left vacant, immobile, and dumb, 'like sepulchrall statues'. It is done with what is surely comic literalness—the souls hanging out like the Homeric (and emblematic) scales between the waiting bodies. Donne may perhaps have meant here that so far their souls are like the pans of the scales, joined though not one thing. But at least the following lines show that no element of contention is intended; and the only other meaningful point of the simile would seem to be the clever parenthesis, 'which to advance their state, / Were gone out'. These powers seek to augment themselves by the closest alliance, not at each other's expense. The notion is that of the perfecting power of the ecstatic union.

The orderly development of the figure is now momentarily interrupted by the introduction of a privileged overhearer of the spiritual communion. It is an amusing and also a pointed device. Donne is able at once to claim that there is a kind of arcanum of love, a soul-language for initiates, and, parenthetically, to assert the perfect oneness of these loving souls. But he has another point too, no less neatly made. This bystander is an initiate, and some way advanced in the mystery—besides being 'refin'd' by love, he has by his good love 'growen all minde'. Yet if he listens carefully here he will learn much; will indeed take 'a new concoction' ('the acceleration of anything towards purity and perfection', Johnson says),[55] and 'part farre purer then he came'. But the lovers who grew all mind in the process, spurning the body, were the strict Neoplatonists. Donne is certainly not condemning them. He only suggests pleasantly that they have still a great deal to learn, and that he is about to show them what it is.

With the opening of the chorus of souls, it is plain that the climax in this first half of the poem is to be the enunciation of the knowledge which has been granted to the lovers in their ecstasy—a revelation concerning their love, of course. Firstly, they see the inadequacy of their previous knowledge. What they love, they realize now, is not sex. Theirs is not the vulgar physical love, whose essence is individuality, differences, and instability, but something which brings together, and indissolubly mingles. 'So to one neutrall thing both sexes fit';[56] which thing is precisely Speroni's hermaphrodite. The positive part of the new knowledge is simply their awareness of the fusing of their souls, and realization of its consequences. As the individual soul is already a mixture, so of these two souls Love has made a further mixture and they each become the other—an analogy from Plotinian metaphysics dresses up the 'one and four' of the theorists. Complementing each other, the deficiencies of their singleness are remedied; as a puny solitary violet grows and reproduces when set in company. The analogy this time is Leone Ebreo's, though more apt in service of the common point because Donne has introduced the emblematic violet. Finally, the results of these ameliorations and the core of the revelation, to the new composite soul is granted self-knowledge, the understanding of its own nature. It is, simply, souls; and souls are such as 'no change can invade'. They are assured (albeit by a sleight of wit) of their own eternal fidelity, that unending mutual enjoyment which Leone declared to be the outcome and guerdon of perfect desire.

One is not unprepared for Donne's return to the incompletely united bodies. But his transition is dramatic, and the rhetoric of memorable cadence. His concern now, in this latter part of the poem, is to develop the assertion that the lovers' state cannot be perfect while their bodies remain in unsatisfied singleness. This he does by stages. We are given first a few simple puffs of the body; then the negative claim that the sexual coupling of the bodies does not actually prevent the union of souls; and finally—save for a few small concluding points —the full affirmation. The treatment in lines 51-56 of the notion that the body is ready instrument of the soul is not remarkable. What is curious is to find Donne all but compromising his argument, and certainly reducing its possible effectiveness, by his apparent adoption of the Augustinian—and Ficinian—dichotomy in this section: 'They are ours, though they are not wee.' This is much more like Ficino's 'the soul is the man' than Speroni's figure of the centaur, and Aquinas's assertion that the man is neither body or soul alone, but a complex of both. It is, I suppose, with the analogy of 'intelligences' and 'spheres'[57] capable of bearing a Thomist construction. 'They are not wee'—we are no more bodies alone than we are souls alone. But there would seem a maladroitness in that way of presenting it unlooked for in so accomplished a rhetorician, and it may be thought more likely that Donne simply balked at professing the full Thomist position. If that is so, we have a rare hint of his private metaphysical views.

The analogy of 'heavens influence' in lines 57-58 is alien to the love-theorists, but remote in neither of its possible senses. The planets, influencing man, commonly do so by the grosser medium of air. And heavenly beings in their earthly visitations take up and wear the air, so as to make themselves visible to men: 'Then as an Angell, face, and wings / Of aire, not pure as it, yet pure doth weare. . . .'[58] The implication is that if the stars, and even God and the angels, do not disdain to work their spiritual ends through a less spiritual medium, then these lovers should not either. Certainly its use cannot frustrate such refined motions.

Donne chooses to support his climax with an analogy produced from the odd notion of intermediary spirits; and the claim is less convincingly made than if he had stated it baldly. His metaphysics are ordinary in doctrine as in production.[59] He has merely made a pleasant (or perhaps tendentious) figure of that physiological explanation of the hypostatic union, following the traditional terminology of man-making 'subtile knyttynges',[60] 'most subtle exhalation', and 'knot between the soul and the . . . body'.[61] The blood, personified, 'labours'; material itself, it deliberately strives to produce something nearer the nature of souls; it is its 'fingers' which knit the human knot. By this little quirk of wit, and an ambiguity (which may only be awkwardness) in the construction of the analogy, Donne does in fact suggest another argument than the expected one. He seems to be saying, 'Man's humanity is incomplete unless blood labours to beget spirits as like souls as it can'—does its best, that is, to produce souls. So 'pure lovers are not completely lovers unless their fused souls, inciting and acting through their blood (affections, passions), labour in begetting, doing their best to produce souls.' But this is at most secondary. What his sources teach, and he presumably means in chief, is that as the soul would be impotent and incomplete were it not linked to the material body by an intermediary, and thus put in touch with the outside world of sense, so pure lovers are impotent and incomplete if their souls do not stoop to use an intermediary, by whose means they can reach sense and each other. These intermediaries are 'affections' and 'faculties'—terms, like 'sense', of apt double import. 'Sense' in particular, with its common sixteenth-century overtone 'sensuality', or 'sexual play',[62] would add the useful implication that it needs nothing short of full physical intercourse to liberate the joint souls of lovers.

There is also the famous figure of the 'great Prince in prison'. One wonders if this is intended to be just a fine and pithy confirmation of the claim that while the bodies do not join the souls cannot. Certainly it would be no novelty to speak of the soul as a Prince, nor of the body as its prison. But it is interesting to find Davies, in *Nosce Teipsum*, developing his long discussion of the interaction of soul and body through a similar figure of a great prince in prison, and meaning something more subtle. 'This cunning mistress and this queen', he says, who lies in 'the body's prison', must look through the body's windows to know the world, and can discourse on and judge nothing but what sense reports to her. Yet the senses are only her instruments, which she uses for the humble task of garnering knowledge, while she 'sits and rules within her private bower', her sole function to 'judge and choose':

Even as our great wise *Empresse*, that now raignes,
By *soveraigne* title over sundrie lands,
Borrowes in meane affaires her *subiects* paines,
Sees by their eyes, and writeth by their hands;

But things of waight and consequence indeed,
Her selfe doth in her chamber them debate,
Where all her Counsellers she doth exceed
As farre in iudgement, as she doth in state.[63]

Thus, while the soul delegates only meaner matters to the sense, it cannot function without sense, any more than could a Prince deprived of her ability to act through executives. And the harm suffered by such an imprisoned Prince would be a loss of precisely that which makes her a Prince, her ruling power. So we may feel that Donne had precise attributes in mind when he called the new soul a great Prince. A Prince's chief attribute is ruling power; this she cannot exercise in prison. The chief attribute of a lover's soul is its power to govern the body of the lover; and this it cannot exercise while in the body's prison—until, that is, it is released by physical intercourse. Hence, until the bodies of the lovers are joined, their joint soul has no kingdom to command. The joint soul of these lovers has not attained its full prerogative until their joined bodies release it to rule. This follows smoothly on the earlier situation. The new composite soul, hovering outside bodies which its 'atomies' formerly occupied, cannot have a body to command unless these bodies are also made one. Until the bodies are made one the subtle knot is not tied, joint soul exists without body, bodies exist without souls, and the lovers are not truly lovers in love's hypostasis. Within the terms of the play of figure, the plea for the coexistence of bodily love with the highest degree of spiritual union has been completely justified. But it is the play of figure which is original, not the plea.

What follows is winding-up, chiefly by means of the comic pretence of the arcana of love. The idea that bodily union might be desired 'as sign of the primary conjunction'[64] is deftly dressed, the body becoming love's book wherein he reveals his spiritual mysteries to uninitiates. We have, again, the point that the speech of the loving souls is intelligible only to another lover—with the weak joke added that it has been a 'dialogue of one', a novel and mysterious sort of *dialogo d'amore*. And the somewhat enigmatic conclusion seems to be an assertion that the lovers' resort to their bodies now will mean no debasing of their love, or sundering of their eternally faithful souls.

Thus we see that if Donne's poem is hardly the seduction-piece of Legouis's 'scholastic Don Juan', it contains no individual metaphysic of love, and can only perversely be regarded as introspective. It is difficult to conceive how Mr. Eliot's 'sensuous apprehension of thought' could be a useful description of the processes which produced 'The Extasie'. Whether Donne was passionately in love when he wrote the poem is surely a profitless question—one remarks only that it is neither the analysis, nor in any direct way the expression, of personal passion. Beyond doubt it is the work of a strongly original and variously gifted personality, with a fine dramatic sense and feeling for language. But these gifts appear to be exercised in that dressing-up, re-presenting of received positions, which Italian critics of the Renaissance regarded as the essential poetic process. Only, Donne's chief vivifying resource is what his age called 'wit'. Certainly 'The Extasie' is a remarkably 'witty' poem.

NOTES

[1] The Poems of John Donne (Oxford, 1912), ii. 41.

[2] Ibid., p. xxxiii.

[3] 'Donne's Extasie Contra Legouis', P.Q., xv (1936), 247-53.

[4] See The Sermons of John Donne, ed. Potter and Simpson, i. 134, and Sermon 5, pp. 236-51.

[5] B. Varchi, 'Lezzione sopra l'Amore', in Lezioni (Fiorenza, 1590), pp. 326-7.

[6] Della Infinità di Amore, in G. Zonta, Trattati d'Amore del Cinquecento (Bari, 1912), p. 222.

[7] Dialoghi d'Amore, ed. S. Caramella (Bari, 1921), p. 6.

[8] Infinità, p. 235.

[9] Leone Ebreo, Dialoghi, p. 49.

[10] G. Betussi, Il Raverta, in Zonta, Trattati, pp. 10-11.

[11] Dialogo di Amore, Opere (Venezia, 1740), i. 3.

[12] B. Gottifredi, Lo Specchio d'Amore, in Zonta, Trattati, p. 297.

[13] T. Tasso, Conclusioni Amorose, in Le Prose Diverse, ed. C. Guasti (Firenze, 1875), ii. 68.

[14] F. Sansovino, Ragionamento nel quale brevemente s'insegna a' giovani uomini la Bella Arte d'Amore, in Zonta, Trattati, p. 180.

[15] Betussi, Raverta, p. 34.

[16] Dialoghi, p. 173.

[17] F. Cattani, I Tre Libri d'Amore (Vinegia, 1561), pp. 119-20.

[18] Leone, Dialoghi, p. 173.

[19] Ibid., p. 176.

[20] J. Weemes, A Treatise of the Foure Degenerate Sonnes (Edinburgh, 1636), pp. 72-73.

[21] Leone, Dialoghi, p. 43.

[22] T. Tasso, Le Considerazioni sopra Tre Canzoni di M. Gio. Battista Pigna, in Guasti, Prose, ii. 92.

[23] S. Speroni, Opere, i. 4.

[24] Betussi, Raverta, p. 95.

[25] Betussi, Raverta, pp. 23, 24.

[26] Leone, Dialoghi, p. 383.

[27] Ibid., pp. 384, 43, 51.

[28] Cattani, *Tre Libri*, p. 111.

[29] M. Ficino, *Sopra lo Amore* (Lanciano, 1914), p. 92.

[30] Cattani, *Tre Libri*, p. 111.

[31] Ibid., p. 112.

[32] The phrase is Varchi's, in 'Dell' Anima', *Lezioni*, p. 721.

[33] I am indebted to M. Étienne Gilson's discussion of this point in ch. ix of *The Spirit of Mediaeval Philosophy* (1936), from pp. 186-8 of which the quotations are taken.

[34] *De Gl'Heroici Furori* (Torino, 1928), p. 89.

[35] *Infinità*, p. 197.

[36] M. Equicola, *Libro di Natura d'Amore* (Vinegia, 1526), f. 110.

[37] *Discorso dell' Anima Umana*, *Opere*, iii. 370.

[38] *Lezioni*, pp. 371, 612.

[39] Betussi, *Raverta*, p. 32.

[40] Varchi, *Lezioni*, p. 381.

[41] *Conclusioni, Considerazioni*, in *Prose*, ii. 67, 89.

[42] *Dialoghi*, p. 50.

[43] Cit. G. Toffanin, *Il Cinquecento* (Milano, 1941), p. 141. See also Castiglione, *Il Libro del Cortegiano*, ed. V. Cian (Firenze, 1947), pp. 89-90.

[44] *Dialoghi*, p. 213.

[45] *Raverta*, p. 140.

[46] *Natura*, f. 111ʳ.

[47] Tullia, *Infinità*, p. 223.

[48] Ibid., p. 224.

[49] *Natura*, f. 197ʳ.

[50] *Lezioni*, p. 338.

[51] *Opere*, i. 6, 22-23.

[52] Cf. Sidney's 'In a Grove Most Rich of Shade', and such conventional descriptions of setting as that for the 'amorous monologue' in Scaliger, *Poetices*, i. 4.

[53] Equicola, *Natura*, f. 164ʳ.

[54] 'To his Lady who had vowed virginity.' Anon., in *A Poetical Rapsody* (1602).

[55] *O.E.D.* under *Concoction*, 2, lists contemporary uses in this sense.

[56] 'The Canonisation'.

[57] Grierson prints 'spheare' following all the manuscripts, whereas the editions give 'spheares'. His explanation of the singular form is that the bodies made one are the sphere in which the two Intelligences meet and command. This is attractive, but an anticipation of Donne's argument. John Hayward's adoption of 'spheares' in the Nonesuch Edition (*Complete Poetry and Selected Prose of John Donne*, 1929) seems justified.

[58] 'Aire and Angells'.

[59] The passage which Grierson cites from *Sermons*, 26. 20. 291 (Alford) in elucidation of this analogy is a simple fragment of the common teaching. In English there is a better account in *Nosce Teipsum* ('The passions of sense'), *The Poems of Sir John Davies*, ed. C. Howard (New York, 1941), pp. 160-1.

[60] Chaucer, *Boece*, in *Works*, ed. F. N. Robinson (1933), p. 440b, l. 18.

[61] Cattani. See p. 144 above.

[62] *O.E.D.*, *Sense* sb. 4.

[63] *Poems*, p. 127. Davies and Donne are likely to have moved in the same circle.

[64] Tasso. See p. 143 above.

The Origins of Stephen Crane's Literary Creed

James B. Colvert

Literary source hunters have experienced little difficulty in suggesting influences upon Stephen Crane's early novels and stories. But where such study should ideally throw light upon the genesis and processes of Crane's art, too often the claims and surmises about his literary origins are so general or so tenuous that they serve more to endarken than enlighten. Spiller, in the *Literary History of the United States*, fairly states the whole case:

> The appearance of an original artist, springing without antecedent into life, is always illusion, but the sources of Crane's philosophy and art are as yet undeciphered. Neither the cold-blooded determinism of his belief nor the sensuous awareness of his writing can be without source, but nowhere in the scant record he has left is there evidence that he, like Garland, read widely in the current books on biological science. A direct influence of Darwin, Spencer, Haeckel, or their American popularizers cannot be established. Rather he seems to have absorbed these influences at second hand through Russian and French writers.[1]

The problem of the "cold-blooded determinism of his belief" aside for the moment, how can the literary historian account for the "illusion" of Crane's appearance as an "original" artist and the amazing rapidity of his apparently untutored growth? In the spring of 1891 he was a Sophomore at Syracuse University, ambitiously planning to end his college career in order to become a writer; by the fall of 1892 he had already formulated the creed of art by which he was to be guided for the remaining eight years of his life and was presumably writing his first novel; by the spring of 1893 the author of *Maggie: A Girl of The Streets*[2] had won the attentions of two of the most influential literary men of his time, Hamlin Garland and William Dean Howells.

Two theories are commonly advanced to explain this phenomenal literary development. First is the popular and persistent notion, perhaps inevitable in view of his unusual literary rise, that Crane had no origins at all, that he was a "natural" genius who had no need for a literary situation in which to develop. An informed contemporary, Howells, could only say that the young author of *Maggie* "sprang into life fully armed,"[3] and Garland, Crane's patron for a time after 1893, propagated for almost twenty years the idea that his protégé was an inexplicable genius, a sort of unconscious recorder of whatever came to him from the outer reaches of a ghostly world. This belief is commonly found in history and criticism even today. He was, a critic wrote in 1941, "an artist who was really not conscious at all. He arrived . . . fully equipped. He had no need to improve."[4] And as late as 1952 a historian asserted that Crane was an artist of "amazing, almost miraculous prescience," and thus "that despair of the academic critic, a highly 'original' writer."[5]

The other view, accepted in part at least by Spiller in the *Literary History of the United States,* is that Crane sprang directly from the tradition of the French and Russian naturalists, a thesis extensively argued in Lars Ahnebrink's study of *The Beginnings of Naturalism in American Fiction.*[6] Ahnebrink attributes Crane's basic concept of fiction and the writer to the European naturalists, particularly Zola, whose *L'Assomoir* and *La Débâcle* he regards as important sources for Crane's first three novels, *Maggie, George's Mother,* and *The Red Badge of Courage.* Turgenev's *Fathers and Sons,* Ahnebrink thinks, probably influenced *George's Mother,* and Ibsen's *An Enemy of the People* perhaps suggested Crane's novelette, *The Monster.*

But there are serious objections to both of these views. The notion that Crane had no literary antecedents contradicts the fundamental principle that every writer is at first dependent upon his times and its traditions, however widely he may later deviate from them in the process of creating something new out of the old. Nor is the second theory much more acceptable. The chief difficulty with the idea that Crane adopted the doctrines and methods of the naturalists is that it assumes, without much evidence, that he read and imitated the writers of this school, an assumption which does not at all square with the fact that Crane's work and the naturalists' differ in many important respects. There are reasons to doubt seriously that the American ever read Zola or the Russians. When Ahnebrink asserts that "even before the composition of *Maggie,* he [Crane] was familiar with some of Zola's work," he ignores the fact that Crane read *Nana*—the only novel by Zola he ever commented on—more than five years after he started writing *Maggie*.[7] No evidence exists that he ever read *L'Assomoir,* and *La Débâcle* he threw aside, according to Thomas Beer, after reading only a few pages.[8] There is no external—and no convincing internal evidence that he knew either Turgenev or Ibsen.

On the contrary, there is good reason to believe that Crane was unusually ill-read. John Barry, the editor of *The Forum* who read Crane's *The Black Riders* in manuscript in 1894, referred to the young poet as "woefully ignorant of books,"[9] and Berryman, who thinks Crane's reading has been understimated, can nevertheless assert that "it is not easy to think of another important prose-writer or poet so ignorant of traditional literature in English as Stephen Crane was and remained."[10] All his life he denied, sometimes with considerable irritation, any connection with the naturalists. "They stand me against walls," he complained about his English acquaintances to James Huneker in 1897, "with a teacup in my hand and tell me how I have stolen all my things from de Maupassant, Zola, Loti, and the bloke who wrote—I forget the name."[11] Except for a reference to the brief period in 1891 when, as a student at Syracuse, he was studying intensely with a view to forming his style, there is little evidence that he ever read much at all, an omission he once defended on the ground that in this way he avoided the risk of unconscious imitation.[12] Unlike Frank Norris, who once referred to himself as "Mr. Norris, Esq. (The Boy Zola)!" Crane seems to owe little, if anything, to nineteenth-century French and Russian naturalism.[13]

How, then, can the literary beginnings of this precocious (but, one supposes, hardly supernatural) young writer be accounted for? "Here came a boy," Beer wrote of the twenty-year-old ex-college student who went into the East Side slums in the spring of 1891 for material for Maggie, "whose visual sense was unique in American writing and whose mind by some inner process had stripped itself of all respect for these prevalent theories which have cursed the national fiction. He was already an ironist, already able to plant his impressions with force and reckless of the consequent shock to a public softened by long nursing at the hands of limited men."[14] But what had stimulated to action his natural rebelliousness and what were the "inner processes" that turned him to slums for the subject of his painfully realistic *Maggie?* From whom had he learned the use of irony, and to whom was he indebted for his interest in painting and his characteristic use of color imagery? What was the origin of his belief that direct personal experience is the only valid material for the writer, and what led him to emphasize so strongly his belief that absolute honesty is a prime virtue of the artist? These questions, it would seem, define the problem of Crane's literary origins, and the answers are to be found in the period of his almost incredibly brief apprenticeship to the craft of fiction in the years 1891-92.

Crane left one of the most important clues to his artistic origins in a letter of 1896 to Lily Brandon Munro, a lady he was once in love with in his Syracuse student days. "You know," he wrote, "when I left you [in the fall of 1892] I renounced the clever school in literature. It seemed to me that there must be something more in life than to sit and cudgel one's brains for clever and witty expedients. So I developed all alone a little creed of art which I thought was a good one. . . . If I had kept to my clever Rudyard-Kipling style, the road might have been shorter, but, ah, it wouldn't be the true road."[15] The significant point here is not so much Crane's rejection of Kipling as a literary mentor as his implicit admission that the Englishman had served him as a model sometime between 1891 and 1892. It seems more than likely that the young American owed to Kipling the basic principles of his artistic beliefs, for Crane's theory of literature matches precisely the esthetic credo of Dick Heldar, the young artist-hero of Kipling's *The Light That Failed,* a novel Crane read sometime before 1892, probably during the spring semester of 1891 at Syracuse University.

Few young writers in a rebellious mood were likely to escape the attraction of Kipling in the first years of the nineties. At the time *The Light That Failed* was appearing in *Lippincott's Magazine* in January of 1891, Kipling was already a best-selling author whose fiction was considered new and unorthodox. His amazing popularity had in fact become a subject for reviewer's verse:

> No matter where I go, I hear
> The same old tale of wonder;
> It's some delusion wild, I fear,
> The world is laboring under.
> Why every friend I've met today
> (I couldn't help but note it)
> Has asked me "Have you read 'Mulvaney'
> Rudyard Kipling wrote it."[16]

Immediately following this is a review of *The Light That Failed* which emphasizes the unorthodoxy of his realistic tale of an artist's adventures as a war correspondent and suggests something of the appeal it must have had for the youthful Crane, then a cub reporter for his brother Townley's Asbury Park news agency: "Bohemian and unconventional as the characters are," the reviewer states, "no one who has seen much of the two classes whence they are chiefly drawn—newspaper correspondents and lady art students—can say they are grossly exaggerated."[17]

There is convincing evidence that Crane not only knew this novel before 1892, but that it indeed made a profound impression upon him. S. C. Osborn notes that Crane's famous image at the end of Chapter IX in *The Red Badge of Courage,* "The sun was pasted against the sky like a wafer," occurs in Kipling's *The Light That Failed* and concludes that the younger writer unconsciously incorporated the idea into *The Red Badge.*[18] There are strong reflections, moreover, of Kipling's early manner—the impressionistic "modern" imagery, the sententious, often flippant, dialogue, and a keen sense of the ironic—in Crane's earliest fiction, *The Sullivan County Sketches,* written in the summers of 1891 and 1892. In these pieces, which comprise all that may be properly called apprentice work, if the first drafts of *Maggie* and a story published in the Syracuse school paper are excepted, Crane put into practice the basic theories of Dick Heldar, the rebellious and unorthodox artist in *The Light That Failed.*

Dick Heldar must have been the apotheosis of all that the nineteen-year-old Crane hoped to become. Dick is an Impressionist painter in revolt against the canons of nineteenth-century respectability. He chooses Bohemian life for the freedom it gives him in his enthusiastic pursuit of fame, and with great determination he seeks the truth about life in the slums of London and on the battlegrounds of remote deserts. He is proud, independent, and free in the expression of iconoclastic opinions.

Crane's orientation was remarkably similar. As a boy he was in perpetual revolt against the respectability of his conventional, middle-class Methodist home life, and at Claverack College, Lafayette, and Syracuse, an indifferent student at all three places, he incurred the displeasure of the faculty for expressing "angular" opinions. He was asked to withdraw from Lafayette at the end of his first semester for refusing to conform to academic regimen. "Away with literary fads and canons," he exclaimed to a friend in the late spring of 1891,[19] and about the same time he began making trips to New York to study life on the Bowery and in the slums. In the fall of 1892, after he was dismissed from the *Tribune* for writing an ironic account of an Asbury Park labor parade, Crane moved into the East Side more or less permanently, where he remained, observing and writing in wretched poverty, for more than two years.

This way of life he led by choice like Kipling's Dick Heldar, from whom he probably got the idea that this privation was valuable, perhaps even indispensable, to his development as an artist. "There are few things more edifying unto Art than the actual belly-pinch of hunger," Kipling explains when he puts Dick into the London slums to starve and paint within walking distance of an affluent friend. "I never knew," Dick says in explaining the value of his experience with poverty, "what I had to learn about the human face before."[20] When he is at last paid for some art work, Dick calls upon his friend and explains that he could not have asked for help because "I had a sort of superstition that this temporary starvation—that's what it was, and it hurt —would bring me more luck later."[21] Crane, as his way of life during this period shows, was of the same belief. One of his nieces, recalling her uncle's misery in the New York slums, was puzzled by his conduct: "We still wonder why he went through such experiences when he was always so very welcome at both our house and Uncle Edmund's. Perhaps he was seeking his own 'Experience in Misery' . . . altho doubtless it came also through his desire to make his own way independently."[22] To these views Crane himself assented, but a more significant explanation lies in his persistent notion that great art is born of the "belly-pinch of hunger":

> It was during this period [he wrote to the editor of Leslie's Weekly about November, 1895] that I wrote "The Red Badge of Courage." It was an effort born of pain—despair, almost; and I believe that this made it a better piece of literature than it otherwise would have been. It seems a pity that art should be a child of pain, and yet I think it is. Of course we have fine writers who are prosperous and contented, but in my opinion their work would be greater if this were not so. It lacks the sting it would have if written under the spur of a great need.[23]

The remarkable kinship in temperament and attitude between Kipling's protagonist and Crane strongly suggests that Dick's ideas about art deeply impressed the young writer. Dick may have inspired Crane in the use of color images for special effects, a stylistic feature which blazes forth in the Sullivan County tales of 1892. For *The Light That Failed* bristles with artist talk about color. Heldar exclaims with sensuous enthusiasm about the scenery of Sudan: "What color that was! Opal and amber and claret and brick-red and sulphur—cockatoo-crest sulphur—against brown, with a nigger black rock sticking up in the middle of it all, and a decorative frieze of camels festooning in front of a pure pale turquoise sky."[24] Crane's interest in painting, it is true, probably originated in his associations with his sister, Mary Helen, who taught art in Asbury Park in the late eighties and early nineties, and with Phebe English, a young art student with whom he fell in love when he was a student at Claverack College.[25] But in *The Light That Failed* he had before him not only an enthusiastic appreciation of the expressive potentialities of color, but also a striking example, in Kipling's "wrathful red disk" images, of how color could be used by the writer to evoke mood and emotional atmosphere.

More important in Crane's literary credo, though, are the principles governing the selection of materials, their treatment, and the attitude of the artist toward them. In *The Light That Failed* Kipling advances and defends the position that real life furnishes the only valid materials for art. "How can you do anything," his hero exclaims, "until you have seen everything, or as much as you can?"[26] Like the blind and ruined Heldar, who met his death following wars to the far corners of the earth, Crane, ill with tuberculosis, wandered away his energies—in the West, Mexico, the Florida swamps, Greece, and Cuba—in quest of experience in the world of action. "I decided," he wrote once in reference to his literary creed of 1892, "that the nearer a writer gets to life the greater he becomes as an artist,"[27] and in 1897, when his career was drawing to a close, he wrote from England to his brother William: "I am a wanderer now and I must see enough."[28] Both Crane and Kipling's hero expressed and acted upon the firm belief that the artist's material is necessarily drawn from personal experience.

Important corollaries for the realist are the convictions that all experience, ugly and unpleasant though it may be, must be faithfully and truthfully reported if the artist is to maintain his integrity. Around this idea Kipling builds one of the key scenes in *The Light That Failed*. Heldar, disappointed because one of his realistic war sketches has been rejected by all the magazines, decides to alter it to conform to the conventional idea of what the soldier is like:

> I lured my model, a beautiful rifleman, up here with drink. . . . I made him a flushed dishevelled, bedevilled scallawag, with his helmet at the back of his head, and the living fear of death in his eye, and the blood oozing out of a cut over his ankle-bone. He wasn't pretty, but he was all soldier and very much man. . . . The artmanager of that abandoned paper said that his subscribers wouldn't like it. It was brutal and coarse and violent. . . . I took my "Last Shot" back. . . . I put him into a lovely red coat without a speck on it. That is Art. I cleaned his rifle—rifles are always clean on service—because that is Art. . . . I shaved his chin, I washed his hands,

and gave him an air of fatted peace. . . . Price, thank Heaven! twice as much as for the first sketch.[29]

"If you try to give these people the thing as God gave it," Dick argues when his friend Torpenhow reprimands him for this practice, "keyed down to their comprehension and according to the powers he has given you . . . half a dozen epicene young pagans who haven't even been to Algiers will tell you, first that your notion is borrowed and, secondly, that it isn't Art!"[30] But Torpenhow destroys the repainted picture and delivers Dick an impassioned lecture on truth and integrity in the practice of art, after which the penitent Heldar concludes, "You're so abominably reasonable!"[31]

This idea Crane was expounding as early as the spring of 1891, about the time he read Kipling's novel. "I became involved," he wrote again in reference to his creed of 1892, "in the beautiful war between those who say that art is man's substitute for nature and we are the most successful in art when we approach the nearest to nature and truth, and those who say—well, I don't know what they say. Then they can't say much but they fight villainously."[32] On another occasion he stated Dick's idea more explicitly: "I cannot see why people hate ugliness in art. Ugliness is just a matter of treatment. The scene of Hamlet and his mother and old Polonius behind the curtain is ugly, if you heard it in a police court. Hamlet treats his mother like a drunken carter and his words when he has killed Polonius are disgusting. But who cares?"[33]

Writing in 1898 about his literary aims, Crane reasserted his belief in this principle and showed how largely it had figured in his career: "The one thing that deeply pleases me in my literary life—brief and inglorious as it is—is the fact that men of sense believe me to be sincere. . . . I do the best that is in me, without regard to cheers or damnation."[34] This echoes the principle oratorically preached to Dick upon the occasion of his moral lapse: "For work done without conviction, for power wasted in trivialities, for labor expended with levity for the deliberate purpose of winning the easy applause of a fashion-driven public, there remains but one end,—the oblivion that is preceded by toleration and cenotaphed with contempt."[35]

These striking parallels in the artistic aims and attitudes of Dick Heldar and Crane strongly suggest that Kipling's novel provided the young American with his basic conception of the art of fiction. Since the evidence for the influence of the naturalists upon Crane's literary theory is unconvincing, and since he knew neither Howells, or Garland's theories of realism and veritism until after 1892, before which time he had read *The Light That Failed*, it seems likely indeed that Kipling is Crane's chief literary ancestor. This belief is further strengthened by the fact that Crane read Kipling's book at the most impressionable period of his literary life. As a rank novice, rebellious against social and literary conventions and searching for a rationale for a new fiction, Crane must have found Kipling's ideas immensely stimulating. "For short, scattered periods Crane read curiously," Berryman states, "and instinct or luck or fate led him early to what mattered."[36] Later, it is true, he found support for his creed in the ideas of Howels, Garland, and the Impressionist painters with whom he was in constant association during his Bohemian New York period. But the book which laid the basic principle was *The Light That Failed*. Here is developed explicitly a whole literary credo which exactly parallels Crane's. In advocating and following closely the principles that art is grounded in actual experience, that absolute honesty in the artist is an indispensable virtue, that all experience, including the ugly and the unpleasant, is material for the artist, Crane, through Kipling, anticipated the "cult of experience" in American fiction which reached its full development in the literary renaissance of the twenties.[37]

NOTES

[1] Robert E. Spiller and others, eds., *Literary History of the United States* (3 vols., New York, 1948), II, 1021.

[2] The book, Spiller writes (*ibid.*, 1022), with which "modern American fiction was born."

[3] Thomas Beer, *Stephen Crane: A Study in American Letters* (New York, 1923), 96.

[4] H. E. Bates, *The Modern Short Story* (New York, 1941), 65.

[5] Edward Wagenknecht, *The Cavalcade of the American Novel* (New York, 1952), 212.

[6] University of Uppsala *Essays and Studies on American Language and Literature*, IX (1950).

[7] Beer, *Stephen Crane: A Study in American Letters*, 148.

[8] *Ibid.*, 97.

[9] John D. Barry, "A Note on Stephen Crane," *The Bookman*, XIII (1901), 148.

[10] John Berryman, *Stephen Crane* (New York, 1950), 24.

[11] Robert W. Stallman, ed., *Stephen Crane: An Omnibus* (New York, 1952), 674. All references to Crane's letters are to this source.

[12] Barry, "A Note on Stephen Crane," 148.

[13] This view is in harmony with that of Albert J. Salvan, a student of Zola who concludes in his study of the naturalist's influence in the United States: "Dans la question toujours délicate d'établir un rapport d'influence définie entre Zola et

Stephen Crane, nous sommes forcés de rester sur une note evasive. Il n'est guère douteux que l'auteur de Maggie manquait d'une connaissance très entendue de la littérature française du XIXe siecle en genéral." *Zola aux Etats-Unis* (Providence, 1943), 163.

[14] Beer, *Stephen Crane: A Study in American Letters*, 77.

[15] Stallman, *Stephen Crane: An Omnibus*, 648.

[16] "The Light That Failed," *The Literary News*, XII (1891), 29.

[17] *Ibid.*, 19.

[18] Scott C. Osborn, "Stephen Crane's Imagery: 'Pasted Like a Wafer,'" *AL*, XXIII (1951), 363. Osborn notes only one occurrence: "The fog was driven apart for a moment, and the sun shone, a blood-red wafer, on the water." *The Writings in Prose and Verse of Rudyard Kipling* (New York, 1897), IX, 63. The image occurs in variations twice more: "A puddle far across the mud caught the last rays of the sun and turned it into a wrathful red disc" (p. 13), and again: "The sun caught the steel and turned it into a savage red disc" (p. 31). See n. 37.

[19] Arthur Oliver, "Jersey Memories —Stephen Crane," *New Jersey Historical Society Proceedings*, n.s., XVI (1931), 454-55.

[20] Rudyard Kipling, *The Light That Failed*, in *The Writings in Prose and Verse of Rudyard Kipling* (New York, 1897), IX, 41.

[21] *Loc cit.*

[22] Edna Crane Sidbury, "My Uncle, Stephen Crane, As I Knew Him," *Literary Digest International Book Review*, IV (1926), 249.

[23] Stallman, *Stephen Crane: An Omnibus*, 591.

[24] *The Light That Failed*, 53.

[25] Joseph J. Kwiat, "Stephen Crane and Painting," *The American Quarterly*, IV (1952), 331.

[26] *The Light That Failed*, 105.

[27] Stallman, *Stephen Crane: An Omnibus*, 627.

[28] *Ibid.*, 663.

[29] *The Light That Failed*, 55-56.

[30] *Ibid.*, 49.

[31] *Ibid.*, 56.

[32] Stallman, *Stephen Crane: An Omnibus*, 648.

[33] Berryman, *Stephen Crane*, 21.

[34] Stallman, *Stephen Crane: An Omnibus*, 679-80.

[35] *The Light That Failed*, 67.

[36] Berryman, *Stephen Crane*, 24.

[37] When this article was in page proof, I saw R. W. Stallman's "The Scholar's Net: Literary Sources," *College English*, XVII (1955), 20-27, in which Mr. Stallman states that Scott C. Osborn, who first pointed out the similarity between Kipling and Crane's wafer image, "failed to explore the related images for what they mean and how they are used. . . . Nor is there any other point of correspondence between *The Light That Failed* and *The Red Badge of Courage*—only this single image (p. 20)."

Shakespeare and the Diction of Common Life

F. P. Wilson

We have heard much in recent years of the necessity of making our-selves Shakespeare's contemporaries. We shall understand him better, it is said, be in less danger of misunderstanding him, if we know as much as we can of the stage for which he wrote, of the actors who performed his plays, of the audience which saw them acted, of the psychological theories of the age, of its economic, political, and social life, of its taste in rhetoric, in language, and in criticism; in short, if we make ourselves good Elizabethans, if possible intelligent Eliza-bethans. I shall not quarrel with this ideal. It is one to which every scholar aspires, and most of this paper is taken up with some of the difficulties. But while it is impossible to exaggerate the difficulties, it is sometimes possible to exaggerate the results. It has been said that nothing but a whole heart and a free mind are needed to understand Shakespeare, and if we interpret this to mean a robust heart and an acute and sensitive mind that is true, and true in an important sense. How little Keats knew of Shakespearian scholarship may be a cooling card for the scholar's fancy. He read Shakespeare not in Malone's edi-tion, but in plain texts without commentary, yet he understood Shake-speare 'to his depths'. If ever man made Shakespeare a part of his life, that man was Keats. He is the great Shakespearian humanist. And if we are ever tempted to forget, his example is a perpetual reminder that while we strive to make ourselves Shakespeare's contemporaries, it is even more important to make Shakespeare our contemporary, to keep him level with life and with our lives.

The title of this lecture was suggested by a man who believed in keeping literature level with life. In the Preface to his *Dictionary* Johnson observes:

> From the authors which rose in the time of Elizabeth, a speech might be formed adequate to all the purposes of use and elegance. If the language of theology were extracted from Hooker and the translation of the Bible; the terms of natural knowledge from Bacon; the phrases of policy, war, and navigation from Raleigh; the dialect of poetry and fiction from Spenser and Sidney; and the diction of common life from Shakespeare, few ideas would be lost to mankind, for want of English words, in which they might be expressed.

Johnson does not say that a lexicographer could find in Shakespeare the diction of common life and nothing else. Shakespeare may have had 'small Latin and less Greek', but he had enough Latin to use English words from that language with confidence. 'With cadent tears fret channels in her cheeks', 'My operant powers their functions leave to do', 'The multitudinous seas incarnadine', these and many other lines contain words or senses of words not yet found earlier than Shakespeare. Within fifteen lines of a speech of Agamemnon's there are four such words.[1] But while he realized the value to his cadence and meaning of the learned word beside the familiar, he was never in danger of becoming an inkhornist. He may use the word 'remuneration' comically in *Love's Labour's Lost* and seriously in *Troilus and Cressida,* or 'festinately' comically in *Love's Labour's Lost* and 'festinate' seriously in *King Lear,* but at no time could the creator of Holofernes have admired the sixteenth-century poet who asked his mistress what thing was 'equipollent to her formosity'.[2] And although he profits from them all, he cannot be attached to any one of the various schemes for enriching the English vocabulary recommended by sixteenth-century grammarians and rhetoricians—whether with inkhorn terms, outlandish terms, archaic words, or dialect. What a Greek writer said of Homer is very true of Spenser but is not in the least true of Shakespeare: 'he did not stop at his own generation, but went back to ancestors; had a word dropped out, he was sure to pick it up, like an old coin out of an unclaimed treasure-house, all for love of words; and again many barbarian terms, sparing no single word which seemed to have in it enjoyment or intensity.'[3] The conditions of Shakespeare's art as a dramatist did not permit him to stray far from popular idiom, but even if they had, his mind was of a cast that would still have found the material upon which it worked mainly in the diction of common life. The best of the Sonnets are evidence of that and all the familiar images in his plays which, as his art matures, flow more and more freely from the less conscious levels of his mind. At the same time his instinct for what was permanent in the colloquial language of his day is stronger than that of any contemporary dramatist. No other Jacobean would have displayed 'a Rogue' with so little use of canting or 'pedlar's French' as does Shakespeare in Autolycus. In the words of Coleridge, his language is that which belongs 'to human nature as *human*, independent of associations and habits from any particular rank of life or mode of employment. . . . It is (to play on Dante's words) in truth the NOBLE *volgare eloquenza*'.[4]

His retentive mind received its stores from books, more still from speech and his own penny of observation. 'It is probable', wrote J. M. Synge, 'that when the Elizabethan dramatist took his inkhorn and sat down to his work he used many phrases that he had just heard, as he sat at dinner, from his mother or his children.'[5] Shakespeare may often have cried 'My tables—meet it is I set it down', as Shaw represents him doing in *The Dark Lady of the Sonnets*. When we find in earlier writers that as in *Love's Labour's Lost* a hat or veil comes over a face 'like a penthouse',[6] that as in *Hamlet* this world is 'a sea of troubles',[7] or even that a man's humour is 'tickle of the sear',[8] we may be in doubt whether these are phrases which Shakespeare had read or overheard, but we cannot doubt that in their boldness and concreteness they are characteristic of what he might have read or heard and of the climate in which his own image-making flourished. So, too, when Sir Thomas Egerton, Lord Keeper, urges the Parliament of 1597 to thank God 'upon the knees of our hearts',[9] we are not surprised at the bold extravagance of the metaphor. Egerton is not clipping the Queen's English: this was the current coinage of the realm. He and his contemporaries did not suffer from 'the Danger of thinking without Images'.[10]

We could not know what wealth Shakespeare had to draw upon or how much by his own invention he added to that wealth until the completion of the great *Oxford Dictionary*, and we shall know more fully if the University of Michigan publishes its Early Modern English Dictionary. Perhaps it is not much of an exaggeration to say that a mere recital of the number of ways in which the Elizabethans could and did refer to their besetting vice of drunkenness would take up the greater part of this hour. Their dictionaries, especially Florio's and Cotgrave's, give us some indication of the wealth of synonym and of the delight these lexicographers took in assembling it. They practised 'copy' (*copia verborum*) even in their dictionaries. Florio calls his second edition 'A New World of Words': it is his voyage of discovery into the land of diction. Watch him exploring the possibilities of two Italian words. Under *tinca:* 'a fish called a Tench. Used also for a freshwater soldier, or unexpert Captain that will have thirty men with him be it but to dig up a Turnip'; and under *squassapennacchio:* 'a tistytosty, a wag-feather, a toss-plume, a swashbuckler'. Shakespeare does not use one of these four words, yet every one is rounded to an actor's palate, every one a moving picture.

Unlike J. M. Synge, Shakespeare needed no 'chink in the floor' to enable him to overhear what was being said in the country-kitchen; he was free of it by birth; but he eavesdropped in the City and at Court and found there talk as fully flavoured. Landor has said that the best language in all countries is that which is spoken by intelligent women, of too high rank for petty affectation, and of too much request in society for deep study.[11] That is the language of Rosaline, of Beatrice, of Rosalind. If Shakespeare ever had a weakness for court affectations, he worked it out of his system in *Love's Labour's Lost*. We hear much of these affectations of speech in Elizabethan literature, of 'Arcadian and Euphuized gentlewomen', but as we should expect there were few affectations in the speech of those who were closest to the Queen. In *Cynthia's Revels* it is not Crites or Arete who drink of the fountain of self-love; and it is not Cynthia. However picked and patterned may be the language of Elizabeth's formal writings, there was no trace of affectation in her private speech or public utterances. Her very oaths identified her with all classes of her people except those who swore by 'yea and nay' or 'indeed la'. In a pious and spirited book which formed half the dowry of Bunyan's wife, Arthur Dent wrote of men who swore less vigorously than his Queen that 'Hell gapeth for them';[12] but fortunately for him his Plain Man's Pathway did not lead him into the Presence. And when she spoke to her people, then, as her great scholar Camden would have wished, she did not follow 'the minion refiners of English'; she spoke not State English, not Court English, not Secretary English, but plain English.[13]

> Though God hath raised me high; yet this I count the glory of my Crown, That I have reigned with your loves. This makes me that I do not so much rejoice, That God hath made me to be a Queen, as, To be a Queen over so thankful a People. . . . There will never Queen sit in my seat, with more zeal to my Country, care for my Subjects; and that sooner with willingness will venture her life for your good and safety, than my self. For it is not my desire to live nor reign longer, than my life and reign shall be for your good.

And though you have had, and may have, many Princes, more mighty and wise, sitting in this State; yet you never had, or shall have, any that will be more careful and loving.[14]

As we read these strong and straightforward sentences we may flatter ourselves that we can read Elizabeth and Shakespeare as good Elizabethans, yet apart altogether from changes in pronunciation the words cannot mean to us what they meant to contemporaries. The words we most value rise from a well of associations fed by a thousand memories, and we cannot rid ourselves of these associations. But we can make an approximation, and in making it the greatest difficulty does not come from obsolete expressions and obscure allusions. When we meet with 'miching mallecho' either we look up a commentary or we pass on. There is a possibility of ignorance here, but not of misunderstanding, unless indeed the commentators mislead us. Nor in some contexts is the danger very great from words which have survived into modern English with very different meanings. Only a very stupid reader would misunderstand when it is said that in the Scotland of Macbeth 'violent sorrow seems A modern ecstasy'. The real danger comes with words to which it is possible to attach the modern meaning and make a sense. But the sense is not Shakespeare's. Sometimes the difference is so slight that the modern meaning does little or no harm. It matters little, to take an example of Henry Bradley's,[15] whether we understand Polonius's 'Still harping on my daughter' to mean 'Now as heretofore harping on my daughter' or, as Shakespeare meant, 'Always harping on my daughter'. It matters more if we forget how the dilatoriness of man has deprived of its urgency such a word as 'presently'.[16] How many a word has lost its vigour by continual usage may be illustrated from a famous passage in *Othello:*

> When you shall these unlucky deeds relate,
> Speak of me as I am; nothing extenuate,
> Nor set down aught in malice: then must you speak
> Of one that loved not wisely but too well;
> Of one not easily jealous, but, being wrought,
> Perplex'd in the extreme.

'These unlucky deeds', 'perplexed in the extreme'. What colourless words, we are tempted to say, and good critics have seen here the irony of understatement. But in Elizabethan English 'unlucky' means or can mean ill-omened, disastrous; and 'perplexed' means or can mean grieved, tortured, the mind on the rack. There is no hyperbole here, but neither is there understatement. In the noble and single magnificence of Othello's speech, the emotion is fully and exactly stated.

Editors have not given us enough help here—Professor Dover Wilson in the later volumes of the New Cambridge Shakespeare is a notable exception—yet since Dr. Onions's *Shakespeare Glossary* of 1911 and the completion of the *Oxford Dictionary* in 1928 much of the evidence has been available. Even with this expert assistance the difficulty of choosing between the many possible meanings of some of the commonest words is often great. It may be important to remember that in addition to bearing its modern meanings the noun 'will' often signifies lust, the carnal passions in control of the reason. It is the last word in the longest speech in which Hamlet rebukes his mother, and it is a climax to the mood of disgust and revulsion which has almost unseated his reason:

> Rebellious hell,
> If thou canst mutine in a matron's bones,
> To flaming youth let virtue be as wax
> And melt in her own fire: proclaim no shame
> When the compulsive ardour gives the charge,
> Since frost itself as actively doth burn,
> And reason pandars will.

And as we should expect, the word is prominent in the plays in which Shakespeare is above all at grips with the sin of lust. 'Redeem thy brother', cries Angelo, 'By yielding up thy body to my will'; of Antony it is said that he 'would make his will Lord of his reason'; and to Troilus eyes and ears are

> Two traded pilots 'twixt the dangerous shores
> Of will and judgement.

So far I have been considering the words apart as if in a dictionary, but let me no longer 'crumble my text into small parts' but draw my observations 'out of the whole text, as it lies entire and unbroken'[17] in Shakespeare himself. For more than a century critics have observed how his line became animated, and his paragraph interanimated, by the rhythms of speech. They have noticed, too, his growing mastery of dramatic prose, and how while never relinquishing its colloquial base it could become upon the lips of Falstaff and Hamlet as quick and forgetive as poetry. And all the time he was slowly working himself free from the over-elaborate use of schemes and tropes inherited by him from his age and by his age from scholastic rhetoric. 'That wonderful poet, who has so much besides rhetoric, is also the greatest poetical rhetorician since Euripides'—these words of Matthew Arnold's[18] remain true of Shakespeare to the end, but there is as much difference between the rhetoric of *Richard III* and *King Lear* as between the verse. An Elizabethan schoolmaster might have set his boys many a speech in Shakespeare's early plays as an exercise in the identification of schemes and tropes, and to name the figures in (say) the soliloquy of Henry VI which begins 'This battle fares like to the morning's war', with its elaborate examples of anaphora with and without climax, would have been well within the capacity of the meanest scholar in Mulcaster's school,[19] although perhaps he would not have observed how the speech is redeemed by the lyricism which cuts across the formalism of the rhetoric. But if the boy had been confronted with *Hamlet* or *King Lear* his task would have been more difficult. There is a development in Shakespeare similar to that which Professor Manly noticed in Chaucer: 'a process of general release from the astonishingly artificial and sophisticated art with which he began and the gradual replacement of formal rhetorical devices by methods of composition based upon close observation of life and the exercise of the creative imagination.'[20] Even in Shakespeare's earliest manner, as in Chaucer's, the natural is ever present with the artificial, but by the turn of the century Shakespeare has forged verse, prose, and rhetoric into the subtlest instrument of dramatic speech the world has known. How this dramatic speech is dependent upon language familiar to all his audience, upon the language of common life, may be illustrated by examining his use of three figures, paronomasia, the image, and the proverb. Paronomasia and the proverb were more valued in his age than in later ages, but command of the image,[21] especially metaphor, has seemed since Aristotle the greatest thing by far for a poet to have.

Johnson recognized that every age has its modes of speech and its cast of thought, but Shakespeare's use of agnomination or paronomasia, or more simply quibbling with words, he could not condone. Camden, too, while quoting Giraldus Cambrensis to the effect that the English and the Welsh 'delighted much in licking the letter, and clapping to gether of Agnominations', felt that 'this merry playing with words' had been 'too much used by some'.[22] There will be few readers of Shakespeare's comic scenes who do not at times agree. The contrast between Speed's verbal wit and Launce's mother-wit is to be remarked: the one perished almost as soon as it was born, and the other is, in its kind, imperishable. Shakespeare inherited a ripe tradition of clowning —it was Tarleton's legacy to the English stage—and in ripe clowning, in 'merry fooling', there is little to choose between his early work and his late. As his art matures, he may bring everything more and more into a unity—Dogberry and Stephano are essential to the action, while Launce is a music-hall turn—but the humour of Launce's talk with his dog is already ripe, as nothing else in that play is ripe. But if being a good Elizabethan means enjoying word-spinning on the level of Speed, few of us can be good Elizabethans. It is some consolation to have Camden on our side, and Camden's greatest pupil who attacked the 'Stage-practice' of 'mistaking words' in *Bartholomew Fair*. Fortunately Shakespeare grew out of the abuse of the practice, and the fool in *Othello* is the last of his characters of whom it can be said: 'How every fool can play upon the word.'

Ben Jonson was inclined to attack all 'Paranomasie or Agnomination'—it is significant that he puts the words into the mouth of his Poetaster—but like most Elizabethans Shakespeare was never willing to relinquish it altogether. The figure played a chief part in their jests and riddles and in the many word-games of which they were so fond. If we wish to see to what good purpose Shakespeare puts the pun we cannot do better than turn to Beatrice and Falstaff. About the time that Shakespeare was creating them, Jonson's friend John Hoskins was blaming 'the dotage of the time upon this small ornament',[23] but there was no longer any question of Shakespeare doting upon it. While the quibble is Speed's only weapon it is one of many in the crammed arsenal of Beatrice's wit and Falstaff's. Beatrice's 'civil count, civil as an orange, and something of that jealous complexion' is gay and stimulating, one of many touches in Shakespeare's greatest exemplar of a love between man and woman that does not abase but sharpens the wits, so that in both sexes the mind and the senses are fully exercised. Falstaff's puns, too, do not merely spin upon themselves. The quibbles in 'thou camest not of the blood royal, if thou darest not stand for ten shillings' are quibbles with sense and are intimately concerned with the action. In this lively lordship over words he shows the agility of his mind. A contemporary proverb said that he who sought for a fine wit in a fat belly lost his labour. That is only one of the many incongruities that are reconciled in this character. A cony-catcher, he hob-nobs with princes of the realm. A coward, he never shows fear or loses presence of mind in the heat of battle. Surrounded by men who would sacrifice their lives for ambition or honour, he believes only in good fellows, sack, and sugar. An old man, he would persuade himself that he is for ever young. Shaken and diseased by his excesses, he is so exuberant with life that he seems to stand for the indestructibility of matter. No wonder he exacted from Dr. Johnson what is perhaps the only apostrophe in his edition of Shakespeare: 'But Falstaff unimitated, unimitable Falstaff, how shall I describe thee?'

To an Elizabethan the play upon words was not merely an elegance of style and a display of wit; it was also a means of emphasis and an instrument of persuasion. An argument might be conducted from step to step—and in the pamphleteers it often is—by a series of puns. The genius of the language encouraged them. 'So significant are our words,' writes Richard Carew, 'that amongst them sundry single ones serve to express divers things; as by *Bill* are meant a weapon, a scroll, and a bird's beak; by *Grave*, sober, a tomb, and to carve.'[24] And we remember Mercutio's dying jest—which is so much more than a jest— 'Ask for me to-morrow, and you shall find me a grave man.' The rich ambiguities of the language were used not merely for fun. Falstaff can jest: 'I would my means were greater, and my waist slenderer'; while in the additions to *The Spanish Tragedy* Hieronimo, in great agony of mind, can implore 'infective night' to 'Grid in my waste of grief with thy large darkness'. So in the famous lines of Lady Macbeth

> If he do bleed,
> I'll gild the faces of the grooms withal,
> For it must seem their guilt

the play upon words is no jest put in to enhance the horror of the scene, nor does it suggest hysteria, for at this point in the play Lady Macbeth is mistress of herself and of the situation. It underlines her determination, it is in Coleridge's words an 'effectual intensive of passion',[25] and it gives to her departure from the stage something of the emphasis and finality of a rhyming couplet.

I have said that the Elizabethans sometimes conducted an argument from step to step by a series of verbal quibbles. In Shakespeare the progression is often indirect and involuntary. This was noticed by Walter Whiter, a friend of Porson's, in his *Specimen of a Commentary on Shakspeare Containing I. Notes on As You Like It. II. An Attempt to Explain and Illustrate Various Passages, on a New Principle of Criticism derived from Mr Locke's Doctrine of the Association of Ideas* (1794), a book which anticipates in a most interesting way much modern work on Shakespeare's imagery. Whiter showed among other things how the images in which Shakespeare's train of thought is clothed may be suggested to his unconscious mind sometimes by similarities of sound, sometimes by words with an equivocal meaning, 'though the signification, in which they are really applied, has never any reference and often no similitude to that which caused their association'.

Whiter's most elaborate researches, in part still unpublished, were made upon the words and images which came to Shakespeare's mind, often involuntarily, from association with the theatre and with masques and pageantry. What is perhaps his most interesting discovery relates to the nexus of images which in varying combinations recurs in play after play to express disgust at false flattery and fawning obsequiousness, a nexus represented by Antony's

> The hearts
> *That spaniel'd me at heels,* to whom I gave
> Their wishes, do *discandy, melt* their *sweets*
> On blossoming Caesar.

But the passage which started Whiter on his inquiries was from the speech in which Apemantus upbraids Timon 'with the contrast between his past and present condition':

> What, think'st
> That the bleak air, thy boisterous *chamberlain,*
> Will put thy *shirt* on *warm*? Will these *moist* trees,
> That have outlived the eagle, page thy heels,
> And skip when thou point'st out?

Hanmer in 1744 had read 'moss'd trees', remembering perhaps the description of the oak in *As You Like It* 'whose boughs were moss'd with age'; and in this reading he has been followed not indeed by the *Oxford Dictionary*[26] but by most, if not all, editors. To make a participial adjective of the past participle 'moss'd', where the metre did not accommodate itself to 'mossy', was not beyond the capacity of any Elizabethan, particularly of Shakespeare, yet there is no evidence that any writer did this before Hanmer did it for the purpose of his emendation. But the seventh canon of criticism for an editor of Shakespeare is, according to Thomas Edwards, that "he may find out obsolete words, or coin new ones; and put them in the place of such as he does not like or does not understand'. By changing 'moist' to 'moss'd' the editors have given the passage a meaning the very opposite to that which Shakespeare intended. The emphasis in *Timon* is not on aged trees. The bleak air, Apemantus means, the trees whose strength is such that they have withstood the harshness of nature longer than the long-lived eagle, the cold brook, the naked creatures of nature, these will not flatter Timon. Whiter did not see that 'moist' in this passage bears the meaning 'full of sap', 'pithy'; but he did see that by an unconscious asssociation of ideas the image of the chamberlain putting his master's shirt on 'warm' or 'aired' impressed the opposite word 'moist' or 'unaired' upon the imagination of the poet, and that while 'moss'd' may be the more elegant epithet, what Shakespeare wrote and intended was 'moist'.[27]

'In the fictions, the thoughts, and the language of the poet,' Whiter writes, 'you may ever mark the deep and unequivocal traces of the age in which he lived, of the employments in which he was engaged, and of the various objects which excited his passions or arrested his attention.' Later and more systematic inquirers have proved, what the researches of Whiter suggest, that the great bulk of Shakespeare's images is taken from everyday things, from the goings-on of familiar life, images as familiar as the chamberlain putting his master's shirt on warm, or that image of heaven peeping 'through the blanket of the dark' which excited Johnson's risibility but does not excite ours.[28] Remoter images there are, for example the simile—to Pope 'an unnatural excursion'—in which Othello likens his determination for revenge to the Pontic sea

> Whose icy current and compulsive course
> Ne'er feels retiring ebb, but keeps due on
> To the Propontic and the Hellespont.

But usually the images are images from sights and sounds and experiences of a kind that came home immediately to the senses of his audience, and even in Othello's simile the emphasis is not on the remote geographical names, as it might have been in Marlowe, but on a natural phenomenon readily grasped by a people that used sea and river as the Elizabethans did. Owing to Shakespeare's instinct for what was permanent and central, his images are perhaps less often obscure than those of some of his contemporaries, but it must sometimes happen that what was obvious to the groundlings of the Globe Theatre because they had seen it with their own eyes or heard it with their own ears becomes apparent to us only after painful research. I take an example from a puzzling passage in *Love's Labour's Lost*. Berowne and the King of Navarre have broken their oaths to renounce love, and when the third perjurer Longaville is unmasked, Berowne observes:

> Thou makest the triumviry, the corner-cap of society,
> The shape of Love's Tyburn that hangs up simplicity.

What image did 'corner-cap' call up in the minds of Shakespeare's audience and by what association of ideas did he proceed from 'corner-cap' to Tyburn? Corner-caps were worn in Shakespeare's time in the universities, in the church, and by the judges of the land, but by an injunction of 1559 these caps were always square, nor do I know of one scrap of evidence that Shakespeare could have seen in England the three-cornered cap which his image so clearly demands. But we may be very sure that a Catholic scholar, Dr. John Story, 'a Romish Canonical Doctor', wore 'a three-cornered cap'. Story was martyred at Tyburn on 1 June 1571, and the execution was recorded in the usual way by ballad, broadside, dying confession, and by pamphlets both official and unofficial. What impressed itself upon the memory of the people was the use in this execution of 'a new pair of Gallows made in triangle manner',[29] and for many a year Tyburn or the gallows was known as 'Dr. Story's corner-cap' or his 'triangle', or simply as his 'cap'. It is not likely that Shakespeare was thinking of Story or of his 'simplicity' or folly; it was sufficient that 'corner-cap' could be associated without difficulty with a triumviry and with Tyburn. Longaville, as the third member of the company or 'society', has made up the triumviry and so recalls the shape of the gallows upon which Love hangs these foolish men who have tried to escape from her in their little academe. To an archaeologist 350 years is a short span, but the historian of manners may find all in doubt after the passage of a generation.

I have mentioned paronomasia, and I have mentioned the image. Let me mention another figure in rhetoric much valued by the Elizabethans. It can best be introduced by quoting a speech made in the Parliament of 1601. After the member for Southwark had begun to speak, had shaken for very fear, stood still a while, and at length sat down, the member for Hereford made this speech on a bill to avoid double payments of debts:

> It is now my chance to speak something, and that without humming or hawing. I think this law is a good law; even reckoning makes long friends; as far goes the penny, as the penny's master. *Vigilantibus non dormientibus jura subveniunt.* Pay the reckoning over night, and you shall not be troubled in the morning. If ready money be *Mensura Publica,* let every man cut his coat according to his cloth. When his old suit is in the wain, let him stay till that his money bring a new suit in the increase. Therefore, I think the law to be good, and I wish it a good passage.[30]

If this were played upon a stage now—those of us who do not read Hansard will say—we could condemn it as an improbable fiction, and indeed Thomas Jones's speech, with its clusters of homely proverbs, is paralleled by many a speech put by the dramatists into the mouths of downright or simple characters; Downright in *Every Man in his Humour,* Basket Hilts in Jonson's only play of rustic humours, *A Tale of a*

Tub, and the goldsmith Touchstone in the citizenly *Eastward Ho* are as full of proverbs as an egg of meat. Shakespeare seldom uses proverbs in this way. He does, however, in two of his earliest plays, use the catch-phrase as a pointer to character or the lack of it, and the Elizabethans made no sharp distinction between catch-phrases and proverbs. Every age has its own catch-phrases, and in every age they are the staple of conversation among those whose wits barely cross the threshold of intelligence. Luce in *The Comedy of Errors* and Jaquenetta in *Love's Labour's Lost* have no conversation outside such pert, ready-made phrases as 'Lord! how wise you are!', 'When? can you tell?', 'With that face?', 'Fair weather after you'. There is a similar dialogue in Lyly's *Mother Bombie* which Shakespeare may be imitating. Lyly calls them 'all the odd blind phrases that help them that know not how to discourse'. Some of them have survived to this day with little change: 'The better for your asking', 'You are such another', 'And therewithal you waked', 'Yea, in my other hose,' and 'quoth you'. Some dramatists exploited the elementary humour which comes from the repetition of a catch-phrase, but in the first quarto of *Hamlet*—the doctrine is Shakespeare's if not the words—the clown is condemned who keeps one suit of jests, like 'You owe me a quarter's wages' or 'Your beer is sour'. The laugh it raised was too easy for Shakespeare, the label it attached to character too superficial, the character to which the label could be attached too shallow. Falstaff has no catch-phrases. His sentiments are a perpetual surprise.

There must still be many a proverb in Shakespeare which his audience recognized as proverbial and which we do not. 'The nature of his work', says Johnson, 'required the use of the common colloquial language, and consequently admitted many phrases allusive, elliptical, and proverbial, such as we speak and hear every hour without observing them; and of which, being now familiar, we do not suspect that they can ever grow uncouth, or that, being now obvious, they can ever seem remote.'[31] When Lovell in *Henry VIII* speaks of 'fool and feather', and the Princess in *Love's Labour's Lost* asks 'What plume of feathers is he that indited this letter?', the collocation was already so well established as to have become proverbial, and for many generations 'he has a feather in his cap' was a periphrasis for a fool. Again, when Falstaff says that if Bardolph were any way given to virtue he would swear by his face and his oath would be 'By this fire, that's God angel', it has been supposed that Shakespeare was borrowing from Chapman in whose *Blind Beggar of Alexandria* a similar expression is to be found. But he was drawing upon the proverbial stock of oaths—the saying is at least as old as the *Misogonus* of about 1570[32]—and his audience received that peculiar delight which comes from the apt application of an old saying to a modern instance, Bardolph's nose.

Sometimes we are left in doubt whether Shakespeare was using a proverb or inventing one. Was Portia's 'a light wife doth make a heavy husband'[33] proverbial or is it Shakespeare's punning variation of 'Light gains make heavy purses'? And when Dekker and Webster use the same sentiment in *Westward Ho*,[34] were they borrowing from Shakespeare or making use of proverbial stock?

Then there are many 'sentences' in Shakespere which are commonplaces of his age yet were never crystallized into a set proverbial form. Hamlet's 'there is nothing either good or bad, but thinking makes it so' is an example. Spenser's 'It is the mind that maketh good or ill' has been cited in evidence, and a closer parallel is found in *Politeuphuia, Wit's Commonwealth*, an anthology of 'sententiae' published in 1597: 'There is nothing grievous if the thought make it not'.[35] Whether Shakespeare kept a commonplace book like Jonson, Bacon, Webster, and most of his contemporaries, is not known. Long before the evidence was discovered by Charles Crawford, J. A. Symonds hinted that Webster kept one.[36] But in Shakespeare there are no ill-fitting joins which betray the borrower. He brings everything into a unity. In the anthology just mentioned we find 'Our good name ought to be more dear unto us than our life',[37] and the sentiment may be as old as civilized man; it is no temporary opinion; but when Iago says to Othello

> Good name in man and woman, dear my lord,
> Is the immediate jewel of their souls

the commonplace takes on a new meaning. The maxim is embedded in the evil in the play: it has become an essential part of a great design.

It is a little difficult to adjust ourselves to the seriousness with which the Elizabethans treated the proverb. Soon after Shakespeare's death it began to lose favour. The decline of the native and homely proverb is suggested by the preference of George Herbert for 'outlandish proverbs', which, in comparison, have 'too much feather and too little point',[38] or by Glanvill's attack on preachers who use 'vulgar Proverbs, and homely similitudes';[39] and before Swift made the graveyard of proverbs and catch-phrases which he called *Polite Conversation* proverbs had almost disappeared from polite literature. This change in taste happened long before Lord Chesterfield called them 'the flowers of the rhetoric of a vulgar man' and said that 'a man of fashion never has recourse to proverbs and vulgar aphorisms'.[40] But to an Elizabethan the proverb was not merely or mainly of use for clouting a hob-nailed discourse; it still retained its place as an important figure in rhetorical training, and the many sixteenth-century collectors and writers who acclimatized foreign proverbs to the English soil were hailed as benefactors who enriched the 'copy' of their native tongue. Proverbs were invaluable for amplifying a discourse, or they added grace and variety to wit-combats. Sometimes they are hardly distinguishable in kind or function from the 'sentence' and the 'example': as Richard Carew said, they prescribed 'under the circuit of a few syllables . . . sundry available caveats'.[41] Preachers, orators, wits, dramatists, found them excellent persuasion. They could strengthen an argument, for they contained in themselves the authority of experience—'it must needs be true what every one says'; they were vivid and epigrammatic so that they stuck in the mind when abstract precepts were forgotten; and the use of a homely proverb might put preacher and congregation, orator or dramatist and audience, upon a friendly and familiar footing, one with each other.

Of the great English poets only Chaucer makes so good use of proverbs as Shakespeare. The contrast between Shakespeare and Jonson is striking. On the title-page of his best and most popular comedy, *The Alchemist*, Jonson put the words:

> —Neque, me ut miretur turba, laboro:
> Contentus paucis lectoribus.

As he despised the 'green and soggy multitude', so he despised their collective wisdom. Ancient proverbs, he said, might illuminate 'A cooper's wit, or some such busy spark',[42] and they have their place in his comedies, but they could serve no serious function in the work of this robust and independent writer. In *Volpone* one proverb, and only one, stands out by reason of its position and the new turn which Jonson gives it. It is the last line of the scene in which the Fox departs in disguise to gloat over the discomfiture of his victims. 'Sir, you must look for curses', says Mosca, to which Volpone replies in one of Jonson's magnificent exits:

> Till they burst;
> The Fox fares ever best, when he is curst.

If we turn to *Sejanus* and *Catiline* we shall not be surprised to find a dearth of proverbs or even proverbial phrases.[43] Gnomic passages there are in plenty, and in the first quarto of *Sejanus* the reader's attention is directed to the tragedy's 'fullness and frequency of sentence' by inverted commas. But English proverbs he rigorously excluded

from the dignity of tragedy. His practice is of a piece with that fundamental contempt for the people which gives to his art so much of its
bent and bias. Of all ancient proverbs, he would most strenuously have
repudiated that which maintained that the voice of the people was the
voice of God. And when in his tragedies his verses 'break out strong
and deep in the mouth',[44] as they often do, they owe little or nothing
of their strength to colloquial English idiom.

In Shakespeare proverbs are used as rhetorical ornaments, as moral
sententiae, and occasionally as a means of building up character. From
Richard's dissimulations in *Henry VI, Part 3*, until he achieves his
throne in *Richard III*, old saws like 'I hear, yet say not much, but think
the more' come pat to his purpose, especially in sardonic aside. He
clothes his 'naked villany' with 'odd old ends'. In Faulconbridge, a
character that sees the worst, seems to approve of it, and follows the
best, bluntness and good humour are strongly marked in the first
scene by the proverbs that pour from his mouth, but as his character
is tested and proved by events his speech, while remaining direct and
vigorous, becomes less proverbial. Richard seeks popularity for his
own ends, Faulconbridge has a native disposition to it, while Coriolanus despises it. To him the 'vulgar wisdoms' of the people are contemptible.

> They said they were an-hungry; sigh'd forth proverbs,
> That hunger broke stone walls, that dogs must eat,
> That meat was made for mouths, that the gods sent not
> Corn for the rich men only: with these shreds
> They vented their complainings.

It is a little ironical that when Aufidius prophesies the doom of Coriolanus he does so with a couple of proverbs: 'One fire drives out one
fire; one nail, one nail.'

What the proverb meant to Shakespeare is best shown not by the
number and variety which he uses, although those so far identified are
indeed many, but by his use of them in the gravest and greatest passages in his plays. Proverbs are mingled with folk-tale and ballad in
the snatches, half sense and half nothing, spoken by the mad
Ophelia: 'They say the owl was a baker's daughter. Lord, we know
what we are, but know not what we may be.' In *King Lear* Shakespeare puts into the mouth of the Fool the silliest catch-phrase—'Cry
you mercy, I took you for a joint-stool'—with poignant effect, and the
Fool's last speech is a reference to the homely, ironical proverb: 'You
would make me go to bed at noon.' Perhaps the most famous proverb
in the whole of Shakespeare is that of the cat who would eat fish but

would not wet her feet, to which Lady Macbeth refers in pluming up her husband's faltering will; but there are others in this play as striking and powerful in their operation. Keats has said that 'nothing ever becomes real till it is experienced. Even a proverb is no proverb to you till your life has illustrated it.'[45] Macbeth has indeed tested the truth of the line, 'It will have blood: they say, blood will have blood', and with what potency is the proverb charged. As moving is the 'what's done is done' of Lady Macbeth. It is one of the many thoughts and deeds which recurr to her broken mind in the sleep-walking scene —'What's done cannot be undone: to bed, to bed, to bed.' They give to her prose the concentration and associative force of poetry.

I have mentioned Jonson's care to exclude popular proverbs from his tragedies, and the reason lies not only in his conception of tragedy as something 'high and aloof'[46] but also in his strict sense of decorum. Shakespeare interprets the Renaissance doctrine of decorum more liberally. His decorum is dramatic, not historical. His tact in translating the manners of the ancient world to the modern stage is superb. He concentrates on what is permanent in spiritual and human values, and if clocks strike and doublets go unbraced, there is no offence for he never sacrifices the dignity of his theme by introducing the trivialities of the present or the pedantries of the past. He is as far from the revolting anachronisms of Heywood's *Rape of Lucrece, a true Roman Tragedy,* in which a Roman senator sings a ditty

> Shall I woe the lovely Molly,
> She's so fair, so fat, so jolly, . . .

as from Jonson's attempts at exact reconstruction of the manners and sentiments of the old Roman world. As the translators of the Bible did not hesitate, when necessary, to change the remote for the familiar, the unknown for the known—the musical instruments of Israel for the cornets, flutes, harps, and sackbuts of Elizabethan England, or the vanities of the attire of Israelitish women for the mufflers, the bonnets, the mantles, the wimples, the crisping pins of the sixteenth century—so Shakespeare writes of the entry of Coriolanus into Rome in words which are also applicable to the triumphal entry of James into the City of London:

> the kitchen malkin pins
> Her richest lockram 'bout her reechy neck,
> Clambering the walls to eye him: stalls, bulks, windows,
> Are smother'd up, leads fill'd and ridges hors'd
> With variable complexions, all agreeing
> In earnestness to see him.

Unlike Jonson, Shakespeare thinks nothing unclean that can deepen and widen his tragic art. He works not by exclusion but by bringing all aspects of life into a sense of order. Other men of his day, Webster or Middleton, tried to be as all-embracing, but the Shakespearian unity is incomparably more sensitive and more closely articulated. The poet's power reveals itself, says Coleridge, in the balance or reconciliation of opposite or discordant qualities. Only the disinterested artist who has no cause to serve (for the moment) except his art can bring himself to balance or reconcile such discordant and opposite qualities as are revealed, for example, in *Antony and Cleopatra*. In this many-sided play he seems to balance nobility and self-indulgence, renunciation and vanity, the glory and the corruption of the flesh, the greatness and the pettiness of the world. In the scene on Pompey's galley, where if anywhere in Shakespeare we find the diction and conduct of common life, the famous triumvirate, 'These three world-sharers, these competitors', drown their schemings and enmities in drink until Lepidus, the weak member of the axis, is carried drunk away, and the first and second parts of the world sing the refrain 'Cup us, till the world go round'. Is this a play then about a set of fools and rogues struggling for power in a world which does not signify? It is, and it would be less rich if it were not. But we remember how these baser elements are balanced by others, and as the play ends it is all 'fire and air'.

I have tried to suggest a few of the ways in which Shakespeare's drama is continually irrigated by the diction of common life. But it does not remain the diction of common life. It is transmuted, and with what nobility let us remind ourselves from his greatest play. When the tempests in Lear's mind and in nature have spent themselves, when 'the great rage . . . is kill'd in him', there is a simplicity in his speech which persists to the end. It is no mannered simplicity such as we sometimes find in Webster when he is trying to write like Shakespeare; but it is as if the fire of genius had reduced language to its elements. The monosyllabic base which some of his contemporaries thought the misfortune of our language he turns into glory. In these sentences there is no gap between the inspiration and the expression, between the mind and the hand, and without wastage they gather up together all the love, terror, and pity that have gone before:

> Pray, do not mock me:
> I am a very foolish fond old man,
> Fourscore and upward, not an hour more nor less;
> And, to deal plainly,
> I fear I am not in my perfect mind.

Methinks I should know you and know this man;
Yet I am doubtful; for I am mainly ignorant
What place this is, and all the skill I have
Remembers not these garments, nor I know not
Where I did lodge last night. Do not laugh at me;
For, as I am a man, I think this lady
To be my child Cordelia.

These are among the words and rhythms in which Shakespeare expresses his vision of good and evil. It is no system of morality which remains in the mind. The play provides symbols for the experience which it gives us—a wheel of fire, or incense of the gods upon such sacrifices—but there are no words to express our experience, or only Shakespeare's words.

NOTES

Annual Shakespeare Lecture of the British Academy, read April 23, 1941.

[1] *Trolius and Cressida*, I. iii. 7-21: conflux, tortive, protractive, persistive.

[2] T. C., *A Pleasant and Delightful History of Galesus, Cymon, and Iphigenia* (1560?), sig. A6.

[3] Dion Chrysostom, translated by A. O. Prickard (*Longinus on the Sublime*, 1906, pp. 93-4).

[4] *Coleridge's Shakespearean Criticism*, ed. T. M. Raysor (1930), i. 149-50.

[5] *Works* (1910), ii. 3-4.

[6] *Love's Labour's Lost*, III. i. 15, and L. Wager, *Mary Magdalene* (1566), l. 585.

[7] *Hamlet*, III. i. 59, and Sir R. Barckley, *Of the Felicity of Man* (1598), pp. 147, 275.

[8] *Hamlet*, II. ii. 321, and *O.E.D.*, s.v. sear, *sb.*[1] I b.

[9] Hayward Townshend, *Historical Collections* (1680), p. 80.

[10] *Unpublished Letters of S. T. Coleridge*, ed. E. L. Griggs (1932), i. 163.

[11] *Imaginary Conversations*, 'Samuel Johnson and John Horne Tooke' (*Works*, ed. T. Earle Welby, 1927, v. 5).

[12] *The Plain Man's Pathway to Heaven* (1601), p. 165.

[13] *Remains* (1605), p. 28.

[14] Townshend, p. 263.

[15] *Shakespeare's England*, ii. 559.

[16] 'By and by' and 'anon' could still mean 'at once', and they sometimes bear their older meaning in the Bible of 1611; but in Shakespeare they can be given the modern meaning of 'soon'. In the 'anon, anon, sir' of the drawer the promise seems to bear the older meaning and the performance the modern.

[17] Cf. George Herbert, *A Priest to the Temple*, ch. 7.

[18] *Merope* (1858), p. xlv.

[19] The Elizabethan equivalent of 'every schoolboy knows'. Cf. F. Hering, *A Modest Defence* (1604), p. 27: 'a meane scholler of *Mul*-

casters schoole will easily tell him that . . .'.

[20] 'Chaucer and the Rhetoricians' (*Proceedings of the British Academy*, 1926, p. 97).

[21] See Note A.

[22] *Remains* (1605), p. 27.

[23] *Directions for Speech and Style*, ed. H. H. Hudson (1935), p. 16.

[24] *Elizabethan Critical Essays*, ed. G. Gregory Smith, 1904, ii. 288.

[25] Op. cit. i. 150.

[26] See under 'mossed', *ppl. a.*, and 'moist', *adj.* 2.

[27] Whiter, pp. 70, 73, 81-2, 138-40. See Note B.

[28] *Macbeth*, I. v. 53; *Rambler*, no. 168. It is a judgement on Johnson that in this essay he should give Lady Macbeth's speech to Macbeth.

[29] *A Declaration of the Life and Death of John Story, late a Romish Canonical Doctor by Profession* (1571), sig. C2. See Note C.

[30] Townshend, p. 283.

[31] *Proposals* (1756), p. 5.

[32] III. i. 240: 'By this fier that bournez thats gods aungell'.

[33] *Merchant of Venice*, v. i. 130.

[34] v. iii.

[35] p. 59b.

[36] 'Vittoria Accoramboni' (*Italian Byways*, 1883, p. 179): 'The sentences, which seem at first sight copied from a commonplace book, are found to be appropriate'; C. Crawford, *Collectanea*, First (1906) and Second (1907) Series.

[37] p. 106b.

[38] *Baconiana* (1679), ed. T. Tenison, p. 93: 'the *Jacula Prudentum*, in Mr. *Herbert*; which latter some have been bold to accuse as having too much Feather, and too little Point.' So Fuller may have thought, but not Jeremy Taylor, who adds Italian proverbs to the margins of *Holy Living*.

[39] *An Essay Concerning Preaching* (1678), p. 77.

[40] Letter to his son, 27 September 1749.

[41] Op. cit. ii. 288.

[42] *A Tale of a Tub*, Prologue.

[43] See Note D.

[44] *News from the New World* (1640, ii. 42).

[45] *Letters*, ed. M. Buxton Forman (1935), p. 318.

[46] *The Poetaster*, 'To the Reader', 1. 238, and again in the 'Ode to Himself' in *Underwoods*.

Supplementary Notes

A

Image in its rhetorical sense is now understood to include metaphor and simile, and I use it so here; but in the sixteenth century the sense was much narrower. Quintilian (v. xi. 24) in discussing 'similitudo' refers to the kind of comparison called by the Greeks εἰκών, which expresses the appearance of things and persons, and advises a more sparing use of it in oratory than of those comparisons or similes which help to prove a point. Something of this survives by what is no doubt a long and devious route in Richard Sherry's *Treatise of Schemes and Tropes* (*c.* 1550), sig. F6: '*Icon*, called of the latines *Imago*, an Image in Englyshe, is muche lyke to a similitude, and if you declare it is a similitude: as if you saye: As an Asse wyll not be driuen from her meat, no not with a club, vntyl she be full: no more wil a warriour reste from murther vntyll he hath fylled his mynd with it. This is a similitude: but if you saye that a man flewe vpon his enemies like a dragon, or lyke a lyon, it is an Image. Howbeit an Image serueth rather to euidence or grauitie, or iocunditie, then to a profe. There is also a general comparacion, speciallye in the kynde demonstratiue, person wyth person, and one thing with an other, for praise or dispraise.' As in Quintilian the examples of 'similitudo' are usually in the elaborate 'ut . . . ita (sic)' form, so in Sherry and usually in Francis Meres's anthology of similes, *Palladis Tamia* (1598), they are expanded into the 'As . . . so' form. This is perhaps what Sherry means by 'if you declare', i.e. 'set out your comparison in full'. In his *Treatise of Schemes and Tropes* and also in his *Treatise of the Figures of Grammar and Rhetoric* (1555), pp. 53 and verso, Sherry's discussion of the image follows his discussion of the example, which he calls comparison with an act done, and his discussion of the similitude or 'comparacion', which he calls comparison with something that is dumb or lifeless. His treatment and instances of these figures correspond in part to those found in the *Epitome Troporum ac Schematum* of Johannes Susenbrotus. The instances of the rhetorical use of image, resemblance, and icon given above are earlier than those in the *O.E.D.*, where the earliest instance of image is dated 1676 and of icon and resemblance 1589: the rhetorical sense of comparation is not given, although comparison in the sense of simile goes back to Wyclif.

B

As he acknowledged on his titlepage, Whiter based his work on the doctrine of association of ideas in Locke's *Essay concerning Human Understanding*, especially the passage quoted on p. 64: 'Ideas, that in themselves are not at all of kin, come to be so united in men's minds, that it is very hard to separate them; they always keep in company, and the one no sooner at any time comes into the understanding, but its associate appears with it; and if they are more than two which are thus united, the whole gang always inseparable shew

themselves together.' By this involuntary association of ideas the poet is supplied with words and ideas suggested to the mind by a principle of union unperceived by himself and independent of the subject to which they are applied (p. 68). Whiter saw and illustrated the value of the principle for the establishment of Shakespeare's text, for the interpretation of his meaning, for deciding upon works of disrupted authorship, and for the light it might throw on 'the employments in which he was engaged, and . . . the various objects which excited his passions or arrested his attention' (p. 73). He even hinted at the presence of recurrent imagery: 'There is scarcely a play of our Author, where we do not find some favourite vein of metaphor or allusion by which it is distinguished' (p. 124). The whole tendency of his work, both in the commentary on certain passages in *As You Like It* and in the more general and more important essay which follows, was to support the readings of the original texts against the emendations of the editors. Many of the readings in *As You Like It* which he defended have been restored by modern editors, though seldom for the same reasons. Whiter is not uniformly happy in his arguments. He had in his nature 'much labour and shrewdness, with a considerable share of credulity' (Francis Jeffrey in a review of Whiter's *Etymologicon Magnum* in the *Monthly Review*, June and July, 1802, cited in the *D.N.B.*), and it is unfortunate that he should have chosen to illustrate the importance of his principle in deciding upon works of disputed authorship by attempting to prove that the Rowley poems, apart from some impurities introduced by the transcriber, are the genuine progeny of a medieval poet. 'Is he a sound man?' is the question asked of

Whiter the philologist in *Lavengro* (ch. 24), and the answer is: 'Why, as to that, I scarcely know what to say; he has got queer notions in his head . . . upon the whole, I should not call him altogether a sound man.'

In his *Etymologicon Magnum* (1800, p. 300) Whiter referred to himself *sine nomine* as 'an obscure writer, who in "A Specimen of a Commentary on Shakespeare" has laboured to enlarge the boundaries of Criticism, by applying a metaphysical principle to the elucidation of Poetic imagery, and figurative description'. He was disappointed with the reception of his book. From an extract from his Journal inserted in his interleaved copy of the *Specimen,* now in the Cambridge University Library, it appears that even his friends were indifferent, an indifference which proceeded perhaps more from 'want of thought than want of feeling. But what is *feeling* but thought?' One of them, however, Raine, a lawyer, considered the book 'as able to form an æra in the style of our language, by which the strength of expression and the grace of composition are preserved without the apparent and perpetually occurring artifice of Johnson and Gibbon'. His diffuse style is overpraised here, as his learning is overpraised in W. B. Donne's statement that he was 'equal to Steevens in acuteness, in black-letter learning to Malone, and immeasurably superior to them both in his perception of the meaning and his sensibility to the metre of Shakespeare' (*British and Foreign Review,* 1844, xvii. 231).

Coleridge and the critics of his generation ignored Whiter as they ignored Maurice Morgann, although both writers anticipated the romantic criticism of Shakespeare if only by their insistence upon the importance of the less conscious workings of the mind. Later editors and critics would not have left Whiter so severely alone if his work had been more often quoted in the Boswell-Malone Variorum edition of 1821. Four of his remarks are quoted or referred to in the commentary on *As You Like It,* but his work left no mark upon the text of that edition. We look in vain for any reference to his criticism of Hanmer's 'moss'd trees'; perhaps Malone would have agreed with the reviewer who wrote: 'From such associations good Lord deliver us! . . . We wish Mr. Whiter would learn to separate his ideas, instead of associating them' (*The Critical Review,* 1795, xiii. 100).

So far as I know, R. W. Babcock was the first modern writer to call attention to Whiter's work on Shakespeare (*The Genesis of Shakespeare Idolatry,* 1931), although he hardly does justice to Whiter's genuine merits. The rediscovery of Whiter has taken place at the moment when the main preoccupation of critics is with Shakespeare's language and imagery, as the rediscovery of Morgann took place when criticism was still mainly preoccupied with Shakespeare's characters. J. Isaacs noticed Whiter's interest in the recurrent association of candy and fawning dogs in *A Companion to Shakespeare Studies* (1934), p. 313. For modern discussions of this nexus of images by writers who did not know that Whiter had to some extent anticipated them, see E. E. Kellett, *Suggestions* (1923), pp. 72-3; G. H. W. Rylands, *Words and Poetry* (1928), pp. 176-8; Caroline F. E. Spurgeon, *Shakespeare's Iterative Imagery* (1931), pp. 13-17, and *Shakespeare's Imagery* (1935), pp. 194-9.

C

In the Arden edition of *Love's Labour's Lost* (1906) H. C. Hart called attention to the expression 'Dr. Story's cap' for Tyburn, and asked the question whether three-cornered caps were worn in Elizabethan England. But he did not notice that a special triangular gallows was used for the first time at Tyburn at Story's execution. Some recollection of this was in the mind of Joseph Healey, translator of Hall's *Mundus Alter et Idem*, when to the words 'hee is forthwith condemned to commence at *Doctor Stories* cappe' he adds in the margin: 'Tiborne was built for him, as some say' (*The Discovery of a New World, c.* 1609, p, 225).

The history of the square cap is discussed by N. F. Robinson, 'The *Pileus Quadratus*' in the *Transactions of the St. Paul's Ecclesiological Society*, v (1905), pp. 1-42, and by E. C. Clark, 'College Caps and Doctors' Hats' in the *Archaeological Journal*, lxi (1904), pp. 33-73. Much is heard of the square cap as a relic of Popish apparel, both in the Vestiarian controversy of the early years of Elizabeth's reign and in the Marprelate controversy. Martin Marprelate often writes contemptuously of 'cater-caps'. And to take a later example Edmund Bolton, in a passage very like some speeches of Candido's in Dekker's *Honest Whore*, part 2, I. iii, and derived perhaps from a common source, observes that 'the square capp is retained not onely in the *Vniuersities*, but also abroad among vs, as well by Ecclesiasticall persons in high places, as by Iudges of the land' (*The City's Advocate*, 1629, p. 41). Philip Stubbes refers to the symbolism which was by some attached to the *pileus quadratus* of the Catholic Church in these words: 'The cornered cappe, say these misterious fellows [the Papists], doth signifie, and represent the whole monarchy of the world, East, West, North, and South, the gouernment whereof

standeth vpon them, as the cappe doth vppon their heades' (*Anatomy of Abuses*, 1583, part 2, ed. Furnivall, p. 115).

In another place (part I, p. 69) Stubbes compares women's 'Lattice cappes with three hornes, three corners I should say' to 'the forked cappes of Popishe Priestes', and just possibly the reference may be to the Italian three-horned biretta, a post-Reformation variation of the four-horned or four-cornered cap (Robinson, 6, and Clark, 36). The new triangular gallows might well have been named after Story even if he had worn a square cap, but if as a 'Romish Canonical Doctor' he was known to wear a three-cornered cap, the coincidence between the shape of the strange cap and the strange gallows would make the invention of Tyburn's new name irresistible. An expression of a similar kind—'Tyburn tippet' for a hangman's rope—is at least as old as Latimer (1549); the phrase appears in the margin of John Cornet's *Admonition to Doctor Story* (1571), a broadside in verse.

The earliest use I have met with of 'cornered' or 'corner' cap is in Gascoigne's *Supposes* (acted 1566), v. iv. 24: 'we will teache maister Doctor to weare a cornerd cappe of a new fashion', where the jest is the usual one of cuckoldry. Lyly, in his *Pap with an Hatchet* of 1589 (Bond III. 401. 31), provides the earliest example yet found of the association of Tyburn with a corner-cap: 'Theres one with a lame wit, which will not weare a foure cornerd cap, then let him put on Tiburne, that hath but three corners.' I have not met with the expression 'Dr. Story's cap' before 1592 (*Defence of Cony-Catching*, ed. G. B. Harrison, p. 6), but it may well have got into print earlier. A late example is in *The Wandering Jew* (1640), where Tyburn is said to wear 'a Three Cornered Cappe' and the criminal to 'ride Westward, at the Sheriffs charges, on Doctor Stories wooden horse of *Troy*'.

Professor Dover Wilson explains 'the corner-cap of society' as a reference to the 'black cap' of the judge. The difficulties are: (1) A corner-cap was the wear of the learned professions, don, divine, as well as judge, and there is nothing in the context to indicate a reference to the corner-cap of a judge. (2) I know of no passage in which corner-cap is used in the sense of the sentence-cap. (*O.E.D.'s* earliest example of 'black cap' is from *Oliver Twist*; it does not give 'sentence-cap'.) According to Robinson (p. 7), in the sixteenth and seventeenth centuries judges wore their corner-caps in the courts at Westminster and during circuit sat in church in them: the wearing of them was not reserved to the sole occasion of pronouncing the death-sentence. (3) The judge's cap was square, and Shakespeare's image requires a three-cornered cap; there are not 'four woodcocks in a dish' until Dumaine has joined the triumvirate.

D

In the whole of *Sejanus* and *Catiline* I find only three homely, familiar proverbs—'laugh and lie down' (*Catiline*, iii. 697), and in oblique reference 'a woman's reason —because it is so' (*Catiline*, ii. 57-

8) and 'Still waters run deep' (*Catiline*, iii. 571-2). The first two are to be found in those scenes of scornful comedy between Fulvia, Galla, and Sempronia which Dryden's Eugenius thought 'admirable of their kind, but of an ill mingle with the rest'. In addition there are two proverbs of a more sententious kind. 'He threatens many, that hath iniur'd one' (*Sejanus*, ii. 476) gets into Apperson's *English Proverbs* from Gabriel Harvey's *Marginalia* (ed. G. C. Moore Smith, 1913, p. 101), where it is found in the form 'He threatenith many, That hurtith any', Harvey took it from the lost *Flowers of Philosophy* (1572) of Sir Hugh Platt, who could have found it in Publilius Syrus. A 'sentence' more often met with is 'Great honors are great burdens' (*Catiline*, iii. 1), of which examples are given in Latin (e.g. *Onus est honos*) and English in Tilley's *Elizabethan Proverb Lore* (1926), no. 346. I suppose that none of the English writers who observed 'watch the watcher' (*Catiline*, iii. 108) or exclaimed 'O age and manners' (*Catiline*, iv. 190) did so without remembering the originals. Of proverbial phrases—to limit these conveniently if mechanically to those mentioned by Apperson or in the *Oxford Book of Proverbs*—I notice only 'to fear no colours' (*Sejanus*, i. 285), 'to have in the wind' (*Sejanus*, ii. 406), and, doubtfully, an oblique reference to 'take counsel of one's pillow' (*Catiline*, ii. 319).

Style and Certitude

Don Cameron Allen

During the early part of the Renaissance in England we come on man universally merry for the last time in the modern world. He dresses like a gamecock and like Chanticleer calls up the sun with his crowing. He struts in the lanes of London, in bower and in hall; and he delights to make grand spectacles at which he is both the observer and the observed. The pen of his major chronicler, Edward Hall, drips color to the five senses and the twentieth century reader is conquered by the passion and the sound. It seems to us that man was, for a moment, putting aside the ancient doubts, that he was becoming more certain of himself, and that a bright new world was seemingly parading before him. His greatest joy was that everything seemed to be fenced about with a perdurability which appeared to have all the blessings of philosophy, politics, and theology. Then suddenly it is all over. There was no noise, no tumult; it was an apocalyptic end. One day they were eating and drinking and listening to the lutanist and the next day they were struck with infinite despair.

No one can say what happened; the age itself was perplexed to know. The transcendental background had collapsed and the disease of reason had set in. With the spread of this infection, the old feeling of personal certitude which depended on the stability of the transcendal norm began to depart. The dikes of philosophy had been cut again, and once more the skeptic's sea rolled westward in Europe. Men now began to talk about life as if it were a dream, something between a sleep and a sleep. Vives compares existence to dreaming that one is rich for a day, and Spenser, as well as his model Du Bellay, perceives in dreams the transitoriness of things. The dreamer of Vives takes dramatic flesh in Shakespeare's *The Taming of the Shrew,* and

John Donne pondering the intricacies of love represents himself as more tormented and more satisfied by what he dreams than by what he knows. The situation of the sensitive European is pathetically summed up by a speaker in Calderon's significantly-named play, *Life is a Dream:*

> What is life? A thing that seems,
> A mirage that falsely gleams
> Phantom joy, delusive rest
> And even dreams themselves are dreams.[1]

Under these circumstances, it is not surprising that Descartes, seeking certainty and attempting to purge his mind of doubts, considered whether or not he was burdened with a dream. At almost the same hour that Descartes was scrutinizing this possibility, Sir Thomas Browne was writing, "it is not a melancholy conceit to think that we are all asleep in this world, and that the conceits of this life are as mere dreams."[2] But Browne was one of the few intellectuals of this age who were able to find a point of rest between reason and faith and so he adds, "to those of the next."

In time, science and the revised theology of the nineteenth century propped up temporarily the sagging backdrop of certainty and so put apart for the while the awful maxim that "we are such stuff as dreams are made on and our little life is rounded with a sleep." But before this progression occurred, much had happened both to the heart and brain of man. The brain was saying dreary things to the heart and the heart was beating faster and more irregularly. The things that men said and the way in which they said them changed, too. The tone and accent of verse and prose alter, for the brain was saying dreary words to the heart and men could hear their hearts pounding in their brains. The phenomenon is of great contemporary interest for it almost convinces one that there is a fixed coincidence between the degree of an artist's positiveness in philosophy and the mode of his expression. The evidences of this spiritual distress and its consequent expression may be observed in the prose of the Jacobeans.

The prose of the joyous period of the early English Renaissance was humanistic prose, the child of a blissful marriage between the Latinity of Cicero, in all of its copiousness and measure, and the native English manner that had been purified by More and his associates of what Ascham called "its augmentations" and "indenture language." Ascham, too, added his stone to the new structure. He might hold for a style that "rose and fell" with the matter and he might praise More for perfecting the historical language of the English; nonetheless, it was his influence that turned many Englishmen to practising as apes of Cicero and that settled the formal prose style of Tudor thinkers, the serious style that culminates in the soaring periods of Hooker. All of this happened in the face of Erasmus' early attack on those who would rather be disciples of Cicero than saints of God. And though we now know that Erasmus was thinking of linguistic purists when he wrote his *Ciceronianus* and of the stylistic procedure only obliquely, we can estimate the shock that this work caused by remembering that the knights of Cicero, as they named themselves, rode at once to the master's aid. On the Continent, Scaliger and Longolius wrote acid replies in long sentences; and in England, Gabriel Harvey attempted to distinguish the true Cicero from the false in his imitation of the polemic of Erasmus. The English opposition to Cicero began, to the contrary, in a sly and cautious manner. Ascham, writing almost in the year of Muretus' declaration of independence, was unaware of the French position; he even tries to moderate between the dead Erasmus and the dead Longolius: "the one seemth to give overmoch, the other over little, to him whom they both loved."[3]

The story of Muretus' and Lipsius' criticism of the style of Cicero and their championing of the rhetorical technique of Tacitus and Seneca has been told in a series of magisterial essays by the late Professor Croll,[4] but the ground for the new direction was more thoroughly prepared in England than we have been inclined to admit. Early in the seventeenth century, the epistles of Seneca and Lipsius were seriously threatening the long reign of Cicero's letters in the public schools. One cannot imagine a schoolmaster like Ascham pausing long over Lipsius' letter to Petrus Villerius in which the Belgian humanist expounds his views with a Judas kiss: "Ciceronem amo. Olim etiam imitatus sum: alius mihi sensus nunc viro."[5] If this sort of heresy could be glossed in the lower forms of the Elizabethan grammar school, orthodoxy must have been breached long before. Such seems to have been the case, for not only are the adjectives with which Muretus and Lipsius hallowed Seneca and Tacitus to be found in English mouths prior to the great vernacular imitation, but a sturdy opposition seems also to have been gathering force.

Thomas Gataker praises the style of Seneca as "eximia, utilia, fortia, sublimia, et arguta, subtiliaque"; and Camden, after calling attention to Tacitus' contracted diction and his "ictus sententiarum," says that there is more to be understood in him than one reads.[6] At an earlier stage of the discussion, Harvey mentions "weightie and speedie Sallust, deep Tacitus, sharp Seneca." The state of affairs is also revealed by the early opposition. Before the close of the sixteenth century, Sergeant Hoskins wrote in his *Directions* that the *sententiae* are better for the bench than the bar.

> Then of all others, why would the writers of these days imprison themselves in the straitness of these maxims? It makes their style like *arena sine calce,* as one saith of such a writer, and doth not he vouchsafe to use them that called them posies for rings? If it be a matter of short direction for life and action, or notes for memory, I intend not to discredit this new trick. But otherwise he that hath a long journey to walk in that pace is like a horse that overreacheth and yet goes slow.[7]

Two years later, Robert Johnson complains about the arrogance of the Neo-stoics which makes them "busie-headed and turbulent," and of the "stranglie brief sentences" of Tacitus.[8]

By the time of James' coronation, this new way of writing had become rooted in English soil. It was the style of the rationalists, the style of the doubters, the style of those who were looking for the causes of things. Here and there, a few meditative writers like Richard Greenham and John Weemes or a few reactionary and well-settled men like David Persons or Thomas Sheafe still clung to the Ciceronian period, but a great Ciceronian is hard to find. Now one must not avoid the seemingly contradictory fact that this rationalistic style crept into the pulpit with Bishop Andrews and was fondled by Dean Donne, Bishop Hall, and others. With the possible exception of Donne, all of these men were certain of their mission and quite capable of sweeping away the doubts that cluster with a dogmatic broom. The momentary preference of some clerics for this style is not too difficult to understand.

There is an elocutionary force in the fragmentation of the Senecan line that is lost in the long sough of the period; or to put the case in the words of Owen Felltham:

> Long and distended clauses, are both tedious to the ear, and difficult for their retaining. A sentence well couched takes both the sense and the understanding. I love not those Cart-rope speeches that are longer than the memory of man can fathom.[9]

But there are other reasons. The attraction of Seneca for the Jacobean divine resided more in his matter than in his form. Seneca was the moralist *par excellence;* his reputation in this respect had carried him triumphantly through the Middle Ages, and Petrarch had introduced him to the Renaissance as the equal of Cicero and the superior of the Greeks in the moral sciences.[10] All of this was further consecrated by the fact that Seneca was a favorite among the Fathers, not only for his almost apostolic doctrine but also for his alleged correspondence with Saint Paul. Tertullian speaks of Seneca with the possessive adjective "noster" and is one of his earliest stylistic disciples. In fact, one can say that much that seems to be Senecan in the pulpit prose of the early seventeenth century is really Tertullian. Bishop Hall, who carried his title of "our English Seneca" with not too much lightness, is obviously partial to Tertullian, whose works he read more completely and quoted more copiously than those of his so-called master. The use of the Senecan manner in the pulpit and in the works of some religious thinkers was motivated by Seneca's reputation as a moral philosopher and by his affiliations with the early Fathers rather than by the adaptability of his nervous, efficient prose to rational speculation. This conclusion may explain in part the echoing of Seneca that we find in secular writers, but it is not the whole explanation.

It has sometimes been said that the Senecan style is the badge of the libertine. There is a certain truth in this observation, but it is not all that may be said. Bacon, who followed the Senecan formularies in his early writings, may have had the instincts of a libertine, but this cannot be said of other secular writers of Senecan English prose. The times made the stoa and, consequently, the manner of the best known stoic attractive. The failure of faith had happened before in the pre-christian era, and on one of these occasions, Zeno had established one place of retreat and Epicurus another. Both of these philosophers had founded systems that tried to poultice the bruises of humanity after it had fallen from another height of positive philosophy. Yet, they were both negative cults and, in the course of time, even they borrowed some of the utilitarian aspects of skepticism, the disease that they were intended to cure. Then, too, they were also diametrically opposed in method to eclecticism (the method of Cicero and the early Renaissance), for it faced all problems, whereas they avoided as many as they could. It was this failure of eclecticism, which is indicated by the inability of Pico della Mirandola, Ficino, and others to create satisfactory *summas*, that is probably as responsible as a change of vogue for the discarding of the Ciceronian prose method. The periodic style is the prose manner of those who have struck a balance, who have a system in which they can trust; hence it is the only style in which Hooker could have written, but it would have been organically discordant to the ultimate purposes of Bacon. Since men were in doubt, and searchingly in doubt, Seneca and Epicurus provided the best stylistic crutches to be found in ancient times. We know that at this particular time the reputation of Epicurus was being refurbished on the Continent and that his atomic doctrines were subsequently to play a great part in the seventeenth century rational explanation of the assembly of the universe; but his style, which was only known through the fragments of Diogenes, had, of course, no influence in an age that was confessedly anti-Greek. We must also not forget that Seneca was the author of the *Natural Questions* and a lost geographical treatise, so he had an additional attraction for the scientific writers who wished to inquire into the causes of things.

Bacon regarded the curt Senecan style as the correct form of expression for the rationalist. He used it in the so-called first essays and in the *Novum organum*. The Ciceronians, he tells us, are more interested in "the sweet falling of clauses than after the weight of matter." Their style hinders "the severe inquisition of truth, and the deep progress into philosophy."[11] The same sort of objections may be found in other men of this time; this is a great falling off from the practices of the Elizabethans; but more interesting yet is the emphasis of the Neo-Senecans. On most subjects they stress the stoic position, but like Bacon they are principally interested in working out the practical approaches to problems that are capable of solution. The doctrine of use is strong in them, and with it goes a stern interest in tangible and positive fact. Their interests and temperaments are reflected in their style. The transcendent contentments of faith have gone with the Ciceronian syntax, and a new nervous style which is consonant with doubt, with speculation, and with utility has taken its place. This seventeenth century position is also seen in the careful avoidance of what we should call "idealistic matters" among these men. "Does it work?" they ask. If it does, it is good. Bishop Hall, as a practical clergyman, might decorate his Christian metaphysics with stoic morality, but the secular Neo-stoics discreetly passed over any discussion of the supra-mundane. It was beyond the realm of the knowable. As a consequence, morality rather than religion seems only too often to be the theme of seventeenth century English writers.

But, as Professor Croll noticed, the terse Senecan style was replaced by a looser style, a baroque style, which is familiarly known to the readers of Sir Thomas Browne and Jeremy Taylor. It is also apparent that Bacon eventually abandoned his earlier prose manner for what he called "methods," a persuasive style more capable of converting the average reader. The real alteration in mode can be detected in men writing towards the middle of the seventeenth century. Lord North, who once prided himself on his "strong and clear" style tells us that he is now placing a line "of easy strain" among his other "tough and pithy" sentences. Lord Chandos can write a long essay on Tacitus without being stained by his dark manner, and Thomas Culpepper can even complain that Tacitus "has trussed up" history.[12] It is perhaps a mistake to call this new variation "the loose Senecan style," for it is rather an outgrowth of the awakened interest in the Church Fathers of the fourth and fifth centuries. When Sir Richard Baker published his *Meditations* in 1636, Sir Henry Wotton named this style in a commendatory epistle.

> I must needs observe and much admire the very Character of your Stile, which seemeth unto mee to have not a little of the African Idea of St. Augustines age, full of sweet Rapture, and of re-searched Conceipts; nothing borrowed; nothing vulgar; and yet all flowing from you (I know not how) with a certaine equall facility. So as I see, your worldly troubles have been but Pressing-yrons to your Heavenly cogitations.[13]

The name, then, that we might give to the style of Browne, of Taylor, and of their fellows is the "African style," a style of which Milton, that forthright and rigid Ciceronian, complained when he wrote about "the knotty Africanisms, the pampered metaphors, the intricate and involved sentences of the fathers."[14] It is the style of those seventeenth century men who had solved their metaphysical problems by clinging to or returning to the traditions of faith, of those who thought that they had erected a bridge between faith and reason, of those who were no longer perplexed by rational doubts.

There is certainly an esthetic of unbelief and it may be observed in the seventeenth century in the equation that seems to exist between the prose style of some men and their sense of certainty. The curt, terse, nervous manner is, in many respects, the characteristic of those seculars who "are troubled with a perplexed doubt" and who have limited themselves to rational speculations about sensible matters. The looser, lax style belongs to men who think that they have solved their difficulties and understand their world. It is the difference between Bacon and Browne. The latter, we remember, loved to lose himself in a "O altitudo," whereas the former remarked that "in divinity many things must be left abrupt and concluded with an 'O altitudo.' " Bacon with his scientific projects and his *Sylva sylvarum* seems not unlike Browne with his natural experiments and his *Vulgar errors;* but Bacon observed all things by the dry light of reason, by the *lumen naturale* whereas Browne, to use Coleridge's phrase, "read the book of nature by the faery light around his head."

NOTES

[1] Trans. by Denis MacCarthy, 2. 2182-7.

[2] Religio medici, *Works* (Ed. Keynes, London, 1928), I, 92.

[3] *The scholemaster* (Ed. Arber, London, 1927), p. 124.

[4] "Attic prose in the seventeenth century," *SP*, XVIII (1921), 79-128; "Juste Lipse et le mouvement anti-Ciceronien," *Revue du Seizieme Siecle*, II (1914), 200-42.

[5] Epistolae, *Opera omnia* (Antverpiae, 1637), II, 75.

[6] Thomas Blount, *Censura celebriorum authorum* (Genevae, 1694), pp. 98, 139.

[7] *Op. cit.* (Ed. Hudson, Princeton, 1935), p. 40.

[8] *Essaies or rather imperfect offers* (London, 1601), sig. D3.

[9] *Resolves* (London, 1677), p. 36.

[10] Epistolae ad viros quosdam, *Opera* (Basel, 1554), pp. 782-3.

[11] Advancement of learning, *Works* (Ed. Ellis, Spedding, Heath, Boston, 1861), VI, 119-20.

[12] *Moral discourses* (London, 1655), p. 46.

[13] Sig. A4r-v.

[14] Of reformation, *Works* (Ed. Ayres, New York, 1931), III, 34.

Symbolism in Medieval Literature

Morton W. Bloomfield

> Unde in nulla scientia, humana industria inventa, proprie lo-
> quendo, potest inveniri nisi litteralis sensus; sed solum in ista
> Scriptura, cujus Spiritus sanctus est auctor, homo vero instrumen-
> tum.—THOMAS AQUINAS, *Quaestiones quodlibetales* vii, a.16.

It is exceedingly fashionable today in the general intellectual flight
from history to interpret literature symbolically or, as it is often called,
"allegorically." The particularity of fact and event is passed over for
the general, the cyclic, and the mythical, which is presumably more
universal and more meaningful. Unless the significance of a literary
work can be subsumed in a system of interpretation—usually Christian,
although not always—it is assumed to have no real meaning.[1] Parallel
to this revolt against history is a revolt against psychology, which is another facet of the same disregard for the unique. Those works which
may easily be interpreted symbolically, such as Melville's *Moby Dick*,
have leaped into new favor, and the great classics of English and American literature are everywhere, as far as is possible, being reinterpreted
along symbolic, usually Christian, lines.

Needless to say, this movement has not left medieval literature untouched, for in the Middle Ages there is at hand a fully worked-out,
even if contradictory, theoretical symbolical system, especially in the
works of the early Fathers. The general awareness in medieval studies
outside theology and the history of theology, at least in English-speaking countries, of the so-called four or three levels of meaning theory
which goes back chiefly to Origen[2] and Philo and the Alexandrine

School[3] and ultimately to the Stoics, dates from the publication of Harry Caplan's article "The Four Senses of Scripture" in *Speculum* in 1929 and of Dr. H. Flanders Dunbar's *Symbolism in Medieval Thought and Its Consummation in the Divine Comedy* in 1929.[4] Since that time, medieval scholars and literary students have increasingly concentrated on interpreting medieval literature in terms of the exegetical method used in medieval biblical criticism, at least in the earlier Middle Ages.[5]

It seems to me that this method, while not totally wrong, is essentially erroneous as a method of understanding most medieval literary works historically, and it is the purpose of this article to discuss briefly the implications and limits of this method in the study of medieval secular literature, especially of the later Middle Ages.

First of all, it must be admitted that meaning is at least partially symbolic. A literary work of any sort and of any period always has some symbolic meaning. Beyond the fact that language itself is a system of sound and written symbols, which is of little significance to my main point, the substance and figures of literature must stand for more than themselves if they are to be fully meaningful. The unique has a meaning of a special sort. If Hamlet is only Hamlet, he is a primary datum; but if he stands for man in a dilemma, or a truth-seeker, or a ditherer, he has another dimension. Although its attention may be captured by it, the human mind comprehends the singular in a special way and not completely intellectually—a limitation, incidentally, of human creatureliness to medieval scholasticism. Meaning in literature comes through the unique but is not equivalent to it.

In this sense, all literature has a *nucleus* and a *cortex* and conveys *sententia*.[6] This is no peculiarity of medieval literature and thought. Historically, of course, medieval man tended to think in Christian categories, and most frequently the *sententia* he put into or discovered in literature was a Christian one. Indeed, no proper understanding of medieval literature is possible without a good knowledge of the Christian categories of thought and beliefs. Yet medieval man was also the heir of late classical antiquity and of barbarian cultures, and their categories of thought, their literary genres, their points of view, were also part of his heritage. He was well aware of a secular tradition which had not been completely transformed by Christianity.

Christianity gave meaning to existence for medieval man, was the framework of his thought generally, and was backed by the state and society with a strength and vigor no longer displayed today. The very form of the universe, with its hierarchy of being, as reflected in nature, in society, in the church, and in the next world, supported a view of a providential and ordered universe. What could be more natural—indeed, inevitable—than to see a Christian *sententia* in secular literature if that literature were to have any deep and important meaning at all. The Bible was, of course, in a class by itself, as the composition of God through various gifted and graced men to reveal his Truth to all men.

What also could be more natural than that students should be taught the letter and the *sensus* and the *sententia*[7] of a text. Although we do not use the terms, we still do so today if the instruction is more than memory work. However, then as now, I suspect, the *sensus* and *sententia* got less emphasis in practice than in theory. A glance at medieval commentaries, especially of the earlier period, on secular works and even occasionally on the Bible shows for the most part an overwhelming interest in the purely grammatical and rhetorical.

The first objection, then, to the symbolic approach is not that it finds a Christian *sententia* in medieval literature but that it assumes that this symbolic method is unique to the period and that there is no essential difference between literary works and theological or pastoral works. It misunderstands the nature of meaning and of literature. It neglects the concrete for the universal and assumes that the concrete exists only for the universal in a work of art,[8] which is not true even of the Bible. It is as if one were to love a woman because she represented eternal beauty or eternal good. Her particularity—her figure, face, skin, and personality—is submerged in her "meaning." She is what Professor Wimsatt would call a "sign," not an icon. There is no "concrete universal" in the world of the symbolists, only the universal.

The second objection is that the emphasis on the symbolic as opposed to the literal[9] approach to the Bible is not characteristic of the later Middle Ages, except perhaps in sermons, which are very conservative and must, of necessity, stress the moral. Although there are warnings earlier against neglect of the literal or historical sense of Scripture,[10] beginning in the twelfth century the symbolic method as applied to biblical exegesis underwent strong attacks, and in the later Middle Ages, except for certain standard interpretations dealing mainly with the prediction of Jesus in the Old Testament and the normal interpretation of any tale or event, the literal sense was the one which received the major attention.[11] In other words, at the time of the rise of the great vernacular literatures, we find a corresponding decline in the emphasis put on the symbolic method in biblical interpretation. In fact, both movements may be viewed as manifestations of a change of attitude in Western man, a new interest in the world of the senses and experience, which is seen in much else and which culminated in the Renaissance and the modern period.

Third, even in the period of its greatest use the symbolic method with its three- or fourfold levels was never mechanically or completely applied to Scripture. These levels should rather be viewed as possible ways of interpreting the manifold meanings in the Bible. All meaning at any time is multiple. The cross, for instance, can stand today for Jesus' sufferings, for Christianity, for the church, for the truth, for good as opposed to evil, and so forth. To attempt to systematize various possible meanings, without understanding what is involved, can lead only to a debased and mechanical interpretation of the highest mysteries. Such attempts reveal a profound misunderstanding of all historical study and, even though the Middle Ages loved system theoretically, medieval history in particular. Besides, in effect, no one can consistently apply the fourfold criterion except to a few hackneyed terms like Jerusalem.

One has only to look at the *Distinctiones*,[12] those symbolic dictionaries chiefly of the twelfth century, to see that there was no science of symbolism. The commonest objects and animals embrace a wide variety of meanings, often contradictory.[13] The meaning could be interpreted only in context, if at all, and even then multiple interpretations would frequently be possible.[14]

It was also at all times recognized that the Bible could be taken symbolically only partially. Much in the Old Testament is literally binding on Christians, and parts of the New Testament must be metaphorically interpreted.[15] Although some parts and elements of the Old Testament were usually interpreted symbolically, there is no evidence whatsoever for a consistent application of any level of meaning interpretation in Scripture. One of the basic arguments for the truth of Jesus' claims is that he fulfils certain Old Testament prophecies and, in general, gives a profound (christological) sense to that collection of divine books. Typology, as it is called, is found in the New Testament itself where Old Testament prophecies and figures are applied to the fulfillment in Christ.[16] Certain other parts of the Bible tend to be morally interpreted. Babylon and Egypt, for example, are always the supreme types of evil. This interpretation is obvious and does not require any special insight or method beyond a normal intelligent reading of the text.

Fourth, the polysemantic school makes no difference between the Bible which was dictated by God in the form of the Holy Ghost and literary works written purely by sinful and erring man. There is very little evidence that the latter were written to be interpreted consistently in a symbolic manner, beyond the normal demands of literary figurative expression.[17] To suppose that medieval man would presume to put himself on the level of God in the writing of literature of whatever sort is surely most astounding. To think that he would write literature, which to him was both for *sentence* and *solace,* merely to convey profound religious truths clothed in many-colored "allegory" seems to me to involve a great misunderstanding of that literature and that man. I do not deny an occasional symbolic reference based on standard biblical interpretations, but to imagine a consistent and elaborate systematic application of a multilayered web of symbolism is unthinkable.

It is also true that certain classical works especially venerated by the Middle Ages, the *Aeneid,* the *Metamorphoses,* for example, were also occasionally interpreted by the symbolic method. Even these special cases, however, did not pass without protest.[18] No medieval writer would ever think of himself on a level with these masters, and the method was chiefly used to Christianize pagan writers. And no one ever maintained that Ovid or Virgil had put the symbolism there himself.

It must be remembered that the advocates of secular literature in the Middle Ages were on the defensive. The pagan worldiness of much of it clashed with Christian otherworldliness, and those who loved the ancient poets were hard put to defend their poetry. The only way out, as the accessus and glosses to many a classical and pagan work show, was to argue strongly for the *utilitas* of such literature, and *utilitas* meant finding a moral meaning.

The medieval scholastics following Aristotle gave, in general, a very low position in the soul to imagination and a very low rank to poetry in the hierarchy of the "sciences."[19] To most, poetry was a branch of logic, but the lowest and weakest branch. This created difficulties, as Thomas' remarks show:

> The science of poetry pertains to those things which because of their lack of truth cannot be grasped by reason; therefore it is necessary that reason be almost beguiled by such similitudes. Theology, however, pertains to those things which are above reason, and so the symbolic method is common to both as neither is proportioned to reason [*In sent.* i. prol. a. 5. 3].

Yet, having quickly removed the problem of certain similarities between poetry and theology, Thomas gives no more thought to this useless art. Those on the defensive were the men who, like Boccaccio, felt that they must defend the claims of poetry and could do so only by arguing that it contained a "sentence." Yet this argument was obviously never taken very seriously by the real thinkers of the Middle Ages, who were content to ignore the so-called claims of poetry as beneath reason and the concern of rational men who did not need *ficta* to see the truth. Reason, authority, and divine revelation were the ways to truth. We have little evidence that the supporters of poetry did in fact interpret their poetry as symbolic, in spite of the theories of some of them.

Then common sense must step in. In a poem like *Piers Plowman,* as in many medieval literary works, the obvious technique is personification, not symbolism. Personification is making what is abstract concrete. It cannot normally have more meanings than what it says. If Mercy kisses Peace, what else does that mean than that peace and mercy embrace?[20] Symbolism is used but not in any wide and consistent pattern.

St. Eucher of Lyons is apparently the only patristic author who admitted that secular works could have levels of meaning.[21] All the other Fathers or theologians I have been able to examine, when they do not tacity assume its applicability only to Scripture, reserve the method exclusively for biblical exegesis.

If the purpose of scholarship is to determine the historical circumstances surrounding a work of art and the probable intention of the author in terms of his background and the evidence of the text itself, then the burden of proof lies with those who would claim a religious symbolic multileveled meaning for medieval literature. If this is not the aim of scholarship, then, of course, there is no objection to finding any meaning or meanings one wants in the literary relics of the past. The really serious reason for opposing this procedure is the historical exactitude which is claimed or implied. One can, if one chooses, interpret a work of literature in any way whatsoever, provided that one does not claim to be thereby revealing the conscious intention of the author.

In view of the fact that the historical trend was moving away from the heavy symbolic interpretation of Scripture and that a secular tradition of entertainment and literature was very much alive in the Middle Ages, it seems to me that to believe that the medieval author would presume to write as God wrote through his chosen servants in Holy Scripture is the height of folly. This, of course, is not to deny that in certain literary works—possibly the *Divine Comedy,* in the case of which there is some evidence for the assumption, although not totally

above question—the multiple method may have been used. It is, however, the task of the historical scholar who makes such a claim to substantiate it in each case. The *Divine Comedy*, if it is an exception, is
almost the exception which proves the rule. It is significant, as Auer-
bach points out,[22] that Dante arrogates to himself, against all precedence, polysemy—a special mission in keeping with his high view of
himself as poet and prophet. Even in the *Divine Comedy*, however, it
is impossible to work out a consistent fourfold scheme of meaning.[23]
The basic and important meaning of the *Divine Comedy* except in the
case of a few obvious symbols is its literal meaning. Individual symbols are often used therein in multiple senses, but this fact is not
equivalent to discovering a consistent four- or threefold level of meaning. And, as we have already admitted, all meaning is, at least to some
extent, symbolic. In every sin there is something of the sin of Adam;
in every goal there is something of the Promised Land.

Nor do I mean to deny that in many medieval works a Christian
meaning is not aimed at or assumed, but this need not imply the acceptance of a multileveled system of symbolism, which in any case for
the most part did not exist. The Christian meaning of medieval literature is usually very clearly underlined by the normal meaning of the
words, as in Chaucer's *Troilus and Criseyde* or the *Divine Comedy*,
where we are expressly told by the authors what the poems mean in
Christian moral, dogmatic, or mystical terms.

The multileveled interpretation cannot be consistently applied to
any work, including the Bible, without involving contradictions, omissions, and denials. The long history of biblical exegesis proves this to
the hilt. To assume that a medieval author would be so proud and un-
perceptive as to take a system which is largely the creation of modern
systematizing scholars and the mere repetition of patristic formulas
and apply it to the composition of secular literature is most unwise.[24]

Literature has ends of its own, and even if in a Christian society
these are fundamentally Christian, they are not exclusively so. If the
work is felt as literature, it would belong to one or more genres which
had traditions of their own generally going back to classical antiquity.
A work of literature cannot have been written fundamentally to expound in Bible-wise the truths of Christianity. These would be assumed by the writers, or if Christian themes were to be the main point
of a work, as in, say, *Piers Plowman*, these are openly discussed or at
least in a normal rhetorical manner.[25]

Fifth, above all, the multileveled system of symbolism provides no
criterion of corrigibility except, as in the case of biblical exegesis, tra-

dition. There is no way, seeing the wide variety of symbolic interpretations of the same thing, to correct any particular interpretation. At the most, one might say a certain interpretation is not right, but of many alternate explanations there is no way of deciding which one is correct, for supporting texts from the wide variety of medieval and patristic theology can be found for each one. Consistency to some extent could, it is true, be used as a criterion of truth; but, as the history of Dante scholarship abundantly shows, it is easy enough to work out a variety of consistent interpretations of at least cantos of a poem, and, in most cases, there is no way of deciding between them. It was this strong subjective element in medieval symbolism, which was so patently misused for various selfish interests in the later Middle Ages, that, along with other factors, led to the strong attacks on and even repudiation of the method from the thirteenth century on, and by the Reformers. In the fourteenth and fifteenth centuries, the gloss on a biblical text was frequently treated as a joke.[26]

Mere assertion and the quotation of a theological or pastoral text are not satisfactory proofs. One cannot perhaps adequately prove any interpretation of literature, but if the words of the text are taken as of primary importance, there is always a court of appeal. With sixteen meanings for the peacock, who is to decide between them?

Finally, the assumption of the organized use of the symbolic method in medieval literature is essentially simplistic. It imposes a non-historical order and system on what was in fact disordered and unsystematic. The theologians of the high Middle Ages were saddled with a theory of levels of meanings from early Christianity and had to give lip service to the principle, but actually there was never any consistent application of that theory anywhere at any time, except for particular biblical passages, in Christian medieval exegesis and, above all, in literary composition.

I would like to conclude with the words of Roger Bacon:

> In sensu litterali jacet tota philosophiæ potestas, in naturis et proprietatibus rerum naturalium, artificialium et moralium; ut per convenientes adaptationes et similitudines eliciantur sensus spirituales. Ut sic simul sciatur [sociatur?] philosophia cum theologia. . . .[27]

NOTES

[1] Unless the system implied by them really gives meaning to the world and man, the general, the cyclic, and the mythical are no more meaningful than the particular, the unique, and the fact. This axiom is

not always kept in mind by the "symbolists." The mere cycles of nature, for instance, are as meaningless as any unique fact unless one is satisfied by a purely biological vision of the world.

I am indebted to Professor Phillip W. Damon for several suggestions which I have used in this paper.

[2] For a recent treatment and defense of Origen's exegetical method see Henri de Lubac, *Histoire et esprit: l'intelligence de l'Écriture d'après Origène* ("Théologie: études publiées sous la direction de la Faculté de Théologie S.J. de Lyon-Fourvière" [Paris, 1950]); see, however, P. Th. Camelot, "La Théologie de l'image de Dieu," *Revue des sciences philosophiques et théologiques,* XL (1956), 453, n. 20, and 455, where the literalness of Origen's biblical exegesis is emphasized.

[3] The Antiochene school, which emphasized the literal more than the spiritual sense (to use inexact but common terms for the sake of convenience), was, however, always opposed to Alexandrine flights of fancy. Its influence, chiefly expressed through Theodore of Mopsuestia (although Ambrosiaster, John Chrysostom, and Junilius must not be neglected), never completely died in the Middle Ages and in the early period is to be found in Ireland and elsewhere, notably England and northern France. See M. L. W. Laistner, "Antiochene Exegesis in Western Europe during the Middle Ages," *HTR,* XL (1947), 19-31; Alberto Vaccari, "La Teoria esegetica della scuola antiochena," *Scritti di erudizione e di filologia,* I (Rome, 1952), 101-42 (reprinted from *Biblica,* 1920 and 1934); and the important article by Bernard Bischoff, "Wendepunkte in der Geschichte der lateinische Exegese im Frühmittelalter," *Sacris erudiri,* V (1954), 189-281. The latter protests against the facile setting of Alexandria against Antioch

in the early Middle Ages. He points out that even Bede, who did much to push the Alexandrine method, was essentially historical in his exegesis. In fact, the whole subject seems to be hopelessly confused. One thing is certain that, except for typology (the veiled prediction of Christ in the Old Testament), at no time did any biblical exegete repudiate the importance and often the primacy of the biblical letter. There are, however, degrees of emphasis.

Even Augustine's *De doctrina Christiana,* which is supposed to have established the fourfold method for the Middle Ages, contains no reference at all to it. In fact, the whole point of that work as regards the Bible is that what is taught is clearly taught, and, if it is occasionally obscure, it is elsewhere in the Bible made very plain. Augustine does refer, it is true, to a four-fold method of interpreting the Bible in *De utilitate credendi* 3 (*PL,* XLII, 68 ff.) and *De genesi ad litteram* 2 (*PL,* XXXIV, 222), but the four meanings are history (the letter), etiology (normal explanation of difficult biblical passages to a Christian), analogy (typology or agreement of the two Testaments), and allegory (figurative meaning, usually typology). The recognition of the figurative meaning of parts of the Old Testament is either typology as found in the New Testament itself or the normal application of a criterion of meaning to a written text. In practice, however, Augustine frequently does indulge in symbolic biblical exegesis. Gregory the Great by his practice did perhaps more to make the early Middle Ages pass over the literal for the figurative (usually moral) meaning of the Bible than anyone else. He had great influence on Bede and Rabanus Maurus, the most important of the early medieval biblical commentators. For some recent discussions of

Augustine's exegetical methods see Maurice Pontet, *L'Exégèse de S. Augustin prédicateur* ("Théologie: études publiées sous la direction de la Faculté de Théologie S.J. de Lyon-Fourvière [Paris, 1944?]), and Allen A. Gilmore, "Augustine and the Critical Method," *HTR*, XXXIX (1946), 141-63. Neither Augustine, Gregory, nor Bede thought of a consistent and continuous multileveled interpretation of Scripture but that the nature of the particular text determined the "level" desired. Bede, for example, gives as an example of tropology I John 3:18, which he says must be taken literally, and of anagogy Matt. 5:8, which also must be taken literally (see his *De tabernacula* i [*PL*, XCI, 410B-411B]).

⁴ There are, of course, earlier treatments of the subject in English; e.g., Frederic W. Farrar, *History of Interpretation: Eight Lectures Preached before the University of Oxford* . . . (London, 1886), and H. Preserved Smith, *Essays in Biblical Interpretation* (Boston, 1921).

⁵ For a good summary of early Christian exegesis and a review of recent literature on the subject see Walter J. Burchardt, "On Early Christian Exegesis," *Theological Studies*, XI (1950), 78-116. The literature on patristic and medieval exegesis is too vast to be suitably summarized here. My comments in this paper should not, of course, be interpreted to mean that I do not believe that traditional biblical exegesis is not of great value in interpreting biblical allusions and symbols when used by medieval authors.

⁶ On the history of *sententia,* see G. Paré, A. Brunet, and P. Tremblay, *La Renaissance du XIIᵉ siècle, les écoles et l'enseignement* ("Publications de l'Institut d'Études Médiévales d'Ottawa." Vol. III [Paris and Ottawa, 1933]), pp. 267 ff. Isidore of Seville interprets it to be an impersonal general *dictum* from which its general, but not only, medieval meaning of "meaning" or "truth" probably derives.

⁷ As at least John of Salisbury and Hugh of St. Victor put it (see Paré, Brunet, and Tremblay, p. 116).

⁸ ". . . All the senses are founded on one—the literal—from which alone can any argument be drawn" (Thomas Aquinas, *ST* i, q.1, a.10). "He [Aristotle] has to do this [criticize the obvious sense of Plato's words] because Plato's method of teaching was faulty; he constantly used figures of speech, teaching by symbols and giving his words a meaning quite other than their literal sense" (Aquinas, *Commentary on De anima* i. 3, lectio 8, trans. K. Foster and S. Humphries [London, 1951], p. 107). Cf. Wyclif (*De benedicta incarnacione* iii, ed. Edward Harris [London: Wyclif Society, 1886], pp. 37 ff., esp. p. 40), who argues for the importance of the literal meaning of Scripture. This attitude can be found everywhere in later Middle Ages (see below, pp. 200-201).

⁹ In the earlier period the word "literal" had a much narrower meaning than it does in the later Middle Ages or today. We include the sense of the "plain meaning of the text" in the term; to the early Middle Ages "literal" tended to be limited to the form of the words. "Most of the Fathers considered the meaning behind a metaphor not a literal but a secondary sense" (R. E. Brown, *The "Sensus plenior" of Sacred Scripture: A Dissertation . . . of St. Mary's University, Baltimore* . . . [Baltimore, 1955], p. 6). This shift in meaning explains some of the confusions in our understanding of what the Fathers mean by their comments on and practice of biblical exegesis. Yet Thomas writes: "Quamvis spiritualia sub figuris rerum corporalium proponantur, non tamen ea quae circa

spiritualia intenduntur per figuras sensibiles, ad mysticum pertinent sensum, sed litteralem; quia sensus litteralis est qui primo per verba intenditur sive proprie dicta, sive figurate" (*In Job* [Parma ed.], XVIII, 6).

[10] See Henri de Lubac, "Sur un vieux distique, La doctrine du 'quadruple sens,'" *Mélanges offerts au A. P. Ferdinand Cavallera . . . à l'occasion de la quarantième année de son professorat à l'Institut catholique* (Toulouse, 1948), p. 352 n.

[11] Our recent awareness of this trend is largely due to the important work of Miss Smalley, *The Study of the Bible in the Middle Ages* (2d ed. rev. and enl.; Oxford, 1952). The author has emphasized the importance of the exegesis of Andrew of St. Victor in the development of later medieval biblical study. Bonaventure writes: "Qui litteram sacrae Scripturae spernit ad spirituales eius intelligentias numquam assurget" (*Breviloquium* Prologue 6).

[12] See M. D. Chenu, "Théologie symbolique et exégèse scolastique aux XII*–XIII* siècles," *Mélanges Joseph de Ghellinck* (Gembloux, 1951), II, 509–26; and Smalley, pp. 246 ff.

[13] Augustine (*De doctrina Christiana* iii. 25) recognizes that one and the same thing (his examples are the lion, serpent, and bread) may have different and even opposing meanings; see also G. G. Coulton, *Art and the Reformation* (2d ed.; Cambridge, England, 1953), Appendix 18, p. 554, who refers to the sixteen meanings for the peacock; and D. W. Robertson, Jr., and Bernard F. Huppé, *Piers Plowman and Scriptural Tradition* (Princeton, 1951), pp. 5–6, who point to the seven meanings of *dormitio*.

[14] Dante in *De monarchia* III, iv, 6, recognizes how easy it is to mis-

interpret the "sensum misticum."

[15] See Jean Daniélou, *Essai sur le mystère de l'histoire* (Paris, 1953). p. 211.

"Si vero aperte fidem predicat vel bonos mores astruit, sive hoc sit ita quod vetat flagitium vel facinus, sive sit ita quod utilitatem vel beneficentiam iubet, sive sit ita quod radicem omnium malorum exstirpat . . . non est ad aliud refferendum quasi figurative dictum, quia per hoc vigor eorum eneruaretur" (Ulrich of Strassburg, *Liber de summo bono* i, tr. 2, cap. 11, ed. J. Daguillon [Paris, 1930], pp. 59–60).

"We must discover first of all, whether the [biblical] expression which we are trying to understand is literal or figurative" (Augustine *De doctrina* iii. 24, trans. John J. Gavigan, *The Fathers of the Church: A New Translation* [New York, 1947]). Gerald of Bologna in his *Summa* Q. XI, a.1, written in 1317, makes this same point (that the Old Testament is not always to be taken allegorically) (see Paul de Vooght, *Les Sources de la doctrine chrétienne . . .* [Bruges, 1954], pp. 425–26).

[16] For a study of the use of typology by the New Testament writers and its general background, see Leonhard Goppelt, *Typos: Die typologische Deutung des Alten Testaments im Neuen* ("Beiträge zur Förderung Christlicher Theologie," ed. Schlatter and Althaus, Vol. II, No. 43 [Gütersloh, 1939]).

St. Thomas Aquinas says that the literal is what the author intends, the spiritual what God intends. In the eyes of God the whole Bible is, however, clear and literal: "Quia vero sensus litteralis est quem auctor intendit, auctor sacrae Scripturae Deus est, qui omnia simul suo intellectu comprehendit: non est inconveniens . . . si etiam secundum litteralem sensum, in una littera

Scripturae, plures sint sensus" (*ST* i, q.1, a.10, in c). This statement implies that only God composes polysemously. See below, next paragraph.

[17] "Auctor sacrae Scripturae est Deus in cujus potestate est ut non solum voces ad significandum accommodet (quod etiam homo facere potest), sed etiam res ipsas" (Aquinas *ST* i, q.1, a.10). Thomas specifically denies a spiritual sense in writings other than the Bible in *Quodl.* vii, a. 16, quoting Gregory the Great, *Moralia* 22. The whole point of the creed is that it is literally true on the authority of faith as interpreted by the church, unlike art, which is only metaphorically true. In one sense the Bible is not symbolic at all but completely literal, i.e., true. Cf. "In caeteris igitur scripturis solae voces significantur, in scriptura divina non solum voces, sed etiam res significativae sunt quamvis non in omnibus" (Conrad of Hirsau, *Dialogus super auctores sive Didascalon*, ed. G. Schepss [Würzburg, 1889], p. 75) and "sciendum est etiam quod in divino eloquio non tantum verba, sed etiam res significare habent" (Hugo of St. Victor, *PL*, CLXXVI, 790).

"In liberalibus disciplinis ubi non res sed dumtaxat verba significant, quisquis primo sensu litterae contentus non est, aberrare videtur mihi" (John of Salisbury, *Polycraticus*, ed. Webb, vii. 12, p. 144). I owe this last reference to Jean Misrahi's excellent review in *Romance Philology*, IV (1951), 350.

[18] See Paré, Brunet, and Tremblay, pp. 119-21. It was Macrobius who probably first suggested for the Middle Ages that the great classical poets consciously used "allegory" (see, on the allegorizing of Virgil, Pierre Courcelle, "Les Pères de l'église devant les enfers virgiliens," *Archives*

d'histoire doctrinale et littéraire du moyen âge, XXII [1955], 5-74). Much earlier, of course, the Stoics and Alexandrines had "allegorized" Homer to their taste and no doubt set a pattern.

[19] See Ernst Robert Curtius, *European Literature and the Latin Middle Ages*, trans. W. R. Trask (London, 1953), p. 224.

[20] See Robert Worth Frank, Jr., "The Art of Reading Medieval Personification Allegory," *ELH*, XX (1953), 237-50, for an excellent discussion of this point as well as other related ones.

[21] See André Pézard, *Dante sous la pluie de feu (Enfer, Chant XV)* ("Études de philosophie médiévale," Vol. XL [Paris, 1950]), pp. 382-84.

[22] See his "Figurative Texts Illustrating Certain Passages of Dante's Commedia," *Speculum*, XXI (1946), 475, n. 5. Cf. "To claim to use the allegory of the theologians (as Dante did in his letter to Can Grande) is to remove *The Divine Comedy* from the category of poetry as his contemporaries understood it" (Joseph A. Mazzeo, "Dante's Conception of Poetic Expression," *Romantic Review*, XLVII [1956], 241; see also his "Dante and the Pauline Modes of Vision," *HTR*, L [1957], 275-306). Dante thought of himself as prophet rather than poet, and perhaps on a level with Paul and Moses (see also Curtius, pp. 221 ff. and 377: ". . . Dante believed that he had an apocalyptic mission").

[23] A recent attempt is by Dorothy L. Sayers in *Introductory Papers on Dante* (London, 1954), who presumes at last to tell the simple truth. She finds most astoundingly that the allegorical (in its narrow meaning of a level) sense has to mean the historical or political level of meaning (pp. 104-5) and gives us only a few generalized clues to this quad-

ruple meaning that she claims to have found in the poem. A number of great Dante scholars have denied that there are systematic levels of meaning in the poem at all. I have never seen this fourfold meaning completely worked out in the case of any litrary work, including Dante's.

²⁴ An easily available fourteenth-century discussion of the problem of multiple meanings (of Scripture) may be found in the second article (pp. 43 ff., esp. pp. 46 ff.) of the recently published *Quaestio de Sacra Scriptura et de veritatibus catholicis* of Henry Totting of Oyta (d. 1397), edited by Albert Lang ("Opuscula et textus, series scholastica," ed. J. Koch and Fr. Pelster [Münster i.W., 1953, editio altera]). Totting was much influenced by English thought of the period—in particular by Scotus, Woodham, and Fitzralph. His discussion of the question is surprisingly modern: he is well aware of the difficulties. He struggles to preserve the validity of the symbolic approach to the Bible. This whole *Quaestio* reveals interestingly some of the doubts raised in Totting's time about scriptural accuracy.

²⁵ See above, p. 202.

²⁶ Cf. The words of the greedy friar in Chaucer's "Summoner's Tale,"

"Glosynge is a glorious thyng, certeyn."

For lettre sleeth, so as we clerkes seyn."

—*Canterbury Tales,* ed. F. N. Robinson (2d ed., III, 1793-94).

²⁷ *Opus tertium,* 24, ed. Brewer, p. 81. Cf. "Freedom of thought was not repressed in the Middle Ages. It was fostered by the allegorical method of interpretation, whereby the philosopher could connect his private theory with established truth" (E. K. Rand, "Medieval Gloom and Medieval Uniformity," *Speculum,* I [1926], 267). Cf. also Erasmus' attacks on the method in his *Praise of Folly.*

Method and Scope of
American Renaissance

F. O. Matthiessen

The starting point for this book was my realization of how great a number of our past masterpieces were produced in one extraordinarily concentrated moment of expression. It may not seem precisely accurate to refer to our mid-nineteenth century as a *re-birth;* but that was how the writers themselves judged it. Not as a re-birth of values that had existed previously in America, but as America's way of producing a renaissance, by coming to its first maturity and affirming its rightful heritage in the whole expanse of art and culture.

The half-decade of 1850-55 saw the appearance of *Representative Men* (1850), *The Scarlet Letter* (1850), *The House of the Seven Gables* (1851), *Moby-Dick* (1851), *Pierre* (1852), *Walden* (1854), and *Leaves of Grass* (1855). You might search all the rest of American literature without being able to collect a group of books equal to these in imaginative vitality. That interesting fact could make the subject for several different kinds of investigation. You might be concerned with *how* this flowering came, with the descriptive narrative of literary history. Or you might dig into its sources in our life, and examine the economic, social, and religious causes *why* this flowering came in just these years. Or you might be primarily concerned with *what* these books were as works of art, with evaluating their fusions of form and content.

By choosing the last of these alternatives my main subject has become the conceptions held by five of our major writers concerning the function and nature of literature, and the degree to which their practice bore out their theories. That may make their process sound too deliberate, but Emerson, Thoreau, and Whitman all commented very explicitly on language as well as expression, and the creative intentions of Hawthorne and Melville can be readily discerned through scrutiny of their chief works. It has seemed to me that the literary accomplishment of those years could be judged most adequately if approached both in the light of its authors' purposes and in that of our own developing conceptions of literature. The double aim, therefore, has been to place these works both in their age and in ours.

In avowing that aim, I am aware of the important books I have not written. One way of understanding the concentrated abundance of our mid-nineteenth century would be through its intellectual history, particularly through a study of the breakdown of Puritan orthodoxy into Unitarianism, and of the quickening of the cool Unitarian strain into the spiritual and emotional fervor of Transcendentalism. The first of those two developments has been best sketched by Joseph Haroutunian, *Piety versus Moralism: The Passing of New England Theology* (1932). The whole movement will be genetically traced in Perry Miller's monumental study of *The New England Mind,* the first volume of which (1939), dealing with the seventeenth century, has already extended the horizons of our cultural past. Another notable book could concentrate on how discerning an interpretation our great authors gave of the economic and social forces of the time. The orientation of such a book would not be with the religious and philosophical ramifications of the transcendental movement so much as with its voicing of fresh aspirations for the rise of the common man. Its method could be the one that Granville Hicks has inherited from Taine, and has already applied in *The Great Tradition* (1933) to our literature since the Civil War. An example of that method for the earlier period is Newton Arvin's detailed examination (1938) of Whitman's emergent socialism.

The two books envisaged in the last paragraph might well be called *The Age of Swedenborg* and *The Age of Fourier*. Emerson said in 1854, 'The age is Swedenborg's,' by which he meant that it had embraced the subjective philosophy that 'the soul makes its own world.' That extreme development of idealism was what Emerson had found adumbrated in Channing's 'one sublime idea': the potential divinity of man. That religious assumption could also be social when it claimed the inalienable worth of the individual and his right to participate in whatever the community might produce. Thus the transition from transcendentalism to Fourierism was made by many at the time, as by Henry James, Sr., and George Ripley and his loyal followers at Brook Farm. *The Age of Fourier* could by license be extended to take up a wider subject than Utopian socialism; it could treat all the radical movements of the period; it would stress the fact that 1852 witnessed not only the appearance of *Pierre* but of *Uncle Tom's Cabin;* it would stress also what had been largely ignored until recently, the anticipation by Orestes Brownson of some of the Marxist analysis of the class controls of action.[1]

But the age was also that of Emerson and Melville. The one common denominator of my five writers, uniting even Hawthorne and Whitman, was their devotion to the possibilities of democracy. In dealing with their work I hope that I have not ignored the implications of such facts as that the farmer rather than the businessman was still the average American, and that the terminus to the agricultural era in our history falls somewhere between 1850 and 1865, since the railroad, the iron ship, the factory, and the national labor union all began to be dominant forces within those years, and forecast a new epoch. The forties probably gave rise to more movements of reform than any other decade in our history; they marked the last struggle of the liberal spirit of the eighteenth century in conflict with the rising forces of exploitation. The triumph of the new age was foreshadowed in the gold rush, in the full emergence of the acquisitive spirit.[2]

The old liberalism was the background from which my writers

emerged. But I have concentrated entirely on the foreground, on the writing itself. I have not written formal literary history—a fact that should be of some relief to the reader, since if it required a volume of this length for five years of that record, the consequences of any extension of such a method would be appalling. Parrington stated in his *Main Currents of American Thought* (1927): 'With aesthetic judgments I have not been greatly concerned. I have not wished to evaluate reputations or weigh literary merits, but rather to understand what our fathers thought . . .' My concern has been opposite. Although I greatly admire Parrington's elucidation of our liberal tradition, I think the understanding of our literature has been retarded by the tendency of some of his followers to regard all criticism as 'belletristic trifling.' I am even more suspicious of the results of such historians as have declared that they were not discussing art, but 'simply using art, in a purpose of research.' Both our historical writing and our criticism have been greatly enriched during the past twenty years by the breaking down of arbitrary divisions between them, by the critic's realization of the necessity to master what he could of historical discipline, by the historian's desire to extend his domain from politics to general culture. But you cannot 'use' a work of art unless you have comprehended its meaning. And it is well to remember that although literature reflects an age, it also illuminates it. Whatever the case may be for the historian, the quality of that illumination is the main concern for the common reader. He does not live by trends alone; he reads books, whether of the present or past, because they have an immediate life of their own.

What constitutes the secret of that life is the subject of this volume. It may be held that my choice of authors is arbitrary. These years were also those of Whittier's *Songs of Labor* (1850), of Longfellow's *Hiawatha* (1855), of work by Lowell and Holmes and Simms, of Baldwin's *Flush Times in Alabama and Mississippi*, of T. S. Arthur's *Ten Nights in a Barroom*. Nor were any of my authors best sellers. The five hundred copies of Emerson's first book, *Nature* (1836), had been disposed of so slowly that a second edition was not called for until 1849; and though his lecturing had made him well known by then, the sales of none of his books ran far into the thousands. Thoreau recorded in his journal that four years after the appearance of his *Week on the Concord and Merrimack* (1849) only 219 copies had been sold; so he had the publisher ship the remainder back to him and said: 'I have now a library of nearly nine hundred volumes, over seven hundred of which I wrote myself. Is it not well that the author should behold the fruits of his labor?' After that *Walden* was considered a great risk, but it managed to go through an edition of two thousand. Whitman set up and printed *Leaves of Grass* for himself, and probably gave away more copies than were bought, whereas Longfellow could soon report (1857) that the total sales of his books had run to over three hundred thousand, and *Fern Leaves from Fanny's Portfolio* (1853), by the sister of N. P. Willis, sold a hundred thousand in its first year. Although *Typee* (1846) was more popular than Melville's subsequent work, it never came within miles of such figures. Hawthorne reported that six or seven hundred copies of *Twice-Told Tales* (1837) had been disposed of before the panic of that year descended. To reach a wider audience he had to wait until *The Scarlet Letter,* and reflecting on the triumphant vogue of Susan Warner's *The Wide, Wide World* (1850), Maria Cummins' *The Lamplighter* (1854), the ceaseless flux of Mrs. E. D. E. N. Southworth's sixty novels, he wrote to Ticknor in 1855: 'America is now wholly given over to a damned mob of scribbling women, and I should have no chance of success while the public taste is occupied with their trash—and should be ashamed of myself if I did succeed. What is the mystery of these innumerable editions of *The Lamplighter,* and other books neither better nor worse?—worse they could not be, and better they need not be, when they sell by the hundred thousand.'

Such material still offers a fertile field for the sociologist and for the historian of our taste. But I agree with Thoreau: 'Read the best books first, or you may not have a chance to read them at all.' And during the century that has ensued, the successive generations of common readers, who make the decisions, would seem finally to have agreed that the authors of the pre-Civil War era who bulk largest in stature are the five who are my subject. That being the case, a book about their value might seem particularly unnecessary. But 'the history of an art,' as Ezra Pound has affirmed, 'is the history of masterwork, not of failures or mediocrity.' And owing to our fondness for free generalization, even the masterworks of these authors have been largely taken for granted. The critic knows that any understanding of the subtle principle of life inherent in a work of art can be gained only by direct experience of it, again and again. The interpretation of what he has found demands close analysis, and plentiful instances from the works themselves. With a few notable exceptions, most of the criticism of our past masters has been perfunctorily tacked onto biographies. I have not yet seen in print an adequately detailed scrutiny even of 'When lilacs last in the dooryard bloom'd,' or of *Moby-Dick.* And such good criticism as has been written has ordinarily dealt with single writers; it has not examined many of the interrelations among the various works of the group.

My aim has been to follow these books through their implications, to observe them as the culmination of their authors' talents, to assess them in relation to one another and to the drift of our literature since, and, so far as possible, to evaluate them in accordance with the enduring requirements for great art. That last aim will seem to many only a pious phrase, but it describes the critic's chief responsibility. His obligation is to examine an author's resources of language and of genres, in a word, to be preoccupied with form. This means nothing rarefied, as Croce's description of De Sanctis' great *History of Italian Literature* can testify: form for De Sanctis 'was not the "form" pathologically felt by aesthetes and decadents: it was nothing else than the entire resolution of the intellectual, sentimental, and emotional material into the concrete reality of the poetic image and word, which alone has aesthetic value.'

The phases of my somewhat complex method of elucidating that concrete reality can be briefly described. The great attraction of my subject was its compactness:[3] for though I made no attempt to confine my study of these authors to the strait jacket of a five-year segment of their careers, the fact remained that Emerson's theory of expression was that on which Thoreau built, to which Whitman gave extension, and to which Hawthorne and Melville were indebted by being forced to react against its philosophical assumptions. The nature of Emerson's achievement has caused me to range more widely in my treatment of him than in that of the others. *Representative Men* has no more right to be called his masterpiece than *Nature* (1836) or *The Conduct of Life* (1860). He wrote no masterpiece, but his service to the development of our literature was enormous in that he made the first full examination of its potentialities. To apply to him his own words about Goethe: he was the cow from which the rest drew their milk. My discussion of his theory has always in view his practice of it, and its creative use by the others. My prime intention is not Sainte-Beuve's: to be 'a naturalist of minds,' to relate the authors' works to their lives. I have not drawn upon the circumstances of biography unless they seemed essential to place a given piece of writing;[4] and whenever necessary, especially in the case of Melville, I have tried to expose the modern fallacy that has come from the vulgarization of Sainte-Beuve's subtle method—the direct reading of an author's personal life into his works.

The types of interrelation that have seemed most productive to understanding the literature itself were first of all the obvious debts, of Thoreau to Emerson, or Melville to Hawthorne. In the next place there were certain patterns of taste and aspiration: the intimate kinship to the seventeenth-century metaphysical strain that was felt by Emerson, Thoreau, and Melville; the desire for a functional style wherein Thoreau and Whitman especially were forerunners of our modern interest. That last fact again suggests one of my chief convictions: that works of art can be best perceived if we do not approach them only through the influences that shaped them, but if we also make use of what we inevitably bring from our own lives. That is an unorthodox postulate for literary history. But if we can see *Moby-Dick* and *Pierre* much more accurately by uncovering Melville's extraordinary debt to Shakespeare, and come closer to Hawthorne's intentions by observing that his psychological assumptions were still fundamentally the same as Milton's, it seems equally clear that Henry James and Eliot can cast light back on Hawthorne, and that one way of judging *Leaves of Grass* is by juxtaposing it with the deliberate counterstatement made by Whitman's polar opposite, Hopkins. I have, therefore, utilized whatever interrelations of this type have seemed to grow organically from my subject. I do not expect the reader to be willing at this point to grant any relevance to the juxtaposition of Whitman with the painters Millet and Eakins, or to that of Thoreau with the theories of the forgotten sculptor Horatio Greenough. It will be my responsibility to demonstrate those relevances.

The phase of my subject in which I am most interested is its challenge to pass beyond such interrelations to basic formulations about the nature of literature. In the chapter, 'Allegory and Symbolism,' Hawthorne and Melville have been its center, but I have attempted, so far as I was able, to write also an account of these two fundamental modes of apprehending reality. In the concluding chapter, 'Man in the Open Air,' the concern was to bring all five writers together through their subject matter, through their varied responses to the myth of the common man. But these serious responses can be better defined if set into contrast with the comic myth of the frontier, especially in its richest expression by George Washington Harris' *Sut Lovingood*. And the function of myth in literature can be clarified by the rediscovery of its necessity by the age of Joyce and Mann. As a final descriptive instance of my method, I have conceived of the two central books on Hawthorne and Melville as composing a single unit in which the chief value would be the aspects of tragedy that could be discerned through its representative practice by these two writers. I have made no pretence of abstracting a general theory of tragedy, but have crystallized out certain indispensable attributes that are common also to the practice of both Shakespeare and Milton.

After this description of my method, it is obvious that the division into four books is merely to indicate the central emphasis of each. This division, with the index, should make it easy for a reader particularly concerned with a single writer to concentrate on his work alone. Since volumes of criticism are now conventionally supposed to be short, I might have concealed the length of mine by printing it as four separate books, spaced, say, a year apart. But that would have defeated one of my main purposes: to make each writer cast as much light as possible on all the others. Moreover, our chief critical need would seem to be that of full-length estimates. I saw no use in adding further partial portraits to those of Parrington and Van Wyck Brooks, but wanted to deal in both analysis and synthesis. That required extensive quotation, since a critic, to be of any use, must back up his definitions with some of the evidence through which he has reached them. Only thus can the reader share in the process of testing the critic's judgments, and thereby reach his own. I trust that the further division into sixty-odd short essays will help the reader to skip wherever he wants. However, when dealing with the work of one writer, I have made as many transitions as practicable to that of the others.

It may be of some help to the reader to know from the start that the structure of the volume is based on recurrent themes. In addition to the types of interrelation I have mentioned, the most dominant of these themes are: the adequacy of the different writers' conceptions of the relation of the individual to society, and of the nature of good and evil—these two themes rising to their fullest development in the treatment of tragedy; the stimulus that lay in the transcendental conviction that the word must become one with the thing; the effect produced by the fact that when these writers began their careers, the one branch of literature in which America had a developed tradition was oratory; the effect of the nineteenth century's stress on seeing, of its identification of the poet with the prophet or seer; the connection, real if somewhat intangible, between this emphasis on vision and that put on light by the advancing arts of photography and open-air painting; the inevitability of the symbol as a means of expression for an age that was determined to make a fusion between appearance and what lay behind it; the major desire on the part of all five writers that there should be no split between art and the other functions of the community, that there should be an organic union between labor and culture.

The avenue of approach to all these themes is the same, through attention to the writers' use of their own tools, their diction and rhetoric, and to what they could make with them. An artist's use of language is the most sensitive index to cultural history, since a man can articulate only what he is, and what he has been made by the society of which he is a willing or an unwilling part. Emerson, Hawthorne, Thoreau, Whitman, and Melville all wrote literature for democracy in a double sense. They felt that it was incumbent upon their generation to give fulfilment to the potentialities freed by the Revolution, to provide a culture commensurate with America's political opportunity. Their tones were sometimes optimistic, sometimes blatantly, even dangerously expansive, sometimes disillusioned, even despairing, but what emerges from the total pattern of their achievement—if we will make the effort to repossess it[5]—is literature for our democracy. In reading the lyric, heroic, and tragic expression of our first great age, we can feel the challenge of our still undiminished resources. In my own writing about that age, I have kept in mind the demands made on the scholar by Louis Sullivan, who found a great stimulus for his architecture in the functionalism of Whitman. 'If, as I hold,' Sullivan wrote, 'true scholarship is of the highest usefulness because it implies the possession and application of the highest type of thought, imagination, and sympathy, his works must so reflect his scholarship as to prove that it has drawn him toward his people, not away from them; that his scholarship has been used as a means toward attaining their end, hence his. That his scholarship has been applied for the good and the enlightenment of all the people, not for the pampering of a class. His works must prove, in short (and the burden of proof is on him), that he is a citizen, not a lackey, a true exponent of democracy, not a tool of the most insidious form of anarchy . . . In a democracy there can be but one fundamental test of citizenship, namely: Are you using such gifts as you possess for or against the people?' These standards are the inevitable and right extension of Emerson's demands in *The American Scholar*. The ensuing volume has value only to the extent that it comes anywhere near measuring up to them.

NOTES

[1] See A. M. Schlesinger, Jr., *Orestes A. Brownson* (1939), and Helen S. Mims, 'Early American Democratic Theory and Orestes Brownson'

(*Science and Society,* Spring 1939).

[2] See Norman Ware, *The Industrial Worker,* 1840-1860 (1924), and E. C. Kirkland, *A History of American Economic Life* (1936).

[3] I have avoided, therefore, the temptation to include a full length treatment of Poe. The reason is more fundamental than that his work fell mainly in the decade of 1835-45; for it relates at very few points to the main assumptions about literature that were held by any of my group. Poe was bitterly hostile to democracy, and in that respect could serve as a revelatory contrast. But the chief interest in treating his work would be to examine the effect of his narrow but intense theories of poetry and the short story, and the account of the first of these alone could be the subject for another book: the development from Poe to Baudelaire, through the French symbolists, to modern American and English poetry. My reluctance at not dealing with Poe here is tempered by the fact that his value, even more than Emerson's, is now seen to consist in his influence rather than in the body of his own work. No group of his poems seems as enduring as *Drum-Taps;* and his

stories, less harrowing upon the nerves than they were, seem relatively factitious when contrasted with the moral depth of Hawthorne or Melville.

[4] I have provided a Chronology of the principal events in the five authors' lives on pages 657-61 [of *American Renaissance*].

[5] Santayana has said that the American mind does not oppose tradition, it forgets it. The kind of repossession that is essential has been described by André Malraux in an essay on 'The Cultural Heritage' (1936): 'Every civilization is like the Renaissance, and creates its own heritage out of everything in the past that helps it to surpass itself. *A heritage is not transmitted; it must be conquered;* and moreover it is conquered slowly and unpredictably. We do not demand a civilization made to order any more than we demand masterpieces made to order. But let us demand of ourselves a full consciousness that the choice made by each of us out of the past—out of the boundless hopes of the men who came before us—is measured by our thirst for greatness and by our wills.'

George Moore and the Nineties

Graham Hough

I am not one who oft or much delights in contemplating the division of literary history into periods: at best it is a barren exercise. Nevertheless it has a certain importance; largely a negative importance. No doubt all history is a seamless web, and everything is continuous with everything else, and our subdivisions are imposed and arbitrary schemes. No doubt these schemes have no substantial existence, and we have no real criterion for deciding that one is right and another wrong; the most we can say is that some are appropriate and useful and others less so. The best-laid scheme cannot give us much positive assistance; but regarded simply as a heuristic mechanism an inappropriate scheme can do a good deal to deform our picture of literary history. It has seemed to me for a long time that the concept of "the Victorian age" has had just this effect. The Victorian age presumably extends from somewhere about the accession of that respectable monarch in 1837 to her death in 1901. But the life of the spirit does not coincide very accurately with the vicissitudes of the temporal power, and as a division of literary history this slice of time makes very little sense. It has presented us with the picture of an age of patient moral and social fervor on the one hand, of the slow decline of the romantic impulse on the other, both fading into a sort of penumbra after the Victorian heyday. This is succeeded by a short space of total eclipse, until the darkness is dispelled by the sudden emergence of the light of Eliot and Pound. What we have here is plainly not a very complete or accurate account of what went on, so we have been persuaded to intercalate a short period called the nineties, just to signalize our recognition of the fact that various changes were taking place. As an alternative I should like to propose for consideration a period extending from about 1880 to 1914, a period distinct in spirit from what we usually think of as Victorianism, a period in which all the foundations of modern literature were being laid, but recognizably distinct from modern literature too. I am not quite sure about 1880; a case might be made for putting the beginning of our period back into the 1870s, perhaps to the publication of Pater's *Renaissance* in 1873; but on balance 1880 is probably about right. It is not until the late seventies that the influence of Pater on style and feeling becomes decisive, or that the influence of French realism begins to make itself felt in the novel. And as for 1914—perhaps it ought to be 1910; but 1914 is such a landmark in cultural as well as political history that it seems the most appropriate point to choose.

A paper on the nineties ideally should not begin by abolishing the nineties, or by merging them in a larger unit; and one may well concede that it is in the nineties that the tendencies of the period find their fullest expression. It is the decade of the one serious poetical *cénacle,* the Rhymers' Club; of the two most characteristic literary magazines, *The Yellow Book* and *The Savoy;* of what is probably the best of the English realist novels, Moore's *Esther Waters;* and of the great social-literary scandal, the Oscar Wilde trial. But a decade is an embarrassing unit in literary history; in general it is far too short to be useful, and there is not a writer of any weight in the nineties whose significant work does not extend outside them. One has only to cite the names of James, Hardy, Conrad, Moore, Gissing, and Yeats. It is sometimes said that the nineties were not an attitude but a state of mind—a state whose peculiar color has been variously described as mauve and greenery-yallery. This is a good enough starting period for period nostalgia, a vision of the poppies and the lilies, the green nightgowns, the blue china, the gas lamps reflected in a Whistlerian Thames, the Sickert music halls, and Sherlock Holmes's Inverness cape. One may become an addict to these historic stimulants, but they do not really tell us very much. And the trouble about the actual achievements of the nineties in their most characteristic forms is that they are so minuscule. The poetry of Dowson and Lionel Johnson, Crackanthorpe's stories and Henry Harland's, will not bear very much weight. Yeats's ninetyish phase is largely proleptic—it looks forward to a much greater achievement of a different kind later on. And Wilde, except as a personality and a portent, seems to me a greatly overrated figure. So if we insist on looking at the nineties by themselves we are presented with a decade where many forces are stirring but not to any very complete purpose.

Having proposed a longer period as the appropriate unit, I should like just to suggest its general characteristics; but only in a very summary fashion, since the bare existence of these twenty-five years as a literary concept has not yet been generally recognized, still less examined. I see three principal developments. First, a greatly increased range and a new freedom in the choice of subjects from actual life; all that we ordinarily call realism. I shall not make any distinction between realism and naturalism, for though in French literary history they are always carefully distinguished, this has no particular relevance to English, and in the controversy of the 1880s the word realism is the one that seems always to have been used. Leaving aside the shocked indignation, of which there was much, we can get an idea of the cautious welcome extended to realism, and the recognition of both its novelty and its foreign origin, from Henry James's remarks on Zola:

> A novelist with a system, a passionate conviction, a great plan— incontestable attributes of M. Zola—is not now easily to be found in England or the United States, where the story-teller's art is almost exclusively feminine, is mainly in the hands of timid (even

when very accomplished) women, whose acquaintance with life is severely restricted, and who are not conspicuous for general views. The novel, moreover, among ourselves, is almost always addressed to young unmarried ladies, or at least always assumes them to be a large part of the novelist's public.

This fact, to a French story-teller, appears, of course, a damnable restriction. . . . Half of life is a sealed book to young unmarried ladies, and how can a novel be worth anything that deals with only half of life? These objections are perfectly valid, and it may be said that our English system is a good thing for virgins and boys, and a bad thing for the novel itself, when the novel is regarded as something more than a simple *jeu d'esprit,* and considered as a composition that treats of life at large and helps us to *know.*

I take this quotation from an advertisement for the series of translations of Zola published by Vizetelly from 1884 onwards. Vizetelly was, of course, the publisher who was most closely associated with the realist movement; he was prosecuted for his publications and eventually imprisoned, in 1888. In subsequent comment on the affair he is generally represented as a sort of martyr for culture, but a further perusal of the advertisement pages I am speaking of leads one to take this with just a small pinch of salt. It may be that Vizetelly was filled only with a pure desire to serve modern letters and to show contemporary society the realities on which it was based, but it is also fairly evident that Vizetelly's Realistic Novels are advertised with half an eye towards a possibly scandalous success; and I mention this because the suggestion that "This is not for young ladies" (or the alternative suggestion that "This will certainly be read by young ladies but their parents ought not to know"), made seriously, or defiantly, or with a behind-the-hand snigger, is a very recognizable element in the literature of this time, quite as recognizable as the high Victorian attitude of Tennyson —

> The prudent partner of his blood
> Lean'd on him, faithful, gentle, good,
> Wearing the rose of womanhood—

and so forth. The advertisement of George Moore's *A Mummer's Wife,* for example, begins with the announcement: "This book has been placed in the Index Expurgatorius of the Select Circulating Libraries of Messrs. Mudie and W. H. Smith and Son."

The second development is a confused set of tendencies that cluster round the notion of art for art's sake. These never amount to a formal doctrine in England, and they hold together in a loose synthesis a number of different ideas, mostly derived from France. Parnassians, symbolists, decadents—these school labels have a tolerably plain meaning in French literary history, but English literary ideas are much less clearly analyzed. Art for art's sake, for what the phrase is worth, goes back to Gautier, and Gautier had been an influence on Swinburne in the 1860s. Transposed into a moral rather than a literary code, it reappears in the preface to Pater's *Renaissance;* and the cult of exquisite sensations, expressed in the languid Paterian rhythms, haunts the production of the nineties and extends some considerable distance into this century. But the strictly literary ideals to which it gave rise remain shifting and uncertain. On the one hand we are constantly hearing echoes of "L'Art," the last poem in *Émaux et Camées,* with its praise of a hard-chiseled perfection of form:

> Lutte avec le carrare,
> Avec le paros dur
>   Et rare,
> Gardiens du contour pur;
>
> Peintre, fuis l'aquarelle,
> Et fixe la couleur
>   Trop frêle
> Au four de l'émailleur.

On the other hand, the quite contrary doctrine of Verlaine's "Art Poètique":

> Il faut aussi que tu n'ailles point
> Choisir tes mots sans quelque méprise:
> Rien de plus cher que la chanson grise
> Ou l'Indécis au Précis se joint.
>
> Car nous voulons la Nuance encore,
> Pas la Couleur, rien que la Nuance!

So that we are left uncertain whether the prevalent ideal is an intaglio cut in the hardest stone or a misty Whistler nocturne. But what these ideals have in common is an insistence on the claims as the artist as artificer against those of the artist as interpreter of life. "The Yellow Dwarf," the pseudonymous book reviewer of *The Yellow Book* (his name, by the way, is borrowed from *Le Nain Jaune,* a Parnassian periodical of the 1860s), makes a great point of the purely aesthetic nature of his criticism, and he is greatly disturbed when he suspects that a work of fiction might have a moral or be intended as a tract for the times. And, as in France, this lightweight aestheticism passes over into symbolism. Whether there is anything in English letters that can be called a symbolist movement I am not sure; but the word seems inevitable, and is not without its uses. Symbolism can be said to occur when the cult of the exquisite, particular sensation, embodied in the perfect form, begins to acquire transcendental overtones, begins to be seen as a means of access to a more authentic world underlying the world of appearances. As a half-sentimental literary idea we see this floating around in a good many places. As a serious conviction, involving the whole moral and literary personality, we see it in the early essays of Yeats.

Now these two tendencies, the realist and the symbolist-aesthetic, are inveterately opposed in France. But in England they show a curious tendency to fuse together. This is because moral ideas in England are commonly clearer and more strongly held than literary ones; a literary controversy tends to shift itself to the moral plane. And morally the two different schools are in fact moving in the same direction. Both place the demands of art outside and above the moral exigencies, and the need for a moral emancipation is so much more pressing in England that it obscures other differences. The movement may be towards fantasy and dream, or it may be towards the recognition of the most sordid social actualities; but these do not feel themselves to be vitally opposed, for they are both expressions of the same need. Moral and psychological adventurousness and the pursuit of an exquisite and refined form go hand in hand in England, and even tend to be seen as much the same thing. George Eliot, we may notice, comes in for equally heavy knocks on both counts—for lumbering bluntness of style and form, and for the ever-present moral superintendence under which her work is seen to labor.

The third very marked feature of the time is a conscious reaction against the English literary tradition. This is something relatively new, at any rate since neo-classical times. It formed no part of the romantic upheaval, though I suppose a foretaste of it may be found in Matthew Arnold's exhortations against English provincialism and complacency. But the reaction I am speaking of has a new flavor, and it continues into the most formative literature of the next decades. It is the beginning of that chronic Francophilia that affects many of the Anglo-American intelligentsia even to our own day. The manifestations that first leap to the mind are the slightly absurd ones—Pater murmuring that Poe was so coarse, he could only read him in Baudelaire's translation; Wilde writing *Salomé* in not very good French; the scraps of French idiom that interlard the pages of Henry James—down to the still current illusions that French coffee is good and the architecture of Paris beautiful. Of course the influence of France was necessary; it was the only one possible. It was an example of that perpetual process of fruitful interchange of which the history of European letters is composed. But there was in this particular wave of French influence an element of affectation. Yeats's use of Mallarmé—whom he cannot possibly have understood—as a name to conjure with provides us with one instance. There went with it a slightly perverse determination to throw overboard some of the most characteristic achievements of the English genius—Moore's dismissal of Shakespeare and the traditional English novel, for example. Without the slightest leaning to that absurdest of attitudes, a literary nationalism, it remains true that the actual achieved body of work in a given language is an inescapable condition for future work. The nineties show signs of wishing to make an escape; and, though this is another subject, and complicated by Anglo-American literary relations, the tendency persisted into the *avant garde* of the twentieth century.

In a period where may of the representative writings are on a very small scale it is difficult to find a typical figure to stand for the central movement of the time. I have a candidate to propose for this office; it is George Moore. There is no particular virtue in being typical; but even if it is the portrait of an age that we are trying to draw there are advantages in examining an individual man, an actual writer, rather than tendencies exhibited in fragments. George Moore has some qualifications that are particularly useful to us in this respect. In the first place, he exists. He is discernible with the naked eye, which can hardly be said for Crackanthorpe or Dowson. Never quite in the center of the picture, he nevertheless played a real part in the literary history of the *fin de siècle*, and in his vivid, outrageous autobiography he has played a considerable part in chronicling it. He has a large body of work to his credit, uneven it is true, but some of it of undeniable excellence, and much of it of peculiar interest. And although his career extends far into this century, he remained remarkably faithful to the intuitions of his earlier years. Even his defects are for our present purpose a recommendation. Moore was not Prince Hamlet, nor was meant to be; almost at times the fool. He was incapable of what in any ordinary acceptation of the term would be called thought. He picks up ideas from everywhere, never understands them quite thoroughly or thinks them out, mixes them up to make a miscellaneous stew, and often pretends to knowledge that he does not really possess.

As an informant on matters of fact he is unreliable in the extreme. To anyone attempting a critical examination of Moore, particularly to anyone who is sensible of his merits, these are highly embarassing qualities. But if we want to feel the form and pressure of the time they are extremely useful ones. He wrote of himself:

> My soul, so far as I understand it, has very kindly taken colour and form from the many various modes of life that self-will and an impetuous temperament have forced me to indulge in. Therefore I may say that I am free from original qualities, defects, tastes, etc. . . . I came into the world apparently with a nature like a smooth sheet of wax, bearing no impress but capable of receiving any; of being moulded into all shapes.

And it is so with his literary development too; he picks up like a magpie all the notions and influences at large in the world around him, spills them out with an air of proud discovery—in fact, as Oscar Wilde said to him, conducts his education in public. If we want to find out what the literary scene looked like to a young man of advanced tastes in the eighties and nineties we can hardly do better than look at his early works. Greater literary personalities will tell us less. The tireless spiritual energy of Yeats, the quick-witted positiveness of Shaw, are too idiosyncratic to tell us much except about their possessors.

The document I wish to look at is the *Confessions of a Young Man*. It was written in 1886; it refers to a period between 1873, when Moore first went to Paris, and 1883, when his first novel appeared; and as we now have it, it was annotated by its author at two later dates. I remember abominating it when I first read it, years ago; and it does indeed give the picture of an intolerable young coxcomb. But I entirely failed to see its significance. It is an account of Moore's literary education, and pretty well the complete account, since he was almost illiterate when he first went to France. It is an education picked up in cafés and studios, the editorial offices of magazines, and the Gaiety bar. We need not stickle for the factual accuracy of the story. The apartment with the red drawing-room, the Buddha, the python, and the Turkish couches is unlikely to have been as Moore describes it in the mid-1870s. It seems to owe far too much to Huysmans's *A Rebours*. And *A Rebours* did not come out till 1884. What we are contemplating in fact is a panoramic view of the formation of a taste and an attitude, of all the varied aesthetic and social influences that went to make it, from the standpoint of 1886. It is a view that still seemed valid to Moore in 1904, and even beyond the limits of our period, in 1916.

The inevitable first reaction to the book is to find it an appalling muddle. Enthusiasms and recantations seem to follow each other in no sort of order. Every opinion is contradicted by its opposite a few pages farther on. There are no dates, and no possibility of making the story into an intelligible chronological sequence. Then one realizes that Moore is perfectly well aware of this and has even made his capriciousness into a sort of principle. "Never could I interest myself in a book," he writes, "if it were not the exact diet my mind required at the time, or in the very immediate future." And later, in excusing himself for lack of sensibility to Shakespeare, "There are affinities in literature corresponding to, and very analogous to, sexual affinities—the same unreasoned attractions, the same pleasures, the same lassitudes. Those we have loved most we are most indifferent to. Shelley, Gautier, Zola, Flaubert, Goncourt! how I have loved you all; and now I could not, would not, read you again." But there are other ways of revealing a sensibility and an attitude than the ordered chronological *Bildungsroman*. This pell-mell jumble of passions and revulsions spreads out, as it were, the contents of Moore's imagination for our inspection; and we can see that the objects displayed, apparently a mere chance assortment, actually fall into two groups. One group is composed of fantasies and dreams, often slightly perverse fantasies and dreams, unchecked by bourgeois ethics or ordinary social reality. The other group consists of equally passionate aspirations after the actualities of life, the tangible realities of contemporary experience and modern urban living. These two enthusiasms sometimes clash violently. Each at times tries to deny the existence of the other, yet both continue to exist—and even in the end come to a kind of reconciliation. They are united, not only as the most staring opposites may be, by the accident of inhering in the same personality, but by a real common factor. The common element is the purely literary one, the need that each passion has to find its fullest and justest verbal expression. Starting with a notable ignorance of both English grammar and the English vocabulary, Moore ultimately finds the ruling passion of his life in the desire to write well.

Fantasy and dream came first, and came even at first in a verbal embodiment. His first literary passion was for the mere name of a novel he heard his parents discussing—*Lady Audley's Secret*. This was followed by the revelation of Shelley, also turned to initially for the same reason. "Lady Audley! What a beautiful name! . . . Shelley! That crystal name, and his poetry also crystalline." Most of the English lyric poets were read soon after. But from Shelley the young Moore had learnt atheism, and he followed this up by a course of the rationalist classics, Lecky and Buckle. It is noticeable that George Eliot comes in with these. She appears as the great agnostic, not as an artist; and the only one of the classic English novelists that Moore mentions with any enthusiasm is Dickens. Then to France, to study painting; not that he had any talent, but France and art became the objects of a romantic devotion, like the names of Lady Audley and Shelley. There were some flirtations with Hugo and Musset; but the first real revelation came from Gautier, from reading *Mademoiselle de Maupin*. It would be hard to exaggerate the influence of this work on the sensibility of the *fin de siècle* in England. It is constantly cited and referred to; and still more often its situations and its spirit are echoed without open acknowledgement. Both his own panegyrics and later scholarship have shown how decisive was the influence of Gautier on Swinburne; and Moore was sufficiently acute to notice it himself. "The 'Hymn to Proserpine' and 'Dolores' are wonderful lyrical versions of Mlle de Maupin," he writes. The frank sensuality, the delight in visible and tangible beauty, combined with the unquiet romantic *Sehnsucht*, the longing for an ideal satisfaction, was a combination of ingredients that the more decorous English romanticism had never supplied. Above all there was the hint of perversity brought in by the epicene nature of the hero-heroine; a double delight, for it was at once a new source of erotic stimulation and a new means to *épater le bourgeois*. Moore expresses the spirit in which it was accepted with uncommon clarity:

> I read "Mlle de Maupin" at a moment when I was weary of spiritual passion, and this great exaltation of the visible above the invisible at once conquered and led me captive. This plain scorn of a world exemplified in lacerated saints and a crucified Redeemer opened up a prospect of new beliefs and new joys in things and new revolts against all that had come to form part and parcel of the commonalty of mankind. Shelley's teaching had been, while accepting the body, to dream of the soul as a star, and so preserve our ideal; but now I saw suddenly, with delightful clearness and intoxicating conviction that by looking with shame and accepting with love the flesh, I might raise it to as high a place within as divine a light as ever the soul had been set in.

It was above all the tone of *Mademoiselle de Maupin* that Moore picked up, and it is a tone that is to echo through much of the literature of the nineties and to give it much of its peculiar flavor. It is a young man's tone, and that of a young man whom our elders would certainly have called a cad. It is rather lightheartedly erotic, and quite openly predatory. It is haunted by sexuality and makes a great deal of its "paganism," yet it does not for a moment suggest the antique world; rather a setting of *deuxsième empire* frou-frou, tea-roses, Parma violets, the minor pleasures of an elegant nineteenth-century Bohemianism. Yet beneath this wordly assurance the note of romantic idealism is never quite absent; the young social and sexual buccaneer is haunted by the ghost of a sad Pierrot sighing after an impossible love. Let us look at a few examples.

Why should I undertake to keep a woman by me for the entire space of her life, watching her grow fat, grey, wrinkled and foolish? Think of the annoyance of perpetually looking after any one, especially a woman! Besides, marriage is antagonistic to my ideal.

(Moore, *Confessions*)

If I were to be the lover of one of these ladies like a pale narcissus, moist with a tepid dew of tears, and bending with willowy languor over the new marble tomb of a spouse, happily and recently defunct, I should be as wretched as the dear departed was in his lifetime.

(Gautier, *Maupin*)

He can read through the slim woman whose black hair, a-glitter with diamonds, contrasts with her white satin; an old man is talking to her, she dances with him, and she refused a young man a moment before. This is a bad sign, our Lovelace knows it; there is a stout woman of thirty-five, who is looking at him, red satin bodice, doubtful taste. He looks away; a little blonde woman fixes her eyes on him, she looks as innocent as a child; instinctively our Lovelace turns to his host. "Who is that little blonde women over there, the right-hand corner?" he asks. "Ah, that is Lady——." "Will you introduce me?" "Certainly." Lovelace has made up his mind.

(Moore, *Confessions*)

All this does not prevent me from positively wanting a mistress. I do not know who she will be, but among the women of my acquaintance I see nobody who could suitably fill this dignified position. Those who may be regarded as young enough are wanting in beauty or intellectual charm; those who are beautiful and young are basely and forbiddingly virtuous, or lack the necessary freedom; and then there is always some husband, some brother, a mother or an aunt, somebody or other, with prying eyes and large ears, who must either be cajoled or given short shrift.

(Gautier, *Maupin*)

I was absorbed in the life of woman—the mystery of petticoats, so different from the staidness of trousers! the rolls of hair entwined with so much art, and suggesting so much colour and perfume, so different from the bare crop; the unnaturalness of the waist in stays! plentitude and slenderness of silk. . . . A world of calm colour with phantoms moving, floating past and changing in dim light —an averted face with abundant hair, the gleam of a perfect bust or the poise of a neck turning slowly round, the gaze of deep translucid eyes. I loved women too much to give myself wholly to one.

(Moore, *Confessions*)

It makes me have a low opinion of women when I see how infatuated they often are with blackguards who despise and deceive them, instead of taking a lover—some staunch and sincere young man who would consider himself very lucky, and would simply worship them; I myself, for example, am such a one. It is true that men of the former kind abound in the drawing-rooms, where they preen themselves for all to behold, and are always lounging on the back of some settee, while I remain at home, my forehead pressed against the window-pane, watching the river shroud itself in haze and the mists rising, while silently setting up in my heart the scented shrine, the peerless temple, in which I am to install the future idol of my soul.

(Gautier, *Maupin*)

I have two points to make in setting these extracts side by side. One is how extraordinarily closely Moore echoes Gautier's tone, and how easy it is to recognize that tone as particularly characteristic of the nineties. We find it again and again in Wilde, in *The Yellow Book* and *The Savoy,* and even, though decorously veiled and entirely without the connivance of the author, in some of the characters of Henry James. The second point is that the attitudes implied here are entirely social and sexual. But *Mademoiselle de Maupin* had a preface—the famous preface which was the manifesto of the art-for-art's-sake movement. Moore does not mention it, but we can hardly suppose that he did not read it. And we later find, by a curious linkage, that he associates *Mademoiselle de Maupin* with Pater's *Marius the Epicurean.* There seems to be little in common between the aesthetic sensuality of Gautier and the spiritualized hedonism of Pater. It may of course be that the one is simply the Oxford version of the other, and Moore partly makes the association on those grounds—with a certain rude psychological insight and a good deal of injustice to what Pater supposed himself to be saying.

Mr. Pater can join hands with Gautier in saying

> je trouve la terre aussi belle que le ciel, et je pense que la correction de la forme est la vertu.

"I think that correctness of form is virtue"; that is the real link that Moore makes between Gautier and Pater. The social and sexual antinomianism is only the correlative of a general pursuit of formal beauty, which can manifest itself as much in the sphere of verbal arrangement as in the sphere of conduct.

> But "Marius the Epicurean" was more to me than a mere emotional influence, precious and rare though that may be, for this book was the first in English prose I had come across that procured for me any genuine pleasure in the language itself, in the combination of words for silver or gold chime, and unconventional cadence, and for all those lurking half-meanings, and that evanescent suggestion, like the odour of dead roses, that words retain to the last of other times and elder usage. . . . "Marius" was the stepping-stone that carried me across the channel into the genius of my own tongue.

I said before that psychological adventurousness and the search for perfection of form go hand in hand. Here we see the process in action. Gautier suggests a style of life; Pater extends it; and at the same time he suggests a style of writing. The cultivation of a mannered exquisiteness of sensation leads directly into the cultivation of prose as a deliberate aesthetic instrument.

After the reading of *Maupin* Moore plunged deep into the waters of aestheticism. Other tales of Gautier followed, and the delicately chiseled nostalgias of *Émaux et Camées*. The inevitable next step was Baudelaire.

> No longer is it the grand barbaric face of Gautier; now it is the clean-shaven face of the mock priest, the slow, cold eye, and the sharp, cunning sneer of the cynical libertine who will be tempted that he may better know the worthlessness of temptation. "Les Fleurs du Mal," beautiful flowers, beautiful in sublime decay. What a great record is yours, and were Hell a reality how many souls would we find wreathed with your poisonous blossoms.

(There is no need to suppose that Moore in 1886 wrote these lines without a tinge of irony.) Bertrand's *Gaspard de la Nuit;* Villiers de l'Isle Adam, whom Moore used to meet at the Nouvelle Athènes; Verlaine; Gustave Kahn's experiments in *verse libre* and faint evocative vocabulary; Ghil's theory of colored vowels, a development of the doctrine of Rimbaud's sonnet, which gave rise to an often quoted passage in *Muslin;* Mallarmé, whose conversation Moore enjoyed, while confessing that he was quite unable to understand either the poetry or the Symbolist theory. Excited by this heady brew, it is not surprising that Moore was unable to appreciate the contemporary experiments in the poetry of common life. When he came to read Coppée he was able to enjoy only his early Parnassian poems.

> But the exquisite perceptivity of Coppèe showed in his modern poems, the certainty with which he raised the commonest subject, investing it with sufficient dignity for his purpose, escaped me wholly, and I could not but turn with horror from such poems as "La Nourrice" and "Le Petit Epicier." I could not understand how anybody could bring himself to acknowledge the vulgar details of our vulgar age.

But a new force was piling up behind the aesthetic screen, and it was soon to burst out. Moore was busy trying to write short stories apparently in the manner of Villiers' *Contes Cruels,* and poems, "Roses of Midnight," in what he believed to be the manner of Baudelaire. One day by chance he read in a magazine an article by Zola (presumably *Le Roman Experimental*). The words *naturalisme, la verité, la science* affronted his eyes. He learnt that one should write with as little imagination as possible, that contrived plot in a novel or a play was illiterate and puerile. It all struck him as a revelation, and he realized the sterile eccentricity of his own aestheticism. He had read a few chapters of *L'Assommoir* when it had appeared in serial form, but like others of his tastes had dismissed it as an absurdity. Now he began to buy up the back numbers of the *Voltaire,* the weekly in which Zola was making propaganda for the naturalist cause.

> The idea of a new art based on science, in opposition to the art of the old world that was based on the imagination, an art that should explain all things and embrace modern life in its entirety, in its endless ramifications, be, as it were, a new creed in a new civilisation, filled me with wonder, and I stood dumb before the vastness of the conception, and the towering height of the ambition.

This mood of enraptured stupefaction did not last; at the time of writing the *Confessions,* in 1886, he is able to look back at the Zola articles and say "Only the simple crude statements of a man of powerful mind, but singulary narrow vision." And a few pages farther on

from the account of the naturalist revelation is a thoroughgoing attack
on Zola's limitations, an attack whose consequences are amusingly
described in the essay "A Visit to Médan." But it is not my purpose to
write the history of Moore's literary opinions in detail. The point is
that from now on the idea of a distinctively modern art, grounding itself on the realities of the contemporary world, lies side by side with
aesthetic fantasy in Moore's mind. It is surprising how easily they
came to lie side by side. On a later page of the *Confessions*, *Mademoiselle de Maupun* and *L'Assommoir* are cited together as the two
books above all from which the respectable circulating-library young
lady must turn away; they are mentioned almost as though they were
the twin pillars of modern letters, in spite of the fact that *Maupun* had
appeared in 1836, and that the two works had nothing whatever in
common, except that neither is exactly the thing *à mettre entre les
mains de toute jeune fille*. And the fact is that naturalism did not drive
out aestheticism, it substituted a new aestheticism of an extended
kind. The immediate effect of the Zola discovery was to send Moore
back to Coppée's modern poems, and to persuade him to modernize
his "Roses of Midnight." But this soon proved to be a hopeless enterprise, and he turns to reflect, not at all on the social and descriptive
implications of naturalism, but on its purely literary qualities. He re-
reads *L'Assommoir* and is impressed by its "strength, height and decorative grandeur," by the "immense harmonic development of the idea,
and the fugal treatment of the different scenes," by "the lordly, river-
like roll of the narrative." In short, it was "the idea of the new aestheticism—the new art corresponding to modern, an ancient art corresponded to ancient life" that captivated him and was to compel his imagination for many years to come.

The later history of Zola's reputation has borne out Moore's intuition. Towards the end of the *Confessions* he writes:

> One thing that cannot be denied to the realists: a constant and in-
> tense desire to write well, to write artistically. When I think of
> what they have done in the matter of the use of words, of the
> myriad verbal effects they have discovered, of the thousand forms
> of composition they have created, how they have remodelled and
> refashioned the language in their untiring striving for intensity of
> expression, for the very osmazome of art, I am lost in ultimate won-
> der and admiration. What Hugo did for French verse, Flaubert,
> Goncourt, Zola, and Huysmans have done for French prose.

It would once have seemed eccentric to talk of Zola in this way,
perhaps did even when Moore was writing. But in later years nobody

has been very interested in Zola the reporter and sociologist; and complaints about the supposed coarseness and crudity of his style have given way, and justly, to admiration for his impressionist painting and the organization of his large set pieces. The massive symbolism in his writing has not passed unnoticed, and the flat opposition between naturalist and symbolist has been much played down. By now, when the professed "scientific" pretensions of *Le Roman Experimental* can no longer be taken seriously, the real nature of Zola's achievement can be seen more clearly, and it is seen much as Moore saw it. In making the transition from Zola's untenable naturalist theory to his far more interesting and comprehensive practice Moore is taking the line that both criticism and fiction itself were to take in the years to come.

But Moore's discipleship to Zola was brief. He soon saw something nearer to his real aim in Flaubert, where the demands of a scrupulous realism are united with an equal scrupulosity of rhythm and phrasing. However great the difference between their achievements, Flaubert's strict attachment to the truth, to be sought only through formal perfection, probably came nearest to embodying Moore's artistic ideal. *A Mummer's Wife* is his only Zolaesque novel; he was annoyed if one did not recognize that *Esther Waters* was in inspiration "pure Flaubert." But strangely, even Flaubert was not the object of Moore's lasting devotion. Talking of his own literary infidelities he says "even a light of love is constant, if not faithful, to her *amant de coeur*"; and the most enduring of his literary passions was for Balzac. "Upon that rock I built my church, and his great and valid talent saved me from the shoaling waters of new aestheticisms, the putrid mud of naturalism, and the faint and sickly surf of the symbolists." It is only in Balzac that he can find an unrestricted romantic imagination united with a complete engagement in the involved turmoil of contemporary life. Essentially a spectator on the sidelines, Moore is fascinated by that colossal vitality; and if for Alisander he is more than a little o'erparted, we can at least recognize in the totality of his work something of his master's passion for the diversity of human experience.

Disorderly and capricious as Moore's expression of his enthusiasms is, it can still tell us something, and something that is of importance beyond his own career. He was more completely involved in French literature than any other writer of the nineties—more even than Symons; and we can see in him a complete microcosm of the French influences that were then reshaping English literature. His experience tells us of the opening of a new chapter in the history of English

fiction. Three steady preoccupations can be discerned among his shifting allegiances: one is with telling the truth about experience instead
of merely devising an agreeable story; the second is with imaginative
freedom in spite of the circulating libraries and the young ladies; the
third is with formal justness and beauty in expression and organization, instead of the labored or slapdash approximations to which the
English novel in all but its highest moments had been prone. Together
they make a break with many of the traditions of English fiction—with
the traditions of picaresque adventure, indiscriminate humor, genial
satire, and reforming zeal. A severer artistic ideal takes their place.
And this break is not merely a matter of Moore's own work. We are
not considering his intrinsic quality at the moment, though my own
conviction is that it is far higher than has been generally recognized;
we are using him simply as a convenient periscope to survey the literary scene of his time. And the lessons he was learning were also being
learnt, wholly or in part, by Hardy, Conrad, and Henry James.

James is a far greater, Hardy and Conrad more central writers than
Moore. It is relatively easy to fit them into a "great tradition" of English fiction. Moore has always his own marked idiosyncrasy, and the
criticism of our time, in its preoccupation with prevalent trends and
successful revolutions rather than with individual quality, has been
inclined to see it as a dead end. This is not, I think, true; and if it is
necessary to justify Moore to the trend-mongers one may do so by
showing that he was leading, if not up the main road, into an area
where the greatest prose experiment of our time has its beginning. We
have seen Moore oscillating between aesthetic reverie and realism, and
if we were to follow the development of his art we should find him in
the end arriving at a style that was to harmonize the two. He manages
in his best work to present in all their uncompromising contingency
the actualities of common experience, and yet to preserve the inevitability of impression, the delicate rightness of diction and rhythm that
he had learned from the high priests of a scrupulous art. At the end of
our period, when Moore was past the threshold of old age, another
Irish writer brought out his youthful confessions; and in it he defined
the function of the poet, the literary artist, as it appeared to his eyes.
It is to be "the mediator between the world of reality and the world of
dreams." No writer in any age has carried farther than James Joyce
the dual allegiance to an exhaustive naturalism on the one hand and a
complex aesthetic symbolism on the other; and I think it is likely that
neither the title nor the content of Joyce's *Portrait of the Artist as a*

Young Man would have been quite the same in 1916 if it had not been for the prior existence of Moore's *Confessions of a Young Man* in 1886. And there are other resemblances more strongly marked. Critics have often spoken about the absolute originality of Joyce's *Dubliners;* and that is a curious instance of how far George Moore's achievements have dropped out of sight—itself perhaps a curious instance of the general failure to recognize the importance of the *fin de siècle* as a formative power in modern literature. For *Dubliners* has an obvious ancestor in Moore's stories in *The Untilled Field.* Joyce's stories have an urban instead of a rural setting, and make far more use of the romantic-ironical contrast. But it is surprising that the closeness of his manner to Moore's has not been observed. Part of it no doubt is a matter of a common discipleship. Moore's debt to Pater's prose has always been achknowledged; and Joyce's use of the same master is obvious, especially in *Portrait of the Artist.* It would be too long to illustrate in detail, but the echoed cadences sometimes reveal themselves in a sentence.

> From without as from within the waters had flowed over his barriers: their tides once more began to jostle fiercely above the crumbled mole.
>
> (Joyce, *Portrait of the Artist*)

> I could see that he believed the story, and for the moment I, too, believed in an outcast Venus becoming the evil spirit of a village that would not accept her as divine.
>
> (Moore, *The Untilled Field*)

Neither of these dying falls would be quite as they are if they had not echoed so often already through Pater's prose. In feeling and treatment too we can see common obligations. "The Window" in *The Untilled Field* and "Clay" in *Dubliners* are both stories about humble old women; and I doubt whether either of them would exist if Flaubert had not written "Un Coeur Simple." But the similarities between the two volumes are so marked and pervasive that I am persuaded the debt is more direct. Moore said later that he began *The Untilled Field* "with the hope of furnishing the young Irish of the future with models"; and reading *Dubliners* beside the earlier book we can hardly doubt that for Joyce he achieved just that. He also said that, as the work progressed, "the first stories begot a desire to paint the portrait of my country"; almost the words in which Joyce described to his publisher the purpose of *Dubliners:* "to write a chapter of the moral history of my country." One could go on to speak of the last story in

Dubliners, "The Dead," and of how extraordinarily close it is in feeling to, say, "The Exile" and "Home Sickness" in Moore's collection. But to do justice to the charity, the gentleness, the centrality of feeling that these two lonely antinomian writers achieve in these beautiful tales would be to desert periods and influences, and would demand quite other tools and another manner. I end on this note just to give a small illustration of what is still often forgotten—how intimate the connection is between the writing of the late nineteenth century and what is most new and living in the twentieth.

The Importance of Shaftesbury

Ernest Tuveson

1

It has generally been acknowledged that the third Earl of Shaftesbury exercised an immense influence on the eighteenth century.[1] His collected works, the *Characteristics*, went through eleven editions between 1711 and 1790; and the list of authors who demonstrated the influence of Shaftesbury would include a majority of those published in the eighteenth century. Yet there is a puzzle about Shaftesbury's effect on his own and later times. It was long assumed that this influence consisted in his originality, the newness of his theory of the "moral sense" in particular, as well as his "preromantic" and supposedly original glorification of external nature. The notable growth in altruism in eighteenth century literature, says Professor C. A. Moore, "is to be traced largely, I think, to the *Characteristics* . . . of Lord Shaftesbury," and he adds, "It has long since been established that his system of philosophy constitutes a turning point in the history of pure speculation, especially in ethics."[2] In more recent years, however, this view has been challenged. Professor R. S. Crane has shown that the essentials of the "moral sense" theory were being preached by "Latitudinarian" divines even before Shaftesbury was born. He writes:

> If we wish to understand the origins and the widespread diffusion in the eighteenth century of the ideas which issued in the cult of sensibility, we must look, I believe, to a period considerably earlier than that in which Shaftesbury wrote and take into account the

propaganda of a group of persons whose opportunities for moulding the thoughts of ordinary Englishmen were much greater than those of even the most aristocratic of deists.[3]

It can be shown as well that the exaltation and adoration of external nature was anticipated by and reflected a complex of ideas that the new science in combination with religion had already prepared.[4]

Must we, then, give up Shaftesbury as "original"? And if we do, how are we to account for the astonishing influence which he exerted? The answers to these questions, I believe, lie along other lines than have usually been suggested. In the world of thought, the whole is greater than the sum of the parts; and if the age that followed Shaftesbury was to a considerable extent *Characteristical,* it was not because his ideas separately were new or startling, but because he constructed of many elements a complete and artistically consistent whole, in a setting which had not previously existed.

As to the "moral sense" theory. There was as Professor Crane indicates, a cloud of divines who to some extent advanced the propositions that virtue is centered in a natural impulse towards humanitarian feeling for and sympathy with one's fellows, and that the exercise of this virtue is accompanied by an inward feeling of satisfaction and joy, while the spectacle of distress produces sympathetic pain. Yet, however striking these statements may be in themselves, we must remember that they were embedded in a context which did much to reduce their revolutionary effect.

Let us consider as examples two influential members of what is loosely called the "Cambridge Platonist" group. John Norris's *The Theory and Regulation of Love* (1694) postulates a "moral Gravity" of the soul, impressed on it by God Himself. This gravity

> will be its *Connaturality* to all Good, or Good in general, that is to God as its primary adequate Object, and to particular Goods only so far as they have something of the common Nature of Good, something of God in them.[5]

The image borrowed from the new philosophy, which makes goodness seem as inevitable in men as the operation of natural law in the cosmos, is striking and apparently radical enough; yet the theory is not what it seems to be. For Norris still sees good as merely participation in a transcendental God. The "moral gravity," it appears, is the result of a spiritual ascent. "From the Original Pravity and Degeneracy of our Nature, among *all* these particular Goods, that which we most eagerly propend to, is *sensual* Good."[6] The "Animal" impressions are formed first, "Sensuality comes to be *Adult* and *Mature,* when our discourses are but *young* and *imperfect.*" When we arrive at an age for reflection we have, therefore, to "unravel the Prejudices of our Youth, and *unlive* our former Life . . .," and we are assured that it is not an easy job. This curious theory, with its mixture of new science, psychology, and old theology, represents in sum a partly scientific, partly Neoplatonic version of the doctrine of original sin. At no time did Norris, despite his seemingly radical phrase "moral gravity," really absorb morality into nature, or identify the end of existence with conduct in this world. Against this view Norris's friend Henry More advanced another account of moral action, also seemingly radical in its imagery.

> For, as the eye, . . . if it be vitiated in it self, cannot rightly discern the Condition of the visible Object it fixes its Sight upon; so the Mind of Man, let him set himself never so diligently to contemplate any *Moral* or *Intelligible* Object, if she be made dim by Moral Corruptions and Impurities, will not be able or free to close with what is best in the Circumstances that lye before her, being held captive by the Vices the Party has not yet purified himself from . . . our being redeemed into an Ability or freedom of chusing what is best, is not from *mere attention* to the Object, but from Purification, *Illumination,* and *real Regeneration* into the *Divine Image.*[7]

Here are two liberal clergymen who speak indeed of "goodness" as "natural," as natural as gravity in the physical world, or as seeing in the animal; yet the images certainly are not to be taken by themselves. Platonized Christianity, though modified by Cartesianism and early Newtonianism, nevertheless did not lose sight of *"Purification, Illumination,* and *real Regeneration"* as essential before the "divine Image" can be complete.

Other preachers, of a later generation, do in fact carry the naturalizing tendency further; but we see, if we read the works of these divines, that the basic Christian pattern is always to be discerned in the background. Isaac Barrow, one of the most extreme of them all, can exclaim:

> In fine, the wisest observers of man's nature have pronounced him to be a creature gentle and sociable, inclinable to and fit for conversation, apt to keep good order, to observe rules of justice, to embrace any sort of vertue, if well managed; if instructed by good discipline, if guided by good example, if living under the influence of wise laws and virtuous governors. Fierceness, rudeness, craft, malice, all perverse and intractable, all mischievous and vitious disposi-

tions do grow among men (like weeds in any, even the best soil) and overspread the earth from neglect of good education; from ill conduct, ill custome, ill example; ('tis the comparison of Saint *Chrysostome*, and of Plutarch.)[8]

The combination of a Father and a pagan philosopher as authorities should remind us that such ideas go back very far and derive from the amalgamation of classical philosophy with Christianity which early began to take place. That man has some—perhaps a fairly large—capacity for goodness was part of orthodox Christian theology. But we must always view such statements against the whole background. Barrow, for instance, frequently points out that the soul must undergo a spiritual awakening before its goodness can be released:

If also being, through divine grace awakened out of that drowsie state (which naturally in great measure hath seised upon all men) he discovereth his moral or spiritual wants, and imperfections; he is then apt to breathe and endeavour a nearer similitude to God. . . .[9]

The sacrifice of the Cross is essential to that "rousing." We must seek divine illumination "to enflame us with ardent love unto thee, and to direct our steps in obedience to thy Laws through the gloomy shades of this world, into that region of eternal light and bliss, where thou reignest in perfect Glory and Majesty, . . ."[10] In the famous sermon "The Nature, Properties and Acts of Charity," which has been considered a very close approach to the theory of natural benevolence, we find him telling his hearers that we cannot disregard any man as "contemptible," for the reason that "Every man is of a divine extraction, and allied to heaven by nature and by grace, as the Son of God, and Brother of God Incarnate."[11] Such a theory of altruism, a version of the great tradition of Christian charity and brotherhood, is still some distance from a consistently naturalistic one. On other occasions he shows his remoteness from the "social" doctrine of Shaftesbury and the eighteenth century when he praises the virtues of solitude quite in the old tradition, implying that in it is to be found the climax of religion; man is "social" by nature because of his potentialities as a son of God, but he manifests the true glory of his nature in his solitary immediate relation to God.

It would be a fatal mistake to assume that the Christian and other worldly elements in the thinking of these preachers were mere vestigial remains, so to speak, hanging on to a new, secular, optimistic opinion about human nature. However great their "latitude"—and of course to such conservatives as Swift it seemed dangerously wide—they were never really out of touch with the great traditional belief that men are destined to recover, by supernatural aid, from a disastrous cosmic fall into a transcendental state. Thus it would be easy, on the basis of isolated passages alone, to place Samuel Parker among the most completely naturalistic benevolists. In attempting to defend the existence of a divinely ordained law of nature against the attacks of skepticism, he cites such facts as strength of parental feeling, and that "as for the Generality of Men their hearts are so tender and their natural affections so humane, that they cannot but pity and commiserate the afflicted with a kind of fatal and mechanical sympathy."[12] Before we conclude that such a remark anticipates the man of feeling, however, we should recall that elsewhere he very emphatically asserts that the instincts are insufficient guides.

> God may possibly have put some secret Notices into the Minds of Men for the greater security of Justice and Honesty in the world; but then, beside that there is no way to prove the Certainty or demonstrate the Obligation of any such inward Record, this plainly resolves the Authority of the Law of Nature into uncertain and unaccountable Principles, or such as may be pretended and, when they are, ought to be admitted without any Proof or Evidence of Reason. . . .[13]

Many other examples might be cited.[14] But in sum they would, I think, show that, while the Latitudinarian preaching certainly had much to do with bringing about a new emphasis on altruism, it did not present a really new concept of human nature.

The Anglican apologists were on the *qui vive* against opinions of many kinds which they regarded as erroneous. They strongly emphasized free will and the possibility of the general access to grace, in opposition to the extreme of "total depravity." They were aware of the fact that for some time there had been a tendency to depreciate "right reason" as a reliable governor of personal conduct. Montaigne could remark that reason, like wax, takes any form imposed on it. Such skeptical idealists as Rochester were led into an attitude resembling romantic irony, seeing in reason a faculty which serves only to make men worse than the animals whose impulses they share; as Mackenzie, much later, puts the view:

> Men must have passions; paint them, if you can;
> Where less the brute enjoys, and more the man.
> To combat passion when our reasons rise,
> Reasons are better passions in disguise. . . .
> The world's dull reason, sober, cool, and pure,
> The world's dull reason is a knave demure.[15]

To combat this attitude, destructive alike of belief in the divine possibilities of the soul and of the concept of the "dignity of man," it was necessary to show that the universe as a whole is "rational" and that human behavior, even though man stands in need of assistance from beyond himself, is not truly anarchic.

The school of Hobbes, of course, powerfully reinforced the tradition of doubt, and it was said that every aspiring bachelor of divinity broke a spear against the steel cap of the sage of Malmesbury. He represented what was thought of as the "naturalistic" school, and the culmination of the skepticism about reason. But he was more easily condemned than answered. The powerful realism or apparent realism, of his demonstration that crass self-interest, however dressed up, is the true motive of all actions, could not be answered except by descending into the deep subrational drives of human nature. To answer Hobbes involved showing that this subrational part of our nature has more than one drive, that it can be good and "social" instead of warring and chaotic.

In answering these and other attacks, the Anglican divines were polemicists, it must be remembered, and the polemicist is notoriously prone to exaggerate in making whatever point he immediately has in hand. Defending religion did for many reasons involve defending the relative natural goodness of human beings; but while this fact certainly is important, it should not obscure our recognition that the polemical treatises and sermons are not representative of the whole views of both preachers and congregations. A most important result of the complex of thought in this time was a largely unconscious drift among these preachers towards a kind of Pelagianism: the proposition that the potentialities of human nature remain, and that corruption has entered from a long accumulation of pejorative changes in customs, educations, etc. Yet theological Pelagianism, although a heresy, remains within religion, and implies need for grace and redemption; and one can say no more than that it hovered in the air, and was hardly more than a vague omen of what was to come.[16] It is undoubtedly true, however, that a vague Christian Pelagianism could easily prepare the way for the powerful secular development of Pelagianism which is dominant in our own time. Contributing to the drift was the great mass of new information about other cultures that had been reaching Western Europe since the time of Henry the Navigator, which was making people realize more and more the real importance of environment and training on personality; this was the age of Locke, and the old faith in innate ideas went out with astounding rapidity.

Before a new sensibility could arise, however, a kind of catalytic agent was necessary to precipitate these undefined and unintegrated elements. That agent was supplied, in considerable part, by Shaftesbury. He did it by combining the spiritual idealism of the divines with the "naturalistic" view of the psychologists, and by applying consistently the full implications of the new world-view in science to the problems of ethics. It is usually said that he defends the "natural goodness" of man. In a general way this is true, but only if we remember that "goodness" has for him a new kind of meaning. It would be more accurate to say that Shaftesbury represents the human being as naturally adapted, with a kind of psychological ethical fitness, to live in his surroundings. The new philosophy depicted a universe of a myriad of parts, harmoniously operating according to immutable laws; it is not a universe in need of transformation or salvation, but one perfect and complete. The sum of these operations represent the *raison d' être* of the whole: the *process* is the final cause, not eternal principles rising above the flux.

It is logical to assume, therefore, that the human being, as an operating part of the great Whole, must be so constructed that in all his action he will, if he behaves "naturally," do those things which will promote his happiness and the happiness of the universe. With Shaftesbury we take the difficult step that this conclusion involves: with Shaftesbury we begin to see conduct in terms of what we should now call "normal" instead of in terms of obedience to divine or natural law; and with Shaftesbury we begin to think of departures from desirable behavior as the "abnormal" and "maladjustment" rather than "sin." The villains become environment and training, rather than the hereditary "degenerate nature of man," as Swift puts it.

Yet Shaftesbury was intensely aware of the fact that, to the human view at least, society in his time was far from being the ideal harmonious system it should be. Mandeville did Shaftesbury a great injustice by caricaturing him as a retiring patrician, favored by a gentle education, viewing through rose-colored glasses a world which he did not understand. The truth is that the noble philosopher remarkably anticipated Rousseau's passionate indictment of the social order, as we see in such passages as this:

> Tho however we may, in passing by, observe, that whilst we see in all other Creatures around us so great a proportionableness, constancy and regularity in all their passions and affections; so great a harmony, and such an adherence to Nature; no failure in the care of the Offspring, or of the Society (if living in Society). . . . Man in

the mean time, vicious and unconsonant man, lives out of all rule and proportion, contradicts his Principles, breaks the Order and Oeconomy of all his Passions, and lives at odds with his whole Species, and with Nature: so that it is next to a Prodigy to see a Man in the World who lives NATURALLY, and as A MAN.[17]

The last clause, of course, has the stinger, for in it Shaftesbury uncompromisingly asserts that it is coming back to nature, not rising above her, that will solve the ethical problem.

Why, then, is there an air of hope about the whole work of Shaftesbury, an air of "enthusiasm" which was to infect future generations? Here the real purpose of the moralist has been misusderstood. It seems that he was not writing a mere complacent defense of the universe, or seeking to rehabilitate the aesthetic side of life as against "mechanism." His real goal was much larger. Shaftesbury, the heir to the great Whig tradition of his grandfather, thought of himself as carrying on, in the field of morals, the work of the reformer. In *The Moralists* (1709) he speaks of the

Grace or Beauty in that original Native Liberty, which sets us free from so many inborn Tyrannys, gives us the Privilege of Ourselves, and makes us our own, and Independent. . . . A sort of Property, which, methinks, is as material to us to the full, as that which secures us our Lands, or Revenues.[18]

Now that security of estate and freedom of thought have been established after the Glorious Revolution, and the way is clear to remove fanaticism from religion, a great prospect for the betterment of life is opening up; the way is open to free men from the perversions engendered by religious dogmas and zeal, from false, derogatory ideas of human nature, and from artificial customs which separate man from nature, God from nature, and all three from the unity in which they should exist. Above all, if men are to be "natural" and therefore happy, they must stop connecting morality with meretricious ideas of the future life, which remove the emphasis from nature and its harmony. But argument and attack were not Shaftesbury's method; rather, he envisioned something like therapy, the treatment of an urbane and insinuating style, the application of raillery rather than the the traditional satire, the artistic presentation of external nature and encouragement of the communion of the mind with landscape untouched by man.

In an age intoxicated by the wonders of mechanism, it was necessary to show how this adaptation of the moral nature to environment could work. If man is to be represented as merely "natural" how can the presence of the impulse to good within the mind be explained without resorting to some such hypothesis as that reason is the "candle of the Lord"? And if good behavior is "natural," how can it be reconciled with so abstruse a faculty as advanced logical thought?

I have suggested that Shaftesbury combined a tradition of spiritual idealism with naturalistic psychology. The first he inherited from the Cambridge Platonists, at least in large part. We have seen how Henry More reduced the moral action to a kind of process, thus showing the influence of the new philosophy. In the *Enchiridion Ethicum*, he describes virtue as "rather a Power than a Habit."[19] This "power" is manifested in a "boniform Faculty," which More calls, borrowing but changing in connotation an Aristotelian phrase, the "very Eye of the Soul." This boniform faculty is the manifestation in action of "right reason," but—most importantly—it does not consist of innate propositions, or reasoning therefrom. Indeed, these things are at best crutches for the numerous race in whom the boniform faculty is regrettably weak. The highest kind of moral judgment consists in a kind of superintuition, but one which is emphatically not a purely natural endowment. It has affinities with the "mens" or "intellectus angelicus" of Ficino's Christian Neoplatonism, and More once defines it as a divine power "by which we are lifted up and cleave unto God," which produces a "ravishing" and supra-worldly pleasure in those lofty spirits who have it. Those who belong to this group can perceive a "symmetry of the passions" as immediately as the average man perceives a parallelism of lines. It appears that More describes a kind of "moral sense"; his emphasis on a "power" rather than a reasoning faculty is part of his movement away from the "clear and distinct ideas" of Descartes, that philosopher who came to seem to him an *ignis fatuus,* and this movement More shared with his age. The idea, nevertheless, remains firmly embedded in a concept of the universe both other worldly and aspirational. The process of moral intuition is the result of an extensive purification of the soul from its corruption by matter.

Shaftesbury's innovation was the naturalization of this moral faculty. The moral intuition, in the successful developed personality, is the original, not final state of man. In other words, the ancient picture is turned upside down: the task of the human being is to retain a natural and original moral sense, instead of to attain it by a long course of redemption. Exactly how could such a natural moral sense be shown to exist? Fortunately, there was available a means of implementing the idea in terms of the master of the new psychology himself.

The older idea that Locke was a complete empiricist has been challenged in recent years.[20] In saying that the soul at birth is like a blank sheet of paper, he meant only that ideas are not somehow mysteriously present in us before we have any contact with the outside world. He did not, however, mean to imply that our ideas are formed by a purely passive action, through the automatic effect of sense impressions. In fact the mind plays the decisive part in cognition. It is autonomous, the ever alert observer, combining, separating, creating order out of the chaos of sensations which constantly are borne in upon it. First it is an *observer:* all mental action, to Locke, is ultimately a matter of "perceiving." He reduces the whole of thought to three kinds of "perception":

1. The perception of ideas in our minds. 2. The perception of signification of signs. 3. The perception of the connexion or repugnance, agreement or disagreement, that there is between any of our ideas.[21]

Certainly the independent power of the mind in the second and third kinds of thinking cannot be denied, and it is possible that it has some creative function even with regard to the first; and when sensations associate themselves arbitrarily, without the mind's ordering control, we have "association of ideas," the manifestation of irrationality and even insanity. By identifying "perception" and "understanding," therefore, Locke placed the pivot of intellectual action in the imagination, and not without reason did Berkeley object to Locke's attempt to show that abstractions can be made, independent of any one image. The image, indeed, is the very center of the mental process. A constant procession of images pass before the mind, even when it is not experiencing directly, and even in sleep.[22]

If Locke had presented a convincing epistemology, he had, it was feared, set forth a wholly inadequate system of ethics—or, some thought, none in fact at all. Practical morality, according to him, depends on the fear of eternal punishment threatened by the Supreme Being for those who disobey His revealed will.[23] Shaftesbury, the disciple of the Cambridge Platonists, objected to the proposition that good and evil are not absolutes but rather mere arbitrary commandments of God, which to be known, must be revealed. Certainly it seemed, further, if good and evil are absolutes, they must have their representative faculty in man's mind; he surely is not left helpless to drift without a moral rudder. Much of Shaftesbury's aversion to his teacher Locke arises from his horror of Locke's calloused attitude to-

wards the moral problem. Yet the calm confidence which earlier philosophers, such as Lord Herbert of Cherbury, had displayed in innate
ideas, was no more. How, without invoking a supernatural and mystical power, could the absolute standard of right and wrong be brought
into relation to human life?

The solution lay at hand in the adaptation of Locke's own system to
moral idealism of the kind Henry More had displayed. If the mind
perceives the connection, repugnance, etc., of ideas derived from sensation, why should not this process apply to morality as well? Why
should not the mind perceive the harmony or repugnance of images of
action and passions, just as it perceives the difference between a
triangle and a circle? And so Shaftesbury, in the *Inquiry concerning
Virtue*, combines the two:

> In a Creature capable of forming general Notions of things, not
> only the sensible things that offer themselves to the sense, are the
> objects of the Affections; but the very *actions* themselves, and the
> affections of Pity, Charity, Kindness, Justice, and so their con-
> traries, being brought into the Mind by reflection, become Ob-
> jects; . . .[24]

The imagination, as in Locke, makes possible the action; the similarity
to Locke's "perception" is evident.

> And thus the several Motions, Inclinations, Passions, Dispositions
> and consequent Carriage and Behavior of Creatures in the various
> Parts of Life, being in several scenes represented to the Mind,
> which readily discerns the good and the ill towards the species or
> Public; it proves afterwards a new work for the affection, either
> virtuously and soundly to incline to, and affect what is just and
> right; and disaffect what is contrary; or, vitiously and corruptly to
> affect what is ill, and disregard or hate what is worthy and good.

The actual "moral sense" is not in itself an emotion. It is an action of
the mind in viewing the "several scenes" of behavior, etc.; the affections follow, and should be properly related as effect to cause. Shaftesbury implies that the actual recognition of good and evil is in itself
sound. The process goes wrong when the affections get out of kilter
with the perceptions, and the wrong passion, or the right passion to
excess becomes attached to an intuition. But a powerful natural impulse should produce the normal kind of reaction: the reflex action
must be distorted by long habit before it goes wrong. The affection in
turn is a drive to action. Here of course something like instrumental
reason has its place. The affection may produce the right intention

but, because of poor judgment, inappropriate action may be taken. It is important, nevertheless, to recognize that "reason" here is a means of implementation rather than the judicial governor of basic decisions.

Shaftesbury's conception of the affections also clearly shows the influence of Locke. The latter reduced emotion to pleasure and pain, which he identified with good and evil for the individual.[25] Things, whether experienced in the present or only as images in reflection, produce thoughts of pain and pleasure, and "our ideas of love and hatred are but the dispositions of the mind, in respect of pleasure and pain in general, however caused in us." The various emotions—love, joy, sorrow, etc.,—are states of mind, "easiness" or "uneasiness." These conscious states of pleasure or pain enable us, among other things, to be sure that we exist separately from the objects which we perceive. Locke even hints at a kind of moral sense: shame, he says, "is an uneasiness of the mind upon the thought of having done something which is indecent, or will lessen the valued esteem which others have for us," and a father delighting in the well-being of his children need only call up that idea into reflection to have pleasure.

Locke, however, had separated knowledge from moral decisions. Morality, he did admit, may be theoretically as certain as knowledge—but only when moral propositions are abstractions.

> And hence it follows that moral knowledge is as capable of real certainty as mathematics. For certainty being but the perception of the agreement or disagreement of our ideas, and demonstration nothing but the perception of such agreement, by the intervention of other ideas or mediums; our moral ideas, as well as mathematical, being archetypes themselves, and so adequate and complete ideas; all the agreement or disagreement which we shall find in them will produce real knowledge, as well as in mathematical figures.[26]

But of course Locke is speaking only of "archetypes," abstracted from concrete events. The kind of adaptation of archetype to experience which Kant was to make lay far in the future, but Shaftesbury as well as other philosophers groped for something of the kind. They thought they had found what they wanted in the seeming fact that men have a capacity for observing the "harmony" among images of passions and actions as certain as their capacity for knowing the existence and differences between things of the outside world. Such a belief fitted in perfectly with the rising conviction that the universe is a great system in which each smallest part operates in perfect mathematical harmony

with all the other parts. It is not surprising that Shaftesbury thought
there could be an "arithmetic" of the moral sense.

The later versions of the *Inquiry* and other works, however, contain
a very important modification of the "moral sense." At first Shaftesbury seemed to identify it with Locke's third, "complex" form of understanding. Later he suggested that moral ideas are more like Locke's
first class of perception, so immediate and direct are the impressions
they make on the mind.

> Is there then, said he, a natural Beauty of *Figures*, and is there not
> as natural a one of Actions? No sooner the Eye opens upon *Fig-
> ures*, the Ear to *Sounds*, than straight the *Beautiful* results, and
> *Grace* and *Harmony* are known and acknowledged. No sooner are
> Actions view'd no sooner the *human Affections* and *Passions* dis-
> cern'd (and they are most of 'em as soon discern'd as felt) than
> straight *an inward* Eye distinguishes and sees the *Fair* and *Shape-
> ly*, the *amiable* and *Admirable*, apart from the Deform'd *the Foul,
> the Odious,* or *the Despicable*. . . .[27]

The addition of the analogy with aesthetic experience makes it even
clearer that the "moral sense" is a naturalized "spiritual eye" of the
kind More and others had described. The point is even more emphatic
in the later editions of the *Inquiry*, which have three added paragraphs, beginning as follows:

> The Case is the same in the *mental* or *moral* subjects, as in the or-
> dinary *Bodys*, or common Subjects of *Sense*. The Shapes, Motions,
> Colours, and Proportions of these latter being presented to our Eye;
> there naturally results a Beauty or Deformity, according to the
> different Measure, Arrrangement, and Disposition of their several
> Parts. . . .[28]

In the next of these added paragraphs, Shaftesbury tells us that the
mind is continually observing other minds; in the third, that as the
forms and images of things continually move before our senses, "even
when we sleep" (a statement obviously suggested by Locke) so the
forms and images of the "moral and intellectual kind" continually
move before the mind, even when the objects themselves are absent.

The extremely "aesthetic" form of the moral sense theory, then, was
an afterthought in Shaftesbury, but it is the form in which his theory
is best known. He was not the first to suggest such an analogy.[29]
There may be several reasons for the desire to reduce the moral sense
to a reflex so immediate. For one thing, the age increasingly was impressed by the essential importance of the direct sense impression.

The fashion for study of epistemology itself betrays this preoccupation, as well as the central place given images in thinking. Again, in this time the standards of taste, at least on the level of forms, seemed absolutely decisive; More, to take one example, often appeals to aesthetic comparisons to make more nebulous matters seem clear-cut. Finally, the desire to take the moral intuition out of the field of "ratiocination" altogether, to remove it from any possible contamination by innate ideas, would tend to make the analogy with immediate sensation tempting.

Many questions remained unanswered. There was, most difficult of all, still the problem of relativism. Granted that there is some kind of innate potentiality for sensing good and bad, are its contents really absolute and immutable, even where development of the personality has been "natural"? These issues, as we shall see, were to prove more than troublesome. But Shaftesbury had made his contribution by combining in a system the deepest desires and beliefs of his age. He had effectually severed morality from righteousness; the supernatural had been absorbed into the natural. He had furthered the process by which, as Panofsky has said, the dualism between Christian and classical "ceased to be real, . . . because the very principle of reality was shifted to the subjective human consciousness."[30]

2

Consequences of the first importance follow from the new *kind* of thinking about man and society and the universe which I have sketched, and in no field more than in literature. In this section I shall try to outline very generally a few of the results of the position Shaftesbury represents (though not necessarily Shaftesbury's direct influence), as we see them in some eighteenth century writing. The full consequences of great changes in thought do not become evident until some time after they have taken place, and the examples cited not unnaturally come several decades after Shaftesbury's death.

Attention has been so completely concentrated on Shaftesbury's "natural goodness" theory that few realize how much of his work is devoted to the study of the "ill" in human nature (the very term is significant in that he does not use "evil" or "sin"). A reading of the *Inquiry*, however, reveals a catalogue of something like case studies in abnormal psychology, presented with an acuteness of insight and a sympathetic power which deserve recognition. Perhaps it was in this field that Shaftesbury was most "original." His two main contributions may be, first, the conception of undesirable behavior as "maladjustment"—to use a modern term; and second, the call for study of states of mind in themselves, impartially and so to speak from within.

The cause of "unsocial" behavior, as we have seen, is described as the disharmony of the moral perception with the drives to action. Shaftesbury's immediate purpose was to show, by imaginative presentation of states of mind, that these dislocations of the personality produce an "uneasiness" such as Locke describes. Thus Shaftesbury departed from the tradition of morality handbooks, with their listings of virtues and vices considered with relation to a given natural or divine law. He did preserve the names of the virtues and vices, but they are only specialized forms of two great basic impulses. In a broader sense Shaftesbury attempted to study the personality to find what causes produce such results—logically enough if the villain is not the will but the external factors which have warped the growth of the mind. Thus he stands in the tradition of objective study of nature—which from Bacon's time on included as a desideratum the natural history of man. The reform of an ill society would require first of all clearing away the false notions about man which have caused infinite mischief. The principal source of "ill" states of mind is the undue strengthening of man's natural and in its place wholly desirable impulse of self-interest. Shaftesbury, describing the basic impulses as self-love and the social sense, combined the two great views of ethics in the Restoration period: the Hobbesian and the Latitudinarian. His style is adapted to the gradations of this self-interest: as he proceeds through the forms which its excess may take, ranging from the slight to the pathological, there is an increasing emotional tension; and at the last, with the "unnatural" emotions, we experience unrelieved horror, which arises from participation with the experiencing mind itself. No one can read these descriptions and feel that the author is the complacent aristocrat of fable.

The progress is from something like "neuroses" to the "psychopathic." Locke pointed out, as he discussed association of ideas, that we all have vagaries in our thinking; the difference between our everyday eccentricities and madness is one of degree. Much the same kind of distinction applies to Shaftesbury's division of the "ill" emotions into those which merely represent over-action of self-interest and those in which the drives to action have become twisted into something tragically self-defeating.

Now if these SELFISH PASSIONS, besides what other ill they are the occasion of, are withal the certain means of losing us our *natural Affections*; then 'tis evident, That they must be the certain means of losing us the chief Enjoyment of Life, and raising in us those horrid and unnatural Passions, and that Savageness of Temper, which makes the GREATEST OF MISERIES, and the most wretched State of Life.[31]

Shaftesbury's isolation of sadism as a psychopathological condition and his serious interest in it, which anticipates later developments in literature, is an example of his method:

> To see the Sufferance of an Enemy with Cruel Delight may proceed from the height of Anger, Revenge, Fear, and other extended Self-Passions: But to delight in the Torture and pain of other Creatures indifferently, Natives or Foreigners, of our own or of another Species, Kindred or no Kindred, known or unknown; to feed, as it were, on Death, and be entertain'd with dying agonys. . . .[32]

He asks whether the unnatural passions may not carry with them a sort of pleasure, barbarous as it is—nevertheless a real kind of satisfaction, from tyranny, sadism, and the like. He grants that this is the fact, but going in subtlety far beyond the crude analysis of Hobbes, finds it is the very perversion of the mind that produces the pleasure:

> For as the cruellest bodily Pains do by Intervals of Assuagement, produce (as has been shewn) the highest bodily Pleasure; so the fiercest and most raging Torments of the Mind, do, by certain Moments of Relief, afford the greatest of mental Enjoyments, to those who know little of the truer kind.[33]

Such a theory is susceptible of other interpretations, however, and this fact perhaps as much as anything illustrates the real weakness in an ethics grounded on the subjective consciousness. The pleasures of perversity were to provide material for the "Satanist" school of writers. The parallel of physical and mental pleasure and pain, and the obvious implication that the most intense pleasure can derive from the extreme pathological, could have startling results. How can we distinguish "true" from "false" pleasure if the test is the quantity of sensation: how can one be "falser" than the other? Shaftesbury's own "arithmetic" of the moral sense would betray him here. Not without reason did Archibald Campbell ridicule the pretensions of those "refined spirits" who affect to follow only a "disinterested moral sense," for, as Campbell says, the self-approval which follows a generous action provides a pleasure and is the real motive of action, however loftily disguised.[34]

Shaftesbury's rhetoric in his character sketches often anticipates later developments in literature. His subsequent shortening and smoothing of the following passage from the 1699 edition of the *Inquiry*, for example, obscure its kinship of mood and language and imagery with descriptions of heroic villains we find in later romantic fiction:

> How thorow and deep must that Melancholy be, where there is nothing softning or pleasing from the side of Friendship to allay or divert it when once risen: no flattering view or imagination of kindness, or affection from any part; but where every thing around is gastly and horrid, every thing in appearance hostile, and, as it were, *bent* against a privat and single being, who is divided from, and at war with the rest of Nature, in a disagreement and irreconciliation with every thing, and with the Order and Government of the Universe? 'Tis thus at last that a Mind becomes a Wilderness where all is laid waste, everything fair and goodly remov'd, and nothing extant but what is dismal and horrid. Now if any thing that but looks desert, or that feels like banishment or expulsion from human Commerce, be so heavy to bear; what must it be to be thus estranged from Mankind, and to be after this manner in a Desert, and in the horridest of Solitudes, even when in the midst of Society; and to live with Mankind as with a foren Species and as with those Creatures that are most remote from Man, and such as he has the most cause to fear?[35]

But there is a deep contradiction in the very use of "unnatural" to describe pathological states of mind. How, in a universe perfectly planned and operating, can there be anything not ultimately harmonious? Shaftesbury was one of the philosopers who encouraged that intoxication with the Whole which was to lead to Voltaire's bitter protest in the letter on the Lisbon earthquake. There must be a *"Resignation, . . .* a Sacrifice and mutual yielding of Natures one to another," and all "Inferiour Natures" must be subjected to the "Superiour Nature of the World." "The Central Powers, which hold the lasting Orbs in their just Poize and Movement, must not be controul'd to save a fleeting Form, and rescue from the Precipice a puny Animal. . . ."[36] Some such scheme, it appears operates in the human as well as all other systems, and the intersection of the majestic, impersonal forces can produce there, too, what seem to finite eyes disasters. He does suggest, with a sly trace of raillery, that even those who see nature as imperfect may have their use. " 'Twas not its [nature's] Intention to leave us without some Pattern of Imperfection; such as we perceive in Minds like these, perplex'd with froward thought."[37]

The theory has, however, a very important potentiality. The study of the "ill" in all its varieties is a means of determining, by contrast, what is "natural." Literary theory soon reflected the concept. But the theory, like others of Shaftesbury's, could be carried to lengths of which the moralist never dreamed. It is one thing to rise to the level of the great over-all Plan and ask with Pope

> If plagues or earthquakes break not Heav'n's design,
> Why then a Borgia, or a Catiline?

It is quite another to look at the matter from the viewpoint of the Borgia or the Catiline, as we do in this passage from the Marquis de Sade:

> C'étaient des monstres, m'objectent les sots. Oui, selon nos moeurs et nôtre façon de penser; mais relativement aux grandes vue de la nature sur nous, ils m'étaient que les instruments de ses desseins; c'était pour accomplir ses lois qu'elle les avait doués de ses caractères féroces et sanguinaires.[38]

Is not the "monster," in being a monster, living according to his nature, and is he not therefore among the new enlightened who seek the "natural"?

The necessity for sympathetic, imaginative representations of the mind and experience is a vital part of Shaftesbury's philosophy. Of the early philosophical writings which Horace mentions in the *Ars Poetica*, he says:

> 'Twas not enough that these Pieces treated fundamentally of *Morals*, and in consequence pointed out *real Characters* and *Manners*: They exhibited 'em *alive*, and set the Countenances and Complexions of Men plainly in view. And by this means they not only taught us to know *Others*; but, what was principal and of highest virtue in 'em, they taught us to know *Our-selves*.[39]

The best poet, Shaftesbury tells an author to whom he addresses "Advice,"

> describes no Qualitys or Virtues; censures no Manners: makes no Encomium, nor gives Characters himself; but brings his actors still in view. 'Tis they who shew themselves. For the poet is a second Maker: a just PROMETHEUS, under Jove.[40]

He is a maker, because, like the Deity, he is a "moral Artist," and it is a fundamental principle in Shaftesbury that the world is to be considered as a work of art. The creation of the poet presents through the imagination a series of scenes, appealing through artful arrangement to the moral sense; the business of the poet is to present the scenes so effectively that the sense will operate of itself, and he should not tell in so many words and abstractions what the "moral" is. Distinguishing the "unnatural" from the "natural" therefore is a matter of arousing response and not giving formal instruction. Aesthetic form is inseparable from truth as images are from thought. One of Shaftesbury's principal differences from his old tutor Locke is the fact that the one was by nature aesthetic in response, the other not; but it was, as we have seen, Locke's own epistemology, with its basis of "perception," that did a vital service in promoting the cult of the imagination. Shaftesbury here as elsewhere began to draw out the consequences of this epistemology.

These forms of art supplement and extend our primary source of knowledge about man—ourselves. Even that "rectification" of society which so much concerned Shaftesbury is found to depend in considerable part on introspection.

> But the knowledg of our Passions in their very Seeds, the measuring well the Growth and Progress of Enthusiasm, and the judging rightly of its natural Force . . . may teach us to oppose more successfully those Delusions which . . . come arm'd with the specious Pretext of moral certainty. . . .[41]

Thus Shaftesbury cast his *Advice to an Author* as a "solioquy," a form to which he gives the highest praise. He expands the Socratic tradition of "Know thyself." Not meditations or essays written with one eye on the audience, he says—but true soliloquy, self-examination to the very depths of the soul, is what is needed. One thinks involuntarily of Rousseau's *Confessions*. He praises *Hamlet* in a significant but neglected piece of criticism as "one continu'd *Moral:* a Series of deep Reflections, drawn from *one* Mouth, upon the Subject of *one* single Accident and Calamity naturally fitted to move Horrour and Compassion."[42] Here, it may be, is the beginning of the change in the tradition of *Hamlet* criticism, wherein the play moves from a tragedy of action to that of an inward and subjective revelation, the *"one"* absorbing everything.

In this tradition is the critic William Richardson, who came much later in the century and was influenced by such followers of Shaftesbury as Lord Kames and Reid (although he refers to Shaftesbury directly, too). In the Introduction to the *Lectures on Shakespeare's Dramatic Characters,* he dilates upon the points made briefly in Shaftesbury. Our "internal feelings" are the beginning of our understanding of human nature. But they are far from sufficient to give us the insight we need.

> We judge of mankind by referring their actions to the passions and principles that influence our own behaviour. We have no other guide, since the nature of the passions and faculties of the mind are [*sic*] not discernible by the senses.[43]

Shaftesbury had lightly assumed that we continually observe other minds, recreating their experience as our inner sense observes the "scenes" representing their characteristics and qualities. But this simple idea, like so many derived from Locke, had all manner of complexities lurking in it. Shaftesbury himself suggested that we need the second maker under Jove to extend our knowledge. Richardson explains that there are many barriers between our minds and those of others. We ourselves are seldom "indifferent" while we observe others; we are biassed, and we can seldom see all that is going on from external actions and signs; our memories are fallible; and the emotions which are weak in us are strong in others, and *vice versa,* so that we unconsciously distort our picture of others' characters.

> If we measure the minds of others precisely by our own, . . . our theories must necessarily be inadequate. But, by considering the copy and portrait of minds different from our own, and by reflecting on these latent and unexerted principles, augmented and promoted by imagination, we may discover many new tints, and uncommon features. Now, that class of poetical writers that excel by imitating the passions, might contribute in this respect to rectify and enlarge the sentiments of the philosopher; and if so, they would have the additional merit of conducting us to the temple of truth, by an easier and more agreeable path, than mere metaphysics.[44]

Thus carrying observers, so to speak, into the very minds of other personalities—as wide a range of personalities as possible—becomes a primary function of art. This vicarious introspection sets, moreover, a new task for literature, one which powerfully encourages a "psychological" approach.

It was inevitable that Shakespeare should become the ideal poet of this new ideal kind. His principal characters come to be seen as types of the relations between the social passions, self-interest, and society; his method is praised as the pattern of that sympathetic imagination which was essential to the poet. A new school of criticism came into being: "An exercise no less adapted to improve the heart, than to inform the understanding," Richardson boasts of his essays. The kind of effect the poet is to produce is indicated in a famous passage from another pioneer critic of this group:

> The reader will perceive that I distinguish between *mental impressions* and the *understanding.* . . . There are none of us unconscious of certain feelings or sensations of mind, which do not seem to have passed through the understanding; the effects, I suppose, of some secret influences from without, acting upon a certain mental sense,

and producing feelings and passions in just correspondence to the force and variety of those influences on the one hand, and to the quickness of our sensibility on the other.[45]

The conception that poetry may produce "certain feelings or sensations of mind, which do not seem to have passed through the understanding" owes much, I think it is clear, to the kind of thinking Shaftesbury did so much to inaugurate.

The new critical method may be seen at work in relation to a peculiar problem which arose from the new secularized Pelagianism. If the fall is really the fall of society, what becomes of those rare spirits who seemingly cannot do anything other than live according to nature—what becomes of them in a world where the great majority live "out of all rule and proportion"? That there is an aesthetic value in this situation Shaftesbury himself hinted.

> The very Disturbances which belong to natural Affection, though they may be wholly contrary to Pleasure, yield still a Contentment and Satisfaction greater than the Pleasures of indulg'd Sense. . . . We continue pleas'd even with this melancholy Aspect or Sense of Virtue. Her Beauty supports it-self under a Cloud, and in the midst of surrounding Calamitys.[46]

The problem is twofold. There is the conflict of the natural man with an unnatural world, and there is the difficulty of ascertaining a desirable balance between sensibility and self-interest. Shaftesbury unmistakably implies that in some cases unbalance of the moral sense and the emotions is due to temperament; there may be need for patterns of imperfection, and he suggests, again, that the moral sense may be too tender. May there be need, also, for patterns of perfection?

Hamlet soon became the image of this dilemma. Mackenzie, who probably led the way in the "sentimental" interpretation of this hero, explains that

> Naturally of the most virtuous and most amiable disposition, the circumstances in which he was placed unhinged those principles of action which, in another situation, would have delighted mankind, and made himself happy. Finding such a character in real life, of a person endowed with feelings so delicate as to border on weakness, with sensibility too exquisite to allow of determined action, he has placed it where it could be best exhibited, in scenes of wonder, of terror, and of indignation, where its varying emotions might be most strongly marked amidst the workings of imagination, and the war of the passions.[47]

Hamlet is, indeed, as Mackenzie says, a new kind of tragedy if we accept this interpretation. The plot and the other characters are reduced to mere contrasting "scenes" against which the sensibility of the hero is exhibited.

In *Mirror* No. 39 Mackenzie goes so far as to suggest that the fall of society is responsible for many of the most affecting tragedies. Unfortunately, "honest ambition" for recognition is accompanied by "delicacy of taste and sentiment" out of place in the present world. In earlier times, when mankind was uncorrupted by excessive luxury and refinement, there could be confidence that recognition would be given where it was due; but now a man of true worth, seeing himself set aside in favor of the worthless and contemptible, gives way to despair, and is "in danger of changing . . . into a morose and surly misanthrope." Mackenzie implies that reason is a power of the mind, one of many potentialities which can be "brought into action as chance or circumstances direct." In the imperfect state of society in which we find ourselves, it is the part of prudence to adjust ourselves with cheerfulness and good humor (the Shaftesburian tone is obvious in the emphasis on these qualities) and "firmly rise above injustice, and refuse to retreat into the passive virtues."

Perhaps it is the absence of the revolutionary or even reforming spirit that is the keynote to Mackenzie's puzzling combination of idealistic sensibility and hard-headed prudence. He condemns at once the unnatural society and the fine spirit who is too "natural" for it. The story of Emilia (*Mirror* No. 101), a girl whose "delicacy and fineness of feeling" lead her to an irreconcilable conflict with Mrs. Grundy, produces no more than an effect of hysterical emotion; the difficulty arises from the ambivalence of the author's attitude, which is at once passionately sympathetic with the sensitive heroine and condemnatory of her perfect sensibility. We miss the single effect of melancholy beauty which unfallen goodness in a fallen society could produce. The Man of Feeling himself represents the dilemma. He has had, significantly, a sheltered life, his remarkable moral sense has unfolded without obstacle, and from his conflict with a selfish and cruel society Mackenzie tries to extract the essence of tragedy. The situation is presented during the stagecoach conversation of chapter 33. The stranger enthusiastically maintains that the "poetical inclination" has at least one advantage—"the causes of human depravity vanish before the romantic enthusiasm [the poet] professes, and many who are not able to reach the Parnassian heights, may yet approach so near as to be bettered by the air of the climate." To which the now disillusioned Harley replies: "I have always thought so; but this is an argument of the prudent against it; they urge the danger of unfitness for the world." The suggestion that the poet, although hopelessly ineffectual in the world as it is, may yet have his function as a "pattern of perfection" both etherealizes the nature of poetry and emphasizes its evocative rather than its communicative aspect.

Richardson's essay on the character of Hamlet shows the relation of his view to the Shaftesbury school:

> On reviewing the analysis now given, a sense of virtue, if I may use the language of an eminent philosopher, without professing myself of his sect, seems to be the ruling principle in the character of Hamlet. In other men, it may appear with the ensigns of high authority: in Hamlet, it possesses absolute power.[48]

So delicate is this sense of virtue that it governs his every action, his every personal relation:

> It even sharpens his penetration; and, if unexpectedly he discerns turpitude or impropriety in any character, it inclines him to think more deeply of their transgression, than if his sentiments were less refined. . . . As it excites uncommon pain and abhorrence on the appearance of perfidious and inhuman actions, it provokes and stimulates his resentment; yet, attentive to justice, and concerned in the interests of human nature, it governs the impetuosity of that unruly passion.

Hamlet's sufferings caused by this acute sensibility occupy an essay devoted to the paradox of the pathological "amiable." The whole play takes on a new character, and to go from Johnson's criticism, with its concern about plot, characterization and outcome, to that of Richardson is to go from one age to another. In Richardson's analysis is the germ of the melancholy of Werther, and there is the anticipation of his death: one can hardly escape the suspicion that Richardson and Mackenzie secretly feel that suicide would have been a really appropriate ending to the play. Strange dilemma! That the most "natural," the most harmonious and sensitive to moral beauty, should so fail, so come to cross purposes with the order of the world! "We love, we almost revere the character of Hamlet; and grieve for his sufferings. But we must at the same time confess, that his weaknesses, are the cause of his disappointments and early death."

That a strong sensibility produces "weakness" in action became a commonplace. In Thomas Whately's *Remarks on Some of the Characters of Shakespeare* it even transforms Macbeth. This critic, significantly, tells us that the emphasis on "fable" in criticism is erroneous, and that "character" is the real center of a play.[49] In line with this principle, he studies *Macbeth* and *Richard III*. The former hero he finds to be a "man of sensibility" led astray by what Shaftesbury would have called the "zeal" introduced by the weird sisters' suggestions. He shows indecision and fear everywhere, as is to be expected from a man of "gentle and amiable qualities." Richard, on the other hand, shows firmness and courage, for he "is totally destitute of every softer feeling."[50] Irresolute, showing the "symptoms of a feeble mind," Macbeth is yet, in an absolute sense, by far the more admirable, for he has a strong sense of virtue, whereas Richard has none. It is not merely the conflict within himself that weakens Macbeth, moreover; it would be easy to turn him the other way and see a Hamlet in him. The conclusion is that the noblest of men are by a strange paradox the weakest of men, and that a strong moral sense means an inevitably tragic life.

More celebrated theories of Hamlet carry on these themes. The sense of the fatal conflict of highly developed sensibility with real facts underlies Goethe's account of the hero, in *Wilhelm Meister*. "The feeling for the good and graceful," we learn, "had unfolded in him together with his consciousness of his high birth." The natural development is strongly emphasized; he was "polished by nature, courteous from the heart." But such a soul, so perfect in itself, comes into inevitable conflict with the necessity for action, for he "is endowed more properly with sentiment than with a character." Hamlet is, when we consider the setting of the discussion in the novel, plainly the image of that conflict which Mackenzie's stranger in the stagecoach suggests.

Coleridge's view is more purely psychological, and more straightforwardly analyzes Hamlet in terms going back to Shaftesbury's modification of the Locke epistemology. There must, in the healthy mind, be a balance between "the impressions of outward objects and the inward operations of the intellect: if there be an overbalance in the contemplative faculty, man becomes the creature of meditation, and loses the power of action."[51] The *Notes on the Tragedies of Shakespeare* makes the process more explicit. "In Hamlet this balance does not exist—his thoughts, images and fancy being far more vivid than his perceptions, and his very perceptions instantly passing thro' the medium of his contemplations, and acquiring as they pass a form and color not naturally their own."[52] It is logical that the stream of images passing before the inner sense could be too vivid and be transformed too much in the process of imaginative working.

The function of Shakespeare thus appeared in a new light. Coleridge sees Shakespeare as providing those "patterns of imperfection" which the new philosophy of man called for: "conceiving characters out of his own intellectual and moral faculties, by conceiving any one intellectual or moral faculty in morbid excess and then placing himself, thus mutilated and diseased, under given circumstances." Among the important results of this new criticism were lifting characters out of plays and making them, as it were, living beings—represented by the tendency to write separate studies of Shakespeare's *dramatis personae;* and the increasing decline of emphasis on dramatic action as such, implicit in Shaftesbury's remark about *Hamlet's* being a long soliloquy and culminating in the romantic aversion to seeing Shakespeare's plays performed. The distant descendant of the theory of the function of the poet is, perhaps, to be seen in T.S. Eliot's theory of the "objective correlative," in his remark that

> If you examine any of Shakespeare's more successful tragedies, you will find this exact equivalence; you will find that the state of mind of Lady Macbeth walking in her sleep has been communicated to you by a skilful accumulation of imagined sensory impressions; the words of Macbeth on hearing of his wife's death strike us as if, given the sequence of events, these words were automatically released by the last event in the series.

Communication of a state of mind by "imagined sensory impressions" is indeed in keeping with Shaftesbury's vision of the poet as a "second maker under Jove"; vicarious experience is the purpose of poetry.

If Hamlet was the supreme symbol of the tragedy of the natural in a degenerate world, there was another figure who as a kind of foil was to loom especially large in romantic literature. William Richardson adumbrates the type in describing Jaques as the frustrated benevolist, but one whose mental history has been different from that of Hamlet. Even the prince, in whom the conflict of his sense of virtue with society is the ruling principle, eventually is led into violence; but his hesitations are "amiable." In Jaques, on the other hand, the result of frustration of a keen sense of benevolence has been less amiable. Richardson starts from the doctrine of the "ruling passion." What if the dominating impulse in a person is the "social and beneficent Affections," and what if those affections are so strong as to be irresistible—and then, as they come into conflict with an uncongenial, selfish world, are twisted into evil ways? The result of this thwarting of the "natural" will be misanthropy. The social affections lead men to society, and society being what it is, to dissipations and regrets. Jaques accordingly turned into a "dissipated and sensual libertine," and, like la Rochefoucauld's old roué (but for different reasons) into a gloomy moralist as well. This "white" melancholy (as distinguished from the "black" melancholy of the true villain) is, then, really a good impulse perverted by its contact with a world to which it should be suited, but, because of the evil of society, is not.[53]

The Byronic hero, I might suggest, often shows this kind of thwarting of the exceptional moral sense.

> With more capacity for love than earth
> Bestows on most of mortal mould and birth,
> His early dreams of good outstripp'd the truth,
> And troubled manhood follow'd baffled youth;
> With thought of years in phantom chase misspent,
> And wasted powers for better purpose lent; . . .
> Too high for common selfishness, he could
> At times resign his own for others' good,
> But not in pity, not because he ought,
> But in some strange perversity of thought,
> That sway'd him onward with a secret pride,
> To do what few or none would do beside. . . .[54]

The few examples sketched above give some idea of the changes which the complex of thought which Shaftesbury pioneered could produce. All of them assume the continued existence of the system of society as it exists. Obviously, however, another road was open. Could it be that a "root and branch" reformation of the social order is necessary to release the supposed normal state of mankind? It would be outside the limits of this paper to show that there is little in Rousseau that is not in Shaftesbury also, but that the French moralist carries things much farther than does the English one. Both were optimists in a deeper sense; it is not that all *is* well, but that all *can* be well in society. They both declare the eternal possibility of living "NATURAL-LY, and as a MAN." The enchanting prospect they offer is that nature is always before and within men, divinely harmonious, beautiful and serene, and that every generation, if it will only awaken from the nightmare dreams of the past, can find happiness and freedom in this life and on this earth.

NOTES

[1] Two recent books deal with Shaftesbury and his influence: A. O. Aldridge, *Shaftesbury and the Deist Manifesto* (Transactions of the American Philosophical Society, 1951); and R. L. Brett, *The Third Earl of Shaftesbury* (London, 1951). Since these studies, as well as the still essential book of Fowler, *Shaftesbury and Hutcheson*, give detailed accounts of this author's life and writings, I am not repeating this material. I am trying only to suggest a new interpretation of Shaftesbury's relationship to his own time, especially to the Cambridge Platonists and to Locke, and to suggest some new lines which study of his influence may take. In suggesting these lines I am not trying to define direct and exact "sources," but rather significant changes which the *kind* of thinking Shaftesbury pioneered helped to produce. It is to be remembered, however, that we can assume nearly every educated man of the eighteenth century had some acquaintance with the *Characteristics* of Lord Shaftesbury, just as nearly every educated person today has some acquaintance with the writings of, say, John Dewey.

[2] "Shaftesbury and the Ethical Poets in England, 1700-1760," *PMLA*, 31 (1916), 264 ff.; and see also W. E. Alderman, "Shaftesbury and the Doctrine of Moral Sense in the Eighteenth Century," *PMLA*, 46 (1931), 1087 ff.

[3] "Suggestions toward a Genealogy of the 'Man of Feeling,'" *ELH*, 1 (1934), 207.

[4] See F. E. L. Priestley, "Newton and the Romantic Concept of Nature," *UTQ*, 17 (1948), 323 ff.; Miss Marjorie Nicolson's books, especially *The Breaking of the Circle* (Evanston, 1950); and an article of the writer, "Space, Diety, and the 'Natural Sublime,'" in *MLQ*, March 1951.

[5] Pages 9-10.

[6] P. 55.

[7] *Ibid.*, pp. 156-8.

[8] *Works of Isaac Barrow*, ed. Tillotson (London, 1696), II: 107-8.

[9] *Ibid.*, 105.

[10] *Ibid.*, I: 11-12.

[11] *Ibid.*, I: 356.

[12] *A Demonstration of the Divine Authority of the Law of Nature, and of the Christian Religion* (London, 1681), 55.

[13] *Ibid.*, 5.

[14] Archbishop Tenison, for example, contrasts the "generous Spirit of Charity," a soul that animates society and makes it possible, with the self-love which is becoming all too prevalent; but this state of affairs is to be expected since St. Paul predicted that "the nigher [men] are to the Last Judgment, the more Criminal they grow." *A Sermon against Self-Love* (London, 1689), 12. It is Christian charity, not benevolence, of which he speaks, and it cannot be equated with the social feeling of Shaftesbury or Rousseau. The idea that the growth of self-interest argues the approach of the Judgment, furthermore, is a very old one among theologians. Again, we find one of the most "liberal" of the Latitudinarians, Archbishop Tillotson, describing how God in His mercy has provided, by the "abundance and *Grace* of the Gospel, so powerful a *Remedy* for this hereditary Disease of our corrupt and de-

generate Nature." *Six Sermons*, 2d ed. (London, 1694), 51. It is "common humanity," to be sure, that makes us concerned for the welfare of our families, etc., but this fact does not argue innate goodness of men.

[15] *The Pursuits of Happiness* (London, 1771).

[16] It is interesting to note that Tillotson carefully guards himself against the imputation of this heresy by emphasizing that the "disease of the depravity of human nature" is transmitted by traduction, from parent to child, and not by imitation. His student Thomas Burnet was one of the first to go the whole way in saying that the fall was a gradual affair, really consisting in the corruption of society.

[17] *Inquiry concerning Virtue*, p. 99. This first, "imperfect" edition, now extremely rare, published though it was without Shaftesbury's knowledge, often gives us more immediately and more impressively the very spirit of its author than does the later, "polished" *Inquiry concerning Virtue, or Merit* as published in the *Characteristics*.

[18] *Characteristics* (London, 1737), II. 252.

[19] *An Account of Virtue: Or, Dr. Henry More's Abridgment of Morals, Put into English*, tr. Edward Southwell (London, 1690), 11.

[20] This assumption may be the most serious fault in Mr. Brett's recent book on Shaftesbury—which otherwise has many acute insights. To oppose Shaftesbury as the champion of the belief that perception involves a "creative process" over against Locke as the philosopher of "passive association" seems to me misleading. The close connection of Shaftesbury's theory with Locke's epistemology has not, so far as I know, been pointed out. Locke in fact is the fountain head of the two great schools of thought about the mental life; on one side, he leads to the romantic psychology and ethics inaugurated by Shaftesbury—on the other, to the Hartley associationist school, depending on which element in his thought is stressed at the expense of the other.

[21] *An Essay concerning Human Understanding*, ed. A. C. Fraser (Oxford, 1914), II: xxi: 5.

[22] The implications for literature of this yoking of the image to thought are of course incalculable. Shaftesbury and Addison immediately show the results. Philocles, in Shaftesbury's *The Moralists*, says that he must have a "kind of material Object," an "Image" in mind before he can love a person or an abstraction; he has been in love, for example, with the "People of old Rome" under the form of a beautiful youth "call'd *the* GENIUS *of the People*." *Characteristics*, II: 242 ff. This should be the lower rung of the Platonic ladder of beauty, which should ascend to the immaterial pure Idea, but the ladder is never completed. Later, when Shaftesbury presents his very important idea of the organic unity of the universe, he cites as an authority Locke's *Essay*, IV: vi: 11, where it is shown that we cannot understand the essence of any object unless we perceive its intricate physical integration into the workings of the universal machine; we perceive a collection of related images. See *The Moralists*, in *ed. cit.*, II: 285 ff. And in one of the most significant passages of all Shaftesbury's works, in the late *Miscellaneous Reflections*, he sets forth his version of the "scale or catalogue of beauty" (the equivalence of the terms is interesting for a Platonist) in the form of greater and greater combinations of

images into patterns, in both the animate and inanimate worlds. *Ed. Cit.*, III: 182-3, footnote. The spirit, the enthusiasm, the language, are Neoplatonic, but the substance has much of Locke in it.

²³ On the objections to Locke's ethics, see my article "The Origins of the 'Moral Sense,'" in *HLQ*, XI (1948), 241-59.

²⁴ P. 27.

²⁵ *Essay*, II: xx.

²⁶ *Essay*, IV: iv: 7.

²⁷ *The Moralists*, in *Characteristics*, II: 414 f.

²⁸ *Characteristics*, II: 28 ff.

²⁹ Thomas Burnet, in three pamphlets directed against Locke (first in 1697, the second and third in 1699), appears to have originated the comparison. He wrote in 1697: "This I am sure of, that the Distinction, suppose of Gratitude and Ingratitude, Fidelity, and Infidelity, . . . and such others, is as sudden without any Ratiocination, and as sensible and piercing, as the difference I feel from the Scent of a Rose, and of Assa-foetida. . . ." For an account of these pamphlets and of Locke's reaction thereto—a reaction which may be assumed in large part to Shaftesbury also—see my article, cited above.

³⁰ *Studies in Iconology* (New York, 1939), 229. It may be well to say a little about the question of Shaftesbury's attitude towards religion, a problem which has rather unnecessarily vexed his critics and biographers from his own century onwards. Of his dislike for and fear of any strong religious belief involving any form of "mystery" or supernatural faith there can be no doubt. It is true that in the preface to Whichcote's *Sermons*, and in some letters he speaks of the Anglican state church in respectful and even affectionate terms; but careful reading of these passages will show,

I think, that it is the absence of "zeal" and the generally good therapeutic effect which belief in providence may have that he means. Of his certainty that the universe is God's creation, in which He is imminent, there is no doubt, either. But no one who takes revealed religion seriously can look on Shaftesbury as a confrere. The really governing fact is that, as I have tried to point out, his basic assumptions about the nature of man rule out original sin and the belief in a supernatural destiny as the true goal of life. And as Swift says, "So I affirm original sin, and that men are now liable to be damned for Adam's sin, to be the foundation of the whole Christian religion." It must be added that Shaftesbury was not argumentative. To attack religion dogmatically would be a manifestation of that very "zeal" which he felt had produced so much damage. Better is the convincing presentation, in imaginative form, of the truth about men, accompanied by a raillery against superstition. Shaftesbury's artistic achievement in the latter form has never been studied satisfactorily.

³¹ *Characteristics*, II: 163.

³² *Ibid.*, II: 164.

³³ *Ibid.*, II: 169.

³⁴ *An Enquiry into the Original of Moral Virtue* (Edinburgh, 1733), 324 ff.

³⁵ Pp. 193-4. The psychological state, the warfare of the mind with itself, is the essence of the horror in this passage, rather than pride, a sense of disobedience to God, or remorse, as in Milton's Satan, or Marlowe's Faustus.

³⁶ *Characteristics*, II: 214-15.

³⁷ *Ibid.*, II: 283.

³⁸ Quoted by Mario Praz, *The Romantic Agony*, tr. Angus Davidson (London, 1951), 98. Diderot, as is well known, expressed similar ideas.

[39] *Ibid.,* I: 194. And so Shaftesbury casts his own work in artistic forms, such as dialogues and "soliloquies," a fact which accounts at once for its suggestiveness and its vagueness. One must always remember that Shaftesbury was, by choice, no systematizer, and that, not isolated statements, but as in creative works, the effect of the whole is what counts.

[40] *Ibid.,* I: 207. The applicability of this statement to Shaftesbury's own work, even the *Inquiry,* is worth noting. He is not a judicial moralist.

[41] *Ibid.,* I: 43. Professor R. D. Havens has pointed out that as early as 1725 Henry Baker wrote a "natural History of myself, truly pointing out the Turn and Disposition of my Soul at the Time it gave them [the poems he was publishing] birth." The shift to introspection, as Professor Havens indicates, is noteworthy. It comes fourteen years after the publication of the *Characteristics,* when the reading of Shaftesbury was ubiquitous. "Unusual Opinions in 1725 and 1726," *PQ,* 30 (1951), 447. In line with this change in presentation of character, attention may be called to Professor Edward Hooker's article "Humour in the Age of Pope," *HLQ,* 11 (1948), 361 ff. The attitude changes from one of condemnation according to an objective standard, to sympathetic depiction of diversity. This change is entirely in accord with Shaftesbury's principle.

[42] *Ibid.,* I: 275-6.

[43] (Sixth edition, London, 1812). For an account of this book and its evolution, see R. W. Babcock, "William Richardson's Criticism of Shakespeare" *JEGP,* 29 (1929), 117 ff.

[44] *Ibid.,* pp. 19-20. On the history of the sympathetic imagination see W. J. Bate, "The Sympathetic Imagination in Eighteenth Century English Criticism," *ELH,* 12 (1945), 144 ff.

[45] Maurice Morgann, *An Essay on the Dramatic Character of Sir John Falstaff* (London, 1825), 6-7.

[46] *Op. cit.,* II: 106.

[47] *Mirror,* No. 99.

[48] *Op. cit.,* 117.

[49] (London, 1785), Introduction.

[50] *Ibid.,* 15.

[51] Bristol Lecture III, in *Coleridge's Shakespearean Criticism,* ed. Raysor (London, 1930), II: 272.

[52] *Ibid.,* I: 37.

[53] Richardson, *op. cit.,* 168 ff.

[54] *Lara,* I: xvii. The last four lines recall Richardson's analysis of that supreme example of misanthropy, Timon at Athens, whose morbid condition is supposed to result from a combination of a ruling passion—desire for eminence—with a strong sense of benevolence. The new casuistry could indeed adopt many forms!

'Dissociation of Sensibility': Modern Symbolist Readings of Literary History

Frank Kermode

The primary pigment of poetry is the IMAGE.

BLAST

The poetic myths are dead; and the poetic image, which is the myth of the individual, reigns in their stead.

C. DAY LEWIS

When the accounts come to be rendered, it may well appear to future historians that the greatest service done by early twentieth-century criticism to contemporary poetry has been this: it has shown poets a specially appropriate way of nourishing themselves from the past. It has shown them that their isolation, and their necessary preoccupation with the Image, do not cut them off from all their predecessors, and that there are ways of looking at the past which provide valuable insights into essentially modern possibilities and predispositions. The need was to bring literary history—and this involved other kinds of history too—to the support of the Image; to rewrite the history of poetry in Symbolist terms. The whole effort crystallised, in 1921, in Mr. Eliot's famous announcement of the doctrine of the dissociation of sensibility, and although this was by no means so original an idea as it has been called, it will necessarily be at the centre of what I have to say about this extremely important phase of my subject.

The doctrine has lately been wilting under well-directed criticism, though there is no doubt that it will continue, whether under the same name or not, whether fallacious or not, to exert a powerful influence for a long time yet. My business here is merely to establish that it has a strong connexion with the development, in the present century, of the theory of the Image, and to ask why it has had such success.

What I say about its value as a key to literary history is really incidental to this.

Mr. Eliot first used the expression 'dissociation of sensibility' in an essay on 'The Metaphysical Poets' (1921), and his last recorded comment upon the theory is in his British Academy lecture on Milton (1947). The first passage, as printed in *Selected Essays*, runs like this: Mr. Eliot has been saying that the dramatic verse of the late Elizabethans and early Jacobeans "expresses a degree of development of sensibility which is not found in any of the prose. . . . In Chapman especially there is a direct sensuous apprehension of thought, or a recreation of thought into feeling, which is exactly what we find in Donne." He then compares a passage of Chapman's and one by Lord Herbert of Cherbury with bits of Tennyson and Browning, and comments:

> The difference is not a simple difference of degree between poets. It is something which had happened to the mind of England between the time of Donne or Lord Herbert of Cherbury and the time of Tennyson and Browning; it is the difference between the intellectual poet and the reflective poet. Tennyson and Browning are poets, and they think; but they do not feel their thought as immediately as the odour of a rose. A thought to Donne was an experience; it modified his sensibility. When a poet's mind is perfectly equipped for its work, it is constantly amalgamating disparate experience; the ordinary man's experience is chaotic, irregular, fragmentary. The latter falls in love, or reads Spinoza, and these two experiences have nothing to do with each other, or with the noise of the typewriter or the smell of cooking; in the mind of the poet these experiences are always forming new wholes.
>
> We may express the difference by the following theory: The poets of the seventeenth century, the successors of the dramatists of the sixteenth, possessed a mechanism of sensibility which could devour any kind of experience. They are simple, artificial, difficult, or fantastic, as their predecessors were; no less nor more than Dante, Guido Cavalcanti, Guinicelli, or Cino. In the seventeenth century a dissociation of sensibility set in, from which we have never recovered; and this dissociation, as is natural, was aggravated by the influence of the most powerful poets of the century, Milton and Dryden.

Observe that there are certain qualifications for poetry described as operative *now*, though possessed by the poets of the seventeenth century and none since (until now?). There are other places in Mr. Eliot's earlier criticism which amplify this statement, but we will content our-selves with his last pronouncement on the subject:

> I believe that the general affirmation represented by the phrase 'dissociation of sensibility' . . . retains some validity; but . . . to lay the burden on the shoulders of Milton and Dryden was a mistake. If such a dissociation did take place, I suspect that the causes are too complex and profound to justify our accounting for the change in terms of literary criticism. All we can say is, that something like this did happen; that it had something to do with the Civil War; that it would be unwise to say it was caused by the Civil War, but that it is a consequence of the same cause which brought about the Civil War; that we must seek the causes in Europe, not in England alone; and for what these causes were, we may dig and dig until we get to a depth at which words and concepts fail us.

In this passage Mr. Eliot seems to be recommending, as a desidera-tum, what had in fact already been done; for by 1947 supplementary enquiries into the dissociation had long ceased to be conducted entire-ly in terms of literary criticism. Almost every conceivable aspect of seventeenth-century life had been examined by scholars anxious to validate the concept, though it is true that the investigators were usu-ally historians of literature by profession. In very general terms it might be said that the notion of a pregnant historical crisis, of great impor-tance in every sphere of human activity, was attractive because it gave design and simplicity to history; and because it explained in a subtly agreeable way the torment and division of modern life. Feeling and thinking by turns, aware of the modern preference for intellect over imagination, a double-minded period measured itself by a serene-ly single-minded one. Poets tried again to be concrete, to charge their thinking with passion, to restore to poetry a truth independent of the presumptuous intellect. They looked admiringly to those early years of the seventeenth century when this was normal, and the scholars at-tended them with explanations of why it was so, and why it ceased to be so. There was, I think, an implicit parallel with the Fall. Man's soul, since about 1650, had been divided against itself, and it would never be the same again—though correct education could achieve something.

It is a measure of Mr. Eliot's extraordinary persuasiveness that thinkers in this tradition have for so long accepted the seventeenth century as the time of the disaster. As we see from his second pro-nouncement, he has himself stuck to this position, although he advises us to look back into earlier history for fuller explanations. Nor is his attitude difficult to understand; it is animated by a rich nostalgia for the great period of Anglican divinity, the period when the Church of England, beset on all sides by determined recusancy, confidently proposed itself as truly Catholic and apostolic—looking back, itself, to a vague past when the folly and arrogance of intellect had not yet begun the process of dissociating Christianity. This period ended with the Civil War, and the end of the first Anglo-Catholicism coincided with the end of an admired poetry and a great drama, both affected, to some extent, by ecclesiastically-determined attitudes, the drama remembering (but how faintly?) its devout origins, 'metaphysical poetry' the *concetto predicabile*. What happens is that the Civil War becomes a kind of allegory, with the Puritans as Pride of Intellect, and the King as Spiritual Unity.

The truth is that, if we look to Europe and not to England alone, we see that there was never much chance that the Church of England would be universally recognised as Catholic, and that 'something' had presumably 'happened' long before to predispose people against such recognition. And this is a characteristic situation. It is not merely a matter of wrong dates; however far back one goes one seems to find the symptoms of dissociation. This suggests that there is little historical propriety in treating it as a seventeenth-century event, even when the historian is serious and respectable enough not to assume that it really was an occurrence like, say, Pride's Purge, after which feeling disappeared from certain mental transactions, leaving a Rump of intellect with which we are still conducting our business. With more thoughtful chroniclers there is usually much emphasis on the dissociative force of science, and on the un-dissociated condition of pre-Baconian and pre-Cartesian philosophy and theology. But it is easy enough to show that scientists were already under Elizabeth incurring odium and the suspicion of atheism for a variety of reasons, all coming in the end to the charge that they were setting nature against God. Bacon's position with respect to religious laws that were apparently contrary to reason is very similar to that of many philosophers, especially those affected by Averroes and the great Aristotelian tradition of Padua, from the thirteenth century onward, to Pomponazzi in the early sixteenth and to Cremonini, an influential teacher who was, incidentally, a friend of that very Lord Herbert of Cherbury who was used as an example of the un-dissociated poet. Obviously the rediscovery of Aristotle involved in some sense a dissociation of Christian thought, tending ultimately to some such escape-device as the 'double-truth' of Averroism, first condemned, by a Church anxious to save rational theology, in the

1270s. And if we were to pursue the dissociation back into the past, we should find ourselves in Athens. Elizabethan 'atheism' was far more than a scientific issue; there was genuine anxiety, a real 'naturalist' movement widely affecting ethical and political conduct. Similarly, the condemnations of the 1270s referred not only to Averroism but to the book on love by Andreas Capellanus, and M. Gilson has spoken of "a sort of polymorphic naturalism stressing the rights of pagan nature" as chracteristic of the period as a whole. It would be quite as reasonable to locate the great dissociation in the sixteenth or the thirteenth century as in the seventeenth; nor would it be difficult to construct arguments for other periods. The truth may be that we shall never find a state of culture worth bothering about (from the literary point of view, that is) in which language is so primitive as to admit no thinking that is not numinous; in which there is no possibility of a naturalist assault on the society's beliefs. The Christian 'West' has never wanted to be as primitive even as the Song of Solomon, and its whole immense allegorical tradition is the result of applying intellectual instruments to the dissection of writings in which thought and feeling are, if they are anywhere, inseparable.

But it seems to me much less important that there was not, in the sense in which Mr. Eliot's supporters have thought, a particular and far-reaching catastrophe in the seventeenth century, than that there was, in the twentieth, an urgent need to establish the historicity of such a disaster. And the attempt to answer the question why there should have been takes us back to the Image. The theory of the dissociation of sensibility is, in fact, the most successful version of a Symbolist attempt to explain why the modern world resists works of art that testify to the poet's special, anti-intellectual way of knowing truth. And this attempt obviously involves the hypothesis of an age which was different, an age in which the Image was more readily accessible and acceptable.

When, in fact, the poets and aestheticians of the Image turn their attention to history, it is in search of some golden age when the prevalent mode of knowing was not positivist and anti-imaginative; when the Image, the intuited, creative reality, was habitually respected; when art was not permanently on the defensive against mechanical and systematic modes of enquiry. Since the order of reality postulated as the proper study of the poet tends, in one way or another, to be granted supernatural attributes, the ideal epoch is usually a religious one. Hence the medievalism of Byzantinism of Hulme and the Decadents, of Yeats and Henry Adams. Hulme, in particular—as we have seen—exposes the whole process; he has to go back, using Worringer as a guide, to a moment of crisis (using one that already existed for historians, but using it in a new way) and achieve the required anti-thesis between his two ages (undissociated and dissociated) by treating all thought between the Renaissance and his own time as of a piece. It was partly because this obviously would not do that the date of the crisis was moved on to 1650. But everybody in the tradition was agreed that there must have been such a crisis; it was necessary to their aesthetic, and the only point of dispute was its date.

There is a passage, to which I have already referred, in Pound's *Make It New,* that illuminates this aspect of the problem.

> When the late T. E. Hulme was trying to be a philosopher . . . and fussing about Sorel and Bergson . . . I spoke to him one day of the difference between Guido's precise interpretative metaphor, and the Petrarchian fustian and ornament, pointing out that Guido thought in accurate terms; that the phrases correspond to definite sensations undergone . . . Hulme took some time over it in silence, and then finally said: "That is more interesting than anything anyone ever said to me. It is more interesting than anything I ever read in a book".

The only aspects of this odd interchange that I want to discuss are those which are relevant to what I am trying to say about the histori-ography of modern Symbolist aesthetics. One is that Pound is de-scribing Cavalcanti as a poet of the integral image, and contrasting him with Petrarch, a poet of the ornamental image, the image ap-pended to discourse, the flower stuck in sand. In the one there is 'a unification of thought and feeling'; in the other, a dissociation of them. Another is Hulme's reaction to what Pound said. The general idea could not have been unfamiliar to him; after all, it was the reason why he was fussing about Bergson. But a man is never more impressed by an argument than when it provides unexpected support for opinions he already holds, and Hulme could not have been less than charmed to discover that Petrarch, of all people—the First Man of that Renais-sance he blamed so strenuously—already exhibited the symptoms of error that characterised the period, whereas Cavalcanti, an older con-temporary of Dante, habituated to the hallowed concept of discontinu-ity, brought up on Original Sin, had precisely those Imagist qualities, that reluctance to glide away into abstraction, which for Hulme was the index of true poetry. Somewhere between Cavalcanti and Petrarch a dissociation of sensibility, it would seem, had set in; and from it, Hulme was willing to add, we have never recovered.

But we have now to remind ourselves that Mr. Eliot claimed for the poets of the seventeenth century the very qualities of Dante, Cavalcanti, and Cino, and believed that the dissociation came after these later poets. It is not in the nature of the concept of dissociation that it should occur at random intervals, any more than it is of the Fall; only on some such theory as Yeats's can it occur more than once. What are we to conclude from this confusion?

The fact is that Mr. Eliot's argument for a general dissociation that can be detected in art is meant to satisfy much the same need as Hulme's, and Yeats's. For Hulme, as we have seen, the Renaissance is the critical moment; men began to ignore the human limitations suggested by the doctrine of Original Sin, and nothing has been right since. Romanticism is just the new disease at the stage of mania. For Yeats the great moment in the present historical phase is 1550; for about a century before that there was a tense perfection, celebrated in some of his most splendid prose; but after that everything changed, art faced in the wrong direction, the artist became more and more an exile. In fact Yeats's history is written in terms of this doctrine, written in a world that offended him socially and imaginatively, a world of 'shopkeeping logicians', the very existence of which he had to explain by exhaustive glosses on every conceivable aspect of the idea of dissociation. My own belief is that Yeats's expression of the whole aesthetic-historical complex is by far the most satisfactory and, in terms of poetry, the most fruitful. But the immediate point is that all these writers search history for this critical moment, and because they share much the same poetic heritage, they are all looking for much the same kinds of rightness and wrongness in historical periods. They seek, in short, a historical period possessing the qualities they postulate for the Image: unity, indissociability; qualities which, though passionately desired, are, they say, uniquely hard to come by in the modern world. That poets and critics so diverse in personality as Pound, Hulme, Yeats and Eliot, should all have made such similar incursions into Symbolist historiography is testimony to the great pressure the idea of the Image has exerted in the formative phase of modern poetic. Mr. Eliot's attempt, distinguished from the others by the accident of his personal concerns in theology, is not essentially different from them. It has only been more successful, partly because of his prestige and persuasive force, partly perhaps because of the growing scholarly tendency to medievalise the Renaissance, so that a later date for the split became more acceptable.

The fact remains that Mr. Eliot's is the version that has had wide currency. Like the others, it is, as I have been trying to show, quite useless historically. It will not do to say that it is partly true, or true in a way, as some people now claim. A once-for-all event cannot happen every few years; there cannot be, if the term is to retain the significance it has acquired, dissociations between the archaic Greeks and Phidias, between Catullus and Virgil, between Guido and Petrarch, between Donne and Milton. As a way of speaking about *periods* the expression is much less useful than even 'baroque'. At its worst, it is merely a way of saying which poets one likes, and draping history over them. At its best it is an interesting primitivism, looking for an unmodern virtue, not as the noble savage was sought in the impossibly remote past or in Tahiti, but in Christian Europe right up to some moment in, or shortly after, what is vaguely called the Renaissance. The most deplorable consequence of the doctrine is that the periods and poets chosen to illustrate it are bound to receive perverse treatment; you must misrepresent them if you propose to make them justify a false theory. If the theory helps to produce good poetry (as it did) this is not worth complaining about, provided that it dies when this work is accomplished. But this theory shows every sign of surviving, and it is therefore a matter of importance to show how it has distorted Donne and Milton, the two poets most affected by it. Once again, the astonishing degree of distortion imposed here is a measure of the power generated by the Image in modern poetic.

Milton and Donne have been involved in an unhappy relationship (existing only in the fantasies of historians) which has seemed to mean that one of them has to be occulted to enable the other to be lit. Milton was to be put out—though it may be noted that Mr. Eliot's change of opinion about Donne was followed by an upward revision of his estimate of Milton. At the time when Donne was being admired for thinking passionately, Milton was being despised for writing monuments to dead ideas in a dead language. Milton, self-conscious postlapsarian that he was, obstinately thought and discoursed *about* feeling, divorcing the body and soul, the form and matter, of the image. Donne, writing before the same Fall, had his intellect at the tip of his senses.

Superficially this argument was attractive because it gave major status to an obscure poet whose diction was inartificial, even colloquial, and who lived in times supposed to be very like modern times, in that the established order was already being threatened by those 'naturalist' forces which eventually dissociated sensibility. There is, of course, a contradiction here: Donne is admired because he was deeply troubled by the new philosophy, and also because he was lucky enough to live just before it became really troublesome. There is also an error of fact: Donne alludes frequently enough to the 'new philosophy,' but nobody who has examined these allusions in their context can seriously believe he was much put out by it, and considering his religious views it would indeed be surprising if he had been. It might have been useful to the dissociationist argument if somebody had been prepared to capitalise this point, by way of emphasising Donne's pre-dissociation status; but there seems to have been a heavy commitment to the view that Donne was important to modern poets because of the ways in which his world resembled theirs, as well as because it was completely different from theirs. As usual, the history is feeble. But pure criticism has had very similar difficulties: Miss Tuve's now famous demonstration that Donne's images have a logical, or at any rate a pseudo-logical function, was a direct affront to the basis of the theory that he was a poet of the modern Image; but it can scarcely have surprised anybody who had read Donne open-eyed and seen how much he depends on dialectical conjuring of various kinds, arriving at the point of wit by subtle syllogistic misdirections, inviting admiration by slight but totally destructive perversities of analogue, which re-route every argument to paradox. Some of this Mr. Eliot perhaps felt when he prematurely prophesied the demise of Donne during the tercentenary celebrations of 1931, and showed how far he had gone towards excluding Donne from the category of unified sensibility, saying outright that in him "there is a manifest fissure of thought and sensibility." Donne is, to say the least, of doubtful value to the Symbolist theory—less use than the poetic and critical experiments of some of his European contemporaries might have been. At first glance, one might be excused for wondering how Donne ever got mixed up with the thoery of dissociation; the explanation of course lies in nineteenth-century thought.

Mr. F. W. Bateson, in a very important critique of the theory, has noticed in passing how little separates Mr. Eliot's formula from the conventional nineteenth-century view, which he exemplifies by Stopford Brooke's opinion that the Restoration saw the end "of a poetry in which emotion always accompanied thought." And something like this view can in fact be found in Coleridge. But after Grosart's edition of 1872 some people were already noticing that Donne wrote poems in which the note of passion, the true voice of feeling, was audible despite the fact that they were love poems unpromisingly couched in terms of alchemy, astronomy and law. It was this discovery of the true voice of feeling in such surroundings that led to what was in effect a late Romantic glorification of Donne. This was contemporary with the Blake revival, the teaching of Pater, and finally with the assimilation of the parallel but more important phenomenon of French Symbolism —in short, with the emergence of the modern Image as it was understood by Symons (a great champion of Donne and the Jacobean drama), and those who came under his influence: Yeats, and later Pound and Eliot. One can watch the older thought-and-feeling formula developing from a Romantic into a characteristically Symbolist hypothesis. George Eliot, who knew Donne by the time she wrote *Middlemarch,* assumes like her master Wordsworth that the true voice comes from artists of higher organic sensibility than other men, but can write in that novel—doubtless unconscious of her role as critical pioneer—that the poet is "quick to discern", but also "quick to feel" because he possesses "a soul in which knowledge passes instantaneously into feeling, and feeling flashes back as a new organ of knowledge".

This period of transition is greatly illuminated in a paper recently published by Mr. J. E. Duncan in the *Journal of English and Germanic Philology.* Anyone who has used the Victorian editions upon which much of our reading in seventeenth-century poetry still depends must have occasionally felt that there was some hallucinatory resemblance between certain observations made by the enthusiastic clerical editors and those of Mr. Eliot. Mr. Duncan has collected a great deal of evidence to show, not only that Donne was well and truly revived long before Eliot's essays, and indeed Grierson's edition, but that even 70 years ago people were talking about the poet in what we recognise as the modern way. By 1911, Courthope, in his *History,* was already complaining that it had probably gone too far. Grierson's great edition of the following year was accepted as merely setting the seal on Donne's reputation. But what is more interesting than this mere setting back of the starting post is the terminology in which the Victorian critics, pleased with their rediscovery of the conceit and of hard-thinking poetry, devised in order to praise the Metaphysical poets. They speak of its intellectual cunning *and* its power of 'sensibility' and then, quite early, we find ourselves approaching, with a sort of unconscious inevitability, the modern formula which combines these two qualities as two sides of a coin. Grosart says that Crashaw's thinking "was so emotional as almost always to tremble into feeling"; Crowley's thought is "made to pulsate with feeling". Symons finds that Donne's "senses speak with unparallelled directness"; Schelling that Donne's contribution to the English lyric was "intellectualised emotion". Poets began to find Donne-like qualities in their own work; in so doing,

Francis Thompson spoke of his own "sensoriness instinct with mind", and the parallel was supported by Symons and by Mrs. Meynell. The familiar comparison between the seventeenth and twentieth centuries began as early as 1900; after that it was easy to play the game of parallel poets, and both Brooke and Bridges were credited with resemblances to Donne. Gosse and Grierson alike saw the similarity between Donne and Baudelaire, and briefly hinted at the parallel between English-Jacobean and French-Symbolist which was later to prove so fertile. Arthur Symons in fact developed the parallel to a considerable extent; he is the link between nineteenth- and twentieth-century orthodoxies of the Image, and of Donne and the seventeenth century.

Long before the great edition of Grierson, which made Donne relatively easy to read, and long before Mr. Eliot's phrase had its remarkable success in the world, powerful aesthetic interests were being satisfied by the conversion of a little-known poet into an English Laforgue; and the same interests demanded a catastrophic start to the modern world shortly after the death of Donne, and before *Paradise Lost*, that great dissociated poem which you must, said Mr. Eliot, read once for the meaning and once for the verse, and which is therefore of no use either to that illiterate audience he desiderates for his unified Symbolist poetry, or for the next best thing, a highly cultivated audience that also likes its art undissociated. The strangest irony in all this—and it is all I have to say about the second of these perverted poets—is that Milton, rather exceptionally, actually believed in and argued for the unity of the soul (a continuum of mind and sense), allowed his insistence on the inseparability of form and matter to lead him into heresy; and believed that poetry took precedence over other activities of the soul because it was simple (undissociated by intellect) sensuous and passionate. But this did not matter; there were overriding reasons why Milton had to be bent or broken. He was the main sufferer in the great experiment of projecting on to an historical scale a developed Romantic-Symbolist theory of the Image. And although, as Mr. Bateson has shown, Mr. Eliot borrowed the phrase 'dissociation of sensibility' from Gourmont's peculiar account of the processes of poetry in the mind of an individual (specifically Laforgue) and applied it to the history of a nation's poetry, it is obvious that behind the theory there is the whole pressure of the tradition I have been discussing. The historical effort of Symbolism has been to identify a period happily ignorant of the war between Image and discourse, an un-dissociated age. In the end, it is not of high importance that any age selected for this role is likely to be found wanting, except of course for the tendency to exclude particular poets and periods from the canon. Hulme could never have justified his selection; Pound was driven to Chinese, and a dubious theory of ideograms; Yeats believed his own theory only in a specially qualified way, admitting that its importance lay in the present and not in the past. This is true of Mr. Eliot also. The essays in which he proposed his theory represent a most fruitful and effective refinement of the Symbolist doctrine, yielding far more than Symons's, for instance, similar though they are in essentials. To attack his position has usually seemed to mean an assault on what most people are content to regard as the main tradition of modern verse.

One such attack, that of Mr. Yvor Winters, seems to me both extremely intelligent and extremely revealing; and it carries me on to the last phase of this essay, a cursory glance at the contemporary relation between Image and discourse. Mr. Winters looks for inconsistencies in Mr. Eliot's criticism, so that he can defend his own position, which is notoriously not a fashionable one. He insists that art is a statement of an understood experience, which it morally evaluates; and that poetry has, in consequence, the same *kind* of meaning as cruder statements of the same sort, so that one would expect it to be paraphrasable. This position is, of course, frankly opposed to a cherished Symbolist doctrine, and Mr. Winters is therefore very hostile to some of Eliot's opinions. For example, the famous sigh for an illiterate audience (analogous, by the way, to Yeats's desire for illiterate actors, and really a hopeless wish for an audience incapable of discourse and so cut off from intellection's universe of death) simply fans Winters' indignation, as does the cognate doctrine that meaning is only the burglar's bait for the housedog of intellect. So, when Eliot writes, in the beautiful essay on Dante, that "clear visual images are given much more intensity by having a meaning—we do not need to know what the meaning is, but in our awareness of the image we must be aware that the meaning is there too," and when Mr. Winters bullies him about this, we have a clear picture of the fundamental opposition between a Romantic-Symbolist criticism and a criticism conscientiously in reaction against it. Mr. Eliot says that a poem can be understood before its 'meaning' is taken, though the 'meaning' is not without importance. Winters replies: "If the meaning is important in the creation of the poem, at any rate, it is foolish to suppose that one can dispense with it in the reading of the poem or that the poet did not take his meaning seriously. Only the frailest barrier exists between the idea of this passage and Poe's theory that the poet should lay claim to a meaning when he is aware of none".

It is no use saying that Mr. Winters has simply misunderstood; he knows very well what Eliot means, as he shows when he traces Eliot's theory of necessary disorder in modern art to Romantic doctrines of organic form, and speaks of *The Waste Land* and *The Cantos* as belonging to the art of revery. He understands the roots of these poems, and even goes so far as to call Pound "a sensibility without a mind", which is, if nothing else, a very just punishment upon abusers of the word 'sensibility'. Mr. Winters, as we should expect, is eccentric in his choice of major modern poets, but he is nevertheless the only critic of any fame who can take for granted the history of the kind of poetry and criticism he is opposed to. In the essay on Eliot he bases a very important argument upon a revealing sentence which is hidden away in the introduction to the *Anabasis* of St. Jean Perse: "There is a logic of the imagination as well as a logic of concepts". (We, I hope, understand what this means, and can see how sharply such a belief separates the modern from the 'Metaphysical' poet.) It is hard to resist Winters' argument that here "the word *logic* is used figuratively", that it indicates nothing but "qualitative progression", "graduated progression of feeling". Yet for all that the argument is false. It indicates no *progression* of any sort. Time and space are exorcised; the emblem of this 'logic' is the Dancer. This misunderstanding, slight as it seems, shows that the difference between these two critics is extremely wide. If you want to mean something, says Mr. Winters, you must mean it in the usual way; in other words, form is not significant. But to Mr. Eliot, and to many others, this is an admission that the speaker has no real notion at all of what art is. "People who do not appreciate poetry," says Mr. Eliot, "always find it difficult to distinguish between order and chaos in the arrangement of images." But Mr. Winters does appreciate poetry. The truth is that he is an anti-Symbolist critic, and this necessarily puts him in opposition to most of his contemporaries. For him, poetry is the impassioned expression on the countenance of *all* science and, as George Eliot called it, an aesthetic teacher. Since he does not believe that it deals in a different order of truth he has not the same difficulties about language, communication and paraphrase as the critics who oppose him.

I draw attention in this sketchy way to Mr. Winters, because he leads us to an understanding of what is one of the main issues of modern poetic. This is the unformulated quarrel between the orthodoxy of

Symbolism and the surviving elements of an empirical-utilitarian tradition which, we are assured, is characteristically English. Yeats had a foot in both camps, the one stubbornly holding to the commonalty of the means of discourse and seeking to define those differences of degree which distinguish poetry, the other talking about images (sometimes indeed forgetting about words and their temporal behaviour altogether, or treating them as physical things like bits of string) and taking poetry to be a different kind of thing, a different mode of cognition, involving, at least as a working hypothesis, a different order of reality from any available to ordinary intellection. The difficulty of the first party is to find some way of talking about poetry and its propositions that does not disqualify it from the serious attention of *honnêtes gens;* for example, Richards's 'pseudo-statement' is asking for trouble, Wellek's theory of genre is too technical. On the other side, nobody can any longer (in the present state of semantics) be so offhand about the linguistic problems of the Image as the French Symbolists were. Indeed a good deal of the best modern criticism is interesting as evidence of the oscillations and tensions in the minds of critics between the claims of the Image and the claims of ordinary discourse.

These tensions are visible also in poetry, and it is possible that in the controlling of them the immediate future of our poetry lies, as well as our criticism and ways of looking at the past. At the moment, perhaps, the movement of the 'thirties away from aesthetic monism, the new insistence on the right to discourse, even to say such things as "We must love one another or die" (as Auden does in an exquisite poem) has ceased. There are good poets who cultivate a quasi-philosophical tone of meditation, but they are careful to have no design upon us, to place their meditation within the confines of reverie; there are others who prefer the ironies of stringently mechanical forms; but no Auden, nobody who wants, apparently, to go that way; and this is a pity. Recently Wallace Stevens has come to be more widely read in this country, and he is a poet who provides a unique, perhaps un-repeatable, solution to the image-and-discourse problem, by making the problem itself the subject of poems:

> Is the poem both peculiar and general?
> There's a meditation there, in which there seems
>
> To be an evasion, a thing not apprehended or
> Not apprehended well. Does the poet
> Evade us, as in a senseless element?

> Evade us, this hot, dependent orator,
> The spokesman at our bluntest barriers,
> Exponent by a form of speech, the speaker
>
> Of a speech only a little of the tongue?

One thing Stevens insists upon, and no poet is now likely to forget it: it is a lesson that Romantic aesthetic has taught once and for all. The poem is

> Part of the *res* and not itself about it.
> The poet speaks the poem as it is,
> Not as it was.

Only by knowing this can the poet be "the necessary angel of the earth." The sentiment is Blake's, but it has become everybody's; yet Stevens's answer to the problem—it is the problem of dissociation—though very complete, and achieving in the late poem called 'The Rock' a most moving comprehensiveness, is not available to all poets, and they must seek their own.

Stevens's problems are the problems also of modern criticism (in its way and of necessity almost as obscure as the poetry). The unique power of the poet, however one describes it, is to make images or symbols, however one understands these,—as somehow visual, or, in the tradition of the new semantics, as the neologisms created by shifting contexts. How are these products related to discourse? Is there any way to talk of poetry without breaking up the monad and speaking of thought and image?

The one thing nearly everybody seems to be agreed upon is that the work of art has to be considered as a whole and that considerations of 'thought' must be subordinated to a critical effort to see the whole as one image; the total work is not *about* anything—"a poem should not mean but *be*"—which is simply a vernacular way of saying what modern critics mean when they speak of it as 'autotelic' (they even speculate as to whether criticism is not also autotelic—the critic as artist once more). Put as simply as this, the position is not much changed since Mallarmé: "nul vestige d'une philosophie, l'éthique ou la métaphysique, ne transparaîtra; j'ajoute qu'il faut incluse et latente . . . le chant jaillit de source innée, antérieure à un concept". And many of the practical difficulties encountered by the holism of French Symbolism recur in modern critics. Take, for example, the problem which must sometimes arise, of what is the whole work of art. Is it the 'Voyage à Cythère' or is it the whole of *Les fleurs du Mal?* Is it 'They that have power to hurt' or the whole collection of Shakespeare's Sonnets? Professor Lehmann considers the first of these problems in his *Symbolist Aesthetic,* and seems to decide that the proper course is to take one poem at a time, since we know that *Les Fleurs du Mal* is not "really a poem with a decisive organization overall" but "poems loosely strung on a string of pre-dominating attitude". But how, it might be asked, can we be sure of this without trying the experiment of reading the whole book as a poem? Where do we get this important bit of information, which determines the whole question in advance? Certainly, on the purist view, from some illicit source—a knowledge of Baudelaire's intention. This may seem very extreme; but on the contrary it turns up with the regularity of an orthodoxy. We are told to read the whole of Shakespeare as one work. Mr. Wilson Knight reads all the Sonnets as one poem; he won his spurs by pioneering the Symbolist criticism of the plays, and is the most thoroughgoing of the holist Symbolist critics, unless we dare to say that Mr. Eliot, in his most famous essay, invites us to treat the whole of literature as one work.

There is a problem here, inherent in the Symbolist approach to poetry, which deserves more serious treatment than it gets, since it concerns the definition of what critics are talking about. In practice, of course, they cut the knot in silence, and assume the discontinuity of the poem they happen to be talking about, and even, for the purposes of exposition, talk about parts of poems as if they were wholes (just as they slyly paraphrase). Occasionally they even justify this practice. Mr. W. K. Wimsatt has several good things to say about the problem in his book *The Verbal Icon,* for instance this:

> Extreme holism is obviously contrary to our experience of literature. (We do not wait until the end of the play or novel to know whether the first scene or chapter is brilliant or dull—no long work in fact would ever be witnessed or read if this were so.) A poem, said Coleridge, the father of holism in English criticism, is a composition which proposes "to itself such delight from the *whole,* as is compatible with a distinct gratification from each component part". The value of a whole poem, while undoubtedly reflecting something back to the parts, has to grow out of parts which are themselves valuable. *The Rape of the Lock* would not come off were not the couplets witty. We may add that good poems may have dull parts; bad poems, bright parts. How minutely this principle could be urged without arriving at a theory of Longinian "sudden flashes", of "cathartically charged images", of Arnoldian touch-

stones, of poetic diction, or of irrelevant local texture, I do not know. Nor what the minimal dimension of wit or local brilliance of structure may be; nor to what extent a loosely constructed whole may be redeemed by the energy of individual chapters or scenes. Yet the validity of partial value as a general principle in tension with holism seems obvious.

Something might be said against this defence of *littérature*, for the 'spatial' view of works of art, and it is worth considering that there are modern works (*Ulysses* is an obvious example) which are deliberately, and for long stretches, extremely tedious, and without any brilliance of local texture. Yet what Mr. Wimsatt says is satisfactory to common sense, and in fact modern holist criticism is closely related, so far as poetry is concerned, to that other Symbolist article which sets up the lyric poem as the norm, so that for the most part only short poems get the full treatment.

Even so, the question of how to treat partial aspects continues to rise and trouble practical critics, and occasionally provides new insights. Mr. Empson, for example, has developed a habit of referring regularly to the whole work in the discussions of its parts; Mr. Ransom has raised a whole theory upon the assertion that the value of 'texture' resides precisely in its irrelevance to the structural concern of the poem, and he is further heretical in allowing no poem to be without some embodied 'prose discourse', providing the logical relevance denied to the 'texture'. Mr. Winters is right, I think, when he calls this an embarrassing doctrine, holding that Ransom "does not know what to do with the rational content, how to account for it or evaluate it." (Mr. Winters of course does know this.) To put the matter so baldly is, of course, to do wrong to Mr. Ransom's intense though urbane efforts to solve an important problem; but my object here is merely to insist that the problem arises quite naturally out of the attempt (which must be made in any modern poetic) to find a place for discourse in a Symbolist poetry. Ransom accepts most of the Symbolist position,—he calls the poetry of the Image 'physical' and the poetry of discourse 'Platonic'—right down to the psychological theory of the artist as isolated or inhibited from action (the check on action he calls 'sensibility') and without a radical reorientation there is simply no room for discourse in the work of art so conceived. The problem comes up again in the associated criticism of Allen Tate. He also believes that art "has no useful relation to ordinary forms of action," and accepts a distinction similar to that of Ransom, finding the virtue of poetry in the *tension* between idea and image, or between abstraction and concretion, or between discourse and the symbol which can have no logical relation to it.

Such formulations, however fruitful they may be in the exegesis which stems from them (and it is arguable that they are not fruitful in this way at all) have the disadvantages, as well as the benefits, of their Romantic-Symbolist heritage. Mr. R. W. Stallman, in his useful account of these critics, asks us to distinguish between their "formalism" and "the aestheticism of the nineties"; but the differences are by no means as decisive as he suggests, and if one were able to construct a normal modern poetic it would be unlikely to contain much, apart from its semantic content, to surprise Arthur Symons. It is true that a new school of critics, the Chicago 'neo-Aristotelians,' are directing us back to the *Poetics* and away from that preoccupation with metaphor (the rhetorical vehicle of the Image) which is an essential component of modern poetic, but one can truly say, without comment on the quality of this criticism, that, from the standpoint of modern orthodoxy, it is clearly tainted with heresy, the heresy of abstraction. What still prevails is the Symbolist conception of the work of art as aesthetic monad, as the product of a mode of cognition superior to, and different from, that of the sciences. Any alternative is likely to be treated as heretical—dubbed, for instance, 'ornamentalist', as degrading the status of the Image, and dealing to another 'dissociation', another over-valuation of ideas in poetry similar to that effected by Hobbes. One result of this orthodoxy is that the practical business of criticism becomes enormously strenuous, despite the technical facilities provided by Richards and Empson; and that there is a good deal of what must be called cheating, for example in the matter of paraphrase. Good modern criticism is much more eclectic in method than most theoretical pronouncements suggest; it must not seem to believe in paraphrase (or, sometimes, in any form of historical approach to the work in question) yet these and similar forbidden techniques are in fact frequently employed. It may be said that the strenuousness, as well as the obscurity, of such modern criticism, is a direct consequence of its Symbolist inheritance.

The effects of this inheritance may be traced also, so far as I know them, in the philosopher-aestheticians whom critics tend to take notice of (it would not be easy to say why they take notice of some and not of others). There are naturally many variations; but, to take two recent books, the 'concrete universal' as proposed by Mr. Wimsatt is the same thing as the Symbol of Mrs. Langer under a slightly different aspect. Mrs. Langer's is comfortably traditional in design, if not in ex-

ecution. It starts from music, where the definition of symbol as "articulate but non-discursive form" does not raise the same problems of
'content' and 'ideas' as it does in literature; so far she shares the
'aestheticism' of the 'nineties'. (It is interesting, by the way, to find her
quoting with approval a passage from Arthur Michel about the dance
which would have pleased Mallarmé and Symons and Yeats—the
dancer is conceived as oscillating "between two external poles of tension, thus transplanting the dancing body from the sensually existing
atmosphere of materialism and real space into the symbolic super-
sphere of tension space"; and he speaks of "the dissolution of the
dancer into swaying tension".) When she arrives at the problem of the
discursive content of poems, Mrs. Langer's answer is that "the poet
uses discourse to create an illusion, a pure appearance, which is a non-
discursive symbolic form". She distinguishes between this position and
that of 'pure poetry' as formulated by Moore and Bremond, accurately
calling the latter's a magical solution; it is magical in so far as it is
Symbolist, and so, perhaps, in its different way, is hers. But hers is
distinguished further by arduous and delightful discriminations. She
gives modified approval to Mr. Pottle's view that "Poetry should be no
purer than the purpose demands", but calls it a philosophical make-
shift; exposes the mass of unphilosophical thinking that vitiates most
attempts to distinguish between poetry and non-poetry; and argues
that to maintain its interest in life poetry has to traffic with "serious
thought". But "the framework of subject-matter" becomes part of the
symbolic whole; something has to be *done* to it, it must, in the Croce-
Collingwood sense, be 'expressed,' and it will then be part of the work
of art which is "a single indivisible symbol, although a highly articulated one".

Mrs. Langer has undoubtedly found a place for 'discourse' in her
'symbol'—so necessary, when the art is one which uses words—and the
success of her books is probably an advance towards the dissociation
of Romantic-Symbolist aesthetic from the anti-intellectualism with
which it has been so persistently and inevitably associated from the
beginning, and so potently since Rimbaud. An age of criticism, for so
we tend to think of our epoch, is comforted by the assurance that reason can somehow get at poems, and that criticism itself should not be
the autotelic act that Wilde as well as some later critics argued it must
be (and as it indeed must, if art is the symbol by definition inexplicable). "The situation," says Mr. Wimsatt, "is something like this: In
each poem there is something (an individual intuition—or a concept)
which can never be expressed in other terms. It is like the square root

of two or like pi, which cannot be expressed by rational numbers, but only as their *limit*. Criticism of poetry is like 1.414. . . or 3.1416. . . , not all it would be, yet all that can be had and very useful."

And this is all the critic can expect. He cannot give up the autonomy of the symbolic work of art, a concept of form which has been near the heart of criticism since Coleridge. And so he cannot expect ever to achieve finality in his own work; he is doomed to be limited, even if he remembers the symbolic origin of the discourse he is extracting for discussion. Not that a good critic would wish it otherwise; he is so accustomed to *defending* poetry on these very grounds, his way of thinking about poetry is, in fact, inclined to be defensive, and even when he is asserting poetry's unique powers there is likely to be a cautious anti-positivism in his tone. Reviewing Mr. Philip Wheelright's recent book *The Burning Fountain*, Mr. M. H. Abrams points out that this excellent writer is "a prisoner of the theory he opposes" because he accepts the opposition between scientific and expressive language. And Mr. Abrams goes on to suggest, in a most sympathetic way, that we ought now to go over to the offensive. "An adequate theory of poetry must be constructed, not by a strategy of defense and limited counter-attack on ground chosen by a different discipline, but by a positive strategy specifically adapted to disclose the special ends and structures and values, not only of poetry as such, but of the rich diversity of individual poems. What is needed is not merely a "metagrammar" and a "paralogic." What is needed, and what the present yeasty ferment in criticism may well portend, is simply, a poetic."

If such a poetic emerges it will still, of course, be Symbolist; but it will have a different place for discourse from any found for it during the nineteenth-century struggle with the positivists. It will owe much to modern semantics, but it will not call the discourse of poetry "pseudo-statement." Nor will its differences from scientific statement be reduced to differences of degree; it will not become statement transfigured by impassioned expression. The new poetic would be remote from the radicalism of Blake, have little to do with the forlorn hopes of Mallarmé, and less with the disastrous *dérèglement* of Rimbaud. We have perhaps learnt to respect order, and felt on our bodies the effect of irrationalism, at any rate when the sphere of action is invaded by certain elements of the Romantic *rêve*. It will be a waking poetic, respecting order. 'Shape' has no chance of interfering with 'form', to use Coleridge's distinction; but among good poets it never had. But 'reason' will return to poetics, and perhaps Mrs. Langer has shown how to find it a *modus vivendi* with the symbol. One notes also that Mr. Wimsatt, as his title suggests, is willing to allow both meanings of 'symbol' to the words of poetry, I mean those of the semasiologist and of the Romantic critic.

But in the end, of course, these matters are solved by poets and not by critics. That is why, I think, Yeats is so important in what I have been saying. He had a matured poet's concern for the relation of symbol to discourse. He understood that one pole of Symbolist theory is sacramentalism, whether Catholic or theurgic:

> Did God in portioning wine and bread
> Give man His thought, or his mere body?

and was willing to see in the discourse, whether of language or gesture, of the dedicated, symbolic values. He, as we have seen, most fully worked out the problems of the Image and of the nature of the poet's isolation; he understood the importance of magic to Symbolist aesthetic; and he also found his solution to that most urgent problem of discourse, assuming that such a statement as "The best lack all conviction", in contact with the vast image out of *Spiritus Mundi*, puts on the knowledge with the power of that image. So the slaves of time, the non-poets, will find a validity in his symbolic poems that is, for them, absent from the pure poetry of the dream. They share with the poet not only the Great Memory, but also the ordinary syntax of the daily life of action. Yeats's sun may be full of angels hymning Jehovah, but it is also a disc shaped somewhat like a guinea. This is not the dissociation of image that is complained of; it is an admission that art was always made *for* men who habitually move in space and time, whose language is propelled onward by verbs, who cannot always be asked to respect the new enclosure laws of poetry, or such forbidding notices as "No road through to action". Somehow, and probably soon, the age of dissociation—which is to say, the age that invented and developed the concept of dissociation—must end.

The Houyhnhnms, the Yahoos, and the History of Ideas

R. S. Crane

I shall be concerned in this essay with two ways of using the history of ideas—or, in the case of one of them, as I shall argue, misusing it—in literary interpretation. The particular issue I have in mind is forced on one in an unusually clear-cut manner, I think, by what has been said of the 'Voyage to the Country of the Houyhnhnms' in the criticism of the past few decades; and for this reason, and also because I wish to add a theory of my own about Swift's intentions in that work to the theories now current, I shall base the discussion that follows almost exclusively on it.

I

With a very few exceptions (the latest being George Sherburn),[1] since the 1920s, and especially since the later 1930s, writers on the fourth Voyage have been mainly dominated by a single preoccupation.[2] They have sought to correct the misunderstanding of Swift's satiric purpose in the Voyage which had vitiated, in their opinion, most earlier criticism of it and, in particular, to defend Swift from the charge of all-out misanthropy that had been levelled against him so often in the past —by Thackeray, for example, but many others also—on the strength of Gulliver's wholesale identification of men with the Yahoos and his unqualified worship of the Houyhnhnms.

It is easy to see what this task would require them to do. It would require them to show that what Gulliver is made to say about human nature in the Voyage, which is certainly misanthropic enough, and what Swift wanted his readers to believe about human nature are, in certain crucial respects at any rate, two different and incompatible things. It would require them, that is, to draw a clear line between what is both Swift and Gulliver and what is only Gulliver in a text in which Gulliver alone is allowed to speak to us.

The resulting new interpretations have differed considerably in emphasis and detail from critic to critic, but they have been generally in accord on the following propositions: The attitudes of Swift and his hero do indeed coincide up to a certain point, it being true for Swift no less than for Gulliver that men in the mass are terrifyingly close to the Yahoos in disposition and behaviour, and true for both of them also that the Houyhnhnms are in some of their qualities—their abhorrence of falsehood, for instance—proper models for human emulation. That, however, is about as far as the agreement goes: it is to Gulliver alone and not to Swift that we must impute the radical pessimism of the final chapters—it is he and not Swift who reduces men literally to Yahoos; it is he and not Swift who despairs of men because they cannot or will not lead the wholly rational life of the Houyhnhnms. Gulliver, in other words, is only in part a reliable spokesman of his creator's satire; he is also, and decisively at the end, one of the targets of that satire—a character designed to convince us, through his obviously infatuated actions, of the absurdity both of any view of man's nature that denies the capacity of at least some men for rational and virtuous conduct, however limited this capacity may be, and of any view of the best existence for man that makes it consist in taking 'reason alone' as a guide. What, in short, Swift offers us, as the ultimate moral of the Voyage, is a compromise between these extremist opinions of Gulliver: human nature, he is saying, is bad enough, but it is not altogether hopeless; reason is a good thing, but a life of pure reason is no desirable end for man.

Now it is evident that however appealing this interpretation may be to those who want to think well of Swift and to rescue him from his nineteenth-century maligners, it is not a merely obvious exegesis of the 'Voyage to the Houyhnhnms,' or one that most common readers, past or present, have spontaneously arrived at. It is not an exegesis, either, that goes at all comfortably with that famous letter of Swift's in 1725 in which he told Pope that his chief aim was 'to vex the world rather than divert it' and that he never would have peace of mind until 'all honest men' were of his opinion. For there is nothing particularly vexing in the at least partly reassuring moral now being attributed to the Voyage or anything which 'honest men' in 1726 would have had much hesitation in accepting. And again, though we must surely agree that there is a significant difference between Gulliver and Swift, why must we suppose that the difference has to be one of basic doctrine? Why could it not be simply the difference between a person who just discovered a deeply disturbing truth about man and is consequently, like Socrates' prisoner in the myth of the cave, more than a little upset and one who, like Socrates himself, has known this truth all along and can therefore write of his hero's discovery of it calmly and with humour?

I introduce these points here not as decisive objections to the new interpretation but rather as signs that it is not the kind of interpretation which (in Johnson's phrase), upon its first production, must be acknowledged to be just. Confirmatory arguments are plainly needed; and a consideration of the arguments that have in fact been offered in support of it will bring us rather quickly to the special problem I wish to discuss.

A good deal has been made, to begin with, of what are thought to be clear indications in the Voyage itself that Swift wanted his readers to take a much more critical view than Gulliver does of 'the virtues and ideas of those exalted Houyhnhnms' and a much less negative view of human possibilities. If he had designed the Houyhnhmns to be for us what they are for Gulliver, namely the 'perfection of nature' and hence an acceptable standard for judging of man, he would surely, it is argued, have endowed them with more humanly engaging qualities than they have; he would surely not have created them as the 'remote, unsympathetic, and in the end profoundly unsatisfying' creatures so many of his readers nowadays find them to be. We must therefore see in Gulliver's worship of the rational horses a plain evidence of the extremist error into which he has fallen. And similarly, if Swift had expected us to go the whole way with Gulliver in his identification of men with the Yahoos, he would hardly have depicted the human characters in his story—especially the admirable Portuguese captain, Don Pedro de Mendez, and his crew—in the conspicuously favourable light in which they appear to us. They are bound to strike us as notable exceptions to the despairing estimate of 'human kind' to which Gulliver has been led by his Houyhnhnm master; and we can only conclude that Gulliver's failure to look upon them as other than Yahoos, whom at best he can only 'tolerate,' is meant as still another sign to us of the false extremism of his attitude.

All this looks at first sight rather convincing—until, that is, we begin to think of other possible intentions that Swift might have had in the Voyage with which these signs would be equally compatible. Suppose that his primary purpose was indeed to 'vex the world' by administering as severe a shock as he could to the cherished belief that man is par excellence a 'rational creature,' and suppose that he chose to do this, in part at least, by forcing his readers to dwell on the unbridgeable gap between what is involved in being a truly 'rational creature' and what not only the worse but also the better sort of men actually are. It is plain what he would have had to do in working out such a design. He would have had to give to his wholly rational beings precisely those 'unhuman' characteristics that have been noted, to their disadvantage, in the Houyhnhnms; to have made them creatures such as we would normally like or sympathize with would have been to destroy their value as a transcendent standard of comparison. And it would have been no less essential to introduce characters, like Don Pedro, who, in terms of ordinary human judgments, would impress us as unmistakably good; otherwise he would have exempted too many of his readers from the shock to their pride in being men which, on this hypothesis, he was trying to produce. He would have had to do, in short, all those things in the Voyage that have been taken as indications of a purpose very different from the one I am now supposing, and much less misanthropic. Clearly, then, some other kind of proof is needed than these ambiguous internal signs before the current view of Swift's meaning can be thought of as more than one possibility among other competing ones.

A good many defenders of this view, especially during the past decade, have attempted to supply such proof by relating the Voyage to its presumed background in the intellectual and religious concerns of Swift and his age; and it is their manner of doing this—of using hypotheses based on the history of ideas in the determination of their author's meaning—that I want to examine in what immediately follows.

They have been fairly well agreed on these three points: in the first place, that Swift's main design in the Voyage was to uphold what they describe as the traditional and orthodox conception of human nature, classical and Christian alike, that 'recognizes in man an inseparable complex of good and evil,' reason and passion, spiritual soul and animal body; secondly, that he conceived the Houyhnhnms and the Yahoos, primarily at least, as allegorical embodiments of these two parts of man's constitution taken in abstraction the one from the other;

and thirdly, that he developed his defence of the orthodox view by directing his satire against those contemporary doctrines, on the one hand, that tended to exalt the Houyhnhnm side of man in forgetfulness of how Yahoo-like man really is, and those doctrines, on the other hand, that tended to see man only as a Yahoo in forgetfulness of his Houyhnhnm possibilities, limited though these are. All this has been more or less common doctrine among critics of the Voyage since Ernest Bernbaum in 1920; there has been rather less agreement on the identity of the contemporary movements of ideas which Swift had in view as objects of attack. It was usual in the earlier phases of the discussion to say simply, as Bernbaum does, that he was thinking, at the one extreme, of the 'sentimental optimism' of writers like Shaftesbury and, at the other, of the pessimism or cynicism of writers like Hobbes and Mandeville. Since then, though, other identifications have been added to the list, as relevant especially to his conception of the Houyhnhnms; we have been told, thus, that he 'obviously' intended to embody in the principles and mode of life of these creatures, along with certain admittedly admirable qualities, the rationalistic errors of the neo-stoics, the Cartesians and the Deists—some or all of these, depending on the critic.

Now if we could feel sure that what was in Swift's mind when he conceived the fourth Voyage is even approximately represented by these statements, we should have little reason for not going along with the interpretation of his design they have been used to support. For if he was indeed engaged in vindicating the 'Christian humanist' view of human nature against those contemporary extremists who made either too much or too little of man's capacity for reason and virtue, then the current view of Gulliver as partly a vehicle and partly an object of the satire is surely correct. Everything depends, therefore, on how much relevance to what he was trying to do in the Voyage this particular historical hypothesis can be shown to have.

Its proponents have offered it as relevant beyond reasonable doubt; which suggests to me that some special assumptions about the application of intellectual history to the exegesis of literary works must be involved here. For they would find it difficult, I think, to justify their confidence in terms merely of the ordinary canons of proof in this as well as other historical fields.

They can indeed show that the hypothesis is a possible one, in the sense that it is consistent with some of the things we know about Swift apart from the Voyage. We know thus that he was a humanistically educated Anglican divine, with traditionalist inclinations in many matters; that he looked upon man's nature as deeply corrupted by the Fall but thought that self-love and the passions could be made, with the help of religion, to yield a positive though limited kind of virtue; that he held reason in high esteem as a God-given possession of man but distrusted any exclusive reliance on it in practice or belief, and ridiculed the Stoics and Cartesians and made war on the Deists; and that he tended, especially in his political writings, to find the useful truth in a medium between extremes. A man of whom these things can be said might very well have conceived the 'Voyage to the Houyhnhnms' in the terms in which, on the present theory, Swift is supposed to have conceived it. And beyond this, it is possible to point to various characteristics in the Voyage itself which *if* the hypothesis is correct, can be interpreted as likely consequences of it. *If* Swift had in fact intended to symbolize, in the sustained opposition of Houyhnhnms and Yahoos, the deep division and conflict within man between his rational and his animal natures, he would undoubtedly have depicted these two sets of creatures, in essentials at least much as they are depicted in the text (though this would hardly account for his choice of horses as symbols of rationality). So too with the supposition that we were meant to see in the Houyhnhnms, among other things, a powerful reminder of how inadequate and dangerous, for weak and sinful human nature, is any such one-sided exaltation of reason as was being inculcated at the time by the Deists, the neo-Stoics, and the Cartesians: it would not be surprising, if that were actually Swift's intention, to find Gulliver saying of 'those exalted quadrupeds,' as he does, that they consider 'reason alone sufficient to govern a rational creature,' that they neither affirm nor deny anything of which they are not certain, and that they keep their passions under firm control, practise 'universal friendship and benevolence,' and remain indifferent to human fear of death and human grief for the death of others.

Now all this is to the good, to the extent at least that without such considerations as these about both Swift and the fourth Voyage there would be no reason for entertaining the hypothesis at all. But can we say anything more than this—so long, that is, as we judge the question by the ordinary standards of historical criticism? In other words, do the considerations I have just summarized tend in any decisive way to establish the hypothesis as fact? The answer must surely be that they do not, and for the simple reason that they are all merely positive and favouring considerations, such as can almost always be adduced in support of almost any hypothesis in scholarship or common life, however irrelevant or false it may turn out to be. It is a basic maxim of scholarly criticism, therefore, that the probability of a given hypothesis is proportionate not to our ability to substantiate it by confirmatory evidence (though there obviously must be confirmatory evidence) but to our inability—after serious trial—to rule it out in favour of some other hypothesis that would explain more completely and simply the particulars it is concerned with. We have to start, in short, with the assumption that our hypothesis may very well be false and then permit ourselves to look upon it as fact only when, having impartially considered all the counter-possibilities we can think of, we find disbelief in it more difficult to maintain than belief. This is a rule which few of us consistently live up to (otherwise we would not publish as much as we do); but there are varying degrees of departure from it; and I can see few signs that its requirements are even approximated to in the current historical discussions of the fourth Voyage. It would be a different matter if these critics had been able to show statements by Swift himself about *Gulliver's Travels* that defy reasonable interpretation except as references to the particular issues and doctrines which the hypothesis supposes were in his mind when he wrote the Voyage. But they have not succeeded in doing this; and they have given no attention at all to the possibility that there were other traditions of thought about human nature in Swift's time (I can think of one such, as will appear later) which he can be shown to have been familiar with and which they ought to have considered and then, if possible, excluded as irrelevant before their hypothesis can be said—again on ordinary scholarly grounds—to be confirmed.

What are, then, the special assumptions about interpretative method in the history of ideas on which, in view of all this, their confidence must be presumed to rest? Their problem has naturally led them, as it would any historian, to make propositions about Swift's thought apart from *Gulliver* and about the thought of Swift's age: what is distinctive is the character of these propositions and the use they are put to in the interpretation of the Voyage. In the eyes of the ordinary historian of ideas inquiring into the intellectual antecedents and causes of this work, the thought of Swift as expressed in his other writings is simply an aggregate of particular statements and arguments, some of which may well turn out to be relevant to an understanding of its meaning; for any of them, however, this is merely a possibility to be tested, not a presumption to be argued from. It is the same, too, with the thought of Swift's age: this, again, in the eyes of the ordinary historian, is nothing more determinate than the sum of things that were being written in the later seventeenth and early eighteenth centuries, from varying points of view and in varying traditions of analysis, on the general theme of human nature; some of these, once more, may well be relevant to the argument developed in the Voyage, but the historian can know what they are only after an unprejudiced inquiry that presupposes no prior limitation on the ideas Swift might have been influenced by or have felt impelled to attack in constructing it. For the ordinary historian, in short, the fact that the 'Voyage to the Houyhnhnms' was written by Swift at a particular moment in the general history of thought about man has only this methodological significance: that it defines the region in which he may most hopefully look for the intellectual stimuli and materials that helped to shape the Voyage; it gives him, so to speak, his working reading-list; it can never tell him—only an independent analysis of the Voyage can do that—how to use the list.

That the critics we are concerned with have taken a different view of the matter from this is suggested by the title of the book in which the current historical theory of Swift's intentions in the Voyage is argued most fully and ingeniously—Kathleen Williams's *Jonathan Swift and the Age of Compromise*. For to think of a period in intellectual history in this way—as the age *of* something or other, where the something or other is designated by an abstract term like 'compromise'—is obviously no longer to consider it as an indefinite aggregate of happenings; it is to consider it rather as a definite system of happenings; something like the plot of a novel in which a great many diverse characters and episodes are unified, more or less completely, by a principal action or theme. It is to assume, moreover, not only that the historian can determine what was the central problem, the basic conflict or tension, the dominant world-view of a century or generation, either in general or in some particular department of thought, but that he can legitimately use his formula for this as a confirmatory premise in arguing the meanings and causes of individual works produced in that age. It is to suppose that there is a kind of probative force in his preferred formula for the period which can confer, a priori, if not a unique at least a privileged relevance on one particular hypothesis about a given work of that period as against other hypotheses that are less easily brought under the terms of the formula, so that little more is required by way of further proof than a demonstration, which is never hard to give, that the work makes sense when it is 'read' as the hypothesis dictates.

These are, I think, the basic assumptions which underlie most of the recent historical discussions of the fourth Voyage and which go far toward explaining the confidence their authors have felt in the correctness of their conclusions. It would be hard, otherwise, to understand why they should think it important to introduce propositions about what was central and unifying in the moral thought of Swift's age; the reason must be that they have hoped, by so doing, to establish some kind of antecedent limitation on the intentions he could be expected to have had in writing the Voyage. And that, indeed, is the almost unavoidable effect of the argument for any reader who closes his mind, momentarily, to the nature of the presuppositions on which it rests. For suppose we agree with these critics that the dominant and most significant issue in the moral speculation of the later seventeenth and early eighteenth centuries was a conflict between the three fundamentally different views of man's nature represented by the orthodox 'classical-Christian' dualism in the middle and, at opposite extremes to this, by the newer doctrines of the rationalists and benevolists on the one side and of the materialists and cynics on the other. Since this is presented as an exhaustive scheme of classification, it will be easy for us to believe that the view of man asserted in the Voyage must have been one of these three. And then suppose we agree to think of Swift as a character in this three-cornered plot, who was predisposed by his humanist education and his convictions as an Anglican divine to adhere to the traditional and compromising view as against either of the modern extremisms. It will be difficult for us now to avoid believing that the 'Voyage to the Houyhnhnms' was therefore more probably than not an assertion of this middle view against its contemporary enemies, and it will be harder than it would be without such an argument from the age to the author to the work, to resist any interpretations of its details that may be necessary to make them accord with that theory of Swift's intentions.

This is likely to be our reaction, at any rate, until we reflect on the peculiar character of the argument we have been persuaded to go along with. There are many arguments like it in the writings of modern critics and historians of ideas in other fields (those who have interpreted Shakespeare in the light of 'the Elizabethan world-picture,' for instance); but they all betray, I think, a fundamental confusion in method. The objection is not that they rest on a false conception of historical periods. There is nothing intrinsically illegitimate in the mode of historical writing that organizes the intellectual happenings of different ages in terms of their controlling 'climates of opinion,' dominant tendencies, or ruling oppositions of attitude or belief; and the results of such synthesizing efforts are sometimes—as in A. O. Lovejoy, for example—illuminating in a very high degree. The objection is rather to the further assumption, clearly implicit in these arguments, that the unifying principles of histories of this type have something like the force of empirically established universal laws, and can therefore be used as guarantees of the probable correctness of any interpretations of individual writings that bring the writings into harmony with their requirements. That this is sheer illusion can be easily seen if we consider what these principles really amount to. Some of them amount simply to assertions that there was a tendency among the writers of a particular time to concentrate on such and such problems and to solve them in such and such ways; there is no implication here that this trend affected all writers or any individual writer at all times; whether a given work of the age did or did not conform to the trend remains therefore an open question, to be answered only by independent inquiry unbiased by the merely statistical probabilities affirmed in the historian's generalization. But there are also principles of a rather different sort, among which we much include, I think, the formula of Swift's critics for the dominant conflict about human nature in his time. These are best described as dialectical constructs, since they organize the doctrinal facts they refer to by imposing on them abstract schemes of logical relationships among ideas which may or may not be identical with any of the various classifications of doctrines influential at the time. Thus the characterization of Swift's age and of Swift himself as a part of that age in our critics derives its apparent exhaustiveness from a pattern of general terms—the concept of 'Christian humanism' and the two contraries of this—which these critics clearly owe to the ethical and historical speculations of Irving Babbitt and his school. Now it may be that this scheme represents accurately enough the distinctions Swift had in mind when he conceived the fourth Voyage; but that would be something of a coincidence, and it is just as reasonable to suppose that he may have been thinking quite outside the particular framework of notions which this retrospective scheme provides. We must conclude, then, that this whole way of using the history of ideas in literary interpretation is a snare and a delusion. From the generalizations and schematisms of the synthesizing historians we can very often get suggestions for new working hypotheses with which to approach the exegesis of individual works. What we cannot get from them is any assurance whatever that any of these hypotheses are more likely to be correct than any others that we have hit upon without their aid.

I should now like to invite the reader's criticism, in the light of what I have been saying, on another view of the intellectual background and import of the fourth Voyage (or a considerable part of it at least) which I have attempted to argue on the basis merely of ordinary historical evidence, independently of any general postulates about Swift or his age.

II

Whatever else may be true of the Voyage, it will doubtless be agreed that one question is kept uppermost in it from the beginning, for both Gulliver and the reader. This is the question of what sort of animal man, as a species, really is; and the point of departure in the argument is the answer to this question which Gulliver brings with him into Houyhnhnmland and which is also, we are reminded more than once, the answer which men in general tend, complacently, to give to it. Neither he nor they have any doubt that only man, among 'sensitive' creatures, can be properly called 'rational'; all the rest— whether wild or tame, detestable or, like that 'most comely and generous' animal, the horse, the reverse of that—being merely 'brutes,' not 'endued with reason.' The central issue, in other words, is primarily one of definition: is man, or is he not, correctly defined as a 'rational creature'? It is significant that Gulliver's misanthropy at the end is not the result of any increase in his knowledge of human beings in the concrete over what he has had before; it is he after all who expounds to his Houyhnhnm master all those melancholy facts about men's 'actions and passions' that play so large a part in their conversations; he has known these facts all along, and has still been able to call himself a 'lover of mankind.' The thing that changes his love into antipathy is the recognition that is now forced upon him that these facts are wholly incompatible with the formula for man's nature which he has hitherto taken for granted—are compatible, indeed, only with a formula, infinitely more humiliating to human pride, which pushes man nearly if not quite over to the opposite pole of the animal world.

What brings about the recognition is, in the first place, the deeply disturbing spectacle of the Houyhnhnms and the Yahoos. I can find nothing in the text that forces us to look on these two sets of strange creatures in any other light than that in which Gulliver sees them— not, that is, as personified abstractions, but simply as two concrete species of animals: existent species for Gulliver, hypothetical species for us. The contrast he draws between them involves the same pair of antithetical terms (the one positive, the other privative) that he has been accustomed to use in contrasting men and the other animals. The essential character of the Houyhnhnms, he tells us, is that they are creatures 'wholly governed by reason'; the essential character of the Yahoos is that 'they are the most unteachable of brutes,' without 'the least tincture of reason.' The world of animals in Houyhnhnmland, in other words, is divided by the same basic differences as the world of animals in Europe. Only, of course—and it is the shock of this that prepares Gulliver for his ultimate abandonment of the definition of man he had started with—it is a world in which the normal distribution of species between 'rational creatures' and irrational 'brutes' is sharply inverted, with horses, whom he can't help admiring, in the natural place of men, and man-like creatures, whom he can't help abhorring, in the natural place of horses.

This is enough in itself to cause Gulliver to view his original formula for his own species, as he says, 'in a very different light.' But he is pushed much farther in the same misanthropic direction by the questions and comments of his Houyhnhnm master, acting as a kind of Socrates. What thus develops is partly a reduction to absurdity of man's 'pretensions to the character of a rational creature' and partly a demonstration of the complete parity in essential nature between men and the Houyhnhnmland Yahoos. There is of course one striking difference—unlike the Yahoos, men are after all possessed of at least a 'small proportion,' a 'small pittance' of reason, some in greater degree than others. But I can see no clear signs in the text that this qualification is intended to set men apart as a third, or intermediate, species for either Gulliver or the reader. For what is basic in the new definition of man as a merely more 'civilized' variety of Yahoo is the fundamentally irrational 'disposition' which motivates his habitual behaviour; and in relation to that his 'capacity for reason' is only an acquired attribute which he is always in danger of losing and of which, as Gulliver says, he makes no other use, generally speaking, than 'to improve and multiply those vices' whereof his 'brethren [in Houyhnhnmland] had only the share that nature allotted them.'

It is clear what a satisfactory historical explanation of this line of argument in the Voyage would have to do. It would have to account for Swift's very patent assumption that there would be a high degree of satirical force, for readers in 1726, in a fable which began with the notion that man is pre-eminently a 'rational creature' and then proceeded to turn this notion violently upside down, and which, in doing so, based itself on a division of animal species into the extremes of 'rational creatures' and irrational 'brutes' and on the paradoxical identification of the former with horses and of the latter with beings closely resembling men. Was there perhaps a body of teaching, not so far brought into the discussion of the Voyage but widely familiar at the time, that could have supplied Swift with the particular scheme of ideas he was exploiting here? I suggest that there was, and also that there is nothing strange in the fact that it has been hitherto overlooked by Swift's critics. For one principal medium through which these ideas could have come to Swift and his readers—the only one, in fact, I know of that could have given him all of them—was a body of writings, mainly in Latin, which students of literature in our day quite naturally shy away from reading: namely, the old-fashioned textbooks in logic that still dominated the teaching of that subject in British universities during the later seventeenth and early eighteenth centuries.[3]

It is impossible not to be impressed, in the first place, by the prominence in these textbooks of the particular definition of man which the Voyage sought to discredit. *Homo est animal rationale:* no one could study elementary logic anywhere in the British Isles in the generation before *Gulliver* without encountering this formula or variations of it (e.g., *Nullus homo est irrationalis*) in his manuals and the lectures he heard. It appears as the standard example of essential definition in the great majority of logics in use during these years at Oxford, Cambridge, and Dublin; and in most of those in which it occurs, it is given without comment or explanation as the obviously correct formula for man's distinctive nature, as if no one would ever question that man is, uniquely and above all, a rational creature. It is frequently brought in many times over, in various contexts, in individual textbooks: I have counted a dozen or so occurrences of it in Milton's *Art of Logic,* and many times that number in the *Institutionum logicarum . . . libri duo* of Franco Burgersdijck (or Burgersdicius), which was one of the most widely used, and also one of the longest lived, of all these writings—it appeared in 1626 and was still prescribed at Dublin when Edmund Burke went there as a Junior Freshman in 1744.[4] I shall have some more to say of Burgersdicius, or 'Burgy' as Burke called him, presently; but it is worth noting that he provides us, in one passage, with the very question on which much of the fourth Voyage was to turn, with the answer Swift was *not* to give to it: 'Quærenti enim, Quale animal est homo? apposite respondetur, Rationale.'

Not only, however, was the definition omnipresent in these books, but there is some evidence that it was thought of, in Swift's time, as the special property of the academic logicians. Locke, for instance, calls it in his *Essay* 'the ordinary Definition of the Schools,' the 'sacred Definition of *Animal Rationale*' of 'the learned Divine and Lawyer'; it goes, he implies, with 'this whole *Mystery* of *Genera* and *Species*, which make such a noise in the Schools, and are, with Justice, so little regarded out of them' (III.iii.10; vi.26; iii.9). And there are other later testimonies to the same effect; among them these opening lines of an anonymous poem of the period after *Gulliver*, once ascribed to Swift— 'The Logicians Refuted':

> Logicians have but ill defin'd
> As rational, the human kind;
> Reason, they say, belongs to man,
> But let them prove it if they can.
> Wise Aristotle and Smiglesius,
> By ratiocinations specious,
> Have strove to prove with great precision,
> With definition and division,
> *Homo est ratione preditum;*
> But for my soul I cannot credit 'em.[5]

But the logicians had more to offer Swift than the great authority which they undoubtedly conferred on the definition 'rational animal.' They could have suggested to him also the basic principle on which the inverted animal world of Houyhnhnmland was constructed, and consequently the disjunction that operated as major premise in his argument about man. Whoever it was, among the Greeks, that first divided the genus 'animal' by the differentiae 'rational' and 'irrational,' there is much evidence that this antithesis had become a commonplace in the Greco-Roman schools long before it was taken up by the writer who did more than any one else to determine the context in which the definition *animal rationale* was chiefly familiar to Englishmen of Swift's time. This writer was the Neoplatonist Porphyry of the third century A.D., whose little treatise, the *Isagoge*, or introduction to the categories of Aristotle, became, as is well known, one of the great sources of logical theorizing and teaching from the time of Boethius until well beyond the end of the seventeenth century. There is no point in going into the details of Porphyry's doctrine: what is important for our purpose here is the new sanction he gave to the older division of animal species through his incorporation of it into the general scheme of differentiae for the category of substance which was later known as the *arbor porphyriana* or Porphyry's tree, especially in the diagrams of it that became a regular feature of the more elementary textbooks. Here it is, set forth discursively, in the crabbed prose of Burgersdicius (I quote the English version of 1697, but the Latin is no better). In seeking the definition of man, he writes, we must first observe that

> Man is a Substance; but because an Angel is also a Substance; *That it may appear how Man differs from an Angel,* Substance ought to be divided into Corporeal and Incorporeal. A Man is a *Body,* an Angel *without a Body:* But a Stone also is a *Body:* That therefore a Man may be distinguished from a Stone divide Bodily or Corporeal Substance into Animate and Inanimate, that is, *with or without a Soul.* Man is a Corporeal Substance Animate, Stone Inanimate. But Plants are also *Animate:* Let us divide therefore again Corporeal Substance Animate into *Feeling and void of Feeling.* Man feels, a Plant not: But a Horse *also feels,* and likewise other Beasts. Divide we therefore Animate Corporeal Feeling Substance into Rational and Irrational; Here therefore *are we to stand,* since it appears that every, and only Man *is Rational.*[6]

And there was, finally, one other thing in these logics that could have helped to shape Swift's invention in the fourth Voyage. In opposing man as the only species of 'rational animal' to the brutes, Porphyry obviously needed a specific instance, parallel to man, of an 'irrational' creature; and the instance he chose—there were earlier precedents for the choice[7]—was the horse. The proportion 'rational' is to 'irrational' as man is to horse occurs more than once in the *Isagoge;* and the juxtaposition, in the same context, of *homo* and *equus* was a frequently recurring cliché in his seventeenth-century followers, as in the passage in Burgersdicius just quoted: other species of brutes were occasionally mentioned, but none of them nearly so often. And any one who studied these books could hardly fail to remember a further point —that the distinguishing 'property' of this favourite brute was invariably given as whinnying *(facultas hinniendi)*; *equus,* it was said again and again, *est animal hinnibile.*

To most Englishmen of Swift's time who had read logic in their youth—and this would include nearly all generally educated men— these commonplaces of Porphyry's tree, as I may call them for short, were as familiar as the Freudian commonplaces are to generally educated people today, and they were accepted, for the most part, in an even less questioning spirit, so that it might well have occurred to a clever satirist then that he could produce a fine shock to his readers' complacency as human beings by inventing a world in which horses appeared where the logicians had put men and men where they had put horses, and by elaborating, through this, an argument designed to shift the position of man as a species from the *animal rationale* branch of the tree, where he had always been proudly placed, as far as possible over toward the *animal irrationale* branch, with its enormously less flattering connotations. But have we any warrant for thinking that this, or something like it, was what Swift actually had in mind? It is clearly possible to describe the Voyage as, in considerable part at least, an anti-Porphyrian satire in the genre of the poem I quoted from earlier, 'The Logicians Refuted.' But is there any evidence that Swift planned it as such?

That the Porphyrian commonplaces had been known to him in their full extent from his days at Trinity College in the early 1680s we can hardly doubt in view of the kind of education in logic he was exposed to there. Among the books which all Junior Freshmen at Dublin in those years were required to study or hear lectures on, we know of three in which the Porphyrian apparatus and examples had a prominent place: the *Isagoge* itself (which was prescribed by the statutes of the College to be read twice over during the year), the older logic of Burgersdicius, and the newer *Institutio logicae* of Narcissus Marsh. It is true that Swift, according to his own later statement, detested this part of the curriculum, and it is true that on one examination in his last year his mark in Philosophy was *Male* (he had a *Bene* in Greek and Latin). But this was an examination in the more advanced branches of the Aristotelian system, and it is likely that he had fared better in the earlier examination in logic, since he had evidently been allowed to proceed with his class. It is possible, moreover, to infer from his occasional use of logical terms in his later writings that, abhorrent as the subject was to him, the time he had been compelled to spend on it as a Junior Freshman was not a total loss. He at least remembered enough of it to allude familiarly in different places to such things as a 'long sorites,' 'the first proposition of a hypothetical syllogism,' and the fallacy of two middle terms in a single syllogism;[8] and if this was possible, there is good reason to suppose that he had not forgotten the much simpler Porphyrian points about genera, species, and definition, 'rational' versus 'irrational' animals, men and horses which he had been introduced to at the same time.

The crucial question, however, is whether he had these notions of the logicians at all actively in mind when, in the 1720s, he conceived and wrote the 'Voyage to the Houyhnhnms.' And here it will be well to take a fresh look at the two much-quoted letters about *Gulliver's Travels* which he sent to Pope in 1725, just after that work was completed. In the first of these, that of September 29, after having told Pope that his chief aim is 'to vex the world rather than divert it' and that he hates and detests 'that animal called man,' he goes on to remark: 'I have got materials towards a treatise proving the falsity of that definition *animal rationale,* and to show it should be only *rationis capax.* Upon this great foundation of misanthropy, though not in Timon's manner, the whole building of my Travels is erected; and I never will have peace of mind till all honest men are of my opinion.' In the second letter, that of November 26, he desires that Pope and 'all my friends' will 'take a special care that my disaffection to the world may not be imputed to my age, for I have credible witnesses . . . that it has never varied from the twenty-first to the f——ty-eighth year of my life.' He then adds a passage which has been read as a retraction of the judgment on humanity expressed in the first letter, though the final sentence makes clear, I think, that it was not so intended: 'I tell you after all, that I do not hate mankind; it is *vous autres* [i.e., Pope and Bolingbroke] who hate them, because you would have them reasonable animals, and are angry for being disappointed. I have always rejected that definition, and made another of my own. I am no more angry with ——than I am with the kite that last week flew away with one of my chickens; and yet I was glad when one of my servants shot him two days after.'

The casual references in both letters to 'that definition'—'*animal rationale*' and 'reasonable animals'—which Swift tells Pope he has 'always rejected' have usually been interpreted by modern critics as allusions to such contemporary philosophical or theological heresies (from Swift's point of view) as the 'optimism' of Shaftesbury or the 'rationalism' of Descartes and the Deists. It is surely, however, a much less far-fetched conjecture, especially in view of the familiar textbook Latin of the first letter, to see in 'that definition' nothing other or more than the 'sacred definition' of the logicians which he had had inflicted on him, by thoroughly orthodox tutors, in his undergraduate days at Dublin.

I find this explanation, at any rate, much harder to disbelieve than any other that has been proposed; and all the more so because of another passage in the first letter which is almost certainly reminiscent of the Trinity logic course in the early 1680s. It is the famous sentence —just before the allusion to 'that definition *animal rationale*' and leading on to it—in which Swift says: 'But principally I hate and detest that animal called man, although I heartily love John, Peter, Thomas, and so forth.' Now to any one at all widely read in the logic textbooks of Swift's time two things about this sentence are immediately evident: first, that the distinction it turns on is the distinction to be found in nearly all these books between a species of animals and individual members of that species; and second, that the names 'John, Peter, Thomas, and so forth' are wholly in line with one of the two main traditions of names for individuals of the species man that had persisted side by side in innumerable manuals of logic since the Middle Ages: not, of course, the older tradition of classical names—Socrates, Plato, Alexander, Caesar—but the newer tradition (which I have noted first in Occam, though it doubtless antedates him) that drew upon the list of apostles—Peter, John, Paul, James, Thomas, in roughly that descending order of preference. (Other non-classical names, like Stephen, Catharine, Charles, Richard, also appear, but much less frequently.)

We can go farther than this, however. For although all three of Swift's names occur separately in divers texts (Thomas least often), the combination 'John, Peter, Thomas, and so forth' was an extremely unusual one. I have met with it, in fact, in only one book before 1725; and I have examined nearly all the logics, both Latin and English, down to that date for which I can find any evidence that they had even a minor circulation in Great Britain. The exception, however, is a book which Swift could hardly have escaped knowing as an undergraduate, since it was composed expressly for the use of Trinity College students by the then Provost and had just recently come 'on the course' when he entered the College in 1682—namely, the *Institutio logicae*, already referred to, of Narcissus Marsh (Dublin, 1679: reissued Dublin, 1681). Early in the book Marsh gives a full-page diagram of Porphyry's tree, with its inevitable opposition of *animal-rationale-homo* and *animal-irrationale-brutum;* and here, as *individua* under *homo*, we find 'Joannes, Petrus, Thomas, &c.' And a little later in the book the same names are repeated in the same order as individual specimens of *homo* in Marsh's analytical table for the category *substantia.*

Was this combination of names, then, Marsh's invention? There is one further circumstance which suggests that it may well have been. We know from his own testimony,[9] as well as from internal evidence, that the source on which he based the greater part of his Dublin logic of 1679 was his own revision, published at Oxford in 1678, of the *Manuductio ad logicam* of the early seventeenth-century Jesuit logician Philippe Du Trieu. Now of the two passages in the Dublin book that contain Swift's three names, the first—the diagram of Porphyry's tree—has no counterpart in the Oxford book of 1678, though it has in

Du Trieu's original text, where the names are 'Petrus' and 'Joannes.' It would seem likely, then, that Marsh first thought of the combination 'John, Peter, Thomas, and so forth' when he revised his earlier revision of Du Trieu for his Trinity students in 1679; and this is borne out by what he did at the same time with the other passage—the table of substance. This he retained almost exactly as it had been in Du Trieu except for the names under *homo:* here, where in 1678 he had reprinted Du Trieu's 'Stephanus, Johannes, Catharine, &c.,' he now wrote 'Johannes, Petrus, Thomas, &c.' Which would seem to imply a certain sense of private property in these particular names in this particular combination.

It is somewhat hard, then, not to conclude that Swift was remembering Marsh's logic as he composed the sentence, in his letter to Pope, about 'John, Peter, Thomas, and so forth.' But if that is true, can there be much doubt, in view of the Porphyrian context in which these names appear in Marsh, as to what tradition of ideas was in his mind when he went on to remark, immediately afterwards, that 'the great foundation of misanthropy' on which 'the whole building' of his *Travels* rested was his proof—against Marsh and the other logicians he had been made to study at Trinity—of 'the falsity of that definition *animal rationale*'?[10]

NOTES

This paper was read, in somewhat different form, at Wadham College, Oxford, in April, 1959, before the Annual Conference of Nonprofessorial University Teachers of English of the British Isles.

[1] See his 'Errors Concerning the Houyhnhnms,' *MP*, LVI (1958), 92-97.

[2] The list of writings that reflect this preoccupation is now a fairly long one; in the present essay I have had in view chiefly the following: Ernest Bernbaum, 'The Significance of "Gulliver's Travels,"' in his edition of that work (New York, 1920); T. O. Wedel, 'On the Philosophical Background of *Gulliver's Travels*,' *SP*, XXIII (1926), 434-50; John F. Ross, 'The Final Comedy of Lemuel Gulliver,' in *Studies in the Comic* ('University of California Publications in English,' Vol. VIII, No. 2, 1941), pp. 175-96; Robert B. Heilman, Introduction to his edition of *Gulliver's Travels* (New York, 1950), especially pp. xii-xxii; Ernest Tuveson, 'Swift: the Dean as Satirist,' *University of Toronto Quarterly*, XXII (1953), 368-75; Roland M. Frye, 'Swift's Yahoo and the Christian Symbols for Sin,' *JHI*, XV (1954), 201-15; W. A. Murray's supplementary note to Frye, *ibid.*, pp. 596-601; Samuel H. Monk, 'The Pride of Lemuel Gulliver,' *Sewanee*

Review, LXIII (1955), 48-71; Irvin Ehrenpreis, 'The Origins of *Gulliver's Travels,*' *PMLA,* LXXII (1957), 880-99 (reprinted with some revisions in his *The Personality of Jonathan Swift* [London, 1958]); Kathleen Williams, *Jonathan Swift and the Age of Compromise* (Lawrence, Kansas, 1958); Calhoun Winton, 'Conversion on the Road to Houyhnhnmland,' *Sewanee Review,* LXVIII (1960), 20-33; Martin Kallich, 'Three Ways of Looking at a Horse: Jonathan Swift's "Voyage to the Houyhnhnms" Again,' *Criticism,* II (1960), 107-24.

    [3] There are useful descriptions of many, though by no means all, of these in Wilbur Samuel Howell, *Logic and Rhetoric in England, 1500–1700* (Princeton, 1956).

    [4] *The Correspondence of Edmund Burke,* ed. by Thomas W. Copeland, I (Cambridge and Chicago, 1958), 4, 7-9, 21, 28.

    [5] *The Busy Body,* No. 5, October 18, 1759. Both the ascription to Swift, which occurs in a note prefixed to this first known printing of the poem, and the later ascription to Goldsmith seem to me highly dubious.

    [6] *Monitio Logica: or, An Abstract and Translation of Burgersdicius his Logick* (London, 1697), pp. 13-14 (second pagination).

    [7] E.g., Quintilian, *Institutio oratoria,* VII.iii.3, 24. For the contrast of man and horse in Porphyry see especially Migne, *PL,* LXIV, col. 128 (Boethius' translation): 'Differentia est quod est aptum natum dividere ea quæ sub eodem genere sunt: rationale enim et irrationale, hominem et equum quæ sub eodem genere sunt animali dividunt.'

    [8] See John M. Bullitt, *Jonathan Swift and the Anatomy of Satire* (Cambridge, Mass., 1953), p. 73. Cf. also Swift, 'A Preface to the B——p of S——m's Introduction,' in *Works,* ed. by Temple Scott, III, 150.

    [9] See his preface 'Ad lectorem' in the 1681 issue (it is missing from some copies but can be found in the Cambridge University Library copy and in that belonging to Archbishop Marsh's Library, Dublin); also the entry for December 20, 1690, in his manuscript diary. I owe this latter reference to Miss Mary Pollard, of Archbishop Marsh's Library. For the rather complicated bibliographical history of Marsh's *Institutio logicae* (the title was altered to *Institutiones logicae* in the reissue of 1681), see her article, 'The Printing of the Provost's Logic and the Supply of Text-books in the late Seventeenth Century,' in *Friends of the Library of Trinity College, Dublin: Annual Bulletin,* 1959-61.

    [10] Since this essay went to press I have discussed some further aspects of the subject in a brief article, 'The Rationale of the Fourth Voyage,' in *Gulliver's Travels: An Annotated Text with Critical Essays,* ed. by Robert A. Greenberg (New York, 1961), pp. 300-7, and in a review of two recent papers on Swift and the Deists, in *PQ,* XL (1961), 427-30.

A Greek Theater of Ideas

William Arrowsmith

Several years ago I made a plea that scholars and critics should recover a feeling for what I called turbulence in Greek tragedy.[1] By turbulence I meant both "the actual disorder of experience as that experience gets into Greek drama" and "the impact of ideas under dramatic test." What I want to do here is to take up the turbulence of ideas, as I see those ideas expressed by Euripidean drama, with the purpose of showing that the Greeks possessed a theater which we should have no difficulty in recognizing as a genuine theater of ideas. By theater of ideas I do not mean, of course, a theater of intellectual *sententiae* or Shavian "talk" or even the theater of the sophist-poet; I mean a theater of dramatists whose medium of thought was the stage, who used the whole machinery of the theater as a way of *thinking*, critically and constructively, about their world.

In such a theater I assume that the emphasis will be upon ideas rather than character and that a thesis or problem will normally take precedence over development of character or heroism; that aesthetic or formal pleasure will be secondary to intellectual rigor and thought; and that the complexity of ideas presented may require severe formal dislocations or intricate blurrings of emotional modes and genres once kept artistically distinct. It is also likely that the moral texture of an action will be "difficult," and that moral satisfaction will not come easily or even at all; that problems may be left unresolved; that is, that the effect of a play may very well be discomfort or even pain, and that the purpose of this discomfort will be to influence the social rather than the individual behavior of the spectator. Beyond this I would expect such a theater to be commonly concerned with the diagnosis and dramatization of cultural crisis, and hence that the universe in which

309

the dramatic action takes place would tend to be either irrational or incomprehensible. All of these characteristics are, of course, abstracted at random from the historical theater of ideas from Hebbel to the present, but in their ensemble they serve to give at least a general sense of the kind of theater of ideas I have in mind.

That such a theater—so specifically modern and anti-traditional a theater—existed among the Greeks is not, I believe, exactly an article of faith among scholars and critics. To be sure, the Greek theater, like any other great theater, made abundant use of ideas, and the Athenians regarded the theater, not as entertainment, but as the supreme instrument of cultural instruction, a democratic *paideia* complete in itself. Aeschylus, for instance, uses ideas with stunning boldness, showing in play after play how the great post-Hesiodic world-order could be compellingly and comprehensively adapted to Athenian history and society; and his theater not only provides a great, and new, theodicy, but dramatically creates the evolving idea of Athens as the supreme achievement of the mind of Zeus and the suffering of mankind. As for Sophocles, I am not of those who believe that he, like Henry James, possessed a mind so fine that no idea could violate it. In Oedipus, for instance, we have Sophocles' image of heroic man, shorn of his old Aeschylean confidence in himself and his world, and relentlessly pursuing the terrible new truth of his, and human, destiny. Oedipus looks into the abyss that yawns beneath him—the frightful knowledge of his nature which fifth-century man had learned from the war, the plague and the atrocities, the sophisitc revolution, and the collapse of the old world-order—and dashes out his eyes at the unbrookable sight. Similarly in Sophocles' Ajax I think we are meant to see a somewhat earlier symbol of the old aristocratic ethos; caught in new and anti-heroic circumstances which degrade him and make him ludicrous, Ajax consistently prefers suicide to a life of absurdity in an alien time.[2] But all this is merely to say that Sophocles, like Aeschylus, uses the perceptions of cultural crisis as framing dramatic ideas or symbolically, not that his theater is in any meaningful sense a theater of ideas. Clearly it is to Euripides—the innovator and experimentalist, the anti-traditional "immoralist" and "stage-sophist"—that we must look for any valid fifth-century theater of ideas.

That the second half of the fifth century B.C. was a period of immense cultural crisis and political convulsion is, fortunately for my purpose here, beyond any real doubt. The evidence itself needs only the barest rehearsal, but it should at least be *there*, the real though sketchy weather of my argument. Let me therefore brush it in.

There is, first of all, the breakdown of the old community, the over-whelming destruction of that mythical and coherent world-order which Werner Jaeger has described so fully in *Paideia*. Political con-vulsion—stasis and revolution—broke out everywhere. If civil war was nothing new among the Greek city-states, civil war on the fifth-century scale was absolutely unprecedented in its savagery: city against city, man against man, father against son. Under such conditions the whole kinship structure on which the polis was theoretically and con-stitutionally founded was irretrievably weakened. In culture the so-phistic revolution ushered in something like a transvaluation of morals. In society there was the rise of a new bourgeoisie provided with new sanctions and new theories of human nature, as well as a politically conscious proletariat. In the arts restless innovation was the rule, and throughout the Hellenic world—in literature, thought, and politics—there took place a vast debate whose very terms vividly report the schism in the culture, especially in the great argument between *physis* (nature) and *nomos* (custom, tradition, and law). Men begin to wonder now whether the laws of the state and the state itself, once thought divinely established, are any longer related to *physis* at large or to human *physis* in particular. Thus the great experience of the late fifth century is what can be called "the loss of innocence." Sophocles, Eurip-ides, Aristophanes, and Thucydides are all, each in his different way, haunted by the disappearance of the old integrated culture and the heroic image of man that had incarnated that culture. There is a new spirit of divisiveness abroad in the Hellenic world; appearance and reality, nature and tradition, move steadily apart under the destructive pressure of war and its attendant miseries. Subjected to harsh necessi-ty, human nature now shows itself in a new nakedness, but also in a startling new range of behavior, chaotic and uncontrollable.

How wrenching that convulsion was, how extreme and catastrophic, is told us by no less an authority than Thucydides himself:

> So bloody was the march of the revolution [in Corcyra], and the impression which it made was the greater as it was one of the first to occur. Later on, one may say, the whole Hellenic world was con-vulsed. . . . The sufferings which revolution entailed upon the cities were many and terrible, such as have occurred and always will occur, as long as the nature of mankind remains the same; though in a severer or milder form, and varying in their symptoms, accord-ing to the variety of the particular cases. In peace and prosperity states and individuals have better sentiments, because they do not find themselves suddenly confronted with imperious necessities; but war takes away the easy supply of daily wants, and so proves a

rough master that brings most men's characters to a level with their fortunes. Revolution thus ran its course from city to city, and the places which it arrived at last, from having heard what had been done before, carried to a still greater excess the refinement of their inventions, as manifested in the cunning of their enterprises and the atrocity of their reprisals. Words had to change their ordinary meaning and to take that which was now given them. Reckless audacity came to be considered the courage of a loyal ally; prudent hesitation, specious cowardice; moderation was held to be a cloak for unmanliness; ability to see all sides of a question, inaptness to act on any. Frantic violence became the attribute of manliness; cautious plotting, a justifiable means of self-defence. The advocate of extreme measures was always trustworthy; his opponent a man to be suspected. . . . Even blood became a weaker tie than party, from the superior readiness of those united by the latter to dare everything without reserve; for such associations had not in view the blessings derivable from established institutions but were formed by ambition for their overthrow; and the confidence of their members in each other rested less on any religious sanction than upon complicity in crime. . . .

The cause of all these evils was the hunger for power arising from greed and ambition; and from these passions proceeded the violence of parties once engaged in contention. The leaders in the cities, each provided with the fairest professions, on the one side with the cry of political equality for the people, on the other of a moderate aristocracy, sought prizes for themselves in those public interests which they pretended to cherish, and, recoiling from no means in their struggles for ascendancy, engaged in the direct excesses; in their acts of vengeance they went to even greater lengths, not stopping at what justice or the good of the state demanded, but making the party caprice of the moment their only standard, and invoking with equal readiness the condemnation of an unjust verdict or the authority of the strong arm to glut the animosities of the hour. Thus religion was in honor with neither party, but the use of fair phrases to arrive at guilty ends was in high reputation. Meanwhile the moderate part of the citizenry perished between the two, either for not joining in the quarrel or because envy would not suffer them to escape.

Thus every form of evil took root in the Hellenic countries by reason of the troubles. The ancient simplicity into which honor so largely entered was laughed down and disappeared; and society became divided into camps in which no man trusted his fellow. To put an end to this, there was neither promise to be depended upon, nor oath that could command respect; but all parties dwelling rather in their calculation upon the hopelessness of a permanent state of affairs, were more intent upon self-defence than capable of confidence. In this contest the blunter wits were most successful. Apprehensive of their own deficiencies and of the cleverness of their antagonists, they feared to be worsted in debate and to be surprised by the combinations of their more versatile opponents, and so at once boldly had recourse to action; while their adversaries, arrogantly thinking that they should know in time, and that it was unneccessary to secure by action what policy afforded, often fell victims to their want of precaution.

Meanwhile Corcyra gave the first example of most of the crimes alluded to; of the reprisals exacted by the governed who had never experienced equitable treatment or indeed anything except outrage from their rulers—when their hour came; of the iniquitous resolves of those who desired to get rid of their accustomed poverty, and ardently coveted their neighbors' possessions; and lastly, of the savage and pitiless excesses into which men who had begun the struggle, not in a class but a party spirit, were hurried by their ungovernable passions. In the confusion into which life was now thrown in the cities, human nature, always rebelling against the law and now its master, gladly showed itself uncontrolled in passion, above respect for justice, and the enemy of all superiority; since revenge would not have been set above religion, and gain above justice, had it not been for the fatal power of envy. Indeed men too often take upon themselves in the prosecution of their revenge to set the example of doing away with those general laws to which all alike can look for salvation in their day of adversity, instead of allowing them to exist against the day of danger when their aid may be required. (III, 82 ff. Trans. Crawley)

Every sentence of that account deserves to be read, slowly and meditatively, with due weight given to every phrase, every word, lest we underread, as we so often do with the classics, and translate the greatest cultural crisis of the Hellenic world into a parochial and ephemeral time of troubles. If Thucydides is to be trusted, the culture of his time had been shaken to the roots, and he feared for its survival.

How did this convulsion of a whole culture affect the idea of a theater as we find that idea expressed by Euripides?

The immediate, salient fact of Euripides' theater is the assumption of a universe devoid of rational order or of an order incomprehensible to men. And the influence of Aristotle is nowhere more obvious than in the fact that this aspect of Euripides' theater is the one least often recognized or acted upon by critics. Yet it is stated both explicitly and implicitly from play to play throughout Euripides' lifetime. "The care of god for us is a great thing," says the chorus of Hippolytus, "if a man believe it. . . . So I have a secret hope of someone, a god who is wise and plans; / but my hopes grow dim when I see / the actions of men and their destinies. / For fortune always veers and the currents of life are shifting, / shifting, forever changing course." "O Zeus, what can I say?" cries Talthybius in *Hecuba*. "That you look on men and care? Or do we, holding that the gods exist, / deceive ourselves with unsubstantial dreams / and lies, while random careless chance and change / alone control the world?" Usually desperate, feeble, and skeptical in the first place, it is the fate of these hopes to be destroyed in action. In *Heracles* the fatal chaos of the moral universe is shown formally; a savage reversal which expresses the flaw in the moral universe splits the entire play into two contrasting actions connected only by sequence. Thus the *propter hoc* structure required by Aristotelian drama is in Euripides everywhere annulled by *created* disorder and formal violence. What we get is *dissonance, diparity, rift, peripeteia;* in Euripides a note of firm tonality is almost always the sign of traditional parody; of the false, the unreal, or lost innocence remembered in anguish. What this assumption of disorder means is: first, that form is not organic; second, that character is not destiny, or at best that only a part of it is; and third, that Aristotelian notions of responsibility, tragic flaw, and heroism are not pertinent.

The central dissonance assumes a variety of forms. But the commonest is a carefully construed clash between myth (or received reality) on the one hand, and fact (or experienced reality) on the other. Λόγῳ μέν . . . ἔργῳ δέ as the Greeks put it, contrasting theory (*logos*) and fact (*ergon*), appearance (or pretence) and reality, legend and truth. In *Alcestis*, for instance, Euripides juxtaposes the traditional, magnanimous Admetus with the shabby egotist who results when a "heroic" character is translated into realistic fifth-century terms. By making Alcestis take Admetus at his own estimate, Euripides delays the impact of his central idea—the exposure of Admetus' *logos* by his *ergon*—until the appearance of Pheres, whose savage "realistic" denunciation of his son totally exposes the "heroic" Admetus. By a similar translation, Euripides' Odysseus becomes a demagogue of *realpolitik*, Agamemnon a pompous and ineffectual field marshal, and Jason a vulgar adventurer. It was, of course, this technique of realism, this systematic exposure and deflation of traditional heroism, which earned Euripides his reputation for debasing the dignity of the tragic stage. And in some sense the charge is irrefutable. Euripides' whole bent is clearly anti-traditional and realistic; his sense of rebelliousness is expressed beyond doubt by the consistency with which he rejects religious tradition, by his restless experiments with new forms and new music, and by his obvious and innocent delight in his own virtuosity—his superior psychology and his naturalistic stagecraft. With justifiable pride he might have seen himself as a dramatic pioneer, breaking new ground, and courageously refusing to write the higher parody of his predecessors which his world—and ours—have demanded of him. There must be, I imagine, very few theaters in the world where the man who writes of "people as they are" is automatically judged inferior to the man who writes of "people as they should be."

But it would be wrong to assume that realism was the whole story or that Euripides was drawn to realism because he knew it would offend the worthies of his day. For it was life, not Euripides, which had abandoned the traditional forms and the traditional heroism. What Euripides reported, with great clarity and honesty, was the widening gulf between reality and tradition; between the operative and the professed values of his culture; between fact and myth; between *nomos* and *physis;* between life and art. That gulf was the greatest and most evident reality of the last half of the fifth century, *the* dramatic subject par excellence, and it is my belief that the theater of Euripides, like Thucydides' history, is a radical and revolutionary attempt to record, analyze and assess that reality in relation to the new view of human nature which crisis revealed. To both Thucydides and Euripides, the crisis in culture meant that the old world-order with its sense of a great humanity and its assumption of an integrated human soul was irrecoverably gone. The true dimensions of the human psyche, newly exposed in the chaos of culture, forbade any return to the old innocence or heroism. Any theater founded on the old psyche or the old idea of fate was to that extent a lie. The task imposed upon the new theater was not merely that of being truthful, of reporting the true dimensions and causes of the crisis, but of coping imaginatively and intellectually with a change in man's very condition.

It is for this reason that Euripides' theater almost always begins with a severe critique of tradition, which necessarily means a critique of his predecessors. Such programmatic criticism is what we expect from any new theater, and in the case of Greek theater, where the dramatist is official *didaskalos,* charged with the *paideia* of his people, it was especially appropriate. Aeschylus and Sophocles were not merely great theatrical predecessors; they were the moral tutors of Athens and their versions of the myths embodied, as nothing else did, the values of tradition and the old *paideia.* Given such authority and power, polemic and criticism were only to be expected, the only possible response; indeed, were it not for the fact that Euripides' criticism has generally been construed as cultural *lèse-majesté*, the point would hardly be worth making. When Shakespeare or Ibsen or Shaw or Brecht criticizes the theater of his immediate predecessors, we applaud; this is what we expect, the aggressive courage a new theater requires. When Euripides does it, it becomes somehow sacrilege, a crime against the classics. We respond, if at all, with outraged traditionalism, automatically invoking that double standard which we seem to reserve for the classics, that apparent homage which turns out to be nothing but respect for our own prejudices.

In Euripides' case, the prejudice is usually justified by the argument that Euripides' criticism of his predecessors is destructive and negative; that his attack on the old order is finally nothing but the niggling rage for exposure, devoid of constructive order. If this argument were sound, it would be impressive; but it is not enough to offer on Euripides' behalf the reply which Morris Cohen is said to have made to a student who accused him of destroying his religious beliefs: "Young man, it is recorded of Heracles that he was required only to *clean* the Augean stables." Not, that is, if we are serious in maintaining that Euripides was a great dramatist. Negative criticism of dead tradition and inert values is often of positive therapeutic effect, but no really great dramatist, it seems to me, can escape the responsibility for imaginative order. Actually the charge that Euripides is negative is based upon misreading of the plays. For one thing Euripides did not always expose myth and tradition; this is his bias, to be sure, but there are exceptions in which the received myth and its values are used to criticize contemporary reality and public policy. The obvious example is the *Trojan Women*. A more revealing instance is the *Iphigenia in Tauris*, in which the cult of Artemis of Brauron is reestablished by Athena at the close of the play in order to lay bare the immense human "blood sacrifice" of the Peloponnesian War.

The point here, I believe, is both important and neglected. Let me try to restate it. Euripides' favorite technique for demonstrating the new dissonance in Athenian culture, the disparity between putative values and real values is simply realism of the pattern λόγῳ μέν . . . ἔργῳ δέ. But it is balanced at times by the converse technique—allowing the myth to criticize the everyday reality—ἔργῳ μέν . . . λόγῳ δέ. And these exceptions are important, since they show us that Euripides' realism is not a matter of simple anti-traditionalism, but consistent dramatic technique. What is basic is the mutual criticism, the mutual exposure that occurs when the incongruities of a given culture—its actual behavior and its myth—are juxtaposed in their fullness. That this is everywhere the purpose of Euripidean drama is clear in the very complaints critics bring against the plays: their tendency to fall into inconsistent or opposed parts (*Heracles, Andromache*); their apparent multidimensionality (*Alcestis, Heracles*), the frequency of the *deus ex machina*. This last device is commonly explained by a hostile criticism as Euripides' penchant for archaism and aetiology, or as his way of salvaging botched plays. Actually it is *always* functional, a part of the very pattern of juxtaposed incongruities which I have been describing. Thus the appearance of any god in a Euripidean play is invariably the sign of *logos* making its epiphany, counterpointing *ergon*. Most Euripidean gods appear only in order to incriminate themselves (or a fellow god), though some—like Athena in the *Iphigenia in Tauris*—criticize the action and the reality which the action mirrors. But it is a variable, not a fixed, pattern, whose purpose is the critical counterpointing of the elements which Euripides saw everywhere sharply and significantly opposed in his own culture: myth confronted by behavior, tradition exposed by, or exposing, reality; custom and law in conflict with nature. What chiefly interested him was less the indictment of tradition, though that was clearly essential, than the *confrontation*, the *dramatic juxtaposition*, of the split in his culture. This was his basic theatrical perception, *his* reality, a perception which makes him utterly different from Aeschylus and Sophocles, just as it completely alters the nature of his theater.

Is that theater merely analytical then, a dramatic description of a divided culture? I think not. Consider this statement: "As our knowledge becomes increasingly divorced from real life, our culture no longer contains ourselves (or only contains an insignificant part of ourselves) and forms a social context in which we are not 'integrated.' The problem thus becomes that of again reconciling our culture with our life, by making our culture a living culture once more. . . ." That happens to be Ionesco on Artaud, but it could just as well be Euripides' description of the nature and purpose of his own theater. The reconciliation of life and culture is, of course, more than any theater, let alone a single dramatist, can accomplish; and it is perhaps enough that the art of a divided culture should be diagnostic, should describe the new situation in its complexity. Only by so doing can it redefine man's altered fate. It is my own conviction that Euripidean theater is critical and diagnostic, and that, beyond this, it accepts the old artistic burden of constructive order, does not restrict itself to analysis alone.

But what concerns me at the moment is the way in which his basic theatrical perceptions altered his theater.

First and most significant after the destruction of *propter hoc* structure is the disappearance of the hero. With the sole exception of *Heracles*—Euripides' one attempt to define a new heroism—there is no play which is dominated by the single hero, as is Sophocles' *Oedipus* or *Ajax*.

Corresponding to the disappearance of the hero is Euripides' "Fragmentation" of the major characters. What we get is typically an agon or contest divided between two paired characters (sometimes there are three): Admetus and Alcestis; Jason and Medea; Hippolytus and Phaedra; Andromache and Hermione; Pentheus and Dionysus, etc. In such a theater, the Aristotelian search for a tragic hero is, of course, meaningless. But the significance of the fragmentation is not easy to assess; it is not enough to say merely that Euripides was temperamentally drawn to such conflict because they afforded him opportunities for psychological analysis. What is striking about the consistently paired antagonists one finds in Euripides is, I think, their obsessional nature. They function like obsessional fragments of a whole human soul: Hippolytus as chastity, Phaedra as sexuality. The wholeness of the old hero is now represented divisively, diffused over several characters; the paired antagonists of the Euripidean stage thus represent both the warring modes of a divided culture and the new incompleteness of the human psyche. Alternatively, as in the *Bacchae*, they embody the principles of conflicting ideas: Pentheus as *nomos*, Dionysus as *physis*.

This fragmentation is also the sign of a new psychological interest. That the convulsion of the late fifth century had revealed new dimensions in the human psyche is sharply expressed by Thucydides, and just as sharply by Euripides. Indeed, Euripides' interest in abnormality and mental derangement is so marked that critics have usually seen it as the very motive of his drama. This, I think, is a mistake. The interest in psychology is strong, but it is always secondary; the real interest lies in the analysis of culture and the relationship between culture and the individual. If I am correct in assuming that Euripides' crucial dramatic device is the juxtaposition and contrast of *logos* and *ergon*, then it follows that the characters of his plays must bear the burden of the cultural disparity involved. I mean: if a myth is bodily transplanted from its native culture to a different one, then the characters of the myth must bear the burden of the transplantation, and that burden is psychological strain. Consider, for example, Euripides' Orestes, a man who murders his mother in an Argos where civil justice already exists; or the heroic Jason translated into the context of a fifth-century Corinth; or an Odysseus or Hermione or Electra cut off from the culture in which their actions were once meaningful or moral, and set in an alien time which *immoralizes* or *distorts* them. The very strain that Euripides succeeds in imposing upon his characters is the mark of their modernity, their involvement in a culture under similar strain. And it is the previously unsuspected range of the human psyche, the discovery of its powers, its vulnerability to circumstance, its incompleteness, and its violence, that interest Euripides, not the psychological process itself. The soliloquy in which Medea meditates the murder of her children is much admired; but Euripides' dramatic interest is in the collapse or derangement of culture—the gap between *eros* and *sophia*—that makes the murder both possible and necessary.

Side by side with cultural strain is the striking loneliness of the Euripidean theater. Loneliness is, of course, a feature of traditional tragedy, but the difference between Euripides and his predecessors in this respect is marked. In Aeschylus the loneliness of human fate is effectively annulled by the reconciliation which closes trilogies and creates a new community in which god and man become joint partners in civilization. In Sophocles the sense of loneliness is extremely strong, but it is always the distinguishing mark of the hero, the sign of the fate which makes him an outcast, exiled from the world to the world's advantage and his own anguish. But in Euripides loneliness is the common fate. Insofar as the characters are fragmented and obsessional, their loneliness is required. The one thing they normally cannot do is communicate, and typically, even such communications as occur (for instance, Heracles' moving reunion with his children) are liable to almost certain destruction by the malevolence of fate. Again and again Euripides gives us those exquisite, painterly groupings which stress the impassable gulf which separates the old from the young, man from god, woman from man, and even hero from hero. The climax of the *Heracles* comes when Heracles, touched by Theseus' *philia*, makes his great decision to live; but the understanding is then immediately and deliberately clouded as Theseus fails to understand the enormous range of his friend's new heroism. The touch is typically and revealingly Euripidean. The gulf seems to close only to widen out again.

From the point of view of traditional tragedy nothing is more strikingly novel than the Euripidean fusion and contrast of comic and tragic effects. Thus at any point in a tragedy the comic, or more accurately, the pathetic or ludicrous, can erupt with poignant effect, intensifying the tragic or toughening it with parody. Nor is this a device restricted to Euripides' so-called "romantic" plays or his tragicomedies; it occurs even in the most powerful and serious tragedies. Tiresias and Cadmus in the *Bacchae*, for instance, are seen simultaneously as tragic and comic, that is, directly pathetic and incongruous: two old mummers of ecstasy; they try to dance for Dionysus as the god requires, but their bodies, like their minds, are incapable of expressing devotion except as a ludicrous mimicry. Aegeus, in *Medea*, has puzzled traditional interpretation from Aristotle on, precisely because he is Euripides' pathetic and ironic embodiment of Athens—that Athens which the chorus hails later as the place

> where Cypris sailed,
> and mild sweet breezes breathed along her path,
> and on her hair were flung the sweet-smelling garlands
> of flowers of roses by the Lovers, the companions
> of Wisdom, her escort, the helpers of men
> in every kind of *arete*.

The irony is not, of course, the cutting irony of exposure, but the gentler irony that comes when *logos* and *ergon* of things not too far apart are juxtaposed: we feel it as a light dissonance. Which is merely another way of saying that the new element of the comic in Euripidean tragedy is just one more instance of the dramatist's insistence upon preserving the multiplicity of possible realities in the texture of his action. In the traditional drama, such dissonance is rightly avoided as an offence against seriousness and tragic dignity; Euripides significantly sees both tragedy and comedy as equally valid, equally necessary. A drama of truth will contrive to contain them both; the complex truth requires it.

It is for this same reason that Euripides accentuates what might be called the multiple moral dimension of his characters. Every one of them is in some sense an exhibit of the sophistic perception that human character is altered by suffering or exemption from suffering; that every human disposition contains the possibilities of the species for good or evil. Aristotle objects, for instance, that Euripides' Iphigenia changes character without explanation. And so, in fact, she does, and so does Alcmene in *Heraclidae*. They change in this way because their function is not that of rounded characters or "heroes" but specifications of the shaping ideas of the play. Besides, if Heraclitus was right, and character is destiny, then the complex or even contradictory destiny which Euripidean drama assumes and describes must mean complex and contradictory characters. But the one kind of character which Euripides' theater cannot afford is that splendid integrated self-knowledge represented by the "old fantastical Duke of dark corners" in *Measure for Measure;* Euripides' theater is all Angelos, Lucios, and Claudios—average, maimed, irresolute, incomplete human nature. The case of Heracles himself, the most integrated hero Euripides ever created, is darkened by Euripides' insistence that we observe, without passing judgment, that even the culture-hero has murder in his heart. This fact does not, of course, compose a tragic flaw, but rather what Nietzsche called "the indispensable dark spring" of action. Moral judgment is, as Euripides tried to show, no less precarious and difficult than the comprehensive description of reality. How could it be otherwise?

This does not mean that Euripides avoids judgment or that his plays are attempts to put the problematic in the place of dramatic resolution. It means merely that his theater everywhere insists upon scrupulous and detailed recreation of the complexity of reality and the difficulty of moral judgment. The truth is concealed, but not impenetrably concealed. There can be little doubt, for instance, that Euripides meant his *Medea* to end in a way which must have shocked his contemporaries and which still shocks today. His purpose was, of course, not merely to shock, but to force the audience to the recognition that Medea, mortally hurt in her *eros,* her defining and enabling human passion, must act as she does, and that her action has behind it, like the sun, the power of sacred *physis.* There is no more savage moral oxymoron in Greek drama. But if Euripides here speaks up for *physis* against a corrupt *nomos,* he is capable elsewhere of defending *nomos* and insisting that those who prostrate themselves before *physis,* like the Old Nurse in *Hippolytus,* are the enemies of humanity. Necessity requires submission, but any necessity that requires a man to sacrifice the morality that makes him human, must be resisted to the end, even if it cost him—as it will—his life. Better death than the mutilation of his specifically human skill, that *sophia* which in Euripides is mankind's claim to be superior to the gods and necessity. Only man in this theater makes morality; it is this conviction, the bedrock classical conviction, that provides the one unmistakable and fixed reference-point in Euripides' dramatic world. Above that point all truths are purposely played off against one another in endless and detailed exactness of observation.

Within this new context of changed reality, Euripides' whole theater of ideas is set.

Several examples.

The *Iphigenia in Tauris* is a play commonly classified as romantic or escapist melodrama, and seems at first, or even second, sight extremely remote from the theater of ideas. Aristotle, for instance, particularly admired its elegant finish and its tightness of structure—especially its famous recognition scene—and he talks about it with the enthusiasm a nineteenth-century critic might have shown for a good "well-made" play. Smooth, urbane, and exciting, the play appears to be pure entertainment, lively and sophisticated but without a thought in its head. Clearly not tragic, its plot is as improbable as it is skillful; situation clearly counts for a great deal, characterization for very little. None of the leading characters, for instance, is given more than deft, generalizing traits, and the very slightness of the characterization draws attention to the virtuosity of the plot and the remarkable facility of execution.

But the romantic atmosphere is by no means absolute; again and again Euripides intrudes into this artificial world the jarring dissonance of a harsh contemporary reality. Quite deliberately, and with odd effect, he evokes and remembers the real war: the vision of the dead and the doomed; the illusion of ambition and the deceptive hope of empire; the exile's yearning for home; the bitter image of a Hellas at peace, remembered with longing from the impossible distance of the present. *Logos* set against *ergon;* form in partial conflict with subject; romantic myth undercut by, and therefore intensifying in turn, the actual world, as though the story of Cinderella were suddenly revealed as set on the outskirts of Auschwitz. If his play is melodrama, it is melodrama subtly but sensibly tilted toward the experience of national tragedy and exploiting that experience symbolically.

Symbolically how? It is perhaps easy for moderns to misunderstand or overread. But I wonder what Athenian, even the most insensitive, could have failed to grasp or respond to the image which this play sets before him, especially in the light of that experience of war which the play so powerfully exploits. *A sister dedicates her brother to death by the sword.* It seems perhaps melodramatic to moderns, but, unless I am badly mistaken, that symbolism is directly addressed to the experience—and the conscience—of a people who, for nearly twenty years, had suffered all the horrors of fratricidal war. The symbolism is available and familiar, and it culminates naturally in the great recognition scene, when Iphigenia, on the point of butchering her brother Orestes, suddenly discovers his true identity. For this scene the whole play was built, and its quite remarkable power is ultimately based, I think, upon the explosive liberation of love which reunites a family or a people grown hostile, estranged, and unfamiliar. Behind the recognition of brother and sister in the play lies a people's recognition, a recognition of *kind*. For Argos, read Hellas; for the history of the house of Atreus, the history of Hellas. What is war but blood sacrifice? Why, the play asks, should Greeks kill Greeks? And to give his argument further point, Euripides introduces Athena to establish in Attica the cult of the civilized Artemis who will put an end to human sacrifice and, by implication, the needless butchery which is war. The symbolism is, of course, the more effective for being unobtrusive, but once felt, it drastically alters the experience of the play. What seems at first romantic escape becomes confrontation and recognition, a true tragicomedy in which the tragic shapes the comic or romantic and the romantic gives poignancy to the tragic. In short, the kind of play we might have expected from the dramatist of the *Alcestis* and the humanist of the *Trojan Women*. Admittedly a fresh political interpretation of its major symbolism does not transform the *Iphigenia in Tauris* into a true drama of ideas; but the existence of a deeply serious and critical intent in a play universally regarded as Euripides' most frivolous "entertainment," is indicative of the dramatist's bent in the "darker" plays.

In the *Orestes*, for instance. Here, if anywhere in Euripides' work, the contrast between *logos* and *ergon* is structural and crucial. The play falls abruptly into two distinct parts. *Ergon* is represented by the body of the play proper, a freely invented account of the events which followed Orestes' matricide; *logos*, by the concluding epiphany of Apollo, an archaizing *deus ex machina*, in which the god foretells the known mythical futures of the characters. These two parts are enjambed with jarring dissonance, since the characters as developed in the play and their mythical futures as announced by Apollo are incompatible. Through this device the play becomes problematic: the spectator is literally compelled, it seems, to choose between his own experience of the play and Apollo's closing words, between *ergon* and *logos*, behavior and myth. Moreover, the choice is a hard one; for, if the experience of the play proper is of almost unbearable bitterness and pessimism, Apollo's arrangements are foolish and traditional to the point of unacceptability. In short, impasse, or so at first sight it might seem. But here, as so often in Euripides, a crux or problem or impasse is the dramatist's way of *confronting* his audience with the necessity of choosing between apparently antithetical realities or positions (Hippolytus or Phaedra? Pentheus or Dionysus? *Physis* or *nomos*? Cold expedience or passionate *eros?* Barbarian or Greek? Victim or oppressor? *Logos* or *ergon?*).[3] Almost without exception, these seemingly necessary choices are finally illusory alternatives, the dramatist's device for stimulating his audience and forcing it on to the critical perception which underlies and comprehends the alternatives, unifying them in a single, complex, synthetic judgment—the judgment which holds each play together and for which the plays were written in the first place. That Euripides' critics have so seldom managed to arrive at this final judgment would seem to indicate that his theatrical strategies were ineffective; on the other hand, Euripides' critics have usually assumed that his consistency of technique necessarily meant a consistent failure to write correct traditional tragedy in the (imagined) manner of Sophocles.

Certainly the impasse between *logos* and *ergon* in the *Orestes* is apparent only. What resolves it is a common purpose in both parts—an ascending curve of exposure, first of the "heroic" Orestes who killed his mother and tried to kill Helen, and then of the traditionally "wise" Apollo who drove Orestes to matricide. The exposures are, in fact, mutual and cumulative, compelling us to see that if Orestes, by any human standard of morality, is mad, Apollo is utterly insane (for madness or incompetence in a god, and a god of radiant reason at that, is a fortiori more dangerous than in a mortal). *Logos* and *ergon*, apparently contradictory, are in fact complementary: depraved and immoral human action in the play proper is mirrored and sanctioned by the callous folly of heaven and the brutality of the myth; Orestes and Apollo mutually create, mutually deserve, each other: murderers both. Man and god project each other; myth influences behavior, and behavior in turn shapes the myth in a vicious circle of moral deterioration. If from this perspective we ask why Euripides freely invents the story of Orestes instead of recreating the traditional matricide, the answer is immediately clear: because he wants to demonstrate through the abortive attempt to kill Helen—a crime in which Apollo significantly plays no part—that Orestes is a murderer born, a man who kills not from necessity but in *freedom*, out of his sickness and hatred. Having demonstrated this, Euripides can proceed to the complementary exposure of Apollo, a god made in the image of Orestes.

Produced just half a century after Aeschylus' *Oresteia*, Euripides' *Orestes* is not only an indictment of the Aeschylean myth, its values and its hero, but a savage critique of Hellenic society in the last decade of the fifth century. If the impasse between *logos* and *ergon* is, as I claim, resolved by a continuous mutual exposure, the purpose of that exposure is a complex and profoundly bitter cultural statement. Euripides seems to be saying something like this: A society whose sacred legend is embodied in a god like Apollo and a man like Orestes runs the risk that its citizens may emulate the myth, revive it, in their own political behavior. That is, Athens and Greek society generally are in danger of realizing their own myths, of at last reconciling *logos* and *ergon*, myth and conduct, in a new synthesis of murderous brutality and insanity—the worst myth fused now with the worst behavior. In earlier plays Euripides critically contrasted myth and behavior with the aim of letting the better expose the worse; here, in the bitterest play of all, he shows how bad behavior and bad myth interact for the defeat of culture and communal life.

That this bleak conclusion is the purpose of the play is supported by the systematic desolation which Euripides visits upon every aspect of moral and political behavior. Thus there is not a character in the play who is not defined either by inhuman devotion to sound principle, by patient treachery, or by nightmare loyalty of complicity or stupidity. Every moral word is consistently inverted or emptied of its meaning, as the action proceeds from madness to "honorable" murder on a wave of sickening heroic rhetoric. As for justice, if Orestes creates none, he gets none either; for human justice here is merely power politics or mob passion, and Apollo rules in heaven. Between health and sickness, heroism and depravity, morality and immorality, every distinction is removed. Politics is either brutal power or demagoguery; the only honorable motives are self-interest and revenge. In short, the world of the *Orestes* is indistinguishable from the culture in convulsion described by Thucydides; point for point, Euripides and Thucydides confirm each other. And, presumptuous or not, I am tempted to see in this frightening play Euripides' apocalyptic vision of the final destruction of Athens and Hellas, or of that Hellas to which a civilized mind could still give its full commitment. In the house of Atreus we have the house of Hellas: the great old aristocratic house, cursed by a long history of fratricidal blood and war, brought down in ruin by its degenerate heirs.

Finally, consider the *Medea*. Traditionally classified as psychological tragedy, it is better interpreted as a genuine drama of ideas. Superficially it is a critique of relations between men and women, Greeks and barbarians, and of an *ethos* of hard, prudential self-interest as against passionate love. At a profounder level it is a comprehensive critique of the quality and state of contemporary culture. Like the *Bacchae*, Euripides' other great critique of culture, the *Medea* is based upon a central key term, *sophia*. Inadequately translated "wisdom," *sophia* is an extremely complex term, including Jason's cool self-interest, the magical and erotic skills of the sorceress Medea, and that ideal Athenian fusion of moral and artistic skills which, fostered by *eros*, creates the distinctive *arete* of the civilized polis. This third sense of *sophia*—nearly synonymous with "civilization" and specifically including the compassion[4] for the suppliant and the oppressed for which Athens was famous and which Aegeus significantly shows to Medea—is the standard by which the actions of Jason and Medea are to be judged. Thus the vivid harmony of *eros* and *sophia* which Athens represents is precisely what Jason and Medea are not. Jason's calculating, practical *sophia* is, lacking *eros*, selfish and destructive; Medea's consuming *eros* and psychological *sophia* (an emotional cunning which makes her a supreme artist of revenge) is, without compassion, maimed and destructive. They are both destroyers, destroyers of themselves, of others, of *sophia*, and the polis.[5] And it is this *destructiveness* above all else which Euripides wants his audience to observe: the spirit of brutal self-interest and passionate revenge which threatens both life and culture, and which is purposely set in sharp contrast to life-enhancing Athens where the arts flourish, where *eros* collaborates with *sophia*, and where creative *physis* is gentled by just *nomoi*. Behind Jason and Medea we are clearly meant to see that spreading spirit of expedience and revenge which, unchecked by culture or religion, finally brought about the Peloponnesian War and its attendant atrocities. For it cannot be mere coincidence that a play like this was performed in the first year of the war.

What of Medea herself? Upon our understanding of her depends the final interpretation of the play. Thus those who find in Medea a barbarian woman whose lack of self-control, hunger for revenge, and male courage set her in firm contrast to the Corinthian women of the chorus, with their Greek praise of *sophrosune* and their fear of excess, usually see the play as a psychological tragedy of revenge. Against this interpretation there are decisive arguments. For one thing, Euripides takes pains to show that Medea is not at all pure barbarian femininity, but rather a barbarian woman who has been partially and imperfectly Hellenized. Thus Medea's first appearance is an intentionally striking one, domniated by her attempt to pass for Greek, to say the right thing; she talks, in fact, the stock language of Greek women, *hēsuchia* and *sophrosune*. Now this may be a pose, but it may just as well be genuine cultural imitation, the sort of thing a barbarian woman in Corinth might be expected to do. But the point is important for, if I am right, this play records the loss of the civilized skills through the conflict of passion; and for this reason Euripides first shows us his Medea making use of those civilized virtues which, in the throes of passion, she promptly loses, reverting to barbarism. Euripides' point is not that Medea qua barbarian is different in nature from Greek women, but that her inhibitions are weaker and her passions correspondingly nearer the surface. Thus she can very quickly be reduced to her essential *physis*, and it is this nakedness of *physis*, shorn of all cultural overlay, that Euripides wants displayed. Unimpeded *eros* (or unimpeded hatred) can be shown in Medea with a concentration and naturalness impossible in a Greek woman, not because Greek women were less passionate, but because their culture required them to repress their passions. If culture is truly effective, the control of passion eventually becomes true self-mastery (*sophrosunē*); where culture is less effective or out of joint (as in the Corinth of this play), *physis* is checked only by fear, and reveals itself in resentment of the punishing authorities and ready sympathy with those who rebel against them. Hence the profound resentment which the chorus in this play feels against male domination. This—and not mere theatrical convention or necessity—is why Medea can so easily convince the chorus to become her accomplices in her "crusade" against Jason and male society. Their control over their passions, while greater than Medea's perhaps, is still inadequate and precarious (as their bitter resentment of men makes clear); and Medea's revenge arouses their fullest sympathy, just as war evokes the barbarian in an imperfectly civilized man. And this is Euripides' point, that "one touch of nature" makes kin of Hellene and barbarian. In Medea's barbarism we have a concentrated image of human *physis* and a symbol of the terrible closeness of all human nature to barbarism. In her inadequate *sophrosunē* and her imperfect *sophia* is represented the norm of Hellenic, and most human, society. Thus when Jason cries out, "No Greek woman would have dared this crime," we are meant, not to agree, but to wonder and doubt, and finally to disbelieve him.

The validity of that doubt and disbelief is immediately confirmed by the appearance of the golden chariot of the Sun in which Medea makes her escape to Athens. In this chariot Euripides does two related things: he first restates, vividly and unmistakably, the triumph of Medea over Jason, and secondly he provides the whole action with a symbolic and cosmological framework which forces the private *agon* of Jason and Medea to assume a larger public significance. And by showing Medea, murderess and infanticide, as rescued by the Sun himself—

traditionally regarded as the epitome of purity, the unstained god who will not look upon pollution—he drives home his meaning with the shock of near sacrilege. As for the chariot of the Sun, it is the visible cosmic force which blazes through Medea's motives and which her whole *pathos* expresses: the blinding force of life itself, stripped of any mediating morality or humanizing screen; naked, unimpeded, elemental *eros;* intense, chaotic, and cruel; the primitive, premoral, precultural condition of man and the world. If that force vindicates Medea as against Jason, her ardor as against his icy self-interest, it is only because her *eros* is elemental and therefore invincible. But she is vindicated only vis-à-vis Jason; and she is not *justified* at all. Of justification there can be no question here, not only because *eros* is, like any elemental necessity, amoral and therefore unjustifiable, but also because Euripides clearly believes the loss of *sophia* to be a tragic defeat for man and human culture.

In the *agon* of Jason and Medea, passion, vengeance, and self-interest expel *sophia*. That *agon,* as we have seen, stands for the Peloponnesian War—the war which Euripides, like Thucydides, feared would expel *sophia* from civilized cities, thereby barbarizing and brutalizing human behavior. At any time, in both individuals and cities, *sophia* is a delicate and precarious virtue; if anywhere in the Hellenic world, *sophia* flourished in Athens, but even there is bloomed precariously (how precariously the plague which overtook the city in the following year proved). And with the coming of Medea to Athens, Euripides seems to imply, comes the spirit of vengeance and passion, endangering *sophia,* that *sophia* whose creation and growth made Athens, in Thucydides' phrase, "the education of Hellas." For Hellas and humanity a new and terrible day dawns at the close of the *Medea*.

In sum, the Greeks possessed a recognizable and developed form of what we should not scruple to call a classical theater of ideas. And there, in substance, my argument rests. Whatever its critical shortcomings may be, its historical basis is, I think, sufficiently secure. If, historically, the theater of ideas tends to occur in times of severe cultural crisis, then we may properly expect it in late-fifth-century Athens, for of all the cultural crises of Hellenism, the late-fifth-century crisis was by far the most profound. Among its casualties are classical tragedy and comedy; the old mythical cosmology and the culture which it mirrored and sanctioned; the gods of the polis; the sense of community on which the polis was based, and therefore in a sense the polis itself. In short, the whole cloth of culture, fabric and design together.

In the fourth century Plato's attempt to repiece the old culture—to reconcile *physis* and *nomos*, myth and behavior, to reweave the moral community of the polis—was heroic but finally unsuccessful. Plato was a great conservative and a great revolutionary, but the Hellas he preserved was only preserved by being radically changed, in fact revolutionized. The old Greek culture—the culture to which the Western world most owes its being and to which it returns for life and freshness when Platonic Hellenism threatens to swamp it—died in the fifth century B.C., and it is this culture in its crisis of disintegration that Euripides records. If Euripides could no longer hold out the old heroic image of man, it is because he preferred to base his theater upon what he actually saw as the prime reality of his time: the new emerging human psyche, tested and defined by crisis, and the apparently uncontrollable chaos of human behavior and therefore the turbulence which any viable culture must know how to contain, but without repressing.

Put it this way. The complex knowledge and experience about politics and culture so evident in *Hecuba* or the *Bacchae* look forward to Plato and also explain Plato's response to the same crisis. Both men share the conviction that war and greed for power have corrupted culture or deranged it; both are convinced that chaotic human nature, as revealed by crisis, cannot be controlled within the framework of existing culture. But Euripides' liberating perception has become Plato's restrictive premise. For Euripides any new cultural order must somehow contain what is uncontrollable in behavior; the failure to allow for turbulence, the failure to democratize its ethics, was what had made the old culture so susceptible to crisis. The Athenian democracy after Pericles could no more make do on aristocratic *sophrosunē* than industrial England could run on knightly chivalry. The solution, however, was not to reorganize society to operate on *sophrosunē* and the old aristocratic ethos but to revise *sophia* and *sophrosunē* in terms of a more democratic view of human nature. It is for this reason that in the *Bacchae* Pentheus' inability to control his inward turmoil is matched by his incompetence to control the public situation. He is an emblem of his age, attempting out of his ignorance of himself and his culture to cope with chaos by means of an inadequate or corrupted aristocratic *sophrosunē*. For whatever the solution to Dionysiac chaos may be, it is not repression, but perhaps a more responsibly Dionysiac (that is to say, liberated and liberating) society. The new polis may not be quite "polymorphously perverse," but it will at least be free, disciplined by experience of inward and outward chaos to a larger self-mastery.

For Plato the ideal polis can only be based upon a coercion that looks like consent. And it is therefore subject to the fate of Euripides' Pentheus, the terrible revenge which *physis* takes upon a *nomos* that cannot enlarge itself to a true human order. In short, the culture envisaged by Plato rests ultimately upon suppression of the natural, and is to that degree profoundly pessimistic and anti-Hellenic. Euripides' specifications for culture rest upon an extremely realistic judgment of human nature and its potentialities for disorder; but because what is chaotic is seen as the thrust of life itself, as something *below* (or *beyond*) good or evil, morally neutral, culture is always a project for hope, for free order, for the creation of new institutions in which man's society will not be in conflict with his nature. The Athens which Euripides had so triumphantly hailed in the great choral ode of the *Medea* may have betrayed what it stood for, but the creative fusion between the passions (*erotes*) and the civilized and artistic skills (the large sense of *sophia*, nearly synonymous with "culture") which produced *arete—here*, however transient, was a paradigm of ideal social order, the polis which made man's fulfillment possible.

That Euripides is an innovator is, of course, not an altogether new idea; Werner Jaeger's word for him is, flatly, revolutionary. But those who regard Euripides as an innovator or a revolutionary rarely see in him much more than a theatrical sophist or the inventor of a realistic and psychological tragedy. So far as I know, nobody has seriously proposed what I am proposing here: that Euripides' theater is no less revolutionary than his ideas, and that these ideas are implicitly expressed in the assumptions of his theater and his dramatic hypotheses. In short, that his theater *is* his ideas; that his radical critique of crisis in culture is not just Sophoclean tragedy turned topical and sophistic, but a wholly new theater, uneasily based upon the forms and conventions of the old. That is, not tragedy at all, but a critical drama related to Aeschylus and Sophocles in much the same way that Hebbel's theater was, at least in theory, related to Schiller's.[6] And for this very reason, I suppose, the argument will be discounted: Why, it will be objected, has a point like this been somehow missed for twenty-five hundred years?

To this question it is possible to make a great many answers. For one thing, the identification of the theater of ideas is of very recent date, even among critics of the theater. For another, classicists have traditionally been—as they remain—hostile or indifferent to literary criticism. For this reason they have very rarely asked the kind of question which might have led them to a literary answer. Instead of giving the dramatist the customary benefit of the doubt, they have assumed that a hostile tradition was generally sound and that Euripides was an interesting aberration but finally too realistic, irreverent and vulgar to fill the bill as a bona fide classic. With deplorable regularity scholars have insisted that it was Euripides' fate to be an imitator or higher parodist of his predecessors, and then, just as regularly, have condemned him for bungling the job. I doubt, in fact, that the history of literature can show a more pathological chapter. Surely no great dramatist of the world has ever received less benefit of the critical doubt or been more consistently patronized; a fourth-rate Broadway hack will normally demand, and get, more courtesy from critics than Euripides has received from six centuries of scholarship. Even when he is praised by comparison with other dramatists, the comparison is inevitably patronizing. We do not honor our greatest classics by asserting their modernity; if classicists and critics compare Euripides to Ibsen, this is more to Ibsen's credit than to Euripides'—though this is *not* the assumption. We pay no honor to Shakespeare when we compliment him on his modernity: we merely reveal the true proportions of our contempt for the classics. Having said that, I can now say without being misunderstood: the theater of Brecht and of Sartre, and even the Theater of the Absurd, are in many ways remarkably like the theater of Euripides.

In any traditional perspective, Euripidean theater is complex and uncomfortably strange, almost exasperating to a taste founded on Aeschylus and Sophocles. Its premises, as we have seen, are unlike, and almost the inversion of those of the traditional Greek theater. Typically it likes to conceal the truth beneath strata of irony because this is the look of truth: layered and elusive. For the same reason it presents its typical actions as problems and thereby involves the audience in a new relation, not as worshippers but as jurors who must resolve the problem by decision. But because the problem is usually incapable of outright resolution, is in fact tragic, the audience is compelled to forfeit the only luxury of making a decision—the luxury of *knowing* that one has decided wisely. Something—innocence, comfort, complacency —is always forfeited, or meant to be forfeited, by the audience of jurors. This suggests that the essential anagnorisis of Euripidean theater is not between one actor and another but between the audience and its own experience, as that experience is figured in the plays. Anagnorisis here is knowing moral choice, exercised on a problem which aims at mimicking the quandary of a culture. As such, it is a pattern of the way in which the psyche is made whole again, and the hope of a culture.

It is thus a difficult theater, and difficulty in literature, as opposed to textual difficulty or a doubtful manuscript reading, has never quickened the pulses of classical scholars. Indeed, the commonest scholarly response to the suggestion of a complex critical reading is that no classical writer could ever have been so unclear as not to be immediately transparent. If he was unclear or unusually complex or at all contorted, he was clearly unclassical; to such a degree has Winckelmann's criterion of "noble simplicity" seized the imagination of classical scholars. To those who believe that Euripides could not possibly have meant more than the little they are willing to understand, there is no adequate reply. But if it is true that critics who interpret great dramatists often seek to involve themselves in the dramatist's greatness, those who deny the dramatist any ideas but their own clearly involve the dramatist in their own dullness. John Finley's words to those who charge that more is read into Thucydides' speeches than the average Athenian citizen could have understood, are appropriate:

> It might be replied that the mass of the people could not have followed speeches of so general a character, but to make such an objection is to misunderstand the mind of the fifth century, indeed of any great period. The plays of Shakespeare and the sermons of early Protestantism give proof enough of the capacity assumed in an ordinary audience or congregation. It could be argued that any era which offers the ordinary man vast horizons of opportunity demands and receives from him a fresh comprehension proportionate to his fresh self-respect. Attic tragedy, even the philosophical and political subjects treated by Aristophanes, cannot be explained on any other assumption.[7]

As for Euripides, if I am right in assuming that his subject was nothing less than the life of Greek and Athenian culture, respect for the intelligence and good faith of the ordinary audience *must* be forthcoming, since it is the premise of culture itself. If Euripides for the most part failed to win the understanding of his audience, as I think he did, the fact does not disprove the intent. It is, I think, not sufficiently recognized that the very scholars who object that literary criticism means importing modern prejudices into an ancient text are themselves usually the worst offenders. Utterly unconsciously they take for granted all the cramping prejudices which a culture like ours can confer upon an uncritical man, and confer them in turn upon antiquity. "The classicist's attitude toward the ancient world," wrote Nietzsche, "is either apologetic or derives from the notion that what our age values highly can also be found in antiquity. The right starting point is the opposite, i.e., to start from the perception of modern absurdity and to look backward from that viewpoint—and many things regarded as offensive in the ancient world will appear as profound necessities. We must make it clear to ourselves that we are acting absurdly when we justify or beautify antiquity: who are *we?*"

Among literary men and critics of literature, as opposed to scholars, it might be assumed that a Greek theater of ideas would find favor, if only as a sanction and precedent for the new intellectual theater. But I suspect that this is not the case, precisely because contemporary critics are so stubbornly and unreasonably convinced that the entire Greek theater from Aeschylus to Euripides is firmly ritualistic. In saying this, I am thinking of the fact that the modern poetic theater, in searching for anti-naturalistic models, turned significantly to Greek drama. What interested contemporaries in Greek drama was, of course, the belief that they would find in it those features—ritual, stylization, gesture, a sacramental sense of life and community—which promised release from the restrictions of the naturalistic theater. They were confirmed in this by the literary vogue of anthropology, and the apparent success of the so-called Cambridge school, especially Francis Cornford and Jane Harrison. But the strongest argument for the ritual view of Greek drama came, I think, from the inability of the classicists themselves to give any substantial meaning to Greek drama. Thus literary men, always a little nervous when confronted with a Greek text and seldom inclined to quarrel with scholarship, eagerly accepted a scholarly view of the Greek plays that at least had the merit of making them mean *something* and which also suited their own theatrical programs. Ritual for them was a "find." For Greek drama it was, as I have tried to show elsewhere, an unqualified disaster.

But because its basis is "need," ritual interpretation is particularly insidious. My own objections to it are threefold; first, the belief that developed tragedy still bears the visible structural and esthetic effects of its origin is a clear case of the genetic fallacy; second, there is so little evidence for it in extant tragedy that its own originator, Gilbert Murray, recanted it; and third, it is really Cornford's argument for comedy—a far sounder argument in view of comedy's late nationalization—that gives it cogency. My critical objection to the ritual approach is that it tends to diminish rather than enhance the literary value of the plays; in short, it tends to make priests of tragedians and worshipers of audiences. This is not, of course, to deny the religious importance of the Greek tragedian or his religious concern. But it is to deny that his subject was prescribed, his treatment wholly conventional or stylized, and his thought unimportant or unadventurous. Whatever value the ritual approach may have for Aeschylus or Sophocles (and I think the value is small) its application has obscured even further the nature and originality of the Euripidean theater of ideas, since it is precisely discursive, *critical* thought, the complex dialectic of Euripidean drama, that ritualist interpretation regularly suppresses. Thus the only result of the ritual criticism of Greek drama has been, in my opinion, a further falsification.

But the essential, the crucial reason for our misunderstanding of Greek drama in general, and Euripidean theater in particular, is one which classicists and literary men alike share with the whole modern world. And this is our special cultural need of the classics, our own crucial myth of classical culture. A tradition is, after all, like love; we "crystallize" it, endow it with the perfections it must have in order to justify our need and our love. And classical Greek culture has for some time stood in relation to modern culture as a measure of our own chaos—a cultural Eden by which we measure our fall from grace and innocence. Thus we view the Greeks with the same envious and needful wonder that Nietzsche and Thomas Mann reserved for Goethe—that integrated soul—and which Euripides' age felt for the age of Aeschylus. To our modern dissonance, the Greeks play the role of old tonality, the abiding image of a great humanity. They are our lost power; lost wholeness; the pure *presence* and certainty of reality our culture has lost.

Against a need like this and a myth like this, argument may be futile. But we should not, I think, be allowed to mythologize unawares. If we first deprive classical culture of its true turbulence in order to make ourselves a myth of what we have lost, and then hedge that myth with false ritual, we are depriving ourselves of that community of interest and danger that makes the twentieth century true kin to the Greeks. We deprive ourselves, in short, of access to what the past can teach us in order to take only what we want. And that is a cultural loss of the first magnitude.

NOTES

[1] See "The Criticism of Greek Tragedy," in *The Tulane Drama Review*, III, No. 3 (Spring, 1959), 31 ff.

[2] Compare Ajax' situation with Thucydides' statement in the Corcyraean excursus: "The ancient simplicity into which honor so largely

entered was laughed down and disappeared."

[3] A dramatic adaptation, I believe, of Protagoras' *antilogoi* (the rhetorical technique of first attacking and then defending a thesis, or of antithetical theses). Thucydides' method of contrasting set speeches (the Mytilenean debate, for instance) is an historian's adaptation of the *antilogoi* and a way of indicating, between the lines, by what is omitted and shared by both speakers, the crucial spoken and unspoken assumptions of politics and ethics. So too in the case of Euripides.

[4] Cf. Euripides' *Electra,* 294–96, where Orestes says: "Compassion is found in men who are *sophoi,* never in brutal and ignorant men. And to have a truly compassionate mind is not without disadvantage to the *sophoi.*"

[5] Just as Medea and Jason between them destroy Creon and his daughter Glauke, so Medea, once she is domiciled in Athens, will attempt to murder Theseus, the son whom Aegeus so passionately desires—a fact which Athenians could be expected to know and hold against Medea, especially in view of Aegeus' generosity to her. Wherever Medea goes, the polis, as represented by the ruling family, is threatened.

[6] A comparison I owe to Eric Bentley's *The Playwright as Thinker* (New York, 1955), p. 27. Hebbel described his new theater in this way: "At its every step there throngs around it a world of views and relations, which point both backwards and forwards, and all of which must be carried along; the life-forces cross and destroy one another, the thread of thought snaps in two before it is spun out, the emotion shifts, the very words gain their independence and reveal hidden meaning, annulling the ordinary one, for each is a die marked on more than one face. Here the chaff of little sentences, adding bit to bit and fiber to fiber, would serve the purpose ill. It is a question of presenting conditions in their organic totality. . . . Unevenness of rhythm, complication and confusion of periods, contradiction in the figures are elevated to effective and indispensable rhetorical means."

[7] John H. Finley, Jr., *Thucydides* (Cambridge, Mass., 1947), pp. 64–65.

Control of Distance
in Jane Austen's *Emma*

Wayne C. Booth

Sympathy and Judgment in Emma

Henry James once described Jane Austen as an instinctive novelist whose effects, some of which are admittedly fine, can best be explained as "part of her unconsciousness." It is as if she "fell-a-musing" over her work-basket, he said, lapsed into "wool-gathering," and afterward picked up "her dropped stitches" as "little masterstrokes of imagination."[1] The amiable accusation has been repeated in various forms, most recently as a claim that Jane Austen creates characters toward whom we cannot react as she consciously intends.[2]

Although we cannot hope to decide whether Jane Austen was entirely conscious of her own artistry, a careful look at the technique of any of her novels reveals a rather different picture from that of the unconscious spinster with her knitting needles. In *Emma* especially, where the chances for technical failure are great indeed, we find at work one of the unquestionable masters of the rhetoric of narration.

At the beginning of *Emma*, the young heroine has every requirement for deserved happiness but one. She had intelligence, wit, beauty, wealth, and position, and she has the love of those around her. Indeed, she thinks herself completely happy. The only threat to her happiness, a threat of which she is unaware, is herself: charming as she is, she can neither see her own excessive pride honestly nor resist imposing herself on the lives of others. She is deficient both in generosity and in self-knowledge. She discovers and corrects her faults only after

336

she has almost ruined herself and her closest friends. But with the reform in her character, she is ready for marriage with the man she loves, the man who throughout the book has stood in the reader's mind for what she lacks.

It is clear that with a general plot of this kind Jane Austen gave herself difficulties of a high order. Though Emma's faults are comic, they constantly threaten to produce serious harm. Yet she must remain sympathetic or the reader will not wish for and delight sufficiently in her reform.

Obviously, the problem with a plot like this is to find some way to allow the reader to laugh at the mistakes committed by the heroine and at her punishment, without reducing the desire to see her reform and thus earn happiness. In *Tom Jones* this double attitude is achieved, as we have seen, partly through the invention of episodes producing sympathy and relieving any serious anxiety we might have, and partly through the direct and sympathetic commentary. In *Emma,* since most of the episodes must illustrate the heroine's faults and thus increase either our emotional distance or our anxiety, a different method is required. If we fail to see Emma's faults as revealed in the ironic texture from line to line, we cannot savor to the full the comedy as it is prepared for us. On the other hand, if we fail to love her, as Jane Austen herself predicted we would[3]—if we fail to love her more and more as the book progresses—we can neither hope for the conclusion, a happy and deserved marriage with Knightley following upon her reform, nor accept it as an honest one when it comes.[4] Any attempt to solve the problem by reducing either the love or the clear view of her faults would have been fatal.

Sympathy Through Control of Inside Views

The solution to the problem of maintaining sympathy despite almost crippling faults was primarily to use the heroine herself as a kind of narrator, though in third person, reporting on her own experience. So far as we know, Jane Austen never formulated any theory to cover her own practice; she invented no term like James's "central intelligence" or "lucid reflector" to describe her method of viewing the world of the book primarily through Emma's own eyes. We can thus never know for sure to what extent James's accusation of "unconsciousness" was right. But whether she was inclined to speculate about her method scarcely matters; her solution was clearly a brilliant one. By showing most of the story through Emma's eyes, the author insures that we shall travel with Emma rather than stand against her. It is not simply that Emma provides, in the unimpeachable evidence of her own conscience, proof that she has many redeeming qualities that do not appear on the surface; such evidence could be given with authorial commentary, though perhaps not with such force and conviction. Much more important, the sustained inside view leads the reader to hope for good fortune for the character with whom he travels, quite independently of the qualities revealed.

Seen from the outside, Emma would be an unpleasant person, unless, like Mr. Woodhouse and Knightley, we knew her well enough to infer her true worth. Though we might easily be led to laugh at her, we could never be made to laugh sympathetically. While the final unmasking of her faults and her humiliation would make artistic sense to an unsympathetic reader, her marriage with Knightley would become irrelevant if not meaningless. Unless we desire Emma's happiness and her reform which alone can make that happiness possible, a good third of this book will seem irredeemably dull.

Yet sympathetic laughter is never easily achieved. It is much easier to set up a separate fool for comic effects and to preserve your heroine for finer things. Sympathetic laughter is especially difficult with characters whose faults do not spring from sympathetic virtues. The grasping but witty Volpone can keep us on his side so long as his victims are more grasping and less witty than he, but as soon as the innocent victims, Celia and Bonario, come on stage, the quality of the humor changes; we no longer delight unambiguously in his triumphs. In contrast to this, the great sympathetic comic heroes often are comic largely because their faults, like Uncle Toby's sentimentality, spring from an excess of some virtue. Don Quixote's madness is partly caused by an excess of idealism, an excess of loving concern for the unfortunate. Every crazy gesture he makes gives further reason for loving the well-meaning old fool, and we can thus laugh at him in somewhat the same spirit in which we laugh at our own faults—in a benign, forgiving spirit. We may be contemptible for doing so; to persons without a sense of humor such laughter often seems a wicked escape. But self-love being what it is, we laugh at ourselves in a thoroughly forgiving way, and we laugh in the same way at Don Quixote: we are convinced that his heart, like ours, is in the right place.

Nothing in Emma's comic misunderstandings can serve for the same effect. Her faults are not excesses of virtue. She attempts to manipulate Harriet not from an excess of kindness but from a desire for power and admiration. She flirts with Frank Churchill out of vanity and irresponsibility. She mistreats Jane Fairfax because of Jane's *good* qualities. She abuses Miss Bates because of her own essential lack of "tenderness" and "good will."

We have only to think of what Emma's story would be if seen through Jane Fairfax' or Mrs. Elton's or Robert Martin's eyes to recognize how little our sympathy springs from any natural view, and to see how inescapable is the decision to use Emma's mind as a reflector of events—however beclouded her vision must be. To Jane Fairfax, who embodies throughout the book most of the values which Emma discovers only at the end, the early Emma is intolerable.

But Jane Austen never lets us forget that Emma is not what she might appear to be. For every section devoted to her misdeeds—and even they are seen for the most part through her own eyes—there is a section devoted to her self-reproach. We see her rudeness to poor foolish Miss Bates, and we see it vividly. But her remorse and act of penance in visiting Miss Bates after Knightley's rebuke are experienced even more vividly. We see her successive attempts to mislead Harriet, but we see at great length and in high color her self-castigation (chaps. xvi, xvii, xlviii). We see her boasting proudly that she does not need marriage, boasting almost as blatantly of her "resources" as does Mrs. Elton (chap. x). But we know her too intimately to take her conscious thoughts at face value. And we see her, thirty-eight chapters later, chastened to an admission of what we have known all along to be her true human need for love. "If all took place that might take place among the circle of her friends, Hartfield must be comparatively deserted; and she left to cheer her father with the spirits only of ruined happiness. The child to be born at Randalls must be a tie there even dearer than herself; and Mrs. Weston's heart and time would be occupied by it. . . . All that were good would be withdrawn" (chap. xlviii).

Perhaps the most delightful effects from our sustained inside view of a very confused and very charming young woman come from her frequent thoughts about Knightley. She is basically right all along about his pre-eminent wisdom and virtue, and she is our chief authority for taking *his* authority so seriously. And yet in every thought about him she is misled. Knightley rebukes her; the reader knows that Knightley is in the right. But Emma?

> Emma made no answer, and tried to look cheerfully unconcerned, but was really feeling uncomfortable, and wanting him very much to be gone. She did not repent what she had done; she still

thought herself a better judge of such a point of female right and refinement than he could be; but yet she had a sort of habitual respect for his judgment in general, which made her dislike having it so loudly against her; and to have him sitting just opposite to her in angry state, was very disagreeable [chap. viii].

Even more striking is the lack of self-knowledge shown when Mrs. Weston suggests that Knightley might marry Jane Fairfax.

Her objections to Mr. Knightley's marrying did not in the least subside. She could see nothing but evil in it. It would be a great disappointment to Mr. John Knightley [Knightley's brother]; consequently to Isabella. A real injury to the children—a most mortifying change, and material loss to them all;—a very great deduction from her father's daily comfort—and, as to herself, she could not at all endure the idea of Jane Fairfax at Donwell Abbey. A Mrs. Knightley for them all to give way to!—No, Mr. Knightley must never marry. Little Henry must remain the heir of Donwell [chap. xxvi].

Self-deception could hardly be carried further, at least in a person of high intelligence and sensitivity.

Yet the effect of all this is what our tolerance for our own faults produces in our own lives. While only immature readers ever really identify with any character, losing all sense of distance and hence all chance of an artistic experience, our emotional reaction to every event concerning Emma tends to become like her own. When she feels anxiety or shame, we feel analogous emotions. Our modern awareness that such "feelings" are not identical with those we feel in our own lives in similar circumstances has tended to blind us to the fact that aesthetic form can be built out of patterned emotions as well as out of other materials. It is absurd to pretend that because our emotions and desires in responding to fiction are in a very real sense disinterested, they do not or should not exist. Jane Austen, in developing the sustained use of a sympathetic inside view, has mastered one of the most successful of all devices for inducing a parallel emotional response between the deficient heroine and the reader.

Sympathy for Emma can be heightened by withholding inside views of others as well as by granting them of her. The author knew, for example, that it would be fatal to grant any extended inside view of Jane Fairfax. The inadequacies of impressionistic criticism are nowhere revealed more clearly than in the suggestion often made about such minor characters that their authors would have liked to make them vivid but didn't know how.[5] Jane Austen knew perfectly well how to make such a character vivid; Anne in *Persuasion* is a kind of Jane Fairfax turned into heroine. But in *Emma*, Emma must shine supreme. It is not only that the slightest glance inside Jane's mind would be fatal to all of the author's plans for mystification about Frank Churchill, though this is important. The major problem is that any extended view of her would reveal her as a more sympathetic person than Emma herself. Jane is superior to Emma in most respects except the stroke of good fortune that made Emma the heroine of the book. In matters of taste and ability, of head and of heart, she is Emma's superior, and Jane Austen, always in danger of losing our sympathy for Emma, cannot risk any degree of distraction. Jane could, it is true, be granted fewer virtues, and *then* made more vivid. But to do so would greatly weaken the force of Emma's mistakes of heart and head in her treatment of the almost faultless Jane.

Control of Judgment

But the very effectiveness of the rhetoric designed to produce sympathy might in itself lead to a serious misreading of the book. In reducing the emotional distance, the natural tendency is to reduce—willynilly—moral and intellectual distance as well. In reacting to Emma's faults from the inside out, as if they were our own, we may very well not only forgive them but overlook them.[6]

There is, of course, no danger that readers who persist to the end will overlook Emma's serious mistakes; since she sees and reports those mistakes herself, everything becomes crystal clear at the end. The real danger inherent in the experiment is that readers will overlook the mistakes as they are committed and thus miss much of the comedy that depends on Emma's distorted view from page to page. If readers who dislike Emma cannot enjoy the preparation for the marriage to Knightley, readers who do not recognize her faults with absolute precision cannot enjoy the details of the preparation for the comic abasement which must precede that marriage.

It might be argued that there is no real problem, since the conventions of her time allowed for reliable commentary whenever it was needed to place Emma's faults precisely. But Jane Austen is not operating according to the conventions, most of which she had long since parodied and outgrown; her technique is determined by the needs of the novel she is writing. We can see this clearly by contrasting the manner of *Emma* with that of *Persuasion*, the next, and last-completed work. In *Emma* there are many breaks in the point of view, because Emma's beclouded mind cannot do the whole job. In *Persuasion*, where the heroine's viewpoint is faulty only in her ignorance of Captain Wentworth's love, there are very few. Anne Elliot's consciousness is sufficient, as Emma's is not, for most of the needs of the novel which she dominates. Once the ethical and intellectual framework has been established by the narrator's introduction, we enter Anne's consciousness and remain bound to it much more rigorously than we are bound to Emma's. It is still true that whenever something must be shown that Anne's consciousness cannot show, we move to another center; but since her consciousness can do much more for us than Emma's, there need be few departures from it.

The most notable shift for rhetorical purposes in *Persuasion* comes fairly early. When Anne first meets Captain Wentworth after their years of separation that follow her refusal to marry him, she is convinced that he is indifferent. The major movement of *Persuasion* is toward her final discovery that he still loves her; *her* suspense is thus strong and inevitable from the beginning. The reader, however, is likely to believe that Wentworth is still interested. All the conventions of art favor such a belief: the emphasis is clearly on Anne and her unhappiness; the lover has returned; we have only to wait, perhaps with some tedium, for the inevitable outcome. Anne learns (chap. vii) that he has spoken of her as so altered "he should not have known her again!" "These were words which could not but dwell with her. Yet she soon began to rejoice that she had heard them. They were of sobering tendency; they allayed agitation; they composed, and consequently must make her happier." And suddenly we enter Wentworth's mind for one time only: "Frederick Wentworth had used such words, or something like them, but without an idea that they would be carried round to her. He had thought her wretchedly altered, and, in the first moment of appeal, had spoken as he felt. He had not forgiven Anne Elliot. She had used him ill"—and so he goes on, for five more paragraphs. The necessary point, the fact that Frederick believes himself to be indifferent, has been made, and it could not have been made without some kind of shift from Anne's consciousness.

At the end of the novel, we learn that Wentworth was himself deceived in this momentary inside view: "He had meant to forget her, and believed it to be done. He had imagined himself indifferent, when he had only been angry." We may want to protest against the earlier suppression as unfair, but we can hardly believe it to be what Miss Lascelles calls "an oversight."[7] It is deliberate manipulation of inside views in order to destroy our conventional security. We are thus made ready to go along with Anne in her long and painful road to the discovery that Frederick loves her after all.

The only other important breaks in the angle of vision of *Persuasion* come at the beginning and at the end. Chapter one is an excellent example of how a skilful novelist can, by the use of his own direct voice, accomplish in a few pages what even the best novelist must take chapters to do if he uses nothing but dramatized action. Again at the conclusion the author enters with a resounding reaffirmation that the Wentworth-Elliot marriage is as good a thing as we have felt it to be from the beginning.

> Who can be in doubt of what followed? When any two young people take it into their heads to marry, they are pretty sure by perseverance to carry their point, be they ever so poor, or ever so imprudent, or ever so little likely to be necessary to each other's ultimate comfort. This may be bad morality to conclude with, but I believe it to be truth; and if such parties succeed, how should a Captain Wentworth and an Anne Elliot, with the advantage of maturity of mind, consciousness of right, and one independent fortune between them, fail of bearing down every opposition?[8]

Except for these few intrusions and one in chapter xix, Anne's own mind is sufficient in *Persuasion,* but we can never rely completely on Emma. It is hardly surprising that Jane Austen has provided many correctives to insure our placing her errors with precision.

The chief corrective is Knightley. His commentary on Emma's errors is a natural expression of his love; he can tell the reader and Emma at the same time precisely how she is mistaken. Thus, nothing Knightley says can be beside the point. Each affirmation of a value, each accusation of error is in itself an action in the plot. When he rebukes Emma for manipulating Harriet, when he attacks her for superficiality and false pride, when he condemns her for gossiping and flirting with Frank Churchill, and finally when he attacks her for being "insolent" and "unfeeling" in her treatment of Miss Bates, we have Jane Austen's judgment on Emma, rendered dramatically. But it has come from someone who is essentially sympathetic toward Emma, so that his judgments against her are presumed to be temporary. His sympathy reinforces ours even as he criticizes, and her respect for his opinion, shown in her self-abasement after he has criticized, is one of our main reasons for expecting her to reform.

If Henry James had tried to write a novel about Emma, and had cogitated at length on the problem of getting her story told dramatically, he could not have done better than this. It is possible, of course, to think of *Emma* without Knightley as *raisonneur*, just as it is possible to think of *The Golden Bowl*, say, without the Assinghams as *ficelles* to reflect something not seen by the Prince or Princess. But Knightley, though he receives less independent space than the Assinghams and is almost never seen in an inside view, is clearly more useful for Jane Austen's purposes than any realistically limited *ficelle* could possibly be. By combining the role of commentator with the role of hero, Jane Austen has worked more economically than James, and though economy is as dangerous as any other criterion when applied universally, even James might have profited from a closer study of the economies that a character like Knightley can be made to achieve. It is as if James had dared to make one of the four main characters, say the Prince, into a thoroughly good, wise, perceptive man, a thoroughly clear rather than a partly confused "reflector."

Since Knightley is established early as completely reliable, we need no views of his secret thoughts. He has no secret thoughts, except for the unacknowledged depths of his love for Emma and his jealousy of Frank Churchill. The other main characters have more to hide, and Jane Austen moves in and out of minds with great freedom, choosing for her own purposes what to reveal and what to withhold. Always the seeming violation of consistency is in the consistent service of the particular needs of Emma's story. Sometimes a shift is made simply to direct our suspense, as when Mrs. Weston suggests a possible union of Emma and Frank Churchill, at the end of her conversation with Knightley about the harmful effects of Emma's friendship with Harriet (chap. v). "Part of her meaning was to conceal some favourite thoughts of her own and Mr. Weston's on the subject, as much as possible. There were wishes at Randalls respecting Emma's destiny, but it was not desirable to have them suspected."

One objection to this selective dipping into whatever mind best serves our immediate purposes is that it suggests mere trickery and inevitably spoils the illusion of reality. If Jane Austen can tell us what Mrs. Weston is thinking, why not what Frank Churchill and Jane Fairfax are thinking? Obviously, because she chooses to build a mystery, and to do so she must refuse, arbitrarily and obtrusively, to grant the privilege of an inside view to characters whose minds would reveal too much. But is not the mystery purchased at the price of shaking the reader's faith in Jane Austen's integrity? If she simply withholds until later what she might as well relate now—if her procedure is not dictated by the very nature of her materials—why should we take her seriously?

If a natural surface were required in all fiction, then this objection would hold. But if we want to read *Emma* in its own terms, the real question about these shifts cannot be answered by an easy appeal to general principles. Every author withholds until later what he "might as well" relate now. The question is always one of desired effects, and the choice of any one effect always bans innumerable other effects. There is, indeed, a question to be raised about the use of mystery in *Emma*, but the conflict is not between an abstract end that Jane Austen never worried about and a shoddy mystification that she allowed to betray her. The conflict is between two effects both of which she cares about a good deal. On the one hand she cares about maintaining some sense of mystery as long as she can. On the other, she works at all points to heighten the reader's sense of dramatic irony, usually in the form of a contrast between what Emma knows and what the reader knows.

As in most novels, whatever steps are taken to mystify inevitably decrease the dramatic irony, and, whenever dramatic irony is increased by telling the reader secrets the characters have not yet suspected, mystery is inevitably destroyed. The longer we are in doubt about Farnk Churchill, the weaker our sense of ironic contrast between Emma's views and the truth. The sooner we see through Frank Churchill's secret plot, the greater our pleasure in observing Emma's innumerable misreadings of his behavior and the less interest we have in the mere mystery of the situation. And we all find that on second reading we discover new intensities of dramatic irony resulting from the complete loss of mystery; knowing what abysses of error Emma is preparing for herself, even those of us who may on first reading have deciphered nearly all the details of the Churchill mystery find additional ironies.

But it is obvious that these ironies could have been offered even on a first reading, if Jane Austen had been willing to sacrifice her mystery. A single phrase in her own name—"his secret engagement to Jane Fairfax"—or a short inside view of either of the lovers could have made us aware of every ironic touch.

The author must, then, choose whether to purchase mystery at the expense of irony. For many of us Jane Austen's choice here is perhaps the weakest aspect of this novel. It is a commonplace of our criticism that significant literature arouses suspense not about the "what" but about the "how." Mere mystification has been mastered by so many second-rate writers that her efforts at mystification seem second-rate.

But again we must ask whether criticism can be conducted effectively by balancing one abstract quality against another. Is there a norm of dramatic irony for all works, or even for all works of a given kind? Has anyone ever formulated a "law of first and second readings" that will tell us just how many of our pleasures on page one should depend on our knowledge of what happens on page the last? We quite properly ask that the books we call great be able to stand up under repeated reading, but we need not ask that they yield identical pleasures on each reading. The modern works whose authors pride themselves on the fact that they can never be read but only re-read may be very good indeed, but they are not *made* good by the fact that their secret pleasures can only be wrested from them by repeated readings.

In any case, even if one accepted the criticism of Jane Austen's efforts at mystification, the larger service of the inside views is clear: the crosslights thrown by other minds prevent our being blinded by Emma's radiance.

The Reliable Narrator and the Norms of Emma

If mere intellectual clarity about Emma were the goal in this work, we should be forced to say that the manipulation of inside views and the extensive commentary of the reliable Knightley are more than is necessary. But for maximum intensity of the comedy and romance, even these are not enough. The "author herself"—not necessarily the real Jane Austen but an implied author, represented in this book by a reliable narrator—heightens the effects by directing our intellectual, moral, and emotional progress. She performs, of course, most of the functions described in chapter vii. But her most important role is to reinforce both aspects of the double vision that operates throughout the book: our inside view of Emma's worth and our objective view of her great faults.

The narrator opens *Emma* with a masterful simultaneous presentation of Emma and of the values against which she must be judged: "Emma Woodhouse, handsome, clever, and rich, with a comfortable home and happy disposition, seemed to unite some of the best blessings of existence; and had lived nearly twenty-one years in the world with very little to distress or vex her." This "seemed" is immediately reinforced by more directly stated reservations. "The real evils of Emma's situation were the power of having rather too much her own way, and a disposition to think a little too well of herself; these were the disadvantages which threatened alloy to her many enjoyments. The danger, however, was at present so unperceived, that they did not by any means rank as misfortunes with her."

None of this could have been said by Emma, and if shown through her consciousness, it could not be accepted, as it must be, without question. Like most of the first three chapters, it is nondramatic summary, building up, through the ostensible business of getting the characters introduced, to Emma's initial blunder with Harriet and Mr. Elton. Throughout these chapters, we learn much of what we must know from the narrator, but she turns over more and more of the job of summary to Emma as she feels more and more sure of our seeing precisely to what degree Emma is to be trusted. Whenever we leave the "real evils" we have been warned against in Emma, the narrator's and Emma's views coincide: we cannot tell which of them, for example, offers the judgment on Mr. Woodhouse that "his talents could not have recommended him at any time," or the judgment on Mr. Knightley that he is "a sensible man," "always welcome" at Hartfield, or even that "Mr. Knightley, in fact, was one of the few people who could see faults in Emma Woodhouse, and the only one who ever told her of them."

But there are times when Emma and her author are far apart, and the author's direct guidance aids the reader in his own break with Emma. The beautiful irony of the first description of Harriet, given through Emma's eyes (chap. iii) could no doubt be grasped intellectually by many readers without all of the preliminary commentary. But even for the most perceptive its effect is heightened, surely, by the sense of standing with the author and observing with her precisely how Emma's judgment is going astray. Perhaps more important, we ordinary, less perceptive readers have by now been raised to a level suited to grasp the ironies. Certainly, most readers would overlook some of the barbs directed against Emma if the novel began, as a serious modern novelist might well begin it, with this description:

> [Emma] was not struck by any thing remarkably clever in Miss Smith's conversation, but she found her altogether very engaging—not inconveniently shy, not unwilling to talk—and yet so far from pushing, shewing so proper and becoming a deference, seeming so pleasantly grateful for being admitted to Hartfield, and so artlessly impressed by the appearance of every thing in so superior a style to what she had been used to, that she must have good sense and deserve encouragement. Encouragement should be given. Those soft blue eyes . . . should not be wasted on the inferior society of Highbury. . . .

And so Emma goes on, giving herself away with every word, pouring out her sense of her own beneficence and general value. Harriet's past friends, "though very good sort of people, must be doing her harm." Without knowing them, Emma knows that they "must be coarse and unpolished, and very unfit to be the intimates of a girl who wanted only a little more knowledge and elegance to be quite perfect." And she concludes with a beautiful burst of egotism: "*She* would notice her; she would improve her; she would detach her from her bad acquaintance, and introduce her into good society; she would form her opinions and her manners. It would be an interesting, and certainly a very kind undertaking; highly becoming her own situation in life, her leisure, and powers." Even the most skilful reader might not easily plot an absolutely true course through these ironies without the prior direct assistance we have been given. Emma's views are not so outlandish that they could never have been held by a female novelist writing in her time. They cannot serve effecitvely as signs of *her* character unless they are clearly disavowed as signs of Jane Austen's views. Emma's unconscious catalogue of her egotistical uses for Harriet, given under the pretense of listing the services *she* will perform, is thus given its full force by being framed explicitly in a world of values which Emma herself cannot discover until the conclusion of the book.

The full importance of the author's direct imposition of an elaborate scale of norms can be seen by considering that conclusion. The sequence of events is a simple one: Emma's faults and mistakes are brought home to her in a rapid and humiliating chain of rebukes from Knightley and blows from hard fact. These blows to her self-esteem produce at last a genuine reform (for example, she brings herself to apologize to Miss Bates, something she could never have done earlier in the novel). The change in her character removes the only obstacle in the way of Knightley's proposal, and the marriage follows. "The wishes, the hopes, the confidence, the predictions of the small band of true friends who witnessed the ceremony, were fully answered in the perfect happiness of the union."

It may be that if we look at Emma and Knightley as real people, this ending will seem false. G. B. Stern laments, in *Speaking of Jane Austen*, "Oh, Miss Austen, it was *not* a good solution; it was a bad solution, an unhappy ending, could we see beyond the last pages of the book." Edmund Wilson predicts that Emma will find a new protégée like Harriet, since she has not been cured of her inclination to "infatuations with women." Marvin Mudrick even more emphatically rejects Jane Austen's explicit rhetoric; he believes that Emma is still a "confirmed exploiter," and for him the ending must be read as ironic.[9]

But it is precisely because this ending is neither life itself nor a simple bit of literary irony that it can serve so well to heighten our sense of a complete and indeed perfect resolution to all that has gone before. If we look at the values that have been realized in this marriage and compare them with those realized in conventional marriage plots, we see that Jane Austen means what she says: this will be a happy marriage because there is simply nothing left to make it anything less than perfectly happy. It fulfils every value embodied in the world of the book—with the possible exception that Emma may never learn to apply herself as she ought to her reading and her piano! It is a union of intelligence: of "reason," of "sense," of "judgment." It is a union of virtue: of "good will," of generosity, of unselfishness. It is a union of feeling: of "taste," "tenderness," "love," "beauty."[10]

In a general way, then, this plot offers us an experience superficially like that offered by most tragicomedy as well as by much of the cheapest popular art: we are made to desire certain good things for certain good characters, and then our desires are gratified. If we depended on general criteria derived from our justified boredom with such works, we should reject this one. But the critical difference lies in the precise quality of the values appealed to and the precise quality of the characters who violate or realize them. All of the cheap marriage plots in the world should not lead us to be embarrassed about our pleasure in Emma and Knightley's marriage. It is more than just the marriage: it is the *rightness* of *this* marriage, as a conclusion to all of the comic wrongness that has gone before. The good for Emma includes both her necessary reform and the resulting marriage. Marriage to an intelligent, amiable, good, and attractive man is the best thing that can happen to this heroine, and the readers who do not experience it as such are, I am convinced, far from knowing what Jane Austen is about —whatever they may say about the "bitter spinster's" attitude toward marriage.

Our modern sensibilities are likely to be rasped by any such formulation. We do not ordinarily like to encounter perfect endings in our novels—even in the sense of "perfectedness" or completion, the sense obviously intended by Jane Austen. We refuse to accept it when we see it: witness the many attempts to deny Dostoevski's success with Alyosha and Father Zossima in *The Brothers Karamazov*. Many of us find it embarrassing to talk of emotions based on moral judgment at all, particularly when the emotions have any kind of affirmative cast. Emma herself is something of a "modern" in this regard throughout most of the book. Her self-deception about marriage is as great as about most other important matters. Emma boasts to Harriet of her indifference to marriage, at the same time unconsciously betraying her totally inadequate view of the sources of human happiness.

> If I know myself, Harriet, mine is an active, busy mind, with a great many independent resources; and I do not perceive why I should be more in want of employment at forty or fifty than one-and-twenty. Woman's usual occupations of eye and hand and mind will be as open to me then, as they are now; or with no important variation. If I draw less, I shall read more; if I give up music, I shall take to carpet-work.

Emma at carpet-work! If she knows herself indeed.

> And as for objects of interest, objects for the affections, which is, in truth, the great point of inferiority, the want of which is really the great evil to be avoided in *not* marrying [a magnificent concession, this] I shall be very well off, with all the children of a sister I love so much, to care about. There will be enough of them, in all probability, to supply every sort of sensation that declining life can need. There will be enough for every hope and every fear; and though my attachment to none can equal that of a parent, it suits my ideas of comfort better than what is warmer and blinder. My nephews and nieces!—I shall often have a niece with me [chap. x].

Without growing solemn about it—it is wonderfully comic—we can recognize that the humor springs here from very deep sources indeed. It can be fully enjoyed, in fact, only by the reader who has attained to a vision of human felicity far more profound than Emma's "comfort" and "want" and "need." It is a vision that includes not simply marriage, but a kind of loving converse not based, as is Emma's here, on whether the "loved" person will serve one's irreducible needs.

The comic effect of this repudiation of marriage is considerably increased by the fact that Emma always thinks of marriage for others as *their* highest good, and in fact unconsciously encourages her friend Harriet to fall in love with the very man she herself loves without knowing it. The delightful denouement is thus what we want not only because it is a supremely good thing for Emma, but because it is a supremely comic outcome of Emma's profound misunderstanding of herself and of the human condition. In the schematic language of chapter v, it satisfies both our practical desire for Emma's well-being and our appetite for the qualities proper to these artistic materials. It is thus a more resounding resolution than either of these elements separately could provide. The other major resolution of the work—Harriet's marriage with her farmer—reinforces this interpretation. Emma's

sin against Harriet has been something far worse than the mere med-
dling of a busybody. To destroy Harriet's chances for happiness—
chances that depend entirely on her marriage—is as close to viciousness as any author could dare to take a heroine designed to be loved.
We can laugh with Emma at this mistake (chap. liv) only because
Harriet's chance for happiness is restored.

Other values, like money, blood, and "consequence," are real
enough in *Emma*, but only as they contribute to or are mastered by
good taste, good judgment, and good morality. Money alone can make
a Mrs. Churchill, but a man or woman "is silly to marry without it."
Consequence untouched by sense can make a very inconsequential
Mr. Woodhouse; untouched by sense or virtue it can make the much
more contemptible Mr. and Miss Elliot of *Persuasion*. But it is a pleasant thing to have, and it does no harm unless, like the early Emma,
one takes it too seriously. Charm and elegance without sufficient moral
force can make a Frank Churchill; unschooled by morality it can lead
to the baseness of Henry Crawford in *Mansfield Park* or of Wickham
in *Pride and Prejudice*. Even the supreme vitures are inadequate in
isolation: good will alone will make a comic Miss Bates or a Mr. Weston, judgment with insufficient good will a comic Mr. John Knightley,
and so on.

I am willing to risk the commonplace in such a listing because it is
only thus that the full force of Jane Austen's comprehensive view can
be seen. There is clearly at work here a much more detailed ordering
of values than any conventional public philosophy of her time could
provide. Obviously, few readers in her own time, and far fewer in our
own, have ever approached this novel in full and detailed agreement
with the author's norms. But they were led to join her as they read,
and so are we.

Explicit Judgments on Emma Woodhouse

We have said in passing almost enough of the other side of the coin—
the judgment of particular actions as they relate to the general norms.
But something must be said of the detailed "placing" of Emma, by direct commentary, in the hierarchy of values established by the novel. I
must be convinced, for example, not only that tenderness for other
people's feelings is an important trait but also that Emma's particular
behavior violates the true standards of tenderness, if I am to savor to
the full the episode of Emma's insult to Miss Bates and Knightley's

reproach which follows. If I refuse to blame Emma, I may discover a kind of intellectual enjoyment in the episode, and I will probably think that any critic who talks of "belief" in tenderness as operating in such a context is taking things too seriously. But I can never enjoy the episode in its full intensity or grasp its formal coherence. Similarly, I must agree not only that to be dreadfully boring is a minor fault compared with the major virtue of "good will," but also that Miss Bates's exemplification of this fault and of this virtue entitle her to the respect which Emma denies. If I do not—while yet being able to laugh at Miss Bates—I can hardly understand, let alone enjoy, Emma's mistreatment of her.

But these negative judgments must be counteracted by a larger approval, and, as we would expect, the novel is full of direct apologies for Emma. Her chief fault, lack of good will or tenderness, must be read not only in relationship to the code of values provided by the book as a whole—a code which judges her as seriously deficient; it must also be judged in relationship to the harsh facts of the world around her, a world made up of human beings ranging in degree of selfishness and egotism from Knightley, who lapses from perfection when he tries to judge Frank Churchill, his rival, down to Mrs. Elton, who has most of Emma's faults and none of her virtues. In such a setting, Emma is easily forgiven. When she insults Miss Bates, for example, we remember that Miss Bates lives in a world where many others are insensitive and cruel. "Miss Bates, neither young, handsome, rich, nor married, stood in the very worst predicament in the world for having much of the public favour; and she had no intellectual superiority to make atonement to herself, or frighten those who might hate her, into outward respect." While it would be a mistake to see only this "regulated hatred" in Jane Austen's world, overlooking the tenderness and generosity, the hatred of viciousness is there, and there is enough vice in evidence to make Emma almost shine by comparison.

Often, Jane Austen makes this apology-by-comparison explicit. When Emma lies to Knightley about Harriet, very close to the end of the book, she is excused with a generalization about human nature: "Seldom, very seldom, does complete truth belong to any human disclosure; seldom can it happen that something is not a little disguised, or a little mistaken; but where, as in this case, though the conduct is mistaken, the feelings are not, it may not be very material.—Mr. Knightley could not impute to Emma a more relenting heart than she possessed, or a heart more disposed to accept of his."

The Implied Author as Friend and Guide

With all of this said about the masterful use of the narrator in *Emma,*
there remain some "intrusions" unaccounted for by strict service to the
story itself. "What did she say?" the narrator asks, at the crucial moment in the major love scene. "Just what she ought, of course. A lady
always does.—She said enough to show there need not be despair—and
to invite him to say more himself." To some readers this has seemed to
demonstrate the author's inability to write a love scene, since it
sacrifices "the illusion of reality."[11] But who has ever read this far in
Emma under the delusion that he is reading a realistic portrayal which
is suddenly shattered by the unnatural appearance of the narrator? If
the narrator's superabundant wit is destructive of the kind of illusion
proper to this work, the novel has been ruined long before.

But we should now be in a position to see precisely why the narrator's wit is not in the least out of place at the emotional climax of the
novel. We have seen how the inside views of the characters and the
author's commentary have been used from the beginning to get the
values straight and to keep them straight and to help direct our reactions to Emma. But we also see here a beautiful case of the dramatized author as friend and guide. "Jane Austen," like "Henry Fielding," is a paragon of wit, wisdom, and virtue. She does not talk about
her qualities; unlike Fielding she does not in *Emma* call direct attention to her artistic skill. But we are seldom allowed to forget about her
for all that. When we read this novel we accept her as representing
everything we admire most. She is as generous and wise as Knightley;
in fact, she is a shade more penetrating in her judgment. She is as
subtle and witty as Emma would like to think herself. Without being
sentimental she is in favor of tenderness. She is able to put an adequate but not excessive value on wealth and rank. She recognizes a
fool when she sees one, but unlike Emma she knows that it is both immoral and foolish to be rude to fools. She is, in short, a perfect human
being, within the concept of perfection established by the book she
writes; she even recognizes that human perfection of the kind *she* exemplifies is not quite attainable in real life. The process of her domination is of course circular; her character establishes the values for us
according to which her character is then found to be perfect. But this
circularity does not affect the success of her endeavor; in fact it insures it.

Her "omniscience" is thus a much more remarkable thing than is ordinarily implied by the term. All good novelists know all about their characters—all that they need to know. And the question of how their narrators are to find out all that *they* need to know, the question of "authority," is a relatively simple one. The real choice is much more profound than this would imply. It is a choice of the moral, not merely the technical, angle of vision from which the story is to be told.

Unlike the central intelligences of James and his successors, "Jane Austen" has learned nothing at the end of the novel that she did not know at the beginning. She needed to learn nothing. She knew everything of importance already. We have been privileged to watch with her as she observes her favorite character climb from a considerably lower platform to join the exalted company of Knightley, "Jane Austen," and those of us readers who are wise enough, good enough, and perceptive enough to belong up there too. As Katherine Mansfield says, "the truth is that every true admirer of the novels cherishes the happy thought that he alone—reading between the lines—has become the secret friend of their author."[12] Those who love "gentle Jane" as a secret friend may undervalue the irony and wit; those who see her in effect as the greatest of Shaw's heroines, flashing about her with the weapons of irony, may undervalue the emphasis on tenderness and good will. But only a very few can resist her.

The dramatic illusion of her presence as a character is thus fully as important as any other element in the story. When she intrudes, the illusion is not shattered. The only illusion we care about, the illusion of traveling intimately with a hardy little band of readers whose heads are screwed on tight and whose hearts are in the right place, is actually strengthened when we are refused the romantic love scene. Like the author herself, we don't care about the love scene. We can find love scenes in almost any novelist's works, but only here can we find a mind and heart that can give us clarity without oversimplification, sympathy and romance without sentimentality, and biting irony without cynicism.

NOTES

[1] "The Lesson of Balzac," *The Question of Our Speech* (Cambridge, 1905), p. 63. A fuller quotation can be found in R. W. Chapman's indispensable *Jane Austen: A Critical Bibliography* (Oxford, 1955). Some important Austen items published too late to be included by Chapman are: (1) Ian Watt, *The Rise of the Novel* (Berkeley, Calif.,

1957); (2) Stuart M. Tave, review of Marvin Mudrick's *Jane Austen: Irony as Defense and Discovery* (Princeton, N.J., 1952) in *Philological Quarterly,* XXXII (July, 1953), 256–57; (3) Andrew H. Wright, *Jane Austen's Novels: A Study in Structure* (London, 1953), pp. 36–82; (4) Christopher Gillie, "*Sense and Sensibility:* An Assessment," *Essays in Criticism,* IX (January, 1959), 1–9, esp. 5–6; (5) Edgar F. Shannon, Jr., "*Emma:* Character and Construction," *PMLA,* LXXI (September, 1956), 637–50.

² See, for example, Mudrick, *op. cit.,* pp. 91, 165; Frank O'Connor, *The Mirror in the Roadway* (London, 1957), p. 30.

³ "A heroine whom no one but myself will much like" (James Edward Austen-Leigh, *Memoir of His Aunt* [London, 1870; Oxford, 1926], p. 157).

⁴ The best discussion of this problem is Reginald Farrer's "Jane Austen," *Quarterly Review,* CCXXVIII (July, 1917), 1–30; reprinted in William Heath's *Discussions of Jane Austen* (Boston, 1961). For one critic the book fails because the problem was never recognized by Jane Austen herself: Mr. E. N. Hayes, in what may well be the least sympathetic discussion of *Emma* yet written, explains the whole book as the author's failure to see Emma's faults. "Evidently Jane Austen wished to protect Emma. . . . The author is therefore in the ambiguous position of both loving and scorning the heroine" ("'Emma': A Dissenting Opinion," *Nineteenth-Century Fiction,* IV [June, 1949], 18, 19).

⁵ A. C. Bradley, for example, once argued that Jane Austen intended Jane Fairfax to be as interesting throughout as she becomes at the end, but "the moralist in Jane Austen stood for once in her way. The

secret engagement is, for her, so serious an offence, that she is afraid to win our hearts for Jane until it has led to great unhappiness" ("Jane Austen," in *Essays and Studies, by Members of the English Association,* II [Oxford, 1911], 23).

⁶ I know of only one full-scale attempt to deal with the "tension between sympathy and judgment" in modern literature, Robert Langbaum's *The Poetry of Experience* (London, 1957). Langbaum argues that in the dramatic monologue, with which he is primarily concerned, the sympathy engendered by the direct portrayal of internal experience leads the reader to suspend his moral judgment. Thus, in reading Browning's portraits of moral degeneration—e.g., the duke in "My Last Duchess" or the monk in "Soliloquy of a Spanish Cloister"— our moral judgment is overwhelmed "because we prefer to participate in the duke's power and freedom, in his hard core of character fiercely loyal to itself. Moral judgment is in fact important as the thing to be suspended, as a measure of the price we pay for the privilege of appreciating to the full this extraordinary man" (p. 83). While I think that Langbaum seriously underplays the extent to which moral judgment remains even after psychological vividness has done its work, and while he perhaps defines "morality" too narrowly when he excludes from it such things as power and freedom and fierce loyalty to one's own character, his book is a stimulating introduction to the problems raised by internal portraiture of flawed characters.

⁷ *Jane Austen and Her Art* (Oxford, 1939), p. 204.

⁸ It seems to be difficult for some modern critics, accustomed to ferreting values out from an impersonal or ironic context without the aid of the author's voice, to make use of

reliable commentary like this when it is provided. Even a highly perceptive reader like Mark Schorer, for example, finds himself doing unnecessary acrobatics with the question of style, and particularly metaphor, as clues to the norms against which the author judges her characters. In reading *Persuasion*, he finds these clues among the metaphors "from commerce and property, the counting house and the inherited estate" with which it abounds ("Fiction and the Matrix of Analogy," *Kenyon Review* [Autumn, 1949], p. 540). No one would deny that the novel is packed with such metaphors, although Schorer is somewhat over-ingenious in marshaling to his cause certain dead metaphors that Austen could not have avoided without awkward circumlocution (esp. p. 542). But the crucial question surely is: What precisely are these metaphors of the countinghouse doing in the novel? *Whose* values are they supposed to reveal? Accustomed to reading modern fiction in which the novelist very likely provides no direct assistance in answering this question, Schorer leaves it really unanswered; at times he seems almost to imply that Jane Austen is unconsciously giving herself away in her use of them (e.g., p. 543).

But the novel is really very clear about it all. The introduction, coming directly from the wholly reliable narrator, establishes unequivocally and without "analogy" the conflict between the world of the Elliots, depending for its values on selfishness, stupidity, and pride—and the world of Anne, a world where "elegance of mind and sweetness of character" are the supreme values. The commercial values stressed by Schorer are only a selection from what is actually a rich group of evils. And Anne's own expressed views again and again provide direct guidance to the reader.

[9] The first two quotations are from Wilson's "A Long Talk about Jane Austen," *A Literary Chronicle: 1920-1950* (New York, 1952). The third is from *Jane Austen*, p. 206.

[10] It has lately been fashionable to underplay the value of tenderness and good will in Jane Austen, in reaction to an earlier generation that overdid the picture of "gentle Jane." The trend seems to have begun in earnest with D. W. Harding's "Regulated Hatred: An Aspect of the Work of Jane Austen," *Scrutiny*, VIII (March, 1940), 346-62. While I do not feel as strongly aroused against this school of readers as does R. W. Chapman (see his *A Critical Bibliography*, p. 52, and his review of Mudrick's work in the *T.L.S.* [September 19, 1952]), it seems to me that another swing of the pendulum is called for: when Jane Austen praises the "relenting heart," she means that praise, though she is the same author who can lash the unrelenting heart with "regulated hatred."

[11] Edd Winfield Parks, "Exegesis in Austen's Novels," *The South Atlantic Quarterly*, LI (January, 1952), 117.

[12] *Novels and Novelists*, ed. J. Middleton Murry (London, 1930), p. 304.

Pastoral Poetry: The Vitality and Versatility of a Convention

Hallett Smith

The Elizabethan poet usually began, as Virgil had done, by writing pastoral poetry. And, since many poets begin and not all of them continue, the proportion of pastoral to the whole literary production of the Elizabethan period is fairly high. There have been many attempts to account for this prominence of the shepherd in the literature of an age of sea dogs and explorers, of courtiers and usurers, of magnificent Leicester, dashing Essex, and staid Burleigh.

One critic maintains that pastoral is always a vehicle for something else: "The pastoral, whatever its form, always needed and assumed some external circumstance to give point to its actual content. The interest seldom arises directly from the narrative itself."[1] Another commentator shakes his head over the whole pastoral tradition and seems to think that in the Elizabethan period it is merely a literary fad which got out of hand. "The exquisitely artificial convention of the pastoral poetry of the late sixteenth century and its stylized vocabulary, at times so dazzling and yet so often monotonous, gave little scope for original expression."[2] A more sensitive critic finds the reason for the popularity of pastoral in artistic considerations: "It was the peculiarly combined satisfaction of freedom and formalism which attracted so many Elizabethans to pastoral."[3] Probably the most commonly held view is that pastoral is merely escape literature, especially attractive at a time when populations are shifting, life is becoming more complex, and the townsman dreams nostalgically of life in the country.

It is certainly true that pastoral was a convention. Shepherds thronged in the entertainments for royalty, in the pageants and devices like those presented at Kenilworth in 1575 and in the royal entertainments of 1578. These shows are in part literature, and they had their influence on works which were more purely literature.[4] But to establish the occasion, and even the fashion, of a work of art is not to explain its significance. The more conventional it is, the more likely it is to have some central core of meaning from which individual treatments may originate. "Originality" cannot be estimated until we know what the convention meant to the writers working in it.

Whatever may be said of other times and places, Elizabethan England saw a meaning in pastoral. This meaning was, or constituted, a positive ideal. It was an ideal of the good life, of the state of content and mental self-sufficiency which had been known in classical antiquity as *otium*. The revival of this ideal is a characteristic Renaissance achievement; it would have been impossible in the Middle Ages, when time spent in neither work nor communion with God was felt to be sinful. By projecting this ideal, poets of the age of Shakespeare were able to criticize life as it is and portray it as it might be. Their shepherds are citizens of the same Arcadia as that inhabited by the shepherds of Milton and Matthew Arnold.

The Elizabethan mind took over its conception of pastoral from many sources. The most general and the most obvious of these sources was the Bible. In Genesis, the first great event after the fall of man is one which involves a shepherd; it is the story of Cain and Abel. What it meant to the Elizabethans is explained by Bacon:

> We see (as the Scriptures have infinite mysteries, not violating at all the truth of the story or letter), an image of the two estates, the contemplative state and the active state, figured in the two persons of Abel and Cain, and in the two simplest and most primitive trades of life; that of the shepherd, (who, by reason of his leisure, rest in a place, and living in view of heaven, is a lively image of a contemplative life,) and that of the husbandman: where we see again the favour and election of God went to the shepherd, and not to the tiller of the ground.[5]

Moreover, David, perhaps the most romantic figure in the Old Testament, was a shepherd, as well as being the principal poet and singer of songs among the ancient Hebrews. Of his psalms, the twenty-third was of course a special favorite. It reflected not only the atmosphere of green pastures but also the doctrine of content as the greatest of God's blessings. "The Lord is my shepherd; I shall not want" was explained by the preachers as a pastoral metaphor expressing the truth of Christian content.[6]

In the New Testament there is the central pastoral imagery of Christ the Good Shepherd, and of course the episode of the shepherds hearing from heaven the good tidings of Christ's birth. As Michael Drayton wrote, "In the Angels Song to Shepheards at our Saviours Nativitie Pastorall Poesie seemes consecrated."[7]

Characteristically, the Renaissance mixed examples of the shepherd from Greek and Roman tradition and history with those from the Bible. In Mantuan's seventh eclogue, Moses and Apollo are mentioned in pastoral roles.[8] Paris, the son of Priam, King of Troy, was the most famous of all classical shepherds because from his actions sprang the whole epic narrative of the siege of Troy. Besides Paris, James Sandford's translation of Cornelius Agrippa (1569) cites Romulus and Remus, Anchises, and the emperor Diocletian as shepherds. Thomas Fortescue's translation from Pedro Mexía, *The Foreste* (1586), adds Galerius and Tamburlaine. A shepherd in Drayton's "Dowsabell," is described as resembling Tamburlaine in looks and Abel in temper.[9]

The Elizabethan attitude toward Paris reveals much of the meaning and significance of pastoral in the poetry of the age. The story of Paris is of course one of the great stories: how a king's son, living as a shepherd, is in love with the nymph Oenone; how he is chosen to be umpire among the three goddesses, Juno, Venus, and Pallas Athena, to decide which of them deserves the golden apple inscribed "For the fairest"; how he decides in favor of Venus and is given as a reward the love of the most beautiful of women, Helen; how he deserts Oenone, brings Helen to Troy, and precipitates the Trojan War with all of its consequences—this plot is surely one of the great achievements of the Western imagination.

Dramatic treatments of the story of Paris are mentioned by Saint Augustine;[10] the subject is inherently dramatic, both for the power of the rival claims of the goddesses and for the world-shaking consequences of Paris' choice. The death of Hector and Achilles, the destruction of Troy, the wanderings of Ulysses and of Aeneas, the founding of Rome (and of Britain, too, as the Elizabethans thought), all resulted from this one simple decision by a shepherd on the hills of Ida.

Purely as plot, then, the story of the shepherd's choice had color and vitality. But it was also symbolic, and an understanding of what was represented to the Elizabethan mind by the offers of Juno, Pallas, and Venus while Paris was trying to make up his mind is essential to an appreciation of poetic treatments of the myth. From classical times on down, the principal myths had been interpreted morally, if not allegorically, and the Judgment of Paris was one which lent itself to such treatment in a very natural way. Athenaeus says, in the *Deipnosophistae,*

"And I for one affirm also that the Judgment of Paris, as told in poetry by the writers of an older time, is really a trial of pleasure against virtue. Aphrodite, for example—and she represents pleasure—was given the preference, and so everything was thrown into turmoil."[11]

Fulgentius, Bishop of Carthage, also moralized the myth of the Judgment of Paris. The three goddesses, he says, represent the three ways of life: the active, the contemplative, and the voluptuous. Jove himself, continues Fulgentius, could not make judgment among the three contending goddesses or the ways of life they represent; it is essentially a human dilemma. A shepherd, in Fulgentius' opinion, is the most suitable of all men to be the judge, though of course, according to the bishop, Paris made a foolish choice. Spenser agrees, and in the July eclogue of *The Shepheardes Calender* goes out of his way to condemn Paris:

> For he was proude, that ill was payd,
> (no such mought shepheards bee)
> And with lewde lust was ouerlayd:
> tway things doen ill agree.[12]

To the Renaissance, Paris' mistake was intended as a powerful warning. Italian treatises on nobility considered the Judgment of Paris story to represent the choice which must actually be made by the young man deciding upon a course of life.[13]

In the most popular of the pastoral romances, the Judgment of Paris is a subject for debate; in Montemayor's *Diana*, for example, Delia and Andronius spend the greater part of a night in arguing the question whether Paris gave the apple to the right goddess or not and whether the inscription on it referred to physical or mental beauty.[14] The shepherds and shepherdesses in Elizabethan pastoral poetry often allude to the Paris story or compare themselves with figures in it. An example is from "Phillidaes Loue-Call to her Coridon, and his replying," by "Ignoto" in *England's Helicon;*[15] another is Willye's compliment to Cuddie, the umpire of the singing match in Spenser's August eclogue:

> Neuer dempt more right of beautye I weene,
> The shepherd of Ida, that iudged beauties Queene.[16]

Drayton's Rowland, on the other hand, compares himself to the deserted Oenone.[17]

Whatever the faults of Paris' decision, the son of Priam remained, for the Elizabethan, the archetype of the shepherd. Spenser's Sir Calidore, when he takes off his armor and puts on shepherd's weeds in order to woo Pastorella, suggests the obvious model, "Phrygian Paris by Plexippus brooke."[18]

The Judgment of Paris had of course been treated in medieval love allegories such as Froissart's *L'Espinette Amoureuse,* Machaut's *Le Dit de la Fontaine Amoureuse,* and Lydgate's *Reson and Sensuallyte;* there had been continental dramas on the subject in the fifteenth and early sixteenth centuries; and most important of all for the English pastoral, the Paris story was a common subject of the pageants—for Queen Margaret at Edinburgh in 1503, for the coronation of Anne Boleyn in 1533, and at a marriage masque in 1566.[19] It also appeared in the emblem-books. In Whitney's *Choice of Emblemes* the account of the Judgment is much abbreviated, but full justice is done to the interpretation.[20]

It is obvious, then, that the major Elizabethan treatment of the Paris story, George Peele's play *The Arraignment of Paris* (1584), is in a well-established tradition. It is in dramatic form, but it is so important as an indication of the significance of pastoral in the Elizabethan mind that it must be discussed briefly here.

In the temptation scene, when the three goddesses in turn offer their rewards to Paris, they are more abstract than personal. Juno offers the shepherd "great monarchies, Empires, and kingdomes, heapes of massye golde, scepters and diadems," symbolized theatrically by the appearance of a golden tree, the fruit of which is diadems. Pallas offers fame, wisdom, honor of chivalry and victory, "but yf thou haue a minde to fly aboue." The reward is symbolized by nine knights in armor treading a warlike Almain. Venus offers Paris the services of Cupid, kisses from herself, and finally (here the reward and the symbol become the same thing) Helen.[21] Paris is constantly a symbolic figure; he is suggestive. I do not mean that the artist had nothing to do with this suggestiveness and that the audience could be counted upon to do it all. A sixteenth-century Italian treatise on painting makes clear the artist's obligation in the matter and uses Paris as an example:

> Hence then the painter may learne how to expresse not onely the proper and naturall motions, but also the accidentall; wherein consisteth no small part of the difficulty of the Arte, namelie in representing diversities of affections and passions in one bodie: A thing much practized, by the ancient Painters (though with greate difficulty) who ever indevored to leaue no iotte of the *life* vnexpressed.

> It is recorded that *Euphranor* gaue such a touch to the counterfeit of *Paris,* that therein the beholder might at once collect, that

hee was *Vmpire* of the three *Goddesses,* the *Courter of Helena,* and the slaier of *Achilles.*[22]

But Paris, with the alternatives clearly before him, chooses Venus. When he defends himself before the court of the gods, in Peele's play, he speaks first as a man, blaming his fault, if any, on the judgment of his eye. Then he adds a *reason:* that it was only for beauty he gave the ball, and if other virtues had been concerned he would have chosen Pallas or Juno. Furthermore, he says, he was tempted more than man ever was, and as a shepherd he was relatively immune to offers other than that of Venus.[23] The simplicity of the shepherd's conditions makes for an invulnerability to appeals in the name of wealth or of chivalry. It is only beauty, of the three ideals represented by the goddesses, which has any significant power in a pastoral life.

Paris is the judge precisely because the conditions of the pastoral life provide the greatest independence, the greatest security. The shepherd is not motivated by ambition or by greed. Free from these two common human passions, he enjoys "content," or the good life. Elizabethan pastoral poetry is essentially a celebration of this ideal of content, of *otium.* The comtemplative state enjoyed a freedom, not only from ambition or greed, but from the vicissitudes of fortune. The popular tradition of the fall of princes, represented in Elizabethan literature by the *Mirror for Magistrates* and the poems added to it, had stressed ominously the dangers in the turn of Fortune's wheel. Kings and princes, the high and mighty, were exhibited in tragic circumstances, the victims of their own high position, their ambition, or their greed. The poetic tragedies of the *Mirror* therefore supported, negatively, the same ideal celebrated by pastoral. Occasionally the warning in a *Mirror* tragedy concludes with a direct endorsement of the quiet life of content. In one of the tragedies in Blenerhasset's *Mirror,* for example, the herdsman who kills Sigebert and is hanged for it concludes with the lesson:

> And happy he, who voyde of hope can leade
> A quiet lyfe, all voyde of Fortunes dread.

This makes the following Induction deal with the question of why it is that formerly the wisest men were content to be shepherds, but now "in these our dayes, non bee Heardmen but fooles, and euery man though his witte be but meane, yet he cannot liue with a contented mind, except he hath the degree of a Lorde."[24]

In order to respond adequately to the appeal of the Elizabethan ideal of the mean estate, content, and *otium,* it is necessary to feel the force of its opposite, a form of ambition which the sixteenth century called most commonly the aspiring mind. Marlowe's Tamburlaine is of course the great representative of the aspiring mind, as he is its philosopher:

> Nature that fram'd vs of foure Elements,
> Warring within our breasts for regiment,
> Doth teach vs all to haue aspyring minds.[25]

But there are many other examples of the concept in Elizabeth England. Mr. Secretary Walsingham, summing up the personal charges against Mary Queen of Scots, said that she had an aspiring mind;[26] and Queen Elizabeth herself, writing a poem about Mary, included the line

> But clowds of tois vntried, do cloake aspiring mindes.[27]

Blue, as the color of the sky, was symbolic of the aspiring mind, according to Lomazzo:

> Persius sat. 1. speaking of Blew garments, sheweth that they belong only to such persons, as aspire vnto high matter: and Cicero vsed sometimes to weare this color, giuing men thereby to vnderstand, that he bare an aspiring minde.[28]

There were many other Roman examples of the aspiring mind; a typical one is Pompey.[29] That the aspiring mind was a dangerous and possibly sinful state is made clear by Du Bartas, who contrasts it to the attitude of the angels.[30] The first example of the aspiring mind, according to Du Bartas, was in the hunter, Nimrod, "that was the first Tyrant of the world, after the time of Noah, the first Admiral of the worlde: his aspiring minde & practises in seeking the peoples fauour, his proud and subtle attempt in building the Tower of Babel, & Gods iust punishment thereof in confounding the language of the builders."[31]

The central meaning of pastoral is the rejection of the aspiring mind. The shepherd demonstrates that true content is to be found in this renunciation. Sidney expresses the preference in terms of a contrast between pastoral and court life:

> Greater was that shepheards treasure,
> Then this false, fine, Courtly pleasure.[32]

In the pastoral episode in Book VI of *The Faerie Queene*, Sir Calidore envies the apparent happiness of the shepherds; he comments that their life seems free from the "warres, and wreckes, and wicked enmitie" which afflict the rest of the world.[33] In reply to this, the sage old Meliboee then answers with an analysis of the pastoral existence which is in effect a definition of "the good life." It consists of four elements: (1) being content with what you have, however small it is—this is the way taught by nature (contrast Tamburlaine's statement that nature teaches us to have aspiring minds); (2) enjoying freedom from envy of others and from excessive care for your own possessions (the flocks multiply without your doing much about it); (3) avoiding the dangers of pride and ambition and also the insomnia that plagues those who hold positions of responsibility (see the testimony of Shakespeare's kings in 2 Henry IV, III, i, 1-31, and IV, v, 20-27; Henry V, IV, i, 266-290); (4) doing what you like. Old Meliboee does not speak from provincial ignorance, either. He once spent ten years at court, but returned to the pastoral life from choice.

The question of the moral validity of pastoral life when compared with life at court is not difficult to answer: the long tradition of dispraise of the court is always, by implication or by direct statement, an endorsement of the pastoral life. But there is a more difficult question when the alternatives are the quiet, retired life of the shepherd on the one hand or a mission of chivalric and honorable achievement on the other. The pastoral romance, both in Sidney and in his sources like Montemayor's Diana, mingles pastoral and heroic elements. The question of the relative value of the two kinds of life is naturally raised. The pastoral sojourn of Erminia in the seventh book of Tasso's Jerusalem Delivered is used as a contrast to the heroic actions of the main part of the poem. It is also obvious that pastoral and heroic put a different light upon the feelings of love; these might or might not be a detriment to the heroic life, but they are sanctioned in the world of pastoral.

The commentators on the sixth book of Spenser's Faerie Queene have been at odds over the meaning of the pastoral interlude there, the Pastorella episode. T. P. Harrison says, "Spenser obviously censures Sir Calidore's pastoral aberration; yet he, like Sidney, is inclined to paint the rural picture sympathetically."[34] The opposite view is expressed by C. S. Lewis:

> The greatest mistake that can be made about this book is to suppose that Calidore's long delay among the shepherds is a pastoral truancy from Spenser's moral intention . . . Courtesy, for the poet, has very little connection with court. It grows "on a lowly stalke"; . . . according to Spenser, courtesy, in its perfect form, comes by nature; moral effort may produce a decent substitute for everyday use, which deserves praise, but it will never rival the real courtesy of those who

> so goodly gracious are by kind
> That every action doth them much commend.[35]

Lewis is certainly right about Spenser's endorsement of the pastoral life, or his justification of Sir Calidore, for the opening stanzas of Canto x make it clear.[36] Spenser's own words do not, however, support conclusively the suggestion that courtesy is wholly natural. When in the beginning of Canto XII the poet makes a kind of apology for the wandering structure of the narrative, he is careful to defend the idea behind it.[37] The pastoral environment is a further test and demonstration of Sir Calidore's courtesy, but it is not its source. Calidore treats his shepherd rival, Coridon, with great generosity and magnanimity.[38] The pastoral ideal, then, is reconcilable somehow with the code of chivalry and honor, even though its emphasis is different. As the climax and goal of a life of heroic effort there is a state of heavenly contemplation not too different from the state of mind of the pastoral ideal. But this state may be reached only after the knightly quest is achieved as we see in the tenth canto of Spenser's Book I.

Closer to pastoral is the Horatian praise of the country gentleman's life, of which there are many examples in Elizabethan poetry. Wyatt's first satire, a translation of Alamanni, and Thomas Lodge's "In Praise of the Countery Life," a translation of Desportes, are typical. This type of poetry, like pastoral, proclaims the moral and emotional advantages of the country over the court. Lodge, for example, sings:

> Amidst the pallace braue puft vp with wanton showes
> Ambicions dwell, and there false fauors finde disguise,
> There lodge consuming cares that hatch our common woes:
> Amidst our painted feelds the pleasant Fayrie lies,
>   And all those powers diuine that with vntrussed tresses,
>   Contentment, happie loue, and perfect sport professes.[39]

This kind of thing moves in the direction of satire, and it will be considered again later in connection with the other elements of satire in the pastoral.

The theme of the Golden Age is one of the great commonplaces of Elizabethan literature.[40] The creation of an Arcadia which is primitive and pastoral, which may be identified with the early period before the birth of Jupiter, and which finally is a country located not so much in central Greece as in some Utopian space, is a result of the work of Polybius, Ovid, and Virgil.[41] There are many sources in antiquity for the theme; it was especially popular among the Stoics, and it was congenial to Stoic thought because it explained the Law of Nature as a survival from the Golden Age.[42] Accordingly, the best example of it may be chosen from Seneca:

> 'Twas in such wise, methinks, they lived whom the primal age produced, in friendly intercourse with gods. They had no blind love of gold; no sacred boundary-stone, judging betwixt peoples, separated fields on the spreading plain; not yet did rash vessels plough the sea; each man knew only his native waters.[43]

Spenser in the Proem to Book V of *The Faerie Queene* follows the convention of idealizing the Golden Age,[44] even though his friend Harvey was of the newer school of Jean Bodin, which thought that the earliest periods of history were the worst and that something like progress had taken place.

The first information given the audience about the pastoral atmosphere in Shakespeare's *As You Like It* compares pastoral life to the Golden Age; the wrestler Charles, informing Oliver, and at the same time the audience, of the circumstances of the banished Duke, says:

> They say he is already in the Forest of Arden, and a many merry men with him; and there they live like the old Robin Hood of England; they say many young gentlemen flock to him every day, and fleet the time carelessly, as they did in the golden world.[45]

The identification of the pastoral life with the conditions of the Golden Age was natural enough. One was a criticism of life by means of adopting the point of view of its simplest and purest elements; the other was a criticism of the present way of life by describing an ideal past.

It is also true that pastoral was considered the earliest form of poetry and would therefore be the natural expression of the earliest blissful age.[46] Not all English opinion agreed with this conventional account, however. George Puttenham, bearing in mind the humanistic use of eclogues for satire, considers that the form cannot be primitive.[47] He insists that the eclogue is a sophisticated form, but he concedes that the pastoral lyric does come down from "the first idle wooings," "the first amorous musicks." The Golden Age, associated with pastoral as we have seen, was supposed to have been an age of free love.[48] It is so celebrated in a song from Tasso's *Aminta* which Samuel Daniel translated under the title "A Pastorall."[49] And since the shepherd is insensitive to the claims of power and wealth, as Paris was, it is sometimes emphasized in pastoral that his susceptibility to love is a cruel bondage. As Montemayor puts it:

The shepherd busied not his thoughts in the consideration of the prosperous and preposterous successe of fortune, nor in the mutabilitie and course of times, neither did the painfull diligence and aspiring minde of the ambitious Courtier trouble his quiet rest: nor the presumption and coye disdaine of the proude and nice Ladie (celebrated onely by the appassionate vowes and opinions of her amorous sutours) once occur to his imaginations. And as little did the swelling pride, and small care of the hawtie priuate man offend his quiet minde. In the field was he borne, bred and brought vp: in the field he fed his flockes, and so out of the limits of the field his thoughts did neuer range, vntill cruell loue tooke possession of his libertie, which to those he is commonly woont to doe, who thinke themselues freest from his tyrannie.[50]

Love in a pastoral environment is first exploited in the second-century Greek romance *Daphnis and Chloe,* written by someone whose name was perhaps Longus. It is the only one of the Greek romances which is pastoral in character, and it is the great forerunner of the Renaissance pastoral romances—those of Sannazarro, Montemayor, and their many imitators. It plays with the adventures in love of two perfectly simple and naïve pastoral people; their innocence of sex along with their captivation by it is presented with amused sophistication by the author for an equally sophisticated reader. S. L. Wolff well describes the peculiar salacious quality of the romance: "Longus with all his art did not—or rather did not try!—to take his emphasis off the teasing succession of Daphnis and Chloe's attempts, and place it wholly or even preponderantly upon their idyllic simplicity, their idyllic environment. *They* are simple enough, but *we* are not; and Longus knows it."[51]

There was an Elizabethan translation of *Daphnis and Chloe,* by Angel Day from the French of Jacques Amyot, in 1587. Day's version does not include the more salacious parts of the Greek romance, substituting instead pastoral lyrics and inserting a pastoral praise of Queen Elizabeth under the title "The Shepheardes Holidaye." Day's language is often colloquial and vivid, especially in descriptive scenes, but his tone is softened and sobered; the conscious absurdity and the conscious aphrodisiac quality of the original are quite lacking.[52] The great translation of *Daphnis and Chloe* into English is not Day's but that of George Thornley in the mid-seventeenth century.

The innocent and naïve, but pagan, lover immediately calls to mind such figures as Shakespeare's Adonis and Marlowe's Hero and Leander. Marlowe especially may have been influenced by Longus, but the significant point here is that pastoral is touching the boundary of still another literary genre, that of Ovidian-mythological poetry. In the Ovidian tradition sexuality was of course an important element, and the shepherds of pastoral, if made creatures of myth (and Paris could be treated as a mythology or pastoral) became suitable subjects for the Ovidian love poem.

The general tendency of English pastoral literature was to subdue the sexual element and make the love scenes romantic and innocent. The innocence of rustic lovers is not exploited for the superior feeling of more worldly readers; what humor there is develops from gentle satire of rude and boorish characters. A conventional comic device is the detailed description of a costume which is inappropriate or absurd.[53] The love is generally idyllic, lending itself to lyrical treatment, fitting in with the idealized setting, timeless and remote.

The element of love in pastoral romance works in two directions—toward lyric simplicity, as I have said, and toward plot complication. The events of pastoral plot usually come from outside and are not the result of the lovers' characters. Brigands, unscrupulous rivals, uncoöperative parents all provide motion and direction for the plot. The oracle, the exposed child, the changeling motif supply a frame for the beginning and conclusion of the story. Essentially, however, there is nothing complex about the course of love itself in the pastoral plot. Fortune and villains provide the difficulties; they do not lie in the nature of love itself. Love expressed as emotion (rather than as plot) is simple and lyric; love used as plot entanglement (not as feeling) is involved and complicated.

Pastoral emphasizes the irrationality of love. That is, it agrees with the general Elizabethan view. Lovers are subject to the whims of fortune (although Fortune is kinder in Arcadia than elsewhere), but there is no blame imputed to anyone for falling in love. It is irrational but unavoidable. The lyric, then, accepts the fate of love but complains at its sorrows just as it rejoices at its pleasures. "Since that in love there is no sound/ Of any reason to be found" is a basic assumption.[54]

Love is simple in essence, but the variety and complexity of its consequences make for a total paradox. Though there is no jot of reason in love, the lover invariably reasons about it. Pastoral provides amply for this paradox. It utilizes for the purpose various devices which taken out of their context seem absurd. The most common perhaps is the "cross-eyed Cupid" situation, in which A loves B, B loves C, C loves D, and D loves A. It is used in Montemayor,[55] and of course it is a device in Lodge's *Rosalynde* and Shakespeare's *As You Like It*, as well as in the woodland part of *A Midsummer Night's Dream*. The paradox is that love itself is so simple; the lyric and plot elements of pastoral romance work together to enforce the contrast between simplicity and complexity.

Another aspect of pastoral love is the contrast between the direct, personal, subjective expression of the feeling and the same feeling seen in some other way, reflected, as in a mirror. In Book XI of the *Diana* Syrenus hears three nymphs singing his own farewell song to Diana—a song which one of them got from a shepherd who heard it long ago and memorized it. A similar effect is produced by having a pastoral lover hang his poems on trees, to be read or recited by others, sometimes in his hearing. There is an absence of self-consciousness in both these devices which makes the paradoxical effect possible. The naïveté of the whole pastoral convention is being utilized.

The ancestry of much pastoral poetry has something to do with its quality. The primitive song-and-dance games of the countryside, which often kept the color of their native surroundings, were in large part wooing ceremonies or complaints of the rejected lover who wore willow at the wedding and was expected to display his sorrows to heighten the merriment of the occasion. There were also celebrations of the beauty of the shepherdess who was crowned queen of the May. These popular customs were beginning to die out in Elizabethan times, or rather to be relegated to the use of children. But the courtly vogue, picking them up, made of them something both sophisticated and naïve. There is an awareness on the part of the Elizabethan poet of pastoral that he is exploiting a quality which works in two ways.[56]

This combination of "distance" and familiarity, of formalism and freedom, gives the Elizabethan love lyric and the song of good life their characteristic tone. Their "Elizabethanness," that quality which makes them popular in the anthologies, which permits enjoyment of them without any concern for the authorship, derives from this suspension.

If we turn to the greatest storehouse of Elizabethan pastoral lyric, the anthology published in 1600 called *England's Helicon*,[57] we may examine the concrete results of the fashion. The compiler of this anthology had under survey the whole body of Elizabethan literature, from *Tottel's Miscellany* on down to the end of the century. He selected poems from translated pastoral romances (Montemayor's *Diana* translated by Bartholomew Yong), from original romances in English (Sidney's *Arcadia*, Greene's *Menaphon*, and Lodge's *Rosalynde*), from the songbooks of Byrd and Morley and Dowland, from plays, from other anthologies (*The Passionate Pilgrim*, 1599), and from manuscripts. His volume has remained popular from 1600 to the present time, and his modern editor says it would be hard for anyone to compile a better anthology of the period without lavish use of Shakespeare and Jonson.[58]

I shall consider the poems in the volume under several headings, without suggesting that these headings constitute rigid "types" or kinds. For purposes of clarity it is easier to talk about pastoral lyrics as complaints, invitations, palinodes, love dialogues, blazons, and dance songs than to group them all together.

More of the poems in *England's Helicon* are complaints than any other kind. Most commonly the shepherd himself is the speaker, although sometimes the complaint is "framed" within the poem as something overheard by the speaker. This latter is an old medieval device, familiar in such poems as Chaucer's *Book of the Duchesse*. The cause of the shepherd's complaint is of course always unrequited love, or a mistress who has proved fickle, and his sorrow is almost always reflected in the change made not only upon himself but also upon his flocks, his dog, upon nature itself. No. 35 (which had already appeared in Weelkes' *Madrigals*, 1957, and *The Passionate Pilgrim*, 1599) begins:

> My Flocks feede not, my Ewes breede not,
> My Rammes speede not, all is amisse:
> Loue is denying, Faith is defying,
> Harts renying, causer of this.[59]

This kind of complaint serves, of course, as a description of the values in pastoral life by bewailing their loss. The emphasis is not so much sentimental, in that sympathy is asked for the lovelorn shepherd, as it is pictorial, in which the "merry jigs," the clear wells, and the happy herds are thrown into strong relief by having their basic attributes reversed.

Quite frequently some object of comparison is found, so that the rhetorical expression of the shepherd's grief can be saved for a climax. This principle of economy is apparent in a fine lyric by Thomas Lodge:

> A Turtle sate vpon a leauelesse tree,
> Mourning her absent pheare,
> With sad and sorrie cheare.[60]

The contrast of bitter and sweet is the complaining shepherd's constant theme; sometimes it is expressed more lavishly, as by Lodge in a poem which he himself described as Italianate in manner.[61]

Sometimes the shepherd's complaint takes the form of a narrative and is elaborated in such a way as to make the effect of a pageant or little drama. In this case the pastoral element is likely to be mere stage setting for the central situation, which derives from medieval allegory or Anacreontic cupid-lore. A good example is No. 126 in *England's Helicon,* by Michael Drayton.[62]

Fifteen of the poems in this pastoral anthology are by Sidney; all are taken from the 1598 folio volume containing the *Arcadia, Astrophel and Stella,* and miscellaneous poems. Actually, fewer than half of the Sidney poems in the *Helicon* are pastoral when taken out of context, but Sidney's name gave prestige to the volume and he was thought of as a writer who had lent seriousness and dignity to the pastoral mode. Thomas Wilson, for example, confessed to a certain embarrassment about his translation of Montemayor's *Diana:* "Soe it may bee said of mee that I shewe my vanitie enough in this litle, that after 15 yeares painfully spent in Vniversitie studies, I shold bestow soe many ydle howres, in transplanting vaine amorous conceipts out of an Exotique language." But his justification was that however vain and frivolous the *Diana* seem, Sir Philip Sidney "did very much affect and imitate the excellent Author there of."[63]

The best known of Sidney's poems in the volume is "Ring out your belles, let mourning shewes be spread," a more elaborate and subtle poem than Drayton's "Antheme" and of the same type; but there is nothing specifically pastoral about the poem. Sidney's characteristic touch and his skill in conveying a mood by indirection are best exemplified in No. 5, called "Astrophell the Sheep-heard, his complaint to his flocke." It begins in the usual mood of the forlorn shepherd, telling his merry flocks to go elsewhere to feed so they may have some defense from the storms in his breast and the showers from his eyes. The poet leaves us uncertain how to interpret this extravagant feeling until the shepherd states to the sheep the extent of his love, in terms the sheep could understand:

> Stella, hath refused me,
>   Stella, who more loue hath proued
> In this caitiffe hart to be,
>   Then can in good eawes be moued
>   Towards Lambkins best beloued.[64]

Sidney is pushing homely pathos to the point at which it is felt as humor also, and the comic tone is underlined two stanzas later:

> Is that loue? Forsooth I trow,
>   if I saw my good dogge greeued:
> And a helpe for him did know,
>   my loue should not be beleeued:
>   but he were by me releeued.

Finally, at the conclusion, the identification of the shepherd's emotions with his pastoral environment, a stock feature of the mode, is used for comic purposes. The complaints of the shepherd-lover are whimsically identified with the bleatings of his sheep.

Parody is not the most difficult art. The "distance" between pastoral and reality (which Panofsky says is intimately connected with that other Renaissance invention, perspective) can easily be foreshortened or flattened out so as to make a fantastic effect. But it is not so easy to make the pathetic and absurd felt at once, as partners in the result. This Sidney was able to do. As Theodore Spencer accurately expresses it, "The pastoral setting, the traditional tone of lament, the rigorous form of the verse have been revitalized not merely by Sidney's superb technique, but by the fact that he has put into them something more than the purely conventional emotion."[65]

The other kind of pastoral complaint besides that of the rejected shepherd is of course that of the betrayed or abandoned shepherdess. She is the Oenone of the Judgment of Paris story. In *England's Helicon* Oenone's complaint from Peele's *Arraignment* is No. 149, the next to the last poem in the book. There are half a dozen other nymph's complaints in the volume, of which the most interesting are Selvagia's song from the *Diana*, as translated by Bartholomew Yong (No. 103), with its graceful return at the end to the chorus of the beginning,

> It is not to liue so long,
> as it is too short to weepe,

and No. 118, "Lycoris the Nimph, her sad Song," from Thomas Morley's *Madrigals to Four Voices* (1594).[66] The varied line length of the second poem and the feminine rhymes suggest the fragility of the nymph and the insecurity she feels. And the poem progresses very prettily from idyllic description to rhetorical exclamation to the final taunt and pout, conveyed by the strikingly simple and direct language of the last two lines. Its sudden transitions of mood are characteristic of the poem-for-music.

Some half dozen of the poems in *England's Helicon* are invitations, a few of them the most attractive and famous poems in the volume. At its best, the invitation poem is simple in language and in versification, preferring short lines and a direct rhetoric. The strategy of the shepherd is to call attention to the beauty and innocence of the pastoral setting and to use these qualities as arguments naturally reinforcing his simple desires:

> Faire Loue rest thee heere,
> Neuer yet was morne so cleere,

> Sweete be not vnkinde,
> Let me thy fauour finde,
> Or else for loue I die.

This (No. 74) is Drayton, who well understands the Elizabethan art of securing a beauty and simplicity which seems almost impersonal. Passion and thought are carefully strained out; the poem must be self-contained and must cast no oblique lights. The humorous and the sentimental attributes of the complaint are entirely lacking. The *aubade* and the May-morning song are cousins to it, but the clearest and simplest form for this state of mind is the pastoral lyric of invitation.

> Come away, come sweet Loue,
> The golden morning breakes:
> All the earth, all the ayre,
> Of loue and pleasure speaks.

This is an anonymous poem, taken from Dowland's *First Booke of Songes or Ayres* (1597). I have cited these two poems of invitation to show that the most famous of them, Marlowe's "The passionate Sheepheard to his loue" (No. 137), is not alone in its class, even though it is superior to all of its kind.[67] The greatness of Marlowe's poem consists in the completeness of his pastoral picture and its total identification with the state of mind which the pastoral lyric of invitation is intended to induce. It includes gowns, shoes, beds of roses, cap, kirtle, slippers, and belt, all rural and simple, but rich and fine; more significantly it includes the entertainments fit for the contented mind: to see the shepherds feed their flocks, to listen to the music of the shallow rivers, and best of all to watch the shepherd swains dancing and singing. These are delights to move *the mind* (as the last stanza in the *Helicon* version specifies), and there is of course no ground for refusal to this invitation—except the one given in the answer ascribed to Ralegh, that the pastoral picture assumes a youthful, single-hearted, timeless world; deny this premise and you destroy the force of the whole thing. Just so, in Spenser's garden of Adonis, there is no disturbing element but Time:

> But were it not, that Time their troubler is,
> All that in this delightfull gardin growes
> Should happy bee, and have immortall blis:
> For here all plenty and all pleasure flowes,
> And sweete Love gentle fitts emongst them throwes,
> Without fell rancor or fond gealosy:
> Franckly each paramor his leman knowes,

Each bird his mate, ne any does envy
Their goodly meriment and gay felicity.[68]

The extreme popularity of Marlowe's poem caused many parodies and imitations of it, one of which is given in the *Helicon* as No. 139; to some extent these parodies show that the original poem ceased to be felt as a pastoral invitation. Modern criticism can more readily approach the famous poem from the point of view of its contemporaries if it takes into account the whole pastoral mode and the special nature of the lyric of invitation.

The palinode, a song in rejection of love, is represented in *England's Helicon* by a few examples. One of them, No. 54, is a definition of love put in such terms as to warn the inexperienced away from it. The poem is an example of those which were not originally pastoral but were doctored by the editor of *England's Helicon* to make them fit the pastoral character of his anthology. Lifting it from *The Phoenix Nest* (1593), the editor added speech tags for two shepherds, Melibeus and Faustus, and substituted phrases like "Sheepheard, what's" for "Now what" and "good Sheepheard" for "I praie thee." A better example of the rejection of love is the well-known ballet of William Byrd, "Though Amarillis daunce in greene" (No. 110). It has a pastoral and rustic atmosphere, since the chorus to each stanza is the humorously resigned exclamation, "Hey hoe, chill loue no more," and the second stanza begins "My Sheepe are lost for want of foode." It is interesting that there is so little of the rejection of love in the anthology. Perhaps a reason is that in the pastoral romances no shepherd ever cures himself of love by philosophy; it can be done only by magic or a drug. Therefore there is no tradition within this mode of a rejection of love, as there is in others. The Ovidian *remedia amoris* or the Platonic "Leave me, O love, which reachest but to dust" has no place in pastoral.[69]

The "blazon," or catalogue of the lady's beauties, is in style if not in origin a pastoral adaptation of one of the main conventions of the Petrarchan sonnet. As such it is subject to the same limitations as those felt by the sonneteers, but perhaps pastoral praise exhausts itself sooner because the comparisons must be those which are possible for a shepherd. Further the naïve quality of the shepherd does not fit with his being an accomplished fine courtier (unless there is allegory, of course; I am here dealing only with the lyric); wit and ingenuity are out of place among sheep-flocks, as Shakespeare points out in *As You Like It*. Accordingly, we get blazons which are effective because of their subdued tone and restraint; they are likely to be plaintive, as for example the one by J. Wotton in *England's Helicon,* No. 41.

The finest and most elaborate blazon in all English pastoral poetry is of course Spenser's praise of Queen Elizabeth in the April eclogue of *The Shepheardes Calendar,* which is printed in *England's Helicon* as No. 6. The comment on this poem has mostly concerned itself with the flattery of royalty and with the versification. Considered purely as a blazon, however, its structure and proportion are very impressive. The style itself is first established, as a "siluer song," and the Muses are invoked for aid. Then comes the justification for the heightened praise: that the lady is "of heauenly race" and therefore without mortal blemish. Within this framework, she is first presented as a picture;[70] the following stanza forms a bridge from her physical beauty to her "heauenly hauiour, her Princely Grace," and this makes possible the association with her of the sun and the moon in the two succeeding stanzas. The summary of this part is the line "Shee is my Goddesse plaine," and we are brought back to the lowly pastoral atmosphere by the shepherd's promise to offer her a milk-white lamb when the lambing season comes. The musical glorification of Eliza then follows, with the Muses trooping to her and playing their instruments, while the Graces (she herself making the fourth) dance and sing. The Ladies of the Lake then come to crown her with olive branches symbolizing peace, and this leads to the lovely flower stanza in which the Queen is again associated with the beauties of earth. As such she is to be attended by the "Sheepheards daughters that dwell on the greene," and we have the pastoral atmosphere reaffirmed. Finally, the attendant maidens are dismissed, with the quaint promise by the shepherd of some plums if they will return when he gathers them.

The most remarkable quality of the poem considered as a pastoral blazon is the firm and sure control the poet exercises over his transitions and the harmonious blending of many motifs. Classic myth, abstract divine qualities, the reality of earth, music, and color—all are here. The poem has an organic motion, wavelike, easy, and natural. Its stability comes from its pastoral inspiration and method.

The gayest pastoral lyrics are the roundelays, jigs, and dance songs, of which *England's Helicon* exhibits a half dozen examples. Spenser is again represented as the most expert maker of this type of poem, thanks to the fact that the editor did not pick up the "Cupid's Curse" roundelay when he was going through Peele's *Arraignment of Paris.* The roundelay from the August eclogue of *The Shepheardes Calendar* is No. 11 in *England's Helicon.* It seems probable that Spenser's poem was written to an already existing tune, "Heigh ho Holiday."[71] Either because of the popularity of the old tune or the success of Spenser's poem, there are several imitations, two of them in the *Helicon*: No. 81 from Lodge's *Rosalynde*, "A Blithe and bonny Country-Lasse," and No. 125 by H. C., "Fie on the sleights that men deuise"[72] These poems were to be sung by two singers, alternating; the editor of *England's Helicon* has removed the speech-tags and has left the indication of how the songs were sung only in the heading to No. 125: "two Nimphes, each aunswering other line for line."

Two shepherds' jigs, "Damaetas Iigge" by John Wotton (No. 28) and "The Sheepheard Dorons Iigge" from Greene's *Menaphon* (1589; No. 32), have the same carefree spirit. The characteristic feeling is that of Wotton's first stanza:

> Iolly Sheepheard, Sheepheard on a hill
> on a hill so merrily,
> on a hill so cherily,
> Feare not Sheepheard there to pipe thy fill,
> Fill euery Dale, fill euery Plaine:
> both sing and say; Loue feeles no paine.

This atmosphere of merriment and naïveté distinguishes some of the *Helicon* poems which are otherwise hard to classify, such as the pleasant narrative poem of Nicholas Breton's "Phillida and Coridon" (No. 12), which merely relates, in short lines appropriate to the fresh and simple feeling of the poem, a pastoral betrothal.[73] Although this poem reads like a mere pretty narrative, it, too, was originally set to music and as a song in three parts was sung to Queen Elizabeth by three musicians "disguised in auncient Countrey attire" as she opened the casement of her gallery window about nine o'clock on a September morning. According to the account published in 1591, the song pleased Her Highness so much, both in words and music, that she commanded a repeat performance and graced it highly "with her chearefull acceptance and commendation."[74]

The royal progress was, incidentally, one of the important sources of pastoral poetry and pageant. In the next year, 1592, the Queen was again entertained with a shepherd's speech at Sudeley, and she would have seen a pastoral play except that the Cotswold weather prevented its production.[75] In 1599 when Elizabeth visited Wilton, she was entertained by a song in praise of Astrea, sung by two shepherds, Thenot and Piers, the words written by her hostess, the Countess of Pembroke.[76] Whether the progress was primarily responsible or not, much of the glorification of Her Majesty took a pastoral form. In fact,

William Empson thinks that "it was this Renaissance half-worship of Elizabeth and the success of England under her rule that gave conviction to the whole set of ideas."[77]

Sometimes the shepherd's complaint was transformed into a song, and, when the naïveté was emphasized and the chorus lines made prominent, something like a comic tone tempered the declaration of love. An example is *Helicon* No. 68, by H. C.

England's Helicon contains several examples of the song of good life to which we have already referred. The editor was no doubt aware that some of his readers would tire of love songs, and he may have been as willing to please them as is the clown Feste in *Twelfth Night,* when he asks the two tippling knights, who have demanded a song, "Would you have a love-song, or a song of good life?" Feste, as a professional entertainer, knows the conventional types of song well enough, though the commentators have not done much to illuminate the passage.

Examples of the good-life song in *Helicon* are No. 10 by Lodge, a piece preferring the shepherd's life to that of kings and worldlings, and No. 104, taken from a songbook of Byrd's. The second poem in *England's Helicon,* mainly a blazon of the shepherd's mistress, begins with two stanzas on the good life, in which it is claimed that

> Good Kings haue not disdained it,
> > but Sheepheards haue beene named:
> A sheepe-hooke is a Scepter fit,
> > for people well reclaimed.
> The Sheepheards life so honour'd is and praised:
> That Kings lesse happy seeme, though higher raised.[78]

The pastoral lyric concerns itself largely, as we have seen, with love and the good life. It is less psychologically and rhetorically complex than the Petrarchan sonnet, less troubled by the sexual paradox than the poetry of the Ovidian-mythological tradition. A few more comments on its treatment of love may be useful. In general, love in the pastoral world is thought of as innocent, chaste, childlike. The final lines of No. 147 in *England's Helicon* (by "Shepherd Tonie") are representative:

> Take hands then Nimphes & Sheepheards all,
> And to this Riuers musiques fall
> Sing true loue, and chast loue
> > begins our Festiuall.

So general is this atmosphere that one wonders if the edtior of the great pastoral anthology realized that one of the poems he took from

Yonge's *Musica Transalpina* (Nos. 131 and 132) exploits a *double entendre* on the word "die." It is curious indeed to encounter here a poem not very far in intention from Dryden's song, "Whil'st Alexis lay prest," in *Marriage à-la-Mode.*

There is little in common between Elizabethan pastoralism and the transparent pretense of Restoration shepherds and shepherdnesses. The Elizabethan view of pastoral is at once more serious and more gay. It emphasizes the value of *otium* and the mean estate, and, possibly because a realization of that value produces a legitimate feeling of freedom, Elizabethan pastoral gaiety is natural, untainted, and harmonious:

> Harke iollie Sheepheards,
>   harke yond lustic ringing:
> How cheerfully the bells daunce,
>   the whilst the Lads are springing?
>
> Goe we then, why sit we here delaying:
> And all yond mery wanton lasses playing?
> How gailie Flora leades it,
>   and sweetly treads it!
> The woods and groaues they ring,
>   louely resounding:
> With Ecchoes sweet rebounding.

This is the note on which the reader of *England's Helicon* in 1600 closed the book.[79]

NOTES

[1] W. W. Greg, *Pastoral Poetry and Drama* (London, 1906), p. 67.

[2] Anonymous review of *England's Helicon*, ed. Hyder E. Rollins, 2 vols. (Cambridge: Harvard University Press), in *TLS*, April 11, 1935, p. 240.

[3] Kathleen Tillotson in *The Works of Michael Drayton*, ed. J. W. Hebel, 5 vols. (Oxford, 1931–1941), V, 4.

[4] See, for example, Thomas Blenerhasset's *Revelation of the True Minerva*, ed. J. W. Bennett (New York, 1941), and I. L. Schulze, "Blenerhasset's *A Revelation,* Spenser's *Sheapheardes Calender,* and the Kenilworth Pageants," ELH, XI (1944), 85–91.

[5] *Sir Francis Bacon, Works,* ed. James Spedding, R. L. Ellis, and D. D. Heath, 15 vols. (Boston, 1860–1864), VI, 138.

[6] See, for example, *Davids Pastorall Poeme: or Sheepeheards Song. Seven Sermons, on the 23. Psalme of Dauid,* by Thomas Jackson (1603).

[7] "To the Reader of his Pastorals" in *Works,* ed. Hebel, II, 517.

[8] *The Eclogues of Baptista Mantuanus,* ed. W. P. Mustard (Baltimore, 1911), p. 97. Translations or

adaptations of this passage are in Alexander Barclay's fifth eclogue (before 1530), lines 469–492; in Turbervile's translation (1567), sig. K2ᵛ; in Spenser's July eclogue in *The Shepheardes Calender* (1579), lines 131–160; and in Francis Sabie's *Pan's Pipe* (1595), sigs. D2ᵛ–D3ʳ.

⁹ *Works,* ed. Hebel, I, 89.

¹⁰ *De civitate Dei,* XVIII, 10.

¹¹ *The Deipnosophists,* XII, 510 c, trans. C. B. Gulick, Loeb Classical Library, 7 vols. (1922–1949), V, 295.

¹² The same point had been emphasized by Horace in *Epistles,* II, 10. The idea was also familiar to Renaissance Platonists and was elaborated by Ficino, for example, in his commentary on Plato's *Philebus.* See P. O. Kristeller, *The Philosophy of Marsilio Ficino* (New York, 1943), pp. 358–359.

¹³ The passage in G. B. Nenna's treatise is so typical, and the reputation of his book in England is so amply attested to by Edmund Spenser, Samuel Daniel, George Chapman, and Angel Day, that it must be quoted: "Now let vs consider what fruit may be gathered by the shadowe of fables, especially of this which I euen now recited. For indeed vnder those vailes we may receiue no lesse pleasant then profitable instruction . . . After that a man is once framed, and that he hath attained to that age, that hee beginneth nowe to discourse within himselfe, what kinde of life hee were best to followe as the most noble in account amongst men: whether that which is grounded vppon knowledge, which the Philosophers were wont to cal a contemplatiue kind of life: or otherwise, yt which guideth a man that addicteth himself only to worldly matters, which they terme actiue: or else that which consisteth wholy in pleasure, which they name delight-

full. Then straightwaie discord entreth: of which three sortes of liues, Soueraigne Iupiter will not giue sentence which is the best, least that in approuing the one, he should condemne the other two; and so the life of man should rather be constrained then free, but hee leaueth them to the judgement of man, to the end that he may as pleaseth him, tie himselfe to that kind of life that shall best like him; it may be, shewing vs thereby, the free choice which is granted to vs by him. Of the which notwithstanding he that is caried away to follow the delightfull kind of life, doth bring vnto him selfe vnspeakeable detriment" (*Nennio, or a Treatise of Nobility,* trans. William Jones, 1595, sig. H3ᵛ).

¹⁴ Trans. Bartholomew Yong (1598), p. 53.

¹⁵ Rollins ed., I, 70.

¹⁶ Lines 137–138.

¹⁷ *Idea The Shepheards Garland* (1593), Eclogue IX, lines 55–60.

¹⁸ *Faerie Queene,* VI, ix, xxxvi.

¹⁹ See C. R. Baskervill, "Early Romantic Plays in England," *MP,* XIV (1916–17), 483; T. S. Graves, "*The Arraignment of Paris* and Sixteenth Century Flattery," *MLN,* XXVIII (1913), 48–49; A. H. Gilbert, 'The Source of Peele's *Arraignment of Paris,"* *MLN,* XLI (1926), 36; and Douglas Bush, *Mythology and the Renaissance Tradition in English Poetry* (Minneapolis, 1932), pp. 51–52.

²⁰ Ed. of 1586, p. 83.

²¹ Sig. Cʳ.

²² G. P. Lomazzo, *A Tracte Containing the Artes of Curious Paintinge,* trans. Richard Haydocke (1598), sig. Bb6ʳ.

²³ Sig. D4ʳ.

²⁴ *Parts Added to the Mirror for Magistrates,* ed. L. B. Campbell (Cambridge, England, 1946), pp. 462–463.

²⁵ Lines 869–871. For evidence

that Tamburlaine was a symbol of this Renaissance spirit before he appeared in Marlowe's play, see my "Tamburlaine and the Renaissance," *Elizabethan Studies in Honor of George F. Reynolds* (Boulder, Colo., 1945), pp. 128–129.

[26] Conyers Read, *Mr. Secretary Walsingham and the Policy of Queen Elizabeth*, 3 vols. (Oxford, 1925), I, 69.

[27] George Puttenham, *The Arte of English Poesie*, ed. Gladys D. Willcock and Alice Walker (Cambridge, England, 1936), p. 248.

[28] *The Artes of Curious Paintinge*, trans. Haydocke, p. 122.

[29] *Fennes Frutes* (1590), sig. E3ᵛ.

[30] *The First Day of the Worldes Creation*, trans. Joshua Sylvester (1595), sig. Elᵛ.

[31] *Babilon*, trans. William L'Isle (1595), sig. A3ᵛ.

[32] "Disprayse of a Courtly life," first published in *A Poetical Rhapsody* (1602), ed. Hyder E. Rollins, 2 vols. (Cambridge: Harvard University Press, 1931, 1932), I, 9–12.

[33] VI, ix, xix.

[34] "The Relations of Spenser and Sidney," *PMLA*, XLV (1930), 720.

[35] *The Allegory of Love* (Oxford, 1936), pp. 350–353.

[36] VI, x, iii.

[37] VI, xii, ii.

[38] VI, ix, xlv.

[39] "Sonnets" appended to *Scillaes Metamorphosis* (1589), sig. D4ʳ.

[40] For the general background, see A. O. Lovejoy and George Boas, *Primitivism and Related Ideas in Antiquity* (Baltimore, 1935); Paul Meissner, "Das goldene Zeitalter in der Englischen Renaissance," *Anglia*, LIX (1935), 351–367; E. Lipsker, *Der Mythos vom goldenen Zeitalter in den Schäferdichtungen Italiens, Spaniens und Frankreichs zur Zeit der Renaissance* (Berlin, 1933).

[41] Erwin Panofsky, "Et in Arcadia Ego," *Philosophy and History*, ed.

Raymond Klibansky and H. J. Paton (Oxford, 1936), pp. 225–227.

[42] See L. I. Bredvold, "The Naturalism of Donne in Relation to Some Renaissance Traditions," *JEGP*, XXII (1923), 471–502.

[43] *Hippolytus*, in *Seneca's Tragedies*, trans. F. J. Miller, Loeb Classical Library, 2 vols. (1916–17), I, 525–539.

[44] V, Proem, ix.

[45] I, i, 109–114.

[46] For a Renaissance account of this historical side of pastoral, see F. M. Padelford, *Selected Translations from Scaliger's Poetics* (New York, 1905), pp. 21–32.

[47] *The Arte of English Poesie*, ed. Willcock and Walker, pp. 37–39.

[48] The differing attitudes possible on this and other points are noticed by Lois Whitney, "Concerning Nature in *The Countesse of Pembrokes Arcadia*," *SP*, XXIV (1927), 207–222.

[49] This is the final poem in Daniel's *Works* (1601); it did not, as Grosart asserts, appear in the *Delia* of 1592 (*Complete Works of Samuel Daniel*, ed. A. B. Grosart, 5 vols. [London, Spenser Society, 1885–1896], I, 260).

[50] *Diana*, trans. Yong, sig. A1ᵛ.

[51] *The Greek Romances in Elizabethan Fiction* (New York, 1912), p. 131.

[52] It is impossible to agree with Wolff that "Angel Day's version is pervaded by this indulgent ridicule of rustic wits, manners, speech and dress" (*ibid.*, p. 122, n. 6). Day presents it all quite seriously.

[53] I have pointed out an example of this in Lodge's *Rosalynde*. See *The Golden Hind*, ed. Roy Lamson and Hallett Smith (New York, 1942), p. 665. There is another in Montemayor's *Diana*, trans. Yong, sig. E6ᵛ.

[54] Montemayor, *Diana*, trans. Yong, sig. D5ʳ.

⁵⁵ *Diana,* trans. Yong, sig. B6ʳ.
⁵⁶ A good account of the popular
dance-song background of Elizabethan pastoral is given in C. R.
Baskervill, *The Elizabethan Jig* (Chicago, 1929), chap. I.
⁵⁷ Edited by H. E. Rollins in two
volumes (Cambridge: Harvard University Press, 1935).
⁵⁸ Rollins, II, 3–4.
⁵⁹ Rollins ed., I, 56.
⁶⁰ Rollins ed., I, 58.
⁶¹ Rollins, I, 85, and II, 134.
⁶² Rollins, I, 167. This poem was
used by Drayton to take the place
of a more direct song of complaint
which he had published in his
second eclogue in *Idea The Shepheards Garland* (1593). The version
as given in *England's Helicon* was
printed in the 1606 edition of Drayton's eclogues and revised further
for publication in 1619 (see *Works*,
ed. Hebel, I, 53, and II, 525). Mrs.
Tillotson remarks that "the song [as
given in *E. H.*] gives a much more
detached and playful impression of
Rowland's love than the song of
Shepheards Garland" (*ibid.,* V,
184).
⁶³ Preface, reproduced in *Revue
Hispanique,* L (1920), 372.
⁶⁴ I have substituted the correct
reading "eawes" of the 1598 folio
for the meaningless "by us" of
England's Helicon.
⁶⁵ "The Poetry of Sir Philip Sidney," *ELH,* XII (1945), 267. Spencer is speaking of a poem not included in *England's Helicon,* the
double sestina "You goat-herd gods."
It is certainly true that a better
selection from Sidney's poetry in
the 1598 folio could be made than
that of the editor of *England's Helicon.*
⁶⁶ Rollins' note (*England's Helicon,* II, 173), is possibly misleading
when it says that the poem was
taken from Morley's book "with
very lavish changes." Rollins de-

pends upon E. H. Fellowes' *English
Madrigal Verse, 1588–1632* (Oxford,
1913), p. 126, for what he calls "the
original." But Dr. Fellowes' text is
a reconstruction from the various
part-books of Morley, and in his
reconstruction Dr. Fellowes is markedly classical. Every variant from
Fellowes' text in *England's Helicon*
can be found in some one of the
part-books. The editor of the *Helicon*
simply made a different reconstruction, pruning away the "Aye me's"
and the like less rigorously. I grant
that he arranged the first line incor-
rectly for the rhyme. The whole
point is of some importance in that
it raises the question of what *are*
the words that make up a poem
when they occur as words to a
madrigal. For Fellowes' method of
reconstruction, and his triumph in
reconstructing a poem by Ben Jonson, see *English Madrigal Verse,* pp.
xv-xvii; most Elizabethans, I am
convinced, were not as firmly sealed
of the tribe of Ben as Dr. Fellowes.
Certainly the editor of *England's
Helicon* was not.
⁶⁷ R. S. Forsythe, in *"The Passionate Shepherd* and English Poetry,"
PMLA, XL (1925), 692–742, provides an elaborate treatment of the
imitations of Marlowe's poetry in
English and some account of earlier
uses of the invitation motif.
⁶⁸ *Faerie Queene,* III, ᴠɪ, xli.
⁶⁹ The poem printed by Albert
Feuillerat (ed., *The Complete
Works of Sir Philip Sidney,* 4 vols.
[Cambridge University Press, 1922–
1926], II, 344–346) from Harleian
MS. 6057, entitled by him "A
Remedie for Love" and said in the
manuscript to be "An old dittie of
Sr Phillipp Sidneyes omitted in the
Printed Arcadia," may seem to be a
contradiction of this statement. Actually, the poem is a version of the
"mock-blazon" on Mopsa which I discuss below, p. 53 [of Smith's book].

[70] The editor of *England's Helicon* apparently liked a more regular line than he found in Spenser. He changes line 6 from "With Damaske roses and Daffadillies set" to "With Daffadils and Damaske Roses set."

[71] See Bruce Pattison, "The Roundelay in the August Eclogue of *The Shepheardes Calender*," *RES*, IX (1933), 54–55, and his *Music and Poetry in the English Renaissance* (London, 1948), pp. 173–174.

[72] This poem, although Rollins (*England's Helicon*, II, 178) says it is known only in the *Helicon*, appears in Thomas Deloney's *Garland of Good Will*, 1631 (*Works*, ed. F. O. Mann [Oxford, 1912], pp. 344–346); whether it was in the *Garland* as entered in 1593 and published in 1596, hence before its publication in the *Helicon*, is not known.

[73] Perhaps the closest parallel to Breton's poem is the "Dowsabell" song in Drayton's eighth eclogue of *Idea The Shepheards Garland*, 1593 (see *Works*, ed. Hebel, I, 88–91). But Drayton's poem is much more "naturalized," with English place names and very specific details about the materials of the shepherds' clothing and equipment. It moves the pastoral environment out of Arcadia to the English countryside. This realism no doubt had a comic effect for the Elizabethans, and Drayton uses a comic meter, that of Chaucer's *Sir Thopas*.

[74] *The Honorable Entertainement gieuen to the Queenes Maiestie in Progresse, at Eluetham in Hampshire, by the right Honorable the Earle of Hertford* (1591), sig. D2ᵛ.

[75] *Speeches Delivered to Her Maiestie this Last Progresse, at the Right Honorable the Lady Rvssels, at Bissam, the Right Honorable the Lorde Chandos at Sudley, at the Right Honorable the Lord Norris, at Ricorte* (Oxford, 1592), sigs. B–Cʳ.

[76] Printed as No. 4 in Davison's *A Poetical Rhapsody* (1602), ed. Rollins, I, 15.

[77] *English Pastoral Poetry* (New York, 1938; American edition of *Some Versions of Pastoral*), p. 34. For a discussion of Elizabeth in this role and a survey of the many relevant works, see E. C. Wilson, *England's Eliza* (Cambridge: Harvard University Press, 1939), chap. IV, "Fayre Elisa, Queene of Shepheardes All."

[78] I have found about forty-five additional Elizabethan poems which would be called "poems of good life."

[79] Part II of Professor Smith's chapter goes on to a critical examination of the pastoral eclogue [editor's note].

Form and Matter in the Publication of Research

R. B. McKerrow

May I as one who has had occasion both as a publisher and an editor to read a very considerable number of books and articles embodying the results of research into English literary history plead for more attention to *form* in the presentation of such work?

I do not know whether advancing age has made me thicker in the head than I used to be or whether I have merely become more impatient—there is so much that one still wants to do and constantly less and less time in which to do it—but it certainly seems to me that there has been a tendency in recent years for the way in which the results of research are set out to become progressively less efficient, especially among the younger students, both in England and in America. And when I say "less efficient" I am not thinking of any high qualities of literary art, but of the simplest qualities of precision and intelligibility. Indeed, I have sometimes wondered whether the fate of "English studies" will not eventually be to be smothered in a kind of woolly and impenetrable fog of wordiness that few or none will be bothered to penetrate.

It may perhaps surprise some readers of *R.E.S.* if I tell them that I have several times been compelled to refuse articles offered to me which seemed, from the evidence of the footnotes, to have been the product of real research, for no other reason than that after several readings I have completely failed to discover the point or points which the author was trying to make. In one or two cases this has perhaps been due to the author's inability to express himself in English at all, but in others the trouble has seemed to be rather due to a complete ignorance of the way in which he should present his material. Being himself fully cognizant of the point at issue and with the way in which his research corrects or supplements views currently held on his subject, the author has apparently assumed that all would become clear to his readers by the mere recital of his investigations without any commentary on the results as they appear to him. But such a mere recital of an investigation will only convey what is intended by the author to a person with the same knowledge and mental outlook as the author himself, and to anyone else may be almost meaningless.

Articles of which I have been unable to make out the point at all I have necessarily rejected, generally after trying them on a friend or two, lest I were at the time more than usually dense; but I must confess to having printed in *R.E.S.* a certain number of articles which I regarded as definitely bad work. These were some which contained good research which I was assured would be useful to those with knowledge of the subject and willing to spend time and effort in puzzling out the bearing of the new matter, but of little if any use to others. Such articles cannot, of course, be lightly rejected. The pity is they could so easily, by a writer of adequate training in presenting his facts, or with sufficient imagination to enable him to dispense with such training, have been made really interesting contributions to knowledge which would have appealed to a wide circle of readers, instead of only being absorbed with difficulty and distaste by the few.

For it is imagination which is, before all else, necessary in presenting a piece of research. It is not to be considered as, so to say, an emanation of the author's brain which has been allowed to escape into the void, a mere fragment of knowledge detached from its originator, but one which is intended to become part of the knowledge of others, and in order that it may do this it must be so shaped and adapted that it may fit with ease and certainty on to the knowledge of others, those others being of course the likely readers.

New facts, skilfully prepared for our easy assimilation, for forming part of our existing aggregate of knowledge, are invariably welcomed, even when the subject is not one in which we are normally much interested, when a badly presented bit of what should be our own special subject may completely fail to make any impression on our consciousness.

We ought, I think, at the start to realize that no readers whom we are likely to have will be nearly as much interested in our views or discoveries as we ourselves are. Most of them will be people who are a little tired, a little bored, and who read us rather out of a sense of duty and a wish to keep up with what is being done than because they have any real interest in the subject; and in return for our reader's complaisance it is our duty as well as our interest to put what we have to say before him with as little trouble to him as possible. It is our duty because we ought to be kind to our fellow creature; it is our interest because if the view that we wish to put before him is clearly and competently expressed, so that he understands without trouble what we are trying to say, he will be gratified at the smooth working of his own intelligence and will inevitably think better of our theory and of its author than if he had had to puzzle himself over what we mean and then in the end doubt whether he had really understood us, so raising in himself an uneasy doubt whether his brains are quite what they used to be!

Now I suggest that if we analyse almost any piece of research which seems to us thoroughly workmanlike and satisfactory from all points of view, we shall almost always find that it falls into five parts in the following order.

1. The *introduction,* in which the author briefly states the present position of research on his subject and the views currently held on it.
2. The *proposal,* in which he describes in outline what he hopes to prove.
3. The *boost,* in which he proceeds to magnify the importance of his discovery or argument and to explain what a revolution it will create in the views generally held on the whole period with which he is dealing. This is, as it were, a taste of sauce to stimulate the reader's appetite.
4. The *demonstration,* in which he sets forth his discovery or argument in an orderly fashion.
5. The *conclusion,* or *crow,* in which he summarizes what he claims to have shown, and points out how complete and unshakeable is his proof.

Of course I am not serious in this! It is not to be supposed necessary that we should *formally* divide our research articles in this way, but it is a real and practical division and there are few research articles which would not be improved by the adoption of such a framework, at least under the surface.

The following points might, I believe, be worth much more serious consideration than seems frequently to be given to them.

1. The subject of a research article should always be a unity. The paper should always deal either with a single subject or with a well-

defined group of subjects of the same general character. Thus a particular literary work might be dealt with in all its aspects, or any one aspect might be dealt with, say, its origin, its date, its popularity, or what not, or its author's life or any one period or incident of it. On the other hand it is seldom well to mix two pieces of research on different scales, an account of a man's works as a whole and of a particular one of his works dealt with in much greater detail. Similarly, an article in which an attempt is made both to give new discoveries in an author's biography and a correction in the bibliography of one of his books will almost certainly turn out an unreadable muddle. These various kinds of discovery may often arise as the result of a single piece of research, but it is much better to put them forward in quite independent articles. Opportunity may always be found to insert a cross-reference from one to the other in order to ensure that students do not overlook the author's other discoveries.

2. Give your book or article a name which tells at once what it is all about. Facetious and cryptic titles should be utterly eschewed. At best they annoy, and at worst they tend to be forgotten and to render the work under which they are concealed untraceable. Fancy names, pastoral and the like, should never be used, however familiar they may be to students versed in the literature of a particular period. Thus Katherine Philips may have been well known to students of her time as the "Matchless Orinda," but one who writes about her by the latter name risks his work being entered in indexes under headings where it will be missed by scholars searching for her under her family name.

3. Remember that though the great majority of your readers are likely to have a considerable knowledge of English Literature as a whole and an expert knowledge of a certain part of it, only a minority are likely to be experts in your particular period or field. In any case very few indeed can be expected to possess the minute knowledge of it which you who have just been devoting all your time to the study of it have or ought to have. (Indeed, if you do not know *much* more than others, why are you writing about it?) Keep this in mind in the whole of your writing and *adjust what you say to the knowledge which you may reasonably expect your readers to have.* This is really the whole secret of exposition, and it is so simple that it seems incredible that writers of research articles should so often be ignorant of it. But they are, they are! If you have a young brother or sister of, say, fifteen years old or so, think that you have him or her before you and that you are trying to explain the point of your article to them and at the same time to prevent them from thinking what an ass you are to be wasting their time and yours about anything so completely futile. If in

your imagination you see their eyes light up and their faces set with a desire to protest or argue, you will know that whether the thesis of your paper is sound or not its presentation is at least on the right lines!

Naturally the method of presenting an argument must depend on the persons for whom it is intended. You need not in an article in *R.E.S.* explain who Ben Jonson or John Dryden or Cynewulf or Layamon were, but it would be unwise to expect all your readers to have precise knowledge as to their dates or the details of their biography. If these are required for your argument it is easy to give them without the reader being moved to indignation by the feeling that he is being treated like a child. In this connection much offence may often be avoided by the insertion of the little phrases "of course," or "as everyone knows"—*e.g.* "Stephen Hawes, who was of course writing in the earliest years of the sixteenth century, and called Lydgate 'master'" gives information which every reader of *R.E.S.* must have known at some time, but of which a few may need to be reminded in an article concerning the poetical associations of Henry VIII's court.

In your introduction, then, take your reader metaphorically by the hand and lead him gently up to the threshold of your research, reminding him courteously and without any appearance of dogmatism, not with the gestures of a teacher but gently as a comrade in study, of what he ought to know in order to understand what you have to tell him—the object of your research. He will be far better able to appreciate your demonstration if he knows what to look for, and to know what to look for if you tell him at once just what the current views of the matter are and how your own differ from them.

4. So far as possible state your facts in chronological order. When a digression is necessary, make quite clear that it *is* a digression, and when you reach the end of it, make quite clear that you are returning to the main course of the story. And always give plenty of dates, *real* dates, not the kind of dates of which many of the historical people seem to be so fond—"about two years before the conclusion of the events which we have described" or "later in the same year," which after reading several earlier pages turns out to be the year in which "the king" attained his majority, necessitating further research to discover what king and in what year and what part of the year he was born and what "majority" meant at the time. But enough! We have all suffered. Keep on remembering that though *you* are perhaps completely familiar with all aspects of your subject, your reader may not be.

5. State your facts as simply as possible, even boldly. No one wants flowers of eloquence or literary ornaments in a research article. On the

other hand do not be slangy, and, especially if you are writing for *R.E.S.*, do not use American slang. We may be interested in it, but we may not always understand it. Only a few days ago I had to beg the author of an excellent article which I was printing to substitute some phrase more intelligible to us over in England for a statement that certain evidence—"is not quite enough to convict of actual skulduggery (and the aroma of high-binding will not down) . . ."

6. Never be cryptic nor use literary paraphrases. Needless mysteries are out of place in research articles. There are plenty of them there already. If they think that you are trying to be superior, most readers will stop reading at once.

7. Do not try to be humorous. Humour is well enough in its place, but nothing more infuriates a man who is looking for a plain statement of facts than untimely humour, especially if he does not know whether the writer is really trying to be humorous or not, a point which some would-be humorists fail to make clear.

8. Do not use ambiguous expressions. The worst of these are perhaps phrasing containing the word "question." If you say "there is no question that Ben Jonson was in Edinburgh in 1618" most people, perhaps all, will take you to mean that he *was* there in that year; and the same if you say "that Jonson was in Edinburgh in 1618 is beyond question" or "does not admit of question." If, however, you say that "there is no question, of Jonson having been in Edinburgh in 1618," most people, though I think not all, will take you to mean that he was *not* there in that year. But there is certainly no question that it would be better to use a phrase the meaning of which is not open to question.

Avoid also the word "doubtless," which has been defined as "a word used when making a statement for the truth of which the speaker is unaware of any evidence."

Do not overtask such expressions as "it is generally admitted that," "there can be no doubt that," "it is well known that" unless you can shift your responsibility on to at least one other person by giving a reference.

9. Always be precise and careful in references and quotations, and never fear the charge of pedantry. After all, "pedant" is merely the name which one gives to anyone whose standard of accuracy happens to be a little higher than one's own!

10. Do not treat the subjects of your research with levity. Above all avoid that hateful back-slapping "heartiness" which caused certain nineteenth-century Elizabethans to refer to "Tom Nash," "Bob Green,"

"Will Shakespeare" and so on, with its horrible flavour of modern gutter journalism which refers in this way to film stars, long-distance fliers, and the like. These Elizabethans had certain qualities which have made it seem worth while to keep their memories green for more than 300 years, and on this account, if for no other, they should be given the courtesy which is their due.

11. Above all, whatever inner doubts you may have as to whether the piece of research upon which you have been spending your time was really worth while, you must on no account allow it to appear that you have ever thought of it otherwise than of supreme importance to the human race! In the first place, unless you yourself believe in what you are doing, you will certainly not do good work, and, secondly, if your reader suspects for a moment that you do not set the very highest value on your work yourself he will set no value on it at all. He will on the other hand be full of fury that you should have induced him to waste his precious time in reading stuff that you do not believe in yourself, an attitude which will completely prevent him from appreciating any real and evident merit which there may be in it. After all, one can never be certain of the value of one's own work. Often in scientific research a discovery which in itself seemed most trivial has led to results of the utmost importance, and though sensational occurrences of this kind may be rarer in literary research than in science, it is still true that what is merely a side-issue in one research may give rise, when critically examined, to results of quite unexpected value.

As a general rule the interest and importance of a piece of research lies either in the facts disclosed or the methods by which they have been brought to light—or in both. To these prior considerations the manner of presentation may indeed be subordinate. Nevertheless good presentation may help enormously in the effective value of good research, while bad presentation may rob it of the recognition which is its due.

Suggested Reading

Bibliography

W. W. Greg, "The Bakings of Betsey," *The Library*, 3d ser., II (1911), 225-259.

Charlton Hinman, *The Printing and Proof-Reading of the First Folio of Shakespeare*, Oxford, 1963.

Textual Criticism

Fredson Bowers, "Textual Criticism," in *Aims and Methods of Scholarship in the Modern Languages and Literature*, ed. James Thorpe, New York, 1963.

Paul Maas, *Textual Criticism*, Oxford, 1958.

Authorship and Dating

"The Case for Internal Evidence," *Bulletin of the New York Public Library*, 1957-1960; a series of articles about methods of proving authorship.

Jacques Barzun and Henry F. Graff, "Verification," in *The Modern Researcher*, New York, 1957.

Biography

W. J. Bate, *John Keats*, Cambridge, Mass., 1963.

James Clifford, ed., *Biography as an Art; Selected Criticism, 1560-1960*, New York, 1960.

Sources and Analogues

Ernst Robert Curtius, *European Literature and the Latin Middle Ages*, trans. Willard R. Trask, New York, 1953.

John Livingston Lowes, "Loveris Maladye of Hereos," *Modern Philology*, XI (1913-14), 491-546.

History of Ideas and the Concept of Period

M. H. Abrams, *The Mirror and the Lamp: Romantic Theory and the Critical Tradition*, New York, 1953.
Ronald S. Crane, "On Writing a History of English Criticism, 1650-1800," *University of Toronto Quarterly*, XXII (1953), 376-391.
A. O. Lovejoy, *Essays in the History of Ideas*, Baltimore, 1948.

Style

Leo Spitzer, *Linguistics and Literary History: Essays in Stylistics*, Princeton, 1948.
Richard M. Ohmann, *Shaw: The Style and the Man*, Middletown, Conn., 1962.

Historical Interpretation

Helen Gardner, *The Business of Criticism*, London, 1959.
A. S. P. Woodhouse, "The Historical Criticism of Milton," *PMLA*, LXVI (1951), 1033-1044.
Marc Bloch, *The Historian's Craft*, trans. Peter Putnam, New York, 1953.
K. R. Popper, *The Poverty of Historicism*, London, 1957.

Form and Convention

Kenneth Burke, *The Philosophy of Literary Form*, rev. ed., New York, 1957.
Moody Prior, "Poetic Drama: An Analysis and a Suggestion," *English Institute Annual, 1949*, 1950.
Yvor Winters, "Problems for the Modern Critic of Literature," *Hudson Review*, IX (1956), 325-386.

Scholarly Prose

Richard D. Altick, "The Philosophy of Composition," in *The Art of Literary Research*, New York, 1963.

Graduate Study and the Profession

Ronald S. Crane, "History Versus Criticism in the University Study of Literature," *The English Journal* (College Edition), XXIV (1935), 645-666.

Stuart P. Sherman, "Professor Kittredge and the Teaching of English," *The Nation,* September 11, 1913; reprinted in *Great Teachers,* ed. Houston Peterson, New Brunswick, New Jersey, 1946.

Notes on Authors

The late R. C. Bald was Professor of English at the University of Chicago. He edited Elizabethan plays and studied literary friendships of the romantic poets as well as the printing of seventeenth-century books. At the time of his death he was completing a full-length biography of John Donne.

Fredson Bowers, Chairman of the English Department at the University of Virginia, has written influential books on bibliography and textual studies, numerous critical articles, and studies of literary history. His book reviews have a devastating thoroughness. Having edited the dramatic works of Thomas Dekker, he is now preparing editions of Marlowe, Beaumont and Fletcher, Hawthorne, and Stephen Crane.

Sir Walter Greg's *A Bibliography of the English Printed Drama to the Restoration* (1939-1959) capped a lifetime of original research in Elizabethan literature. As Librarian of Trinity College, Cambridge, Editor for the Malone Society, and regular contributor to *The Library*, he shaped the thought of two generations of scholars.

Bruce Harkness, Associate Dean of the College of Liberal Arts and Sciences, University of Illinois, is a stulent of modern fiction and an authority on Joseph Conrad.

S. Schoenbaum is currently editing the plays of Thomas Middleton. His revision of Alfred Harbage's *Annals of English Drama* and his teaching at Northwestern University have earned him a reputation for soundness and accuracy.

G. E. Bentley, Jr., who teaches at the University of Toronto, is completing an edition of Blake's manuscripts for the Clarendon Press, the first volume of which set new standards for impressive facsimiles of literary documents.

Donald C. Baker, Associate Professor of English at the University of Colorado, has written articles on Chaucer and other Middle English authors.

Leon Edel, author of a multi-volume life of Henry James, is Professor of English at New York University. He has also written on the modern psychological novel.

Richard Ellmann of Northwestern University is noted for his detailed and imaginative studies of Yeats and Joyce.

Harrison Hayford of the English Department at Northwestern University is co-editor of the definitive edition of *Billy Budd*.

A. J. Smith, who teaches in the University of Swansea, Wales, has written extensively on Donne's poetry.

James B. Colvert of the University of Virginia is preparing a book on the art of Stephen Crane and is editor of a forthcoming edition of Crane's works.

The late F. P. Wilson was general editor of the Oxford History of English Literature, Merton Professor of English, and author of studies of English prose and drama.

Don Cameron Allen, Sir William Osler Professor of English in Johns Hopkins University and editor of *ELH*, has published important books on seventeenth-century poetry and prose. His learning ranges over all of European literature and thought of the Middle Ages and the renaissance.

Morton W. Bloomfield, who teaches at Harvard University, has written on *Piers Plowman* and the history of English. His articles in *Speculum, Modern Philology,* and *PMLA* have stimulated a wide interest in medieval literature.

F. O. Matthiessen, through his classes at Harvard, his books on T. S. Eliot and Henry James, and his studies of classic American authors, was one of the most effective teachers in America.

Graham Hough's versatility enables him to write authoritatively on almost anyone from Spenser to D. H. Lawrence. He is a fellow of Christ's College and University Lecturer at Cambridge.

Ernest Tuveson, Professor of English in the University of California at Berkeley, is an expert on eighteenth-century thought; his principal work is *The Imagination as a Means of Grace: Locke and the Aesthetics of Romanticism,* 1960.

Frank Kermode's *The Romantic Image* influenced the study of twentieth-century literature by emphasizing the continued force of the romantic tradition. His reviews and articles collected in *Puzzles and Epiphanies* (1962) have freshness and trenchancy. He is Professor of English Literature in the University of Bristol.

R. S. Crane, Distinguished Service Professor Emeritus in the University of Chicago, has done important work on Bacon, Locke, Shaftesbury, Hume, and Goldsmith; his studies of literary theory in *The Languages of Criticism and the Structure of Poetry* (1953) have been widely read.

William Arrowsmith, Professor of Classics at the University of Texas, is editor and chief translator of *The Complete Greek Comedy.*

Wayne C. Booth's *Rhetoric of Fiction* won the Christian Gauss award for 1961. He is Dean of the College at the University of Chicago and has contributed regularly to the *Carlton Miscellany.*

Hallett Smith, Professor of English at California Institute of Technology, has exerted a steady influence upon Elizabethan studies through his critical writing and his well-balanced anthologies.

R. B. McKerrow edited the *Review of English Studies* and the works of Thomas Nashe; he was a pioneer in modern bibliography.

F. O. Matthiessen, though his chosen subjects include such authors, was one of the most creative forces in American criticism.

Graham Hough's versatility enables him to write authoritatively on almost anyone from Spenser to D. H. Lawrence. He is a Fellow of Christ's College and University Lecturer at Cambridge.

Ernest Tuveson, Professor of English at the University of California at Berkeley, is an expert on eighteenth-century thought. His principal work is The Imagination as a Means of Grace and the Aesthetics of Romanticism, 1960.

Frank Kermode, The Romantic Image, influenced the study of twentieth-century literature by emphasising the continuous tradition of the romantic sensibility. His reviews and articles collected in Puzzles and Epiphanies (1962) have freshness and trenchancy. He is Professor of English Literature at the University of Bristol.

R. S. Crane, Distinguished Service Professor Emeritus in the University of Chicago, has done important work on Robert Burke, and has done valuable work on the studies of literary theory. His Languages of Criticism and the Structure of Poetry (1953) has been widely read.

William Arrowsmith, Professor of Classics at the University of Texas, is editor and chief translator of The Complete Greek Comedy.

Wayne C. Booth, author of The Rhetoric of Fiction, won the Christian Gauss award for 1961. He is Dean of the College at the University of Chicago and has contributed significantly to the Chicago Anthology.

Hallett Smith, Professor of English at California Institute of Technology, has earned a reputation as an Elizabethan scholar through his critical reviews and his well-balanced attitudes.

B. Rajan, reviewer, editor, the author of English Studies and the work of Thomas Mallet. He was a pioneer in modern bibliography.